Introduction to Financial Accounting

Charles T. Horngren Series in Accounting
Charles T. Horngren, Consulting Editor

Introduction to Financial Accounting

Ninth Edition

Charles T. Horngren
Stanford University

Gary L. Sundem
University of Washington

John A. Elliott
City University of New York—Baruch College

Donna R. Philbrick
Portland State University

Pearson Education International

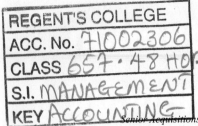
Senior Acquisitions Editor: Wendy Craven
Editorial Director: Jeff Shelstad
Editorial Assistant: Joanna Doxey
Director of Development: Steve Deitmer
Development Editor: Elisa Adams
Assistant Editor: Sam Goffinet
Media Project Manager: Caroline Kasterine
Marketing Director: Eric Frank
Managing Editor, Production: Cynthia Regan
Production Editor: Michael Reynolds
Production Manager, Manufacturing: Arnold Vila
Permissions Coordinator: Charles Morris
Design Manager: Maria Lange
Art Director: Janet Slowik
Interior Design: Craig Ramsdell
Cover Design: Debbie Iverson/Quorum Creative Services
Cover Photo: Moggy/Stone/Getty Images, Inc.
Art Studio: Matrix Art Services
Manager, Print Production: Christy Mahon
Print Production Liaison: Suzanne Duda
Director, Image Resource Center: Melinda Reo
Manager, Rights and Permissions: Zina Arabia
Manager, Visual Research: Beth Brenzel
Image Permissions Coordinator: Debbie Latronica
Photo Researcher: Julie Tesser
Composition/Full-Service Project Management: Progressive Information Technologies
Printer/Binder: Courier,Kendallville

Credits and acknowledgments borrowed from other sources and reproduced, with permission, in this textbook appear on appropriate page within text (or on page P1).

If you purchased this book within the United States or Canada you should be aware that it has been wrongfully imported without the approval of the Publisher or the Author.

Pearson Education LTD.
Pearson Education Singapore, Pte. Ltd
Pearson Education, Canada, Ltd
Pearson Education–Japan
Pearson Education Australia PTY, Limited

Pearson Education North Asia Ltd
Pearson Educación de Mexico, S.A. de C.V.
Pearson Education Malaysia, Pte. Ltd
Pearson Education Upper Saddle River, New Jersey

PEARSON
Prentice
Hall

10 9 8 7
ISBN 0-13-196875-0

To Joan, Scott, Mary, Susie,

Cathy, Liz, Garth, Jens,

Laura, Dawn, Jesse,

and Duncan

Charles T. Horngren is the Edmund W. Littlefield Professor of Accounting, Emeritus, at Stanford University. A graduate of Marquette University, he received his MBA from Harvard University and his Ph.D. from the University of Chicago. He is also the recipient of honorary doctorates from Marquette University and DePaul University.

A Certified Public Accountant, Horngren served on the Accounting Principles Board for six years, the Financial Accounting Standards Board Advisory Council for five years, and the Council of the American Institute of Certified Public Accountants for three years. For six years, he served as a trustee of the Financial Accounting Foundation, which oversees the Financial Accounting Standards Board and the Government Accounting Standards Board.

Horngren is a member of the Accounting Hall of Fame.

A member of the American Accounting Association, Horngren has been its President and its Director of Research. He received its first annual Outstanding Accounting Educator Award. He also received its Lifetime Contribution to Management Accounting Award.

The California Certified Public Accountants Foundation gave Horngren its Faculty Excellence Award and its Distinguished Professor Award. He is the first person to have received both awards.

The American Institute of Certified Public Accountants presented its first Outstanding Educator Award to Horngren.

Horngren was named Accountant of the Year, Education, by the national professional accounting fraternity, Beta Alpha Psi.

Professor Horngren is also a member of the Institute of Management Accountants, where he received its Distinguished Service Award. He was a member of the Institute's Board of Regents, which administers the Certified Management Accountant examinations.

Horngren is the author of these books published by Prentice-Hall: *Cost Accounting: A Managerial Emphasis,* Tenth Edition, 2000 (with George Foster and Srikant Datar); *Introduction to Management Accounting*, Thirteenth Edition, 2006 (with Gary L. Sundem and William O. Stratton); *Introduction to Financial Accounting,* Eighth Edition, 2002 (with Gary L. Sundem, John A. Elliott, and Donna R. Philbrick; *Accounting,* Fifth Edition, 2002 (with Walter T. Harrison, Jr. and Linda Bamber); and *Financial Accounting,* Fourth Edition, 2001 (with Walter J. Harrison, Jr.).

Horngren is the Consulting Editor for the Charles T. Horngren Series in Accounting.

Gary L. Sundem is the Julius A. Roller Professor of Accounting and Co-Chair of the Department of Accounting at the University of Washington, Seattle. He received his B.A. degree from Carleton College and his MBA and Ph.D. degrees from Stanford University.

Professor Sundem was the 1992–93 President of the American Accounting Association. He was Executive Director of the Accounting Education Change Commission, 1989–91, and served as Editor of *The Accounting Review,* 1982–86.

A member of the National Association of Accountants, Sundem is past president of the Seattle chapter. He has served on IMA's national Board of Directors, the Committee on Academic Relations, and the Research Committee.

Professor Sundem has numerous publications in accounting and finance journals including *Issues in Accounting Education, The Accounting Review, Journal of Accounting Research,* and *The Journal of Finance.* He was selected as the Outstanding Accounting

Educator by the American Accounting Association in 1998 and by the Washington Society of CPAs in 1987. He has made more than 200 presentations at universities in the United States and abroad.

John A. Elliott   is the Dean of the Zickin School of Business at Baruch College and Vice President of Baruch College, which is part of the City University of New York (CUNY). He is the Irwin and Arlene Ettinger Professor of Accountancy. He received his B.S. and MBA degrees from the University of Maryland and his Ph.D. degree from Cornell University. Prior to accepting the Deanship at the Zicklin School, he spent 20 years on the faculty at Cornell University's Johnson Graduate School of Management, most recently as Associate Dean for Academic Affairs.

Dean Elliott is a certified public accountant with professional experience as an auditor and consultant for Arthur Andersen & Co. and in the controller's office of the Westinghouse Defense and Space Center. During his career he has taught at six different institutions. His responsibilities have included financial accounting, intermediate accounting, financial statement analysis, taxation, and extensive executive teaching. He is currently teaching introductory financial accounting in the Zicklin Honors MBA program.

His academic publications have appeared in the *Accounting Review,* the *Journal of Accounting Research, Accounting Horizons*, and the *Rand Journal* among others. In 2004 his recent paper on earnings management (with Nelson and Tarpley) received the award from the American Accounting Association for Notable Contributions to Accounting Literature. His research is concentrated on the role of accounting information in financial analysis and contracts.

Donna R. Philbrick   is Professor of Accounting at Portland State University. She received her B.S. degree from the University of Oregon and her MBA and Ph.D. degrees from Cornell University.

Professor Philbrick is a certified public accountant and worked in public accounting prior to returning for her graduate degrees. Before joining the faculty at Portland State, she taught at the University of Oregon and Duke University. She currently teaches financial accounting and financial statement analysis. Professor Philbrick also teaches in the Oregon Executive MBA program and serves on the Academic Committee of that organization.

Professor Philbrick's research has been published in accounting journals including *The Accounting Review, Journal of Accounting Research*, and *Journal of Accounting and Economics*. She served on the Advisory Board of *Accounting Horizons* from 1994 to 2000 and as Associate Editor of that journal from 2000 to 2003.

BRIEF CONTENTS

CONTENTS

PREFACE

"You have to know what something is before you know how to use it."

Introduction to Financial Accounting, 9/E, describes the most widely accepted accounting theory and practice with an emphasis on using and analyzing the information in financial statements.

IFA, 9/E, takes the view that business is an exciting process and that accounting is the perfect window through which to see how economic events affect businesses. Because we believe that accounting aids the understanding of economic events and that accounting builds on simple principles, this book introduces a number of concepts earlier than many other textbooks. We cover these early concepts at the most accessible level and illustrate them with carefully chosen examples from real companies. Our coverage addresses the choices that management makes when preparing financial statements and how these choices affect the way users interpret the information. We also discuss ethical issues throughout the book and in the assignment materials.

This is the ninth edition of this text, and that is a testimonial to its effectiveness. But it also is a testimonial to our former colleagues, students and adoptors who, in each prior edition, have shared their thoughts and suggestions and driven us to change and adapt it to better meet the needs of today's students and adopting faculty.

Our Philosophy

Introduce the simple concepts early, revisit concepts at more complex levels as students gain understanding, and provide appropriate real-company examples at every stage—that's our philosophy. Our goal is for students to be able to read and interpret a real company's financial statements, balance sheet, income statement, and statement of cash flows.

We want students to view accounting as a tool that enhances their understanding of economic events. Students should be asking questions such as "After this transaction, are we better or worse off?" and "What do these statements tell us about the company's financial position and performance?"

Students cannot understand financial statements in isolation. Rather, they must look at all the financial statements within the context of the company's business environment. They need to understand the accrual basis of accounting that underlies the balance sheet and income statement, but they must also understand the importance of cash as presented in the statement of cash flows. We present all three basic financial statements in the first five chapters. By presenting the statement of cash flows as Chapter 5, immediately after the presentation of the basics of accrual accounting, students learn the importance of all three statements and the unique information each statement presents before encountering details about financial reporting practices in the later chapters.

One of our colleagues, Hal Bierman, often focuses on an economic event by asking, "Are you happy or are you sad?" We believe that accounting provides a way to understand what is happening and to answer that question. You might think of the basic financial statements as scorecards in the most fundamental economic contests. Each year the financial statements help you answer the most important questions: Are you happy or sad? Did you make or lose money? Are you prospering or just surviving? Will you have the cash you need for the next big step?

Who Should Use this Book?

Introduction to Financial Accounting, 9/E, presupposes no prior knowledge of accounting and is suitable for any undergraduate or MBA student enrolled in a financial accounting course. It deals with important topics that all business students should study. We have aimed to present relevant subject matter and to present it clearly and accessibly.

This text is oriented to the user of financial statements but gives ample attention to the needs of potential accounting practitioners. *IFA*, 9/E, stresses underlying concepts yet makes them concrete with numerous illustrations, many taken from recent corporate annual reports. Moreover, accounting procedures such as transaction analysis, journalizing, and posting are given due consideration where appropriate. Managers and accountants can develop a better understanding of the economic consequences of a company's transactions by summarizing those transactions into journal entries and T-accounts. However, the ultimate objective is an understanding of financial position and prospects, which we achieve by a focus on the balance sheet equation.

Enhanced Chapter Organization

- Increased emphasis on the Statement of Cash Flows by moving it to Chapter 5, completely revised chapter simplifies the presentation enough for coverage early in the course.
- We combined Chapters 8 and 9 from the last edition to create a new Chapter 9. This change streamlines coverage of liabilities, interest, bonds, and leases.
- We deleted Chapter 14 from the 8th edition, Conceptual Framework and Measurement Techniques, with essential material integrated into other chapters.

Enhanced Emphasis on Financial Statement Analysis

- **NEW Financial Statement Portfolio, located right after Chapter 2!** This insert provides a visual roadmap to financial statement analysis by highlighting key financial ratios and how to derive them from the financial statements. The Financial Statement Portfolio also refers students to appropriate chapters in the book for in-depth coverage of these ratios. A convenient tab gives students easy reference to the Portfolio all semester long.
- **NEW "Interpreting Financial Statements"** sections in each chapter permit students to pause and ponder how to use the information they are learning to better understand the financial position and prospects of a company.
- **NEW "Analyzing and Interpreting Financial Statements" problems at the end of each chapter**. Each problem set includes financial statement research, analyses of Starbucks financial statements, and analysis of other companies' financial statements using the internet.
- **NEW Focus on Starbucks' Annual Report** to illustrate various methods for analyzing financial statements. (See portions of Starbucks 10K in the appendix of this book.) By using one company throughout the book, students get a complete picture of its operations. Problem material at the end of each chapter asks students to analyze Starbucks' financial results.

Retained and Enhanced Features

- Expanded treatment of ethics, with both text coverage and end-of-chapter problems focusing on this important topic in nearly every chapter.
- Critical Thinking Exercises in the assignment material of each chapter that ask students to consider conceptual issues that may have no right answer.
- Business First Boxes in each chapter, new or completely revised. These boxes provide insights into operations at well-known domestic and international companies, accenting today's real-world issues.

Teaching and Learning Support: Because Resources Should Simplify, Not Overwhelm A successful accounting course requires more than a well-written book. Today's classroom requires a dedicated teacher and a fully integrated teaching package. The following material supports this title.

Supplements for Instructors

ONLINE AND TECHNOLOGY RESOURCES

Instructor's Resource Center (www.prenhall.com/horngren): This Prentice Hall resource depository hosts the following resources: Instructor's Manual, Test Item File, TestgGen for PC/MAC, PowerPoints, end of chapter Excel templates and solutions, and Test Item File in Blackboard and WebCT formats.

Instructor Resource Center on CD-ROM—Everything you need where you need it. With a new interface and searchable database, sorting through specific resources has never been easier. The Prentice Hall Instructor Resource Center/CD-ROM increases your effectiveness and saves you time and effort. Harness the power of having all of your resources in one well-organized place. Includes Instructor's Manual, Test Item File, TestGen, Solutions Manual, and Powerpoints.

Test Gen for PC/MAC—This PC/MAC-compatible test generating software, new for the 9th edition is powerful and easy to use. It is preloaded with all of the questions from the new Test Item File and allows users to manually or randomly view test bank questions and drag and drop them to create a test. Add or modify questions using the built-in Question Editor, print up to twenty five variations of a single test, deliver the test on a local area network use the built-in Quiz-master feature, and much more. Technical support is available at media.support@pearsoned.com or 1-800-6-PROFESSOR between 8:00–5:00 P.M. (C.S.T). Test Gen EQ available on Instructor Resource CD-ROM.

PowerPoint Slides: Comprehensive slides designed to aid in presentation of key chapter concepts. Available online and on the Instructor's Resource CD-ROM.

Print Resources

INSTRUCTOR'S RESOURCE MANUAL BY SCOTT YETMAR Contains the following elements for each chapter of the text: chapter overviews, chapter outlines organized by objectives, teaching tips, chapter quiz, transparency masters derived from textbook exhibits, and suggested readings.

SOLUTIONS MANUAL BY TEXT AUTHORS: COMPLETE SOLUTIONS TO END OF CHAPTER PROBLEMS, EXERCISES AND QUESTIONS. Special thanks to Carolyn Streuly for reviewing this material.

TEST ITEM FILE BY ZANE SWANSON The Test Item File includes multiple choice, true/false, exercises, comprehensive problems, short answer problems, critical thinking essay questions, etc. Each test item is tied to the corresponding learning objective, has an assigned difficulty level, and provides a page reference.

Solutions Transparencies on Acetate: Ideal for Classroom Presentations and Lectures.

Supplements for Students

Excel Templates for end of chapter problems—For each chapter, selected problems have readymade templates designed to help students solve problems using excel. Gives students a chance to practice and improve skills. Templates on Companion Website.

Companion Website—An excellent online resource center for students, containing key resources such as PowerPoint presentations, excel templates, and self-study quizzes.

ACKNOWLEDGMENTS

Our appreciation extends to our present and former mentors, colleagues, and students. This book and our enthusiasm for accounting grew out of their collective contributions to our knowledge and experience. We particularly appreciate the following individuals who supplied helpful comments and reviews of drafts of this edition and previous editions.

8th Edition Reviewers

John E. Armstrong, Dominican College

Frances L. Ayres, University of Oklahoma

Paul E. Bayes, East Tennessee State University

Martin J. Birr, Indiana University

Nancy Cassidy, Texas A&M University

Michele J. Daley, Rice University

Allan R. Drebin, Northwestern University

Robert Dunn, Georgia Institute of Technology

Al Hartgraves, Emory University

Gregory D. Kane, University of Delaware

Sungsoo Kim, Rutgers University

April Klein, New York University

Mark J. Myring, Ball State University

Brian M. Nagle, Duquesne University

Elizabeth Plummer, Southern Methodist University

Chandra Seethamraju, Washington University, St. Louis

Bill Shoemaker, University of Dallas

William Smith, Xavier University

Patrick T. Wirtz, University of Detroit Mercy

Previous Reviewers

Frances Ayers, University of Oklahoma; Roderick S. Barclay, University of Texas at Dallas; Ronald S. Barden, Georgia State University; LuAnn Bean, Pittsburg State University; Michele J. Daley, Rice University; Patricia A. Doherty, Boston University; Philip D. Drake, Thunderbird, The American Graduate School of International Management; Allan R. Drebin, Northwestern University; D. Jacque Grinnell, University of Vermont; M. Zafar

Iqbal, California Polytechnic State University-San Luis Obispo; John L. Norman Jr., Keller Graduate School of Management; Renee A. Price, University of Nebraska; and James A. Schweikart, Rhode Island College. We would also like to thank those who gave valuable feedback on previous editions: Roderick S. Barclay, University of Texas at Dallas; Mary Barth, Stanford University; Marianne Bradford, The University of Tennesse; David T. Collins, Bellarmine College; Ray D. Dillon, Georgia State University; Patricia A. Doherty, Boston University; Alan H. Falcon, Loyola Marymount University; Anita Feller, University of Illinois; Richard Frankel, University of Michigan; John D. Gould, Western Carolina University; Leon J. Hanouille, Syracuse University; Al Hartgraves, Emory University; Suzanne Hartley, Franklin University; Peter Huey, Collin County Community College; Yuji Ijiri, Carnegie Mellon University; Joan Luft, Michigan State University; Maureen McNichols, Stanford University; Mohamed Onsi, Syracuse University; Patrick M. Premo, St. Bonaventure University; Leo A. Ruggle, Mankato State University; James A. Schweikart, University of Richmond; Robert Swieringa, Cornell University; Katherene P. Terrell, University of Central Oklahoma; Michael G. Vasilou, DeVry Institute of Technology, Chicago; Deborah Welch, Tyler Junior College; Christine Wiedman, University of Western Ontario; and Peter D. Woodlock, Youngstown State University.

Finally, our thanks to the following people at Prentice Hall: Steve Deitmer, Wendy Craven, Sam Goffinet, Jane Avery, Beth Toland, Richard Bretan, Arnold Vila, Michael Reynolds, Caroline Kasterine, Nancy Welcher.

Comments from users are welcome.

Charles T. Horngren
Gary L. Sundem
John A. Elliott
Donna R. Philbrick

Introduction to Financial Accounting

Accounting: The Language of Business

CHAPTER 1

LEARNING OBJECTIVES

After studying this chapter, you should be able to:

1. Explain how accounting information assists in making decisions.

2. Describe the components of the balance sheet.

3. Analyze business transactions and relate them to changes in the balance sheet.

4. Compare the features of sole proprietorships, partnerships, and corporations.

5. Identify how the owners' equity section in a corporate balance sheet differs from that in a sole proprietorship or a partnership.

6. Describe auditing and how it enhances the value of financial information.

7. Explain the regulation of financial reporting.

8. Evaluate the role of ethics in the accounting process.

Accounting is the language of business. It is the method companies use to communicate financial information to their employees and to the public. Information is important for many decisions. You have probably bought a latte in, or at least walked by, one of Starbucks' 7,000 coffee stores throughout the world. Did you know that you could also buy a share of Starbucks stock, making you a part owner of Starbucks? To buy a latte, you want to know how it tastes. To buy a share of stock, you want to know about the financial condition and prospects of Starbucks Corporation. You would want to own part of Starbucks only if you think it will continue to be successful. To learn this, you need to know accounting. By the time you finish reading this book, you will be comfortable reading the financial reports of Starbucks and other companies. You will be able to use those reports to assess the financial health of these companies.

Starbucks first issued shares of stock to the public in 1992. If you had bought shares at that time, today your investment would be worth $20 for every $1 you invested. Will Starbucks continue to be a good investment? No one can predict with certainty the financial prospects of Starbucks. However, the financial statements included in Appendix A of this book can give you clues. A search of the Internet can provide more information. Yet, only if you understand accounting will you be able to make sense of this financial information.

Starbucks is a young, fast-growing company. It has established a worldwide reputation in a short time. Recently, it was named one of the Top 5 Global Brands of the Year by Brandchannel.com's Readers Choice survey. It has consistently been among *Fortune* magazine's 100 Best Companies to Work For. *Business Ethics* magazine

A group of Japanese teens gathers outside the world's busiest Starbucks in Tokyo's Shibuya shopping district. From Beijing to Bangkok, Starbucks is converting Asian tea lovers into fans of frappuccino and other frothy drinks. Starbucks reports its economic performance in its financial statements. As you read this text, you will learn how to read and analyze the financial statements of Starbucks and other companies, large and small, throughout the world.

selected it among its 100 Best Corporate Citizens. The former chief executive officer of Starbucks, Howard Schultz, was selected by *Business Week* as one of the Top 25 Best Managers in the country. Finally, *Fortune* named Starbucks the Most Admired Brand in the food services category 2 years in a row and ranked it America's eighth most admired company in 2004. Despite all these awards, it is important to know something about Starbucks' financial prospects. Let's look at a few financial facts. Most of these facts are in Appendix A, but you need not find them at this time. You will learn more about them as you proceed through this book.

In 2003, Starbucks' total revenues—the amount the company received for all the items sold—was $4.1 billion, compared with only $700 million in 1996. The net income—the profit that Starbucks made—was $436 million, up from only $42 million in 1996. Total assets—the value of the items owned by Starbucks—grew from less than $900 million to more than $2.7 billion from 1996 to 2003. You can see that the amount of business done by Starbucks has grown quickly. However, there is much more to be learned from the details in Starbucks' financial statements. You will learn about revenues, income, assets, and other details of accounting as you read this book. ■

As we embark on our journey into the world of financial accounting, we explore what it takes for a company such as Starbucks to manage its financial activities and how investors use this accounting information to better understand Starbucks. Keep this in mind: The same basic accounting framework that supported a small coffee company like Starbucks in 1992 supports the larger company today, and indeed it supports businesses big and small, old and new, worldwide.

accounting
The process of identifying, recording, and summarizing economic information and reporting it to decision makers.

financial accounting
The field of accounting that serves external decision makers, such as stockholders, suppliers, banks, and government agencies.

This book is an introduction to financial accounting. **Accounting** is a process of identifying, recording, and summarizing economic information and reporting it to decision makers. **Financial accounting** focuses on the specific needs of decision makers external to the organization, such as stockholders, suppliers, banks, and government agencies. You probably expect to see a bunch of rules and procedures about how to record and report financial information. Well, you are correct. You will see all those. However, our philosophy about financial accounting goes beyond rules and procedures. To use your financial accounting training effectively, you must also understand the underlying business transactions that give rise to the economic information and why the information is helpful in making financial decisions.

We hope that you want to know how businesses work. When you understand that Starbucks' financial reports help its management make decisions about what products to produce and sell, as well as help investors to assess the performance and prospects of Starbucks, you will see why being able to read and interpret these reports is important. Both outside investors and internal managers need this information.

Our goal is to help you understand business transactions—to know how they create accounting information and how decision makers both inside the company (managers) and outside the company (investors) use this information in deciding how, when, and what to buy or sell. In the process, you get to learn about some of the world's premier companies. You may wonder about what it costs to open a new Starbucks store. Are these new stores worth that kind of huge investment? How many people visit each Starbucks store every year? Can Starbucks keep track of them all, and are there enough customers to make the stores profitable? If investors consider purchasing Starbucks stock, what do they need to know to decide whether the current price is a good one? We cannot answer every such question you might ask, but we explore some exciting aspects of business and use business examples to illustrate the uses of accounting information.

In pursuing actual business examples, we consider details about many of the 30 companies in the Dow Jones Industrial Average (the Dow), the most commonly reported stock market index in the world. Well-known companies, such as Coca-Cola, Microsoft, and McDonald's, are among these 30 companies, along with many other large but less familiar companies, such as International Paper and SBC Communications. Exhibit 1-1 lists the 30 Dow companies, and the Business First box on p. 6 describes the Dow Jones

Symbol	Company	Total Sales	Symbol	Company	Total Sales
WMT	Wal-Mart Stores Inc.	$244.5	JNJ	Johnson & Johnson	$36.3
GM	General Motors Corp.	186.8	MSFT	Microsoft Corp.	32.2
XOM	ExxonMobil Corp.	178.9	UTX	United Technologies Corp.	28.0
GE	General Electric Co.	130.7	INTC	Intel Corp.	26.8
C	Citigroup Inc.	92.6	DIS	Walt Disney Co.	25.3
IBM	International Business		IP	International Paper Co.	25.0
	Machines Corp.	81.2	DD	E. I. DuPont de Nemours & Co.	24.0
MO	Altria Group, Inc.	80.4	AXP	American Express Co.	23.8
HD	Home Depot Inc.	58.2	HON	Honeywell International Inc.	22.3
HWP	Hewlett-Packard Co.	56.6	AA	Alcoa Inc.	20.3
BA	Boeing Co.	54.1	CAT	Caterpillar Inc.	20.2
MRK	Merck & Co. Inc.	51.8	KO	Coca-Cola Co.	19.6
JPM	JP Morgan Chase & Co.	43.4	MMM	3M Company	16.3
PG	Procter & Gamble Co.	43.4	MCD	McDonald's Corp.	15.4
SBC	SBC Communications Inc.	43.1	EK	Eastman Kodak Co.	12.8
T	AT&T Corp.	37.8			

Exhibit 1-1
Dow Industrials
Ranked by Total 2002 Sales ($ in billions)

Industrial Average. We also consider some younger and faster-growing companies, such as Starbucks, Cisco, Apple, and Timberland. For now, we start with the basics.

The Nature of Accounting

Accounting organizes and summarizes economic information so decision makers can use it. Accountants present this information in reports called financial statements. To prepare these statements, accountants analyze, record, quantify, accumulate, summarize, classify, report, and interpret economic events and their financial effects on the organization.

A company's accounting system is the series of steps by which it initially records information and converts it into financial statements. Accountants analyze the information needed by managers and other decision makers and create the accounting system that best meets those needs. Bookkeepers and computers then perform the routine tasks of collecting and compiling economic information. The real value of any accounting system lies in the information it provides.

Consider the accounting system at your school. It collects information about tuition charges and payments and tracks the status of each student. Your school must be able to bill individuals with unpaid balances. It must be able to schedule courses and hire faculty to meet the course demands of students. It must ensure that tuition and other cash inflows are sufficient to pay the faculty and keep the buildings warm (or cool) and well lit. If your experience is like that of most students, you can find some flaws with your school's accounting system. Perhaps there are too many waiting lines at registration or too many complicated procedures in filing for financial aid. If you are lucky, you have experienced electronic registration for courses and made all your tuition payments in response to bills received in the mail. The right information system can streamline your life. Every business maintains an accounting system, from the store where you bought this book to the company that issued the credit card you used. MasterCard and Visa maintain fast, complicated accounting systems. At any moment, thousands of credit card transactions occur around the globe, and accounting systems keep track of them all. When you use your charge card, a scanner reads it electronically and transmits the transaction amount over phone lines to the card company's central computer.

Why did the Dow Jones Industrial Average (DJI) fall from nearly 12,000 in January 2000 to near 7,000 at the end of 2002 and then rise again to more than 10,500 by early 2004? What does this mean to investors? To explain this 40 percent drop followed by a large recovery, you need to understand the DJI. However, to fully understand the reasons for the drop, you need to understand accounting—what the financial reports prepared by companies really mean.

The DJI is one of many indices used to describe the performance of stock markets around the world. All indices provide a picture of what is happening on average to the value of securities owned by investors. The Dow began as the average value of an investment in one share of each of 12 stocks and was first published in 1896 by Charles Dow. To calculate it, he simply added the prices of the 12 stocks and divided by 12. It began at 40.94 but fell to an all-time low of 28.48 in August of that year. The calculation today is more complex, but the basic concept is unchanged. Since 1928, the number of stocks in the DJI has been constant at 30, but there have been 41 changes in the composition of the average. These changes reflect the dynamic nature of American industry. The original DJI had several auto and petroleum companies to capture the massive importance of these industries. Among the original twelve companies were U.S. Leather, U.S. Rubber, American Tobacco, Tennessee Coal & Iron, and Laclede Gas. Of these, only Laclede Gas, the Missouri utility, still exists—although it is not included in the Dow. Today, only General Electric remains from the original twelve, although predecessors of ExxonMobil and General Motors were also included. McDonald's replaced American Tobacco in 1985, Wal-Mart replaced Woolworth in 1997, and Home Depot replaced Sears in 1999. Technology companies have only appeared in the DJI in significant numbers recently with Hewlett-Packard, Microsoft, and Intel all added since 1997. Most recently, Pfizer, Verizon, and AIG replaced Eastman Kodak, AT&T, and International Paper in 2004. It is also interesting to note that the largest one-day Dow increase, 15 percent, was in October 1931. The largest drop was in October 1987 when the Dow fell 23 percent.

Although indices such as the DJI give a picture of how stock prices have changed, they do not explain why those changes occurred. Researchers have shown that accounting results affect stock prices. Therefore, most financial analysts rely on companies' financial reports, along with other information, to explain movements in stock prices. For example, the *New York Times* focused on corporate profits in its report on October 6, 2003: "Stocks rose on Monday for the fourth session in a row as investors bet that the economy and corporate profits are on the mend and wait for the earnings season to heat up." Annual and quarterly reports, including balance sheets, income statements, and cash flow statements, provide much of the information investors use. They use this financial information to predict future financial positions and prospects of companies. In this way, they try to anticipate movements in stock prices. The classic advice to investors is to "buy low and sell high." Although this is never easy, accounting information can help investors to approach this ideal. The DJI fell when the economy weakened and companies' profits declined. It rebounded when companies' financial reports indicated that financial results were on the upswing.

Sources: "Stocks Slide Amid Worries About Economy and Corporate Profits," *New York Times*, October 6, 2003; Dow Jones Indexes (http://averages.dowjones.com/jsp/industrialAverages.jsp?sideMenu =true); "The Motley Fool," *The Seattle Times* (February 15, 2004), p. E2.

The computer verifies that your charges are within acceptable limits and approves or denies the transaction. At the same time, the computer also conducts security checks. For example, if your credit card were being used simultaneously to buy groceries in Chicago and to make long distance phone calls in Korea, the system might sense that something is wrong and require you to call a customer service representative before the credit card company approves the charges. Without reliable accounting systems, credit cards simply could not exist.

OBJECTIVE 1

Explain how accounting information assists in making decisions.

Accounting as an Aid to Decision Making

Accounting information is useful to anyone making decisions that have economic consequences. Such decision makers include managers, owners, investors, and politicians. For example,

- When the engineering department of **Apple Computer** developed the iMac, accountants developed reports on the potential profitability of the product, including estimated sales and estimated production and selling costs. Managers used the reports to help decide whether to produce and market the product.
- When QBC Information Services, a small consulting firm with five employees, decides who to promote (and possibly who to fire), the managing partner produces reports on the productivity of each employee and compares productivity to the salary and other costs associated with the employee's work for the year.
- When portfolio managers at **Vanguard Group** consider buying stock in either **General Motors** or **Volvo**, they consult published accounting reports to compare the most recent financial results of the companies. The information in the reports helps the managers decide which company would be the better investment choice.
- When Senator Phil Gramm introduced President Bush's Homeland Security plan, he needed to know how the proposed plan would affect the country's budget. Accounting information helped predict how much the plan would cost and where the money would come from.
- When **Bank of America** considers a loan to a company that wants to expand, it examines the historical performance of the company and analyzes projections the company provides about how it will use the borrowed funds to produce new business.

Accounting helps decision making by showing where and when a company spends money and makes commitments, providing information for evaluating financial performance, and illustrating the financial implications of choosing one plan instead of another. Accounting also helps predict the future effects of decisions, and it helps direct attention to current problems, imperfections, and inefficiencies, as well as opportunities.

Consider some basic relationships in the decision-making process:

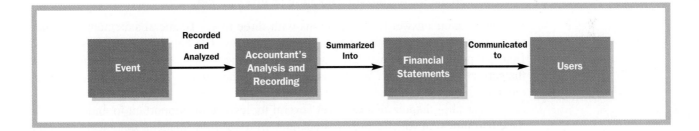

When economic events occur, accountants analyze and record the events. Periodically, accountants summarize the results of the events into financial statements. Users then rely on the financial statements when making their decisions. Our focus includes all four boxes. All financial accounting courses cover the analysis and recording of information and preparing financial statements. We pay more attention to the underlying business processes creating the events and to the way in which the financial reports help decision makers to take action.

Financial and Management Accounting

The financial statements we discuss in this book are common to all areas of accounting. Accountants often distinguish "financial accounting" from "management accounting." The major distinction between financial and management accounting is their use by two different classes of decision makers. Recall that financial accounting serves external decision makers, such as stockholders, suppliers, banks, and government agencies. In contrast, **management accounting** serves internal decision makers, such as top executives, department heads, college deans, hospital administrators, and people at other management levels

management accounting
The field of accounting that serves internal decision makers, such as top executives, department heads, college deans, hospital administrators, and people at other management levels within an organization.

within the organization.[1] The two fields of accounting share many of the same procedures for analyzing and recording the effects of individual transactions.

The most common source of financial information used by investors and others outside the company is the **annual report.** The annual report is a document prepared by management and distributed to current and potential investors to inform them about the company's past performance and future prospects. Firms distribute their annual reports to stockholders automatically. Potential investors may request the report by calling the investor relations department of the company or visiting its Web site.

Most large companies use their annual reports to promote the company, using pleasing photographs extensively to communicate their message. Also, in addition to the financial statements, annual reports include

1. A letter from corporate management
2. A discussion and analysis by management of recent economic events
3. Footnotes that explain many elements of the financial statements in more detail
4. The report of the independent auditors
5. A statement of management's responsibility for preparation of the financial statements
6. Other corporate information

Although all elements of the annual report are important, we concentrate on the principal financial statements and how accountants collect and report this information. You can also find U.S. companies' financial statements in their **Form 10-K** that they file annually with the Securities and Exchange Commission. Appendix A contains excerpts from Starbucks' 10-K, including all its financial statements.

The primary questions concerning a firm's financial success that decision makers want answered are:

What is the financial picture of the organization on a given day?
How well did the organization do during a given period?

Accountants answer these questions with three major financial statements: balance sheet, income statement, and statement of cash flows. The balance sheet focuses on the financial picture as of a given day. The income statement and cash flow statement focus on the performance over time. We discuss the balance sheet in this chapter, the income statement in Chapter 2, and the statement of cash flows in Chapter 5. After introducing the balance sheet, this chapter also explores several topics that are important to understanding the environment in which a business operates. You can find financial statements for most companies on their Web sites, as described in the Business First box on p. 9.

The Balance Sheet

One of the major financial statements prepared by the accounting system is the **balance sheet**, also called the **statement of financial position.** The balance sheet shows the financial status of a company at a particular instant in time. It is essentially a snapshot of the organization at a given date. It has two counterbalancing sections. The left side lists the resources of the firm (everything the firm owns and controls—from cash to buildings, etc.). The right side lists the claims against the resources. The resources and claims form the **balance sheet equation:**

$$\text{Assets} = \text{Liabilities} + \text{Owners' equity}$$

Margin glossary

annual report
A document prepared by management and distributed to current and potential investors to inform them about the company's past performance and future prospects.

Form 10-K
A document that U.S. companies file annually with the Securities and Exchange Commission. It contains the companies' financial statements.

OBJECTIVE 2
Describe the components of the balance sheet.

balance sheet (statement of financial position)
A financial statement that shows the financial status of a business entity at a particular instant in time.

balance sheet equation
Assets = Liabilities + Owners' equity

---

[1]For a book-length presentation of the field, see Charles T. Horngren, Gary L. Sundem, and William O. Stratton, *Introduction to Management Accounting*, 13th ed. (Upper Saddle River, NJ: Prentice-Hall, 2005), the companion volume to this textbook.

BUSINESS FIRST

Until the last decade, annual reports were generally glossy documents produced by companies about 3 months after year-end. In addition to being a primary source of financial information about the company, annual reports also contain much other information (some might call it propaganda) about the company. However, the Internet has changed and continues to change the way investors get information about a company. Today, more information is available more quickly on the Web than on paper.

Most publicly held companies, and certainly the large ones, include their annual reports on their Web site. You can usually find a company's annual report in a segment of its site called "Investors" or "Investor Relations." Often this comes under a heading such as "Corporate Information," "About the Company," or some such title included on the company's home page.

The first step many companies took was to save copies of their annual reports as PDF files that investors could read but could not download into spreadsheets or word processors. An example of such a report is the 2003 annual report of Honda Motor Company, Ltd. (http://world.honda.com/investors/annualreport/). This report on the Web is identical to the paper version. In contrast, Microsoft provides options to download any part of its annual report. To download its balance sheet (the statement introduced in this chapter) for 2003, you can go to http://www.microsoft.com/msft/ar03/downloads/balancesheets.xls. With this file, you can perform any analyses supported by Excel.

There is even a competition for the best annual reports. The League of American Communications Professionals (LACP) rates annual reports based on how well they communicate their messages. Among the categories rated are report cover, letter to shareholders, report narrative, report financials, readability, and clarity. The five top 2002 annual reports, selected from more than 900 entries, were Henkel (Dusseldorf, Germany), Jack In The Box, FEMSA (Monterrey, Mexico), U.S. Department of State, and Lockheed Martin.

Some executives use their company's annual report to educate investors. Warren Buffett, chairman and CEO of Berkshire Hathaway, always includes a long letter explaining his philosophies as well as his company's performance. In 2002, his letter contained 20 pages of insightful comments. In 2001, he even compared financial reporting to his golf game.

Annual reports are venerable documents that have been useful to investors for many years. They are not likely to go away. However, their content and format are both changing. Use of the Internet opens up possibilities for presenting financial information (as well as other information) to investors that were previously impossible. This should lead to better information for those making investment decisions and therefore better functioning capital markets.

Sources: LACP 2002 Annual Report Competition Results, http://www.lacp.com/2002vision/competition.htm; Honda Motor Company, 2003 Annual Report; Microsoft, 2003 Annual Report; Berkshire Hathaway, 2001 and 2002 Annual Reports.

We define the terms in this equation as follows:

Assets are economic resources that the company expects to help generate future cash inflows or reduce or prevent future cash outflows. Examples are cash, inventories, and equipment.

Liabilities are economic obligations of the organization to outsiders, or claims against its assets by outsiders. An example is a debt to a bank. When a company takes out a loan or other type of liability, it generally signs a promissory note that states the terms of repayment. Accountants use the term **notes payable** to describe the existence of promissory notes.

Owners' equity is the owners' claim on the organization's assets. Because debt holders have first claim on the assets, the owners' claim is equal to the assets less the liabilities.

To illustrate the balance sheet, suppose Hector Lopez, a salaried employee of a local bicycle company, quits his job and opens his own bicycle shop, Biwheels Company, on January 2, 20X2. Lopez has heard about the troubles of new businesses that lack money,

assets
Economic resources that a company expects to help generate future cash inflows or help reduce future cash outflows.

liabilities
Economic obligations of the organization to outsiders, or claims against its assets by outsiders.

notes payable
Promissory notes that are evidence of a debt and state the terms of payment.

owners' equity
The owners' claims on an organization's assets, or total assets less total liabilities.

so he invests plenty: $400,000. Then Lopez, acting for the business, borrows $100,000 from a local bank. That gives Biwheels $500,000 in assets, all currently in the form of cash. The opening balance sheet of this new business enterprise follows:

Biwheels Company
Balance Sheet
January 2, 20X2

Assets		Liabilities and Owners' Equity	
Cash	$500,000	Liabilities (note payable)	$100,000
		Lopez, capital	400,000
Total assets	$500,000	Total liabilities and owners' equity	$500,000

Because the balance sheet shows the financial status at a particular point in time, it always includes a particular date. The elements in this balance sheet show the financial status of the Biwheels Company as of January 2, 20X2. The balance sheet lists the company's assets at this point in time ($500,000) on the left. They are balanced on the right by an equal amount of liability and owners' equity ($100,000 liability owed to the bank plus $400,000 paid in by Lopez). The double underscores (double ruling) under the column totals denote final numbers. Note that we always keep the left and right sides in balance.

When someone first starts a business, the owners' equity is equal to the total amount invested by the owner or owners. As illustrated by "Lopez, capital" in the Biwheels Company example, accountants often use the term capital instead of owners' equity to designate an owner's investment in the business. We can emphasize the residual, or "left-over," nature of owners' equity by reexpressing the balance sheet equation as follows:

$$\text{Owners' equity} = \text{Assets} - \text{Liabilities}$$

This shows that the owners' claims are the amount left over after deducting the liabilities from the assets.

Balance Sheet Transactions

entity
An organization or a section of an organization that stands apart from other organizations and individuals as a separate economic unit.

transaction
Any event that both affects the financial position of an entity and that an accountant can reliably record in money terms.

OBJECTIVE 3

Analyze business transactions and relate them to changes in the balance sheet.

Every transaction entered into by a company, or an entity, affects the balance sheet. An **entity** is an organization or a section of an organization that stands apart from other organizations and individuals as a separate economic unit. A **transaction** is any event that affects the financial position of an entity and that an accountant can reliably record in money terms. When accountants record a transaction, they make at least two entries so the total assets always equal the total liabilities plus owners' equity. That is, we must maintain the equality of the balance sheet equation for every transaction. If a balance sheet balances before a transaction, adding or subtracting a single amount would necessarily leave the balance sheet out of balance. An accountant who prepares a balance sheet that does not balance has made a mistake somewhere because the balance sheet must always balance. Because single entries cannot maintain the balance in the balance sheet, we often call the system that records transactions a *double-entry* accounting system, as we explain further in Chapter 3.

Let's take a look at some transactions of Biwheels Company to see how typical transactions affect the balance sheet.

Transaction 1, Initial Investment. The first Biwheels transaction was the investment by the owner on January 2, 20X2. Lopez deposited $400,000 in a business bank account entitled Biwheels Company. The transaction affects the balance sheet equation as follows:

	Assets	=	Liabilities	+	Owners' Equity
	Cash				Lopez, Capital
(1)	+400,000	=			+400,000
					(Owner investment)

This transaction increases both the assets, specifically Cash, and the owners' equity of the business, specifically Lopez, Capital. It does not affect liabilities. Why? Because Lopez's business has no obligation to an outside party because of this transaction. We use a parenthetical note, "Owner investment," to identify the reason for the transaction's effect on owners' equity. The total amounts on the left side of the equation are equal to the total amounts on the right side, as they should be.

Transaction 2, Loan from Bank. On January 2, 20X2, Biwheels Company also borrows from a bank, signing a promissory note for $100,000. The $100,000 increases the business's cash. The effect of this loan transaction on the balance sheet equation is:

	Assets	=	Liabilities + Owners' Equity	
			Note	
	Cash		Payable	Lopez, Capital
(1)	+400,000	=		+400,000
(2)	+100,000	=	+100,000	
Bal.	500,000	=	100,000	400,000
	500,000		500,000	

The loan increases the asset, Cash, and increases the liability, Note Payable, by the same amount, $100,000. After completing the transaction, Biwheels has assets of $500,000, liabilities of $100,000, and owners' equity of $400,000. As always, the sums of the individual account balances (abbreviated Bal.) on each side of the equation are equal.

Transaction 3, Acquire Store Equipment for Cash. On January 3, 20X2, Biwheels acquires miscellaneous store equipment for $15,000 cash. Store equipment is an example of a **long-lived asset**—an asset that the company expects to provide services for more than 1 year.

long-lived asset
An asset that a company expects to provide services for more than 1 year.

	Assets		=	Liabilities + Owners' Equity	
		Store		Note	Lopez,
	Cash	Equipment		Payable	Capital
Bal.	500,000		=	100,000	400,000
(3)	−15,000	+15,000	=		
Bal.	485,000	15,000	=	100,000	400,000
	500,000			500,000	

This transaction, the cash purchase of store equipment, increases one asset, Store Equipment, and decreases another asset, Cash, by the same amount. The form of the assets change, but the total amount of assets is unchanged. Moreover, the right-side items are completely unchanged.

Biwheels can prepare a balance sheet at any point in time, even after every transaction. The balance sheet for January 3, after the first three transactions, would look like this:

Biwheels Company
Balance Sheet January 3, 20X2

Assets		Liabilities and Owners' Equity	
Cash	$485,000	Liabilities (note payable)	$100,000
Store equipment	15,000	Lopez, capital	400,000
Total assets	$500,000	Total liabilities and owners' equity	$500,000

Transaction Analysis

account

A summary record of the changes in a particular asset, liability, or owners' equity.

Accountants record transactions in an organization's accounts. An **account** is a summary record of the changes in a particular asset, liability, or owners' equity, and the account balance is the total of all entries to the account to date. For example, Biwheels' cash account through January 3 shows increases of $400,000 and $100,000 and a decrease of $15,000, leaving an account balance of $485,000. The analysis of transactions is the heart of accounting. For each transaction, the accountant determines (1) which specific accounts the transaction affects, (2) whether it increases or decreases each account balance, and (3) the amount of the change in each account balance. After recording all the transactions for some period, the accountant will summarize these transactions into financial statements that managers, investors, and others use in their decision-making process.

Exhibit 1-2 shows how to analyze a series of transactions using the balance sheet equation. We number the transactions for easy reference. Examine the first three transactions in Exhibit 1-2, the analysis of the transactions that we discussed earlier.

Description of Transactions	Assets				=	Liabilities + Owners' Equity		
	Cash	+	Merchandise Inventory	+	Store Equipment =	Note Payable	+	Accounts Payable +	Lopez, Capital
(1) Initial investment	+400,000				=			+400,000
(2) Loan from bank	+100,000				= +100,000			
(3) Acquire store equipment for cash	−15,000			+15,000	=			
(4) Acquire inventory for cash	−120,000		+120,000		=			
(5) Acquire inventory on credit			+10,000		=		+10,000	
(6) Acquire inventory for cash plus credit	−10,000		+30,000		=		+20,000	
(7) Sale of equipment	+1,000			−1,000	=			
(8) Return of inventory acquired on January 6			−800		=		−800	
(9) Payments to creditors	−4,000				=		−4,000	
Balance, January 12, 20X2	352,000	+	159,200	+	14,000 =	100,000	+	25,200 +	400,000
			525,200					525,200

Exhibit 1-2
Biwheels Company
Analysis of Transactions for January 2–January 12, 20X2

Next, consider how to analyze each of the following additional transactions:

4. January 4. Biwheels acquires bicycles from a manufacturer for $120,000 cash.
5. January 5. Biwheels buys bicycle parts for $10,000 from a manufacturer. Biwheels will sell these parts in addition to the bicycles themselves. The manufacturer requires $4,000 by January 10 and the balance in 30 days.
6. January 6. Biwheels buys more bicycles from another manufacturer for $30,000. This manufacturer requires a cash down payment of $10,000, and Biwheels must pay the remaining balance in 60 days.
7. January 7. Biwheels sells a store showcase to a business neighbor after Lopez decides he dislikes it. Its selling price, $1,000, happens to be exactly equal to its cost. The neighbor pays cash.
8. January 8. Biwheels returns some inventory (which it had acquired on January 6 for $800) to the manufacturer for full credit (an $800 reduction of the amount that Biwheels owes the manufacturer).
9. January 10. Biwheels pays $4,000 to the manufacturer described in transaction 5.
10. January 12. Lopez remodels his home for $35,000, paying by check from his personal bank account.

Use the format in Exhibit 1-2 to analyze each transaction. Try to do your own analysis of each transaction before looking at the entries shown for it in the exhibit. For example, you could cover the numerical entries with a sheet of paper or a ruler and then proceed through each transaction, one by one.

INTERPRETING FINANCIAL STATEMENTS

Transaction 10 does not appear in Exhibit 1-2. Why not?

Answer

Transaction 10 is a personal transaction by Lopez and does not involve Biwheels as a business. Lopez would record it in his personal accounts, but it does not belong in Biwheels' business accounts. It is important for readers of financial statements to identify the entity accounted for in the financial statements—which in our case is Biwheels, a business.

Transaction 4, Purchase Inventory for Cash. Inventory refers to goods held by the company for the purpose of sale to customers. The bicycles are inventory, or Merchandise Inventory, to Biwheels. Inventory increases by the amount paid for the bicycles, and cash decreases by the same amount.

inventory
Goods held by a company for the purpose of sale to customers.

	Assets				Liabilities and Owners' Equity	
	Cash	Merchandise Inventory	Store Equipment		Note Payable	Lopez, Capital
Bal.	485,000		15,000	=	100,000	400,000
(4)	−120,000	+120,000		=		
Bal.	365,000	120,000	15,000	=	100,000	400,000
		500,000			500,000	

Transaction 5, Purchase Inventory on Credit. Companies throughout the world make most purchases on a credit basis instead of a cash basis. An authorized signature of the buyer is usually good enough to ensure payment. We call this practice buying on **open account.** The buyer records the money owed on its balance sheet as an account payable. Thus, an **account payable** is a liability that results from a purchase of goods or services on open account. As Exhibit 1-2 shows for this transaction, the merchandise inventory (an asset account) of Biwheels increases and we add an account payable (a liability account) in the amount of $10,000 to keep the equation in balance. Both total assets and total liabilities and owners' equity increase to $510,000.

open account
Buying or selling on credit, usually by just an "authorized signature" of the buyer.

account payable
A liability that results from a purchase of goods or services on open account.

	Assets			=	Liabilities + Owners' Equity		
	Cash	Merchandise Inventory	Store Equipment		Note Payable	Accounts Payable	Lopez, Capital
Bal.	365,000	120,000	15,000	=	100,000		400,000
(5)		+10,000		=		+10,000	
Bal.	365,000	130,000	15,000	=	100,000	10,000	400,000
		510,000				510,000	

Transaction 6, Purchase Inventory for Cash Plus Credit. This transaction illustrates a **compound entry** because it affects more than two balance sheet accounts (two asset accounts and one liability account in this case). Merchandise inventory increases by the full amount of its cost regardless of whether Biwheels makes its payment in full now, in full later, or partially now and partially later. Therefore, Biwheels' Merchandise Inventory (an asset account) increases by $30,000, Cash (an asset account) decreases by $10,000, and Accounts Payable (a liability account) increases by the difference, $20,000.

compound entry
A transaction that affects more than two accounts.

	Assets			=	Liabilities + Owners' Equity		
	Cash	Merchandise Inventory	Store Equipment		Note Payable	Accounts Payable	Lopez, Capital
Bal.	365,000	130,000	15,000	=	100,000	10,000	400,000
(6)	−10,000	+30,000		=		+20,000	
Bal.	355,000	160,000	15,000	=	100,000	30,000	400,000
		530,000				530,000	

Transaction 7, Sale of Asset for Cash. This transaction increases cash by $1,000 and decreases Store Equipment by $1,000. In this case, the transaction affects asset accounts only. One increases and one decreases, with no change in total assets. Liabilities and owners' equity are unchanged.

	Assets			=	Liabilities + Owners' Equity		
	Cash	Merchandise Inventory	Store Equipment		Note Payable	Accounts Payable	Lopez, Capital
Bal.	355,000	160,000	15,000	=	100,000	30,000	400,000
(7)	+1,000		−1,000	=			
Bal.	356,000	160,000	14,000	=	100,000	30,000	400,000
		530,000				530,000	

Transaction 8, Return of Inventory to Supplier. When a company returns merchandise to its suppliers for credit, the transaction reduces its merchandise inventory account and reduces its liabilities. In this instance, the amount of the decrease on each side of the equation is $800.

		Assets		=	Liabilities + Owners' Equity		
	Cash	Merchandise Inventory	Store Equipment		Note Payable	Accounts Payable	Lopez, Capital
Bal.	356,000	160,000	14,000	=	100,000	30,000	400,000
(8)		−800		=		−800	
Bal.	356,000	159,200	14,000	=	100,000	29,200	400,000
		529,200				529,200	

Transaction 9, Payment to Creditor. A **creditor** is one to whom the company owes money. For Biwheels, the manufacturer who supplied the bikes on credit is a creditor. Payments to the manufacturer decrease both assets (Cash) and liabilities (Accounts Payable) by $4,000.

creditor
A person or entity to whom a company owes money.

		Assets		=	Liabilities + Owners' Equity		
	Cash	Merchandise Inventory	Store Equipment		Note Payable	Accounts Payable	Lopez, Capital
Bal.	356,000	159,200	14,000	=	100,000	29,200	400,000
(9)	−4,000			=		−4,000	
Bal.	352,000	159,200	14,000	=	100,000	25,200	400,000
		525,200				525,200	

Preparing the Balance Sheet

To prepare a balance sheet, we can compute a cumulative total for each account in Exhibit 1-2 at any date. The following balance sheet uses the totals at the bottom of Exhibit 1-2. Observe once again that a balance sheet represents the financial impact of all transactions up to a specific point in time, here January 12, 20X2.

Biwheels Company
Balance Sheet
January 12, 20X2

Assets		Liabilities and Owner's Equity	
Cash	$352,000	Note payable	$100,000
Merchandise		Accounts payable	25,200
inventory	159,200	Total liabilities	$125,200
Store equipment	14,000	Lopez, capital	$400,000
Total	$525,200	Total	$525,200

As noted earlier, Biwheels could prepare a new balance sheet after each transaction. Obviously, such a practice would be awkward and unnecessary. Therefore, companies usually produce balance sheets when needed by managers and at the end of each quarter for reporting to the public.

Exhibit 1-3
Comparative
Consolidated
Condensed Balance
Sheets, September
28, 2003
(Dollars in
thousands)

	Starbucks	Jack In The Box
Assets		
Cash and cash equivalents	$ 200,907	$ 22,362
Inventories	342,944	31,699
Prepaid expenses	55,173	21,056
Property, plant and equipment	1,384,902	866,960
Other assets	745,820	233,873
Total assets	$2,729,746	$1,175,950
Liabilities and Stockholders' Equity		
Accounts payable	$ 168,984	$ 49,491
Long-term debt	4,354	433,984
Other liabilities	473,981	222,153
Total liabilities	647,319	705,628
Total owners' equity	2,082,427	470,322
Total liabilities and owners' equity	$2,729,746	$1,175,950

Examples of Actual Corporate Balance Sheets

To become more familiar with the balance sheet and its equation, consider the condensed balance sheet information for Starbucks and Jack In The Box for 2003 shown in Exhibit 1-3. Both Starbucks and Jack In The Box provide food services, but their strategies are different. Starbucks focuses on coffee, has almost four times as many outlets, and has expanded internationally. Jack In The Box has outlets in only 31 states. From the companies' balance sheets, we learn that Starbucks has 10 times more cash and inventories, but it has only 60 percent more property, plant, and equipment. Therefore, with about one-fourth as many outlets, Jack In The Box has more than twice as much invested in each outlet. Just think about the investment required by a restaurant compared with that in a coffee shop—the difference is logical. We also see that Jack In The Box has more debt, and Starbucks has more owners' equity.

Appendix A at the end of this book contains a complete set of the actual 2003 financial statements of Starbucks Corporation. As you proceed from chapter to chapter, you should examine the pertinent parts of these financial statements. In this way, you will become increasingly comfortable with actual financial reports. For example, the general format and some major items in Starbucks' balance sheet (Appendix A, pp. A12–A13) should be familiar by now. Notice that on September 28, 2003, Starbucks' total assets were $2,729,746,000, the same amount as the total liabilities and shareholders' (owners') equity. Every balance sheet maintains this equality. Details about various items in the balance sheet will gradually become more understandable as each chapter explains the nature of the various major financial statements and examines their components.

Summary Problems for Your Review

PROBLEM

Analyze the following additional transactions of Biwheels Company. Begin with the balances shown for January 12, 20X2, in Exhibit 1-2 on p. 12. Prepare an ending balance sheet for Biwheels Company (e.g., on January 16, after these additional transactions).

		Assets			=		Liabilities + Owners' Equity	
Description of Transaction	Cash	+	Merchandise Inventory	+	Store Equipment =	Note Payable +	Accounts Payable +	Lopez, Capital
Balance, January 12, 20X2	352,000	+	159,200	+	14,000 =	100,000 +	25,200 +	400,000
(i) Payment on bank loan	−10,000				=	−10,000		
(ii) Personal; no effect								
(iii) Acquire inventory, half for cash	−25,000	+	50,000		=		+ 25,000	
(iv) Payment to suppliers	−4,000				=		−4,000	
Balance, January 16	313,000	+	209,200	+	14,000 =	90,000 +	46,200 +	400,000

$$\$536,200 \qquad = \qquad \$536,200$$

Exhibit 1-4
Biwheels Company
Analysis of Additional January Transactions

i. Biwheels pays $10,000 on the bank loan (ignore interest).
ii. Lopez buys furniture for his home for $5,000, using his family's charge account at Macy's.
iii. Biwheels buys merchandise inventory for $50,000. Biwheels pays one-half the amount in cash and owes one-half on open account.
iv. Biwheels pays another $4,000 to its supplier of bicycles.

SOLUTION

See Exhibits 1-4 and 1-5. Note that we ignored transaction 2 because it is wholly personal. However, visualize how this transaction would affect Lopez's personal balance sheet. His assets, Home Furniture, would rise by $5,000 and his liabilities, Accounts Payable, would also rise by $5,000.

PROBLEM

Refer to the Starbucks financial statements reproduced in Appendix A and examine the balance sheets for 2002 and 2003 (pp. A12–A13). Respond to the following questions:

1. As of what date is the 2003 balance sheet prepared?
2. What are total assets for each of the 2 years shown in the balance sheets? What elements explain the difference in the asset levels for the 2 years?
3. Total assets increased by $515,354,000 from September 29, 2002 to September 28, 2003. What was the change in total liabilities plus shareholders' equity over that same time period?

Assets		Liabilities and Owner's Equity	
		Liabilities:	
Cash	$313,000	Note payable	$ 90,000
		Accounts payable	46,200
Merchandise inventory	209,200	Total liabilities	$136,200
Store equipment	14,000	Lopez, capital	400,000
Total	$536,200	Total	$536,200

Exhibit 1-5
Biwheels Company
*Balance Sheet
January 16, 20X2*

4. Of the following items on Starbucks' balance sheet, which are assets, which are liabilities, and which are shareholders' equity: Property, plant and equipment; Cash and cash equivalents; Long-term debt; Inventories; Accounts payable; and Common stock and additional paid-in-capital?

SOLUTION

1. Two balance sheets are presented. The most recent is dated September 28, 2003, and the other is dated September 29, 2002. The more recent one is in the left column. Footnote 1 to the financial statements, "Summary of Significant Accounting Policies," explains that the company uses a fiscal year that ends on the Sunday closest to September 30. Thus fiscal 2003 refers to the year ending September 28, 2003.
2. Total assets increased from \$2,214,392,000 to \$2,729,746,000. All assets except short-term investments increased during this time period. Starbucks recorded increases of more than \$100,000 in cash and cash equivalents, long-term investments, and property, plant and equipment, net.
3. Total liabilities and shareholders' equity increased by the same amount as the increase in total assets: \$515,354,000. The two increases must be the same to keep the balance sheet equation in balance.
4. Property, plant and equipment, cash and cash equivalents, and inventories are assets. The liabilities are long-term debt and accounts payable. Common stock and additional paid-in-capital is a shareholders' equity account.

Types of Ownership

OBJECTIVE 4

Compare the features of sole proprietorships, partnerships, and corporations.

Although most accounting processes are the same for all types of companies, a few differences arise, especially in accounting for owners' equity, because of the legal structure of the company. Therefore, you will find it useful to know something about the three basic forms of ownership structures for business entities: sole proprietorships, partnerships, and corporations.

Sole Proprietorships

sole proprietorship
A business with a single owner.

A **sole proprietorship** is a business with a single owner. Most often, the owner is also the manager. Therefore, sole proprietorships tend to be small retail establishments and individual professional businesses, such as neighborhood restaurants and dentists or attorneys who operate alone. Biwheels started out as a sole proprietorship owned and operated by Hector Lopez. From an accounting viewpoint, each sole proprietorship is a separate entity that is distinct from the proprietor. Thus, the cash in a dentist's business account is an asset of the dental practice, whereas the cash in the dentist's personal account is not. Similarly, Lopez's remodeling of his home (see transaction 10, p. 13) was a personal transaction, not a business transaction.

Partnerships

partnership
A form of organization that joins two or more individuals together as co-owners.

A **partnership** is an organization that joins two or more individuals who act as co-owners. Many auto dealerships are partnerships, as are groups of physicians or accountants who group together to provide services. Partnerships can be gigantic. The largest international accounting firms have thousands of partners. Again, from an accounting viewpoint, each partnership is an individual entity that is separate from the personal activities of each partner.

Corporations

Most large businesses, including all 30 Dow companies listed in Exhibit 1-1 (p. 5), are corporations. **Corporations** are business organizations created under state laws in the United States. The owners of a corporation have **limited liability,** which means that corporate creditors (such as banks or suppliers) ordinarily have claims against the corporate assets only, not against the personal assets of the owners. In contrast, owners in sole proprietorships and partnerships are usually personally liable for any obligations of the business. (An exception is limited liability partnerships, which limit the liability of partners.) Another difference is that the owners of proprietorships and partnerships are typically active managers of the business, whereas large corporations generally hire professional managers.

Most large corporations are **publicly owned.** This means that the company sells shares in its ownership to the public. Purchasers of the shares become shareholders (or stockholders). Large publicly owned corporations often have thousands of shareholders. In contrast, some corporations are **privately owned** by families, small groups of shareholders, or a single individual, with shares of ownership not publicly sold. Corporations in the United States often use one of the abbreviations Co., Corp., or Inc. in their names.

Internationally, organizational forms similar to corporations are common. In the United Kingdom, such companies frequently use the word "limited" (Ltd.) in their names. In many countries whose laws trace back to Spain, they use the initials S.A., which refer to Spanish words that we translate as "society anonymous," meaning that multiple unidentified owners stand behind the company. Not surprisingly, countries in the former Soviet Union have now created legal systems that permit corporate-style companies. They are also creating markets where the owners of these companies can buy and sell their ownership interests.

corporation
A business organization that is created by individual state laws.

limited liability
A feature of the corporate form of organization whereby corporate creditors (such as banks or suppliers) ordinarily have claims against the corporate assets only, not against the personal assets of the owners.

publicly owned
A corporation that sells shares in its ownership to the public.

privately owned
A corporation owned by a family, a small group of shareholders, or a single individual, in which shares of ownership are not publicly sold.

Advantages and Disadvantages of the Corporate Form

The corporate form of organization has many advantages. We have already discussed limited liability. What are some other advantages? One is easy transfer of ownership. To sell shares in its ownership, the corporation usually issues **capital stock certificates** (often called simply **stock certificates**) as formal evidence of ownership. Owners of these shares can sell them to others. Numerous stock exchanges exist in the United States and worldwide to facilitate buying and selling of shares. Investors buy and sell more than 1 billion shares on an average day on the New York Stock Exchange (NYSE), the largest exchange in the world. NASDAQ lists the stock of more than 4,000 companies, primarily smaller, tech-oriented companies, but it also includes Microsoft, Intel, and a few other large companies. Other large exchanges include those in Tokyo, Frankfurt, and London. Just as many Japanese, German, and British firms have shares traded on the NYSE, many U.S. companies list their shares abroad. The London Stock Exchange is one of the most international of the exchanges. Exhibit 1-6 displays just a few of the international companies listed on the London exchange.

capital stock certificate (stock certificate)
Formal evidence of ownership shares in a corporation.

Because owners can easily trade shares of stock, corporations have the advantage of raising ownership capital from hundreds or thousands of potential stockholders. For example, General Electric has millions of stockholders, owning a total of nearly 10 billion shares of stock. More than 20 million shares trade hands daily as investors buy and sell this popular stock.

The corporation also has the advantage of continuity of existence. The life of a corporation is indefinite in the sense that it continues even if its ownership changes. In contrast, proprietorships and partnerships officially terminate on the death or complete withdrawal of an owner.

Company	Country	Company	Country
Foster's Group	Australia	Latvijas Unibanka	Latvia
Arab Insurance Group	Bahrain	Kuala Lumpur Kepong Berhad	Malaysia
Centrais Electricas de Santa Catar	Brazil	Royal Dutch Petroleum Co. NV	Netherlands
Canadian Pacific Railways	Canada	Norsk Hydro ASA	Norway
China Petroleum and Chemical Corp.	China	Telekomunikacja Polska	Poland
Plive d.d.	Croatia	Qatar Telecom	Qatar
Ceske Telecom A.S.	Czech Repubilc	Bank of Ireland	Republic of Ireland
Novo-Nordisk A/S	Denmark	Gazprom	Russia
Suez Cement Company	Egypt	Harmony Gold Mining Co.	South Africa
Nokia Corp.	Finland	Hyundai Motor Co.	South Korea
Euro Disney S.C.A.	France	Telefonica SA	Spain
Bayer AG	Germany	Volvo	Sweden
National Bank of Greece	Greece	Nestle SA	Switzerland
Pick Szeged Rt	Hungary	GVC Corp.	Taiwan
Bajai Auto	India	Boeing Co.	USA
Emblaze Systems	Israel	Ford Motor Co.	USA
Honda Motor Co.	Japan	General Electric	USA
Sony Corp.	Japan	Xerox Corp.	USA

Exhibit 1-6
Sample of Companies Traded on the London Stock Exchange

Finally, the tax laws may favor a corporation or a partnership or a proprietorship. This depends heavily on the personal tax situations of the owners and is beyond the scope of this book.

Regardless of the economic and legal advantages or disadvantages of each type of organization, some small business owners incorporate simply for prestige. That is, they feel more important if they can refer to "my corporation" and if they can refer to themselves as "chairman of the board" or "president" instead of "business owner" or "partner."

Although only 20 percent of U.S. businesses are corporations, they do almost 90 percent of the business. The 72 percent of businesses that are sole proprietorships generate only 5 percent of the business activity. Because of the economic importance of corporations, this book emphasizes the corporate form of ownership.

INTERPRETING FINANCIAL STATEMENTS

Biwheels is organized as a sole proprietorship. What would be the biggest advantage for Mr. Lopez in converting it to a corporation?

Answer
As a sole proprietorship, Mr. Lopez is personally liable for all the liabilities of Biwheels. If it were a corporation, his liability would be limited to the investment he has already made. There may also be tax advantages, and Mr. Lopez would find it easier to sell part of the business by issuing shares if it is a corporation.

Accounting Differences Between Proprietorships, Partnerships, and Corporations

All business entities account for assets and liabilities similarly. However, corporations account for owners' equity slightly differently than do sole proprietorships and partnerships. The basic concepts that underlie the owners' equity section of the balance sheet are the same for all three forms of ownership. That is, owners' equity always equals total assets less total liabilities. However, we often label the owners' equities for proprietorships and partnerships with the word capital. In contrast, we call owners' equity for a corporation **stockholders' equity** or **shareholders' equity.** Examine the possibilities for the Biwheels Company that are shown in Exhibit 1-7.

The accounts for the proprietorship and the partnership show owners' equity as straightforward records of the capital invested by the owners. For a corporation, though, we call the total capital investment by its owners, both at and subsequent to the inception of the business, **paid-in capital.** We record it in two parts: common stock (or capital stock) at par value and paid-in capital in excess of par value. Let's next explore what par value means.

The Meaning of Par Value

Most states require stock certificates to have some dollar amount printed on them. We call this amount **par value** or **stated value.** Typically, a company sells stock at a price that is higher than its par value. The difference between the total amount the company receives for the stock and the par value is called **paid-in capital in excess of par value** or **additional paid-in capital.** This distinction is of little economic importance, and we introduce it here only because you will frequently encounter it in actual financial statements.

Let's take a closer look at par value by altering our Biwheels example. We now assume that Biwheels is a corporation and that Lopez received 10,000 shares of stock for his $400,000 investment. Thus, he paid $40 per share. The par value is $10 per share, and the paid-in capital in excess of par value is $30 per share. The total

Exhibit 1-7
Owners' Equity for Different Organizations

OWNERS' EQUITY FOR A PROPRIETORSHIP (Assume Hector Lopez is the Sole Owner)	
Hector Lopez, capital	$400,000
OWNERS' EQUITY FOR A PARTNERSHIP (Assume Lopez has Two Partners)	
Hector Lopez, capital	$320,000
Alex Handl, capital	40,000
Susan Eastman, capital	40,000
Total partners' capital	$400,000
OWNERS' EQUITY FOR A CORPORATION (Assume Lopez has Incorporated)	
Stockholders' equity:	
Paid-in capital:	
Capital stock, 10,000 shares issued at par value of $10 per share	$100,000
Paid-in capital in excess of par value of capital stock	300,000
Total paid-in capital	$400,000

Exhibit 1-8
Paid-In Capital,
Starbucks and Ford
Motor Company

Starbucks (in thousands) September 28, 2003		Ford Motor Co. (in millions) December 31, 2002	
Stockholders' Equity		Stockholders' Equity	
Common stock and		Common stock, par value $0.01	$ 18
additional paid-in capital	$959,103	Capital in excess of par value	
		of stock	5,420
		Total paid-in capital	$5,438

ownership claim of $400,000 arising from the investment is split between two equity claims, one for $100,000 capital stock at par value and one for $300,000 paid-in capital in excess of par value:

$$\text{Total Paid-in Capital} = \text{Capital Stock at Par} + \text{Paid-in Capital in Excess of Par Value}$$

$$\$400,000 = \$100,000 + \$300,000$$

$$\begin{array}{ccc}
\text{Average Issue Price per Share} & & (\text{Average Issue Price per Share} - \\
\times \text{ Number of Shares Issued} = \text{Par Value per Share} & + & \text{Par Value per Share}) \\
\times \text{ Number of Shares Issued} & + & \times \text{ Number of Shares Issued}
\end{array}$$

$$\$40 \times 10,000 = \$10 \times 10,000 + (\$40 - \$10) \times 10,000$$

Exhibit 1-8 shows the paid-in capital for Starbucks and Ford Motor Company. Notice that Starbucks shows the entire amount of paid-in capital related to common stock on one line. In contrast, Ford separates the par value from the capital in excess of par value. Both companies use the label **common stock** to describe the par value of the stock purchased by the common shareholders. Starbucks uses "additional paid-in capital" and Ford uses "capital in excess of par value" to describe the amount paid-in above the par value. Some companies, such as General Motors, use a less descriptive term, capital surplus, for this amount. Although it would be nice to stick to one phrase for each item in this textbook, the world is full of different words used for identical accounting items. One of our goals is to help you to prepare to read and understand actual financial statements and reports. Therefore, we use many of the synonyms you will encounter when reading financial statements.

The par value per share for Ford is only $0.01, much smaller than the amount investors paid Ford for the common shares. We know this because the capital in excess of par value is much larger than the common stock at par value. The extremely small amount of par value as compared with the additional paid-in capital is common in practice and illustrates the insignificance of par value in today's business world. More and more companies are not disclosing the division between par value and additional paid-in capital. This combined reporting is acceptable because readers of financial statements would learn little of significance from separating the two components. The important thing to recognize is that the total of common stock at par value and additional paid-in capital is the amount that owners actively contributed to the firm. This total includes the contributions of owners who have a "residual" ownership in the corporation, that is, the common stockholders. They have a claim on whatever is left over after all other claimants have been paid. This could be a large amount for a successful company or nothing for an unsuccessful one. Although this account identifies the amount of the stockholders' claims, it shows the amount they paid in, not the amount they might receive now or in the future.

common stock
Par value of the stock purchased by common shareholders of a corporation.

Common stockholders are individuals or firms who buy shares of stock as investments. Sometimes they purchase the stock from the company. In such a case, the company increases both its cash and its paid-in capital. However, the majority of stock transactions occur between stockholders. Often, a broker matches a buyer and seller using the services of one of the stock exchanges such as the NYSE or the NASDAQ. When Mary sells 100 shares of DuPont stock to Carlos, the transaction does not affect DuPont's balance sheet. DuPont does not receive cash, and it issues no new shares. The only effect on DuPont will be to replace Mary with Carlos on the corporate records as an owner of the 100 shares of stock.

Summary Problems for Your Review

PROBLEM

"If I purchase 100 shares of the outstanding stock of Starbucks, I invest my money directly in that corporation. Starbucks must record that event." Do you agree? Explain.

SOLUTION

Stockholders invest directly in a corporation only when the corporation originally issues the stock. For example, Starbucks may issue 100,000 shares of stock at $30 per share, bringing in $3 million to the corporation. This is a transaction between the corporation and the stockholders. It affects the corporate financial position:

Cash $3,000,000   Stockholders' equity $3,000,000

Subsequently, an original stockholder (say, Tong Kim) may sell 100 shares of that stock to another individual (Dawn Matsumoto) for $50 per share. This is a private transaction. The corporation receives no cash. Of course, the corporation records the fact that Matsumoto now owns the 100 shares originally owned by Kim, but the corporate financial position is unchanged. Accounting focuses on the business entity. Private stock trades of the owners have no effect on the financial position of the entity, although the corporation records the owners' identities.

PROBLEM

"One individual can be an owner, an employee, and a creditor of a corporation." Do you agree? Explain.

SOLUTION

The corporation enters contracts, hires employees, buys buildings, and conducts other business. The chairman of the board, the president, the other officers, and all the workers are employees of the corporation. Thus, Bill Gates could own some of the capital stock of Microsoft and also be an employee. Because money owed to employees for salaries is a liability, he could be an owner, an employee, and a creditor. Similarly, Jane Smith could be an employee of a telephone company, a stockholder of the company, and also receive telephone services from the same company. Suppose she has earned wages that the company has not yet paid and she has not yet paid her current telephone bill. She is simultaneously an owner, employee, customer, creditor, and debtor of the company.

Stockholders and the Board of Directors

In sole proprietorships and partnerships, the owners are usually also managers. In contrast, corporate shareholders (that is, the owners) delegate ultimate responsibility for management of the company to professional managers. To make sure managers look out for the shareholders' interests, the shareholders elect a **board of directors,** which in turn is responsible for appointing and monitoring the managers, as shown in the following diagram:

board of directors
A body elected by the shareholders to represent them. It is responsible for appointing and monitoring the managers.

Why is the separation of ownership and management in a corporation desirable? With such separation, stockholders can invest resources but do not need to devote time to managing, and managers can be selected for their managerial skills, not their ability to invest large sums of money in the firm. The board of directors is the link between stockholders and the actual managers. The board's duty is to ensure managers act in the best interests of shareholders. In some of the recent business scandals, shareholders have accused some boards of not fulfilling this responsibility and thereby causing shareholders to lose billions of dollars.

When boards of directors do their duty in monitoring management, the corporate form of organization has proved to be very effective. What might have caused the problems experienced by some companies in the early 2000s? One problem may be the way companies select board members. Shareholders elect the board of directors, but management often selects the slate of candidates. Sometimes, the chairman of the board is also the top manager (**chief executive officer,** or **CEO**). For example, for more than 30 years Henry Ford II was the chairman of the board and the CEO of the Ford Motor Company. Fortunately, he was also the major stockholder, so he had an incentive to look out for the shareholders' interests. Others holding both the chairman and CEO positions may be more beholden to management than to shareholders. In addition, shareholders routinely elect other top managers of the company, such as the president, financial vice president, and marketing vice president, to its board of directors. If management exerts too much influence on the board of directors, the board may not do a good job of monitoring management.

chief executive officer (CEO)
The top manager in an organization.

A majority of members of most effective boards are independent of management's influence, which allows them to better tend to shareholders' interests. Members of a board often include CEOs and presidents of other corporations, university presidents and professors, attorneys, and community representatives. For example, the nine-member board of Oracle in 2003 included three members of Oracle's management, three professors, former senator and presidential aspirant Jack Kemp, a venture capitalist, and another company's CEO. Although boards once often had 15 to 20 members, many companies are moving toward having smaller boards of directors that include fewer members of the company's management team.

Credibility and the Role of Auditing

OBJECTIVE 6
Describe auditing and how it enhances the value of financial information.

The separation of owners and managers in a corporation also creates potential problems in getting truthful information about the performance of a company. Corporate managers have the best access to information about the company, but they may also have incentives to make the company's performance look better than it really is. Perhaps doing so will make it easier to raise money to open new stores, or perhaps it would lead to increases in managers' compensation. Managers often believe that company conditions are better than they really are because managers are optimistic about the good decisions they have made and the plans they are implementing. The problem shareholders face is that they must rely on managers to tell the truth, because shareholders cannot see personally what is going on in the firm.

One way to solve this credibility problem is to introduce an honorable, expert third party. In the area of financial statements this third party is the auditor. The **auditor** examines the information that managers use to prepare the financial statements and provides assurances about the credibility of those statements. On seeing the auditor's assurance that the financial statements fairly present a company's economic circumstances, shareholders and potential shareholders can feel more comfortable about using the information to guide their investing activity.

> *auditor*
> *A person who examines the information used by managers to prepare the financial statements and attests to the credibility of those statements.*

Another way to ensure truthful reporting by managers is by handing out stiff legal penalties for lying. A manager who knowingly misstates performance is subject to both fines and jail sentences under U.S. law. In 2003, legal actions against executives in Enron, WorldCom, Tyco, and other U.S. companies made large headlines. Such legal actions were not limited to the United States. Parmalat in Italy, and Dutch food giant Ahold are just some of the global companies that also faced allegations of improper financial reporting. Authorities hope that these examples will help prevent future executives from issuing misleading information about their companies.

The Certified Public Accountant and the Auditor's Opinion

The desire for third-party assurance about the credibility of financial statements gave rise naturally to a profession dedicated to that purpose. Providing credibility requires individuals who have both the technical knowledge to assess financial statements and the reputation for integrity and independence that assures they will honestly tell shareholders and other interested parties if management has not produced reliable financial statements. Such audit professionals are called certified public accountants (CPAs) in many countries, including the United States, and chartered accountants (CAs) in many others, including most British Commonwealth countries. They are part of a profession of **public accountants** who offer services to the general public on a fee basis. Such services include auditing, preparing income taxes, and management consulting, but we focus here on the audit services.

> *public accountants*
> *Accountants who offer services to the general public on a fee basis, including auditing, tax work, and management consulting.*

In the United States, each state has a Board of Accountancy that sets standards of both knowledge and integrity that public accountants must meet to be called a **certified public accountant (CPA).** Only CPAs have the right to issue official opinions on financial statements in the United States. This regulation is supposed to ensure auditors are qualified and, therefore, allows investors to rely on their opinions.

> *certified public accountant (CPA)*
> *In the United States, a person earns this designation by meeting standards of both knowledge and integrity set by a State Board of Accountancy. Only CPAs can issue official opinions on financial statements in the United States.*

To assess management's financial disclosures, public accountants conduct an **audit,** which is an examination of a company's transactions and the resulting financial statements. The **auditor's opinion** (also called an **independent opinion**) describes the scope and results of the audit, and companies include the opinion with the financial statements in their annual reports. Auditors use a standard phrasing for their opinions, as illustrated by the opinion rendered by a large CPA firm, Deloitte & Touche LLP, for Starbucks Corporation which appears in Exhibit 1-9. Some phrases in this opinion may be unfamiliar now, but they will become more clear as you read further. For now, reflect on the fact that auditors do not prepare a company's financial statements. Instead, the auditor's opinion is the public accountant's judgment that the financial statements prepared by management fairly present economic reality.

> *audit*
> *An examination of a company's transactions and the resulting financial statements.*

> *auditor's opinion (independent opinion)*
> *A report describing the scope and results of an audit. Companies include the opinion with the financial statements in their annual reports.*

Exhibit 1-9
Report of
Independent Auditors

To the Board of Directors and Shareholders of Starbucks Corporation Seattle, Washington

We have audited the accompanying consolidated balance sheets of Starbucks Corporation and subsidiaries (the "Company") as of September 28, 2003, and September 29, 2002, and the related consolidated statements of earnings, shareholders' equity and cash flows for the years ended September 28, 2003, September 29, 2002, and September 30, 2001. These financial statements are the responsibility of the Company's management. Our responsibility is to express an opinion on these financial statements based on our audits.

We conducted our audits in accordance with auditing standards generally accepted in the United States of America. Those standards require that we plan and perform the audit to obtain reasonable assurance about whether the financial statements are free of material misstatement. An audit includes examining, on a test basis, evidence supporting the amounts and disclosures in the financial statements. An audit also includes assessing the accounting principles used and significant estimates made by management, as well as evaluating the overall financial statement presentation. We believe that our audits provide a reasonable basis for our opinion.

In our opinion, such consolidated financial statements present fairly, in all material respects, the financial position of the Company as of September 28, 2003, and September 29, 2002, and the results of its operations and its cash flows for the years ended September 28, 2003, September 29, 2002, and September 30, 2001, in conformity with accounting principles generally accepted in the United States of America.

/s/ DELOITTE & TOUCHE LLP
DELOITTE & TOUCHE LLP
Seattle, Washington
December 19, 2003

The Accounting Profession

To understand auditors and auditors' opinions, you need to know something about the accounting profession. There are many ways to classify accountants, but the easiest and most common way is to divide them into public and private accountants. We already learned that public accountants offer services to the general public for a fee. All other accountants would be **private accountants.** This category consists not only of those individuals who work for businesses, but also of those who work for government agencies, including the Internal Revenue Service (IRS), and other nonprofit organizations.

private accountants
Accountants who work for businesses, government agencies, and other nonprofit organizations.

Public Accounting Firms

Public accountants work for firms that vary in size and in the type of accounting services they perform. There are small proprietorships, where auditing may represent less than 10 percent of annual billings. Billings are the total amounts charged to clients for services rendered to them. These small proprietorships often focus on income tax reporting and bookkeeping services for clients who are not equipped to do their own accounting.

There are also a handful of gigantic firms with more than 2,000 partners and offices located throughout the world. Such enormous firms are necessary because their clients also tend to be enormous. For instance, one large CPA firm reported that its annual audit of one client takes the equivalent of 72 accountants working a full year. Another client has

300 separate corporate entities in 40 countries that it must ultimately consolidate into one set of overall financial statements.

The four largest public international accounting firms are:

- **Deloitte Touche Tohmatsu**
- **Ernst & Young**
- **KPMG**
- **PricewaterhouseCoopers**

Of the companies listed on the NYSE, 97 percent are clients of these four firms. These accounting firms have annual billings in excess of a $1 billion each. A large part of the billings is attributable to auditing services. The top partners in big accounting firms receive compensation on about the same scale as their corporate counterparts. Huge accounting firms tend to receive more publicity than other firms. However, please remember that there are thousands of capable accounting firms, varying in size from sole practitioners to giant international partnerships. The CPAs in all these firms meet the same criteria to enter the accounting profession, and all firms must meet the same minimum standards for auditing and financial reporting.

Regulation of Financial Reporting

Financial statements are the result of a measurement process that rests on a set of principles. If every accountant and every public accounting firm used a different set of measurement rules, investors would find it difficult to use and compare financial statements. For example, consider the recording of an asset such as a machine on the balance sheet. If one accountant listed the purchase cost, another the amount for which the company could sell the used machine, and others listed various other amounts, the readers of financial statements would be confused. It would be as if each accountant were speaking a different language. Therefore, accountants have agreed to apply a common set of measurement principles—that is, a common language—to report information on financial statements.

Generally accepted accounting principles (GAAP) is the term that applies to all the broad concepts and detailed practices to be followed in preparing and distributing financial statements. It includes all the conventions, rules, and procedures that together comprise accepted accounting practice. In this book, we concentrate on the GAAP that exists today in the United States. However, we frequently mention practices from other countries and use financial reports for non-U.S. firms to illustrate the extent of global diversity in practice. Although there is no single, perfect method for measuring an organization's performance, each country has found it useful to narrow the range of practices to a few acceptable ones. The general trend is to reduce international diversity, and governments and accounting groups worldwide are cooperating in this effort.

Accounting principles become "generally accepted" by agreement. Logical analysis is not the only basis for such agreement. Experience, custom, usage, and practical necessity contribute to a set of principles. Yet, there must be some way to codify GAAP so its principles become widely known. Thus, standard setting bodies have arisen throughout the world.

Standard Setting Bodies

The existence of GAAP implies that someone must decide which principles are generally accepted and which are not. In the United States, a private sector body sets GAAP (with government oversight), but in many countries, such as France, the government sets the standards directly.

OBJECTIVE 7
Explain the regulation of financial reporting.

generally accepted accounting principles (GAAP)
The term that applies to all the broad concepts and detailed practices to be followed in preparing and distributing financial statements. It includes all the conventions, rules, and procedures that together comprise accepted accounting practice.

*Financial Accounting
Standards Board (FASB)*
*The private sector body
that is responsible for
establishing GAAP in the
United States.*

FASB Statements
*Name for the FASB's
rulings on GAAP.*

*Securities and Exchange
Commission (SEC)*
*The government agency
charged by the U.S.
Congress with the
ultimate responsibility for
authorizing the GAAP for
companies whose stock
is held by the general
investing public.*

The **Financial Accounting Standards Board (FASB)** is responsible for establishing GAAP in the United States. The FASB is an independent creature of the private sector consisting of seven individuals who work full-time with a staff to support them. A mandatory charge to all public companies, in proportion to their total market values, provides the FASB's annual budget of more than $23 million. The FASB's calls its rulings on GAAP **FASB Statements.**

The U.S. Congress has charged the **Securities and Exchange Commission (SEC)** with the ultimate responsibility for authorizing the GAAP for companies whose stock is held by the general investing public. However, the SEC has delegated much rule-making power to the FASB. This public sector–private sector authority relationship can be sketched as follows:

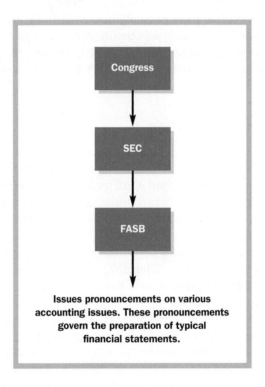

Take a careful look at the preceding three-tiered structure. Note that Congress can overrule both the SEC and the FASB, and the SEC can overrule the FASB. The FASB and the SEC work closely together and seldom have public disagreements. However, on occasion Congress has overruled FASB decisions. Most recently, Congress heeded the pleas of constituents and donors and threatened to overrule the FASB if it required companies to recognize stock options as an expense of doing business. This caused the FASB to rescind such a proposed requirement. In 2001 and 2002, the FASB received much criticism for going along with the wishes of Congress. You can see that the setting of accounting principles is a complex political process involving heavy interactions among the affected parties: public regulators (Congress and the SEC), private regulators (FASB), companies, those in the public accounting profession, representatives of investors, and other interested groups and lobbyists. GAAP is not a set of arcane rules of interest only to accountants. GAAP can affect many people and companies, and it is an important part of a country's public policy.

Until recently, accounting principles were primarily an internal concern for each country. The global economy has changed that. There is a growing interest in adopting a common set of accounting principles throughout the world. The movement seeks to eliminate differences in accounting principles that are not caused by cultural or environmental differences between countries. Leading the way is the **International Accounting Standards Board (IASB),** which was established "to develop, in the public interest, a single set of high quality, understandable and enforceable global accounting standards." The IASB has 12 full-time and 2 part-time members, including one academic, Mary Barth of Stanford University. The board members represent a diversity of geographic and professional backgrounds. Although compliance with international accounting standards is voluntary, a growing number of countries and multinational companies are adopting the methods advocated by the IASB. A significant step for international accounting standards was their recent adoption by the European Union for financial statements prepared after 2005.

International Accounting Standards Board (IASB)
An international body established to develop, in the public interest, a single set of high-quality, understandable, and enforceable global accounting standards.

The motivation for this conformity movement lies in the explosive growth of international commerce. Increasingly, investors commit their money worldwide either as individuals or through retirement accounts or mutual funds. Companies rely on international capital to finance their growth. In September 2002, the NYSE listed shares of 468 non-U.S. companies from 51 countries. This phenomenon is even more pronounced in London where approximately two-thirds of the market value of traded firms on the London Stock Exchange are non-U.K. firms. Examples of major multinational firms that now publish their financial statements in conformity with international accounting standards are Allianz (Germany), Nestlé (Switzerland), Nokia (Finland), Shanghai Petrochemical (China), and Microsoft (United States).

Audit Regulation

Until recently, the audit profession in the United States was primarily self-regulated. The **American Institute of Certified Public Accountants (AICPA)** is the principal professional association in the private sector that regulates the quality of the public accounting profession. In 2002, the U.S. Congress passed the **Sarbanes-Oxley Act**, which gave the government a larger role in regulating the audit profession. Among other things, the act (1) established the Public Company Accounting Oversight Board with powers to regulate many aspects of public accounting and to set standards for audit procedures; (2) prohibited public accounting firms from providing to audit clients certain nonaudit services, such as financial information systems design and implementation and internal audit outsourcing services; and (3) required rotation every 5 years of the lead audit or coordinating partner and the reviewing partner on an audit. Much of the bill also provided regulation of corporate governance with provisions such as requiring boards of publicly held companies to appoint an audit committee composed only of "independent" directors, making CEOs and chief financial officers (CFOs) personally sign a statement certifying the appropriateness and fairness of their companies' financial statements, and increasing the criminal penalties for knowingly misreporting financial information.

American Institute of Certified Public Accountants (AICPA)
The principal professional association in the private sector that regulates the quality of the public accounting profession.

Sarbanes-Oxley Act
A law passed by the U.S. Congress in 2002 that gave the government a larger role in regulating the audit profession.

Despite the government's growing role, the AICPA remains a main force in accounting regulation. It regulates both areas that are essential to certify the credibility of financial statements: (1) technical knowledge appropriately applied, and (2) integrity and independence. To ensure the technical knowledge of CPAs, the AICPA administers and grades a computer-based national examination. The 14-hour, computer-based CPA examination covers auditing and attestation, financial accounting and reporting, regulation, and business environment and concepts. This examination is a significant hurdle to those desiring to enter the profession. As a consequence, passing the exam opens many opportunities to the newly minted CPA.

To ensure proper application of a CPA's technical knowledge, the Public Company Accounting Oversight Board issues generally accepted auditing standards (GAAS), a task previously carried out by the AICPA. These standards prescribe the minimum steps that an auditor must take in examining the transactions and financial statements before it can issue an auditor's opinion. Auditors with sufficient technical knowledge applying GAAS should have a reasonable chance of discovering any errors or omissions, intentional or unintentional, in a company's financial statements. However, in several well-publicized cases, auditors apparently failed to discover some accounting irregularities. Examples include WorldCom, Tyco, Qwest, and others. This has created increased scrutiny on the minimum standards for audits, and this may result in additional required audit procedures.

Professional Ethics

OBJECTIVE 8

Evaluate the role of ethics in the accounting process.

Once an auditor discovers a problem with a company's financial statements, there must be an incentive to report that discovery. Auditors have an obligation to the general public to truthfully report what they find. This is why we call them *public* accountants. This requires integrity and independence from management's influence. To help achieve this, members of the AICPA must abide by a code of professional conduct. The code specifically addresses integrity and independence, as well as providing guidance on other topics. Surveys of public attitudes toward CPAs have consistently ranked the accounting profession as having high ethical standards. However, the corporate scandals in the last few years have caused investors to question some auditors' integrity and independence, especially their independence. This has led to additional government regulation of auditor independence and a revision of the AICPA's independence standards.

Exhibit 1-10 presents some of the AICPA's independence and integrity standards. The full standards contain many more details and guidance for application, but this exhibit illustrates some of the major requirements.

The emphasis on ethics extends beyond public accounting. For example, the Institute of Management Accountants has a code of ethics for management accountants. Auditors and management accountants have professional responsibilities concerning competence, confidentiality, integrity, and objectivity. Professional accounting organizations and state regulatory bodies have procedures for reviewing behavior alleged to violate codes of professional conduct.

Although professions and companies have codes of ethics or codes of conduct, the major influence on the ethical decisions of employees is the "tone at the top." Complete integrity and outspoken support for ethical standards by senior managers is the single greatest motivator of ethical behavior throughout an organization. In the final analysis, however, ethical standards are personal and depend on the values of the individual. Hiring ethical employees is the best way to ensure ethical behavior.

Developing integrity and high ethical standards must start while you are still a student. Some ethics courses teach that there are no uniform standards of right and wrong. They maintain that ethics are relative to the time and place. This is not true in accounting. Although there are some gray areas, there are many definite standards, and it is important for all accountants to adhere to those standards. You will set your moral compass by how you behave as a student and by the early decisions you make on the job.

On April 29, 2004, an ABCNEWS Primetime special documented widespread cheating in high schools and colleges and universities. One poll revealed that 36% of students admit to cheating, and they think more than 70% of their classmates cheat. As one student said, "There's other people getting better grades than me and they're cheating. Why am I not going to cheat? It's kind of almost stupid if you don't." We cannot deny that business executives and government officials have lied and cheated. Many have been

I. INDEPENDENCE: The standards indicate that independence will be impaired if:

- During the period of the professional engagement a covered member a) had or was committed to acquire any direct or material indirect financial interest in the client, b) was a trustee of any trust or executor or administrator of any estate if such trust or estate had or was committed to acquire any direct or material indirect financial interest in the client, c) had a joint closely held investment that was material to the covered member, or d) except as specifically permitted, had any loan to or from the client, any officer or director of the client, or any individual owning 10 percent or more of the client's outstanding equity securities or other ownership interests.
- During the period of the professional engagement, a partner or professional employee of the firm, his or her immediate family, or any group of such persons acting together owned more than 5 percent of a client's outstanding equity securities or other ownership interests.
- During the period covered by the financial statements or during the period of the professional engagement, a partner or professional employee of the firm was simultaneously associated with the client as a a) director, officer, or employee, or in any capacity equivalent to that of a member of management; b) promoter, underwriter, or voting trustee; or c) trustee for any pension or profit-sharing trust of the client.

II. INTEGRITY: The standards indicate that integrity will be impaired by:

- *Knowing misrepresentations in the preparation of financial statements or records.* A member shall be considered to have knowingly misrepresented facts when he or she knowingly a) makes, or permits or directs another to make, materially false and misleading entries in an entity's financial statements or records; or b) fails to correct an entity's financial statements or records that are materially false and misleading when he or she has the authority to record an entry; or c) signs, or permits or directs another to sign, a document containing materially false and misleading information.
- *Conflicts of interest.* A conflict of interest may occur if a member performs a professional service for a client or employer and the member or his or her firm has a relationship with another person, entity, product, or service that could, in the member's professional judgment, be viewed by the client, employer, or other appropriate parties as impairing the member's objectivity.
- *Subordination of judgment.* A member may not knowingly misrepresent facts or subordinate his or her judgment when performing professional services.

caught and have paid the price. However, some have not. Yet, this does not make cheating a path to success. To the contrary. Both businesses and society run better if participants have high integrity. So do colleges and universities. The appropriate attitude is not, as one student offered, "Whether or not you did it, if you can get the jury to say that you're not guilty, you're free." This attitude leads to behavior like that at Enron and WorldCom. Such actions destroy value; they do not create value. You will create more value for yourself if you maintain your integrity as a student, just as you will create more value for your company or organization by maintaining high integrity after your graduate and pursue your career.

To be a successful accountant or manager, you must recognize the ethical dimensions of your situation and act with absolute integrity. *The Wall Street Journal* reports two positive trends—more and more graduates are asking about the ethical standards and practices at companies seeking to hire them, and more and more companies are exploring the ethical commitment of potential employees. Further, despite the criticism of accounting ethics in many of the recent corporate scandals, accountants were responsible for revealing the problems in several cases, as indicated in the Business First box on p. 32.

Companies often rely on accountants to safeguard the ethics of the company. Accountants have a special responsibility to ensure managers act with integrity and that the information disclosed to customers, suppliers, regulators, and the public is accurate. If accountants do not take this responsibility seriously, or if the company ignores the accountants' reports, bad consequences can follow. Just ask WorldCom or Enron. In both companies, an accountant decided to be a "whistle blower," one who reports wrongdoings to his or her supervisor. The WorldCom and Enron whistle-blowers became two of the three 2002 Persons of the Year in *Time* magazine.

In June 2002, Cynthia Cooper, Vice President of Internal Audit for WorldCom, told the company's board of directors that fraudulent accounting entries had turned a $662 million loss into a $2.4 billion profit in 2001. This disclosure led to additional discoveries totaling $9 billion in erroneous accounting entries—the largest accounting fraud in history. Cooper was proud of WorldCom and highly committed to its success. Nevertheless, when she and her internal audit team discovered the unethical actions of superiors she admired, she did not hesitate to do the right thing. She saw no joy when CEO Bernie Ebbers and CFO Scott Sullivan were placed in handcuffs and led away. She simply applied what she had learned when she sat in the middle of the front row of seats in her accounting classes at Mississippi State University. Accountants ask hard questions, find the answers, and act with integrity. Being a whistle-blower has not been easy for Cooper. She is a hero to some, a villain to others. However, regardless of the reaction of others, Cooper knows that she just did what any good accountant should do—no matter how painful it is to tell the truth.

At Enron, Sherron Watkins had a similar experience. An accounting major at the University of Texas at Austin who started her career at Arthur Andersen, Watkins moved out of accounting when she took a position at Enron in 1993. However, in spring of 2001, she moved back into the financial arena, working directly for CFO Andrew Fastow. As she became more familiar with the accounting at Enron, she discovered the off-the-books liabilities that now have become famous. In August, she wrote a memo to CEO Kenneth Lay and had a personal meeting with him, explaining to him "an elaborate accounting hoax." Later she discovered that, rather than the hoax being investigated, her report had generated a memo from Enron's legal counsel titled "Confidential Employee Matter" that included the following: ". . . how to manage the case with the employee who made the sensitive report. . . . Texas law does not currently protect corporate whistle-blowers. . . ." In addition, her boss confiscated her hard drive, and she was demoted. She now regrets that she did not take the matter to higher levels, but she believed that Mr. Lay would take her allegations seriously. In the end, Watkins proved to be right. Although many at Enron knew what was happening, they ignored it. Watkins' accounting background made her both able to spot the irregularities and compelled to report them. Another Enron employee, Lynn Brewer, said that "hundreds, perhaps thousands, of people inside the company knew what was going on, and chose to look the other way." Watkins made the ethical decision and did not simply look the other way.

Sources: "The Party Crasher," *Time,* Jan. 30, 2002–Jan. 6, 2003, pp. 52–56; "The Night Detective," *Time,* Jan. 30, 2002–Jan. 6, 2003, pp. 45–50; M. Flynn, "Enron Insider Shares Her Insights," *Puget Sound Business Journal,* March 7–13, 2003, p. 50.

Career Opportunities for Accountants

Most of you who read this book will not become accountants. You will be intelligent consumers of accounting information in your business and personal lives. Because accounting cuts across all management functions, including purchasing, manufacturing, wholesaling, retailing, and a variety of marketing and transportation activities, it provides an excellent background for almost any manager. Knowledge of accounting is especially important for finance professionals. After the disclosure of accounting problems at Enron, WorldCom, and others, a *Business Week* article indicated that "even professional money managers are scared that they don't know enough accounting." However, accounting's value is not restricted to financial managers. Managers who want to move up in the management structure of a company need to know accounting. In fact, surveys have ranked accounting as the most important business school course for future managers. A major business periodical reported that "more CEOs started out in finance or accounting than in any other area." It is easy to see why accounting is called the language of business.

We hope that many of you will become accountants, at least at the beginning of your career. Because accountants are responsible for collecting and interpreting financial information about the entire company, they develop detailed knowledge about what is occurring and form close relationships with key decision makers. Senior accountants or controllers in a corporation often become production or marketing executives. Why? Because they may have impressed other executives as having acquired general management skills through their dealings with a variety of managers. Others continue in the finance function to become vice-presidents of finance or CFOs. Exhibit 1-11 shows various potential career paths for those hired as staff accountants. Some accountants join a public accounting firm and reach partner after a series of promotions. Others join a business corporation or government agency and proceed up the ladder of success. Many others start in public accounting, even if they do not intend to stay for their entire careers. After being promoted once or twice in pubic accounting, they shift to a controller or treasurer position in government or industry, or even to a CFO position.

Accounting provides exciting career opportunities. It is a great training ground for future managers and executives. Staff accountants in public accounting firms perform

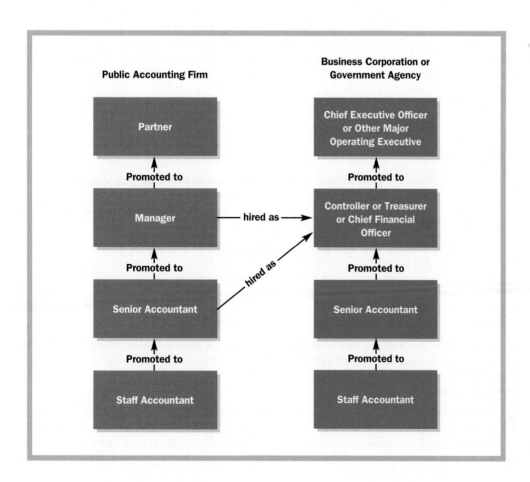

Exhibit 1-11
Common Accounting Career Paths

work for many clients and encounter many different work experiences. Accountants in private companies work with managers throughout the organization and gain a broad understanding of the various functional and product areas. In addition, accountants are well rewarded. Beginning accountants in large public accounting firms earned nearly $40,000 a year in 2003. Partners averaged more than $130,000, whereas CFOs averaged nearly $100,000. Top partners in the international accounting firms and CFOs at some of the largest corporations earn more than $1 million annually.

A Note on Nonprofit Organizations

The major focus of this book is on profit-seeking organizations, such as business firms. However, the fundamental accounting principles also apply to nonprofit organizations. Managers and accountants in hospitals, universities, government agencies, and other nonprofit organizations use financial statements. After all, such organizations must raise and spend money, prepare budgets, and judge financial performance. Some nonprofit organizations, such as the Red Cross or Girl Scouts, are as big as large corporations. Others, such as Bainbridge Island Land Trust or West Seattle Food Bank, serve a specific local interest. There is a growing pressure on nonprofit organizations to disclose financial information to the public. The Governmental Accounting Standards Board (GASB) regulates disclosures for governmental organizations, and the FASB regulates financial reporting for other nonprofit organizations.

Highlights to Remember

1 **Explain how accounting information assists in making decisions.** Financial statements provide information to help managers, creditors, and owners of all types of organizations make decisions. The balance sheet (or statement of financial position) provides a "snapshot" of the financial position of an organization at any instant. That is, it answers the basic question, where are we?

2 **Describe the components of the balance sheet.** The balance sheet equation is Assets = Liabilities + Owners' Equity. This equation must always be in balance. The balance sheet presents the balances of the components of Assets, Liabilities, and Owners' Equity at a specific point in time. Assets are things a company owns, liabilities are what it owes, and owners' equity is the owners' claims on assets less liabilities.

3 **Analyze business transactions and relate them to changes in the balance sheet.** Transaction analysis is the heart of accounting. A transaction is any event that both affects the financial position of an entity and can be reliably recorded in money terms. For each transaction, an accountant must determine what accounts the transaction affects and the amount to record.

4 **Compare the features of sole proprietorships, partnerships, and corporations.** Sole proprietorships and partnerships usually have owners who also act as managers. In corporations, shareholders delegate management of the firm to professional managers. The shareholders elect a board of directors, which in turn appoints and monitors the managers. Owners of corporations have limited liability; their personal assets are not at risk. Corporations are the most important form of business ownership because corporations conduct a majority of the world's business.

5 **Identify how the owners' equity section in a corporate balance sheet differs from that in a sole proprietorship or a partnership.** The ownership equity of a corporation is usually called stockholders' equity. It initially takes the form of common stock at par value (or stated value) plus additional paid-in capital.

6 **Describe auditing and how it enhances the value of financial information.** Separation of ownership from management in corporations creates a demand for auditing, a third-party examination of the financial statements. Auditors evaluate the record-keeping system of the firm and test specific transactions and account balances to provide assurance that the balances fairly reflect the financial position and performance of the company.

7 **Explain the regulation of financial reporting.** In the United States, the FASB determines GAAP, with oversight by the SEC. The IASB is creating an international GAAP that many countries are adopting. The AICPA administers the CPA exam that ensures that professional accountants meet minimum qualification standards. In addition, in 2002, the U.S. Congress passed the Sarbanes-Oxley Act, which increases the government's role in accounting and auditing regulation. As a result of the act, the Public Company Accounting Oversight Board now regulates the accounting profession and sets auditing standards.

8 **Evaluate the role of ethics in the accounting process.** Ethical behavior is critically important in professional activities such as accounting. In public accounting, the value of an audit is directly linked to the credibility of the auditor as an ethical, independent professional who is qualified to evaluate the financial statements of the firm and is also reliably committed to disclosing problems or concerns uncovered in the evaluation.

Accounting Vocabulary

account, p. 12
account payable, p. 14
accounting, p. 4
additional paid-in capital, p. 21
American Institute of Certified
    Public Accountants
    (AICPA), p. 29
annual report, p. 8
assets, p. 9
audit, p. 25
auditor, p. 25
auditor's opinion, p. 25
balance sheet, p. 8
balance sheet equation, p. 8
board of directors, p. 24
capital stock certificate, p. 19
certified public accountant
    (CPA), p. 25
chief executive officer (CEO),
    p. 24
common stock, p. 22
compound entry, p. 14

corporation, p. 19
creditor, p. 15
entity, p. 10
FASB Statements, p. 28
financial accounting, p. 4
Financial Accounting Standards
    Board (FASB), p. 28
Form 10-K, p. 8
generally accepted accounting
    principles (GAAP), p. 27
independent opinion, p. 25
International Accounting
    Standards Board (ISAB),
    p. 29
inventory, p. 13
liabilities, p. 9
limited liability, p. 19
long-lived asset, p. 11
management accounting, p. 7
notes payable, p. 9
open account, p. 14
owners' equity, p. 10

paid-in capital, p. 21
paid-in capital in excess of
    par value, p. 21
par value, p. 21
partnership, p. 18
private accountants, p. 26
privately owned, p. 19
public accountants, p. 25
publicly owned, p. 19
Sarbanes-Oxley Act, p. 29
Securities and Exchange
    Commission (SEC), p. 28
shareholders' equity, p. 21
sole proprietorship, p. 18
stated value, p. 21
statement of financial position,
    p. 8
stock certificate, p. 19
stockholders' equity, p. 21
transaction, p. 10

Assignment Material

The assignment material for each chapter is divided into Questions, Critical Thinking Questions, Exercises, Problems, a Collaborative Learning Exercise, and three projects on Analyzing and Interpreting Financial Statements. The assignment material contains problems based on fictitious companies and problems based on real-life situations. We hope our use of actual companies and news events enhances your interest in accounting.

We identify problems based on real companies by highlighting the name in blue. These problems underscore a major objective of this book: to increase your ability to read, understand, and use published financial reports and news articles. In later chapters, these problems provide the principal means of reviewing not only the immediate chapter but also the previous chapters.

Questions

1-1 Describe accounting.

1-2 "It's easier to learn accounting if you avoid real-world examples." Do you agree? Explain.

1-3 Give three examples of decisions where the decision maker is likely to use financial statements.

1-4 Give three examples of users of financial statements.

1-5 Briefly distinguish between financial accounting and management accounting.

1-6 Describe the balance sheet equation.

1-7 "The balance sheet may be out of balance after some transactions, but it is never out of balance at the end of an accounting period." Do you agree? Explain.

1-8 "When a company buys inventory for cash, total assets do not change. However, when it buys inventory on open account, total assets increase." Explain.

1-9 Explain the difference between a note payable and an account payable.

1-10 List three differences between a corporation and a sole proprietorship or a partnership.

1-11 Explain the meaning of limited liability.

1-12 Why does this book emphasize the corporation instead of the proprietorship or the partnership?

1-13 "International companies with Ltd. or S.A. after their name are essentially the same in organizational form as U.S. companies with Corp. after their name." Do you agree? Explain.

1-14 "The idea of par value is insignificant." Explain.

1-15 Explain the relationship between the board of directors and top management of a company.

1-16 What gives value to an audit?

1-17 What is a CPA, and how does someone become one?

1-18 How is GAAP set in the United States? Internationally?

1-19 What are the most important ethical standards for accountants?

1-20 "The accounting systems described in this book apply to corporations and are not appropriate for nonprofit organizations." Do you agree? Explain.

Critical Thinking Questions

1-21 Double-Entry Accounting
The accounting process in use today is typically called "double-entry" bookkeeping. Discuss the meaning and possible importance of this name.

1-22 Accountants as Historians
Critics sometimes refer to accountants as historians and do not mean it kindly. In what sense are accountants historians, and do you believe this is a compliment or a criticism?

1-23 The Corporation
Some historians were arguing over the most important innovation in the history of business.

Most thought of things and processes such as the railroad, the automobile, the printing press, the telephone, television, or more recently, the computer chip, fiber-optic cable, or even the Internet. One person argued that the really important innovation was the corporation. How would this person argue for this idea?

1-24 The Auditor's Opinion
In reviewing the annual report of a company in which you might invest, you noted that you did not recognize the name of the audit firm that signed the audit opinion. What questions would this raise in your mind, and how might you resolve them?

Exercises

1-25 The Balance Sheet Equation
Laredo Company reported total assets of $5 million and total liabilities of $3 million at the end of 20X3.

1. Construct the balance sheet equation for Laredo Company at the end of 20X3 and include the correct amount for owners' equity.
2. Suppose that during January 20X4 Laredo borrowed $1 million from **Wells Fargo Bank**. How would this affect Laredo's assets, liabilities, and owners' equity?

1-26 Describing Underlying Transactions
Mann's Furniture Company, which was recently formed, is engaging in some preliminary transactions before beginning full-scale operations for retailing household furnishings. The balances

of each item in the company's accounting equation are given next for June 1 and for each of the next 9 business days.

	Cash	Furniture Inventory	Store Fixtures	Accounts Payable	Owners' Equity
June 1	$ 6,000	$18,000	$2,000	$ 4,000	$22,000
2	12,000	18,000	2,000	4,000	28,000
3	12,000	18,000	6,000	4,000	32,000
4	9,000	21,000	6,000	4,000	32,000
5	9,000	26,000	6,000	9,000	32,000
6	12,000	26,000	3,000	9,000	32,000
7	7,000	26,000	9,000	10,000	32,000
8	5,000	26,000	9,000	8,000	32,000
9	5,000	25,600	9,000	7,600	32,000
10	2,000	25,600	9,000	7,600	29,000

State briefly what you think took place on each of the 9 days beginning June 2, assuming that only one transaction occurred each day.

1-27 Describing Underlying Transactions

The balances of each item in LaPaz Company's accounting equation are given next for September 1 and for each of the next 7 business days.

	Cash	Computer Inventory	Store Fixtures	Accounts Payable	Owners' Equity
Sept. 1	$5,000	$ 9,000	$ 7,500	$5,500	$16,000
2	5,000	9,000	10,000	8,000	16,000
3	2,000	9,000	10,000	8,000	13,000
4	2,000	4,000	10,000	3,000	13,000
5	2,000	11,000	10,000	3,000	20,000
8	1,500	11,000	10,000	2,500	20,000
9	1,000	11,000	13,000	5,000	20,000
10	1,000	11,000	12,700	4,700	20,000

State briefly what you think took place on each of the 7 days beginning September 2, assuming that only one transaction occurred each day.

1-28 Prepare Balance Sheet

Atlanta Corporation's balance sheet at March 30, 20X4, contained only the following items (arranged here in random order):

Cash	$10,000	Accounts payable	$ 8,000
Notes payable	10,000	Furniture and fixtures	3,000
Merchandise inventory	40,000	Long-term debt payable	12,000
Paid-in capital	80,000	Building	28,000
Land	14,000	Machinery and equipment	15,000

On March 31, 20X4, these transactions and events took place:

1. Purchased merchandise on account, $4,000.
2. Sold at cost for $1,000 cash some furniture that was not needed.
3. Issued additional capital stock for machinery and equipment valued at $12,000.
4. Purchased land for $25,000, of which $5,000 was paid in cash, the remaining being represented by a 5-year note (long-term debt).
5. The building was valued by professional appraisers at $47,000.

Prepare in good form a balance sheet for March 31, 20X4, showing supporting computations for all new amounts.

1-29 Prepare Balance Sheet

Soho Corporation's balance sheet at November 29, 20X1, contained only the following items (arranged here in random order):

Paid-in capital	$189,000	Machinery and equipment	$ 20,000
Notes payable	21,000	Furniture and fixtures	8,000
Cash	22,000	Land	41,000
Accounts payable	16,000	Building	230,000
Merchandise inventory	29,000	Long-term debt payable	124,000

On the following day, November 30, these transactions and events occurred:

1. Purchased machinery and equipment for $13,000, paying $3,000 in cash and signing a 90-day note for the balance.
2. Paid $6,000 on accounts payable.
3. Sold some land that was not needed for cash of $6,000, which was the Soho Corporation's acquisition cost of the land.
4. The remaining land was valued at $240,000 by professional appraisers.
5. Issued capital stock as payment for $23,000 of the long-term debt, that is, debt due beyond 1 year.

Prepare in good form a balance sheet for November 30, 20X1, showing supporting computations for all new amounts.

1-30 Balance Sheet

General Electric (GE) is one of the largest companies in the world with sales of more than $130 billion. The company's balance sheet on January 1, 2003, had total assets of $575 billion and stockholders' equity (called share owners' equity by GE) of $64 billion.

1. Compute GE's total liabilities on January 1, 2003.
2. As of January 1, 2003, GE had issued 9,969,894,000 shares of common stock. The par value was $.0671 per share. Compute the balance in the account, "Common stock, par value" on GE's balance sheet.

Problems

1-31 Analysis of Transactions

Use the format of Exhibit 1-2 to analyze the following transactions for April of Corner Cleaners. Then prepare a balance sheet as of April 30, 20X1. Corner Cleaners was founded on April 1.

1. Issued 1,000 shares of common stock for cash, $40,000.
2. Issued 500 shares of common stock for equipment, $20,000.
3. Borrowed cash, signing a note payable for $35,000.
4. Purchased equipment for cash, $30,000.
5. Purchased office furniture on account, $10,000.
6. Disbursed cash on account (to reduce the account payable), $4,000.
7. Sold equipment for cash, $8,000.
8. Discovered that the most prominent competitor in the area was bankrupt and was closing its doors on April 30.

1-32 Analysis of Transactions

Consider the following January transactions:

1. On January 1, 20X4, three persons, Xiao, Yergen, and Zimbel, formed XYZ Corporation. XYZ will be a wholesale distributor of PC software. The company issued 10,000 shares of common stock ($1 par value) to each of the three investors for $10 cash per share. Use two stockholders' equity accounts: Capital Stock (at par) and Additional Paid-in Capital.
2. XYZ acquired merchandise inventory of $80,000 for cash.
3. XYZ acquired merchandise inventory of $85,000 on open account.
4. XYZ returned for full credit unsatisfactory merchandise that cost $11,000 in transaction 3.

5. XYZ acquired equipment of $40,000 for a cash down payment of $10,000, plus a 3-month promissory note of $30,000.
6. As a favor, XYZ sells equipment of $4,000 to a business neighbor for cash. The equipment had cost $4,000.
7. XYZ pays $20,000 on the account described in transaction 3.
8. XYZ buys merchandise inventory of $100,000. The company pays one-half of the amount in cash, and owes one-half on open account.
9. Zimbel sells one-half of his common stock to Quigley for $12 per share.

Required
1. By using a format similar to Exhibit 1-2, prepare an analysis showing the effects of January transactions on the financial position of XYZ Corporation.
2. Prepare a balance sheet as of January 31, 20X4.

1-33 Analysis of Transactions

You began a business as a wholesaler of woolen goods. The following events have occurred:

1. On March 1, 20X1, you invested $60,000 cash in your new sole proprietorship, which you call BC Products.
2. You acquired $9,000 inventory for cash.
3. You acquired $8,000 inventory on open account.
4. You acquired equipment for $15,000 in exchange for a $5,000 cash down payment and a $10,000 promissory note.
5. A large retail store, which you had hoped would be a big customer, discontinued operations.
6. You take gloves home for your family. BC's inventory carried the gloves at $600. (Regard this as taking part of your capital out of BC Products.)
7. Gloves that cost $300 in transaction 2 were of the wrong style. You returned them and obtained a full cash refund.
8. Gloves that cost $800 in transaction 3 were of the wrong color. You returned them and obtained gloves of the correct color in exchange.
9. Caps that cost $500 in transaction 3 had an unacceptable quality. You returned them and obtained full credit on your account.
10. You paid $1,000 on the promissory note.
11. You use your personal cash savings of $5,000 to acquire some equipment for BC. You consider this to be an additional investment in your business.
12. You paid $3,000 on open account.
13. Two scarf manufacturers who are suppliers for BC announced a 7 percent rise in prices, effective in 60 days.
14. You use your personal cash savings of $1,000 to acquire a new TV set for your family.
15. You exchange equipment that cost $4,000 in transaction 4 with another wholesaler. However, the equipment received, which is almost new, is smaller and is worth only $1,500. Therefore, the other wholesaler also pays you $2,500 in cash. (You recognize no gain or loss on this transaction.)

Required
1. By using Exhibit 1-2 (p. 12) as a guide, prepare an analysis of BC's transactions for March. Confine your analysis to the effects on the financial position of BC Products.
2. Prepare a balance sheet for BC Products as of March 31, 20X1.

1-34 Analysis of Transactions

Eduardo Gomez, a recent graduate of a law school, was penniless on December 25, 20X3.

1. On December 26, Gomez inherited an enormous sum of money.
2. On December 27, he placed $50,000 in a business checking account for his unincorporated law practice.
3. On December 28, he purchased a home for a down payment of $100,000 plus a home mortgage payable of $250,000.
4. On December 28, Gomez agreed to rent a law office. He provided a $1,000 cash damage deposit (from his business cash), which will be fully refundable when he vacates the premises. This deposit is a business asset. He will make rental payments in advance on the first business day of each month. (The first payment of $700 is not to be made until January 2, 20X4.)
5. On December 28, Gomez purchased a computer for his law practice for $2,000 cash, plus a $2,000 promissory note due in 90 days.

6. On December 28, he purchased legal supplies for $1,000 on open account.
7. On December 28, Gomez purchased office furniture for his practice for $4,000 cash.
8. On December 29, Gomez hired a legal assistant receptionist for $380 per week. She was to report to work on January 2.
9. On December 30, Gomez's law practice lent $2,000 of cash in return for a 1-year note from Gloria See, a local candy store owner. See had indicated that she would spread the news about the new lawyer.

Required

1. Use the format demonstrated in Exhibit 1-2 (p. 12) to analyze the transactions of Eduardo Gomez, lawyer. To avoid crowding, put your numbers in thousands of dollars. Do not restrict yourself to the account titles in Exhibit 1-2.
2. Prepare a balance sheet as of December 31, 20X3.

1-35 Analysis of Transactions

Walgreen Company is a well-known drugstore chain. A condensed balance sheet for May 31, 2003, follows ($ in millions):

Assets		Liabilities and Stockholders' Equity	
Cash	$ 854	Accounts payable	$ 1,956
Inventories	4,020	Other liabilities	2,033
Property and			
other assets	6,085	Stockholders' equity	6,970
Total	$10,959	Total	$10,959

Use a format similar to Exhibit 1-2 to analyze the following transactions for the first 2 days of June ($ amounts are in millions). Then prepare a balance sheet as of June 2.

1. Issued 1,000,000 shares of common stock to employees for cash, $30.
2. Issued 1,500,000 shares of common stock for the acquisition of $45 of special equipment from a supplier.
3. Borrowed cash, signing a note payable for $12.
4. Purchased equipment for cash, $18.
5. Purchased inventories on account, $90.
6. Disbursed cash on account (to reduce the accounts payable), $35.
7. Sold for $2 cash some display equipment at original cost $2.

1-36 Analysis of Transactions

Nike, Inc. had the following condensed balance sheet on August 31, 2003 ($ in millions):

Assets		Liabilities and Owners' Equity	
Cash	$ 998		
Inventories	1,480		
Property, plant,			
& equipment	1,564	Total liabilities	$2,743
Other assets	2,918	Owners' equity	4,217
		Total liabilities and	
Total assets	$6,960	owners' equity	$6,960

Suppose the following transactions occurred during the first 3 days of September ($ in millions):

1. Nike acquired inventories for cash, $17.
2. Nike acquired inventories on open account, $19.
3. Nike returned for full credit, $4, some unsatisfactory shoes that it acquired on open account in August.
4. Nike acquired $12 of equipment for a cash down payment of $3, plus a 2-year promissory note of $9.
5. To encourage wider displays, Nike sold some special store equipment to New York area stores for $40 cash. The equipment had cost $40 in the preceding month.

6. Clint Eastwood produced, directed, and starred in a movie. As a favor to a Nike executive, he agreed to display Nike shoes in a basketball scene. Nike paid no fee.
7. Nike disbursed cash to reduce accounts payable, $16.
8. Nike borrowed cash from a bank, $50.
9. Nike sold additional common stock for cash to new investors, $90.
10. The president of the company sold 5,000 shares of his personal holdings of Nike stock through his stockbroker.

Required
1. By using a format similar to Exhibit 1-2 (p. 12), prepare an analysis showing the effects of the September transactions on the financial position of Nike.
2. Prepare a balance sheet as of September 3.

1-37 Prepare Balance Sheet

Rachel Liebowitz is a realtor. She buys and sells properties on her own account, and she also earns commissions as a real estate agent for buyers and sellers. Her business was organized on November 24, 20X3, as a sole proprietorship. Liebowitz also owns her own personal residence. Consider the following on November 30, 20X3:

1. Liebowitz owes $90,000 on a mortgage on some undeveloped land, which her business acquired for a total price of $175,000.
2. Liebowitz had spent $15,000 cash for a Century 21 real estate franchise. Century 21 is a national affiliation of independent real estate brokers. This franchise is an asset.
3. Liebowitz owes $100,000 on a personal mortgage on her residence, which she acquired on November 20, 20X3, for a total price of $180,000.
4. Liebowitz owes $3,800 on a personal charge account with Nordstrom's Department Store.
5. On November 28, Liebowitz hired Benjamin Goldstein as her first employee. He was to begin work on December 1. Liebowitz was pleased because Goldstein was one of the best real estate salesmen in the area. On November 29, Goldstein was killed in an automobile accident.
6. Liebowitz acquired business furniture for $17,000 on November 25, for $6,000 on open account, plus $11,000 of business cash. On November 26, Liebowitz sold a $1,000 business chair for $1,000 to her next-door business neighbor for cash.
7. Liebowitz's balance at November 30 in her business checking account after all transactions was $9,000.

Prepare a balance sheet as of November 30, 20X3, for Rachel Liebowitz, realtor.

1-38 Bank Balance Sheet

Consider the following balance sheet accounts of Citigroup Inc. (in millions of $):

Assets		Liabilities and Stockholders' Equity	
Cash	$ 18,515	Deposits	$ 374,525
Investment securities	440,550	Other liabilities	595,678
Loans receivable	381,845	Total liabilities	970,203
Other assets	210,540	Stockholders' equity	81,247
		Total liabilities and	
Total assets	$1,051,450	stockholders' equity	$1,051,450

This balance sheet illustrates how Citigroup gathers and uses money. Nearly 80 percent of the total assets are in the form of investments and loans, and more than 35 percent of the total liabilities and stockholders' equity are in the form of deposits, a major liability. That is, these financial institutions are in the business of raising funds from depositors and, in turn, lending those funds to businesses, homeowners, and others. The stockholders' equity is usually tiny in comparison with the deposits (only about 8 percent of total liabilities and stockholders' equity in this case).

1. What Citigroup accounts would be affected if you deposited $1,000?
2. Why are deposits listed as liabilities?
3. What accounts would be affected if the bank loaned John Solvang $45,000 for home renovations?
4. What accounts would be affected if Isabel Ramos withdrew $4,000 from her savings account?

1-39 Airline Balance Sheet

KLM Royal Dutch Airlines is an international airline with a home base at Schiphol Airport in Amsterdam. It is the world's oldest scheduled airline still operating under its original name. It has more than 30,000 employees, 80 percent of them located in the Netherlands. On March 31, 2003, KLM's noncash assets were €7,557 million. Total assets were €8,165 million, and total liabilities were €6,688 million. The symbol € represents the euro, the European currency.

1. Compute the following:
   a. KLM's cash on March 31, 2003.
   b. KLM's stockholders' equity on March 31, 2003.
2. Explain the easiest way to determine KLM's total liabilities and stockholders' equity from the information given in this problem.

1-40 Prepare Balance Sheet

United Technologies Corporation provides a broad range of high-technology products and support services to the building systems and aerospace industries. Those products include Pratt & Whitney aircraft engines, Carrier heating and air conditioning equipment, Otis elevators, and Sikorsky helicopters. United Technologies' September 30, 2003 balance sheet included the following items ($ in millions):

Property, plant, and equipment	$ 4,899
Accounts payable	2,695
Common stock	5,756
Cash	?
Total stockholders' equity	?
Long-term debt	4,650
Total assets	34,062
Inventories	3,963
Other assets	23,779
Other stockholders' equity	?
Other liabilities	16,598

Prepare a condensed balance sheet, including amounts for

1. Cash.
2. Total stockholders' equity.
3. Other stockholders' equity.

1-41 Prepare Balance Sheet

May Department Stores, headquartered in St. Louis, operates Lord & Taylor, Filene's, and six other department store chains. Its balance sheet of February 1, 2003 contained the following items ($ in millions):

Long-term debt	$ 4,035
Cash	(a)
Total shareholders' equity	(b)
Total liabilities	(c)
Common stock	144
Inventories	2,857
Accounts payable	1,099
Property, plant, and equipment	5,466
Additional shareholders' equity	3,891
Other assets	3,592
Other liabilities	2,767
Total assets	11,936

Prepare a condensed balance sheet, including amounts for

(a) Cash. What do you think of its relative size?
(b) Total shareholders' equity.
(c) Total liabilities.

1-42 Presenting Paid-In Capital

Consider excerpts from two balance sheets (amounts in millions):

Citigroup

Common stock ($.01 par value; authorized shares: 6.0 billion), issued shares 5,477,416,254	$ 55
Additional paid-in capital	23,196

IBM

Common stock, par value $.20 per share—shares authorized: 4,687,500,000; shares issued: 1,913,513,218 shares (includes capital in excess of par value)	$14,248

1. How would the presentation of Citigroup stockholders' equity accounts be affected if the company issued 500 million more shares for $30 cash per share?
2. How would the presentation of IBM's stockholders' equity accounts be affected if the company issued 1 million more shares for $60 cash per share? Be specific.

1-43 Presenting Paid-In Capital

Honeywell International Inc., maker of thermostats and a variety of complex control systems, presented the following in its January 1, 2003 balance sheet (in millions).

Common stock—$1.00 par value, 957,599,900 shares issued	?
Additional paid-in capital	$3,409

What amount should be shown on the common stock line? What was the average price per share paid by the original investors for the Honeywell common stock? How do your answers compare with the $24 market price of the stock on January 1, 2003? Comment briefly.

1-44 Presenting Paid-In Capital

Honda Motor Company is the largest producer of motorcycles in the world, as well as a major auto manufacturer. Honda included the following items in its 2003 balance sheet (in millions of Japanese Yen [¥]):

Common stock—authorized 3,600,000,000 shares; issued 974,414,215 shares	¥ 86,067
Additional paid-in capital*	172,529

* Honda actually used the term "capital surplus" instead of the better term, paid-in capital.

1. What is the par value of Honda's common stock?
2. What was the average price per share paid by the original investors for the Honda common stock?
3. How do your answers compare with the ¥4,000 market price of the stock at the end of fiscal 2003? Comment briefly.

1-45 Board of Directors and Audit Committee

Examine the 2003 annual report of General Mills, maker of cereals such as Cheerios, Betty Crocker cake mixes, Progresso soups, and other foods (the Web site is http://media.corporate-ir.net/media_files/NYS/gis/reports/2003_AR.pdf). Turn to the listing of General Mills' Board of Directors near the end of the annual report.

1. How many board members does General Mills have? How many of them are General Mills executives?

2. How many of the nonexecutive directors are executives of other companies? How many are attorneys? How many are academics, government officials, or community advocates? How does the background of board members influence their ability to carry out the responsibilities of the board?

3. How many members of the General Mills' Board of Directors are on the audit committee? Are any audit committee members also General Mills executives? Why would investors want to know the composition of the audit committee?

1-46 Accounting and Ethics

A survey of high school seniors and college freshmen by the AICPA showed that accountants are given high marks for their ethics. Professional associations for both internal accountants and external auditors place much emphasis on their standards of ethical conduct. Discuss why maintaining a reputation for ethical conduct is important for (1) accountants within an organization, and (2) external auditors. What can accountants do to foster a reputation for high ethical standards and conduct?

Collaborative Learning Exercise

1-47 Understanding Transactions

Form groups of three to five students each. Each group should choose one of the companies included in the Dow Jones Industrial Average (Exhibit 1-1), and find its most recent balance sheet. (You might try the company's homepage on the Internet.) Ignore much of the detail on the balance sheet, focusing on the following accounts: cash, inventory, equipment, notes payable, accounts payable, and total stockholders' equity.

Divide the following six assumed transactions among the members of the group:

1. Sold 1 million shares of common stock for a total of $11 million cash (ignore par value).
2. Bought inventory for cash of $3 million.
3. Borrowed $5 million from the bank, receiving the $5 million in cash.
4. Bought inventory for $6 million on open account.
5. Paid $4 million to suppliers for inventory bought on open account.
6. Bought equipment for $9 million cash.

Required

1. The student responsible for each transaction should explain to the group how the transaction would affect the company's balance sheet, using the accounts listed earlier.
2. By using the most recent published balance sheet as a starting point, prepare a balance sheet for the company, assuming the preceding six transactions are the only transactions since the date of the latest balance sheet.

Analyzing and Interpreting Financial Statements

1-48 Financial Statement Research

Select the financial statements of any company, and focus on the balance sheet.

1. Identify the amount of cash (including cash equivalents, if any) shown on the most recent balance sheet.
2. What were the total assets shown on the most recent balance sheet, and the total liabilities plus stockholders' equity? How do these two amounts compare?
3. Compute a) total liabilities and b) total stockholders' equity. (Assume that all items on the right side of the balance sheet that are not explicitly listed as stockholders' equity are liabilities.) Compare the size of the liabilities to stockholders' equity, and comment on the comparison. Write the company's accounting equation, as of the most recent balance sheet date, by filling in the dollar amounts.

1-49 Analyzing Starbucks' Financial Statements

This and similar problems in succeeding chapters focus on the financial statements of Starbucks, contained in the Form 10-K in Appendix A. Starbucks is a worldwide retailer of specialty coffees. As you solve each of these homework problems, you will gradually strengthen your understanding of Starbucks' complete financial statements.

Refer to Starbucks' balance sheet in Appendix A at the end of the book and answer the following questions:

1. How much cash did Starbucks have on September 28, 2003? (Include cash equivalent as part of cash.)
2. List the account titles and amounts from Starbucks' balance sheet that are accounts that were discussed in this chapter.
3. Write the company's accounting equation as of September 28, 2003, by filling in the dollar amounts: Assets = Liabilities + Stockholders' equity. Consider deferred income taxes to be a liability.

1-50 Analyzing Financial Statements Using the Internet: Cisco

Go to www.cisco.com to locate the Cisco annual report. Click on About Cisco. Under Investor Relations, click Annual Reports. Then click the latest annual report. Then click Online Annual Report. Answer the following questions concerning Cisco:

1. Select Letter to Shareholders from the menu. In what languages can you get the letter? Is the message optimistic?
2. Select Corporate Profile from the menu. When was the company founded and by whom? In how many countries does Cisco operate?
3. Now find Cisco's balance sheet under Financial Review. What are Cisco's total assets, total liabilities, and total shareholders' equity? (Treat "Minority interest" as a liability.)
4. How much are Cisco's inventories? Have they increased or decreased in the last year? Do you think that change is good or bad?
5. Find Cisco's list of members of its board of directors. How many directors are there? How many are Cisco executives? How many are academics?
6. Select the Report of Independent Auditors. Who is responsible for the preparation, integrity, and fair presentation of Cisco's financial statements? What is the auditor's responsibility?

Measuring Income to Assess Performance

CHAPTER 2

LEARNING OBJECTIVES

After studying this chapter, you should be able to:

1. Explain how accountants measure income.

2. Determine when a company should record revenue from a sale.

3. Use the concept of matching to record the expenses for a period.

4. Prepare an income statement and show how it is related to a balance sheet.

5. Account for cash dividends and prepare a statement of retained earnings.

6. Explain how the following concepts affect financial statements: entity, reliability, going concern, materiality, cost-benefit, and stable monetary unit.

7. Compute and explain earnings per share, price-earnings ratio, dividend-yield ratio, and dividend-payout ratio.

8. Explain how accounting regulators trade off relevance and reliability in setting accounting standards (Appendix 2).

In 1866, Cadwallander Washburn built his first flour

mill on the banks of the Mississippi River in Minneapolis. Little did he know that in 2004 products produced by his company would continue to satisfy customers worldwide. When you walk down the aisles of a supermarket, notice the cereal section. It is one of the largest displays in the store. The "Big G" cereals such as Cheerios, Wheaties, and Lucky Charms, produced by General Mills, the successor to Mr. Washburn's firm, are prominently displayed. Now look at other parts of the store. General Mills' products surround you. Convenience foods such as Old El Paso Mexican foods, Progresso soups, Green Giant vegetables, and "helper" casseroles; baking supplies such as Betty Crocker cake mixes, Bisquick baking mixes, and Gold Medal flour; snack foods such as Fruit Roll-Ups, Pop Secret microwave popcorn, and Nature Valley granola bars; and refrigerated doughs such as Pillsbury frozen breakfast pastries, Pillsbury frozen waffles, and Totino's frozen pizza, not to mention Yoplait yogurt, Häagen-Dazs ice cream, and many more. General Mills produces all these products. For General Mills to have grown so large and to have so many products, management must have been successful. In this chapter, we see how to measure such success.

How can we measure the overall performance of a company such as General Mills? It has so many products, some doing well and some possibly faltering. When owners and investors want to evaluate the performance of management, they need a measure of profitability for the entire company as well as measures related to segments of the company. The main measure of profitability for a company is its net income—its sales less its expenses—which is the topic of this chapter. In 2003, General Mills had sales of more than $10.5 billion and expenses of about $9.6 billion,

Sales of breakfast cereals contribute to the profitability of General Mills. Most people know that Cheerios and Wheaties are "Big G" cereals, but so are the boxes of Lucky Charms shown here. The company's income statement, described in this chapter, summarizes the profits General Mills makes from Lucky Charms and all the company's other products.

leaving income of approximately $900 million. This means that, on average, when you buy a box of Cheerios for which the store paid $4.00, General Mills ends up with almost $.35 of income. It takes a lot of boxes of cereal, bags of flour, cans of soup, and cartons of yogurt to add up to $10.5 billion of sales. That is why General Mills sells its products in more than 100 countries around the world. In addition, General Mills pays a lot of employees and farmers, uses many buildings and machines, purchases much advertising and other promotion services, and incurs many other expenses—all of which add up to the $9.6 billion of expenses. It takes skillful management to oversee such a large operation, and accounting reports are an important tool of management. It also takes huge amounts of capital to support such operations, and General Mills has raised part of that capital by selling more than 500 million ownership shares to the public. These owners also want financial reports on General Mills' operations to help them evaluate their decision to invest in the firm.

Until now you may have thought of a trip to the grocery store as nothing more than a chance to replenish your food supply. However, from here on you can think about the accounting systems that record sales for the items you buy and identify the expenses required to bring this food to you. It might not make your trip more enjoyable, but it will make it more enlightening. ■

Investors in General Mills eagerly await reports about the company's annual income, as do investors in other companies. Investors care about the price of their shares, and stock prices generally reflect investors' expectations about income. However, actual reported income often differs from what was expected, and stock prices react accordingly. For example, General Mills disclosed on April 25, 2002 that its income would fall short of expectations. Fourth-quarter 2002 income would be $.25 per share instead of the expected $.43, and the new prediction for annual 2003 income was $2.60 instead of the earlier expectation of $2.90. What happened? After the announcement, General Mills' stock price fell from $48 to $43. By the time its actual 2003 income of $2.49 per share was announced, the price had stabilized at about $46 a share. The General Mills example showed the reaction to a company announcement about income, but even rumors about earnings can have a major effect on stock prices. On October 8, 2002, AFX News Limited reported that "Nestlé AG shares were under pressure on rumors the company may issue a profit warning," causing a nearly 5 percent drop in Nestlé's stock price. Although income and stock prices tend to move in the same direction, this relationship is not perfect. Look at Exhibit 2-1, which shows the income and stock price of McDonald's Corporation for the last 14 years. The left vertical axis and the orange bars represent the stock price in dollars per share, and the right vertical axis and green bars are the income in billions of dollars. As income increased, so did the stock price, and when income began to fall, the stock price also fell. However, you can see the stock price "bubble" in the late 1990s, when stock prices in the entire market generally rose faster than income. The recession in 2001 and 2002 brought stock prices for most companies, including McDonald's, more in line with earnings.

Thus, income is a key measure of performance and value. This chapter presents the basics of measuring income, with a special focus on revenues and expenses.

Introduction to Income Measurement

OBJECTIVE 1

Explain how accountants measure income.

Measuring income is important to everyone, from individuals to businesses, because we all need to know how well we are doing economically. Income is like the number on the scoreboard that tells how well the home team is performing. However, measuring income is not as easy as measuring the number of runs scored in a baseball game. Most people regard income as a measure of the increase in the "wealth" of an entity over a period of time. However, there is less agreement on just what wealth is and how we should measure it. Nevertheless, accountants have agreed on a common set of rules for measuring income and wealth that all companies are supposed to apply. Decision makers such as investors can more easily

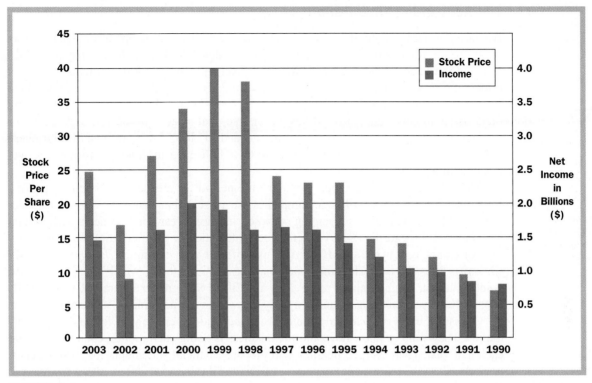

Exhibit 2-1
Relationship Between Stock Price and Net Income for McDonald's Corporation

compare the performance of one company with that of another when both companies use the same "measuring stick," net income. Let's now take a look at the foundations of the rules for measuring income. First, we look at the period over which we measure income.

Operating Cycle

Most companies follow a similar operating cycle. During the **operating cycle,** the company uses cash to acquire goods and services, which in turn it sells to customers. The customers in turn pay for their purchases with cash, which brings us back to the beginning of the cycle. Consider a retail company such as **Wal-Mart:**

operating cycle
The time span during which a company uses cash to acquire goods and services, which in turn it sells to customers, who in turn pay for their purchases with cash.

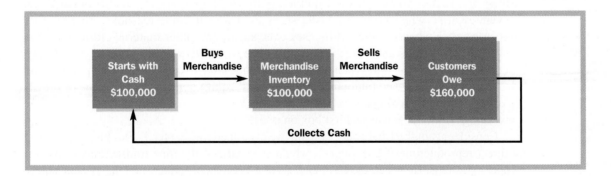

The box for the amounts owed to the entity by customers is larger than the other two boxes because the company's objective is to sell its goods at a price higher than it paid for them. The amount by which the selling price exceeds expenses is profit or income. The total amount of profit earned during a particular period depends on the difference between the selling price and costs and on how much merchandise the company sells.

The Accounting Time Period

Because it is hard to accurately measure the success of an ongoing operation, the only way to be certain of a business's success is to close its doors, sell all its assets, pay all liabilities, and return any leftover cash to the owner. Actually, in the 1400s, Venetian merchant traders did exactly that for each and every voyage. Successful investors might combine their cash to initiate another voyage, whereas investors in failed voyages might have to sell other assets to cover unpaid liabilities. Of course, that system would not be feasible for companies today (imagine a company that needed to close down and restart after every business deal!). Instead, companies need to be able to measure their performances over discrete time periods.

The calendar year is the most popular time period for measuring income or profits. However, about 40 percent of large companies use a **fiscal year** that differs from a calendar year. Established purely for accounting purposes, the fiscal year does not necessarily end on December 31. Instead, the fiscal year-end date is often the low point in annual business activity. For example, Kmart and JCPenney use a fiscal year ending on January 31. Why? Christmas sales and post-Christmas sales are over, and inventories, which are at their lowest point of the year, can be counted more easily and valued with greater accuracy. General Mills ends its fiscal year on the last Sunday in May, a low point in the company's operating cycle.

Of course, users of financial statements cannot wait an entire year for financial information. They want to know how well the business is doing each month, each quarter, and each half year. Therefore, companies also prepare financial statements for these **interim periods.** The SEC requires companies to officially file financial statements every quarter. However, in some countries, authorities require only annual statements.

Revenues and Expenses

Now that we know the "when" and "why" of measuring income, we need to examine the "how." Revenues and expenses are the key components in measuring income. These terms apply to the inflows and outflows of assets that occur during a business's operating cycle. Companies gain assets when they sell products or services and record **sales revenues,** or sometimes simply **sales** or **revenues,** which increase the owner's interest (equity) in the business by the amount of assets received in exchange for the delivery of goods or services to customers. In contrast, companies give up assets when they recognize **expenses,** which decrease the owner's interest. Expenses are measures of the assets that a company gives up or consumes in order to deliver goods or services to a customer. Together revenues and expenses define the fundamental meaning of **income,** which is simply the excess of revenues over expenses. Common synonyms for income are **profits** or **earnings.** Revenues arise when General Mills ships a carton of Cheerios boxes to Safeway. Expenses arise when General Mills uses oats, sugar, and other materials to produce the Cheerios that it ships and when it pays the costs of delivering the products to Safeway. General Mills earns income when it receives revenues that exceed the costs to produce and deliver the Cheerios. The total cumulative owners' equity generated by income or profits is called **retained earnings** or **retained income.** You can learn the importance of income or earnings from the Business First box on p. 51.

Consider again the Biwheels Company we examined in Chapter 1. Exhibit 2-2 is almost a direct reproduction of Exhibit 1-2, which summarized the nine transactions of Hector Lopez's business. However, the company has now been incorporated, and the owners' equity account is no longer Hector Lopez, Capital. In Exhibit 2-2, it is Stockholders' Equity.

Now consider some additional transactions. Suppose Biwheels' sales for the entire month of January amount to $160,000 on open account. The cost to Biwheels of the inventory sold is $100,000. Selling on open account creates an account receivable. **Accounts receivable** (or **trade receivables** or simply **receivables**) are amounts owed to a company by customers as a result of the company's delivering goods or services to them

---

fiscal year
The year established for accounting purposes, which may differ from a calendar year.

interim periods
The time spans established for accounting purposes that are less than 1 year.

revenues (sales, sales revenues)
Increases in owners' equity arising from increases in assets received in exchange for the delivery of goods or services to customers.

expenses
Decreases in owners' equity that arise because a company delivers goods or services to customers.

income (profits, earnings)
The excess of revenues over expenses.

retained earnings (retained income)
Total cumulative owners' equity generated by income or profits.

accounts receivable (trade receivables, receivables)
Amount owed to a company by customers as a result of delivering goods or services and extending credit in the ordinary course of business.

HOW IMPORTANT ARE EARNINGS?

Earnings are a critical measure of company performance, and investors watch earnings carefully. Almost every day the financial press reports on current and prospective earnings. *Barron's* is a financial weekly published by Dow Jones with a Web site at www.barrons.com. The October 21, 2002 issue included an article titled, "Tech Earnings Remain a Farrago Despite IBM Surprise." What does this mean? The reference to farrago tech earnings means that recent reports of net income for technology stocks is a hodgepodge—some stocks up and some down. Earnings for IBM, Yahoo, and Microsoft surged, whereas earnings for others such as Intel, Gateway, and Apple failed to meet expectations.

Thus, meeting earnings expectations is important. Analysts develop earnings predictions for companies, and *Barron's* publishes consensus earnings forecasts. Each week *Barron's* lists the companies who are expected to announce earnings during the next week and reports the expected day of announcement, the earnings level reported in the prior year, and the consensus expectation of analysts for what earnings should be this year. People anticipate these announcements and revise their beliefs about the company when the results become known.

Stocks of companies whose earnings exceed the consensus expectation reported by *Barron's* generally do well, and vice versa. When IBM's earnings exceeded expectations in October 2002, its stock price increased by about 35 percent. Yahoo also beat earnings expectations that month, lifting its stock from under $10 to more than $15, but analysts' doubts about the sustainability of this income immediately began dropping the price again. Microsoft's earnings also exceeded expectations that month, raising its stock from about $44 to about $53.

On the opposite side of the farrago were Intel and Apple. Both had earnings that came in below expectations, with Intel's price dropping by 18 percent and Apple's by nearly 10 percent. Gateway met earnings expectations (or, rather, loss expectations), but decreased its predictions of the company's future income. Its stock dropped nearly 25 percent. You can see that investors take companies' earnings reports seriously.

Source: *Barron's*, October 21, 2002. Web sites for IBM, Microsoft, Yahoo, Intel, Apple, and Gateway.

---

and extending credit in the ordinary course of business. Thus, the January sales increase Biwheels' accounts receivable by $160,000. Delivering merchandise to customers reduces its inventory by $100,000.

Note that we record the January sales and other transactions illustrated here as summarized transactions. The company's sales, purchases of inventory, collections from customers, or disbursements to suppliers do not all take place all at once. Actual accounting systems would record every sale using a cash register, a scanner, or some other data entry device, and would then record summary data daily.

The accounting for the summarized sales transaction has two phases, a revenue phase (10a) and an expense phase (10b):

	Assets		=	Liabilities	+	Stockholders' Equity
	Accounts Receivable	**Merchandise Inventory**				**Retained Earnings**
(10a) Sales on open account	+160,000		=			+160,000 (sales revenues)
(10b) Cost of merchandise inventory sold		−100,000	=			−100,000 (cost of goods sold expenses)

Description of Transactions	Cash	+	Merchandise Inventory	+	Store Equipment	=	Note Payable	+	Accounts Payable	+	Stockholders' Equity
			Assets			**=**	**Liabilities**	**+**			**Stockholders' Equity**
(1) Initial investment	+400,000					=					+400,000
(2) Loan from bank	+100,000					=	+100,000				
(3) Acquire store equipment for cash	−15,000				+15,000	=					
(4) Acquire inventory for cash	−120,000		+120,000			=					
(5) Acquire inventory on credit			+10,000			=			+10,000		
(6) Acquire inventory for cash plus credit	−10,000		+30,000			=			+20,000		
(7) Sale of equipment	+1,000				−1,000	=					
(8) Return of inventory acquired on January 5			−800			=			−800		
(9) Payments to creditors	−4,000					=			−4,000		
Balance January 12, 20X2	352,000	+	159,200	+	14,000	=	100,000	+	25,200	+	400,000
			525,200						525,200		

Exhibit 2-2
Biwheels Company
Analysis of Transactions for January 2, 20X2 to January 12, 20X2 (in $)

To understand this transaction, think of it as two steps occuring simultaneously in the balance sheet equation: an inflow of assets in the form of accounts receivable (10a) in exchange for an outflow of assets in the form of merchandise inventory (10b). This exchange of assets does not affect liabilities, so to keep the equation in balance, stockholders' equity must rise by $60,000 [$160,000 (sales revenues) − $100,000 (cost of goods sold expense)]. Note that **cost of goods sold** expense (also called **cost of sales** or **cost of revenue**) is the original acquisition cost of the inventory that a company sells to customers during the reporting period.

cost of goods sold (cost of sales, cost of revenue)
The original acquisition cost of the inventory that a company sells to customers during the reporting period.

As entries 10a and 10b show, we record revenue from sales as an increase in the asset Accounts Receivable and an increase in Retained Earnings. In contrast, we record the cost of goods sold expense as a decrease in the asset Merchandise Inventory and a decrease in Retained Earnings. You can thus see that revenues are positive entries to the retained earnings account in the stockholders' equity section of the balance sheet, and expenses are negative entries to retained earnings. We illustrate these relationships as follows, where the arrows show the components of the various accounts:

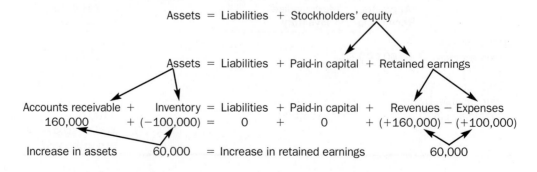

The ultimate purpose of sales is not to generate accounts receivable. Rather, Biwheels wants to eventually collect these receivables in cash. The company may receive some cash shortly after a credit sale, and some customers may delay payments for long periods. You have probably seen ads for furniture where the payments for the furniture are not due until 6 months or even a year after the sale. Suppose Biwheels collects $5,000 of its $160,000 of accounts receivable during January. This summary transaction, call it transaction 11, increases cash and decreases accounts receivable. It does not affect retained earnings.

		Assets		=	Liabilities	+	Stockholders' Equity
	Cash	Accounts Receivable	Merchandise Inventory				Retained Earnings
(11) Collection of accounts receivable	+5,000	−5,000		=			

We next consider how accountants decide when to record revenues in the books and how this affects measures of income.

Measuring Income

Accrual Basis and Cash Basis

There are multiple ways to measure income. We discuss the two most popular methods, the accrual basis and the cash basis. The **accrual basis** recognizes the impact of transactions in the financial statements for the time periods when revenues and expenses occur. That is, accountants record revenue as a company earns it, and they record expenses as the company incurs them—not necessarily when cash changes hands. In contrast, the **cash basis** recognizes the impact of transactions in the financial statements only when a company receives or pays cash.

For many years, accountants debated the merits of accrual-basis versus cash-basis accounting. Supporters of the accrual basis maintained that the cash basis ignores activities that increase or decrease assets other than cash. Supporters of the cash basis pointed out that a company, no matter how well it seems to be doing, can go bankrupt if it does not manage its cash properly. Who is correct? In the end, the debate has been declared a draw. Companies include both an accrual-basis income statement and a cash-basis statement of cash flows in their annual reports. Although companies must prepare cash flow statements, the results are not labeled "income." For the calculation of income over a period of time, the accrual basis won out and is the current standard for income measurement and the best basis for measuring economic performance.

Although both cash and accrual bases have their merits, the accrual basis has the advantage of presenting a more complete summary of the entity's value-producing activities. It recognizes revenues as they are earned and matches costs to revenues. We illustrated this accrual process in our analysis of the sale on open account in transaction 10. We recognized revenue although Biwheels received no cash, and we recorded an expense although Biwheels paid no cash. Let's now take a look at some of the specifics of the accrual basis.

accrual basis
Accounting method that recognizes the impact of transactions on the financial statements in the time periods when revenues and expenses occur.

cash basis
Accounting method that recognizes the impact of transactions on the financial statements only when a company receives or pays cash.

Recognition of Revenues

A major convention accountants use to measure income on an accrual basis is **recognition** of revenues, which is a test for determining whether to record revenues in

OBJECTIVE 2

Determine when a company should record revenue from a sale.

recognition
A test for determining whether to record revenues in the financial statements of a given period. To be recognized, revenues must be earned and realized.

the financial statements of a given period. To be recognized, revenues must ordinarily meet two criteria:

1. *They must be earned.* A company earns revenues when it delivers goods or services to a customer.
2. *They must be realized.* A company realizes revenues when it receives cash or claims to cash in exchange for goods or services. "Claims to cash" usually mean credit or some other promise to pay. To recognize revenue on the basis of a promise to pay, the company must be relatively certain that it will receive the cash.

Revenue recognition for most retail companies, such as **Wal-Mart**, **Safeway**, and **McDonald's**, is straightforward. They both earn and realize revenue at the point of sale — when a customer makes a full payment and takes possession of the goods. Other companies may earn and realize revenue at different times. In such cases, they do not recognize revenue until both earning and realization are complete. Consider the following examples:

- *Newsweek* receives prepaid subscriptions. *Newsweek* realizes revenue when it receives the subscription, but it does not earn the revenue until delivery of each issue.
- A dealer in oriental rugs lets a potential customer take a rug home on a trial basis. The customer has possession of the goods, but the dealer records no revenue until the customer formally promises to accept the rug and pay for it.

INTERPRETING FINANCIAL STATEMENTS

Suppose you are examining the 2004 financial statements of a new theater company. The theater sells a subscription series that allows patrons to attend all nine of its productions that occur monthly from September through May. During August and September, the company sold 1,000 subscriptions for the 2004–2005 season at $180 each and collected the cash. How much revenue from these subscriptions did the theater recognize in its financial statements for the year ended December 31, 2004?

Answer
At December 31, 2004, the theater has produced only four out of nine productions, so the company has earned only four-ninths of the total or $80,000. Its total collections are $180,000, so the theater has realized all $180,000, but because it has earned only $80,000, it recognized and therefore recorded only $80,000 of revenue in 2004.

Matching

We have seen how to recognize revenues on the accrual basis. What about expenses? There are two types of expenses in every accounting period: (1) those linked with the revenues earned that period, and (2) those linked with the time period itself. Some expenses, called **product costs,** are naturally linked with revenues. Cost of goods sold and sales commissions are good examples. If there are no revenues, there is no cost of goods sold or sales commissions. When do we recognize product costs? Accountants match such expenses to the revenues they help produce. We recognize and record expenses in the same period that we recognize their related revenues. This process is known as **matching.**

product costs
Costs that are linked with revenues and are charged as expenses when the related revenue is recognized.

matching
The recording of expenses in the same time period that we recognize the related revenues.

It is difficult to link some other expenses directly to specific revenues. Rent and many administrative expenses are examples. These expenses support a company's operations for a given period, and thus we call them **period costs.** We record period costs as expenses in the period in which the company incurs them. In essence, we match the expenses to the revenues of the period for which we incur the expenses. For example, rent expense arises because of the passage of time, regardless of the sales level. Therefore, rent is a good example of a period cost. Consider a General Mills warehouse. The rent expense for May gives General Mills the right to use the building for the month. General Mills matches the rent expense with May's sales, regardless of whether the sales are high or low.

To help us match expenses with revenues, we record some purchases of goods or services as assets because we want to match their costs with the revenues in future periods. For example, we might buy inventory that we will not sell until a future period. By recording this inventory first as an asset and then expensing it when we sell the item, we match the cost of the inventory with the revenue from the sale of the inventory. Another example is rent paid in advance. Suppose a firm pays annual rent of $12,000 on January 1 for the use of a building. We increase an asset account, prepaid rent, by $12,000 because we have not yet used the rental services. Each month we reduce the prepaid rent account by $1,000 and increase rent expense by $1,000, recognizing the using up of the prepaid rent asset and matching the rent expense with the revenue recorded in each month that we use the building.

period costs
Items supporting a company's operations for a given period. We record the expenses in the time period in which the company incurs them.

Applying Matching

To focus on matching, assume that Biwheels Company has only two expenses other than the cost of goods sold: rent expense and depreciation expense. Rent is $2,000 per month, payable quarterly in advance. Transaction 12 (see Exhibit 2-3, which merely continues Exhibit 2-2) is the payment of $6,000 of store rent, covering January, February, and March of 20X2. (Assume that Biwheels made this initial payment on January 16, although rent is commonly paid at the start of the rental period.)

The rent payment gives the company the right to use store facilities for the next 3 months. The use of the facilities constitutes a future benefit, so Biwheels records the $6,000 in an asset account, Prepaid Rent. Transaction 12, the rent payment, shows no effect on stockholders' equity in the balance sheet equation. Biwheels simply exchanges one asset, cash, for another, prepaid rent.

At the end of January, Biwheels records transaction 13. It recognizes that the company has used 1 month (one-third of the total) of the rental services. Therefore, Biwheels reduces Prepaid Rent by $2,000. It also reduces the Retained Earnings section of Stockholders' Equity by $2,000 as rent expense for January. This recognition of rent expense means that Biwheels has used $2,000 of the asset, Prepaid Rent, in the conduct of operations during January. That $2,000 worth of rent was a period cost for January, and Biwheels recognized it as an expense at the end of that period.

Prepaid rent of $4,000 remains an asset as of January 31. Why? Because without the prepayment, Biwheels would have to pay $2,000 in both February and March for rent. So Biwheels will recover the cost of the prepayment in the sense that its future cash outflows will be $4,000 less than they would have been if Biwheels had not prepaid the rent.

The same matching concept that underlies the accounting for prepaid rent applies to **depreciation,** which is the systematic allocation of the acquisition cost of long-lived or fixed assets to the expense accounts of particular periods that benefit from the use of the assets. These assets are tangible physical assets, such as buildings, equipment, furniture, and fixtures, owned by the entity. Land is not subject to depreciation because it does not deteriorate over time.

In both prepaid rent and depreciation, the business purchases an asset that gradually wears out or is used. As a company uses an asset, it transfers more and more of its original cost from an asset account to an expense account. The sole difference between depreciation and prepaid rent is the length of time taken before the asset loses its usefulness. Buildings, equipment, and furniture remain useful for many years; prepaid rent and other prepaid expenses usually expire within a year.

OBJECTIVE 3

Use the concept of matching to record the expenses for a period.

depreciation
The systematic allocation of the acquisition cost of long-lived or fixed assets to the expense accounts of particular periods that benefit from the use of the assets.

Exhibit 2-3

Description of Transactions	Cash	+	Accounts Receivable	+	Merchandise Inventory	+	Prepaid Rent	+	Store Equiment	=	Note Payable	+	Accounts Payable	+	Paid-in Capital	+	Retained Earnings
(1)–(9) See Exhibit 2-2 Balance, January 12, 20X2	352,000	+			159,200	+		+	14,000	=	100,000	+	25,200	+	400,000		
(10a) Sales on open account (inflow of assets)			+160,000							=							+160,000 (Sales revenu1e)
(10b) Cost of merchandise inventory sold (outflow of assets)					−100,000					=							−100,000 (Increase cost of goods sold expense)
(11) Collect accounts receivable	+5,000		−5,000														
(12) Pay rent in advance	−6,000						+6,000			=							
(13) Recognize expiration of rental services							−2,000			=							−2,000 (Increase rent expense)
(14) Recognize expiration of equipment services									−100	=							−100 (Increase depreciation rent expense)
Balance January 31, 20X2	351,000	+	155,000	+	59,200	+	4,000	+	13,900	=	100,000	+	25,200	+	400,000	+	57,900

583,100 = 583,100

Exhibit 2-3
Biwheels Company
Analysis of Transactions for January 20X2 (in $)

Transaction 14 in Exhibit 2-3 records the depreciation expense for the Biwheels equipment. A portion of the original cost of $14,000 becomes depreciation expense in each month of the equipment's useful life. Assume that Biwheels will use the equipment for 140 months. Under the matching concept, the depreciation expense for January is $14,000 ÷ 140 months, or $100 per month:

	Assets	=	Liabilities	+	Stockholders' Equity
	Store Equipment				Retained Earnings
(14) Recognize depreciation expense	−100	=			−100 (Increase depreciation expense)

In this transaction, Biwheels decreases the asset account, Store Equipment, and also decreases the stockholders' equity account, Retained Earnings. Transactions 13 and 14 highlight the general concept of expense under the accrual basis. We can account for the purchase and use of goods and services, for example, inventories, rent, and equipment, in two basic steps: (1) the acquisition of the assets (transactions 3, 4, 5, and 6 in Exhibit 2-2 and transaction 12 in Exhibit 2-3), and (2) the expiration of the assets as expenses (transactions 10b, 13, and 14 in Exhibit 2-3). As these examples show, when a company uses prepaid expenses and fixed assets, it decreases both total assets and owners' equity. Expense accounts are deductions from stockholders' equity.

Recognition of Expired Assets

You can think of assets such as inventory, prepaid rent, and equipment as costs that a company stores and carries forward to future periods and records as expenses when it uses them. For inventory, we record the expense when the company sells the item and recognizes revenue from the sale. For rent, we recognize the expense in the period to which the rent applies. For equipment, we split the total cost of the long-lived asset into smaller pieces and recognize one piece of that total cost as an expense in each of the periods that benefits from the use of the equipment. In summary, inventory costs are *product costs* that accountants match to the revenue they produce. Rent is a *period cost* that accountants match to the period it benefits. Because equipment benefits many periods, accountants spread its cost over those periods as depreciation expense.

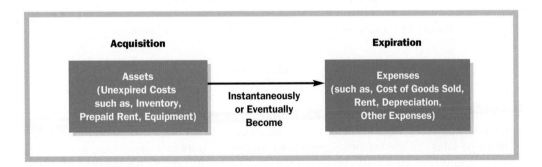

The analysis of the inventory, rent, and depreciation transactions in Exhibit 2-3 distinguishes between acquisition and expiration. Biwheels recorded inventory, rent, and equipment as assets when it acquired them. The unexpired costs of inventory, prepaid rent, and equipment then remain assets until used. When Biwheels uses them, they become expenses. What happens if Biwheels uses assets almost immediately after it acquires them? For example, companies often acquire and use services such as advertising almost simultaneously. Conceptually, these costs are, at least momentarily, assets until the company uses them, at which time it writes them off as expenses. For example, suppose **General Mills** purchased newspaper advertising for Wheaties for $1,000 cash. To abide by the acquisition–expiration sequence, we could analyze the transaction in two phases as in alternative 1 that follows:

	Assets			=	Liabilities	+	Stockholders' Equity	
Transaction	Cash	+ Other Assets	+ Prepaid Advertising =				Paid-in Capital +	Retained Earnings
Alternative 1: Two Phases								
Phase (a) Prepay for advertising	−1,000		+1,000 =					
Phase (b) Use advertising			−1,000 =					−1,000 (Advertising expense)
Alternative 2: One Phase								
Phases (a) and (b) together	−1,000		=					−1,000 (Advertising expense)

In practice, however, so little time passes between the acquisition and use of prepaid advertising and other similar services that accountants do not bother recording them as assets. Instead, accountants use the recording shortcut shown above in alternative 2. When they prepare financial statements, this alternative presents the correct result, although the two-step alternative 1 more accurately portrays the events.

Although this chapter focuses on the income statement, it is important to realize that the income statement is really just a way of explaining changes between one balance sheet and another. It shows how the performance of management moved the company from its beginning position to its end-of-the-period position. The balance sheet equation shows revenue and expense items as subparts of owners' equity. The income statement simply collects all these changes in owners' equity for the accounting period and combines them in one place.

(1) Assets (A) = Liabilities (L) + Stockholders' equity (SE)

(2) Assets (A) = Liabilities   + Paid-in capital + Retained Earnings

(3) Assets (A) = Liabilities   + Paid-in capital + $\dfrac{\text{Cumulative}}{\text{Revenues}} - \dfrac{\text{Cumulative}}{\text{Expenses}}$

Revenue and expense accounts are nothing more than subdivisions of stockholders' equity—temporary stockholders' equity accounts. Their purpose is to summarize the volume of sales and the various expenses so we can measure income.

The analysis of each transaction in Exhibits 2-2 and 2-3 illustrates the dual nature of the balance sheet equation, which always remains in balance. If the items affected are all on one side of the equation, the total amount added must equal the total amount subtracted on that side. If the items affected are on both sides, then equal amounts are simultaneously added or subtracted on each side.

The striking feature of the balance sheet equation is its universal applicability. No one has ever conceived a transaction, no matter how simple or complex, that we cannot analyze via the equation. Business leaders and accountants employ the balance sheet equation constantly to be sure they understand the effects of business transactions they are planning.

is clearly unethical. However, ethical standards and accounting standards often leave much room for individual interpretation and judgment. The most difficult ethical situations arise when there is strong pressure to take an action in the gray area between ethical and unethical or when two ethical standards conflict. Because net income is so important in measuring managerial performance, occasionally managers put pressure on accountants to report higher revenues or lower costs than is appropriate. In 2002, authorities accused executives at Enron, WorldCom, and other companies of manipulating net income, Enron by recognizing excess revenues and WorldCom by omitting required expenses.

One area that requires judgment, and therefore leaves room for ethical conflicts, is depreciation. Suppose you are an accountant for an airline with $15 billion of new airplanes. Management wants to depreciate the airplanes over 30 years—leading to depreciation of $500 million per year. You discover that most airlines depreciate similar airplanes over 15 years, which would mean $1 billion of annual depreciation. Management argues that airplanes such as these will physically last at least 30 years, and there is no reason not to use them for the entire 30-year period. You believe that technological change is likely to make them obsolete in 15 years, but such technological improvements are not assured and may not occur. Before-tax income for the company is $400 million, so increasing depreciation by $500 million will put the company in a loss position. If this happens, banks might ask for repayment of loans and force the company into bankruptcy. Should you prepare an income statement with $500 million of depreciation or insist on the larger depreciation expense?

There is no obviously right answer to this question. The important point is that you recognize the ethical dimensions of this problem and weigh them when forming your opinion. The company might be in dire straits if you refuse to prepare an income statement with the $500 million of depreciation. However, if you truly believe that it is not proper to depreciate the airplanes over 30 years, you cannot ethically prepare an income statement with only $500 million of depreciation. Could management be right and you be wrong about the proper depreciation expense? Is management trying to influence its net income by manipulating its depreciation expense? Accountants must assert their judgments in cases such as this, and recognizing the ethical issues involved is an important part of making those judgments.

Summary Problem for Your Review

PROBLEM

Biwheels' transactions for January were analyzed in Exhibits 2-2 and 2-3. The balance sheet at January 31, 20X2, follows.

Biwheels Company
Balance Sheet January 31, 20X2

Assets		Liabilities and Stockholders' Equity		
Cash	$351,000	Liabilities:		
Accounts receivable	155,000	Note payable		$100,000
Merchandise		Accounts payable		25,200
inventory	59,200	Total liabilities		$125,200
Prepaid rent	4,000	Stockholders' equity		
Store equipment	13,900	Paid-in capital	$400,000	
		Retained earnings	57,900	
		Total stockholders' equity		457,900
		Total liabilities and		
Total assets	$583,100	stockholders' equity		$583,100

Description of Transactions	Cash	+ Accounts Receivable	+ Merchandise Inventory	+ Prepaid Rent	+ Store Equipment	=	Notes Payable	+ Accounts Payable	+ Paid-in Capital	+ Retained Earnings
Assets						=	**Liabilities**		+ **Stockholder's Equity**	
Balance, January 31, 20X2	351,000 +	155,000 +	59,200 +	4,000 +	13,900	=	100,000 +	25,200 +	400,000 +	57,900
(15) Collection of accounts receivable	+130,000	−130,000								
(16) Payments of accounts payable	−15,000					=		−15,000		
(17) Acquisitions of inventory on open account and for cash	−10,000		+90,000			=		+80,000		
(18a) Sales on open account and for cash	+51,000	+125,000				=				+176,000 (Increase sales revenue)
(18b) Cost of inventory sold			−110,000			=				−110,000 (Increase cost of goods sold expense)
(19) Recognize expiration of rental services				−2,000		=				−2,000 (Increase rent expense)
(20) Recognize expiration of equipment services (depreciation)					−100	=				−100 (Increase depreciation expense)
(21a) Borrow from bank	+10,000					=	+10,000			
(21b) Purchase store equipment	−10,000				+10,000	=				
Balance February 28, 20X2	507,000 +	150,000 +	39,200 +	2,000 +	23,800	=	110,000 +	90,200 +	400,000 +	121,800

722,000 = 722,000

Exhibit 2-5
Biwheels Company
Analysis of Transactions for February 20X2 (in $)

The following series of transactions occurred during February:

15. Collections of accounts receivable, $130,000.
16. Payments of accounts payable, $15,000.
17. Acquisitions of inventory on open account, $80,000, and for cash, $10,000.
18. Sales of merchandise for $176,000, of which $125,000 was on open account and $51,000 was for cash. Biwheels carried the sold merchandise in inventory at a cost of $110,000.
19. Recognition of rent expense for February.
20. Recognition of depreciation expense for February.
21. Borrowing of $10,000 from the bank, which Biwheels used to buy $10,000 of store equipment on February 28.

Required

1. Prepare an analysis of transactions, employing the balance sheet equation approach demonstrated in Exhibit 2-3.
2. Prepare a balance sheet as of February 28, 20X2, and an income statement for the month of February.

SOLUTION

1. The analysis of transactions is in Exhibit 2-5. All transactions are straightforward extensions or repetitions of the January transactions.
2. Exhibit 2-6 contains the balance sheet and income statement, which were both described earlier. Notice that the balance sheet lists the ending balances in all the accounts in Exhibit 2-5. The income statement summarizes the revenue and expense entries in retained earnings.

Exhibit 2-6
Biwheels Company
Balance Sheet February 28, 20X2 (before declaring dividends)

Assets		Liabilities and Stockholders' Equity		
Cash	$507,000	Liabilities		
Accounts receivable	150,000	Notes payable	$110,000	
Merchandise		Accounts payable	90,200	$200,200
inventory	39,200			
Prepaid rent	2,000	Stockholders' equity		
Store equipment	23,800	Paid-in capital	$400,000	
		Retained earnings	121,800	521,800
Total	$722,000	Total		$722,000

Biwheels Company
Income Statement for the Month Ended February 28, 20X2

Sales		$176,000
Deduct expenses		
Cost of goods sold	$110,000	
Rent	2,000	
Depreciation	100	112,100
Net income		$ 63,900

Accounting for Dividends and Retained Earnings

OBJECTIVE 5

Account for cash dividends and prepare a statement of retained earnings.

Recall that we record a corporation's revenues and expenses for a particular time period in the stockholders' equity account, Retained Earnings. Because net income is the excess of revenues over expenses, the retained earnings account increases by the amount of net income reported during the period. If expenses exceed revenues, retained earnings decrease by the amount of the period's net loss.

Cash Dividends

In addition to revenues and expenses, we record **cash dividends,** distributions of cash to stockholders, in the Retained Earnings account. These distributions reduce retained earnings. Corporations pay out cash dividends to stockholders to provide a return on the stockholders' investment in the corporation. The ability to pay dividends is fundamentally a result of profitable operations. Retained earnings increase as profits accumulate, and they decrease as a company pays dividends.

Although cash dividends decrease retained earnings, they are not expenses like rent and depreciation. We do not deduct them from revenues because dividends are not directly linked to the generation of revenue or the costs of operating activities. They are transactions with shareholders. For example, assume that on February 28, Biwheels declared and disbursed cash dividends of $50,000 to stockholders. We can analyze this transaction (22) as follows:

	Assets	=	Liabilities	+	Stockholders' Equity
	Cash				Retained Earnings
(22) Declaration and payment of cash dividends	−$50,000	=			−$50,000 (Dividends)

Cash dividends distribute some of the company's assets (cash) to shareholders, thus reducing the economic value of their remaining interest in Biwheels. Of course, companies must have sufficient cash on hand to pay cash dividends.

Transaction 22 presented the payment of a dividend as a single transaction. However, corporations usually approach dividend matters in steps. The board of directors *declares*—announces its intention to pay—a dividend on one date (declaration date), payable to those *stockholders on record* as owning the stock on a second date (record date), and actually *pays* the dividend on a third date (payment date).

Not all companies pay dividends. Starbucks has never paid any dividends. Until 2003, Microsoft also retained all its income to finance future growth, although it now pays a small dividend. McDonald's also paid no dividends during its early, highest growth years, but today it pays dividends. As a successful company grows, the retained earnings account can soar enormously if the company pays no dividends. Retained earnings can easily be the largest stockholders' equity account. Its balance is the cumulative, lifetime earnings of the company less its cumulative, lifetime losses and dividends. For example, on May 25, 2003, General Mills had retained earnings of $3,074 million, whereas total stockholders' equity was only $4,175 million.

Retained Earnings and Cash

The existence of retained earnings and cash enable a board of directors to declare a cash dividend. However, Cash and Retained Earnings are two entirely separate accounts, sharing no necessary relationship. Consider the following illustration:

Step 1. Assume an opening balance sheet of:

Cash	$100	Paid-in capital	$100

Step 2. Purchase inventory for $50 cash. The balance sheet now reads:

Cash	$ 50	Paid-in capital	$100
Inventory	50		
Total assets	$100		

Step 3. Now sell the inventory for $80 cash, which produces a retained earnings of $80 − $50 = $30:

Cash	$130	Paid-in capital	$100
		Retained earnings	30
		Total owners' equity	$130

At this stage, the retained earnings seem to be directly linked to the cash increase of $30. It is, but do not think that retained earnings is a claim against the cash specifically. Remember, it is a claim against total assets. We can clarify this relationship by the transaction that follows.

Step 4. Purchase inventory and equipment, in the amounts of $60 and $50, respectively. Now,

Cash	$ 20	Paid-in capital	$100
Inventory	60	Retained earnings	30
Equipment	50		
Total assets	$130	Total owners' equity	$130

What claim does the $30 in retained earnings represent? Is it a claim on Cash? It cannot be because there is only $20 in Cash, and Retained Earnings is $30. The company reinvested part of the cash in inventory and equipment. This example helps to explain the nature of the Retained Earnings account. It is a residual claim, not a pot of gold. A residual claim means that if the company went out of business and sold its assets for cash, the owners would receive the amount left over after the company paid its liabilities. This might be either more or less than the current balance in the Cash account.

Statement of Retained Earnings

Because owners are interested in tracing the amount of retained earnings in a company, accountants have created a financial statement to do just that. Exhibit 2-7 shows the **statement of retained earnings,** which lists the beginning balance (in this case, January 31) in Retained Earnings, followed by a description of any major changes (in this case, the addition of net income and deduction of dividends) that occurred during the period, and the ending balance (February 28) for the Biwheels Company. Most companies, like Biwheels, will have only two items that affect retained earnings: net income (or loss) and dividends. Other transactions, most having to do with repurchases of a company's own common stock, can affect retained earnings, but they are not common and are usually small in amount.

statement of retained earnings
A statement that lists the beginning balance in retained earnings, followed by a description of any changes that occurred during the period, and the ending balance.

Retained earnings, January 31, 20X2	$ 57,900
Net income for February	63,900
Total	$121,800
Dividends declared	50,000
Retained earnings, February 28, 20X2	$ 71,800

Exhibit 2-7
Biwheels Company
Statement of Retained Earnings for the Month Ended February 28, 20X2

Exhibit 2-8
Biwheels Company
*Statement of Income
and Retained Earnings
for the Month Ended
February 28, 20X2*

Sales		$176,000
Deduct expenses		
Cost of goods sold	$110,000	
Rent	2,000	
Depreciation	100	112,100
Net income		$ 63,900*
Retained earnings, January 31, 20X2		57,900
Total		$121,800
Dividends declared		50,000
Retained earnings, February 28, 20X2		$ 71,800

* Note how the income statement ends here. The $63,900 simultaneously becomes the initial item on the statement of retained earnings portion of this combined statement.

accumulated deficit
*A more descriptive term for
retained earnings when the
accumulated losses plus
dividends exceed
accumulated income.*

**statement of
stockholders' equity**
*A statement that shows all
changes during the year in
each stockholders' equity
account.*

**statement of income and
retained earnings**
*A statement that includes
a statement of retained
earnings at the bottom of
an income statement.*

If Biwheels had a net loss (negative net income), we would *subtract* the amount from the beginning balance of retained earnings. If accumulated losses plus dividends exceed accumulated income, retained earnings would be negative. Many companies with negative retained earnings use the more descriptive term **accumulated deficit.**

More than 95 percent of major companies include the statement of retained earnings as one column in a more comprehensive **statement of stockholders' equity.** This statement shows all the changes during the year in each stockholders' equity account. You can see such a presentation in Starbucks' annual report in Appendix A p. A14.

A few companies add the statement of retained earnings to the bottom of the income statement. In such cases, we call the combined statement a **statement of income and retained earnings.** For example, Exhibit 2-8 is Biwheels' statement of income and retained earnings, which combines the income statement in Exhibit 2-6 with the statement of retained earnings in Exhibit 2-7.

Note how Exhibit 2-8 is anchored to the balance sheet equation:

Assets = Liabilities + Paid-in capital + Retained earnings

[Beginning balance + Revenues − Expenses − Dividends]
[57,900   + 176,000 − 112,100 − $50,000]

Ending Retained Earnings balance = $71,800

INTERPRETING FINANCIAL STATEMENTS

A company's income statement reveals revenues of $50,000 and expenses of $40,000. Its balance sheet showed that retained earnings grew from $15,000 at the beginning of the year to $17,000 at the end of the year. What can you conclude about dividends declared?

Answer
We know that net income = revenue − expenses, so net income is $10,000 = $50,000 − $40,000. Further, end-ing retained earnings = beginning retained earnings + net income − dividends. This means that $17,000 = $15,000 + $10,000 − dividends. Retained earnings would have been $15,000 + $10,000 = $25,000 if the company had declared no dividends, but it was only $17,000. Therefore, the company must have declared $25,000 − $17,000 = $8,000 in dividends.

Summary Problem for Your Review

PROBLEM

The following interpretations and remarks are common misinterpretations of financial statements. Explain fully the fallacy in each:

1. "Sales show the cash coming in from customers, and the various expenses show the cash going out for goods and services. The difference is net income."
2. Consider the following December 31, 2002 accounts of Motorola Inc., a U.S. company that is a leading worldwide provider of wireless communications, semiconductors, and advanced electronic systems, as well as components and services. You may have used one of its cell phones.

Motorola, Inc
Consolidated Balance Sheets
(In millions, except per share amounts)

December 31	2002	2001
Stockholders' equity		
Common stock, $3 par value		
Authorized shares: 2002 and 2001, 4,200		
Issued and outstanding shares: 2002, 2,315.3; 2001, 2,254.0	6,947	6,764
Additional paid-in capital	2,233	1,707
Retained earnings	2,582	5,434
Other	(523)	(214)
Total stockholders' equity	$11,239	$13,691

A Motorola employee commented, "Why can't that big company pay higher wages and dividends, too? It can use its hundreds of millions of dollars of retained earnings to do so."

3. "The total Motorola stockholders' equity measures the amount that the shareholders would get today if the corporation ceased business, sold its assets, and paid off its liabilities."

SOLUTION

1. Cash receipts and disbursements are not the basis for the accrual accounting recognition of revenues and expenses. Sales could easily be credit sales for which the company has not yet received cash, and expenses could be those that the company has incurred but not yet paid out. Depreciation is another example where the expense recognition does not coincide with the payment of cash. Depreciation recorded in today's income statement may result from the use of equipment that the company acquired for cash years ago. Therefore, under accrual accounting, sales and expenses are not equivalent to cash inflows and outflows. To determine net income under accrual accounting, we subtract expenses from revenues (expenses are linked to revenues via matching). This might be quite different from cash inflows minus cash outflows.
2. As the chapter indicated, retained earnings is not cash. It is a stockholders' equity account that represents the accumulated increase in ownership claims due to profitable operations. This claim may be lowered by paying cash dividends, but a growing company will need to reinvest cash in receivables, inventories, plant, equipment, and other assets necessary for expansion. Paying higher wages may make it impossible to compete effectively and stay in business. Paying higher dividends may make it impossible to grow. The level of retained earnings does not lead to a specific wage or dividend policy for the firm.

3. Stockholders' equity is the excess of assets over liabilities. If a company carried its assets in the accounting records at their market value today and listed the liabilities exactly at their market values, the remark would be true. However, the numbers on the balance sheet are historical numbers, not current numbers. Intervening changes in markets and general price levels in inflationary times may mean that the assets are woefully understated. Investors make a critical error if they think that balance sheets indicate current values.

Some Basic Concepts

OBJECTIVE 6

Explain how the following concepts affect financial statements: entity, reliability, going concern, materiality, cost-benefit, and stable monetary unit.

So far, we have looked at three of the four main financial statements. To develop your understanding of these statements we have implicitly used some basic concepts. Now it is time to make some of those concepts explicit. In this section, we discuss the entity, reliability, going concern, materiality, cost-benefit, and stable monetary unit concepts. We discuss some additional concepts that influence the regulation of accounting in Appendix 2.

The Entity Concept. The first basic concept or principle in accounting is the entity concept. As you learned in Chapter 1, an accounting entity is an organization or a section of an organization that stands apart from other organizations and individuals as a separate economic unit. Accounting draws sharp boundaries around each entity to avoid confusing its affairs with those of other entities.

An example of an entity is General Motors Corporation, an enormous entity that encompasses many smaller entities such as Chevrolet and Buick operations. In turn, Chevrolet encompasses many smaller entities such as a Michigan assembly plant and an Ohio assembly plant. Managers want accounting reports that are confined to their particular entities.

The entity concept helps the accountant relate events to a clearly defined area of accountability. For example, do not confuse business entities with personal entities. A purchase of groceries for merchandise inventory is an accounting transaction of a grocery store (the business entity), but the store owner's purchase of a stereo set with a personal check is a transaction of the owner (the personal entity).

reliability
A quality of information that assures decision makers that the information captures the conditions or events it purports to represent.

The Reliability Concept. Users of financial statements want assurance that management did not fabricate the numbers. Consequently, accountants regard reliability as an essential characteristic of measurement. **Reliability** is a quality of information that assures decision makers that the information captures the conditions or events it purports to represent. Reliable data require convincing evidence that can be verified by independent auditors.

The accounting process focuses on reliable recording of events that affect an organization. Although many events may affect a company—including wars, elections, and general economic booms or depressions—accountants recognize only specified types of events as being reliably recorded as accounting transactions.

Suppose a top executive of ExxonMobil is killed in an airplane crash. The accountant would not record this event. Now suppose that ExxonMobil discovers that an employee has embezzled $1,000 in cash. The accountant would record this event. The death of the executive may have considerably more economic or financial significance for ExxonMobil than does the embezzlement, but the monetary effect is hard to measure in any reliable way.

going concern (continuity)
A convention that assumes that ordinarily an entity persists indefinitely.

Going Concern Convention. The **going concern (continuity)** convention is the assumption that ordinarily an entity persists indefinitely. This notion implies that a company will use its existing resources, such as plant assets, to fulfill its general business needs rather than sell them in tomorrow's real estate or equipment markets. For a going concern, it is reasonable to use historical cost to record long-lived assets. Also, for a going concern it is reasonable to report liabilities at the amount to be paid at maturity.

The opposite view of this going concern convention is an immediate liquidation assumption, whereby all items on a balance sheet are valued at the amounts appropriate if the entity were to be liquidated in piecemeal fashion within a few days or months. This liquidation approach to valuation is usually used only when the probability is high that the company will be liquidated.

Materiality Convention. How does an accountant know what to include on the financial statements? There are a lot of rules and regulations about what must appear in those statements. However, some items are trivial enough that they need not be reported. The **materiality** convention asserts that an item should be included in a financial statement if its omission or misstatement would tend to mislead the reader of the financial statements under consideration.

materiality
A convention that asserts that an item should be included in a financial statement if its omission or misstatement would tend to mislead the reader of the financial statements under consideration.

Most large items, such as buildings and machinery, are clearly material. Smaller items, though, may not be so clear-cut. Many acquisitions that a company theoretically should record as assets are immediately written off as expenses because of their insignificance. For example, coat hangers may last indefinitely but never appear in the balance sheet as assets. Many corporations require the immediate write-off to expense of all outlays under a specified minimum, such as $1,000, regardless of the useful life of the asset acquired. The resulting $1,000 understatement of assets and stockholders' equity is considered too trivial to worry about. The FASB regularly includes the following statement in its standards: "The provisions of this statement need not be applied to immaterial items."

When is an item material? There will probably never be a universal, clear-cut answer. What is trivial to General Motors may be material to Evelyn's Boutique. A working rule is that an item is material if its proper accounting would probably affect the decision of a knowledgeable party. In sum, materiality is an important convention, but it is difficult to use anything other than prudent judgment to tell whether an item is material.

Cost-Benefit Criterion. Accounting systems vary in complexity—from the minimum crude records kept by a small business to satisfy government authorities, to the sophisticated budgeting and feedback schemes used to manage huge, multinational corporations. Of course, a system can start out small and get much bigger as is necessary. However, when are changes to an accounting system necessary? The **cost-benefit** criterion states that a system should be changed when the expected additional benefits of the change exceed its expected additional costs. Often the benefits are difficult to measure, but this criterion should always underlie the decisions about the design and change of accounting systems. In fact, the FASB uses a cost-benefit criterion in judging new standards. It safeguards the cost effectiveness of its standards by (1) ensuring a standard does not "impose costs on the many for the benefit of a few," and (2) seeking alternative ways of handling an issue that are "less costly and only slightly less efficient."

cost-benefit
A criterion that states that an accounting system should be changed when the expected additional benefits of the change exceed its expected additional costs.

Stable Monetary Unit. The monetary unit (called the dollar in the United States, the yen in Japan, the euro in the European Union, and various names elsewhere) is the principal means for measuring assets and equities. It is the common denominator for quantifying the effects of a wide variety of transactions. Accountants record, classify, summarize, and report in terms of the monetary unit. The ability to use historical cost accounting depends on a stable monetary unit. A stable monetary unit is simply one that is not expected to change in value significantly over time—that is, a 2005 dollar has about the same value as a 2000 dollar. Although this is not precisely correct, with low levels of inflation, the changes in the value of the monetary unit do not cause great problems.

Four Popular Financial Ratios

OBJECTIVE 7

Compute and explain earnings per share, price-earnings ratio, dividend-yield ratio, and dividend-payout ratio.

earnings per share (EPS)
Net income divided by average number of common shares outstanding during the period.

Now that you know quite a bit about balance sheets and income statements, you are ready to learn how investors use some of the information in these statements. Numbers are hard to understand out of context. Is $10 a lot to pay for a share of stock? Is $1 a good dividend? To show you how investors think about such questions, let's look at a few financial ratios that compare financial statement numbers in ways that help us to understand the economic meaning of the numbers.

We compute a financial ratio by dividing one number by another. For a set of complex financial statements, we can compute literally hundreds of ratios. Every analyst has a set of favorite ratios, but one is so popular that it dwarfs all others: **earnings per share (EPS)** of common stock. EPS is net income divided by the average number of common shares outstanding during the period. In fact, EPS data must appear on the face of the income statement of publicly held corporations. This is the only financial ratio that is required in the body of the financial statements. Let us now examine EPS and three other popular ratios based on financial statement information.

Earnings Per Share

EPS tells investors how much of a period's net income "belongs to" each share of common stock. When the owners' equity is relatively simple, computing EPS is straightforward. For example, consider General Mills. It reported EPS of $2.34, $1.38, and $2.49 in 2001, 2002, and 2003, respectively. The calculation for 2003 follows:

$$\text{EPS} = \frac{\text{Net income}}{\text{Average number of common shares outstanding}}$$

$$\text{2003 EPS} = \frac{\$917,000,000}{369,000,000} = \$2.49$$

The General Mills computation is relatively simple because the company has only one type of capital stock, little fluctuation of shares outstanding throughout the year, and few unusual items affecting the computation of net income. EPS calculations can become more difficult when such complications arise. Investors interested in General Mills might be concerned about the decrease in EPS in 2002. Management gave detailed explanations for this decrease in its 2002 annual report and predicted an increase in 2003 to $2.60. Although 2003 EPS fell short of that prediction, it recovered to a level greater than in 2001. Investors should predict a company's future EPS before deciding whether to buy the company's common shares.

Price-Earnings Ratio

price-earnings (P-E) ratio
Market price per share of common stock divided by earnings per share of common stock.

Another popular ratio is the **price-earnings (P-E) ratio**:

$$\text{P-E ratio} = \frac{\text{Market price per share of common stock}}{\text{Earnings per share of common stock}}$$

The numerator is typically today's market price for a share of the company's stock. The denominator is the EPS for the most recent 12 months. Thus, the P-E ratio varies throughout a given year, depending on the fluctuations in the company's stock price. For example, **General Mills'** P-E ratios at the end of fiscal 2001, 2002, and 2003 were:

2003 P-E	$46.56 ÷ $2.49 = 18.7
2002 P-E	$45.10 ÷ $1.38 = 32.7
2001 P-E	$42.20 ÷ $2.34 = 18.0

Some folks call the P-E ratio the earnings multiple. It measures how much the investing public is willing to pay for a chance to share the company's potential earnings. Note especially that the marketplace determines the P-E ratio. Why? Because the market establishes the price of a company's shares. The P-E ratio may differ considerably for two companies within the same industry. It may also change for the same company through the years. General Mills' P-E increased between 2001 and 2002, but decreased the following year. This is partly due to General Mills' performance and prospects and partly reflects the overall performance in the financial markets. In general, a high P-E ratio indicates that investors predict the company's net income will grow rapidly. Investors apparently believed that General Mills' EPS in 2002 was uncharacteristically low and therefore expected it to grow. By 2003, the market seemed to think the EPS growth would be about the same as in 2001.

Consider **Starbucks'** 2003 P-E of nearly 43 compared with the P-E ratio of 7 for **General Motors** (GM). These ratios tell us that investors expect Starbucks' earnings to grow much more rapidly than GM's. History certainly suggests this is likely. Starbucks' EPS grew more than 25 percent each year during the last four years, whereas GM's EPS declined significantly over that time period. *The Wall Street Journal* publishes P-E ratios daily on its stock pages. The Business First box on p. 72 illustrates the P-E ratios of some of the largest companies in the United States.

INTERPRETING FINANCIAL STATEMENTS

From **Microsoft's** financial statements, you can find that its EPS grew from $.71 in 1999 to $.92 in 2003. At the same time, its stock price fell from $45 per share to $26 per share. What happened to Microsoft's P-E ratio between 1999 and 2003? What would its price have been in 2003 if it had maintained its 1999 P-E ratio?

Answer

Microsoft's P-E in 1999 was $45 ÷ $.71 = 63, and by 2003 it had fallen to $26 ÷ $.92 = 28. If the company had a P-E ratio of 63 in 2003, its price would have been 63 × $.92 = $58, or 223 percent higher than it was.

Dividend-Yield Ratio

Individual investors are usually interested in the profitability of their personal investments in common stock. That profitability takes two forms: cash dividends and market-price appreciation of the stock. The **dividend-yield ratio** is the common dividends per share

dividend-yield ratio
Common dividends per share divided by market price per share.

MARKET VALUE, EARNINGS, AND P-E RATIOS

Business Week Online lists the 50 largest U.S. companies ranked by a variety of criteria. Let's look at some statistics for the 10 largest companies in 2002 ranked by market value:

Company	Market Value in Millions	EPS	Stock Price	P-E Ratio
Microsoft	$280.7	$1.45	$52.51	36.2
General Electric	270.1	1.59	27.15	17.1
Wal-Mart	249.4	1.65	56.40	34.2
ExxonMobil	243.3	1.54	36.00	23.4
Pfizer	199.0	1.37	32.15	23.5
Johnson & Johnson	181.8	2.09	61.11	29.2
Citigroup	179.8	3.22	35.52	11.0
American International	167.0	2.29	63.95	27.9
IBM	128.0	3.30	75.55	22.9
Procter & Gamble	119.9	3.09	92.19	29.8

First, consider what companies are among the 10 largest market cap companies. Just 3 years ago, four of these companies would have been different. Four technology companies (Cisco, Intel, Lucent, and AT&T) fell off the list, replaced by two pharmaceutical companies (Pfizer and Johnson & Johnson), one insurance company (American International), and one consumer products company (Procter & Gamble). Twenty-five years ago, only IBM, General Electric, and ExxonMobil would have been on the list, together with companies such as General Motors, Sears Roebuck, Texaco, Xerox, and Gulf Oil. Microsoft, the largest firm today, would not have been on any type of "largest" list 25 years ago. You can see that large companies do not always stay large and small companies do not always stay small.

Now look at the P-E ratios for these 10 companies. Microsoft and Wal-Mart have the largest P-E ratios, indicating that investors expect their earnings to grow the fastest. Citigroup has the lowest ratio, so apparently investors do not expect large earnings growth from Citigroup. General Electric, a company that had a high P-E ratio not long ago, now has the next lowest of the 10. Although General Electric's market value remains high, it is because of the high current earnings, not because of exceptional expected growth in earnings.

Sources: *Business Week* Online, October 22, 2002; Web sites for Microsoft, General Electric, Wal-Mart, ExxonMobil, Pfizer, Johnson & Johnson, Citigroup, American International, IBM, and Procter & Gamble.

divided by the current market price of the stock. General Mills' recent dividend-yield ratios were:

$$2003 \text{ Dividend-yield} = \$1.10 \div \$46.56 = 2.4\%$$

$$2002 \text{ Dividend-yield} = \$1.10 \div \$45.10 = 2.4\%$$

$$2001 \text{ Dividend-yield} = \$1.10 \div \$42.20 = 2.6\%$$

Investors in common stock who seek regular cash returns on their investments pay particular attention to dividend ratios. For example, an investor who favored high current cash returns would not buy stock in growth companies. Growth companies have conservative dividend policies because they use most of their profit-generated resources to help finance expansion of their operations.

Dividend-Payout Ratio

Analysts are also interested in what proportion of net income a company elects to pay in cash dividends to its shareholders. The formula for computing the **dividend-payout ratio** is given here, followed by General Mills' recent ratios:

dividend-payout ratio
Common dividends per share divided by earnings per share.

$$\text{Dividend-payout ratio} = \frac{\text{Common dividends per share}}{\text{Earnings per share}}$$

2003 Dividend-payout ratio = $1.10 ÷ $2.49 = 44%

2002 Dividend-payout ratio = $1.10 ÷ $1.38 = 80%

2001 Dividend-payout ratio = $1.10 ÷ $2.34 = 47%

General Mills has a relatively high dividend-payout ratio. Until 1993, the company generally paid dividends of less than one-half of its income, but the numbers shown here are representative of the last 10 years. Notice that General Mills maintained its dollar level of dividends in 2002 despite a drop in income by increasing its dividend-payout ratio. Many companies elect to pay a reasonably constant dollar amount in dividends, even if this means variations in its dividend-payout ratio.

Stock Price and Ratio Information in the Press. The business section of most daily newspapers in the United States reports market prices for stocks listed on major stock exchanges, such as the NYSE, American Stock Exchange, or NASDAQ. Many also publish the P-E ratios and dividend yields, based on the most recent annual information on EPS and dividends and the current market price of the stock.

Consider the following stock quotations for General Mills in the Monday, March 8, 2004, issue of *The Wall Street Journal:*

Ytd % Chg	52 Weeks High	Low	Stock (SYM)	Div	Yld %	P-E	Vol 100s	Close	Net Change
5.1	49.66	41.43	GenMills GIS	1.10	2.3	18	16478	47.60	0.60

These data represent trading on Friday, March 5, because the market is not open on weekends. Notice that the fourth column identifies General Mills and shows that its ticker symbol is GIS. All listed stocks have short ticker symbols that identify them. Stock exchanges created these symbols years ago to facilitate communication via ticker tape, but they remain effective for computer communication today.

Reading from left to right, General Mills stock price increased by 5.1 percent between January 1, 2004 and March 5, 2004. The highest price at which General Mills' common stock sold in the preceding 52 weeks was $49.66 per share; the lowest price, $41.43. The current annual dividend is $1.10 per share, and the dividend yield is 2.3 percent based on the day's closing price of the stock. The P-E ratio is 18, also based on the closing price. A total of more than 1.6 million shares were traded on March 5. The closing price—that is, the price of the last trade for the day—was $47.60, which was $.60 higher than the last trade on March 4. That means that the closing price on March 4 was $47.60 − $.60 = $47.00, and shareholders gained $.60 on each share they held on March 5.

Keep in mind that transactions in publicly traded shares are between individual investors in the stock, not between the corporation and the individuals. Thus, a "typical trade" results in the selling of, for example, 100 shares of General Mills stock held by Ms. Johnson in Minneapolis to Mr. Ruiz in Atlanta for $4,760 in cash. These parties would ordinarily transact the trade through their respective stockbrokers. The trade would not directly affect General Mills, except that it would change its records of shareholders to show that Ruiz, not Johnson, holds the 100 shares.

Summary Problem for Your Review

PROBLEM

On February 3, 2002, The Home Depot stock sold for about $49 per share. The company had net income of $3,044 million for the fiscal year ending February 3, 2002, had an average of 2,335 million shares outstanding during the year, and paid dividends of $.11 per share. Calculate and interpret the following:

Earnings per share   Dividend-yield ratio
Price-earnings ratio   Dividend-payout ratio

SOLUTION

$$\text{Earnings per share} = \$3,044 \div \$2,335 = \$1.30$$

$$\text{Price-earnings ratio} = \$49 \div \$1.30 = 37.7$$

$$\text{Dividend-yield ratio} = \$.11 \div \$49 = 0.2\%$$

$$\text{Dividend-payout ratio} = \$.11 \div \$1.30 = 8.5\%$$

The Home Depot had net income of $1.30 for each share of its common stock. Its market price was 37.7 times its earnings. This is relatively high and shows that investors expect significant growth in The Home Depot's earnings. It is not a stock for those who want cash dividends. The Home Depot returns only $.002 per year for every dollar invested today. This is better than some companies, such as Starbucks and Cisco, which pay no dividends, but The Home Depot's dividends are only 8.5 percent of its net income.

Highlights to Remember

1 **Explain how accountants measure income.** Accountants can measure income, the excess of revenues over expenses for a particular time period, on an accrual or cash basis. In accrual accounting, companies record revenue when they earn it and record expenses when they incur them. In cash accounting, companies record revenues and expenses only when cash changes hands. Accrual accounting is the standard basis for accounting today.

2 **Determine when a company should record revenue from a sale.** The concept of revenue recognition means that companies record revenues in the earliest period in which they are both earned and realized. Earning requires delivery of the product or service and realization requires a high probability that the company will receive the promised resources (usually cash). Recording revenues increases stockholders' equity.

3 **Use the concept of matching to record the expenses for a period.** Under matching, companies assign expenses to a period in which it uses the pertinent goods and services to create revenues or when they apparently have no future benefit. Recording expenses decreases stockholders' equity.

4 **Prepare an income statement and show how it is related to a balance sheet.** An income statement shows an entity's revenues and expenses for a particular period of time. The net income (loss) during the period increases (decreases) the amount of retained earnings on the balance sheet.

5 **Account for cash dividends and prepare a statement of retained earnings.** Cash dividends are not expenses. They are distributions of cash to stockholders that reduce retained earnings. Corporations are not obligated to pay dividends, but once the board of directors declares dividends they become a legal liability until paid in cash. A statement of retained earnings shows how net income increases the beginning balance in retained earnings and dividends decrease it to calculate the ending balance.

6 **Explain how the following concepts affect financial statements: entity, reliability, going concern, materiality, cost-benefit, and stable monetary unit.** Authorities achieve comparability of financial statements by adopting concepts and conventions that all companies must use. Such concepts and conventions include: (a) accounting statements apply to a specific entity, (b) all transactions must have reliable measures, (c) companies are assumed to be ongoing (not about to be liquidated), (d) items that are not large enough to be material need not follow normal rules, (e) information should be worth more than it costs, and (f) accountants use the monetary unit for measurement despite its changing purchasing power over time.

7 **Compute and explain EPS, P-E ratio, dividend-yield ratio, and dividend-payout ratio.** Ratios relate one element of a company's economic activity to another. EPS expresses overall earnings on a scale that individual investors can link to their own ownership level. The P-E ratio relates accounting earnings to market prices. The dividend-yield ratio relates dividends paid per share to market prices, and the dividend-payout ratio relates those same dividends to the earnings during the period.

Appendix 2: Cost-Benefit Criterion and Accounting Regulation

When the FASB or IASB sets standards for financial reporting, they must make many judgments. Consider the accounting for the expiration of prepaid expenses. In the case of prepaid rent, it is fairly easy to identify when the prepaid asset provides a benefit to the company. Rent becomes an expense in the period in which a company uses the rented facilities or equipment. However, some of the most difficult issues in accounting center on when a prepaid asset expires and becomes an expense. For example, some accountants believe that companies should first record research and development (R&D) costs as an asset on the balance sheet and then gradually write them off to expense in some systematic manner over a period of years. After all, companies engage in R&D activities because they expect them to create future benefits. However, the FASB in the United States and the IASB internationally have ruled that such costs have vague future benefits that are difficult to measure reliably. Therefore, most companies must treat R&D costs as expenses when incurred. They do not appear on the balance sheet as assets.

The FASB and IASB must frequently make difficult decisions about reporting requirements, such as those for R&D. For example, should companies record an expense when they issue stock options to executives? How should companies measure and disclose the expense for retirement benefits? Should companies show assets and liabilities at historical cost or current market value? The list could go on and on.

Criteria for Accounting Regulation Decisions

How do the FASB and IASB decide that one level of disclosure or one measurement method is acceptable and another is not? They use the same criterion that companies use when deciding whether to change their accounting system—cost-benefit. Accounting should improve decision making. This is a benefit. However, accounting information is an economic good that is costly to produce. The FASB or IASB must choose rules whose decision-making benefits exceed their costs. Just as the cost-benefit criterion mentioned in the chapter states that a company should change its accounting system when the expected additional benefits of the change exceed its expected additional costs, regulators should apply the cost-benefit criterion when setting accounting principles.

OBJECTIVE 8

Explain how accounting regulators trade off relevance and reliability in setting accounting standards.

The costs of providing information to the investing public include costs to both companies and investors. Companies incur costs for data collecting and processing, auditing, and educating employees. In addition, disclosure of sensitive information can lead to lost competitive advantages or increased labor union pressures. These provider costs are often passed along to the user via higher prices, thereby becoming user costs. User costs also include the costs of education, analysis, and interpretation.

The benefits of accounting information are often harder to pinpoint than the costs. For example, countries in the former Soviet Union and in other emerging market economies have been trying to create an infrastructure of financial markets and relevant information to guide their economies. However, the specific benefits of any particular proposal are harder to articulate than the general benefits of an intelligent system of accounting rules and procedures.

Because these benefits can be hard to measure or even see, the FASB has come up with a set of easily identified characteristics of information that lead to increased benefits, as shown in Exhibit 2-9. The IASB is working on a similar framework. The main characteristic of the FASB framework is decision usefulness. If accounting information is not useful in making decisions, it provides no benefit. The rest of the characteristics are helpful in assessing decision usefulness.

Aspects of Decision Usefulness

Relevance and reliability are the two main qualities that make accounting information useful for decision making. Users of financial statements want assurance that management has truthfully reported its financial numbers. Consequently, accountants regard reliability as an essential

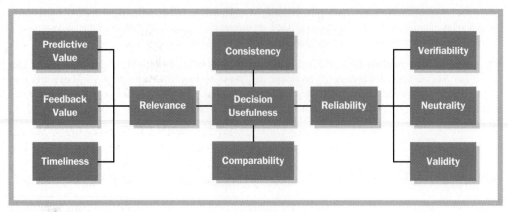

Exhibit 2-9
Qualities that Increase the Value of Information

characteristic of measurement. As defined in the chapter, reliability is a quality of information meaning that it truly captures the conditions or events it purports to represent. Reliable data require convincing evidence that can be verified by independent accountants. The accounting process focuses on reliable recording of events that affect an organization. Although many events may affect a company — including wars, elections, and general economic booms or depressions — the accountant recognizes only specified types of events as being reliable enough to record as accounting transactions.

relevance
The capability of information to make a difference to the decision maker.

Relevance refers to whether the information makes a difference to the decision maker. If information has no impact on a decision, it is not relevant to that decision.

Accounting is filled with trade-offs between relevance and reliability. Consider the $1.7 billion balance sheet value of Weyerhaeuser Company's timberlands, which the company shows at historical cost. Much of the land was purchased more than 50 years ago. The historical cost is reliable, but not very relevant. In contrast, the current value of the land is more relevant, but estimates of this current value are subjective and thus might not be reliable. Which quality is more important? That answer depends on the specific decision being made. However, the most desirable information is both reliable and relevant. The prevailing view in the United States and most of the world is that many current market value estimates, especially for property, plant, and equipment, are not sufficiently reliable to be included in the accounting records, even though they are more relevant. However, in some countries, current market values are routinely used for such assets. In addition, throughout the world, current market values are becoming more acceptable for financial assets and liabilities that can be traded in the financial markets.

verifiability
A quality of information meaning that it can be checked to ensure it is correct.

validity (representational faithfulness)
A correspondence between the accounting numbers and the objects or events those numbers purport to represent.

As you can see in Exhibit 2-9, both relevance and reliability have their own characteristics. For information to be relevant, it must help decision makers predict the outcomes of future events (predictive value) or confirm or update past predictions (feedback value). Relevant information must also be available on a timely basis, that is, before a decision maker has to act.

Reliability is characterized by verifiability (or objectivity), neutrality, and validity. **Verifiability** means that information can be checked to ensure it is correct. It also means that measured amounts have the same value each time the measurement is made. The historical cost of an item is verifiable because we can check the records to verify that the amounts are correct. In contrast, estimates and appraisals are not verifiable. **Validity** (also called **representational faithfulness**) means the information provided represents the events or objects it is supposed to represent. **Neutrality,** or freedom from bias, means that information is objective and is not weighted unfairly. For example, information that focuses heavily on the benefits of one option while ignoring the benefits of another option is not neutral and does not help lead to a fair decision.

neutrality
A quality of information meaning that it is objective and free from bias.

comparability
Conformity across companies with respect to policies and procedures.

The final items affecting decision usefulness are comparability and consistency. **Comparability** requires all companies to use similar concepts and measurements. **Consistency** requires conformity within a company from period to period with unchanging policies and procedures. Information is more useful if it can be compared with similar information about other companies (comparability) or with similar information for other reporting periods (consistency). For example, financial results of two companies are hard to compare if the companies used different methods of accounting for the value of their inventory. Further, we cannot make useful comparisons over time if a company constantly changes its accounting methods.

consistency
Conformity from period to period with unchanging policies and procedures.

The Portfolio is your key to understanding a company's financial position and prospects using the three major financial statements—the balance sheet, the statement of earnings, and the cash flow statement. It shows some of the most important financial ratios used in analyzing Starbucks' financial statements—and the statements of other companies. You can use this tool in your financial statement analysis throughout the course.

Current Ratio $= \dfrac{\$924{,}029}{\$608{,}703} = 1.52$

Starbucks has $1.52 in current assets for each $1 in current liabilities. See Chapter 4.

Consolidated Balance Sheets

In thousands, except share data

	Sept. 28, 2003	Sept. 29, 2002
ASSETS		
Current assets:		
Cash and cash equivalents	$ 200,907	$ 99,677
Short-term investments – Available-for-sale securities	128,905	217,302
Short-term investments – Trading securities	20,199	10,360
Accounts receivable	114,448	97,573
Inventories	342,944	263,174
Prepaid expenses and other current assets	55,173	42,351
Deferred income taxes, net	61,453	42,206
Total current assets	924,029	772,643
Long-term investments – Available-for-sale securities	136,159	– –
Equity and other investments	144,257	102,537
Property, plant, and equipment, net	1,384,902	1,265,756
Other assets	52,113	43,692
Other intangible assets	24,942	9,862
Goodwill	63,344	19,902
TOTAL ASSETS	$2,729,746	$2,214,392

Debt-to-Total-Assets Ratio $= \dfrac{(\$608{,}703 + \$33{,}217 + \$4{,}354 + \$1{,}045)}{\$2{,}729{,}746} = \$.24$

Starbucks' uses $.24 of debt financing for every $1 of total assets. See Chapter 9.

LIABILITIES AND SHAREHOLDERS' EQUITY

	Sept. 28, 2003	Sept. 29, 2002
Current liabilities:		
Accounts payable	$ 168,984	$ 135,994
Accrued compensation and related costs	152,608	105,899
Accrued occupancy costs	56,179	51,195
Accrued taxes	54,934	54,244
Other accrued expenses	101,800	72,289
Deferred revenue	73,476	42,264
Current portion of long-term debt	722	710
Total current liabilities	608,703	462,595
Deferred income taxes, net	33,217	22,496
Long-term debt	4,354	5,076
Other long-term liabilities	1,045	1,036
Shareholders' equity:		
Common stock and additional paid-in capital – Authorized, 600,000,000 shares; issued and outstanding, 393,692,536 and 388,228,592 shares, respectively	959,103	891,040
Other additional paid-in-capital	39,393	39,393
Retained earnings	1,069,683	801,337
Accumulated other comprehensive income/(loss)	14,248	(8,581)
Total shareholders' equity	2,082,427	1,723,189
TOTAL LIABILITIES and SHAREHOLDERS' EQUITY	$2,729,746	$2,214,392

Book Value per Share $= \dfrac{(\$2{,}082{,}427 - 0)}{393{,}692{,}536} = \$5.29$

(The numerator is total stockholders' equity minus book value of preferred stock.) The stockholders' equity associated with each share of Starbucks' common stock is $5.29. See Chapter 10.

Market-to-Book $= \dfrac{\$29.57}{\$5.29} = 1.52$

The price of one share of Starbucks on September 28, 2003, was $29.57. The $5.29 amount is the book value per share. Starbuck's' market value is 1.52 times its book value. See Chapter 10.

$$\text{Gross Profit Percentage} = \frac{\$4{,}075{,}522 - \$1{,}685{,}928}{\$4{,}075{,}522} = 59\%$$

Starbucks' gross margin above the cost of items sold (including occupancy costs) is $.59 out of every $1 of sales. *See Chapter 4.*

Consolidated Statement of Earnings

In thousands, except share data

Fiscal year ended	Sept. 28, 2003
Net revenues	4,075,522
Cost of sales including occupancy costs	1,685,928
Store operating expenses	1,379,574
Other operating expenses	141,346
Depreciation and amortization expenses	237,807
General and administrative expenses	244,550
Income from equity investees	38,396
Operating income	424,713
Interest and other income, net	11,622
Gain on sale of investment	–
Earnings before income taxes	436,335
Income taxes	167,989
Net earnings	$ 268,346
Net earnings per common share – basic	$ 0.69
Weighted average shares outstanding	390,753

$$\text{Return on Sales} = \frac{\$268{,}346}{\$4{,}075{,}522} = 6.6\%$$

For every $1 of sales Starbucks earns net income of 6.6¢. *See Chapter 4.*

$$\text{Earnings Per Share} = \frac{\$268{,}346}{390{,}753} = \$.69$$

This tells shareholders how much of Starbucks' net earnings applies to each share of stock they own. *See Chapter 2.*

$$\text{Price-Earnings Ratio} = \frac{\$29.57}{\$.69} = 42.9$$

The price of one share of Starbucks' stock on September 28, 2003, was $29.57. This ratio reveals how much value the market places on each dollar of Starbucks' current earnings. *See Chapter 2.*

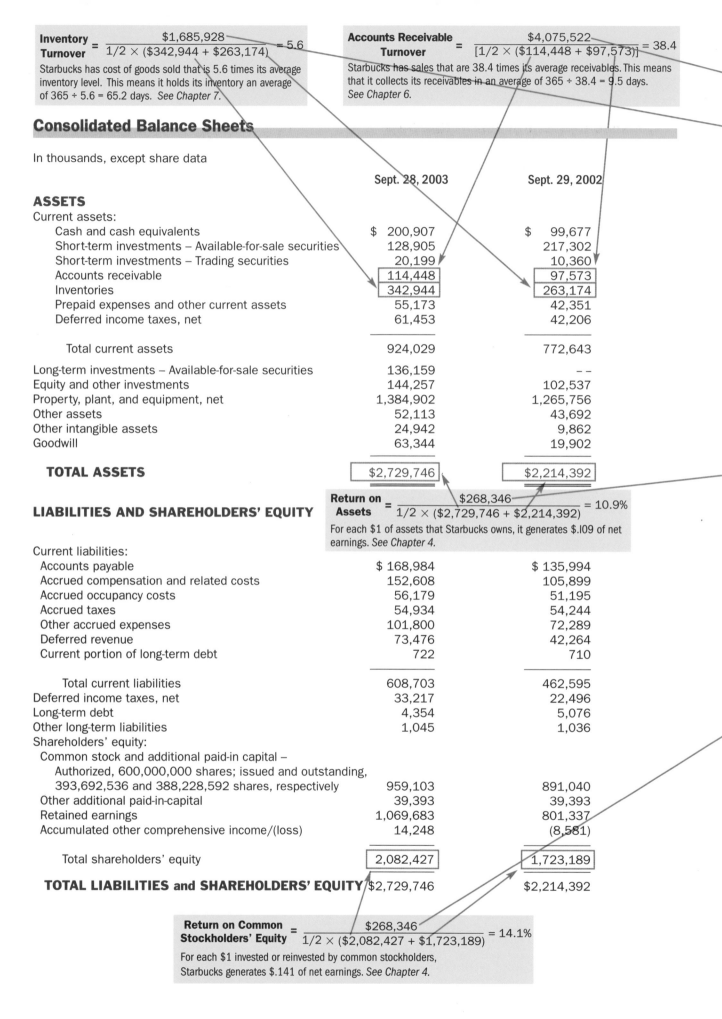

Inventory Turnover $= \dfrac{\$1,685,928}{1/2 \times (\$342,944 + \$263,174)} = 5.6$

Starbucks has cost of goods sold that is 5.6 times its average inventory level. This means it holds its inventory an average of 365 ÷ 5.6 = 65.2 days. *See Chapter 7.*

Accounts Receivable Turnover $= \dfrac{\$4,075,522}{[1/2 \times (\$114,448 + \$97,573)]} = 38.4$

Starbucks has sales that are 38.4 times its average receivables. This means that it collects its receivables in an average of 365 ÷ 38.4 = 9.5 days. *See Chapter 6.*

Consolidated Balance Sheets

In thousands, except share data

	Sept. 28, 2003	Sept. 29, 2002
ASSETS		
Current assets:		
Cash and cash equivalents	$ 200,907	$ 99,677
Short-term investments – Available-for-sale securities	128,905	217,302
Short-term investments – Trading securities	20,199	10,360
Accounts receivable	114,448	97,573
Inventories	342,944	263,174
Prepaid expenses and other current assets	55,173	42,351
Deferred income taxes, net	61,453	42,206
Total current assets	924,029	772,643
Long-term investments – Available-for-sale securities	136,159	– –
Equity and other investments	144,257	102,537
Property, plant, and equipment, net	1,384,902	1,265,756
Other assets	52,113	43,692
Other intangible assets	24,942	9,862
Goodwill	63,344	19,902
TOTAL ASSETS	**$2,729,746**	**$2,214,392**

Return on Assets $= \dfrac{\$268,346}{1/2 \times (\$2,729,746 + \$2,214,392)} = 10.9\%$

For each $1 of assets that Starbucks owns, it generates $.109 of net earnings. *See Chapter 4.*

LIABILITIES AND SHAREHOLDERS' EQUITY		
Current liabilities:		
Accounts payable	$ 168,984	$ 135,994
Accrued compensation and related costs	152,608	105,899
Accrued occupancy costs	56,179	51,195
Accrued taxes	54,934	54,244
Other accrued expenses	101,800	72,289
Deferred revenue	73,476	42,264
Current portion of long-term debt	722	710
Total current liabilities	608,703	462,595
Deferred income taxes, net	33,217	22,496
Long-term debt	4,354	5,076
Other long-term liabilities	1,045	1,036
Shareholders' equity:		
Common stock and additional paid-in capital – Authorized, 600,000,000 shares; issued and outstanding, 393,692,536 and 388,228,592 shares, respectively	959,103	891,040
Other additional paid-in-capital	39,393	39,393
Retained earnings	1,069,683	801,337
Accumulated other comprehensive income/(loss)	14,248	(8,581)
Total shareholders' equity	2,082,427	1,723,189
TOTAL LIABILITIES and SHAREHOLDERS' EQUITY	$2,729,746	$2,214,392

Return on Common Stockholders' Equity $= \dfrac{\$268,346}{1/2 \times (\$2,082,427 + \$1,723,189)} = 14.1\%$

For each $1 invested or reinvested by common stockholders, Starbucks generates $.141 of net earnings. *See Chapter 4.*

Consolidated Statement of Earnings

In thousands, except share data

Fiscal year ended	Sept. 28, 2003
Net revenues	4,075,522
Cost of sales including occupancy costs	1,685,928
Store operating expenses	1,379,574
Other operating expenses	141,346
Depreciation and amortization expenses	237,807
General and administrative expenses	244,550
Income from equity investees	38,396
Operating income	424,713
Interest and other income, net	11,622
Gain on sale of investment	–
Earnings before income taxes	436,335
Income taxes	167,989
Net earnings	$ 268,346
Net earnings per common share – basic	$ 0.69
Weighted average shares outstanding	390,753

Consolidated Statements of Cash Flows

In thousands

Fiscal year ended	Sept. 28, 2003	Sept. 29, 2002
OPERATING ACTIVITIES:		
Net earnings	$ 268,346	$ 212,686
Adjustments to reconcile net earnings to net cash provided by operating activities:		
Depreciation and amortization	259,271	221,141
Gain on sale of investment	—	(13,361)
Provision for impairments and asset disposals	7,784	26,852
Deferred income taxes, net	(5,932)	(6,088)
Equity in income of investees	(22,813)	(19,584)
Tax benefit from exercise of non-qualified stock options	36,590	44,199
Net accretion of discount and amortization of premium on marketable securities	5,996	–
Cash provided/(used) by changes in operating assets and liabilities:		
Inventories	(64,768)	(41,379)
Prepaid expenses and other current assets	(12,861)	(12,460)
Accounts payable	24,990	5,463
Accrued compensation and related costs	42,132	24,087
Accrued occupancy costs	4,293	15,343
Deferred revenue	30,732	15,321
Other operating assets and liabilities	(7,313)	5,465
Net cash provided by operating activities	566,447	477,685
INVESTING ACTIVITIES:		
Purchase of available-for-sale securities	(323,331)	(339,968)
Maturity of available-for-sale securities	180,687	78,349
Sale of available-for-sale securities	88,889	144,760
Purchase of Seattle Coffee Company, net of cash acquired	(69,928)	–
Net additions to equity, other investments, and other assets	(47,259)	(15,841)
Distributions from equity investees	28,966	22,834
Net additions to property, plant, and equipment	(357,282)	(375,474)
Net cash used by investing activities	(499,258)	(485,340)
FINANCING ACTIVITIES:		
Proceeds from issuance of common stock	107,183	107,467
Principal payments on long-term debt	(710)	(697)
Repurchase of common stock	(75,710)	(52,248)
Net cash provided by financing activities	30,763	54,522
Effect of exchange rate changes on cash and cash equivalents	3,278	1,560
Net increase in cash and cash equivalents	101,230	48,427
CASH AND CASH EQUIVALENTS:		
Beginning of period	99,677	51,250
End of period	$ 200,907	$ 99,677

Free Cash Flow = $566,447 – $357,282 = $209,165
Starbucks generated $209,165 more cash from its operations than it needed to invest in maintaining and expanding its property, plant, and equipment. See Chapter 5.

Accounting Vocabulary

accounts receivable, p. 50
accrual basis, p. 53
accumulated deficit, p. 66
cash basis, p. 53
cash dividends, p. 64
comparability, p. 76
consistency, p. 76
continuity, p. 68
cost of goods sold, p. 52
cost of revenue, p. 52
cost of sales, p. 52
cost-benefit, p. 69
depreciation, p. 55
dividend-payout ratio, p. 73
dividend-yield ratio, p. 71
earnings, p. 50
earnings per share (EPS), p. 70
expenses, p. 50
fiscal year, p. 50

going concern, p. 68
income, p. 50
income statement, p. 59
interim periods, p. 50
matching, p. 54
materiality, p. 69
net earnings, p. 59
net income, p. 59
net loss, p. 60
neutrality, p. 76
operating cycle, p. 49
operating statement, p. 59
period costs, p. 55
price-earnings (P-E) ratio,
    p. 70
product costs, p. 54
profits, p. 50
receivables, p. 50
recognition, p. 54

relevance, p. 76
reliability, p. 68
representational faithfulness,
    p. 76
retained earnings, p. 50
retained income, p. 50
revenues, p. 50
sales, p. 50
sales revenues, p. 50
statement of earnings, p. 59
statement of income and
    retained earnings, p. 66
statement of retained
    earnings, p. 65
statement of stockholders'
    equity, p. 66
trade receivables, p. 50
validity, p. 76
verifiability, p. 76

Assignment Material

Questions

2-1 How long is a company's operating cycle?

2-2 What is the difference between a fiscal year and a calendar year? Why do companies use a fiscal year that differs from a calendar year?

2-3 What is the major defect of the cash basis of accounting?

2-4 "Expenses are negative stockholders' equity accounts." Explain.

2-5 What are the two tests for the recognition of revenue?

2-6 Give two examples where revenue is not recognized at the point of sale, one where recognition is delayed because the revenue is not yet earned, and one because it is not yet realized.

2-7 "Expenses are assets that have been used." Explain.

2-8 "The manager acquires goods and services, not expenses per se." Explain.

2-9 "The income statement is like a moving picture; in contrast, a balance sheet is like a snapshot." Explain.

2-10 Give two synonyms for income statement. Why is it important to learn synonyms that are used for various accounting terms?

2-11 Why might a manager put pressure on accountants to report higher revenues or lower expenses than accounting standards allow?

2-12 "Cash dividends are not expenses." Explain.

2-13 "Retained earnings is not a pot of gold." Explain.

2-14 "The statement of retained earnings is often buried in the middle of another financial statement." Explain.

2-15 "An accounting entity is always a separate legal organization." Do you agree? Explain.

2-16 The concepts of materiality and cost-benefit can limit the amount of detailed information included in the financial statements. Explain how an accountant might use each to exclude an item from the statements.

2-17 How do accountants judge whether an item is reliable enough for reporting in the financial statements?

2-18 "Financial ratios are important tools for analyzing financial statements, but no ratios are shown on the statements." Do you agree? Explain.

2-19 "Fast-growing companies have high P-E ratios." Explain.

2-20 Give two ratios that give information about a company's dividends, and explain what each means.

2-21 "Companies with a high dividend-payout ratio are good investments because stockholders get more of their share of earnings in cash." Do you agree? Explain.

2-22 Study Appendix 2. "It is better to be roughly right than precisely wrong." Interpret this statement in light of the qualitative characteristics of accounting.

2-23 Study Appendix 2. "Timing of expense recognition is not important. The important thing is that all expenses are eventually recognized in the income statement." Do you agree? Explain.

2-24 Study Appendix 2. "Neutrality underscores the fundamental approach that should be taken by the FASB." Describe the approach.

2-25 Study Appendix 2. Name three types of costs of producing accounting information.

Critical Thinking Questions

2-26 Quarterly versus Annual Financial Statements
In the United States, it is common to provide abbreviated financial data quarterly with full financial statements provided annually. In some countries only annual data are provided. Discuss the trade-offs.

2-27 Accrual or Cash Basis
Which would you rather have, a cash-basis income statement or an accrual-basis income statement? Why?

2-28 Dividends and Stock Prices
Suppose a company was going to pay out one-half of its total assets in a cash dividend. What would you expect to happen to the value of the company's stock as a result of the dividend?

2-29 Interpretation of the P-E Ratio
Would you rather own a company with a high P-E ratio or a low P-E ratio? Why?

Exercises

2-30 Synonyms and Antonyms
Consider the following terms: (1) expenses, (2) unexpired costs, (3) accumulated deficit, (4) net earnings, (5) prepaid expenses, (6) accounts receivable, (7) statement of earnings, (8) used-up costs, (9) net profits, (10) net income, (11) revenues, (12) retained earnings, (13) sales, (14) statement of financial condition, (15) statement of income, (16) statement of financial position, (17) operating statement, and (18) cost of goods sold.

Group the items into two major categories, those on the income statement and those on the balance sheet. Answer by indicating the numbered items that belong in each group. Specify items that are assets and items that are expenses.

2-31 Special Meanings of Terms
A news story described the disappointing sales of a new model car, the Nova. An auto dealer said: "Even if the Nova is a little slow to move out of dealerships, it is more of a plus than a minus. . . . We're now selling 14 more cars per month than before. That's revenue. That's the bottom line."

Is the dealer confused about accounting terms? Explain.

2-32 Nature of Retained Earnings
This is an exercise on the relationships between assets, liabilities, and ownership equities. The numbers are small, but the underlying concepts are large.

1. Assume an opening balance sheet of:

Cash	$1,000	Paid-in capital	$1,000

2. Purchase inventory for $800 cash. Prepare a balance sheet. A heading is unnecessary in this and subsequent requirements.
3. Sell the entire inventory for $950 cash. Prepare a balance sheet. Where is the retained earnings in terms of relationships within the balance sheet? That is, what is the meaning of the retained earnings? Explain in your own words.
4. Buy inventory for $300 cash and equipment for $800 cash. Prepare a balance sheet. Where is the retained earnings in terms of relationships within the balance sheet? That is, what is the meaning of the retained earnings? Explain in your own words.
5. Buy inventory for $500 on open account. Prepare a balance sheet. Where is the retained earnings and account payable in terms of the relationships within the balance sheet? That is, what is the meaning of the account payable and the retained earnings? Explain in your own words.

2-33 Asset Acquisition and Expiration
The Tremain Company had the following transactions in July:

a. Paid $12,000 cash for rent for the next 6 months on July 1.
b. Paid $3,000 for supplies on July 3.
c. Paid $4,000 cash for an advertisement in the next day's *New York Times* on July 10.
d. Paid $9,000 cash for a training program for employees on July 17. The training was completed in July.

Show the effects on the balance sheet equation in two phases—at acquisition and on expiration at the end of the month of acquisition. Show all amounts in thousands.

2-34 Find Unknowns
The following data pertain to the Francisco Corporation. Total assets at January 1, 20X1 were $110,000; at December 31, 20X1, $124,000. During 20X1, sales were $354,000, cash dividends were $5,000, and operating expenses (exclusive of cost of goods sold) were $200,000. Total liabilities at December 31, 20X1 were $55,000; at January 1, 20X1, $50,000. There was no additional capital paid in during 20X1.

Compute the following:

1. Stockholders' equity, January 1, 20X1 and December 31, 20X1.
2. Net income for 20X1.
3. Cost of goods sold for 20X1.

2-35 Recording Transactions
The Greenville Company had the following transactions during June, 20X4:

a. Collections of accounts receivable, $80,000.
b. Payment of accounts payable, $45,000.
c. Acquisition of inventory, $18,000, on open account.
d. Sale of merchandise, $30,000 on open account and $23,000 for cash. The sold merchandise cost Greenville company $24,000.
e. Depreciation on equipment of $1,000 in June.
f. Declared and paid cash dividends of $12,000.

Use the balance sheet equation format to enter these transactions into the books of Greenville Company. Suppose that Greenville has a cash balance of $15,000 at the beginning of June. What was the cash balance on June 30?

2-36 Income Statement
A statement of an automobile dealer follows:

R. Moss BMW, Inc.
Statement of Profit and Loss
December 31, 20X3

Revenues		
Sales	$1,050,000	
Increase in market value of land and building	$ 200,000	$1,250,000
Deduct expenses		
Advertising	$ 100,000	
Sales commissions	50,000	
Utilities	20,000	
Wages	160,000	
Dividends	100,000	
Cost of cars purchased	700,000	1,130,000
Net profit		$ 120,000

List and describe any shortcomings of this statement.

2-37 Income Statement and Retained Earnings

Borders Group Inc. operates Borders Bookstores. In the year ended January 26, 2003, Borders had revenues of $3,486.1 million and total expenses of $3,374.4 million. Borders' retained earnings were $257.7 million at the beginning of the year and $369.4 million at the end of the year.

1. Compute Borders Group's net income for the year ended January 26, 2003.
2. Compute the amount of cash dividends declared by Borders Group during the year ended January 26, 2003.

2-38 Balance Sheet Equation

(Alternates are 2-39 and 2-53.) Each of the three following columns is an independent case. For each case, compute the amounts ($ in thousands) for the items indicated by letters and show your supporting computations:

	Case 1	Case 2	Case 3
Revenues	$145	$K	$280
Expenses	125	200	240
Dividends declared	—	5	Q
Additional investment by stockholders	—	40	35
Net income	E	20	P
Retained earnings			
Beginning of year	30	60	120
End of year	D	J	130
Paid-in capital			
Beginning of year	15	10	N
End of year	C	H	85
Total assets			
Beginning of year	80	F	L
End of year	95	280	M
Total liabilities			
Beginning of year	A	90	105
End of year	B	G	95

2-39 Balance Sheet Equation

(Alternates are 2-38 and 2-53.) Xcel Energy, provider of gas and electricity to customers in 12 Midwestern and Rocky Mountain states, has the following actual data ($ in millions) for the year 2002:

Total costs	$B
Net income (loss)	($2,218)
Dividends	441
Assets, beginning of period	28,754
Assets, end of period	D
Liabilities, beginning of period	A
Liabilities, end of period	22,004
Shareholders' equity, beginning of period	6,794
Shareholders' equity, end of period	5,254
Retained earnings, beginning of period	2,558
Retained earnings, end of period	C
Total revenues	9,524

Find the unknowns ($ in millions), showing computations to support your answers.

2-40 Nonprofit Operating Statement

Examine the accompanying statement of the Liverpool University Faculty Club. Identify the Liverpool classifications and terms that would not be used by a profit-seeking hotel and restaurant. Suggest terms that the profit-seeking entity would use instead (£ is the British pound).

Liverpool Faculty Club
Statement of Income and Expenses for Fiscal Year

Food Service			
Sales		£548,130	
Expenses			
Food	£287,088		
Labor	272,849		
Operating costs	30,537	590,474	
Deficit			£ (42,344)
Bar			
Sales		£ 90,549	
Expenses			
Cost of liquor	£ 29,302		
Labor	5,591		
Operating costs	6,125	41,018	
Surplus			49,531
Hotel			
Sales		£ 33,771	
Expenses		23,803	
Surplus			9,968
Total surplus from operations			£ 17,155
General income (members' dues, room fees, etc.)			95,546
General administration and operating expenses			(134,347)
Deficit before university subsidy			£ (21,646)
University subsidy			23,000
Net surplus after university subsidy			£ 1,354

2-41 Earnings and Dividend Ratios

Cadbury Schweppes, the British candy and beverage company, had 2002 earnings of £548 million. Cash dividends were £230 million. The company had an average of 2,003 million common shares outstanding. No other type of stock was outstanding. The market price of the stock at the end of the year was approximately £3.294 per share.

Compute (1) EPS, (2) P-E ratio, (3) dividend-yield, and (4) dividend-payout ratio.

2-42 Earnings and Dividend Ratios

ChevronTexaco Corporation is one of the largest oil companies in the world. The company's revenue in 2002 was $98.691 billion. Net income was $1.132 billion. EPS was $1.07. The company's common stock is the only type of shares outstanding.

1. Compute the average number of common shares outstanding during the year.
2. The dividend-payout ratio was 262 percent. What was the amount of dividends per share? Compare this with EPS.
3. The market price of the stock at the end of the year was $66 per share. Compute (a) dividend-yield and (b) P-E ratio.

Problems

2-43 Fundamental Revenue and Expense

Ramanathan Corporation was formed on June 1, 20X2, when some stockholders invested $100,000 in cash in the company. During the first week of June, the company spent $80,000 cash for merchandise inventory (sportswear). During the remainder of the month, total sales reached $115,000, of which $70,000 was on open account. The cost of the inventory sold was $60,000. For simplicity, assume that no other transactions occurred except that on June 28, Ramanathan Corporation acquired $26,000 additional inventory on open account.

1. By using the balance sheet equation approach demonstrated in Exhibit 2-3 (p. 56), analyze all transactions for June. Show all amounts in thousands.

2. Prepare a balance sheet for June 30, 20X2.
3. Prepare two statements for June, side by side. The first should use the accrual basis of accounting to compute net income, and the second, the cash basis to compute the difference between cash inflows and cash outflows. Which basis provides a more informative measure of economic performance? Why?

2-44 Revenue Recognition

Footnote 1 to Microsoft's 2002 annual report contained the following:

Revenue Recognition

"Microsoft . . . recognizes revenue when (i) persuasive evidence of an arrangement exists; (ii) delivery has occurred or services have been rendered; (iii) the sales price is fixed or determinable; and (iv) collectibility is reasonably assured. . . . Revenue from products licensed to original equipment manufacturers (OEMs) is based on the licensing agreement with an OEM and has historically been recognized when OEMs ship licensed products to their customers. Licensing provisions were modified with the introduction of Windows XP in 2002 and revenue for certain products is recorded upon shipment of the product to OEMs. The effect of this change in licensing provisions was not material. Revenue from packaged product sales to distributors and resellers is usually recorded when related products are shipped. However, when the revenue recognition criteria required for distributor and reseller arrangements are not met, revenue is recognized as payments are received. Revenue related to the Company's Xbox game console is recognized upon shipment of the product to retailers. Online advertising revenue is recognized as advertisements are displayed."

1. Explain how Microsoft's revenue recognition policy meets the criteria of being earned and realized.
2. Why might Microsoft change its policy on OEM sales? Will this change speed up or delay the recording of revenue?
3. What does Microsoft mean when the footnote states that this change in licensing provisions was not material?

2-45 Accounting for Prepayments

(Alternates are 2-46, 2-48, 2-50, and 2-52). The Ortiz Company, a wholesale distributor of home appliances, began business on July 1, 20X2. The following summarized transactions occurred during July.

1. Ortiz's stockholders contributed $250,000 in cash in exchange for their common stock.
2. On July 1, Ortiz signed a 1-year lease on a warehouse, paying $60,000 cash in advance for occupancy of 12 months.
3. On July 1, Ortiz acquired warehouse equipment for $100,000. A cash down payment of $40,000 was made, and a note payable was signed for the balance.
4. On July 1, Ortiz paid $24,000 cash for a 2-year insurance policy covering fire, casualty, and related risks.
5. Ortiz acquired assorted merchandise for $35,000 cash.
6. Ortiz acquired assorted merchandise for $190,000 on open account.
7. Total sales were $200,000, of which $30,000 were for cash.
8. Cost of inventory sold was $160,000.
9. Rent expense was recognized for the month of July.
10. Depreciation expense of $2,000 was recognized for the month.
11. Insurance expense was recognized for the month.
12. Collected $35,000 from credit customers.
13. Disbursed $80,000 to trade creditors.

For simplicity, ignore all other possible expenses.

Required
1. By using the balance sheet equation format demonstrated in Exhibit 2-3 (p. 56), prepare an analysis of each transaction. Show all amounts in thousands. What do transactions 8 to 11 illustrate about the theory of assets and expenses? (Use a Prepaid Insurance account, which is not illustrated in Exhibit 2-3.)
2. Prepare an income statement for July on the accrual basis.
3. Prepare a balance sheet for July 31, 20X2.

2-46 Analysis of Transactions, Preparation of Statements

(Alternates are 2-45, 2-48, 2-50, and 2-52.) The Dichev Company was incorporated on April 1, 20X2. Dichev had 10 holders of common stock. Rita Dichev, who was the president and chief executive officer, held 51 percent of the shares. The company rented space in chain discount stores and specialized in selling ladies' accessories. Dichev's first location was in a store that was part of The Old Market in Omaha.

The following events occurred during April:

1. The company was incorporated. Common stockholders invested $150,000 cash.
2. Purchased merchandise inventory for cash, $45,000.
3. Purchased merchandise inventory on open account, $35,000.
4. Merchandise carried in inventory at a cost of $37,000 was sold for cash for $25,000 and on open account for $65,000, for a grand total of $90,000. Dichev (not The Old Market) carries and collects these accounts receivable.
5. Collection of accounts receivable, $18,000. See transaction 4.
6. Payments of accounts payable $30,000. See transaction 3.
7. Special display equipment and fixtures were acquired on April 1 for $36,000. Their expected useful life was 36 months. This equipment was removable. Dichev paid $12,000 as a down payment and signed a promissory note for $24,000. Also see transaction 11.
8. On April 1, Dichev signed a rental agreement with The Old Market. The agreement called for a flat $2,000 per month, payable quarterly in advance. Therefore, Dichev paid $6,000 cash on April 1.
9. The rental agreement also called for a payment of 10 percent of all sales. This payment was in addition to the flat $2,000 per month. In this way, The Old Market would share in any success of the venture and be compensated for general services such as cleaning and utilities. This payment was to be made in cash on the last day of each month as soon as the sales for the month had been tabulated. Therefore, Dichev made the payment on April 30.
10. Employee wages and sales commissions were all paid for in cash. The amount was $34,000.
11. Depreciation expense of $1,000 was recognized ($36,000/36 months). See transaction 7.
12. The expiration of an appropriate amount of prepaid rental services was recognized. See transaction 8.

Required

1. Prepare an analysis of Dichev Company's transactions, employing the equation approach demonstrated in Exhibit 2-3. (p. 56). Show all amounts in thousands.
2. Prepare a balance sheet as of April 30, 20X2, and an income statement for the month of April. Ignore income taxes.
3. Given these sparse facts, analyze Dichev's performance for April and its financial position as of April 30, 20X2.

2-47 Accrual versus Cash-Based Revenues

(Alternate is 2-49.) Refer to the preceding problem. Suppose Dichev measured performance on the cash basis instead of on the accrual basis. Compute the net cash inflows for April. Which measure, accural-based revenue or cash inflows, provides a better measure of accomplishment? Why?

2-48 Analysis of Transactions, Preparation of Statements

(Alternates are 2-45, 2-46, 2-50, and 2-52.) H.J. Heinz Company's actual condensed balance sheet data for April 30, 2003 follow ($ in millions):

Cash	$ 802	Accounts payable	$ 938
Receivables	1,165	Other liabilities	7,088
Inventories	1,153		
Other assets	4,147	Owner's equity	1,199
Property, plant,			
and equipment	1,958		
Total	$ 9,225	Total	$ 9,225

The following summarizes some transactions during May 2003 ($ in millions):

1. Ketchup carried in inventory at a cost of $3 was sold for cash of $3 and on open account of $8, for a grand total of $11.
2. Acquired inventory on account, $6.
3. Collected receivables, $5.
4. On May 2, used $12 cash to prepay some rent and insurance for 12 months.
5. Payments on accounts payable (for inventories), $2.

6. Paid selling and administrative expenses in cash, $1.
7. Prepaid expenses of $1 for rent and insurance expired in May.
8. Depreciation expense of $1 was recognized for May.

Required

1. Prepare an analysis of Heinz's transactions, employing the equation approach demonstrated in Exhibit 2-3 (p. 56). Show all amounts in millions. (For simplicity, only a few transactions are illustrated here.)
2. Prepare a statement of earnings for the month ended May 31 and a balance sheet, May 31. Ignore income taxes.

2-49 Accrual versus Cash-Based Revenue

(Alternate is 2-47.) Refer to the preceding problem. Suppose Heinz measured performance on the cash basis instead of the accrual basis. Compute the net cash inflows during May. Which measure, net income or net cash inflows, provides a better measure of overall performance? Why?

2-50 Analysis of Transactions, Preparation of Statements

(Alternates are 2-45, 2-46, 2-48, and 2-52.) Wm. Wrigley Jr. Company manufactures and sells chewing gum. The company's actual condensed balance sheet data for January 1, 2003 follows ($ in millions):

Cash	$ 279	Accounts payable	$ 98
Receivables	313	Dividends payable	46
Inventories	321	Other liabilities	441
Property, plant,		Owner's equity	1,523
and equipment	836		
Other assets	359		
Total	$2,108	Total	$2,108

The following summarizes some major transactions during January 2003 ($ in millions):

1. Gum carried in inventory at a cost of $45 was sold for cash of $35 and on open account of $40, for a grand total of $75.
2. Collection of receivables, $42.
3. Depreciation expense of $3 was recognized.
4. Selling and administrative expenses of $24 were paid in cash.
5. Prepaid expenses of $5 expired in January. These included fire insurance premiums paid in the previous year that applied to future months. The expiration increases selling and administrative expense and reduces other assets.
6. The January 1 liability for dividends was paid in cash on January 25.

Required

1. Prepare an analysis of Wrigley's transactions, employing the equation approach demonstrated in Exhibit 2-3 (p. 56). Show all amounts in millions. (For simplicity, only a few major transactions are illustrated here.)
2. Prepare a statement of earnings. Also prepare a balance sheet, January 31. Ignore income taxes.

2-51 Prepare Financial Statements

The Vitaly Corporation does not use the services of a professional accountant. At the end of its second year of operations, 20X2, the company's office manager prepared its financial statements. Listed next in random order are the items appearing in these statements:

Accounts receivable	$ 27,400	Office supplies inventory	$ 2,000
Paid-in capital	100,000	Notes payable	7,000
Trucks	33,700	Merchandise inventory	61,000
Cost of goods sold	157,000	Accounts payable	14,000
Salary expense	86,000	Notes receivable	2,500
Unexpired insurance	1,800	Utilities expenses	5,000
Rent expense	19,500	Net income	4,200
Sales	281,000	Retained earnings	
Advertising expense	9,300	January 1, 20X2	18,000
Cash	14,800	December 31, 20X2	22,200

    You are satisfied that the statements in which these items appear are correct, except for several matters that the office manager overlooked. The following information should have been entered on the books and reflected in the financial statements:

a. The amount shown for rent expense includes $1,500 that is actually prepaid for the first month in 20X3.
b. Of the amount shown for unexpired insurance, only $800 is prepaid for periods after 20X2.
c. Depreciation of trucks for 20X2 is $5,000.
d. About $1,200 of the office supplies in the inventory shown earlier was actually issued and used during 20X2 operations.
e. Cash dividends of $4,000 were declared in December 20X2 by the board of directors. The company will distribute these dividends in February 20X3.

Prepare in good form the following corrected financial statements, ignoring income taxes:

1. Income statement for 20X2.
2. Statement of retained earnings for 20X2.
3. Balance sheet at December 31, 20X2.

It is not necessary to prepare a columnar analysis to show the transaction effects on each element of the accounting equation.

2-52 Transaction Analysis and Financial Statements, Including Dividends
(Alternates are 2-45, 2-46, 2-48, and 2-50.) Consider the following balance sheet of a wholesaler of party supplies:

Funco Supplies Company
Balance Sheet December 31, 20X7

Assets		Liabilities and Stockholders' Equity		
		Liabilities		
Cash	$ 340,000	Accounts payable		$ 800,000
Accounts receivable	400,000	Stockholders' equity		
Merchandise inventory	860,000	Paid-in capital	$300,000	
Prepaid rent	40,000	Retained earnings	640,000	
Equipment	100,000	Total stockholders'		
		equity		940,000
Total	$1,740,000	Total		$1,740,000

The following is a summary of transactions that occurred during 20X8:

a. Acquisitions of inventory on open account, $1 million.
b. Sales on open account, $1.5 million; and for cash, $200,000. Therefore, total sales were $1.7 million.
c. Merchandise carried in inventory at a cost of $1.25 million was sold as described in b.
d. The warehouse 12-month lease expired on September 1, 20X8. However, the company immediately renewed the lease at a rate of $84,000 for the next 12-month period. The entire rent was paid in cash in advance.
e. Depreciation expense for 20X8 for the warehouse equipment was $20,000.
f. Collections on accounts receivable, $1.25 million.
g. Wages for 20X8 were paid in full in cash, $200,000.
h. Miscellaneous expenses for 20X8 were paid in full in cash, $70,000.
i. Payments on accounts payable, $900,000.
j. Cash dividends for 20X8 were declared and paid in full in December, $100,000.

Required
1. Prepare an analysis of transactions, employing the equation approach demonstrated in Exhibit 2-3 (p. 56). Show the amounts in thousands of dollars.
2. Prepare a balance sheet, statement of income, and statement of retained earnings. Also prepare a combined statement of income and retained earnings.

3. Reconsider transaction j. Suppose the dividends were declared on December 15, payable on January 31, 20X9, to shareholders of record on January 20. Indicate which accounts and financial statements in requirement 2 would be changed and by how much. Be complete and specific.

2-53 Balance Sheet Equation

(Alternates are 2-38 and 2-39.) **Nordstrom Inc.**, the fashion retailer, had the following actual data for fiscal year ended January 31, 2003 ($ in millions):

Assets, beginning of period	$4,051
Assets, end of period	4,096
Liabilities, beginning of period	A
Liabilities, end of period	D
Other shareholders' equity, beginning of period	339
Other shareholders' equity, end of period	358
Retained earnings, beginning of period	975
Retained earnings, end of period	C
Sales and other revenues	5,975
Cost of sales and all other expenses	5,885
Net earnings	B
Dividends	51

Find the unknowns ($ in millions), showing computations to support your answers.

2-54 Two Sides of a Transaction

For each of the following transactions, show the effects on the entities involved. As was illustrated in the chapter, use the A = L + OE equation to demonstrate the effects. Also name each account affected, show the dollar amount, and indicate whether the effects are increases or decreases. The following transaction is completed as an illustration.

ILLUSTRATION

The Denver General Hospital collects $1,000 from the Blue Cross Health Care Plan.

		A		=	L + OE
Entity	Cash	Receivables	Trucks		Payables
Hospital	+1,000	−1,000		=	
Blue Cross	−1,000			=	−1,000

1. Borrowing of $120,000 on a home mortgage from Fidelity Savings by Lauren Walker.
2. Payment of $10,000 principal on the preceding mortgage. Ignore interest.
3. Purchase of a 2-year subscription to *Time* magazine for $90 cash by Carla Paperman.
4. Purchase of trucks by the U.S. Postal Service for $10 million cash from the U.S. General Services Administration. The trucks were carried in the accounts at $10 million by the General Services Administration.
5. Purchase of U.S. government bonds for $100,000 cash by **Lockheed Corporation**.
6. Cash deposits of $11 on the returnable bottles sold by **Safeway Stores** to a retail customer, Philomena Simon.
7. Collections on open account of $100 by **Sears** store from a retail customer, Kenneth Debreu.
8. Purchase of traveler's checks of $1,000 from **American Express Company** by Michael Sharpe.
9. Cash deposit of $600 in a checking account in **Bank of America** by David Kennedy.
10. Purchase of a **United Airlines** "supersaver" airline ticket for $400 cash by Robert Peecher on June 15. The trip will be taken on September 10.

2-55 Net Income and Retained Earnings

McDonald's Corporation is a well-known fast-food restaurant company. The following data are from the 2002 annual report ($ in millions):

McDonald's Corporation

Retained earnings,		Dividends paid	$ 298
beginning of year	$18,608	Selling, general, and	
Revenues	15,406	administrative expenses	1,713
Interest and other		Franchise restaurants—	
nonoperating expenses	549	occupancy expenses	840
Provision for income taxes	670	Retained earnings,	
Food and paper expense	3,917	end of year	19,204
Payroll and employee benefits	3,078	Occupancy and other	
		operating expenses	3,745

1. Prepare the following for the year:
   a. Income statement. Label the final three lines of the income statement as follows: income before provision for income taxes, provision for income taxes, and net income.
   b. Statement of retained earnings.
2. Comment briefly on the relative size of the cash dividend.

2-56 Earnings Statement, Retained Earnings

Dell is a computer company with headquarters in Austin, Texas. The following amounts were in the financial statements contained in its annual report for the year ended February 1, 2003 ($ in millions):

Total revenues	$35,404	Retained earnings at	
Cash	3,641	beginning of year	$ 1,364
Provision for			
income taxes	905	Cost of revenue	29,055
Accounts payable	5,989	Dividends declared	0
Total assets	15,470	Other expenses	3,322

Choose the relevant data and prepare (1) the income statement for the year and (2) the statement of retained earnings for the year. Label the final three lines of the income statement as follows: income before income taxes, provision for income taxes, and net income.

2-57 Continuity Convention and Liquidation

The following news report appeared in the financial press in late 2002:

> "The Bulgarian national airline Balkan is to be placed in liquidation after its credi-
> tors today rejected a reorganization plan, legal administrators for the carrier said.
> With debts of €92 million to 2,200 creditors, Balkan began bankruptcy procedures
> in March 2001. Creditors today rejected a restructuring for the airline and insisted
> on the sale of its assets to pay off its debts."

Explain how the measurements used in the financial statements of Balkan would differ from those used in a similar airline that had not been placed in liquidation.

2-58 Financial Ratios

(Alternate is 2-59.) Following is a list of three well-known package delivery companies (**UPS** and **FedEx** from the United States and **Deutche Post World Net**, owner of DHL, in Germany) and selected financial data of the sort typically included in letters sent by stock brokerage firms to clients. Note that € is the symbol for the Euro, the European currency.

	Per Share Data			Ratios and Percentages		
Company	Price	Earnings	Dividends	P-E	Dividend-Yield	Dividend-Payout
FedEx	—	$2.79	—	22.9	—	7%
UPS	$54.50	—	—	25.6	1.4%	—
Deutche Post	€15.00	€1.42	—	—	—	26%

The missing figures for this schedule can be computed from the data given.

1. Compute the missing figures and identify the company with:
   a. The highest dividend-yield.
   b. The highest dividend-payout percentage.
   c. The lowest market price relative to earnings.

2. Assume you know nothing about any of these companies other than the data given and the computations you have made from the data. Which company would you choose as:
   a. The most attractive investment? Why?
   b. The least attractive investment? Why?

2-59 Financial Ratios

(Alternate is 2-58.) Following is a list of three well-known petroleum companies and selected financial data of the sort typically included in letters sent by stock brokerage firms to clients. Note that € is the symbol for the Euro, the European currency.

	Per Share Data			Ratios and Percentages		
Company	Price	Earnings	Dividends	P-E	Dividend-Yield	Dividend-Payout
Shell*	€41.95	€2.87	€1.72	—	—	—
ExxonMobil	$39.30	—	—	17.6	2.3%	—
ChevronTexaco	—	$3.10	—	28.9	—	85%

* Royal Dutch Petroleum Company.

The missing figures for this schedule can be computed from the data given.

1. Compute the missing figures and identify the company with:
   a. The highest dividend-yield.
   b. The highest dividend-payout percentage.
   c. The lowest market price relative to earnings.
2. Assume that you know nothing about any of these companies other than the data given and the computations you have made from the data. Which company would you choose as:
   a. The most attractive investment? Why?
   b. The least attractive investment? Why?

2-60 Revenue Recognition and Ethics

Kendall Square Research Corporation (KSR), located in Waltham, Massachusetts, produced high-speed computers and competed against companies such as Cray Research and Sun Microsystems.

In August 1993, the common stock of KSR reached an all-time high of $25.75 a share; by mid-December, it had plummeted to $5.25. Its financial policies were called into question in an article in *Financial Shenanigan Busters,* Winter 1994, p. 3. The main charge was that the company was recording revenues before it was appropriate.

KSR sold expensive computers to universities and other research institutions. Often, the customers took delivery before they knew how they might pay for the computers. Sometimes they anticipated receiving grants that would pay for the computers, but other times they had no prospective funding. KSR also recorded revenue when it shipped computers to distributors who did not yet have customers to buy them and when it sold computers contingent on future upgrades.

Comment on the ethical implications of KSR's revenue recognition practices.

Collaborative Learning Exercise

2-61 Financial Ratios

Form groups of four to six persons each. Each member of the group should pick a different company and find the most recent annual report for that company. (If you do not have printed annual reports, try searching the Internet for one.)

1. Members should compute the following ratios for their company:
   a. EPS
   b. P-E ratio
   c. Dividend-yield ratio
   d. Dividend-payout ratio
2. As a group, list two possible reasons that each ratio differs across the selected companies. Focus on comparing the companies with the highest and lowest values for each ratio, and explain how the nature of the company might be the reason for the differences in ratios.

Analyzing and Interpreting Financial Statements

2-62 Financial Statement Research

Select the financial statements of any company.

1. What was the amount of sales or total revenues, and the net income for the most recent year?
2. What was the total amount of cash dividends for the most recent year?
3. What was the ending balance in retained earnings in the most recent year? What were the two most significant items during the year that affected the retained earnings balance?

2-63 Analyzing Starbucks' Financial Statements

Refer to the Starbucks financial statements in Appendix A (pp. A12–14) at the end of the text and answer the following questions:

1. What was the amount of net revenues (total sales) and net earnings for the year ended September 28, 2003?
2. Compute the increase in retained earnings for the year ended September 28, 2003. Is this number familiar? Where did you see it before?
3. What is Starbucks' EPS for the year ended September 28, 2003? Compute the P-E ratio, assuming the market price for Starbucks' stock was $29 at the time.
4. Suppose the average P-E ratio for companies at that time was 15. Do investors expect Starbucks' EPS to grow faster or slower than average? Explain.

2-64 Analyzing Financial Statements Using the Internet: Outback Steakhouse

Go to the Web site for Outback Steakhouse (www.outback.com). Click on Company Info, Investor Relations, and then Financial Documents. Find and open the most recent annual report.

Answer the following questions:

1. Locate Outback's revenue recognition policy in the Notes to Consolidated Financial Statements. When does Outback recognize revenue? Does it differ for franchise sales (i.e., the sale of a franchise to an investor)? How?
2. Why does Outback have "unearned revenue"? Where is it found in the financial statements?
3. Refer to Outback's Statement of Income. What items comprise its total revenues?
4. What specific items comprise Cost of Sales? Is labor considered part of this line item?
5. Does Outback prepare its income statement using the cash or accrual basis? What items on the balance sheet are clues to answering this question?
6. Do you think Outback Steakhouse is a profit-seeking organization? What clues on the financial statements help you answer this?

Recording Transactions

CHAPTER 3

LEARNING OBJECTIVES

After studying this chapter, you should be able to:

1. Use double-entry accounting.

2. Analyze and journalize transactions.

3. Post journal entries to the ledgers.

4. Prepare and use a trial balance.

5. Close revenue and expense accounts and update retained earnings.

6. Correct erroneous journal entries and describe how errors affect accounts.

7. Explain how computers have transformed processing of accounting data.

Have you ever bought a shirt, a pair of jeans, or any-thing else from a Gap store? If so, your purchase was just one of hundreds of thousands of transactions that Gap Inc. had to record that day. With so many transactions happening, you might think that yours might get lost in the shuffle. Yet, you can read a report on your transaction combined with millions of others in any major newspaper in articles built on press releases such as this one dated August 21, 2003 and time-stamped 4:31 P.M.:

> *Gap Inc. today reported that earnings for the second quarter, which ended August 2, 2003, rose more than three times over last year to $209 million, driven by double-digit percentage increases in sales and gross profit. . . . Earnings per share for the second quarter were $0.22, compared with $0.06 per share for the same period last year. Net income was $209 million, compared with $57 million for the same period last year. . . . Second quarter net sales increased 13 percent to $3.7 billion, compared with $3.3 billion for the same period last year. Comparable store sales were up 10 percent, compared with a prior year decrease of 7 percent.*

Are you not seeing that shirt you bought? The information contained in this news article comes directly from Gap's corporate headquarters and informs investors, stockholders, and other interested parties about the financial performance of the organization. Gap's corporate headquarters gets this information from the company's accounting records. Of course, these records contain every single Gap transaction, including your shirt purchase.

Gap Inc.'s transactions can take many forms—for example, merchandise sales for cash or credit or purchases of inventory for its stores. At the end of the month,

Customers find a variety of clothing products, including the denim products pictured, at Gap stores. Gap Inc. has more than 4,000 casual apparel specialty stores, including Banana Republic and Old Navy locations. Gap records millions of sales transactions each year. These transactions provide the basic information for the company's financial statements.

quarter, or year, accountants compute the totals for each account and use them to prepare the reports that tell the financial story for that period. As you can see from Gap's press release, net sales totaled $3.7 billion for the quarter. After deducting expenses and other items, net earnings came to $209 million, or 5.6 percent of net sales ($209 ÷ $3,700). Now you know that only 5.6 percent of the price Gap receives from its sales was actually net earnings for Gap.

Information in press releases often leads to price changes in a company's stock. Gap's share prices increased by 2.4 percent to close at $19.70 for the week ending August 21, 2003. The earnings release and the results for the quarter were significant information and caused investors to change their valuation of shares of Gap. This was the fourth straight quarter of improved financial results for Gap, and investors apparently took the report as good news. Retailers such as Gap provide information every month on sales levels. Second quarter sales were up 13 percent from the year earlier level. Part of Gap's increase in sales was due to opening new stores. When looking only at stores open for both years, sales increased by 10 percent, still a healthy increase. Thus, the August press release confirmed that Gap's financial results were continuing to improve. By November, the Gap share price reached the low $20s as investors became more convinced that Gap was likely to continue its improved performance.

Methods of processing accounting data have changed dramatically in the last decade or two because computerized systems have replaced manual ones. However, the steps in recording, storing, and processing accounting data have not changed. Switching from pencil-and-paper accounting records to computerized ones is a little like switching from a car with a stick shift to one with an automatic transmission. You spend less time worrying about routine tasks, but you still need to understand how to use the vehicle. Whether a company enters data into the system by pencil, keyboard, or optical scanner, it must enter, summarize, and report the same basic data, and users must interpret the same basic financial statements. ■

To intelligently use the financial statements we learned about in the last two chapters, decision makers need a general understanding of the methods accountants use to record and analyze the data in those reports. This chapter focuses on those methods. In particular, this chapter explains the double-entry accounting system that all companies use to record and process information about their transactions. As you will find, a working knowledge of this system is essential for anyone engaged in business. Ultimately, accounting practices constitute a language that managers in all organizations use to understand the economic progress of their organizations.

The Double-Entry Accounting System

OBJECTIVE 1

Use double-entry accounting.

double-entry system
The method usually followed for recording transactions, whereby every transaction always affects at least two accounts.

In large businesses such as **Gap**, **McDonald's**, and **AT&T**, hundreds or thousands of transactions occur hourly. With so much activity, it might seem easy to lose track of one or two transactions. Even one lost transaction could wreak havoc on a company's accounting (just think of what happens when you miss one transaction in your checking account record) and may lead to some serious consequences. As a result, accountants must record these transactions in a systematic manner. Worldwide, the dominant recording process is a **double-entry system,** in which every transaction affects at least two accounts. Accountants must analyze each transaction to determine which accounts it affects, whether to increase or decrease the account balances, and how much each balance will change. Accountants have used such a system for more than 500 years, as described in the Business First box on p. 93.

DOUBLE-ENTRY ACCOUNTING: FIVE CENTURIES OF PROGRESS

Double-entry accounting is more than 500 years old. In the same decade that Columbus set sail for America, Luca Pacioli, an Italian friar and mathematician, published *Summa de Arithmetica, Geometria, Proportioni, et Proportionalita* ("Everything About Arithmetic, Geometry, and Proportions"), the first book that described a double-entry accounting system. Pacioli did not invent accounting. He simply described the system used by Viennese merchants. His system included journals and ledgers, with accounts for assets (including receivables and inventories), liabilities, equity, income, and expenses. His process included closing the books and preparing a trial balance. All these terms and concepts are still in use today, as described in this chapter. Pacioli also warned that "a person should not go to sleep at night until the debits equaled the credits," a good warning for accountants today.

The last five decades have seen more changes in accounting than did the preceding five centuries. First, automated data processing started replacing manual accounting systems. This, combined with the growth of complex business transactions, made accounting transactions more difficult and less transparent to financial statement users. Then a knowledge-based economy called into question an accounting system that focused mainly on physical assets.

The accounting scandals of the early twenty-first century put double-entry accounting at a crossroads. Were the problems at Enron, WorldCom, Global Crossing, Tyco, Adelphia, and others a symbol that accounting is no longer relevant? Not at all. Now, a few years after the criticisms of accounting peaked, it is clear that reliable accounting systems are more important than ever. The discipline of a double-entry system cannot prevent managers and accountants from entering fraudulent transactions in a company's books, but it does provide a framework for reporting economic results that is essential for disclosing information about a company to investors and potential investors.

In the 1920s, Werner Sombart, a German accountant, made the case that double-entry accounting played a major role in the development of capitalistic, market-based economies. The events of the last decade prove its importance to the smooth functioning of worldwide capital markets. From Pacioli's time until today, double-entry accounting systems have kept confirming their value. To understand a market economy, one must understand the basics of double-entry accounting.

Sources: L. Pacioli, *Summa de Arithmetica, Geometria, Proportioni, et Proportionalita*, 1494; W. Sombart, *Der Moderne Kapitalismus*, 1924.

Recall the first three transactions of the Biwheels Company introduced in Chapter 1:

	A		=	L	+	SE
	Cash	**Store Equipment**		**Note Payable**		**Paid-in Capital**
(1) Initial investment by owner	+400,000		=			+400,000
(2) Loan from bank	+100,000		=	+100,000		
(3) Acquire store equipment for cash	−15,000	+15,000	=			

This balance sheet equation format illustrates the basic concepts of the double-entry system by showing two entries for each transaction. It also emphasizes that the equation Assets = Liabilities + Stockholders' Equity must always remain in balance. Unfortunately, this format is too unwieldy for recording each and every transaction that occurs. In practice, accountants record the individual transactions as they occur and then organize the elements of the transaction into accounts that group similar items together. For example, the cash account collects all elements that affect cash.

The remainder of this chapter describes the elements of a double-entry system, focusing on the ledger and journal and how accountants use them to record, summarize, and report financial information.

Ledger Accounts

ledger
The records for a group of related accounts kept current in a systematic manner.

general ledger
The collection of accounts that accumulate the amounts reported in the major financial statements.

T-account
Simplified version of ledger accounts that takes the form of the capital letter T.

A **ledger** contains the records for a group of related accounts. The ledger may be in the form of a bound record book, a loose-leaf set of pages, or some kind of electronic storage element. It is always kept current in a systematic manner. For simplicity's sake, you can think of a ledger as a book with one page for each account. When you hear about "keeping the books" or "auditing the books," the word *books* refers to the ledger. A firm's **general ledger** is the collection of accounts that accumulate the amounts reported in the firm's major financial statements.

We use ledger accounts that are simplified versions of those used in practice. We call them **T-accounts** because they take the form of the capital letter T. They capture the essence of the accounting process. The vertical line in the T divides the account into left and right sides for recording increases and decreases in the account. The account title is on the horizontal line. For example, consider the format of the Cash account:

Cash	
Left side	Right side
Increases in cash	Decreases in cash

The T-accounts for the first three Biwheels Company transactions are as follows:

Assets			=	Liabilities + Stockholders' Equity		
Cash				**Note Payable**		
Increases		Decreases		Decreases		Increases
(1)	400,000	(3) 15,000				(2) 100,000
(2)	100,000					
Store Equipment				**Paid-in Capital**		
Increases		Decreases		Decreases		Increases
(3)	15,000					(1) 400,000

Note that each numbered transaction affects two accounts, as is the rule under the double-entry system. In practice, we create accounts as we need them. We call the process of creating a new T-account in preparation for recording a transaction opening the account. For transaction 1, we opened Cash and Paid-in Capital. For transaction 2, we opened Note Payable, and for transaction 3, we opened Store Equipment. We know that we need a new account when a transaction requires an entry to an account that we have not yet opened.

Each T-account summarizes the changes in a particular asset, liability, or owners' equity account. Because T-accounts show only amounts and not transaction descriptions, we key each transaction in some way, such as by the numbering used in this illustration, by the date, or by both. This keying helps us to identify the transaction that caused each entry to the ledger.

balance
The difference between the total left-side and right-side amounts in an account at any particular time.

A **balance** is the difference between the total left-side and right-side amounts in an account at any particular time. Asset accounts have left-side balances. Entries on the left side increase asset account balances and entries on the right side decrease them. This process is exactly reversed for liabilities and owners' equity accounts that have right-side balances. Entries on the right side increase their balances and entries on the left side decrease them.

Take a look at the analysis of the entries for each Biwheels transaction. Notice that each transaction generates a left-side entry in one T-account and a right-side entry of the same amount in another T-account. When you analyze a transaction, it is helpful to initially pinpoint the effects (if any) on cash. Did cash increase or decrease? Then think of the effects on other accounts. Usually, it is much easier to identify the effects of a transaction on cash than it is to identify the effects on other accounts.

1. Transaction: Initial investment by owners, $400,000 cash.
   Analysis: The asset **Cash** increases.
   The stockholders' equity **Paid-in-Capital** increases.

Cash		Paid-in Capital	
(1)	(400,000)	(1)	(400,000)

2. Transaction: Loan from bank, $100,000.
   Analysis: The asset **Cash** increases.
   The liability **Note Payable** increases.

Cash		Note Payable	
(1)	400,000	(2)	(100,000)
(2)	(100,000)		

3. Transaction: Acquired store equipment for cash, $15,000.
   Analysis: The asset **Cash** decreases.
   The asset **Store Equipment** increases.

Cash			
(1)	400,000	(3)	(15,000)
(2)	100,000		

Store Equipment	
(3)	(15,000)

Accounts keep a record of the changes in specific assets, liabilities, and owners' equities. Accountants can prepare financial statements at any instant if the account balances are up-to-date. The information accumulated in the accounts provides the necessary summary balances for the financial statements. For example, Biwheels' balance sheet after its first three transactions would contain the following account balances:

Assets		Liabilities + Stockholders' Equity	
Cash	$485,000	Liabilities	
Store		Note payable	$100,000
equipment	15,000	Stockholders' equity	
		Paid-in capital	400,000
Total	$500,000	Total	$500,000

Three of the four accounts have only one transaction, so the transaction amount becomes the account balance. For cash, the balance of $485,000 is the difference between the total increases on the left side of $500,000 (400,000 + 100,000) and the total decreases of $15,000 on the right side.

Debits and Credits

You have just seen that the double-entry system features entries on left sides and right sides of various accounts. Accountants use the term **debit** (abbreviated dr.) to denote an entry on the left side of any account and the term **credit** (abbreviated cr.) to denote an entry on the right side of any account. Many people make the mistake of thinking that

debit
An entry or balance on the left side of an account.

credit
An entry or balance on the right side of an account.

credit means increase and debit means decrease. Trust us—when used in accounting, they do not. Left and right would be much easier and more descriptive to use, but debit and credit are the standard terms for the double-entry system. Some accountants use the word **charge** instead of debit, but there is no such synonym for credit. Just remember that debit refers to left and credit refers to right, and you will be fine.

Accountants use debit and credit as verbs, adjectives, and nouns. "Debit $1,000 to cash," and "credit $1,000 to accounts receivable" are examples of uses as verbs, meaning that you should place $1,000 on the left side of the Cash account and on the right side of the Accounts Receivable account. Similarly, in phrases such as "make a debit to cash" or "cash has a debit balance of $12,000," the word debit is a noun or an adjective that describes the status of a particular account. From this point on you will be seeing debit and credit again and again. Be sure you understand their uses completely before moving on.

Summary Problem for Your Review

PROBLEM

Do you agree with the following statements? Explain.

1. My credit is my most valuable asset.
2. When I give credit, I debit my customer's account.

SOLUTION

Remember that in accounting, debit means left side and credit means right side.

1. As used in this statement, "my credit" refers to "my ability to borrow," not which side of a balance sheet is affected. "My ability to borrow" may indeed be a valuable right, but the accountant does not recognize that ability (as such) as an asset to be measured and reported in the balance sheet. When borrowing occurs, the borrower's assets are increased (debited, increased on the left side) and the liabilities are increased (credited, increased on the right side).
2. Yes. Accounts Receivable is debited (left). "Give credit" in this context means that the seller is allowing the customer to defer payment. The corresponding account payable on the customer's accounting records will be increased (credited, right).

The Recording Process

In the preceding section, we entered Biwheels' transactions 1, 2, and 3 directly in the ledger. In actual practice, the recording process does not start with the ledger. The sequence of five steps in recording and reporting transactions is as follows:

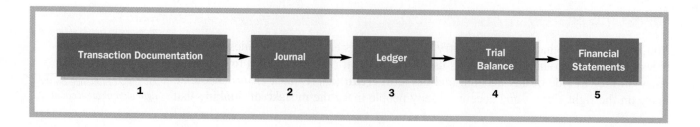

Step 1: The recording process begins with **source documents.** These are the original records of any transaction. Examples of source documents include sales slips or invoices, check stubs, purchase orders, receiving reports, cash receipt slips, and minutes of the board of directors. As soon as a transaction occurs, it generates a source document. For example, when a company sells a product to a customer, it makes a receipt for the sale. Companies keep source documents on file so they can use them to verify the details of a transaction and the accuracy of subsequent records, if necessary.

Step 2: In the second step of the recording process, we place an analysis of the transaction, based on the source documents, in a **book of original entry** called the general journal. The **general journal** is a formal chronological listing of each transaction and how it affects the balances in particular accounts. It is basically a diary of all events (transactions) in an entity's life.

Step 3: The third step is to enter transactions into the ledger. As we have seen, we enter each component into the left side or the right side of the appropriate accounts.

Step 4: The fourth step is the preparation of the **trial balance,** which is a simple listing of the accounts in the general ledger together with their balances. This listing aids in verifying clerical accuracy and in preparing financial statements. Thus, we prepare it as needed, perhaps each month or each quarter as the firm prepares its financial statements. The timing of the first four steps varies. Transactions occur constantly so companies prepare source documents continuously. Depending on the size and nature of the organization, transaction analysis may occur continuously, weekly, or monthly. Basically, the timing of the steps in the recording process must conform to the needs of the users of the data.

Step 5: The final step, the preparation of financial statements, occurs at least once a quarter, every 3 months, for publicly traded companies in the United States. Although companies must produce financial statements only once a quarter for external reporting, some companies prepare financial statements more frequently for management's benefit. For example, Springfield ReManufacturing Corporation in the Ozark Mountains of southern Missouri prepares monthly financial statements. Springfield is a leader in "open book management," in which the company opens its accounting results to everyone in the firm. Management and all employees meet monthly to examine the results in detail. The company provides extensive training to employees on how the accounting process works and what the numbers mean. This new management process has focused the attention of every employee and increased efficiency and profitability at Springfield.

source documents
The supporting original records of any transaction.

book of original entry
A formal chronological record of how the entity's transactions affect the balances in pertinent accounts.

general journal
The most common example of a book of original entry; a complete chronological record of transactions.

trial balance
A list of all accounts in the general ledger with their balances.

Chart of Accounts

To ensure consistency in recording transactions, organizations specify a **chart of accounts,** which is a numbered or coded list of all account titles. This list specifies the accounts (or categories) that the organization uses in recording its activities. We use these account numbers as references in the Post Ref. column of the journal, as Exhibit 3-1 demonstrates. The following is the chart of accounts for Biwheels:

chart of accounts
A numbered or coded list of all account titles.

Account Number	Account Title	Account Number	Account Title
100	Cash	202	Note payable
120	Accounts receivable	203	Accounts payable
130	Merchandise inventory	300	Paid-in capital
140	Prepaid rent	400	Retained earnings
170	Store equipment	500	Sales revenues
170A	Accumulated depreciation,	600	Cost of goods sold
	store equipment	601	Rent expense
	(explained later)	602	Depreciation expense

Exhibit 3-1
Journal Entries—
Recorded in General
Journal and Posted
to General Ledger
Accounts

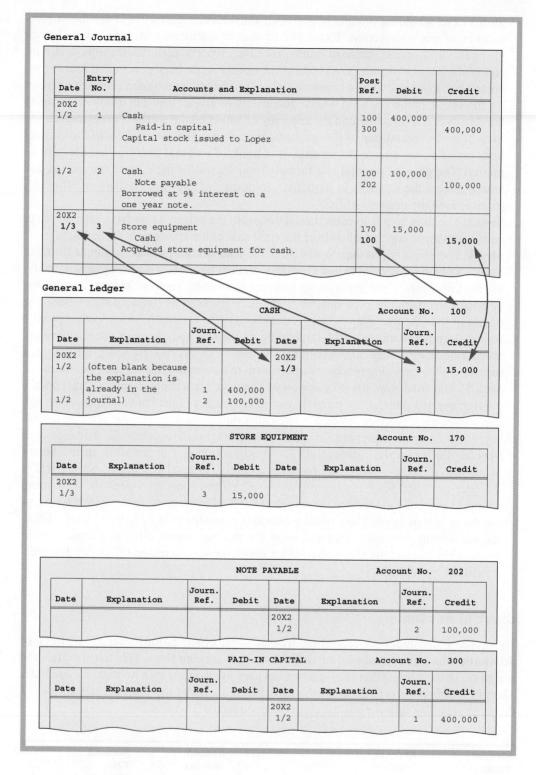

Accountants within a company often become so familiar with the various codes that they think, talk, and write in terms of account numbers instead of account names. Thus, they might journalize Biwheels' entry 3, the acquisition of Store Equipment (Account 170) for Cash (Account 100), as follows:

		dr.	cr.
20X2			
Jan. 3	170.............................	15,000	
	100		15,000

This journal entry employs the accountant's shorthand, which uses codes without account names. Its brevity and lack of explanation would hamper any outsider's understanding of the transaction, but the entry's meaning would be clear to anyone within the organization.

Journalizing Transactions

Let's examine more closely step 2 in the recording process. **Journalizing** is the process of entering transactions into the general journal. A **journal entry** is an analysis of all the effects of a single transaction on the various accounts, usually accompanied by an explanation. For each transaction, this analysis identifies the accounts to be debited and credited. The top of Exhibit 3-1 shows how to journalize the opening three transactions for Biwheels.

We will use the following conventions for recording in the general journal:

1. The date and identification number of the entry make up the first two columns.
2. The next column, Accounts and Explanation, shows the accounts affected. We place at the left margin the title of the account or accounts to be debited. We indent in a consistent way the title of the account or accounts to be credited. Following the journal entry itself is the narrative explanation of the transaction, which can be brief or extensive. The length of the explanation depends on the complexity of the transaction and whether management wants the journal itself to contain all relevant information. Most often, explanations are brief because details are available in the file of supporting documents.
3. The Post Ref. (posting reference) column contains an identifying number that we assign to each account and use for cross-referencing to the ledger accounts.
4. The debit and credit columns are for recording the amounts that we debit (left-entry) or credit (right-entry) for each account. It is customary not to use dollar signs in either the journal or the ledger. You should also note that negative numbers never appear in the journal or the ledger. Instead, the side on which the number appears tells you whether to add or subtract the number in computing an account balance. Debits and credits tell the whole story in the recording process, so be sure you understand them fully.

Posting Transactions to the Ledger

We can call step 3, the transferring of amounts from the journal to the appropriate accounts in the ledger, **posting.** To see how this works, consider transaction 3 for Biwheels (see p. 95). Exhibit 3-1 shows with bold arrows how we post the credit to cash using the information and values from the journal entry. Note that the format of the sample of the general ledger in Exhibit 3-1 provides space for transferring the information in the journal entry, not just the summary information allowed in the simplified T-account format. There are columns for dates, explanations, journal references, and amounts. The structure is repeated for debits on the left side of the page and for credits on the right side.

Because posting is strictly a mechanical process of moving numbers from the journal to the ledger, it is most efficiently done by a computer. The accountant journalizes a transaction in an electronic general journal, and the computer automatically transfers the information to an electronic version of the ledger. Note how cross-referencing

OBJECTIVE 2

Analyze and journalize transactions.

journalizing
The process of entering transactions into the journal.

journal entry
An analysis of the effects of a transaction on the accounts, usually accompanied by an explanation.

OBJECTIVE 3

Post journal entries to the ledgers.

posting
The transferring of amounts from the journal to the appropriate accounts in the ledger.

Exhibit 3-2
Ledger Account
with Running
Balance Column

		Cash		Account No.		100
Date	Explanation		Journ. Ref.	Debit	Credit	Balance
20X2						
1/2	(often blank because the explanation is		1	400,000		400,000
1/2	already in the journal)		2	100,000		500,000
1/3						
			3		15,000	485,000

occurs between the journal and the ledger. **Cross-referencing** is the process of using numbering, dating, and/or some other form of identification to relate each ledger posting to the appropriate journal entry. A single transaction from the journal might be posted to several different ledger accounts. Cross-referencing allows users to find all the components of the transactions in the ledger no matter where they start. It also helps auditors to find and correct errors and reduces the frequency of initial errors.

Ledger entries do not always take the form of Exhibit 3-1. Exhibit 3-2 shows another popular ledger account format, one that has only one date column and one explanation column and also adds an additional column to the presentation to provide a running balance of the account holdings. This format should look familiar to you because it is very similar to the format found in a checkbook. The running balance feature is a useful addition because it provides a status report for an account at a glance. Although most accounting systems are now fully computerized, the reports generated by computers often look much like the paper-based ledgers and journals they replaced. After hundreds of years of use, these formats have become traditional and familiar.

Analyzing, Journalizing, and Posting the Biwheels Transactions

We have seen that accountants review source documents about a transaction, mentally analyze the transaction, record that analysis in a journal entry, and then post the results to the general ledger. We can now apply this process to additional transactions from the Biwheels Company. We will omit explanations for the journal entries because we already presented them in the statement of the transaction. We indicate the posting of the elements of the transaction to the T-accounts by encircling the new number.

4. Transaction: Acquired inventory for cash, $120,000.
      Analysis: The asset **Merchandise Inventory** increases.
                The asset **Cash** decreases.
Journal Entry: Merchandise Inventory. 120,000
              Cash 120,000
      Posting:

	Cash					Merchandise Inventory	
(1)	400,000	(3)	15,000	(4)	120,000	
(2)	100,000	(4)	120,000			

5. Transaction: Acquired inventory on credit, $10,000.
      Analysis: The asset **Merchandise Inventory** increases.
                The liability **Accounts Payable** increases.

Journal Entry: Merchandise inventory 10,000
           Accounts payable.   10,000

Posting:

Merchandise Inventory				Accounts Payable		
(4)	120,000			(5)		(10,000)
(5)	(10,000)					

Transaction 5, like transactions 1, 2, 3, and 4, is a **simple entry** in that the transaction affects only two accounts. Note that the balance sheet equation always remains in balance.

simple entry
An entry for a transaction that affects only two accounts.

6. Transaction: Acquired merchandise inventory for $10,000 cash plus $20,000 trade credit.
    Analysis: The asset **Cash** decreases.
                 The asset **Merchandise Inventory** increases.
                 The liability **Accounts Payable** increases.
Journal Entry: Merchandise Inventory 30,000
           Cash   10,000
           Accounts payable   20,000

Posting:

Cash				Accounts Payable		
(1)	400,000	(3)	15,000	(5)		10,000
(2)	100,000	(4)	120,000	(6)		(20,000)
		(6)	(10,000)			

Merchandise Inventory			
(4)	120,000		
(5)	10,000		
(6)	(30,000)		

Transaction 6 is a **compound entry,** which means that a single transaction affects more than two accounts. Whether transactions are simple (like transactions 1 through 5) or compound, the total of all left-side entries always equals the total of all right-side entries. The net effect is always to keep the accounting equation in balance:

compound entry
An entry for a transaction that affects more than two accounts.

$$\text{Assets} = \text{Liabilities} + \text{Stockholders' equity}$$
$$+30,000 - 10,000 = +20,000$$

7. Transaction: Sold unneeded showcase to neighbor for $1,000 cash.
    Analysis: The asset **Cash** increases.
                 The asset **Store Equipment** decreases.
Journal Entry: Cash 1,000
           Store equipment   1,000

Posting:

Cash				Store Equipment		
(1)	400,000	(3)	15,000	(3)	15,000	(7)	(1,000)
(2)	100,000	(4)	120,000			
(7)	(1,000)	(6)	10,000			

In transaction 7, one asset goes up, and another asset goes down. The transaction affects only one side of the accounting equation because there is no entry to a liability or owners' equity account.

8. Transaction: Returned inventory to supplier for full credit, $800.
    Analysis: The asset **Merchandise Inventory** decreases.
                 The liability **Accounts Payable** decreases.

Journal Entry: Accounts payable 800

Merchandise inventory   800

Posting:

Merchandise Inventory					Accounts Payable				
(4)	120,000	(8)		⦰800⦰	(8)	⦰800⦰	(5)	10,000
(5)	10,000						(6)	20,000
(6)	30,000							

9. Transaction: Paid cash to creditors, $4,000.

Analysis: The asset **Cash** decreases.

The liability **Accounts Payable** decreases.

Journal Entry: Accounts payable 4,000

Cash   4,000

Posting:

Cash					Accounts Payable				
(1)	400,000	(3)	15,000	(8)	800	(5)	10,000
(2)	100,000	(4)	120,000	(9)	⦰4,000⦰	(6)	20,000
(7)	1,000	(6)	10,000				
		(9)	⦰4,000⦰				

Transactions 7, 8, and 9 are all simple entries. In transactions 8 and 9, an asset and a liability both go down.

Revenue and Expense Transactions

Revenue and expense transactions deserve special attention because their relationship with the balance sheet equation is less obvious. Recall that the owners' equity section of the balance sheet equation includes both paid-in capital and retained earnings:

$$\text{Assets} = \text{Liabilities} + \text{Stockholders' equity}$$

$$\text{Assets} = \text{Liabilities} + (\text{Paid-in capital} + \text{Retained earnings})$$

Recall from Chapter 2 that, if we ignore dividends, retained earnings is merely accumulated revenue less accumulated expenses. Therefore, we can group the T-accounts as follows:

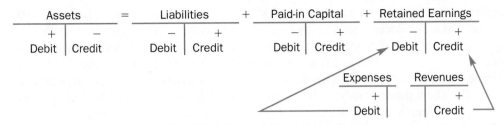

Why don't we simply increase the retained earnings account directly? To do so would make it harder to prepare an income statement because revenue and expense items would be mixed together in the retained earnings account. By accumulating information separately for categories of revenue and expense, we can more easily prepare an income statement.

Expense and revenue accounts are part of retained earnings. You can think of them as separate compartments within the larger retained earnings account. Expense and revenue accounts are types of retained earnings accounts, just as cash and accounts receivable are types of asset accounts.

A revenue account collects items that increase retained earnings. Thus, any credit to revenue is essentially a credit to retained earnings. Therefore, recording sales revenues increases both revenues and retained earnings. The expense account collects items that decrease retained earnings. Thus, a debit to expense is essentially a debit to retained earnings. Although a debit entry increases expenses, it results in a decrease in retained earnings. Thus, recording wage expense increases expenses but decreases retained earnings. Revenue and expense accounts are really "little" stockholders' equity accounts. That is, they are fundamentally a part of stockholders' equity.

We can now examine a few transactions involving revenues and expenses. Consider Biwheels' transactions 10a and 10b in detail:

10a. Transaction: Sales on credit, $160,000.
   Analysis: The asset **Accounts Receivable** increases.
        The stockholders' equity **Sales Revenues** increases.
  Journal Entry: Accounts receivable 160,000
         Sales revenues   160,000
    Posting:

Accounts Receivable		Sales Revenues	
(10a) 160,000			(10a) 160,000

A credit, or right-side, entry in transaction 10a increases the Sales Revenues account, essentially increasing the stockholders' equity account, Retained Earnings. In transaction 10b, a debit, or left-side, entry increases the expense account, Cost of Goods Sold. The effect is to decrease the stockholders' equity account, Retained Earnings.

10b. Transaction: Cost of merchandise inventory sold, $100,000.
   Analysis: The asset **Merchandise Inventory** decreases.
        The stockholders' equity decreases because an expense account, **Cost of Goods Sold,** which is essentially a negative stockholders' equity account, increases.
  Journal Entry: Cost of goods sold 100,000
         Merchandise inventory 100,000
    Posting:

Merchandise Inventory				Cost of Goods Sold	
(4)	120,000	(8)	800	(10b) 100,000	
(5)	10,000	(10b)	100,000		
(6)	30,000				

Before we go on, let's look for a minute at the logic illustrated by transactions 10a and 10b. These transactions illustrate the general relationship of revenue and expense to retained earnings using actual journal entries and showing the effects on the ledger accounts. Revenues increase stockholders' equity because the revenue accounts and the stockholders' equity accounts are right-side balance accounts. Expenses decrease stockholders' equity because expenses are left-side balance accounts. They are offsets to the normal right-side balance of stockholders' equity. Therefore, increases in expenses are decreases in stockholders' equity. The following analysis shows that we could record the $100,000 Cost of Goods Sold expense directly in the Stockholders' Equity account, in the Retained Earnings account, or in an expense account. This third alternative captures the most information.

If we use only a lone stockholders' equity account:

Stockholders' Equity	
Decreases	Increases
(100,000)	

If we use two stockholders' equity accounts without a revenue or expense account:

Paid-in Capital		Retained Earnings	
Decreases	Increases	Decreases	Increases
		(100,000)	

If we create revenue and expense accounts that we will eventually summarize into a single net effect on retained earnings:

Expenses		Revenues	
Increases			Increases
(100,000)			

Exhibit 3-3 presents the rules of debit and credit and the normal balances of the accounts discussed in this section. It demonstrates the basic principles of the balance sheet equation and the double-entry accounting system:

$$\text{Left side} = \text{Right side}$$

$$\text{Debit} = \text{Credit}$$

The exhibit also emphasizes that revenues increase stockholders' equity. Therefore, we record them as credits. In contrast, expenses decrease stockholders' equity, and we record them as debits. Keeping separate accounts for revenues and expenses makes it easier to prepare an income statement. Revenues and expenses comprise the data used to calculate net income (or net loss) on the income statement, thereby providing a detailed explanation of how the period's transactions caused the balance sheet account, retained earnings, to change during the period.

Transaction 11 is the collection of some of the accounts receivable created by transaction 10a:

11. Transaction: Collected cash from debtors, $5,000.
Analysis: The asset **Cash** increases.
The asset **Accounts Receivable** decreases.
Journal Entry: Cash. 5,000
Accounts receivable 5,000
Posting:

	Cash				Accounts Receivable		
(1)	400,000	(3)	15,000	(10a)	160,000	(11)	(5,000)
(2)	100,000	(4)	120,000				
(7)	1,000	(6)	10,000				
(11)	(5,000)	(9)	4,000				

Prepaid Expenses and Depreciation Transactions

Recall from Chapter 2 that prepaid expenses, such as prepaid rent and depreciation expenses, relate to assets having a useful life that will expire some time in the future. Biwheels' transactions 12, 13, and 14 demonstrate the analysis for journalizing and posting of prepaid rent expenses and depreciation of store equipment.

12. Transaction: Paid rent for 3 months in advance, $6,000.
Analysis: The asset **Cash** decreases.
The asset **Prepaid Rent** increases.

Journal Entry: Prepaid rent. 6,000
               Cash   6,000
    Posting:

	Cash				Prepaid Rent	
(1)	400,000	(3)	15,000	(12)	(6,000)	
(2)	100,000	(4)	120,000			
(7)	1,000	(6)	10,000			
(11)	5,000	(9)	4,000			
		(12)	(6,000)			

Transaction 12 represents the prepayment of rent as the acquisition of an asset. It affects only asset accounts—Cash decreases (a credit) and Prepaid Rent increases (a debit). Transaction 13 represents the subsequent expiration of one-third of the asset as an expense.

13. Transaction: Recognized expiration of rental services, $2,000.
    Analysis: The asset **Prepaid Rent** decreases.
             The negative stockholders' equity **Rent Expense** increases.
Journal Entry: Rent expense. 2,000
             Prepaid rent   2,000
    Posting:

	Prepaid Rent				Rent Expense	
(12)	6,000	(13)	(2,000)	(13)	(2,000)	

Remember that, in this transaction, the effect of the $2,000 increase in Rent Expense is a decrease in stockholders' equity on the balance sheet.

Rules of Debit and Credit

Assets		=	Liabilities		+	Owners' Equity			
Assets		=	Liabilities		+	Paid-in Capital		+	Retained Earnings
+	−	=	−	+	+	−	+	−	+
Increase	Decrease		Decrease	Increase		Decrease	Increase	Decrease	Increase
Debit	Credit		Debit	Credit		Debit	Credit	Debit	Credit
Left	Right		Left	Right		Left	Right	Left	Right
Normal Bal.				Normal Bal.			Normal Bal.		Normal Bal.

	Expenses		Revenues	
	+*	−	−	+
	Increase	Decrease	Decrease	Increase
	Debit	Credit	Debit	Credit
	Left	Right	Left	Right
	Normal Bal.			Normal Bal.

*Remember that increases in expenses decrease retained earnings.

Normal Balances

Assets	Debit
Liabilities	Credit
Owners' Equity (overall)	Credit
Paid-in Capital	Credit
Revenues	Credit
Expenses	Debit

Exhibit 3-3
Rules of Debit and Credit and Normal Balances of Accounts

14. Transaction: Recognized depreciation, $100.
Analysis: The asset-reduction account **Accumulated Depreciation, Store Equipment** increases.
The negative stockholders' equity **Depreciation Expense** increases.
Journal Entry: Depreciation expense 100
Accumulated depreciation, store equipment   100
Posting:

Accumulated Depreciation, Store Equipment	Depreciation Expense
(14) (100)	(14) (100)

contra account
A separate but related account that offsets or is a deduction from a companion account. An example is accumulated depreciation.

contra asset
A contra account that offsets an asset.

In transaction 14, we open a new account, Accumulated Depreciation. Although we describe it as an asset-reduction account in our analysis and corresponding journal entry, a more popular term is contra account. A **contra account** is a separate but related account that offsets or is a deduction from a companion account. A contra account has two distinguishing features: (1) it always has a companion account and (2) it has a balance on the opposite side from the companion account. In our illustration, accumulated depreciation is a **contra asset** account because it is a contra account offsetting an asset. Although the normal balance of the asset account is a debit, the normal balance of accumulated depreciation is a credit. The asset and contra asset accounts on January 31, 20X2, are:

Asset:	Store equipment	$14,000
Contra asset:	Accumulated depreciation, store equipment	100
Net asset:	Book value	$13,900

book value (net book value, carrying amount, carrying value)
The balance of an account shown on the books, net of any contra accounts. For example, the book value of equipment is its acquisition cost minus accumulated depreciation.

The **book value**, also called **net book value, carrying amount,** or **carrying value,** is the balance of an account shown on the books, minus the value of any contra accounts. In our example, the book value of Store Equipment is $13,900, the original acquisition cost ($14,000) less the contra account for accumulated depreciation ($100).

A Note on Accumulated Depreciation

accumulated depreciation (allowance for depreciation)
The cumulative sum of all depreciation recognized since the date of acquisition of an asset.

The balance sheet distinguishes between the store equipment's original cost and its accumulated depreciation. As the name implies, **accumulated depreciation** (sometimes called **allowance for depreciation**) is the cumulative sum of all depreciation recognized since the date of acquisition of an asset. Published balance sheets routinely report both the original cost and accumulated depreciation.

Why is there an Accumulated Depreciation account? Why do we not reduce Store Equipment directly by $100? Conceptually, a direct reduction is indeed justified. However, accountants have traditionally preserved the original cost in the original asset account throughout the asset's useful life. They can then readily refer to that account to learn the asset's initial cost. Reports to management, government regulators, and tax authorities might require such information. Moreover, the original $14,000 cost is the height of accuracy—it is a reliable, objective number. In contrast, the Accumulated Depreciation is an estimate, the result of a calculation whose accuracy depends heavily on the accountant's less reliable prediction of an asset's useful life. Recall that we calculated the $100 of depreciation by dividing the $14,000 cost by an assumed useful life of 140 months. We have no assurance concerning how long an asset will be useful. Some cars run for several hundred thousand miles over 20 years, whereas others become impossible to keep running after 10 years of use. In calculating depreciation, we must make estimates that are imperfect, but there is no other way to allocate the cost of the equipment over the periods that it benefits.

In practice, investors can estimate the average age of the assets by dividing accumulated depreciation by the original cost of the assets. For example, recently **Gap, Inc.** had accumulated depreciation of $2,458 million on an original cost of property and equipment of $6,620 million, making it 37 percent depreciated. Most of the Gap's assets must be quite young, which is what we would expect for a fast-growing company. We can compare this with the French retailer **Carrefour**, which has accumulated depreciation of €10,225 million on an original cost of €23,855 million (€ stands for euro, the European currency). Therefore, its assets are 10,225 ÷ 23,855 = 43 percent depreciated. For another comparison, **Sears, Roebuck and Co.** has assets that are 48 percent depreciated.

Summary Problem for Your Review

PROBLEM

An annual report of **Kobe Steel, Ltd.**, one of the world's largest producers of iron and steel, showed (Japanese yen in billions):

Plant and equipment, at cost	¥2,626
Accumulated depreciation	1,618

1. Open T-accounts for (a) Plant and Equipment, (b) Accumulated Depreciation, and (c) Depreciation Expense. Enter these amounts therein.
2. Assume that during the ensuing year Kobe Steel purchased additional plant and equipment for cash of ¥63 billion and incurred depreciation expense of ¥107 billion. Prepare the journal entries, and post to the T-accounts.
3. Show how Kobe Steel would present its plant and equipment accounts in its balance sheet after the journal entries in requirement 2.

SOLUTION

1. Amounts are in billions of Japanese yen.

Plant and Equipment

	2,626		
(a)	63		
Bal.	2,689		

Accumulated Depreciation, Plant and Equipment

			1,618
		(b)	107
		Bal.	1,725

Depreciation Expense

(b)	107

2.
Plant and equipment	63	
Cash		63
Depreciation expense	107	
Accumulated depreciation, plant and equipment		107

3. The plant and equipment section would appear as follows:

Plant and equipment, at cost	¥2,689
Accumulated depreciation	1,725
Plant and equipment, net	¥964

Biwheels' Transactions in the Journal and Ledger

Exhibit 3-4 shows the formal journal entries for Biwheels' transactions 4 through 13 as analyzed in the previous section. The posting reference (Post Ref.) column uses the account numbers from the Biwheels chart of accounts on page 97. These account numbers also appear on each account in the Biwheels general ledger. Exhibit 3-5 shows the Biwheels general ledger in T-account form.

Pause and trace each of the following journal entries to its posting in the ledger in Exhibit 3-5. Recall that the first three journal entries were summarized in Exhibit 3-1, the remainder appear in Exhibit 3-4.

1. Initial investment
2. Loan from bank
3. Acquire store equipment for cash
4. Acquire merchandise inventory for cash
5. Acquire merchandise inventory for credit
6. Acquire merchandise inventory for cash plus credit
7. Sale of equipment on credit
8. Return of merchandise inventory for credit
9. Payments to creditors
10a. Sales on credit
10b. Cost of merchandise inventory sold
11. Collections from debtors
12. Pay rent in advance
13. Recognize expiration of rental services
14. Recognize depreciation

As you trace these items, ask yourself why they appear on the left or right side of each account. You might find it useful to state the relationships explicitly as follows: The initial investment was a debit to Cash and a credit to Paid-in-Capital. The posting shows an entry on the left-hand side of the Cash account, which increases the balance in this asset account. It also shows a right-hand side entry to the Paid-in-Capital account, which increases the balance in this owners' equity account.

In the ledgers that do not keep a running balance column, accountants may update the account balance from time to time as desired. There are many acceptable techniques for updating, and accountants' preferences vary. We will use double horizontal lines, as in Exhibit 3-5, to signify that we have updated these accounts. A single balance immediately below the double lines summarizes all postings above the double lines. We use this single balance as a starting point for computing the next updated balance.

The accounts in Exhibit 3-5 that contain only one lone number do not have a double line. Why? If there is only one number in a given account, this number automatically also serves as the ending balance. For example, the Note Payable entry of $100,000 also serves as the ending balance for the account.

Preparing the Trial Balance

O B J E C T I V E 4

Prepare and use a trial balance.

Once accountants have posted journal entries to the ledger, their next step in the process of recording transactions is the preparation of a trial balance (see step 4 on p. 97). Recall that a trial balance is a list of all accounts with their balances. Accountants prepare it as a test or check—a trial as the name says—before proceeding further. Thus, the purpose of the trial balance is twofold: (1) to help check on the accuracy of postings by proving whether the total debits equal the total credits, and (2) to establish a convenient summary of the balances in all accounts for the preparation of formal financial statements. We can take a trial balance at any time the accounts are up-to-date. For example, we might take a trial balance for Biwheels on January 3, 20X2, after the company's first three transactions:

Exhibit 3-4
General Journal of
Biwheels Company

Date	Entry No.	Accounts and Explanation	Post Ref.	Debit	Credit
20X2	4	Merchandise inventory	130	120,000	
		Cash	100		120,000
	5	Merchandise inventory	130	10,000	
		Accounts payable	203		10,000
		Acquired inventory on credit			
	6	Merchandise inventory	130	30,000	
		Cash	100		10,000
		Accounts payable	203		20,000
		Acquired merchandise inventory for cash plus credit			
		(This is an example of a *compound journal entry*			
		whereby more than two accounts are affected by			
		the same transaction)			
	7	Cash	100	1,000	
		Store equipment	170		1,000
		Sold store equipment to business neighbor			
	8	Accounts payable	203	800	
		Merchandise inventory	130		800
		Returned some inventory to supplier			
	9	Accounts payable	203	4,000	
		Cash	100		4,000
		Payments to creditors			
	10a	Accounts receivable	120	160,000	
		Sales	500		160,000
		Sales to customers on credit			
	10b	Cost of goods sold	600	100,000	
		Merchandise inventory	130		100,000
		To record the cost of inventory sold			
	11	Cash	100	5,000	
		Accounts receivable	120		5,000
		Collections from debtors			
	12	Prepaid rent	140	6,000	
		Cash	100		6,000
		Payment of rent in advance			
	13	Rent expense	601	2,000	
		Prepaid rent	140		2,000
		Recognize expiration of rental service			
	14	Depreciation expense	602	100	
		Accumulated depreciation, store equipment	170A		100
		Recognize depreciation for January			

Biwheels Company

Trial Balance, January 3, 20X2 for the Period January 1–2, 20X2

Account Number	Account Title	Balance Debit	Balance Credit
100	Cash	$485,000	
170	Store equipment	15,000	
202	Note payable		$100,000
300	Paid-in capital		400,000
	Total	$500,000	$500,000

Assets = **Liabilities and Stockholders' Equity**

| (Increases on left, decreases on right) | | (Decreases on left, increases on right) |

Cash — Account No. 100

(1)	400,000	(3)	15,000
(2)	100,000	(4)	120,000
		(6)	10,000
(7)	1,000	(9)	4,000
(11)	5,000	(12)	6,000
1/31 Bal.	351,000		

Accounts Receivable — 120

(10a)	160,000	(11)	5,000
1/31 Bal.	155,000		

Merchandise Inventory — 130

(4)	120,000	(8)	800
(5)	10,000	(10b)	100,000
(6)	30,000		
1/31 Bal.	59,200		

Prepaid Rent — 140

(12)	6,000	(13)	2,000
1/31 Bal.	4,000		

Store Equipment — 170

(3)	15,000	(7)	1,000
1/31 Bal.	14,000		

Accumulated Depreciation, Store Equipment — 170A

		(14)	100

Note Payable — 202

		(2)	100,000

Accounts Payable — 203

(8)	800	(5)	10,000
(9)	4,000	(6)	20,000
		1/31 Bal.	25,200

Paid-in Capital — 300

		(1)	400,000

Retained Earnings — 400

		1/31 Bal.	57,900*

Sales Revenues — 500

		(10a)	160,000

Expense and Revenue Accounts

Cost of Goods Sold — 600

(10b)	100,000

Rent Expense — 601

(13)	2,000

Depreciation Expense — 602

(14)	100

Note: An ending balance is shown on the side of the account with the larger total.

*The details of the revenue and expense accounts appear in the income statement. Their net effect is then transferred to a single account, Retained Earnings, in the balance sheet. In this case, $160,000 − $100,000 − $2,000 − $100 = $57,900.

Exhibit 3-5
General Ledger of Biwheels Company

	Debits	Credits
Cash	351,000	
Accounts receivable	155,000	
Merchandise inventory	59,200	
Prepaid rent	4,000	
Store equipment	14,000	
Accumulated depreciation, store equipment		$ 100
Note payable		100,000
Accounts payable		25,200
Paid-in capital		400,000
Retained earnings		0*
Sales revenues		160,000
Cost of goods sold	100,000	
Rent expense	2,000	
Depreciation expense	100	
Total	$ 685,300	$ 685,300

*If a Retained Earnings balance existed at the start of the accounting period, it would appear here. However, in our example, Retained Earnings was zero at the start of the period.

Exhibit 3-6
Biwheels Company
Trial Balance, January 31, 20X2, for the Period January 1–January 31, 20X2

Obviously, the more accounts there are, the more detailed (and the more essential for checking multiple figures) the trial balance becomes.

Exhibit 3-6 shows the trial balance of the general ledger in Exhibit 3-5. As shown, we normally prepare the trial balance with the balance sheet accounts listed first, assets, then liabilities, and then stockholders' equity. Next come the income statement accounts, Revenues and Expenses. Note that the last stockholders' equity account listed, Retained Earnings, has no balance here because it was zero at the start of the period in our example. All balance sheet accounts except Retained Earnings show their balances as of the date the trial balance is prepared. Retained Earnings shows the balance at the *beginning* of the period. The revenues and expenses for the current period that are on the list constitute the change in retained earnings for the current period. When accountants prepare formal balance sheets, they delete the revenue and expense accounts and add their net effect to the Retained Earnings account to get the ending balance in Retained Earnings.

Deriving Financial Statements from the Trial Balance

As you can see, the trial balance assures the accountant that the debits and credits are equal. It is also the springboard for the last step of the process, preparing the balance sheet and the income statement, as shown in Exhibit 3-7. We summarize the income statement accounts as a single number, net income, which then becomes part of Retained Earnings in the formal balance sheet. Note that the retained earnings in the balance sheet in Exhibit 3-7 is $57,900, although the retained earnings in the trial balance is $0. Why is this the case? Because the January 31 balance sheet shows the ending balance in retained earnings, the beginning balance of zero plus net income during the period. In future periods when we prepare a trial balance, the beginning balance will be the ending balance of the previous period. The beginning balance for February will be $57,900.

Although the trial balance helps alert accountants to possible errors, it may balance even when there are recording errors. For example, an accountant may misread a $10,000 cash receipt on account as a $1,000 receipt and record the erroneous amount

Biwheels Company
Trial Balance
January 31, 20X2

	Debits	Credits
Cash	351,000	
Accounts receivable	155,000	
Merchandise inventory	59,200	
Prepaid rent	4,000	
Store equipment	14,000	
Accumulated depreciation, store equipment		$ 100
Note payable		100,000
Accounts payable		25,200
Paid-in capital		400,000
Retained income		0
Sales revenue		160,000
Cost of goods sold	100,000	
Rent expense	2,000	
Depreciation expense	100	
Total	$685,300	$685,300

Biwheels Company
Balance Sheet January 31, 20X2

Assets		
Cash		$351,000
Accounts receivable		155,000
Merchandise inventory		59,200
Prepaid rent		4,000
Store equipment	14,000	
Less: accumulated depreciation	100	13,900
Total assets		$583,100

Liabilities and Stockholders' Equity		
Liabilities		
Note payable	$100,000	
Accounts payable	25,200	
Total liabilities		$125,200
Stockholders' equity		
Paid-in capital	$400,000	
Retained earnings	57,900	
Total stockholders' equity		457,900
Total liabilities and stockholders' equity		$583,100

Biwheels Company
Income Statement
for the Month Ended January 31, 20X2

Sales revenues		$160,000
Deduct expenses		
Cost of goods sold	$100,000	
Rent	2,000	
Depreciation	100	
Total expenses		102,100
Net income		$ 57,900

Exhibit 3-7
Trial Balance, Balance Sheet, and Income Statement

in both the Cash and Accounts Receivable accounts. Then both Cash and Accounts Receivable would be in error by offsetting amounts of $9,000. Or the accountant might record a $10,000 cash receipt on account as a credit to Sales Revenues instead of a credit reducing Accounts Receivable. Sales Revenues and Accounts Receivable would both be overstated by $10,000. Nevertheless, the trial balance would still show total debits equal to total credits.

Closing the Accounts

After preparing financial statements, accountants must **close the books,** which prepares the ledger accounts to record the next period's transactions. To do this, accountants make closing entries that summarize all balances in the "temporary" stockholders' equity accounts (revenue and expense accounts) and transfer the balances to a "permanent" stockholders' equity account, Retained Earnings. Closing the books essentially creates the proper ending balance in the Retained Earnings account by reducing the amount in each temporary account to zero, so it will be ready to record transactions for the next period, and transferring the amounts in each account to an Income Summary account. Then we transfer the amount in the Income Summary account to the permanent Retained Earnings account.

We illustrate the closing process for Biwheels in Exhibit 3-8. The process closes the revenue accounts in entry C1 and closes the expense accounts in entry C2, transferring the amounts in revenue and expense accounts to the Income Summary account. Then, as a final step, entry C3 transfers the total net income for the period from Income Summary to Retained Earnings. Notice that we opened a new temporary account called Income Summary. We use it only momentarily to keep track of the process. We transfer the revenue and expense amounts into Income Summary, and then immediately transfer the balance to Retained Earnings. Slight variations on this process occur in different companies, but the end result is always the same—revenue and expense account balances are "reset" to zero and the net income generated during the period increases retained earnings.

OBJECTIVE 5

Close revenue and expense accounts and update retained earnings.

close the books
Preparing the ledger accounts to record the next period's transactions by making closing entries that summarize all balances in the revenue and expense accounts and transferring the balances to retained earnings.

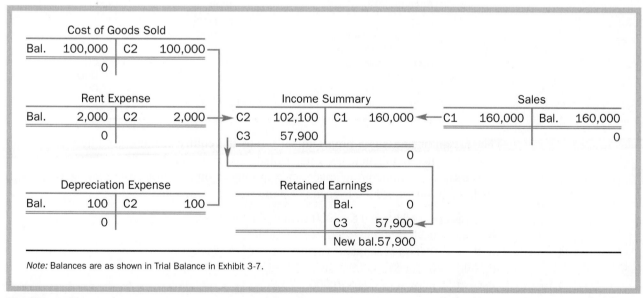

Exhibit 3-8
Closing the Accounts
Data are from Exhibit 3-7

The following analysis gives the journal entries for the closing transactions shown in Exhibit 3-8:

C1. Transaction: Clerical procedure of transferring the ending balances of revenue accounts to the Income Summary account.

Analysis: The stockholders' equity account **Sales** decreases to zero.
The stockholders' equity account **Income Summary** increases.

Journal Entry: Sales 160,000
    Income summary   160,000

C2. Transaction: Clerical procedure of transferring the ending balances of expense accounts to the Income Summary account.

Analysis: The negative stockholders' equity (expense) accounts **Cost of Goods Sold, Rent Expense,** etc., decrease to zero.
The stockholders' equity account **Income Summary** decreases.

Journal Entry: Income summary. 102,100
    Cost of goods sold   100,000
    Rent expense.   2,000
    Depreciation expense   100

C3. Transaction: Clerical procedure of transferring the ending balance of Income Summary account to the Retained Earnings account.

Analysis: The stockholders' equity account **Income Summary** decreases to zero.
The stockholders' equity account **Retained Earnings** increases.

Journal Entry: Income summary 57,900
    Retained earnings   57,900

Summary Problem for Your Review

PROBLEM

The balance sheet of Hassan Used Auto Company, on March 31, 20X1, using the format of the trial balance, follows:

| | Balance | |
Account Title	Debit	Credit
Cash	$ 10,000	
Accounts receivable	20,000	
Automobile inventory	100,000	
Accounts payable		$ 3,000
Notes payable		70,000
Hassan, owner's equity		57,000
Total	$130,000	$130,000

The Hassan business is a proprietorship, thus the equity account used here is Hassan, Owner's Equity. In practice, it is often called Hassan, Capital.

Hassan rented operating space and equipment on a month-to-month basis. During April, the business had the following summarized transactions:

a. Invested an additional $20,000 cash in the business.
b. Collected $10,000 on accounts receivable.
c. Paid $2,000 on accounts payable.
d. Sold autos for $120,000 cash.
e. Cost of autos sold was $70,000.
f. Replenished inventory for $60,000 cash.
g. Paid rent expense in cash, $14,000.
h. Paid utilities in cash, $1,000.

  i. Paid selling expense in cash, $30,000.
  j. Paid interest expense in cash, $1,000.

Required

1. Open the following T-accounts in the general ledger: cash; accounts receivable; automobile inventory; accounts payable; notes payable; Hassan, owner's equity; sales; cost of goods sold; rent expense; utilities expense; selling expense; and interest expense. Enter the March 31 balances in the appropriate accounts.
2. Journalize transactions a through j and post the entries to the ledger. Key entries by transaction letter.
3. Prepare the trial balance at April 30, 20X1.
4. Prepare an income statement for April. Ignore income taxes.
5. Give the closing entries.

SOLUTION

The solutions to requirements 1 through 5 are in Exhibits 3-9 through 3-12. Exhibit 3-9 shows the journal entries. Exhibit 3-10 includes the appropriate opening balances and shows the posting of all transactions to the general ledger. Exhibit 3-11 presents the trial balance and the income statement. The closing entries appear in Exhibit 3-12

Exhibit 3-9
Hassan Used Auto Company
General Journal

ENTRY	ACCOUNTS AND EXPLANATION	POST REF.*	DEBIT	CREDIT
a.	Cash	✓	20,000	
	Hassan, owner's equity	✓		20,000
	Investment in business by Hassan			
b.	Cash	✓	10,000	
	Accounts receivable	✓		10,000
	Collected cash on accounts			
c.	Accounts payable	✓	2,000	
	Cash	✓		2,000
	Disbursed cash on accounts owed to others			
d.	Cash	✓	120,000	
	Sales (or Sales Revenue)	✓		120,000
	Sales for cash			
e.	Cost of goods sold	✓	70,000	
	Automobile inventory	✓		70,000
	Cost of inventory that was sold to customers			
f.	Automobile inventory	✓	60,000	
	Cash	✓		60,000
	Replenished inventory			
g.	Rent expense	✓	14,000	
	Cash	✓		14,000
	Paid April rent			
h.	Utilities expense	✓	1,000	
	Cash	✓		1,000
	Paid April utilities			
i.	Selling expense	✓	30,000	
	Cash	✓		30,000
	Paid April selling expenses			
j.	Interest expense	✓	1,000	
	Cash	✓		1,000
	Paid April interest expense			

* Ordinarily, account numbers are used to denote specific posting references. Otherwise, check marks are used to indicate that the entry has been posted to the general ledger.

Cash

Bal.*	10,000	(c)	2,000
(a)	20,000	(f)	60,000
(b)	10,000	(g)	14,000
(d)	120,000	(h)	1,000
	160,000	(i)	30,000
		(j)	1,000
			108,000†
Bal.	52,000		

Accounts Receivable

Bal.*	20,000	(b)	10,000
Bal.	10,000		

Automobile Inventory

Bal.*	100,000	(e)	70,000
(f)	60,000		
Bal.	90,000		

Accounts Payable

(c)	2,000	Bal.*	3,000
		Bal.	1,000

Notes Payable

		Bal.*	70,000

Cost of Goods Sold

(e)	70,000

Selling Expense

(i)	30,000

Utilities Expense

(h)	1,000

Hassan, Owner's Equity

		Bal.*	57,000
		(a)	20,000
		Bal.	77,000

Sales

		(d)	120,000

Rent Expense

(g)	14,000

Interest Expense

(j)	1,000

*Balances denoted with an asterisk are as of March 31; balances without asterisks are as of April 30. A lone number in any account also serves as an ending balance.
†Subtotals are included in the Cash account. They are not an essential part of T-accounts. However, when an account contains many postings, subtotals ease the checking of arithmetic.

Exhibit 3-10
Hassan Used Auto Company
General Ledger

Account Title	Balance	
	Debit	**Credit**
Cash	$ 52,000	
Accounts receivable	10,000	
Automobile inventory	90,000	
Accounts payable		$ 1,000
Notes payable		70,000
Hassan, owners' equity		77,000*
Sales		120,000
Cost of goods sold	70,000	
Rent expense	14,000	
Utilities expense	1,000	
Selling expense	30,000	
Interest expense	1,000	
Total	$268,000	$268,000

Hassan Used Auto Company
Income Statement for the Month Ended April 30, 20X1

Sales		$120,000
Deduct expenses		
Cost of goods sold	$70,000	
Rent expense	14,000	
Utilities expense	1,000	
Selling expense	30,000	
Interest expense	1,000	116,000
Net income		$ 4,000

* Beginning balance ($57,000) plus additional investment ($20,000).

Exhibit 3-11
Hassan Used Auto Company
Trial Balance and Income Statement, April 30, 20X1

C1.	Sales 120,000		
	Income summary		120,000
C2.	Income summary 116,000		
	Cost of goods sold		70,000
	Selling expense		30,000
	Utilities expense		1,000
	Rent expense		14,000
	Interest expense		1,000
C3.	Income summary.................... 4,000		
	Retained earnings		4,000

Exhibit 3-12
Hassan Used Auto
Company
Closing Entries

Effects of Errors

Now that we have completed all steps of the recording process, let's consider what happens when journal entries have errors. Suppose a journal entry contains an error. How do we correct it? If we discover the error immediately, we can rewrite the entry or reenter the correct data. However, if we detect the error after posting to ledger accounts, we must make a **correcting entry** (as distinguished from a correct entry). Basically, the idea behind correcting entries is to cancel a previous erroneous entry and to add the correct amounts to the correct accounts. We record the correcting entry in the general journal and post it to the general ledger exactly as we would for a regular entry. However, the end result is that we have corrected the balances in the accounts to what they should have been originally. The focus is on the final balances, not on the flow of entries through the accounts. Because we use the balances to prepare the financial statements, they must be correct.

OBJECTIVE

Correct erroneous journal entries and describe how errors affect accounts.

correcting entry
A journal entry that cancels a previous erroneous entry and adds the correct amounts to the correct accounts.

Consider the following examples:

1. A company erroneously debited a repair expense to Equipment on December 27. We discover the error on December 31:

CORRECT ENTRY	12/27 Repair Expense.............. 500	
	Cash	500
ERRONEOUS ENTRY	12/27 Equipment 500	
	Cash	500
CORRECTING ENTRY	12/31 Repair Expense.............. 500	
	Equipment	500

The correcting entry shows a credit to Equipment to cancel or offset the erroneous debit to Equipment. Moreover, the correcting entry debits Repair Expense, adding the amount that should have been added on 12/27. Notice that the credit to Cash was correct, and therefore we did not change it.

2. A collection on account was erroneously credited to Sales on November 2. We discover the error on November 28:

CORRECT ENTRY	11/2 Cash..................... 3,000	
	Accounts Receivable........	3,000
ERRONEOUS ENTRY	11/2 Cash..................... 3,000	
	Sales	3,000
CORRECTING ENTRY	11/28 Sales 3,000	
	Accounts Receivable........	3,000

The debit to Sales in the correcting entry offsets the incorrect credit to Sales. The credit to Accounts Receivable in the correcting entry places the collected amount where it belongs. Essentially, the correcting entry moves the 3,000 from the Sales account to the Accounts Receivable account where it belongs. The debit to Cash in the original entry is correct, and thus we do not change it.

INTERPRETING FINANCIAL STATEMENTS

Suppose that on May 27, 20X3, a manager reported to the accounting department a purchase of equipment for $10,000 cash. The accountant recorded this transaction in the company's books. After the company had prepared its May financial statements, the manager indicated that he had been in error and that the $10,000 was for supplies that his department used up during May. Prepare a correcting entry. Would this situation raise any potential ethical issues? Explain.

Answer

CORRECTING ENTRY Supplies expense 10,000
                                    Equipment   10,000

The "error" kept the $10,000 expense from reducing May's income. This overstatement of income for May might have had a benefit for the manager, perhaps helping him meet a profit target needed for a bonus. The accountant would have an ethical obligation to investigate this transaction to make sure it was truly an error and not an attempt to manipulate May's income.

Some Errors Are Temporary

Accountants' errors that are undetected can affect a variety of items, including revenues and expenses for a given period. Some errors are automatically corrected in the ordinary bookkeeping process in the next period. Such errors misstate net income in both periods, which could easily mislead users of the financial statements. However, by the end of the second period the errors counterbalance or cancel each other out, and they affect the balance sheet of only the first period, not the second.

Consider a payment of $1,000 in December 20X1 for rent. Suppose this was for January 20X2's rent. Instead of recording it as Prepaid Rent, the accountant listed the payment as Rent Expense:

INCORRECT ENTRY	12/X1 Rent expense	1,000	
	Cash		1,000
	One month's rent.		
CORRECT ENTRY	12/X1 Prepaid rent.	1,000	
	Cash		1,000
	Payment for January 20X2's rent.		
	1/X2 Rent Expense	1,000	
	Prepaid rent		1,000
	Expiration of January 20X2's rent.		

The effects of this recording error are (1) to overstate rent expense (which understates pretax income by $1,000) and understate year-end assets by $1,000 (because the prepayment would not be listed as an asset) for the first year and (2) to understate rent expense (which overstates pretax income by $1,000) for the second year. These errors have no effect on the second year's ending assets. Why? Because the same total assets exist whether the accountant records rent as used in January of that year or as used in full the previous year. The total of the incorrect pretax incomes for the 2 years is the same as the total of the correct pretax incomes for the 2 years. The first year's understatement of pretax income by $1,000 counterbalances the second year's overstatement of $1,000. The retained earnings balance at the end of the second year is thus correct on a pretax basis.

Some Errors Persist Until Corrected

Errors that are not automatically corrected in the ordinary bookkeeping process will keep subsequent balance sheets in error until an accountant makes specific correcting entries. For example, overlooking a depreciation expense of $2,000 in only one year would (1) overstate pretax income, assets, and retained earnings by $2,000 in that year, and (2) continue to overstate assets and retained earnings on successive balance sheets for the life of the fixed asset. However, observe that the error would not affect pretax income for subsequent years unless the same error is committed again.

Incomplete Records

A company's accounting records are not always perfect. Someone may steal, lose, or destroy records, forcing accountants to make journal and ledger entries and create financial statements with incomplete information. Luckily, T-accounts can help accountants to discover unknown amounts. For example, suppose the proprietor of a local sports shop asks you for help in calculating her sales for 20X5. She provides the following accurate but incomplete information:

List of customers who owe money	
December 31, 20X4	$ 4,000
December 31, 20X5	6,000
Cash receipts from customers during 20X5	
appropriately credited to customer's accounts	280,000

She further tells you that all sales were on credit, not cash. How can you use T-accounts to solve for the missing credit sales figure? There are two basic steps to follow:

Step 1: Enter all known items into the key T-account. Of course, you need to understand this account and its components to properly work the problem. In this case, we are looking for credit sales, which accountants debit to Accounts Receivable. By substituting S for the unknown credit sales, we get the following T-account values:

Accounts Receivable

Bal. 12/31/X4	4,000	Collections	280,000
	S		
Total debits	(4,000+S)	Total credits	280,000
Bal. 12/31/X5	6,000		

Step 2: Solve for the unknown. Finding this solution is a simple algebraic exercise. We can use the debit and credit relationships we have just learned to solve our problem:

$$\text{Total debits} - \text{Total credits} = \text{Balance}$$
$$(4,000 + S) - 280,000 = 6,000$$
$$S = 6,000 + 280,000 - 4,000$$
$$S = 282,000$$

Obviously, the analyses of missing data become more complicated if there are more entries in a particular account or if there is more than one unknown value. Nevertheless, the key idea is to fill in the account with all known debits, credits, and balances, and then solve for the unknown.

Data Processing and Accounting Systems

OBJECTIVE 7

Explain how computers have transformed processing of accounting data.

data processing
The totality of the procedures used to record, analyze, store, and report on chosen activities.

Data processing is a general term referring to the procedures used to record, analyze, store, and report on chosen activities. An accounting system is a data processing system. Today most accounting systems are computerized. Software packages are available in many sizes and types. Small companies might use QuickBooks, Peachtree, NetLedger, or Microsoft Small Business Manager. Many large companies are building their accounting systems around a larger enterprise resource planning (ERP) system. A variety of companies produce ERP systems, including the large German company SAP and American competitors Oracle, Baan, PeopleSoft, J. D. Edwards, and others. These systems use the basic structure of journal entries and ledger accounts used in this book. They take the drudgery out of bookkeeping, but they have not fundamentally changed the way companies keep their accounting records. Whether you enter transactions data into a book or into a computer, the transaction data in ledgers and journals remain the same. Of course, if you enter journal amounts into a computerized accounting program, the computer can automatically carry out steps such as ledger postings and financial statement preparation.

Computers affect not only the processing of data and preparation of reports. When you check out at a Walgreens drugstore or The Limited clothing store, the cash

DATA PROCESSING USING XBRL

The Internet has created new opportunities for companies to report and exchange financial information. The first step was putting financial statements on the Web in PDF format. This conveyed the information quickly and easily, but it did not allow analysis of the data. Some companies then put the statements in Excel format. This allowed analysis between years and between different statements for the same company, but it did not allow intercompany analyses. To address this issue, an original group of 12 organizations (including **AICPA, Arthur Andersen LLP, Deloitte & Touche LLP, Ernst & Young LLP, Great Plains Software, KPMG LLP, Microsoft Corporation**, and **PricewaterhouseCoopers LLP**) formed XBRL International in August 1999 to create a common XML-based language for the reporting of business information. Today, a consortium of more than 170 companies and agencies supports the efforts. You can view the current status of XBRL on the Web at www.xbrl.org.

XBRL (extensible business reporting language) provides "an XML-based framework that the global business information supply chain will use to create, exchange, and analyze financial reporting information including, but not limited to, regulatory filings such as annual and quarterly financial statements, general ledger information, and audit schedules." XBRL will make it easier to share information. As Robert Elliott, visionary former Chair of the AICPA, said, "While sharing business information has always been necessary, it has been a significant challenge. [XBRL] will revolutionize the way financial information is communicated, accessed and used." Former SEC Chairman Arthur Levitt added: "I would like to see you take [the] XBRL project a step further, providing account classifications for companies in common industries." This is exactly what XBRL is doing.

In 2002, the NASDAQ stock exchange, Microsoft Corp., and PricewaterhouseCoopers LLP developed a pilot program to apply XBRL to 21 NASDAQ-listed companies.

They showed that XBRL will benefit both companies and financial statement users. The companies will enter data only once, using the same database for preparing financial statements for investors and the SEC, Internal Revenue Service tax filings, reports to regulatory agencies, and many other specialized financial reports. Investors will benefit from a streamlined analysis process that will allow easy comparison of financial statement information across companies in a particular industry or in the market in general. To facilitate international application of XBRL, IASB and XBRL International have developed an XBRL taxonomy that models the primary financial statements that a commercial and industrial entity may use to report under International Accounting Standards.

Proponents of XBRL also claim that it can help the quality of financial reporting by making monitoring of reporting easier. Today, the SEC in the United States reviews only 14 percent of the 14,000 filings made by publicly traded companies. If companies submitted financial statements in XBRL format, the SEC could use analytic software to electronically screen nearly all filings. Intraindustry and cross-industry analyses might reveal anomalies that would lead to further investigation of the financial reports. Can this eliminate fraudulent reporting? No, but it might more quickly and easily identify such problems, making accountants and executives think twice before deciding to manipulate their financial numbers.

Sources: XBRL International Web site (http://www.xbrl.org); L. Watson, B. McGuire, and E. Cohen, "Looking at Business Reports Through XBRL-Tinted Glasses," *Strategic Finance* (September 2000), pp. 40–45; "IASC Foundation and XBRL PFS Taxonomy Release," International Accounting Standards Board Press Release, 27 November 2002; "Pilot Program Uses XBRL for Reports," *Financial Executive,* October 2002, p. 8; N. Hannon, "Accounting Scandals: Can XBRL Help?" *Strategic Finance,* August 2002, pp. 61–62.

register often does more than just record a sale. It may be linked to a computer that also records a decrease in inventory. It may activate an order to a supplier if the inventory level is low. If a sale is on credit, the computer may check your credit limit, update the accounts receivable, and eventually prepare your monthly billing. Most important, the computer can automatically enter every transaction into the journal as it occurs, thereby reducing the amount of source document paperwork and potential data-entry errors.

Because computers reduce the need for paperwork and for accountants to analyze every transaction, data processing costs have consistently decreased. Consider the oil companies. ExxonMobil would receive more than 1 million separate sales slips daily if its system were manual. However, today computers record most credit sales by reading the magnetic strips on credit cards. Many gas stations have the card-reading equipment built into the gasoline pumps, eliminating the need for sales clerks. Information about each credit sale is electronically submitted to a central computer, which prepares all billing documents and financial statements. Companies automatically record millions of transactions into their general journals without any paperwork or keyboard entry, producing huge savings in time and money while increasing accuracy.

Computers also reduce the time it takes to close the books and prepare financial statements. IBM announced its financial results for the year ended December 31, 2003 in a Webcast at 8:00 A.M. ET on Thursday, January 15, 2004. It takes only about 2 weeks for a company with some $86 billion in sales to finalize its results. The most recent advance in data processing for financial reporting is the use of extensible business reporting language (XBRL), an extensible markup language (XML)-based computer language that allows easy comparisons across companies. We describe this in the Business First box on page 121.

Highlights to Remember

1 **Use double-entry accounting.** Double-entry accounting refers to the fact that every transaction affects at least two elements in the fundamental accounting equation. For example, we not only keep track of an increase in cash, but also keep track of whether that increase arose from making a sale or borrowing money.

2 **Analyze and journalize transactions.** Recording transactions in the general journal is the first step in the accountant's recording process. The journal provides a chronological record of transactions.

3 **Post journal entries to the ledgers.** After we initially record transactions as journal entries in the general journal, we post the elements of each transaction to the proper accounts in the general ledger. The general ledger accounts accumulate all the transactions affecting the account over time. We determine the balance in a specific general ledger account by adding all debits and all credits and subtracting the totals. This textbook uses a simplified version of general ledger accounts called T-accounts. Accountants at all levels use T-accounts to help think through complex transactions. Accountants use the terms debit and credit repeatedly. Remember that debit simply means "left side" and credit means "right side."

4 **Prepare and use a trial balance.** Trial balances are internal reports that list each account in the general ledger together with the balance in that account as of the trial balance date. Accountants use them for detecting errors in the accounts and in preparing financial statements. Trial balances that fail to balance are inevitably the result of careless or rushed journalizing or posting. The good news is that the out-of-balance condition lets you know that an error has been made.

5 **Close revenue and expense accounts and update retained earnings.** At the end of each accounting period, accountants "close" the temporary revenue and expense accounts. This involves resetting them to zero by transferring their balances for the period into the Retained Earnings account.

6 **Correct erroneous journal entries and describe how errors affect accounts.** Despite precautions, errors sometimes occur in accounting entries. Accountants correct such errors when discovered by making a correcting entry that reverses the error and adjusts account balances so they equal the amounts that would have existed if the correct entry had been made.

7 **Explain how computers have transformed processing of accounting data.** Computers are fast and efficient and enable the performance of repetitive tasks with complete accuracy. Many software packages are available to aid in the processing of accounting transactions. In many parts of the accounting process, human effort and error creation have been eliminated. Computers perform tasks from initial recording of a sale, to journalizing and posting, to creation of trial balances and financial statements, and finally to sending financial information to interested parties over the Web.

Accounting Vocabulary

accumulated depreciation,
  p. 106
allowance for depreciation,
  p. 106
balance, p. 94
book of original entry, p. 97
book value, p. 106
carrying amount, p. 106
carrying value, p. 106
charge, p. 96
chart of accounts, p. 97

close the books, p. 113
compound entry, p. 101
contra account, p. 106
contra asset, p. 106
correcting entry, p. 117
credit, p. 95
cross-referencing, p. 100
data processing, p. 120
debit, p. 95
double-entry system, p. 92
general journal, p. 97

general ledger, p. 94
journal entry, p. 99
journalizing, p. 99
ledger, p. 94
net book value, p. 106
posting, p. 99
simple entry, p. 101
source documents, p. 97
T-account, p. 94
trial balance, p. 97

Assignment Material

Questions

3-1 "Double entry means that amounts are shown in the journal and ledger." Do you agree? Explain.

3-2 "Increases in cash and stockholders' equity are shown on the right side of their respective accounts." Do you agree? Explain.

3-3 "Debit and credit are used as verbs, adjectives, or nouns." Give examples of how debit may be used in these three meanings.

3-4 Name three source documents for transactions.

3-5 "The ledger is the major book of original entry because it is more essential than the journal." Do you agree? Explain.

3-6 "Revenue and expense accounts are really little stockholders' equity accounts." Explain.

3-7 Give two synonyms for book value.

3-8 "Accumulated depreciation is the total depreciation expense for the year." Do you agree? Explain.

3-9 "A trial balance assumes that the amounts in the financial statements are correct." Do you agree? Explain.

3-10 "If debits equal credits in a trial balance, you can be assured that no errors were made." Do you agree? Explain.

3-11 "In double-entry accounting, errors are not a problem because they are self-correcting." Do you agree? Explain.

3-12 Are all data processing systems computerized? Explain.

Critical Thinking Questions

3-13 The Chart of Accounts
You have just joined the accounting staff of a fast-food company. You are surprised that this company has a chart of accounts with twice as many accounts as the company you previously worked for, even though the current client's sales are one-half as large. You are tempted to write a very critical memo to your senior about this issue. You have asked a more experienced friend for advice. What might this friend ask you about these clients?

3-14 The Relation of Expense and Retained Earnings Accounts
A fellow student asked you the following: "I understand that a debit increases an expense account. I also understand that a debit decreases retained earnings. But if an expense account is a part of retained earnings (a 'little' stockholders' equity account), how can a debit entry have a different effect on retained earnings than it does on an expense account?" Provide an explanation to the student.

3-15 Reconstructing Transactions
Your supervisor in the accounting department has asked you to trace transactions from the general journal to the general ledger. You are part way into the task when you find at the top of one page in the general journal that a coffee spill has obliterated part of a transaction. You can see that the debit portion of the transaction was for $1,000 to rent expense, but the credit portion is illegible. How might you go about re-creating what happened?

3-16 Manual versus Computerized Accounting Systems

As a new auditor, you have just been assigned to an audit of a highly computerized accounting system. How would you expect an audit of such a system to differ from the audit of a small company whose records were maintained manually?

Exercises

3-17 Debits and Credits

For each of the following accounts, indicate whether it normally possesses a debit or a credit balance. Use dr. or cr.:

1. Sales
2. Accounts receivable
3. Supplies expense
4. Accounts payable
5. Supplies inventory
6. Retained earnings
7. Depreciation expense
8. Dividends payable
9. Paid-in capital
10. Subscription revenue

3-18 Debits and Credits

Indicate for each of the following transactions whether an accountant will debit or credit the account named in parentheses:

1. Borrowed money from a bank (Notes Payable), $10,000.
2. Bought merchandise on account (Merchandise Inventory), $4,000.
3. Paid Napoli Associates $3,000 owed them (Accounts Payable).
4. Received cash from customers on accounts due (Accounts Receivable), $2,000.
5. Bought merchandise on open account (Accounts Payable), $5,000.
6. Sold merchandise (Merchandise Inventory), $1,500.

3-19 Debits and Credits

For the following transactions, indicate whether the accountant for El Paso Company should debit or credit the accounts in parentheses. Use dr. or cr.:

1. El Paso sold merchandise on credit (Accounts Receivable).
2. El Paso declared dividends and paid them in cash (Retained Earnings).
3. El Paso received interest on an investment (Interest Revenue).
4. El Paso paid wages to employees (Wages Expense).
5. El Paso sold merchandise for cash (Sales Revenue).
6. El Paso acquired a 4-year fire insurance policy (Prepaid Expenses).

3-20 True or False

Use T or F to indicate whether each of the following statements is true or false:

1. Cash payments of accounts payable should be recorded by a debit to Cash and a credit to Accounts Payable.
2. Repayments of bank loans should be charged to Notes Payable and credited to Cash.
3. Inventory purchases on account should be credited to Accounts Payable and debited to an expense account.
4. In general, all debit entries are recorded on the left side of accounts and represent decreases in the account balances.
5. Cash collections of accounts receivable should be recorded as debits to Cash and credits to Accounts Receivable.
6. Credit purchases of equipment should be debited to Equipment and charged to Accounts Payable.
7. In general, entries on the right side of asset accounts represent decreases in the account balances.
8. Increases in liability and revenue accounts should be recorded on the left side of the accounts.
9. Decreases in retained earnings are recorded as debits.
10. Both increases in assets and decreases in liabilities are recorded on the debit sides of accounts.
11. In some cases, increases in account balances are recorded on the right sides of accounts.
12. Asset debits should be on the right and liability debits should be on the left.

3-21 Matching Transaction Accounts

Listed here are a series of accounts that are numbered for identification. Accompanying this problem are columns in which you are to write the identification numbers of the accounts affected by the transactions described. You may use the same account in several answers. For each transaction, indicate which account or accounts are to be debited and which are to be credited.

1. Cash
2. Accounts receivable
3. Inventory
4. Equipment
5. Accumulated depreciation, equipment
6. Prepaid insurance
7. Accounts payable

8. Notes payable
9. Paid-in capital
10. Retained earnings
11. Sales revenues
12. Costs of goods sold
13. Operating expense

	Debit	Credit
(a) Purchased new equipment for cash plus a short-term note	4	1, 8
(b) Bought regular merchandise on credit	_____	_____
(c) Made sales on credit: Inventory is accounted for as each sale is made	_____	_____
(d) Paid cash for salaries and wages for work done during the current fiscal period	_____	_____
(e) Collected cash from customers on account	_____	_____
(f) Paid some old trade bills with cash	_____	_____
(g) Purchased 3-year insurance policy on credit	_____	_____
(h) Paid off note owed to bank	_____	_____
(i) Paid cash for inventory that arrived today	_____	_____
(j) To secure additional funds, 400 new shares of common stock were sold for cash	_____	_____
(k) Recorded the entry for depreciation on equipment for the current fiscal period	_____	_____
(l) Paid cash for ad in today's *Chicago Tribune*	_____	_____
(m) Some insurance premiums have expired	_____	_____

3-22 Prepaid Expenses

Continental AG is a large German supplier of auto parts. Continental had €31.2 million of prepaid expenses on January 1, 2003. (€ stands for Euro, the European currency.) A footnote to the company's financial statements indicates that "this item mainly consists of prepayments of rent, leasing fees, interest and insurance premiums." Assume all these prepayments were for services that Continental used during 2003 and that Continental spent €140 million in cash during 2003 for rent, leasing, and interest, of which €38 million was a prepayment of expenses for 2004.

1. Prepare a journal entry recognizing the use of the €31.2 million of prepaid expenses during the year.
2. Prepare a compound journal entry for the cash payment of €140 million for rent, leasing fees, interest, and insurance premiums during 2003, with the proper amounts going to expense and prepaid expenses.

3-23 Journalizing and Posting

(Alternate is 3-24.) Prepare journal entries and post to T-accounts the following transactions of Haida Charter and Yacht Supplies:

a. Cash sales, $10,000.
b. Collections on accounts, $7,000.
c. Paid cash for wages, $3,000.
d. Acquired inventory on open account, $5,000.
e. Paid cash for janitorial services, $600.

3-24 Journalizing and Posting

(Alternate is 3-23.) Prepare journal entries and post to T-accounts the following transactions of Barbara Losh, realtor:

a. Acquired office supplies of $800 on open account. Use a Supplies Inventory account.
b. Sold a house and collected a $9,000 commission on the sale. Use a Commissions Revenue account.
c. Paid cash of $700 to a local newspaper for current advertisements.
d. Paid $600 for a previous credit purchase of office supplies.
e. Recorded office supplies used of $300.

3-25 Reconstruct Journal Entries

(Alternate is 3-26.) Reconstruct the journal entries (omit explanations) that resulted in the postings to the following T-accounts of Schmidt Network Consultants:

Cash				Equipment			Revenue from Fees	
(a)	60,000	(b)	1,000	(c)	15,000		(d)	85,000
		(c)	5,000					

Accounts Receivable		Note Payable	
(d)	85,000	(c)	10,000

Supplies Inventory			Paid-in Capital		Supplies Expense	
(b)	1,000	(e) 300	(a)	60,000	(e) 300	

3-26 Reconstruct Journal Entries

(Alternate is 3-25.) Reconstruct the journal entries (omit explanations) that resulted in the postings to the following T-accounts of a small computer retailer:

Cash				Accounts Payable			Paid-in Capital	
(a)	45,000	(e)	25,000	(e) 25,000	(b)	90,000	(a)	45,000

Accounts Receivable	
(c)	100,000

Inventory				Cost of Goods Sold		Sales	
(b)	90,000	(d)	57,000	(d) 57,000		(c)	100,000

3-27 Effects of Errors

The bookkeeper of Midwest Legal Services Corporation included the cost of a new computer, purchased on December 30 for $9,000 and to be paid for in cash in January, as an operating expense instead of an addition to the proper asset account. What was the effect of this error ("no effect," "overstated," or "understated"?—use symbols n, o, or u, respectively) on:

1. Operating expenses for the year ended December 31
2. Profit from operations for the year
3. Retained earnings as of December 31 after the books are closed
4. Total assets as of December 31
5. Total liabilities as of December 31

3-28 Effects of Errors

Analyze the effect of the following errors on the net profit figures of Philippines Trading Company (PTC) for 20X7 and 20X8. Choose one of three answers: understated (u), overstated (o), or no effect (n). Problem (a) has been answered as an illustration.

a. Example: Failure to adjust at end of 20X7 for prepaid rent that had expired during December 20X7. PTC charged the remaining prepaid rent in 20X8. 20X7: o; 20X8: u. (Explanation: In 20X7, expenses would be understated and profits overstated. This error would carry forward so expenses in 20X8 would be overstated and profits understated.)

b. PTC omitted recording depreciation on Office Machines in 20X7 only. Correct depreciation was taken in 20X8.

c. During 20X8, PTC purchased $300 of office supplies and debited Office Supplies, an asset account. At the end of 20X8, only $100 worth of office supplies were left. No entry had recognized the use of $200 of office supplies during 20X8.

d. Machinery, cost price $500, bought in 20X7, was not entered in the books until paid for in 20X8. Ignore depreciation; answer in terms of the specific error described.

e. PTC debited 3 months' rent, paid in advance in December 20X7, for the first quarter of 20X8, directly to Rent Expense in 20X7. No prepaid rent was on the books at the end of 20X7.

Problems

3-29 Account Numbers, Journal, Ledger, and Trial Balance

Journalize and post the entries required by the following transactions for Holmstrom Construction Company. Prepare a trial balance as of April 30, 20X6 for the period April 1 – April 30, 20X6. Ignore interest. Use dates, posting references, and the following account numbers:

Cash	100	Note payable	130
Accounts receivable	101	Paid-in capital	140
Equipment	111	Retained earnings	150
Accumulated depreciation,		Revenues	200
equipment	111A	Expenses	300, 301, etc.
Accounts payable	120		

- April 1, 20X6. The Holmstrom Construction Company was formed with $95,000 cash on the issuance of common stock.
- April 2. Holmstrom acquired equipment for $75,000. Holmstrom made a cash down payment of $25,000. In addition, Holmstrom signed a note for $50,000.
- April 3. Sales on credit to a local hotel, $2,200.
- April 3. Supplies acquired (and used) on open account, $200.
- April 3. Wages paid in cash, $700.
- April 30. Depreciation expense for April, $2,000.

3-30 Account Numbers, T-Accounts, and Transaction Analysis

Consider the following ($ in thousands):

Manitoba Computing
Trial Balance December 31, 20X7

Account Number	Account Titles	Balance Debit	Credit
10	Cash	$ 55	
20	Accounts receivable	115	
21	Note receivable	100	
30	Inventory	130	
40	Prepaid insurance	12	
70	Equipment	120	
70A	Accumulated depreciation, equipment		$ 30
80	Accounts payable		135
100	Paid-in capital		65
110	Retained earnings		182
130	Sales		950
150	Cost of goods sold	550	
160	Wages expense	200	
170	Miscellaneous expense	80	
		$1,362	$1,362

The following information had not been considered before preparing the trial balance:

a. The note receivable was signed by a major customer. It is a 3-month note dated November 1, 20X7. Interest earned during November and December was collected at 4 P.M. on December 31. The interest rate is 12 percent per year.

b. The Prepaid Insurance account reflects a 1-year fire insurance policy acquired for cash on August 1, 20X7.

c. Depreciation for 20X7 was $16,000.

d. Manitoba Computing paid wages of $12,000 in cash at 5 P.M. on December 31.

Required

1. Enter the December 31 balances in T-accounts in a general ledger. Number the accounts. Allow room for additional T-accounts.

2. Prepare the journal entries prompted by the additional information. Show amounts in thousands.

3. Post the journal entries to the ledger. Key your postings. Create logical new account numbers as necessary.

4. Prepare a new trial balance, December 31, 20X7.

3-31 Trial Balance Errors

Consider the following trial balance ($ in thousands):

Fort Ward Auto Parts Store
Trial Balance, Year Ended December 31, 20X7

Cash	$ 17	
Equipment	33	
Accumulated depreciation, equipment	15	
Accounts payable	42	
Accounts receivable	14	
Prepaid insurance	1	
Prepaid rent		$ 3
Inventory	129	
Paid-in capital		12
Retained earnings		10
Cost of goods sold	500	
Wages expense	100	
Miscellaneous expenses	80	
Advertising expense		30
Sales		788
Note payable	40	
	$971	$843

List and describe all the errors in the preceding trial balance. Be specific. On the basis of the available data, prepare a corrected trial balance.

3-32 Journal, Ledger, and Trial Balance

(Alternates are 3-34 through 3-39.) The balance sheet accounts of Iowa Farm Implements, Inc. had the following balances on October 31, 20X5:

Cash	$ 39,000	
Accounts receivable	90,000	
Inventory	70,000	
Prepaid rent	2,000	
Accounts payable		$ 25,000
Paid-in capital		160,000
Retained earnings		16,000
	$201,000	$201,000

Following is a summary of the transactions that occurred during November:

a. Collections of accounts receivable, $82,000.

b. Payments of accounts payable, $19,000.

c. Acquisitions of inventory on open account, $80,000.
d. Merchandise carried in inventory at a cost of $70,000 was sold on open account for $86,000.
e. Recognition of rent expense for November, $1,000.
f. Wages paid in cash for November, $8,000.
g. Cash dividends declared and disbursed to stockholders on November 29, $10,000.

Required
1. Prepare journal entries.
2. Enter beginning balances in T-accounts. Post the journal entries to T-accounts. Use the transaction letters to key your postings.
3. Prepare a trial balance on November 30, 20X5 for the month ending November 30, 20X5.
4. Explain why accounts payable increased by so much during November.

3-33 Financial Statements
Refer to problem 3-32. Prepare a balance sheet as of November 30, 20X5, and an income statement for the month of November. Prepare a statement of retained earnings. Prepare the income statement first.

3-34 Journal, Ledger, and Trial Balance
(Alternates are 3-32 and 3-35 through 3-39.) The balance sheet accounts of Renteria Appliance Company had the following balances on December 31, 20X8:

Account Title	Balance	
	Debit	Credit
Cash	$ 36,000	
Accounts receivable	29,000	
Merchandise inventory	120,000	
Accounts payable		$ 35,000
Notes payable		80,000
Paid-in capital		39,000
Retained earnings		31,000
Total	$185,000	$185,000

Operating space and equipment are rented on a month-to-month basis. A summary of January transactions follows:

a. Collected $26,000 on accounts receivable.
b. Sold appliances for $60,000 cash and $50,000 on open account.
c. Cost of appliances sold was $50,000.
d. Paid $19,000 on accounts payable.
e. Replenished inventory for $64,000 on open account.
f. Paid selling expense in cash, $33,000.
g. Paid rent expense in cash, $7,000.
h. Paid interest expense in cash, $1,000.

Required
1. Open the appropriate T-accounts in the general ledger. In addition to the seven accounts listed in the trial balance of December 31, open accounts for Sales, Cost of Goods Sold, Selling Expense, Rent Expense, and Interest Expense. Enter the December 31 balances in the accounts.
2. Journalize transactions a through h. Post the entries to the ledger, keying by transaction letter.
3. Prepare a trial balance, January 31, 20X9, for the month ended January 31, 20X9.

3-35 Journal, Ledger, and Trial Balance
(Alternates are 3-32, 3-34, and 3-36 through 3-39.) Norma Nielsen owned and managed a franchise of Tacoma Espresso, Incorporated. The company's balance sheet accounts had the following balances on September 1, 20X8, the beginning of a fiscal year.

Norma's Tacoma Espresso
Balance Sheet Accounts, September 1, 20X8

Cash	$ 2,600
Accounts receivable	25,200
Merchandise inventory	77,800
Prepaid rent	4,000
Store equipment	21,000

Accumulated depreciation, store equipment		$ 5,750
Accounts payable		45,000
Paid-in capital		30,000
Retained earnings		49,850
	$130,600	$130,600

Summarized transactions for September were:

a. Acquisitions of merchandise inventory on account, $49,000.
b. Sales for cash, $36,250.
c. Payments to creditors, $29,000.
d. Sales on account, $38,000.
e. Advertising in newspapers, paid in cash, $3,000.
f. Cost of goods sold, $40,000.
g. Collections on account, $33,150.
h. Miscellaneous expenses paid in cash, $8,000.
i. Wages paid in cash, $9,000.
j. Entry for rent expense. (Rent was paid quarterly in advance, $6,000 per quarter. Payments were due on February 1, May 1, August 1, and November 1.)
k. Depreciation of store equipment, $250.

Required

1. Enter the September 1 balances in T accounts in a general ledger.
2. Prepare journal entries for each transaction.
3. Post the journal entries to the ledger. Key your postings by transaction letter.
4. Prepare an income statement for September and a balance sheet as of September 30, 20X8.

3-36 Journalizing, Posting, and Trial Balance

(Alternates are 3-32, 3-34, 3-35, and 3-37 through 3-39.) Yoshida Gardens, a retailer of garden supplies and equipment, had the accompanying balance sheet accounts, December 31, 20X7:

Assets			Liabilities and Stockholders' Equity	
Cash		$ 19,000	Accounts payable*	$111,000
Accounts receivable		40,000	Paid-in capital	40,000
Inventory		131,000	Retained earnings	79,000
Prepaid rent		4,000		
Store equipment	$60,000			
Less: Accumulated depreciation	24,000	36,000		
Total		$230,000	Total	$230,000

*For merchandise only.

Following is a summary of transactions that occurred during 20X8:

a. Purchases of merchandise inventory on open account, $550,000.
b. Sales, all on credit, $800,000.
c. Cost of merchandise sold to customers, $440,000.
d. On June 1, 20X8, borrowed $80,000 from a supplier. The note is payable in 4 years. Interest is payable yearly on December 31 at a rate of 15 percent per annum.
e. Disbursed $25,000 for the rent of the store. Add to Prepaid Rent.
f. Disbursed $165,000 for wages through November.
g. Disbursed $75,000 for miscellaneous expenses such as utilities, advertising, and legal help. (Combined here to save space. Debit Miscellaneous expenses.)
h. On July 1, 20X8, lent $20,000 to the office manager. He signed a note that will mature on July 1, 20X9, together with interest at 10 percent per annum. Interest for 20X8 is due on December 31, 20X8.
i. Collections on accounts receivable, $691,000.
j. Payments on accounts payable $471,000.

The following entries were made on December 31, 20X8:

k. Recognized rent expense for 20X8. $3,000 of prepaid rent is applicable to 20X9; the remainder expired in 20X8.

l. Depreciation for 20X8 was $6,000.

m. Wages earned by employees during December were paid on December 31, $6,000.

n. Interest on the loan from the supplier was disbursed. See transaction d.

o. Interest on the loan made to the office manager was received. See transaction h.

Required

1. Prepare journal entries in thousands of dollars.
2. Post the entries to T-accounts in the ledger, keying your postings by transaction letter.
3. Prepare a trial balance for the year ending December 31, 20X8.

3-37 Transaction Analysis, Trial Balance, and Closing Entries

(Alternates are 3-32, 3-34 through 3-36, 3-38, and 3-39.) Buckeye Appliance Repair Service, Inc., had the accompanying balance sheet values on January 1, 20X8

Buckeye Appliance Repair Service, Inc.
Balance Sheet Accounts, January 1, 20X8

Cash	$ 5,000	
Accounts receivable	3,000	
Parts inventory	2,000	
Prepaid rent	2,000	
Trucks	36,000	
Equipment	8,000	
Accumulated depreciation, trucks		$15,000
Accumulated depreciation, equipment		5,000
Accounts payable		1,900
Paid-in capital		17,000
Retained earnings		17,100
Total	$56,000	$56,000

During January, the following summarized transactions occurred:

January 2	Collected accounts receivable, $3,000.
3	Rendered services to customers for cash, $4,200 ($700 collected for parts, $3,500 for labor). Use two accounts, Parts Revenue and Labor Revenue.
3	Cost of parts used for services rendered, $300.
7	Paid legal expenses, $500 cash.
9	Acquired parts on open account, $900.
11	Paid cash for wages, $1,000.
13	Paid cash for truck repairs, $500.
19	Billed customer for services, $3,600 ($800 for parts and $2,800 for labor).
19	Cost of parts used for services rendered, $500.
24	Paid cash for wages, $1,300.
27	Paid cash on accounts payable, $1,500.
31	Rent expense for January, $1,000 (reduce Prepaid Rent).
31	Depreciation for January: trucks, $600; equipment, $200.
31	Paid cash to local gas station for gasoline for trucks for January, $300.
31	Paid cash for wages, $800.

Required

1. Enter the January 1 balances in T-accounts. Leave room for additional accounts.
2. Record the transactions in the journal.
3. Post the journal entries to the T-accounts. Key your entries by date. (Note how keying by date is not as precise as by transaction number or letter. Why? There is usually more than one transaction on any given date.)
4. Prepare a trial balance for the month ended January 31, 20X8.
5. Prepare closing entries.

3-38 Transaction Analysis, Trial Balance

(Alternates are 3-32, 3-34 through 3-37, and 3-39.) McDonald's Corporation is a well-known fast-food restaurant company. Examine the accompanying balance sheet values, which are based on McDonald's annual report and actual terminology.

McDonald's Corporation
Balance Sheet Values, January 1, 2003 ($ in millions)

Cash	$ 330	
Accounts and notes receivable	855	
Inventories	112	
Prepaid expenses	418	
Property and equipment, at cost	26,219	
Other assets	3,672	
Accumulated depreciation		$ 7,635
Notes and accounts payable		636
Other liabilities		13,054
Paid-in capital		1,764
Retained earnings		19,204
Other stockholders' equity*		(10,687)
Total	$31,606	$ 31,606

*These negative stockholders' equity items will be explained in later chapters.

Consider the following assumed partial summary of transactions for 2003 ($ in millions):

a. Revenues in cash, company-owned restaurants, $2,100.
b. Revenues, on open account from franchised restaurants, $500. Open a separate revenue account for these sales.
c. Inventories acquired on open account, $827.
d. Cost of the inventories sold, $820.
e. Depreciation, $226 (Debit Depreciation Expense).
f. Paid rent and insurance premiums in cash in advance, $42 (Debit Prepaid Expenses).
g. Prepaid expenses expired, $37 (Debit Operating Expenses).
h. Paid other liabilities, $148.
i. Cash collections on receivables, $590.
j. Cash disbursements on notes and accounts payable, $747.
k. Paid interest expense in cash, $100.
l. Paid other expenses in cash, mostly payroll and advertising, $1,510 (Debit Operating Expenses).

Required
1. Record the transactions in the journal.
2. Enter beginning balances in T-accounts. Post the journal entries to the T-accounts. Key your entries with the transaction letters used here.
3. Prepare a trial balance, December 31, 2003, for the year ended December 31, 2003.

3-39 Transaction Analysis, Trial Balance
(Alternates are 3-32 and 3-34 through 3-38.) Kellogg Company's major product line is ready-to-eat breakfast cereals. Examine the following condensed balance sheet values, which are based on Kellogg's annual report.

Kellogg Company Balance Sheet Values
January 1, 2003 ($ in millions)

Cash	$ 101	
Accounts receivable	741	
Inventories	603	
Property and equipment, net	2,840	
Other assets	5,934	
Accounts payable		619
Other liabilities		8,705
Paid-in capital		154
Retained earnings		741
Total	$10,219	$10,219

Consider the following assumed partial summary of transactions for 2003 ($ in millions):

a. Acquired inventories for $1,750 on open account.
b. Sold inventories that cost $1,600 for $2,500 on open account.
c. Collected $2,550 on open account.
d. Disbursed $1,650 on open accounts payable.
e. Paid cash of $300 for advertising expenses (use an Operating Expenses account).
f. Paid rent and insurance premiums in cash in advance, $20 (use a Prepaid Expenses account).
g. Prepaid expenses expired, $18 (use an Operating Expenses account).
h. Other liabilities paid in cash, $110.
i. Interest expense of $13 was paid in cash (use an Interest Expense account).
j. Depreciation of $50 was recognized [use an Operating Expenses account; instead of creating an accumulated depreciation account, reduce the Property and Equipment (net) account directly].
k. Additional shares were sold for $10 in cash (record as increase to paid-in capital).

Required
1. Record the transactions in the journal.
2. Enter beginning balances in T-accounts. Post the journal entries to the T-accounts. Key your entries with the transaction letters used here.
3. Prepare a trial balance, December 31, 2003, for the year ended December 31, 2003.
4. Explain why cash increased more than fivefold during 2003.

3-40 Preparation of Financial Statements from Trial Balance

PepsiCo produces snack foods such as Fritos and Lay's potato chips, as well as beverages such as Pepsi and Mug Root Beer. The company had the following trial balance as of December 28, 2002, for the year ended December 28, 2002 ($ in millions):

PepsiCo Trial Balance

	Debits	Credits
Current assets	$ 6,413	
Property and equipment, net	7,390	
Intangible assets, net	5,219	
Other assets	4,452	
Current liabilities		$ 6,052
Long-term debt and other liabilities		8,124
Stockholders' equity*		7,027
Net sales		25,112
Cost of sales	11,497	
Selling, general, and administrative expenses	8,523	
Other expenses	2,095	
Other income		316
Cash dividends	1,042	
Total	$46,631	$46,631

*Includes beginning retained earnings.

1. Prepare PepsiCo's income statement for the year ended December 28, 2002.
2. Prepare PepsiCo's balance sheet as of December 28, 2002.

3-41 Accumulated Depreciation

Johnson Matthey, the British specialty chemical company, had the following balances on its March 31, 2003 balance sheet [£ (British pound) in millions]:

Tangible fixed assets, at cost	£943.7
Accumulated depreciation	342.6
Net tangible fixed assets	£601.1

Suppose that Johnson Matthey depreciates most of its tangible fixed assets over 15 years.

1. What is the approximate average age of Johnson Matthey's tangible fixed assets?
2. Johnson Matthey invested £373.5 in tangible fixed assets during the prior year. Using this information and your answer to part 1, explain whether Johnson Matthey is growing or depleting its supply of fixed assets.

3-42 Journal Entries, Posting

Sony Corporation is a leading international supplier of audio and video equipment. The Sony annual report at the end of the 2002 fiscal year included the following balance sheet items (Japanese yen in billions):

Cash	¥ 713
Receivables	1,118
Prepaid expenses	419
Land	188
Accounts payable, trade	697

Consider the following assumed transactions that occurred immediately subsequent to the balance sheet date (Japanese yen in billions):

a. Collections from customers	¥820
b. Purchase of land for cash	20
c. Purchase of insurance policies on account	12
d. Disbursements to trade creditors	590

1. Enter the five account balances in T-accounts.
2. Journalize each transaction.
3. Post the journal entries to T-accounts. Key each posting by transaction letter.

3-43 Reconstructing Journal Entries, Posting

(Alternate is 3-44.) Gap owns department stores including Old Navy stores. A partial income statement from its annual report for the fiscal year ending in February 1, 2003, showed the following actual numbers and nomenclature ($ in millions):

Net sales	$14,455
Costs and expenses	
Cost of goods sold and occupancy expenses	9,542
Operating expenses	3,901
Interest expense	249
Interest income	(37)
Income taxes	323
Total expenses	13,978
Net earnings	$ 477

1. Prepare six summary journal entries for the given data. Label your entries a through f. Omit explanations. For simplicity, assume that all transactions (except for cost of products sold) were for cash. One-fourth of the cost of retail sales and occupancy was paid in cash. The other three-fourths represented a decrease in inventories.
2. Post to T-accounts in a ledger for all affected accounts. Key your postings by transaction letter.

3-44 Reconstructing Journal Entries, Posting

(Alternate is 3-43) Lowe's Companies, Inc. operates nearly 900 home improvement retail stores in 44 states. It is the fourteenth largest retailer in the United States. A partial income statement from its annual report for the fiscal year ending January 31, 2003 showed the following actual numbers and nomenclature ($ in millions):

Net sales		$26,491
Expenses		
Cost of sales	$18,465	
Selling, general, and administrative expenses	4,730	
Other expenses	937	
Total costs and expenses		24,132
Pretax earnings		$ 2,359

1. Prepare four summary journal entries for the given data. Label your entries a through d. Omit explanations. For simplicity, assume that all transactions except for cost of sales were for cash.
2. Post to T-accounts in a ledger for all affected accounts. Key your postings by transaction letter.

3-45 Plant Assets and Accumulated Depreciation

Georgia-Pacific, the pulp, paper, and building products company, had the following in its January 1, 2003 balance sheet ($ in millions):

Total property, plant, and equipment, at cost	$18,857
Accumulated depreciation	9,535
Property, plant, and equipment, net	$ 9,322

1. Open T-accounts for (a) Property, Plant, and Equipment; (b) Accumulated Depreciation, Property, Plant, and Equipment; and (c) Depreciation Expense. Enter the balance sheet amounts into the T-accounts.
2. Assume that in 2003 Georgia-Pacific purchased or sold no assets and that depreciation expense for 2003 was $950 million. Prepare the journal entry, and post to the T-accounts.
3. Prepare the property, plant, and equipment section of Georgia-Pacific's balance sheet at the end of 2003.
4. Land comprises $566 million of Georgia-Pacific's property, plant, and equipment, and land is not depreciated. Comment on the age of the company's depreciable assets—that is, all property, plant, and equipment except land—at the January 1, 2003 balance sheet date.

3-46 Management Incentives, Financial Statements, and Ethics

Juanita Cirillo was controller of the San Leandro Electronic Components (SLEC) division of a major medical instruments company. On December 30, 2003, Cirillo prepared a preliminary income statement and compared it with the 2003 budget:

San Leandro Electronic Components Division
Income Statement for the Year Ended December 31, 2003
($ in thousands)

	Budget	Preliminary Actual
Sales revenues	$ 1,200	$ 1,600
Cost of goods sold	600	800
Gross margin	600	800
Other operating expenses	450	500
Operating income	$ 150	$ 300

The top managers of each division had a bonus plan that paid each a 10 percent bonus if operating income exceeded budgeted income by more than 20 percent. It was obvious to Cirillo that the SLEC division had easily exceeded the $180,000 of operating income needed for a bonus. In fact, she wondered if it would not be desirable to reduce operating income this year—after all, the higher the income this year, the higher top management is likely to set the budget next year. Besides, if some of December's sales could just be held back and recorded in January, the division would have a running start on next year.

Cirillo had always been a team player, and she saw holding back sales as the best strategy for her team of managers. Therefore, she recorded only $1,500,000 of sales in 2003 — the other $100,000 was recorded as January 2004 sales. Operating income for 2003 then became $250,000 and there was a head start of $50,000 on 2004's operating income.

Comment on the ethical implications of Cirillo's decision.

Collaborative Learning Exercise

3-47 Income Statement and Balance Sheet Accounts
Form teams of two persons each. Each person should make a list of 10 account names, with approximately one-half being income statement accounts and one-half being balance sheet accounts. Give the list to the other member of the team, who is to write beside each account name the financial statement (I for income statement or B for balance sheet) on which it belongs. If there are errors or disagreements in classification, discuss the account and come to an agreement about which financial statement it belongs to.

Analyzing and Interpreting Financial Statements

3-48 Financial Statement Research
Select the financial statements of any company.

1. Prepare an income statement in the following format:
   Total sales (or revenues)
   Cost of goods sold
   Gross margin
   Other expenses
   Income before income taxes
   Be sure to include all revenues in the first line and all expenses (except income taxes) in either Cost of goods sold or Other expenses.
2. Prepare three summary journal entries for the income statement data you prepared. Use the given account titles and label your entries a, b, and c. Omit explanations. For simplicity, assume that all "Other expenses" were paid in cash and all sales are on credit.
3. Post to T-accounts in a ledger for all affected accounts. Key your postings by transaction letter.

3-49 Analyzing Starbucks' Financial Statements
Refer to the financial statements of **Starbucks** in Appendix A at the end of the book. Note the following summarized items (rounded to the nearest million) from the income statement for the year ended September 28, 2003:

Net revenues		$ 4,076
Cost of sales including occupancy costs	$1,686	
Store and other operating expenses	1,521	
Other expenses	445	
Interest and other income (net)	(12)	3,640
Income taxes		168
Net earnings		$ 268

1. Prepare six summary journal entries for the given data. Use Starbucks' account titles and label your entries a through f. Omit explanations. For simplicity, assume all transactions (except for cost of sales) were for cash. Assume cost of sales is 70 percent of the "cost of sales including occupancy costs," whereas occupancy costs are 30 percent.
2. Why are there parentheses around the Interest and other income number?

3-50 Analyzing Financial Statements Using the Internet: Gap
Go to www.gapinc.com. Locate **Gap**'s Annual Reports under Financials and Media. Select the most recent annual report.

Answer the following questions about Gap Inc.:

1. Locate Gap's entry for accumulated depreciation and amortization. Does this represent an expense for Gap? Why does Gap keep track of accumulated depreciation?

2. Gap Inc. does not include a line for depreciation on its Consolidated Statement of Earnings. Where do you suppose depreciation expenses are included among Gap's expenses?

3. Locate Cash and Equivalents at the end of the year on the Consolidated Balance Sheet. How much did cash and cash equivalents increase or decrease during the past year?

4. Locate Shareholders' Equity on the Consolidated Balance Sheets. Consider two amounts: Common Stock at par value and Additional Paid-in Capital. How did these amounts arise?

5. Suppose Gap overstated its merchandise inventory amount in its balance sheet at the end of this year. What is the effect on cost of goods sold, on net earnings, and on ending shareholders' equity? If no other errors are made, what will be the effect on these reported amounts next year?

Accrual Accounting and Financial Statements

CHAPTER 4

LEARNING OBJECTIVES

After studying this chapter, you should be able to:

1. Understand the role of adjustments in accrual accounting.

2. Make adjustments for the expiration or consumption of assets.

3. Make adjustments for the recognition of unearned revenues.

4. Make adjustments for the accrual of unrecorded expenses.

5. Make adjustments for the accrual of unrecorded revenues.

6. Describe the sequence of the final steps in the recording process and relate cash flows to adjusting entries.

7. Prepare a classified balance sheet and use it to assess short-term liquidity.

8. Prepare single- and multiple-step income statements.

9. Use ratios to assess profitability.

Chances are you or someone you know is one of the millions of customers who have purchased outdoor wear or accessories made by Columbia Sportswear, the Oregon-based designer and manufacturer of active outdoor apparel. Columbia offers a wide range of durable and functional outerwear, sportswear, footwear, and accessories and is the leading seller of skiwear in the United States. The company has an international reputation based on quality, performance, functionality, and value—factors that have won over discerning shoppers. Columbia Sportswear's management team is also concerned about these factors, and they take pride in their high ratings for customer satisfaction. However, customer satisfaction alone does not pay their salaries, so managers also need to know whether the company is making a profit. Do managers have to turn to complicated equations and formulas to figure out the company's profit? No, they can turn to Columbia Sportswear's financial statements—just as we can.

Information in Columbia Sportswear's financial statements comes straight from the company's financial accounting system, which provides information useful in assessing the company's financial success. If you want to buy Columbia Sportswear's stock instead of their clothes, you need information about the company's financial position and prospects in order to judge whether it is wise to invest. To read and understand Columbia's financial statements and compare them to the statements of other companies, you must first understand the fundamentals of financial accounting. This includes the use of accrual accounting and the adjusting entries required before financial statements are prepared.

Financial managers in entities as large as IBM and as small as Rosa's Mexican Restaurant, in nonprofit as well as for-profit organizations, and located

Columbia Sportswear distributes and sells products in more than 60 countries and to more than 10,600 retailers internationally. The flagship store is located in downtown Portland, Oregon. Columbia's financial statements reflect the results of all this business activity, using the principles of accrual accounting discussed in this chapter. Company founder Gert Boyle is featured in the poster on the wall.

in France, China, the United States, or elsewhere in the world, must understand the consequences of these adjustments when interpreting financial statements. ▪

Adjustments to the Accounts

Accountants record the majority of a company's transactions in journals and ledgers when they occur. However, no observable event triggers transactions such as depreciation and the expiration of prepaid rent. In fact, they might not seem like transactions at all because we recognize them only at the end of an accounting period. The difference between these transactions and the majority of the transactions we have recorded to date stems from how obvious or explicit they are.

explicit transactions
Observable events such as cash receipts and disbursements, credit purchases, and credit sales that trigger nearly all day-to-day routine entries.

Explicit transactions are observable events, such as cash receipts and disbursements, credit purchases, and credit sales, that trigger nearly all day-to-day routine entries. For every explicit transaction, we can show that an economic event has occurred, and we know that an accountant must make an entry. Entries for these transactions are supported by source documents, for example, sales slips, purchase invoices, employee payroll checks, or other tangible evidence. Note that not all explicit transactions require actual exchanges of goods and services between the entity and another party. For instance, the loss of assets from fire or theft are explicit transactions, even though no market exchange occurs. In all cases, though, a specific observable event triggers the need to record a journal entry.

implicit transactions
Events (such as the passage of time) that do not generate source documents or visible evidence of the event. We do not recognize such events in the accounting records until the end of an accounting period.

The events that trigger implicit transactions are not as obvious. **Implicit transactions** are events, such as the passage of time, that do not generate source documents or any visible evidence that the event actually occurred. Because bookkeepers do not receive specific notification to record such events, we do not formally recognize the events in the accounting records until the end of an accounting period. For example, accountants prepare entries for depreciation expense and expiration of prepaid rent from special schedules or memorandums at the end of an accounting period. An explicit event did not trigger such entries. Accountants recorded the related explicit transaction at the time the company purchased the asset or made the initial rent payment. We call the end-of-period entries that record these implicit events adjustments. **Adjustments** (also called **adjusting entries**) help assign the financial effects of implicit transactions to the appropriate time periods. Thus, adjustments occur at periodic intervals, usually when the financial statements are about to be prepared. We make adjustments by recording journal entries in the general journal and then posting them to the general ledger. After we recognize these adjustments for implicit transactions, we update the balances in the general ledger accounts through the end of the period and use these balances for preparing financial statements.

adjustments (adjusting entries)
End-of-period entries that assign the financial effects of implicit transactions to the appropriate time periods.

accrue
To accumulate a receivable or payable during a given period, even though no explicit transaction occurs, and to record a corresponding revenue or expense.

Adjusting entries are at the heart of accrual accounting. **Accrue** means to accumulate a receivable (asset) or payable (liability) during a given period, even though no explicit transaction occurs. The receivables or payables grow as time passes, but no physical assets change hands. In addition to accumulating the receivable or payable on the balance sheet, we must also recognize a revenue or expense on the income statement. What routine business transactions require accruals? Examples are the wages earned by employees but not yet paid and the interest owed on borrowed money before the interest payment date. First, consider wages. Usually we recognize wage expense when a company pays its employees. However, suppose a company pays wages on Friday, and its accounting period ends on the following Wednesday. Employees have earned three days' wages, but the company has recorded no expense. The accrual adjusting entry for wages payable corrects this. Because accruals are not based on explicit transactions, we do not record them on a day-to-day basis. Thus, we need to make adjusting entries at the end of each accounting period to recognize unrecorded but relevant accruals.

You will see that each adjustment affects both the income statement and the balance sheet. The goal of adjusting entries is to ensure that all the company's assets, liabilities, and owners' equity accounts are properly reflected in the financial statements. In the adjusting process, we consider whether the passage of time or other events has led to the creation of assets, the consumption of assets, or the creation or discharge of liabilities.

Adjustments help match revenues and expenses to a particular period and ensure the balance sheet correctly states assets and liabilities. For example, consider a $22 million annual contract for a baseball star, such as Alex Rodriguez, for the 2006 season. If the team pays all $22 million in cash in 2006, there is an explicit transaction. In contrast, suppose the team pays only $10 million in cash and defers $12 million until 2007 or later. The $10 million cash payment is an explicit transaction that the team records as an expense in 2006. Because there is no explicit transaction for the additional $12 million during 2006, the team does not routinely enter it into the accounting record. However, the player has earned the full $22 million as a result of playing the whole season and the team must eventually pay the remaining $12 million, so a liability exists. Further, the team incurred the entire $22 million for the benefit of the 2006 season, so the $12 million deferred payment is an expense for 2006. Thus, at the end of the period, when the team prepares the 2006 financial statements, an adjustment is necessary to record the deferred $12 million payment as an expense and to record a $12 million liability for its payment.

The principal adjustments arise from four basic types of implicit transactions:

I. Expiration of unexpired costs
II. Earning of revenues received in advance
III. Accrual of unrecorded expenses
IV. Accrual of unrecorded revenues

Let us now examine each of these categories in detail.

I. Expiration of Unexpired Costs

OBJECTIVE 2

Make adjustments for the expiration or consumption of assets.

Some costs expire due to the passage of time. For example, initially a company engages in an explicit transaction that creates an asset. As the company consumes the asset, it must make an adjustment to reduce the asset and to recognize an expense. The key characteristic of unexpired items is that an explicit transaction in the past created an asset, and subsequent implicit transactions serve to adjust the value of this asset.

For example, as illustrated on page 56 of Chapter 2, Biwheels initially records $6,000 of Prepaid Rent as an asset. The company then makes $2,000 adjustments at the end of each month to mark the gradual expiration of the rent costs. The adjusting entry reduces the asset, Prepaid Rent, and increases Rent Expense. Other examples of adjusting for asset expirations include the write-offs to expense of such assets as Office Supplies Inventory or Prepaid Fire Insurance. Consider Office Supplies Inventory. Suppose a company purchases $10,000 of Office Supplies Inventory on March 1, 2005. At the time of the purchase, the company records an increase (debit) to Office Supplies Inventory and a decrease (credit) to Cash. The journal entry to record this explicit transaction is:

Office Supplies Inventory	$10,000	
Cash		$10,000

At the end of March, the company determines that it has used $1,500 of the Office Supplies Inventory. This requires the following adjusting entry to increase Office Supplies Expense (debit) and reduce Office Supplies Inventory (credit):

Office Supplies Expense	$1,500	
Office Supplies Inventory		$1,500

Will failure to record an adjusting entry cause the balance sheet and income statement to be incorrect? Even though the balance sheet will balance, both the income statement and the balance sheet will be in error. If the company fails to make the preceding adjusting entry, assets are overstated and expenses are understated. Understated expenses result in overstated net income and overstated retained earnings, a stockholders' equity account.

Another example of the expiration of unexpired costs is the recording of Depreciation Expense and Accumulated Depreciation. You can review the accounting for depreciation expense on page 106 of Chapter 3.

II. Earning of Revenues Received in Advance

OBJECTIVE 3

Make adjustments for the recognition of unearned revenues.

unearned revenue (revenue received in advance, deferred revenue)
Represents payments from customers who pay in advance for goods or services to be delivered at a future date.

Just as a company acquires assets and recognizes the related expense as the assets are used over time, it often receives revenue in advance and then earns the revenue over time. **Unearned revenue** (also called **revenue received in advance** or **deferred revenue**) represents payments from customers who pay in advance for goods or services that the company promises to deliver at a future date. The company receives cash before it is earned. This commitment is a liability, and the company must record both the receipt of cash and the liability for future services. For instance, airlines often require advance payments for special fare tickets. American Airlines recently showed a balance of more than $2.6 billion in an unearned revenue account labeled Air Traffic Liability. Over time, as customers take the flights they have paid for, American reduces the liability and increases revenue accordingly.

The analysis of adjusting entries for unearned revenue is easier to understand if we visualize the financial positions of both parties to a contract. For example, recall the Biwheels Company's January advance payment of $6,000 for 3 months rent. Compare the financial impact on Biwheels Company with the impact on the owner of the property, who received the rental payment:

	Owner of Property (Landlord, Lessor)				Biwheels Company (Tenant, Lessee)			
	A	=	L	+	SE	A	= L	+ SE
	Cash		Unearned Rent Revenue		Rent Revenue	Cash	Prepaid Rent	Rent Expense
(a) Explicit transaction (advance payment of 3 months' rent)	+6,000	=	+6,000			−6,000	+6,000 =	
(b) January adjustment (for 1 month rent)		=	−2,000		+2,000		−2,000 =	−2,000
(c) February adjustment (for 1 month rent)		=	−2,000		+2,000		−2,000 =	−2,000
(d) March adjustment (for 1 month rent)		=	−2,000		+2,000		−2,000 =	−2,000

The journal entries for (a) and (b) follow:

OWNER (LANDLORD)

(a) Cash	6,000	
Unearned rent revenue		6,000
(b) Unearned rent revenue	2,000	
Rent revenue		2,000
[Entries for (c) and (d) are the same as for (b).]		

BIWHEELS COMPANY (TENANT)

(a) Prepaid rent	6,000	
Cash		6,000
(b) Rent expense	2,000	
Prepaid rent		2,000

[Entries for (c) and (d) are the same as for (b).]

We are already familiar with the analysis from Biwheels' point of view. The $2,000 monthly entries for Biwheels are examples of the first type of adjustment, the expiration of a prepaid asset. From the viewpoint of the owner of the rental property, transaction (a) is an explicit transaction that recognizes the receipt of unearned revenue. The owner increases the cash account and records a liability of an equal amount. Why record a liability? Because the lessor is now obligated to either deliver the rental services or refund the money if the services are not delivered. Sometimes this account is called Rent Collected in Advance instead of Unearned Rent Revenue, as in our example. Regardless of the title, it is a liability account. That is, it is revenue collected in advance that has not been earned, and it obligates the landlord to provide services in the future.

Notice that transaction (a) does not affect the landlord's stockholders' equity because it does not recognize any revenue. The revenue is recognized (earned) only when the owner makes the adjusting entries in transactions (b), (c), and (d). As the liability Unearned Rent Revenue is decreased (debited), the stockholders' equity account Rent Revenue is increased (credited). The net effect is an increase in stockholders' equity at the time the owner recognizes the revenue. If the owner fails to record the adjusting entry represented in (b), liabilities are overstated and revenues are understated. Understated revenues result in understatements of both net income and stockholders' equity. Similarly, if Biwheels fails to record the adjusting entry represented previously, its assets are overstated and its expenses are understated. When expenses are understated, both net income and stockholders' equity are overstated.

By looking at both sides of the Biwheels rent contract, you can see that adjustment categories I and II are really mirror images of each other. Why? If a contract causes one party to record a prepaid expense, it must cause the other party to record unearned revenue. This basic relationship holds for any prepayment situation, from a 2-year fire insurance policy to a 5-year magazine subscription. For example, the magazine buyer initially recognizes a prepaid expense (asset) and uses adjustments to spread the initial cost to an expense account over the term of the subscription. In turn, the seller, the magazine publisher, initially records a liability, Unearned Subscription Revenue, on receipt of payment for the 5-year subscription.

For example, **AOL Time Warner**, publisher of *Time* and other magazines, lists Deferred Revenue of $1.209 billion among its liabilities on December 31, 2002. As the company delivers magazines throughout the life of a subscription, the unearned revenue becomes earned revenue. The initial explicit cash transaction creates a liability on the balance sheet that, thanks to periodic adjustments for the implicit transactions, is later transformed into revenue on the income statement. Another example of companies that receive revenue in advance is franchisors as described in the Business First box on page 144.

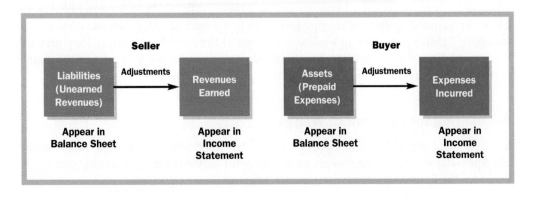

BUSINESS FIRST

FRANCHISES AND REVENUE RECOGNITION

In a franchise arrangement, a central organization, such as **McDonald's** or the **National Basketball Association**, sells the right to use the company name and company products to a franchisee. The franchisee also receives the benefit of advertising through the larger company, along with management assistance and product development. There are more than 500,000 franchise outlets of various types in the United States, with sales totaling more than $1 trillion. It is hard to know exactly how many franchises are out there, but in fast food alone, the largest category, there are more than 200 franchised names.

Franchising raises an interesting accounting problem. How does the central organization account for the franchise fees? At first glance, it might seem clear that companies should record such fees as revenue. However, under accrual accounting, companies should record revenue only after two conditions have been satisfied: (1) the company has completed the "work," that is, it has earned the revenue, and (2) there is reasonable assurance the company will actually collect the fee (it is realized in cash or will be collectible).

Jiffy Lube, a subsidiary of **Pennzoil–Quaker State Company**, is a franchisor of oil change centers with more than 2,200 service centers in the United States and Canada. It provides an example of a company that collects franchise fees before it performs the related work. Jiffy Lube sells its franchisees area development rights, which grant the franchisee the exclusive right to develop Jiffy Lube outlets in a certain area. In return for these rights, Jiffy Lube receives an upfront fee. Should Jiffy Lube record the fee as revenue when it is received? It should not because Jiffy Lube's work is not done until the franchisee actually opens the outlets. In the interim, Jiffy Lube must report the fees as unearned revenue.

McDonald's is perennially named *Entrepreneur Magazine's* number one franchising organization. McDonald's has over 30,000 locations worldwide. In 2002, McDonald's had $41.5 billion in systemwide sales of which franchisees and affiliates generated $30.3 billion. However, when we look at the income statement, we see total revenue of only $15.4 billion—$11.5 billion from company-owned restaurants and $3.9 billion from franchisees and affiliates. Why? McDonald's only recognizes as revenues the franchise fees, not the total sales of its franchisees.

Sources: www.jiffylube.com/company/aboutus.aspx; www.mcdonalds.com/corp/about.html

III. Accrual of Unrecorded Expenses

OBJECTIVE 4

Make adjustments for the accrual of unrecorded expenses.

Wages are an example of a liability that grows moment to moment as employees perform their duties. The services the employees provide represent expenses. It is awkward and unnecessary to make hourly, daily, or even weekly formal recordings in the accounts for many accrued expenses. Remember, these liabilities and related expenses continually grow over the length of a given period, so the cost of such frequent recording would certainly exceed the benefits. This is true, even though computers can perform these tasks somewhat effortlessly. The costs of computing are small, but in this case the benefits are even smaller. Accountants aggregate these costs only when they prepare financial statements, and this rarely needs to be done hourly or daily. Consequently, they make adjustments to bring each accrued expense (and corresponding liability) account up-to-date at the end of the period, just before they prepare the formal financial statements. These adjustments are necessary to accurately match the expense to the period in which they help generate revenues.

Accounting for Payment of Wages

Most companies pay their employees on a predetermined schedule. Assume that **Columbia Sportswear** pays its employees each Friday for services rendered during that week. Consider the following sample calendar for January:

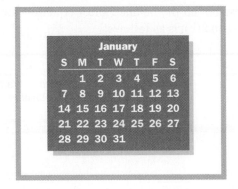

Because wage expense accrues for an entire week before it is paid, wages paid on January 26 are compensation for the week ended January 26. Assume the total wages paid on the four Fridays during January amount to $200,000, which is $50,000 per 5-day workweek, or $10,000 per day. Columbia makes routine entries for wage payments at the end of each week in January. As it pays wages, the company increases Wage Expense and decreases Cash. During the January shown in the preceding calendar, Columbia would pay wages on the 5th, 12th, 19th, and 26th. These events represent explicit transactions, driven by writing payroll checks. At the end of January, the balance sheet shows the summarized amounts of these explicit transactions and their effect on the accounting equation:

	A	=	L	+	SE
	Cash				**Wages Expense**
(a) Routine entries for explicit transactions	−200,000	=			−200,000

Accounting for Accrual of Wages

Assume that Columbia Sportswear prepares financial statements on a monthly basis. In addition to the $200,000 actually paid to employees during the month of January, Columbia owes $30,000 for employee services rendered during the last 3 days of the month. The company will not pay the employees for these services until Friday, February 2. To ensure an accurate accounting of Wages Expense for the month of January, Columbia must make an adjustment. Transaction (a) shows the total of the routine entries for the explicit payment of wages to employees, and transaction (b) shows the entry to accrue wages for Monday, January 29, through Wednesday, January 31. Transaction (b) recognizes both the expense and the liability.

(a) Wages expense	200,000	
Cash		200,000
(b) Wages expense	30,000	
Accrued wages payable		30,000

If Columbia does not record transaction (b), both expenses and liabilities are understated. Understated expenses result in the overstatement of both net income and stockholders' equity.

The total effect of wages on the balance sheet equation for the month of January, including transactions (a) and (b), is as follows:

	A	=	L	+	SE
			Accrued Wages		**Wages**
	Cash		**Payable**		**Expense**
(a) Routine entries for explicit transactions	−200,000	=			−200,000
(b) Adjustment for implicit transaction, the accrual of unrecorded wages		=	+30,000		−30,000
Total effects	−200,000	=	+30,000		−230,000

The adjustment in entry (b) is the first adjusting entry we have examined that shows an expense offset by an increase in a liability instead of a decrease in an asset. The accountant's problem is different for this type of accrual than it was for prepaid rent. With prepaid rent, there is a record in the accounts of an asset, and the accountant might recognize the necessity for an adjustment by asking, is the balance shown on the books correct or is an adjustment required to reduce it? With accrued wages, the accountant's question is a little harder. Is there something that does not appear in the records at all that should appear there? Of course, most end-of-period adjustments are routine. We know to check for expired rent and for accrued wages because we experience these items every period.

On February 2, Columbia will pay off the liability for the work performed during the last 3 days of January, together with the wages expense for February 1 and 2:

Wages expense (February 1 and 2).   20,000
Accrued wages payable   30,000
   Cash   50,000
(To record wages expense for February 1 and 2 and to pay wages for the week ended February 2)

These entries clearly demonstrate the matching principle. The routine entries and the adjusting entries match the wages expense to the periods in which they help generate revenues.

Accrual of Interest

Other examples of accrued expenses include sales commissions, property taxes, income taxes, and interest paid on borrowed money. Interest is the "rent" paid for the use of money, just as rent is paid for the use of buildings. The interest accumulates (accrues) as time passes, regardless of when a company actually pays cash for interest.

Suppose **Columbia Sportswear** borrowed $100,000 on December 31, 2005. The terms of the loan require that Columbia repay the loan amount of $100,000 plus interest at 9 percent on December 31, 2006. By convention, we express interest rates on an annual basis. We can calculate interest for any part of a year as follows:

$$\text{Principal} \times \text{Interest rate} \times \text{Fraction of a year} = \text{Interest}$$

Principal is the amount borrowed ($100,000). The interest rate is expressed as an annual percentage (.09). For the full year, the interest is:

$$\$100,000 \times .09 \times 1 = \$9,000$$

As of January 31, Columbia has had the benefit of the $100,000 bank loan for 1 month or one-twelfth of a year. Columbia owes the bank for the use of this money, and the amount owed has accrued for the entire month of January. The amount of interest owed is $100,000 × .09 × 1/12 = $750. The monthly cost of the loan is $750. The interest is not actually due to be paid until December 31, 2006. However, at the end of January, the company is liable for 1 month of accrued interest. We analyze and record the adjustment in the same way as the adjustment for accrued wages:

	A	=	L	+	SE
			Accrued Interest Payable		**Interest Expense**
Adjustment to accrue January interest not yet recorded		=	+750		−750

The adjusting journal entry is:

Interest expense   750
        Accrued interest payable   750

At the end of January, Columbia owes the bank $100,750, not $100,000. The adjusting entry matches the $750 interest expense with the period in which it occurred. If Columbia omits the adjusting entry, liabilities and expenses will both be understated at the end of January. Would the understatement of interest expense have other financial statement implications? Yes. If interest expense is understated, both net income and stockholders' equity are overstated.

Accrual of Income Taxes

As a company generates income, it accrues income tax expense. Income taxes exist worldwide, although rates and details differ from country to country and from state to state. Corporations in the United States are subject to federal and state corporate income taxes. For many corporations, the federal-plus-state income tax rates hover around 40 percent. Thus, for every dollar of income a company makes, it accrues 40 cents worth of income tax expense. Of course, the company does not pay 40 cents as each dollar is earned. Instead, taxes accrue over the period, and the company makes an adjustment at the end of the period when it prepares financial statements.

Companies use various labels to denote income taxes on their income statements: income tax expense, provision for income taxes, and income taxes are most common. For multinational firms, income tax expense may include tax obligations in every country in which the firm operates. In preparing income statements, almost all U.S. companies calculate a subtotal called **income before taxes** or **pretax income** and then show income taxes as a separate income statement item just before net income. This arrangement is logical because income tax expense is based on income before taxes. The 2003 Columbia Sportswear annual report contains the format adopted by the vast majority of companies.

pretax income
Income before income taxes.

Income before income taxes	$190,669,000
Income tax expense	70,548,000
Net income	$120,121,000

IV. Accrual of Unrecorded Revenues

Just as the realization of unearned revenues is the mirror image of the expiration of prepaid expenses, the accrual of unrecorded revenues is the mirror image of the accrual of unrecorded expenses. Because the company has not received cash, there is no explicit

OBJECTIVE 5

Make adjustments for the accrual of unrecorded revenues.

transaction and nothing is automatically recorded in the accounts. However, according to the revenue recognition principle, revenues affect stockholders' equity in the period they are earned, not the period in which cash is received. Thus, an adjustment is required to recognize revenues earned but not yet received.

Suppose Wells Fargo Bank loaned $100,000 to Columbia Sportswear. As of January 31, Wells Fargo Bank has earned $750 on the loan. The following tabulation shows the mirror-image effect:

	Wells Fargo Bank as a Lender					Columbia Sportswear as a Borrower				
	A	=	L	+	SE	A	=	L	+	SE
	Accrued Interest Receivable				Interest Revenue			Accrued Interest Payable		Interest Expense
January interest	+750	=			+750		=	+750		−750

Another example of accrued revenues and receivables is "unbilled" fees. Attorneys, public accountants, physicians, and advertising agencies may earn hourly fees during a particular month, but not issue bills to their clients until the completion of an entire contract or engagement. Under the accrual basis of accounting, a company should record such revenues in the month in which the revenues are earned, not at a later time. Suppose a law firm renders $10,000 of services during January, but does not bill for these services until March 31. Before the firm prepares financial statements for January, it makes the following adjustment for unrecorded revenues for the month:

	A	=	L	+	SE
	Accrued (Unbilled) Fees Receivable				Fee Revenue
Adjustment for fees earned	+10,000	=			+10,000

The journal entry to record these unrecorded revenues is shown here:

Accrued (unbilled) fees receivable. $10,000
      Fee revenue $10,000

What happens if the law firm does not make this adjusting entry? Assets and revenues are both understated. Understated revenues result in understated net income and stock-holders' equity.

Utility companies often recognize unbilled revenues for utility services provided but not yet billed to customers. In fact, as of December 31, 2002, Northwest Natural, a utility that provides natural gas to more than 500,000 residential and business customers throughout Oregon and Washington, included nearly as many unbilled revenues as accounts receivable among its current assets:

Accounts receivable	$46,936,000
Accrued unbilled revenue	44,069,000

Ethics, Unearned Revenue, and Revenue Recognition

In Chapter 2, you read about the accountant for an airline who was asked to report lower depreciation expense than she believed to be appropriate. If the airline reports $500,000 in depreciation expense, the before tax net income is $400,000. If the accountant records the $1 million in depreciation that she believes to be more accurate, the company reports a before tax net loss of $100,000. Given the concern about presenting an overly optimistic picture of the company to shareholders, the ethical dilemma faced by the accountant is clear.

Now, suppose you are the accountant for a small company that receives a $100,000 cash payment on December 15, in exchange for a commitment to provide various consulting services at a later date. At the time the cash is received, you appropriately record an increase in cash and an increase in the liability Unearned Revenue. As we saw earlier in this chapter, as the company provides the services, the appropriate accounting treatment is to decrease the Unearned Revenue account and recognize revenue on the income statement.

At December 31, you review the contract and conclude that the company has performed $65,000 worth of the $100,000 in consulting services. You propose an adjusting entry to recognize $65,000 in revenue (credit) and to reduce the Unearned Revenue account (debit) by $65,000. Your boss, the CFO of the company, insists that only $10,000 in services have been completed. He argues that recognition of only $10,000 in revenue is a more conservative estimate of the percentage of services performed. In addition, he reminds you that conservatism is one of the principles accountants follow. **Conservatism** means selecting methods of measurement that yield lower net income, lower assets, and lower stockholders' equity. Your boss argues that financial statements are less likely to mislead users if balance sheets report assets at lower rather than higher amounts, report liabilities at higher rather than lower amounts, and if income statements report lower rather than higher net income. He claims that it is unethical to overstate revenue and net income, but that his lower estimate of $10,000 conservatively states revenue and net income.

conservatism
Selecting methods of measurement that yield lower net income, lower assets, and lower stockholders' equity.

You have overheard conversation at the water cooler suggesting that the company expects sales to slow in the coming year and wonder whether that forecast has anything to do with the CFO's estimate. Could the CFO be attempting to "save" revenue to record in the coming year? Should you prepare an income statement that recognizes $10,000 of revenue associated with the service contract or insist on recording $65,000?

The issues in this scenario are complex. It is often difficult to determine exactly when consulting services have been performed. Two people, both acting in good faith, may give different estimates of the completion of these services. The $10,000 is a more conservative estimate of revenue earned. However, by reporting lower net income in the current period, the company will report higher net income in the following period. If the CFO's $10,000 estimate is intended solely to manipulate the company's revenue and earnings trend, use of that estimate is unethical.

O B J E C T I V E 6

Describe the sequence of the final steps in the recording process and relate cash flows to adjusting entries.

The Adjusting Process in Perspective

Chapter 3 presented the various steps in the recording process as follows:

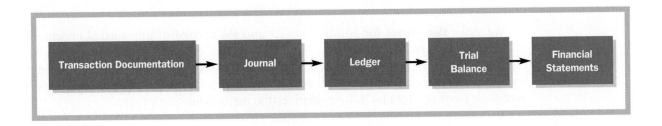

Transaction Documentation → Journal → Ledger → Trial Balance → Financial Statements

This process has a final aim: the preparation of accurate financial statements prepared on the accrual basis. To accomplish this goal, the process must include adjusting entries to record implicit transactions. When we consider the adjustments, we can further divide the final three steps in the recording process as follows:

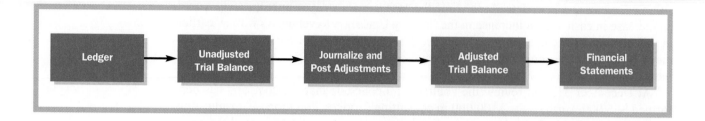

As you review these steps, remember that each adjusting entry affects at least one income statement account, a revenue or an expense, and one balance sheet account, an asset or a liability. No adjusting entry debits or credits cash. Why? If transactions affect cash, they are explicit transactions that companies routinely record as they occur. The end-of-period adjustment process is reserved for implicit transactions that are an important feature of the accrual basis of accounting.

Cash flows—that is, explicit transactions involving cash receipts or disbursements—may precede or follow the adjusting entry that recognizes the related revenue or expense. The diagrams that follow underscore the basic differences between the cash flows and the accrual accounting entries.

Entries for adjustments I and II, expiration of unexpired costs and realization of revenues received in advance, generally occur subsequent to the cash flows. For example, at the time a company receives or disburses cash for rent, only the balance sheet is affected. The subsequent adjusting entry records the later impact on the income statement.

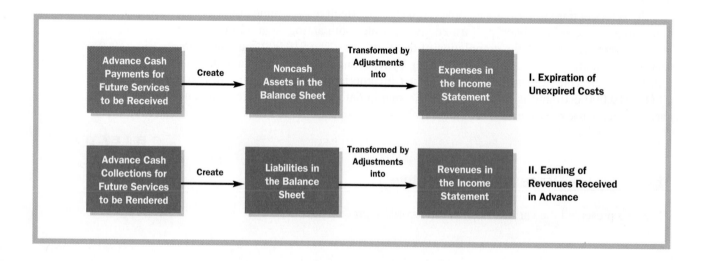

We make the entries for adjustments III and IV, accrual of unrecorded expenses and accrual of unrecorded revenues, before the related cash flows. The income statement is affected before the cash receipts and disbursements occur. The accounting entity computes the amount of goods or services provided or received prior to any cash receipt or payment. Exhibit 4-1 summarizes the major adjusting entries.

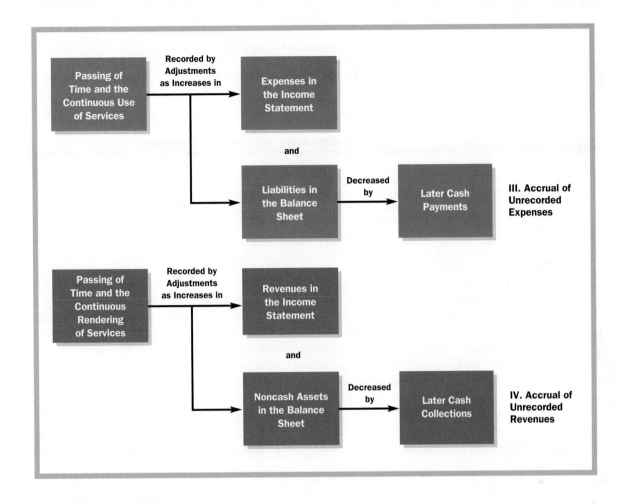

Exhibit 4-1
Summary of Adjusting Entries

Adjusting Entry	Type of Account Debited	Type of Account Credited
I. Expiration of unexpired costs	Expense	Prepaid expense, accumulated depreciation
II. Earning of revenues received in advance	Unearned revenue	Revenue
III. Accrual of unrecorded expenses	Expense	Payable
IV. Accrual of unrecorded revenues	Receivable	Revenue

Summary Problem for Your Review

PROBLEM

Chan Audio Company is a retailer of stereo equipment that began operation on January 1, 20X2. One month later, on January 31, 20X2, the company's unadjusted trial balance consists of the following accounts:

Cash	$ 71,700	
Accounts receivable	160,300	
Note receivable	40,000	
Merchandise inventory	250,200	
Prepaid rent	15,000	
Store equipment	114,900	
Note payable		$100,000
Accounts payable		117,100
Unearned rent revenue		3,000
Paid-in capital		400,000
Sales		160,000
Cost of goods sold	100,000	
Wages expense	28,000	
Total	$780,100	$780,100

Consider the following adjustments on January 31:

a. January depreciation, $1,000.
b. On January 2, Chan paid $15,000 of rent in advance to cover the first quarter of 20X2, as shown by the debit balance in the Prepaid Rent account. Adjust for January rent.
c. Wages earned by employees during January but not paid as of January 31 were $3,750.
d. Chan borrowed $100,000 from the bank on January 1. The company recorded this explicit transaction when the business began, as shown by the credit balance in the Note Payable account. Chan is to pay the principal and 9 percent interest 1 year later (January 1, 20X3). Chan has not yet made an adjustment for the January interest expense.
e. On January 1, Chan made a cash loan of $40,000 to a local supplier, as shown by the debit balance in the Note Receivable account. The promissory note stated that the loan is to be repaid 1 year later (January 1, 20X3), together with interest at 12 percent per annum. On January 31, an adjustment is needed to recognize the interest earned on the note receivable.

Exhibit 4-2
Chan Audio Company
Journal Entries

	Debit	Credit
(a) Depreciation expense	1,000	
Accumulated depreciation, store equipment		1,000
Depreciation for January		
(b) Rent expense	5,000	
Prepaid rent		5,000
Rent expense for January		
$15,000 \div 3 = $5,000		
(c) Wages expense	3,750	
Accrued wages payable		3,750
Wages earned but not paid		
(d) Interest expense	750	
Accrued interest payable		750
Interest for January		
$100,000 \times .09 \times 1/12 = $750		
(e) Accrued interest receivable	400	
Interest revenue		400
Interest earned for January		
$40,000 \times .12 \times 1/12 = $400		
(f) Unearned rent revenue	500	
Rent revenue		500
Rent earned for January, rent per month,		
$3,000 \div 3 = $1,000; for half a month, $500		
(g) Income tax expense	11,200	
Accrued income taxes payable		11,200
Income tax on January income		
.50 \times [160,000 + 400 + 500 - 100,000 - 28,000 - 3,750 - 1,000 - 5,000 - 750]		

f. On January 15, a nearby corporation paid $3,000 cash to Chan as an advance rental for temporary use of Chan's storage space and equipment. The rental agreement covers the 3 months from January 15 to April 15. This $3,000 is the credit balance in the Unearned Rent Revenue account. On January 31, Chan needs to make an adjustment to recognize the rent revenue earned for one-half a month.

g. Chan must accrue income tax expense on January income at a rate of 50 percent of income before taxes.

Required

1. Enter the trial balance amounts in the general ledger. Set up the new asset account, Accrued Interest Receivable, and the new asset reduction account, the contra account, Accumulated Depreciation, Store Equipment. Set up the following new liability accounts: Accrued Wages Payable, Accrued Interest Payable, and Accrued Income

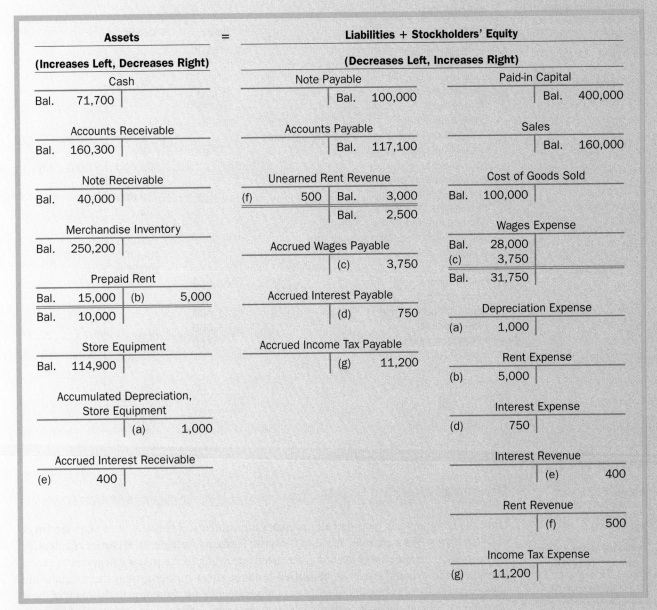

Exhibit 4-3
Chan Audio Company
General Ledger

Taxes Payable. Set up the following new expense and revenue accounts: Depreciation Expense, Rent Expense, Interest Expense, Interest Revenue, Rent Revenue, and Income Tax Expense.

2. Journalize adjustments (a) to (g) and post the entries to the ledger. Identify entries by transaction letter.
3. Prepare an adjusted trial balance as of January 31, 20X2.

SOLUTION

The solutions to requirements 1 through 3 are in Exhibits 4-2, 4-3, and 4-4. Accountants often refer to the final trial balance, Exhibit 4-4, as the adjusted trial balance. Why? All the necessary adjustments have been made; thus, the trial balance provides the data necessary for creating the formal financial statements.

Exhibit 4-4
Chan Audio Company
Adjusted Trial Balance
January 31, 20X2

Account Title	Balance		
	Debit	Credit	
Cash	$ 71,700		
Accounts receivable	160,300		
Note receivable	40,000		
Merchandise inventory	250,200		
Prepaid rent	10,000		
Store equipment	114,900		
Accumulated depreciation, store equipment		$ 1,000	Balance
Accrued interest receivable	400		Sheet
Note payable		100,000	Exhibit 4-5
Accounts payable		117,100	
Unearned rent revenue		2,500	
Accrued wages payable		3,750	
Accrued interest payable		750	
Accrued income taxes payable		11,200	
Paid-in capital		400,000	
Sales		160,000	
Cost of goods sold	100,000		
Wages expense	31,750		
Depreciation expense	1,000		
Rent expense	5,000		Income
Interest expense	750		Statement,
Interest revenue		400	Exhibit 4-8
Rent revenue		500	
Income tax expense	11,200		
Total	$797,200	$797,200	

OBJECTIVE 7

Prepare a classified balance sheet and use it to assess short-term liquidity.

classified balance sheet
A balance sheet that groups the accounts into subcategories to help readers quickly gain a perspective on the company's financial position.

Classified Balance Sheet

Once the company has recorded all necessary adjustments, it is ready to prepare the financial statements. We were introduced to the basic financial statements in earlier chapters. As we have seen, balance sheet accounts are listed according to the major categories of assets, liabilities, and owners' equity. A **classified balance sheet** further groups the accounts into subcategories to help readers quickly gain a perspective on the company's financial position and to draw attention to certain accounts or groups of accounts. Assets are frequently classified into two groups: current assets and noncurrent or long-term assets. Liabilities are similarly classified into current liabilities and noncurrent or long-term liabilities.

Current Assets and Liabilities

Current assets are cash and those other assets that a company expects to convert to cash, sell, or consume during the next 12 months (or within the normal operating cycle if longer than 1 year). Similarly, **current liabilities** are those liabilities that come due within the next year (or within the normal operating cycle if longer than a year). Identifying current assets and liabilities is useful in assessing the company's ability to meet obligations as they become due. For the most part, current assets give rise to the cash needed to pay current liabilities, so the relationship between these categories is important.

Exhibit 4-5 shows the classified balance sheet for Chan Audio Company, which we prepared from the adjusted trial balance for the company (shown in Exhibit 4-4). On a classified balance sheet, companies generally list the current asset accounts in the order in which the assets are likely to be converted to cash during the coming year. Cash thus appears first because it is, obviously, already in the form of cash. In the case of Chan Audio, Accounts Receivable are next because the firm should receive cash payments for these accounts within weeks or months. Note Receivable and Accrued Interest Receivable, the third and fourth accounts, should be converted to cash by the end of the year. Nonmonetary assets, such as inventories and prepaid expenses (in this case, Merchandise Inventory and Prepaid Rent), appear last in the current assets section of the balance sheet. Prepaid Rent is not converted to cash, but is a current asset in the sense that its existence reduces the obligation to pay cash within the next year.

As shown in Exhibit 4-5, we also list current liability accounts in the approximate order in which they will draw on, or decrease, cash during the coming year. Wages tend to be paid weekly or monthly, whereas interest and taxes tend to be paid monthly, quarterly, or annually.

The excess of current assets over current liabilities is **working capital.** In the case of Chan Audio Company, the working capital on January 31, 20X2, is $297,300 ($532,600 − $235,300). Working capital is important because it connects current assets and current liabilities. It normally grows larger as the company grows, so it is proportional to the size of the firm and is frequently evaluated using the current ratio.

current assets
Cash and other assets that a company expects to convert to cash or sell or consume during the next 12 months or within the normal operating cycle if longer than 1 year.

current liabilities
Liabilities that fall due within the coming year or within the normal operating cycle if longer than 1 year.

working capital
The excess of current assets over current liabilities.

Current Ratio

Current assets are an indicator of how much cash a company will have on hand in the near future; current liabilities tell you how much debt the company will have to pay off with

Assets			Liabilities and Owners' Equity		
Current assets			Current liabilities		
Cash		$ 71,700	Accounts payable		$117,100
Accounts receivable		160,300	Unearned rent revenue		2,500
Note receivable		40,000	Accrued wages payable		3,750
Accrued interest receivable		400	Accrued interest payable		750
Merchandise inventory		250,200	Accrued income taxes payable		11,200
Prepaid rent		10,000	Note payable		100,000
Total current assets		$532,600	Total current liabilities		$235,300
Long-term assets			Stockholders' equity		
Store equipment	$114,900		Paid-in capital	$400,000	
Accumulated			Retained earnings	11, 200	411,200
depreciation	1,000	113,900			
Total		$646,500	Total		$646,500

Exhibit 4-5
Chan Audio Company
Balance Sheet, January 31, 20X2

liquidity
An entity's ability to meet its immediate financial obligations with cash and near-cash assets as those obligations become due.

that cash in the near future. Comparing the two amounts helps readers of financial statements assess a business entity's **liquidity,** which is its ability to meet its immediate financial obligations with cash and near-cash assets as those obligations become due.

Investors use the **current ratio** (also called the **working capital ratio**), which we calculate by dividing current assets by current liabilities, to evaluate a company's liquidity. Chan Audio's current ratio, for example, is:

current ratio (working capital ratio)
Current assets divided by current liabilities.

$$\text{Current ratio} = \frac{\$532,600}{\$235,300} = 2.3$$

A current ratio that is too low may indicate the company will have difficulty meeting its short-term obligations. Conversely, a current ratio that is too high may indicate excessive holdings of cash, accounts receivable, or inventories. Excessive holdings of this nature are bad for a company because they tie up money that could be more effectively used elsewhere.

How do we assess this ratio? Is a higher current ratio always better? Other things being equal, the higher the current ratio, the more assurance creditors have about being paid in full and on time. However, as with all ratios, it can be misleading to draw conclusions from the numeric value of the ratio alone. In the case of the current ratio, it is important to consider the composition of current assets and current liabilities before drawing inferences. Suppose that just prior to the end of January, Chan Audio used $70,000 of its cash to pay off part of the outstanding balance in Accounts Payable. The restated current ratio is:

$$\text{Current ratio} = \frac{\$532,600 - \$70,000}{\$235,300 - \$70,000} = 2.8$$

Even though the restated current ratio is higher than the previous value of 2.3, it is difficult to argue that Chan is more liquid as it has only $1,700 in cash. The relative liquidity of Chan under these two different scenarios depends on the company's ability to convert its current assets such as Merchandise Inventory and Accounts Receivable to cash. This illustrates one of the difficulties in interpreting the current ratio; some current assets are less liquid than others and may take longer to convert to cash.

quick ratio (acid test ratio)
Variation of the current ratio that removes less liquid assets from the numerator. Perhaps the most common version of this ratio is (current assets – inventory)/current liabilities.

Variations of the current ratio attempt to distinguish among assets based on their level of liquidity. One common variation of the current ratio is the **quick ratio** (also known as the **acid test ratio**), which removes inventory (and potentially other less liquid assets such as prepaid expenses) from the numerator of the calculation. This provides a more restrictive view of the company's liquidity. For example, in the initial scenario depicted for Chan Audio, the quick ratio is ($532,600 − $250,200)/$235,300 = 1.2. In the second scenario, the quick ratio is ($532,600 − $250,200 − $70,000)/($235,300 − $70,000) = 1.3.

An old rule of thumb was that the current ratio should be greater than 2.0. However, current ratios today are more commonly close to one. In making judgments about a company's liquidity, analysts do not focus on the ratio value in isolation; rather they compare a company's current ratio with those of past years and with those of similar companies. We can make one useful assessment by comparing a company's current ratio with the average ratio in its industry. For example, recently **IBM**'s ratio was 1.2, compared with an industry average of 1.33. Although only slightly greater than 1.0 and below the industry average, IBM's ratio is probably not a cause for concern. It is also common for firms in the utility industry to have low current ratios because of low inventories and stable cash flows. For example, **Verizon**, a regional telephone company, had a current ratio of only 0.77 as of December 31, 2002. On the other hand, **Microsoft**'s current ratio of 4.2 as of June 2003 was more than three times as large as IBM's and 5.5 times as large as Verizon's. You will find more information on working capital and the current ratio in the Business First box on page 157.

Although some people use the current or quick ratio to measure short-term debt-paying ability, a prediction of cash receipts and disbursements is more useful. Whether a company's level of cash is too low or too high really depends on the forecasts of operating

MANAGING WORKING CAPITAL

The traditional view is that large amounts of working capital and high current ratios are good—they show that a company is likely to remain solvent. For years, the rule of thumb for a desirable current ratio was 2.0, indicating twice as many current assets as current liabilities. However, large amounts of working capital may needlessly tie up funds that can be used profitably elsewhere in the company. Each dollar not invested in working capital is a dollar of free cash available for investing in value-adding activities—activities that actually create and deliver products or services to customers. When companies have good investment opportunities, working capital levels tend to be lower. In the 1990s, the booming economy offered such opportunities and holding large amounts of inventories and accounts receivable fell out of fashion. The stated target of some firms was zero working capital and a current ratio of 1.0, and many companies made a concerted effort to reduce working capital and, hence, lower their current ratios.

For example, between January 1998 and January 2000, Gap Inc. reduced its working capital by $394 million, from $839 million to $445 million and reduced its current ratio from 1.85 to 1.25. This meant that Gap had an extra $394 million to invest in new products, corporate acquisitions, or whatever other opportunity presented itself. By year end February 2001, Gap had decreased its working capital even further. In fact, working capital was actually a negative $151 million and they reported a current ratio of 0.95!

As the economy slowed in the early 2000s, the working capital of many companies began to creep back up. As sales levels declined, inventory levels rose and some companies faced an increase in receivables levels because customers took longer to pay. Other companies elected to conserve their cash by delaying capital expenditures and expansion. All these events can result in increased levels of working capital.

Let's look at Gap Inc. again. Between February 2001 and February 2003, Gap experienced an increase in working capital from negative $151 million to $3,013 million, the highest level in more than 10 years. The current ratio jumped from 0.95 as of February 2001, to 1.48 in February 2002, and to 2.11 by February 2003! Examination of Gap's financial statements for the year ending February 2003 indicates that part of the increase in working capital and the current ratio is attributable to an increase in inventory levels. However, Gap's management states that the primary driver of the increase in working capital and the current ratio from February 2002 to February 2003 was an increase in cash due to the issuance of long-term debt and a decrease in capital expenditures.

The main components of working capital for a typical company are accounts receivable plus inventories less accounts payable. Fluctuations in working capital levels must be interpreted with caution. Receivables may grow because of increasing sales, but they can also increase when collection of receivables slows down. Soaring inventories may mean increased ability to deliver orders on time. They may also mean that sales are not keeping up with production or that the company is incurring excessive storage and handling costs for inventory. Companies with large inventories may also lack the ability to adapt products quickly to customers' wishes. You can see that there are mixed signals in measures such as working capital and the current ratio.

Source: www.gapinc.com.

requirements over the coming months. For example, a company such as a small comic book and baseball card retailer might need very little cash on hand because upcoming debts and operating needs will be small in the next few months. Conversely, Marvel Comics, the corporation that produces the comic books sold by the small retailer, will need millions of dollars in cash to meet upcoming debt and short-term operating needs. As a rule, companies should try to keep on hand only the cash necessary to meet disbursement needs and invest any temporary excess cash to generate additional income.

Formats of Balance Sheets

The details and formats of balance sheets and other financial statements vary across companies. Yet, all balance sheets contain the same basic information, regardless of format. For example, consider the balance sheets of Columbia Sportswear for the years ended

December 31, 2002 and December 31, 2003, as shown in Exhibit 4-6. The format and classifications are those actually used by Columbia. Note the absence of a separate subtotal for noncurrent assets and noncurrent liabilities. Some companies prefer to omit these headings when there are only a few items within a specific class.

report format
A classified balance sheet with the assets at the top.

account format
A classified balance sheet with the assets at the left.

Exhibit 4-6 presents a classified balance sheet in the **report format** (assets at top), which is different from the **account format** (assets at left) illustrated in Exhibit 4-5. Either format is acceptable. Non-U.S. companies and U.S. companies in certain industries may use formats that differ from those presented in Exhibits 4-5 and 4-6. Exhibit 4-7 shows a condensed balance sheet for BP Amoco, a British company. Notice that BP Amoco lists fixed assets—that is, noncurrent assets—before current assets and deducts current liabilities from current assets to give a direct measure of working capital (called net current assets or net current liabilities). BP Amoco reports negative working capital of £1,235 million for the year ended December 31, 2002. Again, regardless of the format, balance sheets always contain the same basic information.

Exhibit 4-6
Columbia Sportswear
Company
*Consolidated
Balance Sheets
(In thousands)*

	December 31	
	2003	**2002**
Assets		
Current assets		
Cash and cash equivalents	$264,585	$194,670
Accounts receivable, net	206,024	154,099
Inventories, net	126,808	94,862
Deferred tax asset	17,442	10,840
Prepaid expenses and other current assets	6,028	6,006
Total current assets	620,887	460,477
Property, plant, and equipment, net	126,247	124,515
Intangibles and other assets	24,475	7,825
Goodwill	12,157	—
Total assets	$783,766	$592,817
Liabilities and Shareholders' Equity		
Current liabilities		
Notes payable	$ —	$ 9,835
Accounts payable	62,432	49,370
Accrued liabilities	43,789	35,146
Income taxes payable	8,069	—
Current portion of long-term debt	4,596	4,498
Total current liabilities	118,886	98,849
Long-term debt	16,335	20,636
Deferred tax liability	7,716	613
Total liabilities	142,937	120,098
Shareholders' equity:		
Preferred stock; 10,000 shares authorized; none issued and outstanding	—	—
Common stock; 125,000 shares authorized; 40,253 and 39,737 issued and outstanding	182,188	159,996
Retained earnings	435,364	315,243
Accumulated other comprehensive income (loss)	23,277	(1,156)
Unearned portion of restricted stock issued for future services	—	(1,364)
Total shareholders' equity	640,829	472,719
Total liabilities and shareholders' equity	$783,766	$592,817

Exhibit 4-7
BP Amoco Balance
Sheet
*December 31, 2002
and December 31,
2003 (£ in millions)*

	December 31		
	2002		**2003**
Fixed assets		£ 114,059	£ 123,107
Current assets	45,066		54,465
Current liabilities	46,301		50,584
Net current liabilities		(1,235)	3,881
Total assets less current liabilities		£ 112,824	£ 126,988
Long-term liabilities and provisions		43,415	51,050
Shareholders' interests		£ 69,409	£ 75,938

INTERPRETING FINANCIAL STATEMENTS

Published annual reports typically contain condensed balance sheet information. This level of detail is appropriate for external analysts and investors. Is this same level of detail sufficient for internal use?

Answer

No. Firms prepare detailed balance sheets for their internal use. Suppose that you are the person responsible for managing inventory at **Columbia Sportswear**'s flagship store in Portland, Oregon. Rather than just knowing the total amount of inventory on hand, you would need to know what the inventory levels are for spring merchandise and for summer merchandise, for men's wear and women's wear, and for clothing and accessories. This detail and more is necessary for you to manage your operation and evaluate your performance. Outside investors are more concerned with the overall performance of Columbia Sportswear as a whole relative to competing retailers, so summarized companywide information is sufficient.

Income Statement

We have seen that balance sheets can provide decision makers with information about a company's ability to meet its short-term operating and debt needs. However, investors are also concerned about a company's ability to generate earnings and pay dividends. The income statement provides some of the information necessary to address these concerns. To be most informative, income statements, like balance sheets, may include subcategories that help focus attention on certain accounts or groups of accounts. There are two commonly used formats for income statements prepared for use by outside investors: the single-step income statement and the multiple-step income statement.

Single- and Multiple-Step Income Statements

The adjusted trial balance for Chan Audio Company (Exhibit 4-4) provides the data for the two formats of income statements shown in Exhibit 4-8. The statement in Part A of Exhibit 4-8 is a **single-step income statement.** Notice that it groups all types of revenue together (e.g., sales revenue, interest revenue, and rent revenue) and then lists and deducts all expenses without drawing any intermediate subtotals. The statement in Part B of Exhibit 4-8 is a **multiple-step income statement.** Rather than grouping all revenues together and then subtracting all expenses, the multiple-step income statement combines revenues and expenses to highlight significant relationships, which we discuss here. The Columbia Sportswear income statement in Exhibit 4-9 is a multiple-step income statement. Note that regardless of the presentation format, the net income number is the same. There is no

OBJE8TIVE

Prepare single- and multiple-step income statements.

single-step income statement
An income statement that groups all revenues and then lists and deducts all expenses without drawing any intermediate subtotals.

multiple-step income statement
An income statement that contains one or more subtotals that highlight significant relationships.

Exhibit 4-8 Part A
Chan Audio Company
*Single-Step Income
Statement
Income Statement for
the Month Ended
January 31, 20X2*

Sales		$160,000
Rent revenue		500
Interest revenue		400
Total sales and other revenues		$160,900
Expenses		
Cost of goods sold	$100,000	
Wages	31,750	
Depreciation	1,000	
Rent	5,000	
Interest	750	
Income taxes	11,200	
Total expenses		$149,700
Net income		$ 11,200

Exhibit 4-8 Part B
Chan Audio Company
*Multiple-Step Income
Statement
Income Statement for
the Month Ended
January 31, 20X2*

Sales		$160,000
Cost of goods sold		100,000
Gross profit		$ 60,000
Operating expenses		
Wages	$31,750	
Depreciation	1,000	
Rent	5,000	37,750
Operating income		$ 22,250
Other revenues and expenses		
Rent revenue	$ 500	
Interest revenue	400	
Total other revenue	$ 900	
Deduct: interest expense	750	150
Income before income taxes		$ 22,400
Income taxes (at 50%)		11,200
Net income		$ 11,200

theoretical or practical reason to prefer one of these formats. Experienced readers of financial statements can easily adjust from one to another. As you begin to read and evaluate actual statements, do not let the superficial differences in presentation confuse you.

The majority of U.S. companies employ the multiple-step income statement format in their external financial statements. Let's take a closer look at the subtotals that commonly appear in a multiple-step statement. Most multiple-step income statements start with the separate computation and disclosure of **gross profit** (also called **gross margin**), which is the excess of sales revenue over the cost of the inventory that was sold. Chan reports a gross profit of $60,000 in Exhibit 4-8, Part B, and Columbia Sportswear's 2003 income statement shows a gross profit of $440,685,000.

The next section of a multiple-step income statement usually contains the **operating expenses,** which is a group of recurring expenses that pertain to the firm's routine, ongoing operations. Examples of such expenses are wages, rent, depreciation, and various other operation-oriented expenses, such as telephone, heat, and advertising. We deduct these operating expenses from the gross profit to obtain **operating income** (also called **operating profit** or **income from operations).** Chan reports operating income of $22,250 in Exhibit 4-8, Part B. In Exhibit 4-9, Columbia Sportswear groups all operating expenses together into a category called Selling, General and Administrative, and subtracts them from gross profit. Prior to computing income from operations, Columbia Sportswear also shows a small amount of income from licensing activities. It reports income from operations of $190,189,000 in 2003.

gross profit (gross margin)
The excess of sales revenue over the cost of the inventory that was sold.

operating expenses
A group of recurring expenses that pertain to the firm's routine, ongoing operations.

operating income (operating profit, income from operations)
Gross profit less all operating expenses.

Exhibit 4-9
Columbia Sportswear
Company
*Consolidated
Statements of
Operations
(In thousands)*

	Year Ended December 31		
	2003	**2002**	**2001**
Net sales	$951,786	$816,319	$779,581
Cost of sales	511,101	437,782	422,430
Gross profit	440,685	378,537	357,151
Selling, general, and administrative	252,307	216,085	209,503
Net licensing income	(1,811)	(1,223)	(533)
Income from operations	190,189	163,675	148,181
Interest income	(2,107)	(2,790)	(1,712)
Interest expense	1,627	2,436	4,280
Income before income tax	190,669	164,029	145,613
Income tax expense	70,548	61,511	56,789
Net income	$120,121	$102,518	$88,824

The next grouping in the multiple-step income statement contains nonoperating revenues and expenses, which are revenues and expenses that are not directly related to the mainstream of a firm's operations. The revenues are usually minor in relation to the sales revenue shown in the first section of the multiple-step statement. The expenses are also minor, with the possible exception of interest expense. Some companies make heavy use of debt, which causes high interest expense, whereas other companies incur little debt and have low interest expense. Both Chan Audio Company and Columbia Sportswear separately itemize Interest Expense and Interest Revenue (Columbia Sportswear uses the expression Interest Income in place of Interest Revenue). In contrast, some companies net Interest Expense and Interest Revenue on the income statement. In all financial statements, accountants use the label "net" to denote that some amounts have been offset in computing the final result. Thus, if a company reports net interest, it means that interest revenue and interest expense have been combined into one number, which may result in either an expense or a revenue. Users of financial statements usually regard interest revenue and interest expense as "other" or "nonoperating" items because they arise from lending and borrowing money, activities that are distinct from most companies' ordinary operations of selling goods or services. Of course, exceptions occur in companies in the business of lending and borrowing money: banks, credit unions, insurance companies, and other financial intermediaries.

If nonoperating revenues and expenses appear in a separate category on the income statement, we can easily compare operating income over time or between companies. Comparisons of operating income focus attention on selling the product and controlling the costs of doing so. Success in this arena is the ultimate test of a company's health.

Note where income taxes appear in both of the income statements in Exhibit 4-8 and in Columbia Sportswear's income statement in Exhibit 4-9. Most companies follow the practice of showing income taxes as a separate item immediately above net income, regardless of the grouping of other items on the income statement.

Analysts and investors follow trends in corporate earnings. When observing earnings trends, it is important to distinguish between trends in operating versus nonoperating earnings. There is a distinction between those circumstances when earnings are growing because interest cost is falling or interest revenue is rising and those circumstances when earnings growth is due to dramatic increases in sales. The first two sources of earnings growth depend on outside forces or one-time changes, which may not be sustainable. However, when demand for the product increases, the long-term potential for continued growth is improved. The need to use caution in interpreting changes in earnings is not limited to the distinction between operating and nonoperating earnings. For example, a reduction in research and development expense, an operating expense, will result in an improvement in current period earnings. However, the long-term implications for the company will be negative if research and development is crucial to the development of new products. In more recent years, a number of companies have gotten in trouble for misclassification of revenues or expenses. For example, in the fourth quarter of fiscal year 2000, IBM used $300 million in revenue from the sale of a business to offset ordinary operating expenses, thereby increasing operating earnings and potentially deceiving investors.

Profitability Evaluation Ratios

OBJECTIVE 9

Use ratios to assess profitability.

For experienced managers, the income statement and balance sheet are the "language of business." These managers can compare current period income with that of the previous quarter or prior year. They know their competitors' financial statements inside and out and can evaluate how their company compares with the competition. They know that high earnings may earn them a big bonus. How can individuals who do not have this deep company and industry knowledge use the financial statements to gain insights into the company's performance?

Earlier in this chapter, we saw that ratios such as the current ratio help give meaning to the numbers in the balance sheet. Similarly, ratios using income statement numbers are useful in evaluating a company's **profitability,** which is the ability of a company to provide its investors with a particular rate of return on their investment. If Mary invests $100 in Columbia Sportswear and receives $10 every year as a result, $10 is her return on investment. However, absolute amounts are hard to evaluate. What if Mary had given Columbia Sportswear $200? In that case, a return of $10 would not be as attractive. Thus, it is common to express the return as a **rate of return,** a return per dollar invested. In the case of a $100 investment, a $10 return is a 10 percent rate of return ($10/$100). For a $200 investment, a $10 return is a 5 percent rate of return ($10/$200).

Profitability measures are useful decision-making tools. Investors use them to distinguish among different investment opportunities. Managers know that their company's profitability measures will affect the investment decisions of investors and that high profitability makes it easier to raise capital by selling stock or issuing debt securities. From time to time, managers may have to decide whether to buy another company, a division of a company, or a machine that will be used in manufacturing a new product. In each case, the manager will evaluate the profitability of the project as part of making the decision.

We use trends in profitability measures over time, and within and among industries, as a basis for predictions and decisions. We provide a very brief introduction to four profitability ratios: gross profit percentage, return on sales, return on common stockholders' equity, and return on assets. Chapter 12 expands on the discussion of how to interpret these ratios and introduces additional measures of financial performance.

profitability
The ability of a company to provide investors with a particular rate of return on their investment.

rate of return
The return per dollar invested.

Gross Profit Percentage

A ratio based on gross profit (sales revenue minus cost of goods sold) is particularly useful to a retailer or manufacturer in choosing a pricing strategy and in judging its results. This measure, the **gross profit percentage,** or **gross margin percentage,** is defined as gross profit divided by sales. Chan Audio Company's gross profit percentage for January was (numbers from Exhibit 4-8, Part B):

gross profit percentage (gross margin percentage)
Gross profit (sales − cost of goods sold) divided by sales.

$$\text{Gross profit percentage} = \text{Gross profit} \div \text{Sales}$$
$$= \$60,000 \div \$160,000$$
$$= 37.5\%$$

We can also present this relationship as follows:

	Amount	Percentage
Sales	$160,000	100.0%
Cost of goods sold	100,000	62.5
Gross profit	$ 60,000	37.5%

Gross profit percentages vary greatly by industry. For example, software companies have high gross profit percentages (Microsoft's was 82 percent for the year ending June 30, 2003). Why? Because most costs in the software industry are in research and development and sales and marketing, not in cost of goods sold. In contrast, retail companies have lower gross margin percentages because product costs are their main expense. For example, in 2002, the gross profit percentage for Kroger was 27 percent. Other gross margin percentages fall between the extremes, such as Chico's at 63 percent and Columbia Sportswear at 46 percent.

Return on Sales or Net Profit Margin

Managers carefully follow the **return on sales ratio** (also known as the **net profit margin ratio**), which shows the relationship of net income to sales revenue. This ratio gauges a company's ability to control the level of all its expenses relative to the level of its sales. As with the gross profit percentage, the return on sales tends to vary by industry, but the range is not as great. We can compute Chan Audio's return on sales ratio as follows using numbers from Exhibit 4-8:

return on sales ratio (net profit margin ratio) Net income divided by sales.

$$\text{Return on sales} = \text{Net income} \div \text{Sales}$$
$$= \$11,200 \div \$160,000$$
$$= 7\%$$

Columbia Sportswear reports a return on sales ratio of 12.6 percent for the year ended December 31, 2003.

Return on Common Stockholders' Equity

The **return on common stockholders' equity ratio** (**ROE** or **ROCE**) also uses net income, but compares it with invested capital (as measured by average common stockholders' equity) instead of sales. Many analysts regard this ratio as the ultimate measure of overall accomplishment from the perspective of the shareholder. The return on common stockholders' equity calculation for Chan Audio is:

return on common stockholders' equity ratio (ROE or ROCE) Net income divided by invested capital (measured by average common stockholders' equity).

$$\text{Return on common stockholders' equity} = \text{Net income} \div \text{Average common stockholders' equity}$$
$$= \$11,200 \div 1/2 \,(\text{January 1 balance, } \$400,000$$
$$+ \text{January 31 balance, } \$411,200)$$
$$= \$11,200 \div \$405,600$$
$$= 2.8\% \text{ (for 1 month)}$$

Return on Assets

The **return on assets ratio (ROA)** compares net income with invested capital as measured by average total assets. The company invests its resources in assets, which it uses to generate

return on assets ratio (ROA) Net income divided by average total assets.

revenues and ultimately, net income. The return on assets ratio measures how effectively those assets generate profits. There are numerous variations of the return on assets ratio. Assuming a balance in total assets of $620,000 as of January 1, we can calculate a simplified version of the return on assets ratio for Chan Audio for the month of January as follows:

$$\text{Return on assets} = \text{Net income} \div \text{Average total assets}$$
$$= \$11,200 \div 1/2 \ (\text{January 1 balance}, \$620,000$$
$$+ \text{January 31 balance}, \$646,500)$$
$$= \$11,200 \div \$633,250$$
$$= 1.8\% \ (\text{for 1 month})$$

Other variations of the return on assets ratio are discussed in Chapter 12.

Chan Audio's 37.5 percent gross profit percentage is a bit low compared with the usual 40 to 45 percent for the retail stereo industry. However, Chan Audio has maintained excellent expense control because its 7 percent return on sales, 33.6 percent return on common stockholders' equity (a monthly rate of 2.8% × 12 = 33.6% as an annual rate), and 21.6 percent return on assets (1.8% × 12 = 21.6%) are higher than the 3, 19 and 7 percent annual returns earned by the industry over the same period.

Recent examples of actual annual return on sales, return on common stockholders' equity, and return on assets ratios for firms in different industries are shown here:

	Return on Sales (%)	Return on Common Stockholders' Equity (%)	Return on Assets (%)
Microsoft	27.6	15.7	12.4
Nike	6.7	18.1	10.8
McDonald's	5.8	9.0	3.8
Kroger	2.3	32.8	6.2
Walgreens	3.6	17.8	10.9
Unilever (The Netherlands)	4.4	8.0	4.4
Johnson & Johnson	18.2	28.1	16.7
Starbucks	6.6	14.1	10.9

INTERPRETING FINANCIAL STATEMENTS

Which industry would you expect to have a higher gross margin percentage, the grocery industry or the pharmaceutical industry? Why?

Answer

There are many "right ways" to think about this issue. As noted in the text, Kroger, a grocery store chain, has a gross margin of 27 percent. The grocery industry is a retail activity where stores buy and resell items very quickly. As a result they can accept fairly low margins because they hold the inventory briefly and face little risk of failure. In contrast, the pharmaceutical industry has to develop drugs, seek govern-

ment approval to market them, and then aggressively sell them. Thus, the pharmaceutical industry has very high gross margin percentages. Pfizer has a gross margin percentage of 84 percent. Two issues are important to understand. Cost of goods sold does not include very important selling, general, and administrative costs, which are larger in the pharmaceutical industry than in the grocery industry. More important, the pharmaceutical industry faces huge R&D costs, which GAAP treats as a period cost instead of a product cost. So R&D, which may be 15 percent or more of sales in the pharmaceutical industry, is not part of cost of goods sold and does not affect the gross margin percentage.

Summary Problem for Your Review

PROBLEM

Johnson & Johnson (maker of Tylenol, Band-Aid products, and other health care and personal use products) uses a statement of earnings as follows:

Johnson & Johnson
Statement of Earnings for the year ended December 31, 2003
($ in millions except per share figures)

Sales to customers	$41,862
Cost of products sold	12,176
Gross profit	29,686
Selling, marketing, and administrative expenses	14,131
Research expense	4,684
Purchased in-process research and development expense	918
Interest income	(177)
Interest expense	207
Other expense (income), net	(385)
	19,378
Earnings before provision for taxes on income	10,308
Provision for taxes on income	3,111
Net earnings	$ 7,197
Basic net earnings per share	$ 2.42

1. Is this a single- or multiple-step income statement? Explain your answer.
2. What term would Columbia Sportswear use as a label for the line in Johnson & Johnson's statements having the $10,308 figure? (Refer to the Columbia Sportswear income statement in Exhibit 4-9 on page 161.)
3. Suggest an alternative term for Interest Income.
4. What is the amount of the famous "bottom line" that is so often referred to by managers?
5. Net earnings per share are defined as net earnings divided by the average number of common shares outstanding. Compute the average number of common shares outstanding during the year.

SOLUTION

1. As is often the case, Johnson & Johnson uses a hybrid of single- and multiple-step income statements. However, this one is closer to a multiple-step statement. A pure-bred single-step statement would place interest income with sales to obtain total revenues and would not calculate a gross profit subtotal.
2. Columbia Sportswear would use "income before income tax" to describe the $10,308 figure.
3. Interest revenue.
4. The "bottom line" is net earnings of $7,197 million. The bottom line per average common share outstanding is $2.42.
5. Companies must show net earnings per share on the face of the income statement.

Earnings per share (EPS) = Net earnings ÷ Average number of common shares outstanding

$2.42 = $7,197,000,000 ÷ Average shares

Average shares = $7,197,000,000 ÷ $2.42

Average shares = 2,973,966,942

Highlights to Remember

1 **Understand the role of adjustments in accrual accounting.** At the end of each accounting period, accountants must make adjustments so financial statements recognize revenues and expenses that do not result from explicit transactions.

2 **Make adjustments for the expiration or consumption of assets.** We record many costs initially as assets and recognize them as expenses as time passes. Examples are depreciation and the consumption of prepaid rent.

3 **Make adjustments for the recognition of unearned revenues.** Some companies receive payments for revenue before they earn the revenue. They initially recognize unearned revenue as a liability. As the revenue is earned, the company must reduce the liability and recognize the revenue. Examples are rental payments received in advance or prepaid magazine subscriptions. To clarify these first two types of adjustments, you might view them as mirror images by looking at both sides of the adjustment simultaneously. For example, (a) the expiration of unexpired costs (the tenant's rent expense) is accompanied by (b) the recognition of unearned revenues (the landlord's rent revenue).

4 **Make adjustments for the accrual of unrecorded expenses.** Companies may incur expenses before cash disbursements are made. Such expenses should be included in the income statement of the period when they are incurred, not in the period when they are paid. Examples are the accrual of wages or interest expense.

5 **Make adjustments for the accrual of unrecorded revenues.** Some revenues accrue before there is an explicit transaction leading to a cash flow. Interest revenue may be recorded before there is a legal obligation for payment. Similarly, utilities often provide services before a bill is issued. This results in the recognition of revenue and a receivable before the billing cycle sends out a request for payment. You can also view these final two types of adjustments as mirror images. For example, (a) the accrual of unrecorded expenses (a borrower's interest expense) is accompanied by (b) the accrual of unrecorded revenues (a lender's interest revenue).

6 **Describe the sequence of the final steps in the recording process and relate cash flows to adjusting entries.** The adjusting entries capture expense and revenue elements that either precede or follow the related cash flows. Entries for the expiration of unexpired costs and the recognition of unearned revenues follow the cash flows, whereas entries for the accrual of unrecorded expenses and the accrual of unrecorded revenues precede the cash flows. The adjusting entries provide a mechanism for capturing implicit transactions that do not necessarily generate documents that lead to them being recorded.

7 **Prepare a classified balance sheet and use it to assess short-term liquidity.** Classified balance sheets divide various items into subcategories. Assets and liabilities are separated into current and long-term subcategories that are useful in analysis. For example, the difference between current assets and current liabilities is called working capital. The current ratio, defined as current assets divided by current liabilities, is used to help assess liquidity. The quick or acid test ratio, defined as current assets minus inventory divided by current liabilities, is also useful.

8 **Prepare single- and multiple-step income statements.** Income statements may appear in single- or multiple-step format. Single-step statements group all revenue items together and all expense items together, whereas multiple-step statements calculate various subtotals such as gross profit and operating income. Regardless of the format, published income statements are highly condensed and summarized compared with reports used within an organization.

9 **Use ratios to assess profitability.** Analysts use income statement ratios to assess profitability. Among the most useful are gross margin percentage (or gross profit percentage), return on sales, return on common stockholders' equity, and return on assets.

Accounting Vocabulary

account format, p. 158
accrue, p. 140
acid test ratio, p. 156
adjusting entries, p. 140
adjustments, p. 140

classified balance sheet, p. 154
conservatism, p. 149
current assets, p. 155
current liabilities, p. 155
current ratio, p. 156

deferred revenue, p. 142
explicit transactions, p. 140
gross margin, p. 160
gross margin percentage,
    p. 162

Assignment Material

Questions

4-1 Give two examples of explicit transactions.

4-2 Give two examples of implicit transactions.

4-3 Give two synonyms for unearned revenue.

4-4 Distinguish between the accrual of wages and the payment of wages.

4-5 Give a synonym for income tax expense.

4-6 Explain why income tax expense is usually the final deduction on both single-step and multiple-step income statements.

4-7 "The accrual of previously unrecorded revenues is the mirror image of the accrual of previously unrecorded expenses." Explain by using an illustration.

4-8 What types of adjusting entries are made before the related cash flows? After the related cash flows?

4-9 Why are current assets and current liabilities grouped separately from long-term assets and long-term liabilities?

4-10 "Microsoft is much more profitable than IBM because its current ratio is three times larger than IBM's." Do you agree? Explain.

4-11 "Companies should always strive to avoid negative working capital." Do you agree? Explain.

4-12 Explain the difference between a single-step and a multiple-step income statement.

4-13 Why does interest expense appear below operating income on a multiple-step income statement?

4-14 The term "costs and expenses" is sometimes found instead of just "expenses" on the income statement. Would expenses be an adequate description? Why?

4-15 Name four popular ratios for measuring profitability, and indicate how to compute each of the four.

4-16 "Computer software companies are generally more profitable than grocery stores because their gross profit percentages are usually at least twice as large." Do you agree? Explain.

Critical Thinking Questions

4-17 Accounting Errors

You have discovered an error in which the tenant has "incorrectly" recorded as rent expense a $3,000 payment made on December 1 for rent for the months of December and January. As a young auditor you are not sure whether this must be corrected. You think it is a self-correcting error. What are the issues you should consider?

4-18 What Constitutes Revenue?

You have just started a program of selling gift certificates at your store. In the first month, you sold $5,000 worth and customers redeemed $1,250 of these certificates for merchandise. Your average gross profit percentage is 40 percent. What should you report as gift certificate revenue, and how much gross margin related to the gift certificates will appear in the income statement?

4-19 Operating versus Nonoperating Expenses

You have recently begun a new job as an internal auditor for a large retail clothing chain. The company prepares a multiple-step income statement. You discover that a material amount of salaries expense was erroneously classifed as a nonoperating expense. One of your coworkers argues that the error need not be corrected because the net income number is not affected by the misclassification. You disagree. Defend your position.

4-20 Accounting for Supplies

A company began business on July 1 and purchased $1,000 in supplies including paper, pens, paper clips, and so on. On December 31, as financial statements were being prepared, the accounting clerk asked how to treat the $1,000 that appeared in the supplies inventory account. What should this clerk do?

Exercises

4-21 True or False

Use T or F to indicate whether each of the following statements is true or false:

1. Retained earnings should be accounted for as a current liability item.
2. Deferred revenue will appear on the income statement.
3. Machinery used in the business should be recorded as a noncurrent asset item.
4. A company that employs cash-basis accounting cannot have a Prepaid Expense account on the balance sheet.
5. From a single balance sheet, you can find stockholders' equity for a period of time but not for a specific day.
6. It is not possible to determine changes in the financial condition of a business from a single balance sheet.

4-22 Tenant and Landlord

The Trucano Company, a retail hardware store, pays quarterly rent on its store at the beginning of each quarter. The rent per quarter is $18,000. The owner of the building in which the store is located is the Resing Corporation.

By using the balance sheet equation format, analyze the effects of the following on the tenant's and the landlord's financial position:

1. Trucano pays $18,000 rent on July 1.
2. Adjustment for July.
3. Adjustment for August.
4. Adjustment for September. Also prepare the journal entries for Trucano and Resing for September.

4-23 Customer and Airline

Kimberly Clark (KC), maker of Scott paper products, decided to hold a managers' meeting in Hawaii in February. To take advantage of special fares, KC purchased airline tickets in advance from Alaska Airlines at a total cost of $70,000. These were acquired on December 1 for cash.

By using the balance sheet equation format, analyze the impact of the December payment and the February travel on the financial position of both KC and Alaska. Also prepare journal entries for February for both companies.

4-24 Accrual of Wages

Consider the following calendar:

The Golden Rule Department Store commenced business on September 1. It is open every day except Sunday. Its total payroll for all employees is $8,000 per day. Payments are made each Tuesday for the preceding week's work through Saturday.

By using the balance sheet equation format, analyze the financial impact on the Golden Rule of the following:

1. Disbursements for wages on September 8, 15, 22, and 29.
2. Adjustment for wages on September 30. Also prepare the journal entry.

4-25 Accrued Vacation Pay

Delta Airlines had the following as a current liability on its balance sheet, December 31, 2002:

Accrued salaries and related benefits	$1,365,000,000

The "related benefits" include the liability for vacation pay. Under the accrual basis of accounting, vacation pay is ordinarily accrued throughout the year as workers are regularly paid. For example, suppose a Delta baggage handler earns $1,000 per week for 50 weeks and also gets paid $2,000 for 2 weeks' vacation each year. Accrual accounting requires that the obligation for the $2,000 be recognized as it is earned instead of when the payment is disbursed. Thus, in each of the 50 weeks, Delta would recognize a wage expense (or vacation pay expense) of $2,000/50 = $40.

1. Prepare Delta's weekly adjusting journal entry called for by the $40 example.
2. Prepare the entry for the $2,000 payment of vacation pay.

4-26 Placement of Interest in Income Statement

Two companies have the following balance sheets as of December 31, 20X8:

Jupiter Company

Cash	$ 50,000	Note payable*	$100,000
Other assets	150,000	Stockholders' equity	100,000
Total	$200,000	Total	$200,000

* 8% annual interest.

Saturn Company

Cash	$ 50,000	Stockholders' equity	$200,000
Other assets	150,000		
Total	$200,000		

In 20X9, each company had sales of $600,000 and expenses (excluding interest) of $525,000. Ignore income taxes. Jupiter had not repaid the $100,000 Note Payable as of December 31, 20X9. Neither company incurred any new interest-bearing debt in 20X9.

Did the two companies earn the same net income and the same operating income? Explain, showing computations of operating income and net income.

4-27 Effects of Interest on Lenders and Borrowers

Prudential lent Rodda Paint Company $1,500,000 on April 1, 20X5. The loan plus interest of 10 percent is payable on April 1, 20X6.

1. By using the balance sheet equation format, prepare an analysis of the impact of the transaction on both Prudential's and Rodda's financial position on April 1, 20X5. Show the summary adjustments on December 31, 20X5, for the period April 1 to December 31. Prepare an analysis of the transaction that takes place on April 1, 20X6, when Rodda repays its obligation.
2. Prepare adjusting journal entries for Prudential and Rodda on December 31, 20X5.
3. Prepare the entries that Prudential and Rodda would make on April 1, 20X6 when the loan and interest is repaid. These entries should include interest that accumulates between January 1, 20X6 and April 1, 20X6.

4-28 Identification of Transactions

Valenzuela Corporation's financial position is represented by the nine balances shown on the first line of the following schedule ($ in thousands). Assume that a single transaction took place for each of the following lines, and describe what you think happened, using one short sentence for each line.

	Cash	Accounts Receivable	Inven-tory	Equip-ment	Accounts Payable	Accrued Wages Payable	Unearned Rent Revenue	Paid-in Capital	Retained Earnings
Bal.	19	32	54	0	29	0	0	55	21
(1)	29	32	54	0	29	0	0	65	21
(2)	29	32	54	20	29	0	0	85	21
(3)	29	32	66	20	41	0	0	85	21
(4a)	29	47	66	20	41	0	0	85	36
(4b)	29	47	58	20	41	0	0	85	28
(5)	34	42	58	20	41	0	0	85	28
(6)	14	42	58	20	21	0	0	85	28
(7)	19	42	58	20	21	0	5	85	28
(8)	19	42	58	20	21	2	5	85	26
(9)	19	42	58	19	21	2	5	85	25
(10)	19	42	58	19	21	2	3	85	27

4-29 Effects on Balance Sheet Equation

Following is a list of effects of accounting transactions on the balance sheet equation: Assets = Liabilities + Stockholders' equity.

a. Increase in assets, decrease in liabilities.
b. Increase in assets, increase in liabilities.
c. Decrease in assets, decrease in stockholders' equity.
d. Decrease in assets, decrease in liabilities.
e. Increase in assets, decrease in assets.
f. Increase in liabilities, decrease in stockholders' equity.
g. Decrease in assets, increase in liabilities.
h. Decrease in liabilities, increase in stockholders' equity.
i. Increase in assets, increase in stockholders' equity.
j. None of these.

Required

Which of the relationships previously identified by letter defines the accounting effect of each of the following transactions?

1. The adjusting entry to recognize periodic depreciation.
2. The adjusting entry to record accrued salaries.
3. The adjusting entry to record accrued interest receivable.
4. The collection of interest previously accrued.
5. The settlement of an account payable by the issuance of a note payable.
6. The recognition of an expense that had been paid for previously. A "prepaid" account was increased on payment.
7. The earning of revenue previously collected. Unearned revenue was increased when collection was made in advance.

4-30 Effects of Errors in Adjustments

What will be the effect—understated (u), overstated (o), or no effect (n)—on the income of the present and future periods if the following errors were made. In all cases, assume that amounts carried over into 20X7 would affect 20X7 operations via the routine accounting entries of 20X7.

	Period	
	20X6	*20X7*
1. Revenue has been collected in advance, but earned amounts have not been recognized at the end of 20X6. Instead, all revenue was recognized as earned in 20X7.	_____	_____
2. Revenue for services rendered has been earned, but the unbilled amounts have not been recognized at the end of 20X6.	_____	_____

3. Accrued wages payable have not been recognized
   at the end of 20X6.   _____   _____
4. Prepaid items like rent have been paid (in late 20X6),
   but not adjusted at the end of 20X6. The payments
   have been debited to prepaid rent. They were
   transferred to expense in mid-20X7.   _____   _____

4-31 Effects of Adjustments and Corrections

Listed here are a series of accounts that are numbered for identification. All accounts needed to answer this question are included. The same account may be used in several answers.

1. Cash	16. Accrued wages and salaries payable
2. Accounts receivable	17. Accrued interest payable
3. Notes receivable	18. Unearned subscription revenue
4. Inventory	19. Capital stock
5. Accrued interest receivable	20. Sales
6. Accrued rent receivable	21. Fuel expense
7. Fuel on hand	22. Sales and wages
8. Prepaid rent	23. Insurance expense
9. Prepaid insurance	24. Repairs and maintenance expense
10. Prepaid repairs and maintenance	25. Rent expense
11. Land	26. Rent revenue
12. Buildings	27. Subscription revenue
13. Machinery and equipment	28. Interest revenue
14. Accounts payable	29. Interest expense
15. Notes payable	

Required

Prepare any necessary adjusting or correcting entries called for by the following situations, which were discovered at the end of the calendar year. With respect to each situation, assume that no entries have been made concerning the situation other than those specifically described (i.e., no monthly adjustments have been made during the year). Consider each situation separately. These transactions were not necessarily conducted by one firm. Amounts are in thousands of dollars.

a. A $3,000 purchase of equipment on December 30 was erroneously debited to Accounts Payable. The credit was correctly made to Cash.

b. A business made several purchases of fuel oil. Some purchases ($800) were debited to Fuel Expense, whereas others ($1,100) were charged to an asset account. An oil gauge revealed $400 of fuel on hand at the end of the year. There was no fuel on hand at the beginning of the year. What adjustment was necessary on December 31?

c. On April 1, a business took out a fire insurance policy. The policy was for 2 years, and the full premium of $1,600 was paid on April 1. The payment was debited to Insurance Expense on April 1. What adjustment was necessary on December 31?

d. On December 1, $6,000 was paid in advance to the landlord for 5 months rent. The tenant debited Prepaid Rent for $6,000 on December 1. What adjustment is necessary on December 31 on the tenant's books?

e. Machinery is repaired and maintained by an outside maintenance company on an annual fee basis, payable in advance. The $900 fee for the year beginning October 1 was paid on October 1 and charged to Repairs and Maintenance Expense. What adjustment is necessary on December 31?

f. On November 16, $800 of machinery was purchased, $200 cash was paid down, and a 90-day, 5 percent note payable was signed for the balance. The November 16 transaction was properly recorded. Prepare the adjustment for the interest.

g. A publisher sells subscriptions to magazines. Customers pay in advance. Receipts are originally credited to Unearned Subscription Revenue. On June 1, $24,000 in 1-year subscriptions were collected and recorded. What adjustment was necessary on December 31?

h. On December 30, certain merchandise inventory was purchased for $1,000 on open account. The bookkeeper debited Machinery and Equipment and credited Accounts Payable for $1,000. Prepare a correcting entry.

i. A 120-day, 8 percent, $20,000 cash loan was made to a customer on November 1. The November 1 transaction was recorded correctly. What adjustment is necessary on December 31?

4-32 Working Capital and Current Ratio

Using the Columbia Sportswear balance sheet in Exhibit 4-6 on page 158, compute Columbia's working capital, current ratio, and quick ratio for 2003. Compute the quick ratio as (current assets − inventories) ÷ current liabilities.

4-33 Profitability Ratios

The Nestlé Group, the Swiss chocolate company, sells many other food items in addition to various types of chocolates. Sales in 2001 were SF 89,160 million (where SF means Swiss francs), cost of goods sold was SF 38,521 million, net income was SF 7,564 million, average common stockholders' equity was SF 34,236 million, and average total assets were SF 90,569 million.

Compute Nestlé's gross profit percentage, return on sales, return on average common stockholders' equity, and return on average total assets.

4-34 Impact of Adjusting Entries on Ratios

Exercise 4-31 asked you to write adjusting/correcting entries for transactions (a) through (i). In this problem, consider the effect on the current ratio and return on sales if the adjusting/correcting entries were not made. Indicate whether the failure to record the adjusting/correcting entry will result in these ratios being understated (u), overstated (o), or no effect (n). If additional information is necessary before you can provide the correct response, indicate with (i). Prior to the adjusting entry, the current ratio exceeds 1.0 and the company operated at a profit.

	Current Ratio	Return on Sales
(a)	_____	_____
(b)	_____	_____
(c)	_____	_____
(d)	_____	_____
(e)	_____	_____
(f)	_____	_____
(g)	_____	_____
(h)	_____	_____
(i)	_____	_____

Problems

4-35 Adjusting Entries

(Alternates are 4-37 through 4-39.) Amber Marshall, certified public accountant, had the following transactions (among others) during 20X8:

a. For accurate measurement of performance and position, Marshall uses the accrual basis of accounting. On August 1, she acquired office supplies for $2,000. Office Supplies Inventory was increased, and Cash was decreased by $2,000 on Marshall's books. On December 31, her inventory of office supplies was $900.

b. On September 1, a client gave Marshall a retainer fee of $36,000 cash for monthly services to be rendered over the following 12 months. Marshall increased Cash and Unearned Fee Revenue.

c. Marshall accepted an $8,000 note receivable from a client on October 1 for tax services. The note plus interest of 12 percent per year was due in 6 months. Marshall increased Note Receivable and Fee Revenue by $8,000 on October 1.

d. As of December 31, Marshall had not recorded $600 of unpaid wages earned by her secretary during late December.

For the year ended December 31, 20X8, prepare all adjustments called for by the preceding transactions. Assume that appropriate entries were routinely made for the explicit transactions described earlier. However, no adjustments have been made before December 31. For each adjustment, prepare an analysis in the same format used when the adjustment process was explained in the chapter (i.e., the balance sheet equation format). Also prepare the adjusting journal entry.

4-36 Multiple-Step Income Statement

(Alternates are 4-40 & 4-51.) From the following data, prepare a multiple-step income statement for the Curran Company for the fiscal year ended May 31, 20X6 ($ in thousands except for percentage).

Sales	$ 1,800	Cost of goods sold	$ 1,000
Interest expense	138	Depreciation expense	60
Utilities expense	110	Rent revenue	20
Interest revenue	28	Wage expense	400
Income tax rate	40%		

4-37 Four Major Adjustments

(Alternates are 4-35, 4-38, and 4-39) Leslie Baker, an attorney, had the following transactions (among others) during 20X8, her initial year in law practice:

a. On August 1, Baker leased office space for 1 year. The landlord (lessor) insisted on full payment in advance. Prepaid Rent was increased and Cash was decreased by $24,000 on Baker's books. Similarly, the landlord increased Cash and increased Unearned Rent Revenue.

b. On October 1, Baker received a retainer of $12,000 cash for services to be rendered to her client, a local trucking company, over the succeeding 12 months. Baker increased Cash and Unearned Fee Revenue. The trucking company increased Prepaid Expenses and decreased Cash.

c. As of December 31, Baker had not recorded $500 of unpaid wages earned by her secretary during late December.

d. During November and December, Baker rendered services to another client, a utility company. She had intended to bill the company for $5,400 services through December 31, but failed to do so.

Required

1. For the year ended December 31, 20X8, prepare all adjustments called for by the preceding transactions. Assume that appropriate entries were routinely made for the explicit transactions described earlier. However, no adjustments have been made before December 31. For each adjustment, prepare an analysis in the same format used when the adjustment process was explained in the chapter (i.e., the balance sheet equation format). Prepare two adjustments for each transaction, one for Baker and one for the other party to the transaction. In part c, assume that the secretary uses the accrual basis for her entity.

2. For each transaction, prepare the journal entries for Leslie Baker and the other entities involved.

4-38 Four Major Adjustments

(Alternates are 4-35, 4-37, and 4-39). The Goodyear Tire & Rubber Company included the following items in its December 31, 2002 balance sheet ($ in millions):

Prepaid expenses (a current asset)	$ 448.1
United States and foreign taxes (a current liability)	473.2

1. Analyze the impact of the following transactions on the financial position of Goodyear as of January 31, 2003. Prepare your analysis in the same format used when the adjustment process was explained in the chapter. Also show adjusting journal entries.

a. On January 31, an adjustment of $5 million was made for the rental of various retail outlets that had originally increased Prepaid Expenses but had expired.

b. During December 2002, Goodyear sold tires for $7 million cash to U-Haul, but delivery was not made until January 28, 2003. Unearned Revenue had been increased in December. No other adjustments had been made since then. Prepare the adjustment on January 31.

c. Goodyear had loaned cash to several of its independent retail dealers. As of January 31, the dealers owed $6 million of interest that had been unrecorded.

d. On January 31, Goodyear increased its accrual of federal income taxes by $68 million.

2. Compute the ending balances on January 31, 2003 in prepaid expenses and in U.S. and foreign taxes.

4-39 Four Major Adjustments

(Alternates are 4-35, 4-37, and 4-38.) Alaska Airlines showed the following items in its balance sheet as of December 31, 2002, the end of the fiscal year ($ in millions):

Inventories and supplies	$ 71.9
Prepaid expenses and other current assets	82.0
Air traffic liability	211.61
Accrued wages, vacation, and payroll taxes	87.4

A footnote stated: "Passenger revenue is recognized when the passenger travels. Tickets sold but not yet used are reported as Air Traffic Liability."

The 2002 income statement included ($ in millions):

Passenger revenues	$2,037.7
Wages and benefits expense	858.1

1. Analyze the impact of the following assumed 2003 transactions on the financial position of Alaska. Prepare your analysis in the same format used when the adjustment process was explained in the chapter. Also show adjusting journal entries.
   a. Rented sales offices for 1 year, beginning July 1, 2003, for $6 million cash.
   b. On December 31, 2003, an adjustment was made for the rent in requirement a.
   c. Sold 20 charter flights to Apple Computer for $100,000 each. Cash of $2 million was received in advance on November 20, 2003. The flights were for transporting marketing personnel to business conventions.
   d. As the financial statements were being prepared on December 31, 2003, accountants for both Alaska and Apple Computer independently noted that the first 10 charter flights had occurred in December. The rest will occur in early 2004. An adjustment was made on December 31.
   e. Alaska loaned $30 million to Boeing. Interest of $1.6 million was accrued on December 31.
   f. Additional wages of $30 million were accrued on December 31.
2. At year-end, in addition to liabilities for future charter flights from the transactions described in 1.c and 1.d above, the company had $236 million of collections in advance for flights scheduled in 2004. Compute the proper year-end balance in the Air Traffic Liability account as of December 31, 2003.

4-40 Coldwater Creek Financial Statements

(Alternates are 4-36 and 4-51.) Coldwater Creek is a retailer of women's apparel, jewelry, footwear, gift items, and home merchandise headquartered in Sandpoint, Idaho. Some actual financial data and nomenclature from its February 1, 2003 annual report are given below ($ in thousands). Coldwater Creek does not pay dividends to shareholders.

Net sales	$473,172	Other income, net	$ 170
Gross profit	188,766	Retained earnings	
Income from operations	15,436	Beginning of year	49,873
Selling, general, and		End of year	?
administrative expenses	?	Provision for income taxes	6,249
Cost of sales	?		

1. Compute the missing values. Prepare a combined multiple-step statement of income and retained earnings for the year ended February 1, 2003.
2. Compute the percentage of gross profit on sales and the percentage of net income on sales.
3. The average common stockholders' equity for the year was $100,445 thousand. What was the return on average common stockholders' equity?

4-41 Accounting for Dues

(Alternate is 4-42.) The Stone Beach Golf Club provided the following data from its comparative balance sheets:

	December 31	
	20X8	**20X7**
Dues receivable	$90,000	$75,000
Unearned dues revenue	—	$30,000

The income statement for 20X8, which was prepared on the accrual basis, showed Dues Revenue Earned of $680,000. No dues were collected in advance during 20X8.

Prepare journal entries and post to T-accounts for the following:

1. Earning of dues collected in advance.
2. Billing of dues revenue during 20X8.
3. Collection of dues receivable in 20X8.

4-42 Accounting for Subscriptions

(Alternate is 4-41.) A French magazine company collects subscriptions in advance of delivery of its magazines. However, many magazines are delivered to magazine distributors (for newsstand sales), and these distributors are billed and pay later. The subscription revenue earned for the month of March on the accrual basis was €200,000 (€ refers to the Euro). Other pertinent data were as follows:

	March	
	31	**1**
Unearned subscription revenue	€190,000	€140,000
Accounts receivable	7,000	9,000

Prepare journal entries and post to T-accounts for the following:

1. Collections of unearned subscription revenue of €140,000 prior to March 1.
2. Billing of accounts receivable (a) of €9,000 prior to March 1, and (b) of €80,000 during March (credit Revenue Earned).
3. Collections of cash during March and any other entries that are indicated by the given data.

4-43 Financial Statements and Adjustments

Rockwell Wholesalers, Inc., has just completed its fourth year of business, 20X3. A set of financial statements was prepared by the principal stockholder's eldest child, a college student who is beginning the third week of an accounting course. Following is a list (in no systematic order) of the items appearing in the student's balance sheet, income statement, and statement of retained earnings:

Accounts receivable	$183,100	Advertising expense	$ 98,300
Note receivable	36,000	Cost of goods sold	590,000
Merchandise inventory	201,900	Unearned rent revenue	4,800
Cash	99,300	Insurance expense	2,500
Paid-in capital	620,000	Unexpired insurance	2,300
Building	300,000	Accounts payable	52,500
Accumulated depreciation,		Interest expense	600
building	20,000	Telephone expense	2,900
Land	169,200	Notes payable	20,000
Sales	936,800	Net income	110,500
Salary expense	124,300	Miscellaneous expense	3,400
Retained earnings		Maintenance expense	4,300
December 31, 20X2	164,000		
December 31, 20X3	274,500		

Assume that the statements in which these items appear are current and complete, except for the following matters not taken into consideration by the student:

a. Salaries of $5,200 have been earned by employees for the last half of December 20X3. Payment by the company will be made on the next payday, January 2, 20X4.
b. Interest at 10 percent per annum on the Note receivable has accrued for 2 months and is expected to be collected by the company when the Note is due on January 31, 20X4.
c. Part of the building owned by the company was rented to a tenant on November 1, 20X3, for 6 months, payable in advance. This rent was collected in cash and is represented by the item labeled Unearned Rent Revenue.
d. Depreciation on the building for 20X3 is $6,100.

e. Cash dividends of $60,000 were declared in December 20X3, payable in January 20X4.

f. Income tax at 40 percent applies to 20X3, all of which is to be paid in the early part of 20X4.

Required

Prepare the following corrected financial statements:

1. Multiple-step income statement for the year ended December 31, 20X3.
2. Statement of retained earnings for the year ended December 31, 20X3.
3. Classified balance sheet at December 31, 20X3. (Show appropriate support for the dollar amounts you compute.)

4-44 Mirror Side of Adjustments

Problem 4-35 described some adjustments made by Amber Marshall, CPA. Prepare the necessary adjustment as it would be made by the client in transactions (b) and (c) and by the secretary in transaction (d). For our purposes, assume that the secretary keeps personal books on the accrual basis.

4-45 Mirror Side of Adjustments

Problem 4-38 described some adjustments made by Goodyear Tire & Rubber Company. Prepare the necessary adjustment as it would be made by (a) landlords, (b) U-Haul, (c) retail dealers, and (d) U.S. and foreign governments. Assume that all use accrual accounting.

4-46 Mirror Side of Adjustments

Problem 4-39 described some adjustments made by Alaska Airlines. The adjustments are lettered (a) through (f). Repeat the requirements for each adjustment as it would be made by the other party in the transaction. Specifically, (a) and (b) landlord, (c) and (d) Apple Computer, (e) Boeing, and (f) employees. Assume that all use accrual accounting.

4-47 Journal Entries and Posting

Nike, Inc., has many well-known products, including footwear. The company's balance sheet included ($ in millions):

	May 31	
	2003	**2002**
Prepaid expenses	266.2	260.5
Income taxes payable	107.2	83.0

Suppose that during the fiscal year ended May 31, 2003, $180 million cash was disbursed and charged to Prepaid Expenses. Similarly, $287.9 million was disbursed for income taxes and charged to Income Taxes Payable.

1. Assume that the Prepaid Expenses account relates to outlays for miscellaneous operating expenses, for example, supplies, insurance, and short-term rentals. Prepare summary journal entries for (a) the disbursements and (b) the expenses for fiscal 2003.
2. Assume that there were no other accounts related to income taxes. Prepare summary journal entries for (a) the disbursements and (b) the expenses for fiscal 2003.

4-48 Advance Service Contracts

Diebold, Incorporated, a manufacturer of automated teller machines, showed the following current liability on the balance sheet on December 31, 2002 ($ amounts in thousands):

	December 31	
	2002	**2001**
Deferred income	$86,281	$81,011

A footnote to the financial statements stated: "Deferred income is recognized for customer service billings in advance of the period in which the service will be performed and is recognized in income on a straight-line basis over the contract period."

1. Prepare summary journal entries for the creation in 2001, and subsequent earning in 2002, of the deferred income of $81,011. Use the following accounts: Accounts Receivable, Deferred Income, and Income from Advance Billings.

2. A 1-year job contract was billed to Keystone Bank on January 1, 2002, for $36,000. Work began on January 2. The full amount was collected on February 15. Prepare all pertinent journal entries through February 28, 2002. ("Straight-line" means an equal amount per month.)

4-49 Journal Entries and Adjustments

NW Natural is a public utility in Oregon. An annual report included the following footnote: "Utility revenue from gas sale and transportation is recognized when the gas is delivered to and received by the customer. Estimated revenues are accrued for gas deliveries not billed to customers from meter reading dates to month end (unbilled revenue) and are reversed the following month when actual billings occur." The income statements showed ($ in thousands):

For year ended December 31

	2003	2002
Gross operating revenues	$611,256	$641,376
Operating income (loss)	102,272	116,258

The balance sheets showed as part of current assets ($ in thousands):

	December 31	
	2003	2002
Accounts receivable	$52,213	$46,936
Accrued unbilled revenues	59,109	44,069

Prepare the adjusting journal entry for (a) the unbilled revenues at the end of 2003 and (b) the eventual billing and collection of the unbilled revenues in 2004. Ignore income taxes.

4-50 Classified Balance Sheet, Current Ratio and Quick Ratio

Gateway is a producer of personal computers. The company's balance sheet for December 31, 2002 (slightly modified) contained the following items ($ in thousands):

Property and equipment, net	$ 481,011
Accrued compensation and royalties	56,684
Cash & cash equivalents	465,603
Noncurrent assets	49,732
Other noncurrent liabilities	127,118
Inventories	88,761
Other current liabilities	240,315
Other current assets	602,073
Accounts payable	278,609
Marketable securities	601,118
Accounts receivable	?
Intangibles, net	23,292
Accrued liabilities	364,741
Stockholders' equity	1,441,940

1. Prepare a December 31, 2002 classified balance sheet for Gateway. Include the correct amount for accounts receivable.
2. Compute the company's working capital, current ratio and quick ratio. Compute the quick ratio as (current assets − inventory) ÷ current liabilities.
3. Comment on the company's current and quick ratios. In 2001, the current ratio was 1.85 and the quick ratio was 1.75.
4. During 2002, Gateway increased its marketable securities by $166,063. Suppose the company had not increased its marketable securities but had instead increased its long-term investments (classified as Noncurrent Assets) by $166,063. How would this have affected Gateway's current ratio? How would it have affected the company's liquidity?

4-51 Multiple-Step Income Statement

(Alternates are 4-36 and 4-40.)Intel Corporation is one of the largest companies in the United States. Its annual report for the year ended December 27, 2003 contained the following data and actual terms ($ in millions):

Cost of sales	$13,047	Gross margin	$17,094
Research & development	4,360	Interest and other income	(192)
Marketing, general and		Provision for taxes	1,801
administrative	4,278	Purchased in-process R&D	5
Impairment of goodwill	617	Losses on equity securities,	
Amortization and impairment		net	283
of intangibles	301	Sales	?

Prepare a multiple-step statement of income. Include the correct amount for Sales.

4-52 Single-Step Income Statement

Harley-Davidson is the parent company of Harley-Davidson Motor, Buell Motorcycle, and Harley-Davidson Financial Services. It is most well known for producing heavyweight, custom, and touring motorcycles as well as parts, accessories, and apparel. Harley-Davidson Financial Services provides wholesale and retail financing and insurance programs to dealers and customers. A recent Harley-Davidson annual report contained the following items ($ in thousands) for the year ending December 31, 2003:

Other expense, net	$ 6,317	Selling, administrative and	
Cost of goods sold	2,958,708	engineering expense	$ 684,175
Financial services income	279,459	Interest income, net	23,088
Retained earnings at end		Provision for income taxes	405,107
of year	3,074,037	Cash dividends declared	58,986
Financial services expense	111,586	Net sales revenue	4,624,274

1. Prepare a combined single-step statement of income and retained earnings for the year.
2. Compute the percentage of gross profit on sales and the percentage of net income on sales.
3. The average stockholders' equity for the year was $2,595,303. What was the percentage of net income on average stockholders' equity

4-53 Retail Company Financial Statements

The Home Depot, Incorporated is one of the world's largest retailers. The annual report for the year ended February 2, 2003 included the data (slightly modified) shown below ($ in millions). Unless otherwise specified, the balance sheet amounts are the balances as of February 2, 2003.

Sales	$58,247	Interest expense	$ 37
Cash dividends declared	492	Long-term debt	1,321
Merchandise inventories	8,338	Cash	2,188
Paid-in capital	3,831	Accrued salaries payable	809
Other current assets	254	Short-term investments	65
Retained earnings		Provision for income taxes	2,208
Beginning of year	12,799	Property and equipment, net	17,168
End of year	15,971	Other noncurrent assets	926
Accounts payable	4,560	Selling, general & admin. expenses	12,278
Cost of merchandise sold	40,139	Other noncurrent liabilities	853
Other current liabilities	1,441	Other income	79
Deferred revenue	998	Income taxes payable	227
Receivables	1,072		

1. Prepare a combined multiple-step statement of income and retained earnings.
2. Prepare a classified balance sheet.

3. The average common stockholders' equity for the year was $18,942 million. What was the percentage of net income to average common stockholders' equity?
4. The average total assets for the year were $28,203 million. What was the percentage of net income to average total assets?
5. Compute (a) gross profit percentage and (b) percentage of net income to sales.

4-54 Preparation of Financial Statements from Trial Balance

Procter & Gamble is one of the largest consumer products companies in America. The (slightly modified) trial balance as of June 30, 2003 appears here:

Procter & Gamble Company
Trial balance as of June 30, 2003 ($ in millions)

	Debits	Credits
Cash and cash equivalents	$ 5,912	
Investment securities	300	
Receivables	3,038	
Inventories	3,640	
Deferred income taxes	843	
Prepaid expenses	1,487	
Property, plant, and equipment, at cost	23,542	
Accumulated depreciation, property, plant, and equipment		$10,438
Trademarks and other intangibles, net	2,375	
Goodwill	11,132	
Other noncurrent assets	1,875	
Debt due within 1 year		2,172
Accounts payable		2,795
Accrued payroll and other liabilities		5,512
Taxes payable		1,879
Long-term debt		11,475
Deferred income tax		1,396
Other noncurrent liabilities		2,291
Preferred stock		1,580
Common stock, $1 par value		1,297
Retained earnings (June 30, 2002)		11,980
Additional paid-in capital		2,931
Accumulated other comprehensive income*	2,006	
Reserve for ESOP debt retirement*	1,308	
Net sales		43,377
Cost of goods sold	22,141	
Selling, administrative, and general expenses	13,383	
Interest expense	561	
Other nonoperating income, net		238
Income taxes	2,344	
Cash dividends declared	3,474	
Total	$99,361	$99,361

*Part of stockholders' equity.

1. Prepare Proctor & Gamble's income statement for the year ended June 30, 2003, using a multiple-step format.
2. Prepare Proctor & Gamble's income statement for the year ended June 30, 2003, using a single-step format. Which format for the income statement is more informative? Why?
3. Prepare Proctor & Gamble's classified balance sheet as of June 30, 2003.

4-55 Adjusting Entries and Ethics

By definition, adjusting entries are not triggered by an explicit event. Therefore, accountants must initiate adjusting entries. For each of the following adjusting entries, discuss a potential unethical behavior that an accountant or manager might undertake:

   a. Recognition of expenses from the prepaid supplies account.
   b. Recognition of revenue from the unearned revenue account.
   c. Accrual of interest payable.
   d. Accrual of fees receivable.

Collaborative Learning Exercise

4-56 Implicit Transactions

Form groups of from three to six "players." Each group should have a die and a paper (or board) with four columns labeled:

1. Expiration of unexpired costs.
2. Recognition of unearned revenues.
3. Accrual of unrecorded expenses.
4. Accrual of unrecorded revenues.

The players should select an order in which they want to play. Then, the first player rolls the die. If this player rolls a 5 or 6, the die passes to the next player. If the second player rolls a 1, 2, 3, or 4, this person must, within 20 seconds, name an example of a transaction that fits in the corresponding category; for example, if a 2 is rolled, the player must give an example of recognition of unearned revenues. Each time a correct example is given, the player receives one point. If someone doubts the correctness of a given example, the player can challenge it. If the remaining players unanimously agree that the example is incorrect, the challenger gets a point and the player giving the example does not get a point for a correct example and is out of the game. If the remaining players do not unanimously agree that the answer is incorrect, the challenger loses a point and the player giving the example gets a point for a correct example. If a player fails to give an example within the time limit or gives an incorrect example, this person is out of the game (except for voting when an example is challenged), and the remaining players continue until everyone has failed to give a correct example within the time limit. Each correct answer should be listed under the appropriate column. The player with the most points is the group winner.

    When all groups have finished a round of play, a second level of play can begin. The groups can get together and list all examples for each of the four categories by group. Discussion can establish the correctness of each entry; the faculty member or an appointed discussion leader will be the final arbitrator of the correctness of each entry. Each group gets one point for each correct example and loses one point for each incorrect entry. The group with the most points is the overall winner.

Analyzing and Interpreting Financial Statements

4-57 Financial Statement Research

Select any two companies.

1. For each company, determine the amount of working capital and the current ratio.
2. Compare the current ratios. Which company has the larger ratio, and what do the ratios tell you about the liquidity of the companies?
3. Compute the gross margin percentage, the return on sales, and the return on common stockholders' equity.
4. Compare the profitability of the two companies.

4-58 Analyzing Starbucks' Financial Statements

This problem develops skills in preparing adjusting journal entries. Refer to the financial statements of Starbucks (Appendix A at the end of the book). Note the following balance sheet items:

	September 28, 2003	September 29, 2002
Prepaid expenses and other current assets	$ 55,173,000	$ 42,351,000
Other accrued expenses	101,800,000	72,289,000

Suppose that during the year ended September 28, 2003, $31,200,000 cash was disbursed and charged to Prepaid Expenses and $61,600,000 of accrued liabilities were paid in cash.

1. Assume that the Prepaid Expenses account relates to outlays for miscellaneous operating expenses, for example, supplies, insurance, and short-term rentals. Prepare summary journal

entries for (a) the disbursements and (b) the expenses (for our purposes, debit Operating Expenses) for the year ended September 28, 2003. Post the entries to the T-accounts.

2. Prepare summary journal entries for (a) the disbursements and (b) the expenses related to the accrued liabilities for the year ended September 28, 2003. (For our purposes, debit Operating Expenses.) Post the entries to the T-accounts.

4-59 Analyzing Financial Statements Using the Internet

Go to http://www.columbiasportswear.com to find Columbia Sportswear's home page. Select Who We Are then Investor Info from the menu. Then select Annual Reports and click on the most recent annual report.

Answer the following questions:

1. Name one item on Columbia Sportswear's balance sheet that most likely represents unexpired (prepaid) costs. Name one item that most likely represents the accrual of unrecorded expenses.
2. Does Columbia Sportswear prepare a single- or multiple-step income statement? How can you tell?
3. Determine Columbia Sportswear's gross profit percentage for the past 2 years. Is the change favorable? What does Columbia Sportswear's management say about the change? (Hint: Look in Management's Discussion and Analysis.) If nothing was said, why do you think management chose not to comment? How do you think management determines the reason that gross profit changed, given the condensed nature of the income statement?
4. Calculate Columbia Sportswear's current ratio for the past 2 years. Did this ratio improve or decline? Does management offer any comment about any particular problems that could have affected this ratio? Should management be concerned about changes in the current ratio?
5. Where can you find evidence in Columbia Sportswear's annual report that the financial statements were prepared using GAAP?

Statement of Cash Flows

CHAPTER 5

LEARNING OBJECTIVES

After studying this chapter, you should be able to:

1. Identify the purposes of the statement of cash flows.

2. Classify activities affecting cash as operating, investing, or financing activities.

3. Compute and interpret cash flows from financing activities.

4. Compute and interpret cash flows from investing activities.

5. Use the direct method to calculate cash flows from operations.

6. Use the indirect method to explain the difference between net income and net cash provided by (used for) operating activities.

7. Understand why we add depreciation to net income when using the indirect method for computing cash flow from operating activities.

8. Show how the balance sheet equation provides a conceptual framework for the statement of cash flows.

If you watched nothing but commercials on television, you would think the only thing **Nike** spends its money on is getting athletes to endorse the company's products. We are all familiar with Nike's first endorsement—Michael Jordan of Chicago Bulls basketball fame—but there have been countless others. Runners, hockey players, and college and professional football players have all appeared in Nike's commercials or signed other endorsement deals, not to mention swimmers, tennis players, and just about any other sports figure imaginable. Golfer Tiger Woods' deal was for tens of millions of dollars over several years. In 2002, Nike made a major commitment to the World Cup of soccer, internally called Football Zero Two or FZT. The company set out to create "a new generation of performance product that would take Nike to a new level of play." The ultimate result of this strategy occurred 49 minutes into the World Cup game between Brazil and Turkey. The World Cup MVP, Renaldo, scored the winning goal to send Brazil to the finals. He did it wearing a special edition of the Nike Mercurial Vapor soccer shoe. When he saw the shoe for the first time a couple days before the game, Renaldo decided he had to have a pair. Nike supplied the shoes, Renaldo wore them, and the rest is history.

Of course, the company behind the famous Nike "swoosh" needs cash to make the endorsements happen. A quick look at the company's balance sheet tells you Nike has plenty—more than $634 million at last count. However, if you truly want to see where Nike spends its cash, you should pay attention to one specific financial report—the statement of cash flows.

Nike reports the cash provided or used by the company for operating, investing, and financing activities, giving you a complete picture of how Nike generated

Athletes and nonathletes around the world recognize the Nike "swoosh," shown here on both the jersey and the stockings. Nike pays much cash for athlete endorsements and other promotional activities, in addition to paying cash to buy and sell shoes and other apparel. Tracing the flow of cash through a company is an important part of understanding its financial position and prospects. We learn about the statement of cash flows, the financial report that focuses on cash, in this chapter.

On July 26, 2003, Cisco had $8.5 billion in cash and short-term investments, about 23% of its total assets of about $37 billion. On December 31, 2002, Ford Motor Company had about $12 billion in cash and another $18 billion in highly liquid marketable securities, more than 10% of total assets. In managing our personal lives, we need to do cash planning so we will have the money we need when we need it, and the corporate world is no different. However, these amounts seem to far exceed normal needs for liquidity. Investors might reasonably ask why companies commit such significant asset levels to such low-return investments as cash and U.S. Treasury notes and bonds.

There are conventional answers. Cash and cash equivalents provide flexibility. Merger transactions, something both Cisco and Ford do regularly, often require cash. In cyclical industries, such as autos, cash helps you through the money-losing years when car and truck sales drop sharply. In unstable industries such as hardware for computer networks, cash can prevent financial insolvency when sales drop. You might describe the cash levels as precautions against bad economic times, as the minimum level to cover ongoing transactions, or as the speculative amounts needed to fund major unspecified investments.

Even in the lean times of 2000 through 2003, Cisco generated cash from operations averaging more than $6 billion each year. Because of the slow demand for its products, Cisco did not have investment uses for all the cash being generated. Cisco does not pay dividends, so it had a choice of accumulating cash, starting to pay dividends, or buying back stock. It chose the first and last of the options.

Ford's cash and marketable securities grew by about $12 billion in 2002, mainly because it generated $15 billion more cash from operations than it used in investing activities. Ford's management faced the question of whether this was too much cash or whether it provided an appropriate safety net. Apparently, they felt a need for a larger safety net.

Although Cisco and Ford have lived with high cash levels, other companies are devoted to operating with as little cash as possible. The CFO of Verizon says, "I hate cash on hand. It is anathema to me." Firms that take such strategies typically use short-term debt to manage ups and downs in the cash flow cycle. They set up collection and cash management processes so they can pay down any existing debt whenever cash balances are above the minimum.

Sources: Cisco Systems, Inc. 2003 Annual Report; Ford Motor Company, 2002 Annual Report.

the money and where it has gone. For example, in recent years, operations such as selling merchandise have provided millions in cash for Nike ($917 million in 2003). In contrast, investing and financing activities have used cash, primarily because Nike invested heavily in property, plant, and equipment and spent millions of dollars to buy back shares of its own stock. The net result of these activities in 2003 was an increase in cash of $58.5 million over the previous year's balance. ∎

The primary importance of cash makes the statement of cash flows one of the central financial statements. It explains the changes that occur in the firm's cash balance during the year. The statement of cash flows allows both investors and managers to keep their fingers on the pulse of any company's lifeblood—cash. Attitudes toward holding cash vary, as indicated in the Business First box above. Some managers and investors like the safety of large stores of cash, whereas others minimize cash holdings because they provide only small returns to the company.

Companies that lose too much cash become critically ill. The business equivalent of critical illness is bankruptcy. Bankruptcy is loosely used to refer to companies that are unable to meet their obligations. It also refers to firms that seek court protection from their debts under federal law. Court protection allows a firm to delay paying certain obligations while it negotiates with its creditors to reorganize its business and settle its debts. Enron and United Airlines are recent examples of large and seemingly successful companies that entered bankruptcy and either liquidated entirely or reorganized large portions of their business. We observed bankruptcies among many large companies in the economic downturn of 2001–2002.

Although managers and investors benefit from watching cash flows, until recently many countries did not require a statement of cash flows. For example, India did not require such a statement until 2001. Today, both the IASB and FASB require a statement of cash flows. In this chapter, we examine cash flow statements and explain how managers and investors use the information in such statements.

Overview of Statement of Cash Flows

The **statement of cash flows** (or **cash flow statement**) reports the cash receipts and cash payments of an entity during a particular period and classifies them as financing, investing, and operating flows. Like the income statement, it summarizes activities over a span of time, so we label it with the exact period covered. Furthermore, like the income statement, which shows details about how operating activities produce changes in retained earnings, the statement of cash flows details the changes in one balance sheet account, the cash account.

statement of cash flows (cash flow statement)
One of the basic financial statements that reports the cash receipts and cash payments of an entity during a particular period and classifies them as financing, investing, and operating flows.

Purposes of Cash Flow Statement

Why do managers and investors use a statement of cash flows?

1. It helps them understand the relationship of net income to changes in cash balances. Cash balances can decline despite positive net income and vice versa.
2. It reports past cash flows as an aid to:
   a. Predicting future cash flows.
   b. Evaluating how management generates and uses cash.
   c. Determining a company's ability to pay interest, dividends, and debts when they are due.
3. It identifies specific increases and decreases in a firm's productive assets.

OBJECTIVE 1

Identify the purposes of the statement of cash flows.

Balance sheets show the status of a company at a single point in time. In contrast, statements of cash flows and income statements show the performance of a company over a period of time. Both explain why the balance sheet items have changed. As the following diagram shows, these statements thus link the balance sheets in consecutive periods:

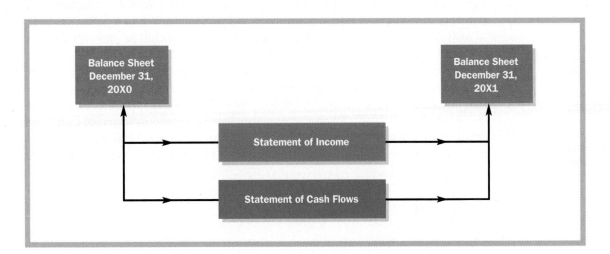

The statement of cash flows explains where cash came from during a period and where it went. Let's first be clear on what we mean by cash. Our use of the term refers not

cash equivalents
Highly liquid short-term investments that a company can easily and quickly convert into cash, such as money market funds and Treasury bills.

Classify activities affecting cash as operating, investing, or financing activities.

operating decisions
Decisions that are concerned with the major day-to-day activities that generate revenues and expenses.

cash flows from operating activities
The first major section of the cash flow statement. It helps users evaluate the cash impact of management's operating decisions.

operating activities
Transactions that affect the purchase, processing, and selling of a company's products and services.

financing decisions
Decisions concerned with whether to get cash or repay debt.

cash flows from financing activities
The section of the statement of cash flows that helps users understand management's financing decisions.

financing activities
A company's transactions that obtain resources as a borrower or issuer of securities or repay creditors and owners.

only to the currency and bank accounts that we all call cash, but also to cash equivalents. **Cash equivalents** are highly liquid short-term investments that a company can easily and quickly convert into cash, such as money market funds and Treasury bills. Hereafter, when we refer to cash, we mean both cash and cash equivalents.

Typical Activities Affecting Cash

Managers affect cash by three types of decisions: operating, financing, and investing decisions. **Operating decisions** are concerned with the major day-to-day activities that generate revenues and expenses. To evaluate the cash impact of such decisions, we can use the first major section of the statement of cash flows labeled **cash flows from operating activities. Operating activities** are transactions that affect the purchase, processing, and selling of a company's products and services. For example, making sales and collecting accounts receivable are both operating activities. Recording an expense for cost of goods sold, purchasing inventory, and paying accounts payable are also operating activities. The thing all these transactions have in common is that they are an integral part of the major income-generating activities of the company.

Managers make **financing decisions** when they decide whether to get cash or repay debt. For example, financial managers decide whether to borrow money from a bank or to repay previous borrowings. They also decide whether to issue additional capital stock or to buy back previously issued stock. To understand financing decisions, we use the section of the statement of cash flows labeled **cash flows from financing activities. Financing activities** are a company's transactions that obtain resources as a borrower or issuer of securities or repay creditors and owners.

After raising capital, managers must decide how to invest the capital raised. These **investing decisions** include the choices to (1) acquire or dispose of plant, property, equipment, and other long-term productive assets, and (2) provide or collect cash as a lender or as an owner of securities. The statement of cash flows covers the results of investing decisions in a section labeled **cash flows from investing activities. Investing activities** are transactions that acquire or dispose of long-lived assets—assets that the company expects to provide services for more than a year. Thus, purchasing property or equipment is an investing activity, but purchasing inventory or prepaying rent are operating activities. Why? Because a company will generally use property and equipment for multiple years, whereas it will use inventory and prepaid rent within 1 year. You should note that financing and investing activities are really opposite sides of the same coin. For example, when a company issues stock for cash to an investor, the issuing company treats it as a financing activity and the investor treats it as an investing activity.

Exhibit 5-1 shows typical operating, investing, and financing activities reported in a statement of cash flows. The relationship of these activities to cash should be fairly obvious and straightforward. What is not always obvious is the classification of these activities as operating, investing, or financing. Take interest payments and dividend payments, for example. These both represent cash flows to those who supply capital to the firm. You might think they should be treated the same. However, after much debate, the FASB decided to classify interest payments as cash flows associated with operations and dividend payments as financing cash flows. This classification maintains the long-standing distinction that transactions with the owners (dividends) cannot be treated as expenses, whereas interest payments to creditors are expenses.

Preparing a Statement of Cash Flows

To see how various activities affect the statement of cash flows, consider the activities of Biwheels Company for January 20X2. We reproduce the company's transactions analyzed by the balance sheet equation in Exhibit 5-2 and the balance sheet and income statement in Exhibit 5-3. We use these statements and the transactions underlying them to prepare

Cash Inflows | **Cash Outflows**

Operating activities

Cash Inflows	Cash Outflows
Collections from customers	Cash payments to suppliers
Interest and dividends collected	Cash payments to employees
Other operating receipts	Interest and taxes paid
	Other operating cash payments

Investing activities

Sale of property, plant, and equipment	Purchase of property, plant, and equipment
Sale of securities that are not cash equivalents	Purchase of securities that are not cash equivalents
Receipt of loan repayments	Making loans

Financing activities

Borrowing cash from creditors	Repayment of amounts borrowed
Issuing equity securities	Repurchase of equity shares (including the purchase of treasury stock)
Issuing debt securities	Payment of dividends

Exhibit 5-1
Typical Operating, Investing, and Financing Activities

a statement of cash flows for Biwheels for January 20X2. Notice that the cash balance for Biwheels increased from $0 at the beginning of the month to $351,000 at the end of the month. Because the statement of cash flows explains the causes for the changes in cash, the first step in developing the statement is always to compute the amount of the change, in this case an increase of $351,000. We next examine the three sections of the statement of cash flows that combine to explain this $351,000 increase.

Cash Flows from Financing Activities

Although most companies list operating activities as the first section of the cash flow statement, it is better to begin our discussion with the more easily described and understood section of the cash flow statement, cash flows from financing activities. This section shows cash flows to and from providers of capital. The easiest way to determine cash flows from financing activities is to examine changes in the cash account in the balance sheet equation (or T account) and identify those associated with financing activities. Biwheels had two such transactions in January, as shown in Exhibit 5-2:

Transaction 1, Initial Investment, $400,000
Transaction 2, Loan from Bank, $100,000

Both of these transactions are cash inflows, that is, increases in cash. Therefore, Biwheels' cash flows from financing activities total $500,000:

Biwheels Company
Cash Flows from Financing Activities
for the Month of January 20X2

Proceeds from initial investment	$400,000
Proceeds from bank loan	100,000
Net cash provided by financing activities	$500,000

If you did not have access to the balance sheet equation entries, you could also look at the changes in Biwheels' balance sheet during January. Note that all balance sheet

investing decisions
Decisions that include the choices to (1) acquire or dispose of plant, property, equipment, and other long-term productive assets, and (2) provide or collect cash as a lender or as an owner of securities.

cash flows from investing activities
The section of the statement of cash flows that helps users understand management's investing decisions.

investing activities
Transactions that acquire or dispose of long-lived assets.

OBJE3TIVE

Compute and interpret cash flows from financing activities.

Assets = **Liabilities** + **Stockholders' Equity**

Description of Transactions	Cash	+	Accounts Receivable	+	Merchandise Inventory	+	Prepaid Rent	+	Store Equipment	=	Note Payable	+	Accounts Payable	+	Paid-In Capital	+	Retained Earnings
(1) Initial investment	+400,000									=					+400,000		
(2) Loan from bank	+100,000									=	+100,000						
(3) Acquire store equipment for cash	−15,000								+15,000	=							
(4) Acquire inventory for cash	−120,000				+120,000					=							
(5) Acquire inventory on credit					+10,000					=			+10,000				
(6) Acquire inventory for cash plus credit	−10,000				+30,000					=			+20,000				
(7) Sale of equipment	+1,000								−1,000	=							
(8) Return of inventory acquired on January 5					−800					=			−800				
(9) Payments to creditors	−4,000									=			−4,000				
(10a) Sales on open account			+160,000							=							+160,000
(10b) Cost of merchandise inventory sold					−100,000					=							−100,000
(11) Collect accounts receivable	+5,000		−5,000							=							
(12) Pay rent in advance	−6,000						+6,000			=							
(13) Recognize expiration of rental services							−2,000			=							−2,000
(14) Depreciation									−100	=							−100
Balance January 31, 20X2	351,000	+	+155,000	+	+59,200	+	+4,000	+	+13,900	=	100,000	+	+25,200	+	+400,000	+	+57,900

583,100

583,100

Exhibit 5-2
Biwheels Company
Analysis of Transactions for January 20X2 (in $)

Exhibit 5-3
Biwheels Company
Income Statement
and Balance Sheet

Income Statement for the Month Ended January 31, 20X2

Sales (revenues)		$160,000
Deduct expenses		
Cost of goods sold	$100,000	
Rent	2,000	
Depreciation	100	
Total expenses		102,100
Net income		$ 57,900

Balance Sheet January 31, 20X2

Assets		Liabilities and Stockholders' Equity		
Cash	$351,000	Liabilities		
Accounts receivable	155,000	Note payable		$100,000
Merchandise		Accounts payable		25,200
inventory	59,200	Total liabilities		$125,200
Prepaid rent	4,000	Stockholders' equity		
Store equipment	13,900	Paid-in capital	$400,000	
		Retained earnings	57,900	
		Total stockholders'		
		equity		457,900
		Total liabilities and		
Total assets	$583,100	stockholders' equity		$583,100

accounts were zero at the beginning of the month. You can compute the increases in notes payable and paid-in capital as follows:

	Balance, January 1, 20X2	Balance, January 31, 20X2	Increase (Decrease)
Notes Payable	$0	$100,000	$100,000
Paid-in Capital	0	400,000	400,000

If Hector Lopez had invested $200,000 in 20X1 and the remaining $200,000 on January 2, 20X2, the cash inflow for January 20X2 from Lopez's investment would have been only $200,000:

	Balance, January 1, 20X2	Balance, January 31, 20X2	Increase (Decrease)
Paid-in Capital	$200,000	$400,000	$200,000

Two general rules for financing activities are:

- Increases in cash (cash inflows) stem from increases in liabilities or paid-in capital
- Decreases in cash (cash outflows) stem from decreases in liabilities or paid-in capital

You can see a list of some financing activities and their effect on cash in the first part of Exhibit 5-4. For example, selling common shares increases cash (+), paying dividends decreases cash (−), and converting debt into common stock has no effect on cash.

Cash Flows from Investing Activities

The section of the cash flow statement called cash flows from investing activities lists cash flows from the purchase or sale of plant, property, equipment, and other long-lived

OBJECTIVE 4

Compute and interpret cash flows from investing activities.

Exhibit 5-4
Analysis of Effects
of Financing and
Investing
Transactions
on Cash

Type of Transaction	Increase (+) or Decrease (−) in Cash
Financing Activities	
Increase long- or short-term debt	+
Reduce long- or short-term debt	−
Sell common or preferred shares	+
Repurchase common shares	−
Pay dividends	−
Convert debt to common stock	No effect
Investing Activities	
Purchase fixed assets for cash	−
Purchase fixed assets by issuing debt	No effect
Sell fixed assets for cash	+
Purchase investment securities of other firms that are not cash equivalents	−
Sell investment securities in other firms that are not cash equivalents	+
Make a loan to another company or person	−
Collect a loan	+

assets. It is usually the second section in the statement. To determine the cash flows from investing activities, you need to look at transactions that increase or decrease long-lived assets, loans, or securities that are not cash equivalents. Biwheels has only one such asset, store equipment. There were two cash transactions relating to store equipment during January:

Transaction 3, Acquire Store Equipment for Cash, $15,000
Transaction 7, Sale of Asset [Store Equipment] for Cash, $1,000

The first of these transactions is a use of cash, or a cash outflow. The second is a source of cash, or a cash inflow. The investing activities section of Biwheels' cash flow statement is:

Biwheels Company
Cash Flows from Investing Activities
for the Month of January 20X2

Purchase of store equipment	$(15,000)
Proceeds from sale of store equipment	1,000
Net cash used by investing activities	$(14,000)

Notice that we place the cash outflows in parentheses. Because there is a net cash outflow, investing activities used cash during January. This contrasts with financing activities, which provided cash.

The second part of Exhibit 5-4 shows types of investing activities and their effects on cash. For example, selling investment securities (except for securities that are cash equivalents) increases cash (+) and making a loan decreases cash (−). Notice that buying or selling securities that are cash equivalents does not change cash. It simply turns one type of cash into another type of cash.

If you did not have access to the transactions listed in the balance sheet equation, you would need to look at changes in the long-lived assets, loans, and other investments on the balance sheet. Two general rules for investing activities are:

- Increases in cash (cash inflows) stem from decreases in long-lived assets, loans, and investments
- Decreases in cash (cash outflows) stem from increases in long-lived assets, loans, and investments

Consider Biwheels' only long-lived asset, store equipment. Changes in such assets generally result from three possible sources: (1) asset acquisitions, (2) asset disposals, and (3) depreciation expense for the period:

$$\text{Increase in assets} = \text{Acquisitions} - \text{Disposals} - \text{Depreciation expense}$$

Asset acquisitions and disposals may involve cash, but depreciation does not. Thus, it is important to identify how much of the change in the asset values resulted from the charging of depreciation. From the balance sheet, we learn that Biwheels' store equipment increased from $0 to $13,900 in January. From the income statement, we know that depreciation expense was $100. Thus, we know that the net acquisitions (that is, acquisitions less disposals) were $14,000:

$$\$13,900 = \text{Acquisitions} - \text{Disposals} - \$100$$
$$\text{Acquisitions} - \text{Disposals} = \$13,900 + \$100 = \$14,000$$

Only by knowing more about either the actual acquisitions or disposals can we break down net acquisitions into acquisitions and disposals. If we could determine from further analysis that Biwheels' acquisitions were $15,000, we would know that disposals must have been $15,000 − $14,000 = $1,000. Management has no problem examining financial records directly to determine the details, but investors have a more difficult time obtaining such details.

INTERPRETING FINANCIAL STATEMENTS

A company raises $1 million by selling common stock and puts $400,000 into marketable securities that are cash equivalents and uses the other $600,000 to buy equipment. What are the effects on the cash flow statement?

Answer

The $1 million appears as cash provided by financing activities. The $600,000 appears as a use of cash in the investing section. Because the marketable securities are cash equivalents, the $400,000 does not appear in the investing section; instead, it is simply a rearrangement of the form in which the company holds cash. The net increase in cash from this transaction is $400,000, or $1 million of financing less $600,000 of investing.

Noncash Investing and Financing Activities

Sometimes financing or investing activities do not affect cash, but are similar to transactions that have a cash flow effect. Companies must list such activities in a separate schedule accompanying the statement of cash flows. In our example, Biwheels Company did not have any noncash investing or financing activities. However, suppose Biwheels' purchase of the store equipment was not for cash, but was financed as follows:

A. Biwheels acquired $8,000 of the store equipment by issuing common stock.
B. Biwheels acquired the other $7,000 of store equipment by signing a note payable for $7,000.

Also consider one other possible transaction:

C. Biwheels converted $50,000 of its original note payable to common stock. That is, Biwheels issued $50,000 of common stock in exchange for a reduction of $50,000 in the note payable.

These items would affect the balance sheet equation as follows:

	Cash	+	Store Equipment	=	Note Payable	+	Paid-in Capital
A.	0		+$8,000	=			+$ 8,000
B.	0		+$7,000	=	+$ 7,000		
C.	0			=	−$50,000		+$50,000

None of these transactions affect cash; therefore, they do not belong in a statement of cash flows. However, each transaction could just as easily involve cash. For example, in the first transaction, the company might issue common stock for $7,000 cash and immediately use the cash to purchase the fixed asset. The cash inflow and outflow would then appear on the statement of cash flows. Because of the similarities between these noncash transactions and ones involving cash, readers of statements of cash flows want to be informed of such noncash activities. Companies must report such items in a schedule of noncash investing and financing activities. Biwheels Company's schedule for these hypothetical transactions would be:

Schedule of noncash investing and financing activities	
Common stock issued to acquire store equipment	$ 8,000
Note payable for acquisition of store equipment	$ 7,000
Common stock issued on conversion of note payable	$50,000

Summary Problem for Your Review

PROBLEM

Examine the entries to Biwheels' balance sheet equation for February 20X2 in Exhibit 2-5 (p. 62) and the final February transaction, transaction 22, declaration and payment of dividends of $50,000 (p. 64).

1. Identify the items that belong in the financing and investing sections of the statement of cash flows for February.
2. Assume that Biwheels has two additional transactions during February:
   a. Bought shares of common stock of Pacific Cycle for $12,000 cash.
   b. Bought a $30,000 storage shed for $8,000 cash and signed a note payable for the remaining $22,000. The company financed the $8,000 for the cash down payment by borrowing $8,000 cash from the bank.

How would these transactions affect the financing and investing sections of Biwheels' February statement of cash flows?

3. Prepare the financing and investing sections of Biwheels' statement of cash flows including all transactions in numbers 1 and 2. Interpret the information you learn from these two sections.

SOLUTION

1. Only transaction 21, borrowing of $10,000 from the bank and using that $10,000 to buy store equipment, and transaction 22, payment of cash dividends of $50,000,

involve financing or investing activities. The $10,000 loan is a financing activity, the $10,000 paid to buy the store equipment is an investing activity, and the $50,000 of dividends paid is a financing activity.

2. The $12,000 paid for Pacific Cycle shares is an investing activity. The purchase of the storage shed has three effects: (1) the $8,000 paid in cash is an investing activity, (2) the $8,000 borrowed from the bank is a financing activity, and (3) the $22,000 acquisition for a note payable is a noncash investing and financing activity.

3. The statement of cash flows would include the following. Note that we combined the two borrowings from the bank into one line: $10,000 + $8,000 = $18,000.

Biwheels Company
Cash Flows from Financing and Investing Activities
for the Month of February 20X2

Cash Flows from Investing Activities	
Acquisition of store equipment	$(10,000)
Purchase of Pacific Cycle common shares	(12,000)
Acquisition of storage shed	(8,000)
Net cash used for investing activities	$(30,000)
Cash Flows from Financing Activities	
Borrowing from banks	$ 18,000
Payment of dividends	(50,000)
Net cash used by financing activities	$(32,000)
Noncash Investing and Financing Activities	
Note payable financing for purchase of storage shed	$ 22,000

From these sections of the cash flow statement, we learn that in February Biwheels used a total of $62,000 in cash for investing and financing activities. Either the company used cash generated by operations or it depleted its cash balance to support these activities. Of the $30,000 spent for investing activities, $18,000 increased long-lived assets and $12,000 increased Biwheels' investment in the securities of another company, Pacific Cycle. We also learn that the $18,000 in cash inflows from financing was entirely debt financing, borrowing from banks. The company did not sell or buy back any shares of its common stock. The $50,000 cash outflow for dividends was larger than the additional borrowing, resulting in a net cash outflow of $32,000 from financing activities. Finally, Biwheels also invested another $22,000 in the storage shed and financed it with debt in the form of a note payable. This consisted of a financing activity and an investing activity, but there was no affect on cash.

Cash Flow from Operating Activities

Analyzing the results of financing and investing activities informs investors about management's ability to make financial and investment decisions. However, users of financial statements are even more concerned with assessing management's operating decisions. They focus on the first major section of cash flow statements, cash flows from operating activities (or cash flows from operations). This section shows the cash effects of transactions that affect the income statement.

Approaches to Calculating the Cash Flow from Operating Activities

We can use either of two approaches to compute cash flows from operating activities (or cash flows from operations). The **direct method** subtracts operating cash disbursements

direct method
A method for computing cash flows from operating activities that subtracts operating cash disbursements from cash collections to arrive at cash flows from operations.

Exhibit 5-5

Analysis of Effects
of Operating
Transactions
on Cash

Type of Transaction	Increase (+) or Decrease (−) in Cash
Operating Activities	
Sales of goods and services for cash	+
Sales of goods and services on credit	No effect
Collection of accounts receivable	+
Receive dividends or interest	+
Recognize cost of goods sold	No effect
Purchase inventory for cash	−
Purchase inventory on credit	No effect
Pay accounts payable	−
Accrue operating expenses	No effect
Pay operating expenses	−
Accrue taxes	No effect
Pay taxes	−
Accrue interest	No effect
Pay interest	−
Prepay expenses for cash	−
Record the using of prepaid expenses	No effect
Charge depreciation	No effect

indirect method

A method for computing cash flows from operating activities that adjusts the previously calculated accrual net income from the income statement to reflect only cash receipts and cash disbursements.

from cash collections to arrive at cash flows from operations. The **indirect method** adjusts the previously calculated accrual net income from the income statement to reflect only cash receipts and cash disbursements. Both methods show the same amount of cash provided by (or used for) operating activities. The only difference is the format of the statement.

The FASB prefers the direct method because it is a straightforward listing of cash inflows and cash outflows and is easier for investors to understand. However, 99% of all U.S. companies use the indirect method. Why? Because it links cash flows directly with net income, emphasizing how income and cash flows differ. We discuss the direct method first because, as a newcomer to accounting, you will probably find it easier to understand. However, to understand cash flow statements for real companies, you also need to understand the indirect method that most companies use.

Consider first the types of cash flows that accountants classify as operating activities. Exhibit 5-5 lists many such activities. These cash flows are associated with revenues and expenses on the income statement. Notice that recording revenues from the sales of goods or services does not necessarily increase cash. Only sales for cash immediately increase cash. There is no cash effect of credit sales until the customer actually pays. Biwheels must collect its accounts receivable to generate any cash. Similarly, cash received for services to be performed is an operating cash flow even though a company may not earn the revenue until a later period.

The cash effects of expenses are similar. Sometimes—prepaid rent is an example—the cash outflow precedes the recording of the expense on the income statement. For example, Biwheels paid $6,000 in cash for prepaid rent in January and recorded the purchase as an asset. The company then records rent expense when it later uses the rented facilities. In contrast, sometimes the cash outflow follows the recording of the expense, as with payment of wages.

Let's examine the cost of goods sold expense. We often record this expense in three steps: (1) purchase of inventory on credit, (2) payment of accounts payable, and (3) delivery of goods to the customer and thus the recording of an expense. Consider a bicycle seat that Biwheels bought on credit for $30 on January 7. Biwheels sold the seat on January 29 and paid the supplier on February 7. Two transactions occurred during January:

1. January 7: the balance sheet accounts Merchandise Inventory and Accounts Payable increased by $30.
2. January 29: the balance sheet account Merchandise Inventory decreased by $30, and Biwheels recorded a $30 cost of goods sold expense on the income statement. (Note that Biwheels would also record the sale on January 29, but we are focusing here on the expense part of the transaction.)

At the end of January, no cash transaction had occurred. Neither purchasing inventory on credit nor charging cost of goods sold expense affects cash. On February 7, the only cash transaction occurs: Biwheels pays $30 of cash to the supplier, thereby reducing its accounts payable by $30. The end result of the three expense-related transactions is a $30 expense and a $30 payment. However, Biwheels recorded the expense in January and the cash outflow in February. January's income statement would have a $30 expense, but January's cash flow statement would have no related cash outflow. In February, the situation would be reversed. The cash flow statement would have a $30 outflow, but there would be no expense on the income statement. Notice in Exhibit 5-5 that there is no effect on cash when we recognize cost of goods sold or purchase inventory on credit, but there is a decrease in cash when we pay accounts payable or purchase inventory for cash.

Now that you know some of the operating transactions that affect cash and how the cash inflow or outflow can occur at a different time than the recording of the related revenue or expense, let's examine the two formats used for showing the cash flow effects of operations.

Cash Flow from Operations — The Direct Method

The direct method consists of a listing of cash receipts (inflows) and cash disbursements (outflows). The easiest way to construct the statement of cash flows from operations using the direct method is to examine the Cash column of the balance sheet equation. The following entries from Exhibit 5-2 affect cash:

OBJECTIVE 5

Use the direct method to calculate cash flows from operations.

Entry	Cash Effect
(1) Initial investment	+400,000
(2) Loan from bank	+100,000
(3) Acquire store equipment for cash	−15,000
(4) Acquire inventory for cash	**−120,000**
(6) Acquire inventory for cash plus credit	**−10,000**
(7) Sales of equipment	+1000
(9) Payments to creditors	**−4,000**
(11) Collect accounts receivable	**+5,000**
(12) Pay rent in advance	**−6,000**

We know from the previous sections that transactions 1, 2, 3, and 7 were financing and investing activities. Thus, the remaining transactions affecting cash must be operating activities. Therefore, the cash flows from operating activities include transactions 4, 6, 9, 11, and 12, which are in bold italics. The statement follows:

Biwheels Company
Cash Flows from Operating Activities
for the Month of January 20X2

Cash payments for inventory (transactions 4 and 6)	$(130,000)
Cash payments to creditors for accounts payable (transaction 9)	(4,000)
Cash collections on accounts receivable (transaction 11)	5,000
Cash payment for rent (transaction 12)	(6,000)
Net cash used by operating activities	$(135,000)

A more common format for this statement lists the cash collections first. It also combines the cash payment for inventory and cash payments to creditors for accounts payable on one line, cash payments to suppliers:

Biwheels Company
Cash Flows from Operating Activities
for the Month of January 20X2

Cash collections	$ 5,000
Cash payments to suppliers	(134,000)
Cash payments for rent	(6,000)
Net cash used by operating activities	$(135,000)

Notice the small cash inflow from operations. All sales in January were credit sales, and Biwheels collected only $5,000 during the month. Operating cash outflows that exceed cash inflows are common in young, growing companies. Companies pay for items such as rent and inventories in advance of receiving cash for the sales that result from the use of these resources.

Cash Flow from Operations—The Indirect Method

OBJECTIVE

Use the indirect method to explain the difference between net income and net cash provided by (used for) operating activities.

The direct method gives a straightforward picture of where a company gets cash and how it spends cash. However, it does not address the issue of how the cash flows from operating activities differ from net income. To do this, we use the indirect method. We can construct the indirect method cash flow statement for Biwheels from January's income statement and the January 1 and January 31 balance sheets in Exhibit 5-3. (Note that all January 1 balances are zero.) Each income statement item has a parallel item or items in the statement of cash flows. Each sale eventually results in cash inflows; each expense entails cash outflows at some time. When the cash inflow from a sale or the cash outflow for an expense occurs in one accounting period and we record the sales revenue or expense in another, net income can differ from the cash flows from operations. The indirect method highlights such differences by beginning with net income and then listing all adjustments necessary to compute cash flows from operating activities. Exhibit 5-6 illustrates the indirect method, and we next explain the entries in this exhibit.

If all sales were for cash and all expenses were paid in cash as incurred, the cash flows from operating activities would be identical to the net income. Thus, you can think of the first line of Exhibit 5-6, net income, as what the cash flow from operating activities would be if revenues equaled cash inflows and expenses equaled cash outflows. The subsequent adjustments recognize the differences in timing between revenues and cash inflows and between expenses and cash outflows.

The first adjustment is to add the depreciation expense to net income. We do this because we deducted depreciation of $100 when computing the net income of $57,900, but it does not represent an operating cash outflow in January. Depreciation is an expense, but

Exhibit 5-6
Biwheels Company
Cash Flows from Operating Activities—Indirect Method for the Month of January 20X2

Net income	$ 57,900
Adjustments to reconcile net income to net cash provided (used) by operating activities	
Depreciation	100
Net increase in accounts receivable	(155,000)
Net increase in inventory	(59,200)
Net increase in accounts payable	25,200
Net increase in prepaid rent	(4,000)
Net cash provided by (used for) operating activities	$(135,000)

Net Income		Adjustments		Cash Flows from Operating Activities	
A. Sales revenues	$ 160,000	Increase in accounts receivable	$(155,000)	Cash collections from customers	$ 5,000
B. Cost of goods sold	(100,000)	Increase in inventories Increase in accounts payable	(59,200) 25,200	Cash payments to suppliers	(134,000)
C. Rent expense	(2,000)	Increase in prepaid rent	(4,000)	Cash payments for rent	(6,000)
D. Depreciation	(100)	Depreciation	100		0*
Net income	$ 57,900	Total adjustments	$(192,900)	Net cash provided by (used for) operating activities	$(135,000)

*Depreciation is not a cash flow.

Exhibit 5-7
Biwheels Company
Comparison of Net Income and Cash Provided by Operating Activities

the related cash flow occurred as an investing activity when Biwheels purchased the equipment. Because we deducted $100 of depreciation in computing January's net income, adding it back simply cancels the deduction. There is no cash flow effect of depreciation.

To highlight the effect of depreciation, let's for a moment assume that Biwheels received all $160,000 of revenue in cash and paid all $102,000 of nondepreciation expenses in cash. The income statement and statement of cash flows from operating activities would be as follows:

Income Statement		Cash Flows from Operating Activities	
Sales	$160,000	Cash inflows from sales	$160,000
Nondepreciation expenses	(102,000)	Cash outflows for expenses	(102,000)
Depreciation	(1 00)	Net cash provided by operating activities	$ 58,000
Net income	$ 57,900		

The only difference between net income and cash provided by operating activities in this example is the $100 of depreciation. To compute the net cash provided by operating activities, we simply add the $100 to the net income: $57,900 + $100 = $58,000. The center column of line D of Exhibit 5-7 shows depreciation is one of the adjustments to net income when computing cash provided by operating activities.

Let's examine depreciation more closely. Suppose depreciation were $500 rather than $100. Net income would be $57,500, and net cash provided by operating activities would be $57,500 + $500 = $58,000. Net cash provided by operating activities did not change. That is, the amount of depreciation has no effect on the cash provided by operating activities. To calculate cash flows, we add back to net income exactly the same amount we subtracted for depreciation, essentially canceling the earlier deduction.

Depreciation represents an expense for which there is never an operating cash flow. The related cash flow was an investing outflow. We see other examples of such an expense in later chapters, but for now this is the only expense of this type to concern us. The remaining adjustments represent situations where only timing creates differences between net income and cash flows from operations. That is, the timing of revenues or expenses differs from that of the related operating cash inflows or outflows.

We next consider revenues. The sales revenues of $160,000 shown on the income statement immediately affect the accounts receivable account on the balance sheet and eventually

OBJECTIVE 7

Understand why we add depreciation to net income when using the indirect method for computing cash flow from operating activities.

will affect cash. If all sales were for cash, sales would not affect accounts receivable, the associated cash flows would occur at the time of sale, and the cash inflow would equal the sales. However, Biwheels' sales are all on open account. Thus, the sale initially increases accounts receivable, and the cash inflow occurs when Biwheels collects the receivables. You can compute the amount of cash collections from income statement and balance sheet data in one of two ways. First, you can compute the total collections Biwheels could possibly collect in the month, which is the accounts receivable balance at the beginning of the month plus the sales of the month. From this you subtract the amount that Biwheels has not yet collected, the accounts receivable at the end of the month. This gives collections in January of $5,000:

Beginning accounts receivable	$ 0
+ Sales	160,000
Potential collections	$160,000
− Ending accounts receivable	155,000
Cash collections from customers	$ 5,000

Alternatively, you can start with the sales for the month. If accounts receivable had remained unchanged (that is, accounts receivable at the end of the month equaled the accounts receivable at the beginning of the month), cash collections would equal sales. If accounts receivable increased, collections fell short of the sales, causing net income to be higher than cash flows from operations. If accounts receivable decreased, that means collections exceeded sales, causing net income to be lower than cash flows from operations. In January, Biwheels' accounts receivables increased from $0 to $155,000, so cash collections were only $5,000:

Sales	$160,000
Decrease (increase) in accounts receivable*	(155,000)
Cash collections from customers	$ 5,000

* The format "decrease (increase)" means that decreases are positive amounts and increases are negative amounts.

Because Biwheels' accounts receivable increased in January, we need to deduct the $155,000 from net income to get cash provided by operating activities. Line A in Exhibit 5-7 shows this adjustment.

If accounts receivable had decreased, it would mean that collections exceeded sales. We would then add the decrease in accounts receivable to the sales to determine the cash collections.

INTERPRETING FINANCIAL STATEMENTS

Suppose all $160,000 of Biwheels' sales were for cash. Compute the cash collections from customers using the formula sales plus or minus the changes in accounts receivable. Explain.

Answer

If all sales were in cash, accounts receivable would have remained at $0. Because there was no increase or decrease in accounts receivable, there would be no adjustment of sales to get cash collections from customers:

Sales	$ 160,000
Decrease (increase) in accounts receivable	0
Cash collections from customers	$ 160,000

Just as we adjusted sales to compute cash collections from customers, we can adjust the cost of goods sold line in the income statement to compute cash outflow for payments to suppliers. To do this, we look at one income statement account, cost of goods sold, and two balance sheet accounts, inventory and accounts payable. We adjust cost of goods sold to get cash payments to suppliers in two steps:

| Cost of Goods Sold | 1. Adjusted to Get → | Purchases | 2. Adjusted to Get → | Payments to Suppliers |

These two steps yield the following:

Step 1

Ending inventory, January 31	$ 59,200
+ Cost of goods sold in January	100,000
Inventory available in January	$ 159,200
− Beginning inventory, January 1	0
Inventory purchased in January	$ 159,200

Step 2

Inventory purchased in January	$ 159,200
+Beginning accounts payable, January 1	0
Total amount to be paid	$ 159,200
− Ending accounts payable, January 31	(25,200)
Amount paid in cash during January	$ 134,000

In step 1, we compute the amount of inventory purchased in January, independent of whether we purchase the inventory for cash or credit. The calculation requires taking the amount of inventory used in January (that is, the cost of goods sold), plus the amount of inventory left at the end of January, less the amount that was already in inventory at the beginning of the month. If Biwheels had bought all its inventory for cash, we could stop at this point. Its cash outflow to suppliers would have been equal to the amount purchased, $159,200. However, because Biwheels purchased some inventory on credit, we must take step 2. If Biwheels had paid off all its accounts payable by the end of January, it would have paid an amount equal to the beginning accounts payable plus the purchases in January, a total of $159,200. Yet, $25,200 remained payable at the end of January, meaning that of the $159,200 of potential payments, Biwheels paid only $159,000 − $25,200 = $134,000 in January.

From these two steps, we can determine the two adjustments to cost of goods sold needed to adjust net income to a cash flow number:

Cost of goods sold in January	$100,000
Increase (decrease) in inventory during January	59,200
Decrease (increase) in trade accounts payable during January	(25,200)
Payments to suppliers during January	$134,000

Purchases that build up inventory require cash, but do not affect the cost of goods sold. Thus, *if there had been no change in accounts payable in January,* the cash outflow for payments to suppliers would have exceeded the cost of goods sold by the $59,200 increase in inventory: $100,000 cost of goods sold + $59,200 increase in inventory = $159,200 of inventory purchased. However, because accounts payable increased by $25,200, Biwheels did not pay the entire $159,200 in January. Of the $159,200 potential cash outflow, Biwheels will pay $25,200 in the future, so the company paid only $159,200 − $25,200 = $134,000 in January.

Now consider the adjustment to net income required to compute cash provided by operating activities. Exhibit 5-7 shows this in line B. First, remember that we subtract cost of goods sold in computing net income just as we subtract the cash payments to suppliers in determining cash provided by operating activities. Any adjustment showing a cash outflow greater than the cost of goods sold will lead to cash provided by operations that is less than net income. Because the increase in inventory caused the cash outflow to exceed the cost of goods sold by $59,200, net income will be $59,200 more than cash provided by operations. In contrast, the increase in accounts payable caused the cash outflow to fall short of cost of goods sold by $25,200, which results in net income that is $25,200 less than cash provided by operations.

Before considering line C in Exhibit 5-7, let's create a general approach to adjustments. Then we can apply the approach to that line.

- Adjust for revenues and expenses not requiring cash
    Add back depreciation
    Other adjustments of this type are introduced in later chapters
- Adjust for changes in noncash assets and liabilities relating to operating activities
    Add decreases in assets
    Deduct increases in assets
    Add increases in liabilities
    Deduct decreases in liabilities

Adjustments so far have included adding back the $100 of depreciation (the only revenue or expense not requiring cash), deducting the $155,000 increase in accounts receivable (an asset), deducting the $59,200 increase in inventory (an asset), and adding the $25,200 increase in accounts payable (a liability). Take time now to verify that each of these adjustments is consistent with the preceding general rules.

Now let's consider the rent expense. Notice that prepaid rent, an asset account, increased from $0 at the beginning of the month to $4,000 at the end of the month. Thus, we need to deduct a $4,000 adjustment for rent, as shown in line C of Exhibit 5-7. This $4,000 balance is the result of paying $6,000 in cash for rent, but charging only $2,000 as an expense. This means that Biwheels' cash outflow exceeded the expense by $4,000, as shown in the adjustment we made.

To summarize, look again at Exhibit 5-7. The comparison of net income to cash flows from operating activities in Exhibit 5-7 begins with the net income of $57,900 from the bottom of the first column, adds (deducts) the adjustments of $(192,900) in the middle column, and ends with the $(135,000) net cash used for operating activities in the right-hand column. The left-hand column calculates net income, the right-hand column calculates cash flows from operations, and the middle column shows line-by-line adjustments. Although Biwheels had a healthy net income of $57,900, it used $135,000 of cash to support its operations. Such depletion of cash cannot continue indefinitely, regardless of how much income Biwheels generates. However, Biwheels is like other young, growing companies. It is using cash to build up its business in anticipation of positive cash flows being provided by operating activities in the future.

Reconciliation Statement

When a company uses the direct method for reporting cash flows from operating activities, users of the financial statements might miss information that relates net income to operating cash flows. Thus, the FASB requires direct-method statements to include a supplementary schedule reconciling net income to net cash provided by operations. Such a supplementary statement is basically an indirect method cash flow statement. In essence, companies that choose to use the direct method must also report using the indirect method. In contrast, those using the indirect method never explicitly report the information on a direct-method statement. The supplementary statement included with direct-method cash flow statements would be identical to the body of Exhibit 5-6, but it would be labeled "Reconciliation of Net Income to Net Cash Provided by Operating Activities." No wonder 99% of firms use the indirect method!

The Statement of Cash Flows and the Balance Sheet Equation

To better understand how the cash flow statement relates to the other financial statements, let's examine the balance sheet equation. The balance sheet equation provides the conceptual basis for all financial statements, including the statement of cash flows. The equation can be rearranged as follows:

OBJE**8**TIVE

Show how the balance sheet equation provides a conceptual framework for the statement of cash flows.

$$\text{Assets} = \text{Liabilities} + \text{Stockholder's equity}$$
$$\text{Cash} + \text{Noncash assets (NCA)} = \text{L} \quad + \text{SE}$$
$$\text{Cash} = \text{L} \quad + \text{SE} \quad - \text{NCA}$$

Any change (Δ) in cash must be accompanied by a change in one or more items on the right side to keep the equation in balance:

$$\Delta\text{Cash} = \Delta\text{L} + \Delta\text{SE} - \Delta\text{NCA}$$

Therefore:

$$\text{Change in cash} = \text{Change in all noncash accounts}$$

or

$$\text{What happened to cash} = \text{Why it happened}$$

The statement of cash flows focuses on the changes in the noncash accounts as a way of explaining how and why the level of cash has increased or decreased during a given period. Thus, the major changes in the accounts on the right side of the equation appear in the statement of cash flows as causes of the change in cash. The left side of the equation measures the net effect of the change in cash.

This same analysis can help explain the direct and indirect methods of reporting cash from operating activities. Exhibit 5-8 lists all of Biwheels' January transactions that are operating activities. However, we have rearranged the columns in the format of the revised balance sheet equation:

$$\Delta\text{Cash} = \Delta\text{L} + \Delta\text{SE} - \Delta\text{NCA}$$

We list only the transactions that appear in the operating cash flows section of the statement of cash flows. Recall that operating activities are transactions that affect the purchase, processing, and selling of products or services.

Notice that the entries in the column on the left side of the equals sign (those in the boxes) are those that appear on the direct method statement of cash flows from operations. They are the direct cash flows and total an outflow of $135,000. The changes in each

Exhibit 5-8

Biwheels Company
Analysis of Operating Transactions for January 20X2 (in $)

Description of Transactions	Cash = Cash	Liabilities = Accounts Payable	+ Stockholders' Equity Retained Earnings	Noncash Assets − Accounts Receivable	− Merchandise Inventory	− Prepaid Rent	− Store Equipment
(4) Acquire inventory for cash	−120,000				+120,000		
(5) Acquire inventory on credit		+10,000			+10,000		
(6) Acquire inventory for cash plus credit	−10,000	+20,000			+30,000		
(8) Return of inventory acquired on January 5		−800			−800		
(9) Payments to creditors	−4,000	−4,000					
(10a) Sales on open account			+160,000	+160,000			
(10b) Cost of merchandise inventory sold			−100,000		−100,000		
(11) Collect accounts receivable	+5,000			−5,000			
(12) Pay rent in advance	−6,000					+6,000	
(13) Recognize expiration of rental services			−2,000			−2,000	
(14) Depreciation			−100				−100
Total Changes	−135,000	25,200	57,900	+155,000	+59,200	+4,000	−100

account (that is, the last line for each column) on the right side of the equation (those circled) appear on the indirect method statement. They also must total $135,000. Therefore, you can see that the direct and indirect method statements must always have the same totals. They differ only in format. The direct method statement is a listing of all changes in cash, whereas the indirect method statement shows the reasons for those changes. The following summarizes this analysis:

$$\Delta Cash = \Delta L + \Delta SE - \Delta NCA$$
$$\text{Direct method} = \text{Indirect method}$$

Examples of Statements of Cash Flows

Exhibit 5-9 shows the complete January statement of cash flows for Biwheels. It shows that the total cash balance increased by $351,000, mainly due to $500,000 generated by financing activities. Of the $500,000 raised, operations used $135,000 and investing activities used $14,000, leaving the $351,000 balance.

You are now prepared to read most of the significant items on a real corporation's statement of cash flows. Consider Exhibit 5-10, Nike's statement of cash flows. Items that we have discussed are in italics. Some terminology is slightly different from what we have used, but the meanings should be clear. Notice that Nike did almost the opposite of Biwheels. It generated substantial cash from operations and used that cash for both investing and financing activities. The three largest Nike cash flows that we have not discussed are all repayments of financing: $80.3 million to reduce long-term debt, $431.5 million to reduce notes payable, and $226.9 million for repurchase of stock. We discussed issuing debt and common stock. These are just the reverse—using cash to reduce liabilities and paying cash to shareholders to buy back their shares.

Cash Flows from Operating Activities		
Net income	$ 57,900	
Adjustments to reconcile net income to net		
cash provided by (used for) operating activities		
Depreciation	100	
Net increase in accounts receivable	(155,000)	
Net increase in inventory	(59,200)	
Net increase in accounts payable	25,200	
Net increase in prepaid rent	(4,000)	
Net cash provided by (used for) operating activities		$(135,000)
Cash Flows from Investing Activities		
Purchase of store equipment	$ (15,000)	
Proceeds from sale of store equipment	1,000	
Net cash provided by (used for) investing activities		$ (14,000)
Cash Flows from Financing Activities		
Proceeds from initial investment	$ 400,000	
Proceeds from bank loan	100,000	
Net cash provided by (used for) financing activities		$ 500,000
Net increase in cash		$ 351,000
Cash, January 2, 20X2		0
Cash, January 31, 20X2		$ 351,000

Exhibit 5-9
Biwheels Company
Statement of Cash Flows for January 20X2

Exhibit 5-10
Nike, Inc.
Statement of Cash Flows (in millions) for the Year ended May 31, 2002

CASH PROVIDED (USED) BY OPERATIONS		
Net income	$ 663.3	
Income charges not affecting cash		
Depreciation	223.5	
Deferred income taxes	15.2	
Amortization and other	53.1	
Income tax benefit from exercise of stock options	13.9	
Changes in certain working capital components		
Increase in accounts receivable	(135.2)	
Decrease (increase) in inventories	55.4	
Decrease in other current assets and income taxes receivable	16.9	
Increase in accounts payable, accrued liabilities, and income taxes payable	175.4	
Cash provided by operations		$1,081.5
CASH PROVIDED (USED) BY INVESTING ACTIVITIES		
Additions to property, plant and equipment	$(282.8)	
Disposals of property, plant and equipment	15.6	
Increase in other assets	(39.1)	
Increase in other liabilities	3.5	
Cash used by investing activities		$ (302.8)
CASH PROVIDED (USED) BY FINANCING ACTIVITIES		
Proceeds from long-term debt issuance	329.9	
Reductions in long-term debt	(80.3)	
Decrease in notes payable	(431.5)	
Proceeds from exercise of stock options and other stock issuances	59.5	
Repurchase of stock	(226.9)	
Dividends—common and preferred	(128.9)	
Cash used by financing activities		(478.2)
Effect of exchange rate changes		(29.0)
Net increase in cash and equivalents		271.5
Cash and equivalents, beginning of year		304.0
Cash and equivalents, end of year		$ 575.5

Summary Problem for Your Review

PROBLEM

Examine the entries to Biwheels' balance sheet equation for February 20X2 in Exhibit 2-5 (p. 62) and the balance sheet and income statement in Exhibit 2-6 (p. 63).

1. Prepare a statement of cash flows from operating activities for February using the direct method.
2. Prepare a statement of cash flows from operating activities for February using the indirect method.
3. Give a one-line explanation of the insight most readily learned from each of the two statements.

SOLUTION

1. See Exhibit 5-11. The numbers come directly from the first column of Exhibit 2-5. The cash collections are $130,000 collected on accounts receivable and the $51,000

Cash collections from customers	$181,000
Cash payments to suppliers	(25,000)
Net cash provided by operating activities	$156,000

Exhibit 5-11
Biwheels Company
*Statement of Cash
Flows from Operating
Activities—Direct
Method
February 20X2*

Adjustments to reconcile net income to net	
cash provided by (used for) operating activities	
Depreciation	100
Net decrease in accounts receivable	5,000
Net decrease in inventory	20,000
Net increase in accounts payable	65,000
Net increase in prepaid rent	2,000
Net cash provided by (used for) operating activities	$156,000

Exhibit 5-12
Biwheels Company
*Statement of Cash
Flows from Operating
Activities—Indirect
Method
February 20X2*

cash sales. The payments to suppliers include $15,000 paid on accounts payable and $10,000 for cash purchases.

2. See Exhibit 5-12. The net income and add-back of depreciation come from the income statement. The remainder of the adjustments are differences between January 31 and February 28 balances on the balance sheet.

3. The direct-method statement shows the large excess of cash collections over cash payments. The indirect-method statement shows that the cash flow from operations exceeded net income by $156,000 − $63,900 = $92,100 due primarily to the large increase in accounts payable and the depletion of inventory.

The Importance of Cash Flow

Both the income statement and the statement of cash flows report on changes the company experiences during the period. Both are measures of performance over the period. You might wonder why accounting authorities require both. Why should the company not pick the better one? The problem is that each fills a different but critical information need. The income statement shows how a company's owners' equity increases (or decreases) as a result of operations. It matches revenues and expenses using the accrual concepts and provides a valuable measure of economic performance. In contrast, the statement of cash flows explains changes in the cash account rather than owners' equity. The focal point of the statement of cash flows is the net cash flow from operating activities. Frequently, this is called simply cash flow. It measures a firm's performance in maintaining a strong cash position. In addition, users of financial statements often compare the cash flows from operating, investing, and financing activities. The Business First box on p. 206 describes the significance for managers of some of these comparisons.

A concept that has received notice recently is **free cash flow**—generally defined as cash flows from operations less capital expenditures. This is the cash flow left over after undertaking the firm's operations and making the investments necessary to ensure its continued operation. Some also subtract dividends, assuming they are necessary to keep the shareholders happy. Companies that cannot generate enough cash from operations to cover their investments need to raise more capital, either by selling assets

free cash flow
*Generally defined
as cash flows from
operations less
capital expenditures.*

The three sections of the statement of cash flows are related in certain ways, depending on the company's industry and stage in its growth cycle. The following table suggests eight relationships. The table uses a plus sign (+) to indicate that cash was provided by the activity and a minus sign (−) to indicate that the activity used cash. The basic activities of operations, investing, and financing are each discussed as follows:

Relationship	1	2	3	4	5	6	7	8
Operating cash flow	+	+	+	+	−	−	−	−
Investing cash flow	+	−	+	−	+	−	+	−
Financing cash flow	+	+	−	−	+	+	−	−

What are the most natural or common relationships? Generally, stable or growing companies make continuous, new investments (shown by a negative (−) for investing cash flow). The healthiest of these companies usually also have a positive cash flow from operations. Thus, they fit relationship 2 or 4. Companies in earlier stages of growth, where operations do not generate enough cash to meet the voracious needs of the investment activities, fit relationship 2. Starbucks was in this situation in 2002 and 2003. Relationship 4 describes a firm that is probably more mature, with operating cash flow sufficient to both cover growth and repay debt. Microsoft has been in this situation for the last several years, and most established, profitable companies exhibit this relationship.

Some younger, growing firms that are not yet generating positive cash from operations fit relationships 6 and 8. Many biotech companies are in this situation until their initial products start generating operating inflows. Those still raising capital are in relationship 6. Icos and Zymogenetics, two fast-growing Seattle-based companies, are examples. Another biotech company, Boston Biomedica, fit relationship 8 in 2001 and 2002, with net cash outflows for financing activities

because it is paying back debt while raising little or no funds. If profitability is just around the corner for such companies, this may be fine. However, companies with negative operating cash flows cannot continue indefinitely.

In contrast to the growth perspectives previously discussed, relationships 1, 3, 5, and 7 describe a shrinking firm that is realizing cash from the sale or retirement of assets. This is not generally a healthy situation. Companies undergoing a bankruptcy restructuring may fall into one of these categories. CMGI, the high-flying technology company that suffered in the dot.com meltdown, fit relationship 7 in 2001, as did telecom company Global Crossing during its restructuring in 2002. Both were selling assets to be able to pay debt obligations because operations were not generating enough cash. The remaining relationships, 1, 3, and 5, are not common. In relationship 5, a company might be both selling assets and raising capital to provide cash for operations. Apparently, both management and some investors must think there are future prospects for positive cash flow from operations. In relationships 1 and 3, the company is selling assets despite positive cash flow from operations. Relationship 3 is more likely in that a company may be using cash generated from operations and sales of assets to retire debt. However, any relationship with cash being generated by investing activities probably bodes ill for the future.

No pattern is fully revealing by itself. Each requires analysis. What has the past pattern been, and what is projected for the future? What is the strategic plan behind the pattern? Classifying the pattern is just the first step in understanding the company.

Sources: Starbucks 2003 Annual Report; Microsoft 2003 Annual Report; Icos 2002 Annual Report; Zymogenetics 2002 Annual Report; Boston Biomedica 2002 Annual Report; CMGI 2002 Annual Report.

or by issuing debt or equity. If investment is for growth, this situation may be acceptable. If the investment is merely to maintain the status quo, the company is probably in trouble. In recent years, many utilities, such as Aquila Corporation and Dynegy, Inc., have resorted to selling off assets because they could not generate enough free cash flow to meet their needs. Biwheels Company has a large negative free cash flow for January, $(135,000) − $14,000 = $(149,000) meaning that it cannot maintain its current plans without raising substantial capital or improving its cash flow from operations.

The Crisis of Negative Cash Flow

Although investors make important economic decisions on the basis of net income, the so-called bottom line, sometimes earnings numbers do not tell the full story of what is really happening inside a company. Take the case of Prime Motor Inns, once one of the world's largest hotel operators. At its peak, Prime reported earnings of $77 million on revenues of $410 million. Moreover, revenues had increased by nearly 11% from the preceding year. Despite its impressive earnings performance, Prime lacked the cash to meet its obligations and filed for Chapter 11 bankruptcy. Under bankruptcy protection, a firm's obligations to its creditors are frozen as management figures out how to pay those creditors. How can a firm with $77 million in earnings file for bankruptcy about a year later?

Although the company's business was owning and operating hotels, much of Prime's reported $77 million of earnings arose from selling hotels. When buyers found it difficult to obtain outside financing for these hotel sales, Prime financed the sales itself by accepting notes and mortgages receivable from buyers rather than receiving cash. Of course, Prime soon ran out of hotels to sell. In the year that Prime reported $77 million of net income, an astute analyst would have noted that Prime had a net cash *outflow* from operations of $15 million. Analyzing the cash flow statement focuses attention on important relationships such as this one.

Prime emerged from bankruptcy with 75 hotels—roughly one-half the 141 hotels it had prior to bankruptcy—and a new name, Prime Hospitality Corporation. The new company kept its great stock symbol, "PDQ," and investors who bought the new shares for about $1.50 when the reorganization occurred have done well. Today Prime Hospitality operates 238 hotels located in 33 states including AmeriSuites and Wellesley Inn & Suites. Its stock price peaked at more than $20 per share and now is at about $10.

INTERPRETING FINANCIAL STATEMENTS

What pattern in the cash flow statement would have helped to alert the careful analyst to a potential problem at Prime Hospitality Corporation?

Answer

Prime was reporting large profits under accrual accounting, but operating cash flow was negative. Prime was financing sales by accepting notes and mortgages from buyers. This predicament would have been evident from the significant increases in these notes and mortgages receivable as compared with prior years.

Summary Problems for Your Review

PROBLEM

The Buretta Company has prepared the data in Exhibit 5-13.

In December 20X2, Buretta paid $54 million cash for a new building acquired to accommodate an expansion of operations. The company financed this purchase partly by

Exhibit 5-13
Buretta Company
Financial Statements
(in millions)

**Income Statement and Statement of Retained Earnings
for the Year Ended December 31, 20X2**

Sales		$100
Less cost of goods sold		
Inventory, December 31, 20X1	$ 15	
Purchases	105	
Cost of goods available for sale	$120	
Inventory, December 31, 20X2	47	73
Gross profit		$ 27
Less other expenses		
General expenses	$ 8	
Depreciation	8	
Property taxes	4	
Interest expense	3	23
Net income		$ 4
Retained earnings, December 31, 20X1		7
Total		$ 11
Dividends		1
Retained earnings, December 31, 20X2		$ 10

**Balance Sheets
for December 31**

Assets	20X2	20X1	Liabilities and Stockholders' Equity	20X2	20X1
			Accounts payable	$ 39	$14
Cash	$ 1	$20	Accrued property		
Accounts receivable	20	5	tax payable	3	1
Inventory	47	15	Long-term debt	40	0
Prepaid expenses	3	2	Common stock	70	70
Fixed assets, net	91	50	Retained earnings	10	7
			Total liabilities and		
Total assets	$162	$92	stockholders' equity	$162	$92

a new issue of long-term debt for $40 million cash. During 20X2, the company also sold fixed assets for $5 million cash. The assets were listed on Buretta's books at $5 million. All sales and purchases of merchandise were on credit.

Because the 20X2 net income of $4 million was the highest in the company's history, Alice Buretta, the chairman of the board, was perplexed by the company's extremely low cash balance.

1. Prepare a statement of cash flows from the Buretta data in Exhibit 5-13. Ignore income taxes. You may want to use Exhibit 5-9 (p. 203) as a guide. xUse the direct method for reporting cash flows from operating activities.
2. Prepare a supporting schedule that reconciles net income to net cash provided by operating activities.
3. What does the statement of cash flows tell you about Buretta Company? Does it help you reduce Alice Buretta's puzzlement? Why?

SOLUTION

1. See Exhibit 5-14. We can compute cash flows from operating activities as follows ($ in millions):

Exhibit 5-14
Buretta Company
*Statement of Cash
Flows for the Year
Ended December 31,
20X2 (in Millions)*

Cash flows from operating activities		
Cash collections from customers (a)		$ 85
Cash payments		
Cash paid to suppliers (b)	$(80)	
General expenses (c)	(9)	
Interest paid (d)	(3)	
Property taxes (e)	(2)	(94)
Net cash used by operating activities		$(9)
Cash flows from investing activities		
Purchase of fixed assets (building)	$(54)	
Proceeds from sale of fixed assets	5	
Net cash used by investing activities		(49)
Cash flows from financing activities		
Long-term debt issued	$ 40	
Dividends paid	(1)	
Net cash provided by financing activities		39
Net decrease in cash		$(19)
Cash balance, December 31, 20X1		20
Cash balance, December 31, 20X2		$ 1

Sales	$100
Less increase in accounts receivable	(15)
(a) Cash collections from customers	$ 85
Cost of goods sold	$ 73
Plus increase in inventory	32
Purchases	$105
Less increase in accounts payable	(25)
(b) Cash paid to suppliers	$ 80
General expenses	$ 8
Plus increase in prepaid general expenses	1
(c) Cash payment for general expenses	$ 9
(d) Cash paid for interest	$ 3
Property taxes	$ 4
Less increase in accrued property tax payable	(2)
(e) Cash paid for property taxes	$ 2

2. Exhibit 5-15 reconciles net income to net cash provided by operating activities.
3. The statement of cash flows shows where cash has come from and where it has gone. Operations used $9 million of cash. Why? The statement in Exhibit 5-14, which uses the direct method, shows the result clearly: $94 million in cash paid for operating activities exceeded $85 million in cash received from customers. The reconciliation using the indirect method, in Exhibit 5-15, shows why, in a profitable year, operating cash flow could be negative. The three largest items differentiating net income from cash flow are changes in inventory, accounts receivable, and accounts payable. Sales during the period were not collected in full because accounts receivable rose sharply, by $15 million—a 300% increase. Similarly, Buretta spent cash on inventory growth, although it financed much of that growth by increased accounts payable. In summary, the items in parentheses in Exhibit 15-15, large increases in accounts receivable ($15 million) and inventory ($32 million), plus an increase in prepaid expenses ($1 million), show that Buretta used $48 million of cash. In contrast, the sum of the items not in parentheses show that Buretta generated only $39 million in cash, that is, $4 million + $8 million + $25 million + $2 million. Thus, the company used a net amount of $9 million in operations ($39 million − $48 million).

Exhibit 5-15
Supporting Schedule
to Statement of
Cash Flows
*Reconciliation of Net
Income to Net Cash
Provided by Operating
Activities for the Year
Ended December 31,
20X2 (in Millions)*

Net income (from income statement)	$ 4
Adjustments to reconcile net income to net cash	
provided by operating activities	
Add: Depreciation, which was deducted	8
in the computation of net income	
but does not decrease cash	
Deduct: Increase in accounts receivable	(15)
Deduct: Increase in inventory	(32)
Deduct: Increase in prepaid general expenses	(1)
Add: Increase in accounts payable	25
Add: Increase in accrued property tax payable	2
Net cash used by operating activities	$ (9)

Investing activities also consumed cash because Buretta invested $54 million in a building, and it received only $5 million from sales of fixed assets, leaving a net use of $49 million. Financing activities did generate $39 million cash, but that was $19 million less than the $58 million used by operating and investing activities ($58 million = $9 million used in operations + $49 million used in investing).

Alice Buretta should no longer be puzzled. The statement of cash flows shows clearly that cash payments exceeded receipts by $19 million. However, she may still be concerned about the depletion of cash. Either the company must change operations so they do not require so much cash, it must curtail investment, or it must raise more long-term debt or ownership equity. Otherwise, Buretta Company will soon run out of cash.

PROBLEM

To understand how cash flow and net income vary during the life cycle of a business, consider the following example that portrays the 4-year life of a short-lived merchandising company, CB International. The first year the entrepreneurs bought twice as much as they sold because they were building their base inventory levels. CB International's suppliers offered payment terms that resulted in CB paying 80% of each year's purchases during that year and 20% in the next year. Sales were for cash with a sales price equal to twice the cost of the item. Selling expenses were constant over the life of the business and CB International paid them in cash as incurred. At the end of the fourth year, CB International paid the suppliers in full and sold all the inventory. Use the following summary results to prepare four income statements and statements of cash flows from operations using both direct and indirect methods for CB International, one for each year of its life.

	Year 1	Year 2	Year 3	Year 4
Purchases	2,000 units	1,500 units	1,500 units	1,000 units
$1 each	$2,000	$1,500	$1,500	$1,000
Sales	1,000 units	1,500 units	2,000 units	1,500 units
$2 each	$2,000	$3,000	$4,000	$3,000
Cost of sales	$1,000	$1,500	$2,000	$1,500
Selling expense	$1,000	$1,000	$1,000	$1,000
Payments to suppliers*	$1,600	$1,600	$1,500	$1,300

*.8 × 2,000 = 1,600; (.2 × 2,000) + (.8 × 1,500) = 1,600; (.2 × 1,500) + (.8 × 1,500) = 1,500; (.2 × 1,500) + (1.0 × 1,000) = 1,300.

SOLUTION

	Year 1	Year 2	Year 3	Year 4	Total
Income statement					
Sales	$2,000	$3,000	$4,000	$3,000	$12,000
Cost of sales	1,000	1,500	2,000	1,500	6,000
Selling expenses	1,000	1,000	1,000	1,000	4,000
Net income	$ 0	$ 500	1,000	$ 500	$ 2,000
Cash flows from operations:					
direct method					
Collections	$2,000	$3,000	$4,000	$3,000	$12,000
Payments on account	1,600	1,600	1,500	1,300	6,000
Payments for selling efforts	1,000	1,000	1,000	1,000	4,000
Cash flow from operations	$ (600)	$ 400	$1,500	$ 700	$ 2,000
Cash flows from operations:					
indirect method					
Net income	$ 0	$ 500	$1,000	$ 500	$ 2,000
− Increase in inventory	(1,000)				(1,000)
+ Decrease in inventory			500	500	1,000
+ Increase in accounts payable	400				400
− Decrease in accounts payable		(100)		(300)	(400)
Cash flow from operations	$ (600)	$ 400	$1,500	$ 700	$ 2,000

Balance Sheet Accounts at the end of	Year 1	Year 2	Year 3	Year 4
Merchandise inventory	$1,000	$1,000	$500	$0
Accounts payable	$ 400	$ 300	$300	0

This problem illustrates the difference between accrual-based earnings and cash flows. Observe that significant cash outflows occur for operations during the first year because payments to acquire inventory far exceed collections from customers. In fact, it is not until the third year that cash flow from operations exceeds net earnings for the year.

Highlights to Remember

1 Identify the purposes of the statement of cash flows. The statement of cash flows focuses on the changes in cash and the activities that cause those changes. Accrual-based net income is a useful number, but we also ask: How did our cash position change? How much of the change in cash was caused by operations, how much by investing activities, and how much by financing activities.

2 Classify activities affecting cash as operating, investing, or financing activities. Operating activities are the typical day-to-day activities of the firm in acquiring or manufacturing products, selling them to customers, and collecting the cash. Investing activities involve buying and selling plant, property, and equipment. It might include buying a whole company as well as specific assets. Financing activities involve raising or repaying capital such as borrowing from a bank, issuing bonds, or paying dividends to shareholders.

3 Compute and interpret cash flows from financing activities. Financing activities are transactions that obtain or repay capital. Cash flows from financing activities show whether a company borrows or repays money, issues additional securities, pays dividends, or buys back shares from stockholders.

4 Compute and interpret cash flows from investing activities. Investing activities are transactions that acquire or sell long-lived assets such as property or equipment. Cash flows from investing activities show where management has elected to invest any funds raised or generated.

5 Use the direct method to calculate cash flows from operations. The direct method explicitly lists all cash inflows and cash outflows from operating activities. We can find the relevant cash flows in the cash column in the balance sheet equation.

6 Use the indirect method to explain the difference between net income and net cash provided by (used for) operating activities. The more commonly used method for calculating the cash flow from operations is the indirect method, which starts with net income and adjusts it for the differences, typically account by account, between accrual income and operating cash flow. Both the direct and indirect method yield the same result. The advantage of the indirect method is that it explicitly addresses the differences between net income and net cash from operations.

7 Understand why we add depreciation to net income when using the indirect method for computing cash flow from operating activities. Under the indirect method, we add depreciation to net income because it is an expense not requiring the use of cash. Because we deduct depreciation when computing net income, adding it back simply eliminates the effect of deducting this noncash item. This adding back of depreciation sometimes causes some people to think of depreciation as a source of cash. This is not the case. Increasing depreciation does not affect cash flow.

8 Show how the balance sheet equation provides a conceptual framework for the statement of cash flows. The balance sheet equation is the conceptual base of all financial statements. By reconstructing the equation with cash alone on the left side of the equals sign, we can see how the right-hand entries provide an explanation for the changes in cash. Increases in liabilities or stockholders' equity or decreases in noncash assets increase cash, whereas decreases in liabilities or stockholders' equity or increases in noncash assets decrease cash.

Accounting Vocabulary

cash equivalents, p. 186
cash flow statement, p. 185
cash flows from financing
    activities, p. 186
cash flows from investing
    activities, p. 187

cash flows from operating
    activities, p. 186
direct method, p. 193
financing activities, p. 186
financing decisions, p. 186
free cash flow, p. 205

indirect method, p. 194
investing activities, p. 187
investing decisions, p. 187
operating activities, p. 186
operating decisions, p. 186
statement of cash flows, p. 185

Assignment Material

Special note: The following exercises and problems do not involve the indirect method, and therefore can be solved without reading pages 196–201: 5-31 through 5-37, and 5-41 through 5-51.

Questions

5-1 "The statement of cash flows is an optional statement included by most companies in their annual reports." Do you agree? Explain.

5-2 What are the purposes of a statement of cash flows?

5-3 Define cash equivalents.

5-4 What three types of activities are summarized in the statement of cash flows?

5-5 Name four major operating activities included in a statement of cash flows.

5-6 Name three major investing activities included in a statement of cash flows.

5-7 Name three major financing activities included in a statement of cash flows.

5-8 Where does interest received or paid appear on the statement of cash flows?

5-9 Which of the following financing activities increase cash: increase long-term debt, repurchase common shares, pay dividends? Which decrease cash?

5-10 Which of the following investing activities increase cash: purchase fixed assets by issuing debt, sell fixed assets for cash, collect a loan, and purchase equipment for cash? Which decrease cash?

5-11 Explain why increases in liabilities increase cash and increases in assets decrease cash.

5-12 Why are noncash investing and financing activities listed on a separate schedule accompanying the statement of cash flows?

5-13 A company acquired a fixed asset in exchange for common stock. Explain how this transaction should be shown, if at all, in the statement of cash flows. Why is your suggested treatment appropriate?

5-14 Suppose a company paid off a $1 million short-term loan to one bank with the proceeds from an identical loan from another bank. The change in the short-term debt account would be zero. Should anything appear in the statement of cash flows? Explain.

5-15 What are the two major ways of computing net cash provided by operating activities?

5-16 Where does a company get the information included in the direct-method cash flow statement?

5-17 What types of adjustments reconcile net income with net cash provided by operations?

5-18 Why is there usually a difference between the cash collections from customers and sales revenue in a period's financial statements?

5-19 What two balance sheet accounts explain the difference between the cost of goods sold and the cash payments to suppliers?

5-20 "Net losses mean drains on cash." Do you agree? Explain.

5-21 Demonstrate how the fundamental balance sheet equation can be recast to focus on cash.

5-22 The indirect method for reporting cash flows from operating activities can create an erroneous impression about noncash expenses (such as depreciation). What is the impression, and why is it erroneous?

5-23 An investor's newsletter had the following item: "The company expects increased cash flow in 2005 because depreciation charges will be substantially greater than they were in 2004." Comment.

5-24 "Depreciation is an integral part of a statement of cash flows." Do you agree? Explain.

5-25 A company operated at a profit for the year, but cash flow from operations was negative. Why might this occur? What industry or industries might find this a common occurrence?

5-26 A company operated at a loss for the year, but cash flow from operations was positive. Why might this occur? What industry or industries might find this a common occurrence?

Critical Thinking Questions

5-27 Cash Flow Patterns and Growth

You are considering an investment in a company that has negative cash flow from operations, negative cash flow from investing, and positive cash flow from financing. All the financing in the current year is from short-term debt with various covenants. What does this pattern of cash flow tells you about the client's circumstance. How does this affect your investment decision?

5-28 Microsoft and Cash Generation

As of early 2004 Microsoft was generating increasing amounts of cash from operating activities each year and was unable to fully use it in business growth. Hence, the levels of liquid investments were increasing. What would you imagine Microsoft's management might have been considering as a means of using more than one-half of its assets that were in cash and liquid investments?

5-29 Amazon and Negative Cash Flow from Operations

In 2002, Amazon.com, the industry leader in online sales of books and other consumer products, had positive cash flow from operations for the first time. In fact, its $174 million cash flow from operations exceeded its $125 million cash used for investing activities. What does this tell you about the stage of growth that Amazon is in?

5-30 Failures to Generate Cash Flow from Operations

You are discussing your investment strategies with a colleague who says, "I would never invest in a company that is not generating both positive earnings and positive cash flow from operations." How do you respond?

Exercises

5-31 Financing Activities

During 20X8, the Bremerhavn Shipping Company refinanced its long-term debt. It spent €160,000 to retire long-term debt due in 2 years and issued €200,000 of 15- year bonds at par (€ signifies euro, the European monetary unit). It then bought and retired common shares for cash of €35,000. Interest expense for 20X8 was €23,000, of which it paid €21,000 in cash; the other €2,000 was still payable at the end of the year. Dividends declared and paid during the year were €11,000.

Prepare a statement of cash flows from financing activities.

5-32 Investing Activities

Far-East Trading Company issued common stock for $320,000 on the first day of 20X5. The company bought fixed assets for $160,000 and inventory for $65,000. Late in the year, it sold fixed assets for their book value of $20,000. It sold one-half the inventory for $55,000 during the year. On December 15, the company used excess cash of $60,000 to purchase common stock of Repulski Company, which Far-East regarded as a long-term investment.

Prepare a statement of cash flows from investing activities for Far-East Trading Company.

5-33 Noncash Investing and Financing Activities

Poulsbo Bay Company had the following items in its statement of cash flows:

Note payable issued for acquisition of fixed assets	$191,000
Retirement of long-term debt	565,000
Common stock issued on conversion of preferred shares	340,000
Purchases of marketable securities	225,000
Mortgage assumed on acquisition of warehouse	630,000
Increase in accounts payable	42,000

Prepare a schedule of noncash investing and financing activities, selecting appropriate items from the preceding list.

5-34 Cash Received from Customers

Sigma University Press, Inc., had sales of $750,000 during 20X1, 80% of them on credit and 20% for cash. During the year, accounts receivable increased from $60,000 to $90,000, an increase of $30,000. What amount of cash was received from customers during 20X1?

5-35 Cash Paid to Suppliers

Cost of goods sold for Sigma University Press, Inc., during 20X1 was $500,000. Beginning inventory was $100,000, and ending inventory was $150,000. Beginning trade accounts payable were $24,000, and ending trade accounts payable were $45,000. What amount of cash did Sigma pay to suppliers?

5-36 Cash Paid to Employees

Sigma University Press, Inc., reported wage and salary expenses of $195,000 on its 20X1 income statement. It reported cash paid to employees of $180,000 on its statement of cash flows. The beginning balance of accrued wages and salaries payable was $18,000. What was the ending balance in accrued wages and salaries payable? Ignore payroll taxes.

5-37 Simple Cash Flows from Operating Activities

Orion Strategy, Inc., provides consulting services. In 20X6, net income was $185,000 on revenues of $470,000 and expenses of $285,000. The only noncash expense was depreciation of $35,000. The company has no inventory. Accounts receivable increased by $5,000 during 20X6, and accounts payable and salaries payable were unchanged.

Prepare a statement of cash flows from operating activities. Use the direct method. Omit supporting schedules.

5-38 Net Income and Cash Flow

Refer to Problem 5-37. Prepare a schedule that reconciles net income to net cash flow from operating activities.

5-39 Depreciation and Cash Flows

(Alternate is 5-55.) Ocean View Cafe had sales of $880,000, all received in cash. Total operating expenses were $570,000. All except depreciation were paid in cash. Depreciation of $100,000 was included in the $570,000 of operating expenses. Ignore income taxes.

1. Compute net income and net cash provided by operating activities.
2. Assume that depreciation is tripled. Compute net income and net cash provided by operating activities.

5-40 Identify Operating, Investing, and Financing Activities

The following listed items were found on a recent statement of cash flows for AT&T. For each item, indicate which section of the statement should contain the item—the operating, investing, or financing section. Also, indicate whether AT&T uses the direct or indirect method for reporting cash flows from operating activities.

a. Dividends paid
b. Proceeds from long-term debt issuance
c. Net income (loss)
d. Capital expenditures net of proceeds from sale or disposal of property, plant, and equipment
e. Issuance of common shares
f. Retirements of long-term debt
g. Increase in inventories
h. Depreciation and amortization
i. Increase in short-term borrowing—net

Problems

5-41 Cash Flows from Financing Activities

Eli Lilly and Company is a global, research-based corporation that develops, manufactures, and markets pharmaceuticals, medical instruments, diagnostic products, and agricultural products. Its 2002 sales exceeded $11 billion. Lilly's 2002 statement of cash flows included the following items, among others ($ in millions):

Dividends paid	$ (1,335.8)
Purchase of common stock and other capital transactions	(385.2)
Purchase of property and equipment	(1,130.9)
Depreciation and amortization	493.0
Stock issuances	64.6
Decrease in short-term borrowings	(18.0)
Increase in inventories	(285.1)
Additions to long-term debt	1,259.6
Net income	2,707.9
Repayments of long-term debt	(7.2)

Prepare the section "Cash flows from financing activities" from Eli Lilly's 2002 annual report. All items necessary for that section appear in the preceding. Some items from other sections have been omitted.

5-42 Cash Flows from Investing Activities

KLM Royal Dutch Airlines transports approximately 12 million passengers and more than 460 million tons of freight annually. Its revenues in fiscal 2003 topped €10 billion, where € is euros, the monetary unit of Europe. The company's statement of cash flows for fiscal 2003 contained the following items (euros in millions):

Net capital expenditure on intangible fixed assets	€ (28)
Net income (loss)	(416)
Capital expenditures on aircraft	(637)
Decrease in long-term debt	(259)
Investments in affiliated companies	(33)
Increase in long-term debt	121
Disposals of aircraft	308
Net capital expenditures on other tangible fixed assets	(53)
Sales of investments	7
Change in operating working capital	280

Prepare the section "Cash flows from investing activities" for KLM for the 2003 fiscal year. All items from that section are included in the preceding, along with some items from other sections of the statement of cash flows.

5-43 Noncash Investing and Financing Activities
The Vidarc Company operates a chain of video game arcades. Among Vidarc's activities in 20X8 were:

1. The firm traded four old video games to another amusement company for one new "Guerilla Fighter" game. The old games could have been sold for a total of $6,000 cash.
2. The company paid off $50,000 of long-term debt by paying $20,000 cash and signing a $30,000 6-month note payable.
3. The firm issued debt for $60,000 cash, all of which was used to purchase new games for its Northwest Arcade.
4. The company purchased the building in which one of its arcades was located by assuming the $100,000 mortgage on the structure and paying $20,000 cash.
5. Debt holders converted $60,000 of debt to common stock.
6. The firm refinanced debt by paying cash to buy back an old issue at its call price of $21,000 and issued new debt at a lower interest rate for $21,000.

Prepare a schedule of noncash investing and financing activities to accompany a statement of cash flows.

5-44 Statement of Cash Flows, Direct Method
Northwest Communications had cash and cash equivalents of $200 million on December 31, 2003. The following items are on the company's statement of cash flows ($ in millions) for the first 6 months of 2004:

Receipts from customers	$ 9,355
Interest paid, net	(140)
Capital expenditures for property and equipment	(1,710)
Purchase of treasury stock	(193)
Sales of marketable securities	191
Retirement of long-term debt	(160)
Payments to suppliers and employees	(7,499)
Issuance of common stock for employee stock plans	251
Dividend payments	(17)
Issuance of long-term debt	135
Other investing activity	(134)
Taxes paid	(167)

Prepare a statement of cash flows for the first 6 months of 2004 using the direct method. Include the balance of cash and cash equivalents at year-end 2003 and calculate the cash balance at June 30, 2004. Omit the schedule reconciling net income to net cash provided by operating activities and the schedule of noncash investing and financing activities.

5-45 Prepare a Statement of Cash Flows, Direct Method
(Alternate is 5-46.) Pools, Inc. is a wholesale distributor of prefabricated swimming pools. Its cash balance on December 31, 20X6, was $176 thousand, and net income for 20X7 was $314 thousand. Its 20X7 transactions affecting income or cash follow ($ in thousands):

a. Sales of $1,500 were all on credit. Cash collections from customers were $1,400.
b. The cost of items sold was $800. Purchases of inventory totaled $850; inventory and accounts payable were affected accordingly.
c. Cash payments on trade accounts payable totaled $825.
d. Accrued salaries and wages: totaled $190 and paid in cash, $200.
e. Depreciation was $45.
f. Interest expense, all paid in cash was $11.
g. Other expenses, all paid in cash totaled $100.
h. Income taxes accrued were $40; income taxes paid in cash were $35.
i. Plant and facilities were bought for $435 cash.
j. Long-term debt was issued for $110 cash.
k. Cash dividends of $41 were paid.

Prepare a statement of cash flows for 20X7 using the direct method for reporting cash flows from operating activities. Omit supporting schedules.

5-46 Prepare a Statement of Cash Flows, Direct Method

(Alternate is 5-45.) Kobe Exports, Inc., is a wholesaler of Asian goods. By the end of 20X5, the company's cash balance had dropped to ¥7 million, despite net income of ¥254 million in 20X5. Its transactions affecting income or cash in 20X5 were (¥ in millions):

a. Sales were ¥2,510, all on credit. Cash collections from customers were ¥2,413.
b. The cost of items sold was ¥1,599.
c. Inventory increased by ¥56.
d. Cash payments on trade accounts payable were ¥1,653.
e. Payments to employees were ¥305; accrued wages payable decreased by ¥24.
f. Other operating expenses, all paid in cash, were ¥94.
g. Interest expense, all paid in cash, was ¥26.
h. Income tax expense was ¥105; cash payments for income taxes were ¥108.
i. Depreciation was ¥151.
j. A warehouse was acquired for ¥540 cash.
k. Equipment was sold for ¥47; original cost was ¥206, accumulated depreciation was ¥159.
l. The firm received ¥28 for issue of common stock.
m. Long-term debt was retired for ¥25 cash.
n. The company paid cash dividends of ¥98.

Prepare a statement of cash flows for 20X5 using the direct method for reporting cash flows from operating activities. Calculate the cash balance as of January 1, 20X5. Omit supporting schedules.

5-47 Prepare Statement of Cash Flows from Income Statement and Balance Sheet

(Alternate is 5-49.) During 20X4, Arroyo Manufacturing Company declared and paid cash dividends of $10,000. Late in the year, the company bought new metal-working machinery for a cash cost of $125,000, financed partly by its first issue of long-term debt. Interest on the debt is payable annually. The company sold several old machines for cash equal to their aggregate book value of $5,000. It paid taxes in cash as incurred. The following data are in thousands:

Arroyo Manufacturing Company
Income Statement for the Year
Ended December 31, 20X4

Sales		$371
Cost of sales		209
Gross margin		162
Salaries	$82	
Depreciation	40	
Cash operating expenses	15	
Interest	2	139
Income before taxes		23
Income taxes		8
Net income		$ 15

Arroyo Manufacturing Company
Balance Sheets

	December 31		Increase
	20X4	**20X3**	**(Decrease)**
Assets			
Cash and cash equivalents	$ 97	$ 45	$ 52
Accounts receivable	45	60	(15)
Inventories	57	62	(5)
Total current assets	199	167	32
Fixed assets, net	190	110	80
Total assets	$389	$277	$112
Liabilities and Stockholders' Equity			
Accounts payable	$ 26	$ 21	$ 5
Interest payable	2	—	2
Long-term debt	100	—	100
Paid-in capital	220	220	—
Retained earnings	41	36	5
Total liabilities and stockholders' equity	$389	$277	$112

Prepare a statement of cash flows for 20X4. Use the direct method for reporting cash flows from operating activities. Omit supporting schedules. Assume that Arroyo paid expense items in cash unless balance sheet changes indicate otherwise.

5-48 Statement of Cash Flows, Direct Method

The **J. M. Smucker Company** had net sales of $1,311 million from selling products such as jam (Smuckers), peanut butter (Jif), and vegetable oils (Crisco) for the year ending April 30, 2003. The income statement showed operating expenses of $1,147 million, other expenses of $9 million, and income taxes of $59 million. Assume depreciation and amortization affect operating expenses and that other noncash items affect other expenses. The company's statement of cash flows, prepared under the indirect method, also contained the following items (where negative numbers represent cash outflows):

	(in Millions)
Issuance of common stock	$ 7
Dividends paid	(34)
Additions to property, plant, and equipment	(49)
Business acquired	(11)
Disposal of property, plant, and equipment	7
Net income	96
Depreciation and amortization	34
Changes in operating assets and liabilities	
Trade receivables	(43)
Inventories	(12)
Accounts payable and accrued liabilities	56
Income taxes	23
Other	12

1. Prepare the statement of cash flows for J.M. Smucker using the direct method. Omit the schedule reconciling net income to net cash provided by operating activities.
2. Discuss the relation between operating cash flow and investing and financing needs.

5-49 Prepare Statement of Cash Flows from Income Statement and Balance Sheet

(Alternate is 5-47.) Firenze S.A. had the following income statement and balance sheet items (euro in millions):

Income Statement for the Year Ended
December 31, 20X1

Sales	€910
Cost of goods sold	(540)
Gross margin	€370
Operating expenses	(220)
Depreciation	(60)
Interest	(15)
Income before taxes	€ 75
Income taxes	(25)
Net income	€ 50
Cash dividends paid	(30)
Total increase in retained earnings	€ 20

Balance Sheets

	December 31		Increase
	20X1	**20X0**	**(Decrease)**
Assets			
Cash	€ 20	€ 60	€ (40)
Accounts receivable	240	150	90
Inventories	450	350	100
Total current assets	710	560	150
Fixed assets, gross	890	715	175
Accumulated depreciation	(570)	(550)	(20)
Fixed assets, net	320	165	155
Total assets	€1,030	€725	€305
Liabilities and			
stockholders' equity			
Trade accounts payable	€ 520	€300	€220
Long-term debt	245	180	65
Stockholders' equity	265	245	20
Total liabilities and			
stockholders' equity	€1,030	€725	€305

During 20X1, Firenze purchased fixed assets for €315 million cash and sold fixed assets for their book value of €100 million. Operating expenses, interest, and taxes were paid in cash. No long-term debt was retired.

Prepare a statement of cash flows for 20X1. Use the direct method for reporting cash flows from operating activities. Omit supporting schedules.

5-50 Statement of Cash Flows, Direct Method, Interest Expense, Australia

CSR Limited is a leading supplier of building and construction materials headquartered in Sydney, Australia. The company's 2003 revenues exceeded A$7.2 billion, where A$ is the Australian dollar. The items at the top of p. 220 appeared in CSR's 2003 statement of cash flows (in millions).

1. Prepare a statement of cash flows for CSR Limited using the direct method. Include the proper amount for the net increase in cash. One item, interest paid, is included in a different section of the statement than it would be on a U.S. statement of cash flows. Place it in the section that makes the cash flows in each section total to the amounts given.
2. Where would the interest paid be shown in a statement of cash flows in the United States?
3. Explain why CSR places interest paid where it does.
4. Explain why the FASB in the United States requires the interest paid to be placed in the section you indicated in requirement 2.

Receipts from customers	A$7,572.7
Payments to suppliers and employees	(6,281.3)
Dividends and interest received	78.3
Net cash from operating activities	1,172.1
Purchase of property, plant, and equipment	(315.2)
Proceeds from sale of property, plant, and equipment	97.7
Net proceeds from borrowings	666.2
Dividends paid	(245.1)
Other investing activities	(897.6)
Income taxes paid	(197.6)
Net cash used in investing activities	(1,115.1)
Proceeds from issue of shares	42.8
Interest paid	(111.4)
Repurchase of shares	(6.7)
Net cash from financing activities	345.8
Net increase in cash	?

5-51 Statement of Cash Flows, Japan

Kansai Electric supplies power to an area of Japan that includes Osaka and Kyoto. Its operating revenues exceed ¥2.5 trillion, and its assets exceed ¥7 trillion. Instead of a statement of cash flows, Kansai Electric provides a statement of receipts and expenditures:

Statement of Receipts and Expenditures, Year Ended March 31
(in Billions of Yen)

Cash balance at beginning of the period	¥ 72
Receipts	
Operating revenues	2,545
Nonoperating revenues	109
Bond issue	236
Increase in loans	1,546
Total receipts	4,436
Expenditures	
Operating expenses	1,954
Nonoperating expenses	140
Repayments of bonds	262
Repayments of loans	1,419
Cost of construction	672
Total expenditures	4,447
Cash balance at end of the period	¥ 61

From the information in the statement of receipts and expenditures, prepare a statement of cash flows using the direct method.

5-52 Reconcile Net Income and Net Cash Provided by Operating Activities

(Alternate is 5-56.) Refer to Problem 5-45. Prepare a supporting schedule that reconciles net income to net cash provided by operating activities.

5-53 Cash Provided by Operations

Clorox Company is a leading producer of laundry additives, including Clorox liquid bleach. In fiscal 2003, net sales of more than $4 billion were double the 1997 level, and these operations produced earnings of $514 million. To calculate net earnings, Clorox recorded $191 million in depreciation.

Other items of revenue and expense not requiring cash increased cash flow from operations by $164 million. Dividends of $193 million were paid during 2003. Among the changes in balance sheet accounts during 2003 were ($ in millions):

Accounts receivable	$17	Decrease
Inventories	11	Increase
Prepaid expenses	1	Increase
Accounts payable	84	Decrease
Income taxes payable	71	Increase
Other accrued liabilities	54	Decrease

Compute the net cash provided by operating activities using the indirect method.

5-54 Cash Flows from Operating Activities, Indirect Method

Sumitomo Metal Industries, Ltd., is a leading diversified manufacturer of steel products. During the year ended March 31, 2003, Sumitomo earned ¥17.1 billion on revenues of approximately ¥1,224.6 billion (or approximately U.S.$10 billion). The following summarized information relates to Sumitomo's statement of cash flows:

	(Billions of Yen)
Depreciation and amortization	¥ 93.0
Repayments of long-term debt	324.2
Proceeds from long-term debt	197.1
Other noncash revenues and expenses, net	16.4
Decrease in receivables	30.6
Decrease in inventories	30.7
Other decreases in cash from operations due to changes in current assets and liabilities	29.5
Additions to property and equipment	59.3
Increase in payables	2.8

Compute the net cash provided by operating activities. All the information necessary for that task is provided, together with some information related to other elements of the cash flow statement. Note that the format does not include parentheses to differentiate elements that increase cash from those that decrease cash, but the distinction should be clear from the captions (except for "Other noncash revenues and expenses, net, which is a net noncash expense).

5-55 Depreciation and Cash Flows

(Alternate is 5-39.) The following condensed income statement and reconciliation schedule are from the annual report of Tang Company ($ in millions):

Sales	$380
Expenses	350
Net income	$ 30

Reconciliation Schedule of Net Income to
Net Cash Provided by Operating Activities

Net income	$ 30
Add noncash expenses	
Depreciation	25
Deduct net increase in noncash operating working capital	(17)
Net cash provided by operating activities	$ 38

A shareholder has suggested that the company switch from straight-line to accelerated depreciation on its annual report to shareholders, maintaining that this will increase the cash flow provided by operating activities. According to the stockholder's calculations, using accelerated methods would increase depreciation to $45 million, an increase of $20 million; net cash flow from operating activities would then be $58 million.

1. Suppose Tang Company adopts the accelerated depreciation method proposed. Compute net income and net cash flow from operating activities. Ignore income taxes.
2. Use your answer to requirement 1 to prepare a response to the shareholder.

5-56 Reconcile Net Income and Net Cash Provided by Operating Activities
(Alternate is 5-52.) Refer to Problem 5-46. Prepare a supporting schedule to the statement of cash flows that reconciles net income to net cash provided by operating activities.

5-57 Indirect Method: Reconciliation Schedule in Body of Statement
Refer to Problem 5-47. Prepare a statement of cash flows that includes a reconciliation of net income to net cash provided by operating activities in the body of the statement.

5-58 Cash Flows, Indirect Method
The Salinas Company has the following balance sheet data ($ in millions):

| | December 31 | | | | December 31 | | |
	20X1	20X0	Change		20X1	20X0	Change
Current assets				Current liabilities			
Cash	$ 15	$ 21	$ (6)	(summarized)	$101	$ 26	$ 75
Receivables, net	50	15	35	Long-term debt	150	—	150
Inventories	94	50	44	Stockholders' equity	208	160	48
Total current assets	$159	$ 86	$ 73				
Plant assets (net of							
accumulated depreciation)	300	100	200				
				Total liabilities and			
Total assets	$459	$186	$273	stockholders' equity	$459	$186	$273

Net income for 20X1 was $60 million. Net cash inflow from operating activities was $96 million. Cash dividends paid were $12 million. Depreciation was $40 million. Fixed assets were purchased for $240 million, $150 million of which was financed via the issuance of long-term debt outright for cash.

Roberto Salinas, the president and majority stockholder of the Salinas Company, was a superb operating executive. He was imaginative and aggressive in marketing and ingenious and creative in production. However, he had little patience with financial matters. After examining the most recent balance sheet and income statement, he muttered, "We've enjoyed 10 years of steady growth; 20X1 was our most profitable ever. Despite such profitability, we're in the worst cash position in our history. Just look at those current liabilities in relation to our available cash! This whole picture of the more you make, the poorer you get, just does not make sense. These statements must be cockeyed."

1. Prepare a statement of cash flows for 20X1 using the indirect method.
2. By using the statement of cash flows and other information, write a short memorandum to Salinas, explaining why there is such a squeeze on cash.

5-59 Prepare Statement of Cash Flows
The Rosenberg Company has assembled the accompanying (a) balance sheets, and (b) statement of income and retained earnings for 20X4.

Rosenberg Company
Balance Sheets as of December 31 (in Millions)

	20X4	20X3	Change
Assets			
Cash	$ 5	$ 20	$(15)
Accounts receivable	47	33	14
Inventory	70	50	20
Prepaid general expenses	4	3	1
Plant assets, net	202	150	52
	$328	$256	$ 72
Liabilities and shareholders' equity			
Accounts payable for merchandise	$ 74	$ 60	$ 14
Accrued tax payable	3	2	1
Long-term debt	50	—	50
Capital stock	100	100	—
Retained earnings	101	94	7
	$328	$256	$ 72

Rosenberg Company
Statement of Income and Retained Earnings for the Year Ended
December 31, 20X4 (in Millions)

Sales		$275
Less cost of goods sold		
Inventory, December 31, 20X3	$ 50	
Purchases	185	
Cost of goods available for sale	$235	
Inventory, December 31, 20X4	70	165
Gross profit		$110
Less other expenses		
General expense	$ 51	
Depreciation	40	
Taxes	10	101
Net income		$ 9
Dividends		2
Net income of the period retained		$ 7
Retained earnings, December 31, 20X3		94
Retained earnings, December 31, 20X4		$101

On December 30, 20X4, Rosenberg paid $98 million in cash to acquire a new plant to expand operations. This was partly financed by an issue of long-term debt for $50 million in cash. Plant assets were sold for their book value of $6 million during 20X4. Because net income was $9 million, the highest in the company's history, Jacob Rosenberg, the chief executive officer, was distressed by the company's extremely low cash balance.

1. Prepare a statement of cash flows for 20X4 using the direct method for reporting cash flows from operating activities.
2. Prepare a schedule that reconciles net income to net cash provided by operating activities.
3. What is revealed by the statement of cash flows? Does it help you reduce Mr. Rosenberg's distress? Why? Briefly explain to Mr. Rosenberg why cash has decreased even though net income was $9 million.

5-60 Balance Sheet Equation

Refer to Problem 5-59, requirement 1. Support your financial statement by using a form of the balance sheet equation. Step by step, show in equation form how each item in the statement of cash flows affects cash.

5-61 Comprehensive Statement of Cash Flows

During the past 30 years, Adirondack Toys, Inc., has grown from a single-location specialty toy store into a chain of stores selling a wide range of children's products. Its activities in 20X4 included the following:

a. The company purchased 40% of the stock of Lake Placid Toy Company for $3,848,000 cash.

b. The organization issued $1,906,000 in long-term debt; $850,000 of the proceeds was used to retire debt that became due in 20X4 and was listed on the books at $900,000.

c. The firm purchased property, plant, and equipment for $1,986,000 cash, and sold property with a book value of $576,000 for $500,000 cash.

d. The company signed a note payable for the purchase of new equipment; the obligation was listed at $516,000.

e. Executives exercised stock options for 8,000 shares of common stock, paying cash of $170,000.

f. On December 30, 20X4, the firm bought Sanchez Musical Instruments Company by issuing common stock with a market value of $297,000.

g. The company issued common stock for $3,300,000 cash.

h. The firm withdrew $800,000 cash from a money market fund that was considered a cash equivalent.

i. The company bought $249,000 of treasury stock to hold for future exercise of stock options.

j. Long-term debt of $960,000 was converted to common stock.

k. Selected results for the year follow:

Net income	$ 672,000
Depreciation and amortization	615,000
Increase in inventory	72,000
Decrease in accounts receivable	19,000
Increase in accounts and wages payable	7,000
Increase in taxes payable	35,000
Interest expense	144,000
Increase in accrued interest payable	15,000
Sales	9,739,000
Cash dividends received from investments	152,000
Cash paid to suppliers and employees	8,074,000
Cash dividends paid	240,000
Cash paid for taxes	390,000

Prepare a statement of cash flows for 20X4 using the direct method. Include a schedule that reconciles net income to net cash provided by operating activities. Also include a schedule of noncash investing and financing activities.

5-62 Statement of Cash Flows, Direct and Indirect Methods

Nordstrom, Inc., the Seattle-based fashion retailer, had the following income statement for the year ended January 31, 2003 ($ in millions):

Net sales		$5,975
Costs and expenses		
Cost of sales	$3,971	
Selling, general, and administrative	1,814	
Interest (net)	82	
Less: Other income	(74)	
Total costs and expenses		$5,793
Earnings before income taxes		$ 182
Income taxes		92
Net earnings		$ 90

The company's net cash provided by operating activities, prepared using the indirect method, was ($ in millions):

Net earnings	$ 90
Adjustments to reconcile net earnings to net cash provided by operating activities	
Depreciation, amortization, and other	288
Changes in	
Accounts receivable	(58)
Merchandise inventories	(117)
Prepaid expenses	1
Accounts payable	(10)
Accrued salaries and wages	24
Other accrued expenses	17
Income taxes payable	44
Net cash provided by operating activities	$279

Prepare a statement showing the net cash provided by operating activities using the direct method. Assume that Nordstrom received all "other income" in cash and that prepaid expenses and accrued salaries and wages and other accrued expenses relate to selling, general, and administrative expenses.

5-63 Free Cash Flow

A condensed version of the Kellogg Company statement of cash flows appears in Exhibit 5-16. Use that statement to answer the following two questions.

1. What was Kellogg's free cash flow for each of the 3 years shown?
2. What does the free cash flow tell us about Kellogg's ability to generate sufficient cash flow from operations to cover ongoing investing activities and pay dividends to its shareholders?

5-64 Miscellaneous Cash Flow Questions

McDonald's Corporation is a well-known provider of food services around the world. McDonald's statement of cash flows for 2002 is reproduced with a few slight modifications as Exhibit 5-17 on p. 227. Use that statement and the additional information provided to answer the following questions:

1. In the financing activities section, all parentheses for 2002 have been removed. Which numbers should be put in parentheses?
2. In the investing activities section, all parentheses for 2002 have been removed. Which numbers should be put in parentheses?
3. The 2002 values for the change in cash and cash equivalents and for beginning and end-of-year balances have been omitted and replaced with the letters A, B, and C. Provide the proper values for these three missing numbers.
4. Retained earnings at December 31, 2001 was $18,608.3 million. Compute the retained earnings balance at December 31, 2002.
5. Comment on the relation between cash flow from operations and cash used for investing activities.

5-65 Interpretation of the Statement of Cash Flows and Ethics

Brookline, Inc., was a successful producer of athletic shoes in the late-1990s. The company's peak year was 2000. Since then, both sales and profits have fallen. The following information is from the company's 2003 annual report ($ in thousands):

	2003	2002	2001
Net income	$1,500	$4,500	$7,500
Accounts receivable (end of year)	900	1,800	6,000
Inventory (end of year)	1,050	2,100	2,850
Net cash provided by operations	675	1,050	2,250
Capital expenditures	900	1,050	1,350
Proceeds from sales of fixed assets	2,700	1,500	2,250
Net gain on sales of fixed assets plus net extraordinary gains	2,250	1,800	2,400

Exhibit 5-16
Kellogg Company
and Subsidiaries
*Consolidated Statement
of Cash Flows, Year
Ended December 31*

(Millions)	2002	2001	2000
Operating Activities			
Net earnings	$ 720.9	$ 473.6	$587.7
Items in net earnings not requiring (providing) cash			
Depreciation and amortization	348.4	438.6	290.6
Other noncash expenses	111.9	36.7	59.9
Changes in operating assets and liabilities	265.3	259.4	27.0
Other	(446.6)	(76.3)	(84.3)
Net cash provided by operating activities	999.9	1,132.0	880.9
Investing Activities			
Additions to properties	(253.5)	(276.5)	(230.9)
Acquisitions of businesses	(2.2)	(3,858.0)	(137.2)
Dispositions of businesses	60.9	—	—
Property disposals	6.0	10.1	4.8
Other	—	(19.4)	(16.0)
Net cash used in investing activities	(188.8)	(4,143.8)	(379.3)
Financing Activities			
Reductions of notes payable	(447.3)	(519.6)	(331.6)
Issuances of notes payable	354.9	549.6	294.0
Issuances of long-term debt	—	5,001.4	—
Reductions of long-term debt	(439.3)	(1,608.4)	(4.8)
Net issuances of common stock	100.9	26.4	4.5
Common stock repurchases	(101.0)	—	—
Cash dividends	(412.6)	(409.8)	(403.9)
Other	—	.6	—
Net cash used in financing activities	(944.4)	3,040.2	(441.8)
Increase (decrease) in cash and cash equivalents	$(133.3)	$ 28.4	$ 59.8

During 2004, short-term loans of $9 million became due. Brookline paid off only $2.25 million and was able to extend the terms on the other $6.75 million. Accounts payable continued at a very low level in 2004, and the company maintained a large investment in corporate equity securities, enough to generate $900,000 of dividends received in 2004. Brookline neither paid dividends nor issued stock or bonds in 2004. Its 2004 statement of cash flows was as follows:

Brookline, Inc.
Statement of Cash Flows for the Year Ended December 31, 2004 (in thousands)

Cash flows from operating activities	
Net income	$ 1,050
Adjustments to reconcile net income to net cash provided by operating activities	
Depreciation and amortization	600
Net decrease in accounts receivable	150
Net decrease in inventory	225
Investment revenue from equity investments, less $900 of dividends received	(600)
Gains on sales of fixed assets	(2,100)
Extraordinary loss on building fire	1,200
Net cash provided by operating activities	$ 525

Cash flows from investing activities

Purchase of fixed assets	$ (600)	
Insurance proceeds on building fire	3,000	
Sale of plant assets	3,750	
Purchase of corporate equity securities	(2,250)	
Net cash provided by investing activities		3,900
Cash flows from financing activities		
Principal payments on short-term debt to banks	$(2,250)	
Purchase of treasury stock	(900)	
Net cash used for financing activities		(3,150)
Net increase in cash		1,275
Cash, December 31, 2003		1,800
Cash, December 31, 2004		$3,075

1. Interpret the statement of cash flows for Brookline.
2. Describe any ethical issues relating to the strategy and financial disclosures of Brookline.

(In Millions)	2002	2001
Operating Activities		
Net income	$ 893.5	$1,636.6
Adjustments to reconcile to cash provided by operations		
Depreciation and amortization	1,050.8	1,086.3
Changes in operating working capital items		
Accounts receivable	1.6	(104.7)
Inventories, prepaid expenses and other current assets	(38.1)	(62.9)
Accounts payable	(11.2)	10.2
Taxes and other liabilities	448.0	270.4
Other	545.5	(147.6)
Cash provided by operations	2,890.1	2,688.3
Investing Activities		
Property and equipment expenditures	2,003.8	(1,906.2)
Purchases of restaurant businesses	548.4	(331.6)
Sales of restaurant businesses and property	369.5	375.9
Other	283.9	(206.3)
Cash used for investing activities	2,466.6	(2,068.2)
Financing Activities		
Net short-term borrowings (repayments)	606.8	(248.0)
Long-term financing issuances	1,502.6	1,694.7
Long-term financing repayments	750.3	(919.4)
Treasury stock purchases	670.2	(1,068.1)
Common stock dividends	297.4	(287.7)
Other	310.9	204.8
Cash used for financing activities	511.2	(623.7)
Cash and equivalents increase (decrease)	A	(3.6)
Cash and equivalents beginning of year	B	421.7
Cash and equivalents at end of year	$ C	$ 418.1

Exhibit 5-17
McDonald's Corporation
Consolidated Statement of Cash Flows, Years Ended December 31

Collaborative Learning Exercise

5-66 Items in the Statement of Cash Flows

Form groups of four to six students each. Each member of the group should select a different company, find its statement of cash flows for a recent year, and make a list of the items included in each section of the statement: operating, investing, and financing activities. Be ready to explain the nature of each item.

1. As a group, make a comprehensive list of all items the companies listed under cash flows from operating activities. Identify those that are essentially the same but simply differ in terminology, and call them a single item. For each item, explain why and how it affects cash flows from operating activities. Note whether any of the companies selected use the direct method for reporting cash flows from operating activities. (Most companies use the indirect method, despite the fact that the FASB prefers the direct method.) If any use the direct method, separate the items listed under the direct method from those listed under the indirect method.
2. Make another comprehensive list of all items listed under cash flows from investing activities. Again, combine those that are essentially identical and differ only in terminology. For each item, explain why and how it affects cash flows from investing activities.
3. Make a third comprehensive list, this time including all items listed under cash flows from financing activities. Again, combine those that are essentially identical and differ only in terminology. For each item, explain why and how it affects cash flows from financing activities.
4. Reconvene as a class. For each of the three sections on the statement of cash flows, have groups sequentially add one item to the list of items included in the statement, simultaneously explaining why it is included in that section. Then identify the items that appear on nearly all cash flow statements and those that are relatively rare.

Analyzing and Interpreting Financial Statements

5-67 Financial Statement Research

Identify an industry and select two companies within that industry.

1. Determine whether cash flow from operations is stable through time.
2. Relate cash flow from operations to investing and dividend payment needs.
3. Compare cash flow from operations to net income. Explain why they differ.

5-68 Analyzing Starbucks's Financial Statements

Examine Starbucks' statement of cash flows in Appendix A, p. A13.

1. Explain why Starbucks' net cash provided by operating activities was nearly $90 million more in the year ended September 28, 2003, than it was in the year ended September 29, 2002. Would you expect a similar increase in the next year? Why or why not?
2. Explain to a nonaccountant what Starbucks did with the $566 million of cash generated by operating activities during the year ended September 28, 2003.
3. Suppose a friend of yours commented, "Starbucks must have poor financial management. It made nearly $270 million in the year ended September 28, 2003, and it generated more than $566 million in cash from operations, yet it paid no dividends. It's shareholders got nothing." Answer your friend's question.

5-69 Analyzing Financial Statement Using the Internet: Nike

Go to www.nikebiz.com, then select Investors to locate Nike's most current financial information.

1. Take a look at Nike's Condensed Consolidated Statement of Cash Flows. Does Nike use the direct or indirect method? How can you tell?
2. Locate Management's Discussion and Analysis. Look under the section titled Liquidity and Capital Resources. What does management have to say about cash provided by operations?

3. Which is larger—cash provided (or used) by operations or net income for the period? Why is the cash provided by operations different from the amount of net income for the year?
4. Why does Nike add depreciation and amortization to net income in the operating activities section?
5. What is the primary reason for cash used (provided) by investing activities in the most recent fiscal period?
6. What is the primary reason for cash used (provided) by financing activities in the most recent fiscal period?

Accounting for Sales

CHAPTER 6

LEARNING OBJECTIVES

After studying this chapter, you should be able to:

1. Recognize revenue items at the proper time on the income statement.

2. Account for cash and credit sales.

3. Compute and interpret sales returns and allowances, sales discounts, and bank credit card sales.

4. Manage cash and explain its importance to the company.

5. Estimate and interpret uncollectible accounts receivable balances.

6. Assess the level of accounts receivable.

7. Develop and explain internal control procedures.

8. Prepare a bank reconciliation (Appendix 6).

Not many companies seek the permission of the Central Intelligence Agency (CIA) when naming products. Yet that is precisely what System Development Laboratories did in 1977 when it created a new type of database while working on a confidential project for the U.S. government. Called the "Oracle," this new relational database structure became the world's most popular form, and for the company, now called Oracle Corporation, it was an explosive sales success story. Revenues for its most recent fiscal year-end approached $10 billion for software sales worldwide.

Recording and managing this sales revenue is important to Oracle's success. For every sale generated, the company must either collect cash or record an accounts receivable from the customer. The accounts receivable must then be collected so the company has adequate cash to continue its operations. On average, it took Oracle 84 days to convert sales to cash in 2002. This was longer than the 77 days required 3 years earlier.

Managing accounts receivable and collecting cash is a key activity for Oracle. The faster the company collects the cash, the less it will need to borrow (and the less interest it will pay). However, many customers need to obtain credit from their suppliers. Companies that push to collect cash too quickly may drive potential customers elsewhere. Oracle is one of many companies that has created a financing division to assist their customers. In 2002, Oracle's financing division financed about 13% of its sales. Oracle has a "standard practice of providing long-term financing outside of one year to creditworthy customers." Similar financing transactions are a common feature of buying or leasing an automobile. Ford Credit and General Motors Acceptance Corporation provide low interest or zero interest car loans. In 2002, this was an important factor supporting auto sales in a difficult market.

Oracle supplies the software that powers the Internet. Its revenues from software licenses and servicing customers were just short of $10 billion in 2003, making Oracle second only to Microsoft in its industry.

In a recent analysis of Oracle, a security analyst presented a prominent graph displaying the revenue growth in each part of Oracle's business. Such trends in revenue help analysts to understand what happened in the last year or the last quarter and to predict what may occur in the future. Thus, recording sales revenue in the right time period is essential to measuring the rate of increase or decrease. For Oracle, whose company name means "source of wisdom," efficient and accurate measurement of revenues and tracking of accounts receivables is smart business. ■

Recognition of Sales Revenue

OBJECTIVE 1

Recognize revenue items at the proper time on the income statement.

Why is the timing of revenue recognition so important? It is critical to the measurement of net income. Revenue recognition affects net income in two ways. First, it directly affects net income because it is one element of the calculation net income = revenue − expense. Second, it indirectly affects net income because it determines when a company recognizes certain expenses. Under the matching principle, a company reports the cost of the items sold in the same period in which it recognizes the related revenue.

The timing of changes in sales and net income is especially important because of the profound effects they have on stock prices. For example, the Business First box on page 233 shows how growing earnings drove increases in Intel's stock price. Moreover, managers often receive higher salaries or greater bonuses for increasing sales and net income. Therefore, they prefer to recognize sales revenue as soon as possible. Owners and potential investors, however, want to be sure the economic benefits of the sale are certain before recognizing revenue. In other words, financial statement users want to be sure that the company will actually receive payment before they recognize the accounting effects of a completed sale. These different perspectives make accountants carefully assess when to recognize revenue.

Accrual-basis accounting uses a two-pronged test for revenue recogniton: (1) goods or services must be delivered to the customers, that is, the revenue must be earned; and (2) cash or an asset virtually assured of being converted into cash must be received, that is, the revenue must be realized. Most companies recognize revenue at the point of sale. Suppose you buy a compact disc at a local music store. Both revenue recognition tests are generally met at the time of purchase. You receive the merchandise, and the store receives cash, a check, or a credit card slip. Because the store can readily convert both checks and credit card slips to cash, it recognizes revenue at the point of sale regardless of which of these three methods of payment you use.

Of course, the two revenue recognition tests are not always met at the same time. In such cases, we recognize revenue only when both tests have been met. Consider magazine subscriptions. The realization test is met when the publisher receives cash. However, the publisher does not earn revenues until magazines are delivered. Therefore, we delay revenue recognition until the time of delivery.

INTERPRETING FINANCIAL STATEMENTS

Refer to the **Starbucks** financial statements in the final appendix, and the description of revenue recognition that is included in Note 1: Summary of Significant Accounting Policies. Describe how Starbucks recognizes revenue using the categories of revenue in the Consolidated Statements of Earnings.

Answer

Starbucks reports two major categories of revenue: retail and specialty. Retail refers to over-the-counter sales in stores, and revenue is recognized as cash is collected for retail sales. The exception occurs when customers purchase prepaid "stored value" cards. Purchases of these cards are recorded initially as a liability "deferred revenue," and revenue is then recognized as customers use their cards at retail stores. Specialty revenue is the label given to bulk sales of coffee not through company-operated stores. Specialty revenue is generally recognized upon shipment to the customer. Note that the vast majority of the revenue is from retail sales.

THE INTEL DECADE OF THE 1990S . . . AND THE RECKONING IN THE NEW MILLENIUM

Would you like to invest in a stock whose price increases 54-fold in just 10 years? Anyone who bought Intel's stock in 1990 already has. Intel stock purchased for $100 in March 1990 sold for about $5,400 in March 2000.

If you had been able to read and understand Intel's financial statements in 1990, could you have predicted this large increase in stock price? Unfortunately, you probably could not. You also could not have predicted in March 2000 that by November 2003 your $5,400 would have collapsed to $2,475. Of course the good news is that $2,475 was a huge improvement from the fall of 2002 when your investment hit a low point of $1,125. If understanding financial statements were sufficient for making good investment decisions, there would be a lot of rich accountants in this world. However, looking at Intel's financial statements from 1990 through 2000 helps explain why the company did so well over that period. Understanding what made Intel successful helps you predict whether that success will continue.

Intel's revenues increased from $3.9 billion in 1990 to $33.7 billion in 2000, a rate of growth of more than 24% per year. Meanwhile, earnings per share grew from $.10 to $1.51. This growth in earnings per share is even more rapid than the revenue growth, nearly 31% per year.

To support this growth in sales and earnings, Intel continued to invest heavily, spending over $3.9 billion in 2000 on R&D in addition to another $2.4 billion on plant, property, and equipment.

Will Intel return to its former success? We cannot know for sure, but there are some clues in the past. In 2000, Intel had nearly $14 billion in cash. That cash helped Intel fund its expansion plans during a very difficult period. Over the ensuing years, Intel maintained its annual commitment to new investment in R&D. In the fall of 2003, Intel again has almost $14 billion in cash, after falling to much lower levels of cash early in the decade. The microprocessor industry is cyclical, which means that sales throughout the industry rise and fall. Sales, of course, are the driving force behind any company's success. In Intel's case a major factor in its change in value was that the growth in sales reversed. Sales grew by 14% per year at the end of the 1990s, only to fall even faster in the early part of the next decade. In the fall of 2003, the market value of Intel was twice its level a year prior and earnings per share had almost tripled. Stay tuned.

Sources: Intel Annual Reports for 2000 and 2003.

Sometimes accountants must make a judgment call on when the recognition criteria are met. A classic example is accounting for long-term contracts. Suppose Oracle signs a $40 million consulting contract with the U.S. government for the antiterrorism program. Oracle signs the contract and immediately begins work on January 2, 20X4. The completion date is December 31, 20X5. The government will pay Oracle upon completion of the project. Oracle expects to complete one-half of the project each year. When should Oracle record the $40 million of revenue on its income statement?

The most common answer is that Oracle earns one-half of the revenue each year, so it should record $20 million of the revenue annually. Generally, companies can count on the government and major corporations to make payments on their contracts. Therefore, they can recognize revenues on such contracts as the work is performed. Because payment is virtually certain, revenues are realized as the company earns them. Using this **percentage-of-completion** method, we recognize revenue on long-term contracts as production occurs, and under the matching principle we also recognize the associated expenses. When Oracle recognizes one-half of the revenue, it also recognizes one-half of the expected expenses.

percentage-of-completion method
Method of recognizing revenue on long-term contracts as production occurs.

Measurement of Sales Revenue

After deciding when to recognize revenue, accountants must determine the amount of revenue to record. In other words, how should accountants measure revenue?

OBJECTIVE 2

Account for cash and credit sales.

A cash sale increases Sales Revenue, an income statement account, and increases Cash, a balance sheet account. Accountants record a credit sale on open account much like a cash sale, except that the balance sheet account Accounts Receivable is increased instead of Cash. To measure revenue, accountants approximate the net realizable value of the asset inflow from the customer. That is, they measure revenue in terms of the cash equivalent value of the asset (either cash or accounts receivable) received.

A $100 sale will be recorded differently depending on the asset received:

Cash	100	
Sales revenue		100
OR		
Accounts receivable	100	
Sales revenue		100

In fact, there are many reasons why prices are not what they appear to be, and ultimately, the revenue earned may not equal the original sales price. Why? Merchants give discounts for prompt payment and for high-volume purchases. Sometimes, the customer is unable or unwilling to pay the full amount owed. The accounting system must deal with all these issues. Managers also use accounting information about sales and collections to determine how company policy is affecting its relationship with the customer. Do sales increase when the company offers more generous discounts and payment terms?

Merchandise Returns and Allowances

OBJECTIVE 3

Compute and interpret sales returns and allowances, sales discounts, and bank credit card sales.

sales returns (purchase returns)
Products returned by the customer.

sales allowance (purchase allowance)
Reduction of the original selling price.

gross sales
Total sales revenue before deducting sales returns and allowances.

net sales
Total sales revenue reduced by sales returns and allowances.

Suppose a store recognizes revenue for a given sale at the point of that sale, but later the customer returns the merchandise. The purchaser may be unhappy with the product's color, size, style, or quality, or simply may have a change of heart. The store (supplier, vendor) calls these **sales returns**; the customer calls them **purchase returns.** Such merchandise returns are minor for manufacturers and wholesalers, but are major for retail department stores. For instance, returns of 12% of gross sales are not abnormal for stores such as **Marshall Fields** or **Macys**.

Sometimes, instead of returning merchandise, the customer demands a reduction of the selling price (the original price previously agreed to). For example, a customer may complain about scratches on a household appliance or about buying a cordless phone for $40 on Wednesday and seeing the same item on sale for $35 on Thursday. Sellers often settle such complaints by granting a **sales allowance**, which is essentially a reduction of the original selling price (the purchaser calls this a **purchase allowance**).

Sales allowances and returns have an effect on net sales, but not on gross sales. **Gross sales** are the initial revenues or asset inflows based on the initial sales price. We decrease gross sales by the amount of the returns and allowances to calculate the **net sales**. Instead of reducing the revenue (or sales) account directly, managers of retail stores typically use a contra account, Sales Returns and Allowances, which combines both returns and allowances in a single account. Managers use a contra account to watch changes in the level of returns and allowances. For instance, a change in the percentage of returns in fashion merchandise may signal changes in customer tastes. Similarly, sellers of fashion or fad merchandise may find tracking of sales returns to be especially useful in assessing the quality of products and services from various suppliers. Also, properly using sales figures for commissions or bonuses may require that the manager knows which sales staff members have especially high rates of sales returns or allowances. Because returns happen after the sales, managers employ separate tracking of returns and allowances to avoid going back and changing the original entries for the sale, a messy and unreliable process.

How would a retailer adjust gross sales by accounting for sales returns and allowances? Suppose your local outlet of The Disney Store has $900,000 gross sales on credit and $80,000 sales returns and allowances. The analysis of transactions would show:

	A	=	L	+	SE
Credit sales on open account	+900,000 [Increase Accounts Receivable]	=			+900,000 [Increase Sales]
Returns and allowances	−80,000 [Decrease Accounts Receivable]	=			−80,000 [Increase Sales Returns and Allowances]

The journal entries (without explanations) are:

Accounts receivable	900,000	
Sales		900,000
Sales returns and allowances	80,000	
Accounts receivable		80,000

The income statement would begin:

Gross sales	$900,000
Deduct: Sales returns and allowances	80,000
Net sales	$820,000
or	
Sales, net of $80,000 returns and allowances	$820,000

How would an analyst or manager react to this information differently than they would upon seeing simply that net sales were $820,000? About 9% of our sales are either being returned or lost through price reductions. How has this pattern changed through time? What can we do to reduce the amount of extra service costs we incur to handle these special transactions?

Cash and Trade Discounts

In addition to returns and allowances, cash and trade discounts also reduce reported sales. **Trade discounts** offer one or more reductions to the gross selling price for a particular class of customers. An example is a discount for large-volume purchases. The seller might not offer a discount on the first $10,000 of merchandise purchased per year, but a 2% discount on the next $10,000 worth of purchases and a discount of 3% to a customer on all sales in excess of $20,000. The gross sales revenue recognized from a trade discount sale is the price received after deducting the discount.

trade discounts
Reductions to the gross selling price for a particular class of customers.

Companies set trade discount terms to be competitive in industries where such discounts are common or to encourage certain customer behavior. For example, manufacturers with seasonal products (gardening supplies, snow shovels, fans, Christmas gifts, and so on) might offer price discounts on early orders and deliveries to smooth out production throughout the year and to minimize the manufacturer's cost of storing the inventory. In deciding to accept early delivery, the buyer must weigh the storage costs it will incur against the reduced price the discount provides.

In contrast to trade discounts, **cash discounts** are rewards for prompt payment. Sellers quote the terms of the discount in various ways on the invoice:

cash discounts
Reductions of invoice prices awarded for prompt payment.

Credit Terms	Meaning
n/30	The full billed price (net price) is due on the thirtieth day after the invoice date.
1/5, n/30	A 1% discount can be taken for payment within 5 days of the invoice date; otherwise, the full billed price is due in 30 days.
15 E.O.M.	The full price is due within 15 days after the end of the month of sale; an invoice dated December 20 is due January 15.

For example, a manufacturer sells $30,000 of computer equipment to Oracle on terms 2/10, n/60. Therefore, Oracle may remit $30,000 less a cash discount of $0.02 \times \$30,000$, or $30,000 - \$600 = \$29,400$, if it makes payment within 10 days after the invoice date. Otherwise, it must pay the full $30,000 within 60 days.

Cash discounts encourage prompt payment and thus reduce the manufacturer's need for cash. Early collection also reduces the risk of bad debts. Moreover, favorable credit terms with attractive cash discounts are a way to compete with other sellers. Of course, once one seller grants such terms, competitors tend to do likewise.

Should purchasers take cash discounts? The answer is usually yes, but the decision depends on the relative costs of interest. Suppose Oracle decides not to pay the $30,000 invoice for 60 days. It has the use of $29,400 for an extra 50 days $(60 - 10)$ for an "interest" payment of $600. Think of this as if Oracle had two choices. It could borrow the money from the bank and pay 10% interest per year. Interest for 50 days on $29,400 is $403 ($29,400 \times 10\% \times 50 \div 365$). Alternatively, Oracle could delay payment for 50 days and pay the higher invoice price. Notice that it is much cheaper to borrow the money, and that is what most companies should do. The total invoice is $600 higher than the discount price, and the interest is only $403.

You could also calculate the annual interest rate equivalent of the discount using the following logic. If you pay $600 to use the money for 50 days, you pay 2.04% for the 50 days ($600 \div \$29,400$). During a year, there are 7.3 periods of 50 days ($365 \div 50$ days). If the interest rate is 2.04% for 50 days, it is 14.9% for the year (2.04% per period $\times 7.3$ periods per year). Most well-managed companies, such as Oracle, can borrow for less than 14.9% interest per year, so they design their accounting systems to take advantage of all cash discounts automatically. Usage of cash discounts varies through time and from one industry to another. You may be familiar with some gas stations that offer a lower price for cash payment, whereas other stations do not.

Why might a manager elect to pass up cash discounts? If a company's credit rating is poor, it may have trouble borrowing at interest rates lower than the annual rates implied by the cash discount terms offered by its suppliers. A manager in such a company would be wise to pass up the discount and pay only when the supplier requires payment.

Recording Charge Card Transactions

In a sense, companies offer cash discounts when they accept charge cards such as VISA, MasterCard, American Express, Carte Blanche, or Diner's Club. Why? These credit card companies charge retailers a fee, and the retailers receive an amount less than the listed sales price. Why do retailers accept these cards? There are three major reasons: (1) to attract credit customers who would otherwise shop elsewhere, (2) to get cash immediately instead of waiting for customers to pay in due course, and (3) to avoid the cost of tracking, billing, and collecting customers' accounts.

Retailers deposit VISA slips in their bank accounts daily (just like cash), or they use electronic devices to direct cash immediately to their bank accounts. This service costs money (in the form of service charges on every credit sale), and this cost is included in calculating net sales revenue. Card companies' service charges are typically from 1% to 4% of gross sales, although large-volume retailers bear less cost as a percentage of sales. A sample arrangement for a large-volume retailer might be 4.3 cents per transaction plus 1.08% of the gross sales using charge cards.

Suppose VISA charges a company a straight 3% of sales for its credit card services. Credit sales of $10,000 will result in cash of only $9,700 [$10,000 − (0.03 × $10,000), or $10,000 − $300]. Management can tabulate the $300 amount separately for control purposes:

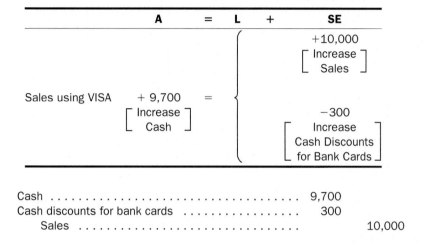

	A	=	L	+	SE
					+10,000 [Increase Sales]
Sales using VISA	+ 9,700 [Increase Cash]	=			−300 [Increase Cash Discounts for Bank Cards]

Cash	9,700	
Cash discounts for bank cards	300	
Sales		10,000

By accounting for these cash discounts separately, managers can continuously evaluate whether the costs they incur are justified.

Accounting for Net Sales Revenue

Because we record cash discounts and sales returns and allowances as deductions from Gross Sales, a detailed income statement might contain multiple elements as follows (numbers assumed):

Gross sales		$1,000
Deduct		
Sales returns and allowances	270	
Cash discounts on sales	20	290
Net sales		$ 710

Reports to shareholders typically omit details and show only net revenues. For example, **Starbucks** reports net revenue of $4,075 million on its income statement. In many countries outside the United States, the word **turnover** is used as a synonym for sales or revenues. Thus, **BP**, the huge British integrated petroleum company, began its 2003 income statement with "Group Turnover . . . £236,045 million" instead of "Net Revenues . . . £236,045 million."

An important feature of the income statement is the fact that returns, allowances, and most discounts are offsets to gross sales. Management may design an accounting system to use one account, Sales, or several accounts, as shown in the preceding sample income statement. When using only one account, all returns, allowances, and cash discounts decrease the sales account directly. When using a separate account for cash discounts on sales, the following analysis illustrates the possible outcomes of the $30,000 sale on terms 2/10, n/60 from our **Oracle** example:

turnover
A synonym for sales or revenues in many countries outside the United States.

	A	=	L +	SE
1. Sell at terms of 2/10, n/60	+ 30,000	=		+ 30,000
	Increase Accounts Receivable			Increase Sales
Followed by either 2 or 3				
2. Either collect $29,400 ($30,000 less 2%)	+ 29,400	=		−600
	Increase Cash			Increase Cash Discounts on Sales
	−30,000			
	Decrease Accounts Receivable			
or				
3. Collect $30,000	+ 30,000	=		(No effect)
	Increase Cash			
	−30,000			
	Decrease Accounts Receivable			

The journal entries follow:

```
1. Accounts receivable  ....................  30,000
      Sales  ............................               30,000
2. Cash  ................................  29,400
      Cash discounts on sales  .................     600
         Accounts receivable  ...................            30,000
   OR
3. Cash  ................................  30,000
      Accounts receivable  ...................               30,000
```

Summary Problem for Your Review

PROBLEM

Carlos Lopez, marketing manager for Fireplace Distributors, sold 12 wood stoves to Woodside Condominiums, Inc. The sales contract was signed on April 27, 20X1. The list price of each wood stove was $1,200, but a 5% quantity discount was allowed. The wood stoves were to be delivered on May 10, and a cash discount of 2% of the amount owed was offered if payment was made by June 10. Fireplace Distributors delivered the wood stoves as promised and received the proper payment on June 9.

1. How much revenue should be recognized in April, in May, and in June? Explain.
2. Suppose Fireplace Distributors has a separate account titled "Cash Discounts on Sales." What journal entries would be made on June 9 when the cash payment is received?
3. Suppose Fireplace Distributors has another account titled "Sales Returns and Allowances." Suppose further that one of the wood stoves had a scratch and Fireplace Distributors allowed Woodside to deduct $100 from the total amount due. What journal entries would be made on June 9 when the cash payment is received?

SOLUTION

1. Revenue of $13,680 (12 × $1,200 less a 5% quantity discount of $720) would be recognized in May and none in April or June. The key to recognizing revenue is whether the revenue is earned and the asset received from the buyer is realized. The revenue is not earned until the merchandise is delivered. Therefore, revenue cannot be recognized in April because nothing was delivered then. Provided that Woodside Condominiums has a good credit rating, the receipt of cash is reasonably ensured before the cash is actually received. Therefore, recognition of revenue need not be delayed until June. On May 10, both revenue recognition tests were met, and the revenue would be recorded on May's income statement. However, if Woodside had a poor credit rating, the revenue would not be recognized and recorded until it was received in June.

2. The original revenue recorded was $13,680. The 2% cash discount is 2% × $13,680 = $273.60. Therefore, the cash payment is $13,680 − $273.60 = $13,406.40:

Cash	13,406.40	
Cash discounts on sales	273.60	
Accounts receivable		13,680.00

3. The only difference from requirement 2 is a $100 smaller cash payment and a $100 debit to sales returns and allowances:

Cash	13,306.40	
Cash discounts on sales	273.60	
Sales returns and allowances	100.00	
Accounts receivable		13,680.00

Cash

Many companies combine cash and cash equivalents on their balance sheets. Recall that cash equivalents are highly liquid short-term investments that can easily and quickly be converted into cash. For example, the 2003 balance sheet of **Oracle** begins with "Cash and cash equivalents . . . $4,737 million." Oracle describes its cash equivalents as " . . . highly liquid investments in time deposits of major banks, commercial paper, United States government agency discount notes, money market mutual funds and other money market securities with original maturities of 90 days or less." Although this is a long complex list of items, they all share one characteristic: Oracle will have cash in hand when the securities mature (within no more than 90 days), or Oracle can sell these marketable items to other people and receive cash immediately.

Cash means the same thing to organizations that it does to individuals. It is not just paper money and coins, but also includes other items that a bank will accept for deposit, including money orders, and checks. Banks do not accept postage stamps, IOUs, or post-dated checks as cash. Of course, not all items a bank does accept for deposit are treated the same. For example, although a bank may credit all deposits to the accounts of bank customers on the date received, the bank may not provide the depositor with access to the funds from a deposited check until the check "clears" through the banking system (until payment is actually made from the check writer's account). If the check fails to clear because its writer has insufficient funds, the bank deducts the amount of the check from the depositor's account.

In the discussion of cash, we talked about a deposit being "credited" to the account of the customer of the bank. A manager of the company making the deposit was confused

OBJECTIVE 4

Manage cash and explain its importance to the company.

by the term "credited." He regarded the deposit as a debit to cash. Why would a banker say the account is "credited?" Deposits in the bank are assets to the depositor. When a company receives a check and deposits it in its account, the company debits its account to show the increase in the asset Cash-in-bank. The offsetting credit might be to Sales if the check came from a sales transaction or to Accounts Receivable if it arose from collection of an account. In contrast, for the bank, the depositor's account is a liability. When the bank receives the check, it credits its liability account Deposits to acknowledge the increase in the amount it owes the depositor.

Compensating Balances

compensating balances
Required minimum cash balances on deposit when money is borrowed from banks.

Is the entire cash balance in a bank account available for unrestricted use? Frequently not. Banks often require companies to maintain **compensating balances,** which are required minimum balances on deposit to compensate the bank for providing loans. The size of the minimum balance may depend on the amount borrowed, the amount of credit available, or both.

Compensating balances increase the effective interest rate that the borrower pays. For a loan of $100,000 at 10% per year, the annual interest will be $10,000. With a 10% compensating balance, the borrower can use only $90,000 of the loan, raising the effective interest rate on the usable funds to 11.1% ($10,000 ÷ $90,000).

To ensure that financial statements provide a true picture concerning cash, annual reports must disclose any significant compensating balances. For example, a footnote in the annual report of North Carolina Natural Gas Corporation disclosed a requirement for keeping a compensating balance "of 10% of the annual average loan outstanding" in its bank account. Without such disclosures, analysts and investors might think that a company has more cash available than it really does.

Management of Cash

Cash is usually a small portion of the total assets of a company. Yet, we manage cash especially carefully. Why? First, although the cash balance may be small at any one time, the flow of cash can be enormous. Weekly receipts and disbursements of cash may be many times as large as the cash balance. Second, because cash is the most liquid asset, it is enticing to thieves and embezzlers. If someone steals a $200 jacket, they may only be able to get $40 from selling stolen goods, but if they steal $200 of cash, they have $200. Companies that do not watch their cash may find that someone walked off with it.

Third, adequate cash is essential to the smooth functioning of operations. Companies need it for everything from routine purchases to major investments, from purchasing lunch for a visiting business partner to purchasing another company. Finally, because cash itself does not earn income, it is important not to hold excess cash. The treasury department is responsible for managing the levels of cash efficiently and for ensuring that the company deposits unneeded cash in income-generating accounts.

reconcile a bank statement
To verify that the bank balance for cash is consistent with the accounting records.

Most organizations have detailed, well-specified procedures for receiving, recording, and disbursing cash. They immediately deposit cash in a bank account, and they periodically reconcile the company's books with the bank's records. To **reconcile a bank statement** means to verify that the bank balance and the accounting records are in agreement. The two balances are rarely identical. A company records a deposit when it sends money to the bank and records a payment when it writes a check. The bank, however, may receive or record the deposit several days after the company recorded it because it was in the mail, was deposited on a bank holiday or weekend, and so on. The bank typically receives and processes a check written by a company days, weeks, or even months after the company issued it.

The major internal control procedures set up to safeguard cash include the following:

1. Have different individuals receive cash than those who disburse cash.
2. Have different individuals handle cash than those who access accounting records.
3. Record cash receipts immediately and deposit them.
4. Make disbursements using serially numbered checks and require proper authorization by someone other than the person writing the check.
5. Reconcile bank accounts monthly.

Why are such internal controls necessary? Consider a person who handles cash and makes entries into the accounting records. That person could take $200 in cash and cover it up by making the following entry in the books:

Operating expenses	200	
Cash		200

Besides guarding against dishonest actions, internal control procedures help ensure that accounting records are accurate. For example, suppose a company writes a check, but does not record it in the books. With serially numbered checks, it is possible to trace items from the checkbook to a bank statement and identify the unrecorded check.

Credit Sales and Accounts Receivable

Cash sales are important for some companies, but most sales in today's world are on credit. Credit sales create a new set of problems for measuring revenue and managing the company's assets. Recall that credit sales on open account increase accounts receivable, which are amounts owed to the company by its customers as a result of delivering goods or services. Accounts receivable arise when the company grants credit to its customer on an ongoing basis. This means the company agrees to accept payment in the future for goods or services delivered today.

Uncollectible Accounts

Granting credit entails both costs and benefits. The main benefit is the boost in sales and profit that a company generates when it extends credit. Many potential customers would not buy if credit were unavailable, or they would buy from a competitor that offered credit. One cost is administration and collection of the credit amount. Before a company grants credit, it reviews the customer's credit and payment history to decide whether to accept the customer. It must then track what a customer owes, send periodic bills, deposit payments, record the payment in the customer's account, and so forth. These steps require clerical time and effort. Another cost is the delay in receiving payment. The seller must finance its activities in other ways while awaiting payment. Perhaps the most significant cost is **uncollectible accounts** or **bad debts**—receivables that some credit customers are either unable or unwilling to pay. Accountants often label this major cost of granting credit that arises from uncollectible accounts as **bad debts expense.**

The extent of nonpayment of debts varies. It often depends on the credit risks that managers are willing to accept. For instance, many smaller local establishments will accept a higher level of risk than will larger national stores such as Sears. The small stores know their customers personally. The extent of a nonpayment can also depend on the industry. For example, the problem of uncollectible accounts is especially difficult in the health care field. The Bayfront Medical Center of St. Petersburg, Florida, once reported bad debts equal to 21% of gross revenue.

uncollectible accounts (bad debts)
Receivables determined to be uncollectible because debtors are unable or unwilling to pay their debts.

bad debts expense
The cost of granting credit that arises from uncollectible accounts.

Deciding When and How to Grant Credit

Competition and industry practice affect whether and how companies offer credit. The final decision is based on cost-benefit trade-offs. In other words, companies offer credit only when the additional earnings on credit sales exceed the costs of offering credit. Suppose 5% of credit sales are bad debts, administrative costs of a credit department are $5,000 per year, and $20,000 of credit sales (with earnings of $8,000 before credit costs) are achieved. Assume that none of the credit sales would have been made without granting credit. Offering credit is worthwhile because the earnings of $8,000 exceeds the credit costs of $6,000 [(5% × $20,000) + $5,000].

Measurement of Uncollectible Accounts

OBJECTIVE 5

Estimate and interpret uncollectible accounts receivable balances.

Uncollectible accounts require special accounting procedures and thus deserve special attention here. Consider an example. Suppose Compuport has credit sales of $100,000 (200 customers averaging $500 each) during 20X1. Collections during 20X1 were $60,000. The December 31, 20X1 accounts receivable of $40,000 includes the accounts of 80 different customers who have not yet paid for their 20X1 purchases. During 20X1, there were no bad debts, but it turns out that 40% of the year's sales are still unpaid at year-end and some may never be paid. The outstanding balances are:

Customer	Amount Owed
1. Jones	$1,400
2. Slade	125
⦚	⦚
42. Monterro	600
⦚	⦚
79. Weinberg	700
80. Porras	11
Total receivables	$40,000

How should Compuport account for these receivables? Should we assume they will all be collected? If we assume some will not be, how do we decide which are collectible and which are not? Of course, we would never have initially made a credit sale to someone we really believed would not pay us.

There are two basic ways to record uncollectibles: by waiting to see which ones are unpaid or by making estimates today of the portion that will not be collected. The methods are called the specific write-off method and the allowance method.

Specific Write-Off Method

specific write-off method
This method of accounting for bad debt losses assumes all sales are fully collectible until proved otherwise.

A company that rarely experiences a bad debt might use the **specific write-off method,** which assumes that all sales are fully collectible until proved otherwise. If uncollectibles are small and infrequent, this practice will not misstate the economic situation in a material way. When Compuport identifies a specific customer account as uncollectible, it will reduce the Account Receivable. Because Compuport deems no specific customer's account to be uncollectible at the end of 20X1, its December 31, 20X1, balance sheet would simply show Accounts Receivable of $40,000.

Now assume that during the next year, 20X2, Compuport identifies Jones and Monterro as customers who are not expected to pay. When the chances of collection from specific customers become dim, Compuport recognizes the amounts in the particular accounts as bad debts expense:

Specific Write-Off Method	A	=	L +	SE
20X1 Sales	+100,000	=		+100,000
	⌈ Increase Accounts Receivable ⌋			⌈ Increase Sales ⌋
20X2 Write-off	−2,000	=		−2,000
	⌈ Decrease Accounts Receivable ⌋			⌈ Increase Bad Debts Expense ⌋

Unfortunately, the specific write-off method has been justifiably criticized because it fails to apply the matching principle of accrual accounting. The $2,000 bad debts expense recorded using the specific write-off method in 20X2 is related to (or caused by) the $100,000 of 20X1 sales. Matching requires recognition of the bad debts expense at the same time as the related revenue, that is, in 20X1, not 20X2. As a result of not matching expenses to revenues, the specific write-off method produces two errors in reported earnings. First, 20X1 income is overstated by $2,000 because no bad debts expense is charged to that year. Second, 20X2 income is understated by $2,000. Why? Because 20X1's bad debts expense of $2,000 is charged in 20X2. Equally important, the accounts receivable balance in 20X1 overstates the real asset by $2,000. Compare the specific write-off method with a correct matching of revenue and expense:

	Specific Write-Off Method: Matching Violated		Matching Applied Correctly	
	20X1	20X2	20X1	20X2
Sales revenue	100,000	0	100,000	0
Bad debts expense	0	2,000	2,000	0

The principal arguments in favor of the specific write-off method are based on cost-benefit concerns and materiality. Basically, the method is simple and extremely inexpensive to use. Moreover, no great error in measurement of income or accounts receivable occurs if amounts of bad debts are small and similar from one year to the next.

Allowance Method

Most accountants do not use the specific write-off method because it violates the matching principle and bad debts are neither small nor similar from year to year. Instead, accountants use an alternate method that estimates the amount of uncollectible accounts to be matched to the related revenue and appropriately measures the amount of the accounts receivable that will be collected. This method, known as the **allowance method,** has two basic elements: (1) an estimate of the amounts that will ultimately be uncollectible; and (2) a contra account, which contains the estimated uncollectible amount and is deducted from the total accounts receivable. We usually call the contra account **allowance for uncollectible accounts** (or **allowance for doubtful accounts, allowance for bad debts,** or **reserve for doubtful accounts**). It contains the amount of receivables estimated to be uncollectible from as-yet unidentified customers. In other words, using this contra account allows accountants to recognize bad debts in general during the

allowance method
Method of accounting for bad debt losses using estimates of the amount of sales that will ultimately be uncollectible and a contra asset account, allowance for doubtful accounts.

allowance for uncollectible accounts (allowance for doubtful accounts, allowance for bad debts, reserve for doubtful accounts)
A contra asset account that measures the amount of receivables estimated to be uncollectible.

proper period, before they identify specific uncollectible accounts from specific individuals in the following period.

Returning to our example, suppose that Compuport knows from experience that it will not collect about 2% of sales. Therefore, we can estimate that 2% × $100,000 = $2,000 of the 20X1 sales will be uncollectible. However, on December 31, 20X1, we do not know which customers will fail to pay their accounts. (Of course, all $2,000 must be among the $40,000 of accounts receivable at year-end because Compuport has already collected the other $60,000.) Compuport can still acknowledge the $2,000 worth of bad debt in 20X1, before it identifies the specific accounts of Jones and Monterro in 20X2. The effects of the allowance method on the balance sheet equation in the Compuport example follow:

	A	=	L +	SE
Allowance method				
20X1 Sales	+100,000	=		+100,000
	⌈ Increase			⌈ Increase ⌉
	Accounts			⌊ Sales ⌋
	⌊ Receivable ⌋			
20X1 Allowance	−2,000	=		−2,000
	⌈ Increase ⌉			⌈ Increase ⌉
	Allowance for			Bad Debts
	Uncollectible			⌊ Expense ⌋
	⌊ Accounts ⌋			
20X2 Write-off	+2,000	=		(No effect)
	⌈ Decrease ⌉			
	Allowance for			
	Uncollectible			
	⌊ Accounts ⌋			
	−2,000			
	⌈ Decrease ⌉			
	Accounts			
	⌊ Receivable ⌋			

The associated journal entries are:

20X1 Sales	Accounts receivable	100,000	
	Sales		100,000
20X1 Allowances	Bad debts expense	2,000	
	Allowance for uncollectible accounts		2,000
20X2 Write-offs	Allowance for uncollectible accounts	2,000	
	Accounts receivable, Jones		1,400
	Accounts receivable, Monterro		600

Note in the 20X2 write-off journal entry that Compuport makes two credit entries, one for $1,400 for Jones and one for $600 for Monterro. This emphasizes that accounts receivable records are maintained for each individual customer. Similarly note that the 20X1 increase of $100,000 to accounts receivable represents many (200 in this example) individual sales to specific customers.

The principal arguments favoring the allowance method are its superiority in measuring accural accounting income in any given year and in measuring the accounts receivable asset realistically. That is, under this method we deduct from 20X1 sales the $2,000 of those sales that we believe we will never collect. This matches the bad debt expense to the sales that generated the bad debts. In addition, we report the year-end account receivable at the collectible amount of $38,000.

The allowance method results in the following presentation in the Compuport balance sheet, December 31, 20X1:

Accounts receivable	$40,000
Less: Allowance for uncollectible accounts	2,000
Net accounts receivable	$38,000

Oracle discloses its allowance for bad debts in the caption for Trade Receivables:

($ in millions)	2002	2001
Oracle		
Trade receivables, net of allowances of $413 in 2002 and $403 in 2001	$2,036	$2,432

The allowance method relies on historical experience and information about economic circumstances (growth versus recession, interest rate levels, and so on) and customer composition. Of course, companies revise estimates when conditions change. For example, if a local employer closed or drastically reduced employment and many local customers were thus suddenly unemployed, Compuport might increase expected bad debts. Oracle discloses the following:

> *We make judgements as to our ability to collect outstanding receivables and provide allowances for the portion of receivables when collection becomes doubtful. Provisions are made based upon a specific review of all significant outstanding invoices. For those invoices not specifically reviewed, provisions are provided at differing rates, based upon the age of the receivable. In determining these percentages, we analyze our historical collection experience and current economic trends.*

Applying the Allowance Method Using a Percentage of Sales

How do managers and accountants estimate the percentage of bad debts in the allowance method? In our example, Compuport managers determined a 2% rate of bad debts, for a total of $2,000 (2% × $100,000), based on experience. Expressing the amount of bad debts as a percentage of total sales is known as the **percentage of sales method,** which relies on historical relationships between credit sales and uncollectible debts.

percentage of sales method
An approach to estimating bad debts expense and uncollectible accounts based on the historical relations between credit sales and uncollectibles.

To apply the percentage of sales method, we look at the relationship between the general ledger item Accounts Receivable and its supporting detail. Each time we make a sale on account, we record the amount in the general ledger. We also record it in a separate, supporting ledger called a subsidiary ledger. We maintain a separate page in the subsidiary ledger for each customer, recording both sales and payments. On December 31, 20X1, the sum of the balances of all customer accounts in the subsidiary ledger must equal the accounts receivable balance in the general ledger. We illustrate this process in Exhibit 6-1, panel A.

Note that the use of the allowance account enables us to record bad debt expense without identifying specific accounts that will be uncollectible. In 20X2, after exhausting all practical means of collection, Compuport decides the Jones and Monterro accounts are uncollectible. Recording the $2,000 write-off for Jones and Monterro in 20X2 reduces their individual subsidiary accounts, reduces the general ledger Accounts Receivable account, and eliminates the Allowance for Uncollectible accounts as shown in Panel B of Exhibit 6-1.

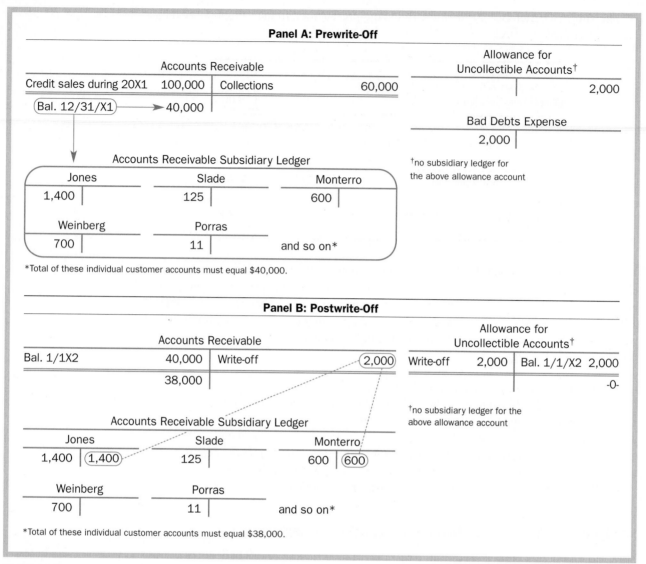

Exhibit 6-1
Compuport General Ledger, December 31, 20X1

INTERPRETING FINANCIAL STATEMENTS

How does the ultimate write-off of the Monterro and Jones accounts affect total assets reported on the balance sheet?

Answer

Convince yourself that the ultimate write-off has no effect on total assets:

	Before Write-Off	After Write-Off
Accounts receivable	$40,000	$38,000
Allowance for uncollectible accounts	2,000	—
Book value (net realizable value)	$38,000	$38,000

Applying the Allowance Method Using a Percentage of Accounts Receivable

As with the percentage of sales method, we use historical experience to apply the **percentage of accounts receivable method.** However, we base estimates of uncollectible accounts on the historical relations of uncollectibles to year-end gross accounts receivable, not on the relationship to total sales made during the year.

We use the Allowance for Bad Debts contra account to show the approximate amount of bad debts contained in the end-of-period accounts receivable. Under the percentage of accounts receivable method, we calculate additions to the Allowance for Bad Debts to achieve a desired ending balance in the Allowance account. Consider the historical experience in the following table.

percentage of accounts receivable method An approach to estimating bad debts expense and uncollectible accounts at year-end using the historical relations of uncollectibles to end-of-period accounts receivable.

	Accounts Receivable at End of Year	Bad Debts Deemed Uncollectible and Written Off in Subsequent Year
20X1	$100,000	$ 3,500
20X2	80,000	2,450
20X3	90,000	2,550
20X4	110,000	4,100
20X5	120,000	5,600
20X6	112,000	2,200
Six-year total	$612,000	$ 20,400
Average (divide by 6)	$102,000	$ 3,400
Average percentage not collected = 3,400 ÷ 102,000 = 3.33%		

At the end of 20X7, assume the accounts receivable balance is $115,000. We compute the 20X7 addition to the Allowance for Bad Debts as follows:

1. Divide average bad debt losses of $3,400 by average ending accounts receivable of $102,000 to calculate the historical average uncollectible percentage of 3.33.
2. Apply the percentage from step 1 to the ending Accounts Receivable balance for 20X7 to determine the ending balance that should be in the Allowance account at the end of the year: 3.33% × $115,000 receivables at the end of 20X7 is $3,830.
3. Prepare an adjusting entry to bring the Allowance to the appropriate amount determined in step 2. Suppose the books show a $700 credit balance in the Allowance account at the end of 20X7. Then the adjusting entry for 20X7 is $3,830 − $700, or $3,130, to record the Bad Debts expense. The journal entry is:

```
Bad debts expense  . . . . . . . . . . . . . . . . . . . . . . . . .   3,130
    Allowance for bad debts  . . . . . . . . . . . . . . . . . .            3,130
    To bring the Allowance to the level
      justified by bad debt experience during
      past 6 years
```

The percentage of accounts receivable method differs from the percentage of sales method in two ways: (1) the percentage is based on the ending accounts receivable balance instead of sales, and (2) the dollar amount calculated using the percentage is the appropriate ending balance in the allowance account, not the amount added to the account for the year.

Applying the Allowance Method Using the Aging of Accounts Receivable

We can refine the percentage of accounts receivable approach by considering the composition of the end-of-year accounts receivable based on the age of the debt. This

Name	Total	1–30 Days	31–60 Days	61–90 Days	More Than 90 Days
Oxwall Tools	$ 20,000	$20,000			
Chicago Castings	10,000	10,000			
Estee	20,000	15,000	$ 5,000		
Sarasota Pipe	22,000		12,000	$10,000	
Ceilcote	4,000			3,000	$1,000
Other accounts (each detailed)	39,000	27,000	8,000	2,000	2,000
Total	$115,000	$72,000	$25,000	$15,000	$3,000
Historical bad debt percentages		0.1%	1%	5%	90%
Bad debt allowance to be provided	$ 3,772 =	$ 72 +	$ 250 +	$ 750 +	$2,700

Exhibit 6-2
Aging of Accounts Receivable—Compuport—20X7

aging of accounts receivable method directly incorporates the customers' payment histories. As more time elapses after the sale, collection becomes less likely. The seller may send the buyer a late notice 30 days after the sale and a second reminder after 60 days, make a phone call after 90 days, and place the account with a collection agency after 120 days. Companies that analyze the age of their accounts receivable for credit management purposes naturally incorporate this information into estimates of the allowance for uncollectibles. For example, the $115,000 balance in Accounts Receivable on December 31, 20X7, for Compuport might be aged as shown in Exhibit 6-2.

This aging schedule in Exhibit 6-2 produces a different target balance for the Allowance account than the balance that resulted from the percentage of accounts receivable method: $3,772 versus $3,830. Similarly, the journal entry is slightly different. Given the same $700 credit balance in the Allowance account, the journal entry to record the Bad Debts Expense is $3,772 − $700, or $3,072:

```
Bad debts expense  . . . . . . . . . . . . . . . . . . . . . . .   $3,072
        Allowance for uncollectible accounts . . . . . . . . .            $3,072
    To bring the Allowance to the level justified by
    prior experience using the aging method.
```

Whether the percentage of sales, percentage of accounts receivable, or aging of accounts receivable method is used to estimate bad debts expense and the Allowance for Uncollectible Accounts, the subsequent accounting for write-offs is the same—a decrease in Accounts Receivable and a decrease in the Allowance for Uncollectible Accounts.

Bad Debt Recoveries

Infrequently, a customer will pay an account that a company has previously written off as uncollectible. When such **bad debt recoveries** occur, we want to be sure to capture the customer's true payment history. We can accomplish this in two steps. First, we reverse the write-off, and then we handle the collection as a normal receipt on account. Return to the earlier Compuport example and assume that we wrote off Monterro's account for $600 in February 20X2 and collected in October 20X2. The following journal entries produce a complete record of the transactions in Monterro's individual accounts receivable account.

```
20X1   Accounts receivable  . . . . . . . . . . . . . . . . . . . . . . . . . . . . .  600
            Sales  . . . . . . . . . . . . . . . . . . . . . . . . . . . . . . . . . . . . .         600
        To record sales of $600 to Monterro,
        a specific customer
```

Feb. 20X2	Allowance for uncollectible accounts	600	
	Accounts receivable		600
	To write off uncollectible account		
	of Monterro		
Oct. 20X2	Accounts receivable	600	
	Allowance for uncollectible accounts		600
	To reverse February 20X2 write-off of		
	account of Monterro		
	Cash	600	
	Accounts receivable		600
	To record the collection on account		

Note that these 20X2 entries have no effect on the level of bad debt expense estimated for 20X1. At the end of 20X1, using one of the three estimation methods we just examined, Compuport estimated bad debt expense and end-of-period uncollectibles. We do not change these estimates, even if future uncollectibles are greater or less than expected. The errors in estimate affect future periods but do not produce adjustments of prior periods. Briefly, in 20X2 Compuport believed that Monterro would be a nonpaying customer. This was not ultimately the case, and the records now reflect Monterro's payment, and the fact that it was delayed.

INTERPRETING FINANCIAL STATEMENTS

Refer to the consolidated balance sheets for **Starbucks** and determine the total account receivables on Starbucks' books at September 28, 2003.

receivable were $119,257 ($114,448 + $4,809) before making adjustments for amounts that will ultimately prove to be bad debts (numbers are in thousands).

Answer

Starbucks reports accounts receivable of $114,448, net of allowances of $4,809. This means that total accounts

Assessing the Level of Accounts Receivable

You now know how to account for bad debts, but you should realize that the management issue is how to control bad debts at the proper level. The more credit a company provides, the greater the chances of bad debts occurring. Management and financial analysts like to monitor the firm's ability to control accounts receivable. Can the firm generate increasing sales without excessive growth in receivables? Do bad debt expenses rise sharply when sales grow, indicating a reduction in the credit quality of the store's customers?

One measure of the ability to control receivables is the **accounts receivable turnover.** We calculate this ratio by dividing the credit sales by the average accounts receivable for the period during which the sales were made:

Accounts receivable turnover = Credit sales ÷ Average accounts receivable

This ratio indicates how rapidly collections occur. Suppose you sold $100 of merchandise each day, 365 days per year, and you collected cash for every sale 10 days after the sale. In this instance, annual sales would be $36,500 (365 × $100) and average accounts receivable would be $1,000 (10 days × $100 per day), giving an accounts receivable turnover of 36.5 ($36,500 divided by $1,000). If the turnover were 12, it would indicate that receivables are collected after 1 month on average. Higher turnovers indicate that

OBJECTIVE 6

Assess the level of accounts receivable.

accounts receivable turnover
Credit sales divided by average accounts receivable.

Exhibit 6-3
Accounts Receivable
Ratios

Industry	Median Levels	
	Accounts Receivable Turnover	Days to Collect Accounts Receivable
Automobile retailer	60.7	6.01
Department stores	73.9	4.94
Furniture retailer	82.0	4.45
Jewelry retailer	27.3	13.37
Bookstores	38.0	9.61

Source: RMA, Annual Statement Studies for 2003.

a company collects its receivables quickly—lower turnovers indicate slower collection cycles. Competitive conditions in the industry often drive the ratio. Changes in the ratio provide important guidance concerning changes in the company's policies, changes in the industry's competive environment, or changes in general economic conditions. For example, a decline in the general level of economic activity will slow collections across the board, and this turnover measure will tend to fall for all firms.

Suppose credit sales (or sales on account) for Compuport in 20X8 were $1 million and beginning and ending accounts receivable were $115,000 and $112,000, respectively.

$$\text{Accounts receivable turnover} = \$1,000,000 \div (0.5 \times (\$115,000 + \$112,000)) = 8.81$$

We can also assess receivables levels in terms of how long it takes to collect them. This alternative to the turnover ratio has an appealing direct interpretation. How long does it take to get my money after I make a sale? **The days to collect accounts receivable**, or **average collection period**, is calculated by dividing 365 by the accounts receivable turnover. For our example:

days to collect accounts receivable (average collection period)
365 divided by accounts receivable turnover.

$$\text{Days to collect accounts receivable} = 365 \text{ days} \div \text{Accounts receivable turnover}$$
$$= 365 \text{ days} \div 8.81$$
$$= 41.4 \text{ days}$$

There is significant variability in accounts receivable turnover levels among industries, as shown in Exhibit 6-3. Although these are calculated with total sales rather than just credit sales, the higher accounts receivable turnovers for automobile retailers and department stores are also a result of the way customers finance their purchases. For automobiles, customers generally finance through banks or through the credit arms of the automobile manufacturer. For department stores, national credit cards, such as VISA and MasterCard, often provide credit. In both industries, the seller receives cash quickly. Other industries more frequently use direct granting of credit by the selling firm. In other words, outside credit providers tend to pay off the sellers quickly, but when the sellers themselves provide the credit, payments come in much more slowly. In fact, if department stores provided their own credit to customers, as used to be the case, their accounts receivable turnover would drop sharply.

Summary Problem for Your Review

PROBLEM

The balance sheet of VF Corporation, the large apparel company that recently purchased Nautica Enterprises, showed accounts receivable at January 4, 2003 of $587,859,000, net of allowances of $48,227,000. Suppose a large discount chain that owed VF $2 million announced bankruptcy on January 5, 2003. VF decided that chances for collection were virtually zero and immediately wrote off the account. Show the accounts receivable and allowance account balances after the write-off, and explain the effect of the write-off on income for the year beginning January 5, 2003.

SOLUTION

The write-off does not affect the net accounts receivable. Nevertheless, both gross accounts receivable and the allowance balance change. Gross accounts receivable were $636,086,000 at January 4 and the allowance was $48,227,000, giving a net accounts receivable of $587,859,000. When Nautica takes the write-off, gross accounts receivable go down by $2 million, but the allowance does also, with the following result:

Gross receivables ($636,086,000 − $2,000,000)	$634,086,000
Less allowance for doubtful accounts	
($48,227,000 − $2,000,000)	46,227,000
Net receivables	$587,859,000

Overview of Internal Control

We previously discussed bank reconciliations and cash management processes that are examples of internal controls. Companies use such controls to protect their assets and to help managers maintain accurate financial records. **Internal control** is a system of checks and balances that ensures all company actions are proper and have the general approval of

OBJECTIVE 7

Develop and explain internal control procedures.

internal control
System of checks and balances that ensures all actions occurring within the company are proper and have the general approval of top management.

top management. For example, we do not want a highly placed manager to expose the company to huge speculative losses from unauthorized trading of exotic derivatives securities. Here internal controls tie daily decisions to corporate strategy. Nor should a salesperson at a clothing store be able to walk out of the store with holiday gifts for the family without paying for them. Here internal control refers to the protection of firm assets from theft and loss. An electronic tag on a leather coat is an internal control device and so is the requirement that two people approve checks over $2,000.

In its broadest sense, internal control refers to both administrative control and accounting controls:

administrative controls
All methods and procedures that facilitate management planning and control of operations.

1. **Administrative controls** include the plan of organization, for example, the formal organizational chart spelling out who reports to whom. It includes methods and procedures that facilitate management planning and control of operations. Examples are departmental budgeting procedures, reports on performance, and procedures for granting credit to customers.

accounting controls
The methods and procedures for authorizing transactions, safeguarding assets, and ensuring the accuracy of the financial records.

2. **Accounting controls** include the methods and procedures for authorizing transactions, safeguarding assets, and ensuring the accuracy of the financial records. Good accounting controls help to maximize efficiency and to minimize waste, unintentional errors, and fraud.

We focus on internal accounting controls, which should provide reasonable assurance concerning:

1. Authorization. Managers execute transactions in accordance with management's general or specific intentions.
2. Recording. Accountants accurately record authorized transactions.
3. Safeguarding. There are appropriate restrictions on access to assets.
4. Reconciliation. Accountants regularly verify records against other independently kept records and/or confirm them by physical counts or examinations.
5. Valuation. Accountants periodically review recorded amounts for impairment of values and necessary write-downs.
6. Operational Efficiency. Good internal control prevents errors and fraud while promoting efficient actions.

The first three general objectives—authorization, recording, and safeguarding—relate to a system of accountability to prevent errors and irregularities. The fourth and fifth objectives—reconciliation and valuation—aid in detecting errors and irregularities. The last objective recognizes that an internal control system's purpose is as much a positive one (promoting efficiency) as a negative one (preventing errors and fraud).

The Accounting System

accounting system
A set of records, procedures, and equipment that routinely deals with the events affecting the financial performance and position of the entity.

An entity's **accounting system** is a set of records, procedures, internal controls, and equipment to collect, organize, and report the continuous flow of information about the events affecting the entity's financial performance and position. Chapters 3 and 4 provided an overview of the heart of the accounting system—source documents, journal entries, postings to ledgers, trial balances, adjustments, and financial reports. The system handles repetitive, voluminous transactions, which fall primarily into four categories:

1. Cash disbursements
2. Cash receipts
3. Purchase of goods and services, including employee payroll
4. Sales or other rendering of goods and services

The volume of the physical records is often staggering. For example, telephone and credit card companies process millions of transactions daily. Computers and data processing systems make it possible. Well-designed and well-run accounting systems are positive contributions to organizations and the economy. Credit card companies, for example, use sophisticated systems to evaluate transactions on your credit card, and may refuse a credit transaction that seems likely to be fraudulent use of your card by an unauthorized party. Although such refusals sometimes inconvenience a legitimate card holder, they more frequently foil criminal use. Another example is FedEx Corporation, which created a dominant position in the overnight delivery market by developing an efficient system for continuous tracking of an item from pickup to delivery. Finally, Wal-Mart's extraordinary success as a low-price retailer is due in part to its integrated inventory control and ordering system that allows its computer to interact automatically with suppliers such as Procter & Gamble to generate orders and reduce delivery times.

Checklist of Internal Control

Good systems of internal control have certain features in common. We have summarized these features in a checklist of internal controls that a manager might use to create or evaluate specific procedures for cash, purchases, sales, payroll, and the like. This checklist incorporates the guidance found in much of the systems and auditing literature:

1. **Reliable Personnel with Clear Responsibilities.** The most important control element is personnel. Incompetent or dishonest individuals undermine any system. Thus, good procedures to hire, train, motivate, and supervise employees are essential. Companies should give individuals authority, responsibility, and duties commensurate with their abilities, interests, experience, and reliability. The wrong, lowest-cost talent may prove expensive in the long run not only because of fraud, but also because of poor productivity.

   Assessing responsibility means tracking actions far down into the organization. It means having sales clerks sign sales slips, inspectors sign initial packing slips, and workers sign time cards and requisitions. Grocery stores often assign each cashier a separate money tray so management can reward efficiency and easily trace shortages.

   The National Mass Retailing Institute estimates that retailers lose about 2% of sales to theft and mistakes. Employee theft causes much larger losses than shoplifting.

2. **Separation of Duties.** Separation of duties makes it hard for one person, acting alone, to defraud the company. This is why movie theaters have a cashier selling tickets and an usher taking them. The cashier takes in cash, the usher keeps the ticket stubs, and a third person compares the cash with the number of stubs.

   Suppose management suspects collusion between the cashier and the usher. Describe actions that the third person's audit would not detect. How might management detect such collusion? The ticket seller can pocket the cash and issue a fake ticket. The usher can accept the fake ticket and allow entry. Separation of duties alone does not prevent collusive theft. Better supervision of the ticket seller and the usher is the primary method of preventing such collusion.

   Here are two more examples where failure to separate duties allows easy theft.

   • In a computer system, a person with custody of assets should not have access to programming or any input of records. In a classic example, a programmer in a bank rounded transactions to the next lower cent instead of the nearest cent and had the computer put the fraction of a cent into his account. For example, a customer amount of $10.057 became $10.05, and the programmer's account received $.007. With millions of transactions, the programmers' account grew very large.

   • Generally, the same individual should not authorize payments and also sign the check in payment of the bill. Similarly, an individual who handles cash receipts should not have the authority to indicate which accounts receivable should be written off as uncollectible. The latter separation of powers prevents the following embezzlement: a bookkeeper opens the mail, removes a $1,000 check from a customer, and somehow cashes it. To hide the theft, the bookkeeper prepares the following journal entry to write off an amount owed by a customer:

Allowance for bad debts	1,000	
Accounts receivable		1,000

3. **Proper Authorization.** General authorizations are usually written policies, such as definite limits on what price to pay (whether to fly economy or first class), on what price to receive (whether to offer a sales discount), on what credit limits to grant to customers, and so forth. Specific authorizations require that a superior manager explicitly approve deviations from the limits set by general authorization. For example, a manager has to approve overtime or the board of directors has to approve large expenditures for capital assets.

4. **Adequate Documents.** Companies have a variety of documents and records, from source documents (such as sales invoices and purchase orders) to journals and ledgers. Immediate, complete, and tamper-proof recording of data is the goal. Companies minimize recording errors by optically scanning bar-coded data, by prenumbering and accounting for all source documents, by using devices such as cash registers, and by designing forms for ease of recording. When a merchant offers a customer a free item if a red star comes up on the cash register receipt, it is partly a way to ensure that sales clerks actually ring up the sale, and for the proper amount.

5. **Proper Procedures.** Most organizations use procedures manuals to specify the flow of documents and provide information and instructions to facilitate record keeping. Well-designed routines permit specialization of effort, division of duties, and automatic checks on each step in the routine.

6. **Physical Safeguards.** Companies minimize losses of cash, inventories, and records by using safes, locks, guards, guard dogs, and special lighting, and allowing limited access to sensitive areas. For example, many companies require all visitors to sign a register and wear a name tag, and they may restrict access to certain places by having card scanners that grant admission only to authorized personnel.

7. **Vacations and Rotation of Duties.** Rotating employees and requiring them to take vacations ensures at least two employees know how to do each job so an absence due to illness or a sudden resignation does not create major problems. Further, the practice of having another employee periodically perform their duties discourages employees from engaging in fraudulent activities that their substitute might discover. A company might accomplish rotation of duties by the common practice of having employees such as receivables and payables clerks periodically exchange duties. In addition, a receivables clerk may handle accounts from A to C for 3 months, and then be rotated to accounts M to P for 3 months, and so forth.

8. **Independent Check.** All phases of the system should undergo periodic review by outsiders, for example, by independent public accountants and internal auditors. By first evaluating the system of internal control and testing the extent to which employees follow the appropriate procedures, the auditor decides on the likelihood of undetected errors. When internal controls are weak, auditors will examine many transactions to provide reasonable assurance that they discover any existing errors. If internal controls are strong, the auditor can use a smaller sample to develop confidence in the accuracy of the accounting records.

9. **Cost-Benefit Analysis.** Highly complex systems can strangle people in red tape, impeding instead of promoting efficiency. The right investments in the accounting system can produce huge benefits. For example, the accounting firm of KPMG completed a study of office automation for a client. After examining the jobs of 2,600 white-collar workers, KPMG quantified a cost-benefit relationship: "A single investment of $10 million would result in a productivity savings equal to $8.4 million every year."

THE $346,770 OVERDRAFT

Karen Smith was amazed when her credit union notified her that her account was overdrawn by $346,770. How could that kind of money turn up missing? Did she mistakenly add three extra zeros to a check? No, she left her bank card in her wallet, locked inside her van during a high school football game on a Friday night. Two thieves broke into the van, stole the bank card, and visited local cash machines.

Think about how bank internal control procedures should stop thieves. Automated teller machines (ATMs) require the use of a customer's specific personal identification number (the "pin" number). As a secondary precaution, ATM machines normally restrict withdrawals to a maximum amount, perhaps $200 per day, per account. Thieves cannot randomly guess pin numbers. The computer tracks "unauthorized" accesses. After several incorrect pin numbers, the ATM keeps the card and notifies the user to reclaim it at the bank.

Nonetheless, these thieves hit the jackpot. Karen stored her pin number on her social security card, in the stolen wallet. Luckier yet, the Oregon TelCo Credit Union was updating some computer programs and their $200 limit per account per day was inoperative. To access all the funds in Karen's account, the thieves put the card in and withdrew $200, time after time. Eventually, the ATM ran out of bills, but the thieves visited many more on a circuitous, five-county, 500-mile route.

A third internal control should have limited the thieves to the balance in Karen's account. Something else went wrong. Most financial institutions permit immediate withdrawal of only certified checks or checks drawn on accounts at the institution. Deposits may be unavailable for days while the institution verifies that the check is written on a good bank against a bonafide account with sufficient funds. Checks on in-state institutions may take 2 days to "clear," whereas out-of-state checks take 3 or 4 days. Deposits into an ATM machine are generally unavailable until the next banking day so the bank can verify the deposit, subject to the rules just described.

Unfortunately, the TelCo system was giving immediate credit for deposits made into automated tellers. The thieves "deposited" $820,500 by inserting empty deposit envelopes and recording large deposits on the ATM keypad. They exhausted the cash in the ATM machines in their five-county area by 2:30 A.M. on Monday and headed to Reno to buy a new truck and enjoy their wealth.

One piece of TelCo's internal control worked. Hidden cameras photographed the thieves. The perpetrators, David Gallagher and his wife Terry, were easily identified. David has been in prison five times and has 21 felony convictions. Federal sentencing guidelines could bring up to 63 years in prison.

Source: New York Times, (February 12, 1995) p. 36.

As many companies implement complex procedures to improve internal control, a few have taken a reverse course. They have decided that the increased costs of additional scrutiny are not worth the expected savings from catching mistakes or crooks. For example, an aerospace manufacturer routinely pays the invoice amounts without checking supporting documentation except on a random-sampling basis. An aluminum company sends out a blank check with its purchase orders, and then the supplier fills out the check and deposits it.

No internal control is perfect as illustrated in the Business First box above. The goal is not total prevention of fraud or implementation of operating perfection; instead, the goal is the design of a cost-effective tool that helps achieve efficient operations and minimizes temptation.

Management's Responsibility

Although outside auditors attest to the financial reports of an entity, management bears the primary responsibility for a company's financial statements. Annual reports of publicly held companies in the United States contain an explicit statement of management's responsibility for its financial statements. These **management reports** state that management is responsible

management reports
Explicit statements in annual reports of publicly held companies that management is responsible for all audited and unaudited information in the annual report.

for all audited and unaudited information in the annual report. Management must also prepare a statement on the adequacy of internal controls, and the independent auditors must give their opinion on management's statement and the controls themselves. Management's statement also includes a description of the composition and duties of the audit committee, as well as the duties of the independent auditor. You can review an example for **Starbucks** in the Appendix.

The Audit Committee. Management's primary responsibility for the entity's financial statements extends upward to the board of directors. Most boards have an **audit committee,** which oversees the internal accounting controls, financial statements, and financial affairs of the corporation.

audit committee
A committee of the board of directors that oversees the internal accounting controls, financial statements, and financial affairs of the corporation.

Audit committee members must be "outside" board members who are not managers of the company. They are considered to be more independent than the "inside" directors — employees who serve as part of the corporation's management. Starbucks has a typical board composition. Of nine directors in 2003, three are also members of management and six are "outside" directors. The audit committee includes only outside directors. The committee provides contact and communication among the board, the external auditors, the internal auditors, the financial executives, and the operating executives.

Highlights to Remember

1 **Recognize revenue items at the proper time on the income statement.** Revenue is generally recognized when two tests are met: (1) the revenue is earned, and (2) the asset received in return is realized. Most often, revenue is recognized at the point of sale, when the product is delivered to the customer. In offering products for sale, many special practices produce differences between the price at which a product is offered and the final price that a customer is charged. The term net sales represents the final proceeds to the seller — gross sales less offsetting amounts for returns, allowances, and cash discounts.

2 **Account for cash and credit sales.** At the moment a sale occurs, we record the full amount of the sale so sales revenue for the year shows our full level of economic activity, regardless of whether the sale is on account or for cash, as long as the revenue recognition criteria are met. To do so, we increase an asset account and increase the sales revenue account. For credit sales we also need to maintain detailed records about the individual customers in a subsidiary account.

3 **Compute and interpret sales returns and allowances, sales discounts, and bank credit card sales.** We may not ultimately collect the total sales we initially record. Various discounts or allowances may be recorded and shown as reductions of gross sales to arrive at net sales on the income statement. Sales returns and allowances arise when merchandise is returned or discounts are given due to damaged goods or errors in filling the order. Customers sometimes receive a cash discount as a result of prompt payment. Similarly, bank cards create a known discount to compensate the bank for its collection services.

4 **Manage cash and explain its importance to the company.** Cash is the fuel that runs a company and must be available to meet obligations as they come due. Cash creates a number of procedural problems for the firm. Protecting cash from theft or loss, adequately planning for the availability of cash as needed, and reconciling the firm's accounting records with the bank's records are just some of these problems.

5 **Estimate and interpret uncollectible accounts receivable balances.** Potential uncollectible accounts reduce the amount of accounts receivable reported on the balance sheet. Reporting the uncollectible portion of credit sales requires estimates that may be based on a percentage of sales, a percentage of accounts receivable, or an aging of accounts receivable. These estimates permit the financial statements to (1) properly reflect asset levels on the balance sheet, and (2) properly match bad debts expense with revenue on the income statement.

6 **Assess the level of accounts receivable.** Companies and analysts use ratios to assess the level of accounts receivable. The accounts receivable turnover ratio and the days to collect accounts receivable both relate the average dollar value of accounts receivable to the level of credit sales during the year. Comparisons with other companies in the same industry or examination of a particular company over time draw attention to unusual circumstances and possible problems.

7 **Develop and explain internal control procedures.** It is tempting to delegate internal control decisions to accountants. However, managers at all levels have a major responsibility for the success of internal controls. To help monitor internal control, boards of directors appoint audit committees, which

oversee accounting controls, the financial statements, and general financial affairs of the company. Managers and accountants should recognize that the role of an internal control system is as much a positive one (enhancing efficiency) as a negative one (reducing errors and fraud). The following general characteristics form a checklist that serves as a starting point for judging the effectiveness of internal control:

a. Reliable personnel with clear responsibilities
b. Separation of duties
c. Proper authorization
d. Adequate documents
e. Proper procedures
f. Physical safeguards
g. Vacations and rotation of duties
h. Independent check
i. Cost-benefit analysis

8 **Prepare a Bank Reconciliation.** see Appendix 6.

Appendix 6: Bank Reconciliations

OBJECTIVE 8

Prepare a bank reconciliation.

Exhibit 6-4 displays a bank statement for account number 96848602, one of thousands of the bank's deposits. Together, these accounts form the subsidiary ledger that supports the bank's general ledger account Deposits, a liability.

The supporting documents for the detailed checks on the statement are canceled checks; for additional deposits, deposit slips. Notice that the minimum balance, $33.39, is negative. This indicates an overdraft, which is a negative account balance arising from the bank's paying a check even though the depositor had insufficient funds available when the check was presented. Overdrafts are permitted as an occasional courtesy by the bank, although the bank may levy a fee (e.g., $10 or $30) for each overdraft.

Exhibit 6-5 shows selected records for another depositor in another bank. The bank balance on December 31 is an asset (Cash) on the depositor's books and a liability (Deposits) on the bank's books. The terms debit and credit as used by banks may seem strange. Banks credit the depositor's account for additional deposits because the bank has a liability to the depositor. Banks debit the account for checks written by the depositor and paid by the bank. When the $2,000 check drawn by the depositor on January 5 is paid by the bank on January 8, the bank's journal entry would be:

```
Jan. 8 Deposits . . . . . . . . . . . . . . . . . . . . . . .    2,000
         Cash  . . . . . . . . . . . . . . . . . . . . . . .              2,000
        To decrease the depositor's account
```

A monthly bank reconciliation is conducted by the depositor to make sure all cash receipts and disbursements are accounted for. Bank reconciliations take many forms, but the objective is to explain all differences in the cash balances shown on the bank statement and in the depositor's general ledger at a given date. By using the data in Exhibit 6-5:

Bank Reconciliation, January 31, 20X2	
Balance per books (also called *balance per check register, register balance*)	$ 8,000
Deduct: Bank service charges for January not recorded on the books (also include any other charges by the bank not yet deducted)*	20
Adjusted (corrected) balance per books	$ 7,980
Balance per bank (also called *bank statement balance, statement balance*)	$10,980
Add: Deposits not recorded by bank (also called *unrecorded deposits, deposits in transit*), deposit of 1/31	7,000
Total	$17,980
Deduct: Outstanding checks, check of 1/29	10,000
Adjusted (corrected) balance per bank	$ 7,980

*Note that new entries on the depositor's books are required for all previously unrecorded additions and deductions made to achieve the adjusted balance per books.

Exhibit 6-4
An Actual Bank
Statement

Seafirst Bank
University Branch
4701 University Way NE
Seattle WA 98145

		Account Number
Richard B. Sandstrom	777	96848602
2420 Highline Rd.		Statement Period
Redmond WA 98110		11-21-03 to 12-20-03

SUMMARY OF YOUR ACCOUNTS

CHECKING

First choice Minimum Balance	96848602
Beginning Balance	368.56
Deposits	5,074.00
Withdrawals	3,232.92
Service Charges/Fees	16.00
Ending Balance	2,193.64
Minimum Balance on 12-9-03	**−33.39**

CHECKING ACTIVITY

Deposits

Posted	Amount	Description
11-21	700.00	Deposit
11-25	1,810.00	Payroll Deposit
12-10	1,810.00	Payroll Deposit
12-16	754.00	Deposit

Withdrawals

Ck No.	Paid	Amount
1606	12-02	1134.00
1607	11-28	561.00
1609*	12-09	12.00
1617*	12-05	7.00
1629*	11-26	10.00
1630	11-25	16.95
1639*	12-02	96.00
1641*	12-09	1025.00
1642	12-05	50.00
1643	12-15	236.25
1644	12-17	84.72

* = Gap in check sequence.
Total number of checks = 11.

The bank reconciliation indicates that an adjustment is necessary on the books of the depositor:

Jan. 31	Bank service charge expense	20	
	Cash		20
	To record bank charges for printing checks.		

The popular reconciliation format has two major sections. The first section begins with the balance per books, that is, the balance in the Cash T-account. Adjustments are made for items not entered on the books but already entered by the bank, such as deduction of the $20 service charge. These

Exhibit 6-5
Comparative Cash
Balances, January
31, 20X2

Depositor's Records

Cash in Bank

(receivable from bank)

1/1/X2 Bal.	11,000	1/5	2,000
1/10	4,000	1/15	3,000
1/24	6,000	1/19	5,000
1/31	7,000	1/29	10,000
	28,000		20,000
1/31/X2 Bal.	8,000		

Bank's Records

Deposits

(payable to depositor)

1/8	2,000	1/1/X2 Bal.	11,000
1/20	3,000	1/11	4,000
1/28	5,000	1/26	6,000
1/31	20*		
	10,020		21,000
		1/31/X2 Bal.	10,980

*Service charge for printing checks.

Date	Depositor's General Journal	Debit	Credit
1/5	Accounts payable	2,000	
	Cash		2,000
	Check No. 1.		
1/10	Cash	4,000	
	Accounts receivable		4,000
	Deposit slip No. 1.		
1/15	Income taxes payable	3,000	
	Cash		3,000
	Check No. 2.		
1/19	Accounts payable	5,000	
	Cash		5,000
	Check No. 3.		
1/24	Cash	6,000	
	Accounts receivable		6,000
	Deposit No. 2.		
1/29	Accounts payable	10,000	
	Cash		10,000
	Check No. 4.		
1/31	Cash	7,000	
	Accounts receivable		7,000
	Deposit No. 3.		

adjustments are then recorded in the records of the company. No additions are shown in the illustrated section, but an illustrative addition would be the bank's collection of a customer receivable on behalf of the company. The second section begins with the balance per bank. Adjustments are made for items not entered by the bank, but already entered in the company's books. These items normally adjust automatically as deposits and checks reach the bank for processing. After adjustments, each section should end with identical adjusted cash balances. This is the amount that should appear as Cash in Bank on the depositor's balance sheet.

Accounting Vocabulary

accounting controls, p. 252
accounting system, p. 252
accounts receivable turnover, p. 249
administrative controls, p. 252
aging of accounts receivable, p. 248
allowance for bad debts, p. 243
allowance for doubtful accounts, p. 243
allowance for uncollectible accounts, p. 243
allowance method, p. 243
audit committee, p. 256
average collection period, p. 250

bad debt recoveries, p. 248
bad debts, p. 241
bad debts expense, p. 241
cash discounts, p. 235
compensating balances, p. 240
days to collect accounts receivable, p. 250
gross sales, p. 234
internal control, p. 252
management reports, p. 255
net sales, p. 234
percentage of accounts receivable method, p. 247
percentage of completion method, p. 233

percentage of sales method, p. 245
purchase allowance, p. 234
purchase returns, p. 234
reconcile a bank statement, p. 240
reserve for doubtful accounts, p. 243
sales allowance, p. 234
sales returns, p. 234
specific write-off method, p. 242
trade discounts, p. 235
turnover, p. 237
uncollectible accounts, p. 241

Assignment Material

Questions

6-1 Describe the timing of revenue recognition for a defense contractor on a $50 million long-term government contract with work spread evenly over 5 years.

6-2 Why is the realizable value of a credit sale often less than that of a cash sale?

6-3 Distinguish between a sales and a purchase return.

6-4 Distinguish between a cash discount and a trade discount.

6-5 "Trade discounts should not be recorded by the accountant." Do you agree? Explain.

6-6 "Retailers who accept VISA or MasterCard are foolish because they do not receive the full price for merchandise they sell." Comment.

6-7 Describe and give two examples of cash equivalents.

6-8 "A compensating balance essentially increases the interest rate on money borrowed." Explain.

6-9 "Cash is only 3% of our total assets. Therefore, we should not waste time designing systems to manage cash. We should use our time on matters that have a better chance of affecting our profits." Do you agree? Explain.

6-10 It is common in sub shops and pizza parlors around the Baruch College campus to find signs that say "Your purchase is free if the clerk does not give you a receipt" or "Two free lunches if your receipt has a red star." What is management trying to accomplish with these free offers?

6-11 "The cash balance on a company's books should always equal the cash balance shown by its bank." Do you agree? Explain.

6-12 List five internal control procedures used to safeguard cash.

6-13 "If everyone were honest, there would be no need for internal controls to safeguard cash." Do you agree? Explain.

6-14 What is the cost-benefit relationship in deciding whether to offer credit to customers, and whether to accept bank credit cards?

6-15 If a company accepts bank credit cards, why might it accept specific cards instead of all of them? For example, some retailers accept VISA and MasterCard, but not American Express or Diner's Club, while the exact opposite is true for some restaurants.

6-16 Distinguish between the allowance method and the specific write-off method for bad debts.

6-17 The El Camino Hospital uses the allowance method in accounting for bad debts. A journal entry was made for writing off the accounts of Jane Jensen, Eunice Belmont, and Samuel Maze Do you agree with this entry? If not, show the correct entry and the correcting entry.

Bad debts expense 14,321
   Accounts receivable 14,321

6-18 "The Allowance for Uncollectible Accounts account has no subsidiary ledger, but the Accounts Receivable account does." Explain.

6-19 "Under the allowance method, there are three popular ways to estimate the bad debts expense for a particular year." Name the three.

6-20 What is meant by "aging of accounts"?

6-21 Describe why a write-off of a bad debt should be reversed if collection occurs at a later date.

6-22 What is the relationship between the average collection period and the accounts receivable turnover?

6-23 Distinguish between the percentage of sales approach to applying the allowance method and the aging of accounts receivable approach.

6-24 Distinguish between internal accounting control and internal administrative control.

6-25 "The primary responsibility for internal controls rests with the outside auditors." Do you agree? Explain.

6-26 What is the primary responsibility of the audit committee?

6-27 Prepare a checklist of important factors to consider in judging an internal control system.

6-28 "The most important element of successful control is personnel." Explain.

6-29 What is the essential idea of separation of duties?

Critical Thinking Questions

6-30 Revenue Recognition
A newly created weekly free newspaper has approached your bank seeking a loan. Although the newspaper is free, it gets significant revenue from advertising. In the first 2 months of operations, it reported profits of $10,000. It has receivables of $70,000 on $200,000 of advertising revenue. Some of the revenue reported for these 2 months included special promotional pricing that gave advertisers 4 months of ads for the price of 2. All this promotional revenue was included in the income statement for 2 months. Comment on the reported profit.

6-31 Using the Income Statement to Evaluate Sales Success
The net income of a company is the result of many factors. Sometimes managers want to measure the performance of one part of the organization separate from the effects of other parts. How might a company evaluate the success of its sales efforts using a classified income statement? Assume that the sales department is responsible for pricing and thus influences both the total amount sold and the margin on the items sold.

6-32 Criteria for Revenue Recognition
We generally treat revenue as earned when the company delivers merchandise to the customer. At that moment, what additional uncertainty remains about the proper amount of revenue that will ultimately be realized?

6-33 Revenue Recognition and Evaluation of Sales Staff
Revenue on an accrual-accounting basis must be both earned and realized before it is recognized in the income statement. Revenue in cash-basis accounting must be received in cash. Is accrual-basis or cash-basis recognition of revenue more relevant for evaluating the performance of a sales staff? Why?

Exercises

6-34 Revenue Recognition, Cash Discounts, and Returns
University Bookstore ordered 1,000 copies of an introductory economics textbook from **Prentice-Hall** on July 17, 20X0. The books were delivered on August 12, at which time a bill was sent requesting payment of $40 per book. However, a 2% discount was allowed if Prentice-Hall received payment by September 12. University Bookstore sent the proper payment, which was received by Prentice-Hall on September 10. On December 18, University Bookstore returned 60 books to Prentice-Hall for a full cash refund.

1. Prepare the journal entries (if any) for Prentice-Hall on (a) July 17, (b) August 12, (c) September 10, and (d) December 18. Include appropriate explanations.
2. Suppose this was the only sales transaction in 20X0. Prepare the revenue section of Prentice-Hall's income statement.

6-35 Revenue Recognition
Cascade Logging Company hired Dmitri Construction Company to build a new bridge across the Logan River. The bridge would extend a logging road into a new stand of timber. The contract called for a payment of $11 million on completion of the bridge. Work was begun in 20X0 and completed in 20X2. Total costs were:

20X0	$3 million
20X1	3 million
20X2	4 million
Total	$10 million

1. Suppose the accountant for Dmitri Construction Company judged that Cascade Logging might not be able to pay the $11 million. How much revenue would you recognize each year?
2. Suppose Cascade Logging is a subsidiary of a major wood products company. Therefore, receipt of payment on the contract is reasonably certain. How much revenue would you recognize each year?

6-36 Sales in Britain

The first line of the 2002 income statement of Cadbury Schweppes, the British candy and beverage company, showed:

Turnover	£5,298,000,000

The current assets on the company's balance sheet were shown as follows:

Current Assets	
Stocks [inventories]	£ 528,000,000
Trade debtors	
Due within 1 year	970,000,000
Due after 1 year	82,000,000
Investments	297,000,000
Cash at bank and in hand	175,000,000
Total current assets	£2,052,000,000

1. What term is used in the United States for the item called "trade debtors" on the Cadbury Schweppes balance sheet?
2. By using the account titles given in this exercise, make a journal entry for the sale of £100,000 of chocolates to Harrod's Department Store.

6-37 Compensating Balances

Gemini Company borrowed $100,000 from First Bank at 9% interest. The loan agreement stated that a compensating balance of $10,000 must be kept in the Gemini checking account at First Bank. The total Gemini cash balance at the end of the year was $45,000.

1. How much usable cash did Gemini Company receive for its $100,000 loan?
2. What was the real interest rate paid by Gemini?
3. Prepare a footnote for the annual report of Gemini Company explaining the compensating balance.

6-38 Sales Returns and Discounts

San Jose Electronics Wholesalers had gross sales of $900,000 during the month of March. Sales returns and allowances were $40,000. Cash discounts granted were $30,000.

Prepare an analysis of the impact of these transactions on the balance sheet equation. Also show the journal entries. Prepare a detailed presentation of the revenue section of the income statement.

6-39 Gross and Net Sales

Midwest Metal Products, Incorporated, reported the following in 20X8 ($ in thousands):

Sales	$700
Cash discounts on sales	20
Sales returns and allowances	40

1. Prepare the revenue section of the 20X8 income statement.
2. Prepare journal entries for (a) initial revenue recognition for 20X8 sales, (b) sales returns and allowances, and (c) collection of accounts receivable. Assume that all sales were on credit and all accounts receivable for 20X8 sales were collected in 20X8. Omit explanations.

6-40 Cash Discounts Transactions

Video Specialties is a wholesaler that sells on terms of 2/10, n/30. It sold video equipment to Video City for $300,000 on open account on January 10. Payment (net of cash discount) was received on January 19. By using the equation framework, analyze the two transactions for Video Specialties. Also prepare journal entries.

6-41 Entries for Cash Discounts and Returns on Sales

The Sonoma Wine Company is a wholesaler of California wine that sells on credit terms of 2/10, n/30. Consider the following transactions:

June 9	Sales on credit to Sierra Wines, $30,000
June 11	Sales on credit to Marty's Liquors, $10,000
June 18	Collected from Sierra Wines
June 26	Accepted the return of six cases from Marty's, $1,000
July 10	Collected from Marty's
July 12	Sierra returned some defective wine that it had acquired on June 9 for $100; Sonoma issued a cash refund immediately

Prepare journal entries for these transactions. Omit explanations. Assume the full appropriate amounts were exchanged.

6-42 Credit Terms, Discounts, and Annual Interest Rates

As the struggling owner of a new Korean restaurant, you suffer from a habitual shortage of cash. Yesterday the following invoices arrived:

Vender	Face Amount	Terms
Cornation Produce	$ 600	n/30
Rose Exterminators	90	EOM
Nebraska Meat Supply	900	15, EOM
John's Fisheries	1,000	1/10, n/30
Garcia Equipment	2,000	2/10, n/30

1. Write out the exact meaning of each of the terms.
2. You can borrow cash from the local bank on a 10-, 20-, or 30-day note bearing an annual interest rate of 16%. Should you borrow to take advantage of the cash discounts offered by the last two vendors? Why? Show computations. For interest rate computations, assume a 360-day year.

6-43 Accounting for Credit Cards

La Roux Designer Clothing Store has extended credit to customers on open account. Its average experience for each of the past 3 years has been:

	Cash	Credit	Total
Sales	$500,000	$300,000	$800,000
Bad debts expense	—	5,000	5,000
Administrative expense	—	10,000	10,000

Edith La Roux is considering whether to accept bank cards (e.g., VISA, MasterCard). She has resisted because she does not want to bear the cost of the service, which would be 4% of gross sales.

The representative of VISA claims that the availability of bank cards would have increased overall sales by at least 10%. However, regardless of the level of sales, the new mix of the sales would be 50% bank card and 50% cash.

1. How would a bank card sale of $200 affect the accounting equation? Where would the discount appear on the income statement?
2. Should La Roux adopt the bank card if sales do not increase? Base your answer solely on the sparse facts given here.
3. Repeat requirement 2, but assume that total sales would increase 10%.

6-44 Trade-Ins versus Discounts

Many states base their sales tax on gross sales less any discount. Trade-in allowances are not discounts, so they are not deducted from the sales price for sales tax purposes. Suppose Michio Nagata had decided to trade in his old car for a new one with a list price of $20,000. He will pay cash of $13,000 plus sales tax. If he had not traded in a car, the dealer would have offered a discount of 15% of the list price. The sales tax is 7%.

How much of the $7,000 price reduction should be called a discount? How much a trade-in? Mr. Nagata wants to pay as little sales tax as legally possible.

6-45 Uncollectible Accounts

During 20X8, the Rainbow Paint Store had credit sales of $800,000. The store manager expects that 2% of the credit sales will never be collected, although no accounts are written off until 10 assorted steps have been taken to attain collection. The 10 steps require a minimum of 14 months.

Assume that during 20X9, specific customers are identified who are never expected to pay $14,000 that they owe from the sales of 20X8. All 10 collection steps have been completed.

1. Show the impact on the balance sheet equation of the preceding transactions in 20X8 and 20X9 under (a) the specific write-off method and (b) the allowance method. Which method do you prefer? Why?
2. Prepare journal entries for both methods. Omit explanations.

6-46 Specific Write-Off versus Allowance Methods

The Empire District Electric Company serves customers in the region where the states of Kansas, Missouri, Arkansas, and Oklahoma come together. Empire District uses the allowance method for recognizing uncollectible accounts. The company's January 1, 2003 balance sheet showed accounts receivable of $21,993,819. The footnotes revealed that this was net of uncollectible accounts of $679,000.

1. Suppose Empire District wrote off a specific uncollectible account for $8,000 on January 2, 2003. Assume this was the only transaction affecting the accounts receivable or allowance accounts on that day. Give the journal entry to record this write-off. What would the balance sheet show for accounts receivable at the end of the day on January 2.
2. Suppose Empire District used the specific write-off method instead of the allowance method for recognizing uncollectible accounts. Compute the accounts receivable balance that would be shown on the January 1, 2003, balance sheet.

6-47 Bad Debts

Prepare all journal entries for 20X2 concerning the following data for a medical clinic that performs elective laser surgery that corrects vision. Such procedures are not covered by third-party payers such as Blue Cross or Medicare. Consider the following balances of a medical clinic on December 31, 20X1: Receivables from individual patients, $200,000; and Allowance for Doubtful Receivables, $50,000. During 20X2, total billings to individual patients were $2.5 million. Past experience indicated that 15% of such individual billings would ultimately be uncollectible. Write-offs of receivables during 20X2 were $360,000.

6-48 Bad Debt Allowance

Myrick Appliance had sales of $1,000,000 during 20X8, including $600,000 of sales on credit. Balances on December 31, 20X7, were Accounts Receivable, $90,000, and Allowance for Bad Debts, $8,000. Data for 20X8: collections on accounts receivable were $560,000. Bad debts expense was estimated at 2% of credit sales, as in previous years. Write-offs of bad debts during 20X8 were $10,000.

1. Prepare journal entries concerning the preceding information for 20X8.
2. Show the ending balances of the balance sheet accounts, December 31, 20X8.

3. Based on the given data, would you advise Alice Myrick, the president of the store, that the 2% estimated bad debt rate appears adequate?

6-49 Bad Debt Recoveries

Seneca Department Store has many accounts receivable. The Seneca balance sheet, December 31, 20X1, showed Accounts Receivable, $950,000 and Allowance for Uncollectible Accounts, $40,000. In early 20X2, write-offs of customer accounts of $25,000 were made. In late 20X2, a customer, whose $6,000 debt had been written off earlier, won a $1 million sweepstakes cash prize. The buyer immediately remitted $6,000 to Seneca. The store welcomed the purchaser's money and return to high credit standing.

Prepare the journal entries for the $25,000 write-off in early 20X2 and the $6,000 receipt in late 20X2.

6-50 Subsidiary Ledger

An appliance store made credit sales of $800,000 in 20X4 to 1,000 customers: Schumacher, $5,000; Cerruti, $7,000; others, $788,000. Total collections during 20X4 were $720,000 including $5,000 from Cerruti, but nothing was collected from Schumacher. At the end of 20X4, an allowance for uncollectible accounts was provided of 2% of credit sales.

1. Set up appropriate general ledger accounts plus a subsidiary ledger for Accounts Receivable. The subsidiary ledger should consist of two individual accounts plus a third account called Others. Post the entries for 20X4. Prepare a statement of the ending balances of the individual accounts receivable to show that they reconcile with the general ledger account.
2. On March 24, 20X5, the Schumacher account was written off. Give the journal entry.

6-51 Accounts Receivable Turnover and Average Collection Period

Vulcan Materials Company had recent sales of $2.7 billion. Beginning and ending accounts receivable for the fiscal year were $334 million and $343 million, respectively.

Compute Vulcan's accounts receivable turnover and average collection period for the fiscal year. Assume all sales are on open account.

6-52 Internal Control Weaknesses

Identify the internal control weaknesses in each of the following situations, and indicate what change or changes you would recommend to eliminate the weaknesses:

a. The internal audit staff of MacDougall Aerospace, Inc., reports to the controller. However, internal audits are undertaken only when a department manager requests one, and audit reports are confidential documents prepared exclusively for the manager. Internal auditors are not allowed to talk to the external auditors.
b. Alice Walker, president of Northwestern State Bank, a small-town midwestern bank, wants to expand the size of her bank. She hired Fred Howell to begin a foreign loan department. Howell had previously worked in the international department of a London bank. The president told him to consult with her on any large loans, but she never specified exactly what was meant by "large." At the end of Howell's first year, the president was surprised and pleased by his results. Although he had made several loans larger than any made by other sections of the bank and had not consulted with her on any of them, the president hesitated to say anything because the financial results were so good. Walker certainly did not want to upset the person most responsible for the bank's excellent growth in earnings.
c. Michael Grant is in charge of purchasing and receiving watches for Blumberg, Inc., a chain of jewelry stores. Grant places orders, fills out receiving documents when the watches are delivered, and authorizes payment to suppliers. According to Blumberg's procedures manual, Grant's activities should be reviewed by a purchasing supervisor. However, to save money, the supervisor was not replaced when she resigned 3 years ago. No one seems to miss the supervisor.

6-53 Assignment of Duties

Music Supplies, Inc., is a distributor of several popular lines of musical instruments and supplies. It purchases merchandise from several suppliers and sells to hundreds of retail stores. Here is a partial list of the company's necessary office routines:

1. Verifying and comparing related purchase documents: purchase orders, purchase invoices, receiving reports, etc.
2. Preparing vouchers for cash disbursements and attaching supporting purchase documents.

3. Signing vouchers to authorize payment (after examining vouchers with attached documents).
4. Preparing checks for 1 to 3.
5. Signing checks (after examining voucher authorization and supporting documents).
6. Mailing checks.
7. Daily sorting of incoming mail into items that contain money and items that do not.
8. Distributing the mail: money to cashier, reports of money received to accounting department, and remainder to various appropriate offices.
9. Making daily bank deposits.
10. Reconciling monthly bank statements.

The company's chief financial officer has decided that no more than five people will handle all these routines, including himself as necessary.

Prepare a chart to show how these operations should be assigned to the five employees, including the chief financial officer. Use a row for each of the numbered routines and a column for each employee: Financial Officer, A, B, C, D. Place a check mark for each row in one or more of the columns. Observe the rules of the textbook checklist for internal control, especially separation of duties.

6-54 Simple Bank Reconciliation

Study Appendix 6. St. Luke's Hospital has a bank account. Consider the following information:

a. Balances as of July 31: per books, $47,000; per bank statement, $32,880.
b. Cash receipts of July 31 amounting to $9,000 were recorded and then deposited in the bank's night depository. The bank did not include this deposit on its July statement.
c. The bank statement included service charges of $120.
d. Patients had given the hospital some bad checks amounting to $11,000. The bank marked them NSF and returned them with the bank statement after charging the hospital for the $11,000. The hospital had made no entry for the return of these checks.
e. The hospital's outstanding checks amounted to $6,000.

Required
1. Prepare a bank reconciliation as of July 31.
2. Prepare the hospital journal entries required by the given information.

Problems

6-55 Allowance for Credit Losses

Tompkins Trustco Inc., a multibank holding company headquartered in Ithaca, New York, included the following in the footnotes to its 2002 annual report:

The following is a summary of changes in the reserve for loan/lease losses ($ in thousands):

	2002
Reserve at beginning of year	$10,706
Loans/leases charged off	(1,721)
Recoveries	484
Provision charged to operations	2,235
Reserve at end of year	$11,704

1. Terminology in bank financial statements sometimes differs slightly from that in statements of industrial companies. Explain what is meant by "reserve for loan/lease losses," "provision charged to operations," and "loans/leases charged off" in the footnote.
2. Prepare the 2002 journal entries to record the writing off of specific credit losses, the recovery of previously written off credit losses, and the charge for credit losses against 2002 income. Omit explanations.
3. Suppose the bank analyzed its loans at the end of 2002 and decided that a reserve for losses equal to $10 million was required. Compute the provision that would be charged in 2002.
4. The bank had income before income taxes of $34,340 thousand in 2002. Compute the income before income taxes if the reserve for losses at the end of 2002 had been $10 million?

6-56 Aging of Accounts

Consider the following analysis of Accounts Receivable, February 28, 20X9:

Name of Customer	Total	Remarks
Ng Nurseries	$ 20,000	25% over 90 days, 75% 61–90 days
Michael's Landscaping	8,000	75% 31–60 days, 25% under 30 days
Shoven Garden Supply	12,000	60% 61–90 days, 40% 31–60 days
Bonner Perennial Farm	20,000	All under 30 days
Hjortshoj Florists	4,000	25% 61–90 days, 75% 1–30 days
Other accounts (each detailed)	80,000	50% 1–30 days, 30% 31–60 days, 15% 61–90 days, 5% over 90 days
Total	$144,000	

Prepare an aging schedule, classifying ages into four categories: 1 to 30 days, 31 to 60 days, 61 to 90 days, and over 90 days. Assume that the prospective bad debt percentages for each category are 0.2%, 0.8%, 10%, and 80%, respectively. What is the ending balance in the Allowance for Uncollectible Accounts?

6-57 Percentage of Ending Accounts Receivable

Consider the following data:

	Accounts Receivable at End of Year	Accounts Receivable Deemed Uncollectible and Written Off During Subsequent Years
20X1	$210,000	$ 8,000
20X2	170,000	6,000
20X3	195,000	7,000
20X4	230,000	9,000
20X5	275,000	13,000
20X6	240,000	9,800

The unadjusted credit balance in Allowance for Uncollectible Accounts at December 31, 20X7, is $600. By using the percentage of ending accounts receivable method, prepare an adjusting entry to bring the Allowance to the appropriate amount at December 31, 20X7 when the Accounts Receivable balance is $250,000. Base your estimate of the percentage on the actual loss experience in the prior 6 years.

6-58 Estimates of Uncollectible Accounts

Rashid Company has made an analysis of its sales and accounts receivable for the past 5 years. Assume all accounts written off in a year related to sales of the preceding year and were part of the accounts receivable at the end of that year. That is, no account is written off before the end of the year of the sale, and all accounts remaining unpaid are written off before the end of the year following the sale. The analysis showed:

	Sales	Ending Accounts Receivable	Bad Debts Written Off During the Year
20X1	$ 680,000	$ 90,000	$12,000
20X2	750,000	97,000	12,500
20X3	750,000	103,000	14,000
20X4	850,000	114,000	16,500
20X5	840,000	110,000	17,600

The balance in Allowance for Uncollectible Accounts on December 31, 20X4, was $15,900.

1. Determine the bad debts expense for 20X5 and the balance of the Allowance for Uncollectible Accounts for December 31, 20X5, using the percentage of sales method.
2. Repeat requirement 1 using the percentage of ending accounts receivable method.

6-59 Percentage of Sales and Percentage of Ending Accounts Receivable

Teton Equipment Company had credit sales of $6 million during 20X7. Most customers paid promptly (within 30 days), but a few took longer; an average of 1.4% of credit sales were never paid. On December 31, 20X7, accounts receivable were $470,000. The Allowance for Bad Debts account, before any recognition of 20X7 bad debts, had a $1,200 debit balance.

Teton produces and sells mountaineering equipment and other outdoor gear. Most of the sales (about 80%) come in the period of March through August; the other 20% is spread almost evenly over the other 6 months. Over the last 6 years, an average of 18% of the December 31 accounts receivable has not been collected.

1. Suppose Teton Equipment uses the percentage of sales method to calculate an allowance for bad debts. Present the accounts receivable and allowance accounts as they should appear on the December 31, 20X7, balance sheet. Give the journal entry required to recognize the bad debts expense for 20X7.
2. Repeat requirement 1, except assume that Teton Equipment uses the percentage of ending accounts receivable method.
3. Which method do you prefer? Why?

6-60 Average Collection Period

Consider the following:

	20X8	20X7	20X6
Sales	$2,000,000	$2,500,000	$2,400,000

	December 31		
	20X8	20X7	20X6
Accounts receivable	$ 175,000	$ 190,000	$ 185,000

Of the total sales, 80% are on account.

Compute the days to collect accounts receivable for the years 20X7 and 20X8. Comment on the results.

6-61 Bank Cards

VISA and MasterCard are used to pay for a large percentage of retail purchases. The financial arrangements are similar for both bank cards. A news story said:

> If a cardholder charges a $600 briefcase, for instance, the merchant deposits the sales draft with his bank, which immediately credits $600 less a small transaction fee (usually 2% of the sale) to the merchant's account. The bank that issued the customer his card then pays the merchant's bank $600 less a 1.5% transaction fee, allowing the merchant's bank a 0.5% profit on the transaction.

1. Prepare the journal entry for the sale by the merchant.
2. Prepare the journal entries for the merchant's bank concerning (a) the merchant's deposit and (b) the collection from the customer's bank that issued the card.
3. Prepare the journal entry for the customer's bank that issued the card.
4. The national losses from bad debts for bank cards are about 1.8% of the total billings to card-holders. If so, how can the banks justify providing this service if their revenue from processing is typically 1.5% to 2.0%?

6-62 Student Loans

An annual report of the University of Washington includes information about its receivables from student loans in a footnote to the financial statements ($ in thousands):

	Year 1		Year 2	
Student loans				
Federal programs	$30,905		$33,109	
Less—allowances	2,793	$28,112	2,378	$ 30,731
University funds	$ 4,748		$ 4,999	
Less—allowances	337	4,411	271	4,728
Total, net		$32,523		$ 35,459

1. Compare the quality of the loans under federal programs with the quality of those using university funds. Compare the quality of the loans outstanding at the end of year 2 with the quality of those outstanding at the end of year 1.
2. By using the allowance method, which accounts would be affected by an allowance for bad debts of an appropriate percentage of $200,000 of additional new loans in year 2 from university funds? Choose a percentage.

6-63 Hospital Bad Debts

EquiMed, Inc., a medical management company based in State College, Pennsylvania, owned, operated, and managed 35 radiation oncology centers. Notes to a recent earnings statement reported the following about net revenue ($ in thousands):

Gross revenues	$159,944
Less provision for contractual adjustments	60,829
Net revenues	$ 99,115

1. Prepare a reasonable footnote to accompany the preceding presentation. What do you think is the purpose of contractual adjustments?
2. Prepare the summary journal entries for the $159,944 and the $60,829.

6-64 Discounts and Doubtful Items

Eli Lilly, a major pharmaceutical company, includes the following in its 2002 balance sheet ($ amounts in millions): Accounts receivable (net of allowances of $66.4): $1,670.3.

1. Compute the ratio of the allowance for doubtful items to gross accounts receivable for December 31, 2002. In 1995, this ratio was 3.5%, and it was 3.2% in 1998. What are some possible reasons for the changes in this ratio?
2. Independent of the actual balances, prepare a journal entry to write off an uncollectible account of $100,000 on January 2, 2003.

6-65 Uncollectible Accounts

Nike, Inc., is a worldwide supplier of athletic products. Its balance sheet on May 31, 2003, included the following data ($ in millions):

Accounts receivable, less allowance for doubtful accounts of $87.9	$2,101.1

1. The company uses the allowance method for accounting for bad debts. The company added $33 million to the allowance during the year ending May 31, 2003. Write-offs of uncollectible accounts were $25.5 million. Show (a) the impact on the balance sheet equation of these transactions and (b) the journal entries.
2. Calculate the allowance balance on May 31, 2002.
3. Suppose Nike had used the specific write-off method for accounting for bad debts. By using the same information as in requirement 1, show (a) the impact on the balance sheet equation and (b) the journal entry.
4. How would these Nike balance sheet amounts have been affected if the specific write-off method had been used up to that date? Be specific.

6-66 Uncollectible Accounts

Oracle is the world's largest supplier of database software. Its balance sheet included the following presentation:

	May 31	
	2003	**2002**
	($ in millions)	
Trade receivables, net of allowance for doubtful accounts of $376 as of May 31, 2003 and $413 as of May 31, 2002	$1,920	$2,036

During 2003, Oracle added $128 million to its allowance for estimated doubtful accounts. (a) Calculate the write-offs of uncollectible accounts, and show (b) the impact on the balance sheet equation of these transactions and (c) the journal entries.

6-67 Allowance for Doubtful Accounts and 10-K Disclosures

The following schedule is taken from page 14 of the 10-K filing of Ford Motor Company for the year ending December 31, 2002. The 10-K is a required filing that companies must make with the SEC each year for their common stock to be traded publicly in the United States. It includes more detail than is often found in the annual report that is sent to all shareholders. This schedule describes exactly what occurred in the allowance for doubtful accounts. Use the information in the schedule at the top of the next page to reproduce the journal entries affecting the allowance for doubtful accounts during the year ending December 31, 2002.

Item 1. Business

The following tables show actual credit losses net of recoveries, which is referred to as net credit losses, and loss-to-receivables ratios (calculated as net credit losses divided by average net receivables) for Ford Credit's worldwide owned and managed portfolios, for the various categories of financing during the years indicated (in millions):

	Years Ended or at December 31,		
	2002	**2001**	**2000**
Owned			
Net credit losses			
Retail installment and lease*	$2,292	$2,052	$1,283
Wholesale	40	33	14
Other	30	24	–
Total	$2,362	$2,109	$1,297
Loss-to-receivables**			
Retail installment and lease*	2.04%	1.74%	1.10%
Wholesale	0.25	0.12	0.05
Total including other	1.72%	1.36%	0.84%
Managed			
Net credit losses			
Retail installment and lease*	$2,740	$2,272	$1,410
Wholesale	46	34	15
Other	30	24	–
Total	$2,816	$2,330	$1,425
Loss-to-receivables**			
Retail installment and lease*	1.73%	1.45%	1.00%
Wholesale	0.13	0.10	0.05
Total including other	1.39%	1.20%	0.81%

* Includes net credit losses on operating leases. ** Includes net investment in operating leases.

Shown below is an analysis of Ford Credit's allowance for credit losses related to owned finance receivables and operating leases for the years indicated (dollar amounts in billions):

	2002	2001	2000
Balance, beginning of year	$2.8	$1.6	$1.5
Provision charged to operations	3.0	3.4	1.6
Deductions			
Losses	2.9	2.5	1.6
Recoveries	(0.5)	(0.4)	(0.3)
Net losses	2.4	2.1	1.3
Other changes, principally amounts relating to finance receivables sold and translation adjustments	0.2	0.1	0.2
Net deductions	2.6	2.2	1.5
Balance, end of year	$3.2	$2.8	$1.6
Allowance for credit losses as a percentage of end-of-period net receivables*	2.51%	1.89%	1.03%

* Includes net investment in operating leases.

In 2002, higher net credit losses resulted largely from the continuation of a weak economy in the United States, and the continuation of a high level of personal bankruptcy filings.

6-68 Sales, Accounts Receivable, and Ethics

Writing in *Corporate Cashflow*, Howard Schillit described how the market value of Comptronix fell from $238 million to $67 million in a few hours when it was revealed that management had "cooked the books." Comptronix provided contract manufacturing services to makers of electronic equipment. Its 1991 financial results looked strong.

	1991	1990	Change
Sales	$102.0 million	$70.2 million	+ 45%
Accounts receivable	12.6 million	12.0 million	+ 5%
Accounts receivable turnover	8.1	5.9	

However, the relationship between sales and accounts receivable sent signals to knowledgeable analysts.

1. Discuss the relationship that you would expect between sales and accounts receivable in a normal situation.
2. What unethical actions might cause sales to grow so much faster than accounts receivable? What unethical actions might cause the opposite, that is, for accounts receivable to grow faster than sales?
3. What is the most likely type of "cooking the books" that occurred at Comptronix?

6-69 Audit Committee Role

In a recent court decision, a U.S. corporation was required to delegate certain responsibilities to its audit committee. The audit committee was required to:

1. Consult with its independent auditors before deciding any significant or material accounting question or policy.
2. Retain independent auditors to perform quarterly reviews of all financial statements prior to public issuance.
3. Conduct internal audits, with personnel reporting directly to the audit committee (internal auditors must report quarterly to the audit committee).
4. Retain or dismiss independent and internal auditors.

5. Consult with the independent auditors on their quarterly reviews of financial statements.
6. Review all monthly corporate and division financial statements and the auditor's management letter.
7. Receive quarterly reports from independent auditors on internal control deficiencies.
8. Review and approve all reports to shareholders and the SEC before dissemination.

The court also ruled that the audit committee must be composed of at least three outside directors who have no business dealings with the firm other than directors' fees and expense reimbursements.

a. Prepare a partial corporation organization chart to depict these requirements. Use boxes only for Audit Committee, Independent Auditors, Internal Auditing, Finance Vice-President, and Board of Directors. Connect the appropriate boxes with lines: solid lines for direct responsibility, and dashed lines for information and communications. Place numbers on these lines to correspond to the eight items specified by the court decision.
b. Identify the main elements of the chapter checklist of internal control that seem most relevant to this system design.

6-70 Embezzlement of Cash Receipts

Braxton Company is a small wholesaler of pet supplies. It has only a few employees.

The owner of Braxton Company, who is also its president and general manager, makes daily deposits of customers' checks in the company bank account and writes all checks issued by the company. The president also reconciles the monthly bank statement with the books when the bank statement is received in the mail.

The assistant to Braxton Company's president renders secretarial services, which include taking dictation, typing letters, and processing all mail, both incoming and outgoing. Each day the assistant opens the incoming mail and gives the president the checks received from customers. The vouchers attached to the checks are separated by the assistant and sent to the bookkeeper, along with any other remittance advices that have been enclosed with the checks.

The bookkeeper makes prompt entries to credit customers' accounts for their remittances. From these accounts, the bookkeeper prepares monthly statements for mailing to customers.

Other employees include marketing and warehouse personnel.

For the thefts described next, explain briefly how each could have been concealed and what precautions you would recommend for forestalling the theft and its concealment:

1. The president's assistant takes some customers' checks, forges the company's endorsements, deposits the checks in a personal bank account, and destroys the check vouchers and any other remittance advices that have accompanied these checks.
2. The same action is taken in 1, except that the vouchers and other remittance advices are sent intact to the bookkeeper.

6-71 Film Processing

Write not more than one page about the possible areas where internal controls should be instituted in the following business described briefly. Keep in mind the size of the business, and do not suggest controls of a type impossible to set up in a firm of this sort. Make any reasonable assumptions about management duties and policies not expressly described.

You have a film-developing service on Long Island, with 10 employees driving their own cars 6 days a week to contact about 40 places each, where film is left to be picked up and developed. Drivers bring film in one day and return the processed film the second or third day later. Stores pay the driver for his charges made on film picked up at their store, less a percentage for their work as an agency. The driver then turns this cash in to the Long Island office, where all film is developed and books are kept. From 6 to 10 employees work at the office in Long Island, depending on the volume of work. You run the office and have one full-time accounting-clerical employee. Route drivers are paid monthly by miles of route covered.

6-72 Appraisal of Internal Control System

From the *San Francisco Chronicle*:

> *The flap over missing ferry fares was peacefully—and openly—resolved at a meeting of the Golden Gate Bridge District finance committee yesterday.*
> *Only a week ago, the subject was a matter of furious dispute in which bridge manager Dale W. Luehring was twice called a liar and there were prospects of a closed meeting on personnel matters.*

But yesterday, after a week of investigation, the meeting turned out to be public after all, and attorney Thomas M. Jenkins revealed the full total of stolen ferry tickets equaled $26.20.

The controversy began when auditor Gordon Dahlgren complained that there was an auditing "problem" and that he had not been informed when four children swiped $13.75 worth of tickets February 28. Committee chairman Ben K. Lerer, of San Francisco, ordered a full investigation.

Jenkins said the situation was complicated because children under 5 have been allowed to ride the ferry without a ticket, but after May 1 everyone will have to have a ticket, allowing for a closer audit.

Secondly, Jenkins explained, the "vault" in which tickets are deposited was proved insecure (resulting in two thefts totaling $26.20 worth of tickets) but has been replaced.

In the future, it was decided, all thefts of cash or tickets must be reported immediately to the California Highway Patrol or the local police, the bridge lieutenant on duty, the general manager, the security officer, the auditor-controller, and the transit manager.

In addition, employees must make a full written report within 24 hours to the president of the district board, the chairman of the finance-auditing committee, the auditor-controller, the attorney, the bus transit manager, the water transit manager, the toll captain, and the chief of administration and security.

What is your reaction to the new system? Explain, giving particular attention to applicable criteria for appraising an internal control system.

6-73 Casino Skimming

An article in *The Wall Street Journal* reported that about $7 million in quarters disappeared from the slot machines of four casinos of Argent Corporation in an 18-month period. The coins weighed nearly 150 tons, and the odds against such a payout to players of the slot machines is one in 3,875,000,000,000,000,000,000,000,000,000,000,000,000,000,000,000,000—an extremely unlikely event, to say the least. The disappearance was part of the biggest known skim operation ever. Skimming is taking a portion of gambling revenues before they can be counted for tax purposes.

Internal control is especially important in casinos. Meters in the slot machines record the winnings paid to customers. Coins are taken immediately to the slot counting room when machines are emptied. In the counting rooms, coins are weighed, and a portion is returned to the change booths.

What items in the chapter checklist of internal control seem especially important concerning slot machine operations? How could the money from slot machine operations have been stolen in such large amounts?

6-74 Employee Dishonesty

Consider the following true newspaper reports of dishonesty:

a. At a small manufacturer, supervisors had access to time cards and gave out W-2 forms each year. The supervisors pocketed $80,000 a year in the paychecks for phantom workers.
b. A manager at a busy branch office of a copying service had a receipt book of his own. Jobs of $200 and $300 were common. The manager stole cash by simply giving customers a receipt from his book instead of one of the company's numbered forms.
c. A purchasing agent received tiny kickbacks on buttons, zippers, and other trims used at a successful dress company. The agent got rich, and the company was overcharged $10 million.

Specify what control or controls would have helped avoid each of the listed situations.

6-75 Internal Control Weaknesses

Identify the internal control weaknesses in each of the following situations.

a. Rodney Williams, a football star at the local university, was hired by D. A. Mount to work in the accounting department of Mount Electronics during summer vacation. Providing summer jobs is one way Mount supports the team. After a week of training, Williams opened the mail containing checks from customers, recorded the payment in the books, and prepared the bank deposit slip.

b. Jim Sanchez manages a local franchise of a major 24-hour convenience store. Sanchez brags that he keeps labor costs well below the average for such stores by operating with only one clerk. He has not granted a pay increase in 4 years. He loses a lot of clerks, but he can find replacements.

c. Martha McGuire operates an **Exxon** service station. Because it takes much extra time for attendants to walk from the gas pumps to the inside cash register, McGuire placed a locked cash box next to the pumps and gave each attendant a key. Cash and credit card slips are placed in the cash box. Each day the amounts are counted and entered in total into the cash register.

d. Lazlo Perconte trusts his employees. The former manager purchased fidelity bonds on employees who handle cash. Perconte decided that such bonds showed a lack of trust, so he ceased purchasing them. Besides, the money saved helped Perconte meet his budget for the year.

6-76 Cooking the Books

In *The Accounting Wars,* author Mark Stevens presents a chapter on "Book Cooking, Number Juggling, and Other Tricks of the Trade." He quotes Glen Perry, a former chief accountant of the SEC's Enforcement Division: "Companies play games with their financial reports for any number of reasons, the most common being the intense pressure on corporate management to produce an unbroken stream of increasing earnings reports." Stevens then lists Perry's "terrible 10 of accounting frauds — ploys used to misrepresent corporate financial statements":

1. Recognition of revenues before they are realized.
2. Recognition of rentals to customers as sales.
3. Inclusion of fictitious amounts in inventories.
4. Improper cutoffs at year-end.
5. Improper application of last-in-first-out (LIFO).
6. Creation of fraudulent year-end transactions to boost earnings.
7. Failure to recognize losses through write-offs and allowances.
8. Inconsistent accounting practices without disclosures.
9. Capitalization or improper deferral of expenses.
10. Inclusion of unusual gains in operating income.

Suppose you were a division manager in a major corporation. Give a brief specific example of each of the 10 methods.

6-77 Straightforward Bank Reconciliation

Study Appendix 6. The City of Royalton has a checking account with First National Bank. The city's cash balance on February 28, 20X1, was $30,000. The deposit balance on the bank's books on February 28, 20X1, was also $30,000. The following transactions occurred during March.

Date	Check Number	Amount	Explanation
3/1	261	$11,000	Payment of previously billed consulting fee
3/6	262	9,000	Payment of accounts payable
3/10		12,000	Collection of taxes receivable
3/14	263	14,000	Acquisition of equipment for cash
3/17		16,000	Collection of license fees receivable
3/28	264	8,000	Payment of accounts payable
3/30	265	21,000	Payment of interest on municipal bonds
3/31		25,000	Collection of taxes receivable

All cash receipts are deposited via a night depository system after the close of the municipal business day. Therefore, the receipts are not recorded by the bank until the succeeding day.

On March 31, the bank charged the City of Royalton $100 for miscellaneous bank services.

1. Prepare the journal entries on the bank's books for check 262 and the deposit of March 10.
2. Prepare the journal entries for all March transactions on the books of the City of Royalton.
3. Post all transactions for March to T-accounts for the City's Cash in Bank account and the bank's Deposit account. Assume only checks 261 to 263 have been presented to the bank in March, each taking 4 days to clear the bank's records.

4. Prepare a bank reconciliation for the City of Royalton, March 31, 20X1. The final three City of Royalton transactions of March had not affected the bank's records as of March 31. What adjusting entry in the books of the City of Royalton is required on March 31?

5. What would be the cash balance shown on the balance sheet of the City of Royalton on March 31, 20X1?

6-78 Semicomplex Bank Reconciliation

Study Appendix 6. An employee, Sylvia Nelson, has a personal bank account. Her employer deposits her weekly paycheck automatically each Friday. The employee's check register (checkbook) for October is summarized as follows:

Reconciled cash balance, September 30, 20X1			$ 100
Additions			
Weekly payroll deposits	October		
	3		800
	10		800
	17		800
	24		800
Deposit of check received for gambling debt	25		475
Deposit of check received as winner of cereal contest	31		400
Subtotal			$4,175
Deductions			
Checks written No. 325–339	1–23	$3,300	
Check No. 340	26	70	
Check No. 341	30	90	
Check No. 342	31	340	3,800
Cash in bank, October 31, 20X1			$ 375

The bank statement is summarized in Exhibit 6-6. Note that NSF means "not sufficient funds." The check deposited on October 25 bounced; by prearrangement with Nelson, the bank automatically lends sufficient amounts (in multiples of $100) to ensure that her balance is never negative.

1. Prepare Nelson's bank reconciliation, October 31, 20X1.
2. Assume Nelson keeps a personal set of books on the accrual basis. Prepare the compound journal entry called for by the bank reconciliation.

6-79 Ethics and Bank Reconciliations

Study Appendix 6. The Springfield Chamber of Commerce recently hired you as an accounting assistant. On assuming your position on September 15, one of your first tasks was to reconcile the August bank statement. Your immediate supervisor, Ms. Ratelli, had been in charge of nearly all accounting tasks, including paying bills, preparing the payroll, and recording all transactions in the books. She has been very helpful to you, providing assistance on all the tasks she has asked you to do. The reconciliation was no different. Without assistance, you were able to locate the following information from the bank statement and the Chamber's books:

Balance per books	$16,610
Balance per bank statement	16,500
Bank service charges	30
NSF check returned	3,000
Deposit in transit	4,600
Outstanding checks	9,850

You also found a deposit on the bank statement of $3,300 that was incorrectly recorded as $3,030 on the Chamber's books.

When you could not reconcile the book and bank balances, you asked Ms. Ratelli for help. She responded that an additional $2,600 deposit was in transit.

Exhibit 6-6
Bank Statement
of Sylvia Nelson

SUMMARY OF YOUR CHECKING ACCOUNTS	
Beginning balance	$ 100.00
Deposits	4,575.00
Withdrawals	3,845.00
Service charges/fees	25.00*
Ending balance	805.00
Minimum balance on 10-28	**−80.00**

*$10.00 for returned check;
  $15.00 monthly service charge.

CHECKING ACTIVITY

Deposits

Posted	Amount	Description
10-03	800.00	Payroll deposit
10-10	800.00	Payroll deposit
10-17	800.00	Payroll deposit
10-24	800.00	Payroll deposit
10-25	475.00	Deposit
10-28	100.00	Automatic loan
10-31	800.00	Payroll deposit

Withdrawals

Ck. No.	Paid	Amount
325–339 Various dates in October. These would be shown by specific amounts, but are shown here as a total.		$3,300.00
340	10–27	70.00
NSF	10–28	475.00

Total number of checks = 16

1. Assume the information you obtained without Ms. Ratelli's help is accurate and complete. Prepare the August bank reconciliation with the original information, showing that the book and the bank balances do not reconcile.
2. Prepare a reconciliation using the new number, $7,200, for deposits in transit.
3. Why might Ms. Ratelli have instructed you to add $2,600 to the deposits in transit? What might she be trying to hide? If there were deceit, when might it be discovered?
4. What actions would you take if you were the accounting assistant?
5. By coincidence, you noticed a $2,600 cancelled check, signed by Ms. Ratelli, to an individual whose name you did not recognize. How would this change your answer to number 4?

Collaborative Learning Exercise

6-80 Revenue Recognition

Form groups of three to six students. Each student should pick one of the six industries listed as follows. The Standard Industrial Classification (SIC) number is provided for each industry. This number may be helpful in locating companies in that industry, especially if using search routines in electronic media.

Members of each group should learn as much as possible about the revenue recognition issues in their industry. Select at least two companies in the industry, and examine the description of each company's revenue recognition policies in the footnotes (usually in footnote 1 or 2) to the financial statements. Two possible companies are listed for each industry, but do not feel restricted to using the companies listed.

After the individual research on a particular industry, get together as a team and report on what each member has learned. Compare and contrast the issues relating to when revenue is earned and realized in each industry. Discuss why issues that are important in one industry are unimportant in another.

- 2721—Periodicals Publishing and Printing
  Marvel Entertainment Group
  Readers Digest Association
- 4512—Air Transportation, Scheduled
  Alaska Air Group
  Southwest Airlines Company
- 4911—Electric Services
  Duke Power
  Puget Sound Energy
- 6311—Life Insurance
  Allstate Corporation
  USLIFE, Incorporated
- 7811—Motion Picture, Videotape Production
  Dick Clark Productions
  Walt Disney Company
- 8062—General Medical and Surgical Hospitals
  Columbia/HCA Healthcare
  Regency Health Services

Analyzing and Interpreting Financial Statements

6-81 Financial Statement Research

Select an industry and choose two companies within that industry.

Calculate the accounts receivable turnover and days to collect accounts receivable for the two companies for 2 years and comment on the results.

6-82 Analyzing Starbucks' Financial Statements

Refer to Starbucks' financial statements (Appendix A).

1. Starbucks combines cash and cash equivalents on the balance sheet. Define cash equivalents and give an example.
2. Calculate the days to collect accounts receivable for the year ended September 28, 2003, assuming all sales were on account.

6-83 Analyzing Financial Statements Using the Internet: Oracle

Go to http://www.sec.gov/ to search for Oracle in the EDGAR database or go to the Oracle Web site. Find Oracle Corporation's latest 10K filing (annual report).

Answer the following questions about the company:

1. Under Part I, Item 1, how does Oracle categorize its software products? What do the categories contain?
2. Under the Research and Development accounting policy in the Notes to Consolidated Financial Statements is Oracle allowed to fully expense its software research and product development costs? What guidelines are followed in this area? What financial statement accounts reflect adherence to these guidelines? How important is R and D?
3. Turn to the Notes to Consolidated Financial Statements. Does Oracle finance sales to its customers on a long-term basis?
4. Examine Oracle's balance sheet. Which method of accounting for uncollectible accounts does the company use? How can you tell?

Inventories and Cost of Goods Sold

CHAPTER 7

LEARNING OBJECTIVES

After studying this chapter, you should be able to:

1. Link inventory valuation to gross profit.

2. Use both perpetual and periodic inventory systems.

3. Calculate the cost of merchandise acquired.

4. Compute income and inventory values using the four principal inventory valuation methods.

5. Calculate the impact on net income of LIFO liquidations.

6. Use the lower-of-cost-or-market method to value inventories.

7. Show the effects of inventory errors on financial statements.

8. Evaluate the gross profit percentage and inventory turnover.

9. Determine inventory costs for a manufacturing company (Appendix 7).

Have you ever gone to your local hardware store

and been frustrated because they did not have what you wanted? A goal of The Home Depot is to help you avoid this frustration. They do it by keeping a large inventory—40,000 to 50,000 different items, more than three times the number at a typical hardware store. As former CEO and Chairman Bernie Marcus said, one of the three main values at The Home Depot is assortment—"everything a do-it-yourselfer needs to complete a project."

Inventory requires a large investment by retail companies—$8.3 billion at The Home Depot, about 28% of the company's total assets—and accounting for this inventory is important. By carefully monitoring inventory levels, The Home Depot makes sure it does not lose sales by having too little inventory and does not lose money by investing in too much inventory. ▪

In Chapter 6, we learned how to account for sales revenues. Of course, when a company sells a product, it also incurs costs. For example, The Home Depot must buy the tools it sells. Similarly, a Toyota dealership has to pay for every car it sells. The company must recognize the cost of tools or Toyotas sold along with the related revenues.

Determining the cost of the Toyota sold is easy enough—you look up the cost on the invoice for the specific car you sold. Unfortunately, the calculations are not always that simple. Because The Home Depot purchases products such as tools in quantity and holds them in inventory, it is often difficult to trace the precise cost of a single product. As a result, companies must develop procedures to determine the value of their inventories and the cost of goods sold. The Home Depot had sales of $58.2 billion in the year ended February 2, 2003, with cost of goods sold of $40.1 billion. This provides a gross margin of $18.1 billion or 31% of sales.

The aisles of The Home Depot are stacked high with products so customers can find what they need. These products are the company's inventories, and managing its inventories is essential to The Home Depot. Recording this inventory on its balance sheet and recognizing cost of goods sold when a customer buys an item are important steps in measuring the company's assets and income. We learn about inventory accounting in this chapter.

This chapter examines various methods for valuing and accounting for inventories that companies such as Toyota or The Home Depot use to calculate cost of sales, inventory, and gross margin measures. You will find different inventory accounting practices around the globe, and multiple methods exist even in the same country or in the same industry. These differences make it hard to compare one firm to another. By understanding these differences, you are better able to evaluate the profitability of different companies. You are able to distinguish between apparent differences that arise solely from different accounting practices and real economic differences that distinguish two firms based on their profitability.

Gross Profit and Cost of Goods Sold

OBJECTIVE 1

Link inventory valuation to gross profit.

For merchandising firms, an initial step in assessing profitability is gross profit (also called profit margin or gross margin), which you learned in Chapter 4 is the difference between sales revenues and cost of the goods sold. Sales revenues must cover the cost of goods sold and provide a gross profit sufficient to cover all other costs, including R&D, selling and marketing, administration, and so on. As illustrated in Exhibit 7-1, companies report products being held prior to sale as inventory, a current asset in the balance sheet. When they sell the goods, the cost of the inventory becomes an expense, Cost of Goods Sold or Cost of Sales, in the income statement. We deduct this expense from Net Sales to determine Gross Profit, and we deduct additional expenses from Gross Profit to determine Net Income.

The Basic Concept of Inventory Accounting

In theory, accounting for inventory and cost of goods sold is very simple. Suppose Christina sells T-shirts. Periodically, she orders many shirts of various sizes and colors. They sell, she orders more, and her business operating cycle continues on in this way. After a year, Christina prepares financial statements to evaluate her success. To calculate the value of inventory

Exhibit 7-1
Merchandising Company (Retailer or Wholesaler)

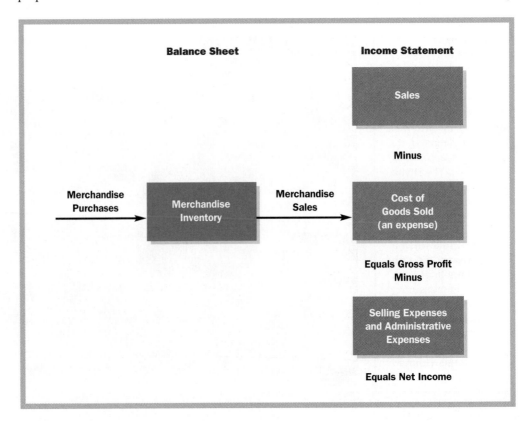

INVENTORY MANAGEMENT AND MERCHANDISING

The Home Depot is on a roll. Following its founding in Atlanta just 25 years ago, its growth has been phenomenal. Its annual report indicates that during 2003, The Home Depot created more net new jobs than any other established U.S. company. Twenty-two million people visit a Home Depot store each week. In 2003, The Home Depot sold enough flooring to pave a two-lane road from NYC to Atlanta to LA and back. It sold enough paint to cover the square footage of Manhattan. It recently eclipsed Sears Roebuck as the nation's second-largest retailer (behind Wal-Mart). It had already replaced Sears on the Dow Jones Industrial Average. The company has generated revenue growth of 23% per year for the 5 years ending in 2003, and earnings per share grew 35% per year. This is impressive, as seen in the following data:

5-Year Average Growth Rates

	Revenue	EPS
The Home Depot	23%	35%
Wal-Mart	17	19
JCPenney	(6)	(8)

The Home Depot attends to details. Of its 50,000 items, including precut Venetian blinds, tool rentals, Christmas trees, and pretzels, 70% are responses to customer suggestions. Concluding a 2-year test, washers, dryers, and refrigerators were added to its product line in 2001. It is now the third largest appliance retailer in the United States.

When General Electric (GE) experienced shortages in light bulb inventories, Bernie Marcus, The Home Depot founder and CEO, immediately cut a deal with Phillips, the Dutch electronics company, to replace GE as light bulb supplier. The Home Depot also seeks new opportunities. In surveys of customers, they found GE was named the third best brand for water heaters, despite the fact that GE did not make water heaters. Solution: Pay GE a royalty for use of the name, pay Rheem to manufacture water heaters with the GE name, and become the exclusive distributor for a great product. They played a similar game with riding lawn mowers, contracting with John Deere to manufacture a mower with the Scott brand. They got quality, Scott got a royalty, and their mower sold for 5% less than the competitors'.

The Home Depot uses technology. Inventory tracking and order placement occurs through wireless pen-based PCs that staff wheel up and down aisles to transmit current inventory counts and to execute orders based on a database of sales history and forecasts. The Home Depot's credit approvals take less than a second, an industry standard. They pioneered self-checkout in their industry. In 2003, they introduced a touch screen point-of-sale system and added 5,000 miles of cable and 90,000 new devices to upgrade technology. Every store has information feeds enabling cashiers to fix jammed register tapes by watching a 20-second training film at their register. The Home Depot's associates received 21 million hours of training in 2003 to support their ability to serve customers knowledgeably.

Of course, today no one is safe from competition. Lowe's is running hard as the second player in this market. Although it is only one-half the size of The Home Depot, its own 5-year growth rates are impressive. Revenue growth was 30% and EPS growth was 48%. Stay tuned.

Sources: The Home Depot 2003 Annual Report; Wal-Mart 2003 Annual Report; JCPenny 2003 Annual Report; "Profit in a Big Orange," *Forbes,* January 24, 2000.

on hand, she counts all the inventory items remaining at year-end. She then develops a **cost valuation** by assigning a specific value from the historical cost records to each item in ending inventory. If the shirts cost $5.00 each and there are 100 shirts remaining in inventory, Christina's total ending inventory is $500. Suppose she had no shirts at the beginning of the year, and total purchases for the year were $26,000. Her cost of goods sold would thus be $25,500 ($26,000 of available shirts minus $500 of unsold shirts). Notice that the key to calculating the cost of goods sold is accounting for the remaining inventory.

Unfortunately, determining the cost of goods sold and accounting for inventory are not this simple in practice. The Business First box above points out some of the inventory issues for The Home Depot. In the following sections, we show you some of the problems that can arise and how to deal with these problems. We also show you the

cost valuation
Process of assigning specific historical costs to items counted in the physical inventory.

major techniques for measuring inventories that various companies use. As a manager or investor, you want to know how inventory accounting can affect reported earnings. Especially important is how economic events, such as inflation, or management decisions, such as increasing or decreasing inventory levels, affect inventory values and thereby affect earnings. However, first let's look at the two major types of systems for keeping inventory records.

Perpetual and Periodic Inventory Systems

OBJECTIVE 2

Use both perpetual and periodic inventory systems.

perpetual inventory system
A system that keeps a running, continuous record that tracks inventories and the cost of goods sold on a day-to-day basis.

physical count
The process of examining and identifying all items in inventory. We then value the inventory by assigning a specific cost to each item.

There are two main systems for keeping merchandise inventory records: perpetual and periodic. We have used the **perpetual inventory system** in prior examples in this text. It keeps a continuous record of inventories and cost of goods sold. This daily record helps managers control inventory levels and prepare interim financial statements. In addition to this continuous record-keeping process, companies periodically physically count and value the inventory. A **physical count** is the process of examining and identifying all items in inventory. We then value the inventory by assigning a specific cost to each item. Companies should conduct a physical count at least once a year to check on the accuracy of the continuous records. Accountants developed the perpetual system to provide managers with information to aid in pricing or ordering. At first it was extremely cumbersome and expensive to maintain constant records, but computerized inventory systems and optical scanning equipment at checkout counters make implementation of perpetual inventory systems inexpensive today in many industries.

Previous chapters have used the perpetual system to record inventory transactions without referring to it by name. It works as follows:

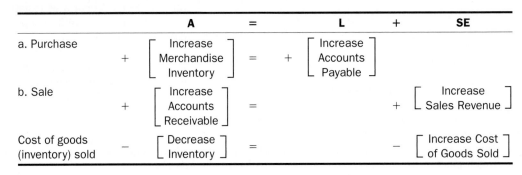

	A	=	L	+	SE
a. Purchase	+ [Increase Merchandise Inventory]	=	+ [Increase Accounts Payable]		
b. Sale	+ [Increase Accounts Receivable]	=		+	[Increase Sales Revenue]
Cost of goods (inventory) sold	− [Decrease Inventory]	=		−	[Increase Cost of Goods Sold]

In the perpetual inventory system, the journal entries are:

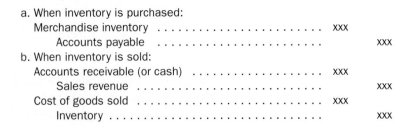

```
a. When inventory is purchased:
   Merchandise inventory ....................... xxx
      Accounts payable  .......................        xxx
b. When inventory is sold:
   Accounts receivable (or cash) ............... xxx
      Sales revenue .............................       xxx
   Cost of goods sold ........................... xxx
      Inventory .................................        xxx
```

Thus, in the perpetual inventory system, we record the sale of an item and the accompanying inventory reduction simultaneously.

periodic inventory system
The system in which the cost of goods sold is computed periodically by relying solely on physical counts without keeping day-to-day records of units sold or on hand.

inventory shrinkage
Inventory reductions from theft, breakage, or losses of inventory.

In contrast, the **periodic inventory system** does not involve a day-to-day record of inventories or of the cost of goods sold. Instead we compute the cost of goods sold and an updated inventory balance only at the end of an accounting period, when we take a physical count of inventory. The physical count allows management to remove damaged or obsolete goods from inventory and thus helps reveal **inventory shrinkage,** which refers to losses of inventory from theft, breakage, and loss. Inventory shrinkage can be quite large in some businesses. We used this periodic inventory system in the example of Christina's T-shirt business.

Under the periodic system, calculations for the cost of goods sold start with the **cost of goods available for sale.** This is the sum of the opening inventory for the period plus purchases during the period. We subtract the ending inventory from the cost of goods available for sale to compute the cost of goods sold. Thus, the periodic system computes cost of goods sold as a residual amount. The logic is that if we had inventory available and it is no longer here, then we sold it. Of course, practically speaking, if someone stole the item, its cost will also be included in cost of sales.

cost of goods available for sale
Sum of beginning inventory plus current year purchases.

Unlike the perpetual system, which computes cost of goods sold instantaneously as a company sells goods, under the periodic system, we delay computing cost of goods sold until we make a physical count:

$$\underbrace{\text{Beginning inventory} + \text{Purchases}}_{\text{Goods available for sale}} - \underbrace{\text{Ending inventory}}_{\text{Inventory left over}} = \underbrace{\text{Cost of goods sold}}_{\text{Cost of goods sold}}$$

Exhibit 7-2 compares the perpetual and periodic inventory systems. The two methods produce the same cost of goods sold figure for annual financial statements. However, the perpetual system also provides managers with continuous assessments of inventory levels and helps them to restock their shelves with the right merchandise in a timely and effective manner. Most companies find these benefits justify the higher cost of implementing the perpetual system, especially since those costs have fallen with the use of computerized systems.

Physical Inventory

Good inventory control procedures require a physical count of items held in inventory at least annually in both periodic and perpetual inventory systems. The physical count is an imposing, time-consuming, and expensive process. You may have seen "Closed for Inventory" signs. To simplify counting and valuation, firms often choose fiscal accounting periods so the year ends when inventories are low. For example, The Home Depot, Kmart, and JCPenney all have late January or early February year-ends, which follow the holiday season.

The physical inventory is so important to income determination that external auditors usually observe the client's physical count and confirm the accuracy of the subsequent valuation. Some audit firms hire outside experts to assist them. For example, assessing a jeweler's inventory might require an expert to test the color, size, clarity,

Periodic System		Perpetual System
Beginning inventories		Cost of goods sold (kept on a
(by physical count)	xxx	day-to-day basis instead of
Add: Purchases	xxx	determined periodically)*
Cost of goods available for sale	xxx	
Less: Ending inventories		
(by physical count)	xxx	
Cost of goods sold	xxx	

*Such a condensed figure does not preclude the presentation of a supplementary schedule similar to that on the left.

Exhibit 7-2
Inventory Systems

and imperfections in the diamonds on hand. Similarly, the client and auditor might rely on an engineer to measure the physical dimensions of an electric utility's coal pile so they can accurately estimate the volume and weight without actually weighing the coal itself.

A classic case of inventory fraud is the Salad Oil Swindle of 1963. Late that year an obscure company named **Allied Crude Vegetable Oil and Refining** was unable to repay its loans. Collateral for the loans had been $175 million worth of vegetable oil supposedly stored in 40 converted gasoline storage tanks in Bayonne, New Jersey. Investigation revealed that, instead of being filled with vegetable oil, the tanks contained seawater, soap stock, and "sludge."

Allied used ingenious techniques to hide their shortfall from the watchful auditors. Because the 40 storage tanks were connected by pipes, Allied pumped a small quantity of vegetable oil from tank to tank during the week required to complete the inventory count. The auditors counted the same vegetable oil over and over. Moreover, the company never completely filled any tank with oil. Allied welded shut all but one opening to each tank. Beneath this working opening, the company then welded a pipe and filled the pipe with a few hundred pounds of real oil. When the auditors took samples, they were actually testing what was in this pipe, not what was in the tank. The tank itself was filled with seawater. After authorities discovered the fraud, they opened a faucet on one tank, and water poured out for 12 days.

Cost of Merchandise Acquired

OBJECTIVE 3
Calculate the cost of merchandise acquired.

Regardless of whether you use the periodic or perpetual system, the basis of inventory accounting is the cost of the merchandise a company purchases to then sell. What makes up that cost? To be more specific, does that cost include all or part of the following: invoice price, transportation charges, trade and cash discounts, cost of handling and placing in stock, storage, purchasing department, receiving department, and other indirect charges? In practice, accountants usually consider the cost of merchandise to include only the invoice price plus the directly identifiable inbound transportation charges less any offsetting discounts. Accountants treat the costs of the purchasing and receiving departments as period costs and charge them on the income statement as they occur.

Transportation Charges

F.O.B. destination
Seller pays freight costs from the shipping point of the seller to the receiving point of the buyer.

F.O.B. shipping point
Buyer pays freight costs from the shipping point of the seller to the receiving point of the buyer.

freight in (inward transportation)
An additional cost of the goods acquired during the period, which is often shown in the purchases section of an income statement.

The major cost of transporting merchandise is typically the freight charges from the shipping point of the seller to the receiving point of the buyer. When the seller bears this cost, the sales invoice reads free onboard or **F.O.B. destination.** When the buyer bears this cost, it reads **F.O.B. shipping point.**

In theory, we should add any transportation costs borne by the buyer to the cost of the inventory acquired. In practice, though, it is not always easy to identify the transportation costs associated with specific inventory items. Companies tend to order several different items and have them shipped at the same time.

Sometimes managers want to keep freight costs separate from other inventory costs. For example, management may want to see how freight costs change over time and to compare costs using rail service to costs using trucks. Consequently, accountants frequently use a separate transportation cost account, calling it Freight In, Transportation In, Inbound Transportation, or Inward Transportation. **Freight in** (or **inward transportation**) appears in the purchases section of an income statement as an additional cost of the goods acquired during the period. It becomes part of the cost of goods available for sale, and because it increases cost of goods sold, Freight In affects the gross profit section of an income statement for the buyer.

INTERPRETING FINANCIAL STATEMENTS

Suppose that Huang Company bought several items of inventory that were shipped in a single load. Should total freight costs be assigned to each of the components of the shipment based on weight, value, number of items, volume of the item, or some other process?

Answer

Each of these bases of assignment might be correct in certain cases. For example, if you thought of coal as the product, weight would be a very good basis for assigning delivery costs. If you thought of jewelry, you might have

thought of assigning costs based on the number of items and their value because outbound transportation costs would depend on packing and handling of the item and insurance for its value in case it were lost or damaged. Thus, assigning inbound transportation costs would require extensive analysis to pick the best approach, followed by a lot of clerical work to apply the technique. Because of these difficulties and the modest benefit to the company from all this work, most companies do not assign freight costs to inventories. Instead, they charge them to expense when incurred.

Returns, Allowances, and Discounts

In Chapter 6, you learned about sales returns, allowances, and discounts. The accounting for purchase returns, purchase allowances, and cash discounts on purchases is just the opposite of their sales counterparts. Using the periodic inventory system, suppose a company's gross purchases are $960,000 and purchase returns and allowances are $75,000. The summary journal entries are:

Purchases	960,000	
Accounts payable		960,000
Accounts payable	75,000	
Purchase returns and allowances		75,000

Suppose also that the company takes cash discounts of $5,000 on payment of the remaining $960,000 − $75,000 = $885,000 of payables. The summary journal entry is:

Accounts payable	885,000	
Cash discounts on purchases		5,000
Cash		880,000

To calculate cost of goods sold, we deduct Cash Discounts on Purchases and Purchase Returns and Allowances from Purchases.

Car dealers sometimes sell cars "below cost" or "$100 below invoice." Do dealers lose money on such sales? Probably not, because gross invoice cost to the dealer and final cost of goods sold may differ. Dealers receive incentives from the manufacturers such as volume discounts or special discounts to push particular models. The dealer's invoice shows the list price before discounts and allowances, not the final net dealer cost.

A detailed gross profit section in the income statement is often arranged as in Exhibit 7-3. Although management may find such detail valuable, summary information is much more common in the annual report to shareholders:

Net sales	$1,570
Cost of goods sold	870
Gross profit	$ 700

Exhibit 7-3
Detailed Gross Profit
Calculation
($ in thousands)

Gross sales			$1,740
Deduct: Sales returns and allowances		$ 70	
Cash discounts on sales		100	170
Net sales			$1,570
Deduct: Cost of goods sold			
Merchandise inventory, December 31, 20X1		$ 100	
Purchases (gross)	$960		
Deduct: Purchase returns and allowances	$75		
Cash discounts on purchases	5	80	
Net purchases		$880	
Add: Freight in		30	
Total cost of merchandise acquired		910	
Cost of goods available for sale		$1,010	
Deduct: Merchandise inventory, December 31, 20X2		140	
Cost of goods sold			870
Gross profit			$ 700

Comparing Accounting Procedures for Periodic and Perpetual Inventory Systems

Suppose GoodEarth Products, Incorporated, has a balance of $100,000 in merchandise inventory at the beginning of 20X2 (December 31, 20X1). A summary of transactions for 20X2 follows:

a. Purchases	$990,000
b. Purchase returns and allowances	80,000

Net purchases were therefore $990,000 less $80,000, or $910,000. The physical count of the ending inventory for 20X2 led to a cost valuation of $140,000. Note how we use these figures to compute the $870,000 cost of goods sold:

$$\underset{\text{inventory}}{\text{Beginning}} + \text{Net purchases} - \underset{\text{inventory}}{\text{Ending}} = \underset{\text{goods sold}}{\text{Cost of}}$$

$$\underbrace{\$100,000 + \$910,000}_{\substack{\text{Cost of goods} \\ \text{available for sale}}} - \underset{\substack{\text{Cost of goods} \\ \text{left over}}}{\$140,000} = \underset{\substack{\text{Cost of} \\ \text{goods sold}}}{\$870,000}$$

$$\$1,010,000 - \$140,000 = \$870,000$$

The periodic and perpetual procedures would record these transactions differently. As the left side of Exhibit 7-4 shows, in the perpetual system we directly increase the Inventory account by the $990,000 purchases (entry a) and decrease it by the $80,000 in returns and allowances (entry b) and the $870,000 cost of goods sold (entry c). We would increase the Cost of Goods Sold account daily as sales occur. The following T-accounts reflect how these items would appear in the general ledger:

Inventory					Cost of Goods Sold	
Balance 12/31/X1	100	(b)	80	(c)	870	
(a)	990	(c)	870			
Balance 12/31/X2	140			Balance 12/31/X2	870	

Perpetual Records			Periodic Records		
a. Gross purchases:	Inventory 990		Purchases 990		
	Accounts payable ...	990	Accounts payable ...		990
b. Returns and allowances:	Accounts payable 80		Accounts payable 80		
	Inventory	80	Purchase returns and allowances		80
c. As goods are sold:	Cost of goods sold 870		No entry		
	Inventory	870			
d. At the end of the accounting period:	d1.⎱ No entry d2.⎰		d1. Cost of goods sold 1,010		
			Purchase returns and allowances 80		
			Purchases		990
			Inventory		100
			d2. Inventory 140		
			Cost of goods sold ..		140

Exhibit 7-4
GoodEarth Products, Incorporated
Comparison of Journal Entries for Perpetual and Periodic Inventory Systems ($ Amounts in Thousands)

These summary amounts of $990,000 in purchases and $80,000 in returns and allowances represent many smaller transactions. GoodEarth Products would record each transaction as it occurs. Similarly, GoodEarth would make smaller daily entries as each sale occurs. Although the method seems to create the correct $140,000 final inventory balance, recall that the company will also conduct a physical count to verify the number. Often there are minor differences between the valuation determined by the physical count and the value shown in the perpetual record. Such differences, often due to clerical error or shrinkage, result in appropriate adjustments to increase or decrease inventory and cost of sales. If the physical count had yielded a value of $135,000, we would make the following journal entry (in thousands):

Inventory shrinkage expense $5	
Inventory	5

Under the periodic system in the right side of Exhibit 7-4, we record purchases and purchase returns and allowances in separate accounts, as entries a and b indicate. We call the system "periodic" because we do not compute the cost of goods sold or the inventory amount on a daily basis. Entries d1 and d2 at the bottom of Exhibit 7-4 show how we update these accounts during the eventual periodic calculation of cost of goods sold.

Entry d1 transfers the beginning inventory balance, purchases, and purchase returns and allowances, totaling $1,010,000, to cost of goods sold. This is the cost of goods available for sale. Next, we physically count the ending inventory and compute its cost. Entry d2 recognizes the $140,000 ending inventory and reduces the $1,010,000 cost of goods available for sale by $140,000 to obtain a final cost of goods sold of $870,000. The following T-accounts show how these journal entries affect the general ledger accounts:

Inventory			Cost of Goods Sold		
Balance 12/31/X1 100	(d1)	100	(d1)	1,010	(d2)	140
(d2) 140					
Balance 12/31/X2 140			Balance 12/31/X2 870		

Notice that both systems reach the same result, Inventory of $140 and Cost of Goods Sold of $870.

Principal Inventory Valuation Methods

OBJECTIVE 4

Compute income and
inventory values using the
four principal inventory
valuation methods.

Each period, accountants must divide the cost of beginning inventory and merchandise acquired between cost of goods sold and cost of items remaining in ending inventory. Under a perpetual system, we must determine a cost for each item sold. Under a periodic system, we instead must only determine the specific costs of the items remaining in ending inventory. In both systems, we must determine the costs of individual items by some inventory valuation method. Four principal inventory valuation methods are generally accepted in the United States: specific identification; first-in, first-out (FIFO); last-in, first-out (LIFO); and weighted-average. In this section, we explain and compare these methods.

If unit prices and costs did not fluctuate, all four inventory methods would show identical results. However, prices change, and these changes raise central issues concerning cost of goods sold (income measurement) and inventories (asset measurement). As a simple example of the valuation method choices facing management, consider Emilio, a new vendor of a cola drink at the fairgrounds, who begins the week with no inventory. He buys one can of cola on Monday for 30¢, a second can on Tuesday for 40¢, and a third can on Wednesday for 56¢. He then sells one can on Thursday for 90¢.

As Exhibit 7-5 shows, Emilio's choice of an inventory method can significantly affect the amount reported as cost of goods sold (and hence gross profit and net income) and ending inventory. The gross profit for Monday through Thursday ranges from 34¢ to 60¢, depending on the method chosen. By using Exhibit 7-5 as a guide, we now examine each of the four methods in detail.

specific identification method

This inventory method concentrates on the physical linking of the particular items sold with the cost of goods sold that we report.

Specific Identification

The **specific identification method** concentrates on physically linking the particular items sold with the cost of goods sold that we report. Emilio could mark each can with its cost and record that cost as cost of goods sold when he hands the can to a customer.

	(1) Specific Identification			(2) FIFO	(3) LIFO	(4) Weighted Average
	(1A)	(1B)	(1C)			
Income Statement for the Period Monday through Thursday						
Sales	90	90	90	90	90	90
Deduct cost of goods sold						
1 30¢ (Monday) unit	30			30		
1 40¢ (Tuesday) unit		40				
1 56¢ (Wednesday) unit			56		56	
1 weighted-average unit						
[(30 + 40 + 56) ÷ 3 = 42]						42
Gross profit for Monday through Thursday	60	50	34	60	34	48
Thursday's ending inventory, 2 units						
Monday unit @ 30¢		30	30		30	
Tuesday unit @ 40¢	40		40	40	40	
Wednesday unit @ 56¢	56	56		56		
Weighted-average units @ 42¢						84
Total ending inventory on Thursday	96	86	70	96	70	84

Exhibit 7-5
Emilio's Cola Sales
Comparison of Inventory Methods (All Monetary Amounts Are in Cents)

If he reached for the Monday can instead of the Wednesday can, the specific identification method would show different results. Thus, Exhibit 7-5 indicates that gross profit for operations of Monday through Thursday could be 60¢, 50¢, or 34¢, depending on the particular can Emilio hands to the customer. He could choose which can to sell and affect reported results by doing so. Because the specific item handed to the customer determines the cost of goods sold, the specific identification method may permit managers to manipulate income and inventory values by filling a sales order from a number of physically equivalent items with different historical costs. This would be true for Emilio. Each can is identical. It would not be true for a car dealer for whom each car has its unique identification number indicating its features such as color, style, engine, sound system, and so forth.

This method is relatively easy to use for expensive low-volume merchandise, such as custom artwork, diamond jewelry, and automobiles. However, most organizations have vast segments of inventories that have too many items insufficiently valuable per unit to warrant such individualized attention. However, the use of bar codes and scanning equipment is making specific identification economically feasible for more and more companies.

FIFO

FIFO refers to **first-in, first-out.** The FIFO method is a cost assignment method and does not track the actual physical flow of individual items, except by coincidence. For identical units, it assigns the cost of the earliest acquired units to cost of goods sold. Picture Emilio putting each new can of cola at the back of the cooler to chill and selling the oldest, coldest can first. Thus, under FIFO, we assume that Emilio sells the Monday can of cola first—regardless of the actual can he delivers. As a result, we assign the costs of the newer cans to the units in ending inventory.

first-in, first-out (FIFO)
This method of accounting for inventory assigns the cost of the earliest acquired units to cost of goods sold.

By using the more recent costs to measure the ending inventory, FIFO provides inventory valuations that closely approximate the actual market value of the inventory at the balance sheet date. In addition, in periods of rising prices, FIFO leads to higher net income. Note that gross profit is 60¢ in Exhibit 7-5 under FIFO because we charge the oldest, cheapest unit as cost of goods sold. Higher reported incomes may favorably affect investor attitudes toward the company. Similarly, higher reported incomes may lead to higher salaries, higher bonuses, or higher status for the management of the company. Unlike specific identification, FIFO specifies the order in which acquisition costs become cost of goods sold, so management cannot affect income by choosing to sell one identical item instead of another.

LIFO

LIFO refers to **last-in, first-out.** Whereas FIFO associates the most recent costs with ending inventories, LIFO assigns the most recent costs to cost of goods sold. The LIFO method assumes that a company sells the stock acquired most recently before it sells older stock. Picture Emilio putting each newly-acquired can into the top of a cooler. At each customer purchase, he sells the top can. This is the physical flow that corresponds to the LIFO cost system. Thus, under LIFO, we assume that Emilio sells the Wednesday can of cola—regardless of the actual can he delivers from the cooler.

last-in, first-out (LIFO)
This inventory method assigns the most recent costs to cost of goods sold.

LIFO provides an income statement perspective in the sense that net income measured using LIFO combines current sales prices and current acquisition costs. In a period of rising prices and constant or growing inventories, LIFO yields lower net income as shown by the 34¢ of gross margin in Exhibit 7-5. Why is lower net income such an important feature of LIFO? In the United States, LIFO is an acceptable inventory accounting method for income tax purposes. When a company reports lower income to the tax authorities, it pays lower taxes, so it is not surprising that almost two-thirds of U.S. corporations use LIFO for at least some of their inventories. However, the Internal Revenue Code requires companies that use LIFO for tax purposes to also use it for financial reporting purposes.

You might think of LIFO as the good news/bad news method. Lower income taxes provide the good news, but the accompanying bad news is lower reported profits. During a period of higher inflation some years ago, *The Wall Street Journal* reported that many small firms changed from FIFO to LIFO. As an example, Chicago Heights Steel Company "boosted cash by 5% to 10% by lowering income taxes when it switched to LIFO." When Becton, Dickinson and Company changed to LIFO, its annual report stated that its "change to the LIFO method . . . for both financial reporting and income tax purposes resulted in improved cash flow due to lower income taxes paid." Indeed, some observers maintain that executives are guilty of serious mismanagement by not adopting LIFO when FIFO produces significantly higher taxable income.

LIFO and Inflation Inflation is a key factor driving companies to use LIFO. When inflation is low, as it has been for a decade, the tax and income differences are also small. The inventory method chosen matters little. Low inflation has been the norm in the United States during most of the last hundred years, but in 1974, the inflation rate in the United States reached double digits for the first time. In response, more than 40 U.S. corporations switched from FIFO to LIFO, deciding the benefit of lower income taxes exceeded the cost of reporting lower profits. These tax savings were not trivial. For example, by switching from FIFO to LIFO, DuPont saved more than $200 million in taxes in 1974, and it anticipated greater savings in the future.

Why did some firms remain on FIFO? Some firms should choose FIFO because for them it lowers taxes. Even when prices were rising in general, some industries, such as computers, faced declining costs and prices, so FIFO minimized reported income and taxes. For those who could have lowered taxes by using LIFO, possible reasons to remain on FIFO include the high bookkeeping costs of implementing the switch, reluctance by management to make an accounting switch reducing reported income and possibly reducing management bonuses, fear that banks would view the reduction in income unfavorably in loan negotiations, and belief that lower reported income would result in a lower stock price.

LIFO and Timing of Purchases LIFO also permits management to influence reported income by the timing of purchases of inventory items. Consider Emilio's case. Suppose that acquisition prices increase from 56¢ on Wednesday to 68¢ on Thursday, the day of the sale of the one unit. How does the acquisition of one more unit on Thursday affect net income? Under LIFO, cost of goods sold would change to 68¢, and profit would fall by 12¢. In contrast, under FIFO, cost of goods sold and gross profit would be unchanged.

	LIFO		FIFO	
	As in Exhibit 7-5	If One More Unit Acquired	As in Exhibit 7-5	If One More Unit Acquired
Sales	90¢	90¢	90¢	90¢
Cost of goods sold	56¢	68¢	30¢	30¢
Gross profit	34¢	22¢	60¢	60¢
Ending inventory				
First purchase, Monday	30¢	30¢		
Second purchase, Tuesday	40¢	40¢	40¢	40¢
Third purchase, Wednesday		56¢	56¢	56¢
Fourth purchase, Thursday				68¢
	70¢	126¢	96¢	164¢

Weighted Average

The **weighted-average method** computes a unit cost by dividing the total acquisition cost of all items available for sale by the number of units available for sale. Picture Emilio dropping his cooler and not knowing which can was on top. Exhibit 7-5 shows the calculations Emilio would make to average the costs of these units. The average cost is 42¢ [(30 + 40 + 56) ÷ 3].

To better understand the weighted-average method, assume that Emilio bought two cans instead of one on Monday at 30¢ each. To get the weighted average, we must consider not only the price paid, but also the number of units purchased as follows:

Weighted average = Cost of goods available for sale ÷ Units available for sale

Weighted average = $[(2 \times 30¢) + (1 \times 40¢) + (1 \times 56¢)] \div 4$

$$= 156¢ \div 4$$

$$= 39¢$$

The weighted-average method produces a gross profit somewhere between that obtained under FIFO and that under LIFO (48¢ as compared with 60¢ and 34¢ in Exhibit 7-5).

Cost Flow Assumptions

Because the actual physical flow of identical products is less important to the financial success of most businesses than is the flow of the units' costs, the accounting profession has concluded that companies may choose any of the four methods to record cost of goods sold. Basically, the units are all the same, but their costs differ, so managing the assignment of these differing costs is more important than is tracing where each specific unit goes. Because three of the four methods are not linked to the physical flow of merchandise, accountants often refer to inventory methods as cost flow assumptions. For example, when we decide to match the cost of the first inventory item purchased with the sales revenue from the first item sold to calculate the gross profit from the sale, we are adopting the FIFO cost flow assumption.

Notice that the cost flow assumptions do not affect the cumulative gross profit over the life of a company. Suppose Emilio sells his remaining inventory for 90¢ per can on Friday and enters a more attractive business. Exhibit 7-6 shows Friday's gross profit and the cumulative gross profit for the entire week. As you can see, the gross profit for Friday varies with the cost flow assumption used. However, the last line of the exhibit shows that the cumulative gross profit over the life of Emilio's business

weighted-average method
This inventory method computes a unit cost by dividing the total acquisition cost of all items available for sale by the number of units available for sale.

	(1) Specific Identification			(2) FIFO	(3) LIFO	(4) Weighted Average
	(1A)	(1B)	(1C)			
Sales, 2 units @ 90 on Friday	180	180	180	180	180	180
Cost of goods sold (Thursday ending inventory from Exhibit 7-5)	96	86	70	96	70	84
Gross profit, Friday only	84	94	110	84	110	96
Gross profit, Monday through Thursday (from Exhibit 7-5)	60	50	34	60	34	48
Gross profit, Monday through Friday (3 cans sold)	144	144	144	144	144	144

Exhibit 7-6
Income Statements for Friday Only and for Monday Through Friday for Emilio's Cola Sales (all monetary amounts are in cents)

would be the same $1.44 under any of the inventory methods. What makes the choice of method important is the need to match particular costs to particular periods during the life of the business in order to prepare periodic financial statements and evaluate performance.

Inventory Cost Relationships

Note that all four methods work with the same basic numbers. Nothing in our choice of methods affects accounts payable. We record inventory purchases at cost and recognize a liability in the same way under all these methods. All that changes is how we allocate those costs between inventory and cost of sales.

Recall that during a period of rising prices, FIFO yields higher inventory and higher gross profit than does LIFO. This result is consistent with the balance sheet equation that requires that A = L + OE. If inventory is higher under FIFO (higher assets) and the equation is to balance, either liabilities or owners' equity must also be higher. Higher gross profit under FIFO implies higher net income and higher owners' equity (OE in the equation).

There are, of course, relationships other than those of the accounting equation that come into play in the various inventory methods. Consider also the link between cost of goods sold and the valuation of ending inventory. Emilio's three cola cans had a total cost of goods available for sale of $1.26. At the end of the period, Emilio must allocate this $1.26 either to cans sold or to cans in ending inventory. The higher the cost of goods sold, the lower the ending inventory. Exhibit 7-7 illustrates that interdependence. At one

Exhibit 7-7
Emilio's Cola Sales, Monday Through Thursday
Diagram of Inventory Methods
All monetary amounts are in cents.

extreme, FIFO treats the 30¢ cost of the first can acquired as cost of goods sold and 96¢ as ending inventory. At the other extreme, LIFO treats the 56¢ cost of the last can acquired as cost of goods sold and 70¢ as ending inventory.

The Consistency Convention

Although companies can choose just about any inventory cost flow assumption they want, they have to be consistent over time and stick with whatever they choose. The FASB has referred to **consistency** as "conformity from period to period with unchanging policies and procedures." Interpreting financial performance over time involves comparing the results of different periods. If accounting methods for inventory were changed often, meaningful comparisons over time would be impossible.

consistency
Conformity from period to period with unchanging policies and procedures.

Occasionally, a change in market conditions or other circumstances may justify a change in inventory method. With its auditor's approval, a firm may change method. However, the firm has to note the change in its financial statements, and the auditor must also refer to the change in the audit opinion. This alerts financial statement readers to the possible effects of the change on their analysis.

Summary Problem for Your Review

PROBLEM

Examine Exhibit 7-8. The company uses the periodic inventory system. By using these facts, prepare a columnar comparison of income statements for the year ended December 31, 20X2. Compare the FIFO, LIFO, and weighted-average inventory methods. Assume that other expenses are $1,000. The income tax rate is 40%.

SOLUTION

See Exhibit 7-9.

Exhibit 7-8
Facts for Summary Problem

	Purchases	Sales	Inventory
December 31, 20X1			200 @ $5 = $1,000
January 25	170 @ $6 = $1,020		
January 29		150*	
May 28	190 @ $7 = $1,330		
June 7		230*	
November 20	150 @ $8 = $1,200		
December 15		100*	
Total	510	$3,550	480*
December 31, 20X2			230 @ ?

*Selling prices were $9, $11, and $13, respectively, providing total sales of:

	150 @ $ 9 = $1,350	
	230 @ $11 = $2,530	
	100 @ $13 = $1,300	
Total sales	480 $5,180	

Summary of costs:

Beginning inventory	$1,000
Purchases	$3,550
Cost of goods available for sale	$4,550

	FIFO		LIFO		Weighted Average
Sales, 480 units		$5,180		$5,180	$5,180
Deduct cost of goods sold					
Beginning inventory, 200 @ $5	$1,000		$1,000		$1,000
Purchases, 510 units (from Exhibit 7-8)*	3,550		3,550		3,550
Available for sale, 710 units†	$4,550		$4,550		$4,550
Ending inventory, 230 units‡					
150 @ $8	$1,200				
80 @ $7	560	1,760			
or					
200 @ $5			$1,000		
30 @ $6			180	1,180	
or					
230 @ $6.408					1,474
Cost of goods sold, 480 units		2,790		3,370	3,076
Gross profit		$2,390		$1,810	$2,104
Other expenses		1,000		1,000	1,000
Income before income taxes		$1,390		$ 810	$1,104
Income taxes at 40%		556		324	442
Net income		$ 834		$ 486	$ 662

*Always equal across all three methods.

†These amounts will not be equal in general across the three methods because beginning inventories will generally be different. They are equal here only because beginning inventories were assumed to be equal.

‡Under FIFO, the ending inventory is composed of the last purchases plus the second-last purchases, and so forth, until the costs of 230 units are compiled. Under LIFO, the ending inventory is composed of the beginning inventory plus the earliest purchases of the current year until the costs of 230 units are compiled. Under weighted average, the ending inventory and cost of goods sold are accumulations based on an average unit cost. The latter is the cost of goods available for sale divided by the number of units available for sale: $4,550 ÷ 710 = $6.408.

Exhibit 7-9
Comparison of Inventory Methods for the Year Ended December 31, 20X2

Characteristics and Consequences of LIFO

LIFO is just another method, but it is very widely used in the United States, has strong tax benefits for certain companies, and has some unusual features in application. Because of its dominant role in inventory accounting in the United States, we give LIFO a little extra attention in this section. Actually, few companies outside the United States use LIFO. For example, Brazil and Australia prohibit its use, and Canadian companies cannot use it for tax purposes. The most popular method worldwide is the average cost method, and the next most common choice is FIFO.

Holding Gains and Inventory Profits

LIFO's income statement orientation provides a particular economic interpretation of operating performance in inflationary periods, based on replacement of inventory. A merchant such as Emilio is in the business of buying and selling on a daily basis. To continue in business, he must be able to maintain his stock of cola and must make sufficient profit on each transaction to make it worth his while to run his soda stand. So, before he can feel he has really made a profit, he will need to restock his inventory and be ready for the next day. If he must spend 56¢ to replace the can he sold, we call this 56¢ cost of acquiring the item today the **replacement cost** of the inventory. Under LIFO, we calculate his profit to be 34¢ because we use that recent inventory acquisition cost of 56¢ to measure cost of goods sold. So LIFO approximates a replacement cost view of the transaction.

replacement cost
The cost at which an inventory item could be acquired today.

In contrast, FIFO measures profit using the 30¢ can acquired on Monday as cost of goods sold and reports a profit of 60¢. The difference between the 60¢ FIFO profit and the 34¢ LIFO profit is 26¢, which is also the difference between the historical cost of 30¢ under FIFO and the replacement cost of 56¢ under LIFO. This 26¢ difference occurs because prices are rising. We call it a **holding gain** or an **inventory profit.** The idea is that between Monday and Thursday, Emilio's first can of cola acquired for 30¢ became more valuable as prices rose, and because he held it as inventory during those days he experienced a 26¢ gain.

Because LIFO matches the most recent acquisition costs with sales revenue, LIFO cost of goods sold typically offers a close approximation to replacement cost, and reported net income rarely contains significant holding gains. In contrast, FIFO reports a profit of 60¢ including the economic profit of 34¢ calculated as sales price less replacement costs, plus the inventory profit or holding gain of 26¢ that arose because the value of the inventory item rose with the passage of time.

This issue is more than an accounting complexity of academic interest. Whenever government officials begin to reconsider the tax law, this issue takes center stage. For example, a recent reduction in U.S. capital gains taxes relies on the notion that holding gains are economically different from true economic profit and should be taxed less.

holding gain (inventory profit) Increase in the replacement cost or other measure of current value of the inventory held during the current period.

LIFO Layers

The ending inventory under LIFO will have one total value, but it may contain prices from many different periods. For example, Emilio's ending inventory contained two cans, one acquired on Monday at 30¢ and one acquired on Tuesday at 40¢. We call each distinct cost element of inventory a **LIFO layer** or a **LIFO increment**—an addition to inventory at an identifiable cost level. As a company grows, the LIFO layers pile on top of one another over the years. Suppose Emilio's business grew for years, ending each year with two more cans in inventory than were there the year before. Each year would have an identifiable LIFO layer, much like the annual rings on a tree. After 4 years of inventory growth and rising prices, his ending inventory might be structured as follows:

LIFO layer (LIFO increment) A separately identifiable additional segment of LIFO inventory.

Year 1	Layer 1—1 can @ .30	
	Layer 2—1 can @ .40	.70
Year 2	Layer 3—2 cans @ .45	.90
Year 3	Layer 4—2 cans @ .50	1.00
Year 4	Layer 5—2 cans @ .55	1.10
Total inventory—8 cans		$3.70

Many LIFO companies show inventories that have ancient layers going back as far as 1940, when companies first used LIFO. Reported LIFO inventory values may therefore be far below the market value or current replacement value of the inventory. This means that the book values reported on the balance sheet will have little relevance to investors interested in assessing the value of the assets of the company. Although LIFO better presents the economic reality on the income statement, FIFO provides more up-to-date valuations on the balance sheet.

Lifo Inventory Liquidations

The existence of old LIFO layers can cause problems in income measurement when inventories decrease after a period of rising prices. Examine Exhibit 7-10. Suppose Harbor Electronics bought 100 units of inventory at $10 per unit on December 31, 20X0 to begin its business operations. The company bought and sold 100 units each year, 20X1 through 20X4, at the purchase and selling prices shown. The example assumes replacement costs and sales prices rise by the same amount, with a difference between the two of $3 per unit. In 20X5, Harbor sold 100 units, but purchased none.

OBJECTIVE 5
Calculate the impact on net income of LIFO liquidations.

Year	Purchase Price Per Unit	Selling Price Per Unit	Revenue	FIFO			LIFO		
				Cost of Goods Sold	Gross Profit	Ending Inventory	Cost of Goods Sold	Gross Profit	Ending Inventory
20X0	$10	—	—	—	—	$1,000	—	—	$1,000
20X1	12	$15	$1,500	$1,000	$500	1,200	$1,200	$300	1,000
20X2	14	17	1,700	1,200	500	1,400	1,400	300	1,000
20X3	16	19	1,900	1,400	500	1,600	1,600	300	1,000
20X4	18	21	2,100	1,600	500	1,800	1,800	300	1,000
20X5		23	2,300	1,800	500	0	1,000	1,300	0
Total			$9,500	$7,000	$2,500		$7,000	$2,500	

Exhibit 7-10

Harbor Electronics

Effect of Inventory Liquidations under LIFO (Purchases and sales of 100 Units 20X1 through 20X4, Purchases but No Sales in 20X0; Sales but No Purchases in 20X5)

LIFO liquidation

A decrease in the physical amount in inventory causing old, low LIFO inventory acquisition costs to become the cost of goods sold, resulting in a high gross profit.

LIFO reserve

The difference between a company's inventory valued at LIFO and what it would be under FIFO.

Compare the gross profit each year under LIFO with that under FIFO in Exhibit 7-10. LIFO gross profit was consistently less than FIFO gross profit because prices were rising, and the LIFO cost of goods sold reflected the latest prices, whereas the FIFO did not. What happened in 20X5? The old 20X0 inventory became the cost of goods sold under LIFO because Harbor depleted its inventory. As a result, gross profit under LIFO soared to $1,300, well above the FIFO gross profit, which was stable at $500. In general, when the physical amount of inventory decreases, under LIFO the cost of goods sold consists of old, low inventory acquisition costs associated with old LIFO layers. This is called a **LIFO liquidation.** This treatment can create a very low cost of goods sold and high gross profit. For example, LIFO inventory liquidations by **Alcoa** increased its 2002 net income by $40 million, nearly 10% of its $420 million net income. In a sense, a LIFO liquidation means that the current year's income includes the cumulative inventory profit from years of increasing prices. An analyst tracking Alcoa's profitability would want to know that its profits in 2002 were not due solely to producing and selling aluminum that year. It was partly due to the company's inventory accounting process.

The effect of LIFO liquidations is potentially large, and security analysts estimate the effect of the choice between LIFO and FIFO on net income. The difference between a company's LIFO inventory level and what it would be under FIFO, its **LIFO reserve,** is helpful in making these estimates. Most companies that use LIFO explicitly measure and report their LIFO reserve on the balance sheet itself or in the footnotes.

Refer to Exhibit 7-10. What is the Harbor Electronics' LIFO reserve at the end of 20X1? It is $1,200 − $1,000 = $200, the difference in the LIFO and FIFO ending inventories. Note that it is the same as the difference in gross profit of $200 in 20X1. What about year 20X2? The LIFO reserve is $400 (FIFO ending inventory of $1,400 less LIFO ending inventory of $1,000). This difference represents the cumulative effect on earnings (or gross profit) during the first 2 years the company was in business. The specific effect on earnings during 20X2 is the change in the LIFO reserve, or $200. Exhibit 7-11 summarizes these effects.

From Exhibit 7-11, note that the annual difference between gross profit using FIFO and that using LIFO is the yearly change in the LIFO reserve. Finally, when Harbor sells all the inventory in 20X5, the liquidation of the LIFO inventory leads to recognition of higher earnings under LIFO than under FIFO by the amount of the LIFO reserve. LIFO recognizes inventory profits when a company reduces its inventory levels. The balance of the LIFO reserve at any point in time indicates the cumulative difference between FIFO and LIFO gross profit over all prior years.

Exhibit 7-11
Harbor Electronics
*Annual and Cumulative
Effects of LIFO Reserve*

Year	Ending Inventory		LIFO Reserve	Change in Reserve	Gross Profit Effect	
	FIFO	LIFO			Current	Cumulative
X0	$1,000	$1,000	$ 0	$ 0	$ 0	$ 0
X1	1,200	1,000	200	200	200	200
X2	1,400	1,000	400	200	200	400
X3	1,600	1,000	600	200	200	600
X4	1,800	1,000	800	200	200	800
X5	0	0	0	(800)	(800)	0

How significant are the effects of LIFO? **Ford Motor Company** reported 2003 inventory of $9.2 billion. Ford used LIFO for about one-third of its inventories. If it had used FIFO for all inventories, the total inventory would have been $1.0 billion higher (an 11% difference). This means that over time, Ford has reported lower income on its tax returns by $1.0 billion and paid lower taxes of approximately $400 million ($1.0 billion times the approximate tax rate of 40%) as a result of its decision to use LIFO instead of FIFO.

This savings amounts to an interest-free loan from the government. If Ford ever goes out of business, the sale of old inventory items will create a large LIFO liquidation, and all these delayed taxes will become due. In the meantime, Ford has the use of some $400 million it has not yet had to pay in taxes.

Adjusting from LIFO to FIFO

As mentioned earlier, **Ford Motor Company** uses LIFO, and therefore, reports different cost of goods sold and inventory levels than it would if it had used FIFO. Ford reported the following in 2003:

Ford Motor Company ($ in Millions)

	2003 Inventory		Cost of Goods Sold
	Beginning	Ending	
LIFO	$6,977	$ 9,181	$129,821
LIFO reserve	957	996	(39)*
FIFO	$7,934	$10,177	$129,782

*Change in LIFO reserve is an increase of $996 − $957 = $39. Therefore, cost of goods sold is $39 less under FIFO then under LIFO.

Note that Ford's LIFO reserve increased from $957 million to $996 million during the year. This increase of $39 million in the LIFO reserve is exactly the amount by which the cost of goods sold for the year under LIFO is more than the cost of goods sold under FIFO.

Why is the LIFO cost of goods sold higher? Because costs are rising and under LIFO the new higher costs flow directly to Ford's cost of goods sold reported in the earnings statement. In contrast, if Ford had used FIFO, the new higher costs flow into ending inventory, whereas cost of goods sold includes the older lower costs. Cumulatively, this process has happened year after year for Ford. The change in the LIFO reserve from one year to the next answers the question, "How much did this year's LIFO cost of goods sold differ from what the cost of goods sold would have been if FIFO were used?"

INTERPRETING FINANCIAL STATEMENTS

In contrast to the effect on cost of goods sold in a specific year, we can examine the cumulative effect of the inventory accounting choice over time. The end-of-year level of the LIFO reserve allows us to answer the question, "During the years that Ford has used LIFO, what has been the total, cumulative effect on cost of goods sold over all those years?" To see this, do the mental experiment of having Ford sell all its 2003 year-end inventory for $12,000 million. How would profit from this liquidation differ between LIFO and FIFO given inventory levels that would exist at year-end 2003 under each method?

Answer

This complete liquidation would produce higher profits under LIFO. These higher profits in the final liquidation year are equal to the cumulative amount by which gross profits were lower under LIFO in past years. The hypothetical liquidation of Ford inventories would show (in millions):

	LIFO	FIFO	Difference
Sales	$ 12,000	$ 12,000	—
Cost of goods sold	9,181	10,177	996
Gross profit	$ 2,819	$ 1,823	($ 996)

Summary Problem for Your Review

PROBLEM

"When prices are rising, FIFO produces profits that confuse economic profit and holding gains because more resources are needed to maintain operations than previously." Do you agree? Explain.

SOLUTION

FIFO profits certainly combine economic profits and holding gains, but well-trained analysts and managers know that. LIFO gives a better measure of "distributable" income than FIFO. Recall Emilio's Cola Sales example in Exhibit 7-5. The gross profit under FIFO was 60¢, and under LIFO it was 34¢. The 60¢ − 34¢ = 26¢ difference is a fool's profit because it must be reinvested to maintain the same inventory level as previously. It arises from a profit on holding inventory as prices change instead of buying at wholesale and selling at retail. Therefore, the 26¢ cannot be distributed as a cash dividend without reducing the current level of operations.

OBJECTIVE 6

Use the lower-of-cost-or-market method to value inventories.

lower-of-cost-or-market method (LCM)
A comparison of the current market price of inventory with historical cost derived under one of the four primary methods and choosing the lower of the two as the inventory value.

Lower-of-Cost-or-Market Method

Sometimes companies cannot easily sell obsolete or damaged inventory items at amounts equal to or above their historical cost. In such a case, the historical cost overstates the value of the inventory. To avoid overstating the inventory, we use the **lower-of-cost-or-market method (LCM).** LCM requires that we compare the current market price of inventory with historical cost derived under whichever of the four primary methods we are using and we then report the lower of the two as the inventory value.

LCM is an example of conservatism. **Conservatism** means selecting methods of measurement that yield lower net income, lower assets, and lower stockholders' equity. We illustrated conservatism in accounts receivable with the use of an allowance for bad debts. We estimated and recorded losses on uncollectible accounts before they were certain. With inventories, conservatism dictates that we use the LCM method.

Accountants believe that erring in the direction of conservatism is better than erring in the direction of overstating assets and net income. The accountant's conservatism balances management's optimism. Management prepares the financial statements, but the conservatism principle moderates management's human tendency to hope for, and expect, the best.

conservatism
Selecting the methods of measurement that yield lower net income, lower assets, and lower stockholders' equity.

Role of Replacement Cost

When applying LCM, the definition of market price is complex. Accountants generally think of the market price as the replacement cost of the inventory item, that is, what it would cost to buy the inventory item today. Keep in mind, though, that using this method for LCM assumes that when replacement costs decline in the wholesale market, so do the retail selling prices. Consider the following example. The Ripley Company has 100 units in its ending FIFO inventory on December 31, 20X1. Ripley tentatively computed its gross profit for 20X1 as follows:

Sales		$ 2,180
Cost of goods available for sale	$1,980	
Ending inventory of 100 units, at cost	790	
Cost of goods sold		1,190
Gross profit		$ 990

Assume a sudden decline in replacement costs of our inventory during the final week of December from $7.90 per unit to $4 per unit. If we assume that the sales price will drop along with the market price, an inventory write-down of ($7.90 − $4.00) × 100 units, or $390, is in order. A **write-down** reduces the recorded historical cost of an item in response to a decline in value. When a write-down occurs, the new $4 per unit replacement cost becomes, for accounting purposes, the unexpired cost of the inventory. Thus, if replacement prices subsequently rise to $8 per unit in January 20X2, the assigned cost of each unit will remain $4. In short, the lower-of-cost-or-market method would regard the $4 cost of December 31 as the "new historical cost" of the inventory. The required journal entry is:

write-down
A reduction in the recorded historical cost of an item in response to a decline in value.

Loss on write-down of inventory (or cost of goods sold)	390	
Inventory		390
To write down inventory from $790 cost to $400 market value		

The write-down of inventories increases cost of goods sold in 20X1 by $390. Therefore, reported income for 20X1 would be lowered by $390:

	Before $390 Write-Down	After $390 Write-Down	Difference
Sales	$ 2,180	$ 2,180	
Cost of goods available	$ 1,980	$ 1,980	
Ending inventory	790	400	−$390
Cost of goods sold	$ 1,190	$ 1,580	+$390
Gross profit	$ 990	$ 600	−$390

Why is $390 written down? LCM holds that, of the $790 historical cost, $390 is considered to have expired during 20X1 because Ripley cannot justifiably carry forward the entire $790 cost to the future as an asset. However, if the market replacement cost falls but selling prices remain the same, the items still have their original earnings power. No loss has occurred, and no reduction in the book value of the inventory is necessary.

Exhibit 7-12

The Ripley Company

Effects of Lower-of-Cost-or-Market

	Cost Method		Lower-of-Cost-or-Market Method	
	20X1	**20X2**	**20X1**	**20X2**
Sales	$2,180	$ 800	$2,180	$ 800
Cost of goods available	$1,980	$ 790	$1,980	$ 400
Ending inventory	790	—	400*	—
Cost of goods sold	$1,190	$ 790	$1,580	$ 400
Gross profit	$ 990	$ 10	$ 600	$ 400

Combined gross profit for 2 years
    Cost method: $990 + $10 = $1,000
    Lower-of-cost-or-market method: $600 + $400 = $1,000

*The inventory is shown here after being written down by $390, from $790 to $400. For internal purposes, many accountants prefer to show the write-down separately, presenting a gross profit before write-down of inventory, the write-down, and a gross profit after write-down.

Conservatism in Action

Compared with a pure cost method, the lower-of-cost-or-market method reports less net income in the period of decline in the market value of the inventory and more net income in the period of sale. The lower-of-cost-or-market method affects how much income the Ripley Company reports in each year, but not the total income over the company's life. Exhibit 7-12 underscores this point. Suppose Ripley goes out of business in early 20X2. That is, it acquires no more units. There are no sales in 20X2 except for the disposal of the inventory at $8 per unit (100 × $8 = $800). The LCM method will affect neither combined gross profit nor combined net income for the two periods, as the bottom of Exhibit 7-12 reveals.

A full-blown lower-of-cost-or-market method is rarely encountered in practice. Why? Because it is expensive to get the correct replacement costs of hundreds or thousands of different products in inventory. Further, the benefit from doing so does not justify the cost. Auditors do watch for price trends in the industry that might indicate a serious concern. In particular, they watch for subclasses of inventory that are obsolete, shopworn, or otherwise of only nominal value and apply LCM to such inventory.

Effects of Inventory Errors

OBJECTIVE 7

Show the effects of inventory errors on financial statements.

Inventory errors can arise from many sources. For example, incorrect physical counts might arise because accountants missed goods that were in receiving or shipping areas instead of in the inventory stockroom. Or a clerk might hit a 5 on the keyboard instead of a 6.

An undiscovered inventory error usually affects two reporting periods. The error will cause misstated amounts in the period in which the error occurred, but the effects will then be counterbalanced by identical offsetting amounts in the following period. Consider the income statements in Exhibit 7-13, which assume the physical count of ending 20X7 inventory is in error. The counters reported inventory to be $60,000, but it is really $70,000. That means that 20X7 pretax income will be $10,000 too low, and net income will be $6,000 too low.

Think about the effects of the uncorrected error on the following year, 20X8, shown in Panel B. We assume that the operations during 20X8 are a duplication of those of 20X7, except that the ending inventory is correctly counted as $40,000. The beginning inventory will be $60,000 instead of the correct $70,000. Therefore, counterbalancing errors in 20X8 will exactly offset the errors in 20X7. Thus, the retained earnings at the end of 20X8 shows a cumulative effect of zero. Why? Because the net income in 20X7 is understated by $6,000, but the net income in 20X8 is overstated by $6,000.

Exhibit 7-13
Effects of Inventory
Errors (in thousands)

PANEL A

20X7	Correct Reporting		Incorrect Reporting*		Effects of Errors
Sales		$980		$980	
Deduct: Cost of goods sold					
Beginning inventory	$100		$100		
Purchases	500		500		
Cost of goods available for sale	$600		$600		
Deduct: Ending inventory	70		60		Understated by $10
Cost of goods sold		530		540	Overstated by $10
Gross profit		$450		$440	Understated by $10
Other expenses		250		250	
Income before income taxes		$200		$190	Understated by $10
Income tax expense at 40%		80		76	Understated by $4
Net income		$120		$114	**Understated by $6**
Ending balance sheet items					
Inventory		$ 70		$ 60	Understated by $10
Retained earnings includes					
current net income		120		114	Understated by $6
Income tax liability[†]		80		76	Understated by $4

*Because of error in ending inventory.
[†]For simplicity, assume that the entire income tax expense for the year will not be paid until the succeeding year. Therefore, the ending liability will equal the income tax expense.

PANEL B

20X8	Correct Reporting		Incorrect Reporting*		Effects of Errors
Sales		$980		$980	
Deduct: Cost of goods sold					
Beginning inventory	$ 70		$ 60		Understated by $10
Purchases	500		500		
Cost of goods available for sale	$570		$560		Understated by $10
Deduct: Ending inventory	40		40		
Cost of goods sold		530		520	Understated by $10
Gross profit		$450		$460	Overstated by $10
Other expenses		250		250	
Income before income taxes		$200		$210	Overstated by $10
Income tax expense at 40%		80		84	Overstated by $4
Net income		$120		$126	**Overstated by $6**
Ending balance sheet items					
Inventory		$ 40		$ 40	**Correct**
Retained earnings includes					
Net income of previous year		120		114	Counterbalanced and
Net income of current year		120		126	thus now correct
Two-year total		$240		$240	in total
Income tax liability					
End of previous year		80		76	Counterbalanced and
End of current year		80		84	thus now correct in total[†]
Two-year total		$160		$160	

*Because of error in beginning inventory.
[†]The $84 really consists of the $4 that pertains to income of the previous year plus $80 that pertains to income of the current year.

The complete analyses for 20X7 and 20X8 show the full detail of the inventory error, and they provide us with a handy rule of thumb. If ending inventory is understated, retained earnings is understated. If ending inventory is overstated, retained earnings is overstated. These relations are clear from the balance sheet equation.

Summary Problem for Your Review

PROBLEM

At the end of 20X1, an error was made in the count of physical inventory that understated the ending inventory value by $1,000. The error went undetected. The subsequent inventory at the end of 20X2 was done correctly. Assess the effect of this error on income before tax, taxes, net income, and retained earnings for 20X1 and 20X2, assuming a 40% tax rate.

SOLUTION

	20X1	20X2
Beginning inventory	OK	$1,000 too low
Purchases	OK	OK
Goods available for sale	OK	$1,000 too low
Ending inventory	$ 1,000 too low	OK
Cost of goods sold	$1,000 too high	$1,000 too low

Note that 20X1 Ending inventory becomes 20X2 Beginning inventory, reversing the effects on Cost of goods sold. The 20X1 Cost of goods sold being too high causes 20X1 income before tax to be too low by $1,000. Therefore, taxes will be too low by .40 × $1,000 = $400, and net income will be too low by $600, causing retained earnings to be too low by $600 also. In 20X2, the effects reverse and by year-end retained earnings is correctly stated.

Cutoff Errors and Inventory Valuation

cutoff error
Failure to record transactions in the correct time period.

The accrual basis of accounting should include the physical counting and careful valuation of inventory at least once yearly. Auditors routinely search for **cutoff errors,** which are failures to record transactions in the correct time period. For example, suppose a company with a periodic inventory system conducts a physical inventory on December 31. Inventory purchases of $100,000 arrive in the receiving room during the afternoon of December 31. Accountants include the acquisition in Purchases and Accounts Payable, but the people counting the inventory exclude it from the ending inventory valuation. Such an error would understate ending inventory, thereby overstating cost of goods sold and understating gross profit. However, if accountants did not record the acquisition (and thus add it to Purchases) until January 2, the errors in both inventory count and purchases would understate both the ending inventory and Accounts Payable as of December 31. However, cost of goods sold and gross profit would be correct because the errors would understate Purchases and the ending inventory by the same amount.

The general approach to recording purchases and sales is keyed to the legal transfer of ownership. Auditors are especially careful about cutoff tests because the pressure for profits sometimes causes managers to postpone the recording of bona fide purchases of goods and services. Similarly, the same managers may deliberately include sales orders near year-end (instead of bona fide completed sales) in revenues. For example, consider the case of **Datapoint**, a maker of small computers and telecommunications equipment. A news story reported: "Datapoint's hard-pressed sales force was still logging orders that might not hold up after shipment." In other words, Datapoint's managers recorded revenue from orders that the company had not yet shipped. This is an example of how pressure for performance can lead to ethical lapses. In the wake of an accounting scandal, Datapoint's president declared a 3-week "amnesty period" during which managers could remove scheduled shipments from the sales account, no questions asked.

A similar news story referred to difficulties at **McCormick & Company**, a firm known for its spices: "The investigation also found that improprieties included the company's accounting for sales. In a longstanding practice, the company recorded as sales, goods that had been selected and prepared for shipment rather than waiting until after they had been shipped as is the customary accounting practice." Sometimes managers will accelerate the recognition of revenues in order to meet a sales- or profit-based target and therefore earn a bonus. This is an obvious ethical lapse.

The Importance of Gross Profits

We began this chapter by discussing gross profits, which are the result of sales revenue less the cost of goods sold. Management and investors are intensely interested in gross profit and how it changes over time. In comparing the gross profits of two firms, it is sometimes important to examine which inventory method they have used to calculate their gross profit.

OBJECTIVE 8

Evaluate the gross profit percentage and inventory turnover.

Gross Profit Percentage

Analysts often express gross profit as a percentage of sales. Consider the following information on a past year for a hypothetical **Safeway** grocery store:

	Amount	Percentage
Sales	$10,000,000	100%
Net cost of goods sold	7,500,000	75%
Gross profit	$ 2,500,000	25%

The **gross profit percentage** —gross profit divided by sales—here is 25%. The following table illustrates the extent to which gross profit percentages vary among industries.

gross profit percentage
Gross profit as a percentage of sales.

Industry	Gross Profit Percentage
Auto retailers	12.9%
Auto manufacturers	19.3
Jewelry retailers	45.4
Grocery retailers	23.5
Grocery wholesalers	18.6
Drug manufacturers	46.5

Source: RMA, Annual Statement Studies 2002/2003.

What accounts for this wide variation in gross profit percentage? The nature of the business has a lot to do with it. **Wholesalers** sell in larger quantities and incur fewer selling costs because they sell to retail companies instead of individuals. As a result of competition and high volumes, they have smaller gross profit percentages than do retailers. **Retailers** sell directly to the public—to individual buyers. Among retailers, jewelers have

wholesaler
An intermediary that sells inventory items to retailers.

retailer
A company that sells items directly to the public, to individual buyers.

Nothing is more important than your health, and nothing is more contentious than how much drugs cost, who should pay for them, and where in the world they will be available. Eli Lilly, a major pharmaceutical company with worldwide sales of $12.6 billion, addressed the question, "Are Drug Prices Fair?" in its 1999 annual report. You may or may not agree with them that the answer is yes. They restate the question as two questions: Can patients afford needed prescription drugs? Can pharmaceutical companies afford to conduct the research necessary to find new, effective drugs?

They stressed that today's medicines are more expensive than in the past, but they do more than ever before. Modern medicines are more cost effective than other treatments. A year's treatment with new antipsychotic drugs costs about the same as 1 week of hospitalization for a patient with schizophrenia and improves the patient's quality of life. Much of the public outcry over pharmaceutical costs is not about the specific cost of a specific drug, but about the total cost of all drugs. In a recent year when total costs of drugs rose 12%, 3% of the increase was due to an increase in unit costs of specific existing drugs and 9% was due to expanded use of existing drugs and to new drugs being introduced. New drugs improve our ability to manage disease or attack previously untreatable medical conditions.

Lilly also cites the high cost of developing new treatments. They spend 18% of sales on R&D. To develop three new drugs requires testing 15,000 compounds. A new drug costs $500 million to develop. Lilly's answer to the debate is that pharmaceuticals are a good value in the fight against disease and preserving the quality of life. Today we are learning a great deal about genetics, gene mapping, and how genetic makeup causes treatments to succeed for one patient and fail for another. All of these have the potential to alter the costs of finding successful treatments and using them effectively for the right patients.

"Who should pay?" is answered very differently around the world. In the United States, corporate-sponsored health care plans cover many employees, but companies are putting maximums on their contributions and asking employees to pay more. Many issues about how much insurance should pay, what insurance should pay for, and how companies are changing their policies are currently being pursued in courts. Some countries have government-funded medical care, but we all face the important question of what is a reasonable cost to incur and who will decide. This is ultimately a question of how many resources the country has and for whose benefit will those resources be used. Should people have access to prenatal vitamins, prescription pain relief, or heart transplants? Costs per patient and benefits to society differ radically across these options.

The worldwide availability issue also has multiple parts. Pharmaceutical companies in the developed world are for-profit companies and have often ignored solutions to important diseases in lesser-developed countries because the affected populations could not pay. Merck's expensive decision some years ago to pursue successfully a cure for a major disease prevalent almost exclusively in Africa is one of several exceptions. Pharmaceutical companies have often conducted studies on the effectiveness of drugs in lesser-developed countries because regulations were more lenient, while denying patients access to the successful drugs in those same countries because patients could not cover the costs.

Sometimes humanitarian groups or political pressure has helped encourage compromises that extend the availability of drugs to poor populations. For example, the Gates Foundation has invested more than $1.6 billion to speed vaccine development and provide immunization to the world's poor. Such support gets attention, and Glaxo Smith Kline's vaccine subsidiary is paying attention. Its vaccine sales exceed $2 billion per year, and it has 20 novel vaccines in clinical trials, including a malaria vaccine to prevent a disease that kills three children per minute in developing countries. When the Gates Foundation absorbs some of the risk of failure by funding research, more R&D can and will occur.

Source: 1999 and 2003 Lilly Annual Reports, p. 13; *Business Week*, April 26, 2004, p. 65.

almost twice the gross profits of grocers because of extensive personal selling. Drug manufacturers earn high gross profits because of high drug prices, caused by the need for substantial R&D outlays (sometimes more than 15% of sales) and allowed by patent protection on specific drugs. The Business First box above discusses some of the reasons a pharmaceutical company such as Eli Lilly has high gross margins. In contrast, auto manufacturers face more direct competition and earn lower gross profit percentages.

It is also important to note that R&D is a cost of developing a drug, and therefore, pharmaceutical companies must incur such costs to generate any sales from a drug. However, accounting practice treats the R&D costs as a period cost when incurred instead of a product cost to be matched to future sales of the drug. We do this because it is impossible to know, as a company incurs R&D costs, whether they will ultimately produce a viable drug whose therapeutic value will allow recovery of the costs of developing it.

Estimating Intraperiod Gross Profit and Inventory

To avoid costly physical counts of inventory, some companies use the gross profit percentage to estimate ending inventory balances for monthly or quarterly reports. For example, suppose past sales of a particular The Home Depot store have usually resulted in a gross profit percentage of 30%. The accountant assumes that gross profit continues to be 30% of sales and estimates the cost of goods sold for quarterly sales of $10 million as follows (in millions):

$$\text{Sales} - \text{Cost of goods sold} = \text{Gross profit}$$
$$S - CGS = GP$$
$$\$10.0 - CGS = .30 \times \$10.0 = \$3.0$$
$$CGS = \$7.0$$

If we know the store's beginning inventory is $5 million and purchases are $7.1 million, we can then estimate ending inventory to be $5.1 million as follows (in millions):

$$\text{Beginning inventory} + \text{Purchases} - \text{Ending inventory} = CGS$$
$$BI + P - EI = CGS$$
$$\$5.0 + \$7.1 - EI = \$7.0$$
$$EI = \$5.1$$

Gross Profit Percentage and Turnover

Retailers often attempt to increase total profits by increasing sales levels. They may lower prices and hope to increase their total gross profits by selling their inventories more quickly, replenishing, selling again, and so forth. In essence, they are accepting a lower gross profit per unit, but expecting to increase total sales more than enough to compensate. With a high volume of sales activity, a smaller gross margin per unit sold provides high total profits. This is one of the reasons that stores such as Costco, Wal-Mart, and The Home Depot do well.

To relate sales levels to inventory levels we measure **inventory turnover**—cost of goods sold divided by the average inventory held during a given period. Average inventory is usually the sum of beginning inventory and ending inventory divided by 2. For The Home Depot store in the previous example, the average inventory is ($5.0 million + $5.1 million)/2 = $5.05 million. The quarterly inventory turnover is computed as follows:

inventory turnover
The cost of goods sold divided by the average inventory held during the period.

$$\text{Inventory Turnover} = \text{Cost of goods sold} \div \text{Average inventory}$$
$$= \$7.0 \text{ million} \div \$5.05 \text{ million} = 1.4$$

Suppose sales double if The Home Depot lowers its prices by 5%. Sales revenue on the current level of business drops from $10 million to (0.95 × $10 million), or $9.5 million. But the store sells twice as many units, so total revenue becomes 2 × $9.5 million, or $19 million. How profitable is this store? Cost of goods sold doubles from $7 million to $14 million. Total gross profit is $19 million − $14 million = $5 million. So gross profit during the quarter is $2 million higher as a result of the lower price. The inventory turnover doubles: $14 million divided by $5.05 million (the unchanged average inventory) is 2.8. However, the gross profit percentage falls from 30% to 26% ($5 million divided by $19 million).

Is the company better off? Maybe. Certainly, the current month's gross profit is larger. However, long-term strategic concerns raise the question: is this new sales level sustainable? For some products, when prices fall, consumers sharply increase purchases and stockpile the extras for later consumption. There is little increase in underlying demand, just a shift of future purchases to the present. Therefore, the current good sales could result in terrible future sales.

Another strategic question is: What will the competition do? If The Home Depot's increased sales came at a competitor's expense, the competitor's response may be a similar decrease in prices. The competition might recover most of its old customers, with each buying a little more at the new price than they did at the old. Assuming all competitors decrease prices similarly, the whole market would see, not a doubling of sales, but perhaps a 20% sales growth. In that case, The Home Depot store would be no better off overall because the 20% sales growth would just cover the 5% price reduction.

Exhibit 7-14 illustrates two principles. Panel A shows that if a firm can increase inventory turnover while maintaining a constant gross profit percentage, it should do so. To increase inventory turnover means that you support sales levels with less inventory. You can do this by more frequently restocking, for example. However, as Panel B shows, if the increased inventory turnover results from sales growth driven by a decrease in sales price, the gross margin percentage may fall. The desirability of the change depends on whether the sales gain could offset the decreased margin. In The Home Depot store example, when a 5% price reduction produces only a 20% increase in units sold, the new gross margin of $3 million is just equal to the initial gross margin. Any sales increase less than 20% would result in a decreased gross margin. However, at any sales increase greater than 20%, the new gross margin would exceed the original $3 million. For example, at a 50% increase in sales volume, the new gross margin of $3.75 million exceeds the original by $3.75 million − $3 million = $.75 million. Basically, the lesson of Exhibit 7-14 is that you cannot focus on only one number or measure of company performance. Paying too much attention to one measure could cause you to miss the fact that another was falling fast.

Earlier you saw the industry variability in gross margin percentages. The same variability applies to inventory turnover percentages, as the following table illustrates:

Industry	Gross Profit Percentage	Inventory Turnover
Auto retailers	12.9%	6.3
Auto manufacturers	19.3	5.3
Jewelry retailers	45.4	1.3
Jewelry manufacturers	28.2	3.0
Grocery retailers	23.5	18.1
Grocery wholesalers	18.6	13.9
Drug manufacturers	46.5	4.3
Drugstores	26.2	9.7
Drug wholesalers	25.2	8.2
Computer and software retail	37.8	19.0
Semiconductor manufacturers	33.1	4.9
Computer manufacturers	35.4	6.0

Source: RMA, Annual Statement Studies, 2002/2003.

As you can see, the industries with the highest gross profit percentages tend to have the lowest inventory turnover. This reflects the observation earlier that firms must have total gross margins high enough to cover other selling and administrative costs. The lower turnover for jewelers and drug manufacturers means that they need higher gross profit margin percentages to cover the high costs of selling or research.

The inventory turnover measure is especially effective for assessing companies in the same industry. If one industry member has a higher turnover than another, it is probably

Exhibit 7-14
The Home Depot
Store
*Effects of Increased
Inventory Turnover
($ in Millions)*

	Unit Sales Increase			
	Original	**20%**	**50%**	**100%**
PANEL A				
No change in sales price				
Sales	$10.00	$12.00	$15.00	$20.00
Cost of goods sold (70%)	7.00	8.40	10.50	14.00
Gross margin (30%)	$ 3.00	$ 3.60	$ 4.50	$ 6.00
Inventory turnover	1.4	1.7	2.1	2.8
PANEL B				
5% reduction in sales price				
Sales (95% of above)	$ 9.50	$11.40	$14.25	$19.00
Cost of goods sold (as above)	7.00	8.40	10.50	14.00
Gross margin (26% of sales)	$ 2.50	$ 3.00	$ 3.75	$ 5.00
Inventory turnover (as above)	1.4	1.7	2.1	2.8

more efficient. That is, the higher turnover indicates an ability to use smaller inventory levels to attain high sales levels. This is good, because it reduces the investment in inventory. Such a company has fewer products sitting on display shelves or in warehouses and uses less capital in maintaining, moving, and displaying inventory items.

When calculating ratios, be sure to keep the accounting methods in mind. Consider the data for Ford Motor Company given earlier on page 297. By using LIFO and FIFO results for Ford Motor Company, we can calculate the inventory turnover and gross profit percentages (sales of $138,442 million) to be:

LIFO

$$\text{Gross profit percentage: } (\$138,442 - \$129,821) \div \$138,442 = 6.23\%$$

$$\text{Inventory turnover: } \$129,821 \div ((\$6,977 + \$9,181) \div 2) = 16.07$$

FIFO

$$\text{Gross profit percentage: } (\$138,442 - \$129,782) \div \$138,442 = 6.26\%$$

$$\text{Inventory turnover: } \$129,782 \div ((\$7,934 + \$10,177) \div 2) = 14.33$$

In Ford's case, LIFO decreased the gross profit percentage in the current year slightly and increased the inventory turnover significantly relative to FIFO. The modest change in the gross profit percentage is because the 2003 *change* in the LIFO reserve was small relative to the large size of cost of sales. In contrast, the significant change in inventory turnover is due to the *total* LIFO reserve being large relative to the size of the inventory level. Notice that the FIFO ending inventory balance is 11% larger than the LIFO inventory balance.

Gross Profit Percentages and Accuracy of Records

Auditors, including those from the IRS, use the gross profit percentage to help satisfy themselves about the accuracy of records. For example, the IRS compiles gross profit percentages by types of retail establishment. If a company shows an unusually low percentage compared with similar companies, IRS auditors may suspect that the company has tried to avoid taxes by failing to record all cash sales. Similarly, managers watch changes in gross profit percentages to judge operating profitability and to monitor how well a company is controlling employee theft and shoplifting.

Suppose an internal revenue agent, a manager, or an outside auditor had gathered the following data for a particular jewelry company for the past 3 years ($ in millions):

	20X3	20X2	20X1
Net sales	$350	$325	$300
Cost of goods sold	210	165	150
Gross profit	$140	$160	150
Gross profit percentage	40%	49%	50%

Comparing these data helps to see if there are any changes worth investigating. As you can see, the gross profit percentage for the jewelry company was fairly steady for 2 years. However, the decline in the percentage in year three could be a sign of trouble. Obviously, many factors might cause a decline in the percentage, and not all of them are cause for concern. Possible explanations include the following:

1. Competition has intensified, resulting in intensive price wars that reduced selling prices.
2. The mix of goods sold has shifted so, for instance, the $350 million of sales in 20X3 is composed of relatively more products bearing lower gross margins, for example, more costume jewelry bearing low margins and less diamond jewelry bearing high margins.
3. Shoplifting or embezzling has soared out of control. For example, a manager may be pocketing and not recording cash sales of $70 million. After all, given cost of sales of $210 million, sales in 20X3 would have been $210 × 2 = $420 million if the company had maintained its 50% margin. Similarly, given sales of $350 million, we would have expected costs to be about $175 million, not $210 million.

Reports to Shareholders

Analysis of gross profits is important to investors. Consider a quarterly report to shareholders of **Superscope, Incorporated**, a manufacturer and distributor of stereophonic equipment that encountered rocky times several years ago. The company presented the following condensed income statement for a 3-month period ($ in thousands):

	Current Year	Previous Year
Net sales	$40,000	$40,200
Cost and expenses		
Cost of sales	33,100	28,200
Selling, general, and administrative	11,200	9,900
Interest	2,000	1,200
Total costs and expenses	46,300	39,300
Income (loss) before income tax		
provision (benefit)	(6,300)	900
Income tax provision (benefit)	(3,000)	200
Net income (loss)	$ (3,300)	$ 700

Although the statement does not show the amount of gross profit, you can readily compute the gross profit percentages as ($40,000 − $33,100) ÷ $40,000 = 17% and ($40,200 − $28,200) ÷ $40,200 = 30%. To show how seriously these percentages are considered, the chairman's letter to shareholders began as follows:

> *I shall attempt herein to provide you with a candid analysis of the Company's present condition, the steps we have instituted to overcome current adversities, and the potential which we believe can, in due course, be realized by the Company's realistic positive determination to regain profitability.*
>
> *In the second quarter the Company's gross profit margins decreased to 17% compared to 30% in the corresponding quarter of a year ago.*

*For the first six months gross profit margins were 22%, down from 31%
for the corresponding period of a year ago.*

*Essentially, the gross profits and consequential operating losses in
the second quarter, as reflected in the condensed financial statements
appearing in this report, resulted from lower than anticipated sales volume and from the following second quarter factors: liquidation of our
entire citizens band inventory; increases in dealer cash discounts and
sales incentive expenses; gross margin reductions resulting from sales of
slow moving models at less than normal prices; and markdown of slow
moving inventory on hand to a realistic net realizable market value.*

Internal Control of Inventories

In many organizations, inventories are more easily accessible than cash. Therefore, they
can become a favorite target for thieves.

Retail merchants must contend with inventory shrinkage, a polite term for shoplifting by
customers and embezzling by employees. The accounting firm Ernst & Young estimates that
U.S. retailers lose $46 billion annually to inventory shrinkage, the largest percentage of it due
to employee theft. Consider the following footnote from the 2003 annual report of Dollar
General, a chain of about 6,650 discount stores in 27 states, primarily in the Southeast and
Midwest: "The Company's provision for inventory shrinkage, calculated at the retail value of
the inventory, as a percentage of net sales, decreased to 3.05 percent in the second quarter of
2003 from 3.61 percent in 2002." Average inventory shrinkage for all retailers is about 1.8%.
Some department stores have suffered shrinkage losses of 4% to 5% of their sales volume.
This is large when compared with the typical net profit margin of 5% to 6%.

A management consulting firm has demonstrated how widespread shoplifting has
become. The firm concentrated on a midtown New York City department store. Researchers
followed 500 randomly-selected shoppers from the moment they entered the store to the time
they departed. Forty-two shoppers, or 1 out of every 12, took something. They stole $300
worth of merchandise, an average of $7.15 each. Similar experiments were conducted in
Boston (1 of 20 shoplifted), in Philadelphia (1 of 10), and again in New York (1 of 12).

Experts on controlling inventory shrinkage generally agree that the best deterrent is an
alert employee at the point of sale. Retail stores also use sensitized tags on merchandise; if
not detached or neutralized by a salesclerk, these miniature transmitters trip an alarm as the
culprit begins to leave the store. Many libraries use a similar system to safeguard their
books. Macy's in New York has continuous surveillance with more than 50 television cameras. Some stores have actors pose as shoplifters, who are then subjected to fake arrests. If
potential thieves see the arrests, they may be deterred. Such ploys have helped reduce but not
eliminate thefts by customers at major retail chains. Retailers must also scrutinize their own
personnel because employees account for almost 50% of inventory shortages.

The imposing magnitude of retail inventory shrinkage demonstrates how management
objectives may differ among industries. For example, consider the grocery business,
where net income is about 1% of sales. You can readily see why store managers often put
more effort into controlling inventory shrinkage than to boosting gross sales volume. The
trade-off is clear: if the operating profit is 2% of sales, offsetting a $1,000 increase in
shrinkage requires a $50,000 boost in gross sales.

Shrinkage in Perpetual and Periodic Inventory Systems

Measuring inventory shrinkage is straightforward for companies that use a perpetual
inventory system. Shrinkage is simply the difference between the cost of inventory identified by a physical count and the inventory balance in the company's general ledger.
Consider the following example:

Sales	$100,000
Cost of goods sold (perpetual inventory system)	80,000
Beginning inventory	15,000
Purchases	85,000
Ending inventory, per general ledger	20,000
Ending inventory, per physical count	18,000

Shrinkage is $20,000 − $18,000 = $2,000. The total cost of goods sold becomes $80,000 + $2,000 = $82,000. The journal entries under a perpetual inventory system would be:

Inventory shrinkage expense	2,000	
Inventory		2,000
To adjust ending inventory to its balance per physical count		
Cost of goods sold	2,000	
Inventory shrinkage expense		2,000
The transfer inventory shrinkage to cost of goods sold		

By definition, a periodic inventory system has no continuing balance of the inventory account. Cost of goods sold automatically includes inventory shrinkage in cost of goods sold. Why? Beginning inventory plus purchases less ending inventory measures all inventory that has flowed out, whether it went to customers, shoplifters, or embezzlers, or was simply lost or broken. Our example would show:

Beginning inventory	$ 15,000
Plus: Purchases	85,000
Goods available for sale	$100,000
Less: Ending inventory, per physical count	18,000
Cost of goods sold	$ 82,000

Summary Problem for Your Review

PROBLEM

Hewlett-Packard (HP) designs, manufactures, and services a broad array of products including perhaps your calculator or printer. Some results of product sales for the year ended October 31, 2003 were ($ in millions):

Sales of products	$58,939
Cost of merchandise sold	43,689
Beginning merchandise inventory	5,797
Ending merchandise inventory	6,065

1. Calculate the 2003 gross profit and gross profit percentage for HP.
2. Calculate the inventory turnover ratio.
3. What gross profit would have been reported if inventory turnover in 2003 had been 8, the gross profit percentage remained the same as that calculated in requirement 1, and the level of inventory was unchanged?

SOLUTION

(Monetary amounts are in millions.)

  1. Gross profit = Sales − Cost of merchandise sold

$$= \$58,939 - 43,689$$

$$= \$15,250$$

$$\text{Gross profit percentage} = \text{Gross profit} \div \text{Sales}$$
$$= \$15{,}250 \div \$58{,}939$$
$$= 25.9\%$$

2. $\text{Inventory turnover} = \text{Cost of merchandise sold} \div \text{Average merchandise inventory}$
$$= \$43{,}689 \div [(\$6{,}065 + \$5{,}797) \div 2]$$
$$= \$43{,}689 \div \$5{,}931$$
$$= 7.4$$

3. To respond to this question you must first see that a higher inventory turnover given a constant average inventory implies an increase in sales. Increased sales with a constant gross profit percentage implies increased total gross profit. With these relationships in mind, answering the question is a process of working backward based on the ratios and relationships.

$$\text{Cost of merchandise sold} = \text{Inventory turnover} \times \text{Average merchandise inventory}$$
$$= 8 \times \$5{,}931$$
$$= \$47{,}448$$

$$\text{Gross profit percentage} = (\text{Sales} - \text{Cost of merchandise sold}) \div \text{Sales}$$
$$25.9\% = (S - \$47{,}448) \div S$$
$$.259 \times S = S - \$47{,}448$$
$$S - (.259 \times S) = \$47{,}448$$
$$S \times (1 - .259) = \$47{,}448$$
$$S = \$47{,}448 \div (1 - .259)$$
$$S = \$64{,}032$$

$$\text{Gross profit} = \text{Sales} - \text{Cost of merchandise sold}$$
$$= \$64{,}032 - \$47{,}448$$
$$= \$16{,}584$$

As you would expect given our calculations, the gross profit percentage remains at 25.9% ($16,584 \div 64,032$).

Highlights to Remember

1 **Link inventory valuation to gross profit.** We link inventory valuation to gross profit because the inventory valuation involves allocating the cost of goods available for sale between cost of goods sold (used in computing gross profit, sales less cost of goods sold, on the income statement) and ending inventory (a current asset on the balance sheet).

2 **Use both perpetual and periodic inventory systems.** Under the perpetual inventory system, we continuously track inventories and cost of goods sold by recording cost of goods sold at the time of each sale. Under the periodic inventory system, we compute cost of goods sold using an adjusting entry at year-end. Accountants conduct a physical inventory at the end of each period under either system. They count the goods on hand and calculate a cost for each item from purchase records. Under the periodic system, the physical inventory is the basis for the year-end adjusting entry to recognize cost of goods sold. Under the perpetual system, the physical inventory is used to confirm the accounting records. Differences, if any, lead to adjustments to cost of goods sold and ending inventory.

3 **Calculate the cost of merchandise acquired.** The cost of merchandise acquired is the invoice price of the goods plus directly identifiable inbound transportation costs less any cash or quantity discounts and less any returns or allowances.

4 **Compute income and inventory values using the four principal inventory valuation methods.** Valuation of inventories involves the assignment of specific historical costs of acquisition either to units sold or to units remaining in ending inventory. Four major inventory valuation methods are in use in the United States: specific identification, weighted average, FIFO, and LIFO. Specific identification is most common for low-volume, high-value products such as automobiles, boats, or jewelry. FIFO attributes the most recent, current prices to inventory items. LIFO attributes the most recent, current prices to cost of sales. When prices are rising and inventories are constant or growing, LIFO net income is less than FIFO net income. LIFO is popular in the United States among companies who face rising prices, for whom lower profits under LIFO mean lower taxes. The U.S. tax law allows companies to use LIFO for tax purposes only if they use it also for financial reporting purposes. Weighted average provides results between LIFO and FIFO for both the income statement cost of sales and the balance sheet inventory number.

5 **Calculate the impact on net income of LIFO liquidations.** LIFO liquidation refers to the relatively higher profits generated under LIFO when reductions in inventory levels cause companies to use older, lower inventory costs in calculating cost of goods sold. Notice that, even with declining inventories, with rising costs the cumulative taxable income is always less under LIFO than it is under FIFO until complete liquidation occurs because the inventory valuation is less and the cumulative cost of goods sold is higher.

6 **Use the lower-of-cost-or-market method to value inventories.** Conservatism leads to the lower-of-cost-or-market method, which treats cost as the maximum value of inventory. Companies must reduce inventory carrying amounts to replacement cost (with a corresponding increase in cost of goods sold) when acquisition prices fall below historical cost levels.

7 **Show the effects of inventory errors on financial statements.** The nature of accrual accounting for inventories creates a self-correcting quality about errors in counting or valuing the ending inventory. This occurs because the ending inventory in one period becomes the beginning inventory of the subsequent period.

8 **Evaluate the gross profit percentage and inventory turnover.** Financial analysts and managers use gross profit percentages as a measure of profitability and inventory turnover as a measure of efficient asset use. They compare these measures with prior levels to examine trends and with current levels of other industry members to assess relative performance.

Appendix 7: Inventory in a Manufacturing Environment

OBJECTIVE 9

Determine inventory costs for a manufacturing company.

In this chapter, we examined inventory accounting from the viewpoint of a merchandiser. When a company manufactures products, the cost of inventory is a combination of the acquisition cost of raw material, the wages paid to workers who combine the raw materials into finished products, and an allocation of the costs of space, energy, and equipment used by the workers as they transform the various elements into a finished product.

Consider how we accumulate costs in a manufacturing environment for Packit, a company that makes backpacks. The raw materials are heavy fabric, glue, and thread. The transformation occurs when workers use cutters to make the panels that other workers sew and glue together. The costs of manufacture include depreciation on the manufacturing building, depreciation on the sewing machines and cutters, and utilities to support the effort in the form of heat, power, and light. The finished goods are backpacks.

The accounting process is easiest to understand when calculating the cost of a complete year of production. In the following example, Packit produced 10,000 backpacks during its first year in business at a total cost of $800,000, providing a cost per backpack of $80.00 ($800,000 ÷ 10,000 units). At year-end, if Packit has sold all 10,000 backpacks, the financial statements would include $800,000 in cost of goods sold.

Packit Company—Year 1

Beginning inventory	—
Fabric purchased and used	$200,000
Wages paid to workers	300,000
Thread and glue used	50,000
Depreciation on building and equipment	220,000
Utilities	30,000
Total costs to manufacture	$800,000
Cost per backpack ($800,000 ÷ 10,000)	$ 80.00

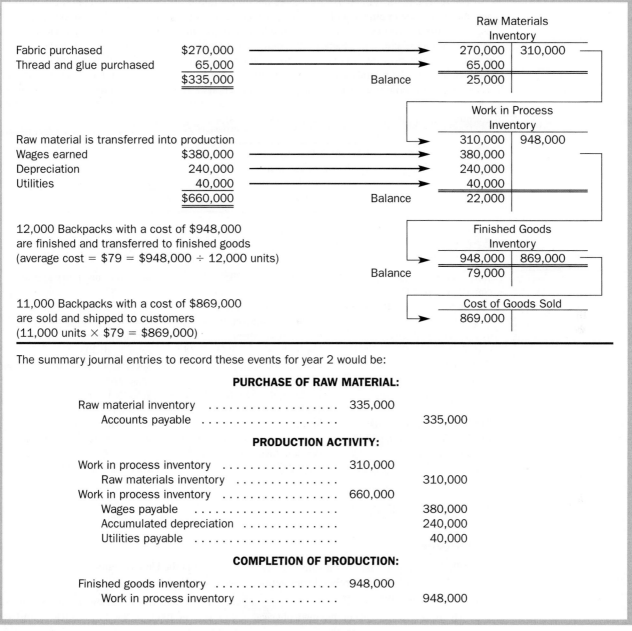

The summary journal entries to record these events for year 2 would be:

PURCHASE OF RAW MATERIAL:

Raw material inventory	335,000	
Accounts payable		335,000

PRODUCTION ACTIVITY:

Work in process inventory	310,000	
Raw materials inventory		310,000
Work in process inventory	660,000	
Wages payable		380,000
Accumulated depreciation		240,000
Utilities payable		40,000

COMPLETION OF PRODUCTION:

Finished goods inventory	948,000	
Work in process inventory		948,000

Exhibit 7-15
Packit Company Accounting for Manufacturing Costs—Year 2

raw material inventory
Includes the cost of materials held for use in the manufacturing of a product.

work in process inventory
Includes the cost incurred for partially completed items, including raw materials, labor, and other costs.

finished goods inventory
The accumulated costs of manufacture for goods that are complete and ready for sale.

In the preceding example, Packit transformed all materials acquired during the year into finished products and sold all those products before year-end. In reality, if we take a snapshot of the typical backpack manufacturer at year-end, we would observe bolts of fabric, spools of thread, and gallons of glue waiting to be put into production. We call these items held for use in the manufacturing of a product **raw material inventory.** In addition, we would also observe fabric already cut but not assembled and some partially completed backpacks. We refer to the material, labor, and other costs accumulated for partially completed items as **work in process inventory.** When manufacture is complete and the goods are ready to deliver to customers, we call the inventory **finished goods inventory.** Exhibit 7-15 shows the accounting system for managing these costs for Packit's second year of production. During this second year, Packit completed 12,000 backpacks and sold 11,000. Some remain in the assembly process at year-end, and Packit holds unused fabric, thread, and glue in preparation for future production.

The schematic in Exhibit 7-15 captures the production process. You might think of each of the accounts as corresponding to a physical reality. The raw material is stored in a locked room, ready for use. The work in process is located in the production room, and as it is finished it is physically transferred to a storage site. When Packit sells goods, they remove the items sold from that storage site and give them to the customer in exchange for cash or an account receivable. Raw materials, work in process, and finished goods are all forms of inventory and appear on the balance sheet as current assets. They are simply in different stages of completion. The act of sale converts the asset into an expense that Packit will report on its income statement. At the end of year 2, Packit will show total inventory on its balance sheet of $126,000, as follows:

Raw materials inventory	$ 25,000
Work in process inventory	22,000
Finished goods inventory	79,000
Total inventory	$126,000

Accounting Vocabulary

conservatism, p. 299
consistency, p. 293
cost of goods available for sale, p. 283
cost valuation, p. 281
cutoff error, p. 302
finished goods inventory, p. 313
first-in, first-out (FIFO), p. 289
F.O.B. destination, p. 284
F.O.B. shipping point, p. 284
freight in, p. 284
gross profit percentage, p. 303

holding gain, p. 295
inventory profit, p. 295
inventory shrinkage, p. 282
inventory turnover, p. 305
inward transportation, p. 284
last-in, first-out (LIFO), p. 289
LIFO increment, p. 295
LIFO layer, p. 295
LIFO liquidation, p. 296
LIFO reserve, p. 296
lower-of-cost-or-market method (LCM), p. 298
periodic inventory system, p. 282

perpetual inventory system, p. 282
physical count, p. 282
raw material inventory, p. 313
replacement cost, p. 294
retailer, p. 303
specific identification method, p. 288
weighted-average method, p. 291
wholesaler, p. 303
work in process inventory, p. 313
write-down, p. 299

Assignment Material

Questions

7-1 When a company records a sales transaction, it also records another related transaction. Explain the related transaction.

7-2 "There are two steps in conducting a physical count of inventories." What are they?

7-3 Distinguish between the perpetual and periodic inventory systems.

7-4 "An advantage of the perpetual inventory system is that a physical count of inventory is unnecessary. The periodic method requires a physical count to compute cost of goods sold." Do you agree? Explain.

7-5 Distinguish between F.O.B. destination and F.O.B. shipping point.

7-6 "Freight out should be classified as a direct offset to sales, not as an expense." Do you agree? Explain.

7-7 Name the four inventory cost flow assumptions or valuation methods that are generally accepted in the United States. Give a brief phrase describing each.

7-8 For which of the following items would a company be likely to use the specific identification inventory method?

a. Corporate jet aircraft
b. Large sailboats
c. Pencils
d. Diamond rings
e. Timex watches
f. Automobiles
g. Books
h. Compact discs

7-9 If a company uses a FIFO cost flow assumption, will it report the same cost of goods sold using the periodic inventory method that it reports using the perpetual method? Why or why not?

7-10 Why is LIFO a good news/bad news inventory method?

7-11 "Purchases of inventory at the end of a fiscal period can have a direct effect on income under LIFO." Do you agree? Explain.

7-12 "Gamma Company has five units of inventory, two purchased for $4 each and three purchased for $5 each. Thus, the weighted-average cost of the inventory is ($4 + $5) ÷ 2 = $4.50 per unit." Do you agree? Explain.

7-13 Assume that the physical level of inventory is constant at the beginning and end of the year and that the cost of inventory items is rising. Which will produce a higher ending inventory value, LIFO or FIFO?

7-14 Will LIFO or FIFO produce higher cost of goods sold during a period of falling prices? Explain.

7-15 What is consistency, and why is it an important accounting principle?

7-16 "There is a single dominant reason why more and more U.S. companies have adopted LIFO." What is the reason?

7-17 "An inventory profit is a fictitious profit." Do you agree? Explain.

7-18 LIFO produces absurd inventory valuations. Why?

7-19 "Conservatism always results in lower reported profits." Do you agree? Explain.

7-20 "Accountants have traditionally favored taking some losses but no gains before an asset is exchanged." What is this tradition or convention called?

7-21 What does market mean in inventory accounting?

7-22 "The lower-of-cost-or-market method is inherently inconsistent." Do you agree? Explain.

7-23 "Inventory errors are counterbalancing." Explain.

7-24 Express the cost of goods sold section of the income statement as an equation.

7-25 "Gross profit percentages help in the preparation of interim financial statements." Explain.

7-26 The branch manager of a national retail grocery chain has stated, "My managers are judged more heavily on the basis of their merchandise-shrinkage control than on their overall sales volume." Why? Explain.

Critical Thinking Questions

7-27 Deciding on a Discount Policy
You are debating with your boss about whether to give customers a 2% discount for quantity purchases. You favor the idea, but your boss says, "Why give money away? If the customer buys more, we are out 2%." How do you reply?

7-28 Effect of Overstating Inventories
Phar Mor was a large, rapidly growing pharmacy chain that proved to have overstated assets by more than $400 million. Top executives accomplished the overstatement by inflating the company's inventories at numerous store locations. How would this affect the income statements of Phar Mor?

7-29 Purchasing Operations and LIFO versus FIFO
Suppose a company bases its evaluation of the purchasing officer for a refinery on the gross margin on the oil products produced and sold during the year. During the year, the price of a barrel of oil increased from $20 to $30. The value of the inventory of oil at the beginning of the year is $20 or less per barrel. On the last day of the year, the purchasing agent is contemplating the purchase of additional oil at $30 per barrel. Is the agent more likely to purchase additional oil if the company uses the FIFO or LIFO method for its inventories? Explain.

7-30 Periodic versus Perpetual Inventory Systems
The Zen Bootist manufactures sheepskin slippers, mittens, gloves, jackets, and leather sandals to sell at craft fairs and similar events. The majority of the company's transactions occur over the winter gift-giving season. As the business has grown, the owner has become concerned about how to account for certain items and has asked your advice about whether to use the periodic or perpetual inventory system. What do you say?

Exercises

7-31 Gross Profit Section
Given the following, prepare a detailed gross profit section for Goodman's Jewelry Wholesalers for the year ended December 31, 20X8 ($ in thousands):

Cash discounts on purchases	$ 6	Cash discounts on sales	$ 5
Sales returns and allowances	40	Purchase returns and allowances	27
Gross purchases	650		
Merchandise inventory,		Merchandise inventory,	
December 31, 20X7	103	December 31, 20X8	185
Gross profit	355	Freight in	50

7-32 Gross Margin Computations and Inventory Costs

On January 15, 20X4, Isabelle Muir valued her inventory at cost, $40,000. Her statements are based on the calendar year, so you find it necessary to establish an inventory figure as of January 1, 20X4. You find that from January 2 to January 15, sales were $71,200; sales returns, $2,300; goods purchased and placed in stock, $54,000; goods removed from stock and returned to suppliers, $2,000; freight in, $500. Calculate the inventory cost as of January 1, assuming that goods are priced to provide a 24% gross profit.

7-33 Journal Entries

Coppola Company had sales of $19 million during the year. The goods cost Coppola $15 million. Give the journal entry or entries at the time of sale under the perpetual and periodic inventory systems.

7-34 Valuing Inventory and Cost of Goods Sold

Aberdeen Metals Ltd. had the following inventory transactions during the month of March:

3/1 beginning inventory	4,000 units @ £2.00	£8,000
Week 1, purchases	2,000 units @ £2.10	4,200
Week 2, purchases	2,000 units @ £2.20	4,400
Week 3, purchases	1,000 units @ £2.30	2,300
Week 4, purchases	1,000 units @ £2.50	2,500

On March 31, a count of the ending inventory was completed, and 5,500 units were on hand. By using the periodic inventory system, calculate the cost of goods sold and ending inventory using LIFO, FIFO, and weighted-average inventory methods.

7-35 Entries for Purchase Transactions

The Schubert Company is a Swiss wholesaler of office supplies. Its unit of currency is the Swiss franc (CHF). Schubert uses a periodic inventory system. Prepare journal entries for the following summarized transactions (omit explanations):

Aug. 2   Purchased merchandise on account, CHF 350,000, terms 2/10, n/45.
Aug. 3   Paid cash for freight in, CHF 15,000.
Aug. 7   Schubert complained about some defects in the merchandise acquired on August 2. The supplier hand-delivered a credit memo granting an allowance of CHF 30,000.
Aug. 11   Cash disbursement to settle purchase of August 2.

7-36 Cost of Inventory Acquired

On July 5, Feltham Company purchased on account a shipment of sheet steel from Northwest Steel Co. The invoice price was $200,000, F.O.B. shipping point. Shipping cost from the steel mill to Feltham's plant was $10,000. When inspecting the shipment, the Feltham receiving clerk found several flaws in the steel. The clerk informed Northwest's sales representative of the flaws, and after some negotiation, Northwest granted an allowance of $15,000.

To encourage prompt payment, Northwest grants a 2% cash discount to customers who pay their accounts within 30 days of billing. Feltham paid the proper amount on August 1.

1. Compute the total cost of the sheet steel acquired.
2. Prepare the journal entries for the transaction. Omit explanations.

7-37 Entries for Periodic and Perpetual Systems

Rajiv Co. had an inventory of $110,000, December 31, 20X7. Data for 20X8 follow:

Gross purchases	$960,000
Cost of goods sold	890,000
Inventory, December 31, 20X8	100,000
Purchase returns and allowances	80,000

By using the data, prepare comparative journal entries, including closing entries, for both a perpetual and a periodic inventory system.

7-38 Entries for Purchase Transactions

Equatorial Imports uses a periodic inventory system. Prepare journal entries for the following summarized transactions for 20X1 (omit explanations). For simplicity, assume the beginning and ending balances in accounts payable were zero.

1. Purchases (all using trade credit), $880,000.
2. Purchase returns and allowances, $50,000.
3. Freight in, $74,000 paid in cash.
4. Payment for all credit purchases, less returns and allowances and cash discounts on purchases of $18,000.

7-39 Journal Entries, Periodic Inventory System

Refer to the data in the preceding problem. Inventories were December 31, 20X0, $71,000 and December 31, 20X1, $120,000. Sales were $1,250,000. Prepare summary journal entries for 20X1 for sales and cost of goods sold. Omit explanations.

7-40 Journal Entries, Periodic Inventory System

Consider the following data taken from the adjusted trial balance of the Vancouver Boat Company, December 31, 20X3 ($ in millions):

Purchases	$130	Sales	239
Sales returns		Purchase returns and	
and allowances	5	allowances	6
Freight in	14		
Cash discounts		Cash discounts	
on purchases	1	on sales	8
Inventory (beginning			
of year)	25	Other expenses	80

Prepare summary journal entries. The ending inventory was $45 million.

7-41 Reconstruction of Transaction

Apple Computer, Inc. produces the well-known Macintosh computer. Consider the following account balances ($ in millions):

	September 27, 2003	September 28, 2002
Inventories	$56	$45

The cost of the inventories purchased (or produced) during the 12 months between September 28, 2002 and September 27, 2003 was $4,510,000,000. The income statement for the 2003 fiscal year had an item "cost of sales." Compute its amount.

7-42 Reconstruction of Records

An earthquake caused heavy damage to the Eurasia Antique Store on May 3, 20X8. All merchandise was destroyed. Some accounting data are missing. In conjunction with an insurance investigation, you have been asked to estimate the cost of the inventory destroyed. The following data for 20X8 before the earthquake are available:

Cash discounts on purchases	$ 2,000	Inventory, December 31, 20X7	$ 38,000
Gross sales	280,000	Purchase returns and allowances	8,000
Sales returns and allowances	24,000	Inward transportation	4,000
Gross purchases	160,000	Gross profit percentage on net sales	45%

7-43 Cost of Inventory Destroyed by Fire

Lin Company's insurance agent requires an estimate of the cost of merchandise lost by fire on March 9. Merchandise inventory on January 1 was $65,000. Purchases since January 1 were $195,000; freight in, $15,000; purchase returns and allowances, $10,000. Sales are made at a gross margin of 20% of sales and totaled $200,000 up to March 9. What was the cost of the merchandise destroyed?

7-44 Inventory Shortage

An accounting clerk of the Plumlee Company absconded with cash and a truck full of electronic merchandise on May 14, 20X4. The following data have been compiled for 20X4:

Beginning inventory, January 1	$ 55,000
Sales to May 14, 20X4	280,000
Average gross profit rate	25%
Purchases to May 14, 20X4	200,000

Compute the estimated cost of the missing merchandise.

7-45 Inventory Errors

At the end of his first business year, Clifford Reyna counted and priced the inventory. A few very high-value items were hidden in a dark corner of the storage shelves and Clifford understated his 20X5 ending inventory by $20,000. His business financial statements and his tax return were affected. Assume a 40% tax rate.

1. Calculate the effect on taxable income, taxes, net income, and retained earnings for 20X5.
2. Repeat requirement 1 for 20X6, assuming the 20X6 ending inventory is correctly calculated.

7-46 Decision about Pricing

Custom Gems, Inc., a retail jewelry store, had gross profits of $1,320,000 on sales of $2,400,000 in 20X3. Average inventory was $1,080,000.

1. Compute inventory turnover.
2. Jerry Siegl, owner of Custom Gems, is considering whether to become a "discount" jeweler. For example, Jerry believes that a cut of 20% in average selling prices would increase inventory turnover in 20X4 to 1.5 times per year. Beginning and ending inventory would be unchanged. Suppose Jerry's beliefs are valid. What would his new gross profit percentage be? Would the total gross profit in 20X4 have improved? Show computations.

7-47 LIFO and FIFO

The inventory of the Shenandoah Gravel Company on June 30 shows 1,000 tons at $9 per ton. A physical inventory on July 31 shows a total of 1,100 tons on hand. Revenue from sales of gravel for July totals $102,000. The following purchases were made during July:

July 8	5,000 tons @ $10 per ton
July 13	1,000 tons @ $11 per ton
July 22	900 tons @ $12 per ton

1. Compute the inventory cost as of July 31 using (a) LIFO and (b) FIFO.
2. Compute the gross profit using each method.

7-48 Lower-of-Cost-or-Market

(Alternate is 7-74.) Fujita Company uses the inventory method "cost or market, whichever is lower." There were no sales or purchases during the periods indicated, although selling prices generally fluctuated in the same directions as replacement costs. Fujita makes adjustments for LCM each quarter. At what amount would you value merchandise on the dates that follow?

	Invoice Cost	Replacement Cost
December 31, 20X1	$200,000	$185,000
April 30, 20X2	200,000	190,000
August 31, 20X2	200,000	220,000
December 31, 20X2	200,000	180,000

7-49 Reconstruction of Transactions

Consider the following account balances of Costco Wholesale Corporation, the Seattle-based warehouse store operator ($ in millions):

	August 31 2003	September 1 2002
Merchandise inventories	$3,339	$3,127

On Costco's income statement for the fiscal year 2003, the cost of the merchandise sold was $37,325 million. Compute the net cost of the acquisition of inventory for the fiscal year ending August 31, 2003.

7-50 Gross Profit Percentage

Toys "Я" Us operates more than 1,500 stores in the United States and abroad. Like most retailers, the managers of Toys "Я" Us monitor the company's gross margin percentage. The following information is from the company's income statement (in millions):

	For the Year Ended		
	February 1, 2003	February 2, 2002	February 3, 2001
Sales	$11,305	$11,019	$11,332
Cost of sales	7,799	7,604	7,815

Compute the gross profit percentage for each of the 3 years. Comment on the changes in gross profit percentage.

7-51 Profitability and Turnover

Island Building Supply began 20X1 with inventory of $240,000. Island's 20X1 sales were $1,200,000, purchases of inventory totaled $1,035,000, and ending inventory was $330,000.

1. Prepare a statement of gross profit for 20X1.
2. What was Island Building Supply's inventory turnover?

Problems

7-52 Detailed Income Statement

(Alternate is 7-55.) Following are accounts taken from the adjusted trial balance of the Backbay Bathroom Supply Company, December 31, 20X5. The company uses the periodic inventory system.

Sales salaries and commissions	$160	Freight in	$ 50
Inventory, December 31, 20X4	200	Miscellaneous expenses	13
Allowance for bad debts	14	Sales	1,091
Rent expense, office space	10	Bad debts expense	8
Gross purchases	600	Cash discounts on purchases	15
Depreciation expense, office equipment	3	Inventory, December 31, 20X5	300
Cash discounts on sales	16	Office salaries	46
Advertising expense	45	Rent expense, selling space	90
Purchase returns and allowances	40	Income tax expense	42
Delivery expense	20	Sales returns and allowances	50
		Office supplies used	6
		Depreciation expenses, trucks, and store fixtures	29

Prepare a detailed income statement for 20X5. All amounts are in thousands.

7-53 Perpetual Inventory Calculations

Kennedy Electric is a wholesaler for commercial builders. The company uses a perpetual inventory system and a FIFO cost-flow assumption. The data concerning Kennedy Electric for the year 20X8 follows:

	Purchased	Sold	Balance
December 31, 20X7			120 @ $5 = $600
February 10, 20X8	80 @ $6 = $ 480		
April 14		60	
May 9	110 @ $7 = $ 770		
July 14		120	
October 21	100 @ $8 = $ 800		
November 12		75	
Total	290 $2,050	255	

Calculate the ending inventory balance in units and dollars.

7-54 Gross Profit and Turnover

Retailers closely watch a number of financial ratios, including the gross profit (gross margin) percentage and inventory turnover. Suppose the results for the furniture department in a large store in a given year were:

Sales	$4,000,000
Cost of goods sold	2,400,000
Gross profit	$1,600,000
Beginning inventory	$ 850,000
Ending inventory	750,000

1. Compute the gross profit percentage and the inventory turnover.
2. Suppose the retailer is able to maintain a reduced inventory of $600,000 throughout the succeeding year. What inventory turnover would have to be obtained to achieve the same $1,600,000 gross profit? Assume that the gross profit percentage is unchanged.
3. Suppose the retailer maintains inventory at the $600,000 level throughout the succeeding year, but cannot increase the inventory turnover from the level in requirement 1. What gross profit percentage would have to be obtained to achieve the same total gross profit?
4. Suppose the average inventory of $800,000 is maintained. Compute the total gross profit in the succeeding year if there is:
   a. A 10% increase of the gross profit percentage, that is, 10% of the percentage, not an additional 10 percentage points, and a 10% decrease of the inventory turnover.
   b. A 10% decrease of the gross profit percentage and a 10% increase of the inventory turnover.
5. Why do retailers find the preceding types of ratios helpful?

7-55 Detailed Income Statement

(Alternate is 7-52.) Sears, Roebuck & Company is a major retailer. The company's annual report contained the following actual data for the year ended December 31, 2002 ($ in millions):

Net revenues	$41,366
Cost of sales	25,646
Selling and administrative	9,249
Provision for uncollectible accounts	2,261
Depreciation	875
Other operating expenses	111
Interest expense (net)	1,143
Other income, net	372
Income before income taxes	$2,453

The balance sheets included the following actual data ($ in millions of dollars):

	December 31	
	2002	**2001**
Allowance for doubtful accounts	$ 1,836	$ 1,166
Inventories	5,115	4,912

Consider the following additional assumed data ($ in millions of dollars):

Gross purchases	$26,124	Freight in	$1,100
Cash discounts on sales	850	Sales returns and allowances	2,100
Purchase returns and allowances	1,200	Cash discounts on purchases	180

Prepare a detailed multistep income statement that ends with profit (or loss) before tax.

7-56 Comparison of Inventory Methods

(Alternates are 7-67 and 7-69.) Contractor Supply Company is a wholesaler for commercial builders. The company uses a periodic inventory system. The data concerning Kemtone cooktops for the year 20X8 follow:

	Purchases	Sold	Balance
December 31, 20X7			110 @ $50 = $5,500
February 10, 20X8	80 @ $60 = $ 4,800		
April 14		60	
May 9	120 @ $70 = $ 8,400		
July 14		120	
October 21	100 @ $80 = $ 8,000		
November 12		80	
Total	300 $21,200	260	
December 31, 20X8			150 @ ?

The sales during 20X8 were made at the following selling prices:

60 @ $ 90 =	$ 5,400
120 @ 100 =	12,000
80 @ 110 =	8,800
260	$26,200

1. Prepare a comparative statement of gross profit for the year ended December 31, 20X8, using FIFO, LIFO, and weighted-average inventory methods.
2. By how much would income taxes differ if Contractor Supply Company had used LIFO instead of FIFO for Kemtone cooktops? Assume a 40% income tax rate.

7-57 Effects of Late Purchases

(Alternates are 7-68 and 7-70.) Refer to the preceding problem. Suppose 100 extra units had been acquired on December 30, 20X8 for $80 each, a total of $8,000. How would net income and income taxes have been affected under FIFO and under LIFO? Show a tabulated comparison.

7-58 LIFO, FIFO, and Lower-of-Cost-or-Market

Altobelli Company began business on March 15, 20X0. The following are Altobelli's purchases of inventory.

March 17	100 units @ $10	$1,000
April 19	50 units @ $12	600
May 14	100 units @ $13	1,300
Total		$2,900

On May 25, the company sold 130 units, leaving inventory of 120 units. Altobelli Company's accountant was preparing a balance sheet for June 1, at which time the replacement cost of the inventory was $12 per unit.

1. Suppose Altobelli Company uses LIFO, without applying lower-of-cost-or-market. Compute the June 1 inventory amount.
2. Suppose Altobelli Company uses lower-of-LIFO-cost-or-market. Compute the June 1 inventory amount.
3. Suppose Altobelli Company uses FIFO, without applying lower-of-cost-or-market. Compute the June 1 inventory amount.
4. Suppose Altobelli Company uses lower-of-FIFO-cost-or-market. Compute the June 1 inventory amount.

7-59 Inventory Errors

(Alternate is 7-66.) The following data are from the 20X1 income statement of the Persian Rug Emporium ($ in thousands):

Sales		$1,650
Deduct cost of goods sold		
Beginning inventory	$ 390	
Purchases	820	
Cost of goods available for sale	$1,210	
Deduct: Ending inventory	370	
Cost of goods sold		840
Gross profit		$ 810
Other expenses		610
Income before income taxes		$ 200
Income tax expense at 40%		80
Net income		$ 120

The ending inventory was overstated by $15,000 because of errors in the physical count. The income tax rate was 40% in 20X1 and 20X2.

1. Which items in the income statement are incorrect and by how much? Use O for overstated, U for understated, and N for not affected. Complete the following tabulation:

	20X1	20X2
Beginning inventory	N	O $15
Ending inventory	?	?
Cost of goods sold	?	?
Gross margin	?	?
Income before income taxes	?	?
Income tax expense	?	?
Net income	?	?

2. What is the dollar effect of the inventory error on retained earnings at the end of 20X1 and at the end of 20X2?

7-60 LIFO, FIFO, Prices Rising and Falling

The Steinberg Company has a periodic inventory system. Inventory on December 31, 20X1, consisted of 10,000 units @ $10 = $100,000. Purchases during 20X2 were 13,000 units. Sales were 12,000 units for sales revenue of $20 per unit.

1. Prepare a four-column comparative statement of gross margin for 20X2:
   a. Assume purchases were at $12 per unit. Assume FIFO and then LIFO.
   b. Assume purchases were at $8 per unit. Assume FIFO and then LIFO.

2. Assume an income tax rate of 40%. Suppose all transactions were for cash. Which inventory method in question 1a would result in more cash for Steinberg Company and by how much?
3. Repeat question 2. Which inventory method in question 1b would result in more cash for Steinberg Company and by how much?

7-61 LIFO, FIFO, Cash Effects

In 20X8, McFarland Company had sales revenue of £330,000 for a line of woolen scarves. The company uses a periodic inventory system. Pertinent data for 20X8 included:

Inventory, December 31, 20X7	14,000 units @ £6	£ 84,000
January purchases	22,000 units @ £7	154,000
July purchases	30,000 units @ £8	240,000
Sales for the year	30,000 units	

1. Prepare a statement of gross margin for 20X8. Use two columns, one assuming LIFO and one assuming FIFO.
2. Assume a 40% income tax rate. Suppose all transactions were for cash. Which inventory method would result in more cash for McFarland Company, and by how much?

7-62 FIFO and LIFO

Two companies, the Lastin Company and the Firstin Company, are in the scrap metal warehousing business as arch competitors. They are about the same size, and in 20X1, coincidentally encountered seemingly identical operating situations. Only their inventory accounting systems differed. Lastin uses LIFO, and Firstin uses FIFO.

Their beginning inventory was 10,000 tons; it cost $50 per ton. During the year, each company purchased 50,000 tons at the following prices:

- 30,000 @ $60 on March 17
- 20,000 @ $70 on October 5

Each company sold 45,000 tons at average prices of $100 per ton. Other expenses in addition to cost of goods sold, but excluding income taxes, were $600,000. The income tax rate is 40%.

1. Compute net income for the year for both companies. Show your calculations.
2. As a manager, which method would you prefer? Why? Explain fully. Include your estimate of the overall effect of these events on the cash balances of each company, assuming all transactions during 20X1 were direct receipts or disbursements of cash.

7-63 Effects of LIFO and FIFO

The Delhomme Company is starting in business on December 31, 20X0. In each half year, from 20X1 through 20X4, it expects to purchase 1,000 units and sell 500 units for the amounts listed next. In 20X5, it expects to purchase no units and sell 4,000 units for the amount indicated in the following table:

	20X1	20X2	20X3	20X4	20X5
Purchases					
First 6 months	$1,000	$2,000	$3,000	$3,000	0
Second 6 months	2,000	2,500	3,000	4,000	0
Total	$3,000	$4,500	$6,000	$7,000	0
Sales (at selling price)	$5,000	$5,000	$5,000	$5,000	$20,000

Assume that there are no costs or expenses other than those shown earlier. The tax rate is 40%, and taxes for each year are payable on December 31 of each year. Delhomme Company is trying to decide whether to use periodic FIFO or LIFO throughout the 5-year period.

1. What was net income under FIFO for each of the 5 years? under LIFO? Show calculations.
2. Explain briefly which method, LIFO or FIFO, seems more advantageous, and why.

7-64 Effects of LIFO on Purchase Decisions

The M. J. Chan Corporation is nearing the end of its first year in business. The following purchases of its single product have been made:

	Units	Unit Price	Total Cost
January	1,000	$10	$ 10,000
March	1,000	10	10,000
May	1,000	11	11,000
July	1,000	13	13,000
September	1,000	14	14,000
December	4,000	15	60,000
	9,000		$118,000

Sales for the year will be 5,000 units for $120,000. Expenses other than cost of goods sold will be $30,000.

The president is undecided about whether to adopt FIFO or LIFO for income tax purposes. The company has ample storage space for up to 7,000 units of inventory. Inventory prices are expected to stay at $15 per unit for the next few months.

1. What would be the net income before taxes, the income taxes, and the net income after taxes for the year under (a) FIFO or (b) LIFO? Income tax rates are 40%.
2. If the company sells its year-one year-end inventory in year 2 @ $24 per unit and goes out of business, what would be the net income before taxes, the income taxes, and the net income after taxes under (a) FIFO and (b) LIFO? Assume that other expenses in year two are $30,000.
3. Repeat requirements 1 and 2, assuming that the 4,000 units @ $15 purchased in December were not purchased until January of the second year. Generalize on the effect on net income of the timing of purchases under FIFO and LIFO.

7-65 Changing Quantities and LIFO Reserve
Consider the following data for the year 20X8:

	Units	Unit Cost
Beginning inventory	2	*
Purchases	3	24
	3	28
Ending inventory	2	†

*FIFO, $20; LIFO, $16.
†To be computed.

1. Prepare a comparative table computing the cost of goods sold, using columns for FIFO and LIFO. In a final column, show (a) the difference between FIFO and LIFO inventories (the LIFO reserve) at the beginning of the year and at the end of the year, and (b) how the change in this amount explains the difference in cost of goods sold.
2. Repeat requirement 1, except assume that the ending inventory consisted of (a) four units, (b) zero units.
3. In your own words, explain why, for a given year, the increase in the LIFO reserve measures the amount by which cost of goods sold is higher under LIFO than FIFO.

7-66 Inventory Errors, 3 Years
(Alternate is 7-59.) The Collins Company had the data at the top of p. 325 for three successive years ($ in millions). In early 20X4, a team of internal auditors discovered that the ending inventory for 20X1 had been overstated by $10 million. Furthermore, the ending inventory for 20X3 had been understated by $5 million. The ending inventory for December 31, 20X2, was correct.

1. Which items in the income statement are incorrect and by how much? Prepare a tabulation covering each of the 3 years.
2. Is the amount of retained earnings correct at the end of 20X1, 20X2, and 20X3? If it is erroneous, indicate the amount and whether it is overstated (O) or understated (U).

	20X3	20X2	20X1
Sales	$200	$160	$170
Deduct: Cost of goods sold			
Beginning inventory	15	25	40
Purchases	135	100	90
Cost of goods available for sale	150	125	130
Ending inventory	30	15	25
Cost of goods sold	120	110	105
Gross profit	80	50	65
Other expenses	70	30	30
Income before income taxes	10	20	35
Income tax expense at 40%	4	8	14
Net income	$ 6	$ 12	$ 21

7-67 Comparison of Inventory Methods

(Alternates are 7-56 and 7-69.) Dell Computer Company produces computers. The following data and descriptions are from the company's annual report ($ in millions):

	January 31	February 1
	2003	**2002**
Inventories	$306	$278

Assume that Dell uses the periodic inventory system. Suppose a division of Dell had the accompanying data concerning the purchase and resale of computers ($ are not in millions):

	Units	Total
Inventory (February 1, 2002)	100	$ 40,000
Purchase (February 20, 2002)	200	100,000
Sales, March 17, 2002 (at $900 per unit)	150	
Purchase (June 25, 2002)	160	96,000
Sales, November 7, 2002 (at $1,000 per unit)	160	

1. For these computers only, prepare a tabulation of the cost of goods sold section of the income statement for the year ended January 31, 2003. Support your computations. Show your tabulation for four different inventory methods: (a) FIFO, (b) LIFO, (c) weighted-average, and (d) specific identification. For requirement d, assume that the purchase of February 20 was identified with the sale of March 17. Also assume that the purchase of June 25 was identified with the sale of November 7.
2. By how much would income taxes differ if Dell used (a) LIFO instead of FIFO for this inventory item and (b) LIFO instead of weighted-average? Assume a 40% tax rate.

7-68 Effects of Late Purchases

(Alternates are 7-57 and 7-70.) Refer to the preceding problem. Suppose the Dell division acquired 60 extra computers @ $700 each on January 30, 2003, a total of $42,000. How would gross profit and income taxes be affected under FIFO—that is, compare FIFO results before and after the purchase of 60 extra computers—and under LIFO—that is, compare LIFO results before and after the purchase of 60 extra computers. Show computations and explain.

7-69 Comparison of Inventory Methods

(Alternates are 7-56 and 7-67.) Texas Instruments is a major producer of semiconductors and other electrical and electronic products. Semiconductors are especially vulnerable to price fluctuations. The following are from the company's annual report ($ in millions):

	December 31	
	2002	**2001**
Inventories	$790	$751

Texas Instruments uses a variety of inventory methods, but for this problem assume it uses only FIFO.

Net revenues for the fiscal year ended December 31, 2002, were $8,383 million. Cost of revenues was $5,313 million.

Assume Texas Instruments had the accompanying data concerning one of its semiconductors. Assume a periodic inventory system.

	In	Out	Balance
December 31, 2001			80 @ $5 = 400
February 25, 2002	50 @ $6 = $ 300		
March 29		60*	
May 28	80 @ $7 = $ 560		
June 7		90*	
November 20	90 @ $8 = $ 720		
December 15		50*	
Total	220 $1,580	200	
December 31, 2002			100 @ ?

*Selling prices were $10, $12, and $14, respectively.

	60 @ $10 = $ 600
	90 @ 12 = 1,080
	50 @ 14 = 700
Total sales	200 $2,380

Summary of costs to account for:

Beginning inventory	$ 400
Purchases	1,580
Cost of goods available for sale	$1,980
Other expenses for this product	$ 600
Income tax rate, 40%	

1. Prepare a comparative income statement for the 2002 fiscal year for the product in question. Use the FIFO, LIFO, and weighted-average inventory methods.
2. By how much would income taxes have differed if Texas Instruments had used LIFO instead of FIFO for this product?
3. Suppose Texas Instruments had used the specific identification method. Compute the gross margin (or gross profit) if the ending inventory had consisted of (a) 90 units @ $8 and 10 units @ $7; and (b) 60 units @ $5 and 40 units @ $8.

7-70 Effects of Late Purchases

(Alternates are 7-57 and 7-68.) Refer to the preceding problem. Suppose Texas Instruments had acquired 50 extra units @ $8 each on December 30, 2002, a total of $400. How would income before income taxes have been affected under FIFO? That is, compare FIFO results before and after the purchase of 50 extra units. Under LIFO? That is, compare LIFO results before and after the purchase of 50 extra units. Show computations and explain.

7-71 Classic Switch from LIFO to FIFO

Effective January 1, 1970, Chrysler Corporation adopted the FIFO method for inventories previously valued by the LIFO method. The 1970 annual report stated: "This . . . makes the financial statements with respect to inventory valuation comparable with those of the other United States automobile manufacturers."

The Wall Street Journal reported:

> The change improved Chrysler's 1970 financial results several ways. Besides narrowing the 1970 loss by $20 million it improved Chrysler's working capital. The change also made the comparison with 1969 earnings look somewhat more favorable because, upon restatement, Chrysler's 1969 profit was raised by only $10.2 million from the original figures.

Finally, the change helped Chrysler's balance sheet by boosting inventories, and thus current assets, by $150 million at the end of 1970 over what they would have been under LIFO. As Chrysler's profit has collapsed over the last two years and its financial position tightened, auto analysts have eyed warily Chrysler's shrinking ratio of current assets to current liabilities.

To get the improvements in its balance sheet and results, however, Chrysler paid a price. Roger Helder, vice president and comptroller, said Chrysler owed the government $53 million in tax savings it accumulated by using the LIFO method since it switched from FIFO in 1957. The major advantage of LIFO is that it holds down profit and thus tax liabilities. The other three major auto makers stayed on the FIFO method. Mr. Helder said Chrysler now has to pay back that $53 million to the government over 20 years, which will boost Chrysler's tax bills about $3 million a year.

Given the content of this chapter, do you think the Chrysler decision to switch from LIFO to FIFO was beneficial to its stockholders? Explain, being as specific as you can.

7-72 LIFO, FIFO, Purchase Decisions, and Earnings per Share

Iowa Seed Corn Supplies, a company with 100,000 shares of common stock outstanding, had the following transactions during 20X1, its first year in business:

Sales	1,100,000 pounds @ $5
Purchases	900,000 pounds @ $2
	300,000 pounds @ $3

The current income tax rate is a flat 50%; the rate next year is expected to be 40%.

It is December 20 and Lane Braxton, the president, is trying to decide whether to buy the 400,000 pounds he needs for inventory now or early next year. The current price is $4 per unit. Prices on inventory are expected to remain stable; in any event, no decline in prices is anticipated.

Braxton has not chosen an inventory method as yet, but will pick either LIFO or FIFO. Other expenses for the year will be $1.4 million.

1. By using LIFO, prepare a comparative income statement assuming the 400,000 pounds (a) are not purchased and (b) are purchased. The statement should end with reported earnings per share.
2. Repeat requirement 1, using FIFO.
3. Comment on the preceding results. Which method should Braxton choose? Why? Be specific.
4. Suppose that in year two the tax rate drops to 40%, prices remain stable, 1.1 million pounds are sold @ $5, enough pounds are purchased at $4 so the ending inventory will be 700,000 pounds, and other expenses are reduced to $800,000.
   a. Prepare a comparative income statement for the second year showing the impact of each of the four alternatives on net income and earnings per share for the second year.
   b. Explain any differences in net income that you encounter among the four alternatives.
   c. Why is there a difference in ending inventory values under LIFO, even though the same amount of physical inventory is in stock?
   d. What is the total cash outflow for income taxes for the 2 years together under the four alternatives?
   e. Would you change your answer in requirement 3 now that you have completed requirement 4? Why?

7-73 Eroding the LIFO Base

Many companies on LIFO are occasionally faced with strikes or material shortages that necessitate a reduction in their normal inventory levels to satisfy current sales demands. A few years ago, several large steel companies requested special legislative relief from the additional taxes that ensued from such events.

A news story stated:

As steelworkers slowly streamed back to the mills this week, most steel companies began adding up the tremendous losses imposed by the longest strike in history. At a significant number of plants across the country, however, the worry wasn't losses but profits—"windfall" bookkeeping profits that for some companies may mean painful increases in corporate income taxes.

These outfits have been caught in the backfire of a special mechanism for figuring up inventory costs on tax returns. It's known to accountants as LIFO, or last in, first out. Ironically, it's designed to slice the corporate tax bill in a time of rising prices.

Biggest Bite—Most of the big steel companies—16 out of the top 20—as well as 40 percent of all steel warehousers, use LIFO accounting in figuring their taxes. But the tax squeeze from paper LIFO profits won't affect them all equally. It will put the biggest bite on warehousers that kept going during the strike—and as a result, the American Steel Warehouse Assn. may ask Congress for a special tax exemption on these paper profits. . . .

Companies such as Ryerson and Castle have been caught because they have had to strip their shelves bare in order to satisfy customer demands during the strike. And they probably won't be able to rebuild their stocks by the time they close their books for tax purposes.

To see how this situation can happen, consider the following example. Suppose a company adopted LIFO in 1976. At December 31, 2003, its LIFO inventory consisted of three "layers":

From 1976	110,000 units @ $1.00	$110,000
From 1977	50,000 units @ 1.10	55,000
From 1978	30,000 units @ 1.20	36,000
		$201,000

In 2004, prices rose enormously. Data follow:

Sales	500,000 units @ $3.00 =	$1,500,000
Purchases	340,000 units @ $2.00 =	$ 680,000
Operating expenses		$ 500,000

A prolonged strike near the end of the year resulted in a severe depletion of the normal inventory stock of 190,000 units. The strike was settled on December 28, 2004. The company intended to replenish the inventory as soon as possible. The applicable income tax rate is 60%.

1. Compute the income taxes for 2004.
2. Suppose the company had been able to meet the 500,000-unit demand out of current purchases. Compute the income taxes for 2004 under those circumstances.

7-74 Lower-of-Cost-or-Market

(Alternate is 7-48.) **Eastman Kodak Company**'s annual report stated: "Inventories are stated at the lower of cost or market. The cost of most inventories in the U.S. is determined by the last-in, first-out (LIFO) method." Assume severe price competition in 2003 necessitated a write-down on December 31 for a class of camera inventories with a LIFO cost of $13 million. The appropriate valuation at market was deemed to be $8 million.

1. Assume sales of this line of camera for 2003 were $20 million, and cost of goods sold was $14 million, and that the product line was terminated in early 2004 and the remaining inventory was sold for $8 million. Prepare a statement of gross margin for 2003 and 2004. Show the results under a strict LIFO cost method in the first two columns and under a lower-of-LIFO-cost-or-market method in the next two columns.
2. Assume Kodak did not discontinue the product line. Instead, a new marketing campaign spurred market demand. Replacement cost of the cameras in the December 31 inventory was $9 million on January 31, 2004. What inventory valuation would be appropriate on January 31, 2004 if Kodak still holds the inventory it held on December 31, 2003?

7-75 LIFO Liquidation

Maytag Corporation reported 2002 pretax operating income of $359.495 million. Footnotes to Maytag's financial statements read: "Inventories are stated at the lower of cost or market. Inventory costs are primarily determined by the last-in, first-out (LIFO) method." The footnote showed that if the FIFO method of inventory accounting, which approximates current cost, had been used for all inventories, they would have been $86.094 million and $83.829 million higher than reported at December 31, 2002 and 2001, respectively.

1. Calculate the 2002 pretax income that Maytag would have reported if the FIFO inventory method had been used.
2. Suppose Maytag's income tax rate is 34%. What were Maytag's income taxes using LIFO? What would they have been if Maytag had used FIFO?
3. Was Maytag's use of LIFO a good choice from a tax perspective? What is the cumulative financial effect of the choice?

7-76 LIFO Reserve

Brunswick Corporation reported LIFO inventories of $546.9 million on January 1, 2003. A footnote to the financial statements indicated that the "LIFO cost was $85.7 million lower than the FIFO cost of inventories."

1. Has the cost of Brunswick's inventory generally been increasing or decreasing? Explain.
2. Suppose Brunswick sold its entire inventory for $700 million the subsequent year and did not replace it. Compute the gross profit from the sale of this inventory (a) as Brunswick would report it using LIFO and (b) as it would have been reported if Brunswick had always used FIFO instead of LIFO. Which inventory method creates higher gross profit? Explain.

7-77 Inventory Errors

IBM had inventories of $3.1 billion at December 31, 2002, and $4.3 billion a year earlier.

1. Suppose the beginning inventory for fiscal 2002 had been overstated by $10 million because of errors in physical counts. Which items in the financial statements would be incorrect and by how much? Use O for overstated, U for understated, and N for not affected. Assume a 40% tax rate.

	Effect on Fiscal Year	
	2002	2001
Beginning inventory	O by $30	N
Ending inventory	?	?
Cost of sales	?	?
Gross profit	?	?
Income before taxes on income	?	?
Taxes on income	?	?
Net income	?	?

2. What is the dollar effect of the inventory error on retained earnings at the end of fiscal 2002 and 2001?

7-78 LIFO Liquidation

Lancaster Colony Corporation produces specialty foods under the Marzetti label, candles labeled Candle-lite, and glass called Indiana Glass, as well as other products. The company's 2003 pretax income was $180.8 million. It reported the following inventories:

	Inventories	
(in millions)	2003	2002
Finished goods and work in process	$116.4	$104.6
Raw materials and supplies	43.0	43.7
Inventories, at LIFO cost	159.4	148.3
Excess of FIFO over LIFO cost	7.4	14.5
Total inventories at FIFO	$166.8	$162.8

In 2003 and 2002, inventory quantities were reduced, resulting in liquidations of LIFO inventory quantities carried at the lower costs prevailing in prior years. The effects of these liquidations increased pretax income by $7.1 million in 2003 and $3.3 million in 2002.

1. What would Lancaster Colony's pretax income have been in 2003 if they had purchased enough inventory to avoid liquidating any LIFO inventory layers?
2. What would Lancaster Colony have reported as pretax income for 2003 had they used FIFO to account for all their inventories?
3. How does the change in the LIFO reserve relate to the effect of the LIFO liquidation?

7-79 Year-End Purchases and LIFO

A company engaged in the manufacture and sale of dental supplies maintained an inventory of gold for use in its business. The company used LIFO for the gold content of its products.

On the final day of its fiscal year, the company bought 10,000 ounces of gold at $380 per ounce. Had the purchase not been made, the company would have penetrated its LIFO layers for 8,000 ounces of gold acquired at $250 per ounce.

The applicable income tax rate is 40%.

1. Compute the effect of the year-end purchase on the income taxes of the fiscal year.
2. On the second day of the next fiscal year, the company resold the 10,000 ounces of gold to its suppliers. What do you think the IRS should do if it discovers this resale? Explain.

7-80 Comparison of Gross Profit Percentages and Inventory Turnover

JCPenney and Kmart are competitors in the retail business, although they target slightly different markets. The gross margin for each company and average inventory follow for the indicated years (both have January year-ends; 2003 refers to the year ending in January of 2003).

JCPenney

	2003	2000	1995
	(in millions)		
Retail sales	$32,347	$32,510	$20,380
Cost of goods sold*	22,573	23,374	13,970
Gross profit	9,774	9,136	6,410
Average inventory	4,938	6,004	3,711

Kmart

	2003	2000	1995
	(in millions)		
Retail sales	30,762	$35,925	$34,025
Cost of goods sold*	26,258	28,102	25,992
Gross profit	4,504	7,823	8,033
Average inventory	5,311	6,819	7,317

*Both companies classify costs of occupancy, buying, and warehousing with cost of goods sold.

Calculate gross profit percentages and inventory turnovers for 2003, 2000, and 1995 for each company and compare them. What trends do you observe? Which company appears to perform better? To what extent do their different performances seem to relate to their relative positions in the retail market?

7-81 Gross Profit on Korean Income Statement

Samsung, the huge Korean conglomerate, had the following results in 2002 and 2003 (in billions of Korean won, KRW).

	2003	2002
Net sales	KRW59,569	KRW46,444
Cost of goods sold	36,952	32,657
Average inventory	3,954	3,611

Compute the gross profit, gross profit percentage, and inventory turnover for Samsung in 2002 and 2003. Comment on the change in gross profit percentage between 2002 and 2003.

7-82 LIFO and Ethical Issues

Yokohama Company is a wholesaler of musical instruments in San Francisco. Yokohama has used the LIFO inventory method since 1971. Near the end of 2004, the company's inventory of a particular instrument listed three LIFO layers, two of which were from earlier years and one from 2004 purchases:

	No. of Units	Unit Cost
Layer one	4,000	$40
Layer two	2,500	50
2004 Purchases	30,000	60
Total available	36,500	

In 2004, Yokohama sold 32,500 units, leaving 4,000 units in inventory.

On December 27, 2004, Yokohama had a chance to buy a minimum of 15,000 units of the instrument at a unit cost of $70. The offer was good for 10 days, and delivery would be immediate on placing the order.

Helen Yamaguchi, chief purchasing manager of Yokohama, was trying to decide whether to make the purchase and, if it is made, whether to make it in 2004 or 2005. The controller had told her that she should buy immediately because the company would save almost $80,000 in taxes. The combined federal and state income tax rate is 45%.

1. Explain why nearly $80,000 of taxes would be saved.
2. Are there any ethical considerations that would influence this decision? Explain.

7-83 Inventory Shrinkage

Lola, owner of Park Hardware Company, was concerned about her control of inventory. In December 20X7, she installed a computerized perpetual inventory system. In April, her accountant brought her the following information for the first 3 months of 20X8:

Sales	$700,000
Cost of goods sold	590,000
Beginning inventory (per physical count)	135,000
Merchandise purchases	630,000

Lola had asked her public accounting firm to conduct a physical count of inventory on April 1. The CPAs reported inventory of $140,000.

1. Compute the ending inventory shown in the books by the new perpetual inventory system.
2. Provide the journal entry to reconcile the book inventory with the physical count. What is the corrected cost of goods sold for the first 3 months of 20X8?
3. Do your calculations point out areas about which Lola should be concerned? Why?

7-84 Cheating on Inventories

The Wall Street Journal reported: "Cheating on inventories is a common way for small businesses to chisel on their income taxes. . . . A New York garment maker, for example, evades a sizable amount of income tax by undervaluing his firm's inventory by 20% on his tax return. He hides about $500,000 out of a $2.5 million inventory."

The news story concluded: "When it's time to borrow, business owners generally want profits and assets to look fat." The garment maker uses a different fiscal period for financial statements to his bank. "After writing down the inventory as of Dec. 31, he writes it up six months later when the fiscal year ends. In this way, he underpays the IRS and impresses his banker. Some describe that kind of inventory accounting as WIFL — Whatever I Feel Like."

1. At a 40% income tax rate, what amount of federal income taxes would the owner evade according to the news story?

2. Consider the next year. By how much would the ending inventory have to be understated to evade the same amount of income taxes?

Use the following table and fill in the blanks:

	Honest Reporting		Dishonest Reporting	
	First Year	Second Year	First Year	Second Year
Beginning inventory	$ 3,000,000	$?	$ 3,000,000	$?
Purchases	10,000,000	$10,000,000	10,000,000	10,000,000
Available for sale	13,000,000	?	13,000,000	?
Ending inventory	2,500,000	2,500,000	2,000,000	?
Cost of goods sold	$10,500,000	$?	$11,000,000	$?
Income tax savings @ 40%*	$ 4,200,000	$?	$?	$?
Income tax savings for 2 years together	$?		$?	

*This is the income tax effect of only the cost of goods sold. To shorten and simplify the analysis, sales and operating expenses are assumed to be the same each year.

7-85 Manufacturing Costs

Study Appendix 7. Sam Teasdale made custom T-shirts for himself and his friends for years before trying to treat it seriously as a business. January 1, 20X1, he decided to become more serious. He bought some screening equipment for $5,000 that he figured was good for 10,000 screenings. He decided to use units of production depreciation. He acquired 2,000 shirts for $6,000 and rented a studio for $500 per month. During the month, he paid an assistant $1,600 and together they created three designs, screened 1,500 shirts, and sold 1,200 at $9 each. At month-end, there were 500 shirts unused, 300 finished shirts ready for sale, and Sam was trying to figure out how he was doing.

1. Calculate the cost of goods sold and the value of ending inventory (including raw material and finished goods).
2. Prepare an income statement for Sam's first month of operations. Assume a 30% tax rate.

Collaborative Learning Exercise

7-86 Understanding Inventory Methods

Form groups of three students each. (If there are more than three students in a group, extras can be paired up.) Each student should select or be assigned one of these three inventory methods:

1. Specific identification
2. FIFO
3. LIFO

Consider the following information from the annual report of Levitz Corporation, one of the largest specialty retailers of furniture in the United States that filed for bankruptcy in 1997. Hence, no updated financial results are available, although the company continues to do business. Levitz uses the LIFO method to account for its inventories ($ amounts are in thousands).

For the year ended March 31, 1997	
Sales	$966,855
Cost of goods sold (using LIFO)	533,555
Other operating expenses	417,283
Operating income	$ 16,017
Purchases of inventory	$562,125
At March 31, 1997	
Inventories @ LIFO	$169,488
Inventories @ FIFO	180,688
At March 31, 1996	
Inventories @ LIFO	$140,918
Inventories @ FIFO	151,918

Assume that Levitz had exactly the same physical sales in fiscal 1998 as in fiscal 1997, but prices were 5% higher. Thus, fiscal 1998 sales were 1.05 × $966,855 = $1,015,198. Assume that other operating expenses in fiscal 1998 were exactly the same as in fiscal 1997. Further assume Levitz bought just enough inventory in fiscal 1998 to replace what the company sold, but because of a 5% price increase on April 1, purchases of inventories in fiscal 1998 were $560,233. (Note that if there had been no price increase, the purchases of inventories would have equaled last year's cost of goods sold, $533,555.) FIFO inventory on March 31, 1998, was $181,088.

1. Compute operating income for Levitz for the year ended March 31, 1998, using the inventory method to which you were assigned. Those using the LIFO and FIFO methods have all the information needed for the calculations. Those using specific identification must make some assumptions, and their operating income numbers will depend on the assumptions made.
2. Explain to the other members of the group how you computed the operating income, including an explanation of how you chose the assumptions you made.

Analyzing and Interpreting Financial Statement

7-87 Financial Reporting Research

Select an industry and identify two firms within that industry.

1. Identify the inventory accounting method used by each.
2. Calculate gross profit percentages and inventory turnovers for 2 years for each firm. Comment on the comparison and any trends.

7-88 Analyzing Starbucks' Financial Statements

Refer to the financial statements for Starbucks in Appendix A. Assume that Starbucks uses the periodic inventory procedure.

1. Compute the amount of merchandise inventory purchased during the year ended September 28, 2003. (Hint: Use the inventory T-account.) Assume that 80% of the costs listed under "Cost of sales including occupancy costs" are cost of sales. The other 20% are occupancy costs.
2. Compute the inventory turnover for Starbucks for the year ended September 28, 2003.
3. Calculate the gross margin percentage for each of the last 3 years. Comment on any changes.

7-89 Analyzing Financial Statements Using the Internet: Deckers Outdoor Corporation

Go to Deckers Outdoor Corporation's latest annual report information on its Web site. Deckers Outdoor Corporation is the exclusive licensee for the manufacture of Teva footwear. Use the latest 10K filing to find financial report data.

Answer the following questions about Deckers:

1. Under Item 6, what percentage of revenues does Teva represent? Have revenues related to Teva products increased or decreased over the past few years?
2. Read the Summary of Significant Accounting Policies section of the Notes to Consolidated Financial Statements. How are inventories valued and accounted for? Why do you think the company uses this particular costing method?
3. Locate the income statement. How much gross profit is reported for the most recent year? Has this amount increased or decreased compared with the previous year? What explanation does management give for the changes? (Hint: Look in the Management's Discussion and Analysis section.)

Long-Lived Assets and Depreciation

CHAPTER 8

LEARNING OBJECTIVES

After studying this chapter, you should be able to:

1. Distinguish a company's expenses from expenditures that it should capitalize.

2. Measure the acquisition cost of tangible assets such as land, buildings, and equipment.

3. Compute depreciation for buildings and equipment using various depreciation methods.

4. Recalculate depreciation in response to a change in estimated useful life or residual value.

5. Differentiate financial statement depreciation from income tax depreciation.

6. Explain the effect of depreciation on cash flow.

7. Account for expenditures after acquisition.

8. Compute gains and losses on the disposal of fixed assets and consider the impact of these gains and losses on the statement of cash flows.

9. Account for the impairment of tangible assets.

10. Account for various intangible assets.

11. Explain the reporting for goodwill.

12. Interpret the depletion of natural resources.

www.prenhall.com/horngren

It was the late 1960s, and Don Fisher, similar to most people of his generation, liked blue jeans and music. Also, similar to many of his peers, he was annoyed that existing clothing stores had disorganized and poorly stocked jeans departments, so he decided to do something about it. He opened a store that sold only blue jeans and music, and called it "Gap" in reference to the generation gap that was the buzz of the times.

That was 1969. As of fiscal year 2002, which ended February 1, 2003, Gap Inc. operated 4,252 stores, including Gap, Banana Republic, and Old Navy locations. Growth slowed during fiscal 2002, with the opening of only 81 new stores, compared with more than 500 per year in the prior 2 years. Gap leases most of these stores, but it still must make a tremendous investment in long-lived assets such as shelves and fixtures to operate each location. For example, the balance sheet asset category for Property and Equipment lists leasehold improvements, which are long-term investments to improve leased facilities, totaling $2.2 billion and furniture and equipment totaling $3.4 billion. During fiscal 2002 Gap spent more than $300 million in cash to purchase property and equipment and acquire lease rights. These assets have useful lives that vary, but they all last longer than the average pair of blue jeans. ■

By now, you should understand how to account for short-lived assets, such as inventory. We match their costs to the single period in which we recognize the associated revenues. What about assets that a company does not use quickly? Many long-lived assets, such as buildings and heavy machinery, produce revenues in multiple periods, and companies must spread the costs of such assets across all those periods. To qualify for the treatment discussed in this chapter, companies must

This store in San Francisco is one of 4,000 specialty stores operated by Gap. Every store has tables, shelves, displays, and walls—expensive assets to support the sales effort. We learn about accounting for property, plant, and equipment, as well as intangible assets, in this chapter.

actually use the assets in their day-to-day operations and not hold them with the intent to resell. For example, a company should classify an unused building or land that it holds for speculative purposes as an investment rather than as property, plant, and equipment.

How important are long-lived assets? Depending on the industry, they can be the most important assets a company owns. For example, consider the net plant and equipment accounts (the main long-lived asset accounts) in the balance sheets of the following companies ($ in millions):

Company	Total Assets	Plant and Equipment		
		Plant and Equipment, net	Percentage
Decker's	$ 122	$ 4	3
Microsoft	52,150	1,903	4
Time Warner	115,450	12,150	11
Gap Inc.	9,902	3,777	38
Starbucks	2,730	1,385	51
ExxonMobil	152,644	94,940	62
Empire District	970	794	82

Why do these numbers vary so greatly? Because different types of businesses require different types of assets. Decker's "designs, manufactures, and markets innovative function-oriented footwear and apparel" under such brand names as Teva, Simple, Ugg, and Picante. The company outsources most of the manufacturing to Asian and Costa Rican subcontractors. It has little need for fixed assets. Time Warner (previously known as AOL Time Warner) and Microsoft are high-tech companies that rely heavily on intellectual property. Microsoft's balance sheet shows significant current and long-term investments, but little property, plant, and equipment (frequently referred to as PP&E). Time Warner's balance sheet shows a significant portion of its assets are in the form of intangible noncurrent assets, whereas very little is in the form of property, plant, and equipment. Gap may lease its stores, but, as noted previously, the "leasehold" improvements to the stores and the fixtures and equipment to outfit them are quite expensive. Similar to Gap, Starbucks' annual report shows a substantial investment in leasehold improvements and furniture and fixtures. However, 25% of Starbucks' PP&E is in the form of roasting and store equipment. ExxonMobil has extensive property, plant, and equipment, including oil wells, drilling rigs, buildings, and gas pumps. Empire District is a utility company, with most of its assets in the form of electric generation plant and equipment.

As you can imagine, accounting for long-lived assets presents some interesting and unique concerns. The main issue is when to charge the cost of a long-lived asset as an expense on the income statement. For example, if an asset lasts 10 years, how much of its cost should we assign to each of the 10 years the company uses the asset? The answer to this question depends on the method chosen for recording depreciation. We explore a number of methods, each of which is a systematic and rational system for allocating the cost of the asset over its useful life.

This chapter shows how to account for long-lived assets. Much of this chapter focuses on depreciation—both understanding the nature of depreciation and learning about the various depreciation methods. We start off, though, with a look at long-lived assets in general.

Overview of Long-Lived Assets

Most business entities hold major assets such as land, buildings, equipment, natural resources, and patents. These long-lived assets help produce revenues over many periods by facilitating the production of goods or services and their sale to customers. Because

BUSINESS FIRST

VALUING RECORDED AND UNRECORDED ASSETS

It is important to know the strengths and weaknesses of the historical-cost accounting model. Accounting for long-lived assets has both. These assets are fairly valued at cost because cost is usually observable, verifiable, and reliable. Companies can calculate depreciation in one of many ways to allocate the acquisition cost over the useful life of the asset. From the moment of acquisition throughout the life of the assets, book value may be out of touch with market value, and the depreciation expense may be unrelated to the change in market value for the period. These characteristics of historical accounting are very serviceable as long as we remember the strengths and weaknesses of the model.

The bigger problem is that the accounting model does not treat certain things as assets, even though they provide undeniable future benefits to the company and represent significant expenditures by corporate America. Baruch Lev, Professor at New York University and one of the leaders of the so-called "Intangibles Movement," reports that in the late 1990s, "the annual U.S. investment in intangible assets—R&D, business processes and software, brand enhancement, employee training, etc.—was roughly $1.0 trillion, almost equal to the $1.2 trillion total investment of the manufacturing sector in physical assets. Further, intangible capital currently constitutes between one-half and two-thirds of corporate market value, of both old and New Economy enterprises."

Much of the money spent on intangible capital goes for the development of human capital, expenditures for advertising, and R&D. Ed Michaels of McKinsey & Company says, "For many companies today, talented people are the prime source of competitive advantage." Investors and analysts realize this, and the extraordinary stock prices once attached to Cisco, Microsoft, and Intel are in part a recognition of what the very able employees of those firms can do. However, the financial statements do not (and cannot independently and reliably) report a value for these assets. A key reason is that the firm does not own these talented employees, it only "rents" them. Talent is always susceptible to being lured away. How do the financial statements help us to assess these elements? Companies with great human capital grow faster and earn more than the others. We can measure their growth and earnings and compare them using financial accounting outcomes.

Coca-Cola sells for more per ounce than does RC Cola or Branson Cola or a number of other very tasty competitors. Part of the reason is the century of advertising and impression making that is Coke's history. The brand name is an asset, and yet the financial statements do not reflect it. In the United States, we expense advertising costs as incurred and do not reflect the internal generation of an asset. Note that this is not as true elsewhere. Companies in the United Kingdom often report an asset on their balance sheet representing the value of the "brand." Again, the accounting process provides information on the amount companies currently spend on these efforts, and we can assess its effectiveness by looking at the outcomes. When Coke grows rapidly and earns high profits, we can see the evidence of a devoted workforce and a great brand.

Sources: Lev, Baruch, "Rethinking Accounting," *Financial Executive*, March/April, 2002, p. 36; Lev, Baruch, *Intangibles: Management, Measurement and Reporting*, Brookings Institution Press, 2001; Byrne, John, "The Search for the Young and Gifted: Why Talent Counts," *Business Week*, October 4, 1999, 108–109.

these assets are necessary in a company's day-to-day operations, companies do not sell them in the ordinary course of business. However, replacement of these assets is an essential part of the successful operation of a business. Keep in mind that one company's long-lived asset might be another company's short-lived asset. For example, a delivery truck is a long-lived asset for most companies, but a truck dealer would regard a delivery truck as short-lived merchandise inventory.

Long-lived assets are divided into tangible and intangible categories. **Tangible assets** (also called **fixed assets** or **plant assets**) are physical items that you can see and touch. Examples are land, natural resources, buildings, and equipment. In contrast, **intangible assets** are not physical in nature. They generally consist of contractual or legal rights or economic benefits, such as patents, trademarks, and copyrights. Intangible assets are becoming increasingly important to companies, as described in the Business First box.

tangible assets (fixed assets, plant assets)
Physical items that can be seen and touched, such as land, natural resources, buildings, and equipment.

intangible assets
Contractual or legal rights or economic benefits, such as franchises, patents, trademarks, copyrights, and goodwill, that are not physical in nature.

depletion
The process of allocating the cost of natural resources to the periods in which the resources are used.

amortization
When referring to long-lived assets, it usually means the allocation of the costs of intangible assets to the periods that benefit from these assets.

OBJECTIVE

Distinguish a company's expenses from expenditures that it should capitalize.

expenditures
Purchases of goods or services, whether for cash or credit.

capitalize
To add a cost to an asset account, as distinguished from expensing the cost immediately.

As you might guess, we account for different types of long-lived assets quite differently. Land is unique—it does not wear out or become obsolete. Therefore, we report land in the financial records at its historical cost and do not depreciate it. Most other long-lived assets wear out, become inadequate for a given company's use, or become obsolete. As a company uses these assets over time, accountants convert their historical cost to expense.

In practice, accountants use various words to describe the allocation of costs over time. For tangible assets such as buildings, machinery, and equipment, they call the allocation depreciation. For natural resources, they call it **depletion.** Finally, they use **amortization** to refer to the allocation of the costs of intangible assets to the periods that benefit from these assets.

Contrasting Long-Lived Asset Expenditures with Expenses

When a company purchases an asset, management must decide whether the asset will be used only within the current accounting year or whether it will be used over a number of years. We call all purchases of goods or services, whether for cash or on credit, **expenditures.** Companies **capitalize** expenditures for assets that benefit more than the current accounting year; that is, they add the purchase price to an asset account rather than expensing it immediately. Capital expenditures add new assets or increase the capacity, efficiency, or useful life of existing assets. They become expenses in the future, when the company uses the assets. In contrast, expenditures that provide a benefit lasting one year or less become expenses in the current year.

The Decision to Capitalize

There are no hard and fast rules about which expenditures to capitalize, but the topic gets the attention of both the public accounting firms and the income tax authorities. Consider whether to classify an engine repair as an asset or an expense. The public accountant might want to call it an expense, whereas an income tax auditor might want to call it an asset. Why? Because public accountants watch for tendencies to understate current expenses through the unjustified charging of a repair to an asset account. Public accountants guard against earnings patterns that are unusually high and increasing, which can mislead investors. In contrast, the income tax auditor is looking for unjustified charges to an expense account. Such charges reduce taxable income below its proper level, thereby reducing taxes collected by the government.

Wherever doubt exists, accountants tend to charge an expense instead of an asset account for repairs, parts, and similar items. Why? Many of these expenditures are minor, so the cost-benefit test of record keeping and the concept of materiality justify this choice. For instance, many companies charge to expense all expenditures that are less than a specified minimum such as $100, $1,000, or $5,000.

Ethics: Capitalization versus Expense

Because decisions about whether to expense or capitalize expenditures require judgment, this is an area that management may inappropriately influence in order to increase reported net income. Suppose that you run the internal audit department of a large U.S. corporation. As part of the routine internal audit work, one of your staff members uncovers $2 billion in disbursements that the company has reported as capital expenditures. No one in the department is able to find authorization for capital spending in that amount. You begin to suspect that the $2 billion really represents operating costs that accountants have shifted to capital expenditure accounts, making the company appear more profitable. The choice of whether to capitalize or expense the $2 billion has a material effect on the company's financial performance. When you question the person in charge of capital spending about the transaction, he states that the expenditure represents "prepaid capacity," a term that is not familiar to you in spite of your extensive background in accounting. Accountants at various levels within the organization repeatedly stonewall your efforts to obtain clarification of these expenditures. Ultimately, you decide to undertake a detailed investigation. When you reveal your intentions to your company's CFO, he asks you to delay the investigation until after the current quarter, indicating that he intends to take care of the problem in the subsequent quarter.

Now you are faced with a difficult decision. Should you pursue the investigation despite the CFO's request to delay? After all, the CFO is your boss, and he and others higher up in the organization have suggested that you postpone or abandon your investigation. You have no hard evidence of wrongdoing, and if the CFO does in fact correct the problem prior to year-end, the annual financial results will be correctly stated. However, the evasiveness of company executives when questioned about these capital expenditures and the lack of documentation for them suggests that the $2 billion disbursement is just the tip of the iceberg. If you and your staff pursue this investigation and find inappropriate accounting for capital expenditures, the findings could be very detrimental to the company and your fellow employees.

This is a situation similar to the one that confronted Cynthia Cooper and her audit staff at WorldCom. We know what decision Ms. Cooper made. She and her audit team contacted the head of WorldCom's audit committee and KPMG, WorldCom's new outside auditors. Further investigation revealed one of the biggest accounting scandals in U.S. history. On June 25, 2002, WorldCom disclosed that it had wrongly treated $3.8 billion in operating costs, primarily access fees that WorldCom paid to other phone companies for the use of their lines, as capital expenditures. Rather than immediately expensing these costs, WorldCom capitalized the $3.8 billion as an asset. This allowed WorldCom to expense the $3.8 billion as depreciation on the income statement over time rather than expensing it immediately. The decision to capitalize rather than expense these costs enhanced the company's net income in the period in which it capitalized the costs, but it would decrease future periods' income as WorldCom depreciated the capitalized costs.

Acquisition Cost of Tangible Assets

Accounting for a long-lived asset begins with its purchase. The acquisition cost of long-lived assets is the cash-equivalent purchase price, including incidental costs to complete the purchase, to transport the asset, and to prepare it for use.

OBJECTIVE 2

Measure the acquisition cost of tangible assets such as land, buildings, and equipment.

Land

The acquisition cost of land includes charges to the purchaser for the cost of land surveys, legal fees, title fees, transfer taxes, and even the demolition costs of old structures that must be torn down to get the land ready for its intended use. Consider the following example for the acquisition of a piece of land that is to be used as the site of a new building. There is an existing building on the land that will be torn down.

Purchase price	$500,000
Closing costs, including attorney's fees	9,500
Title search and transfer taxes	1,000
Costs of demolition of old building	6,000
Costs of clearing, grading, and filling in preparation for new building	19,000
Assumption of unpaid property taxes	10,000
Proceeds from the sale of materials salvaged from the old building	(2,500)
Total acquisition cost	$543,000

Under historical-cost accounting, companies report land in the balance sheet at its original cost. Of course, after years of rising real estate values and inflation, the carrying amount of land is often far below its current market value. Should land acquired and held since 1940 still appear at its 1940 cost on balance sheets prepared nearly 65 years later? Accountants do exactly that. International accounting standards permit periodic revaluation of certain assets. However, the FASB requires companies in the United States to be conservative and carry land and other long-lived assets at their original historical cost.

Buildings and Equipment

The cost of buildings, plant, and equipment should include all costs of acquisition and preparation for use. Consider the following example for used packaging equipment:

Invoice price, gross	$100,000
Deduct 2% cash discount for payment within 30 days	(2,000)
Invoice price, net	$ 98,000
State sales tax at 8% of $98,000	7,840
Transportation costs	3,000
Installation costs	8,000
Repair costs prior to use	7,000
Total acquisition cost	$123,840

As you can see, several individual costs make up the total acquisition cost. We capitalize the total of $123,840 and add it to the Equipment account. Why do we include repair costs in the amount that we capitalize as the acquisition cost of the asset? Normally, we would expense repair costs in the income statement as incurred. The difference is that repair costs incurred prior to the first use of an asset are part of getting the asset ready to use and, therefore, we include them in the acquisition cost on the balance sheet. In contrast, after the machine is in use, we should charge repair costs as expenses in the income statement.

Companies may surrender assets other than cash in exchange for fixed assets. This practice was particularly common in the dot.com and high-tech sectors during the boom years of the late 1990s. Start-up companies that did not have sufficient cash, but whose stock was highly valued, frequently paid for assets using stock. This type of exchange of goods or services in which the assets or liabilities exchanged are not cash is a **nonmonetary exchange.** For example, the owner of a piece of land might sell it in exchange for stock because the owner could either sell the stock immediately or hold the stock in hopes that it would increase in value. According to GAAP, we record a nonmonetary exchange at the fair market value of the asset, land in this example, or the fair market value of the stock, whichever is the more reliably determinable.

nonmonetary exchange
An exchange of goods or services in which the assets or liabilities exchanged are not cash.

Fair market value of an asset is the price for which a company could sell the asset to an independent third party. When a stock trades actively, we typically assume that the fair market value of the stock is the best indicator of the value of the transaction. After all, if we asked four different appraisers to appraise the land, they would probably arrive at four different values. Suppose that Woodside Corporation sold land to Tryon Company in exchange for shares of Tryon stock. Tryon is a publicly traded stock whose share price is observable each day. An appraiser valued the land at $100,000, whereas the stock had a market value at the time of the sale of $108,000. Tryon would record the following entry:

fair market value
The value of an asset based on the price for which a company could sell the asset to an independent third party.

Land	$108,000	
Paid-in-capital		$108,000
Purchase of land in exchange for $108,000 of common stock.		

Basket Purchases

Frequently, companies acquire more than one type of long-lived asset for a single overall purchase price. The acquisition of two or more types of assets for a lump-sum cost is sometimes called a **basket purchase.** The acquisition cost of a basket purchase is split among the assets purchased according to some estimate of the relative sales value for the assets. For instance, suppose Gap Inc. acquires land and a building for $1 million. How much of the $1 million should Gap allocate to land and how much to the building? If an independent appraiser indicates that the market values of the land and the building are $480,000 and $720,000, respectively, the cost would be allocated as follows:

basket purchase
The acquisition of two or more types of assets for a lump-sum cost.

	(1)	(2)	(3)	(2) × (3)
	Appraised Value	**Weighting**	**Total Cost to Allocate**	**Allocated costs**
Land	$ 480,000	480/1,200 (or 40%)	$1,000,000	$ 400,000
Building	720,000	720/1,200 (or 60%)	1,000,000	600,000
Total	$1,200,000			$1,000,000

Allocating a basket purchase cost to the individual assets can significantly affect future reported income if the useful lives of various assets differ. In our example, if less cost is allocated to the land, more cost is allocated to the building, which is depreciable. In turn, depreciation expenses are higher, operating income is lower, and fewer income taxes are paid. Within the bounds of the law, tax-conscious managers load as much cost as possible on depreciable assets instead of land.

Depreciation of Buildings and Equipment

After purchasing long-lived assets, we must depreciate them. Those new to accounting frequently misunderstand depreciation. It is not a process of valuation. In everyday use, we might say that an auto depreciates in value, meaning that its current market value declines. However, to an accountant, depreciation is not a technique for approximating current values such as replacement costs or resale values. It is simply a system for cost allocation. For purposes of financial reporting, companies in the United States freely select the depreciation method they believe best portrays their economic circumstance. In fact, GAAP simply requires that the depreciation method be systematic and rational. In contrast, government (often tax) authorities in countries such as Japan, Germany, and France specify depreciation methods.

Depreciation is one of the key factors distinguishing accrual accounting from cash-basis accounting. If a company purchases a long-lived asset for cash, strict cash-basis accounting would treat the entire cost of the asset as an expense in the period of acquisition. In contrast, accrual accounting initially capitalizes the cost and then allocates it in the form of depreciation over the periods the asset is used. This more effectively matches expenses with the revenues produced.

The amount of the acquisition cost to be depreciated or allocated over the total useful life of the asset is the **depreciable value.** It is the difference between the total acquisition cost and the estimated residual value. The **residual value,** also known as **terminal value, disposal value, salvage value,** and **scrap value,** is the amount a company expects to receive from sale or disposal of a long-lived asset at the end of its useful life. The **useful life** of an asset is the shorter of the physical life of the asset (before it wears out) or the economic life of the asset. The useful life of an asset and its physical life need not be the same. The physical life of an asset depends on the wear and tear it takes while in use. At some point, a company can no longer use a piece of equipment in the production process due to deterioration. However, it may decide to replace equipment prior to the end of its physical life. Such replacement depends on economic factors rather than physical ones. For example, given the rapidly increasing speed and decreasing cost of computers in more recent times, most companies replace them long before they physically wear out. That is, their economic life is shorter than their physical life. Both the residual value and useful

OBJECTIVE 3

Compute depreciation for buildings and equipment using various depreciation methods.

depreciable value
The amount of the acquisition cost to be allocated as depreciation over the total useful life of an asset. It is the difference between the total acquisition cost and the estimated residual value.

residual value (terminal value, disposal value, salvage value, scrap value)
The amount a company expects to receive from disposal of a long-lived asset at the end of its useful life.

useful life
The shorter of the physical life or the economic life of an asset.

THE USE OF ESTIMATES AND THE IMPACT ON EARNINGS

At first glance, it may seem that the assignment of estimated useful lives and residual values to fixed assets is not a decision of critical importance. However, one of the accounting scandals of the 1990s involved Waste Management, a company with assets of almost $20 billion and net income of $822 million in 2002. The company provides waste management services, including collection, transfer, disposal, and recycling. After going public in the early 1970s, Waste Management was obsessed with its stock price. In 1998, the company revealed that it had been using overly aggressive accounting estimates and tactics in an effort to keep earnings up. Waste Management's business requires a big investment in fixed assets, resulting in substantial depreciation expense. To reduce depreciation expense and thereby increase earnings, Waste Management made unrealistic assumptions regarding the estimated useful lives and estimated residual values of its fixed assets. For example, the company assigned garbage trucks a useful life of between 12 and 14 years and a residual value of $25,000. Normal practice in the industry is an 8 to 10-year life and a residual value of zero. Similarly, the company assigned a useful life of 15 to 20 years and a nonzero residual value to dumpsters, compared with a 12-year-life and zero residual value industry standard. In addition, Waste Management claimed they had the ability and intent to expand their landfills. Although typically land does not depreciate, a landfill has a useful life equal to the length of time it takes to fill, and companies depreciate the cost of the landfill over this time period. By claiming the ability to expand the landfills (when in fact expansions were unlikely), Waste Management was effectively extending the useful life. The net effect of these estimates was to reduce the total amount of depreciation taken (by overestimating the estimated residual value) and to spread the depreciation on dumpsters, garbage trucks, and landfills out over a longer period of time. The use of these accounting "tricks" resulted in an increase in pretax earnings of approximately $3.5 billion during the years 1991 through 1997.

Ultimately the SEC investigated Waste Management's accounting for fixed assets, resulting in adjustments to reported earnings for the years in question.

Sources: Elkind, Peter, "Garbage in, garbage out," *Fortune*, May 25, 1998, pp. 130–138; Bailey, Jeff, "Waste Management Takes Charges, Write-Downs of $3.54 Billion," *The Wall Street Journal*, February 25, 1998, p. A4; Waste Managmement 2002 annual report (http://www.wm.com/newwm/press/annualreports/2002Annual.pdf).

life are estimates, and how management makes these estimates can greatly effect a company's net income, as pointed out in the Business First box above.

Depreciation methods differ primarily in the amount of cost allocated to each period. A list of depreciation amounts for each year of an asset's useful life is a **depreciation schedule.** We use the following symbols and amounts to compare the various depreciation schedules for a $41,000 delivery truck purchased by Chang Company on January 1, 20X3:

depreciation schedule
The listing of depreciation amounts for each year of an asset's useful life.

Symbols	Amounts for Illustration
Let	
C = total acquisition cost on January 1, 20X3	$41,000
R = estimated residual value	$ 1,000
n = estimated useful life (in years or miles)	4 years
	200,000 miles
D = amount of depreciation expense	Various

straight-line depreciation
A method that spreads the depreciable value evenly over the useful life of an asset.

Straight-Line Depreciation

Straight-line depreciation spreads the depreciable value evenly over the useful life of an asset. It is by far the most popular method for financial reporting purposes. In fact,

	Balances at End of Year			
	1	2	3	4
Equipment (at original acquisition cost)	$41,000	$41,000	$41,000	$41,000
Less: Accumulated depreciation (the portion of original cost that has already been charged to operations as expense)	10,000	20,000	30,000	40,000
Net book value (the portion of original cost that has not yet been charged to operations)	$31,000	$21,000	$11,000	$ 1,000

Exhibit 8-1
Straight-Line Depreciation Schedule

a recent survey showed that more than 95% of major companies use straight-line depreciation for at least some of their fixed assets.

Exhibit 8-1 shows the balance sheet values for Chang Company's truck using straight-line depreciation. At the end of the fourth year, the truck has a remaining net book value of $1,000, which is the original estimated residual value. The annual depreciation expense charged to Chang's income statement is:

$$\text{Depreciation expense} = \frac{(\text{Acquisition cost} - \text{Estimated residual value})}{\text{Years of estimated useful life}}$$

$$D = \frac{(C - R)}{n}$$

$$D = \frac{(\$41,000 - 1,000)}{4}$$

$$D = \$10,000 \text{ per year}$$

Depreciation Based on Units

In some cases, time is not the limiting factor on the useful life of an asset. When physical wear and tear determines the useful life of the asset, accountants may base depreciation on units of service or units of production instead of units of time (years). Depreciation based on units of service is **unit depreciation** and, in some circumstances, this depreciation method results in a better matching of costs and revenues. In our example, Chang's truck has a useful life of 200,000 miles, so depreciation computed on a mileage basis is:

unit depreciation
A depreciation method based on units of service or units of production when physical wear and tear is the dominating influence on the useful life of the asset.

$$\text{Depreciation expense per unit of service} = \frac{(\text{Acquisition cost} - \text{Estimated residual value})}{\text{Estimated units of service}}$$

$$D = \frac{(C - R)}{n}$$

$$D = \frac{(\$41,000 - \$1,000)}{200,000 \text{ miles}}$$

$$D = \$.20 \text{ per mile}$$

If employees drive the truck 65,000 miles in the first year of use, depreciation expense for that year will be: 65,000 × $.20 = $13,000.

For some assets, such as transportation equipment, unit depreciation may have more logical appeal than the straight-line method. However, the unit depreciation method is not widely used, probably for several reasons:

1. Unit-based depreciation frequently produces approximately the same yearly depreciation amounts as does straight-line depreciation.
2. Straight-line depreciation is easier. Under straight-line, we can determine the entire depreciation schedule at the time of acquisition; however, under unit depreciation, we must keep detailed records of units of service to determine the amount depreciated each year.

Declining-Balance Depreciation

accelerated depreciation
Any depreciation method that writes off depreciable value more quickly than the ordinary straight-line method based on expected useful life.

double-declining-balance (DDB) method
A common form of accelerated depreciation. It is computed by doubling the straight-line rate and multiplying the resulting DDB rate by the beginning book value.

Any pattern of depreciation that writes off depreciable value more quickly than does the ordinary straight-line method is considered **accelerated depreciation.** A number of accelerated depreciation methods are possible. One such method is the **double-declining-balance (DDB) method,** also known as 200% declining-balance-method. We compute DDB depreciation as follows:

1. Compute the straight-line rate by dividing 100% by the years of useful life. Then double the straight-line rate. In our example, the straight-line rate is 100% ÷ 4 years = 25%. The DDB rate is 2 × 25%, or 50%.
2. To compute the depreciation on an asset for any year, ignore the residual value and multiply the asset's net book value at the beginning of the year by the DDB rate. Remember that you cannot depreciate an asset below its estimated residual value. Consideration of the residual value may require adjustments to the method. We discuss these adjustments later in the chapter.

We can apply the DDB method to Chang Company's truck as follows:

$$\text{DDB rate} = 2 \times (100\% \div n)$$

$$\text{DDB rate, 4-year life} = 2 \times (100\% \div 4) = 50\%$$

$$\text{DDB depreciation} = \text{DDB rate} \times \text{Beginning net book value}$$

For year 1: $D = .50\ (\$41{,}000)$
$\qquad = \$20{,}500$
For year 2: $D = .50\ (\$41{,}000 - \$20{,}500)$
$\qquad = \$10{,}250$
For year 3: $D = .50\ (\$41{,}000 - \$20{,}500 - \$10{,}250)$
$\qquad = \$5{,}125$
For year 4: $D = .50\ (\$41{,}000 - \$20{,}500 - \$10{,}250 - \$5{,}125)$
$\qquad = \$2{,}563$

In this example, the depreciation amount for each year is one-half the preceding year's depreciation. However, this halving is a special case that happens only with a 4-year life asset. Remember, the basic approach of DDB is to apply the depreciation rate to the beginning net book value. Although we illustrated the declining-balance method with DDB, other versions use different multiples. For example, the 150% declining-balance method simply multiples the straight-line rate by 1.5 instead of doubling it.

Comparing and Choosing Depreciation Methods

Exhibit 8-2 compares the results of straight-line and DDB depreciation for Chang Company's truck. Note that the DDB method provides $38,438 of total depreciation and does not allocate the full $40,000 depreciable value to expense. To compensate for this fact, some companies that use DDB change to the straight-line method part way

	Straight-Line*		Declining-Balance at Twice the Straight-Line Rate (DDB)[†]		Modified DDB—Switch to Straight-Line in Year 4[‡]	
	Annual Depreciation	Book Value	Annual Depreciation	Book Value	Annual Depreciation	Book Value
At acquisition		$41,000		$41,000		$41,000
Year 1	$10,000	31,000	$20,500	20,500	$20,500	20,500
Year 2	10,000	21,000	10,250	10,250	10,250	10,250
Year 3	10,000	11,000	5,125	5,125	5,125	5,125
Year 4	10,000	1,000	2,563	2,562	4,125	1,000
Total	$40,000		$38,438		$40,000	

*Depreciation is the same each year, 25% of ($41,000 − $1,000).

[†]100% ÷ 4 = 25%. The DDB rate is 50%. Then 50% of $41,000; 50% of ($41,000 − $20,500); 50% of [$41,000 − ($20,500 + $10,250)]; etc. Unmodified, this method will never fully depreciate the existing book value.

[‡]The switch to straight-line occurs in year four, and the depreciation amount is the amount needed to reduce the book value to the final salvage value.

Exhibit 8-2
Depreciation: Two Popular Methods
(Assume Equipment Costs $41,000, 4-Year Life, Estimated Residual Value of $1,000)

through the asset's depreciable life. We illustrate this in the rightmost columns of Exhibit 8-2.

To decide when to change, we calculate straight-line depreciation over the remaining life of the asset given the remaining undepreciated cost. We change methods in the year when the straight-line depreciation first equals or exceeds the amount in the original DDB schedule. For Chang Company's truck, DDB gives depreciation of $5,125 in year 3. Straight-line depreciation for year 3, based on net book value at that point, would be ($10,250 − $1,000) ÷ 2 = $4,625. Therefore, we continue using DDB in year 3 because it gives a higher depreciation amount than does straight-line. After recording DDB depreciation of $5,125 in year 3, the undepreciated book value is $5,125. DDB gives depreciation expense of $2,563 in year 4 [.5 × $5,125]. With 1 year remaining and a $1,000 salvage value, straight-line depreciation for year 4 is $4,125 [($5,125 − $1,000) ÷ 1 year] as shown in the second column from the right of Exhibit 8-2. Because $4,125 exceeds $2,563, the switch occurs for year 4.

If the residual value is large enough, it is also possible that application of DDB will result in fully depreciating an asset prior to the end of its useful life. In this case, we would use an adjustment mechanism (not shown here) similar to that depicted in Exhibit 8-2.

Companies do not necessarily use the same depreciation method for all types of depreciable assets. Although Starbucks uses straight-line depreciation for all assets, a recent Nike annual report states: "Depreciation for financial reporting purposes is determined on a straight-line basis for buildings and leasehold improvements over 2 to 40 years and principally on a declining-balance basis for machinery and equipment over 2 to 15 years."

How does a company choose among the alternatives? In some cases, tradition leads one company to select the method used by other companies in its industry to enhance comparability. Sometimes one method provides far superior matching of expense and revenue, as unit depreciation would for certain types of equipment and manufacturing processes. Sometimes companies choose the method most consistent with the life cycle cost of the asset. Suppose a type of equipment requires little maintenance in the first years of its life, but increasing maintenance later. Accelerated depreciation with decreasing depreciation charges each year, plus rising maintenance costs each year, would provide a somewhat constant cost per year. Thus, the choice depends on the nature of the industry, as well as the equipment and the goals of management.

Summary Problem for Your Review

PROBLEM

"The net book value of plant assets that appears on the balance sheet is the amount that would be spent today for their replacement." Do you agree? Explain.

SOLUTION TO PROBLEM

No. Net book value of the plant assets on the balance sheet is the result of deducting accumulated depreciation from original cost. It is a result of cost allocation, not valuation. This process does not attempt to reflect all the technological and economic events that may affect replacement value. Consequently, there is no assurance that net book value will approximate replacement cost.

Changes in Estimated Useful Life or Residual Value

OBJECTIVE 4

Recalculate depreciation in response to a change in estimated useful life or residual value.

A company estimates the useful life and residual value of an asset at the time of its acquisition. The information on which these estimates are based may improve with time. If new information becomes known and the use of the revised estimate would result in a significant change in depreciation expense, the company must adopt the new estimate and revise the depreciation schedule. Accounting for changes in estimated useful life or residual value is prospective in nature. In other words, the company does not go back and revise the depreciation expense taken in prior periods. Rather, depreciation expense is recomputed for the period in which the estimate is revised and all future periods.

Refer to the straight-line depreciation schedule for Chang Company's truck as shown in Exhibit 8-2. Chang originally estimated a residual value of $1,000 and a useful life of 4 years for the truck. Suppose that at the beginning of year 4, Chang determines that it will continue to use the truck for 3 more years rather than 1 more year. As of the beginning of year 4, Chang has recorded a total of $30,000 in depreciation expense, $10,000 in year 1, $10,000 in year 2, and $10,000 in year 3. The net book value of the truck at the beginning of year 4 is $11,000 as shown in Exhibit 8-2. Chang still expects the residual value to be $1,000. Therefore, Chang must allocate the remaining $10,000 in allowable depreciation expense over a total of 3 years. ($10,000/3 = $3,333.33). The revised depreciation schedule for Chang is given here:

	Annual Depreciation	Book Value
At acquisition		$41,000
Year 1	$10,000	31,000
Year 2	10,000	21,000
Year 3	10,000	11,000
Year 4	3,333	7,667
Year 5	3,333	4,334
Year 6	3,334*	1,000
Total	$40,000	

*$1 difference due to rounding

Contrasting Income Tax and Shareholder Reporting

In accounting for long-lived assets, reporting to stockholders and reporting to the income tax authorities often differ. Reports to stockholders must abide by GAAP. In contrast, reports to income tax authorities must abide by the income tax rules and regulations. Many tax rules are consistent with GAAP, but often the two vary. Therefore, keeping two sets of records is neither immoral nor unethical; it is necessary.

OBJECTIVE 5

Differentiate financial statement depreciation from income tax depreciation.

Depreciation for Tax Reporting Purposes

Congress changes the U.S. tax rules in some way almost every year. However, since 1986 companies have used the Modified Accelerated Cost Recovery System (MACRS) for computing depreciation for tax reporting. The MACRS depreciation schedule is based on the declining-balance depreciation method discussed previously. However, tax depreciation and financial reporting depreciation differ. One important difference is that MACRS often provides useful lives for tax purposes that are shorter than the useful lives used for financial reporting purposes. Remember that the shorter the life, the earlier a company can record depreciation expense. Higher expenses reported for tax purposes mean lower taxable net income, which means lower income taxes. MACRS allows for higher depreciation and lower taxes in the early years of an asset's service life than does the straight-line method commonly used for financial reporting. This is reversed in the later years of an asset's life. However, because of the time value of money, the company benefits from the delay in paying taxes.

Shareholder Reporting

Although companies typically choose MACRS for tax purposes, most use straight-line depreciation for shareholder reporting. Tax authorities may use special rates, short lives, or immediate write-off to accelerate the tax benefits of investing in long-lived assets. In contrast, the depreciation method for shareholder reporting matches the costs of an asset to all periods in which that asset generates revenues.

There are several practical reasons for adopting straight-line depreciation for financial reporting, namely, simplicity, convenience, and reporting of higher earnings in early years than would be reported under accelerated depreciation. Managers tend not to choose accounting methods that hurt reported earnings in the early years of long-lived assets. In Chapter 7 we noted that many firms choose LIFO, which reduces earnings in a period of rising prices. However, they do so because they are required to use LIFO for financial reporting if they elect LIFO for tax purposes. That conformity feature does not exist for depreciation, so firms often use straight-line for financial reporting and MACRS for tax reporting.

Depreciation and Cash Flow

Too often, nonaccountants confuse the relationships among depreciation expense, income tax expense, cash, and accumulated depreciation. For example, the business press frequently contains misleading quotations such as ". . . we're looking for financing of $3.75 billion. Of that, about 60% will be recovered in depreciation and amortization." As another example, consider a *Business Week* news report concerning an airline company: "And with a hefty boost from depreciation and the sale of $6 million worth of property, its cash balance rose by $10 million in the year's first quarter."

These statements imply that depreciation somehow generates cash. It does not. Depreciation simply allocates the original cost of an asset to the periods in which the company uses the asset—nothing more and nothing less. Furthermore, accumulated

OBJECTIVE 6

Explain the effect of depreciation on cash flow.

Exhibit 8-3

Acme Service
Company
Income Statement and
Statement of Cash
Flows ($ in Thousands)

	Before Taxes		After Taxes	
	Straight-Line Depreciation	Accelerated Depreciation	Straight-Line Depreciation	Accelerated Depreciation
Income Statement				
Sales	$103	$103	$103	$103
Operating expenses	53	53	53	53
Depreciation expense	10	20	10	20
Pretax income	40	30	40	30
Income tax expense (40%)	—	—	16	12
Net income	$ 40	$ 30	$ 24	$ 18
Statement of Cash Flows				
Cash collections	$103	$103	$103	$103
Cash operating expenses	53	53	53	53
Cash tax payments	—	—	16	12
Cash provided by operations*	$ 50	$ 50	$ 34	$ 38

*Sometimes called *cash flow from operations*, net cash provided by operations, or just *cash flow*. It is simply cash collected on sales less all operating expenses requiring cash and less cash paid for income taxes.

depreciation is merely the portion of an asset's original cost that has already been written off to depreciation expense in prior periods—not a pile of cash waiting to be used.

Effects of Depreciation on Cash

To illustrate depreciation's relationship to cash, consider Acme Service Company, which began business with cash and common stock equity of $100,000. On the same day, Acme acquired equipment for $40,000 cash. The equipment had an expected 4-year life and an estimated residual value of zero. The first year's operations generated cash sales of $103,000 and cash operating expenses of $53,000.

Assume straight-line depreciation of $10,000 and accelerated depreciation of $20,000 in the first year. Note from the first two columns of Exhibit 8-3 that the reported pretax income differs as a result of the depreciation method chosen, but cash flow from operations is the same. Comparing the pretax amounts stresses the role of depreciation expense most vividly. Why? Because before taxes, changes in the depreciation method affect only the accumulated depreciation and retained earnings accounts. Depreciation does not affect the before-tax ending cash balances.

Now suppose that for financial reporting purposes, GAAP allowed Acme to write off the entire $40,000 in the first year. What are the company's pretax income and the cash provided by operations? Pretax income is only $10,000. However, the increase in cash remains at $50,000. Why? Because cash received from sales of $103,000 and cash expenses of $53,000 do not change, leaving the $50,000 cash provided by operations unchanged.

Effects of Depreciation on Income Taxes

Now consider the after-tax portions of Exhibit 8-3 in the two rightmost columns. Depreciation is a deductible noncash expense for income tax purposes. Thus, the higher the depreciation a company deducts on its tax return in any given year, the lower the taxable income, and the lower the cash paid for income taxes. In short, if tax depreciation expense is higher, taxes are lower and the company keeps more cash for use in the business.

To emphasize the relationship between depreciation and cash and to simplify the comparison, we assume the depreciation method used for financial reporting is the same as for tax purposes. From the last two columns of Exhibit 8-3, you can see that Acme would pay $16,000 of income taxes in the first year using straight-line depreciation, but only $12,000 using accelerated depreciation. Therefore, compared with the straight-line depreciation method, the accelerated method conserves $4,000 in cash. Depreciation does not generate cash, but it does have a cash benefit if it results in lower taxes.

Summary Problems for Your Review

PROBLEM

"Accumulated depreciation provides cash for the replacement of fixed assets." Do you agree with this quotation from a business magazine? Explain.

SOLUTION

Accumulated depreciation does not generate cash. It is the amount of the asset already used and in no way represents a stockpile of cash for replacement.

PROBLEM

Review the important chapter illustration in the section, "Depreciation and Cash Flow," on page 348. Suppose Acme Service had acquired the equipment for $80,000 instead of $40,000. The estimated residual value remains zero and the useful life remains 4 years.

1. Prepare a revised Exhibit 8-3. As in Exhibit 8-3, assume the same depreciation method is used for financial reporting and tax reporting. Assume an income tax rate of 40% and round all income tax computations to the nearest thousand.
2. Indicate the major items affected by these changes. Also tabulate all differences between the final two columns in your revised exhibit as compared with Exhibit 8-3.

SOLUTION

1. The revised income statements and statement of cash flows information are in Exhibit 8-4.

	Before Taxes		After Taxes	
	Straight-Line Depreciation	Accelerated Depreciation	Straight-Line Depreciation	Accelerated Depreciation
Income Statement				
Sales	$103	$103	$103	$103
Operating expenses	53	53	53	53
Depreciation expense	20	40	20	40
Pretax income	30	10	30	10
Income tax expense (40%)	—	—	12	4
Net income	$ 30	$ 10	$ 18	$ 6
Statement of Cash Flows				
Cash collections	$103	$103	$103	$103
Cash operating expenses	53	53	53	53
Cash tax payments	—	—	12	4
Cash provided by operations	$ 50	$ 50	$ 38	$ 46

Exhibit 8-4
Acme Service Company
Income Statement and Statement of Cash Flows ($ in Thousands)

2. The following comparisons of Exhibits 8-4 and 8-3 are noteworthy. The change in depreciation does not affect sales, cash operating expenses, or cash provided by operations before income taxes. Because of higher depreciation, net income is lower in all four columns of Exhibit 8-4 than it was in Exhibit 8-3. Comparison of the final two columns of the exhibits follows:

	As Shown in		
	Exhibit 8-4	**Exhibit 8-3**	**Difference**
Straight-line depreciation	20	10	10 Higher
Accelerated depreciation	40	20	20 Higher
Income tax expense based on			
Straight-line depreciation	12	16	4 Lower
Accelerated depreciation	4	12	8 Lower
Net income based on			
Straight-line depreciation	18	24	6 Lower
Accelerated depreciation	6	18	12 Lower
Cash provided by operations based on			
Straight-line depreciation	38	34	4 Higher
Accelerated depreciation	46	38	8 Higher

Especially noteworthy is the phenomenon that higher depreciation not only decreases net income, but also decreases cash outflows for income taxes. As a result, cash provided by operations increases.

Expenditures After Acquisition

OBJECTIVE 7

Account for expenditures after acquisition.

improvement (betterment, capital improvement) An expenditure that is intended to add to the future benefits provided by an existing fixed asset.

In addition to the initial investment, companies incur ongoing expenditures associated with the operation of long-lived assets. For example, repairs and maintenance costs are necessary to maintain a fixed asset in operating condition. Repairs include the occasional costs of restoring a fixed asset to its ordinary operating condition after breakdowns, accidents, or damage. Maintenance includes the routine recurring costs of activities such as oiling, polishing, painting, and adjusting. Accountants generally compile these costs in a single account and regard them as expenses of the current period.

In contrast, an **improvement** (sometimes called a **betterment** or a **capital improvement**) is an expenditure that increases the future benefits provided by an existing fixed asset by decreasing its operating cost, increasing its rate of output, improving its safety, reducing its rate of pollution, or prolonging its useful life. Repairs and maintenance maintain the level of an asset's future benefits, whereas improvements increase those benefits. We generally capitalize improvements. Examples of capital improvements or betterments include the rehabilitation of an apartment house that will allow increased rents and the rebuilding of a machine that increases its speed or extends its useful life.

Suppose Chang Company's $41,000 delivery truck with a 4-year life and $1,000 residual value presented earlier in the chapter experiences a major overhaul costing $7,000 at the start of year three. Chang depreciated the truck using straight-line depreciation during the first 2 years of use. If this overhaul extends the useful life of the truck from 4 to 5 years, the accounting is:

1. Increase the book value of the asset (now $41,000 − $20,000 = $21,000) by $7,000. Thus, we add the $7,000 to Equipment.
2. Revise the depreciation schedule to spread the revised book value of the asset over the remaining 3 years, as follows (assume Chang continues to use straight-line depreciation):

	Original Depreciation Schedule		Revised Depreciation Schedule	
	Year	Amount	Year	Amount
	1	$10,000	1	$10,000
	2	10,000	2	10,000
	3	10,000	3	9,000*
	4	10,000	4	9,000
			5	9,000
Accumulated depreciation		$40,000		$47,000†

*New depreciable amount is [($41,000 − $20,000 + $7,000) − $1,000 residual value] = $27,000. New depreciation expense is $27,000 divided by remaining useful life of 3 years, or $9,000 per year.

†Recapitulation:
Original cost	$41,000
Major overhaul	7,000
	48,000
Less residual	1,000
Depreciable cost	$47,000

Gains and Losses on Sales of Tangible Assets

Earlier in this chapter you learned how to account for property, plant, and equipment assets at the date of acquisition, how to account for expenditures related to the assets during their useful lives, and how to compute depreciation. However, companies sometimes sell an asset before the end of its useful life. When they sell assets, gains or losses are inevitable. We measure these gains or losses by the difference between the proceeds received and the net book value (net carrying amount) of the asset being sold.

OBJECTIVE 8

Compute gains and losses on the disposal of fixed assets and consider the impact of these gains and losses on the statement of cash flows.

Recording Gains and Losses

Consider Chang Company's delivery truck from our earlier example. Suppose Chang sells the truck for $21,000 in cash at the very beginning of year three. Chang depreciated the asset using straight-line depreciation during the first 2 years of its life. Because its net book value is also $21,000, there would be no gain or loss on the transaction. Chang simply exchanges one asset, equipment, carried on the books at $21,000 for another asset, cash, of $21,000. Chang would eliminate the equipment asset and its accumulated depreciation from the records and record the cash received. The sale would have the following effects:

A					=	L	+	SE
+$21,000	−	$41,000	+	$20,000	=	$0	+	$0
[Increase Cash]		[Decrease Equipment]		[Decrease Accumulated Depreciation]				

Note that the disposal of the equipment requires the removal of its carrying amount or book value, which appears in two accounts, Equipment and Accumulated Depreciation. We remove the original acquisition cost of $41,000 from the Equipment account and the $20,000 in accumulated depreciation on the truck from the Accumulated Depreciation account. Remember that a reduction in the balance in Accumulated Depreciation increases assets, hence the + sign associated with Accumulated Depreciation in the illustration.

Suppose the selling price was $27,000 instead of $21,000. The sale would produce a gain of $6,000, the difference between the sale proceeds and the net book value of the asset being sold:

Sale proceeds		$27,000
Less book value		
Cost	$41,000	
Accumulated depreciation	20,000	21,000
Gain		$ 6,000

This sale would have the following effects on the accounting equation:

		A			=	L	+	SE
+$27,000	−	$41,000	+	$20,000	=	$0	+	$6,000
⎡ Increase ⎤		⎡ Decrease ⎤		⎡ Decrease ⎤				⎡Increase SE⎤
⎣ Cash ⎦		⎣ Equipment ⎦		⎢ Accumulated ⎥				⎢ Gain on ⎥
				⎣ Depreciation ⎦				⎢ Sale of ⎥
								⎣ Equipment ⎦

Now suppose the selling price were $17,000 instead of $21,000. The sale would produce a $4,000 loss with the following effects:

		A			=	L	+	SE
+$17,000	−	$41,000	+	$20,000	=	$0	−	$4,000
⎡ Increase ⎤		⎡ Decrease ⎤		⎡ Decrease ⎤				⎡Decrease SE⎤
⎣ Cash ⎦		⎣ Equipment ⎦		⎢ Accumulated ⎥				⎢ Loss on ⎥
				⎣ Depreciation ⎦				⎢ Sale of ⎥
								⎣ Equipment ⎦

Exhibit 8-5 shows the T-account presentations and journal entries for these transactions. Note again that we must eliminate both the original cost of the equipment and the accompanying accumulated depreciation when we sell the asset. The net effect is to eliminate the $21,000 carrying amount of the equipment (cost of $41,000 less accumulated depreciation of $20,000).

Sale at $27,000:

			Cash		Equipment		Gain on Sale of Equipment
			27 |		* 41 | 41		| 6
Cash	27						
Accumulated depreciation	20				Accumulated		
Equipment		41			Depreciation,		
Gain on sale of equipment		6			Equipment		
					20 | * 20		

Sale at $17,000:

			Cash		Equipment		Loss on Sale of Equipment
			17 |		* 41 | 41		4 |
Cash	17						
Accumulated depreciation	20				Accumulated		
Loss on sale of equipment	4				Depreciation,		
Equipment		41			Equipment		
					20 | * 20		

*Beginning balance.

Exhibit 8-5
Journal and Ledger Entries
Gain or Loss on Sale of Equipment ($ in Thousands)

Income Statement Presentation

In most instances, gains or losses on the disposition of plant assets are not significant enough to appear as separate line items on the income statement. In such cases, companies include these gains and losses as a part of "other income" or "other expense" on the income statement and do not separately identify them. The following three lines from a recent **DuPont** income statement illustrate this treatment ($ amounts in millions):

Sales	$24,006
Other income	516
Total	$24,522

Footnote 2 to DuPont's financial statements reveals that Other Income includes a gain of $30 million arising from the sale of assets. The $30 million is "not significant" in the sense that it is not a material transaction for analysts to understand in evaluating the company. The focus is on the ongoing selling activity of chemicals and other products. To put things in perspective, DuPont had more than $34 billion in assets on December 31, 2003.

Some companies follow DuPont's example and list other income, including gains from the sale of assets, with sales revenue at the very top of the income statement. Others exclude the gain (or loss) from the computation of major profit categories such as gross profit or operating profit. **NW Natural**, a natural gas distribution company headquartered in Portland, Oregon, took this approach in its 2002 income statement. The company subtracted other expense of $14.9 million after calculating gross profit and operating income. Footnotes reveal that this other expense account includes "interest income; gain on sale of assets . . .," as well as other income and expense items. When interpreting a company's income statement, it is important to know which approach a company has taken with regard to other income and other expense categories.

Asset Sales and the Statement of Cash Flows

The sale of fixed assets has implications for the statement of cash flows. Sales of fixed assets are investing activities. The previous examples demonstrate three different scenarios. In the first case (case A), Chang's truck sells for exactly its net book value of $21,000. In the second case (case B), it sells for $27,000 in cash resulting in a gain of $6,000. In the final case (case C), it sells for $17,000 in cash creating a loss of $4,000. In each case, the investing section of the statement of cash flows shows the actual cash received, labeled as "Proceeds from the sale of fixed assets." This is the only impact on the cash flow statement unless Chang Company uses the indirect method for presenting cash flows from operating activities. Because the indirect method starts with net income and because gains or losses from the sale of fixed assets affect net income but are not cash items, we must remove these gains or losses from net income to calculate operating cash flows.

Suppose Chang Company uses the indirect method and has net income of $50,000 before accounting for the sale of the truck. To simplify the illustration, we assume no tax effects. The following table depicts the effects of the sale of the truck on net income:

	Income Before Sale	Gain (Loss)	Income After Sale
Case A: Sale at $21,000	$50,000	0	$50,000
Case B: Sale at $27,000	$50,000	$6,000	$56,000
Case C: Sale at $17,000	$50,000	($4,000)	$46,000

Net income includes the gain or loss on the sale of the truck. Therefore, the reconciliation of net income and cash flows from operating activities must remove the gain or loss from net income. In case A, the $50,000 in reported net income does not include any gain or loss on the sale of the truck. Therefore, in arriving at cash flows from operating activities, we do not adjust net income. In case B, net income of $56,000 includes a $6,000 noncash gain, which we must deduct from net income to arrive at net cash provided by operating activities. Subtracting the $6,000 gain does not imply a use of cash. It simply offsets the effect of the $6,000 gain included in net income. In case C, net income of $46,000 includes the $4,000 loss. Like depreciation expense, this loss is a noncash expense. The company did not pay someone $4,000 in cash to take possession of the truck! Therefore, we must add back to net income the loss on the sale of the truck to offset its earlier deduction. The net cash provided by operating activities is the same in each case. The sale of the truck did not affect operating cash flows.

INTERPRETING FINANCIAL STATEMENTS

In January 2005, Olsson Company sells a building that had an original historical cost of $850,000 and accumulated depreciation of $575,000 at the time of sale. The building sells for cash and Olsson Company records a pretax gain of $75,000. Indicate how these facts affect the statement of cash flows, prepared on an indirect method basis, for the year ended December 31, 2005. Ignore any tax consequences.

Answer

The gain of $75,000 is deducted from net income in the operating section of Olsson's statement of cash flows. This is necessary because the gain represents noncash revenue that was included in net income. Olsson Company also shows cash proceeds from the sale of the building in the investing section of the statement of cash flows. The amount of cash received on the sale of the building is $350,000. The $350,000 is derived as follows:

Net book value of building at the date of the sale = $850,000 − $575,000 = $275,000

Gain on sale = Selling price − net book value

$75,000 = Selling price − $275,000

$350,000 = Selling price

Summary Problem for Your Review

PROBLEM

Refer to Exhibit 8-2 on page 345. Suppose the estimated residual value had been $5,000 instead of $1,000.

1. Compute depreciation for each of the first 2 years using straight-line and double-declining-balance (DDB) methods.
2. Assume that the company uses DDB depreciation and sells the equipment for $20,000 cash at the end of the second year. Compute the gain or loss on the sale. Show the effects of the sale in equipment and accumulated depreciation T-accounts. Where and how would the sale appear in the income statement? Where and how would the sale appear in the statement of cash flows?
3. Assume that the company uses straight-line depreciation and sells the equipment for $20,000 cash at the end of the second year. Compute the gain or loss on the sale. Compare this amount to the gain or loss computed in the previous question.

SOLUTION

1.	Straight-Line Depreciation = (C − R) ÷ n	DDB Depreciation = Rate* × (Beg. Book Value)
Year 1	$36,000 ÷ 4 = $9,000	.50 ($41,000) = $20,500
Year 2	$36,000 ÷ 4 = $9,000	.50 ($41,000 − $20,500) = $10,250

*Rate = 2(100% ÷ n) = 2(100% ÷ 4) = 50%.

2.		
Selling price		$20,000
Net book value of equipment sold is		
$41,000 − ($20,500 + $10,250), or		
$41,000 − $30,750 =		10,250
Gain on sale of equipment		$ 9,750

The effect of removing the book value is a $10,250 decrease in assets. Note that the effect of a decrease in accumulated depreciation (by itself) is an increase in assets:

Equipment			
Acquisition cost	41,000	Cost of equipment sold	41,000

Accumulated Depreciation, Equipment			
Accumulated depreciation on equipment sold	30,750	Depreciation for	
		Year 1	20,500
		Year 2	10,250
			30,750

The $9,750 gain may be shown as a separate item on the income statement as Gain on Sale of Equipment or Gain on Disposal of Equipment. Alternatively, it may be combined with similar transactions as Other Gains and Losses. On the statement of cash flows, we show the $20,000 cash as an inflow from investing activities. If we use the direct method for reporting cash flows from operating activities, there is no further entry. If we use the indirect method, we must deduct the $9,750 gain from net income in computing cash flows from operating activities.

3.		
Selling price		$20,000
Net book value of equipment sold is		
$41,000 − ($9,000 + $9,000) =		23,000
Loss on sale of equipment		$ 3,000

Even though the sales price is the same as in number 2, there is a loss of $3,000 instead of a gain of $9,750 because the book value is $12,750 higher. The amount of the gain or loss on equipment being disposed of depends on the depreciation method used.

Impairment of Tangible Assets

Events or circumstances may arise that result in the impairment of property, plant, and equipment. An asset is considered to be **impaired** when it ceases to have economic value to the company at least as large as the carrying value (book value) of the asset. The FASB requires companies to review assets for possible impairment.

impaired
When an asset ceases to have economic value to the company at least as large as the book value of the asset.

OBJECTIVE 9

Account for the impairment of tangible assets.

recoverability test

A test for asset impairment that compares the total expected future net cash flows from the use of the asset and its eventual disposal with the net book value of the asset.

Impairment of Assets Held for Use

Suppose that Gap Inc. owns equipment that is carried on its books at a net book value of $150,000. Due to a change in store design and product demand, Gap determines the asset must be reviewed for impairment. The first step in the process is to perform a **recoverability test** that compares the total expected future net cash flows from the use of the asset and its eventual disposal with the carrying value of the asset. If the total expected future net cash flows are less than the carrying value, the asset is considered to be impaired. If the total expected future net cash flows are greater than the carrying value, the asset is not impaired. Gap estimates the total expected future net cash flows to be $127,000. Because this is less than $150,000 there is evidence of impairment. Thus Gap proceeds to the second step, which is computation of the impairment loss.

The impairment loss is the amount by which the carrying value of the asset exceeds its fair value. If there is an active market for the asset being evaluated, the market price is used as the fair value. In the absence of an active market, Gap must estimate the market value of the expected future net cash flows. Notice that Gap used the total of all expected future net cash flows to determine whether impairment occurred. However, it uses the current market value of those expected future net cash flows to calculate the magnitude of the loss. The current market value of the expected future cash flows will be less than their total because of uncertainty and the fact that a dollar today is worth more than a dollar in the future. Assume that the estimated current market value of the asset is $105,000. Therefore, Gap must record an impairment loss of $45,000.

Net book value of the equipment	$150,000
Minus: Fair value (market value) of the equipment	105,000
Impairment loss	$ 45,000

The entry to record the impairment loss is:

Loss on impairment	$45,000	
Accumulated depreciation		$45,000

Gap reports this loss as part of continuing operations. If the dollar amount is large enough, the loss may appear as a separate line item on the income statement. If it is relatively small in magnitude, it is likely to be combined with other expenses. The new book value of the asset is $105,000. Even if the fair value of the equipment increases above $105,000, Gap cannot write the asset back up. Once the impairment loss has been recorded, it may not be restored.

In fact, footnote 1 in Gap Inc.'s 2003 annual report states: "Upon indication that the carrying value of such (long-lived) assets may not be recoverable, we recognize an impairment loss in our operating expenses on the Consolidated Statements of Operations. We recorded a charge for the impairment of store assets of $22.6 million, $39.9 million and $13.9 million during fiscal 2003, 2002 and 2001, respectively."

Impairment of Assets to Be Disposed Of

A company may have long-lived assets that it is holding for resale. These assets are also subject to a test for impairment, although the test is somewhat different than that discussed for assets in use. The recoverability test is still the first step. However, the impairment loss, if any, is the excess of the carrying value of the asset over the fair value less the cost to sell. A second difference is that impairment losses taken on assets held for sale can be recovered. Suppose that the asset discussed previously is not used by Gap; rather Gap has the asset for sale and expects to sell it within the year. The following facts apply:

Net book value of the equipment	$150,000
Total future expected net cash flows	127,000
Market value of the asset	105,000
Estimated costs to sell	7,500

The recoverability test establishes that the asset is impaired. Gap computes the fair value of the equipment to be the market value of the asset minus the estimated costs to sell or $97,500 = $105,000 − $7,500. The impairment loss is:

Net book value of the equipment	$150,000
Minus: Fair value of the equipment	97,500
Impairment loss	$ 52,500

If the fair value of the asset subsequently increases from $97,500 to $110,000, Gap will write the asset back up to $110,000. Assets held for resale can be written up following an impairment loss, as long as the write-up never results in a value in excess of the net book value of the asset at the time of the original impairment.

Intangible Assets

We now turn our attention to another group of long-lived assets—intangibles. These assets are not physical items, but instead are rights or claims to expected benefits that are often contractual in nature. The FASB significantly altered the accounting for intangible assets in 2001.

OBJECTIVE 10
Account for various intangible assets.

The accounting for intangible assets depends on two factors: (1) whether a company acquires the intangible from an external party or develops it internally, and (2) whether the intangible asset has a finite or indefinite life. Consider the first of these issues. A company's balance sheet lists an intangible asset only if the company purchased the rights to the asset from an external party. It does not list equally valuable assets created by internal expenditures. For example, suppose **Pfizer** paid $5 million to another company for a drug patent developed by that company. Pfizer would record the $5 million as an intangible asset and amortize that cost over the useful life of the patent. In contrast, suppose Pfizer spent $5 million to internally develop and patent a new drug. Pfizer would charge this $5 million to expense, and it would not recognize the patent as an asset.

Why does this discrepancy exist between externally acquired and internally developed items? Recall that one of the criteria for recognition of an asset is that the future benefits provided by that asset can be quantified with a reasonable degree of precision. The FASB believes that it is difficult for management to value the results of its internal research and development efforts honestly and objectively. As a result, GAAP requires companies to expense the costs of internal research, advertising, and employee training immediately, despite the fact that the company surely expects future benefits. However, when one company purchases the results of another company's efforts, the negotiated purchase price realistically measures the value. From the purchaser's perspective, that negotiated price is a verifiable historical cost.

This discrepancy has generated significant debate. More recent years have seen an increase in the number of firms in the economy that are "knowledge-based" businesses. The value of these firms lies in intangibles such as internal research and development activities and intellectual capital. However, under existing accounting principles, if a company does not acquire these resources externally, it cannot record them as assets. Some analysts believe that R&D and perhaps other expenditures for intellectual capital should be capitalized and they make the adjustment themselves, as shown in the Business First box on page 358.

There is one exception to the automatic expensing of internal research and development costs. Computer software companies capitalize some of the costs of developing and producing software that they intend to sell or lease, and then amortize these capitalized amounts over the estimated product life. Companies in this industry expense R&D costs up to the

Under GAAP, most companies must immediately expense internal R&D expenditures. Why? The FASB decided that it is hard to determine whether R&D will be valuable, and, if it is valuable, it is hard to estimate the value and predict the period of time over which a company will realize this value. Some analysts believe it is important to treat R&D as an asset to fully understand the total commitment of resources a company has made. They assume a useful life and develop a hypothetical value for R&D.

To illustrate, consider the following data for Eli Lilly. R&D spending in the 5-year period 1998 to 2002 rose from $1.739 billion in 1998 to $2.149 billion in 2002 and totaled more than $9.9 billion. Suppose Lilly capitalized these amounts each year as incurred and then amortized them over the subsequent 4 years on a straight-line basis (25% per year). Under this procedure, the $1.739 billion spent in 1998 would appear as an asset of $1.739 billion at year-end and would give rise to amortization of $434.75 million in each of the next 4 years. By the end of 2002, it would be fully amortized and would not appear as an asset.

Consider Lilly's financial statements for 2002 ($ amounts are in millions). If Lilly was allowed to capitalize R&D, we can calculate the 2002 R&D expense of $1,944.0 million and R&D asset of $5,280.25 million as shown below.

Under capitalization, how would the financial statements differ from what Eli Lilly reported under GAAP? Net earnings for 2002 would be higher because R&D expense on the income statement would be $1,944 million, instead of the $2,149 million actually recorded in 2002. This lowers the R&D expense by about $205 million. On the balance sheet, assets would be higher by $5.28 billion or about 28% greater than the actual reported assets of $19.0 billion. Of course, if assets are higher, there needs to be an offsetting effect on the other side of the balance sheet equation, and retained earnings and some liabilities for taxes would also be higher.

Lilly and other pharmaceutical companies are extreme cases because R&D typically represents more than 15% of sales (about 19.4% for Lilly in 2002). Some young, biotech start-ups have even more substantial R&D spending on a proportional basis. Indeed, some of these start-ups have no sales, and if they expense R&D immediately for accounting purposes, they sometimes have essentially no assets. Yet these companies may have very high market values because the ideas they have generated have great potential. Research-intensive firms and young start-up firms are two examples where adjustments to the data from the historical-cost accounting model are often useful for analyzing the firm. The 4-year amortization period in this example is arbitrary and was chosen in part to simplify the example. In various industries, different assumptions might be appropriate depending on how quickly technology is changing.

(all dollar amounts in millions)

Year of R&D Expenditure	R&D Expenditure	2002 Income Statement R&D Expense	% of R&D Spending Unamortized at End of 2002	Balance Sheet Asset—12/31/02
1998	$ 1,739	$ 434.75	0	$ 0.00
1999	1,784	446.00	25	446.00
2000	2,018	504.50	50	1,009.00
2001	2,235	558.75	75	1,676.25
2002	2,149	—	100	2,149.00
Total 2002 Value		$1,944.00		$5,280.25

Source: http://lilly.com/investor/annual-report/lillyar2002complete.pdf

time when the company considers the software product to be technologically feasible. After that point, and prior to the time the product actually goes into production, R&D costs are capitalized. This exception can have a significant impact on the financial statements of companies in the software development industry. The balance sheet of BMC Software, Inc. for the year ended March 31, 2003 shows $192.7 million in capitalized software development costs, net of accumulated amortization. The $192.7 million is almost 7% of BMC's total assets. For the same time period, amortization of software development costs totaled $107.6 million, slightly more than 8% of total sales revenue.

Once a company has capitalized a purchased intangible asset, the remaining question is how to account for that asset going forward. The accounting treatment depends on whether the asset is considered to have a finite life or an indefinite life. Companies do not amortize intangible assets deemed to have indefinite lives. Instead, they evaluate these assets periodically for decreases in value. In contrast, companies amortize finite-lived intangible assets over their estimated useful lives. The useful life of an intangible asset is the shorter of its economic useful life or its legal life, if any. Because of obsolescence, the useful lives of intangible assets are often shorter than their legal lives. To gain a better understanding of this process, we now examine some specific intangible assets that have finite lives and hence are subject to amortization.

INTERPRETING FINANCIAL STATEMENTS

A major pharmaceutical company acquires a biotechnology company that is heavily involved in research and development activities. The research and development of the biotech firm has resulted in only one patented process. However, it has an extensive research pipeline. It is this pipeline that is of most interest to the pharmaceutical company. The total purchase price is $100 million. An independent valuation of the fair market value of the one patent acquired in the transaction set the value at $15 million. The remainder of the purchase price is attributable to the pipeline, which is commonly called "Purchased In-process Research and Development." How should the pharmaceutical company account for this acquisition?

Answer

The company would record the patent as an intangible asset valued at $15 million. It is evident that the pharmaceutical company believes the research pipeline has future benefit or it would not have been willing to pay $100 million. The accounting treatment of in-process R&D acquired in an acquisition has been a matter of considerable disagreement in recent years. Some argue that these costs, or a portion of these costs, should be treated as an asset. After all, one of the criteria for recognition of an asset is the provision of future benefits. However, under current GAAP, the $85 million of purchased in-process R&D must be expensed by the pharmaceutical company, due to the uncertainty of the benefits to be derived from those expenditures.

Examples of Intangible Assets

Patents are grants by the federal government to the inventor of a product or process, bestowing (in the United States) the exclusive right to produce and sell a given product, or use a process, for up to 20 years. After that time, others can manufacture the product or use the process. Suppose a company acquires a newly patented product from an inventor for $170,000. Although the remaining legal life of this patent is 20 years, because of fast-changing technology, the economic life of the patent is only 5 years. Amortization is taken over the shorter of the economic or legal life — $170,000 ÷ 5 = $34,000 per year, instead of $170,000 ÷ 20 = $8,500 per year.

patents
Grants by the federal government to an inventor, bestowing (in the United States) the exclusive right for 20 years to produce and sell a given product, or to use a process.

Copyrights are exclusive rights to reproduce and sell a book, musical composition, film, or similar creative item. In the United States, the federal government issues these rights and provides protection to a company or individual for the life of the creator plus 70 years. The initial costs of obtaining copyrights from the government are nominal; however, a company may pay a large sum to purchase an existing copyright from the owner. For example, a publisher of paperback books will sometimes pay the author of a popular

copyrights
Exclusive rights to reproduce and sell a book, musical composition, film, or similar creative item.

novel in excess of $1 million for the writer's copyright. In 1985, Michael Jackson purchased the rights to more than 250 Beatles songs for $47.5 million! Although copyrights have a long legal life, their economic lives may be no longer than 2 or 3 years, so amortization occurs accordingly.

Trademarks are distinctive identifications of a manufactured product or of a service, taking the form of a name, a sign, a slogan, a logo, or an emblem. An example is an emblem for Coca-Cola or the Prentice-Hall logo on the spine of this book. Trademarks, trade names, trade brands, secret formulas, and similar items are property rights with economic lives depending on their length of use. If you look at Coca-Cola's balance sheet you see no accounting recognition of its secret formula. It was internally developed, not purchased, so it is not recorded. In fact, the story is that Coca-Cola chose to keep the formula a secret instead of patenting it because they did not want the patent protection to expire and leave others free to produce the product. The Coca-Cola balance sheet also does not report an intangible asset for the Coca-Cola trademark, although Coke has spent millions of advertising dollars creating public awareness of the brand and millions more dollars protecting it from infringement. Coca-Cola's balance sheet does show an account entitled trademarks. What does this account represent? The trademarks of such companies as *Fanta* and *Minute-Maid*, which were acquired by Coca-Cola, are listed as intangible assets. Similarly, PepsiCo includes a trademark value for *Gatorade* among its intangible assets because it purchased the trademark rights when it bought Quaker Oats Company.

Franchises and **licenses** are legal contracts that grant the buyer the right to sell a product or service in accordance with specified conditions. An example is a local McDonald's franchise. The buyer obtains the right to use the McDonald's name, to acquire branded products such as cups and bags, and to share in advertising and special promotions. In exchange, the franchisee promises to follow McDonald's procedures and maintain standards of quality, cleanliness, and pricing. Other private sector companies may award franchises for car dealerships, hotel operations, or gasoline stations. These types of franchise agreements typically have a finite life. Therefore, franchisees should capitalize the upfront franchise fee and amortize the fee over its useful life.

Government agencies may grant franchises or operating licenses to a company, awarding it the right to use publicly held property in the operation of its business. Examples include the use of public property for the placement of telephone or electric utility lines, or the use of the airwaves for broadcasting purposes. The lengths of the franchises vary from 1 year to perpetuity. As mentioned previously, one of the factors that determines the accounting for externally acquired intangible assets is whether the asset has a finite or an indefinite life. The FASB used a broadcast license as an explicit example of an intangible asset that might have an indefinite life. Broadcast licenses have a 5-year legal life, but may be renewed indefinitely at a nominal cost to the broadcaster.

A **leasehold** is the right to use a fixed asset (such as a building or some portion thereof) for a specified period of time beyond 1 year. Companies often classify leaseholds with plant assets on the balance sheet, although they are technically intangible assets. A company that owns its own plant clearly counts that plant as a tangible asset. However, if a company leases its plant, then it owns only the right to use the leased plant, not the plant itself. Because the leasehold provides future benefits (in this case, the use of the plant) but does not give the company ownership of the plant, it is an intangible asset. Leases of this type are discussed in Chapter 9.

Related to a leasehold is a **leasehold improvement,** which occurs when a lessee (tenant) spends money to add new materials or improvements to a leased property. These improvements become part of the leased property, and revert to the lessor at the end of the lease. A leasehold improvement can take various forms. Examples are the installation of new fixtures, panels, walls, and air-conditioning equipment that the lessee must leave on the premises when a lease expires. Companies generally amortize the costs of leasehold improvements over the life of the lease, even if the physical life of the leasehold

trademarks
Distinctive identifications of a manufactured product or of a service taking the form of a name, a sign, a slogan, a logo, or an emblem.

franchises (licenses)
Privileges granted by a government, manufacturer, or distributor to sell a product or service in accordance with specified conditions.

leasehold
The right to use a fixed asset for a specified period of time, typically beyond 1 year.

leasehold improvement
Investments by a lessee in items that are not permitted to be removed from the premises when a lease expires, such as installation of new fixtures, panels, walls, and air-conditioning equipment.

improvement is longer. For example, Gap Inc. amortizes its leasehold improvements over the life of the lease, not to exceed 12 years.

Impairment of Intangible Assets

The rules governing impairment of limited life intangible assets are the same as those for long-lived tangible assets discussed earlier in this chapter. Indefinite life intangibles other than goodwill are also subject to impairment testing. However, the rules are slightly different. No recoverability test is required. Rather, the carrying value of the intangible asset is compared with its fair value. If the carrying value is less than the fair value, no impairment has occurred. If the carrying value is greater than the fair value, an impairment loss for the difference must be recognized.

Goodwill

All of the intangible assets discussed so far are separately identifiable. In other words, these are assets that one company could sell to another. Goodwill is an intangible asset that cannot be separated from the company that owns it and therefore the company cannot sell or transfer it. **Goodwill** arises when one company buys another company. It is the excess of the cost of the acquired company over the fair market value of its identifiable net assets. We discuss goodwill in more detail in Chapter 11.

O B J E C T I V E **11**

Explain the reporting for goodwill.

goodwill
The excess of the cost of an acquired company over the fair market value of its indentifiable net assets.

Assume that Millard Corporation purchases Tigner Company for a total of $10 million in cash. At the time of the acquisition, Tigner has total assets with a fair market value of $19 million and total liabilities with a fair market value of $13 million. Therefore, the fair market value of the assets less the liabilities of Tigner is $6 million. Nevertheless, Millard has agreed to pay $10 million for Tigner. Chapter 11 discusses the reasons why one company might pay a premium for another and how it would allocate the purchase price to various assets and liabilities. In our example, Millard accounts for the business combination with a summary journal entry that looks like this (in millions of dollars):

Goodwill	4	
Total Assets of Tigner	19	
Total Liabilities of Tigner		13
Cash		10

Millard records goodwill as a noncurrent asset on its books.

Prior to 2001, GAAP in the United States required companies to amortize goodwill over a period of time not to exceed 40 years. However, in 2001 the FASB eliminated the amortization of goodwill and instead required companies to review goodwill for impairment each year. The details of the steps required to test goodwill for impairment are beyond the scope of this textbook. However, if a company determines that the goodwill is not worth its carrying value, the company must write down the goodwill to its current value, which in some cases might be zero. For example, when AOL purchased Time Warner in 2000, AOL recorded almost $130 billion in goodwill. In early 2002, AOL estimated that the current value of goodwill was $54.2 billion less than the recorded value and recorded a noncash pretax charge for the impairment of goodwill. This impairment loss reduced AOL's first quarter net loss of $1 million to a net loss of more than $54 billion! During the fourth quarter of 2002, the company recorded an additional noncash charge of almost $45 billion for the further impairment of goodwill. Due to the rules governing the change in accounting, the $54 billion first quarter impairment loss was treated as the cumulative effect of a change in accounting method, whereas the $45 billion fourth quarter impairment loss was treated as a loss from continuing operations. After this $99 billion impairment loss, AOL Time Warner reported a net loss of $98.7 billion for 2002.

The AOL annual report detailed the following changes in goodwill over the year ending December 31, 2002. All dollar amounts are in millions.

Goodwill, January 1, 2002	$ 127,420
Additional goodwill and adjustments	8,450
Cumulative effect of accounting change for goodwill impairment	(54,199)
Fourth quarter impairment	(44,685)
Goodwill, December 31, 2002	$ 36,986

Depletion of Natural Resources

OBJECTIVE 12

Interpret the depletion of natural resources.

Our final group of long-lived assets is natural resources, such as minerals, oil, and timber (sometimes called wasting assets). Depletion is the accounting measure used to allocate the acquisition cost of natural resources. Depletion differs from depreciation because depletion focuses specifically on the physical use and exhaustion of the natural resources, whereas depreciation focuses more broadly on any reduction of the economic value of a fixed asset, including physical deterioration and obsolescence.

The costs of natural resources are usually classified as fixed assets. However, buying natural resources is actually like buying massive quantities of inventories under the ground (iron ore) or above the ground (timber). Depletion expense is the measure of that portion of this "long-term inventory" that is used up in a particular period. For example, a coal mine may cost $20 million and originally contain an estimated 1 million tons of usable coal. The depletion rate would be $20 million ÷ 1 million tons = $20 per ton. If 100,000 tons were mined during the first year, the depletion would be 100,000 × $20, or $2 million for that year. Each year the amount of coal extracted would be measured, and the amount of depletion recorded would be based on that usage.

As our coal mine example shows, depletion is measured on a units-of-production basis. The annual depletion may be accounted for as a direct reduction of the asset, or it may be accumulated in a separate contra account similar to accumulated depreciation. Environmental laws and ethical responsibility often lead a firm to expend substantial amounts to return the site to a safe and attractive condition after exhausting the natural resources. When calculating the depletion per unit, companies should add these expected future costs in computing the total costs subject to depletion. Therefore, the depletion per unit would include not only the original cost of the resources, but also future restoration costs. The portion of depletion that represents future costs for site restoration can be added to a Liability for Restoration account that grows as extraction continues.

Highlights to Remember

1 **Distinguish a company's expenses from expenditures that it should capitalize.** Accountants must choose between capitalizing or expensing each expenditure. They should capitalize expenditures with benefits extending beyond the current year and should expense the others.

2 **Measure the acquisition cost of tangible assets such as land, buildings, and equipment.** The acquisition cost includes both an asset's purchase price and all incidental costs necessary to get it ready for use.

3 **Compute depreciation for buildings and equipment using various depreciation methods.** Depreciation is a systematic allocation of historical costs over the useful life of the asset. Three common depreciation methods discussed in the text are straight-line, DDB, and unit depreciation. Straight-line

is a constant amount per year of use. We calculate it by dividing depreciable value (cost less residual value) by the shorter of physical or economic life. DDB is a declining-balance method that records the largest annual amount in the first full year of use and declining amounts thereafter. The annual depreciation charge is a percentage of the book value at the beginning of the year. For DDB the percentage is twice the percentage used for straight-line, that is, $2 \times (100\% \div \text{years of life})$. Unit depreciation is based on the physical use of the asset, for example miles for a vehicle. The cost per unit is the depreciable value divided by the estimated units of use from the asset. We multiply this cost per unit by the actual units of use to determine the annual depreciation.

4 **Recalculate depreciation in response to a change in estimated useful life or residual value.** New information may cause the initial estimate of useful life or residual value to be revised. If the use of the new estimate would result in a significant change in depreciation expense, the new estimate must be adopted and the depreciation schedule revised. A change in estimate is treated as a prospective adjustment. The company does not go back and revise the depreciation expense taken in prior periods. Rather, depreciation expense for the period in which the estimate is revised and all future periods is recomputed based on the revised estimate.

5 **Differentiate financial statement depreciation from income tax depreciation.** Financial reports to shareholders often differ from the reports to tax authorities. Rules governing financial statement presentation produce information useful to investors and managers. Tax rules governing determination of tax obligations achieve political and economic goals and give taxpayers the right to make certain choices with an eye to maximizing expenses and therefore minimizing the tax obligation. Keeping two sets of records to satisfy these two purposes is necessary, not illegal or unethical.

6 **Explain the effect of depreciation on cash flow.** By itself, depreciation does not provide cash. However, depreciation is deductible for income tax purposes. Therefore, the larger the depreciation reported on the tax return in any given year, the lower the annual pretax income and subsequent income taxes, and the greater the amount of cash that a company may keep instead of disbursing it to the income tax authorities.

7 **Account for expenditures after acquisition.** Companies should immediately expense any expenditures that represent routine repairs or maintenance of fixed assets. In contrast, they should capitalize improvements that increase the future benefits provided by a fixed asset, adding the amount to the value of the asset.

8 **Compute gains and losses on the disposal of fixed assets and consider the impact of these gains and losses on the statement of cash flows.** Gains and losses on disposal of fixed assets arise because the proceeds of the sale are not identical to the book value of the asset sold (original historical cost less accumulated depreciation). If the proceeds exceed the book value, the company realizes a gain on its income statement. If the proceeds are less, it records a loss. On the statement of cash flows, the cash proceeds from sales of fixed assets constitute cash provided by investing activities. Under the direct method, they have no effect on our calculation of cash flows from operations. When using the indirect method, the starting point is net income, which includes any gains or losses from asset sales. To adjust net income in calculating net cash provided by operating activities, we subtract gains from, or add losses to, net income.

9 **Account for the impairment of tangible assets.** Events or circumstances may arise that cause an asset to have an economic value to the company that is smaller than the carrying value of that asset. The FASB has implemented a two-step process to test for the impairment of tangible assets. The first step is a recoverability test, which compares the total expected future net cash flows from the asset and its eventual disposition to the carrying value of the asset. If the carrying value is greater than the future cash flows, the asset is considered to be impaired. If the assets are held for use, the impairment loss is the amount by which the carrying value of the asset exceeds its fair value as measured by the market value of the expected future net cash flows. If the assets are held for resale purposes, the impairment loss is the amount by which the carrying value of the asset exceeds its fair value less the cost to sell.

10 **Account for various intangible assets.** Intangible assets are not physical in nature. Instead, they are legal or contractual rights. Examples include, patents, trademarks, and copyrights. Companies capitalize such assets when purchased from external parties. Some purchased intangibles have finite lives. Companies amortize these intangibles on a straight-line basis over their useful lives. The unamortized book value appears on the balance sheet as an asset. Other purchased intangible assets have indefinite lives. Companies do not amortize these intangibles, but they review them regularly for impairment and write them down if their fair market value is less than their book value. Companies do not capitalize internally created intangible assets. Instead, they expense such outlays as incurred.

11 **Explain the reporting for goodwill.** Goodwill is an intangible asset measured as the excess of the purchase price of an acquired company over the fair market value of its identifiable net assets. Companies do not amortize goodwill, but they must write it down when they deem its value to be impaired.

12 **Interpret the depletion of natural resources.** Depletion refers to the accounting process for allocating the cost of natural resources over the periods of extraction. Companies typically use the units-of-production method to allocate the cost of acquiring natural resources. In some cases, there are future costs to be incurred to minimize the environmental damage by returning the site to an acceptable condition. Accountants estimate those future costs and include them in the annual depletion charges to appropriately match the full cost to the revenues generated over time.

Accounting Vocabulary

accelerated depreciation, p. 344
amortization, p. 338
basket purchase, p. 341
betterment, p. 350
capital improvement, p. 350
capitalize, p. 338
copyrights, p. 359
depletion, p. 338
depreciable value, p. 341
depreciation schedule, p. 342
disposal value, p. 341
double-declining-balance (DDB) method, p. 344

expenditures, p. 338
fair market value, p. 340
fixed assets, p. 337
franchises, p. 360
goodwill, p. 361
impaired, p. 355
improvement, p. 350
intangible assets, p. 337
leasehold, p. 360
leasehold improvement, p. 360
licenses, p. 360
nonmonetary exchange, p. 340

patents, p. 359
plant assets, p. 337
recoverability test, p. 356
residual value, p. 341
salvage value, p. 341
scrap value, p. 341
straight-line depreciation, p. 342
tangible assets, p. 337
terminal value, p. 341
trademarks, p. 360
unit depreciation, p. 343
useful life, p. 341

Assignment Material

Questions

8-1 Distinguish between *tangible* and *intangible assets*.

8-2 Distinguish between *amortization*, *depreciation*, and *depletion*.

8-3 "The cash discount on the purchase of equipment is income to the buyer during the year of acquisition." Do you agree? Explain.

8-4 "When an expenditure is capitalized, we credit the stockholders' equity account." Do you agree? Explain.

8-5 "Accumulated depreciation is a sum of cash being accumulated for the replacement of fixed assets." Do you agree? Explain.

8-6 "The accounting process of depreciation is allocation, not valuation." Explain.

8-7 Criticize: "Depreciation is the loss in value of a fixed asset over a given span of time."

8-8 "Keeping two sets of books is immoral." Do you agree? Explain.

8-9 Compare the choice between straight-line and accelerated depreciation with the choice between FIFO and LIFO. Give at least one similarity and one difference.

8-10 "Most of the money we'll spend this year for replacing our equipment will be generated by depreciation." Do you agree? Explain.

8-11 "Accelerated depreciation saves cash but shows lower net income." Explain.

8-12 Contrast repairs and maintenance expenditures with expenditures for capital improvements or betterments.

8-13 The manager of a division reported to the president of the company: "Now that our major capital improvements are finished, the division's expenses will be much lower." Is this really what this manager means to say? Explain.

8-14 "The gain on sale of equipment should be reported fully on the income statement." Explain what the complete reporting would include.

8-15 Name and describe four kinds of intangible assets.

8-16 "We account for internally acquired patents differently than we account for externally acquired patents." Explain the difference.

8-17 "Accountants sometimes are too concerned with physical objects." Explain.

8-18 "Accountants cannot capitalize improvements made to leased property by a tenant because they become part of the leased property and therefore belong to the lessor." Do you agree? Explain.

8-19 XYZ Company's only transaction in 20X1 was the sale of a fixed asset for $20,000 cash. The income statement included only "Gain on sale of fixed asset, $5,000." Correct the following statement of cash flows.

Cash flows from operating activities	
Gain on sale of fixed assets	$ 5,000
Cash flows from investing activities	
Proceeds from sale of	
fixed assets	20,000
Total increase in cash	$25,000

8-20 The Lawrence Company sold fixed assets with a book value of $5,000 and recorded a gain of $4,000. How should the company report this on the statement of cash flows prepared using the indirect method.

8-21 "In a basket purchase, all assets that are part of the purchase must be depreciated over the same useful lives." Do you agree? Explain.

8-22 "The recoverability test determines the magnitude of the impairment loss on a piece of equipment used in the manufacturing process." Do you agree? Explain.

Critical Thinking Questions

8-23 Production Facilities and Depreciation

A manager complained about the amount of depreciation charged on the plant for which she was responsible: "The market value of my plant just continues to increase, yet I am hit with large depreciation charges on my income statement and the value of my plant and equipment on the balance sheet goes down each year. This doesn't seem fair." Comment on this statement, focusing on the relation of asset values on the balance sheet to market values of the assets.

8-24 Research and Development and the Recognition of Intangible Assets

In the United States, expenditures for most R&D are charged directly to expense. In some other countries, companies can recognize such costs as assets. Suppose you are manager of an R&D department. Which method of accounting for R&D would be most consistent with the information you use for decision making? Explain.

8-25 Capital Investment and the Statement of Cash Flows

Growing companies often need capital to purchase or build additional facilities. There are many potential sources of such capital. Describe how an investor might use the statement of cash flows to learn how a company financed its capital expansion.

8-26 Accounting Valuation of Fixed Assets

Consider two types of assets held by Weyerhaeuser Company: timber-growing land purchased in 1910 when the company was known as Weyerhaeuser Timber Company, and machinery purchased and installed at its paper processing plant in Saskatchewan, Canada, in 2002. How close do you suppose the December 31, 2003 balance sheet value of each asset is to the market value of the asset at that date?

Exercises

8-27 Computing Acquisition Costs

On January 1, 20X2, Edmonton University acquired a 20-acre parcel of land immediately adjacent to its existing facilities. The land included a warehouse, parking lots, and driveways. The university paid $600,000 cash and also gave a note for $3 million, payable at $300,000 per year plus interest of 10% on the outstanding balance.

The university demolished the warehouse at a cash cost of $150,000 so it could be replaced with a new classroom building. For construction of the building, the university made a cash down payment of $3 million and gave a mortgage note of $7 million. The mortgage was payable at $250,000 per year plus interest of 10% on the outstanding balance.

1. Calculate the cost that Edmonton University should add to its Land account and its Building account.

2. Prepare journal entries (without explanations) to record the preceding transactions.

8-28 Government Equipment

An office of the IRS acquired some used computer equipment. Installation costs were $8,000. Repair costs prior to use were $9,000. The purchasing manager, with a salary of $54,000 per annum, spent 1 month evaluating equipment and completing the transaction. The invoice price was $400,000. The seller paid its salesman a commission of 4% and offered the buyer a cash discount of 2% if the invoice was paid within 60 days. Freight costs were $4,400, paid by the purchaser. Repairs during the first year of use were $10,000.

Compute the total capitalized cost to be added to the Equipment account. The seller was paid within 60 days.

8-29 Basket Purchase

On February 21, 20X2, Speed-Tune, an auto service chain, acquired an existing building and land for $720,000 from a local gas station that had failed. The tax assessor had placed an assessed valuation of $200,000 on the land and $400,000 on the building as of January 1, 20X2.

Land	$200,000
Building	400,000
Total	$600,000

How much of the $720,000 purchase price should be attributed to the building? Why?

8-30 Basket Purchase of Sports Franchise

Paul Allen, co-founder of Microsoft, purchased the Seattle Seahawks, an NFL football team. Assume a total purchase price of $300 million. The largest assets are the franchise and the player contracts. Assume that for reporting to the IRS, the franchise has an indefinite useful life whereas the contracts have a 5-year useful life. Other assets are relatively minor. Suppose the seller shows the following book values of the assets ($ in millions):

Player contracts	$30
Franchise	50
Total book value	$80

As Allen, if you have complete discretion for tax purposes, how much of the $300 million price would you allocate to the player contracts? Explain.

8-31 Journal Entries for Depreciation

(Alternates are 8-32 and 8-33.) On January 1, 20X1, the Dayton Auto Parts Company acquired nine identical assembly robots for a total of $594,000 cash. The robots had an expected useful life of 10 years and an expected residual value of $54,000 in total. Dayton uses straight-line depreciation.

1. Set up T-accounts and prepare the journal entries for the acquisition and for the first annual depreciation charge. Post to T-accounts.
2. On December 31, 20X3, Dayton sold one of the robots for $42,000 in cash. The robot had an original cost of $66,000 and an expected residual value of $6,000. Prepare the journal entry for the sale.
3. Refer to requirement 2. Suppose Dayton had sold the robot for $52,000 cash instead of $42,000. Prepare the journal entry for the sale.

8-32 Journal Entries for Depreciation

(Alternates are 8-31 and 8-33.) The Alaska Airlines balance sheet dated June 30, 2003 included the following ($ in millions):

Property and equipment	
Flight equipment	$2,279.8
Ground property and equipment	441.7
Deposits for future flight equipment	80.3
Less accumulated depreciation and amortization	(870.1)
Net Property and Equipment	$1,931.7

Assume that on July 1, 2003, Alaska acquired some new maintenance equipment for $880,000 cash. The equipment had an expected useful life of 5 years and an expected residual value of $80,000. Alaska uses straight-line depreciation.

1. Prepare the journal entry that would be made annually for depreciation on the new equipment.
2. Suppose Alaska sold some of the equipment they originally purchased on July 1, 2003. The equipment being sold had an original cost of $220,000 and an expected residual value of $20,000. Alaska sold the equipment for $160,000 cash 2 years after the purchase date. Prepare the journal entry for the sale.
3. Refer to requirement 2. Suppose Alaska had sold the equipment for $110,000 cash, instead of $160,000. Prepare the journal entry for the sale.

8-33 Journal Entries for Depreciation

(Alternates are 8-31 and 8-32.) The Coca-Cola Company's balance sheet of December 31, 2003 included the following ($ in millions):

Property, plant, and equipment	$9,622
Less allowances for depreciation	3,525
	$6,097

Note that the company uses "allowances for" instead of "accumulated" depreciation. Assume that on January 1, 2004, Coca-Cola acquired some new bottling equipment for $1.8 million cash. The equipment had an expected useful life of 5 years and an expected residual value of $300,000. Coca-Cola uses straight-line depreciation.

1. Prepare the journal entry that Coca-Cola would make annually for depreciation on the new equipment.
2. Suppose Coca-Cola sold some of the equipment they had purchased on January 1, 2004. The equipment being sold had an original cost of $60,000 and an expected residual value of $5,000. Coca-Cola sold the equipment for $32,000 cash 2 years after the purchase date. Prepare the journal entry for the sale
3. Refer to requirement 2. Suppose Coca-Cola had sold the equipment for $40,000 cash, instead of $32,000. Prepare the journal entry for the sale.

8-34 Simple Depreciation Computations

A company acquired the following assets:

a. Conveyor, 5-year useful life, $38,000 cost, straight-line method, $5,000 expected residual value.
b. Truck, 3-year useful life, $18,000 cost, DDB method, $1,500 expected residual value.

Compute the first 3 years of depreciation for each asset.

8-35 Unit Depreciation Method

The Rockland Transport Company has many trucks that have an estimated useful life of 250,000 miles. The company computes depreciation on a mileage basis. Suppose Rockland purchases a new truck for $80,000 cash. Its expected residual value is $5,000. Its mileage during year 1 is 60,000 and during year 2 is 90,000.

1. What is the depreciation expense for each of the 2 years?
2. Compute the gain or loss if Rockland sells the truck for $40,000 at the end of year two.

8-36 Fundamental Depreciation Approaches

(Alternates are 8-37 through 8-39.) U-Haul acquired new trucks for $1.2 million. Their estimated useful life is 4 years, and estimated residual value is $200,000.

Prepare a depreciation schedule similar to Exhibit 8-2, p. 345 comparing straight-line and DDB depreciation.

8-37 Units-of-Production, Straight-Line, and DDB

(Alternatives are 8-36, 8-38, and 8-39.) Yukon Mining Company buys special drills for $440,000 each. Each drill can extract about 150,000 tons of ore, after which it has a $40,000 residual value. Yukon bought one such drill in early January 20X1. Projected tonnage figures for the drill are 60,000 tons in 20X1, 45,000 tons in 20X2, and 45,000 tons in 20X3. The drill is scheduled for sale at the end of the third year at the $40,000 residual value. Yukon is considering unit depreciation, straight-line, or DDB depreciation for the drill.

Compute depreciation for each year under each of the three methods.

8-38 Comparison of Popular Depreciation Methods

(Alternates are 8-36, 8-37, and 8-39.) Port Angeles Cedar Company acquired a saw for $32,000 with an expected useful life of 5 years and a $2,000 expected residual value. Prepare a tabular comparison (similar to Exhibit 8-2, p. 345) of the annual depreciation and book value for each year under straight-line and DDB depreciation. If these two methods were available for tax reporting purposes, which would a company prefer to use?

8-39 Fundamental Depreciation Policies

(Alternates are 8-36 through 8-38.) Suppose the printing department of Safeco Insurance acquired a new press for $280,000. The equipment's estimated useful life is 8 years and estimated residual value is $20,000.

Prepare a depreciation schedule similar to Exhibit 8-2, p. 345, comparing straight-line and DDB. Show all amounts in thousands of dollars (rounded to the nearest tenth). Limit the schedule to the first 3 years of useful life. Show the depreciation for each year and the book value at the end of each year. (Note that this is a comparison of methods used for reporting to shareholders. Such methods may differ from those used for reporting to the income tax authorities.)

8-40 Balance Sheet Presentation of PPE

Boeing had the following items listed under property, plant, and equipment as of December 31, 2003 ($ in millions):

Construction in progress	$ 943
Land	457
Net property, plant, and equipment	8,432
Machines and equipment	10,824
Accumulated depreciation	?
Buildings	9,171

Prepare the property, plant, and equipment section of Boeing's December 31, 2003 balance sheet in proper form. Include the appropriate amount for accumulated depreciation.

8-41 Accumulated Depreciation

Oregon Steel Mills reported the following items on its December 31, 2003 balance sheet ($ in thousands):

Property, plant, and equipment, net	$477,581
Accumulated depreciation	440,607

1. Compute Oregon Steel's historical cost of property, plant, and equipment on December 31, 2003.
2. If Oregon Steel uses an 18-year economic life for computing straight-line depreciation on most of its assets, are most of their assets more than or less than 9 years old? Explain how you can determine this.

8-42 Revision of Useful Life and Residual Value Estimates

Nowling Company buys a machine for $75,000 on January 1, 2004. A residual value of $5,000 and a useful life of 10 years are estimated at the acquisition date. Nowling uses straight-line depreciation. Early in 2008, Nowling discovers that a competitor has come out with a new product that will reduce demand for Nowling's product. As a result, it estimates that the machine will no longer be of use after 2010. Nowling believes it will be able to sell the machine to a scrap dealer for $2,000 at that time.

Prepare a depreciation schedule similar to Exhibit 8-2, p. 345 comparing the original depreciation schedule (for 2004 through 2013) with the depreciation schedule based on the revised estimates of useful life and residual value (for 2004 through 2010). Show all amounts in thousands of dollars (rounded to the nearest tenth).

8-43 Depreciation, Income Taxes, and Cash Flow

Fleck Company began business with cash and common stockholders' equity of $150,000. The same day, December 31, 20X1, the company acquired equipment for $50,000 cash. The equipment had an expected useful life of 5 years and an expected residual value of $5,000. The first year's operations generated cash sales of $180,000 and cash operating expenses of $100,000.

1. Prepare an analysis of income and cash flow for the year 20X2, using the format illustrated in Exhibit 8-3 (p. 348). Assume (a) straight-line depreciation and (b) DDB depreciation. Assume an income tax rate of 40%. Fleck pays income taxes in cash. The company uses the same depreciation method for reporting to shareholders and to income tax authorities.
2. Examine your answer to requirement 1. Does depreciation provide cash? Explain as precisely as possible.
3. Suppose Fleck doubled its 20X2 depreciation under straight-line and DDB methods. How would this affect the before-tax cash flow? Be specific.

8-44 MACRS versus Straight-Line Depreciation

Chicago Machinery bought special tooling equipment for $1.8 million. The useful life is 5 years, with no residual value. For tax purposes, assume MACRS specifies a 3-year, DDB depreciation schedule. Chicago Machinery uses the straight-line depreciation method for reporting to shareholders.

1. Explain the two factors that account for the acceleration of depreciation for tax purposes.
2. Compute the first year's depreciation (a) for shareholder reporting and (b) for tax purposes. (Ignore complications in the tax law that are not introduced in this chapter.)

8-45 Leasehold Improvements

Pizza Hut has a 10-year lease on space in a suburban shopping center. Near the end of the sixth year of the lease, Pizza Hut exercised its rights under the lease, removing walls and replacing floor coverings and lighting fixtures. Pizza Hut would not be able to remove these improvements at the end of the lease term. The cost was $120,000. The useful life of the redesigned facilities was predicted to be 12 years.

What accounts would be affected by the $120,000 expenditure? What would be the annual amortization?

8-46 Classic Case from the Business Press

A news story concerning Chrysler Corporation stated:

> Yet the $7.5 billion that John J. Riccardo, its money man, estimates the company will need to finance a recovery over the next five years is huge by any standard. But, says Riccardo, "half is charged to the P&L [profit and loss] as incurred, so we're looking for $3.75 billion. Of that, about 60% will be recovered in depreciation and amortization. That leaves a balance of $1.5 billion over the five years, to be financed through earnings, borrowings, and divestitures. Over the period, that overall number is manageable."

Explain or comment on the following:

1. "Half is charged to the P&L as incurred, so we're looking for $3.75 billion."
2. "Of that, about 60% will be recovered in depreciation and amortization."

8-47 Capital Expenditures

Consider the following transactions:

a. Acquired building for a down payment plus a mortgage payable.
b. Paid plumbers for repair of leaky faucets.
c. Acquired new air-conditioning system for the building.
d. Paid interest on building mortgage.
e. Paid principal on building mortgage.
f. Paid cash dividends.
g. Replaced damaged front door (not covered by insurance).
h. Paid travel expenses of sales personnel.
i. Paid janitorial wages.
j. Paid security guard's wages.

Required

Answer by letter:

1. Indicate which transactions are capital expenditures.
2. Indicate which transactions are expenses in the current year.

8-48 Capital Expenditures

Consider each of the following transactions. For each one, indicate whether it is a capital expenditure (C) or an expense in the current year (E).

a. Paid a consultant to advise on marketing strategy.
b. Installed new lighting fixtures in a leased building.
c. Paid for routine maintenance on equipment.
d. Developed a patent that cost $50,000 in R&D.
e. Paid for overhaul of machinery that extends its useful life.
f. Acquired a patent from General Electric for $40,000.
g. Paid for a tune-up on one of the autos in the company's fleet.

8-49 Repairs and Improvements

Yakima Wheat Company acquired harvesting equipment for $90,000 with an expected useful life of 5 years and a $10,000 expected residual value. Yakima Wheat used straight-line depreciation. During its fourth year of service, expenditures related to the equipment were as follows:

1. Oiling and greasing, $200.
2. Replacing belts and hoses, $450.

3. Major overhaul during the final week of the year, including the replacement of an engine. The useful life of the equipment was extended from 5 to 7 years. The cost was $21,000. The residual value is now expected to be $11,000, instead of $10,000.

Indicate in words how each of the three items would affect the income statement and the balance sheet in the fourth year. Prepare a tabulation that compares the original depreciation schedule with the revised depreciation schedule.

8-50 Disposal of Equipment

The Outpatient Clinic of Eastside Hospital acquired X-ray equipment for $29,000 with an expected useful life of 5 years and a $4,000 expected residual value. The hospital uses straight-line depreciation. The clinic sold the equipment at the end of the fourth year for $12,000 cash.

1. Compute the gain or loss on the sale. Show the effects of the sale on the balance sheet equation, identifying all specific accounts by name. Where and how would the sale appear on the income statement?
2. (a) Show the journal entry for the transaction in requirement 1. (b) Repeat 2a, assuming that the cash sales price was $7,000 instead of $12,000.

8-51 Gain or Loss on Sale of Fixed Assets

Luigi's Pizza Company purchased a delivery van in early 20X1 for $45,000 and depreciated it on a straight-line basis over its useful life of 5 years. Estimated residual value was $5,000. The company sold the van in early 20X4 after recognizing 3 years of depreciation.

1. Suppose Luigi's Pizza received $25,000 cash for the van. Compute the gain or loss on the sale. Prepare the journal entry for the sale of the van.
2. Suppose Luigi's Pizza received $17,000 cash for the van. Compute the gain or loss on the sale. Prepare the journal entry for the sale of the van.

8-52 Gain or Loss on Disposal of Equipment—Cash Flow Implications

Icarus Software Company sold five computers. It had purchased the computers 5 years ago for $120,000, and accumulated depreciation at the time of sale was $90,000.

1. Suppose Icarus received $30,000 cash for the computers. How would the the company show the sale on its statement of cash flows?
2. Suppose Icarus received $40,000 cash for the computers. How would the company show the sale on its statement of cash flows (including the schedule reconciling net income and net cash provided by operating activities).
3. Redo requirement 2 assuming cash received was $20,000.

8-53 Various Intangible Assets and Impairment

(Alternative is 8-54.) Consider the following:

1. On December 29, 20X1, a publisher acquires the paperback copyright for a book by Steven King for $3 million. Most sales of this book are expected to take place uniformly during 20X2 and 20X3. What is the amortization for 20X2?
2. In 20X1, Company C spent $6 million in its research department, which resulted in new valuable patents. In December 20X1, Company D paid $6 million to an outside inventor for some valuable new patents. How would the income statements for the year ended December 31, 20X1 for each company be affected? How would the balance sheets as of December 31, 20X1 be affected?
3. On December 28, 20X8, Black Electronics Company purchased a patent for a calculator for $420,000. The patent has 10 years of its legal life remaining. Technology changes fast, so Black Electronics expects the patent to be worthless in 4 years. What is the amortization for 20X9?
4. (a) During the fiscal year ending December 31, 20X3, Samela Corporation paid $10 million in cash for Haddock Company. At the time of the acquisition, the total assets of Haddock had a fair market value of $22 million and the total liabilities had a fair market value of $16 million. What journal entry would Samela Corporation make to record the acquisition of Haddock?
   (b) On December 31, 20X4, Samela Corporation performed a review to determine if the goodwill recorded in the initial transaction had become impaired. The review indicated that the fair value of the goodwill was $3 million. Does Samela need to make a journal entry to recognize the impairment of goodwill? If so, prepare the entry.

8-54 Various Intangible Assets

(Alternative is 8-53.) Consider the following:

1. On December 29, 2000, Sony Corporation purchased a patent on some broadcasting equipment for $800,000. The patent has 16 years of its legal life remaining. Because technology moves rapidly, Sony expects the patent to be worthless at the end of 5 years. What is the amortization for 2001?

2. (a) Amgen, a biotech firm with almost $5 billion in revenues, spent more than $1,000 million in its research departments in 2002. These expenditures resulted in valuable new patents.

(b) Suppose that in December 2002, Amgen had paid $1,000 million to various outside companies for the same new patents. How would alternatives (a) and (b) affect Amgen's income statement for the year ended December 31, 2002? How would they affect Amgen's balance sheet on December 31, 2002?

3. IBM included $834 million of software in its "Investments and Sundry Assets" account on its 2002 balance sheet. The notes indicated that "Costs that are related to the conceptual formulation and design of licensed programs are expensed as R&D . . . the company capitalizes costs that are incurred to produce the finished product after technological feasibility is established. The annual amortization of the capitalized amounts is performed using the straight-line method and is applied over periods ranging up to three years." Suppose that IBM spends the same amount on this activity every year and that it amortizes all such software over 3 years on a straight-line basis. How would the income statement and balance sheet change if IBM changed the maximum term to 4 years and then amortized every dollar of capitalized software over 4 years?

8-55 Computation of Impairment on Long-Lived Assets

Vincent Corporation acquired an office building that it rents to a variety of small businesses. The building had an original cost of $15 million, and at the end of 20X5 it had a carrying value of $11 million. Due to a change in zoning regulations effective January 20X6, Vincent believes the building has become less desirable and expects rental rates to decline. Vincent deems it necessary to review the building for possible impairment.

The total expected future net cash flows are estimated to be $9 million. The market value of the building has decreased from $19 million to $7.5 million as a result of the zoning change.

Compute the amount of the impairment loss, if any, that Vincent should recognize on the building.

8-56 Depletion

A zinc mine contains an estimated 900,000 tons of zinc ore. The mine cost $14.4 million. The tonnage mined during 20X4, the first year of operations, was 120,000 tons.

1. What was the depletion for 20X4?
2. Suppose that in 20X5 a total of 100,000 tons were mined. What depletion expense would be charged for 20X5?

Problems

8-57 Popular Depreciation Methods

(Problem 8-71 is an extension of this problem.) The annual report of Alaska Airlines contained the following footnote:

> *PROPERTY, EQUIPMENT, AND DEPRECIATION—Property and equipment are recorded at cost and depreciated using the straight-line method over the estimated useful lives, which are as follows:*

Aircraft and other flight equipment	10–20 years
Buildings	10–30 years
Capitalized leases and leasehold improvements	Term of lease
Other equipment	3–15 years

Consider a Boeing 727-100 airplane that Alaska acquired for $30 million. Its useful life is 20 years, and its expected residual value is $6 million. Prepare a tabular comparison of the annual depreciation and book value for each of the first 3 years of service life under straight-line and DDB depreciation. Show all amounts in thousands of dollars (rounded to the nearest thousand). (Note that this is a comparison of methods used for reporting to shareholders. Such methods may differ from those used for reporting to the income tax authorities.) *Hint*: See Exhibit 8-2, p. 345.

8-58 Depreciation Practices

The annual report of General Mills, maker of *Wheaties*, *Cheerios*, and *Betty Crocker* baking products, for the year ended May 25, 2003 contained the following ($ in millions):

	2003	2002
Total land, buildings, and equipment	$4,929	$4,618
Less accumulated depreciation	1,949	1,854
Net land, buildings, and equipment	$2,980	$2,764

During fiscal 2003, depreciation expense was $365 million, and General Mills acquired land, buildings, and equipment worth $711 million. Assume that no gain or loss arose from the disposition of land, buildings, and equipment and that General Mills received cash of $130.0 million from such disposals.

Compute (1) the gross amount of assets written off (sold or retired), (2) the amount of accumulated depreciation associated with the assets sold or retired, and (3) the book value of the assets sold or retired. *Hint*: The use of T-accounts may help your analysis.

8-59 Depreciation

Asahi Kasei Corporation, has sales nearly the equivalent of $9 billion U.S. dollars. The company included the following in its balance sheet (yen in millions):

Property, plant and equipment, net of accumulated depreciation	
(Notes 8 & 9)	
Buildings	¥158,424
Machinery and equipment	156,156
Land	63,150
Construction in progress	22,089
Other	15,374
Total property, plant, and equipment	¥415,193

Footnote 8 contains the following:

Accumulated depreciation comprises the following (yen in millions):	
Buildings	¥ 216,865
Machinery and equipment	875,757
Other	86,795
Total accumulated depreciation	¥1,179,417

Footnote 2 says: "Depreciation is provided under the declining-balance method for property, plant, and equipment, except for buildings which are depreciated using the straight-line method, at rates based on estimated useful lives of the assets, principally, ranging from five years up to sixty years for buildings and from four years up to twenty-two years for machinery and equipment."

1. Compute the original acquisition cost of each of the five categories of assets listed under property, plant, and equipment.
2. Explain why Asahi Kasei shows no accumulated depreciation for land or construction in progress.
3. Suppose Asahi Kasei had used straight-line instead of declining-balance depreciation for all asset categories. How would this affect the preceding values shown for property, plant, and equipment?

8-60 Reconstruction of Plant Asset Transactions

The Ford Motor Company's footnotes included ($ in millions):

Ford Motor Company

| | December 31 | |
	2003	2002
Property		
Land, plant, and equipment	$60,113	$52,981
Less accumulated depreciation	(30,112)	(26,568)
Net land, plant, and equipment	30,001	26,413
Special tools, net	11,992	9,939
Net property	$41,993	$36,352

The notes to the income statement for 2003 revealed depreciation and amortization of $5,472 million. The account Special Tools, net is increased by new investments in tools, dies, jigs, and fixtures necessary for new models and production processes. Ford then amortizes these investments over various periods and reduces the account directly.

Hint: Analyze with the help of T-accounts.

1. Assume that Ford spent $3,000 million on special tools in 2003. There were no disposals of special tools. How much amortization did Ford record on special tools in 2003?
2. Given your answer to requirement 1, estimate the cost of the new acquisitions of land, plant, and equipment. Assume all disposals of plant and equipment involved fully depreciated assets with zero book value.

8-61 Average Age of Assets

SBC Communications, Inc. provides local phone services in 13 states, including California, Texas, and Illinois. It is the No. 2 local phone company in the United States after Verizon. SBC recently combined its wireless operations with BellSouth to form Cingular, the No. 2 wireless company behind Verizon Wireless. In addition, SBC provides long distance service and Internet access in select markets. The company had the following on its December 31, 2002 balance sheet ($ in millions):

Total property, plant, and equipment	$131,755
Less: Accumulated depreciation	83,265
	$ 48,490

A footnote states that "property, plant, and equipment is depreciated using straight-line methods over their estimated economic lives." Annual depreciation expense is approximately $8,500 million.

1. Estimate the average useful life of SBC's depreciable assets.
2. Estimate the average age of SBC's depreciable assets on December 31, 2002.

8-62 Depreciation, Income Tax, and Cash Flow

(Alternates are 8-63 and 8-64) Sanchez Metal Products Company had the following balances, among others, at the end of December 20X1: Cash, $300,000; Equipment, $400,000; Accumulated Depreciation, $100,000. Total revenues (all in cash) were $900,000. All operating expenses except depreciation were for cash and totaled $600,000. Straight-line depreciation expense was $50,000. Depreciation expense would have been $100,000 if Sanchez had used accelerated depreciation.

1. Assume zero income taxes. Fill in the blanks in the accompanying table. Show the amounts in thousands.

Table for Problem 8-62
($ Amounts in Thousands)

	1. Zero Income Taxes		2. 40% Income Taxes	
	Straight-Line Depreciation	Accelerated Depreciation	Straight-Line Depreciation	Accelerated Depreciation
Revenues (all cash)	$	$	$	$
Cash operating expenses				
Cash provided by operations before income taxes				
Depreciation expense				
Pretax income				
Income tax expense				
Net income	$	$	$	$
Supplementary analysis				
Cash provided by operations before income taxes	$	$	$	$
Income tax payments				
Net cash provided by operations	$	$	$	$

2. Repeat requirement 1, but assume an income tax rate of 40%. Assume also that Sanchez uses the same depreciation method for reporting to shareholders and to income tax authorities.
3. Compare your answers to requirements 1 and 2. Does depreciation provide cash? Explain as precisely as possible.
4. Refer to requirement 2. Assume that Sanchez had used straight-line depreciation for reporting to shareholders and to income tax authorities. Indicate the change (increase or decrease and amount) in the following balances if Sanchez had used accelerated depreciation for shareholder and tax reporting instead of straight-line: Cash, Accumulated Depreciation, Pretax Income, Income Tax Expense, and Retained Earnings.
5. Refer to requirement 1 where there are zero taxes. Suppose depreciation was doubled under both straight-line and accelerated methods. How would this affect cash? Be specific.

8-63 Depreciation, Income Taxes, and Cash Flow

(Alternates are 8-62 and 8-64.) A recent annual report of Wal-Mart, a major retailing company, listed the following property and equipment including leaseholds ($ in millions):

Property and equipment, at cost	$ 67,051
Less: Accumulated depreciation	15,147
Property and equipment, net	$ 51,904

The cash balance was $2,758 million.

Depreciation expense during the year was $3,432 million. The condensed income statement follows ($ in millions):

Revenues	$246,525
Expenses	232,881
Operating income	$ 13,644

For purposes of this problem, assume that all revenues and expenses, excluding depreciation, are for cash. Thus, cash operating expenses in millions of dollars were $232,881 − $3,432 = $229,449.

Table for Problem 8-63
($ Amounts in Millions)

	1. Zero Income Taxes		2. 40% Income Taxes	
	Straight-Line Depreciation	Accelerated Depreciation	Straight-Line Depreciation	Accelerated Depreciation
Revenues (all cash)	$	$	$	$
Cash operating expenses				
Cash provided by operations before income taxes				
Depreciation expense				
Pretax income				
Income tax expense				
Net income	$	$	$	$
Supplementary analysis				
Cash provided by operations before income taxes	$	$	$	$
Income tax payments				
Net cash provided by operations	$	$	$	$

1. Wal-Mart uses straight-line depreciation. If accelerated depreciation had been used, depreciation would have been $5,432. Assume zero income taxes. Fill in the blanks in the accompanying table ($ in millions).
2. Repeat requirement 1, but assume an income tax rate of 40%. Assume also that Wal-Mart uses the same depreciation method for reporting to shareholders and to income tax authorities
3. Compare your answers to requirements 1 and 2. Does depreciation provide cash? Explain as precisely as possible.

4. Refer to requirement 2. Assume that Wal-Mart had used straight-line depreciation for reporting to shareholders and to income tax authorities. Indicate the change (increase or decrease and amount) in the following balances if Wal-Mart had used accelerated depreciation for shareholder and tax reporting instead of straight-line during that year: Cash, Accumulated Depreciation, Pretax Income, Income Tax Expense, and Retained Earnings. What would be the new balances in Cash and Accumulated Depreciation?

5. Refer to requirement 1 where there are zero taxes. Suppose Wal-Mart increased depreciation by an extra $2,500 million under both straight-line and accelerated methods. How would cash be affected? Be specific.

8-64 Depreciation, Income Taxes, and Cash Flow

(Alternates are 8-62 and 8-63.) The French auto company, PSA Peugeot Citroen, sells the majority of its cars outside France. The company's annual report showed the following balances (euros in millions):

Revenues	€50,288
Operating expenses	(47,884)
Operating income	€ 2,404

PSA Peugeot Citroen had depreciation expense of €1,974 million (included in operating expenses). The company's ending cash balance was €7,666 million.

PSA Peugeot Citroen reported its property and equipment in the following way (€ in millions):

Property, plant, and equipment, at cost	€28,691
Less: Accumulated depreciation	17,230
Net property and equipment	€11,461

For purposes of this problem, assume all revenues and expenses, excluding depreciation, are for cash.

Table for Problem 8-64
(Amounts in millions of Euros)

	1. Zero Income Taxes		2. 60% Income Taxes	
	Straight-Line Depreciation	Accelerated Depreciation	Straight-Line Depreciation	Accelerated Depreciation
Revenues (all cash)	€	€	€	€
Cash operating expenses				
Cash provided by operations before income taxes				
Depreciation expense				
Pretax income				
Income tax expense				
Net income	€	€	€	€
Supplementary analysis				
Cash provided by operations before income taxes	€	€	€	€
Income tax payments				
Net cash provided by operations	€	€	€	€

1. PSA Peugeot Citroen used straight-line depreciation. If accelerated depreciation had been used, depreciation would have been €2,474 million. Assume zero income taxes. Fill in the blanks in the accompanying table (in millions of euros).

2. Repeat requirement 1, but assume an income tax rate of 60%. Assume also that PSA Peugeot Citroen uses the same depreciation method for reporting to shareholders and to income tax authorities.

3. Compare your answers to requirements 1 and 2. Does depreciation provide cash? Explain as precisely as possible.

4. Refer to requirement 2. PSA Peugeot Citroen used straight-line depreciation for reporting to shareholders and to income tax authorities. Indicate the change (increase or decrease and amount) in the following balances if PSA Peugeot Citroen had used accelerated depreciation for

shareholder and tax reporting instead of straight-line: Cash, Accumulated Depreciation, Pretax Income, Income Tax Expense, and Retained Earnings. What would be the new balances in Cash and Accumulated Depreciation?

5. Refer to requirement 1 where there are zero taxes. Suppose the company had doubled its depreciation under both straight-line and accelerated methods. How would this affect cash? Be specific.

8-65 Depreciation, Income Taxes, and Cash Flow

Mr. Brandt, president of the Bremen Shipping Company, read a newspaper story that stated: "The Frankfurt Steel Company had a cash flow last year of 1,500,000 DM, consisting of 1,000,000 DM of net income plus 500,000 DM of depreciation. New plant facilities helped the cash flow, because depreciation was 25% higher than in the preceding year." "Cash flow" is frequently used as a synonym for "cash provided by operations," which, in turn, is cash revenue less cash operating expenses and income taxes. (DM stands for deutsch mark, the German unit of currency at the time this statement was made.)

Brandt was encouraged by the quotation because Bremen Shipping Company had just acquired a vast amount of new transportation equipment. These acquisitions had placed a severe financial strain on the company. Brandt was heartened because he believed that the added cash flow from the depreciation of the new equipment should ease the financial pressures on the company.

The income before income taxes of the Bremen Shipping Company last year (20X8) was 200,000 DM. Depreciation was 200,000 DM; it will also be 200,000 DM on the old equipment in 20X9.

Revenue in 20X8 was 2.1 million DM (all in cash), and operating expenses other than depreciation were 1.7 million DM (all in cash).

The company expects the new equipment to help increase revenue by 1 million DM in 20X9. Operating expenses other than depreciation will increase by 800,000 DM.

1. Suppose depreciation on the new equipment for financial reporting purposes is 100,000 DM. What would be the cash flow from operations (cash provided by operations) for 20X9? Show computations. Ignore income taxes.
2. Repeat requirement 1, assuming that the depreciation on the new equipment is 50,000 DM. Ignore income taxes.
3. Assume an income tax rate of 30%. (a) Repeat requirement 1; (b) repeat requirement 2. Assume that the same amount of depreciation is shown for tax purposes and for financial reporting purposes.
4. In your own words, state as accurately as possible the effects of depreciation on cash flow. Comment on preceding requirements 1, 2, and 3 to bring out your points. This is a more important requirement than requirements 1, 2, and 3.

8-66 Rental Vehicles

The **AMERCO System** is the holding company for **U-Haul International** and its subsidiaries. The 2003 annual report included the following footnote:

> *Property, plant and equipment are carried at cost and are depreciated on a straight-line basis over the estimated useful lives of the assets. . . . Maintenance is charged to operating expenses as incurred, while renewals and betterments are capitalized. Major overhaul costs are amortized over the estimated period benefited. Gains and losses on dispositions are netted against depreciation expense when realized.*

1. Assume that U-Haul acquires some new trucks on October 1, 2003, for $70 million. The useful life is 1 year. Expected residual values are $52 million. Prepare a summary journal entry for depreciation for 2003. The fiscal year ends on December 31.
2. Prepare a summary journal entry for depreciation for the first 9 months of 2004.
3. Assume that U-Haul sells the trucks for $58 million cash on September 30, 2004. Prepare the journal entry for the sale. U-Haul considers the trucks to be "revenue-earning equipment."
4. What is the total depreciation expense on these trucks for 2004? If U-Haul could have exactly predicted the $58 million proceeds when it originally acquired the trucks, what would depreciation expense have been in 2003? In 2004? Explain.

8-67 Nature of Research Costs

Katherine Mori, a distinguished scientist of international repute, had developed many successful drugs for a well-established pharmaceutical company. Having an entrepreneurial spirit, she persuaded the board of directors that she should resign her position as vice-president of research and launch a subsidiary company to produce and market some powerful new drugs for treating arthritis. However, she did not predict overnight success. Instead, she expected to gather a first-rate research team that might take 3 to 5 years to generate any marketable products. Furthermore, she admitted that the risks were so high that conceivably no commercial success might result. Nevertheless, she had little trouble obtaining an initial investment of $5 million. The Mori Pharmaceuticals Company was 80% owned by the parent and 20% by Katherine.

Katherine acquired a team of researchers and began operations. By the end of the first year of the life of the new subsidiary, it had expended $2 million on research activities, mostly for researchers' salaries, but also for related research costs.

The subsidiary had developed no marketable products, but Katherine and other top executives were extremely pleased about the overall progress and were very optimistic about developing such products within the next 3 or 4 years.

How would you account for the $2 million? Would you write it off as an expense in year one? Could it be capitalized as an intangible asset? If so, would you carry it indefinitely? Or would you write it off systematically over 3 years or some longer span? Why? Explain, giving particular attention to the idea of an asset as an unexpired cost.

8-68 Meaning of Book Value

Chavez Company purchased an office building 20 years ago for $1.3 million, $500,000 of which was attributable to land. The mortgage has been fully paid. The current balance sheet follows:

Cash		$ 300,000	Stockholders' equity	$1,000,000
Land		500,000		
Building at cost	$800,000			
Accumulated depreciation	600,000			
Net book value		200,000		
Total assets		$1,000,000		

The company is about to borrow $1.8 million on a first mortgage to modernize and expand the building. This amounts to 60% of the combined appraised value of the land and building before the modernization and expansion.

Prepare a balance sheet after the loan is made and the building is expanded and modernized. Comment on its significance.

8-69 Capital Expenditures

Disputes sometimes arise between the taxpayer and the IRS concerning whether legal costs should be deductible as expenses in the year incurred or be considered as capital expenditures because they relate to defining or perfecting title to business property.

Consider two examples from court cases:

Example 1
Several years after Rock set up his stone-quarrying business, Smalltown passed an ordinance banning it. Rock spent $1,000 to invalidate the ordinance.

Example 2
Now suppose Rock decided to expand his business. He applied to Smalltown for a permit to build an additional crusher. It was denied because an ordinance prohibited the expansion of nonconforming uses, including quarrying. Rock sued to invalidate the ordinance and won after spending $2,000. He then built the crusher.

Indicate whether each example should be deemed (a) an expense or (b) a capital expenditure. Briefly explain your answer.

8-70 Change in Service Life

Prior to its acquisition by United Airlines, an annual report of TWA contained the following footnote:

> *Note 2, Change in accounting estimate. TWA extended the estimated useful lives of Boeing 727-100 aircraft from principally sixteen years to principally twenty years. As a result, depreciation and amortization expense was decreased by $9,000,000.*

The TWA annual report also contained the following data: depreciation, $235,518,000; net income, $42,233,000.

The cost of the 727-100 aircraft subject to depreciation was $800 million. Residual values were predicted to be 10% of acquisition cost.

Assume a combined federal and state income tax rate of 46% throughout all parts of these requirements.

1. Was the effect of the change in estimated useful life a material difference? Explain, including computations.
2. The same year's annual report of Delta Air Lines contained the following footnote:
   Depreciation—Substantially all the flight equipment is being depreciated on a straight-line basis to residual values (10% of cost) over a 10-year period from dates placed in service.
   The Delta annual report also contained the following data: depreciation, $220,979,000; net income, $146,474,000. Suppose Delta had used a 20-year life instead of a 10-year life. Assume a 46% applicable income tax rate. Compute the new depreciation and net income.
3. Suppose TWA had used a 10-year life instead of a 20-year life on its 727-100 equipment. Estimated residual value is 10%. Compute the new depreciation and net income. For purposes of this requirement, assume that the equipment cost $800 million and has been in service 1 year and that reported net income based on a 20-year life was $42,233,000.

8-71 Disposal of Equipment

(Alternate is 8-72.) Alaska Airlines acquired a new Boeing 727-100 airplane for $26 million. Its expected residual value was $6 million. The company's annual report indicated that straight-line depreciation was used based on an estimated service life of 20 years. Assume the company records gains or losses, if any, in Other Income (Expense).

Show all amounts in millions of dollars.

1. Assume that Alaska sold the equipment at the end of the sixth year for $22 million cash. Compute the gain or loss on the sale. Show the effects of the sale on the balance sheet equation, identifying all specific accounts by name. Where and how would the sale appear on the income statement?
2. (a) Show the journal entries for the transaction in requirement 1. (b) Repeat 2a, assuming that the cash sales price was $19 million instead of $22 million.

8-72 Disposal of Property and Equipment

(Alternate is 8-71.) Rockwell Automation is a leading provider of industrial automation power and controls. The company's annual report indicated that both accelerated and straight-line depreciation were used for its property and equipment. In addition, the annual report said: "Gains or losses on property transactions are recorded in income in the period of sale or retirement."

Rockwell received $4 million for property that it sold.

1. Assume that Rockwell originally acquired the total property in question for $65 million and received the $4 million in cash. There was a loss of $8.5 million on the sale. Compute the accumulated depreciation on the property and equipment sold. Show the effects of the sale on the balance sheet equation, identifying all specific accounts by name.
2. (a) Show the journal entry and postings to T-accounts for the transaction in requirement 1. (b) Repeat 2a, assuming that the cash sales price was $14 million cash instead of $4 million.

8-73 Gain on Airplane Crash

A few years ago, a Delta Air Lines 727 crashed in Dallas. The crash resulted in a gain of $.11 per share for Delta. How could this happen? Consider the accounting for airplanes. Airlines insure their craft at market value, $6.5 million for Delta's 727. However, the planes' book values are often much less because of large accumulated depreciation amounts. The book value of Delta's 727 was only $962,000.

1. Suppose Delta received the insurance payment and immediately purchased another 727 for $6.5 million. Compute the effect of the insurance payment on pretax income. Also compute the effect on Delta's total assets.
2. Do you think a casualty should generate a reported gain? Why?

8-74 Disposal of Equipment

Airline Executive reported on an airline as follows:

> *Lufthansa's highly successful policy of rolling over entire fleets in roughly ten years—before the aircrafts have outlived their usefulness—got started in a "spectacular" way when seven first-generation 747s were sold. The 747s were bought six to nine years earlier for $22–28 million each and sold for about the same price.*

1. Assume an average original cost of $25 million each, an average original expected useful life of 10 years, a $2.5 million expected residual value, and an average actual life of 8 years before disposal. Use straight-line depreciation. Compute the total gain or loss on the sale of the seven planes.
2. Prepare a summary journal entry for the sale.

8-75 Software Development Costs

Microsoft, Incorporated, is one of the largest producers of software for personal computers. Special rules apply to accounting for the costs of developing software for sale or lease. Companies expense such costs until the technological feasibility of the product is established. Thereafter, they should capitalize these costs and amortize them over the life of the product.

One of Microsoft's divisions began working on some special business applications software. Suppose the division had spent $800,000 on the project by the end of 20X1, but it was not yet clear whether the software was technologically feasible.

On July 1, 20X2, after spending another $400,000, management decided that the software was technologically feasible. During the second half of 20X2, the division spent another $1 million on this project. In December 20X2, the company announced the product, with deliveries to begin in March 20X3. The division incurred no R&D costs for the software after December 20X2.

1. Prepare journal entries to account for the R&D expenses for the software for 20X1 and 20X2. Assume that the division paid all expenditures in cash.
2. Would any R&D expenses affect income in 20X3?

8-76 Basket Purchase and Intangibles

A tax newsletter stated: "When a business is sold, part of the sales price may be allocated to tangible assets and part to a 'covenant not to compete.' How this allocation is made can have important tax consequences to both the buyer and seller."

A large law firm, organized as a professional services corporation, purchased a successful local firm for $100,000. The purchase included both tangible assets, which have an average remaining useful life of 10 years, and a 3-year covenant not to compete. Suppose the buyer has legally supportable latitude concerning how to allocate this amount, as follows:

	Allocation One	Allocation Two
Covenant	$ 72,000	$ 48,000
Tangible assets	28,000	52,000
Total for two assets	$100,000	$100,000

1. For income tax purposes, which allocation would the buyer favor? Why?
2. For shareholder reporting purposes, which allocation would the buyer favor? Why?

8-77 Depreciation Policies and Ethics

Some companies have depreciation policies that differ substantially from the norm of their industry. For example, Cineplex Odeon depreciated its theater seats, carpets, and related equipment over 27 years, much longer than most of its competitors. Another example is Blockbuster Entertainment, which depreciated the videotapes it rents over 36 months. Others depreciate them over a period as short as 9 months.

Growing companies can increase their current income by depreciating fixed assets over a longer period of time. Sometimes companies lengthen the depreciable lives of their fixed assets when a boost in income is desired. Comment on the ethical implications of choosing an economic life for depreciation purposes, with special reference to the policies of Cineplex Odeon and Blockbuster.

Collaborative Learning Exercise

8-78 Accumulated Depreciation

Form groups of at least four students (this exercise can be done as an entire class, if desired). Individual students, on their own, should select a company and find the fixed asset section of its most recent balance sheet. From the balance sheet (and possibly the footnotes) find the original acquisition cost of property, plant, and equipment (the account title varies slightly by company) and the accumulated depreciation on property, plant, and equipment. Compute the ratio of accumulated depreciation to original acquisition cost. Also note the depreciation method used and the average economic life of the assets, if given. (For an extra bonus, find a company that uses accelerated depreciation for reporting to shareholders; such companies are harder to find.)

When everyone gets together, make four columns on the board or on a piece of paper. Find the 25% of the companies with the highest ratios and list them in the first column. Then list the 25% with the next highest ratios in the second column, and so on. As a group, make a list of explanations for the rankings of the companies. What characteristics of the company, its industry, or its depreciation methods distinguish the companies with high ratios from those with low ratios?

Analyzing and Interpreting Financial Statements

8-79 Financial Statement Research

Select two distinct industries and identify two companies in each industry.

1. Identify the depreciation methods used by each company.
2. Calculate gross and net plant, property, and equipment as a percentage of total assets for each company. What differences do you observe between industries? Within industries?
3. Do the notes disclose any unusual practices with regard to long-lived assets?

8-80 Analyzing Starbucks' Financial Statements

Refer to the financial statements of Starbucks in the Appendix, especially footnote 1. Depreciation and amortization expense was $237,807,000 for the year ended September 28, 2003 according to the Consolidated Statement of Earnings.

1. What lives does Starbucks use for depreciating and amortizing its assets?
2. Suppose Starbucks extended the lives of all its depreciable assets by 50% so depreciation was smaller each year. Estimate the effect of this on net earnings reported in the year 2003. Assume that the average tax rate in the current income statement applied to this change in depreciation and that depreciation for financial reporting purposes was the same as that for tax purposes.

8-81 Analyzing Financial Statements Using the Internet

Go to www.gapinc.com to find Gap Inc.'s home page. Select Financials and Media and enter the site. Then, select Annual Reports, and click on the most recent annual report.

Answer the following questions about Gap:

1. Read the Notes to Consolidated Financial Statements. What is the nature of Gap's operations? What type of property and equipment would you expect Gap to include in the property and equipment section of its balance sheet?
2. In which section of its financial statements does Gap provide information on the method of depreciation and amortization used? What other disclosures concerning depreciable assets are available in this same location?

3. Does Gap have any intangible assets? What type are they? What time period is used for cost allocation?

4. What does the amount listed on the balance sheet for property and equipment represent — cost, market, or some other amount? If Gap purchases no additional property and equipment assets, what will happen to the net book value over time?

5. How much depreciation and amortization expense did Gap report, as shown in its most recent annual report? Why is this amount not obvious from looking at the income statement? Which financial statement provides the depreciation and amortization amount?

Liabilities and Interest

CHAPTER 9

LEARNING OBJECTIVES

After studying this chapter, you should be able to:

1. Account for current liabilities.

2. Measure and account for long-term liabilities.

3. Account for bond issues over their entire life.

4. Value and account for long-term lease obligations.

5. Evaluate pensions and other postretirement benefits.

6. Interpret deferred tax liabilities.

7. Use ratio analysis to assess a company's debt levels.

8. Compute and interpret present and future values (Appendix 9).

Maybe you have never heard of May Department Stores Company, but you have probably shopped in one of its stores. May is a $14 billion retailer operating under 14 trade names including: Foley's, Hecht's, Robinsons-May, Filene's, Lord & Taylor, and Kaufmann's. The company owns more than 800 stores across the United States. In times of rapid expansion, May borrows money to open new stores. For example, in the fiscal year ended February 3, 2001 the company borrowed more then $1 billion in the form of bonds and notes as part of a huge expansion that increased its number of stores from 408 in 1999 to 839 in February 2003. Its total debt in early 2001 was nearly $7 billion. However, by 2002 and 2003 the economy had slowed, and so had May's expansion plans. Instead of borrowing more money, May paid back nearly $500 million in the year ending February 1, 2003. In this chapter, we learn how companies account for the money they borrow.

Why would May Company want to acquire so much debt? Why does any company borrow money? They borrow because management believes that remaining competitive requires continual growth. If the company can use the borrowed funds to continue increasing sales and earnings per share, both management and shareholders will benefit.

Companies are not the only ones that borrow money. For example, when individuals seek to buy a car or a house, lenders assess the buyer's financial position carefully and pay special attention to the size of the down payment the buyer will make. The larger the down payment, the more "equity" the borrower has in the purchase, and the more comfortable the lender is in making the loan. Similarly, potential investors in the common stock or bonds of a company carefully evaluate the amount of debt the company has relative to the amount of stockholders' equity to assess the

This Lord & Taylor's store in New Orleans is one of many types of department stores owned by May Department Stores Company. May Company must buy, build, or lease a store and acquire its inventory before it generates any sales from the store. To expand its number of stores, May Company borrows money, creating a liability. In this chapter, we see how to account for such liabilities.

potential risk of their investment. Thus, a major element of GAAP in the United States is the careful definition of what constitutes a liability and how best to disclose the liabilities to readers of financial statements. ▪

Liabilities in Perspective

As we learned earlier, liabilities are a company's obligations to pay cash or to provide goods and services to other companies or individuals. Liabilities include wages due to employees, payables to suppliers, taxes owed the government, interest and principal due to lenders, obligations from losing a lawsuit, and so on. Such obligations usually arise from a transaction with an outside party such as a supplier, a lending institution, or an employee. Accrual accounting recognizes expenses as they occur, not necessarily when a company pays for them in cash. A liability arises whenever an organization recognizes an obligation before paying it.

Investors, financial analysts, management, and creditors consider existing liabilities of the firm when valuing the firm's common stock, when evaluating a new loan to the company, and when making many other decisions. Problems arise when companies appear to have excessive debt or seem unable to meet existing obligations. For example, suppliers who normally sell on credit may evaluate a customer's debt level. If they conclude that debt is excessive, they might refuse to ship new items or may ship only collect on delivery (COD). Also, lenders may refuse to provide new loans, and customers, worried that the company will not be around long enough to honor warranties, may prefer to buy elsewhere. Of course, once creditors and customers go, a company's future is bleak. Debt problems can snowball quickly. Because poorly managed debt can cause huge problems, users of financial statements pay close attention to debt levels. Let's look at how the May Department Store Company reports its liabilities. Exhibit 9-1 shows its balance sheet presentation of liabilities.

As is common practice, May classifies its liabilities as either current or long-term (noncurrent), which helps financial statement readers interpret the immediacy of the company's obligations. In Chapter 4, we learned that current liabilities are obligations that fall due within the coming year or within the company's normal operating cycle (if that cycle is longer than a year). In contrast, **long-term liabilities** are those that fall due more than 1 year beyond the balance sheet date. Companies pay some long-term obligations gradually, in yearly or monthly installments. You can see from Exhibit 9-1 that May Company includes the current portion of these long-term obligations ($239 million in 2004) as a part of the company's current liabilities.

In the general ledger, companies keep separate accounts for different liabilities, such as wages, salaries, commissions, interest, and similar items. In the annual report, though, they

long-term liabilities
Obligations that fall due beyond 1 year from the balance sheet date.

Exhibit 9-1
May Department Stores Company
Consolidated Balance Sheets as of January 31, 2004 and February 1, 2003 (dollars in millions)

	2004	2003
Current liabilities		
Short-term debt	$ —	$ 150
Current maturities of long-term debt	239	139
Accounts payable	1,191	1,099
Accrued expenses	975	1,014
Income taxes payable	280	264
Total current liabilities	2,685	2,666
Long-term debt	3,797	4,035
Deferred income taxes	773	710
Other liabilities	507	377
Total debt	$ 7,762	$7,788

often combine these liabilities and show them as a single current liability labeled "accrued liabilities" or "accrued expenses payable." Sometimes they omit the adjective accrued and call these liabilities simply "taxes payable," "wages payable," and so on. Similarly, some omit the term "payable" and simply use "accrued wages" or "accrued taxes" and so on. May separately reports income taxes payable, but lumps all remaining accrued expenses together.

Accountants generally measure liabilities in terms of the amount of cash needed to pay off an obligation or the cash value of products or services to be delivered. For current liabilities, which we examine next, measurement is relatively easy, and the accounting process is straightforward.

Accounting for Current Liabilities

We record some current liabilities as a result of a transaction with an outside entity, such as a lender or supplier. We record other liabilities with an adjusting journal entry to acknowledge an obligation arising over time, such as interest or wages. Let's take a look at the accounting procedures for several different types of current liabilities.

OBJECTIVE 1
Account for current liabilities.

Accounts Payable

Accounts payable are amounts owed to suppliers. They are the largest current liability for May Company. More than 90% of major U.S. companies show accounts payable as a separate line item under current liabilities on their balance sheet. However, a few combine accounts payable with accrued liabilities. Large sums of money flow through these accounts payable systems. Therefore, accountants carefully design data processing and internal control systems for these transactions. The key is to ensure that the company writes checks only for legitimate obligations of the company.

Internal control systems generally require managers to make all payments by check. Why? Prenumbered checks make record keeping easy, and companies can thus trace exactly where their money is going.

Good systems also require source documents to support all checks. First, there must be a **purchase order,** which specifies the quantities and prices of items ordered. Second is the **receiving report,** which indicates the items received and their condition. Then accountants match the purchase order and receiving report to the **invoice,** a bill from the seller. This process permits periodic, systematic reviews to ensure that nothing does go wrong, and it leaves a paper trail that is easy to follow in case anything should go wrong. Because multiple people are involved, the system often avoids errors or detects them early before their consequences are large. Systems can also allow checks only to approved vendors and require a high-level employee to approve all additions to the vendor list. Some corporations use computers to generate automatic payments when a supplier's computer has provided the proper source information.

purchase order
A document that specifies the items ordered and the price to be paid by the ordering company.

receiving report
A document that specifies the items received by the company and the condition of the items.

invoice
A bill from the seller to a buyer indicating the number of items shipped, their price, and any additional costs (such as shipping) along with payment terms, if any.

Notes Payable

When companies take out loans, they must sign promissory notes. A **promissory note,** often simply called a note payable, is a written promise to repay the loan principal plus interest at specific future dates. Most promissory notes are payable to banks.

Balance sheet presentation of notes payable varies. Notes that are payable within 1 year are included with current liabilities; others are long-term liabilities. May Company reports notes payable combined with commercial paper under "short-term debt," and by 2004 the company had no more debt of this type. **Commercial paper** is a debt contract issued by prominent companies that borrow directly from investors. The liability created by commercial paper always falls due in 9 months or less, usually in 60 days after issuance. Other

promissory note
A written promise to repay principal plus interest at specific future dates.

commercial paper
A short-term debt contract issued by prominent companies that borrow directly from investors.

line of credit
An agreement with a bank to provide automatically short-term loans up to some preestablished maximum.

companies combine notes payable with borrowings on a line of credit. A **line of credit** sets up a predetermined maximum amount that a company can borrow from a given lender without significant additional credit checking or other time-consuming procedures. Lines of credit benefit lenders and borrowers. The lender gets the advantage of not having to run credit checks and prepare extensive paperwork every time the borrower wants a loan. The borrower gets the advantage of having a preset amount of borrowing available. Coca-Cola explained its $2.6 billion of loans and notes payable on its 2003 balance sheet as follows:

> *Loans and notes payable consist primarily of commercial paper issued in the United States. On December 31, 2003, we had approximately $2,234 million outstanding in commercial paper borrowings. . . . In addition, we had $1,576 million in lines of credit . . . available as of December 31, 2003, of which approximately $246 million was outstanding.*

Coca-Cola borrows more in the commercial paper market than it does from banks because the interest rates are lower in the commercial paper market. However, only companies with the visibility and creditworthiness of Coca-Cola can issue commercial paper.

Accrued Employee Compensation

Accrued liabilities are expenses that a company has recognized on the income statement but not yet paid. Our first example of an accrued liability is obligations to employees for payment of wages. Many companies have a separate current liability account for such items, with a label such as salaries, wages, and commissions payable, but May Company combines this liability with the other accrued expenses.

In earlier chapters, we assumed that an employee earned, for example, $100 per week and, in turn, received $100 in cash on payday. In reality, however, payroll accounting is never that easy. For example, employers must withhold some employee earnings and pay them instead to the government, insurance companies, labor unions, charitable organizations, and so forth.

Consider the withholding of income taxes and the employees' portion of Social Security taxes (also called Federal Insurance Contributions Act or FICA taxes). Suppose that a particular May Company department store has a $100,000 monthly payroll and, for simplicity, assume that the only amounts it withholds are $15,000 for income taxes and $7,000 for Social Security taxes. The withholdings are not additional employer costs. They are simply part of the employee wages and salaries that the store pays to third parties, instead of directly to the employees. The journal entry for this $100,000 payroll is:

Compensation expense	100,000	
Salaries and wages payable		78,000
Income tax withholding payable		15,000
Social Security withholding payable		7,000

Companies must also deal with payroll taxes and fringe benefits. These are employee-related costs in addition to salaries and wages. Payroll taxes are amounts paid to the government for items such as the employer's portion of Social Security, federal and state unemployment taxes, and workers' compensation taxes. Fringe benefits include employee pensions, life and health insurance, and vacation pay. At many organizations, the fringe benefits exceed 30% of salary. Thus, a person who earns $30,000 per year in salary, effectively costs the company $39,000 ($30,000 + 30% of $30,000). A company must accrue liabilities for each of these costs. If the company has not yet paid them at the balance sheet date, it must include them among its current liabilities.

Note that there are two parts to Social Security taxes. Employers withhold one part from the employees' wages and pay a similar amount themselves. Suppose the May Company pays an employer's FICA tax equal to the $7,000 withheld from the employee and also pays 10% of gross wages into a retirement account. The following journal entry summarizes the effect on May Company's financial statements:

Employee benefit expense	17,000	
Employer Social Security payable		7,000
Pension liability payable		10,000

Income Taxes Payable

In nearly every country in the world, corporations must pay income taxes as a percentage of their earnings. Instead of paying one lump sum at tax time, corporations make periodic installment payments based on their estimated tax for the year. Therefore, the accrued liability for income taxes at year-end is generally much smaller than the annual income tax expense.

To illustrate, suppose a corporation has an estimated taxable income of $100 million for the calendar year 20X0. At a 40% tax rate, the company's estimated taxes for the year are $40 million. It would make payments as follows:

	April 15	June 15	September 15	December 15
Estimated taxes (in millions)	$10	$10	$10	$10

The company must file a final income tax return and make a final payment by March 15, 20X1. Suppose the actual taxable income for the year was $110 million instead of the estimated $100 million. Total tax would then be $44 million. On March 15, the corporation must pay the $4 million additional tax on the extra $10 million of taxable income. The accrued liability on December 31, 20X0, would appear in the current liability section of the balance sheet as:

Income taxes payable	$4,000,000

For simplicity, the illustration assumed equal quarterly payments. However, the estimated taxable income for a calendar year may change as the year unfolds. The corporation must change its quarterly payments accordingly. Regardless of how a company changes its estimates, there will nearly always be a tax payment or refund due on March 15, and there will be an accrual adjustment at year-end.

Current Portion of Long-Term Debt

A company's long-term debt often includes payments due within a year that should be reported as current liabilities. The journal entry for recognizing the current portion of long-term debt reclassifies a noncurrent liability as a current liability. Using the May Company illustration in Exhibit 9-1, the reclassification journal entry for long-term debt that becomes due in fiscal 2005 would be:

Long-term debt	239,000,000	
Current maturities of long-term debt		239,000,000

Sales Tax

When retailers collect sales taxes, they are collecting on behalf of the state or local government. For example, suppose customers pay a 7% sales tax on sales of $10,000. The total collected from the customers must be $10,000 + $700, or $10,700. The transaction would affect the balance sheet as follows:

A	=	L	+	SE
+ 10,700	=	+ 700		+ 10,000
⌈ Increase Cash ⌉ │ or Accounts │ ⌊ Receivable ⌋		⌈ Increase ⌉ │ Sales Tax │ ⌊ Payable ⌋		⌈ Increase ⌉ ⌊ Sales ⌋

The sales shown on the income statement would be $10,000, not $10,700. The sales tax never affects the income statement. The $700 received for taxes affects the current liability account Sales Tax Payable and appears on the balance sheet until the company pays it to the government. The journal entries (without explanations) are:

```
Cash or accounts receivable  . . . . . . . . . . . . . .   10,700
    Sales  . . . . . . . . . . . . . . . . . . . . . . . . . . .              10,000
    Sales tax payable  . . . . . . . . . . . . . . . . . .                       700
Sales tax payable  . . . . . . . . . . . . . . . . . . . . .      700
    Cash  . . . . . . . . . . . . . . . . . . . . . . . . . . .                      700
```

Product Warranties

Some current liabilities are difficult to measure precisely. For example, a sales warranty creates a liability, but warranty claims will arise in the future and accountants must estimate their amount. If warranty obligations are material, a company must accrue them when it sells products because the obligation arises at the time of sale, not when the customer receives actual repair services. Ford describes its warranty accounting as follows: "Estimated costs related to product warranty are accrued at the time of sale."

Companies usually base the estimated warranty expenses on past experience replacing or remedying defective products. Although estimates should be close, they are rarely precisely correct. Assume that a company has $20 million in sales and has found that warranty expense averages about 3% of sales. The accounting entry related to the $20 million in sales is:

```
Warranty expense  . . . . . . . . . . . . . . . . . . . .   600,000
    Liability for warranties
    (or some similar title)  . . . . . . . . . . . . . .              600,000
To record the estimated liability for warranties
arising from current sales; the provision is 3%
of current sales of $20 million, or $600,000
```

When a warranty claim arises, we make an entry such as the following:

```
Liability for warranties  . . . . . . . . . . . . . . . . . . . .   1,000
    Cash, accounts payable, accrued wages payable,
    and similar accounts  . . . . . . . . . . . . . . . . . .              1,000
To record the acquisition of supplies,
outside services, and employee services
to satisfy claims for repairs
```

If the estimate for warranty expense is accurate, the entries for all claims will total about $600,000. If additional information makes it clear that the claims will differ from $600,000, we adjust the liability accordingly. For example, suppose we get information that quality problems are causing excessive warranty claims so we expect total claims to be $700,000 rather than the original estimate of $600,000. We then need to add $100,000 to the Liability for Warranties account and charge an extra $100,000 to Warranty Expense.

Returnable Deposits

Occasionally, customers must make money deposits that are to be returned in full. Well-known examples of returnable deposits are those for returnable containers such as soft drink bottles, oil drums, or beer kegs. Also, many landlords require security deposits that are to be returned in full at the end of a lease, as long as the tenants do not cause any damage to the property.

Companies that receive deposits record them as a form of payable, although the word "payable" may not be a part of their specific labeling. The accounting entries by the recipients of deposits have the following basic pattern (numbers assumed in thousands of dollars):

1. Deposit received	Cash	100	
	Deposits (payable)		100
2. Deposit returned	Deposits	100	
	Cash		100

The account Deposits is a current liability of the company receiving the deposit.

Unearned Revenue

In Chapter 4, you learned that unearned revenue is revenue that a company collects before it delivers services or goods. These unearned revenues are current liabilities because they require a company either to deliver the product or service or to make a full refund. Examples include lease rentals, magazine subscriptions, insurance premiums, advance airline or theater ticket sales, and advance repair service contracts. The journal entries to record $100,000 of prepayments for services and the subsequent performance of those services and appropriate revenue recognition are as follows:

Cash	100,000	
Unearned sales revenues		100,000
To record advance collections from customers		
Unearned sales revenues	100,000	
Sales		100,000
To record sales revenues when services are performed for customers who paid in advance		

Companies use a variety of labels for revenues collected in advance of their being earned. For example, Dow Jones & Company lists "Unexpired subscriptions," and Monster Worldwide, Inc., operator of the largest job-search Web site, uses "Deferred Revenues."

INTERPRETING FINANCIAL STATEMENTS

Consider a basketball team that sells season tickets for $100 each, collected at the beginning of the season. The accounting period is a calendar year, but typically 40% of the games occur in November and December, whereas the other 60% occur in January and February. The team sells all of its 15,000 seats to season ticket holders for the 2004 to 2005 season. Indicate how these facts would affect the income statement and the balance sheet for 2004 and the income statement for 2005.

($600,000) in 2004, so the 2004 income statement would show only $600,000 of revenue. The 2004 balance sheet would show a current liability of 60% × $1,500,000 = $900,000, labeled Revenue Received in Advance or Unearned Service Revenue. This $900,000 is deferred, and the team will recognize it as income on the 2005 income statement when it earns the revenue by playing the remaining games.

Answer
In 2004, the team would collect $100 × 15,000 = $1,500,000. However, it would earn only 40% of it

This concludes our discussion of current liabilities. Now let's proceed to long-term liabilities.

OBJECTIVE

Measure and account for long-term liabilities.

bonds
Formal certificates of debt that include (1) a promise to pay interest in cash at a specified annual rate, plus (2) a promise to pay the principal at a specific maturity date.

nominal interest rate (contractual rate, coupon rate, stated rate)
A contractual rate of interest paid on bonds.

face amount
The loan principal or the amount that a borrower promises to repay at a specific maturity date.

negotiable
Legal financial contracts that can be transferred from one lender to another.

private placement
A process whereby bonds are issued by corporations when money is borrowed from a few sources, not from the general public.

liquidation
Converting assets to cash and paying off outside claims.

mortgage bond
A form of long-term debt that is secured by the pledge of specific property.

debenture
A debt security with a general claim against all assets, instead of a specific claim against particular assets.

subordinated debentures
Debt securities whose holders have claims against only the assets that remain after satisfying the claims of other general creditors.

Long-Term Liabilities

Long-term liabilities are obligations that are not due for at least a year. How exactly do lenders and borrowers measure the value of such obligations? They use the time value of money, which refers to the fact that a dollar you expect to pay or receive in the future is not worth as much as a dollar you have today. If you are not comfortable with the concept and computations involving the time value of money, especially present values, it is important to study Appendix 9 carefully. As you will see, accounting has embraced present value approaches in valuing bonds, leases, pensions, and other long-term liabilities. We start with an analysis of bonds and notes.

Corporate Bonds

Many corporations have heavy demands for borrowed capital, so they often borrow from the general public by issuing corporate bonds in the financial markets. **Bonds** are formal certificates of debt that include (1) a promise to pay interest in cash at a specified annual rate, often called the **nominal interest rate, contractual rate, coupon rate,** or **stated rate,** plus (2) a promise to pay the principal (often called the **face amount** or par value) of the loan at a specific maturity date. Bonds generally pay interest every 6 months. Fundamentally, bonds are individual promissory notes issued to many lenders.

We often call bonds **negotiable** financial instruments or securities because one lender can transfer them to another. Sometimes companies create bonds to borrow directly from a financial institution such as a pension plan or insurance company. We call bonds issued for these purposes **private placements** because the general public does not hold or trade them. Private placements provide more than half the capital borrowed by corporations in the United States. They are popular because they are generally easy to arrange and because they allow the lender to evaluate the creditworthiness of the borrower very carefully and directly. Borrowers and lenders can tailor specific features of the loan agreement to meet their special needs.

Specific Bond Characteristics

There are many ways that issuers can tailor bonds to their needs. In this section, we discuss just some of the provisions companies can put into bonds.

Preference in Liquidation—Mortgage Bonds and Subordinated Debentures

Bond provisions help determine bondholders' priority for claims when a company is in **liquidation,** which means converting assets to cash and paying off outside claims. For example, **mortgage bonds** are secured by the pledge of specific property. In case of default, these bondholders have the first right to proceeds from the sale of that property.

In contrast, debenture holders have a lower priority claim to recover their loan amount. A **debenture** is a debt security with a general claim against the company's total assets, instead of a particular asset. At liquidation, a debenture bondholder shares the available assets with other general creditors, such as trade creditors who seek to recover their accounts payable claims, with one exception. If debenture bonds are **subordinated,** the bondholders have claims against only the assets that remain after satisfying the claims of other general creditors.

To clarify these ideas, suppose a liquidated company had a single asset, a building, that it sells for $110,000 cash. The liabilities total $160,000 as follows:

Liabilities	
Accounts payable	$ 50,000
First mortgage bonds	80,000
Subordinated bonds	30,000
Total liabilities	$160,000

The mortgage bondholders, having a direct claim on the building, will receive their full $80,000. The trade creditors (the company's suppliers, to whom the company owes money) will receive the remaining $30,000 for their $50,000 claim ($0.60 on the dollar). The subordinated debenture claimants will get what is left over—nothing.

Now suppose the $30,000 of bonds were not subordinated. The bondholders would have a general claim on assets equivalent to that of the company's suppliers. The company would then use the $30,000 of cash remaining after paying $80,000 to the mortgage holders to settle the remaining $80,000 claims of the suppliers and bondholders proportionally as follows:

Liabilities		Payments	
Accounts payable	$ 50,000	$5/8 \times 30,000 =$	18,750
First mortgage bonds	80,000		80,000
Unsubordinated bonds	30,000	$3/8 \times 30,000 =$	11,250
	$160,000		$110,000

In order of priority, we have the mortgage bond, then unsubordinated debentures and accounts payable, and finally the subordinated debenture. Because interest rates are higher for riskier bonds, you can see that mortgage bonds would have the lowest interest rate and debentures would have the next lowest. Subordinated debentures would carry the highest interest rate.

Protection of Bondholders—Bond Covenants Many bonds contain **protective covenants** or simply **covenants.** Covenants generally restrict the ability of the borrower to take certain actions or give the lender the ability to force early payment under certain conditions. For example, a covenant might require immediate repayment of the loan if the borrower misses an interest payment, it may restrict sales of particular properties, or it may restrict the payment of dividends unless the borrower has generated additional earnings since issuing the debt. In general, covenants protect the bondholders' interests. Based on the concept of less risky bonds paying lower interest, you can see that these covenants have the ability to make the bond safer and therefore lower the interest rate.

protective covenant (covenant)
A provision stated in a bond, usually to protect the bondholders' interests.

Covenants often give bondholders the right to demand repayment of the loan principal if the company fails to meet some requirement in the convenants. These requirements may include maintaining a sufficient level of retained earnings (which can serve to limit dividend payments), a sufficient ratio of stockholders' equity to debt, or sufficient levels of cash and accounts receivable, or they may prohibit the issuance of additional debt without first repaying the existing debt.

For example, Gap Inc. indicated that its borrowings are subject to "financial and other covenants, including, but not limited to, limitations on capital expenditures, liens and cash dividends, and maintenance of certain financial ratios including a fixed-charge coverage ratio and an asset coverage ratio. Violation of these covenants could . . . require the immediate repayment of [borrowings]." Even colleges and universities issue bonds with covenants. Louisiana's Centenary College violated its covenants in 2003, but at this writing the bondholders have not demanded repayment (although they could, if they wanted to). The Gap and Centenary examples illustrate the ways in which organizations tailor bonds to specific borrowers and situations. In general, the more covenants there are, the more restricted the borrower is, and the more attractive the arrangement is to the lender. You can find more information on bond covenants in the Business First box on p. 392.

BUSINESS FIRST

BOND COVENANTS

A bond is a promise to pay interest and to repay principal at specific times. However, investors have learned that to control the risk that a borrower will be unable to pay in the future, it is useful to limit the borrower's freedom in a number of ways by writing restrictions into the bond contract. These covenants take many forms and may limit the ability to pay dividends, the ability to borrow additional amounts, and/or specify maintenance of certain ratios, such as debt-to-equity, current ratio, and so on.

For such covenants to be powerful, they typically require the borrower to provide the lender with audited financial statements every quarter and require the auditor to assure that no violations of the covenants have occurred. If a company violates a covenant, the debt typically comes due immediately. Although the lender may not require repayment in full when this happens, the default provides the opportunity for the lender to renegotiate the terms of the loan. That may involve earlier repayment, a higher interest rate, issuance of common stock, or some other remedy.

Covenants tend to evolve in response to observed risks. It is currently common for bonds to have a "change of control" feature, which means that when the ownership of the equity (common stock) of a company changes hands, the bonds become immediately due and payable. This feature might be called the RJR provision because it became common after Kohlberg, Kravis, Roberts & Co. (KKR), a leveraged buyout firm, acquired

R.J. Reynolds Tobacco Company (RJR) for $31.4 billion in a hostile takeover in 1989 (the largest corporate takeover ever until the mid-1990s). RJR had various bonds outstanding when KKR acquired it. In the transaction, KKR issued many additional bonds that were equal to RJR's existing bonds in seniority. In the process, the new company became very debt heavy, and investors worried that the merged company would not be able to repay the existing bondholders. Existing bonds fell some 14% in value on the day KKR and RJR announced the takeover. Thereafter, many lenders inserted a change-of-control feature into their bonds to ensure they had the right to get their full face (maturity) value back whenever a takeover occurred.

Recent increases in junk bonds and mezzanine bonds, both issued by more risky borrowers, have led lenders to focus more on covenants that protect their investments. For example, some covenants restrict the amount of capital investment by the borrower. One lender to retail operations requires growth in same-store sales before allowing investment in expanding the number of stores. In general, the more risky the debt, the more covenants the lender will require. Although covenants protect lenders, they can also severely restrict the flexibility of the borrower. Debt with covenants is certainly a double-edged sword.

Sources: Kravis, Roberts & Co. Web site (www.kkr.com); Burns, Mairin, "Lenders Raise Flags About Red-Hot Mezz: Covenants, Expense Belie 'Miracle Cure' Status," *Investment Dealers Digest* (October 27, 2003).

callable bonds
Bonds subject to redemption before maturity at the option of the issuer.

call premium
The amount by which the redemption price of a callable bond exceeds face value.

sinking fund bonds
Bonds that require the issuer to make annual payments to a sinking fund.

sinking fund
A pool of cash or securities set aside for meeting certain obligations.

Callable, Sinking Fund, and Convertible Bonds Additional bond provisions make bonds more or less attractive. Some bonds are **callable,** which means that the issuer has the option to redeem them before maturity. Typically, the redemption price exceeds the face value of the bond by an amount referred to as a **call premium.** To illustrate, consider a $1,000 bond issued in 2004 with a 2024 maturity date, which is callable any time after 2014 for a price of $1,050. The call premium is $50 per $1,000 bond. Callable bonds are good for the borrower because the borrower has a choice to redeem the bond early or wait to maturity. However, it creates uncertainty for the lender, who might therefore require a higher interest rate on callable bonds. The call premium compensates the lender for the risk of unexpected early redemption.

Sinking fund bonds require the issuer to make annual payments into a sinking fund. A **sinking fund** is a pool of cash or securities set aside solely for meeting certain obligations. It is an asset generally listed under "other assets." The sinking fund helps assure the bondholders that the company will have enough cash to repay the bond's principal at maturity. These provisions increase the attractiveness of the bond to lenders and therefore lower the interest rate.

Convertible bonds are bonds that bondholders may exchange for other securities, usually for a preset number of shares of the issuing company's common stock. Because of the conversion feature, convertible bondholders are willing to accept a lower interest rate than on a similar bond without the conversion privilege.

convertible bonds
Bonds that may, at the holder's option, be exchanged for other securities.

Bond Interest Rates, Bond Discount, and Bond Premium

The interest rate is a key factor for all bonds. Recall that the nominal interest rate or coupon rate determines the amount of each semiannual interest payment. In addition, we are concerned with the **market rate,** which is the rate available on investments in similar bonds at a moment in time. It is the amount of interest that investors require if they are to purchase the bond. If the market rate differs from the coupon rate, the issuing company will not receive the face amount when it issues the bond. When the market rate exceeds the coupon rate, the bond sells at a discount—the **bond discount** (or **discount on bonds**) is the amount by which the face amount exceeds the proceeds from the bond. When the coupon rate exceeds the market rate, the bond sells at a premium—the **bond premium** (or **premium on bonds**) is the excess of the proceeds over the face amount. Note that premiums and discounts do not reflect the creditworthiness of the issuer. Instead, they simply reflect differences in the nominal rate and the market rate. These differences often result from changes in market interest rates between the time a company sets the terms of the bond and when it actually issues the bond.

market rate
The rate available on investments in similar bonds at a moment in time.

bond discount (discount on bonds)
The excess of face amount over the proceeds on issuance of a bond.

bond premium (premium on bonds)
The excess of the proceeds over the face amount of a bond.

Consider a $1,000 2-year bond with a coupon rate of 10% that pays interest every 6 months until maturity and pays the face amount at maturity. Exhibit 9-2 shows the bond's values at three different market interest rates. It calculates the present value of the

	Present Value Factor	Total Present Value	Sketch of Cash Flows by Period 0	1	2	3	4
Valuation at market rate of 10% per year, or 5% per half-year							
Principal, 4-Period line, Table 9A-2							
.8227 × $1,000 = $822.70	.8227	822.70					1,000
Interest, 4-Period line, Table 9A-3							
3.5460 × $50 = $177.30	3.5460	177.30		50	50	50	50
Total		1,000.00					
Valuation at market rate of 12% per year, or 6% per half-year							
Principal	.7921	792.10					1,000
Interest	3.4651	173.25		50	50	50	50
Total		965.35					
Valuation at market rate of 8% per year, or 4% per half-year							
Principal	.8548	854.80					1,000
Interest	3.6299	181.50		50	50	50	50
Total		1,036.30					

Exhibit 9-2
Computation of Market Value of $1,000 Face Value, 10% Coupon, 2-Year Bond
(in dollars)

annuity of interest payments and adds that to the present value of the repayment of face value at maturity. Note that:

1. Although we express the quoted bond interest rates as annual rates, companies generally pay bond interest semiannually. Thus, a 10% bond really pays 5% interest each semiannual period. A 2-year bond has 4 periods, a 10-year bond has 20 periods, and so on.
2. The higher the market rate of interest, the lower the present value of the bond payments.
3. When the market interest rate equals the coupon rate of 10%, the bond is worth the face value of $1,000. We say such a bond is issued at par.
4. When the market interest rate of 12% exceeds the 10% coupon rate, the bond sells at a *discount*. The company receives $965.35, $34.65 less than the par value of $1,000.
5. When the market interest rate of 8% is less than the 10% coupon rate, the bond sells at a *premium*. The company receives $1,036.30, $36.30 more than the par value of $1,000.

The bond discount or bond premium depends on the market interest rate at the time the company issues the bond. After issuance, market rates may vary. Bondholders can sell their bonds in the marketplace, and the price they will receive depends on the current market rate for similar bonds, not the market rate in effect at the time of issue. We call the current market rate for a bond the **yield to maturity.** It is the interest rate at which all contractual cash flows for interest and principal have a present value equal to the current price of the bond.

What determines the market interest rate or the yield to maturity? Many factors, including general economic conditions, industry conditions, risks of the use of the proceeds, and specific features of the bonds. However, we can summarize these in three basic components: the real interest rate, the inflation premium, and the firm specific risk component.

1. The **real interest rate** is the return that investors demand because they are delaying their consumption. If you could have a dollar now or later, now is better most of the time. Most people would say the real rate of interest historically has been in the 3% range.
2. The **inflation premium** is the extra interest that investors require because the general price level may increase between now and the time they receive their money. This is an expectation, and peoples' expectations vary widely. In some countries inflation rates routinely exceed 100% per year, whereas in the United States recent inflation rates have been closer to 3% per year or less.
3. Finally, there is the **firm-specific risk,** referring to the risk that the firm will not repay the loan or will not pay the interest on time. In either event, the investor could lose everything, and at a minimum will have to pursue legal avenues to collect the money due. This amount ranges widely from 1% or 2% for firms with very good credit ratings to 10% or more for firms facing financial distress.

The first two of these reflect general economic conditions. Only the third is a result of company-specific conditions. Thus, creditors look carefully at the riskiness of the companies in which they invest. For example, compare a $1,000 bond issued by the U.S. government with $1,000 bonds issued by **AT&T** and **TimeWarner**. In 2004, the U.S. government bond paid interest of about 4.5% per year. At the same time the AT&T bonds paid 6.4%, and the TimeWarner bonds 7.6%. From this we can conclude that AT&T bonds are riskier than U.S. government bonds, and TimeWarner bonds are even more risky.

Assessing the Riskiness of Bonds

Although assessing the riskiness of bonds is essential, many creditors cannot spend the time to do an in-depth analysis of each bond offering. Thus, commercial services have developed evaluation systems to rate bonds according to their creditworthiness. **Mergent, Inc.** (formerly **Moody's**) and **Standard & Poor's** (S&P), a division of **McGraw-Hill**, are perhaps the best known.

yield to maturity
The interest rate at which all contractual cash flows for interest and principal have a present value equal to the current price of the bond.

real interest rate
The return that investors demand because they are delaying their consumption.

inflation premium
The extra interest that investors require because the general price level may increase between now and the time they receive their money.

firm-specific risk
The risk that the firm will not repay the loan or will not pay the interest on time.

Higher rated bonds are safer, and companies with better ratings generally pay lower interest rates. For example, examine the following average interest rates for bonds in each rating category. The rates, for June of each year, are from the Mergent Bond Record. Aaa is the highest rating and Baa is the lowest rating shown.

Rating	Aaa	Aa	A	Baa
2003	4.97	5.72	5.92	6.19
1998	6.53	6.78	6.88	7.13
1993	7.33	7.51	7.74	8.07
1988	9.86	10.13	10.42	11.00

Note that rates increase from left to right as ratings decrease. Investors will accept a lower yield for debt issued by the least risky companies. In addition, rates in every category have fallen steadily since 1988.

To assign the ratings, Mergent often interviews management in addition to analyzing financial data such as sales levels, profitability, and the debt level. In the United States, debt obligations are legally enforceable, and many examples exist where creditors have forced a company to liquidate to pay interest or to repay principal. This is what caused the collapse of Enron, WorldCom, Global Crossing, and many other companies in the economic downturn of the early 2000s.

Financial analysts must adapt to the realities facing specific companies. In Japan, for example, debt ratios tend to be much higher than they are in the United States. This difference partly reflects banking practices. Japanese banks lend very large sums to the biggest and most creditworthy corporations. Although the transaction has the form of debt, it tends to be part of a very long-term relationship between bank and customer. The banks end up with long-term rights that look somewhat like the rights of a U.S. shareholder.

Issuing and Trading Bonds

A syndicate (special group) of investment bankers called **underwriters** generally sells a corporation's bonds. That is, the syndicate buys the entire issue of bonds from the corporation, thus guaranteeing that the company will obtain the funds it needs. The syndicate then sells the bonds to the general investing public. The investment banker who manages the underwriting syndicate often helps the company set the terms of the bond contract—terms such as the time to maturity, interest payment dates, interest rates, and size of the bond issue. After a company initially issues bonds, the bondholders can often trade the bonds in markets or on exchanges such as the NYSE. You can find corporate bond prices in newspaper business sections. For example, on April 26, 2004, *The Wall Street Journal* included the following information on Abbott Laboratories and Cox Communications bonds:

underwriters
A group of investment bankers that buys an entire bond or stock issue from a corporation and then sells the securities to the general investing public.

	Coupon	Maturity	Last Price	Yield
Abbott Laboratories	3.750	Mar 15,2011	95.526	4.513
Cox Communications	7.125	Oct 12, 2012	110.791	5.506

Bonds typically have a face value of $1,000, but we usually express their values in terms of percentages of face value. Abbott's 3.750% coupon bonds maturing in 2011 sell for $955.26 (95.526% of $1,000) and have a yield to maturity of 4.513%. The yield is above the coupon so the price is less than $1,000. In contrast, the Cox Communications bond has a yield of 5.506% and a coupon of 7.125%, so its price of $1,107.91 is greater than $1,000.

Now that you understand the basics of bonds, let's look at how we account for them.

Bond Accounting

OBJECTIVE 3

Account for bond issues over their entire life.

The body of a company's balance sheet usually summarizes the various types of bonds and other long-term debt on one line. However, most companies show details about bonds in the footnotes. In Exhibit 9-1, **May Company** showed $3,797 million of long-term debt on its balance sheet, and a footnote elaborated as follows:

(dollars in millions)	January 31, 2004
Unsecured notes and sinking-fund debentures due 2004–2036	$3,970
Mortgage notes and bonds due 2004–2020	18
Capital lease obligations	48
Total debt	4,036
Less: Current maturities of long-term debt	239
Long-term debt	$3,797

Some other companies show more details. For example, **Coca-Cola** recently listed eight specific bonds and notes (six dollar-based and two euro-based) plus an "other" category for total long-term debt of nearly $3 billion. Many international companies borrow around the world. At the beginning of 2003, for example, **ExxonMobil** had $255 million of Eurobond obligations, $317 million of Canadian dollar obligations, and an additional $298 million of assorted "foreign currency obligations," which together comprise 13% of its long-term debt.

To understand what these accounts mean, we look at how a company records the issuance of bonds, how it recognizes interest payments, and how it records the retirement of bonds.

Bonds Issued at Par

Suppose that on December 31, 2003, Delta Company issued 10,000 2-year, 10% debentures, at par. That means the company received exactly the amount of the bond principal or face value, and the market rate is equal to the coupon rate of 10%. Because bonds typically have a principal or face value of $1,000 each, the total issue is for 10,000 × $1,000 = $10 million. (Notice that this bond is identical to those valued in Exhibit 9-2 on page 393.) The interest expense equals the amount of the interest payments, 5% × $10 million = $500,000 each 6 months for a total of $2,000,000 over the four semi-annual periods. Exhibit 9-3 shows how the bonds affect Delta's balance sheet equation throughout their life, assuming the company does not retire them before maturity.

Exhibit 9-3
Bond Transactions:
Issued at Par
(*$ in thousands*)

	A	=	L	+	SE
	Cash		**Bonds Payable**		**Retained Earnings**
Issuer's records					
1. Issuance	+10,000	=	+10,000		
2. Semiannual interest (repeated twice a year for 2 years)	−500	=			−500 ⎡Increase Interest Expense⎤
3. Maturity value (final payment)	−10,000	=	−10,000		

The journal entries for the issue are

```
1. Cash  ......................  10,000,000
        Bonds payable  .............                10,000,000
   To record proceeds upon issuance of 10%
   bonds maturing on December 31, 2005.
2-5. Interest expense  ............   500,000
        Cash  ....................                 500,000
   To record four payments of interest, one
   each six-month period.
6. Bonds payable  ...............  10,000,000
        Cash  ....................                10,000,000
   To record payment of maturity value of
   bonds and their retirement.
```

Entry 1 is at issue, entries 2 through 5 are the four identical interest payments, and entry 6 is the repayment of principal at maturity.

The issuer's balance sheet at June 30, 2004, December 31, 2004, and June 30, 2005 (after the respective semiannual interest payments) shows:

Bonds payable, 10% due December 31, 2005	$10,000,000

Bonds Issued at a Discount

Now suppose Delta issues its 10,000 bonds when annual market interest rates are 12%, which is a 6% rate for each six-month period. From Exhibit 9-2 we can see that Delta receives $965.35 for each bond, for total proceeds of $10,000 \times \$965.35 = \$9,653,500$. Therefore, the company recognizes a discount of $\$10,000,000 - \$9,653,500 = \$346,500$ at issuance. The discount results from the fact that the company has use of only $9,653,500, not $10,000,000. The journal entry at issue is:

```
Cash  ....................  9,653,500
Discount on bonds payable  .....   346,500
        Bonds payable  ..........                10,000,000
```

The discount on bonds payable is a contra account. The bonds payable account usually shows the face amount, and we deduct the discount amount from the face amount to get the amount shown on the balance sheet, often referred to as the net carrying amount, the net liability, or simply the book value:

Issuer's Balance Sheet	December 31, 2003
Bonds payable, 10% due December 31, 2005	$10,000,000
Deduct: Discount on bonds payable	346,500
Net liability (book value)	$ 9,653,500

For bonds issued at a discount, interest takes two forms—semiannual cash outlays of $5\% \times \$10$ million $= \$500,000$ plus an "extra" lump-sum cash payment of $346,500 at maturity (total payment of $10,000,000 at maturity when Delta actually borrowed only $9,653,500). For the issuer, the $346,500 is another cost of using the borrowed funds over the four semiannual periods. For the investor, the $346,500 represents extra interest revenue in addition to the coupon payments. The issuer should spread the extra $346,500 over all four periods, not simply charge it at maturity. We call the spreading of the discount over the life of the bonds **discount amortization.**

discount amortization
The spreading of bond discount over the life of the bonds as interest expense.

For 6 Months Ended	(1) Beginning Net Liability	(2) Interest Expense* @ 6%**	(3) Nominal Interest† @ 5%	(4) Discount Amortized (2) − (3)	(5) Ending Unamortized Discount	(6) Ending Net Liability $10,000,000 − (5)
12/31/03	—	—	—	—	$346,500	$ 9,653,500
6/30/04	$9,653,500	$ 579,207	$ 500,000	$ 79,207	267,293†	9,732,707
12/31/04	9,732,707	583,959	500,000	83,959	183,334	9,816,666
6/30/05	9,816,666	588,997	500,000	88,997	94,337	9,905,663
12/31/05	9,905,663	594,337	500,000	94,337	0	10,000,000§
		$2,346,500	$2,000,000	$346,500		

*Market interest rate when issued times beginning net liability, column (1).

**To avoid rounding errors, an unrounded actual effective rate slightly under 6% was used. The table used to calculate the proceeds of the issue has too few significant digits to calculate the exact present value of a number as large as $10 million. The more exact issue price would be $9,653,489.

†Nominal (coupon interest) rate times par value (face value) for 6 months.

‡$346,500 − $79,207 = $267,293; $267,293 − $83,959 = $183,334; etc.

§This is the face amount that Delta will repay on December 31, 2005, when the bond matures.

Exhibit 9-4
Effective Interest Amortization of Bond Discount

effective interest amortization (compound interest method)
An amortization method that uses a constant interest rate.

How much of the $346,500 should Delta amortize each semiannual period? The FASB requires companies to use **effective interest amortization,** also called the **compound interest method.** The key to effective interest amortization is that each period bears an interest expense equal to the carrying value of the debt (the net liability or the face amount less unamortized discount) multiplied by the market interest rate in effect when Delta issued the bond. The product is the interest expense for the period. The difference between the interest expense and the cash interest payment is the amount of discount amortized for the period.

Exhibit 9-4 shows the effective interest amortization schedule for our example. Notice that we do not amortize the same amount of discount each period. The interest expense each period is the market rate of interest at issue times the book value of the bond at the beginning of the period [see column (2)]. Interest expense increases each semiannual period as the carrying value of the bond increases until it equals the maturity value. The cash payment is a constant $500,000, and the difference between the interest expense and the cash payment is the amount of discount amortized.

The balance sheet disclosure of the bond payable is the ending net liability, calculated as the difference between the face or par value and the unamortized discount. The balance sheet values each 6 months, after payment of the interest payment due on that date, are:

Delta's Balance Sheets	December 31, 2003	June 30, 2004	December 31, 2004	June 30, 2005	December 31, 2005*
Bond.s payable, 10% due 12/31/05	$10,000,000	$10,000,000	$10,000,000	$10,000,000	$10,000,000
Deduct: Unamortized discount	346,500	267,293	183,334	94,337	—
Net liability	$ 9,653,500	$ 9,732,707	$ 9,816,666	$ 9,905,663	$10,000,000

*Before payment at maturity.

Exhibit 9-5 shows the balance sheet equation for the effective interest method of amortizing the bond discount. The journal entries follow:

12/31/03	1. Cash	9,653,500	
	Discount on bonds payable	346,500	
	Bonds payable		10,000,000

	A	=	L		+	SE
	Cash		**Bonds Payable**	**Discount on Bonds Payable**		**Retained Earnings**
1. Issuance	+9,654	=	+10,000	−346 ⌈ Increase ⌊ Discount		
Semiannual interest for 6 months ended:						
2. 6/30/04	−500	=		+79		−579
3. 12/31/04	−500	=		+84 ⌈ Decrease		−584 ⌈ Increase
4. 6/30/05	−500	=		+89 ⌊ Discount		−589 ∣ Interest
5. 12/31/05	−500	=		+94		−594 ⌊ Expense
6. Maturity value, 12/31/05 (final payment)	−10,000	=	−10,000	0		
Bond-related totals	− 2,346	=	+ 0	+ 0	+	−2,346

Exhibit 9-5
Delta Company
Balance Sheet Equation Effects of Effective Interest Amortization of Bond Discount
(Rounded to Thousands of Dollars)

6/30/04	2. Interest expense	579,207	
	Discount on bonds payable		79,207
	Cash		500,000
12/31/04	3. Interest expense	583,959	
	Discount on bonds payable		83,959
	Cash		500,000
6/30/05	4. Interest expense	588,997	
	Discount on bonds payable		88,997
	Cash		500,000
12/31/05	5. Interest expense	594,337	
	Discount on bonds payable		94,337
	Cash		500,000
12/31/05	6. Bonds payable	10,000,000	
	Cash		10,000,000

Bonds Issued at a Premium

Accounting for bonds issued at a premium is not difficult after you have mastered bond discounts. The key idea remains that the interest expense is the market rate of interest at issue times the book value of the bond. Bond premiums differ from bond discounts in the following ways:

1. The cash proceeds *exceed* the face amount.
2. We *add* the amount of the account Premium on Bonds Payable to the face amount of the bond to determine the net liability reported in the balance sheet.
3. Amortization of the bond premium causes interest expense to be *less than* the cash payment for interest.

To illustrate, suppose Delta issued the 10,000 bonds when annual market interest rates were 8% (and semiannual rates, 4%). From Exhibit 9-2 on page 393, we can see that Delta receives $1,036.30 for each bond, for total proceeds of 10,000 × $1,036.30 = $10,363,000. Exhibit 9-6 shows how to apply the effective interest method to the bond premium. The key concept remains the same as that for amortization of a bond discount: the interest expense (column 2) equals the net liability each period (column 1) multiplied

For 6 Months Ended	(1) Beginning Net Liability	(2) Interest Expense* @ 4%**	(3) Nominal Interest† @ 5%	(4) Premium Amortized (3) − (2)	(5) Ending Unamortized Premium	(6) Ending Net Liability $10,000,000 + (5)
12/31/02	—	—	—	—	$ 363,000	$ 10,363,000
6/30/03	$10,363,000	$ 414,517	$ 500,000	$ 85,483	277,517†	10,277,517
12/31/03	10,277,517	411,098	500,000	88,902	188,615	10,188,615
6/30/04	10,188,615	407,542	500,000	92,458	96,157	10,096,157
12/31/04	10,096,157	403,843	500,000	96,157	0	10,000,000
		$1,637,000	$2,000,000	$363,000		

*Market interest rate when issued times beginning net liability, column (1).
**To avoid rounding errors, an unrounded actual effective rate slightly under 4% was used.
†Nominal (coupon interest) rate times par value (face value) for 6 months.
†$363,000 − $85,483 = $277,517; $277,517 − $88,902 = $188,615; etc.

Delta's Balance Sheets	December 31, 2003	June 30, 2004	December 31, 2004	June 30, 2005	December 31, 2005*
Bonds payable, 10% due 12/31/05	$10,000,000	$10,000,000	$10,000,000	$10,000,000	$10,000,000
Add: Premium on bonds payable	363,000	277,517	188,615	96,157	0
Net liability	$10,363,000	$10,277,517	$10,188,615	$10,096,157	$10,000,000

*Before payment at maturity.

Exhibit 9-6
Effective Interest Amortization of Bond Premium

by the market interest rate in effect when the bond was issued. Balance sheets show the net liability calculated as the face amount plus unamortized premium.

Exhibit 9-7 shows the effects on the balance sheet equation, and the journal entries are as follows:

12/31/03	1. Cash		10,363,000	
		Premium on bonds payable		363,000
		Bonds payable		$10,000,000
6/30/04	2. Interest expense		414,517	
		Premium on bonds payable	85,483	
		Cash		500,000
12/31/04	3. Interest expense		411,098	
		Premium on bonds payable	88,902	
		Cash		500,000
6/30/05	4. Interest expense		407,542	
		Premium on bonds payable	92,458	
		Cash		500,000
12/31/05	5. Interest expense		403,843	
		Premium on bonds payable	96,157	
		Cash		500,000
12/31/05	6. Bonds payable		10,000,000	
		Cash		10,000,000

Companies frequently issue bonds between interest payment dates. When this occurs, the company makes an adjustment to the bond price to allow for the interest between the issue date and the first interest payment date.

	A	=	L		+	SE
	Cash		Bonds Payable	Premium on Bonds Payable		Retained Earnings
Issuer's records						
1. Issuance	+10,363	=	+10,000	+363 ⌈ Increase ⌊ Premium		
2. Semiannual interest 6 months ended						
6/30/04	−500	=		−85		−415 ⌈ Increase
12/31/04	−500	=		−89 ⌈ Decrease		−411 Interest
6/30/05	−500	=		−93 ⌊ Premium		−407 Expense
12/31/05	−500	=		−96		−404
3. Maturity value, 12/31/05						
(final payment)	−10,000	=	−10,000	0		
Bond-related totals	− 1,637	=	+ 0	+ 0	+	−1,637

Exhibit 9-7
Delta Company
*Balance Sheet Equation Effects of Effective Interest Amortization of Bond Premium
(Rounded to Thousands of Dollars)*

Cash Flow Statement Effects

The issuance of bonds is a financing activity, so companies show the cash received as a cash inflow from financing activities on the statement of cash flows. Semiannual interest payments are operating cash outflows, as are all interest payments. Payments at maturity are financing cash outflows. The amortization of bond discounts and premiums does not affect cash. Thus, it does not appear on a direct method statement of cash flows from operations. However, suppose a company uses the indirect method. The amortization of bond discount would be like depreciation, a noncash expense. You would add the amortization of bond discount to (or deduct the amortization of bond premium from) net income to get cash flow from operating activities. Such an adjustment in the indirect method of reporting cash flows from operations is necessary to adjust interest expense as reported on the income statement to the actual cash payment for interest.

Summary Problem for Your Review

PROBLEM

Suppose that on December 31, 2004, ExxonMobil issued $12 million of 10-year, 10% debentures. Assume that the annual market interest rate at issuance was 14%.

1. Compute the proceeds from issuing the debentures.
2. Prepare an analysis of the following items: (a) issuance of the debentures; (b) first two semiannual interest payments; and (c) payment of the maturity value. Use the balance sheet equation (similar to the presentation in Exhibit 9-5, p. 399). Round to the nearest thousand dollars. Use a bond discount account.
3. Prepare journal entries for the items in requirement 2. Use a bond discount account.

SOLUTION

1. Because the market interest rate exceeds the nominal rate, the proceeds will be less than the face amount. Proceeds are the present value (PV) of the 20 interest payments of $600,000 and the $12 million maturity value at 7% per semiannual period:

PV of interest payments: 10.5940 × $600,000	$6,356,400
PV of maturity value: .2584 × $12,000,000	3,100,800
Total proceeds	$9,457,200

2. See Exhibit 9-8.

3. 12/31/04: Cash   9,457,200
            Discount on bonds payable   2,542,800
                 Bonds payable   12,000,000
   6/30/05: Interest expense   662,004
                 Discount on bonds payable   62,004
                 Cash   600,000
   12/31/05: Interest expense   666,344
                 Discount on bonds payable   66,344
                 Cash   600,000
   12/31/14: Bonds payable   12,000,000
                 Cash   12,000,000

	A	=	L		+	SE
			Bonds	**Discount on**		**Retained**
	Cash		**Payable**	**Bonds Payable**		**Earnings**
ExxonMobil's records						
1. Issuance	+9,457		+12,000	−2,543 ⌈ Increase ⌉		
2. Semiannual interest				⌊ Discount ⌋		
6 Months ended						
6/30/05	−600			+62 ⌈Decrease⌉		−662* ⌈ Increase ⌉
12/31/05	−600			+66 ⌊ Discount ⌋		−666*	Interest
						⌊ Expense ⌋
3. Maturity value						
(final payment)	−12,000		−12,000			
Bond-related totals†	−14,543		0	0		−14,543

*7% × 9,457 = 662; 7% × (9,457 + 62) = 666.
†Totals after payment at maturity and all 20 entries for discount amortization and interest payments are made.

Exhibit 9-8
Analysis of ExxonMobil's Bond Transactions
(In Thousands of Dollars)

Early Extinguishment

You have seen how companies account for bonds they hold until maturity. However, some companies redeem or pay off their bonds either by purchases on the open market or by exercising their rights to redeem callable bonds. We call it an **early extinguishment** when a company chooses to redeem its own bonds before maturity. When a company extinguishes debt early, it recognizes the difference between the cash paid and the net carrying amount of the bonds (face less unamortized discount or plus unamortized premium) as a gain or loss.

early extinguishment
When a company chooses to redeem its own bonds before maturity.

	A	=	L		+	SE
	Cash		**Bonds Payable**	**Discount on Bonds Payable**		**Retained Earnings**
Redemption, December 31, 2004	−9,600	=	−10,000	+183 ⎡Decrease⎤ ⎣Discount ⎦	+217	⎡ Gain on ⎤ ⎢ Early ⎥ ⎣Extinguishment⎦

Exhibit 9-9
Delta Company
Analysis of Early Extinguishment of Debt on Issuer's Records
(Rounded to Thousands of Dollars)

Consider the bonds Delta issued at a discount (see Exhibit 9-4, page 398). Suppose Delta purchases all its bonds on the open market for $96 per $100 of face value on December 31, 2004 (after paying all interest payments and recording amortization for 2004):

Carrying amount		
Face or par value	$10,000,000	
Deduct: Unamortized discount on bonds*	183,334	$9,816,666
Cash required, 96% of $10,000,000		9,600,000
Difference, gain on early extinguishment of debt		$ 216,666

*See Exhibit 9-4. Of the original $346,500 discount, Delta has amortized $79,207 + $83,959 = $163,166, leaving $183,334 of the discount unamortized.

Exhibit 9-9 presents an analysis of the transaction. Delta would show the $216,666 gain on extinguishment of debt on its income statement. The journal entry on December 31, 2004, is:

Bond payable	10,000,000	
Discount on bonds payable		183,334
Gain on early extinguishment of debt		216,666
Cash		9,600,000

To record open market acquisition of entire issue of 10% bonds at 96.

Noninterest-Bearing Notes and Bonds

Some notes and bonds do not provide semiannual interest payments. Instead, they simply pay a lump sum at a specified date. For example, consider **zero coupon bonds.** These bonds provide no cash interest payments during their life. Issuers of zero coupon bonds prefer to pay and purchasers prefer to receive all the interest at maturity—they do not want to pay or receive semiannual payments of interest in the meantime. The name, zero coupon, is completely descriptive. To call such notes noninterest-bearing, however, is misleading. Investors demand interest revenue. Otherwise, why would they bother investing in the first place? Therefore, companies sell zero coupon bonds and notes for less than the face or maturity value. The investor determines a bond's market value at the issuance date by calculating the present value of its maturity value, using the market rate of interest for notes having similar terms and risks. The issuer amortizes the discount as interest over the life of the note.

zero coupon bond
A bond or note that pays no cash interest during its life.

Instead of collecting semiannual or other periodic payments, banks often discount both long- and short-term notes when making loans. Consider a 2-year, "noninterest-bearing," $10,000 face value note issued by Gamma Company on December 31, 2003, when annual market interest rates were 10% (which is 5% semiannually). In exchange for a promise to pay $10,000 on December 31, 2005, the bank provides Gamma with cash equal to the present value of the $10,000 payment:

$$\text{PV of \$1.00 from Table 9A-2, 5\% column, 4-period row} = 0.8227$$
$$\text{PV of \$10,000 note} = \$10,000 \times .8227 = \$8,227$$

implicit interest (imputed interest)
An interest expense that is not explicitly recognized in a loan agreement.

The note requires no specific interest payments. However, there is **implicit interest** (or **imputed interest**), which is a form of interest expense that is not explicitly recognized as such in a loan agreement. The imputed interest amount is based on an **imputed interest rate,** which is the market rate that equates the proceeds of the loan with the present value of the loan payments.

imputed interest rate
The market interest rate that equates the proceeds from a loan with the present value of the loan payments.

In this example, the $10,000 payment on December 31, 2005 will consist of $8,227 repayment of principal and $1,773 ($10,000 − $8,227) of imputed interest. At issue, Gamma shows the note on its balance sheet as follows:

Note payable, due December 31, 2005	$10,000
Deduct: Discount on note payable	1,773
Net liability	$ 8,227

Exhibit 9-10 shows how Gamma recognizes interest expense for each semiannual period. Each amortization of the discount decreases the discount account and increases the net carrying amount. The appropriate journal entries follow:

12/31/03	Cash	8,227	
	Discount on note payable	1,773	
	Note payable		$10,000
6/30/04	Interest expense	411	
	Discount on note payable		411
12/31/04	Interest expense	432	
	Discount on note payable		432
6/30/05	Interest expense	454	
	Discount on note payable		454
12/31/05	Interest expense	476	
	Discount on note payable		476
	Note payable	10,000	
	Cash		10,000

	A	=	L		+	SE
			Notes Payable	**Discount on Notes Payable**		**Retained Earnings**
	Cash					
Proceeds of loan	+ 8,227	=	+10,000	−1,773 ⌈Increase		
				⌊Discount		
Semiannual amortization						
6 Months ended:						
6/30/04		=		+411		−411
12/31/04		=		+432 ⌈Decrease		−432 ⌈Increase
				⌊Discount		Interest
6/30/05		=		+454		−454 ⌊Expense
12/31/05		=		+476		−476
Payment of note	−10,000	=	−10,000			
Note-related totals	− 1,773	=	+ 0	+ 0	+	−1,773

Exhibit 9-10
Analysis of Transactions of Borrower, Discounted Notes

Accounting for Leases

On page 396, we saw that May Department Stores Company has a long-term liability called Capital Lease Obligations. Why do we treat some leases as liabilities, but not others? Because sometimes a company signs a lease that gives it most of the privileges of ownership. Essentially, it uses the lease as the method of financing the asset, so its payment obligations are similar to those of debt. Other times a company signs a lease that simply gives it permission to use the asset for a specific period of time—which qualifies as a simple rental expense.

OBJECTIVE 4

Value and account for long-term lease obligations.

Leasing is a big business. Companies can acquire almost any asset imaginable via a lease contract. A **lease** is a contract whereby a **lessor** (owner) grants the use of property to a **lessee** in exchange for regular payments. Legal title to the property remains with the lessor, but the lessee uses the property as it would use property it owns. Our discussion focuses on leasing from the lessee's point of view. From an accounting perspective, whether we record a lease as a liability depends on whether it is a capital lease or an operating lease.

lease
A contract whereby an owner (lessor) grants the use of property to a second party (lessee) for rental payments.

lessor
The owner of property who grants usage rights to the lessee.

Operating and Capital Leases

Accountants categorize leases into two categories, capital and operating. **Capital leases** transfer most of the risks and benefits of ownership to the lessee. Many such leases are similar to installment sales in which the purchaser pays the price of an item over time along with interest payments. Accountants require companies to record such leased items as if the lessee had borrowed the money and purchased the leased asset. In other words, the economic substance of the transaction prevails over the legal form. The property becomes an asset, and the obligation to pay for it becomes a liability.

lessee
The party that has the right to use leased property and makes lease payments to the lessor.

capital lease
A lease that transfers most risks and benefits of ownership to the lessee.

The lease structure determines whether a lease is treated as an operating or capital lease for accounting purposes. Under U.S. GAAP, a lease is a capital lease if it meets one or more of the following conditions:

1. The lessor transfers ownership of the asset to the lessee by the end of the lease term.
2. The lease contains a **bargain purchase option**—that is, a provision that the lessee can purchase the asset from the lessor at the end of the lease for substantially less than the asset's fair value.
3. The lease term equals or exceeds 75% of the estimated economic life of the property.
4. At the start of the lease term, the present value of minimum lease payments is at least 90% of the property's fair value.

bargain purchase option
A provision that the lessee can purchase the asset from the lessor at the end of the lease for substantially less than the asset's fair value.

All other leases are **operating leases.** An example is an office or a car rented by the day, week, or month. Companies account for operating leases as ordinary rent expenses. Operating leases do not affect any balance sheet accounts other than cash when the company makes the lease payment and retained earnings through the charging of the payment as an expense. Managers cannot choose how to treat an existing lease. However, some managers do structure leases so they do not meet any of the criteria of a capital lease. This keeps them from appearing on the balance sheet.

operating lease
A lease that should be accounted for by the lessee as ordinary rent expenses.

Consider a simple example to see how the accounting differs for operating and capital leases. Suppose the Bestick Company can acquire a truck with a useful life of 4 years and no residual value under either of the following conditions:

Buy Outright	or	Capital Lease
Borrow $50,000 cash and agree to repay it in four equal installments at 12% interest compounded annually Use the $50,000 to purchase truck		Rental cost of $16,462 per year, payable at the end of each of 4 years; ownership transfers to Bestick at the end of the lease.

There is no basic difference between an outright purchase or an irrevocable (noncancellable) capital lease for 4 years. The Bestick Company uses the asset for its entire useful life and must pay for repairs, property taxes, and other operating costs under either plan.

Companies pay most lease rentals at the start of each payment period, but to ease our computations we assume that each payment of $16,462 will occur at the end of the year. To make the comparison between capital leasing and purchasing, we need to calculate payments on the $50,000 loan in the purchase option:

$$\text{Let } X = \text{loan payment}$$
$$\$50,000 = \text{PV of annuity of } \$X \text{ per year for 4 years at } 12\%$$
$$\$50,000 = 3.0373X$$
$$X = \$50,000/3.0373$$
$$X = \$16,462 \text{ per year}$$

Note that this loan payment is exactly equal to the lease payment. Thus, from Bestick's perspective, both buying outright and capital leasing create an obligation for four $16,462 payments that have a present value of $50,000.

Suppose Bestick treats this lease contract as an operating lease. At the end of each year the journal entry would be:

```
Rent expense  ..........................  16,462
    Cash  .............................          16,462
To record lease payment
```

No leasehold asset or lease liability would appear on the balance sheet.

Now suppose Bestick accounts for the lease as a capital lease. Then it must place both a leasehold asset and a lease liability on its balance sheet at the present value of future lease payments, initially $50,000 in this illustration. The signing of the capital lease requires the following journal entry:

```
Truck leasehold  .........................  50,000
    Capital lease liability, current  ............          10,462
    Capital lease liability, long-term  ..........          39,538
To record lease creation.
```

Note that the $50,000 liability has two components. The current liability is the payment due in the next year less the first year's interest: $16,462 − (12% × 50,000) = $10,462. The remainder, $50,000 − $10,462 = $39,538, is a long-term liability.

Bestick then amortizes the asset over 4 years. Straight-line amortization, the most common method, is $50,000 ÷ 4 = $12,500 annually.

The yearly journal entries for the leasehold amortization expense are:

```
Leasehold amortization expense  ............  12,500
    Truck leasehold  .....................          12,500
```

In addition, Bestick must record the annual lease payment. Each lease payment consists of interest expense plus an amount that reduces the outstanding liability. We use the effective interest method, as Exhibit 9-11 demonstrates. The yearly journal entries for lease payments are:

	Year 1		Year 2		Year 3		Year 4	
Interest expense	6,000		4,745		3,339		1,764	
Lease liability	10,462		11,717		13,123		14,698	
Cash		16,462		16,462		16,462		16,462

End of Year	(1) Capital Lease Liability at Beginning of Year	(2) Interest Expense at 12% per Year	(3) Cash for Capital Lease Payment	(4) (3)-(2) Reduction in Lease Liability	(5) (1)-(4) Capital Lease Liability at End of Year
1	50,000	$6,000	$16,462	10,462	$39,538
2	39,538	4,745	16,462	11,717	27,821
3	27,821	3,339	16,462	13,123	14,698
4	14,698	1,764	16,462	14,698	0

Exhibit 9-11
Analytical Schedule of Capital Lease Payments for Bestick Company

The following items from the January 1, 2004 balance sheet of Northwest Airlines illustrate leased assets and the associated liabilities. Note that the amount of the asset is substantially less than the amount of the liability.

Northwest Airlines
(Selected Items in Millions)

	January 1	
	2004	**2003**
Assets		
Flight equipment under capital leases:		
Flight equipment	$418	$464
Less accumulated amortization	168	175
Total equipment under capital leases	$250	$289
Liabilities		
Long-term obligations under capital leases	$354	$386

INTERPRETING FINANCIAL STATEMENTS

Explain why the $250 million net asset value of capital leases for Northwest Airlines on January 1, 2004, is not the same as the $354 million of obligations under capital leases.

Answer

When a company initiates a lease, the amounts of the capital leased asset and the capital lease obligation are identical. Their values first diverge and then converge over time because of the accounting process. Companies typically amortize assets using the straight-line basis. In contrast, they reduce the liability each period using the effective interest method. Under this method, each lease payment includes the payment of interest and the reduction of principal. Because interest is largest in the early period of the loan, reductions in the principal of the loan start off small. Hence, we expect the liability to exceed the asset in most cases.

Differences in Income Statements

Exhibit 9-12 summarizes the major differences between the accounting for operating leases and the accounting for capital leases. The cumulative expenses are the same, $65,848, but the timing differs. Relative to the operating lease approach, the capital lease approach tends to produce heavier charges in the early years. The longer the lease, the

	Operating Lease Method	Capital Lease Method			Differences	
Year	(a) Lease Payment*	(b) Amortization of Asset†	(c) Interest Expense‡	(d) (b) + (c) Total Expense	(e) (a) − (d) Difference in Pretax Income	(f) Cumulative Difference in Pretax Income
1	$16,462	$12,500	$ 6,000	$18,500	$(2,038)	$(2,038)
2	16,462	12,500	4,745	17,245	(783)	(2,821)
3	16,462	12,500	3,339	15,839	623	(2,198)
4	16,462	12,500	1,764	14,264	2,198	0
Cumulative expenses	$65,848	$50,000	$15,848	$65,848	$ 0	

*Rent expense for the year under the operating-lease method.
†$50,000 ÷ 4 = $12,500.
‡From Exhibit 9-11.

Exhibit 9-12
Bestick Company
Comparison of Annual Expenses: Operating versus Capital Leases

more pronounced the differences will be in the early years. Therefore, immediate reported income is lower under the capital lease approach.

An operating lease affects the income statement as rent expense, which is the amount of the lease payment. A capital lease affects the income statement as amortization (of the asset) plus interest expense (on the liability).

However, treatment varies across the globe. Many countries, including Austria, Brazil, Sri Lanka, and Taiwan, do not require lease capitalization. However, the IASB requires practices similar to those in the United States, so international divergence is decreasing.

Differences in Balance Sheets and Cash Flow Statements

The difference between operating and capital leases on the balance sheet is straightforward. At the inception of the lease, operating leases do not affect the balance sheet, whereas capital leases create both an asset and a liability.

The effects on the statement of cash flows are not as obvious. Operating leases affect only cash flows from operations. All cash payments for operating leases are operating cash outflows. In contrast, capital leases affect both operating and financing cash flows. The cash lease payment has two components, interest expense and reduction of the lease liability. For Bestick Company, the first year's lease payment of $16,462 includes an interest expense of $6,000 and a reduction in the lease liability of $10,462, as you can see in Exhibit 9-11. The $6,000 interest expense is an operating cash outflow. The lease reduction of $10,462 is a financing cash outflow. In the second year, the operating cash outflow is $4,745, and the financing cash outflow is $11,717. Notice that the operating cash outflow systematically declines throughout the life of the lease, whereas the financing cash outflow grows.

Summary Problem for Your Review

PROBLEM

Suppose the Sanchez Company enters into a lease to use a machine for 3 years with payments at the end of each year. Lease payments for the 3-year term of the lease are as follows:

Year 1	$ 40,000
Year 2	40,000
Year 3	40,000
Total lease payments	$120,000

Sanchez treats the lease as a capital lease and uses an interest rate of 10%.

1. Calculate the amount Sanchez should record as the carrying value of the capital leased asset and the capital lease liability as of the beginning of the lease on 12/31/X0.
2. How will Sanchez record the first year's payment?
3. How will the lease affect the first year's income statement?
4. How will the lease affect the first year's statement of cash flows?

SOLUTION

1. The present value of a 3-year annuity of $40,000 per year at 10% will be the initial value of the asset and the liability. From Table 9A-3, the present value factor is 2.4869.

$$2.4869 \times \$40,000 = \$99,476$$

2. The first year's payment will be for $40,000, part of which is interest and part of which is principal repayment. The interest portion is .10 × 99,476 = 9,948. The journal entry is:

Interest expense	9,948	
Capital lease liability	30,052	
Cash		40,000

3. The first year's income statement will show an expense of $9,948 for interest. It will also show amortization expense on the capital leased asset, assuming straight-line amortization, of $99,476 ÷ 3 = $33,159.
4. The total cash outflow for the first year is $40,000. The interest portion, $9,948, will be an operating cash outflow. The reduction of the lease obligation of $30,052 will be a financing cash outflow.

Other Long-Term Liabilities, Including Pensions and Deferred Taxes

We next explore some other long-term liabilities that commonly appear on balance sheets—pensions, other postretirement benefits, deferred taxes, restructuring liabilities, and contingent liabilities.

Pensions and Other Postretirement Benefits

Many U.S. companies provide benefits for retired employees. Accountants place these benefits into two categories: **pensions,** which are payments to former employees after they retire, and **other postretirement benefits,** primarily health insurance, but also including any other benefits. Pensions are further divided into defined contribution plans and defined benefit plans. Let's first consider pensions.

Pensions Accounting for defined contribution pension plans is straightforward. Employers contribute money directly into a fund that belongs to the employees. An employee's retirement pay will depend on the amount in the fund at the time he or she retires. If the fund has performed well, the employee's payments are higher than if the fund has performed poorly. The company has no obligation beyond its initial contribution. In essence, all the risks and rewards associated with fund performance rest with the employee.

OBJECTIVE 5

Evaluate pensions and other postretirement benefits.

pensions
Payments to former employees after they retire.

other postretirement benefits
Benefits provided to retired workers in addition to a pension, such as life and health insurance.

In contrast, defined benefit plans create a liability for the company. Why? Because such a plan guarantees employees an amount of retirement pay, normally a certain percentage of their last few years of pay, with the percentage usually depending on their years of service. The company is obligated to make these pension payments. We measure the obligation as the present value of the expected future pension payments to currently retired employees and to employees who will retire in the future. This present value depends on many assumptions, such as when current employees will retire, what their salaries will be at the time, their life expectancies, and the interest rate used to calculate present values. Companies report the total value of this pension obligation in footnotes to their financial statements. For example, **May Department Stores Company** reported an obligation of $821 million in the footnotes to its financial statements on January 31, 2004.

Companies could simply accrue pension liabilities without setting assets aside. However, if a company then went bankrupt, current workers and retirees would be left without pension benefits. To avoid this, U.S. tax laws provide incentives for companies to make payments into a pension fund that is separate from the company's assets and controlled by a trustee. The money in this fund is available only to pay future pensions. Footnotes to the financial statements reveal the fair value of the assets in the pension fund. If the fair value of the assets is less than the present value of a company's pension obligations, a company lists a net liability on its balance sheet. The fair value of May Company's pension fund assets on January 31, 2004, was $597 million, leaving a net liability of $821 million − $597 million = $224 million. (There are additional adjustments to the net liability that are beyond the scope of this text.)

How do companies account for pension expenses year by year? They must apply the matching principle, so they charge the pension expense to the years an employee works. Each year that an employee gets claim to additional retirement pay, the additional claim is an expense of the year the employee works, not the year the company distributes the retirement pay. Thus, a company's pension expense each year is essentially equal to the increase in the pension liability, although this is complicated slightly by some measurement issues that are beyond the scope of this text. Consider the May Company's experience in the year ended January 31, 2004. Pension expense was $108 million. In addition, May Company paid $84 million cash into the pension fund. We would account for this as follows (in millions):

	A	=	L	+	SE	
	Cash		**Pension Liability**		**Retained Earnings**	
Current pension expense	−84	=	+24		−108	⎡Increase⎤ Pension ⎣Expense⎦

The journal entry would be:

Pension expense.	108,000,000	
Cash		84,000,000
Pension liability		24,000,000

To record pension expense for the year. Of the $108 million expense, $84 million was paid in cash to the pension fund.

May Company includes its liability for pensions among "other liabilities."

Other Post-Retirement Benefits Accounting for the expense of health insurance and similar postretirement benefits is similar to accounting for pensions. The key difference is that most companies do not set aside specific assets on behalf of employees. Instead, they record the full present value of expected payments as a liability. Companies recognize any increase in the liability as a current expense.

May Company's liability for other postretirement benefits, included in other liabilities on the balance sheet and explained in the footnotes, was $49 million on February 1, 2003. During the next year, the company paid $5 million for health insurance and other benefits to retirees, and the liability at January 31, 2004 was $50 million. Therefore, the postretirement benefits expense for the year was $6 million. (Without the $6 million expense, the liability would have fallen to $44 million because the company paid off $5 million of the liability during the year.) The summary journal entries to record the $6 million expense and the $5 million payment are:

Other postretirement benefits expense	$6,000,000	
Postretirement benefits liability		$6,000,000
Postretirement benefits liability	$5,000,000	
Cash		$5,000,000

Liabilities for pensions and other postretirement benefits can be huge. For example, in 2003 Ford Motor Company had an excess of pension liabilities over funded assets of nearly $12 billion and other postretirement benefits liabilities of more than $28 billion. This was about 27% of Ford's total assets and more than three times its stockholders' equity of $11.7 billion. In contrast, some companies have overfunded their pensions and other postretirement benefits. Medtronic, the Minneapolis-based medical technology company, had net assets of more than $200 million as a "prepaid postretirement benefits" account in 2003. It is important to recognize that the funding status of a pension plan can change very quickly. Because most companies invest their pension assets in the stock and bond markets, the value of the pension assets fluctuates with the market.

Internationally, practice concerning pensions and other postretirement benefits varies widely. For example, many countries provide the majority of retirement income through individual savings or through tax-supported government programs akin to the U.S. Social Security Administration. In these cases, actual company pensions are rare, so there is nothing to report. In roughly one-half of the 45 countries examined in a recent survey, it was common practice for an independent outside trustee to manage pension funds, similar to U.S. practice. In the United States, the Pension Benefit Guarantee Corporation guarantees minimal retirement benefits to more than 44 million U.S. workers, even if their company goes bankrupt and leaves a severely underfunded pension liability.

Deferred Taxes

We have previously seen that delaying the payment of taxes from the time a company earns income to when it pays cash leads to short-term taxes payable. Another source of difference between income tax expense and income tax payments arises because U.S. income tax rules and the GAAP requirements for financial reporting differ. Sometimes the difference between GAAP reporting and tax laws forces companies to record some income tax expense long before they pay the taxes. This creates a **deferred income tax liability.** (Some companies also have deferred tax assets, which are beyond the scope of our coverage.) For example, May Company reported income tax expense of $278 million in the year ending February 1, 2003. However, May paid only $244 million in income taxes and deferred the remainder to future years. The situation reversed in the year ended January 31, 2004, when May paid $269 million to the government but had an income tax expense of only $205 million.

The differences between income tax expense and income taxes actually paid arise because accountants designed GAAP to provide useful information to investors, whereas Congress wrote the tax code to generate revenue for the government. Revenue recognition and expense recognition rules for tax purposes can differ from GAAP rules on two dimensions: (1) whether to recognize an item (permanent differences) and (2) when to recognize it (temporary or timing differences).

OBJECTIVE 6

Interpret deferred tax liabilities.

deferred income tax liability
An obligation arising because of predictable future taxes, to be paid when a future tax return is filed.

To save their companies money, good managers struggle to pay the least amount of income tax at the latest possible moment permitted within the law. As a result, they delay the reporting of taxable revenue as long as possible, while deducting tax-deductible expense items as quickly as possible. Corporations pay taxes to the government as follows:

$$\text{Taxes paid or payable} = \text{Income tax rate} \times (\text{Taxable revenue} - \text{Tax-deductible expenses})$$

tax rate
The percentage of taxable income paid to the government.

The **tax rate** is the percentage of taxable income paid to the government. U.S. corporate tax rates range from 15% on incomes of less than $50,000 to 35% on incomes of more than $335,000. Many states also levy an income tax, with tax rates varying from state to state. To simplify our illustrations, we generally assume a flat tax rate of 40%. This is a reasonable approximation of the combination of the federal 35% statutory (legally set) rate plus a state tax rate. We provide two illustrations, one permanent difference, municipal bond interest, and one temporary difference, depreciation.

permanent differences
Revenue or expense items that are recognized for tax purposes but not recognized under GAAP, or vice versa.

Permanent Differences **Permanent differences** arise when a company recognizes a revenue or expense item for either tax or financial reporting purposes but not for both. For example, suppose a company owns a bond issued by the city of New York and periodically receives interest on it. For financial reporting, the company reports this interest revenue on the income statement. Under federal law, bondholders do not pay taxes on interest received from municipal bonds issued by cities, states, and towns. Therefore, the interest revenue will never appear on the company's tax return. Dealing with this permanent difference is straightforward. We include the interest revenue for financial reporting, but we never recognize an income tax expense related to this revenue on our financial statements, and we never have to pay income tax on the revenue received.

Suppose a company with a 40% tax rate reports $100 of pretax income, of which $20 is revenue from nontaxable municipal bonds. It will pay taxes on only $100 − $20 = $80 of income, resulting in taxes of $80 × 40% = $32. As a percentage of reported income, the tax rate appears to be $32 ÷ $100 = 32%, rather than the 40% nominal tax rate.

temporary differences (timing differences)
Differences between net income and taxable income that arise because some revenue and expense items are recognized at different times for tax purposes than for financial reporting purposes.

Temporary Differences A **temporary** or **timing difference** arises when a company recognizes some revenue and expense item at a different time for tax purposes than for financial reporting purposes. A common temporary difference arises with depreciation. Many companies use accelerated depreciation for tax purposes and straight-line depreciation for financial reporting. Suppose Webster Company earns $40,000 per year before deducting depreciation and taxes, and pays taxes at a rate of 40% of taxable income. Webster acquires a $10,000 asset with a 2-year useful life. It can deduct the $10,000 immediately for tax purposes and will depreciate it at $5,000 per year for financial reporting.

Exhibit 9-13 shows that Webster will pay taxes of $12,000 the first year and $16,000 the second, a total of $28,000 or 40% of the $70,000 total income. What should Webster

Exhibit 9-13
Webster Company
Income for Financial Reporting and Income Tax Return

	Financial Reporting		Income Tax Returns	
	Year 1	Year 2	Year 1	Year 2
Income before depreciation and taxes	$40,000	$40,000	$40,000	$40,000
Depreciation	5,000	5,000	10,000	0
Pretax income	$35,000	$35,000	$30,000	$40,000
Taxes payable at 40%			$12,000	$16,000

report as income tax expense each year for financial reporting purposes? One approach is to report the amount Webster actually pays to the government each year, but the FASB does not permit this alternative. Instead, it requires Webster to report the amount that it would have paid if the pretax income used for financial reporting had also been reported to the tax authorities. If taxable income had been $35,000 each year, the tax would have been 40% × $35,000 = $14,000 annually. Therefore, the income statement for financial reporting would show:

	Year 1	Year 2	2-Year Totals
Pretax income	$35,000	$35,000	$70,000
Tax expense (40% of $35,000)	14,000	14,000	28,000
Net income	$21,000	$21,000	$42,000

This method matches the income tax expense with the financial reporting revenues and expenses to which it relates.

How do we account for this income tax expense? The tax payable to the government in year one is $12,000, but we record a tax expense of $14,000. Think of it as a current payable for the $12,000 currently owed to the government and a $2,000 liability that arises because of predictable future taxes. This $2,000 liability is a deferred tax liability because it will be paid only when a future tax return is filed. The journal entry is:

Income tax expense	14,000	
Deferred tax liability		2,000
Cash (or taxes payable)		12,000

We show the deferred tax liability of $2,000 on the balance sheet. It equals the tax rate of 40% times the $5,000 timing difference in depreciation expense ($5,000 on the books versus $10,000 on the tax return).

Remember that differences between reported income and taxable income result in deferral of taxes, not cancellation of taxes. Thus, we recognize a liability for future taxes equal to today's tax savings. In year two, the tax payable to the government is $16,000, but the company again records a tax expense of $14,000. Therefore, the company pays the $2,000 that it treated as a deferred tax liability in year one. The journal entry in the second year is:

Income tax expense	14,000	
Deferred tax liability	2,000	
Cash (or taxes payable)		16,000

In this example, we create the deferred tax liability in year one and reverse it in year two. However, if we depreciate an asset over 10 years, the deferred tax liability would take 10 years to reverse.

The balance sheet of nearly every company contains deferred tax liabilities. For example, May Company had deferred income taxes of $773 million on January 31, 2004, as shown in Exhibit 9-1 on p. 384, due primarily to the timing of depreciation. If May Company had used straight-line depreciation for both financial and tax reporting, it would have already paid $773 million more to the government in taxes. As it stands, it will still pay the $773 million, but it has delayed the payment and thereby could earn interest on the money in the meantime. In a recent survey of international practice, 60% of the countries surveyed required the use of deferred taxes when financial reporting of expenses differed from the timing of reporting of corresponding tax deductions. Because both the FASB and IASB require companies to report deferred taxes, this percentage is likely to increase quickly.

Summary Problem for Your Review

PROBLEM

The Solar Kitchen Corporation began business on January 1, 20X0, to manufacture and sell energy-efficient additions to provide solar-heated eating areas next to existing kitchens. Because of good styling and marketing to an energy-conscious public, sales soared. During 20X0, the following transactions occurred:

1. On January 1, Solar Kitchen sold 1,000 new shares of common stock at $100 per share.
2. The company immediately invested one-half of the proceeds from the stock sale in tax-free municipal bonds yielding 6% per annum. It held the bonds throughout the year, resulting in interest revenue of $50,000 \times .06 = \$3,000$.
3. Sales for the year were $450,000, with expenses of $380,000 reported under GAAP (exclusive of income tax expense).
4. Tax depreciation exceeded depreciation included in preceding item 3 by $30,000.

Required
1. Calculate earnings before tax for shareholder reporting.
2. Calculate income tax payable to the tax authorities and income tax expense for shareholder reporting using a 40% tax rate.
3. Make the appropriate journal entry. Assume the 40% tax rate is expected to be maintained.

SOLUTION

1. Earnings before taxes for shareholder reporting are:

Sales revenue	$450,000
Interest revenue	3,000
Less operating expenses	(380,000)
Pretax income	$ 73,000

2. Tax calculations:

	Reporting to Tax Authorities	Reporting to Shareholders
Earnings before tax	$73,000	$73,000
Permanent differences		
Nontaxable interest revenue	(3,000)	(3,000)
Subtotal	70,000	70,000
Timing differences		
Depreciation	(30,000)	—
Earnings on which tax is based	40,000	70,000
Tax rate	.40	.40
Income tax payable	$16,000	
Income tax expense reported to shareholders		$28,000

3.	Income tax expense	28,000	
	Income tax payable		16,000
	Deferred tax liability		12,000

Restructuring Liabilities

In the last decade, many companies recorded restructuring charges, and some recognized significant liabilities for future costs. A **restructuring** is a significant makeover of part of the company. It typically involves closing one or more plants, reducing the size of the workforce, and terminating or relocating various activities. For example, Hewlett-Packard (HP) recorded $800 million in restructuring charges in 2003, following recognition of $1,780 million of such costs in the prior year. By year-end 2003, HP had already paid for much of the restructuring. It reported a liability of $807 million for the remaining costs. Note that the charge against the income statement is in anticipation of costs the company expects to incur as it executes the plan. The liability at year-end is for the remaining unexecuted costs. The company may classify it as current or long-term, depending on when it expects to incur the costs. HP listed $709 million as a current liability and $98 million as a long-term liability.

restructuring
A significant makeover of part of the company typically involving the closing of plants, firing of employees, and relocation of activities.

Contingent Liabilities

The liabilities you have learned about so far are all concrete. We are confident about the existence of the liability, even if we have to estimate its amount. In contrast, a **contingent liability** is a potential (possible) liability that depends on a future event arising out of a past transaction. If the probability that the event will occur is high and the company can reasonably estimate the amount of the obligation, the company should list the liability and its amount on its balance sheet. More often, a contingent liability has an indefinite amount. A common example is a lawsuit. These are possible obligations of indefinite amounts. Why? Because if a judge rules against the company, it will be obligated to pay an amount that is currently unknown. However, the judge may rule in the company's favor, in which case there is no obligation.

contingent liability
A potential liability that depends on a future event arising out of a past transaction.

If the probability that the future event will occur does not meet a probability threshold, or if a company cannot estimate the dollar amount of the potential liability, it does not report a dollar amount on its balance sheet. In this situation, some companies list contingent liabilities without a dollar amount on the balance sheet after long-term liabilities, but before stockholders' equity. For example, Hewlett-Packard called this "Commitments and Contingencies" on its balance sheet with no amount specified and included a five-page footnote explaining its position on various lawsuits. Other companies discuss environmental issues, product safety, potential strikes, and any other contingent event that might affect the company. The Business First box on p. 416 describes an example of the evolution of a contingent liability to a definite liability—one where the final amount of the liability remains unknown more than 20 years after Dow Corning first reported it as a contingent liability.

Debt Ratios and Interest-Coverage Ratios

We have emphasized the link between the interest rate paid to lenders and the risk associated with the loan. When people take out loans to buy a car or a house, the interest rate on the loan is smaller if the down payment is larger. Lenders believe that the higher the down payment, the less risk they bear. How does this concept work for corporations? Potential creditors often use debt ratios to measure the extent to which a company has used borrowing to finance its activity. The more the borrowing and the less the stockholder's equity, the riskier it is to lend money to the firm.

OBJECTIVE 7
Use ratio analysis to assess a company's debt levels.

$$\text{Debt-to-equity ratio} = \frac{\text{Total liabilities}}{\text{Total shareholders' equity}}$$

$$\text{Long-term-debt-to total-capital ratio} = \frac{\text{Total long-term debt}}{\text{Total shareholders' equity} + \text{Total long-term debt}}$$

$$\text{Debt-to-total-assets ratio} = \frac{\text{Total liabilities}}{\text{Total assets}}$$

$$\text{Interest-coverage ratio} = \frac{\text{Pretax income} + \text{Interest expense}}{\text{Interest expense}}$$

debt-to-equity ratio
Total liabilities divided by total shareholders' equity.

long-term-debt-to-total-capital ratio
Total long-term debt divided by total shareholders' equity plus total long-term debt.

BUSINESS FIRST

CONTINGENT LIABILITIES AT DOW CORNING, INC.

A well-known product liability issue involved Dow Corning, Inc. In the 1980s, the company began facing many accusations from patients who were unhappy with silicone breast implants made by the company and surgically installed for reconstructive or cosmetic purposes. The accusations became lawsuits over time, and the company was confronted with a major product liability. Throughout the 1980s, Dow Corning regularly reported on its ongoing litigation. However, the lawsuits being heard in court were still fairly few, and no one knew how they might be resolved. So for several years the financial statements disclosed the litigation in some detail, but the balance sheet and income statement did not show specific numbers.

In 1991, the company recorded $25 million of pretax costs; in 1992, it recorded another $69 million. Remember that each of these amounts was intended to be a best estimate of future costs to be incurred. The product from which the claims stemmed had been produced and delivered years before. In fact, production of all silicone implants ceased in 1992. However, the liability estimates provided through 1992 were woefully inadequate. In 1993, Dow Corning recorded another pretax charge of $640 million. Combined with expected insurance coverage exceeding $600 million, the expected total cost of litigation exceeded $1.2 billion. Dow Corning and other manufacturers joined together to structure a settlement that would properly compensate plaintiffs, minimize legal costs, and allow the companies to survive. The deal required an agreement between the plaintiffs,

the companies, and the insurance carriers. In late 1994, agreement seemed close. Dow Corning provided another pretax charge of $241 million. Combined with additional expected insurance costs, the amounts set aside for injured parties approached $2 billion from Dow Corning and another similar amount from other manufacturers. There were more than 19,000 pending lawsuits on this product.

In May 1995, Dow Corning declared bankruptcy. The company claimed that too many plaintiffs were unwilling to agree to the settlement. Bankruptcy changes the company's whole litigation situation and leaves the final outcome very much in doubt. In 1998, Dow Corning recorded another pretax charge of $1.1 billion as its estimate of total additional costs to be incurred on all claims in bankruptcy, including the breast implant controversy. That is the last time Dow has charged a significant amount for implant costs. In 2003, Dow Corning earned $177 million on sales of nearly $2.9 billion. It had a liability of $2.2 billion labeled "Implant Reserve," representing the present value of expected future settlements. Its total stockholder' equity was $842 million. Its true liability is still being played out in the courts, which are still ruling on pending reorganization plans and discharge of plaintiff claims. However, the facts to date show the difficulty of predicting the cost of litigation. Any time your initial estimate of $25 million is off by a factor of 100, you know your prediction methods have a problem or two.

Source: Dow Corning annual reports for 1991 through 2003.

---

debt-to-total-assets ratio
Total liabilities divided by total assets.

interest-coverage ratio
Pretax income plus interest expense divided by interest expense.

Note that the first three ratios are alternate ways of expressing the proportion of the firm's resources obtained by borrowing. The higher the proportion, the riskier the firm and the higher the interest rate it must pay. The fourth ratio, the interest-coverage ratio, more directly measures the firm's ability to meet its interest obligation. It measures the amount of income available in relation to the company's interest expense. The lower the ratio, the more likely the company will have difficulty meeting its interest obligations.

Debt burdens vary greatly from firm to firm and industry to industry. For example, retailing companies, utilities, and transportation companies tend to have debt of more than 60% of their assets, which gives a debt-to-equity ratio of 1.5. May Company has a debt-to-equity ratio of 1.9. Computer companies and drug companies generally have much lower debt levels. Microsoft's debt-equity ratio is .3. Debt-to-equity ratios that were believed to be too high a few years ago are becoming commonplace today. The average debt-to-equity ratio for major U.S. industrial companies grew from about 1.5 in 1960 to nearly 2.5 today.

INTERPRETING FINANCIAL STATEMENTS

In comparing two companies, you observe that one company has little debt with a debt-to-total-assets ratio of 20%. The second company has a much higher ratio of 80%. How would you expect their interest-coverage ratios to compare?

Answer

A low debt-to-total-assets ratio is generally associated with a high interest-coverage ratio. Why? Because low relative debt means low interest costs. Interest costs are low for two reasons: (1) a small amount of debt on which to pay interest, and (2) low interest rates because a small amount of borrowing creates less risk than large borrowings. All else equal, when debt levels and interest costs are low, we expect interest coverage to be high.

Highlights to Remember

1 **Account for current liabilities.** Liabilities are obligations to pay money or to provide goods or services. An entity's liability level is important to analysts because unpaid liabilities may produce difficulties ranging from an inability to raise additional capital to forced liquidation. To help assess debt levels, financial statements typically separate liabilities requiring payment within 1 year as current liabilities. Accounting for current liabilities is a straightforward extension of procedures covered in earlier chapters. Companies record transactions as they occur, and accruals at the end of a period capture incomplete transactions such as accruing interest, wages, utilities, or taxes.

2 **Measure and account for long-term liabilities.** Long-term liabilities involve more complex contracts that convey many rights and responsibilities over long periods of time. Companies initially record bonds, a common long-term liability, at the amount received from investors at issue. During the life of the bond, a company recognizes interest expense each period.

3 **Account for bond issues over their entire life.** The value of bonds at issue is the present value of their future interest payments plus the present value of their principal payment, both at the market rate of interest appropriate to the company's risk level and the current level of expected inflation. During the life of a bond, companies recognize interest expense using the effective interest method each period. They determine the interest paid or payable by multiplying the coupon rate of interest specified in the bond contract by the par value. They determine the interest expense by multiplying the market interest rate when the bond was issued times the book value of the bond. The difference between the two is the amount of the bond discount or premium that the company amortizes during the period. Amortizing a bond discount increases interest expense and amortizing a bond premium decreases it.

4 **Value and account for long-term lease transactions.** Leases are contracts that grant the lessee the right to use property owned by the lessor. Because many leases involve long time periods and place many of the risks of ownership on the lessee, GAAP contains rules to classify some leases as capital leases. Companies account for a capital lease as if they had purchased the asset. They create both an asset and a liability when they sign a capital lease. The initial asset and liability values are both equal to the present value of payments required under the lease. The companies amortize the asset over its economic life, and they divide the lease payments into interest expense and loan repayment portions using the effective interest amortization method. During the life of the lease, the book value of the liability is typically larger than the book value of the asset because of the different amortization methods used. On the statement of cash flows, the portion of the lease payment representing interest is an operating cash outflow, and the portion representing a reduction in the lease liability is a financing cash outflow.

5 **Evaluate pensions and other postretirement benefits.** Companies must recognize measurable obligations for future pension payments and other postretirement benefits. Historical precedent leads to footnote disclosure for much of the pension information. On the income statement, the matching principle leads companies to record annually the change in their liability for future obligations for pensions and other postretirement benefits. In essence, companies record the change in the liability as an expense during the current period. Pension disclosures involve footnote presentations of the present value of the obligation, as well as the value of pension assets set aside with a trustee on behalf of the employees. For life and health insurance obligations to future retirees, companies generally do not set aside assets. Thus, financial statements present a significant liability equal to the present value of anticipated future payments for life and health insurance. Both pensions and insurance obligations depend on complex forecasts of future costs, retiree life expectancies, and so forth.

6 **Interpret deferred tax liabilities.** Deferred tax liabilities arise because tax deductions such as depreciation expense on the company's tax return often preceed the charging of the related expense on the company's books. When this happens, the immediate tax payable is less than it would appear to be if one examined the financial reports. To help investors understand the long-run tax obligations of the company, companies report tax expense as if they were paying taxes on the net income reported to shareholders. The company recognizes a deferred tax liability to reflect predictable higher taxes in the future, when these timing differences in the recording of depreciation expense will reverse.

7 **Use ratio analysis to assess a company's debt levels.** Debt ratios and interest coverage ratios are two measures used to evaluate the level of a company's indebtedness. The more debt a company has, the more problems it will face if cash flow is inadequate to meet liabilities as they fall due.

Appendix 9: Compound Interest, Future Value, and Present Value

OBJECTIVE 8

Compute and interpret present and future values (Appendix 9).

principal
The amount borrowed or the amount to be repaid.

interest
The cost the borrower pays the lender to use the principal.

interest rate
A specified percentage of the principal. It is used to compute the amount of interest.

simple interest
The interest rate multiplied by an unchanging principal amount.

compound interest
The interest rate multiplied by a changing principal amount. The unpaid interest is added to the principal to become the principal for the new period.

future value
The amount accumulated, including principal and interest.

Interest is the cost of using money. This appendix teaches you what you need to know about interest to understand the accounting for long-term liabilities. Our discussion of interest uses amounts from interest tables to solve problems; however, many of you will be using Excel, another spreadsheet, or financial calculators to make these calculations. The mechanism is not important, but the principles are paramount to understanding these liabilities.

When you borrow money, the amount borrowed is the loan **principal. Interest** is the cost the borrower pays the lender to use the principal. It is the rental charge for cash, just as you pay rental charges to use an automobile or an apartment. Investing money is basically the same as making a loan. The investor gives money to a company, and that company acts as a borrower. For the investor, interest is the return on investment or the fee for lending money. Contracts that bear interest have many forms, from simple short-term promissory notes to multimillion-dollar issues of bonds.

Calculating the amount of interest depends on the **interest rate**—a specified percentage of the principal—and the interest period—the time period over which the borrower uses the principal.

We calculate **simple interest** by multiplying an interest rate by an unchanging principal amount. If the borrower pays interest in cash at the end of each period, the principal amount does not change, and simple interest is appropriate. However, more common is **compound interest,** which we calculate by multiplying an interest rate by a principal amount that increases each time interest is accrued but not paid. We add the accumulated interest to the principal, and the total becomes the new principal for the next period.

Future Value

Consider an example. Suppose Christina's T-shirt business has $10,000 in cash that it does not need at this moment. Instead of holding the $10,000 in her business checking account, which does not pay interest, Christina deposits $10,000 in an account that pays 10% yearly interest, compounded annually. She plans to let the $10,000 remain in the account and earn interest for 3 years. After 3 years, she will withdraw all the money. The amount Christina will have in the account after 3 years, including principal and interest, is the **future value** of the $10,000 investment.

Let's compute the future value of Christina's investment after 3 years. Compound interest provides interest on interest. That is, we add interest payments to the principal each period, and the following period Christina earns interest on both the original principal amount and the amount of added interest. Christina earns interest in year one on $10,000: 10% × $10,000 = $1,000. If she does not withdraw the interest, the principal for year two includes the initial $10,000 deposit plus the $1,000 of interest earned in the first year, $11,000. She earns interest in year two on the $11,000: 10% × $11,000 = $1,100. In the third year she will earn interest on $12,100: $12,100 × 10% = 1,210. The future value (FV) of the $10,000 deposit at the end of 3 years with compound interest at 10% is $13,310:

	Principal	Compound Interest	Balance End of Year
Year 1	$10,000	$10,000 × .10 = $1,000	$11,000
Year 2	11,000	11,000 × .10 = 1,100	12,100
Year 3	12,100	12,100 × .10 = 1,210	13,310

More generally, suppose you invest S dollars for two periods and earn interest at an interest rate i. After one period, the investment would be increased by the interest earned, Si. You would have $S + Si = S(1 + i)$. In the second period, you would again earn interest ($i[S(1 + i)]$). After two periods, you would have:

$$[S(1 + i)] + (i[S(1 + i)]) = S(1 + i)(1 + i) = S(1 + i)^2$$

The general formula for computing the FV of S dollars in n years at interest rate i is

$$FV = S(1 + i)^n$$

In general, n refers to the number of periods the funds are invested. Periods can be years, months, days, or any other time period. However, the interest rate must be consistent with the time period. That is, if n refers to days, i must be expressed as i% per day.

The "force" of compound interest can be staggering. For example:

	Future Values at End of		
Compound Interest	10 Years	20 Years	40 Years
$10,000 × (1.10)^{10} = $10,000 × 2.5937 =	$25,937		
$10,000 × (1.10)^{20} = $10,000 × 6.7275 =		$67,275	
$10,000 × (1.10)^{40} = $10,000 × 45.2593 =			$452,593

Calculating future values and compound interest by hand is tedious and time consuming. Fortunately, there are tables, calculators, or software that will do much of the work for you. We use tables in this appendix. For example, Table 9A-1 shows the future values of $1 for various periods and interest rates. In the table, each number is the solution to the expression $(1 + i)^n$. Each column represents a specific interest rate, i, and each row represents a number of periods, n. Notice that the 3-year, 10% future value factor is 1.3310 (the third row, seventh column). We calculated this number as $(1 + .10)^3$. This is consistent with our preceding example where we show that $10,000 grows to $13,310 over 3 years ($10,000 × 1.3310 = $13,310).

Suppose you want to know how much $800 will grow to if left in the bank for 9 years at 8% interest. Multiply $800 by $(1 + .08)^9$. You can find the value for $(1 + .08)^9$ in the 9-year row and 8% column of Table 9A-1.

$$\$800 \times 1.9990 = \$1,599.20$$

The examples in this text use the factors from Table 9A-1 and similar tables in this appendix, which we have rounded to four decimal places. If you use tables with different rounding, or if you use a hand calculator or personal computer, your answers may differ slightly from those given because of a small rounding error.

Present Value

Accountants generally use present values instead of future values to record long-term liabilities. The **present value (PV)** is the value today of a future cash inflow or outflow.

Suppose you invest $1.00 today. As you learned in the discussion of future values, the $1.00 will grow to $1.06 in 1 year at 6% interest—that is, $1 × 1.06 = $1.06. At the end of the second year, its value is ($1 × 1.06) × 1.06 = $1 × (1.06)^2 = $1.124.

present value
The value today of a future cash inflow or outflow.

Table 9A-1
Future Value of $1

$$FV = (1 + i)^n$$

Periods	3%	4%	5%	6%	7%	8%	10%	12%	14%	16%	18%	20%	22%	24%	25%
1	1.0300	1.0400	1.0500	1.0600	1.0700	1.0800	1.1000	1.1200	1.1400	1.1600	1.1800	1.2000	1.2200	1.2400	1.2500
2	1.0609	1.0816	1.1025	1.1236	1.1449	1.1664	1.2100	1.2544	1.2996	1.3456	1.3924	1.4400	1.4884	1.5376	1.5625
3	1.0927	1.1249	1.1576	1.1910	1.2250	1.2597	1.3310	1.4049	1.4815	1.5609	1.6430	1.7280	1.8158	1.9066	1.9531
4	1.1255	1.1699	1.2155	1.2625	1.3108	1.3605	1.4641	1.5735	1.6890	1.8106	1.9388	2.0736	2.2153	2.3642	2.4414
5	1.1593	1.2167	1.2763	1.3382	1.4026	1.4693	1.6105	1.7623	1.9254	2.1003	2.2878	2.4883	2.7027	2.9316	3.0518
6	1.1941	1.2653	1.3401	1.4185	1.5007	1.5869	1.7716	1.9738	2.1950	2.4364	2.6996	2.9860	3.2973	3.6352	3.8147
7	1.2299	1.3159	1.4071	1.5036	1.6058	1.7138	1.9487	2.2107	2.5023	2.8262	3.1855	3.5832	4.0227	4.5077	4.7684
8	1.2668	1.3686	1.4775	1.5938	1.7182	1.8509	2.1436	2.4760	2.8526	3.2784	3.7589	4.2998	4.9077	5.5895	5.9605
9	1.3048	1.4233	1.5513	1.6895	1.8385	1.9990	2.3579	2.7731	3.2519	3.8030	4.4355	5.1598	5.9874	6.9310	7.4506
10	1.3439	1.4802	1.6289	1.7908	1.9672	2.1589	2.5937	3.1058	3.7072	4.4114	5.2338	6.1917	7.3046	8.5944	9.3132
11	1.3842	1.5395	1.7103	1.8983	2.1049	2.3316	2.8531	3.4785	4.2262	5.1173	6.1759	7.4301	8.9117	10.6571	11.6415
12	1.4258	1.6010	1.7959	2.0122	2.2522	2.5182	3.1384	3.8960	4.8179	5.9360	7.2876	8.9161	10.8722	13.2148	14.5519
13	1.4685	1.6651	1.8856	2.1329	2.4098	2.7196	3.4523	4.3635	5.4924	6.8858	8.5994	10.6993	13.2641	16.3863	18.1899
14	1.5126	1.7317	1.9799	2.2609	2.5785	2.9372	3.7975	4.8871	6.2613	7.9875	10.1472	12.8392	16.1822	20.3191	22.7374
15	1.5580	1.8009	2.0789	2.3966	2.7590	3.1772	4.1772	5.4736	7.1379	9.2655	11.9737	15.4070	19.7423	25.1956	28.4217
16	1.6047	1.8730	2.1829	2.5404	2.9522	3.4259	4.5950	6.1304	8.1372	10.7480	14.1290	18.4884	24.0856	31.2426	35.5271
17	1.6528	1.9479	2.2920	2.6928	3.1588	3.7000	5.0545	6.8660	9.2765	12.4677	16.6722	22.1861	29.3844	38.7408	44.4089
18	1.7024	2.0258	2.4066	2.8543	3.3799	3.9960	5.5599	7.6900	10.5752	14.4625	19.6733	26.6233	35.8490	48.0386	55.5112
19	1.7535	2.1068	2.5270	3.0256	3.6165	4.3157	6.1159	8.6128	12.0557	16.7765	23.2144	31.9480	43.7358	59.5679	69.3889
20	1.8061	2.1911	2.6533	3.2071	3.8697	4.6610	6.7275	9.6463	13.7435	19.4608	27.3930	38.3376	53.3576	73.8641	86.7362
21	1.8603	2.2788	2.7860	3.3996	4.1406	5.0338	7.4002	10.8038	15.6676	22.5745	32.3238	46.0051	65.0963	91.5915	108.4202
22	1.9161	2.3699	2.9253	3.6035	4.4304	5.4365	8.1403	12.1003	17.8610	26.1864	38.1421	55.2061	79.4175	113.5735	135.5253
23	1.9736	2.4647	3.0715	3.8197	4.7405	5.8715	8.9543	13.5523	20.3616	30.3762	45.0076	66.2474	96.8894	140.8312	169.4066
24	2.0328	2.5633	3.2251	4.0489	5.0724	6.3412	9.8497	15.1786	23.2122	35.2364	53.1090	79.4968	118.2050	174.6306	211.7582
25	2.0938	2.6658	3.3864	4.2919	5.4274	6.8485	10.8347	17.0001	26.4619	40.8742	62.6686	95.3962	144.2101	216.5420	264.6978
26	2.1566	2.7725	3.5557	4.5494	5.8074	7.3964	11.9182	19.0401	30.1666	47.4141	73.9490	114.4755	175.9364	268.5121	330.8722
27	2.2213	2.8834	3.7335	4.8223	6.2139	7.9881	13.1100	21.3249	34.3899	55.0004	87.2598	137.3706	214.6424	332.9550	413.5903
28	2.2879	2.9987	3.9201	5.1117	6.6488	8.6271	14.4210	23.8839	39.2045	63.8004	102.9666	164.8447	261.8637	412.8642	516.9879
29	2.3566	3.1187	4.1161	5.4184	7.1143	9.3173	15.8631	26.7499	44.6931	74.0085	121.5005	197.8136	319.4737	511.9516	646.2349
30	2.4273	3.2434	4.3219	5.7435	7.6123	10.0627	17.4494	29.9599	50.9502	85.8499	143.3706	237.3763	389.7579	634.8199	807.7936

Once you know how to calculate the future value of S dollars invested at a known interest rate *i* for *n* periods, you can reverse the process to calculate the present value of a future amount. Let *PV* be the present value, or value today, and *FV* be the future value, the value at some future date. Using the equation for future value

$$FV = PV(1 + i)^n$$

we can rearrange terms to compute the present value, *PV*:

$$PV = \frac{FV}{(1 + i)^n}$$

If you expect to receive $1.00 in 1 year, it is worth $1 ÷ 1.06 = $.9434 today. Suppose you invest $.9434 today. In 1 year, you will have $.9434 × 1.06 = $1.00. Thus, $0.9434 is the present value of $1.00 a year hence, at 6%. If you will receive the dollar in 2 years, its present value is $1.00 ÷ (1.06)² = $.8900. If you invest $.89 today at 6% interest, it will grow to $1.00 at the end of 2 years. The general formula for the PV of an FV that you will receive or pay in *n* periods at an interest rate of *i*% per period is:

$$PV = \frac{FV}{(1 + i)^n} = FV \times \frac{1}{(1 + i)^n}$$

Table 9A-2 gives factors for $1/(1 + i)^n$ (which is the present value of $1.00) at various interest rates over several different periods. You may hear present values called **discounted values,** interest rates called **discount rates,** and the process of finding the present value called **discounting.** You can think of present values as discounting (decreasing) the value of a future cash inflow or outflow. Why do we discount the value? Because you will receive or pay the cash in the future, not today, so it is worth less in today's dollars.

Assume a prominent city issues a 3-year noninterest-bearing note payable that promises to pay a lump sum of $1,000 exactly 3 years from now. You desire a rate of return of exactly 6%, compounded annually. We use the phrase **rate of return** to refer to the amount an investor earns expressed as a percentage of the amount invested. How much should you be willing to pay now for the 3-year note? The situation is sketched as follows:

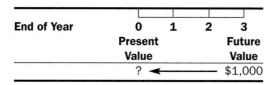

The factor in the period 3 row and 6% column of Table 9A-2 is .8396. The present value of the $1,000 payment is $1,000 × .8396 = $839.60. You should be willing to pay $839.60 for the $1,000 that you will receive in 3 years.

Suppose we compound interest semiannually instead of annually. How much should you be willing to pay now? Remember to pay attention to the number of periods involved, not just the number of years. The 3 years become six interest payment periods. The rate per period is one-half the annual rate, or 6% ÷ 2 = 3%. The factor in the period 6 row and 3% column of Table 9A-2 is .8375. You should now be willing to pay $1,000 × 0.8375, or only $837.50 instead of $839.60. Why do you pay less? Because with more frequent compounding the original investment will grow faster.

To see how present values work, let's return to our example. Suppose Christina's financial institution promised to pay her a lump sum of $13,310 at the end of 3 years for her investment. How much does she need to deposit to earn a 10% rate of return, compounded annually? Using Table 9A-2, the period 3 row and the 10% column show a factor of .7513. Multiply this factor by the future amount and round to the nearest dollar:

$$PV = .7513 \times \$13,310 = \$10,000$$

Present Value of an Ordinary Annuity

An ordinary **annuity** is a series of equal cash flows that take place at the end of successive periods of equal length. In other words, an annuity pays you the same amount at the end of each period for a set

discounted values
Another name for present values.

discount rates
Interest rates used to compute present values.

discounting
The process of finding the present value.

rate of return
The amount an investor earns expressed as a percentage of the amount invested.

annuity
Equal cash flows to take place during successive periods of equal length.

Table 9A-2
Present Value of $1

$$PV = \frac{1}{(1+i)^n}$$

Periods	3%	4%	5%	6%	7%	8%	10%	12%	14%	16%	18%	20%	22%	24%	25%
1	.9709	.9615	.9524	.9434	.9346	.9259	.9091	.8929	.8772	.8621	.8475	.8333	.8197	.8065	.8000
2	.9426	.9246	.9070	.8900	.8734	.8573	.8264	.7972	.7695	.7432	.7182	.6944	.6719	.6504	.6400
3	.9151	.8890	.8638	.8396	.8163	.7938	.7513	.7118	.6750	.6407	.6086	.5787	.5507	.5245	.5120
4	.8885	.8548	.8227	.7921	.7629	.7350	.6830	.6355	.5921	.5523	.5158	.4823	.4514	.4230	.4096
5	.8626	.8219	.7835	.7473	.7130	.6806	.6209	.5674	.5194	.4761	.4371	.4019	.3700	.3411	.3277
6	.8375	.7903	.7462	.7050	.6663	.6302	.5645	.5066	.4556	.4104	.3704	.3349	.3033	.2751	.2621
7	.8131	.7599	.7107	.6651	.6227	.5835	.5132	.4523	.3996	.3538	.3139	.2791	.2486	.2218	.2097
8	.7894	.7307	.6768	.6274	.5820	.5403	.4665	.4039	.3506	.3050	.2660	.2326	.2038	.1789	.1678
9	.7664	.7026	.6446	.5919	.5439	.5002	.4241	.3606	.3075	.2630	.2255	.1938	.1670	.1443	.1342
10	.7441	.6756	.6139	.5584	.5083	.4632	.3855	.3220	.2697	.2267	.1911	.1615	.1369	.1164	.1074
11	.7224	.6496	.5847	.5268	.4751	.4289	.3505	.2875	.2366	.1954	.1619	.1346	.1122	.0938	.0859
12	.7014	.6246	.5568	.4970	.4440	.3971	.3186	.2567	.2076	.1685	.1372	.1122	.0920	.0757	.0687
13	.6810	.6006	.5303	.4688	.4150	.3677	.2897	.2292	.1821	.1452	.1163	.0935	.0754	.0610	.0550
14	.6611	.5775	.5051	.4423	.3878	.3405	.2633	.2046	.1597	.1252	.0985	.0779	.0618	.0492	.0440
15	.6419	.5553	.4810	.4173	.3624	.3152	.2394	.1827	.1401	.1079	.0835	.0649	.0507	.0397	.0352
16	.6232	.5339	.4581	.3936	.3387	.2919	.2176	.1631	.1229	.0930	.0708	.0541	.0415	.0320	.0281
17	.6050	.5134	.4363	.3714	.3166	.2703	.1978	.1456	.1078	.0802	.0600	.0451	.0340	.0258	.0225
18	.5874	.4936	.4155	.3503	.2959	.2502	.1799	.1300	.0946	.0691	.0508	.0376	.0279	.0208	.0180
19	.5703	.4746	.3957	.3305	.2765	.2317	.1635	.1161	.0829	.0596	.0431	.0313	.0229	.0168	.0144
20	.5537	.4564	.3769	.3118	.2584	.2145	.1486	.1037	.0728	.0514	.0365	.0261	.0187	.0135	.0115
21	.5375	.4388	.3589	.2942	.2415	.1987	.1351	.0926	.0638	.0443	.0309	.0217	.0154	.0109	.0092
22	.5219	.4220	.3418	.2775	.2257	.1839	.1228	.0826	.0560	.0382	.0262	.0181	.0126	.0088	.0074
23	.5067	.4057	.3256	.2618	.2109	.1703	.1117	.0738	.0491	.0329	.0222	.0151	.0103	.0071	.0059
24	.4919	.3901	.3101	.2470	.1971	.1577	.1015	.0659	.0431	.0284	.0188	.0126	.0085	.0057	.0047
25	.4776	.3751	.2953	.2330	.1842	.1460	.0923	.0588	.0378	.0245	.0160	.0105	.0069	.0046	.0038
26	.4637	.3607	.2812	.2198	.1722	.1352	.0839	.0525	.0331	.0211	.0135	.0087	.0057	.0037	.0030
27	.4502	.3468	.2678	.2074	.1609	.1252	.0763	.0469	.0291	.0182	.0115	.0073	.0047	.0030	.0024
28	.4371	.3335	.2551	.1956	.1504	.1159	.0693	.0419	.0255	.0157	.0097	.0061	.0038	.0024	.0019
29	.4243	.3207	.2429	.1846	.1406	.1073	.0630	.0374	.0224	.0135	.0082	.0051	.0031	.0020	.0015
30	.4120	.3083	.2314	.1741	.1314	.0994	.0573	.0334	.0196	.0116	.0070	.0042	.0026	.0016	.0012
40	.3066	.2083	.1420	.0972	.0668	.0460	.0221	.0107	.0053	.0026	.0013	.0007	.0004	.0002	.0001

Table 9A-3
Present Value of Ordinary Annuity of $1

$$PV_A = \frac{1}{i}\left[1 - \frac{1}{(1+i)^n}\right]$$

Periods	3%	4%	5%	6%	7%	8%	10%	12%	14%	16%	18%	20%	22%	24%	25%
1	.9709	.9615	.9524	.9434	.9346	.9259	.9091	.8929	.8772	.8621	.8475	.8333	.8197	.8065	.8000
2	1.9135	1.8861	1.8594	1.8334	1.8080	1.7833	1.7355	1.6901	1.6467	1.6052	1.5656	1.5278	1.4915	1.4568	1.4400
3	2.8286	2.7751	2.7232	2.6730	2.6243	2.5771	2.4869	2.4018	2.3216	2.2459	2.1743	2.1065	2.0422	1.9813	1.9520
4	3.7171	3.6299	3.5460	3.4651	3.3872	3.3121	3.1699	3.0373	2.9137	2.7982	2.6901	2.5887	2.4936	2.4043	2.3616
5	4.5797	4.4518	4.3295	4.2124	4.1002	3.9927	3.7908	3.6048	3.4331	3.2743	3.1272	2.9906	2.8636	2.7454	2.6893
6	5.4172	5.2421	5.0757	4.9173	4.7665	4.6229	4.3553	4.1114	3.8887	3.6847	3.4976	3.3255	3.1669	3.0205	2.9514
7	6.2303	6.0021	5.7864	5.5824	5.3893	5.2064	4.8684	4.5638	4.2883	4.0386	3.8115	3.6046	3.4155	3.2423	3.1611
8	7.0197	6.7327	6.4632	6.2098	5.9713	5.7466	5.3349	4.9676	4.6389	4.3436	4.0776	3.8372	3.6193	3.4212	3.3289
9	7.7861	7.4353	7.1078	6.8017	6.5152	6.2469	5.7590	5.3282	4.9464	4.6065	4.3030	4.0310	3.7863	3.5655	3.4631
10	8.5302	8.1109	7.7217	7.3601	7.0236	6.7101	6.1446	5.6502	5.2161	4.8332	4.4941	4.1925	3.9232	3.6819	3.5705
11	9.2526	8.7605	8.3064	7.8869	7.4987	7.1390	6.4951	5.9377	5.4527	5.0286	4.6560	4.3271	4.0354	3.7757	3.6564
12	9.9540	9.3851	8.8633	8.3838	7.9427	7.5361	6.8137	6.1944	5.6603	5.1971	4.7932	4.4392	4.1274	3.8514	3.7251
13	10.6350	9.9856	9.3936	8.8527	8.3577	7.9038	7.1034	6.4235	5.8424	5.3423	4.9095	4.5327	4.2028	3.9124	3.7801
14	11.2961	10.5631	9.8986	9.2950	8.7455	8.2442	7.3667	6.6282	6.0021	5.4675	5.0081	4.6106	4.2646	3.9616	3.8241
15	11.9379	11.1184	10.3797	9.7122	9.1079	8.5595	7.6061	6.8109	6.1422	5.5755	5.0916	4.6755	4.3152	4.0013	3.8593
16	12.5611	11.6523	10.8378	10.1059	9.4466	8.8514	7.8237	6.9740	6.2651	5.6685	5.1624	4.7296	4.3567	4.0333	3.8874
17	13.1661	12.1657	11.2741	10.4773	9.7632	9.1216	8.0216	7.1196	6.3729	5.7487	5.2223	4.7746	4.3908	4.0591	3.9099
18	13.7535	12.6593	11.6896	10.8276	10.0591	9.3719	8.2014	7.2497	6.4674	5.8178	5.2732	4.8122	4.4187	4.0799	3.9279
19	14.3238	13.1339	12.0853	11.1581	10.3356	9.6036	8.3649	7.3658	6.5504	5.8775	5.3162	4.8435	4.4415	4.0967	3.9424
20	14.8775	13.5903	12.4622	11.4699	10.5940	9.8181	8.5136	7.4694	6.6231	5.9288	5.3527	4.8696	4.4603	4.1103	3.9539
21	15.4150	14.0292	12.8212	11.7641	10.8355	10.0168	8.6487	7.5620	6.6870	5.9731	5.3837	4.8913	4.4756	4.1212	3.9631
22	15.9369	14.4511	13.1630	12.0416	11.0612	10.2007	8.7715	7.6446	6.7429	6.0113	5.4099	4.9094	4.4882	4.1300	3.9705
23	16.4436	14.8568	13.4886	12.3034	11.2722	10.3711	8.8832	7.7184	6.7921	6.0442	5.4321	4.9245	4.4985	4.1371	3.9764
24	16.9355	15.2470	13.7986	12.5504	11.4693	10.5288	8.9847	7.7843	6.8351	6.0726	5.4509	4.9371	4.5070	4.1428	3.9811
25	17.4131	15.6221	14.0939	12.7834	11.6536	10.6748	9.0770	7.8431	6.8729	6.0971	5.4669	4.9476	4.5139	4.1474	3.9849
26	17.8768	15.9828	14.3752	13.0032	11.8258	10.8100	9.1609	7.8957	6.9061	6.1182	5.4804	4.9563	4.5196	4.1511	3.9879
27	18.3270	16.3296	14.6430	13.2105	11.9867	10.9352	9.2372	7.9426	6.9352	6.1364	5.4919	4.9636	4.5243	4.1542	3.9903
28	18.7641	16.6631	14.8981	13.4062	12.1371	11.0511	9.3066	7.9844	6.9607	6.1520	5.5016	4.9697	4.5281	4.1566	3.9923
29	19.1885	16.9837	15.1411	13.5907	12.2777	11.1584	9.3696	8.0218	6.9830	6.1656	5.5098	4.9747	4.5312	4.1585	3.9938
30	19.6004	17.2920	15.3725	13.7648	12.4090	11.2578	9.4269	8.0552	7.0027	6.1772	5.5168	4.9789	4.5338	4.1601	3.9950
40	23.1148	19.7928	17.1591	15.0463	13.3317	11.9246	9.7791	8.2438	7.1050	6.2335	5.5482	4.9966	4.5439	4.1659	3.9995

Exhibit 9-14
PV of 3 Annual
$1,000 Payments

	End of Year 6% *PV* Factor	Present Value	0	1	2	3
First payment	.9434	$ 943.40 ◄— $1,000				
Second payment	.8900	890.00 ◄————————— $1,000				
Third payment	.8396	839.60 ◄————————————————— $1,000				
		$2,673.00				

period of time. We denote its present value as PV_A. Assume that you buy a note from a municipality that promises to pay $1,000 at the end of each of 3 years. How much should you be willing to pay for this note if you desire a rate of return of 6%, compounded annually?

You could solve this problem using Table 9A-2. First, find the present value of each payment you will receive, and then add the present values as in Exhibit 9-14. You should be willing to pay $943.40 for the first payment, $890.00 for the second, and $839.60 for the third, a total of $2,673.00.

Table 9A-3 provides a shortcut method for calculating the present value of an annuity. We can calculate the present value in Exhibit 9-14 as follows:

$$PV_A = (\$1,000 \times .9434) + (\$1,000 \times .8900) + (\$1,000 \times .8396)$$
$$= \$1,000 \, (.9434 + .8900 + .8396)$$
$$= \$1,000(2.6730)$$
$$= \$2,673.00$$

The three terms in parentheses are the first three numbers from the 6% column of Table 9A-2, and their sum is in the third row of the 6% column of Table 9A-3: .9434 + .8900 + .8396 = 2.6730. This shortcut is especially valuable if the cash payments or receipts extend over many periods. Consider an annual cash payment of $1,000 for 20 years at 6%. The present value, calculated from Table 9A-3, is $1,000 × 11.4699 = $11,469.90. To use Table 9A-2 for this calculation, you would have to perform 20 calculations and then add up the 20 products.

You can calculate the factors in Table 9A-3 using the following general formula:

$$PV_A = \frac{1}{i}\left[1 - \frac{1}{(1+i)^n}\right]$$

Applied to our illustration:

$$PV_A = \frac{1}{.06}(1 - .83962) = \frac{.16038}{.06} = 2.6730$$

In particular, note that the higher the interest rate, the lower the present value factor in Table 9A-3. Why? Because, at a higher interest rate, you would need to invest less now to obtain the same stream of future annuity payments. For example, for a 10-year annuity the factor declines from 7.7217 for 5% to 6.1446 for 10%.

Summary Problems for Your Review

PROBLEM

To make sure you have the hang of present values, use Table 9A-2 to obtain the present values of:

1. $1,600, @ 20%, to be received at the end of 20 years.
2. $8,300, @ 10%, to be received at the end of 12 years.
3. $8,000, @ 4%, to be received at the end of 4 years.

SOLUTION

1. $1,600 (.0261) = $41.76.
2. $8,300 (.3186) = $2,644.38.
3. $8,000 (.8548) = $6,838.40.

PROBLEM

To make sure you understand present values of annuities, use Table 9A-3 to obtain the present values of the following ordinary annuities:

1. $1,600 to be received at the end of each year for 20 years, assuming interest at 20%.
2. $8,300 to be received at the end of each year for 12 years, assuming interest at 10%.
3. $8,000 to be received at the end of each year for 4 years, assuming interest at 4%.

SOLUTION

1. $1,600 (4.8696) = $7,791.36.
2. $8,300 (6.8137) = $56,553.71.
3. $8,000 (3.6299) = $29,039.20.

Accounting Vocabulary

annuity, p. 421
bargain purchase option, p. 405
bond discount, p. 393
bond premium, p. 393
bonds, p. 390
call premium, p. 392
callable bonds, p. 392
capital lease, p. 405
commercial paper, p. 385
compound interest, p. 418
compound interest method, p. 398
contingent liability, p. 415
contractual rate, p. 390
convertible bonds, p. 393
coupon rate, p. 390
covenant, p. 391
debenture, p. 390
debt-to-equity ratio, p. 415
debt-to-total-assets ratio, p. 416
deferred income tax liability, p. 411
discount amortization, p. 397
discount on bonds, p. 393
discount rates, p. 421
discounted values, p. 421
discounting, p. 421

early extinguishment, p. 402.
effective interest amortization, p. 398
face amount, p. 390
firm-specific risk, p. 394
future value, p. 418
implicit interest, p. 404
imputed interest, p. 404
imputed interest rate, p. 404
inflation premium, p. 394
interest, p. 418
interest-coverage ratio, p. 416
interest rate, p. 418
invoice, p. 385
lease, p. 405
lessee, p. 405
lessor, p. 405
line of credit, p. 386
liquidation, p. 390
long-term-debt-to-total-capital ratio, p. 415
long-term liabilities, p. 384
market rate, p. 393
mortgage bond, p. 390
negotiable, p. 390
nominal interest rate, p. 390
operating lease, p. 405

other postretirement benefits, p. 409
pensions, p. 409
permanent differences, p. 412
premium on bonds, p. 393
present value, p. 419
principal, p. 418
private placement, p. 390
promissory note, p. 385
protective covenant, p. 391
purchase order, p. 385
rate of return, p. 421
real interest rate, p. 394
receiving report, p. 385
restructuring, p. 415
simple interest, p. 418
sinking fund, p. 392
sinking fund bonds, p. 392
stated rate, p. 390
subordinated debentures, p. 390
tax rate, p. 412
temporary differences, p. 412
timing differences, p. 412
underwriters, p. 395
yield to maturity, p. 394
zero coupon bond, p. 403

Assignment Material

Questions

9-1 Distinguish between current liabilities and long-term liabilities.

9-2 Name and briefly describe five items that are often classified as current liabilities.

9-3 "Withholding taxes really add to employer payroll costs." Do you agree? Explain.

9-4 "Product warranties expense should not be recognized until actual repair services are performed. Until then you don't know which products might require warranty repairs." Do you agree? Explain.

9-5 Distinguish between a mortgage bond and a debenture. Which is safer?

9-6 Distinguish between subordinated and unsubordinated debentures.

9-7 "Protective covenants protect the shareholders' interests in cases of liquidation of assets." Do you agree? Explain.

9-8 Bond covenants usually restrict the borrower's rights in various ways. An example might be a restriction that no additional long-term debt could be issued unless the debt-to-total assets ratio was below .5. Who benefits from such a covenant? How?

9-9 Many callable bonds have a call premium for "early" calls. Who does the call premium benefit—the issuer or the purchaser of the bond? How?

9-10 "The face amount of a bond is what you can sell it for." Do you agree? Explain.

9-11 "The quoted bond interest rates imply a rate per annum, but the bond markets do not mean that rate literally." Explain.

9-12 A company plans to issue bonds with a nominal rate of 10%. At what market rates will the bonds be issued at a discount? At what market rates will they be issued at a premium?

9-13 "When a bond is issued at a discount, there are two components of interest expense." Explain.

9-14 What are the three main differences between accounting for a bond discount and accounting for a bond premium?

9-15 "A company that issues zero coupon bonds recognizes no interest expense until the bond matures." Do you agree? Explain.

9-16 Certain leases are essentially equivalent to purchases. A company must account for such leases as if the asset had been purchased. Explain.

9-17 "A capital lease results in both an asset and a liability on a company's balance sheet." Explain.

9-18 "A capital lease and operating lease are recorded differently on the balance sheet, but their effect on the income statement is the same." Do you agree? Explain.

9-19 Discuss which characteristics of a lease are evaluated in deciding whether it is a capital lease.

9-20 "Because a company never knows how much it will have to pay for pensions, no pension liability is recognized. Pension obligations are simply explained in a footnote to the financial statements." Do you agree? Explain.

9-21 Compare and contrast permanent differences and temporary differences between GAAP and tax reporting.

9-22 "Differences in tax and GAAP rules lead to more depreciation being charged on tax statements than on financial reports to the public." Do you agree? Explain.

9-23 "It is unethical for big companies to recognize a large income tax expense on their income statements reported to the public but to pay a small amount to the government." Do you agree? Explain.

9-24 "A contingent liability is a liability having an estimated amount." Do you agree? Explain.

9-25 Refer to Appendix 9. How are Table 9A-2 (p. 422) and Table 9A-3 (p. 423) related to each other?

Critical Thinking Questions

9-26 Lenders and Covenants
Why would a lender want to add a covenant specifying a maximum debt-to-total-assets ratio to a loan contract ?

9-27 Lottery Winnings
The New York Lottery provides prizes that start at $3 million and rise each time someone fails to win the lottery. Participants in the lottery are permitted to choose to receive a lump-sum payment or 26 payments as an annuity. A recent winner of $20 million was surprised to receive a check for less than $10 million? How could you explain this to the winner?

9-28 Refinancing Bonds
Your treasurer is new to the job and has just noticed that your bonds are trading below par (i.e., at a discount). This officer recommends that you retire the bonds by issuing new bonds because you will have a gain in the process and will reduce your interest payments. Do you believe you should accept the treasurer's recommendation?

9-29 Cash Interest versus Interest Expense
As a lender, you are contemplating a covenant that is based on the interest-coverage ratio. A young member of your organization with a new MBA degree has suggested that you calculate the ratio

using actual cash interest payments each period instead of interest expense each period. You have been asked to discuss this proposal. What do you say?

Exercises

9-30 Liabilities on the Balance Sheet

Krispy Kreme Company, the rapidly expanding doughnut company, had the following items on its February 2, 2003 balance sheet (in thousands):

Cash and cash equivalents	$32,203
Accounts payable	14,055
Deferred income taxes	9,849
Retained earnings	102,403
Accrued expenses	20,981
Prepaid expenses	3,478
Revolving line of credit, long-term	7,288
Short-term debt	12,275
Current maturities of long-term debt	3,301
Arbitration award*	9,075
Long-term debt, net of current portion	49,900
Other long-term obligations	5,218

* Krispy Kreme must pay this in the next year.

Prepare the liabilities section of Krispy Kreme's balance sheet. Include only the items that are properly included in liabilities. Separate current and long-term liabilities.

9-31 Accrued Employee Compensation

Welton Company had total compensation expense for March of $24,000. The company paid $20,000 to employees during March, and it will pay the remainder in April.

1. Prepare the journal entry for recording the compensation expense for March.
2. Suppose salaries and wages payable were $2,000 at the beginning of March. Compute salaries and wages payable at the end of March.

9-32 Sales Taxes

Most of the food sold in retail stores in California is not subject to sales taxes (e.g., candy), but some items are (e.g., soft drinks). Apparently, the candy lobbyists were more effective than soft drinks lobbyists when dealing with the state legislature. Most cash registers are designed to record taxable sales and nontaxable sales and automatically add the appropriate sales tax.

The sales for the past week in the local Safeway store were $140,000 cash, of which $40,000 was taxable at a rate of 7%. By using the $A = L + SE$ equation, show the impact on the entity, both now and when the sales taxes are paid at a later date. Also prepare corresponding journal entries.

9-33 Product Warranties

During 20X4, the Cedeno Appliance Company had cash sales of $800,000. The company estimates that the cost of servicing products under warranty will average 3% of sales.

1. Prepare journal entries for sales revenue and the related warranty expense for 20X4. Assume all sales are for cash.
2. The liability for warranties was $11,600 at the beginning of 20X4. Expenditures (all in cash) to satisfy warranty claims during 20X4 were $20,400, of which $4,500 was for products sold in 20X4. Prepare the journal entry for the warranty expenditures.
3. Compute the balance in the Liability for Warranties account at the end of 20X4.

9-34 Unearned Revenues

The Reader's Digest Association, Inc., one of the largest publishers of magazines in the world, had unearned revenues of $415 million on its June 30, 2003 balance sheet. Suppose that during July, Reader's Digest delivered magazines with a sales value of $30 million to prepaid subscribers and sold subscriptions for $37 million cash.

1. Prepare journal entries for the new subscriptions and the deliveries to prepaid subscribers.
2. Compute the amount in the unearned revenue account at the end of July 2003.

9-35 Priorities of Claims

Sterling Real Estate Corporation is being liquidated. It has one major asset, an office building, which was converted into $18 million cash. The stockholders' equity has been wiped out by past losses. The following claims exist: accounts payable, $3 million; debentures payable, $5 million; and first mortgage payable, $13 million.

1. Assume that the debentures are not subordinated. How much will each class of claimants receive?
2. If the debentures are subordinated, how much will each class of claimants receive? How much will each class receive if the cash proceeds from the sale of the building amount to only $14.5 million?

9-36 Discounted Present Value and Bonds

On December 31, 20X1, Tan Company issued a 3-year $1,000 bond that promises an interest rate of 12%, payable 6% semiannually. Compute the discounted present value of the principal and the interest as of December 31, 20X1, if the market rate of interest for such securities is 12%, 14%, and 10%, respectively. Show your computations, including a sketch of cash flows. Round to the nearest dollar.

9-37 Criteria for Capital Leases

Indicate which of the following leases would be a capital lease and which would be operating leases.

a. Rental of an automobile on a 3-month lease for $500 per month. The auto will be returned to the dealer after the 3 months.
b. Rental of a crane for $8,000 per month on a 6-year lease, with an option to buy for $10,000 at the end of the 6 years when its fair value is $150,000.
c. Rental of a computer for $1,000 per month on a 5-year lease. At the end of 5 years, the computer is expected to have a fair market value of zero.
d. Rental of 10 forklifts for $1,400 per month on an 8-year lease. The value of the forklifts at the end of 8 years is uncertain, but the total economic life is not expected to be more than 10 years.
e. Rental of a warehouse for $10,000 per month, renewable annually.

9-38 Accounting for Pensions

Hrbeck Company's current pension expense is $800,000, of which it pays $250,000 in cash to a trustee. By using the balance sheet equation format, show which accounts are affected by these data. Prepare the corresponding journal entry.

9-39 Deferred Taxes

Procter & Gamble (P&G) Company's net sales in 2003 exceeded $43 billion. On its income statement, P&G reported the following ($ in millions):

Earnings before income taxes	$7,530
Income taxes	2,344
Net earnings	$5,186

Taxes due on 2003 taxable income and payments to the government for income taxes related to operations in 2003 were $2,281 million. Assume that the income tax expense and these income tax payments were the only tax-related transactions during 2003.

1. Prepare the journal entry that recognizes the $2,344 million income tax expense and the $2,281 million income tax payment.
2. Compute the change in the deferred income tax liability account for 2003.

9-40 Various Liabilities

1. Maytag Corporation sells electric appliances, including automatic washing machines. Experience in recent years has indicated that warranty costs average 3.0% of sales. Sales of washing machines for April were $3.0 million. Cash disbursements and obligations for warranty service on washing machines during April totaled $82,000. Prepare the journal entries prompted by these facts.
2. Pepsi-Cola Company of New York gets cash deposits for its returnable bottles. In November, it received $105,000 cash and disbursed $95,000 for bottles returned. Prepare the journal entries concerning the receipts and returns of deposits.
3. Citibank received a $4,000 savings deposit on April 1. On June 30, it recognized interest thereon at an annual rate of 4%. On July 1, the depositor closed her account with the bank. Prepare the bank's necessary journal entries.

4. The Greenbriar Theater sold, for $150,000 cash, a "season's series" of tickets in advance of December 31 for five plays, each to be held in successive months, beginning in January.
   a. What is the effect on the balance sheet of December 31? What is the appropriate journal entry for the sale of the tickets?
   b. What is the effect on the balance sheet of January 31? What is the related journal entry for January?
5. Suppose a tabloid newspaper has lost a lawsuit. Damages were set at $600,000. The newspaper plans to appeal the decision to a higher court. The newspaper's attorneys are 90% confident of a reversal of the lower court's decision. What liability, if any, should be shown on the newspaper's balance sheet?

9-41 Exercises in Compound Interest
Study Appendix 9. Then answer the following questions:

1. You deposit $6,000. How much will you have in 4 years at 8%, compounded annually? At 12%?
2. A savings and loan association offers depositors a $6,000 lump-sum payment 4 years hence. How much will you be willing to deposit if you desire an interest rate of 8% compounded annually? How much at an interest rate of 12%?
3. Repeat requirement 2, but assume the interest rates are compounded semiannually.

9-42 Exercises in Compound Interest
Study Appendix 9. A reliable friend has asked you for a loan. You are pondering various proposals for repayment.

1. Repayment of a $20,000 lump sum 4 years hence. How much will you lend if your desired rate of return is (a) 10% compounded annually, (b) 20% compounded annually?
2. Repeat requirement 1, but assume the interest rates are compounded semiannually.
3. Suppose the loan is to be paid in full by equal payments of $5,000 at the end of each of the next 4 years. How much will you lend if your desired rate of return is (a) 10% compounded annually and (b) 20% compounded annually?

9-43 Compound Interest and Journal Entries
Study Appendix 9. A Munich company has bought some equipment on a contract entailing a €200,000 cash down payment and an €800,000 lump sum to be paid at the end of 4 years. The same equipment can be bought for €788,000 cash. (€ refers to the euro, a unit of currency).

1. Prepare the journal entry for the acquisition of the equipment.
2. Prepare journal entries at the end of each of the first 2 years. Ignore entries for depreciation.

9-44 Exercises in Compound Interest
Study Appendix 9. Then answer the following questions:

1. It is your sixtieth birthday. You plan to work 5 more years before retiring. Then you want to spend $20,000 for a Mediterranean cruise. What lump sum do you have to invest now to accumulate the $20,000? Assume your minimum desired rate of return is:
   a. 5%, compounded annually
   b. 10%, compounded annually
   c. 20%, compounded annually
2. You want to spend $3,000 on a vacation at the end of each of the next 5 years. What lump sum do you have to invest now to take the five vacations? Assume that your minimum desired rate of return is:
   a. 5%, compounded annually
   b. 10%, compounded annually
   c. 20%, compounded annually

9-45 Exercises in Compound Interest
Study Appendix 9. Then answer the following questions:

1. At age 60, you find that your employer is moving to another location. You receive termination pay of $100,000. You have some savings and wonder whether to retire now.
   a. If you invest the $100,000 now at 8%, compounded annually, how much money can you withdraw from your account each year so at the end of 5 years there will be a zero balance?
   b. If you invest it at 10%?
2. At 16%, compounded annually, which of the following plans is more desirable in terms of present value? Show computations to support your answer.

| Year | Annual Cash Inflows | |
	Mining	Farming
1	$100,000	$ 20,000
2	80,000	40,000
3	60,000	60,000
4	40,000	80,000
5	20,000	100,000
	$300,000	$300,000

9-46 Basic Relationships in Interest Tables

Study Appendix 9. Then answer the following questions:

1. Suppose you borrow $20,000 now at 16% interest compounded annually. The borrowed amount plus interest will be repaid in a lump sum at the end of 6 years. How much must be repaid? Use Table 9A-1 and basic equation: FV = Present amount × Future value factor.
2. Repeat requirement 1 using Table 9A-2 and the basic equation: PV = Future amount × Present value factor.
3. Assume the same facts as in requirement 1, except that the loan will be repaid in equal installments at the end of each of 5 years. How much must be repaid each year? Use Table 9A-3 and the basic equation: PV_A = Future annual amounts × Conversion factor.

9-47 Discounted Present Value and Leases

Study Appendix 9. Suppose Wal-Mart signed a 10-year lease for a new store location. The lease calls for an immediate payment of $25,000 and annual payments of $20,000 at the end of each of the next 9 years. Wal-Mart expects to earn 16% interest, compounded annually, on its investments. What is the present value of the lease payments?

Problems

9-48 Accounting for Payroll

For the week ended January 27, the Sierra Manufacturing Company had a total payroll of $200,000. The company withheld three items from employees' paychecks: (1) Social Security (FICA) tax of 7.1% of the payroll; (2) income taxes, which average 22% of the payroll; and (3) employees' savings that are deposited in their Credit Union, which are $10,000. Sierra paid all three items on January 30.

1. Use the balance sheet equation to analyze the transactions on January 27 and January 30.
2. Prepare journal entries for the recording of the items in requirement 1.
3. In addition to the payroll, Sierra pays (1) payroll taxes of 9% of the payroll, (2) health insurance premiums of $12,000, and (3) contributions to the employees' pension fund of $16,000. Prepare journal entries for the recognition and payment of these additional expenses.

9-49 Convertible Bonds

Sometimes companies find it desirable to include a convertibility option to sell bonds at a reasonable interest rate. In 2003, Siemens AG, the huge German electronics company, issued €2.5 billion of convertible bonds with a coupon rate of 1.375%, which is less interest than Siemens would have paid if the bonds were not convertible. Each €1,000 bond can be converted into 17.8 common shares of Siemens stock.

In 2003, Siemens had revenues of more than €70 billion and a net income of about €1 billion. The company pays dividends of about €1 per share. The market price of a share of Siemens common stock is approximately €52.

1. Compute the annual interest received by the holders of the convertible bonds.
2. Suppose the price of one share of Siemens common stock quickly rose to €60. If you held some of the Siemens convertible bonds, would you immediately convert your bonds to common stock? Why or why not?
3. Suppose the maturity date of the convertible bonds was rapidly approaching. Would you convert your holdings of the convertible bonds if the price of Siemens stock were €60 per share? If the price were €50 per share? Explain.

9-50 Bonds Issued at Par

On December 31, 2003, Clay Computers issued $30 million of 5-year, 10% debentures at par.

1. Compute the proceeds from issuing the debentures.
2. Using the balance sheet equation format, prepare an analysis of this bond transaction. Show entries for the issuer concerning (a) issuance, (b) first semiannual interest payment, and (c) payment of maturity value.
3. Show all the corresponding journal entries keyed as in requirement 2.
4. Show how the bond-related accounts would appear on the balance sheet as of December 31, 2003 and June 30, 2004. Assume that the semiannual interest payment due on the balance sheet date has been recorded.

9-51 Bonds Issued at Par

On December 31, 2003, BC Fisheries, Inc. issued $15 million of 10-year, 6% debentures at par.

1. Compute the proceeds from issuing the debentures.
2. By using the balance sheet equation format, prepare an analysis of this bond transaction. Show entries for the issuer concerning (a) issuance, (b) first semiannual interest payment, and (c) payment of maturity value.
3. Show the corresponding journal entries for (a), (b), and (c) in requirement 2.
4. Show how the bond-related accounts would appear on the balance sheet as of December 31, 2003 and June 30, 2004. Assume that the semiannual interest payment due on the balance sheet date has been recorded.

9-52 Bond Discount Transactions

(Alternates are 9-53 and 9-55.) On March 1, 2003, Midwest Gas issued $100 million of 20-year, 9% debentures. Proceeds were $91.191 million, implying a market interest rate of 10%. Show all amounts in thousands of dollars.

1. By using the balance sheet equation format, prepare an analysis of bond transactions. Assume effective interest amortization. Show entries for the issuer concerning (a) issuance, (b) first semi-annual interest payment, and (c) payment of maturity value.
2. Show all the corresponding journal entries for (a), (b), and (c) in requirement 1.
3. Show how the bond-related accounts would appear on the balance sheets as of March 1, 2003 and March 1, 2004. Assume the March 1 interest payment and amortization of bond discount have been made.

9-53 Bonds Issued at a Discount

(Alternates are 9-52 and 9-55.) On January 1, 2004, Metro Transit issued $10 million of 5-year, 6% debentures. The market interest rate at issuance was 8%.

1. Compute the proceeds from issuing the debentures.
2. By using the balance sheet equation format, prepare an analysis of this bond transaction. Show entries for the issuer concerning (a) issuance, (b) first semiannual interest payment, and (c) payment of maturity value. Round to the nearest thousand.
3. Show the corresponding journal entries for (a), (b), and (c) in requirement 2.
4. Show how the bond-related accounts would appear on the balance sheets as of January 1, 2004 and July 1, 2004. Assume Metro Transit has already recorded the semiannual interest payment and amortization due on the balance sheet dates.

9-54 Bond Amortization Schedule

Consider the bond in Problem 9-53: A $10 million issue of 5-year, 6% debentures when the market interest rate was 8%. It was issued on January 1, 2004.

1. Prepare a table showing the interest expense and the unamortized discount and ending liability balance for each semiannual period. Use Exhibit 9-4 on p. 398 as an example. (*Hint*: Use a spreadsheet.)
2. Prepare the journal entry for recording interest for the 6-month period ended June 30, 2007.

9-55 Bond Discount Transactions

(Alternates are 9-52 and 9-53.) Assume that on December 31, 2004, Trondheim Tool and Die issued NKR 10 million of 10-year, 10% debentures. Proceeds were NKR 7,881,000; therefore, the market rate of interest was 14%. (NKR is the Norwegian kroner.)

1. By using the balance sheet equation format, prepare an analysis of transactions for Trondheim. Key your transactions as follows: (a) issuance, (b) first semiannual interest using effective interest amortization of bond discount, and (c) payment of maturity value. Round all amounts to the nearest thousand.

2. Prepare corresponding journal entries for (a), (b), and (c) in requirement 1.
3. Show how the bond-related accounts would appear on Trondheim's balance sheets as of December 31, 2004 and June 30, 2005. Assume that Trondheim has already recorded the semiannual interest payments and amortization.

9-56 Bonds Issued at a Premium

(Alternate is 9-57.) On January 1, 2004, New South Wales Travel issued $4 million of 5-year, 10% debentures. The market interest rate at issuance was 8%.

1. Compute the proceeds from issuing the debentures.
2. By using the balance sheet equation format, prepare an analysis of this bond transaction. Show entries for the issuer concerning (a) issuance, (b) first semiannual interest payment, and (c) payment of maturity value. Round to the nearest thousand.
3. Show the corresponding journal entries for (a), (b), and (c) in requirement 2.
4. Show how the bond-related accounts would appear on the balance sheets as of January 1, 2004 and July 1, 2004. Assume the semiannual interest payments and amortization due on the balance sheet date have been recorded.

9-57 Bond Premium Transactions

(Alternate is 9-56.) Assume that on December 31, 20X4, Green Bay Woolens issued $10 million of 10-year, 10% debentures. Proceeds were $11,359,000; therefore, the market rate of interest was 8%.

1. By using the balance sheet equation format, prepare an analysis of transactions for Green Bay Woolens. Key your transactions as follows: (a) issuance, (b) first semiannual interest using effective interest amortization of bond premium, and (c) payment of maturity value. Round all amounts to the nearest thousand.
2. Prepare corresponding journal entries for (a), (b), and (c) in requirement 1.
3. Show how the bond-related accounts would appear on Green Bay Woolens' balance sheets as of December 31, 20X4 and June 30, 20X5. Assume that the semiannual interest payment and amortization have been recorded.

9-58 Early Extinguishment of Debt

On December 31, 2003, Sunnyside Cruises issued $20 million of 10-year, 12% debentures. The market interest rate at issuance was 14%. On December 31, 2004 (after all interest payments and amortization had been recorded for 2004), the company purchased all the debentures for $19 million. Throughout their life, the debentures had been held by a large insurance company.

Show all amounts in thousands of dollars. Round to the nearest thousand.

1. Compute the gain or loss on early extinguishment.
2. By using the balance sheet equation, present an analysis of the December 31, 2004, transaction on the issuer's books.
3. Show the appropriate journal entry.
4. At what price on December 31, 2004 could Sunnyside Cruises redeem the bonds and realize a $500,000 gain?

9-59 Early Extinguishment of Debt

On December 31, 2005, a Geneva real estate holding company issued SFR 10 million of 10-year, 8% debentures. The market interest rate at issuance was 8%. Suppose that on December 31, 2006 (after all interest payments had been recorded for 2006), the company purchased all the debentures for SFR 9 million. The debentures had been held by a large insurance company throughout their life. (SFR represents Swiss francs.)

Show all amounts in thousands of francs.

1. Compute the gain or loss on early extinguishment.
2. By using the balance sheet equation, present an analysis of the December 31, 2004, transaction on the holding company's books.
3. Show the appropriate journal entry.

9-60 Noninterest-Bearing Notes

On January 2 a local bookstore borrowed from a bank on a 1-year note. The face value of the note was $40,000. However, the bank deducted its interest "in advance" at 10% of the face value.

Show the effects on the borrower's records at inception and at the end of the year:

1. By using the balance sheet equation, prepare an analysis of transactions.
2. Prepare journal entries.
3. What was the real rate of interest?

9-61 Zero Coupon Bonds

The U.S. Treasury requires issuers of "deep-discount" or "zero coupon" debt securities to use an effective interest approach to amortization of discount. Similarly, buyers of such securities must record interest income under the effective interest rate method. This law replaced an old tax law that permitted straight-line amortization of bond discount.

1. Assume that Mattel, maker of Barbie Dolls and other toys, issues a 10-year zero coupon bond having a face amount of $20,000,000 to yield 10%. For simplicity, assume that the 10% yield is compounded annually. Prepare the journal entry for the issuer.
2. Prepare the journal entry for interest expense for the first full year and the second full year using (a) straight-line and (b) effective interest amortization.
3. Assume an income tax rate of 35%. How much more income tax for the first year would the issuer have to pay because of applying effective interest instead of straight-line amortization?
4. What kinds of borrowers might prefer these investments over bonds that pay interest immediately?

9-62 Zero Coupon Bonds

The state of Illinois issues zero coupon bonds as part of its Illinois College Savings Bonds series. In late 2002, the state issued 9 million such bonds with a total $45 million maturity value. Each bond had a maturity value of $5,000, and bonds ranged in price from $4,750 for a 3-year bond to $1,800 for a 22-year bond. Consider one of the 22-year zero coupon bonds issues on October 1, 2002 for $1,800.

1. Compute the market interest rates for the 22-year zero coupon bond. How does this compare with the rate on the 3-year bonds?
2. Prepare the state of Illinois' journal entry for one 22-year bond at issuance. Do not use a discount account.
3. Prepare the state's journal entry for recording interest expense on the 22-year bonds for 2002. Round to the nearest dollar. Remember that the bond was outstanding only 3 months in 2002.
4. Compute the liability that Illinois would show on its balance sheet for this bond on December 31, 2002.

9-63 Capital Lease

The Kansas City Meat Packing Company acquired packaging equipment on a capital lease for annual lease payments of $40,000 at the end of each of 3 years. The implicit interest rate was 18% compounded annually.

1. Compute the present value of the capital lease.
2. Prepare journal entries at the inception of the lease and for each of the 3 years. Distinguish between the short and long-term classifications of the lease liability.

9-64 Comparison of Operating and Capital Lease

Refer to the preceding problem. Compare income statement and balance sheet effects of treating the lease as a capital lease rather than an operating lease. Ignore income taxes. You can do this by filling in the blanks in the following table.

	Operating Lease	Capital Lease	Difference
Total expenses			
Year 1	?	?	?
Year 2	?	?	?
Two years together	?	?	?
End of year 1			
Total assets	?	?	?
Total liabilities	?	?	?
Retained earnings	?	?	?
End of year 2			
Total assets	?	?	?
Total liabilities	?	?	?
Retained earnings	?	?	?

9-65 Capital or Operating Lease

On December 31, 20X8, Posada Wood Products Company has been offered an electronically controlled automatic lathe (a) outright for $100,000 cash or (b) on a noncancelable lease whereby rental payments would be made at the end of each year for 3 years. The lathe will become obsolete and worthless at the end of 3 years. The company can borrow $100,000 cash on a 3-year loan payable at maturity at 10% compounded annually.

1. Compute the annual rental payment, assuming that the lessor desires a 10% rate of return per year.
2. Suppose the lease could be accounted for as an operating lease. What annual journal entry would the company make?
3. The lease is a capital lease. Prepare an analytical schedule of each lease payment. Show the lease liability at the beginning of the year, and interest expense, lease payment, and lease liability at the end of the year.
4. Prepare an analysis of transactions for the capital lease, using the balance sheet equation format.
5. Prepare yearly journal entries for the capital lease.

9-66 Leases

The following information appeared in a footnote to the 2002 annual report of Delta Air Lines, Incorporated:

> *The following table summarizes, as of December 31, 2002, our minimum rental commitments under capital leases and noncancelable operating leases with initial or remaining terms of more than 1 year:*

	Capital Leases	Operating Leases
Years Ending December 31	($ in Millions)	
2003	$40	$ 1,277
2004	31	1,203
2005	24	1,176
2006	16	1,128
2007	15	1,042
After 2007	46	6,918
Total minimum lease payments	$172	$12,744
Less: Lease payments that represent interest	45	
Present value of future minimum capital lease payments	$127	

1. Suppose the minimum capital lease payments are made in equal amounts on March 31, June 30, September 30, and December 31 of each year. Compute the interest and principal to be paid on capital leases during the first half of fiscal 2003. Perform calculations in millions with two decimal places. Assume an interest rate of 8% per annum, compounded quarterly.
2. Prepare the journal entries for the lease payments in requirement 1 on March 31 and June 30, 2003.
3. Suppose some of the operating leases were capital leases and assume the payments on these leases were $1,000 million per year for 15 years made annually at year-end. If these operating leases were capitalized at 8%, how much would long-term debt increase? Do calculations to the closest million.

9-67 Leases

Consider footnote 7 from the 2003 annual report of FedEx:

> Footnote 7:
>
> *We utilize certain aircraft, land, facilities, and equipment under capital and operating leases that expire at various dates through 2039. . . . A summary of future minimum lease payments under capital leases and noncancellable operating leases (principally aircraft and facilities) with an initial or remaining term in excess of one year at May 31, 2003 is as follows (in millions):*

	Capital Leases	Operating Leases
2004	$ 44	$ 1,368
2005	125	1,285
2006	102	1,192
2007	11	1,155
2008	11	1,045
Thereafter	238	8,342
Total	$531	$14,387

1. Compute the net present value of the operating lease payments as of May 31, 2003. Use a 10% implicit interest rate. For ease of computation, assume each payment is made on May 31 of the designated year (i.e., the first $1,368 million payment is made on May 31, 2004) and that the final payment, labeled "Thereafter," is made on May 31, 2009.
2. Suppose FedEx were to capitalize the operating leases examined in requirement 1. Show the journal entries necessary to:
   a. Capitalize the leases on June 1, 2003. Ignore any prior period adjustments, and do not break the lease obligation into current and long-term portions.
   b. Record the first payment on May 31, 2004.
3. FedEx's total liabilities on May 31, 2003, were $8,097 million, and its total stockholders' equity was $7,266 million. Compute its total debt-to-equity ratio. Then, suppose FedEx capitalized its operating leases using the present value calculated in requirement 1. Recompute the debt-to-equity ratio. What difference does capitalizing the operating leases make to the debt-to-equity ratio? Explain.

9-68 Capital Leases

The Home Depot is the leading retailer in the home improvement industry and one of the 10 largest retailers in the United States. The company included the following on its February 1, 2004 balance sheet and footnotes ($ in millions):

Capital lease assets	$352
Capital lease obligations (long term)	$318
Capital lease obligations (current)	7
Total capital lease obligations	$311

Total capital lease payments scheduled for the fiscal year ended February 1, 2005 are $52,000,000.

1. Prepare the journal entry for the $52,000,000 lease payments. Remember that the lease payments will include the principal payments due for the year plus interest expense accrued for the year.
2. Suppose that the capital lease assets have an average remaining life of 20 years and that no new leases are signed in the fiscal year ending February 1, 2005. Compute the balance in the capital lease asset account and the total in the capital lease obligations account (long-term and current combined) at February 1, 2005.
3. Explain why the amount in the capital lease assets account is not equal to the amount in the lease obligations accounts.

9-69 Pension Liabilities

General Motors had pension obligations of approximately $92 billion and obligations for postretirement benefits other than pensions of $57 billion at the beginning of 2003. The fair value of plan assets in the pension plan was $57 billion, and the fair value of plan assets for postretirement benefits other than pensions was $6 billion. Total stockholders' equity was $7 billion. The total market value of General Motors is approximately $23 billion.

1. Comment on the confidence that employees might have about receiving the benefits due to them.
2. Recognizing pensions and other postretirement benefits as liabilities on the balance sheet has been a controversial topic. Do you think this is important information to disclose to shareholders? Why or why not?

9-70 Deferred Taxes

Cadbury Schweppes is a major global company in beverages and confectionery based in London. It is the third largest soft drink company in the world, after Coca-Cola and PepsiCo. More recent sales were more than £5 billion (where £ is the British pound). The company's income statement included the following, using Cadbury Schweppes' terminology (£ in millions):

Profit on ordinary activities	
before taxation	£830
Tax on profit on ordinary activities	(255)
Profit on ordinary activities	
after taxation	£575

As a result of operations, the deferred tax liability account increased by £56 million. Assume there was no change in taxes payable.

1. Compute the income taxes paid to the government.
2. Prepare the journal entry to record taxes on ordinary activities.
3. Explain why the amount of income taxes paid to the government was not the same as the amount of income taxes recorded on the income statement.

9-71 Deferral of Taxes and Reversal of Temporary Differences

Castillo Company bought an asset for $200,000 on January 1, 20X0. The asset has a 10-year life and zero salvage value. Castillo uses straight-line depreciation for financial reporting purposes and DDB depreciation for tax purposes. The DDB schedule switches to straight-line depreciation for the remaining book value when the resulting straight-line depreciation exceeds the amount of depreciation on the original DDB schedule. This results in the following depreciation charges:

Year	Straight-line Depreciation	DDB Depreciation
20X0	$20,000	$40,000
20X1	20,000	32,000
20X2	20,000	25,600
20X3	20,000	20,480
20X4	20,000	16,384
20X5	20,000	13,107
20X6	20,000	13,107
20X7	20,000	13,107
20X8	20,000	13,107
20X9	20,000	13,107

The company's tax rate is 40%.

1. Compute the amount in the deferred tax account at the end of each year.
2. Is the deferred tax account an asset or a liability? Explain.
3. What is the amount in the deferred tax account at the end of the life of the asset? Explain what caused the deferred tax account to reach this value at the end of the asset's life.

9-72 The Income Tax Footnote

Yum! Brands Inc. operates many franchised food outlets, including Pizza Hut, Taco Bell, A&W, and KFC. The company had 2002 operating revenues of nearly $8 billion and income before income taxes of $858 million. Footnote 22 to the financial statements provided the following:

The details of our income tax provision (benefit) are set forth below:

	2002	2001
	($ in millions)	
Current		
Federal	$137	$200
Foreign	93	75
State	24	38
	254	313
Deferred		
Federal	29	(29)
Foreign	(6)	(33)
State	(2)	(10)
	21	(72)
Net tax expense	$275	$241

1. Provide the journal entries to record income tax expense for 2002.
2. Compute net income for 2002.

9-73 Debt-to-Equity Ratios

The total debt and stockholders' equity for three companies follows. The companies are described as follows:

- AT&T provides long-distance phone service and is a large, well-established company.
- Micron Technology is a fast-growing producer of memory products for electronic systems.
- Amgen is a biotechnology company pioneering the development of products based on advances in recombinant DNA.

(in millions)	Total Debt		Stockholders' Equity	
	2002	1992	2002	1992
AT&T	$42,960	$17,122	$12,312	$20,313
Micron Technology	1,189	213	6,306	511
Amgen	6,170	440	18,286	934

1. Compute debt-to-equity ratios for each company for 1992 and 2002.
2. Discuss the differences in the ratios across firms.
3. Discuss the changes in individual company ratios from 1992 to 2002.

9-74 Review of Chapters 8 and 9

Albertson's Inc., based in Boise, Idaho, operates nearly 2,500 food and drugstores in 37 states. The company's annual report for fiscal 2003 contained the following ($ in millions):

Albertson's, Inc.

	January 30	January 31
	2003	2002
Property, plant, and equipment, at cost	$15,187	$15,035
Less accumulated depreciation and amortization	6,158	5,753
Net property, plant, and equipment	$ 9,029	$ 9,282
Long-term debt due within 1 year	$ 105	$ 123
Long-term debt	4,950	5,060

Purchases of buildings, machinery, and equipment during fiscal 2003 were $1,258 million and depreciation expense was $966 million. (The use of T-accounts should help your analysis.)

1. Compute the dollar amounts of:
   a. Accumulated depreciation relating to properties and plants disposed of during fiscal 2003.
   b. Original acquisition cost of properties and plants disposed of during fiscal 2003.
2. Compute the dollar amount of the net increase or decrease in long-term debt.

9-75 Liabilities for Frequent Flier Miles and Ethics

Most airlines in the United States have frequent flier programs that grant free flights if a customer accumulates enough flight miles on the airline. For example, United Airlines offers a free domestic flight for every 25,000 miles flown on United. Delta Air Lines describes its program as follows in a footnote to the financial statements:

> We record an estimated liability for the incremental cost associated with providing free transportation under our SkyMiles frequent flier program when a free travel award is earned. The liability is recorded in accounts payable, deferred credits and other accrued liabilities in our Consolidated Balance Sheets. It is adjusted periodically based on awards earned, awards redeemed, changes in the SkyMiles program and changes in estimated incremental costs.

In a recent annual report, American Airlines reported a liability of $1.2 billion for free flights, representing approximately 9.3 million flights owed to customers, an average of $129 per flight. However, some airlines maintain that the true liability is closer to $10 per flight, including only the cost of food, insurance, and other miscellaneous expenses. They argue that all other costs would be incurred even in the absence of the person traveling free.

Suppose airlines use one estimate of the cost of these "free" flights for their internal decision making and another for computing the liability for their publicly reported balance sheet. Comment on the ethical issues.

9-76 Present Value and Sports Salaries

Study Appendix 9. "Rangers break the bank, sign Alex Rodriguez for 10 years, $252 million" read the headline in the December 12, 2000 Dallas newspaper. The contract has several parts: (1) a $10 million signing bonus paid over 5 years at $2,000,000 per year; (2) salary of $21 million per year for 2001, 2002, 2003, and 2004; (3) salary of $25 million per year for 2005 and 2006; and (4) salary of $27 million per year for 2007 through 2010.

Assume that Rodriguez signed the contract on December 1, 2000, that the Rangers made each payment on December 1 of the respective years, and that the appropriate discount rate is 10%.

1. What was the present value of the contract on the day it was signed?
2. How much present value (as of December 1, 2000) did Rodriguez lose by receiving the $10 million payment over 5 years instead of immediately?
3. Do you agree that the contract was worth $252 million? Explain.

Collaborative Learning Exercises

9-77 Characteristics of Bonds

Form groups of three to six persons each. Each person should select a company that has long-term debt in the form of bonds (or debentures). Pick one of the company's bonds, and note the interest rate on the bond. If the company does not list bonds individually, you may need to select one of the groups of bonds that it presents.

Find out as much as you can about the factors that might explain the bond's interest rate. Among the items to look for are characteristics of the bond, such as the size of the issue, the length of the term, and any special features such as subordination, convertibility, and covenants, and characteristics of the company, such as its industry, its debt-to-equity ratio, and its interest-coverage ratio. Also, try to find out when the bond was issued and the level of prevailing interest rates at the time of issue. (Companies do not usually show the issue date in the footnotes to their financial statements. You might try looking at past annual reports to see when the bonds first appeared on the financial statement.) Prevailing interest rates may be represented by the rates on U.S. Treasury securities. Note the amount by which the interest rate of the bond exceeds the rate of a U.S. Treasury security of the same duration.

After individual students have performed their independent research, you should get together and compare results. Do the factors you have identified explain the differences in rates across the companies? How do the factors relate to the riskiness of the bonds? Is the amount by which the bond interest rate exceeds the U.S. Treasury rate related to the bond's riskiness?

9-78 Accounting for Pensions

Form groups of two or more students. Divide each group into two debate teams. Each team should be assigned one of the two following positions:

1. Pensions and other postretirement benefits are legitimate liabilities of a company and should be recognized as such on their balance sheets. They are expenses of the periods in which the benefiting employees work, so the obligation to pay them should be accrued at that time.
2. Pensions and other postretirement benefits are not legal liabilities of a company and should not be included among their liabilities on the balance sheet. They are essentially expenses in the period when the benefits are paid.

One team defending each proposition can be given 5 to 10 minutes to present its case, followed by approximately 2 minutes each for rebuttals. Then a general class discussion of the issues can follow. The class might take a vote on which group made the most convincing argument.

Analyzing and Interpreting Financial Statements

9-79 Financial Statement Research

Select any two companies from the airline industry, and find each company's footnote describing its leases. (Possible companies include Alaska Airlines, American Airlines, Continental Airlines, Delta Airlines, Northwest Airlines, United, and US Airways, but do not feel restricted to these.) Compute each company's debt-to-equity ratio under each of three assumptions:

1. With leases as reported
2. With all leases treated as operating leases
3. With all leases treated as capital leases

For this calculation assume all operating lease payments due after the fifth year are spread evenly over years 6 through 15. That is, one-tenth of the remaining lease payments will be made each of the next 10 years. Use a 10% interest rate for computing the present value of the operating leases. Comment on the differences made by the three treatments of leases. Also, comment on the differences in ratios between the two companies.

9-80 Analyzing Starbucks' Financial Statements

Refer to Starbucks' financial statements in Appendix A. Focus on the liabilities section of the balance sheet and footnote 10.

1. Compute the following three ratios at September 28, 2003 and September 29, 2002. Assess the changes in these ratios.
   a. Debt-to-equity ratio
   b. Debt-to-total-assets ratio
2. Comment on Starbucks' amount of long-term liabilities compared to its amount of current liabilities.

9-81 Analyzing Financial Statements Using the Internet: May Department Stores

Go to www.mayco.com to find May Department Stores' financial information. Select About May, and click on Investor relations and then on the annual report.

Answer the following questions about May and its long-term debt:

1. Locate the discussion of Lease Obligations in the Notes to Consolidated Financial Statements. What percentage of its store space does May own? What type of leases does May report?
2. How do the operating lease payments affect May's financial statements? Explain how these operating leases are considered "invisible debt."
3. What items comprise May's long-term debt? Is any portion of that debt considered "current"? Where is the current portion reported on the financial statements? Was any long-term debt issued in the most recent year?
4. Describe who is eligible for May's pension and other postretirement benefits. How are these items reported on the financial statements? What discount rate is used for determining the present value of these items? Does this rate differ from the rate used a year ago? If so, what difference does that make on the present value of the obligations?

Stockholders' Equity

CHAPTER 10

LEARNING OBJECTIVES

After studying this chapter, you should be able to:

1. Describe the rights of shareholders.

2. Differentiate among authorized, issued, and outstanding shares.

3. Contrast bonds, preferred stock, and common stock.

4. Identify the economic characteristics of and accounting for stock splits.

5. Account for both large- and small-percentage stock dividends.

6. Explain and report stock repurchases and other treasury stock transactions.

7. Record conversions of debt for equity or of preferred stock into common stock.

8. Use the rate of return on common equity and book value per share.

United Parcel Service (UPS) has a distinctive brown fleet of trucks and a distinguished position as the world's largest package delivery company. The company delivers more than 12.5 million packages each business day in more than 200 countries from 1.7 million shippers to 6 million recipients. In the United States, it delivers more than 6% of the gross domestic product and delivers to 97% of U.S. households. To do this requires about 150,000 delivery vehicles including more than 500 aircraft, worldwide.

UPS is poised to be one of the key beneficiaries of the shift to Web-based businesses. UPS ships more than 55% of the goods purchased over the Internet. The firm continues to serve old-line, bricks-and-mortar companies, but the nature of the business is being transformed to a "time-definite" service. Companies once shipped items without knowing their precise arrival day or time. Today, UPS assures a package's time of arrival and provides the ability to monitor its progress constantly. Customers have efficient electronic access to the information that allows them to request a pickup, track an order, and serve a customer. They rely on UPS for full logistics support for ordering, scheduling, shipping, and receiving.

In addition to its package delivery service and logistical support, UPS has a company called **UPS Capital** that lends businesses money, finances inventory, and even buys accounts receivable. It has the capability to offer warehousing and order fulfillment services for small to medium-size firms through UPS e-Logistics. To support this worldwide service requires very modern, high-tech processing. UPS Worldport is a 4 million square foot automated facility near their air hub in Louisville, Kentucky. Overhead cameras read smart labels and have the capacity to guide sorting of 304,000

UPS employees like the man pictured here control UPS through their voting rights as shareholders. The public has relied on UPS for delivery services for almost a century but has only had access to UPS stock since it became public in 1999.

PUBLIC COMPANIES

The SEC was formed by the Securities Acts of 1933 and 1934 in response to economic and political pressure associated with the Stock Market Crash of 1929 and the Great Depression. The SEC regulates accounting practices and ensures publicly traded securities provide information to shareholders on a timely basis. It has delegated its authority for setting accounting standards to the FASB. On rare occassions, the SEC overrules FASB as it did with accounting for oil and gas exploration. On other occassions, the SEC is one of many contributors to the public discussions that the FASB facilitates as it debates future accounting practice. The SEC defines public companies based on the number of shareholders that the company has. Public companies that have many shareholders who buy and sell shares in public markets such as the NYSE, must file quarterly and annual reports with the SEC (forms 10-Q and 10-K, respectively) and also file special reports (form 8-K) whenever something material happens to the company. The SEC Web site (www.sec.gov) indicates that "Companies with more than $10 million in assets whose securities are held by more than 500 owners must file annual and other periodic reports." These reports are accessible in the SEC Web site, and Web sites of individual companies often link to SEC filings, usually in a section called "Investor Relations."

Security analysts closely monitor the quarterly results of public companies. We often observe large changes in market value and significant selling or buying of shares based on the results of one quarter of business. Some investors and managers believe this motivates an excessively short-term view in management decision making. They think a "closely held" private company has much more freedom to take the long view. Private companies can make investements that will take years to bear fruit and can accept short-term negative results in search of longer-term successes.

When a company such as UPS chooses to have an initial public offering (IPO) and allow its shares to trade widely, it is agreeing to comply with costly and complicated SEC rules in exchange for access to a large pool of capital. Recall that UPS raised $5.5 billion of capital when it went through its IPO.

The majority of companies that most of us know are well-established companies that issued their common stock years ago. However, entrepreneurs are continually forming corporations. Silicon Valley in California, Silicon Alley in New York City, and other high-tech locations originated thousands of new ventures during the 1990s. Most of these firms failed, but a few are thriving, including **Amazon**, **e-Bay**, and **Yahoo**.

A complicated marketplace exists for funding of new ventures. New corporations often start with a few investors and then seek additional funding as their original ideas prove to be doable, exciting, and profitable. Groups of investors called venture capitalists support exciting ideas early in the process. If a company successfully implements these ideas, it may issue additional shares to the public through an IPO. An underwriting firm generally manages the IPO, and it sells shares to individual investors and to institutional investors such as pension funds, insurance companies, and mutual funds. Regardless of who owns the firm and whether it is public or private, the accounting procedures are very similar.

Source: www.sec.gov.

packages per hour. To do this requires 122 miles of conveyor belts, 4,500 miles of fiber-optic cable, and databases able to process 59 million transactions per hour.

UPS has only been a public company since November 10, 1999. When UPS chose to "go public," it found a receptive audience, raising some $5.5 billion by selling more than 109 million shares at approximately $50 per share. In the U.S., the SEC regulates public companies, as described in the Business First box above. UPS used the proceeds of the sale not only to fund its aggressive growth and development plans, but also to purchase shares from employee-shareholders. The company had been employee owned for years, and the public offering allowed employees to realize the value of their long-term investment in the company. Even now, employees and retirees own most of the outstanding shares. Every executive officer has more than 25 years of service with UPS. During its first months of public trading, share prices touched $75 per share before falling as low as $49 and settling in the $53 area by summer's end in 2000. In the first half of 2004, the share price fluctuated between $68 and $75 per share. ■

Thus far, we have focused on transactions affecting assets and liabilities. Now we examine stockholders' equity in more detail. After all, stockholders such as those of UPS want to know details about their interests. Moreover, stockholders supply a significant portion of the capital that corporations employ, so knowing the rights and responsibilities of stockholders is important to understanding how companies raise capital.

The accounting equation must balance. If we know the amounts of assets and liabilities, the stockholders' equity is the residual, the difference between the assets and liabilities. This is why we call the stockholders the residual claimants to the corporation. When a company goes out of business, sells its assets, and pays creditors out of the proceeds, the stockholders receive whatever is left. It is now time to address issues relating to how we classify and report transactions between a company and its shareholders and how analysts use this information to evaluate the company.

We show the owners' equity section of the UPS annual report in Exhibit 10-1. Some of what appears there is no surprise because common stock and retained earnings are old friends at this point. However, UPS has two classes of common stock and in addition has preferred stock that is authorized but unissued, additional paid-in-capital, accumulated other comprehensive loss, deferred compensation arrangements, and treasury stock. Most of the items in stockholders' equity arise from explicit transactions between the company and its shareholders.

The retained earnings reflects the historic profitability of UPS that has enabled it to finance much of its exceptional growth by retaining earnings in the business. Assets of the company reported in the balance sheet total $26 billion and total stockholder's equity of $12.5 billion represents almost one-half of that. Note that these accounting values do not correspond to the market value of UPS. It was selling for $63 per share in August 2003, which means its total market value was $70.7 billion ($63 per share times 1,123 million shares held by investors). This is more than five times its book value.

A number of the accounting practices for shareholders' equity are based on legal characteristics of corporations, so we make frequent reference to the rights and privileges of shareholders and the consequences of various financing decisions on the firm and its owners. UPS is unusual in having two classes of common stock. Employees hold the class A common stock, and it is not publicly traded. However, it is directly convertible into class B shares. During 2002, employees converted 133 million shares of class A stock to class B stock, probably so the employee could sell the shares and receive cash. At $63 per share, this represents a sale of $8.4 billion in ownership by long-term employees to new investors.

Why create two classes of stock? The class A shares have 10 votes per share, whereas the class B shares have 1 vote per share. Note that this means that employees control many decisions that the firm will make. This also means that the employees will continue to be able to control decision making in the company long after they fall below 50% ownership.

Exhibit 10-1
UPS Shareowners' Equity
In millions except per share amounts

	December 31	
	2002	**2001**
Preferred stock, no par value; authorized—200 shares, none issued	$ —	$ —
Class A common stock, par value $.01; authorized, 4,600 shares; issued 642 and 772 in 2002 and 2001	7	8
Class B common stock, par value $.01 per share; authorized 5,600 shares; issued 482 and 349 in 2002 and 2001	4	3
Additional paid-in capital	387	414
Retained earnings	12,495	10,162
Accumulated other comprehensive loss	(438)	(339)
Deferred compensation arrangements	84	47
	12,539	10,295
Less: Treasury stock (1 share in 2002 and 2001)	(84)	(47)
	$ 12,455	$ 10,248

Internationally, there are substantial differences in the structure of corporate/business activity and in accounting procedures used to disclose results. For example, in many countries large corporations are primarily privately owned by a few individuals, instead of having broad public ownership and public financial reporting as in the United States. In many countries banks provide the majority of financing, so large public issuances of shares are rare. Many formerly planned economies have been transitioning from state-owned-and-operated business entities into private ones. In many countries the government remains the largest employer because it owns many economic entities such as power producers, phone providers, and airlines, not to mention the mail system, which remains a government monopoly even in the United States. From an accounting perspective, the key point is that diverse legal structures and financing practices produce significant international variation in accounting for stockholders' equity.

Background on Stockholders' Equity

OBJECTIVE 1

Describe the rights of shareholders.

Corporations are entities with perpetual life created in accordance with state laws. The corporate charter specifies the rights of stockholders (or shareholders) that generally include the right to (1) vote, (2) share in corporate profits, (3) share in any assets left at liquidation, and (4) acquire more shares of subsequent issues of stock. The extent of an individual stockholder's power is determined by the number and type of shares held.

Corporations hold annual meetings of shareholders, where they take votes on important matters. For example, the shareholders elect the board of directors. They may also vote on changing employee bonus plans, choosing outside auditors, making decisions to merge, and handling similar matters. Large corporations make heavy use of the proxy system. A **corporate proxy** is a written authority granted by individual shareholders to others (usually members of corporate management) to cast the shareholders' votes. By using a proxy, shareholders may express (vote) their preference without traveling to the site of the annual meeting.

corporate proxy
A written authority granted by individual shareholders to others to cast the shareholders' votes.

The ultimate power to manage a corporation almost always resides with the common shareholders, but shareholders of publicly owned corporations usually delegate that power to the company's top managers. The modern large corporation frequently has a team of professional managers, from the chairman of the board downward. Increasingly, companies are requiring top managers to own a significant number of shares in the firm. When managers own shares directly or hold stock options to acquire shares, they are more likely to share a common economic interest with shareholders. When the company's stock rises in value, the managers benefit personally.

preemptive rights
The rights to acquire a pro rata amount of any new issues of capital stock.

Stockholders also generally have **preemptive rights,** which are the rights to acquire a proportional amount of any new issues of capital stock. Whenever a company issues new shares of stock, more people can become owners, in which case each existing shareholder's percentage of ownership decreases. The preemptive privilege allows present shareholders to purchase additional shares directly from the corporation before it can sell new shares to the general public. In this way, the shareholders are able to maintain their percentage of ownership.

Perhaps the most important right of common shareholders is limited liability, which means that creditors of the corporation have claims only on the assets owned by the corporation, not on the assets of the owners of the corporation. In contrast, the creditors of a partnership have potential rights against the savings, homes, and automobiles of the individual partners.

OBJECTIVE 2

Differentiate among authorized, issued, and outstanding shares.

Authorized, Issued, and Outstanding Stock

A company incorporates in accordance with state law. It creates articles of incorporation that detail the number and types of capital stock that it can issue. We call these

CORPORATE GOVERNANCE

Recent large-scale frauds in corporate America lead to the passage of the Sarbanes-Oxley legislation in 2002. The act creates a new Public Company Accounting Oversight Board (PCAOB) with broad power to register, inspect, investigate, and discipline public accounting firms and set standards for public audits. The five members of the PCAOB are appointed by the SEC in consultation with the Chairman of the Federal Reserve Board and the Secretary of the Treasury. Two must be CPAs, and the other three must not be. The act set specific rules on behavior of registered public accounting firms, including requiring rotation of the lead partner on an audit every 5 years. It prohibits public accounting firms from performing most "nonaudit" services for their audit clients. These services include financial information systems design and implementation, bookkeeping, and internal audit functions. Following passage of the bill a survey of CEOs indicated that they expected enhanced audits and compliance with other rules under Sarbanes-Oxley to increase their costs significantly. A major new cost will be compliance with internal control certification provisions contained in section 404 of the bill. Each annual report must include an "internal control report," including managements' assertions and supporting attestation by the auditor. The SEC now requires every company to adopt a code of ethics for senior financial officers.

Sarbanes-Oxley, together with SEC regulations and other responses, significantly changed the environment for corporate governance. The historical legal notion was that the shareholders elected a board of directors to represent them and to oversee the functioning of professional managers. The various frauds revealed problems in the system. Some directors were neither as qualified nor as hard working as the shareholders expected. Managers, especially the CEO, often selected their friends for board membership, creating a board that was not a critical independent component of the corporate governance structure. Shareholders could vote for or against nominees, but they could not chose candidate A over candidate Z. The post–Sarbanes-Oxley environment is producing increased independence between directors and management, and specifically requires that an independent director, who is professionally qualified for the role, must chair the audit committee of the board. We are also seeing an increase in the number of cases where the CEO does not also chair the board of directors. This concept of a nonexecutive chair has been common in other countries for some years. These changes are transforming the composition of boards of directors and the way shareholders influence the management of corporations.

---

authorized shares. When the company receives cash in exchange for stock certificates, the shares become **issued shares.** We call shares that are issued and held by the stockholders **outstanding shares.**

Sometimes a company buys back shares of stock from its own shareholders. It might buy them to reduce shareholder claims permanently, a procedure we discuss later in the chapter. More often, companies plan to hold the shares for later use, usually to grant them as part of employee bonuses or stock purchase plans. We call such temporarily held shares **treasury stock.** They are issued, but because the company holds them, they are no longer outstanding. For example, as of December 31, 2002, UPS had authorized 10.20 billion shares in total for class A and class B. Issued shares totaled 1,124 million, of which UPS had reacquired 1 million shares that it lists as treasury stock.

authorized shares
The total number of shares that may legally be issued under the articles of incorporation.

issued shares
The aggregate number of shares sold to the public.

outstanding shares
Shares remaining in the hands of shareholders.

treasury stock
A corporation's issued stock that has subsequently been repurchased by the company and not retired.

Number of Shares (in Millions)	
Authorized	10,200
Deduct: Unissued	9,076
Issued	1,124
Deduct: Shares held in treasury	1
Total shares outstanding	1,123

Accounting for Stock Issuance

To account for a stock issuance, we record the receipt of cash and create a common stock account to represent the ownership interest. In 2003, **UPS** stock was selling for around $63 per share, so a stock issuance of 1 million additional shares could be recorded as:

Cash	63,000,000	
Common Stock		63,000,000

Many companies, however, separate their common stock recognition into two categories—par value and additional paid-in capital. Legally, par value was originally a measure of protection for creditors because it established the minimum legal liability of a stockholder. In this way, the creditors would be assured the corporation would have at least a minimum amount of ownership capital, for example, $10 for each share issued. A corporation could not issue stock for less than its par value.

UPS shares have a par value of $.01 each. Thus, the actual entry to record issuance of 1 million additional shares would separate out par value as follows:

Cash	63,000,000	
Common stock at par		10,000
Additional paid-in capital		62,990,000

In practice, corporations usually set the par values far below the full market price of the shares when issued, as is the case with UPS. Some companies call this minimum capital "stated value" rather than "par value." Similarly, the language used to describe additional paid-in capital varies widely. For economic purposes, most of these distinctions are of little importance. However, you encounter them in annual reports and should understand their meaning. The following illustrates the diversity of practice:

Company	Par Value per Share	Name for Additional Paid-in Capital
AT&T	$1.00	Additional paid-in capital
Coca-Cola	.25	Capital surplus
McDonald's	.01	Additional paid-in capital
Motorola	3.00	Additional paid-in capital
PepsiCo	.0167	Capital in excess of par value
Qualcomm	.0001	Paid-in capital

Cash Dividends

Dividends are proportional distributions of income to shareholders in a company, usually in the form of cash. In the United States, companies tend to pay dividends in equal amounts each quarter, although the board may declare, change, or eliminate a dividend at any time. Some firms tend to pay a special, larger dividend once per year.

declaration date
The date the board of directors declares a dividend.

Companies do not automatically pay dividends. A company's board of directors votes to approve each dividend. We call the date on which the board formally announces that it will pay a dividend the **declaration date.** On this date, the dividend becomes a liability. The board specifies a future date as the **date of record.** All stockholders owning stock on that date will receive the dividend. A person who holds the stock on the declaration date, but sells before the date of record, will not receive the dividend. The actual **payment date** is the day the company mails the checks; it usually follows the date of record by a few days or weeks.

date of record
The date that determines which shareholders will receive a dividend.

payment date
The date dividends are paid.

A company records entries for dividends at two times, when it creates the liability and when it pays the dividend:

DATE OF DECLARATION

Sept. 26	Retained earnings	20,000	
	Dividends payable		20,000
	To record the declaration of dividends to be		
	paid on November 15 to shareholders of record		
	as of October 25		

DATE OF PAYMENT

Nov. 15	Dividends payable	20,000	
	Cash		20,000
	To pay dividends declared on September 26 to		
	shareholders of record as of October 25		

If a company prepares a balance sheet between declaration and payment, the dividend payable will appear as a liability. The amount of cash dividends declared by a board of directors depends on many factors, primarily the market expectations, the current and predicted earnings, and the corporation's current cash position and financial plans concerning spending on plant assets and repayments of debts. Remember that payment of cash dividends requires cash. Thus, the single biggest factor affecting the size of dividends is the availability of cash that the company has not otherwise committed. It is also true that investors expect companies that have historically paid regular dividends to continue to do so. General Electric is an example. Its dividend has recently increased each year, from quarterly payments of $.08 per share in 1995 to $.19 per share in 2003. Investors also expect that companies that have not paid dividends because cash was better used to finance expansion will continue to identify growth opportunities requiring additional investment. e-Bay is an example of a growing company that does not pay cash dividends.

What other factors might affect the company's decision to pay a dividend? In some states, the dividend decision depends on the amount of retained earnings because state law forbids dividend payments exceeding the company's accumulated net income. A similar limitation may occur because of bond covenants that restrict dividend payments. Ultimately, investors carefully watch changes in dividend patterns. If a company has maintained a series of uninterrupted dividends over a span of years, it will make an effort to continue such payments, even in the face of net losses. In fact, companies occasionally borrow money for the sole purpose of maintaining dividend payments. Elimination and initiation of payments are big events that cause investors to pause and consider carefully what the company's decision means about the future. This careful consideration is necessary because the meaning of dividend changes can be confusing. Consider a company that initiates or increases a dividend. The good news is that it has resources to distribute to shareholders while continuing to grow and do business. The bad news is that it does not have hugely profitable investments to make in its ongoing business that require all the cash it can generate.

Preferred Stock

The two most common types of stock are common stock and preferred stock. Common stock, as the name implies, is the most basic type. All corporations have it, and the shareholders who own it have the rights discussed earlier. **Preferred stock** offers owners different rights and preferential treatment. Usually preferred shareholders have a right to receive a cash dividend each year and their right to dividends takes precedent over any dividend claims of common shareholders. Often the amount of the preferred dividend is expressed as the product of the dividend rate times the par value. A $100 par, 5% preferred would pay a $5 dividend.

OBJECTIVE 3

Contrast bonds, preferred stock, and common stock.

preferred stock
Stock that offers owners different rights and preferential treatment.

Stock represents a contract between the company and its owners, and the terms of preferred stock can include almost any arrangement the parties select. For example, preferred stock owners do not usually have voting rights, but they do have a preferred claim on assets. Therefore, at liquidation, preferred stockholders receive any available company assets, up to the amount of their liquidation value, before common stockholders receive anything.

Preferred stock is like common stock in that dividends are not a legal obligation until the board of directors declares them. Unlike common stock, the amount of the preferred stock dividend is generally specified and does not change over time. Although UPS has authorized preferred shares, none are currently outstanding.

Cumulative Dividends

cumulative
A characteristic of preferred stock that requires that undeclared dividends accumulate and must be paid in the future before common dividends.

dividend arrearages
Accumulated unpaid dividends on preferred stock.

What happens when the board votes to skip a preferred stock dividend? Just because a company can decide not to pay the dividend now may not mean that the company has completely avoided the obligation. Preferred stock dividends are often **cumulative.** Cumulative preferred stock requires that undeclared dividends accumulate and the company must pay them in the future before it can pay any common dividends. From the standpoint of a common shareholder, accumulated unpaid dividends, called **dividend arrearages,** are somewhat like debt obligations. Why? Because a company must pay them before the common shareholders can receive dividends. Moreover, in the event of liquidation, a company must pay cumulative unpaid preferred dividends before common stockholders receive any cash.

To illustrate the operation of cumulative preferred stock, consider Exhibit 10-2. Panel A contains the stockholders' equity of Acumulado Corporation on December 31, 20X0, and panel B shows the consequences of subsequent years of net income and dividends.

Acumulado's board of directors elected not to declare and pay preferred dividends in 20X1 and 20X2. This decision makes economic sense, given that Acumulado Corporation posted losses both years. You may be thinking that the company had more than enough in retained earnings to be able to pay the dividends despite the losses, but retained earnings is not the same as cash. The large retained earnings balance resulted from many prior years of profitable operations, but in those prior years the company has

Exhibit 10-2
Acumulado
Corporation Preferred
Dividends

PANEL A

Stockholders' Equity, December 31, 20X0	
Preferred stock, no par, cumulative, $5 annual dividend per share	
Issued and outstanding, 1,000,000 shares	$ 50,000,000
Common stock, no par, 5,000,000 shares	100,000,000
Retained earnings	400,000,000
Total stockholders' equity	$550,000,000

PANEL B

	Net Income	Preferred Dividends Declared	Preferred Dividends In Arrears	Common Dividends Declared	Ending Balance, Retained Earnings
20X0					$400,000,000
20X1	$(4,000,000)	—	$ 5,000,000	—	396,000,000
20X2	(4,000,000)	—	10,000,000	—	392,000,000
20X3	21,000,000	$ 3,000,000	12,000,000	—	410,000,000
20X4	49,000,000	17,000,000	—	$ 2,000,000	440,000,000
20X5	32,000,000	5,000,000	—	17,000,000	450,000,000

reinvested the cash generated by operations into productive business assets. When a firm encounters losses such as Acumulado experienced in 20X1 and 20X2, cash flow may be reduced, and there is often insufficient cash available to pay dividends.

Even though the company skipped making the $5 million annual preferred dividend payments, its obligation to make those payments remained and accumulated, becoming $10 million by the end of 20X2. When operating results improved in 20X3, the board declares and paid a partial dividend of $3 million, leaving $2 million additional arrearages, which raised the total arrearage to $12 million. In 20X4, Acumulado had a banner year and improved profitability and cash flow enough to pay a full dividend and more. Dividends to preferred shareholders of $17 million cover not only the 20X4 dividend, but also all accumulated dividends in arrears. With accumulated preferred dividends now completely paid, the firm may pay a dividend to the common shareholders for the first time in 4 years. Note that the ending balance in retained earnings in each year is equal to the beginning balance, plus net income (or minus a net loss) minus dividends declared.

Would you rather own cumulative or noncumulative preferred stock? In the preceding example, a holder of noncumulative preferred stock would receive nothing in 20X1 or 20X2, $3 million in 20X3 and $5 million in 20X4. In contrast, the owner of cumulative shares received $3 million in 20X3 and $17 million in 20X4. The cumulative feature is certainly preferred, but as with most choices, it is not free. Because cumulative preferred shares are more secure, they typically pay a lower dividend than noncumulative shares. The cumulative feature must be explicit in the contract. It is not automatic. Most buyers of preferred shares do insist on cumulative status.

Preference in Liquidation

In addition to the cumulative dividend feature, preferred stock usually has a specific liquidating value. The stock certificate generally states the exact **liquidating value**, which is often the same as par value. Because par value often defines the liquidating value and may define the amount of the dividend, it is economically important for preferred stock. The company has to pay the full liquidating value (plus dividends in arrears, if any) to all preferred stockholders before it distributes any assets to common stockholders when the company is liquidated. Of course, before preferred shareholders receive any assets, the company must also pay off all debt obligations.

liquidating value
A measure of the preference to receive assets in the event of corporate liquidation.

Consider an illustration of the liquidation of assets when short- and long-term debt, preferred stock, and common stock are all present. Exhibit 10-3 shows how to distribute cash to different claimants. The priority of the claims generally decreases as you

(in thousands)	Account Balances	Assumed Total Cash Proceeds to Be Distributed						
		$1,500	$1,000	$500	$450	$350	$200	$100
Accounts payable	$ 100	$ 100	$ 100	$100	$100	$100	$100	$ 50*
Unsubordinated debentures	100	100	100	100	100	100	100	50*
Subordinated debentures	200	200	200	200	200	150		
Preferred stock ($100 par value and $120 liquidating value per share)	100	120	120	100	50			
Common stock and retained earnings	500	980	480					
Total liabilities and shareholders' equity	$1,000							
Total cash proceeds distributed		$1,500	$1,000	$500	$450	$350	$200	$100

*Ratio of 50:50 because each has a $100,000 claim.

Exhibit 10-3
Liquidation of Claims Under Various Alternatives
(in thousands)

move down the chart. The first column presents the book values. The next seven columns show the distributions to each class of claimant under different circumstances.

As you can see, when there is not enough cash to go around, common stockholders are always the last to get paid and often wind up getting nothing. However, in those instances when there is actually excess cash left over, common stockholders get that excess. This illustrates the risks and rewards of stock ownership. When things go well, common shareholders do very well. When things go badly, common shareholders are the first to suffer. Keep in mind, though, that both common and preferred stockholders are protected by limited liability. They do not have to add additional personal assets to the company when it cannot pay off its debts.

Other Features of Preferred Stock

In addition to being cumulative and having liquidation value, preferred stock may have other features. As with our discussion of debt, each feature affects the attractiveness of the stock issue. If you add the cumulative feature to a 5% preferred, investors will pay more for a share of preferred stock. Another way to express the same idea is to say that if you add the cumulative feature to a preferred share, you reduce the size of the fixed dividend that investors require to be willing to invest in the preferred stock.

Each of the following features can also affect the attractiveness of the preferred stock. For example, a participating preferred stock ordinarily receives a fixed dividend, but it can receive higher dividends when the company has a very good year—one in which common stockholders receive especially large dividends. **Participating** means that holders of these shares participate in the growth of the company because they share in the growing dividends. A **callable** preferred stock gives the issuing company the right to purchase the stock back from the owner on payment of the **call price,** or **redemption price.** This call price is typically set 5% to 10% above the par value or issuance price of the stock, to compensate investors for the fact that the stock can be bought back at the issuer's choice.

A **convertible** preferred stock gives the owner the option to exchange the preferred share for shares of common stock. Because the ability to convert the stock can be quite valuable in future years if common stock prices grow significantly, convertible securities typically carry a lower dividend rate. For example, a regular preferred stock with an 8% dividend might sell for the same price as a 7% convertible preferred stock.

It is not possible to describe every imaginable kind of preferred stock because individual investors and issuers have the opportunity to develop a unique security that exactly meets their needs, and they can adapt that security to the particular market conditions they face at the time. In fact, the investment banking community works hard to develop new types of preferred stock that exactly fit the particular needs of certain investors and therefore provide less expensive capital for the issuing company.

Comparing Bonds and Preferred Stock

Preferred stocks are actually quite similar to bonds. Both are contracts between an investor and an issuer that spell out each party's rights and responsibilities. Preferred stocks and bonds each pay a specific return to the investor. However, they differ greatly as to the size and nature of those returns. We call the return to bondholders "interest," and it appears on the earnings statement as an expense. In the United States, interest income is taxable to the recipient and tax deductible to the issuing company. In contrast, the specific return to preferred shareholders is a "dividend" and represents a distribution of profits. Dividends do not reduce net earnings and are not tax deductible to the issuer. Dividends reduce the retained earnings account directly. For the recipient,

participating
A characteristic of preferred stock that provides increasing dividends when common dividends increase.

callable
A characteristic of bonds or preferred stock that gives the issuer the right to redeem the security at a fixed price.

call price
(redemption price)
The price at which an issuer can buy back a callable preferred stock or bond, which is typically 5% to 10% above the par value.

convertible
A characteristic of bonds or preferred stock that gives the holder the right to exchange the security for common stock.

dividends may be fully taxed, partly taxed, or untaxed, depending on whether the stockholder is an individual or a corporation and depending on the quantity of stock that is owned. The most recent tax law created a low, 15% tax rate on most dividends received by individuals. Some preferred dividends are not eligible for this low tax rate, especially those issued by real estate investment trusts and others that are backed by securities held in a trust.

Preferred stocks and bonds also differ in that bonds have specific maturity dates, at which time the company must repay the principal amount, but most preferred stock has an unlimited life. From the investor's perspective, such preferred stock is riskier than bonds because it never matures and the company is not required to declare dividends. It is not always easy to determine whether a security is a debt or an equity instrument. Some preferred stock, for example, does have a mandatory redemption date. This makes it more similar to a bond. The FASB recently issued an opinion that classifies preferred stock that has a manadatory redemption date as if it were debt.

Summary Problem for Your Review

PROBLEM

From the following data, prepare a detailed statement of stockholders' equity for Sample Corporation, December 31, 20X1:

Additional paid-in capital, preferred stock	$ 50,000
Additional paid-in capital, common stock	1,000,000
9% preferred stock, $50 par value, callable at $55, authorized 20,000 shares, issued and outstanding 12,000 shares	
Common stock, stated value $2 per share, authorized 500,000 shares, issued 400,000 shares	
Dividends payable	90,000
Retained earnings	2,000,000

SOLUTION

Dividends payable is a liability. Therefore, it does not appear on a statement of stockholders' equity:

Sample Corporation Statement of Stockholders' Equity, December 31, 20X1

9% preferred stock, $50 par value, callable at $55, authorized 20,000 shares, issued and outstanding 12,000 shares		$ 600,000
Common stock, stated value $2 per share, authorized 500,000 shares, issued 400,000 shares of which 25,000 shares are held in the treasury		800,000
Additional paid-in capital		
Preferred	$ 50,000	
Common	1,000,000	1,050,000*
Retained earnings		2,000,000
Total stockholders' equity		$4,450,000

*Many presentations would not show the detailed breakdown of additional paid-in capital into preferred and common portions.

Additional Stock Issuance

Existing companies occasionally issue additional shares to investors, executives, or current shareholders. There are several motivations and several procedures for additional stock issues. When a firm simply wants to raise additional equity capital, the process is much like the original stock issue described earlier. Investors provide cash and receive additional new shares in exchange. Other procedures for increasing the number of shares held by investors—stock options, restricted stock, stock splits, and stock dividends—are examined next.

Stock Options

stock options
Special rights usually granted to employees to purchase a corporation's capital stock.

Stock options are rights to purchase a specific number of shares of a corporation's capital stock at a specific price for a specific time period. Companies often give them to employees as part of their compensation. The idea is that employees who hold options make money only if they stay with the company and the value of the stock increases, in which case the shareholders also make money. Shareholders can benefit from stock options because they motivate employees to work hard and to make decisions that increase the value of their shares. In addition, stock options are especially valuable to executives and other employees because they can gain the benefits of stock price increases without bearing the risks of price declines. The company typically gives (or grants) the option to an employee with the provision that the employee must remain with the company for a period of time before the options become **vested options.** Once vested, the employee may exercise the options anytime before they expire, usually for another 5 years or so.

vested options
Options for which the holders have the power to exercise their options.

Stock options are a method of employee compensation like salaries and wages. It is logical to treat them as an expense. Measurement of the exact value of options at the time of grant is difficult because the future is unknowable. Because the executives cannot sell these options to others, there are no market prices to use as guides. In 2003, GAAP does not require an entry at the time of grant. However, footnotes in the financial statements must reveal the number and type of options outstanding and an assessment of their value. Accounting authorities have assumed that, when investors and analysts have access to information on the value of the options granted, they can fully understand the significance of the option grants, even if the income statement does not include an expense item.

This accounting practice has been one of the most contentious of the last decade. A joint project between the FASB and IASB supported expensing, and this requirement is scheduled to take effect June 15, 2005. The main issue to iron out is how to value the options. Today's practice of assigning a value of zero is already changing because many companies are choosing to recognize an expense when they grant options, even though they are not required to do so.

Expensing stock options will have a significant effect on the income of many companies. *Business Week* estimated that, if companies had expensed options during 1996, earnings would have decreased by an average of only 2%. In 2002, that percentage would have soared to 23%. We can expect that a change in reporting practice will actually cause many companies to reconsider their compensation practices and may actually reduce the use of options. In a *Business Week* article (4/26/04), Bear Stern's accounting expert Pat McConnell was quoted as estimating that the effect of expensing options in 2003 would have been an 8% reduction in reported earnings. She predicted a 3% income reduction in 2004 and even less in 2005. The declining effects over time show both improving profits in an economic recovery and reducing usage of options due, in part, to the accounting change.

UPS has an incentive stock option program. During 2002, they granted 5.8 million options with an average exercise price of $60.22. Employees can exercise the options for a limited period of time commencing 5 years after the date of issue. For example, suppose UPS granted options to purchase 30,000 shares of $.01 par value common stock at $60 per share, the market price on the date of grant. The options can be exercised over a 3-year span, beginning 5 years from the date of grant. How would the granting of these options affect UPS's income statement? Under today's rules, there would be no effect. Under the proposed FASB standards, UPS would estimate the value of the options at the grant date and charge that as a compensation expense. Suppose the estimated value of the options when UPS granted them in 2002 was $7 per share. The 2002 journal entry would be

Compensation expense, stock options	$210,000	
Additional paid-in capital		$210,000

Now, suppose executives exercise all options 5 years after the date of grant. The journal entry in 2007 would be:

Cash	1,800,000	
Common stock		300
Additional paid-in capital		1,799,700
To record issue of 30,000 shares upon exercise of options to acquire them @ $60 per share		

Note that the journal entry is indistinguishable from the issuance of new shares at the exercise price, which may differ significantly from the market price in 2007. Suppose the market price in 2007 were $54. An executive would simply buy shares in the open market instead of exercising the option and paying $60. UPS would record no transaction. However, if the market price were $70, the executive would exercise the option to buy at $60 and have the opportunity to either sell immediately and capture the $10 per share gain or hold the shares in hopes of further appreciation. Instead of recording the issuance of new shares for $70 × 30,000 = $2,100,000, UPS would record common stock and additional paid-in capital of only $60 × 30,000 = $1,800,000. Note, however, that UPS already recorded $210,000 of capital in 2002, so the total capital contributed for these shares is $2,010,000, of which employees contributed $1,800,000 in cash in 2007 and $210,000 in services in 2002.

INTERPRETING FINANCIAL STATEMENTS

Starbucks created a stock option plan in 1991. Their annual report indicates that the "Bean Stock" made employees into partners by giving the employees ownership in the company and sharing the rewards of financial success. To date, Starbucks has not recorded the issuance of such options as expense, although its 2003 footnotes reveal that net income would have declined by $37 million if they had done so. By what percentage would net earnings have declined in 2003 if Starbucks had recorded these options as an expense? If you were Howard Schultz, creator and chairman of Starbucks, would you continue the stock option program, even if an expense was recorded in the income statement and net earnings declined by this percentage in the future?

Answer

The reduction in net earnings would be a 14% decline ($37 million ÷ $268 million). There are arguments on both sides about continuing to offer options. Starbucks originally created the program to engage their partners (employees). Their strategy has long depended on employees who truly welcomed and served customers, creating a memorable experience as well as great coffee. If these partners lost their passion for the job because options were eliminated, what would that do for the Starbucks experience? Would Starbucks cease to become a favorite destination, an experience as well as a place to buy coffee? If options fuel the Starbucks experience and help grow sales, it would be foolish to eliminate them. However, ultimately, it is a cost–benefit question. What else could Starbucks do to maintain the partnership with employees at lower economic cost. Does the new accounting help managers better understand the exact cost of granting options?

Time will tell. Microsoft, an industry leader, has decided against using stock options in the future. However, most technology companies continue to use them. Even under today's voluntary standard for expensing options, more and more companies are expensing them. They believe the options provide cost-effective incentives to their employees. The original justification for stock options, aligning management and shareholder incentives, still exists. However, the decision to issue them is becoming a more explicit cost–benefit trade-off.

Restricted Stock

restricted stock
Stock paid to employees
that generally has
constraints such as not
being able to sell it until it
vests and then generally
being able to sell it only
back to the company at the
current market price.

Many companies are beginning to use restricted stock instead of options to motivate their employees. Granting **restricted stock** is like paying employees with common stock instead of cash, although the employees cannot sell the stock until it vests and then generally can sell it only back to the company at the current market price. When a company issues restricted stock, it records a salary and wage expense equal to the value of the stock and adds an equal amount to paid-in-capital. Employees get an asset that will increase and decrease in value exactly in proportion to the shareholders' increases and decreases in value. In addition, employees holding restricted stock receive the same dividends that common stockholders receive.

A major benefit of restricted stock over stock options is that it is still worth something, even when stock prices fall sharply. A major problem for many high-tech companies that lost 90% of their value in the early 2000s is that their stock options became worthless and are likely to remain so. When the stock market was rising annually, the recipient of stock options got something that turned out to be very valuable. As the stock market fell in 2000 to 2002, it became evident that stock options did not always pay off. Proponents of restricted stock believe it is better than options because it truly aligns managerial benefits with shareholder benefits. In contrast, stock options pay off for managers the most when the company earns very large returns but do not penalize managers for very low returns. Therefore managers receiving stock options may have incentives to undertake riskier projects than shareholders might prefer.

Stock Splits and Stock Dividends

Stock options and restricted stock put additional shares in the hands of employees. Companies can also issue new shares to current shareholders in several other ways. We examine two of these ways: the stock split and the stock dividend.

Accounting for Stock Splits

O B J E C T I V E

Identify the economic characteristics of and accounting for stock splits.

stock split
Issuance of additional
shares to existing
stockholders for no
payments by the
stockholders.

A **stock split** refers to the issuance of additional shares to existing shareholders without any additional cash payment to the firm. Issuance of one additional share for each share currently owned is a "two-for-one" split. For example, suppose the Allstar Equipment Company has 100,000 shares outstanding with a market value of $150 per share and par value of $10 per share. The total market value of the stock is thus $15 million. Suppose Allstar Equipment gives each shareholder an additional share for each share owned. The total number of shares would increase to 200,000. If nothing else about the company changes (assets, liabilities, and equity all stay the same), the total value of the outstanding stock should still be $15 million. With 200,000 shares outstanding, though, the market value per share should drop to $75. Shareholders are as well off as they were before because they have paid no additional money and they still have the same proportional ownership interest in the company.

So why bother? Good question, and one for which there is no perfect answer. Many companies do split their stock. A common result is that stock price falls 50% in a 2-for-1 split. Thus, one good explanation for issuing a split is that it causes the stock price to fall on a per share basis. If investors like to invest $1,000 to $20,000 at a time, and stocks trade in units of 100 shares, you can see that investors would prefer stocks trading in a range between $10 and $200 per share. Most stocks do trade in that range, and companies that split are often at the high end of that range. However, there is no rule about share prices. Berkshire Hathaway is an example of a company whose common stock trades at more than $84,000 per share at this writing. For more about Berkshire Hathaway, see the Business First Box on page 455.

Some people argue that the stock split is a way to communicate with shareholders and remind them that their company is growing. It is true that after two stock splits, investors realize that they have four times as many shares as they originally bought. However, we

As **Berkshire Hathaway** has grown, it has not split its stock. At the current price of approximately $84,000 per share, many investors cannot even afford one share. At one point, a brokerage firm contemplated creating a trust arrangement that would buy shares of Berkshire Hathaway and sell claims on those shares. The trust would divide each Berkshire Hathaway share into say 50 or 100 derivative shares that would sell for 2% of original share value (1/50) or 1% of original share value (1/100). The brokerage firm would reap a small fee for the service they provided. In response, Berkshire Hathaway created a class B share that was 1/30 of a regular share with some slightly different rights as to voting and exchange of shares. The description of these class B shares shown below appears on the Berkshire Hathaway Web site: As predicted, the class B shares sell at $2,800, approximately 1/30th of the class A shares (30 × $2,800 = $84,000). This makes Berkshire Hathaway shares available to many more potential shareholders.

BERKSHIRE HATHAWAY INC.
1440 Kiewit Plaza
Omaha, Nebraska 68131
Telephone (402) 346-1400
Warren E. Buffett, Chairman

Memo

From: Warren Buffett
Subject: Comparative Rights and Relative Prices of Berkshire Class A and Class B Stock
Date: February 2, 1999, UPDATED July 3, 2003

Comparison of Berkshire Hathaway Inc. Class A and Class B Common Stock

Berkshire Hathaway Inc. has two classes of common stock designated Class A and Class B. A share of Class B common stock has the rights of 1/30th of a share of Class A common stock except that a Class B share has 1/200th of the voting rights of a Class A share (rather than 1/30th of the vote). Each share of a Class A common stock is convertible at any time, at the holder's option, into 30 shares of Class B common stock. This conversion privilege does not extend in the opposite direction. That is, holders of Class B shares are not able to convert them into Class A shares. Both Class A & B shareholders are entitled to attend the Berkshire Hathaway Annual Meeting which is held the first Monday in May.

The Relative Prices of Berkshire Class A and Class B Stock

The Class B can *never* sell for anything more than a tiny fraction above 1/30th of the price of A. When it rises above 1/30th, arbitrage takes place in which someone—perhaps the NYSE specialist—buys the A and converts it into B. This pushes the prices back into a 1:30 ratio.

On the other hand, the B can sell for less than 1/30th the price of the A since conversion doesn't go in the reverse direction. All of this was spelled out in the prospectus that accompanied the issuance of the Class B.

When there is more demand for the B (relative to supply) than for the A, the B will sell at roughly 1/30th of the price of A. When there's a lesser demand, it will fall to a discount.

In my opinion, *most* of the time, the demand for the B will be such that it will trade at about 1/30th of the price of the A. However, from time to time, a different supply-demand situation will prevail and the B will sell at some discount.

In my opinion, again, when the B is at a discount of more than say, 2%, it offers a better buy than the A. When the two are at parity, however, anyone wishing to buy 30 or more B should consider buying A instead.

Source: Berkshire Hathaway website (www.BerkshireHathaway.com)

PANEL A: ALTERNATE JOURNAL ENTRIES

Option 1. Issue 100,000 new $10.00 par value shares	Additional paid-in capital	1,000,000	
	Common stock		1,000,000
Option 2. Exchange 200,000 new $5.00 par value shares for the old ones	No entry		

PANEL B: ALTERNATE OUTCOMES

	Common Stock	Additional Paid-in-Capital	Retained Earnings	Owners' Equity
Option 1	$1,000,000	$4,000,000	$6,000,000	$11,000,000
Split, retain par	1,000,000	(1,000,000)		
Result	2,000,000	$3,000,000	$6,000,000	$11,000,000
Option 2	$1,000,000	$4,000,000	$6,000,000	$11,000,000
No change				

PANEL C: COMMON OUTCOMES

For both treatments, total owners' equity is the same at $11,000,000
For both treatments, the total market value of the firm should remain constant and the two-for-one stock split should cut price per share in half

Exhibit 10-4
Comparing Two Approaches to Stock Splits
Allstar Equipment

would expect a similar pleased reaction from an investor who still had the same original 100 shares that were now valued at four times their purchase price.

Would the accountant need to do anything to acknowledge Allstar's stock issuance of 100,000 additional shares? Yes. There are now twice as many shares outstanding. If the company retains a par value of $10 per share, we would need to add $1 million to the common stock account. Typically we transfer this from additional paid-in capital. This transfer does not change total owner's equity. It merely rearranges it. Sometimes the company decides to adjust par value by exchanging existing shares for twice as many new shares that carry a reduced par value. Assume that Allstar does not just issue an additional share for each current share. Instead, investors return the 100,000 shares of common stock at $10 par value to Allstar in exchange for 200,000 shares of common stock at $5 par value. Nothing changes in the stockholders' equity section, except the description of shares authorized, issued, and outstanding. The aggregate par value is unchanged, no cash has changed hands, each owner has the same proportionate interest as before, and each has the same relative voting power.

Panel A of Exhibit 10-4 shows the journal entries for the two approaches to stock splits. Panel B shows the effect on shareholders' equity. As noted in panel C, in both cases, total shareholders' equity is unchanged and the total market value of the firm should also be unchanged, which implies that the market price of an individual share should be one-half of its prior value.

stock dividends
Distribution to stockholders of a small number of additional shares for every share owned without any payment to the company by the stockholders.

Accounting for Stock Dividends

Stock dividends are also issuances of additional shares to existing shareholders without additional cash payment, but the number of new shares issued is usually smaller than it is in a split, and there is no change in par value. For example, a 10% stock dividend is the issuance of 1 new share for every 10 shares currently owned.

OBJE**5**TIVE

Account for both large- and small-percentage stock dividends.

Large-Percentage Stock Dividends Companies issuing large-percentage stock dividends issue new shares and increase the common stock account for the par value of the newly issued shares. U.S. accounting principles require companies to account for large-percentage stock dividends (typically those 20% or higher) at par or stated value. That means that an accounting entry simply transfers the par or stated value of the new shares from the retained earnings account to the common stock account.

As in the case of stock splits, the market value of the outstanding shares tends to adjust completely when a firm issues a stock dividend, provided that the firm lowers the per share dividend proportionately. Consider the Allstar Equipment Company and the effect of possible stock dividends on share price. The original $150 share price would fall to $125 with a 20% stock dividend [$15,000,000 ÷ (100,000 shares + 20,000 shares)] and to $75 with a 100% dividend. The total value of the company stays at $15 million in all cases.

Suppose the Allstar Equipment Company chose to double the number of outstanding shares by issuing a 100% stock dividend. The total amount of stockholders' equity would be unaffected. However, its composition would change as shown in panel A of Exhibit 10-5. From a shareholder's perspective, this is essentially identical to a two-for-one stock split. Thus, accountants often refer to this as a two-for-one stock split "accounted for as a dividend." There is no economic difference between the 100% stock dividend and the two-for-one stock split. The accounting differs only with regard to where the amount added to common stock at par value comes from—from additional paid-in capital for a stock split and from retained earnings for a stock dividend. Firms often prefer to account for a stock split as a stock dividend because it saves clerical costs. The company does not need to receive permission for a change in par value, and it does not have to exchange stock certificates. It simply sends out certificates for the additional shares.

However, the company does have an economic decision to make. What happens to the cash dividend? One possibility is to adjust the cash dividend proportionately. For a 100% stock dividend or a two-for-one stock split, this means that the cash dividend per share is cut in half and total cash dividends remain unchanged. It is at least as common for the

Exhibit 10-5
Stock Dividends
*Allstar Example:
Originally 100,000
Shares; $10 Par Value
and $150 Market Value
per Share*

PANEL A: LARGE STOCK DIVIDEND (100%)

Issue 100,000 new $10 Par Value Shares Accounted for at Par

Retained earnings $1,000,000
    Common stock $1,000,000

	Common Stock	Additional Paid-in-Capital	Retained Earnings	Owners' Equity
Original	$1,000,000	$4,000,000	$6,000,000	$11,000,000
100% Dividend	1,000,000		(1,000,000)	
Result	$2,000,000	$4,000,000	$5,000,000	$11,000,000

PANEL B: SMALL STOCK DIVIDEND (2%)

Issue 2,000 new $10 Par Value Shares Accounted for at Market

Retained Earnings $300,000
    Common Stock   20,000
    Additional Paid-in-Capital   280,000

	Common Stock	Additional Paid-in-Capital	Retained Earnings	Owners Equity
Original	$1,000,000	$4,000,000	$6,000,000	$11,000,000
2% Dividend	20,000	280,000	(300,000)	
Result	$1,020,000	$4,280,000	$5,700,000	$11,000,000

company to increase the total cash dividend being paid. Investors watch this issue carefully to assess the company's belief about future cash flow and future investment opportunity.

Small-Percentage Stock Dividends When the firm issues a stock dividend of less than 20%, accountants require the firm to account for the dividend at market value, not at par value. This rule is hard to defend. It is partly the result of tradition and partly due to the fact that small-percentage stock dividends are more likely to accompany increases in the total dividend payments or other changes in the company's financial policies. Security analysts argue that the decision to increase total dividends communicates management's conviction that future cash flows will rise to support these increased distributions. This is a positive statement about the firm's prospects.

Panel B of Exhibit 10-5 illustrates the effects of a 2% stock dividend. As before, the individual shareholder receives no assets from the corporation, and the corporation receives no cash from the shareholder. Also, because the overall number of shares and the number of shares held by each investor have both increased proportionally, the shareholders' fractional ownership interests are unchanged. The major possible economic effect of a stock dividend is to signal increased cash dividends. Suppose the board of the company in our example consistently voted to pay cash dividends of $1 per share. Often companies maintain this cash dividend per share after a small stock dividend. The recipient of the stock dividend can now expect a future annual cash dividend of $1 × 1,020 = $1,020 instead of $1 × 1,000 = $1,000. In this case, when a company maintains its dividend rate per share, announcing a stock dividend of 2% has the same economic effect as announcing an increase of 2% in the cash dividend.

The company records small-percentage stock dividends (under 20%), by transferring the market value of the additional shares from retained earnings to common stock and additional paid-in capital. We refer to this transfer as a "capitalization of retained earnings." It is an accounting signal to the shareholders that the company is investing $300,000 for the long term in productive assets such as plant, property, and equipment. U.S. practice concerning the use of market values in accounting for small-percentage stock dividends is arbitrary and is not consistently adopted worldwide. For example, companies in Japan record small stock dividends at par value. The Japanese practice is one most accountants would support.

Summary Problem for Your Review

PROBLEM

Charlie Company distributes a 2% stock dividend on its 1 million outstanding $5 par common shares. The stockholders' equity section before the dividend was:

Common stock, 1,000,000 shares @ $5 par	$ 5,000,000
Additional paid-in capital in excess of par	20,000,000
Retained earnings	75,000,000
Total stockholders' equity	$100,000,000

The common stock was selling on the open market for $150 per share when Charlie Company distributed the dividend. How will the stock dividend affect the stockholders' equity section? If net income were $10.2 million next year, what would be the earnings per share before considering the effects of the stock dividend and after considering the effects of the stock dividend?

SOLUTION

	Before 2% Stock Dividend	Changes	After 2% Stock Dividend
Common stock, 1,000,000 shares @ $5 par	$ 5,000,000	+(20,000 @ $5)	$ 5,100,000
Additional paid-in capital	20,000,000	+[20,000 @ ($150 − $5)]	22,900,000
Retained earnings	75,000,000	−(20,000 @ $150)	72,000,000
Total	$100,000,000		$100,000,000

Earnings per share before considering the effects of the stock dividend would be $10,200,000 ÷ 1,000,000, or $10.20. After the dividend: $10,200,000 ÷ 1,020,000, or $10.

Note that the dividend has no effect on net income, the numerator of the earnings-per-share computation. However, it does affect the denominator and causes a mild dilution that, in theory, should cause a slight decline in the market price of the stock.

Why Use Stock Splits and Dividends?

Experts debate the importance of stock splits and stock dividends even as companies continue to use them. We have reviewed the arguments surrounding the use of stock splits and stock dividends to control the price per share. Wal-Mart, for example, split two-for-one on seven occasions since 1980, usually when its shares sold for about $50. In the summer of 2004, it was selling at $55 per share; the price would have been more than $7,000 per share without the splits.

Often a stock split or stock dividend accompanies other announcements, such as new corporate investment strategies or changes in cash dividend levels. Suppose the firm has traditionally paid a special cash dividend at year-end, but plans to expand production substantially, which absorbs available cash and makes the payment of this special dividend difficult. The firm might combine the announcement of the planned expansion with an announcement of a small stock dividend. The small-percentage stock dividend does not draw on cash immediately, but provides stockholders with an increase in future cash dividends in proportion to the percentage of new shares issued. The Business First box on page 460 illustrates these issues with a recent Microsoft press release.

Fractional Shares

Corporations ordinarily issue shares in whole units. When shareholders are entitled to stock dividends in amounts equal to fractional units, corporations issue additional shares for whole units plus cash equal to the market value of the fractional amount.

For example, suppose a corporation issues a 3% stock dividend. A shareholder has 160 shares. The market value per share on the date of issuance is $40. Par value is $2. The shareholder would be entitled to .03 × 160 = 4.8 shares. The company would issue four shares plus .8 × $40 = $32 cash. The journal entry is:

```
Retained earnings (4.8 × $40) ...................  192
    Common stock, at par (4 × $2)  ..............        8
    Additional paid-in capital (4 × $38) ............      152
    Cash (.8 × $40) .........................       32
To issue a stock dividend of 3% to a holder
of 160 shares
```

MICROSOFT DECLARES ANNUAL DIVIDEND AND ANNOUNCES TWO-FOR-ONE SPLIT ON COMMON STOCK

REDMOND, Wash. — Jan. 16, 2003 — *Microsoft Corp. today announced that its Board of Directors declared an annual dividend and approved a two-for-one split on Microsoft common stock. The annual dividend of $0.16 per share pre-split ($0.08 post-split) is payable March 7, 2003, to shareholders of record at the close of business on Feb. 21, 2003. As a result of the stock split, share-holders will receive one additional common share for every share held on the record date of Jan. 27, 2003.*

"Declaring a dividend demonstrates the board's con-fidence in the company's long-term growth opportunities and financial strength. We are especially pleased to be able to return profits to our shareholders, while maintain-ing our significant investment in research and develop-ment and satisfying our long-term capital requirements," said John Connors, chief financial officer at Microsoft.

Upon completion of the split, the number of common shares outstanding will be approximately 10.8 billion. The additional shares will be mailed or delivered on or about Feb. 14, 2003, by the company's transfer agent, Mellon Investor Services. This is the ninth time Microsoft's common stock has split since the company's initial public offering on March 13, 1986.

"We believe that the split, combined with an annual dividend, will make Microsoft stock even more attractive to a broader range of investors. We see enormous poten-tial for growth in the software and technology sector, and remain committed to attracting investors who share this enthusiasm and take a long-term view of the company's growth opportunities," Connors said.

In connection with the dividend, the company is intro-ducing a Direct Stock Purchase Program and a Dividend Reinvestment Program, offering both new investors and current stockholders the option of receiving Microsoft's annual dividend in cash or having it automatically rein-vested. This program is administered by Mellon Investor.

Source: Microsoft Web site (www.microsoft.com).

The Investor's Accounting for Dividends and Splits

So far, we have focused on how the corporation deals with stock splits and dividends. What about the stockholder? Consider the investor's recording of the transactions described so far. Suppose Jesse bought 1,000 shares of the original issue of Allstar Equipment Company stock for $50 per share:

Investment in Allstar common stock	50,000	
Cash		50,000

To record investment in 1,000 shares of an original issue of Allstar Equipment Company common stock at $50 per share.

If Jesse sold the shares to Katrina at a subsequent price other than $50, Jesse would record a gain or loss and Katrina would carry the shares at the amount she paid Jesse. Meanwhile, the stockholders' equity of Allstar Equipment Company would be com-pletely unaffected by this sale by one investor to another. The company would simply change its underlying shareholder records to delete Jesse and add Katrina as a share-holder.

The following examples show how Jesse would record the stock split, cash divi-dends, and stock dividends, treating each as an independent event, not as sequential events. Note that several events that produced journal entries for Allstar do not cause entries for Jesse:

a. Stock split at 2-for-1:	No journal entry, but Jesse would make a memorandum in the investment account to show that he now owns 2,000 shares at a cost of $25 each, instead of 1,000 shares at a cost of $50 each

b. Cash dividends of $2 per share:

Cash 2,000
    Dividend income 2,000
To record cash dividends on Allstar Equipment Company stock

or:

Alternatively, Jesse might use the following two entries:

Date of declaration:

Dividends receivable 2,000
    Dividend income 2,000
To record dividends declared by Allstar Equipment Company

Date of receipt:

Cash 2,000
    Dividends receivable 2,000
To record the receipt of cash dividends

c. Stock dividends of 2%

No journal entry, but Jesse would make a memorandum in the investment account to show that [assuming the stock split in (a) had not occurred] he now owns 1,020 shares at an average cost of $50,000 ÷ 1,020, or $49.02 per share

d. Stock split in form of a 100% dividend:

No journal entry, but Jesse would make a memorandum in the investment account to show that [assuming the stock splits and stock dividends in (a) and (c) had not occurred] he now owns 2,000 shares at an average cost of $25 instead of 1,000 shares @ $50. Note that this memorandum has the same effect as the memorandum in (a).

Summary Problems for Your Review

PROBLEM

Metro-Goldwyn-Mayer (MGM) declared and distributed a 3% stock dividend. The applicable market value per share was $7.75. The par value of the 966,000 additional shares issued was $1.00 each. In addition, the total cash paid to shareholders in lieu of issuing fractional shares was $70,000. Prepare the appropriate journal entry.

SOLUTION

Retained earnings 7,556,500
    Common stock, $1.00 par value 966,000
    Capital in excess of par value 6,520,500
    Cash 70,000
To record 3% stock dividend, total shares issued, 966,000 at $7.75, a total market value of $7,486,500. In addition, cash of $70,000 was paid in lieu of issuing fractional shares, so the total charge to retained earnings was $70,000 + (966,000 × $7.75) = $7,556,500.

The account title Capital in Excess of Par Value was the description that MGM actually used.

PROBLEM

Baker Company splits its $10 par common stock five for one. How will the split affect its balance sheet and its earnings per share? Assume 2,000 shares are originally outstanding. How would your answer change if the company said that it "accounted for" the split as a stock dividend?

SOLUTION

The total amount of stockholders' equity would be unaffected, but there would be 10,000 outstanding shares at $2 par, instead of 2,000 shares at $10 par. Earnings per share would be one fifth of that previously reported, assuming no change in total net income applicable to the common stock.

If the question were framed as "the company recently issued a five-for-one stock split accounted for as a stock dividend," then the par value per share would be retained, and a journal entry would increase the par value account for common stock by $80,000 (8,000 additional shares times $10 par value per share) and reduce retained earnings by $80,000.

Retained earnings	80,000	
Common stock at par		80,000

Repurchase of Shares

OBJECTIVE 6

Explain and report stock repurchases and other treasury stock transactions.

So far, we have seen how companies sell shares and how they sometimes issue additional shares to current shareholders. You should not think, though, that stock always flows out of a company. Sometimes companies repurchase shares, usually for one of two purposes: (1) to reduce shareholder claims permanently, called retiring stock, and (2) to hold shares temporarily for later use, most often to be granted as part of employee option, bonus, or stock purchase plans. As we learned earlier in this chapter, we call temporarily held shares treasury stock or treasury shares.

Why do companies repurchase their own stock? There are many possible reasons. Management may believe the stock is undervalued by the market. Or the company may want to change the proportion of debt and equity in use to finance the firm. Buying back shares increases the relative importance of debt. A company may also need shares to distribute to employees as part of a stock option or employee stock purchase plan. Finally, it may simply have more cash than it requires for ongoing investment in new projects, and the board of directors may decide to return some capital to its shareholders. It could pay higher dividends, but often the board prefers repurchasing shares. Why? For one thing, buybacks allow the company to return cash to shareholders without creating expectations of permanent increases in dividends. Further, buybacks put the cash in the hands of shareholders who want it, because shareholders decide whether to sell or not sell their shares.

By repurchasing shares, a company liquidates some shareholders' claims, and total stockholders' equity decreases by the amount of the repurchase. The purpose of the repurchase determines which stockholders' equity accounts are affected. We next discuss accounting for permanent and temporary repurchases using the illustration of the Allstar Equipment Company. Recall that Allstar shares have a market value of $150 per share. We also need to know Allstar's book value per share. A company's book value is the recorded value of its assets less liabilities, which equals its stockholders' equity. Allstar's total stockholders' equity of $11 million combines the original purchase price of shares in the past (par value plus additional paid-in capital) with the periodic earnings of the firm that have remained in the business (retained earnings). Allstar's book value per share is its total shareholders' equity divided by number of outstanding shares, $11,000,000 ÷ 100,000 = $110.

Retirement of Shares

Once a company has repurchased shares, it may retire them or hold them for reissue. Suppose the board of Allstar Company purchases and retires 5% of its outstanding shares at $150 per share for a total of 5,000 shares × $150, or $750,000 cash. Allstar originally issued these shares at $50 per share. The repurchase reduces total stockholders' equity by $750,000. How much of this do we charge against the common stock, additional paid-in capital, and retained earnings accounts? We reduce the common stock and additional paid-in capital accounts by the amount of capital contributed by the original purchasers of the shares that were retired. In addition, the company cancels the stock certificates and no longer considers the shares either outstanding or issued. We illustrate this in panel A of Exhibit 10-6.

The following journal entry reverses the original paid-in capital and charges the additional amount to retained earnings:

Common stock	50,000	
Additional paid-in capital	200,000	
Retained earnings	500,000	
Cash		750,000

To record retirement of 5,000 shares of stock for $150 cash per share. The paid-in capital is $50 per share ($10 par value + $40 additional paid-in capital), so we reduce retained earnings by the additional $100 per share.

Exhibit 10-6
Stock Repurchase
Allstar Example

PANEL A: REPURCHASED SHARES RETIRED

	Before Repurchase of 5% of Outstanding Shares	Changes Because of Retirement	After Repurchase of 5% of Outstanding Shares
Common stock, 100,000 shares @ $10 par	$ 1,000,000	$-(5,000 \text{ shares @ } \$10 \text{ par}) = -\$50,000$	$ 950,000
Additional paid-in capital	4,000,000	$-(5,000 \text{ shares @ } \$40) = -\$200,000$	3,800,000
Total paid-in capital	5,000,000		4,750,000
Retained earnings	6,000,000	$-(5,000 \text{ @ } \$100*) = -\$500,000$	5,500,000
Stockholders' equity	$11,000,000		$10,250,000
Book value per common share:			
$11,000,000 ÷ 100,000	$ 110.00		
$10,250,000 ÷ 95,000			$ 107.90

*$150 acquisition price less the $50 (or $10 + $40) originally paid in.

PANEL B: REPURCHASED SHARES HELD AS TREASURY STOCK

	Before Repurchase of 5% of Outstanding Shares	Changes Because of Treasury Stock	After Repurchase of 5% of Outstanding Shares
Common stock, 100,000 shares @ $10 par	$ 1,000,000		$ 1,000,000
Additional paid-in capital	4,000,000		4,000,000
Total paid-in capital	$ 5,000,000		$ 5,000,000
Retained earnings	6,000,000		6,000,000
Total	$11,000,000		$11,000,000
Deduct:			
Cost of treasury stock		$750,000	750,000
Stockholders' equity			$10,250,000

Book value per common share is calculated on shares outstanding and is identical to the values in panel A.

Note how the book value per share of the outstanding shares has declined from $110.00 to $107.90. We call this phenomenon **dilution**—a reduction in shareholders' equity per share or EPS that arises from changes among shareholders' proportionate interests. As a rule, boards of directors avoid dilution unless expected future profits will more than compensate for a temporary undesirable reduction in book value per share.

Some companies have a multiyear plan to repurchase and retire shares. For example, Hormel Company, producers of Jennie-O Turkey products, Dinty Moore canned foods, and Spam, in addition to Hormel brands, retired almost 500,000 shares of stock in 2002 as part of such a repurchase plan. A footnote to Hormel's financial statements disclosed the following:

> *During the year the company repurchased 484,537 shares of its common stock at an average price per share of $21.21 under a repurchase plan approved in September 1998. . . . Total shares purchased under the 10 million share repurchase plan approved in 1998 are 9,943,228 shares. On October 2, 2002, the company announced the approval of the repurchase of up to an additional 10 million shares of its common stock.*

When Hormel has repurchased all 20 million shares, it will have retired about 15% of its common stock.

Treasury Stock

Now suppose Allstar's board of directors decides not to retire the 5,000 repurchased shares but to hold them temporarily as treasury stock. Perhaps the company needs the shares for an employee stock purchase plan or for executive stock options. The repurchase still decreases stockholders' equity. It is NOT an asset. Why? Because a company cannot own part of itself.

If treasury stock is not an asset, then what is it? The Treasury Stock account is a contra account to Owners' Equity, just as Accumulated Depreciation is a contra account to related asset accounts. Like retiring shares, purchasing treasury stock decreases stockholders' equity by $750,000 (5,000 shares purchased at $150 per share). Unlike the accounting for retirements, common stock at par value, additional paid-in capital, and retained earnings remain untouched by treasury stock purchases. The separate treasury stock account is deducted from total stockholders' equity. Panel B of Exhibit 10-6 shows Allstar's stockholders' equity section. Companies do not pay dividends on treasury stock because shares held in the treasury are not outstanding shares:

Shares issued	100,000
Less: Treasury stock	5,000
Total shares outstanding	95,000

Companies usually resell treasury shares at a later date, perhaps through an employee stock purchase plan. Exhibit 10-7 shows the outcomes when Allstar reissues these treasury shares above or below the acquisition cost. We show in panel A journal entries for reissue at $180 (above the $150 acquisition cost) and in panel B the result for reissue at $120 (below the $150 acquisition cost). In panel C, we present the different shareholder equity sections for each outcome.

The specific accounting practices for transactions in the company's own stock vary from company to company. Some companies use a last-in, first-out (LIFO) cost flow assumption for treasury shares, some use a first-in, first-out (FIFO) assumption, and some use average cost. Some companies have multiple paid-in-capital accounts and track changes from treasury stock shares in a special account called additional paid-in-capital from treasury stock transactions. However, one rule remains constant: treasury stock

Exhibit 10-7
Reissuance of
Treasury Shares
*Allstar Repurchased
5,000 Shares for $150
per Share Creating a
Treasury Stock Balance
of $750,000*

PANEL A: REISSUE AT $180 PER SHARE

Cash	900,000	
Treasury stock		750,000
Additional paid-in-capital		150,000

PANEL B: REISSUE AT $120 PER SHARE

Cash	600,000	
Additional paid-in-capital	150,000	
Treasury stock		750,000

PANEL C: COMPARATIVE BALANCES

	With 5,000 Shares in Treasury @ $150	Reissued @ $180	Reissued @ $120
Common stock	$ 1,000,000	$ 1,000,000	$ 1,000,000
Additional paid-in-capital	4,000,000	4,150,000	3,850,000
	5,000,000	5,150,000	4,850,000
Retained earnings	6,000,000	6,000,000	6,000,000
Deduct treasury stock	(750,000)		
	$10,250,000	$11,150,000	$10,850,000

transactions never produce expenses, losses, revenues, or gains in the income statement. Why? A corporation's own capital stock is part of its capital structure. It is not an asset of the corporation. A company cannot make profits or losses by buying or selling its own common stock.

There is no important difference between unissued shares and treasury shares. In our example, Allstar could accomplish the same objective by (1) acquiring 5,000 shares, retiring them, and issuing 5,000 "new" shares; or (2) acquiring 5,000 shares and reselling them. Although some account balances within stockholders's equity would differ under these alternatives, neither the number of shares outstanding nor the total stockholders' equity would change. Starbucks was an active repurchaser of stock in 2003, spending $76 billion to repurchase 3.3 million shares. More than 8 million shares were issued due to the exercise of stock options, and another 743,000 shares were issued for other reasons as shown in the statement of shareholders' equity.

Effects of Repurchases on Earnings Per Share

Repurchasing shares, whether they are retired or put in treasury, reduces the number of shares outstanding. This tends to increase EPS. For example, suppose that Allstar generates net income of $950,000 each year and that using $750,000 to repurchase shares would not reduce future net income. Under these circumstances, repurchasing shares increases EPS by $.50:

EPS = net income ÷ average number of shares outstanding				
Before repurchase	$950,000	÷	100,000 shares =	$ 9.50
After repurchase	$950,000	÷	95,000 shares =	$10.00

In contrast, using $750,000 to pay dividends leaves the number of shares unchanged at 100,000 and the EPS at $9.50.

INTERPRETING FINANCIAL STATEMENTS

As a manager, would you choose to distribute cash to your investors as a dividend or via share repurchase? How does this decision affect the financial statements?

Answer
The text raises several issues. One question pertains to the future. If you begin paying dividends, investors will expect you to continue to do so. Thus, you would want to assess future cash flow and your ability and desire to continue dividend payments before initiating dividends. A one-time distribution is probably better as a share repurchase, as are distributions that are likely to be highly variable over time. The new tax law that reduced taxes on dividends received by individuals has reduced

the size of the tax benefit that investors previously received from share repurchase. Historically, shareholders often preferred repurchases because they could choose to participate or not and if they did participate they had low capital gains tax rates that applied only to their gains.

As a manager, you would note that neither decision affects the income statement or total financing cash flows. You might also note that dividends reduce only retained earnings, whereas the effect of share repurchases depends on the book value of the shares, the market value of the shares, and whether they are retired or held in treasury. Ultimately, the financial statement effects of this choice are minor.

Other Issuances of Common Stock

OBJECTIVE 7
Record conversions of debt for equity or of preferred stock into common stock.

Companies do not always receive cash when they issue common stock. A company may issue shares for other assets or in exchange for its own corporate security—a bond or preferred stock.

Noncash Exchanges

Often a company issues its stock to acquire land, a building, or common stock of another company, or to compensate a person or company for services received. The buyer and seller should both record the transaction at the "fair value" of either the securities or the exchanged assets or services, whichever is easier to determine objectively.

Conversion of Securities

Some companies issue bonds or preferred stock that allow the owner to convert them into common stock of the issuer. The conversion feature makes the securities more attractive to investors and increases the price the issuer receives (or, equivalently, reduces the interest or dividend it must pay). If the owner of convertible securities exercises the conversion privilege, the issuer simply adjusts the accounts as if the common stock were issued initially. This may have significant effects on the company's proportion of debt and equity, and it may eliminate some substantial cash commitments previously associated with interest or dividend payments.

For example, suppose Purchaser Company paid $160,000 for an investment in 5,000 shares of the $1 par value convertible preferred stock of Issuer Company in 20X1. In 20X8, Purchaser Company converted the preferred stock into 10,000 shares of Issuer Company common stock ($1 par value). Exhibit 10-8 shows the effect on the accounts of Issuer Company.

Purchaser Company also experiences a change in form of the investment, with no change in historical cost. The carrying value, or book value, of the investment remains $160,000. To show that the investment is now common stock instead of preferred stock,

	Assets	=	Liabilities	+		Stockholders' Equity		
	Cash				Preferred Stock	Additional Paid-in Capial, Preferred	Common Stock	Additional Paid-in Capital Common
Issuance of preferred (20X1)	+160,000	=			+5,000	+155,000		
Conversion of preferred (20X8)		=			−5,000	−155,000	+10,000	+150,000

The journal entries would be as follows:

On Issuer's Books

```
20X1 Cash  . . . . . . . . . . . . . . . . . . . . . . . . . . . . . . . . . . . . . .   160,000
            Preferred stock, convertible  . . . . . . . . . . . . . . . . . . . . .            5,000
            Additional paid-in capital, preferred  . . . . . . . . . . . . . . .          155,000
         To record issuance of 5,000 shares of $1 par
         preferred stock convertible into two common
         shares for one preferred share
20X8 Preferred stock, convertible  . . . . . . . . . . . . . . . . . . . . . . .     5,000
     Additional paid-in capital, preferred  . . . . . . . . . . . . . . . . . .   155,000
            Common stock  . . . . . . . . . . . . . . . . . . . . . . . . . . . . . .           10,000
            Additional paid-in capital, common  . . . . . . . . . . . . . . . .          150,000
         To record the conversion of 5,000 preferred
         shares to 10,000 common shares
```

Exhibit 10-8
Analysis of Convertible Preferred Stock

Purchaser Company might transfer the $160,000 from one investment account to another. Alternatively, it might change subsidiary records that document the composition of a single general ledger account called Investments.

Tracking Stock

Sometimes companies issue tracking stock based on one part of the company. Tracking stock is similar to common stock. The company can produce separate financial statements for the subunit, it can pay dividends on the tracking stock, and it can issue stock options to employees based on the tracking stock. Tracking shares trade on stock markets just as common shares do. General Motors (GM) created early examples by issuing tracking shares for its subsidiaries Electronic Data Systems (EDS) and Hughes Electronic Corporation. GM purchased both EDS and Hughes, and it wanted to make it obvious that EDS and Hughes were not cyclical, low P/E car manufacturing activities. Lately, tracking shares have become a popular way to highlight a fast-growing subunit of the business.

In 1998, Sprint created two securities to represent the ownership in the firm, FON and PCS. PCS was tied to its wireless business, FON was the rest. In connection with the restructuring, Sprint reclassified each of its publicly traded shares into one share of FON and one-half a share of PCS. The 2002 10-K filed with the SEC indicates that Sprint "tracking stock policies provide that the Board, in resolving material matters in which the holder of FON stock and PCS stock have potentially divergent interests, will act in the best interests of Sprint and all of its common shareholders after giving fair consideration to the potentially divergent interests of the holders of the separate classes of Sprint common stock." At one point, an ultimately failed merger of Worldcom and

Sprint lead to lawsuits by the PCS shareholders because they believed the proposed merger terms did not treat them fairly. In a presentation on May 13, 2003, Sprint Chairman and CEO Gary Forsee acknowledged that " . . . we believe a recombination of the stocks is likely at some point."

A problem with tracking shares is that they do not represent voting rights in a separate company, and the board of directors of the parent company has great freedom in making decisions that favor or harm the investors in one or the other of the units. For example, when GM converted the tracking shares on EDS to real shares in a separate company and separated it from GM, it first extracted a $500 million payment from EDS. The total market value of EDS fell by that $500 million, and the holders of the tracking stock suffered the loss. The EDS shareholder lawsuit against GM for damages failed. Such lawsuits are not uncommon.

Retained Earnings Restrictions

The most closely watched part of stockholders' equity, both by shareholders and creditors, is retained earnings. Boards of directors can make decisions that benefit shareholders but hurt creditors. For example, directors might pay excessive dividends that jeopardize payments of creditors' claims. To protect creditors, state laws or contractual obligations often restrict dividend-declaring power. Moreover, boards of directors can voluntarily restrict their declarations of dividends.

States typically do not permit boards to declare dividends if those dividends would cause stockholders' equity to be less than total paid-in capital. Therefore, retained earnings must exceed the cost of treasury stock. If there is no treasury stock, retained earnings must be positive. This restriction limits dividend payments and thus protects the position of the creditors. For example, consider the following ($ in millions):

	Before Dividends	After Dividend Payments of $10	After Dividend Payments of $4
Paid-in capital	$25	$25	$25
Retained earnings	10	—	6
Total	$35	$25	$31
Deduct:			
Cost of treasury stock	6	6	6
Stockholders' equity	$29	$19	$25

restricted retained earnings (appropriated retained earnings) *Any part of retained earnings that may not be reduced by dividend declarations.*

reserve *Has one of three meanings: (1) a restriction of dividend-declaring power as denoted by a specific subdivision of retained earnings, (2) an offset to an asset, or (3) an estimate of a definite liability of indefinite or uncertain amount.*

Without restricting dividends to the amount of retained earnings in excess of the cost of treasury stock, the corporation could pay a dividend of $10 million. This would reduce the stockholders' equity below the paid-in capital of $25 million. With the restriction, unrestricted retained earnings (and maximum legal payment of dividends) is $10 million − $6 million, or $4 million. In this case, the existence of treasury stock creates a restriction on the company's ability to declare dividends. Most companies with restrictions of retained earnings disclose them by footnotes. Occasionally, restrictions appear as a line item on the balance sheet called **restricted retained earnings, appropriated retained earnings,** or reserves. The term "reserve" can be misleading. Accountants never use the word reserve to indicate cash set aside for a particular purpose; instead, they call such assets a fund. The term **reserve** has one of three broad meanings in accounting: (1) restrictions of dividend declarations, (2) an offset to an asset, or (3) an estimate of a definite liability of indefinite or uncertain amount. An acknowledgment of a restriction on dividend payments is contained in the following reference from a recent annual report of Coherent, Inc., the world's leading manufacturer of lasers:

> *The Company's domestic lines of credit are generally subject to standard covenants related to financial ratios, profitability and dividend payments.*

In the United States, retained earnings reserves tend to arise through state law or contractual agreements. Some other countries, among them France, Germany, the Netherlands, and Japan, allow companies to set up purely discretionary reserves. The idea is to disclose specific intentions of management. An international company might use a "reserve for plant expansion" to communicate an intention to reinvest future earnings in new technology rather than increase dividends.

Other Components of Stockholders' Equity

Two other elements commonly appear in stockholders' equity and deserve brief mention here. The UPS shareholders' equity in Exhibit 10-1 included a deduction of $438 million labeled Accumulated Other Comprehensive Loss. The major portion of this item relates to foreign currency translation adjustments. These amounts arise when a company has subsidiary companies in another country. The process of translating Mexican pesos or Japanese yen into U.S. dollars gives rise to some adjustments that affect shareholders' equity. These are discussed briefly in Chapter 12. Another potential contributor to other comprehensive income relates to certain unrealized investment gains and losses that we also discuss in Chapter 12.

The other element of UPS shareholders' equity that we have not discussed explicitly is the Deferred compensation arrangements. UPS is one of many companies that enhances the commitment of its employees to work hard and provide good service by rewarding them with shares of stock. Here, employees have delayed their right to receive shares for purposes of estate planning and tax management. UPS recognizes the obligation to deliver shares in the future in a Deferred Compensation Arrangements account and includes the number of shares to be issued in the future in calculations of EPS.

Financial Ratios Related to Stockholders' Equity

Analysts answer many questions pertaining to stockholders' equity by using ratios. One important question is: how effectively does the company use resources provided by the shareholders? To assess this, analysts relate the net income generated by the firm to the historic investment by its shareholders. We define the **rate of return on common equity (ROE)** as:

OBJECTIVE 8

Use the rate of return on common equity and book value per share.

rate of return on common equity (ROE)
Net income less preferred dividends divided by average common equity.

$$\text{Rate of return on common equity} = \frac{(\text{Net income} - \text{Preferred dividends})}{\text{Average common equity}}$$

The rate of return on common equity is of great interest to common stockholders because it focuses on the company's profitability based on the book value of the common equity. The denominator is the average of the beginning and ending common equity balances. Note that the common equity balance is the total stockholders' equity less the preferred stock at book value (or at liquidating value if it exceeds the book value). The calculations for Calvin Company are in Exhibit 10-9, with panel A presenting comparative stockholders' equity for 2 years together with earnings information and panel B using that information to calculate ROE.

Exhibit 10-9
Calvin Company
Owners' Equity

PANEL A		
	December 31	
	20X2	**20X1**
Stockholders' equity		
10% preferred stock, 100,000 shares,		
$100 par	$ 10,000,000	$ 10,000,000
Common stock, 5,000,000 shares,		
$1 par	5,000,000	5,000,000
Additional paid-in capital	35,000,000	35,000,000
Retained earnings	87,000,000	83,000,000
Total stockholders' equity	$137,000,000	$133,000,000
Net income for the year ended		
December 31, 20X2	$ 11,000,000	
Preferred dividends @ $10 per share	1,000,000	
Net income available for common stock	$ 10,000,000	

PANEL B: ROE

$$\text{Rate of return on common equity} = \frac{\text{Net income} - \text{Preferred dividends}}{\text{Average common equity}}$$

$$= \frac{\$11,000,000 - \$1,000,0000}{\frac{1}{2}[(\$133,000,000 - \$10,000,000) + (\$137,000,000 - \$10,000,000)]}$$

$$= \frac{\$10,000,000}{\frac{1}{2}(\$123,000,000 + \$127,000,000)}$$

$$= \frac{\$10,000,000}{\$125,000,000} = 8.0\%$$

ROE varies considerably among companies and industries and from year to year, as follows:

	2002	1999	1996	1993
UPS	28.0	9.0	n/a	n/a
McDonald's	10.1	20.4	19.5	19.0
IBM	15.4	38.5	24.8	*
PepsiCo	36.9	32.4	16	27
ExxonMobil[†]	15.5	12.6	16.0	12.3
DaimlerChrysler[‡]	12.8	14.2	31	*

*Denotes a loss year.
n/a, denotes that UPS was a private company prior to 1999.
[†]ExxonMobil values in 2002 and 1999, premerger values for Mobil for 1996 and 1993.
[‡]DaimlerChrysler values in 2002 and 1999, premerger values for Chrysler for 1996 and 1993.

ROE patterns often spark questions that increase your understanding of the company. For example, why was UPS's ROE so much higher in 2002 than in 1999? Further exploration reveals that UPS had a large charge in 1999 for taxes that reduced earnings significantly that year. McDonald's was reasonably stable from 1993 through 1999 but fell sharply in 2002. Why? Because the company reported significant reductions in profit margins. IBM and DaimlerChrysler have highly variable ROE, in part due to losses in 1993. This variability might arise from difficult business activity, but may also relate to changes in accounting practice. For example, the changes in accounting practice for postretirement benefits in 1993 that caused many companies to record very large one-time expense items. Chrysler recorded a $5 billion charge for the accounting change in 1993 and would have had ROE of more than 30% that year without the change. However, further investigation of IBM reveals that its 1993 loss had little to do with the accounting change.

A second ratio is book value per share. When preferred stock is present, the calculation of the **book value per share of common stock** adjusts for the preferred. The calculation for Calvin Company using 20X2 data from panel A of Exhibit 10-9 follows:

book value per share of common stock Stockholders' equity attributable to common stock divided by the number of shares outstanding.

$$\text{Book value per share of common stock} = \frac{\text{Total stockholders' equity} - \text{Book value of preferred stock}}{\text{Number of common shares outstanding}}$$

$$= \frac{\$137{,}000{,}000 - \$10{,}000{,}000}{5{,}000{,}000} = \$25.40$$

The market value of a stock is usually more than its book value, but not always. This relationship is often captured by calculating a **market-to-book ratio** equal to market price per share divided by book value per share. Consider UPS. It had a market value of $63 and a book value of $11.09 on January 1, 2003. This gives a market-to-book ratio of 5.7 to 1. Other comparisons are shown below (taken from Yahoo's financial site in August 2003), with each company's ratios compared with an industry average.

market-to-book ratio Market value per share divided by book value per share.

	Market to Book Ratios	
	Company	Industry
UPS	5.7	5.03
McDonald's	2.52	4.02
IBM	5.29	5.73
PepsiCo	7.34	7.38
ExxonMobil	2.97	2.62
DaimlerChrysler	.92	2.11

Shareholders value a stock based on what they believe the future earning power will be, not based on the historical cost of assets. Book values are balance sheet values, which show the historical cost of assets. Comparing market values with book values often helps highlight the causes behind the difference in values. Note that PepsiCo has the highest market-to-book ratio, and has a significant brand name that is associated with quality and allows it to earn high returns. At the other extreme, DaimlerChrysler is competing in a commodity industry with a low industry level, and its Chrysler division in the United States has had disappointing results. The pharmaceutical industry is typically high on this dimension, both because of its high profitability and because the practice of expensing research and development means that the book value of pharmaceutical firms does not reflect the value of patented drugs. For example, Pfizer's market-to-book ratio is 8.0, and the industry ratio is 6.8.

What do these differences in values mean in the real world? A market value well above the book value may be appropriate if the company has many unrecorded assets or appreciated assets as in the pharmaceutical industry. PepsiCo's high market-to-book ratio presumably reflects investors' beliefs that it will be able to continue its long-term pattern of rapid sales growth and high return on equity.

Highlights to Remember

1 **Describe the rights of shareholders.** On the balance sheet, stockholders' equity is the book value of the residual interests of a corporation's owners. By incorporating, the company provides limited liability for its owners and provides them with various rights, including the right to vote for the board of directors.

Among equity holders, preferred shareholders have more senior claims to dividends and may have other special rights, including cumulative dividends, participating dividends, conversion privileges, and preference in liquidation. Preferred stocks are similar to bonds in many ways.

2 **Differentiate among authorized, issued, and outstanding shares.** Authorized shares are those that the company is legally able to issue based on the articles of incorporation of the corporation. Issued shares are those that the company has distributed to shareholders and must be equal to, or less than, the authorized number. Outstanding shares are those that the company has issued and has not repurchased for the treasury and must be equal to, or less than, the issued shares.

3 **Contrast bonds, preferred stock, and common stock.** Bonds, preferred stock, and common stock are all claims on the assets of the corporation. Bonds are the senior claim and are specific legal obligations with required dates for payment of interest and repayment of principal. Preferred stock may have many specific rights attached to it, but dividends become obligations only when the board of directors declares them, and preferred stock typically has no maturity date. Preferred shareholders typically receive dividends and repayment of principal before common shareholders. We often call common stock the residual claim because common shareholders typically receive what is left after paying all other obligations. In liquidation of a failed company, common shareholders may receive little or nothing. However, when a company grows rapidly and prospers, the value of the common stock will increase much more than the value of either bonds or preferred stock.

4 **Identify the economic characteristics of and account for stock splits.** Stock splits alter the number of shares held by the owners, without altering the economic claims of the shareholders. As a result, no change typically occurs in the total market value of the company, but the value of individual shares changes in proportion to the size of the split or dividend. A two-for-one split would typically cause the market price per share to decline by 50%. Stock splits require either a transfer from additional paid-in-capital to common stock or a change in par value of the common stock and no journal entry.

5 **Account for both large- and small-percentage stock dividends.** Accounting for stock dividends involves rearranging the owners' equity account balances. We can rearrange par value accounts, paid-in capital accounts, and retained earnings without changing the total owners' equity. The exact procedure depends on whether the par value of the new shares changes and on the number of additional shares issued. Similarly, a rearrangement of owners' equity arises when convertible preferred shareholders exchange their shares for common shares.

6 **Explain and report stock repurchases and other treasury stock transactions.** Companies sometimes acquire treasury stock, which are shares of their own stock purchased in the open market. These shares may later be retired, resold, or used to meet obligations under option agreements. Transactions in the company's own stock never give rise to gains and losses and do not affect the income statement. Such transactions with the shareholders give rise only to changes in the equity accounts.

7 **Record conversions of debt for equity or of preferred stock into common stock.** Generally, when investors convert debt or preferred stock into common stock, we transfer the book values of the debt or preferred stock into owners' equity. Part is shown as par or stated value and the remainder as additional-paid-in capital.

8 **Use the rate of return on common equity and book value per share.** Security analysts use the return on common stockholders' equity as a primary ratio to assess the effectiveness of management and the profitability of the firm. Higher is better. Analysts often compare the market value per share with the book value per share. A high ratio of market value to book value generally means good growth prospects and possibly unrecorded assets, such as internally developed patents.

Accounting Vocabulary

appropriated retained earnings, p. 468
authorized shares, p. 445
book value per share of common stock, p. 471
call price, p. 450
callable, p. 450
convertible, p 450
corporate proxy, p. 444
cumulative, p. 448
date of record, p. 446
declaration date, p. 446

dilution, p. 464
dividend arrearages, p. 448
issued shares, p. 445
liquidating value, p. 449
market-to-book ratio, p. 471
outstanding shares, p. 445
participating, p. 450
payment date, p. 446
preemptive rights, p. 444
preferred stock, p. 447
rate of return on common equity (ROE), p. 469

redemption price, p. 450
reserve, p. 468
restricted retained earnings, p. 468
restricted stock, p. 454
stock dividends, p. 456
stock options, p. 452
stock split, p. 454
treasury stock, p. 445
vested options, p. 452

Assignment Material

Questions

10-1 What is the purpose of preemptive rights?

10-2 "Common shareholders have limited liability." Explain.

10-3 Can a share of common stock be outstanding but not authorized or issued? Why?

10-4 "Treasury stock is unissued stock." Do you agree? Explain.

10-5 "Cumulative dividends are liabilities that must be paid to preferred shareholders before any dividends are paid to common shareholders." Do you agree? Explain.

10-6 "The liquidating value of preferred stock is the amount of cash for which it can currently be exchanged." Do you agree? Explain.

10-7 What are convertible securities?

10-8 In what way is preferred stock similar to debt and to common stock?

10-9 Which are riskier—bonds or preferred stock? Why? Whose perspective are you taking—the issuer's or the investor's?

10-10 Why do some accountants want to record an expense when a company grants stock options to its employees?

10-11 Why do you suppose companies offer their employees stock options instead of simply paying higher salaries?

10-12 "The only real dividends are cash dividends." Do you agree? Explain.

10-13 "A 2% stock dividend increases every shareholder's fractional portion of the company by 2%." Do you agree? Explain.

10-14 "A stock split can be achieved by means of a stock dividend." Do you agree? Explain.

10-15 "When companies repurchase their own shares, the accounting depends on the purpose for which the shares are purchased." Explain.

10-16 "When a company retires shares, it must pay the stockholders an amount equal to the original par value and additional capital contributed for those shares plus the stockholders' fractional portion of retained earnings." Do you agree? Explain.

10-17 Why might a company decide to buy back its own shares instead of paying additional cash dividends?

10-18 "Treasury stock is not an asset." Explain.

10-19 "Gains and losses are not possible from a corporation's acquiring or selling its own stock." Do you agree? Explain.

10-20 What is the proper measure for an asset newly acquired through an exchange (e.g., an exchange of land for securities)? Explain.

10-21 Why does a conversion option make bonds or preferred stock more attractive to investors?

10-22 Restrictions on dividend-declaring power may be voluntary or involuntary. Give an example of each.

10-23 Why might a board of directors voluntarily restrict its dividend-declaring power?

10-24 "A company's ROE indicates how much return an investor makes on the investment in the company's shares." Do you agree? Explain.

10-25 "A common stock selling on the market far below its book value is an attractive buy." Do you agree? Explain.

Critical Thinking Questions

10-26 Company Share Prices and Intentions to Repurchase Shares
Your friend has thought about repurchases of common stock by the issuing company and has concluded that this is unethical. Specifically, this friend says that the company knows more than you do and if the company decides to repurchase shares, they are taking advantage of shareholders. How do you respond?

10-27 The Prohibition on Income Recognition from Trading in the Company's Shares
Your friend has considered stock repurchases and thinks that it is proper for the company to buy its own shares and subsequently reissue them, recognizing a profit in doing so that should be reported on the income statement. How do you respond?

10-28 The Meaning of Par Value
Your friend has decided that par value is a meaningless notion and complicates accounting practice without adding value to the financial statements. How do you respond?

10-29 Changes in Stock Prices When the Shares Are Split
Your friend has developed a stock investing strategy that suggests you should always buy the shares of companies when they split their stock or issue large stock dividends. How do you respond?

Exercises

10-30 Distinctions Between Terms

Disposal Services, Inc., a waste management company, had 3 million shares of common stock authorized on August 31, 20X2. Shares issued were 2.1 million. There were 250,000 shares held in the treasury. How many shares were issued and outstanding? How many shares were unissued? Label your computations.

10-31 Distinctions Between Terms

On December 31, 2002, IBM Corporation had 4,688 million shares of common stock authorized. There were 1,921 million shares issued, and 199 million shares held as treasury stock. How many shares were issued and outstanding? How many shares were unissued? Label your computations.

10-32 Preferences as to Assets

The following are account balances of Reliable Autos, Inc. ($ in thousands): common stock and retained income, $300; accounts payable, $300; preferred stock (5,000 shares; $20 par and $24 liquidating value per share), $100; subordinated debentures, $300; and unsubordinated debentures, $200. Prepare a table showing the distribution of the cash proceeds on liquidation and dissolution of the corporation. Assume cash proceeds of ($ in thousands): $1,400, $1,000, $800, $600, $500, and $200, respectively.

10-33 Issuance of Common Shares

Kawasaki Heavy Industries is a large Japanese company that makes ships, aircraft engines, and many other products in addition to motorcycles. Its 2000 sales of ¥1,150 billion were equivalent to $10,831 million. Kawasaki's balance sheet includes (yen in millions):

Common stock of ¥50 par value, 1,390,595,964 shares issued in 2000	
Total paid-in-capital	106,109

1. Assume all 1,390,595,964 shares had been issued at the same time. Prepare the journal entry.
2. Is the relationship between the size of the common stock and the size of the capital surplus different from what one might expect to find for a U.S. company? Explain.

10-34 Cumulative Dividends

The Ute Data Services Corporation was founded on January 1, 20X1.

Preferred stock, no par, cumulative $5 annual dividend per share	
Issued and outstanding, 1,000,000 shares	$ 40,000,000
Capital stock, no par, 6,000,000 shares	90,000,000
Total stockholders' equity	$130,000,000

The corporation's subsequent net incomes (losses) were:

20X1	$ (5,000,000)
20X2	(4,000,000)
20X3	15,000,000
20X4	20,000,000
20X5	13,000,000

Assume the board of directors declared dividends to the maximum extent permissible by law. The state prohibits dividend declarations that cause negative retained earnings.

1. Tabulate the annual dividend declarations on preferred and common shares. There is no treasury stock.
2. How would the total distribution to common shareholders change if the preferred were not cumulative?

10-35 Cumulative Dividends

In recent years, the Winslow Company had severe cash flow problems. In 20X4, the company suspended payment of cash dividends on common stock. In 20X5, it ceased payment on its $4 million of outstanding 7% cumulative preferred stock. No common or preferred dividends were paid in 20X5 or 20X6. In 20X7, Winslow's board of directors decided that $1.0 million was available for cash dividends.

Compute the preferred stock dividend and the common stock dividend for 20X7.

10-36 Cash Dividends

If you have a credit card, you have probably dealt with First Data Corporation without knowing it. First Data maintains data for more than 325 million credit and debit cards and processes more than 1 million credit and debit card transactions every hour. In 1999, First Data declared dividends of $.04 per share paid to an average of 892 million shares. In 2002, the dividend had grown to $.07 on 753 million shares. First Data paid dividends every quarter, but for simplicity assume they declared dividends only once in 2002, on November 15, payable on December 15, to stockholders of record on December 1.

Prepare the journal entries relating to the declaration and payment of 2002 dividends by First Data. Include the date on which each journal entry would be made.

10-37 Stock Options

Lyndon Systems granted its top executives options to purchase 4,000 shares of common stock (par $1) at $20 per share, the market price today. The options may be exercised over a 4-year span, starting 3 years hence. Suppose all options are exercised 3 years hence, when the market value of the stock is $30 per share.

Prepare the appropriate journal entry on the books of Lyndon Systems.

10-38 Stock Split

An annual report of Dean Foods Company included the following in the statement of consolidated retained earnings:

Charge for stock split	$4,401,000

The balance sheets before and after the split showed:

	After	Before
Common stock $1 par value	$13,203,000	$8,802,000

Define stock split. What did Dean Foods do to achieve its stock split? Does this conflict with your definition? Explain fully.

10-39 Reverse Stock Split

According to a news story, "The shareholders of QED approved a 1-for-10 reverse split of QED's common stock." Accounting for a reverse stock split applies the same principles as accounting for a regular stock split. QED Exploration, Incorporated was an oil development company operating in Texas and Louisiana. QED's stockholders' equity section before the reverse split included:

Common stock, authorized 30,000,000 shares, issued 23,530,000 shares	$ 287,637
Additional paid-in capital	3,437,547
Retained income	2,220,895
Less treasury stock, at cost, 1,017,550 shares	(305,250)
Total stockholders' equity	$5,640,829

1. Prepare QED's stockholders' equity section after the reverse stock split.
2. Comment on possible reasons for a reverse split.

10-40 Stock Dividends

> **Company Release- 07/23/2003 10:27**
> **Tompkins Trustco, Inc. Announces Cash and Stock Dividends**
> **Ithaca, New York July 23, 2003 (Business Wire)**

> *Tompkins Trustco, Inc. (TMP- American Stock Exchange) announced today that its Board of Directors approved payment of a regular quarterly cash dividend of $0.30 per share, payable on August 15, 2003, to common shareholders of record on August 5, 2003. The Board also approved the payment of a 10% stock dividend payable on August 15, 2003, to common shareholders of record on August 5, 2003.*

At June 30 Tompkins reported 7,397,133 shares issued with a par value of $.10 per share. At June 30, 24,529 shares were in treasury. The share price was $45 when the stock dividend was issued. Assume no treasury shares were acquired or sold after June 30.

Prepare the journal entry to record Tompkins Trustco's stock dividend.

10-41 Treasury Stock

During the first 6 months of 2003, Tompkins Trustco repurchased 83,050 of its own shares at an average price of $42.53 per share and held them in the treasury. At December 31, 2002, the balance in the treasury stock account was $466,000. Par value was $1 per share.

1. Prepare the journal entry for the 2003 purchase of treasury shares.
2. Give the balance in the Treasury Stock Account at June 30, 2003.
3. In fact, Tompkins Trustco did not add the repurchased shares to treasury stock. Instead, they cancelled the shares and returned them to unissued status. This is accounted for with a debit to capital stock at par value and a debit to paid in surplus for the remainder. Give the actual entry Tompkins made.

10-42 Book Value and Return on Equity

Reach Company had net income of $11 million in 20X8. The stockholders' equity section of its 20X8 annual report follows ($ in millions):

	20X8	20X7
Stockholders' equity		
8% Preferred stock, $50 par value, 400,000 shares authorized, 300,000 shares issued	$ 15.0	$ 15.0
Common stock, $1 par, 5 million authorized, 2 million and 1.8 million issued	2.0	1.8
Additional paid-in capital	32.0	30.0
Retained earnings	69.0	65.2
Total stockholders' equity	$118.0	$112.0

1. Compute the book value per share of common stock at the end of 20X8.
2. Compute the rate of return on common equity for 20X8.
3. Compute the amount of cash dividends on common stock declared during 20X8. (*Hint:* Examine the retained earnings T-account.)

10-43 Financial Ratios and Stockholders' Equity

Consider the following data for New York Bankcorp:

	December 31	
	20X2	**20X1**
Stockholders' equity		
Preferred stock, 200,000 shares,		
$20 par, liquidation value $22	$ 4,000,000	$ 4,000,000
Common stock, 4,000,000 shares,		
$2 par	8,000,000	8,000,000
Additional paid-in capital	5,000,000	5,000,000
Retained income	3,000,000	1,400,000
Total stockholders' equity	$20,000,000	$18,400,000

Net income was $2.4 million for 20X2. The preferred stock is 10%, cumulative. The regular annual dividend was declared on the preferred stock, and the common shareholders received dividends of $.20 per share. The market price of the common stock on December 31, 20X2 was $10.00 per share.

Compute the following statistics for 20X2: rate of return on common equity, earnings per share of common stock, price-earnings ratio, dividend-payout ratio, dividend-yield ratio, and book value per share of common stock.

10-44 Stockholders' Equity Section
The following are data for the Roselli Corporation on December 31, 2008.

6% cumulative preferred stock, $40 par value,	
callable at $42, authorized 100,000 shares,	
issued and outstanding 100,000 shares	$ 4,000,000
Treasury stock, common (at cost)	4,000,000
Additional paid-in capital, common stock	9,000,000
Dividends payable	100,000
Retained income	12,000,000
Additional paid-in capital, preferred stock	2,000,000
Common stock, $2.50 par value per share,	
authorized 1.8 million shares, issued 1.2 million	
shares of which 60,000 are held in the treasury	3,000,000

Prepare a detailed stockholders' equity section as it would appear in the balance sheet at December 31, 20X8.

10-45 Effects on Stockholders' Equity
Indicate the effect (+, −, or 0) on total stockholders' equity of General Services Corporation for each of the following:

1. Declaration of a stock dividend on common stock.
2. Sale of 100 shares of General Services by Jay Smith to Tom Jones.
3. Operating loss for the period of $800,000.
4. Issuance of a stock dividend on common stock.
5. Failing to declare a regular dividend on cumulative preferred stock.
6. Declaration of a cash dividend of $50,000 in total.
7. Payment of item 6.
8. Purchase of 10 shares of treasury stock for $1,000 cash.
9. Sale of treasury stock, purchased in item 8, for $1,200.
10. Sale of treasury stock, purchased in item 8, for $800.

Problems

10-46 Dividends and Cumulative Preferred Stock
Renton Interiors, Inc., maker of seats and other interior equipment for Boeing aircraft, started 20X8 with the following balance sheet.

6% Cumulative convertible preferred stock, par value $10 a share, authorized 150,000 shares; issued 52,136 shares	$ 521,360
Common stock, par value $.20 a share, authorized 2,000,000 shares, issued 1,322,850 shares	264,570
Additional paid-in capital	2,063,351
Retained earnings	2,463,951
Less: Treasury stock, at cost	
Preferred stock, 11,528 shares	(80,249)
Common stock, 93,091 shares	(167,549)
Total stockholders' equity	$5,065,434

1. Suppose Renton Interiors had paid no dividends, preferred or common, in the prior year, 20X7. All preferred dividends had been paid through 20X6. Management decided at the end of 20X8 to pay $.04 per share common dividends. Calculate the preferred dividends that would be paid during 20X8. Prepare journal entries for recording both preferred and common dividends. Assume no preferred or common shares were issued or purchased during 20X8.
2. Suppose 20X8 net income was $440,000. Compute the 20X8 ending balance in the Retained Earnings account.

10-47 Dividend Reinvestment Plans

Many corporations have automatic dividend reinvestment plans. Individual shareholders may elect not to receive their cash dividends. Instead, an equivalent amount of cash is invested in additional stock (at the current market value) that is issued to the shareholder.

The Coca-Cola Company had the following data at December 31, 2002 ($ in millions):

Coca-Cola Company

Common stock: authorized 5,600,000,000 shares; $.25 par value; issued 3,490,818,627 shares	$ 873
Capital surplus	3,857
Reinvested earnings	24,506
Accumulated other comprehensive income	(3,047)
	26,189
Less treasury stock, at cost (1,019,839,490 shares)	14,389
	$11,800

1. Coca-Cola declared a quarterly cash dividend of $.20 per share. Suppose holders of 10% of the company's shares decided to reinvest in the company under an automatic dividend reinvestment plan instead of accepting the cash. The market price of the shares on issuance was $40 per share. Prepare the journal entry (or entries) for these transactions. (*Note:* No dividends are paid on shares held in the treasury.)
2. A letter to the editor of *Business Week* commented:

   Stockholders participating in dividend reinvestment programs pay taxes on dividends not really received. If a company would refrain from paying dividends only to take them back as reinvestments, it would save paperwork, and the stockholder would save income tax.

   Do you agree with the writer's remarks? Explain in detail.

10-48 Dividends

(Alternate is 10-49.)

1. The Minneapolis Company issued 400,000 shares of common stock, $5 par, for $25 cash per share on March 31, 20X1. Prepare the journal entry.
2. Minneapolis Company declared and paid a cash dividend of $1 per share on March 31, 20X2. Prepare the journal entry.

3. Minneapolis Company had retained earnings of $9 million by March 31, 20X5. The market value of the common shares was $50 each. A common stock dividend of 5% was declared; the shares were issued on March 31, 20X5. Prepare the journal entry. Also present a tabulation that compares the stockholders' equity section before and after the declaration and issuance of the stock dividend. Also include at the bottom of the tabulation the effects on the overall market value of the stock, the total shares outstanding, and the number of shares and percentage of ownership of an individual owner who originally bought 5,000 shares.

4. What journal entries would be made by the investor who bought 5,000 shares of the Minneapolis common stock and held this investment throughout the time covered in requirements 1, 2, and 3?

5. Refer to requirement 4. Suppose the investor sold 200 shares for $58 each the day after receiving the stock dividend. Prepare the investor's journal entry for the sale of the shares.

10-49 Dividends

(Alternate is 10-48.)

1. Garcia Company issued 600,000 shares of common stock, $1 par, for $9 cash per share on December 31, 20X5. Prepare the journal entry.

2. Garcia Company declared and paid a cash dividend of $.50 per share on December 31, 20X6. Prepare the journal entry. Assume only the 600,000 shares from part 1 are outstanding.

3. Garcia Company had retained earnings of $7 million by December 31, 20X9. The market value of the common shares was $30 each. A common stock dividend of 2% was declared; the shares were issued on December 31, 20X9. Prepare the journal entry. Also present a tabulation that compares the stockholders' equity section before and after the declaration and issuance of the stock dividend. Also include at the bottom of the tabulation the effects on the overall market value of the stock, the total shares outstanding, and the number of shares and percentage of ownership of an individual owner who originally bought 6,000 shares.

4. What journal entries would be made by the investor who bought 4,000 original-issue shares of Garcia Company common stock and held this investment throughout the time covered in requirements 1, 2, and 3?

5. Refer to requirement 4. Suppose the investor sold 200 shares for $33 each the day after receiving the stock dividend. Prepare the investor's journal entry for the sale of the shares.

10-50 Sony Owners' Equity

Sony Corporation is a prominent Japanese electronics company. The following numbers are all expressed in millions of yen (¥). Net income for 2002 was ¥15,310 and Sony paid cash dividends ¥22,992. During the year, Sony had favorable changes to comprehensive income of 52,974 in addition to net income. Sony issued a new tracking stock for ¥9,529 that included a ¥5,612 credit to Additional paid-in capital. Sony paid ¥468 to purchase treasury stock and reissued some treasury shares with an original cost of ¥373 for ¥395. In addition to the transaction specified previously, various other transactions gave rise to the following journal entry:

Common stock	187	
Additional paid-in capital	188	
Retrained earnings	166	
Cash, convertible debt, etc		541

The stockholders' equity at the beginning of the year was:

Common stock, par value Y50 per share	¥ 472,002
Additional paid-in capital	962,401
Retained earnings	1,217,110
Accumulated other comprehensive income	(328,567)
Treasury stock (at cost)	(7,493)
Total stockholders' equity	¥2,315,453

1. Prepare journal entries for (a) the newly issued tracking shares and (b) the purchase and sale of treasury shares. Omit explanations.

2. Prepare a statement of stockholders' equity at the end of the year.

10-51 Meaning of Stock Splits

A letter of January 31 to shareholders of United Financial, a California savings and loan company, said:

> Once again, I want to take the opportunity of sending you some good news about recent developments at United Financial. Last week the board raised United's quarterly cash dividend 12 percent and then declared a 5-for-4 stock split in the form of a 25 percent stock dividend. The additional shares will be distributed on March 15 to shareholders of record February 15.

On March 16, the board approved a merger between National Steel Corporation and United Financial. The agreement called for a cash payment of $33.60 on each outstanding United Financial share. The original National Steel offer (in early February) was $42 per share for the 5.8 million shares outstanding.

1. As a recipient of the letter of January 31, you were annoyed by the five-for-four stock split. Prepare a letter to the chairman indicating the reasons for your displeasure.
2. Prepare a response to the unhappy shareholder in requirement 1.
3. A shareholder of United Financial wrote to the chairman in early March: "I'm confused about the change in the agreed upon price per share. I owned 100 shares and thought I'd receive $4,200. Now the price has dropped from $42.00 to $33.60." Prepare a response to the shareholder.

10-52 Stock Dividend and Fractional Shares

The Soderstrom Company declared and distributed a 5% stock dividend. The stockholders' equity before the dividend was:

Common stock, 10,000,000 shares, $1 par	$ 10,000,000
Additional paid-in capital	40,000,000
Retained earnings	50,000,000
Total stockholders' equity	$100,000,000

The market price of Soderstrom's shares was $10 when the stock dividend was distributed. Soderstrom paid cash of $30,000 in lieu of issuing fractional shares.

1. Prepare the journal entry for the declaration and distribution of the stock dividend.
2. Show the stockholders' equity section after the stock dividend.
3. How did the stock dividend affect total stockholders' equity? How did it affect the proportion of the company owned by each shareholder?

10-53 Issuance and Retirement of Shares, Cash Dividends

On January 2, 20X1, Chippewa Investment Company began business by issuing 10,000 shares at $1 par value for $100,000 cash. The cash was invested, and on December 26, 20X1 all investments were sold for $114,000 cash. Operating expenses for 20X1 were $4,000, all paid in cash. Therefore, net income for 20X1 was $10,000. On December 27, the board of directors declared a $.20 per share cash dividend, payable on January 15, 20X2 to owners of record on December 31, 20X1. On January 30, 20X2, the company bought and retired 1,000 of its own shares on the open market for $8.00 each.

1. Prepare journal entries for issuance of shares, declaration and payment of cash dividends, and retirement of shares.
2. Prepare a balance sheet as of December 31, 20X1.

10-54 Issuance, Splits, Dividends

(Alternate is 10-55.)

1. Lopez Company issued 100,000 shares of common stock, $5 par, for $36 cash per share on December 31, 20X1. Prepare the journal entry.
2. Lopez Company had retained earnings of $4 million by December 31, 20X5. The board of directors declared a two-for-one stock split and immediately exchanged two $2.50 par shares for each

share outstanding. Prepare the journal entry, if any. Present the stockholders' equity section of the balance sheet before and after the split.

3. Repeat requirement 2, but assume that instead of exchanging two $2.50 par shares for each share outstanding, one additional $5 par share was issued for each share outstanding. Lopez said they issued a two-for-one stock split "accounted for as a stock dividend."

4. What journal entries would be made by the investor who bought 2,000 shares of Lopez Company common stock and held this investment throughout the time covered in requirements 1, 2, and 3?

10-55 Issuance, Splits, Dividends

(Alternate is 10-54.) AT&T's December 31, 2002 balance sheet showed total shareowners' equity of $12,312 million and indicated the following detail:

Common stock, par value $1.00 per share	$783,000,000

1. Suppose AT&T had originally issued 200 million shares of common stock, $1 par, for $14 cash per share many years ago, for instance, on December 31, 19X1. Prepare the journal entry.

2. Suppose AT&T had accumulated earnings of $5 billion by December 31, 19X5. The board of directors declared a two-for-one stock split and immediately exchanged two $.50 par shares for each share outstanding. Prepare the journal entry, if any. Present the stockholders' equity section of the balance sheet before and after the split.

3. Repeat requirement 2, but assume that one additional $1 par share was issued by AT&T for each share outstanding (instead of exchanging shares).

4. What journal entries would be made by the investor who bought 2,000 shares of AT&T common stock and held this investment throughout the time covered in requirements 1, 2, and 3?

10-56 Stock Split and 100% Stock Dividend

The Rubin Company wants to double its number of shares outstanding. The company president asks the controller how a two-for-one stock split differs from a 100% stock dividend. Rubin has 300,000 shares ($1 par) outstanding at a market price of $30 per share.

The current stockholders' equity section is:

Common shares, 300,000 issued and outstanding	$ 300,000
Additional paid-in capital	2,300,000
Retained income	4,500,000

1. Prepare the journal entry for a two-for-one stock split.

2. Prepare the journal entry for a 100% stock dividend.

3. Explain the difference between a two-for-one stock split and a 100% stock dividend.

10-57 Treasury Stock

(Alternate is 10-64.) Minnesota Mining and Manufacturing Company (3M) presented the following data in its 2002 annual report:

	December 31	
	2002	2001
	(in millions)	
Stockholders' equity		
Common stock $.01 per share	$ 5	$ 5
Capital in excess of par	291	291
Retained earnings	12,748	11,914
Treasury stock	(4,767)	(4,633)
Other	(2,284)	(1,491)
Stockholders' equity, net	$ 5,993	$ 6,086

1. During 2002, 3M reacquired 7.9 million treasury shares for $942 million. Give the journal entry to record this transaction.
2. 3M also issued some treasury shares as part of their employee stock option and investment plans. What was the cost of treasury shares issued in 2002?
3. Suppose that on January 1, 2003, 3M used cash to reacquire 100,000 shares for $65 each and held them in the treasury. Prepare the stockholders' equity section after the acquisition of treasury stock. Also prepare the journal entry.
4. Suppose the 100,000 shares of treasury stock are sold for $90 per share. Prepare the journal entry.
5. Suppose the 100,000 shares of treasury stock are sold for $50 per share. Prepare the journal entry.

10-58 Treasury Shares

During 2002 outstanding common shares of **General Electric** (GE) increased from 9,925,938,000 to 9,969,894,000. GE declared dividends of $7,266,000,000. The treasury stock account had a beginning balance of $26,916,000,000 and an ending balance of $26,627,000,000, representing 1,175,318,000 shares in 2002 and 1,219,274,000 in 2001. Treasury shares were sold for $595 million more than their cost. Retained income rose from $68,701 million to $75,553 million.

1. Did GE issue any new, previously unissued shares during 2002?
2. Compute the net cash received from sale of the treasury shares during 2002.
3. Compute GE's net income for 2002.
4. Comment on the decision to buy treasury stock instead of using the same dollars to pay additional cash dividends.

10-59 Treasury Shares in Switzerland

Nestlé N.A., the Swiss food and beverage company, is 22% owned by U.S. citizens. It reported the following in its 2002 end-of-year balance sheet (in millions of CHF, swiss frames):

Shareholders' funds		
Share capital	CHF	404
Share premium and reserves		36,993
Less: Treasury shares		(2,578)
Total equity		CHF 34,819

During 2002, Nestlé purchased 1,837,972 of its own shares for CHF 606 million. Sales of 1,103,167 shares generated CHF 392 million. Assume no other changes in Nestlé's holdings of its own shares. The balance in the Own shares account at the beginning of year was CHF 2,794 million.

1. Restate Nestlé's Shareholders' funds section of its balance sheet using terms more commonly used in the United States.
2. Prepare journal entries for Nestlé's purchase of its own shares during the year.
3. Prepare journal entries for Nestlé's reissue of 275 shares for the exercise of stock options. Assume the exercise price was CHF 200 per share and that the reissued shares were all among those purchased during the year.
4. Comment on the average price paid for the shares repurchased this year compared with the proceeds from resale of shares.

10-60 Repurchase of Shares and Book Value per Share

ExxonMobil repurchased common shares during 2002 and, as a result, the Treasury stock account increased by $4,480,000,000. The market price of ExxonMobil shares averaged $37.70 per share during the year. The condensed 2002 shareholders' equity section of the balance sheet showed (dollars in millions):

Common stock, no par	$ 4,217
Earnings reinvested	100,961
Treasury stock	(24,077)
Other	(6,504)
Total stockholders' equity	$ 74,597

1. Estimate the number of shares repurchased for the treasury.
2. Compute the book value per share at December 31, 2002, assuming 6,700 million shares outstanding.
3. Compute the book value per share, assuming the 2002 treasury stock purchase did not occur.

10-61 Retirement of Shares

Houston Financial Systems, Inc., has the following:

Common stock, 6,000,000 shares @ $2 par	$ 12,000,000
Paid-in capital in excess of par	48,000,000
Total paid-in capital	$ 60,000,000
Retained Earnings	10,000,000
Stockholders' equity	$ 70,000,000
Overall market value of stock @ assumed $40	$240,000,000
Book value per share = $70,000,000	
÷ 6,000,000 = $11.67	

The company used cash to reacquire and retire 200,000 shares for $40 each. Prepare the stockholders' equity section before and after this retirement of shares. Also prepare the journal entry.

10-62 Disposition of Treasury Stock

Chirac Company bought 10,000 of its own shares for $10 per share. The shares were held as treasury stock. This was the only time Chirac had ever purchased treasury stock.

1. Chirac sold 5,000 of the shares for $12 per share. Prepare the journal entry.
2. Chirac sold the remaining 5,000 shares later for $9 per share. Prepare the journal entry.
3. Repeat requirement 2, assuming the shares were sold for $7 instead of $9 per share.
4. Did you record gains or losses in requirements 1, 2, and 3? Explain.

10-63 Effects of Treasury Stock on Retained Earnings

Assume that Ming Company has retained earnings of $9 million, paid-in capital of $24 million, and cost of treasury stock of $6 million.

1. Tabulate the effects of dividend payments of (a) $4 million and (b) $1 million on retained earnings and total stockholders' equity.
2. Why do states forbid the payment of dividends if retained earnings does not exceed the cost of any treasury stock on hand? Explain, using the numbers from your answer to requirement 1.

10-64 Treasury Stock

(Alternate is 10-57.) Capetown Company has the following [in rands (R), the South African unit of currency]:

Common stock, 2,000,000 shares @ R3 par	R 6,000,000
Paid-in capital in excess of par	34,000,000
Total paid-in capital	R40,000,000
Retained income	18,000,000
Stockholders' equity	R58,000,000
Overall market value of stock @ assumed R40	R80,000,000
Book value per share = R58,000,000	
÷ 2,000,000 = R29	

1. The company used cash to reacquire 100,000 shares for R40 each and held them in the treasury. Prepare the stockholders' equity section after the acquisition of treasury stock. Also prepare the journal entry.
2. Suppose all the treasury stock is sold for R50 per share. Prepare the journal entry.

3. Suppose all the treasury stock is sold for R30 per share. Prepare the journal entry.
4. Recalculate book value after each preceding transaction.

10-65 Treasury Stock

The following information was provided in footnote 7 of the 2003 H. J. Heinz annual report.

Shareholders' Equity

(in thousands)	Cumulative Preferred Stock $1.70 First Series $10 Par Amount	Common Stock Issued Amount	Common Stock Issued Shares	In Treasury Amount	In Treasury Shares	Additional Capital Amount
Balance May 1, 2002	$110	$107,774	431,096	$(2,893,198)	(80,192)	$348,605
Conversion of preferred into common stock	(4)	—	—	164	6	(160)
Stock options exercised	—	—	—	7,755	311	838
Other, net	—	—	—	5,773	227	27,259
Balance April 30, 2003	$106	$107,774	431,096	$(2,879,506)	(79,648)	$376,542
Authorized Shares— April 30, 2003	11		600,000			

The preferred stock outstanding is convertible into common stock.

Provide summary journal entries to account for the treasury stock transactions during the period May 1, 2002 through April 28, 2003. Omit the journal entry for "Other, net."

10-66 Convertible Securities

Suppose Boston Company had paid $150,000 to Hartford Company for an investment in 10,000 shares of the $5 par value preferred stock of Hartford Company. The preferred stock was later converted into 10,000 shares of Hartford Company common stock ($1 par value).

1. Using the balance sheet equation, prepare an analysis of transactions of Boston Company and Hartford Company.
2. Prepare the journal entries to accompany your analysis in requirement 1.

10-67 Issue of Common Shares

Intermec Corporation, a leader in the field of bar code data collection, issued the following common shares during a recent year:

a. Through a public offering, 780,000 shares were issued for net cash of $10,765,977, an average price of $13.80 per share.
b. As part of an employee stock purchase plan, 16,900 shares, at $218,093 or $12.90 per share, were issued.
c. For the exercise of stock options 88,283 shares, at $355,275 or $4.02 per share, were issued.

The stockholders' equity section of Intermec's balance sheet at the beginning of the year was the following:

Common stock: authorized 10,000,000 shares with $.60 par value, issued and outstanding 4,510,908 shares	$ 2,706,545
Additional paid-in capital	4,603,092
Retained earnings	8,128,230
Total stockholders' equity	$15,437,867

Net income for the year was $4,008,991. No dividends were paid.

1. Prepare journal entries for the common stock issues in a, b, and c. Omit explanations.
2. Present the stockholders' equity section of the balance sheet at the end of the year.

10-68 Noncash Exchanges

Suppose Cartier Company acquires some equipment from Marseilles Company in exchange for issuance of 10,000 shares of Cartier's common stock. The equipment was carried on Marseilles's books at the €520,000 original cost less accumulated depreciation of €100,000. Cartier's stock is listed on the Paris Stock Exchange; its current market value is €50 per share. Its par value is €1 per share.

1. By using the balance sheet equation, show the effects of the transaction on the accounts of Cartier Company and Marseilles Company.
2. Show the journal entries on the books of Cartier Company and Marseilles Company.

10-69 Covenants and Leases and Buying and Selling Stock

Mitchell Energy and Development Corporation was one of the country's largest oil and gas producers. It was purchased by Devon Energy in 2001. Some years ago, the notes to its financial statements reveal the existence of certain debt agreement restrictions on the level of consolidated stockholders' equity as well as on various asset-to-debt ratios:

> The bank credit agreements contain certain restrictions which, among other things, require consolidated stockholders' equity to be equal to at least $300,000,000 and require the maintenance of specified financial and oil and gas reserve and/or asset value to debt ratios.

1. Given the existence of the asset-to-debt covenants, is Mitchell more likely to be able to enter into operating leases or capital leases without violating the covenants?
2. If Mitchell Energy and Development had refused to agree to these conditions at the time of the debt issues, how would it have affected the market price of the debt they issued?
3. In May 2001, Mitchell issued 4.68 million additional shares at $53 per share. Give the journal entry to record the issue, assuming no par stock.
4. In August 2001, Devon Energy agreed to buy Mitchell Energy by giving each shareholder in Mitchell Energy $31 in cash and .585 shares of Devon Energy. Devon's shares were valued at $50.76. How much profit would an investor who bought 1,000 shares in May 2001 make when the merger was complete?

10-70 Financial Ratios

Consider the following data from two companies in very different industries. Adobe Systems is a software company. Empire District is an electric utility serving the Midwest. (Amounts except earnings per share and market price are in thousands.)

	Total Assets	Total Liabilities	Net Income	Earnings per Share	Market Price per Share
Adobe Systems	$1,052,000	$ 378,000	$191,000	$ .96	$39
Empire District	653,000	391,000	28,300	1.29	21

1. Compute the market-to-book ratio and the rate of return on stockholders' equity for both Adobe Systems and Empire District.
2. Explain what might cause the differences in these ratios between the two companies.

10-71 Shareholders' Equity Section

Enron Corporation was a worldwide energy company with annual revenues in excess of $40 billion in 1999. Its main activities were in natural gas and electricity. Enron's collapse was one of the most spectacular elements of the recent past. Enron filed for bankruptcy protection on December 2, 2001, and 2 years later its common stock shares were trading at $.04 per share. Events surrounding Enron led to the failure of its audit firm, Arthur Andersen, and criminal actions against members of its management team are continuing. The data here are from the company's 1999 annual report ($ in millions).

For the year ended December 31	1999	1998
Other	895	70
Common stock held in treasury, 1,337,714 shares		
and 9,333,322 shares, respectively	(49)	(195)
Common stock, no par value, 1,200,000,000		
shares authorized, 716,865,081 shares and 671,094,552		
shares issued, respectively	6,637	5,117
Retained earnings	2,698	2,226
Preferred stock, cumulative, no par value, 1,370,000		
shares authorized, 1,296,184 shares and 1,319,848		
shares issued, respectively	130	132
Accumulated other comprehensive income	(741)	(162)

1. Prepare Enron's shareholders' equity section of the 1999 balance sheet. Include the amount for total stockholders' equity.
2. Enron paid $355 million of cash dividends on common stock and $66 million of cash dividends on preferred stock in 1999. Compute Enron's net income for 1999.
3. Explain Enron's net acquisition or disposition of treasury shares during 1999. Include the increase or decrease in total number of shares and the average cost per share of those acquired or sold. What is the average purchase price (cost) of the shares remaining in the treasury at the end of 1999?
4. Calculate book value per share at December 31, 1999 and the market-to-book ratio on that date, given a market price per share of about $45.
5. The price per share peaked in 2000 at about $91. Estimate the loss in total market value for Enron from its peak until December 2003. Assume 716 million shares outstanding.

10-72 Stock Options and Ethics

Bristol-Myers Squibb is one of the largest pharmaceutical companies in the world. In 2002, the company granted executives options to purchase 40,112,732 shares of common stock. Suppose all shares were granted with an exercise price of $37.55 per share, which was the market price of the stock on the date the options were granted, and all options could be exercised anytime between 3 and 5 years from the grant date, provided that the executive still works for Bristol-Myers Squibb.

Assume at the same time the stock options were issued Bristol-Myers Squibb also issued warrants with the same $37.55 exercise price that are exercisable any time in the next 5 years. The company received $12 for each such warrant.

1. How much expense was recorded at the issue of each stock option?
2. How much value was there to the executive for each stock option issued?
3. How much did it cost the firm for each stock option that was issued?
4. Might the fact that individual executives hold stock options affect their decisions about declaring dividends? Comment on the ethics of this influence.

Collaborative Learning

10-73 Price to Book and ROE

Form groups of three to six students each. Each student should pick two companies, preferably from different industries. Find the appropriate data and compute the market-to-book ratio and the ROE for each company.

Assemble the group and list the companies selected, together with their market-to-book ratio and ROE. Rank the companies from highest to lowest on price to book ratio. Then rank them on ROE.

Explain why companies rank as they do in each list. Are the rankings similar; that is, is the ranking based on market-to-book similar to the rankings on ROE? Explain why you would or would not expect similarity in the rankings.

Analyzing and Interpreting Financial Statements

10-74 Financial Statement Research

Select a company and use its financial statements to answer the following questions:

1. Identify each transaction that affected stockholders' equity during the most recent 2 years.
2. Indicate which accounts were affected and by how much.
3. List any transactions that appear unusual. For example, many companies have a change in shareholders' equity that arises from tax benefits related to stock options. This and a few other common transactions are beyond our scope in this introductory course.

10-75 Starbucks' Annual Report

Use Starbucks' financial statements and notes contained in Appendix A to answer the following questions:

1. Prepare the journal entries to record any dividends declared in the year ended September 28, 2003.
2. Give the journal entries Starbucks used to record the issuance stock in the year ended September 28, 2003.
3. What was the average price per share of stock issued in the year ended September 28, 2003?

10-76 Analyzing Financial Statements Using the Internet: United Parcel Service

Go to www.ups.com to find the home page of United Parcel Service (UPS). Select UPS Investor Relations. Click on Financials to locate UPS's latest annual report.

Answer the following questions about UPS:

1. Identify the classes of stock that UPS has authorized as of the end of its most recent fiscal period, with their par values. Have all the shares in each category been issued? Can you tell if the shares were issued above par? How?
2. How many additional shares of common stock is UPS able to issue as of its most recent balance sheet date? If these shares were all issued and outstanding, how would the values reported on the balance sheet change? Does UPS have any treasury stock?
3. What is the cause of any changes in the Common stock accounts during the period?
4. Did UPS declare any stock splits or stock dividends during its most recent 2-year comparative reporting period? If so, what effect did these have on the number of shares of stock outstanding? Why do you think UPS would want to declare a stock split or stock dividend?
5. Does UPS have a stock option plan? Prior to December 31, 1998, how did UPS account for its common stock held for awards and distributions? What effect did Financial Accounting Standards No. 123 and Accounting Principles Board Opinion No. 25 have on how UPS accounts for its stock options?

Intercorporate Investments and Consolidations

CHAPTER 11

LEARNING OBJECTIVES

After studying this chapter, you should be able to:

1. Explain why corporations invest in one another.

2. Account for short-term investments in debt securities and equity securities.

3. Report long-term investments in bonds.

4. Contrast the equity and market methods of accounting for investments.

5. Prepare consolidated financial statements.

6. Incorporate minority interests into consolidated financial statements.

7. Explain the economic meaning and financial reporting of goodwill.

Deciding to buy and finance a new car is one of the

most important decisions you can make as a consumer. If you have gone through this process, you realize that automakers sell financing (auto loans) as well as automobiles. Wherever you buy a Ford car, you can also "buy" your financing through a fully owned subsidiary, Ford Credit. Just what is the relationship between Ford Motor Company and Ford Credit? They are separate entities, each with its own financial records. However, they are so closely related that authorities require them to combine financial records when preparing financial statements for the public.

On June 16, 2003, Ford Motor Company celebrated the 100th anniversary of its founding by Henry Ford and 11 other investors. Twelve years after the founding, Henry Ford gave a one-line speech to celebrate their successful mass production of automobiles. He said simply "A million of anything is a great many." At that time the company's production lines could produce one Model T every 10 seconds. In 2003, as they celebrated 100 years, total auto production by Ford reached its 300 millionth vehicle.

Exhibit 11-1 provides a brief timeline of Ford's 100-year history. Acquisitions have been a consistent pattern in the life of the company, beginning with the acquisition of Lincoln as an entry into the luxury car market in 1922. This pattern of acquiring prestige brands continued in 1989 with the purchase of Jaguar and in 1999 with the purchase of Volvo. Ford also created some significant businesses internally. The company formed Ford Credit in 1959 and created Motorcraft, its parts supplier, in 1961. All of these companies are wholly owned subsidiaries that Ford consolidates into one set of financial statements.

This Jaguar is manufactured by Ford Motor Company and is easily financed for the buyer by Ford Credit. Ford Motor owns both Jaguar and Ford Credit and presents consolidated financial statements that include all such owned companies.

Exhibit 11-1
Ford Motor
Company and Its
First 100 Years

1903	Henry Ford and 11 investors found the company
1914	Production capacity reached one Model T every 10 seconds; wages of $5 per day were paid, twice the prevailing wage
1915	Henry Ford acknowledged production of millionth car in one line speech: "A million of anything is a great many."
1922	Acquired Lincoln to enter luxury auto market
1956	Sold first shares to the public
1959	Formed Ford Credit
1961	Formed Motorcraft
1979	Acquired 25% of Mazda
1987	Acquired control of Aston Martin
1989	Acquired Jaguar
1994	Hertz becomes wholly owned subsidiary
1999	Acquired Volvo
2000	Acquired Land Rover
2001	Spun-off Visteon
2002	Sold approximately $1 billion of noncore businesses
2003	Manufactured 300 millionth vehicle
June 16, 2003	Celebrated 100th anniversary

Exhibit 11-2
Overview from 2002,
Ford Motor Company
Annual Report

A global overview

Primary Brands	AUTOMOTIVE CORE BRANDS				PREMIER AUTOMOTIVE GROUP	
	Ford	LINCOLN AMERICAN LUXURY	MERCURY	mazda	ASTON MARTIN	JAGUAR
Dealers, Customers, and Competitors	• Approximately 13,000 dealers worldwide • 137 markets worldwide • Major competitors: DaimlerChrysler, Fiat, General Motors, Honda, Nissan, Toyota, Volkswagen, Hyundai/Kia • Major customers: Hewlett-Packard, Phillip Morris International, GlaxoSmithKline, Astra Merck, CNF Logistics, GE, Budget, other commercial accounts, governments, and millions of individuals	• 1,561 dealers worldwide • 38 markets worldwide • Major competitors: General Motors, DaimlerChrysler, Toyota, Nissan, Honda, BMW • Major customers: Hertz, Budget, Hewlett-Packard, CNA, Carey Limousine, Boston Coach, other commercial accounts, and thousands of individuals	• 2,141 dealers worldwide • 15 markets worldwide • Major competitors: DaimlerChrysler, General Motors, Honda, Nissan, Toyota, Volkswagen • Major customers: McDonald's, Hertz, Budget, Hewlett-Packard, CNA, GE, other commercial accounts, and thousands of individuals	• 6,131 dealers worldwide • 145 markets worldwide • Major competitors: Toyota, Nissan, Honda, Mitsubishi, General Motors, DaimlerChrysler, Volkswagen • Major customers: Sekisui House, LDS Church, AstraZeneca, Hertz, other commercial vehicle accounts, and thousands of individuals	• 100 dealers worldwide • 25 markets worldwide • Major competitors: Lamborghini, Ferrari, Porsche • Major customers: individuals	• 787 dealers worldwide • 66 markets worldwide • Major competitors: DaimlerChrysler (Mercedes), BMW, Toyota (Lexus), Porsche • Major customers: Johnson & Johnson, GE, BP, Hertz, other commercial accounts, and thousands of individuals
2002 Highlights	• 5,457,445 vehicle retail sales worldwide • Sales mix: 62% North America 29% Europe 5% Asia-Pacific 3% South America 1% Rest-of-World	• 159,651 vehicle retail sales worldwide • Sales mix: 99% North America 1% Rest-of-World	• 274,875 vehicle retail sales worldwide • Sales mix: 98% North America 2% Rest-ofWorld	• 964,800 vehicle retail sales worldwide** • Sales mix: 39% Asia-Pacific 36% North America 20% Europe 5% Rest-of-World	• 1,551 vehicle retail sales worldwide • Sales mix: 30% North America 30% Europe 30% UK 10% Rest-of-World	• 130,330 vehicle retail sales worldwide • Sales mix: 50% North America 41% Europe 7% Asia-Pacific 2% Rest-of-World

Not all of Ford's companies are wholly owned. In 1979, Ford acquired 25% of Mazda, a Japanese manufacturer. It later increased its ownership interest to 33%. As we see in this chapter, the accounting for a 33% interest in an affiliate is different than the accounting for a wholly owned or even majority-owned subsidiary.

Exhibit 11-2 provides a global overview of the breadth of the Ford Motor Company's activities and brands.

Pick up the annual report of almost any major company (and even most middle-size companies) and you find *consolidated financial statements*. This term means that the books of two or more separate legal entitles have been combined into the statements presented. Ford describes its statements as follows: "Our financial statements include consolidated majority-owned subsidiaries. Affiliates that we do not control, but have significant influence over operating and financial policies, are accounted for using the equity method."

The process of consolidating financial statements used to be an accountant's nightmare. It took days and sometimes nights for many accountants. The consolidated statements filled pages of green 13-column worksheets. Today, thanks to computers and sophisticated software packages, some companies consolidate statements in hours.

Why did Ford buy Jaguar and part of Mazda? Why not all of Mazda? Is the accounting different for 100% ownership than for 33%? We are not able to answer all the strategic questions, but we address some of the questions and explain how the accounting differs between these two cases, and why. ■

		FINANCIAL SERVICES		**CUSTOMER SERVICES**		
VOLVO	**LAND ROVER**	**Ford Credit**	**Hertz**	**QualityCare** Auto Service	**Motorcraft** ACCESSORIES	**Ford** EXTENDED SERVICE PLAN
• 2,500 dealers worldwide • 100 markets worldwide • Major competitors: BMW, Mercedes-Benz, Audi, Lexus • Major customers: GlaxoSmithKline, Johnson & Johnson, Hertz, Coca-Cola, other commercial accounts, and thousands of individuals	• 1,808 dealers worldwide • 142 markets worldwide • Major competitors: Toyota, Nissan, General Motors, DaimlerChrysler, BMW • Major customers: Enterprise Rent-A-Car, BP, Hertz, and thousands of individuals	• Operations in 36 countries • Nearly 300 locations worldwide • 12,500 dealerships worldwide use Ford Credit financing • More than 11 million customers • Major competitors: major banks and credit unions • Major customers: dealers, automotive loan and lease customers, and commercial accounts	• Hertz and Its affiliates, associates, and independent licensees represent what the company believes is the largest worldwide general used car rental brand, based upon revenues, and one of the largest industrial and construction equipment rental businesses in North America, based on revenues • Operations in more than 150 countries and jurisdictions • Approximately 7,000 worldwide locations • Major competitors: Alamo, Avis, Budget, Dollar, Thrifty, Enterprise Rent-A-Car; Europcar, National • Major customers: commercial accounts Including numerous Fortune 500 companies, as well as millions of Individual customers worldwide	• Quality service in Ford, Lincoln, and Mercury dealerships worldwide • Major competitors: Pep Boys, Penske, Midas, Goodyear, Jiffy Lube, Firestone, Master Care • Major customers: Ford, Lincoln, and Mercury owners as well as large and small commercial accounts with fleets of Ford Motor Company branded vehicles	**Motorcraft** • Available in Ford, Lincoln, and Mercury franchised dealers worldwide, Ford Authorized Distributors, and select major retail accounts • Major U.S. competitors: NAPA, Dana, Moog • Major customers: Ford, Lincoln and Mercury vehicle owners **Genuine Ford Accessories** • Available in Ford, Lincoln, and Mercury franchised dealers, Ford Authorized Distributors • Major competitors: Small aftermarket companies and installers in dealers' selling area • Major customers: Ford, Lincoln, and Mercury vehicle owners	**ESP** • 5,000 Ford Lincoln Mercury dealers • Major customers: Ford, Lincoln, and Mercury dealership customers, commercial accounts, fleets of Ford Motor Company branded vehicles **APCO** • Volvo, Land Rover, Mazda and competitive make dealers • Major customers: Volvo, Land Rover, Mazda and competitive make dealership customers **ESP & APCO** • Major competitors: Independent Service Contract providers
• 406,695 vehicle retail sales worldwide • Sales mix: 60% Europe 30% North America 10% Rest-of-World	• 174,593 vehicle retail sales worldwide • Sales mix: 61% Europe 25% North America 14% Rest-of-World	• Nearly $198 billion In assets managed • More than 4 million vehicle financing contracts	• 75% Revenue from US. • 25% Revenue from Rest-of-World • $5 billion revenue	• Over 25 million customers served	**Motorcraft** • Expanded line of remanufactured engines and transmissions **Genuine Ford Accessories** • Growing lineup of electronics equipment: DVD players, alarms and remote starts, dealership lot protection	**ESP & APCO** • Over 2 million vehicle service contracts

An Overview of Corporate Investments

OBJECTIVE 1

Explain why corporations
invest in one another.

When a firm has an excess of cash, smart managers should invest the cash instead of letting it remain idle in the company's checking account. Just as it makes sense for individuals to invest their extra money, it makes sense for a corporation to earn interest income by investing temporarily idle cash. These investments can take on many different forms.

In many instances, companies invest in both short- and long-term debt securities issued by governments, banks, or other corporations. They also invest in corporate equities that may be classified as marketable securities. For example, Ford classified $17.4 billion of marketable securities as current assets on its 2002 automotive balance sheet and also owned $807 million in securities classified as investments by its Financial Services subsidiary as of December 31, 2002.

Corporate Marriage and Divorce

Corporate mergers can be a little like marriages. The challenge is to combine and retain the right combination of people and products to succeed over the long haul. Many companies acquire other companies on a regular basis. For example, Cisco, Microsoft, Intel, Oracle, and other technology companies often buy smaller, innovative young companies to capture their new ideas and, often, their talented employees.

In other cases, firms buy large similar companies hoping to integrate the two firms and create cost savings from eliminating duplications. For example, British Petroleum acquired AMOCO in 1999 and then ARCO in 2000. The resulting company, now called simply BP, is one of the largest companies in the world. In this instance, three companies with very similar operations created the opportunity for major savings when BP eliminated many redundant, repetitive activities and applied best practices throughout the combined entity.

When Sir John Browne, CEO of BP, announced the ARCO purchase, his presentation to analysts ran 18 pages. He initially announced the acquisition in London and followed that announcement with a separate briefing for the investment community in New York. He indicated that the success in merging AMOCO with British Petroleum had enabled this second major acquisition to occur so quickly. The arrangement involved giving each shareholder of ARCO .82 shares of BP in exchange for one share of ARCO. He indicated key reasons for this acquisition:

1. ARCO has significant ownership interests in Alaska, which blend well and efficiently with BP/AMOCO interests in that region.
2. ARCO refining and marketing activity in the lower 48 states blends well with BP/AMOCO and does not overlap, giving the combined entity 13% of the U.S. gasoline market.
3. The combination grows the combined position worldwide in natural gas production by 60%.
4. Estimated total annual savings on operating costs by combining the entities were $1.5 billion.

BP has continued a process of growth through acquisition. In early 2000, it acquired Castrol, a company that controlled 5% of the worldwide lubricants business and was the leading lubricant brand in more than 50 countries. Days later, BP acquired the 18% of Vastar that ARCO did not already own, making Vastar a wholly owned subsidiary.

More recently, in October 2003, BP announced the acquisition of a 50% interest in TNK, a significant Russian petroleum country. As we see later in this chapter, the choice of a 50% interest has significant consequences for how BP accounts for the results of operations for TNK.

Just as not all marriages work, not all business combinations work. This outcome is disturbingly common. *Forbes* (October 30, 2000) cited a study by the accounting firm KPMG that concluded that more than one-half of all deals destroy shareholder value and an additional one-third offer no benefit. By this reckoning, only one-sixth of business combinations succeed. KPMG found that smaller companies were more likely to be successful with mergers. *Forbes* speculated that it may be because smaller companies are more careful and less likely to do deals to impress the public or create growth for the sake of growth. What if the combination does not work? At the worst, the combined company's assets are sold off, the proceeds are distributed to creditors, and the company disappears. See the Business First box on the next page for insights from the Forbes article on creating successful acquisitions.

Sometimes companies sell parts of themselves when they purchase another company. In some cases, the disposition is for strategic reasons, and in others regulators demand it. For example, when BP bought ARCO its plan included the disposition of $3 billion in assets. Because the U.S. government challenged BP's acquisition of ARCO, BP agreed to sell ARCO's Alaskan assets and some of its assets in the North Sea in order to obtain regulatory approval of the transaction.

Another more recent merger in the petroleum industry united Conoco and Phillips Petroleum Company to form ConocoPhillips in 2002. Part of the merged company's strategic plan included reducing the number of gasoline stations it owned. In October 2003, the company announced agreement to sell its Circle K chain of convenience stores that often included branded gasoline outlets.

Not all disposals of parts of a company involve sales. Merck, a prominent pharmaceutical company, more recently spun off its Medco unit. This means that Merck distributed its shares in Medco directly to Merck shareholders so they became the owners of Medco. Merck no longer had any influence or control over Medco. This action separated two very dissimilar businesses. Merck focused on being a high-margin company that developed and then manufactured branded, patent-protected drugs, whereas Medco was a low-margin company that managed the distribution of pharmaceutical drugs to patients.

Spin-offs often separate dissimilar business segments to create opportunities for more creative and innovative growth. They allow managers of the spun-off company to be compensated more directly based on the performance of the new, often smaller, company. Historically, companies that were spun off have performed well and investors who held the shares they received in the spin-off or who acquired the companies when they were initially available as separate firms have earned substantial profits. A more recent study of 146 spin-offs over 30 years concluded that investments in shares of spun-off firms outperformed the stock market by an average of 35% in their first 3 years as separate companies.

After companies create intercorporate linkages, their accountants must develop ways to report on the financial results of these complicated entities. In 1994, Ford increased its ownership in Hertz from 49% to 100%. That change in ownership significantly altered the way Ford accounts for the relationship. In 1996, Ford increased its ownership of Mazda from 25% to 33%, but this change did not alter the fundamental accounting for the relationship. As we will see, current accounting procedures for intercorporate linkages are tied directly to the percentage of ownership, with 20% and 50% being the critical percentages at which accounting treatment changes.

Once the company chooses an accounting procedure that determines how a relationship is to be measured, there is also a question about *where* it is to be reported on the balance sheet, among current or long-term assets. Investments are classified on a balance sheet according to purpose or intention. An investment should be carried as a current asset if it is a short-term investment, one the owner expects to convert to cash. Other investments are classified as noncurrent assets and usually appear as either (1) a separate investments category between current assets and property, plant, and equipment; or (2) a part of other assets below the plant assets category.

CREATING SUCCESSFUL ACQUISITIONS

How does a company increase the odds that its business combination will be one of the successful ones? The **KPMG** study referred to in the text cites shoddy due diligence, a lack of synergy between the two companies, too little planning, and lousy execution as common reasons for failure. The recipe for a successful acquisition is to avoid these pitfalls. More specifically, the *Forbes* article recommends:

1. Do not wait for a deal to come to you. Investment bankers and company brokers represent companies that want to be acquired. They create a packet of information and make presentations to possible acquirers. *Forbes* advises a more active approach, looking for the right partner and being willing to convince them to be acquired instead of choosing among companies who are formally for sale.

2. Stick to your knitting. Expansion should be aimed at doing what you already do more effectively or at modest expansions of the scope of the business. There have been periodic episodes in which conglomerate mergers were popular. These involve buying very diverse businesses on the grounds that management is management and larger is better. These mergers have failed at an even higher rate than usual.

3. Know what you are buying. "Due diligence" is the phrase for carefully investigating the target company. It refers to the corporate equivalent of kicking the tires or having a mechanic examine a potential car purchase. Common important questions include: What is the order backlog? Will critical employees stay? Is the debt subject to a change of ownership clause? Is the company subject to unrecorded liabilities such as environmental pollution or extensive periods of deferred maintenance that leave plant, property, and equipment in need of repair? What are customers and competitors doing? The list is long.

4. Learn their tribal customs. Perhaps the biggest problem that mergers face is that the two companies have very different work cultures. This is easily illustrated with international examples. Consider a U.S. company headed by a rapid decision maker. Although the U.S. buyer might be willing to sign an agreement immediately, a Swiss seller might want to think about it awhile. Although the U.S. buyer might be able to act alone, a Chinese seller might expect to bring many managers into the negotiation to be sure that a consensus was reached. The process for sealing the deal is suggestive about ongoing managerial expectations that differ around the world and even coast to coast in the United States.

5. Start integration well before the deal is closed. If the most difficult task is the merger of workforces and overcoming cultural differences, the preparation for these tasks must start early and receive total attention.

Notice that the accounting issues do not make the list of do's and don'ts. There are important steps in bringing the financial accounting for the combining companies together, but they are rarely critical to their success.

Source: "The Race to Embrace," *Forbes*, October 30, 2000, pp. 184–191.

OBJECTIVE 2

Account for short-term investments in debt securities and equity securities.

short-term investment
A temporary investment in marketable securities of otherwise idle cash.

marketable securities
Any notes, bonds, or stocks that can readily be sold.

short-term debt securities
Largely notes and bonds with maturities of 1 year or less.

Short-Term Investments

As its name implies, a **short-term investment** is a temporary investment of otherwise idle cash in marketable securities. **Marketable securities** are notes, bonds, or stocks that can be easily sold. A company's short-term investment portfolio (total of securities owned) usually consists of short-term debt securities and short-term equity securities. The investments are highly liquid (easily convertible into cash) and have stable prices.

Ordinarily, companies expect to convert items classified as short-term investments into cash within a year after the date on the balance sheet on which they appear. In actuality some of these securities are not converted into cash and are held beyond a 12-month period. Nevertheless, we classify these investments as current assets if management intends to convert them into cash when needed. The key point is that conversion to cash is immediately available at the option of management.

Short-term debt securities consist largely of government- and business-issued notes and bonds with maturities of 1 year or less. They pay a fixed amount of interest, which is usually why investors purchase them. Typically, debt security investments include short-term

	Amortized Cost	Unrealized		Book/Fair Value
		Gains	Losses	
Trading	$143	$ —	$ —	$143
Available-for-sale-				
U.S. government and agency	163	9	—	172
Municipal	1	—	—	1
Government—non-U.S.	20	—	—	20
Corporate debt	172	10	—	182
Mortgage-backed	215	9	—	224
Equity	46	20	7	59
Total	617	48	7	658
Held-to-maturity				
U.S. government	6	—	—	6
Total	$766	$48	$ 7	$807

Exhibit 11-3

Ford Motor Company, Financial Services Sector Marketable and Other Securities Footnote
Investments in Securities at December 31, 2002 ($ in Millions)

obligations of banks, called **certificates of deposit,** and **commercial paper,** consisting of short-term notes payable issued by large corporations with top credit ratings. They also include **U.S. Treasury obligations,** which refer to interest-bearing notes, bonds, and bills issued by the federal government. All these debt securities may be held until maturity or may be resold in securities markets.

Short-term equity securities consist of capital stock (shares of ownership) in other corporations. Companies, as well as individuals, regularly buy and sell equity securities on the NYSE or other stock exchanges. If the investing firm intends to sell the equity securities it holds within 1 year or within its normal operating cycle, then we classify the securities as short-term investments.

At acquisition, companies record these securities at cost. How they are reported after acquisition depends on whether they are classified as trading securities, available-for-sale securities, or held-to-maturity securities. You can see these three categories in the footnote to Ford's 2002 financial statements shown in Exhibit 11-3.

Trading securities are short-term investments, including both debt and equity securities, that the company buys with the intent to resell them shortly. Companies list such securities among current assets on their balance sheets and measure them at market value (or fair value). As shown in Exhibit 11-3, $143 million of Ford's short-term investments in its Financial Services operations are trading securities (see top row).

Held-to-maturity securities are debt securities that the company purchases with the intent to hold them until they mature. They are shown on the balance sheet at amortized cost, not market value. In Chapter 9, we examined the amortization of premiums and discounts on bonds payable by the issuer of the debt. Corporations that invest in bonds use the same approach, as illustrated later in this chapter. Unlike trading securities, which are always classified as short term because of the owner's intention, held-to-maturity securities are classified according to the time remaining until they mature. If the time to maturity is less than 1 year they are short-term investments, and thus current assets. Otherwise, they are long-term investments, and thus noncurrent assets. Only $6 million of Ford's Financial Services investments are held-to-maturity securities.

Available-for-sale securities include all debt and equity securities that are neither trading securities nor held-to-maturity securities. They include equity securities that the company does not intend to sell in the near future and debt securities that the company neither plans to sell shortly nor to hold to maturity. Ford provides separate lines under this category for many different types of securities held by its Financial Services operations. Note that most are debt securities of one type or another issued by the U.S. Treasury, municipalities, foreign governments, or corporations. The amount reported on the balance sheet is the market value of $658 million, which is $41 million greater than the original $617 million cost of these securities.

certificates of deposit
Short-term obligations of banks.

commercial paper
Short-term notes payable issued by large corporations with top credit ratings.

U.S. Treasury obligations
Interest-bearing notes, bonds, and bills issued by the U.S. government.

short-term equity securities
Capital stock in other corporations held with the intention to liquidate within 1 year as needed.

trading securities
Current investments in equity or debt securities held for short-term profit.

held-to-maturity securities
Debt securities that the investor expects to hold until maturity.

available-for-sale securities
Investments in equity or debt securities that are not held for active trading but may be sold before maturity.

The total investments by the Financial Services operations of Ford, the amount shown in various parts of Ford's balance sheet, is the $807 million shown at the bottom of the far right-hand column of Exhibit 11-3. It is the market value of trading securities and available-for-sale securities combined with the amortized cost of the held-to-maturity securities.

Changes in Market Prices of Securities

You now know how short-term investments are shown on the balance sheet. How do we account for the returns on these investments?

Held-to-maturity investments are easiest to account for because interest revenue is the only return reported on such securities. Changes in market value are ignored. Interest revenue appears directly on the income statement, increasing income and therefore increasing stockholders' equity.

Returns on trading securities and available-for-sale securities come in two forms: (1) dividend or interest revenue, and (2) changes in market value. The former are recorded on the income statement when earned for all securities. However, we treat changes in market value differently for trading securities than for available-for-sale securities. As the market value of *trading* securities changes, companies report the gains from increases in price and the losses from decreases in price in the income statement. In contrast, the gains and losses that arise as market values of *available-for-sale* securities rise and fall are not shown on the income statement. Instead, we add such unrealized gains and losses to a separate account in the stockholders' equity section of the balance sheet. This account increases stockholders' equity for securities whose price has increased since purchase. It decreases stockholders' equity for securities that have experienced a drop in prices. Ford shows $7 million of unrealized losses and $48 million of unrealized gains on available-for-sale securities, for a net increase in stockholders' equity of $41 million.

Notice that increases in prices of both trading securities and available-for-sale securities increase stockholders' equity, and decreases in prices decrease stockholders' equity. For trading securities, the increase or decrease is included in retained earnings because the gains and losses are included in net income. For available-for-sale securities, the increase or decrease is in a separate account included in owners' equity. Ford calls this separate account "net holding gain" in 2002, whereas in 2001 it was a "net holding loss." Travelers calls it "net unrealized gain (loss) on investment securities," whereas Washington Mutual, a rapidly growing bank, uses the label "net unrealized gain from securities." You will generally find the details of these amounts in the footnotes and in the Statement of Changes in Shareholders' Equity, with only a summary line in the Income Statement or the Balance Sheet.

market method
Method of accounting that reports market values of publicly traded securities in the balance sheet; for trading securities changes in market value affect the income statement; for available-for-sale securities changes affect owners' equity directly.

We call this method of accounting for trading securities and available-for-sale securities the market method. Under the **market method,** the reported asset values in the balance sheet are the market values of the publicly traded securities. In the following example, we ignore tax effects. Suppose two companies acquire identical assets at the same price on the same day, but one company reported them as trading securities and the other reported them as available-for-sale securities. The two companies would report identical asset values on their balance sheets, but they would differ in how they report changes in those market values. Assume the portfolio of assets purchased by the two companies cost $50 million and had the market values at the end of four subsequent periods shown in Exhibit 11-4 ($ in millions).

Exhibit 11-4 shows the results for four periods. Most companies present the market value directly as a single line on the balance sheet. The notes provide the linkage to cost and the amount of unrealized gain or (loss).

The unrealized gain (loss) for trading securities affects net income and therefore also increases (decreases) retained earnings. Over the four periods, the loss of $5 million and subsequent gains of $2 million and $7 million provide a cumulative net increase in retained earnings of $4 million by the end of period 4 ($9 million of gains less $5 million of losses).

	End of Period			
	1	**2**	**3**	**4**
Assumed market value	50	45	47	54
Asset presentation—both methods				
Short-term investment at cost	50	50	50	50
Unrealized gain (loss)	0	(5)	(3)	4
Carrying value/fair value	50	45	47	54
For trading securities				
Income statement presentation				
Unrealized gain (loss) on changes in market	0	(5)	2	7
For available-for-sale securities				
Owners' equity presentation				
Unrealized gain (loss)	0	(5)	(3)	4

Exhibit 11-4
Financial Statement Presentation
Trading Securities and Available-for-Sale Securities ($ in millions)

Notice that we use the term unrealized gain (loss) to describe three different items: (1) the adjustment to historical cost to arrive at fair value on the balance sheet, (2) the effect on net earnings for trading securities, and (3) the separate account in owners' equity for available-for-sale securities. This is common, and you will need to determine the precise meaning of the term from its context.

The journal entries for the two classes of securities for periods 2, 3, and 4 would appear as follows, without explanations:

PERIOD	**TRADING SECURITIES**			**AVAILABLE-FOR-SALE-SECURITIES**		
2	Unrealized Loss*	5		Unrealized Gain or Loss**	5	
	Marketable Securities		5	Marketable Securities		5
3	Marketable Securities	2		Marketable Securities	2	
	Unrealized Gain*		2	Unrealized Gain or Loss**		2
4	Marketable Securities	7		Marketable Securities	7	
	Unrealized Gain*		7	Unrealized Gain or Loss**		7

*an income statement account
**a balance sheet account

INTERPRETING FINANCIAL STATEMENTS

In Exhibit 11-4, the carrying value on the balance sheet is identical for both trading and available-for-sale securities. However, the numbers shown for trading and available-for-sale securities in the bottom half of the table are the same in period two, but not in periods three and four. Explain.

Answer
The carrying values on the balance sheet are the same, but for trading securities gains and losses appear in the income statement. The income statement amounts show the *change* in market value each period. In contrast, available-for-sale securities do not affect the income statement. Instead, owners' equity reflects the difference between market value and cost at the end of each period. In the second period, the change in market value is also the end-of-period difference between cost and market, so both securities show ($5). However, in period three, the change shown in the income statement for trading securities is $2 based on the increase in value *during the period*. For available-for-sale securities, the difference between market and cost is ($3), which is the net *cumulative* result of the ($5) loss in period two and the $2 gain in period three.

Comprehensive Income

For many companies, especially some in high-tech industries, it is common to invest in other companies and to treat the investment as an available-for-sale security. The change in the economic value of the investor is not fully revealed in the income statement of the investor. Why? Because the increase or decrease in value of these securities is shown only on the balance sheet: among assets because the market value of the asset is reported, and in owners' equity because the difference between cost and market is included in owners' equity. To understand the changes during the year, comprehensive income is calculated as part of the statement of owner's equity. Two similar firms, one with trading securities and one with available-for-sale securities would not have comparable net earnings but would have comparable comprehensive income reported. Comprehensive income includes net income, changes in the value of available-for-sale securities and a few other items beyond the scope of this text.

In the balance sheet, included in owners' equity, Ford reports Accumulated other comprehensive income (loss) of $(6,531) million in 2002 and $(5,913) million in 2001. These are cumulative amounts, which means the accumulated other comprehensive loss increased by $618 million during 2002. Unrealized gains on available-for-sale securities were offset by other comprehensive income items that are beyond the scope of this discussion.

Long-Term Investments in Bonds

OBJECTIVE 3

Report long-term investments in bonds.

Chapter 9 explained the basic approach issuing firms use to account for bonds payable. Recall that the issuer amortizes bond discounts and premiums as periodic adjustments of interest expense. Investing firms use a similar method to account for bonds held to maturity. However, although the issuer typically keeps a separate account for unamortized discounts and premiums, investors do not (although they could if desired).

Bonds-Held-to-Maturity

Exhibit 11-5 should look familiar. It is basically the same as Exhibit 9-4 on page 398, except that our perspective has changed from issuer to that of investor. Therefore, we use the phrase *book value* to refer to the first column instead of the label net liability used in Exhibit 9-4. Recall that book value is a general term referring to the amount reported in the financial statements under GAAP.

Exhibit 11-5 shows the values for 10,000 2-year bonds paying interest semiannually with a face value of $1,000 each and a 10% coupon rate (5% interest every 6 months). The bonds were issued to yield 12%. Because they pay only a 10% coupon interest rate, they are sold at a discount. Therefore, despite the face value of $10,000,000, an investor acquiring the whole issue would initially pay only $9,653,500. Interest (rental payment for the $9,653,500) takes two forms—four semiannual cash receipts of $500,000 (5% × $10 million), plus an extra lump-sum receipt of $346,500 ($10 million face value less amount paid at issue) at maturity.

The extra $346,500 to be paid at maturity (the amount of the discount) relates to the use of the proceeds over the 2 years. Therefore, like the issuer, the investor amortizes the discount:

	6/30/04	12/31/04	6/30/05	12/31/05
Semiannual interest revenue:				
Cash interest payments, .05 × $10 million	$500,000	$500,000	$500,000	$500,000
Amortization of $346,500 discount*	79,207	83,959	88,997	94,337
Semiannual interest revenue	$579,207	$583,959	$588,997	$594,337

*For the amortization schedule, see column 4 of Exhibit 11-5. Note that $79,207 + $83,959 + $88,997 + $94,337 = $346,500.

For 6 Months Ended	(1) Beginning Book Value	(2) Effective Interest @6%*	(3) Nominal Interest @ 5%	(4) Discount Amortized (2)–(3)	Period End Values		
					Face Amount	Unamortized Discount	Ending Book Value
12/31/03	—	—	—	—	$10,000,000	$346,500	$9,653,500
6/30/04	$9,653,500	$579,207	$500,000	$79,207	10,000,000	267,293†	9,732,707
12/31/04	9,732,707	583,959	500,000	83,959	10,000,000	183,334†	9,816,666
6/30/05	9,816,666	588,997	500,000	88,997	10,000,000	94,337	9,905,663
12/31/05	9,905,663	594,337	500,000	94,337	10,000,000	0	10,000,000

*To avoid rounding errors, an unrounded actual effective rate slightly under 6% was used.
†$346,500 − $79,207 = $267,293; $267,293 − $83,959 = $183,334; etc.

Exhibit 11-5
Effective Interest Amortization of Bond Discount

As Exhibit 11-5 shows, the discount is used to make up the difference between the coupon interest rate of 10% and the market interest rate of 12%. Amortization of a discount increases the interest revenue of investors. (Investor accounting for bonds issued at a premium is similar, except that amortization of premium decreases the interest revenue of investors.)

Exhibit 11-6 shows how the investor and the issuer account for the bonds throughout the bonds' lives. Note that interest revenue and interest expense are identical in each period.

	Investor's Records			Issuer's Records		
12/31/03	1. Investment in bonds	9,653,500		1. Cash	9,653,500	
	Cash		9,653,500	Discount on bonds payable	346,500	
				Bonds payable		10,000,000
6/30/04	2. Cash	500,000		2. Interest expense	579,207	
	Investment in bonds	79,207		Discount on bonds payable		79,207
	Interest revenue		579,207	Cash		500,000
12/31/04	Cash	500,000		Interest expense	583,959	
	Investment in bonds	83,959		Discount on bonds payable		83,959
	Interest revenue		583,959	Cash		500,000
6/30/05	Cash	500,000		Interest expense	588,997	
	Investment in bonds	88,997		Discount on bonds payable		88,997
	Interest revenue		588,997	Cash		500,000
12/31/05	Cash	500,000		Interest expense	594,337	
	Investment in bonds	94,337		Discount on bonds payable		94,337
	Interest revenue		594,337	Cash		500,000
12/31/05	3. Cash	10,000,000		3. Bonds payable	10,000,000	
	Investment in bonds		10,000,000	Cash		10,000,000

Exhibit 11-6
Accounting for Bonds

PANEL A: INVESTOR'S LOSS

Carrying amount		
Face or par value	$10,000,000	
Deduct: Unamortized discount on bonds*	183,334	$9,816,666
Cash received		9,600,000
Difference, loss on sale		$ 216,666

*The remaining discount is $88,997 + $94,337 = $183,334, or $346,500 − $79,207 − $83,959 = $183,334.

PANEL B: JOURNAL ENTRIES AT DECEMBER 31, 2004

Investor's Records			Issuer's Records		
Cash	9,600,000		Bonds payable	10,000,000	
Loss on disposal			Discount on		
of bonds	216,666		bonds payable		183,334
Investment in bonds		9,816,666	Gain on early		
To record the sale of bonds			extinguishment		216,666
on the open market			Cash		9,600,000

Exhibit 11-7
Early Extinguishment

Early Extinguishment of Investment

Suppose in our example that the issuer buys back all its bonds on the open market for $9.6 million on December 31, 2004 (after all interest payments and amortization were recorded for 2004). The investor's loss is calculated in panel A of Exhibit 11-7. The journal entries for the investor and the issuer are shown in panel B.

Recall that this same extinguishment of debt was initially analyzed from the issuer's viewpoint in Chapter 9. Note that for the issuer to extinguish the bonds early, either the bond must grant the issuer the right to repay the debt early or the investor must choose to sell the bonds back to the issuer.

The Market and Equity Methods for Intercorporate Investments

OBJECTIVE 4

Contrast the equity and market methods of accounting for investments.

affiliated company
A company that has 20% to 50% of its voting shares owned by another company.

equity method
Accounting for an investment at acquisition cost, adjusted for the investor's share of dividends and earnings or losses of the investee subsequent to the date of investment.

Many companies invest in the equity securities of another company. The accounting for equity securities from the issuer's point of view was discussed in Chapter 10. The investor's accounting depends on the relationship between the "investor" and the "investee." The question is: How much can the investor influence the operations of the investee? For example, the holder of a small number of shares in a company's stock cannot affect how the company invests its money, conducts its business, or declares and pays its dividends. We call this type of investor a passive investor. Such investors use the market method described earlier, and report the investment at market value and record dividends as income when received.

As investors acquire more substantial holdings of a company's stock, they have increased influence. A stockholder with 2% or 3% ownership of a company has little difficulty making appointments to speak with company management. At 5% ownership, U.S. law requires the investor to report the ownership publicly in a filing with the SEC. As ownership interest rises to 20% and beyond, the investor begins to affect decisions, to appoint directors, and so on.

Once the investor has "significant influence," a term that GAAP defines as 20% to 50% ownership, the market method no longer reflects the economic relationship between the potentially active investor and the investee (or **affiliated company**). In the United States, such an investor must use the **equity method,** which records the investment at acquisition cost and makes adjustments for the investor's share of dividends and earnings or losses experienced by the investee after the date of investment. As a result, the investor's share of the investee's earnings increases the book value at which the investment is carried and reported. Likewise, dividends received from the investee and the investor's share of the investee's losses reduce this carrying amount.

Many companies have "significant influence" levels of stock ownership in other, usually smaller, companies. For example, Corning, Inc., a technology company that is the world's leader in fiber-optic cable, holds such ownership in 19 companies. One such company is the South Korean glass company, Samsung Corning, in which Corning recently held exactly a 50% interest. In total, Corning's consolidated statement of operations for 2002 showed equity in earnings of associated companies of $116 million.

Let us take a look at an example of how the market and equity methods might be applied. Suppose Buyit Corporation invests $80 million in each of two companies, Passiveco and Influential. Influential has a total market value of $200 million, generates earnings of $30 million, and pays dividends of $10 million. Because of its $80 million investment, Buyit owns 40% ($80 million ÷ $200 million) of Influential and must account for that investment using the equity method. Passiveco, however, has a total market value of $800 million, generates earnings of $120 million, and pays dividends of $40 million. Buyit thus owns only 10% ($80 million ÷ $800 million) of Passiveco and must use the market method to account for this investment.

We compare the methods in Exhibit 11-8. Panel A shows the effects on the balance sheet equation, and panel B shows the different journal entries for the two cases. The example assumes that the market values of Passiveco and Influential do not change during the period.

PANEL A: EFFECTS ON THE BALANCE SHEET EQUATION

	Market Method—Passiveco*				Equity Method—Influential**			
	A		=	L + SE	A		=	L + SE
	Cash	Investments		Liab.	SE	Cash	Investment		Liab.	SE
1. Acquisition	−80	+80	=			−80	+80	=		
2. a. Net income of Passiveco	No entry and no effect									
b. Net income of Influential							+12	=		+12
3. a. Dividends from Passiveco	+ 4		=		+4					
b. Dividends from Influential						+ 4	− 4	=		
Effect for year	−76	+80	=		+4	−76	+88	=		+12

*Passiveco: Under the market method, the investment account is unaffected. The dividend increases the cash amount by $4 million. Dividend revenue increases stockholders' equity by $4 million.
**Influential: Under the equity method, the investment account has a net increase of $8 million for the year. The dividend increases the cash account by $4 million and reduces investments. Investment revenue increases stockholders' equity by $12 million.

PANEL B: JOURNAL ENTRIES

Cost Method—Passiveco			Equity Method—Influential		
1. Investment in Passiveco	80		1. Investment in Influential	80	
Cash		80	Cash		80
2. No entry			2. Investment in Influential	12	
			Investment revenue† · · · · · · · ·		12
3. Cash	4		3. Cash	4	
Dividend revenue† · · · · · · · · · ·		4	Investment in Influential		4

†Frequently called "equity in earnings of affiliated companies."
†Frequently called "dividend income."

Exhibit 11-8
Comparing Market and Equity Methods (in million of dollars)

Under the market method, Buyit recognizes income from Passiveco when dividends are received. Although the income statement and retained earnings are affected, Buyit's investment account is unaffected by the event. Under the equity method, Buyit recognizes income as it is earned by Influential instead of when dividends are received. Cash dividends from Influential do not affect net income; they increase cash and decrease the investment balance. Buyit's claim on Influential grows by its share of Influential's net income and the dividend is a partial liquidation of Buyit's "claim." It would be double-counting to include the $4 million of dividends as income after the $12 million of income is already recognized in Buyit's income statement as it is earned.

The major reason for using the equity method instead of the market method is that the equity method does a better job of recognizing increases or decreases in the economic resources that the investor can influence. The reported net income of an "equity" investor (an investor who owns more than 20% of a company and thus uses the equity method) is increased by its share of net income or decreased by its share of net loss recognized by the investee.

Why does GAAP not permit shares accounted for under the equity method to be carried as an asset valued at market price? One explanation is that market prices are only good estimates of sales prices when small transactions occur. For example, 1.8 million of the 153 million outstanding shares of Tricon changed hands on February 3, 2000, a typical day. An investor who wanted to sell 100, 1,000, or even 10,000 shares could do so at about the $29 per share market price observed that day. However, if an investor owned 30% of Tricon and wanted to sell those 46 million shares, it could have a huge effect on the market price, potentially driving it down sharply. Thus, quoted market prices are not good measures of the value of large ownership interests. In addition, observed market prices may not be good estimates of the value of larger equity interests because the investor and investee have significant business relationships. For example, they may be customer and supplier or have joint R&D enterprises, or they may have overlapping boards of directors. In such cases, sale of a large investment interest might also mean significant changes to future business relationships and therefore changes in the value of the investee.

Summary Problem for Your Review

PROBLEM

The following is a summary of material from a recent Dow Chemical annual report ($ in millions):

	$:
Marketable securities and interest-bearing deposits	706
	:
Total current assets	8,847
Investments:	
Investment in nonconsolidated affiliates	1,359
Other investments	2,872
Noncurrent receivables	390
Total investments	4,621
Properties	24,276
Less: Accumulated depreciation	15,786
Net property	8,490
Goodwill	1,834
Deferred charges and other assets	1,707
Total	$25,499

Note that the statements are somewhat compressed and no detail for current assets is shown.

1. Suppose "Marketable securities" included a $24 million portfolio of equity securities. Their market values on the following March 31, June 30, and September 30 were $20, $23, and $28 million, respectively. Compute the following:
   a. Carrying amount of the portfolio on each of the three dates.
   b. Gain (loss) on the portfolio for each of the three quarters.
2. Suppose the $2,872 million of "Other investments" included a $9 million investment in the debentures of an affiliate that was being held to maturity. The debentures had a par value of $10 million and a 10% nominal rate of interest, payable June 30 and December 31. Their market rate of interest when the investment was made was 12%. Prepare the Dow journal entry for the semiannual receipt of interest on June 30.
3. Suppose Dow's 20% to 50% owned companies had net income of $200 million. Dow received cash dividends of $70 million from these companies. No other transactions occurred. Prepare the pertinent journal entries. Assume that on average Dow owns 40% of the companies.

SOLUTION

1. Amounts are in millions.
   a. Market: $20, $23, and $28.
   b. $20 − $24 = $4 loss; $23 − $20 = $3 gain; $28 − $23 = $5 gain. Gain or loss would be reported in the income statement for trading securities or in the stockholders' equity section for securities available for sale.

2.

Cash	500,000	
Other Investments (in bonds)	40,000	
Interest revenue		540,000

Six months' interest earned is
.5 × .12 × $9,000,000 = $540,000
Amortization is $540,000 − cash received of
.5 × .10 × $10,000,000 = $540,000 − $500,000

3.

Investments in 20% to 50% owned companies	80,000,000	
Investment revenue		80,000,000

To record 40% share of $200 million income

Cash	70,000,000	
Investments in 20% to 50% owned companies		70,000,000

To record dividends received from 20% to 50% owned companies

OBJECTIVE 5

Prepare consolidated financial statements.

parent company
A company owning more than 50% of the voting shares of another company, called the subsidiary company.

subsidiary
A corporation owned or controlled by a parent company through the ownership of more than 50% of the voting stock.

Consolidated Financial Statements

So far we have dealt with partial ownership of one company by another. Sometimes, though, as in the case of Ford and Jaguar, one company buys 100% of another company. In other cases, one company buys a majority (more than 50%) share of a second company and effectively takes control of that second company. In these cases a parent–subsidiary relationship exists. The **parent company** is the owner, and the **subsidiary** is the "owned" company that is fully owned or controlled by the parent. Keep in mind that subsidiaries are not folded into the parent company, but instead remain separate legal entities from their parents. One parent can have numerous subsidiaries. Ford Motor Company actually has some 60 different subsidiaries just in the United States, as well as several others, including Jaguar, outside the United States.

Why have subsidiaries? Why not integrate the smaller companies into the larger parent to create a single legal entity? The reasons include limiting the liabilities in a risky venture, saving income taxes, conforming with government regulations with respect to a part of the business, doing business in a foreign country, and expanding in an orderly way while retaining the ability to subsequently sell or spin off the separate corporate subsidiary. For example, there are often tax advantages for the sellers when an acquisition involves the capital stock of a going concern instead of its individual assets.

Sometimes foreign subsidiaries face more favorable treatment from their country of residence than a foreign parent corporation would experience. When Merck spun off Medco, the transaction was easier and less costly because Medco was an existing separate subsidiary corporation.

So how do we account for subsidiaries if they are separate legal entities? We start by keeping records for the subsidiary that are independent of the parent's, then we combine the financial positions and earnings reports of the parent company with those of its subsidiaries to create **consolidated statements.**

consolidated statements
Combinations of the financial positions and earnings reports of the parent company with those of various subsidiaries into an overall report as if they were a single entity.

The Acquisition

To illustrate consolidated financial statements, consider two companies: the parent (P) and a subsidiary (S). Initially, they are separate companies with assets of $650 million and $400 million, respectively. P acquires all the stock of S by purchasing the shares from their current owners for $213 million paid in cash. The transaction is illustrated in panel A of Exhibit 11-9. Exhibit 11-9 shows the balance sheets of the two companies before and after this transaction in panel B. Panel C shows the journal entries for the acquisition. Figures in this and subsequent tables and discussion are in millions.

This purchase transaction is a simple exchange of one asset for another, from P's perspective. In terms of the balance sheet equation, cash declines by $213, and the asset account, Investment in S, increases by the same amount (remember that amounts are in millions). The subsidiary S is entirely unaffected from an accounting standpoint, although it now has one centralized owner with unquestionable control over economic decisions S may make in the future. In this example, the purchase price and the "Investment in S" equal the stockholders' equity of the acquired company. Note that the $213 purchase price is paid to the former owners of S as private investors. The $213 is not an addition to the existing assets and stockholders' equity of S. That is, the books of S are unaffected by P's investment and P's subsequent accounting thereof. S still exists as a separate legal entity, but with a new owner, P.

Each legal entity keeps its own set of books. Interestingly, no books are kept for the consolidated entity. Instead, working papers are used to prepare the consolidated statements as shown schematically in Exhibit 11-10.

How do we consolidate the financial statements? Basically, we add up the individual financial statement values of the parent and the subsidiary. Consider a consolidated balance sheet prepared immediately after P's acquisition of S. The consolidated statement shows the details of all assets and liabilities of both the parent and the subsidiary. The Investment in S account on P's books represents P's investment in S, which is really composed of all the assets and liabilities of S. This same amount is represented in S's books by stockholders' equity. If the consolidated statements simply add the individual balance sheet values of S and P, the $213 amount is represented twice, once as P's Investment in S account, and again in S's stockholders' equity. The consolidated statements cannot count this amount twice because true assets and liabilities will be misstated. We avoid this double-counting by eliminating the investment in S on P's books, and the stockholders' equity on S's books.

On the work sheet for consolidating the balance sheets, the entry to eliminate the double-counting of ownership interest in journal format is:

Stockholders' equity (on S books)   213
    Investment in S (on P books)   213

Exhibit 11-9
Before and After the
Acquisition, Parent
(P) Buys Subsidiary
(S) for $213
($ in millions)

PANEL A: THE EVENTS

100% Purchase of S by P

Before Purchase

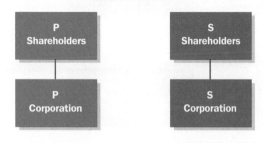

Purchase

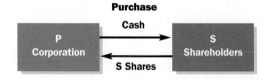

P Pays Cash to Shareholders in S

After Purchase

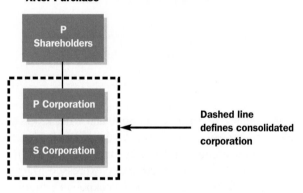

Dashed line
defines consolidated
corporation

PANEL B: THE BALANCE SHEETS

	Before Purchase		After Purchase	
	S	P	S	P
Cash	$100	$300	$100	$ 87
Net plant	300	350	300	350
Investment in S				213
Total assets	$400	$650	$400	$650
Accounts payable	$187	$100	$187	$100
Bonds payable	—	100	—	100
Stockholders' equity	213	450	213	450
Total liabilities and SE	$400	$650	$400	$650

The following journal entries occur:

PANEL C: THE JOURNAL ENTRIES

P Books

Investment in S 213
   Cash 213

S Books

No entry

Exhibit 11-10
Preparing
Consolidated
Statements

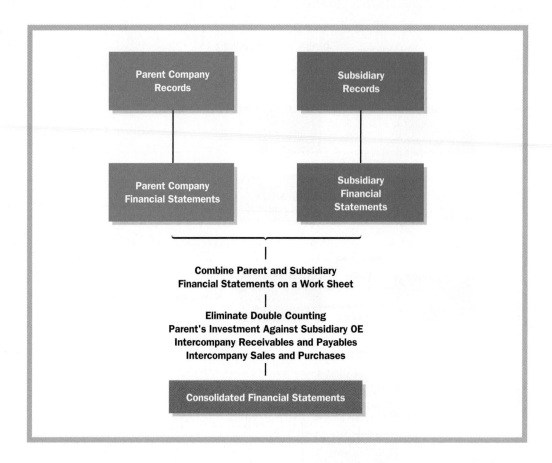

Separately, after the purchase, P has assets of $650 and S has assets of $400, so you might think the consolidated company would have assets totaling $1,050. However, when we consolidate and eliminate the double-counting of the investment amount in S, the consolidated assets are $1,050 − $213, or $837. The consolidated result, expressed in terms of the accounting equation, shows consolidated liabilities of $387 and stockholder's equity of $450 as follows:

100% Ownership

	Assets			=	Liabilities	+	Stockholders' Equity
	Investment in S	+	Cash and Other Assets	=	Accounts Payable, etc.	+	Stockholders' Equity
P's accounts, Jan. 1							
Before acquisition			650	=	200	+	450
Acquisition of S	+213		−213	=			
S's accounts, Jan. 1			400	=	187	+	213
Intercompany							
eliminations	−213			=			−213
Consolidated, Jan. 1	0	+	837	=	387	+	450

After Acquisition

After the initial acquisition, P accounts for its long-term investment in S by the same equity method used to account for an unconsolidated ownership interest of 20% through 50%. Suppose S has a net income of $50 million for the subsequent year (year one). The parent company P using the equity method accounts for the net income of its subsidiary by increasing its Investment in S account and its Stockholders' Equity account (in the form of retained earnings) by 100% of $50 million.

The income statements for the year are (numbers in millions assumed):

	P	S	Consolidated
Sales	$900	$300	$ 1,200
Expenses	800	250	1,050
Operating income	$100	$ 50	$ 150
Investment revenue*	50	—	
Net income	$150	$ 50	

*Pro rata share (100%) of subsidiary net income, often called equity in earnings of affiliate or subsidiary.

P's parent-company-only income statement would show its own sales and expenses plus its proportional share of S's net income (as the equity method requires). This is shown in the leftmost column of the preceding table. The income statement for P shows the same $150 million net income as the consolidated income statement. The difference is that P's "parent-only" income statement shows its 100% share of S as a single $50 million item, whereas the consolidated income statement combines the detailed revenue and expense items for P and S. The journal entry on P's books is:

```
Investment in S . . . . . . . . . . . . . . . . . . . . . . . . . . . . . . . . .   50
     Investment revenue* . . . . . . . . . . . . . . . . . . . . . . . . .        50
*Or "equity in net income of subsidiary."
```

To avoid counting the $50 million net income twice—once as S's net income and again as P's investment revenue—P must eliminate it in consolidation. Thus, after P records this year's net income, the amount that will eliminate the investment in S on the work sheet used for consolidating the balance sheets is $213 + $50 = $263, which is P's new Investment in S balance and S's new Stockholders' Equity.

Exhibit 11-11 reflects the changes in P's accounts, S's accounts, and the consolidated accounts ($ in millions). Consolidated statements sum the individual accounts of two or more separate legal entities. We prepare them periodically via work sheets.

Intercompany Eliminations

When accountants consolidate the financial records of two companies, they must avoid double-counting any items. Exhibit 11-11 emphasizes elimination of the parent's investment account and the subsidiary's owners' equity. In many cases, the parent and subsidiary do business together, which leads to another type of double-counting. For example, suppose S charges P $12 for products that cost S $10, and the sale is made on credit. The following journal entries are made by each firm on its separate books:

P's Records			S's Records		
Merchandise inventory	12		Accounts receivable	12	
Accounts payable		12	Sales revenue		12
			Cost of goods sold	10	
			Merchandise Inventory		10

However, has anything happened economically? No—as far as the consolidated entity is concerned, the product is just moved from one location to another. If P paid cash to S, the cash just shifts from "one pocket to another." So this transaction is not an important one from the perspective of the consolidated company, and it should be eliminated. It is important that each separate legal entity keeps track of its own transactions for its own records. When we consolidate, we eliminate the intercompany receivable and payable, eliminate the costs and revenues, and ensure the inventory is carried at its cost to the consolidated company, $10. We eliminate these items with the following consolidation journal entries on the consolidation work sheet.

	Assets			=	Liabilities	+	Stockholders' Equity
	Investment in S	+	Cash and Other Assets	=	Accounts Payable, etc.	+	Stockholders' Equity
P's account							
Beginning of year	+213	+	437	=	200	+	450
Operating income			+100	=			+100*
Share of S income	+50			=			+50*
End of year	263	+	537	=	200	+	600
S's accounts							
Beginning of year			400	=	187	+	+213
Net income			+50	=			+50*
End of year			450	=	187	+	263
Intercompany eliminations	−263			=			−263
Consolidated, end of year	0	+	987	=	387	+	600

*Changes in the retained earnings portion of stockholders' equity.

Exhibit 11-11
Consolidation Work Sheet

Accounts payable (P)	12	
Accounts receivable (S)		12
Sales revenue (S)	12	
Cost of goods sold (S)		10
Merchandise Inventory (P)		2

The parenthetical letters show whose records contain the account balances. Remember, these entries are not recorded on the individual records of either company, only in the consolidation work sheet.

Minority Interests

OBJECTIVE 6

Incorporate minority interests into consolidated financial statements.

minority interests
The outside shareholders' interests, as opposed to the parent's interests, in a subsidiary corporation.

Our example of the consolidation of P and S assumes P purchased 100% of S. However, in reality, companies often purchase less than 100% of a subsidiary. One company can control another with just 51% of the shares. For example, Corning owns more than 50% but less than 100% of many companies. Corning consolidates each company into its consolidated financial statements, but recognizes the claim on some of the consolidated assets held by other owners. These claims are called **minority interests.** Minority interests represent the claims of nonmajority shareholders in the assets and earnings of a company that are consolidated into the accounts of the major shareholder. On the consolidated 2002 earnings statement, Corning shows a reduction of net income of $98 million due to "Minority interests." On the consolidated balance sheet, Corning shows a $59 million of "Minority interests." Note that the labels are identical: "minority interests." Thus it is up to you, the reader, to know that the $98 million on the income statement is the current year increase, whereas the $59 million on the balance sheet is the cumulative effect.

To apply this concept to our example, assume that our parent company (P) bought only 90% of S. Exhibit 11-12, using the basic figures of the previous example, shows the overall approach to a consolidated balance sheet immediately after the acquisition. In panel A, the graphic shows that some shareholders of S continue to have a minority interest in the consolidated entity. P pays $192 million for 90% of S (0.90 × $213 million). The minority interest is 10%, or $21 million. (All dollar amounts are rounded to the nearest million.) Panel B illustrates that the investment is shown at cost on P's records and in consolidation we show the minority interest at $21 million. You can think of the minority

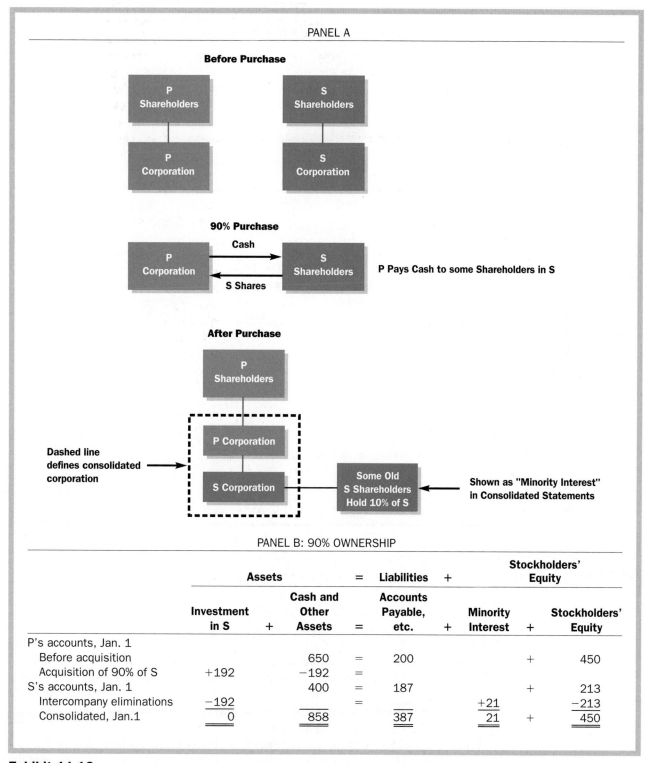

Exhibit 11-12

90% Purchase of S: P Pays Cash to Some S Shareholders; Some S Shareholders Retain Minority Interest

interest as representing the interests of those shareholders who own the 10% of the subsidiary stockholders' equity that is not owned by the parent company.

The 90% acquisition is assumed to occur on January 1. Suppose S has net income of $50 million for the year. P and S follow the same procedures in their individual income statements, regardless of whether S is 100% owned or 90% owned. P reports either

PANEL A: THE INCOME STATEMENT

	P	S	Consolidated
Sales	$900	$300	$1,200
Expenses	800	250	1,050
Operating income	$100	$ 50	$ 150
Investment Revenue*	45	—	
Net income	$145	$ 50	
Minority interest (10%) in subsidiary's net income			5
Net income to consolidated entity			$ 145

*Pro rata share (90%) of subsidiary net income, often called equity in earnings of affiliate or subsidiary.

PANEL B: THE BALANCE SHEET

	Assets		=	Liabilities	+		Stockholders' Equity	
	Investment in S	+	Cash and Other Assets =	Accounts Payable, etc.	+	Minority Interest	+	Stockholders' Equity
P's accounts								
Beginning of year, before acquisition			650 =	200			+	450
Acquisition	+192		−192 =					
Operating income			+100 =					+100
Share of S income	+45		=					+45
End of year	237	+	558 =	200			+	595
S's accounts								
Beginning of year			400 =	187			+	213
Net income			+50 =					+50
End of year		+	450 =	187				+263
Intercompany eliminations	−237		=			+26**		−263
Consolidated, end of year	0	+	1,008 =	387	+	26**	+	595

**Beginning minority interest plus minority interest in net income: 21 + .10(50) = 21 + 5 = 26.

Exhibit 11-13
Effect of 90% Ownership During the Year

100% or 90% of S's earnings as a line item on P's income statement labeled something like equity in earnings of subsidiary. However, the presence of a minority interest changes the consolidated income statement. In consolidation, all the income is combined and then the 10% share due to minority shareholders is subtracted. We illustrate this in panel A of Exhibit 11-13. Note that the parent-only income statement shows net income of $145, as does the consolidated income statement in the far right column.

Panel B shows how the minority interest from the income statement during the year increases the level of the minority interest on the balance sheet at year-end. Note that the minority interest of $21 that existed on January 1 has been increased by $5 during the year to reflect the minority shareholders' 10% interest in the year's net income of $50. As indicated in the intercompany elimination near the bottom of panel B, the eliminating entry on the work sheet used for consolidating the balance sheets is:

Stockholders' equity (on S books)	263	
Investment in S (on P books)		237
Minority interest (on consolidated statements)		26

Defining Control

Intercorporate investments occur worldwide, and different countries have made different choices about how to define control and about when to consolidate the financial results of two related companies. Consolidation is appropriate when one entity can direct the use of the assets of another company. In Australia, the decision to consolidate two firms relies on a combination of factors, including not only whether one firm owns 50% of another, but also whether it can control the membership of the board of directors and whether other investors own significant concentrated blocks of stock. Thus, an Australian parent company might own only 40% of a subsidiary company but might consolidate it because the parent has sufficient influence over the board of directors.

In the United States, GAAP specifies three methods for accounting for intercorporate investments, and currently "bright line" tests are used to choose among them. For ownership of less than 20%, the market method is used, higher than 50%, consolidation is generally required, and between the two, the equity method is used. As this is being written, the FASB is debating whether to modify U.S. GAAP. If it does, it will no doubt move toward the more common and flexible definitions of control currently in use internationally.

Summary Problem for Your Review

PROBLEM

1. Review the section on minority interests, pp. 508-510. Suppose P buys 60% of the stock of S for a cost of .60 × $213, or $128 million. The total assets of P consist of this $128 million plus $522 million of other assets, a total of $650 million. The S assets and equities are unchanged from the amount given in Exhibit 11-9 on p. 509. Prepare an analysis showing what amounts would appear in a consolidated balance sheet immediately after the acquisition.
2. Suppose S has a net income of $50 million for the year, and P has an operating income of $100 million. Other details of their income statements are as described in the example on p. 510. Prepare an analysis showing what amounts would appear in a consolidated income statement and year-end balance sheet.

SOLUTION

1.

	Assets			= Liabilities +		Stockholders' Equity	
	Investment in S	+	Cash and Other Assets =	Accounts Payable, etc.	+	Minority Interest +	Stockholders' Equity
P's accounts, January 1: Before acquisition			650 =	200		+	450
Acquisition of 60% of S	+128		−128 =				
S's accounts, January 1			400 =	187		+	213
Intercompany eliminations	−128		=			+85	−213
Consolidated, January 1	0	+	922 =	387	+	85 +	450

2.

	P	S	Consolidated
Sales	$900	$300	$1,200
Expenses	800	250	1,050
Operating income	$100	$ 50	$ 150
Pro rata share (60%) of unconsolidated			
subsidiary net income	30	—	
Net income	$130	$ 50	
Outside interest (40%) in consolidated			
subsidiary net income (minority			
interest in income)			20
Net income to consolidated entity			$ 130

	Assets			= Liabilities +		Stockholders' Equity	
	Investment in S	+	Cash and Other Assets =	Accounts Payable, etc.	+	Minority Interest +	Stockholders' Equity
P's accounts							
Beginning of year	128	+	522* =	200		+	450
Operating income			+100 =			+	+100
Share of S income	+30		=				+30
End of year	158	+	622 =	200		+	580
S's accounts							
Beginning of year			400 =	187		+	213
Net income			+50 =				+50
End of year			450 =	187		+	263
Intercompany							
eliminations	−158		=			+105†	−263
Consolidated,							
end of year	0	+	1,072 =	387	+	105 +	580

*650 beginning of year − 128 for acquisition = 522.
†85 beginning of year + .40 × (50) = 85 + 20 = 105.

Purchase Price Not Equal to Book Value

OBJECTIVE 7

Explain the economic meaning and financial reporting of goodwill.

When one company acquires another, the amount paid is usually higher and sometimes lower than the net book value of the assets owned by the acquired company and reported on its books. So far, we have assumed that the amount paid was the same as the book value if the investor purchased 100% of the investee or in proportion to the book value if it purchased less than 100%. If the acquiring company pays more or less than book value, it uses the actual amount paid as the basis for accounting for the acquisition.

In the unusual case where the acquiring company pays less than the book value, it must lower the book values of the acquired company's net assets on the consolidated balance sheet so they add up to no more than the purchase price. This accounting assumes the book value of the assets must be greater than their fair market values; otherwise, the acquiring company would have paid more for them.

The more common case is where the acquiring company pays more than book value. In such a case, consolidation requires a two-step adjustment. First, the initial consolidated statement must show all acquired assets and liabilities at their fair market value — taking care to make sure the total net asset value does not exceed the purchase price. Second, if the purchase price exceeds even the fair market value of the acquired net assets, the consolidated statement must show an asset called goodwill. **Goodwill** is the

goodwill
The excess of the cost of an acquired company over the sum of the fair market value of its identifiable individual assets less the liabilities.

excess of the cost of an acquired company over the sum of the fair market value of its identifiable individual assets less the liabilities.

Why do companies pay more than the fair value of the net assets when acquiring a company? Imagine a newspaper. It has simple assets—a building, desks and computers, a printing press, and some paper and ink. Yet newspapers are almost always purchased for far more than the value of these physical assets. The reason is that they have existing contracts, subscribers, advertising customers, and name recognition, so the going concern, the familiar newspaper, is worth more than the collection of physical assets. If the existing newspaper continued and you bought similar assets and created a new competing newspaper, profits would be a long-time coming.

Goodwill can be a significant portion of consolidated assets. Ford reported $5.6 billion of goodwill at December 31, 2002. This is 2% of the total consolidated assets of Ford. At December 31, 2002, Corning reported $1.7 billion of goodwill or 15% of consolidated assets. The Walt Disney Company had $17 billion in goodwill on total assets of $50 billion, or 34%.

Accounting for Goodwill

To see the impact of goodwill on the consolidated statements, refer to our example where P acquired a 100% interest in S. Suppose P paid $253 million rather than $213 million. Upon examining S's assets, accountants found that a building with a book value of $20 million had a fair market value of $35 million. Fair market values of all other assets equaled their book values. This means that, of the $40 million excess of purchase price over book value of net assets, we can attribute $15 million to identifiable assets (the building), and the remaining $25 million is goodwill. The eliminating entry on the work sheet for consolidating the balance sheet, illustrated in Exhibit 11-14, is (in millions of dollars):

Stockholders' equity (on S books)	213
Goodwill (on consolidated balance sheet)	25
Building (added to S's book value only on consolidated balance sheet)	15
Investment in S (on P's books)	253

Subsequent to the acquisition, under U.S. GAAP, the goodwill will decrease only if the acquiring company does not maintain the value of the goodwill. If the value of the goodwill decreases—called **impairment of goodwill**—the consolidated company must

impairment of goodwill reductions of the goodwill account because the value of the goodwill falls below its current carrying amount.

	Assets				=	Liabilities	+	Stockholders' Equity
	Investment in S	+	Cash and Other Assets	+ Goodwill	=	Accounts Payable, etc.	+	Stockholders' Equity
P's accounts								
Before acquisition			650		=	200	+	450
Acquisition of S	+253		−253		=			
S's accounts			400		=	187	+	213
Intercompany eliminations	−253		+15**	+25*	=			−213
Consolidated	0	+	812	25*	=	387	+	450

*The 25 million "goodwill" would appear in the consolidated balance sheet as a separate intangible asset account. It is often shown as the final item in a listing of assets.

**The $15 million increase to cash and other assets shows the increase due to the market value of the building exceeding its book value.

Exhibit 11-14
Creating Goodwill as of Jan. 1

reduce the goodwill account by the amount of the decrease in value and charge that amount as an expense. In contrast, the consolidated company will depreciate any amount of purchase price assigned to an identifiable asset over the remaining life of that asset. Thus, a company that plans to maintain the value of the goodwill and wants to report high net income prefers to assign the excess of the purchase price over the book value to goodwill rather than to identifiable assets.

Goodwill has been a controversial topic. Practice varies significantly worldwide. In some countries, companies never recognize goodwill as an asset. Where companies do recognize goodwill, some countries require companies to amortize it over a particular number of years, whereas others allow it to remain on the books perpetually.

GAAP for Goodwill Recently Changed

Accounting for goodwill in the United States recently changed. Examining this change can help you see the significance of this accounting choice. Prior practice required companies to amortize goodwill over a period not to exceed 40 years. For **Disney**, amortization was $604 million in 2001. In 2001, Disney reported a loss of $41 million. In 2002, it reported profit of $1,326 million. Approximately one-half of the change resulted from the fact that Disney amortized goodwill in 2001 but not in 2002. In early 2002, as most firms converted to the new standard, it was common for firms to have positive earnings comparisons simply because they amortized goodwill in 2001 and not in 2002.

The rules for transition are important whenever accounting methods change. In this instance, 2001 and 2002 were transition years. Authorities no longer required amortization. Instead, the FASB introduced specific rules for evaluation of the continuing value of the goodwill. When the value was impaired, companies had to write-down goodwill, often significantly affecting earnings. In general, this means that the goodwill value on the books will be the lower of historical cost or justifiable market value. Details for actually estimating the market value and possible impairment of goodwill are beyond the scope of this book.

Disney reports that after completing its evaluation of the value of goodwill, it concluded there was no impairment. In contrast, **Corning** recognized impairment of $400 million or about 25% of total goodwill. **Ford** reported impairment charges of $939 million in 2002. This was almost four times the prior year amortization and represented about 20% of the value of the goodwill. Not only did the impairment lead to a reduction in Ford's goodwill asset, it also created a $939 reduction of 2002 earnings in the form of an impairment charge.

Goodwill and Abnormal Earnings

As you might suspect, the final price paid by the purchaser of an ongoing business is the culmination of a bargaining process. Therefore, the exact amount paid for goodwill is subject to the negotiations concerning the total purchase price. A popular logic for determining the maximum price follows.

Goodwill is the price paid for "excess" or "abnormal" earning power. The steps to value the abnormal earning power are summarized in panel A of Exhibit 11-15. Essentially we determine the market value of the identifiable assets of an ordinary company (M in this case) and treat that as the reasonable cost of acquiring the ordinary earnings the company generates ($80,000 in this case). The market value is 10 times earnings. Company N has identical assets worth $800,000, but also has location, human resource, or reputation advantages that allow it to earn an extra $20,000 more than Company M. We calculate a price for these abnormal earnings using a multiple of six. The multiples of 10 times earnings and 6 times abnormal earnings are arbitrary. Actual values differ from year to year and from company to company. But the multiple for abnormal earnings will always be smaller because these earnings are not worth as much per dollar as ordinary earnings. Abnormal earnings are likely to be harder to maintain. The total value of Company N is $920,000, as shown in panel B of Exhibit 11-15.

Exhibit 11-15
Valuation of Goodwill

PANEL A: COMPUTATION OF VALUES

	Ordinary Company M	Extraordinary Company N
1. Fair market value of identifiable assets, less liabilities	$800,000	$800,000
2. Normal annual earnings on net assets at 10%	80,000	80,000
3. Actual average annual earnings for past 5 years (including for Company N an excess or abnormal return of $20,000)	80,000	100,000
4. Maximum price paid for normal annual earnings is 10 times line 2	800,000	800,000
5. Maximum price paid for abnormal annual earnings (which are riskier and thus less valuable per dollar of expected earnings) is six times $20,000	—	120,000*
6. Maximum price a purchaser is willing to pay for the company (line 1 plus line 5)	800,000	920,000

*This is the most the purchaser is willing to pay for goodwill.

PANEL B: VALUE OF COMPANY

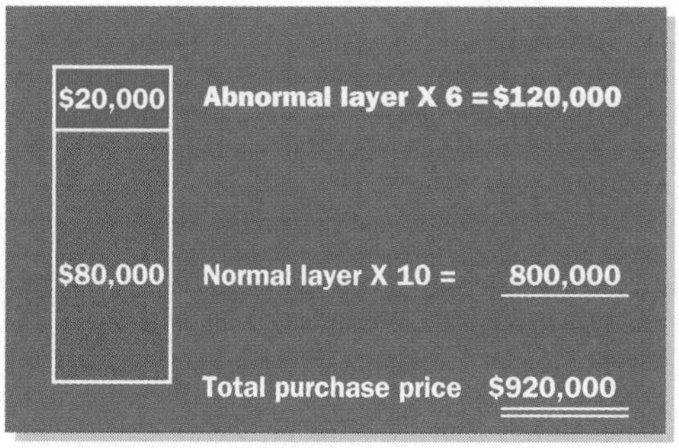

$20,000	Abnormal layer X 6 = $120,000
$80,000	Normal layer X 10 = 800,000
	Total purchase price $920,000

Perspective on Consolidated Statements

Exhibit 11-16 provides summarized financial statements for Ford Motor Company for 2002. The circled items 1 through 6 in the exhibit deserve special mention:

1. The headings indicate that these are consolidated financial statements (i.e, they are for Ford Motor Company and Subsidiaries).
2. Minority interests typically appear on the balance sheet, just above stockholders' equity. For Ford, the minority interest is too small to appear as a line item. In the income statement, the "Minority interests in net income (loss) of subsidiaries" appears as $367 million and is deducted to arrive at a final net loss of $(980) million.
3. "Equity in net assets of affiliated companies" appear with automotive assets in the amount of $2,470 million. On the income statement, the caption "Equity in net loss of affiliated companies" describes the loss associated with these affiliates in the amount of $(91) million.
4. Goodwill for Ford totals $5,557 million. The automotive sector shows $4,805 million of goodwill and an additional $752 million is included in Financial Services. Note 7 indicates that "Effective January 1, 2002 we adopted SFAS No. 142, Goodwill and Other Intangible Assets, which eliminates amortization of goodwill and certain other intangible assets, but requires annual testing for impairment." The note continues to identify write-downs of goodwill associated with Kwik-Fit, a European vehicle repair business, and with Hertz'

Exhibit 11-16

Ford Motor Company and Subsidiaries

Summarized Consolidated Financial Statements for the Year Ended December 31, 2002 (in Millions)

Ford Motor Company and Subsidiaries

① *Consolidated Statements of Income for the year ending December 31, 2002*

Automotive		
Sales	$134,425	
Total costs and expenses	134,956	
Operating income	(531)	
Net interest income (expense)	(534)	
③ Equity in net income (loss) of affilated companies	(91)	
Income before income taxes— Automotive		(1,156)
Financial Services		
Revenues	$ 28,161	
Total costs expenses	26,052	
Income before income taxes—Financial Services		$ 2109
Total Company		
Income before income taxes		953
Provision for income taxes		302
Income before minority interests		651
② Less Minority interests in net income of subsidiaries		367
Income from continuous operations		284
⑤ Loss from discontinued operations		(262)
Cumulative effect of change in accounting principles		(1,002)
Net income		$ (980)

Ford Motor Company and Subsidiaries

① *Consolidated Balance Sheets as of December 31, 2002*

Assets	
Automotive	
Total current assets	$ 40,764
③ Equity in net assets of affiliated companies	2,470
Property, net	36,364
④ Goodwill	4,805
Other assets	23,387
Total automotive assets	107,790
Financial Services	
Total Financial Services assets	187,432
Total assets	295,222
Liabilities and stockholders' equity	
Automotive	
Total current liabilities	45,292
Long-term debt	13,607
② Minority interests in net assets of subsidiaries	0
Other liabilities	57,497
Deferred income taxes	303
Total automotive liabilities	116,699
Financial Services	
Total Financial Services liabilities	172,933
Total stockholders' equity	5,590
Total liabilities and stockholders' equity	295,222

industrial and construction equipment rental business totaling almost $1 billion. The notes also provide extensive detail about the consequences of the new FASB standard and comparative data for prior years as if it had been in effect for earlier years as well.

5. When a company commits to dispose of businesses it becomes important to segregate the items associated with that business so that financial statements can be analyzed in terms of ongoing activity. Ford has $2,504 of assets of discontinued and held-for-sale operations split between the automotive and financial sectors and not shown separately

in these summarized statements. Included in total liabilities (but not detailed here) are $969 million in obligations associated with those operations that will be assumed by the buyer when sale is complete. On the income statement, $262 million of losses on discontinued operations appear below income from continuing operations.

To help you understand the relationship between the consolidated financial statements and Ford's actual corporate structure, consider the simplified version of Ford Motor Company shown in the following diagram.

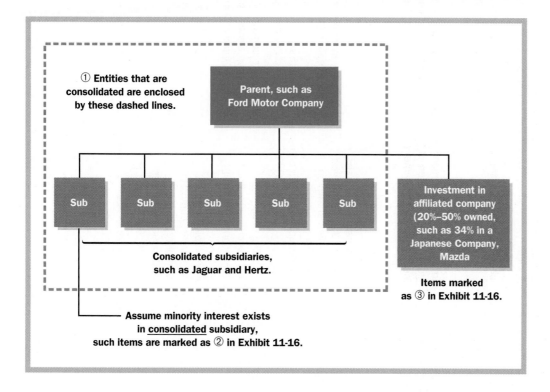

The FASB requires that all subsidiaries be consolidated. This is, all subsidiaries, regardless of their line of business or the parent company's line of business, are an integral part of the complete consolidated entity. As a result, the FASB believes that not consolidating some subsidiaries would result in significant amounts of the overall company's assets, liabilities, revenues, and expenses being left out, which would make the consolidated statements less useful.

There are exceptions to the general rule, but they are rare. One exception is that a subsidiary will not be consolidated if control is likely to be temporary or if that control does not rest with the majority owner. This exception actually applies to Ford. The company sometimes owns dealerships that it plans to resell quickly to a new dealer. Because the ownership of these dealerships is temporary, Ford does not consolidate them. Ford's statements reflect the consolidations of a manufacturing company with a financing company. Ford has chosen to structure the statements to separate clearly these two parts of its economic activity. The assets and liabilities of the Financial Services activity are listed separately as are the revenue and expense components. The footnotes provide additional detail on both segments of the business. Financial analysts pay particular attention to understanding the distinct parts of a business as they make predictions about the future.

Equity Affiliates, Minority Interest, and the Statement of Cash Flows

A company with equity affiliates (firms for which the investor uses the equity method) may use the direct method or the indirect method to prepare its cash flow statement. If it uses the direct method, no special problem arises because only the cash received from the affiliate as a dividend appears as an operating cash flow. However, if the indirect method

Item in Exhibit 11-16	Percentage of Ownership	Type of Accounting	Balance Sheet Effects	Income Statement Effects	Major Journal Entries
①	100%	Consolidation	Individual assets, individual liabilities added together For subsidiaries purchased for more than the fair value of identifiable net assets, goodwill is shown	Individual revenues, individual expenses added together If goodwill exists, it must be checked for impairment	None, except in work sheets for preparing consolidated statements; to eliminate reciprocal accounts, to avoid double-counting, and to recognize any goodwill
②	Greater than 50% and less than 100%	Consolidation	Same as 1, but recognition given to minority interest in liability section	Same as 1, but recognition given to minority interest near bottom of statement when consolidated net income is computed	Same as 1, but recognition of minority interests is included in work sheet entries
③	20% to and including 50%	Equity method	Investment carried at cost plus pro rata share of subsidiary earnings less dividends received	Equity in earnings (losses) of *affiliated* or *associated* companies shown on one line as addition to (deduction from) income	Investment . . . . xx Equity in earnings . . . . . . xx To record earnings Cash . . . . xx Investment . . . . xx To record dividends received
	Less than 20%	Market method	Investment carried at market	For trading securities, annual changes affect the income statement	Marketable securities . . . . . . xx Income statement gain . . . . . . xx To record appreciation
				For available-for-sale securities, cumulative unrealized gains and losses appear in owners' equity	Marketable securities . . . . . . xx Stockholders' equity . . . . xx To record appreciation

Exhibit 11-17
Summary of Accounting for Equity Securities

is used, net earnings are increased by the investor's share of its affiliates' earnings or are decreased by its share of the affiliates' loss. To calculate cash flow from operations, we must adjust reported income. Suppose the investor had net income of $7.6 million, including equity in earnings of an affiliate of $2.5 million, and received $1.3 million in dividends from the affiliate. Cash flow from the affiliate is $1.3 million. Because net earnings include $2.5 million, the indirect method must adjust net earnings by $2.5 million − $1.3 million = $1.2 million, the amount of the equity in earnings that was not received in cash.

Summary of Accounting for Equity Securities

Exhibit 11-17 summarizes the basic relationships in intercorporate investments. Take a few moments to reconcile the Ford financial statements in Exhibit 11-16 with Exhibit 11-17. In particular, note that minority interests arise only in conjunction with consolidated subsidiaries. Why? Because consolidated balance sheets and income statements assume that the parent company owns and controls 100% of the detailed assets, liabilities, sales, and expenses of the subsidiary companies. Thus, if a minority interest were not recognized, the stockholders' equity and net income of the consolidated enterprise would overstate the claims of the parent company shareholders.

In contrast, minority interests do not arise in connection with the equity method accounting for investments in affiliated companies. Why? Because no detailed assets, liabilities, revenues, and expenses of the affiliated companies are included in the consolidated statements. The investor's interests in these companies have been recognized on a proportional basis only.

As we have seen, the accounting for investments in common stock depends on the nature of the investment:

1. Investments that represent more than a 50% ownership interest are usually consolidated. A subsidiary is a corporation controlled by another corporation. The usual condition for control is ownership of a majority (more than 50%) of the outstanding voting stock.
2. The equity method is generally used for a 20% through 50% interest because such a level of ownership creates a presumption that the owner has the ability to exert significant influence. Under the equity method, the cost at date of acquisition and the income statement are adjusted for the investor's share of the earnings or losses of the investee subsequent to the date of investment. Dividends received from the investee reduce the carrying amount of the investment.
3. Marketable equity securities are generally carried at market value when ownership is below 20%. These investments are passive in the sense that the investor exerts no significant influence on the investee. Unrealized gains and losses appear in the income statement for trading securities and in stockholders' equity for available-for-sale securities.

Highlights to Remember

1 **Explain why corporations invest in one another.** Corporate investments arise for many reasons. Smaller investments are intended to create a relationship that leads to communication and sharing of information. As investments rise in size, the investor obtains more influence over the investee leading to changes in the behavior of both parties. When investments exceed 50% ownership of the investee, the investor obtains control sufficient to dictate behavior. The owner totally controls decision making and dictates what is made, to whom it is sold, from whom parts are purchased, how activity is financed, whether dividends are paid, what new assets are purchased, and so on.

2 **Account for short-term investments in debt securities and equity securities.** The accounting for intercorporate investments depends on the purpose of the investment, on whether it is an equity or debt security, and on the level of control the investor has over the issuer of the security. For short-term debt

securities and short-term equity securities, accounting is at market. Trading securities are held to be resold, and the gains and losses from changes in market value go directly to the income statement. Marketable securities that are available-for-sale are reported at market in the balance sheet, but gains and losses are carried in a separate account in stockholders' equity until the securities are sold.

3 **Report long-term investments in bonds.** When the investor's intention is to hold debt securities to maturity, the investor's accounting uses the effective interest rate method in the same manner that the issuer does. That is, discount and premium are amortized to affect interest revenue.

4 **Contrast the equity and market methods of accounting for investments.** For equity securities held for the long term, the accounting is linked to the investor's level of control of the issuer of the equity security. For ownership interests of less than 20%, accounting for equity securities requires classification as either available for sale or trading. The accounting is based on fair value.

As the ownership interest ranges from 20% to 50%, the increasing control the investor can exert over the issuer leads to earnings recognition in the income statement, proportional to the percentage of ownership. The investment account is increased by this share of the issuer's earnings (or decreased by a proportionate share of losses). When dividends are received, the investment account is decreased with no effect on earnings. This is called the equity method.

5 **Prepare consolidated financial statements.** As the ownership interest exceeds 50%, the investor controls the subsidiary. Consolidation is appropriate, which involves combining all the assets and liabilities of the related corporate entities. For 100%-owned subsidiaries, the main concern is the elimination of intercompany transactions: sales, receivables, and payables.

6 **Incorporate minority interests into consolidated financial statements.** Minority interests are the rights of other shareholders in consolidated subsidiaries that are more than 50% owned and therefore consolidated, but are not 100% owned. Minority interests are treated much like the equity interests of an investor. On the income statement, the minority interests are deducted in arriving at net income available to common shareholders of the consolidated entity. On the balance sheet, the minority interests are an historical measure of the claims of minority shareholders on the assets of consolidated subsidiaries.

7 **Explain the economic meaning and financial reporting of goodwill.** Goodwill refers to the excess of the purchase price of an acquired company over the market value of its identifiable net assets. Economically, it arises because the acquired firm has created the ability to earn extraordinary returns by creating market power. The market power might take the form of an exceptional brand name, such as Coca-Cola has developed. Because of the brand recognition, Coca-Cola can sell soft drinks at higher prices and earn higher returns than unbranded colas. Under U.S. GAAP we do not amortize goodwill. Goodwill is written off (reduced) only when management concludes that the value of the goodwill has declined (is impaired).

Accounting Vocabulary

affiliated company, p. 500
available-for-sale securities,
  p. 495
certificates of deposit, p. 495
commercial paper, p. 495
consolidated statements,
  p. 504
equity method, p. 500

goodwill, p. 512
held-to-maturity securities,
  p. 495
impairment of goodwill p. 514
market method, p. 496
marketable securities, p. 494
minority interests, p. 508
parent company, p. 503

short-term debt securities, p. 494
short-term equity securities,
  p. 495
short-term investment, p. 494
subsidiary, p. 503
trading securities, p. 495
U.S. Treasury obligations,
  p. 495

Assignment Material

Questions

11-1 Why is *marketable securities* an ill-chosen term to describe short-term investments?

11-2 Distinguish among trading securities, available-for-sale securities, and held-to-maturity securities.

11-3 "The cost method is applied to investments in short-term securities." Do you agree? Explain.

11-4 "Increases in the market price of short-term investments become gains on the income statement; decreases become losses." Do you agree? Explain.

11-5 Suppose an investor buys a $1,000 face value bond for $950, a discount of $50. Will amortization of the discount increase or decrease the investor's interest income? Explain.

11-6 What is the equity method?

11-7 "The equity method is usually used for long-term investments." Do you think this is appropriate? Explain.

11-8 Contrast the *market* method with the *equity* method.

11-9 What criterion is used to determine whether a parent–subsidiary relationship exists?

11-10 Why have subsidiaries? Why not have the corporation take the form of a single legal entity?

11-11 Suppose Company A buys 100% of the common shares of Company B for cash. How does Company B record the receipt of this cash on its books?

11-12 Why does a consolidated balance sheet require "eliminating entries"?

11-13 "A consolidated income statement will show more income than a parent company-only statement when both the parent and subsidiary have positive net income." Do you agree? Explain.

11-14 What is a minority interest?

11-15 Distinguish between *control of* a company and *significant influence over* a company.

11-16 "Goodwill is the excess of purchase price over the book values of the individual asset acquired." Do you agree? Explain.

11-17 Does GAAP require amortization of goodwill against net income? If not, when does goodwill decrease?

11-18 Why might a company prefer to own 19.9% interest in an affiliate instead of a 20.1% interest?

11-19 When is there justification for not consolidating majority-owned subsidiaries?

11-20 Suppose P company received $20,000 in cash dividends from Y company, a 40%-owned affiliated company. Y company's net income was $80,000. How will P's statement of cash flows show these items using the direct method?

11-21 Why do minority interests arise in connection with consolidated statements, but not with investments in affiliated companies?

11-22 Would you expect the consolidated income statement to report higher net income than shown in the parent's separate financial statements?

Critical Thinking Questions

11-23 Consequences of Marking to Market

As president of a young technology company, you and your chief financial officer are discussing your great success in investing in other high-growth companies in your industry. When you raised $20 million in capital, you actually needed $10 million immediately so you invested the other $10 million in a portfolio of dynamic companies. Over the last year, the value of these companies doubled. You are trying to figure out how next year's reported income will compare with this year's if you liquidate that portfolio and invest it in the core business.

11-24 Scoping Out an Acquisition Strategy

You recently hired a young MBA who is advising you that you should grow more aggressively and suggesting that you should do so by acquiring other small companies. Your cookware and tableware importing business has been quite successful, but you are not sure that this new employee's plan to acquire a series of retail cooking/kitchenware stores makes sense. What issues would you raise in discussing this proposal?

11-25 Accounting Consequences of Changing Ownership Interest

You own 19% of a company that you do business with and are considering buying another 5% of the company. They provide a great product and great service. Their share price has been rising because of their potential. However, they are currently not profitable from an accounting perspective because they are doing a great deal of research and development. You have asked your CFO to advise you about the consequences of this increase in your ownership position. What would you expect the CFO to say?

11-26 Transactions Between Companies

Your company has sales of $100 million and profits of $10 million. A similar, smaller company with sales of $25 million and profits of $5 million appears to be an attractive merger candidate. You currently buy 50% of the smaller company's production. The CEO has indicated that this would be a great acquisition because it would increase sales by 25% and profits by 50%. As CFO what issues do you raise concerning this proposed purchase and the CEO's analysis.

Exercises

11-27 Trading Securities

The McMillan Company has a portfolio of trading securities consisting of common and preferred stocks. The portfolio cost $160 million on January 1. The market values of the portfolio were ($ in millions): March 31, $150; June 30, $140; September 30, $152; and December 31, $160.

1. Prepare a tabulation showing the balance sheet presentations and income statement presentations for interim reporting purposes.
2. Show the journal entries for quarters 1, 2, 3, and 4.

11-28 Available-for-Sale Securities

The MacGregor Company has a portfolio of securities identical to that of the McMillan Company (see Exercise 11-27). However, MacGregor classified the portfolio as available-for-sale securities. The portfolio cost $160 million on January 1. The market values of the portfolio were ($ in millions): March 31, $150; June 30, $140; September 30, $152; and December 31, $160.

1. Prepare a tabulation showing the balance sheet presentations and income statement presentations for interim reporting purposes.
2. Show the journal entries for quarters 1, 2, 3, and 4.

11-29 Bond Discount Transactions

On December 31, 20X1, a company purchased $1 million of 5-year, 10% debentures for $926,400. The market interest rate was 12%.

1. Using the balance sheet equation format, prepare an analysis of bond transactions for the investor. Assume effective interest amortization. Show entries for the investor concerning (a) purchase, (b) first semiannual interest payment, and (c) payment of maturity value.
2. Show the corresponding journal entries for preceding (a), (b), and (c).
3. Show how the bond investment would appear on the balance sheets as of December 31, 20X1, and June 30, 20X2.

11-30 Bond Premium Transactions

On December 31, 20X1, the Guzman Company purchased $2 million of 10-year, 10% debentures for $2,271,830. The market interest rate was 8%.

1. Using the balance sheet equation format, prepare an analysis of transactions for the investor's records. Key your transactions as follows: (a) purchase, (b) first semiannual interest payment using effective interest amortization of bond premium, and (c) payment of maturity value.
2. Prepare sample journal entries for preceding (a), (b), and (c).
3. Show how the bond-related accounts would appear on the balance sheets as of December 31, 20X1, and June 30, 20X2.

11-31 Market Method or Equity Method

Yukon Outdoor Equipment acquired 25% of the voting stock of Bearpaw Snowshoes for $50 million cash. In year one, Bearpaw had a net income of $28 million and paid a cash dividend of $12 million.

1. Using the equity and the market methods, show the effects of the three transactions on the accounts of Yukon Outdoor Equipment. Use the balance sheet equation format. Also show the accompanying journal entries. Assume constant market value for Bearpaw.
2. Which method, equity or market, would Yukon use to account for its investment in Bearpaw? Explain.

11-32 Equity Method

Company X acquired 40% of the voting stock of Company Y for $90 million cash. In year one, Y had a net income of $50 million and paid cash dividends of $20 million.

Prepare a tabulation that uses the equity method of accounting for X's investment in Y. Show the effects on the balance sheet equation. What is the year-end balance in the Investment in Y account under the equity method?

11-33 Consolidated Statements

Able and Baker companies had the following balance sheets at December 31, 20X8 ($ in thousands):

	Able	Baker
Assets		
Cash	$ 500	$100
Net plant	1,700	400
Total assets	$2,200	$500
Liabilities and stockholders' equity		
Accounts payable	175	$ 80
Long-term debt	425	220
Stockholders' equity	1,600	200
Total liabilities and stockholders' equity	$2,200	$500

On January 1, 20X9, Able purchased 100% of the common stock of Baker for $200,000.

1. Prepare a balance sheet for Able Company immediately after its purchase of Baker Company.
2. Prepare a balance sheet for the consolidated entity immediately after the purchase of Baker Company.
3. Suppose Able Company had net income of $250,000 in 20X9 (before recognizing its share of Baker's income) and Baker Company had net income of $50,000 in 20X9. Neither company sold items to the other. What was the 20X9 consolidated net income?

11-34 Minority Interest
Suppose P company owns 95% of S company and S company earns $200,000. What is the amount of the minority interest shown in P company's consolidated income statement? What is the amount of the minority interest shown in S company's individual income statement?

11-35 Goodwill
Megasoft, Inc. purchased 100% of the common shares of Zenatel for $470,000 on January 1, 20X7. Zenatel's balance sheet just before the acquisition was ($ in thousands):

Cash	$ 90
Net fixed assets	220
Total assets	$310
Liabilities	$240
Stockholders' equity	70
Total liabilities and stockholders' equity	$310

The fair market value of Zenatel's assets and liabilities was equal to their book values.

1. Compute the amount of goodwill Megasoft would recognize on this purchase. Where would this goodwill appear on Megasoft's financial statements?
2. Megasoft's 20X7 net income from all operations excluding those of Zenatel were $150,000. Zenatel had a net loss of $10,000. Compute consolidated net income for 20X7.
3. Repeat requirement 2 assuming Megasoft concluded goodwill was impaired by $25,000.
4. How much goodwill appears on the consolidated balance sheet after requirement 3?

11-36 Affiliated Companies
Suppose P company owns 30% of S company. S company earns $200,000 and pays total dividends of $50,000 to its shareholders. What appears in the consolidated income statement of P company as a result of S company's activity? What would be the change in the account titled Investment in equity affiliates on P company's balance sheet?

11-37 Consolidations in Japan
A few years ago, Japan's finance ministry issued a directive requiring the 600 largest Japanese companies to produce consolidated financial statements. The previous practice had been to use parent company-only statements. A story in *Business Week* said,

> *Financial observers hope that the move will help end the tradition-honored*
> *Japanese practice of "window dressing" the parent company financial results by*
> *shoving losses onto hapless subsidiaries, whose red ink was seldom revealed. . . .*
> *When companies needed to show a bigger profit, they would sell their product to*
> *subsidiaries at an inflated price. . . . Or the parent company charged a higher rent*
> *to a subsidiary company using its building.*

Could a parent company follow the quoted practices and achieve window dressing in its parent-only financial statements if it used the equity method of accounting for its intercorporate investments? Explain.

Problems

11-38 Trading Securities

Before its 2002 acquisition by Royal Dutch Shell, Pennzoil Company held a portfolio of trading equity securities that cost $660,100,000 and had a market value of $955,182,000 on January 1. Assume that the same portfolio was held until the end of the first quarter of the subsequent year. The market value of the protfolio was $980,160,000 at January 31, $940,000,000 at February 29, and $960,000,000 at March 31.

1. Prepare a tabulation showing the balance sheet presentation and income statement presentation for monthly reporting purposes.
2. Show the journal entries for January, February, and March.
3. How would your answer to requirement 1 change if the securities were classified as available for sale?

11-39 Short-Term Investments

The VanDankan Company has the following footnote to its financial statements:

> Note 4: Short-Term Investments
>
> *The company holds the following short-term investments at December 31*
> *(in thousands):*

	Cost	Market Value
Trading securities		
U.S. government bonds	$670,000	$660,000
Held-to-maturity securities		
Bonds issued by Beta Corporation	540,000	560,000
Available-for-sale securities		
Common shares of Gamma Corp.	300,000	770,000

1. Compute the amount that VanDankan would show on its balance sheet for short-term investments.
2. Suppose the market values of the three securities at the beginning of the year had been:

U.S. government bonds	$685,000
Bonds issued by Beta Corp.	550,000
Common shares of Gamma Corp.	710,000

Prepare journal entries to recognize the changes in market values that would be recorded in VanDankan's books during the year.

11-40 Early Extinguishment of an Investment

On December 31, 20X2, an insurance company purchased $10 million of 10-year, 10% debentures for $8,852,950. On December 31, 20X3 (after all interest payments and amortization had been recorded for 20X3), the insurance company sold all the debentures for $9.1 million. The market interest rate at purchase when the bonds were issued was 12%.

1. Compute the gain or loss on the sale for the insurance company (i.e., the investor).
2. Prepare the appropriate journal entries for the insurance company (i.e., the investor).

11-41 Consolidated Statements, Minority Interests

Consider the following for Chow Company (the parent) as of December 31, 20X8:

	Chow	Subsidiary*
Assets	$800,000	$200,000
Liabilities to creditors	$300,000	$ 80,000
Stockholder's equity	500,000	120,000
Total	$800,000	$200,000

*70% owned by Chow.

The $800,000 of assets of Chow includes an $84,000 investment in the 70% owned subsidiary. The $84,000 includes Chow's pro rata share of the subsidiary's net income for 20X8. Chow's sales were $870,000 and operating expenses were $802,000. These figures exclude any pro rata share of the subsidiary's net income. The subsidiary's sales were $550,000 and operating expenses were $510,000. Prepare a consolidated income statement and a consolidated balance sheet. Assume neither Chow or its subsidiary sold items to the other.

11-42 Consolidated Financial Statements and Minority Interest

The parent company owns 80% of the common stock of Company S-1 and 60% of the common stock of Company S-2. The balances as of December 31, 20X4, in the condensed accounts follow:

	($ in thousands)		
	Parent	S-1	S-2
Sales in 20X4	300,000	80,000	100,000
Investment in subsidiaries*	65,000	—	—
Other assets	135,000	90,000	20,000
Liabilities to creditors	100,000	20,000	5,000
Expenses in 20X4	280,000	90,000	90,000
Stockholders' equity, including current net income	100,000	70,000	15,000

*Carried at equity in subsidiaries.

Prepare a consolidated balance sheet as of December 31, 20X4, and a consolidated income statement for 20X4 ($ in millions of dollars). Assume none of the companies sold items to each other.

11-43 Consolidated Financial Statements

Company P acquired a 100% voting interest in Company S for $120 million cash at the start of the year. Immediately before the business combination, each company had the following condensed balance sheet accounts ($ in millions):

	P	S
Cash and other assets	$500	$160
Accounts payable, etc.	$200	$ 40
Stockholders' equity	300	120
Total liab. & stk. eq.	$500	$160

1. Prepare a tabulation of the consolidated balance sheet accounts immediately after acquisition. Use the balance sheet equation format.
2. Suppose P and S have the following results for the year:

	P	S
Sales	$600	$180
Expenses	450	170

Prepare income statements for the year for P, S, and the consolidated entity. Assume neither P nor S sold items to the other.

3. Present the effects of the operations for the year on P's accounts and on S's accounts, using the balance sheet equation. Also tabulate the consolidated balance sheet accounts at the end of the year. Assume that liabilities are unchanged.
4. Suppose S paid a cash dividend of $10 million. What accounts in requirement 3 would be affected and by how much?

11-44 Minority Interests

This alters the preceding problem. However, this problem is self-contained because all the facts are reproduced as follows. Company P acquired an 70% voting interest in Company S for $84 million cash at the start of the year. Immediately before the business combination, each company had the following condensed balance sheet accounts ($ in millions):

	P	S
Cash and other assets	$500	$160
Accounts payable, etc.	$200	$ 40
Stockholders' equity	300	120
Total liab. & stk. eq.	$500	$160

1. Prepare a tabulation of the consolidated balance sheet accounts immediately after acquisition. Use the balance sheet equation format.
2. Suppose P and S have the following results for the year:

	P	S
Sales	$600	$180
Expenses	450	170

Prepare income statements for the year for P, S, and the consolidated entity. Assume neither P nor S sold items to the other.
3. Using the balance sheet equation format, present the effects of the operations for the year on P's accounts and on S's accounts. Also tabulate consolidated balance sheet accounts at the end of the year. Assume that liabilities are unchanged.
4. Suppose S paid a cash dividend of $10 million. What accounts in requirement 3 would be affected and by how much?

11-45 Goodwill and Consolidations

This alters problem 11-44. However, this problem is self-contained because all the facts are reproduced as follows. Company P acquired a 100% voting interest in Company S for $150 million cash at the start of the year. Immediately before the business combination, each company had the following condensed balance sheet accounts ($ in millions):

	P	S
Cash and other assets	$500	160
Accounts payable, etc.	$200	$ 40
Stockholders' equity	300	120
Total liab. & stk. equity	$500	$160

Assume the fair values of the individual assets and liabilities of S were equal to their book values.

1. Prepare a tabulation of the consolidated balance sheet accounts immediately after the acquisition. Use the balance sheet equation format.
2. Suppose the book values of the S individual assets are equal to their fair market values except for equipment. The net book value of equipment is $40 million and its fair market value is $50 million. The equipment has a remaining useful life of 5 years. Straight-line depreciation is used.
   a. Describe how the consolidated balance sheet accounts immediately after the acquisition would differ from those in requirement 1. Be specific as to accounts and amounts.
   b. By how much will consolidated income differ in comparison with the consolidated income that would be reported if all equipment had fair value equal to its book value on S's books as in requirement 1?

11-46 Purchased Goodwill

Consider the following balance sheets ($ in millions):

	Company A	Company B
Cash	150	15
Inventories	60	25
Plant assets, net	60	30
Total assets	270	70
Common stock and paid-in surplus	70	30
Retained earnings	200	40
Total liab. & stk. equity	270	70

Company A paid $100 million to Company B stockholders for all their stock. The "fair value" of the plant assets of Company B is $50 million. The fair value of cash and inventories is equal to their carrying amounts. Companies A and B continued to keep separate books.

1. Prepare a tabulation showing the balance sheets of companies A and B, intercompany eliminations, and the consolidated balance sheet immediately after the acquisition.
2. Suppose that $60 million instead of $50 million of the total purchase price of $100 million could logically be assigned to the plant assets. How would the consolidated accounts be affected?
3. Refer to the facts in requirement 2. Suppose Company A had paid $120 million instead of $100 million. State how your tabulation in requirement 2 above would change.

11-47 Effects of Goodwill on the Income Statement

1. Philip Morris purchased General Foods for $5.6 billion. Only $1.7 billion of the purchase price could be assigned to identifiable individual assets and liabilities. How much goodwill was created in the purchase?
2. Philip Morris changed its name to Altria in 2002 to emphasize that it was no longer primarily a tobacco company. It owned Miller Brewing Company and Kraft Foods, as well as operating a financing subsidiary. As a result of numerous acquisitions through time, its 2002 balance sheet showed $37,871 million in goodwill. On its income statement in 2001 goodwill amortization was $1,104 million, while in 2002 only $7 million of goodwill impairment was recorded. In 2002, net earnings were $11,102 million versus $8,500 million in 2001 for a 31% increase. How much of the increase was due to the change in accounting practice that eliminated goodwill amortization?
3. During 2002, Altria sold its wholly owned and consolidated Miller Brewing subsidiary to the South African Brewing Company (SAB) in exchange for SAB stock. Altria is now an owner of more than a 20% equity interest in SAB and will account for this equity interest in the future by recognizing its proportional share of SAB earnings as equity in earnings of an affiliate in its income statement. In 2002, this transaction gave rise to a gain of $2,631 million before income taxes of approximately $900 million. Estimate 2002 net earnings for Altria if neither the change in goodwill amortization nor the sale of Miller had occurred, and contrast the percentage change to the original 31% increase.

11-48 Allocating Total Purchase Price to Assets

Two Hollywood companies had the following balance sheet accounts as of December 31, 20X7 ($ in millions):

	Cinemon	Bradley Productions		Cinemon	Bradley Productions
Cash and receivables	$ 30	$ 22	Current liabilities	$ 50	$ 20
Inventories	120	3	Common stock	100	10
Plant assets, net	150	95	Retained earnings	150	90
Total assets	$300	$120	Total liab. and stk. eq.	$300	$120
Net income for 20X7	$ 19	$ 4			

On January 4, 20X8, these entities combined. Cinemon issued $180 million of its shares (at market value) in exchange for all the shares of Bradley, a motion picture division of a large company.

The inventory of films acquired through the combination had been fully amortized on Bradley's books.

During 20X8, Bradley received revenue of $21 million from the rental of films from its inventory. Cinemon earned $20 million on its other operations (i.e., excluding Bradley) during 20X8. Bradley broke even on its other operations (i.e., excluding the film rental contracts) during 20X8.

1. Prepare a consolidated balance sheet for the combined company immediately after the combination. Assume $80 million of the purchase price was assigned to the inventory of films.
2. Prepare a comparison of Cinemon's consolidated net income between 20X7 and 20X8, where the cost of the film inventories would be amortized on a straight-line basis over 4 years. What would be the net income for 20X8 if the $80 million were assigned to goodwill instead of the inventory of films and goodwill was not amortized?

11-49 Prepare Consolidated Financial Statements

From the following data, prepare a consolidated balance sheet and an income statement for Midlands Data Corporation. All data are in millions and pertain to operations for 20X2 or to balances on December 31, 20X2:

Short-term investments at cost, which approximates current market	$ 35
Income tax expense	90
Accounts receivable, net	110
Minority interest in subsidiaries	90
Inventories at average cost	390
Dividends declared and paid on preferred stock	10
Equity in earnings of affiliated companies	20
Paid-in capital in excess of par	82
Interest expense	25
Retained earnings	218
Investments in affiliated companies	100
Common stock, 10 million shares, $1 par	10
Depreciation and amortization	20
Accounts payable	200
Cash	55
First mortgage bonds, 10% interest, due December 31, 20X8	80
Property, plant, and equipment, net	120
Preferred stock, 2 million shares, $50 par, dividend rate is $5 per share, each share is convertible into one share of common stock	100
Accrued income taxes payable	30
Cost of goods sold and operating expenses, exclusive of depreciation and amortization	710
Subordinated debentures, 11% interest, due December 31, 20X9	100
Minority interest in subsidiaries' net income	20
Goodwill	100
Net sales and other operating revenue	960

11-50 Minority Interest

The consolidated financial statement of Anchor Gaming, Inc., include the accounts of Colorado Grande Enterprises, Inc., an 80%-owned subsidiary. Anchor Gaming makes gambling machines and runs casinos. Colorado Grande Enterprises operates the Colorado Grande Casino in Cripple Creek, 45 miles from Colorado Springs. Colorado Grande Enterprises is Anchor Gaming's only consolidated subsidiary with minority interests. A recent Anchor Gaming income statement contained the following:

Income before minority interest and taxes	$56,987,737
Taxes	21,000,702
Minority interest in earnings of consolidated subsidiary	310,607
Net income	$35,676,428

Anchor Gaming's Minority interest in consolidated subsidiary account listed $672,955 at the beginning of the year. Colorado Grande Enterprises paid no dividends during the year. Anchor Gaming did not buy or sell any of its interest in Colorado Grande Enterprises during the year.

1. Compute the net income of Colorado Grande Enterprises for the year.
2. What proportion of Anchor Gaming's $35,676,428 net income was contributed by Colorado Grande Enterprises?
3. Compute Anchor Gaming's balance in "Minority interest in Consolidated subsidiary" at the end of the year.
4. Comment on the reason for including a line for minority interest in the income statement and balance sheet of Anchor Gaming.

11-51 Discontinued Operations

This problem is an extension of problem 11-50. In 2002, International Game Technology (IGT) acquired Anchor Gaming. After reviewing the transaction and assessing the mix of assets, IGT decided to dispose of Anchor Gaming's interest in Colorado Grande Enterprises because operation of casinos did not fit IGT's strategy.

1. The Consolidated Statement of Income for the year ended September 28, 2002 showed Income from discontinued operations, net of tax of $7,639. Footnotes disclosed this and indicated that financial statements reflected the casino operations as discontinued operations for all periods presented. Yet the income statements for 2001 and 2000 showed no income from discontinued operations. Discuss.
2. How might the decision to discontinue operations affect the balance sheet of IGT?
3. Total assets acquired in the transaction, other than those associated with the discontinued casino operations, were $1,673,593, including identifiable intangible assets of $231,129 and goodwill of $825,953. Comment on the distinction between identifiable intangible assets and goodwill.

11-52 Equity Method and Cash Flows

Moscow Resources Company owns a 40% interest in Siberia Mining Company. Moscow uses the equity method to account for the investment. During 20X6, Siberia had net income of 100 million rubles and paid cash dividends of 60 million rubles. Moscow's net income, including the effect of its investment in Siberia, was 486 million rubles.

1. In reconciling Moscow's net income with its net cash provided by operating activities, the net income must be adjusted for Moscow's pro rata share of the net income of Siberia. Compute the amount of the adjustment. Will it be added to or deducted from net income?
2. Under the direct method, will the dividends paid by Siberia affect the amounts Moscow lists under operating, investing, or financing activities. By how much? Will the amount(s) be cash inflows or cash outflows?

11-53 Effect of Transactions Under the Equity Method

Coca-Cola's 2002 financial statements revealed that it has extensive equity method investments including Coca-Cola Hellenic Bottling Company, Coca-Cola Amatil Limited, and Coca-Cola Enterprises. In total, the balance sheet showed equity investments of $5,128 million at December 31, 2001 and $4,737 million at December 31, 2002. During 2002 Coca-Cola included equity income of $384 million in its income statement, and its cash flow statement indicates that approximately $128 million in dividends was received from equity investees.

1. Compute the approximate reduction in Coca-Cola's equity investment asset that cannot be explained by either increases due to its share in earnings or decreases due to dividends received. You may find a T-account will help your analysis.
2. Coca-Cola uses the indirect method to construct its cash flow statement. Indicate how these transactions with equity investees would be shown in the statement of cash flows.

11-54 Equity Method, Consolidation, and Minority Interest

On January 2, 20X6, Jordan Shoe Company purchased 40% of Sports Clothing Company (SCC) for $2.0 million cash. Before the acquisition, Jordan had assets of $10 million and stockholders' equity of $8 million. SCC had stockholders' equity of $5 million and liabilities of $1 million, and the fair values of its assets and liabilities were equal to their book values.

SCC reported 20X6 net income of $400,000 and declared and paid dividends of $100,000. Assume that Jordan and SCC had no sales to one another. Separate income statements for Jordan and SCC were as follows:

	Jordan Shoe Company	Sports Clothing Company
Sales	$12,500,000	$4,400,000
Expenses	11,100,000	4,000,000
Operating income	$ 1,400,000	$ 400,000

1. Prepare the journal entries for Jordan Shoe (a) to record the acquisition of SCC and (b) to record its share of SCC net income and dividends for 20X6.
2. Prepare Jordan Shoe's income statement for 20X6 and calculate the balance in its investments in SCC as of December 31, 20X6.
3. Suppose Jordan had purchased 80% of SCC for $4 million. Using the balance sheet equation format, prepare a tabulation of the consolidated balance sheet immediately after acquisition. Prepare the journal entries for both Jordan and SCC to record the acquisition, Omit explanations.
4. Prepare a consolidated income statement for 20X6, using the facts of requirement 3 above.

11-55 Equity Investments and Minority Interests

Corning has significant equity investments, and several of its consolidated subsidiaries have minority interests outstanding. Corning's consolidated income statement for 2002 shows (dollars in millions):

Loss from continuing operations before minority interest and equity earnings	($1,994)
Minority interests	98
Equity in earnings of associated companies	116
Loss from continuing operations	($1,780)

1. Assuming each of the equity companies is 40% owned by Corning, estimate the 2002 earnings for these companies.
2. Assuming each of the minority interests is a 20% interest, estimate the 2002 earnings of these companies.
3. Corning prepares a cash flow statement using the indirect method. On it, the loss from continuing operations is adjusted by $25 million for equity in earnings of associated companies in excess of dividends received. Estimate dividends received from equity investees.
4. Corning's cash flow statement also adjusts for $98 million labeled "minority interests, net of dividends paid." Estimate dividends paid to minority investors.

11-56 Goodwill and Intangibles

Gannett Co. owns many media companies, including numerous small-town papers and the national newspaper, USA Today. In 2002, revenues totaled $6.4 billion with net income of $1,160 million, up from $831 million in the prior year.

1. Gannett's 2002 balance sheet showed goodwill of $8.8 billion out of total assets of $13.7 billion. Express goodwill as a percentage of total assets and indicate what that suggests about Gannett's growth. Did Gannett grow by starting new newspapers or by acquiring them?
2. During 2002, Gannett complied with new FASB rules and ended the amortization of goodwill, which had contributed to a $241 million charge for amortization of goodwill and other intangibles in 2001. In contrast, amortization of other intangibles was $7 million in 2002. Calculate the increase in net earnings from 2001 to 2002 as reported by Gannett. Compute the increase in net earnings if there had been no change in accounting rules and amortization of goodwill and other intangibles in 2002 was the same as in 2001. There was no goodwill impairment. Comment.

11-57 The Value of a Stock for Stock Exchange

On October 27, 2003, the following appeared in a news release:

> Bank of America Corporation and FleetBoston Financial Corporation today announced a definitive agreement to merge, creating the nation's premier financial services company. The company will bring unmatched convenience, innovation and resources to customers and clients throughout the nation and around the world.
>
> The merger, to be accomplished through a stock-for-stock transaction, establishes a new Bank of America that will serve approximately 33 million consumer relationships, with leading market shares throughout the Northeast, Southeast, Midwest, Southwest and West regions of the United States . . .

> *Under terms of the agreement, FleetBoston Financial stockholders will receive .5553 shares of Bank of America common stock for each of their shares. The exchange ratio was derived from the share price of Bank of America at the close of business on October 22, 2003, to establish the transaction's value at almost $47 billion, or $45 per FleetBoston Financial share.*

Following this announcement, FleetBoston shares rose sharply and Bank of America shares dropped approximately 10%

Discuss these events. How is this different than Bank of America agreeing to pay $45 per share in cash?

11-58 Intercorporate Investments and Statements of Cash Flow

The 20X6 balance sheet of Global Resources Corp. contained the following three assets:

	20X6	20X5
Long-term debt investments held to maturity	$ 166,000	$ 166,000
Investment in Alberta Mining Company, 43% owned	$ 981,000	$ 861,000
Investment in Sutter Gold Company, 25% owned	$1,145,000	$1,054,000

The long-term-debt investments were shown at cost, which equaled maturity value. Interest income was $14,000 for these debt investments, which had been owned for several years. The equity method was used to account for both Alberta Mining and Sutter Gold. Results for 20X6 included:

	Alberta Mining Company	Sutter Gold Company
Global Resources Corp. pro rata share of net income	$120,000	$100,000
Cash dividends received by Global Resources Corp.	$ 40,000	$ 0

Global Resources reported net income of $696,000 and depreciation of $130,000 in 20X6.

A schedule that reconciles net income to net cash provided by operating activities contained the following:

Net income	$696,000
Depreciation	130,000
Increase in noncash working capital	(15,000)

Note: The increase in noncash working capital is the net change in current assets and liabilities other than cash.

Given the available data, complete the reconciliation of net income to cash from operations.

11-59 Intercorporate Investments and Ethics

Hans Rasmussen and Alex Renalda were best friends at a small undergraduate college and they fought side by side in the jungles of Vietnam. On returning to the United States, they went their separate ways to pursue MBA degrees, Hans to a prestigious East Coast business school and Alex to an equally prestigious West Coast school. However, 30 years later, their paths crossed again.

By 1999, Alex had become president and CEO of Medusa Electronics after 21 years with the firm. Hans had started working for American Airlines, but had left after 9 years to start his own firm, Rasmussen Transport. In April 1999, Rasmussen Transport was near bankruptcy when Hans approached his old friend for help. Alex Renalda answered his friend's call, and Medusa Electronics bought 19% of Rasmussen Transport.

In 2002, Rasmussen was financially stable and Medusa was struggling. In fact, Alex Renalda thought his job as CEO might be in jeopardy if Medusa did not report income up to expectations. Late in 2002, Alex approached Hans with a request—quadruple Rasmussen's dividends so Medusa could recognize $760,000 of investment income. Medusa had listed its investment in Rasmussen as an available-for-sale security, so changes in the market value of Rasmussen were recorded directly in stockholders' equity. However, dividends paid were recognized in Medusa's income statement. Although Rasmussen had never paid dividends of more than 25% of net income, and it had plenty of use for excess cash, Hans felt a deep obligation to Alex. Thus, he agreed to a $4 million dividend on net income of $4.17 million.

1. Why does the dividend policy of Rasmussen Transport affect the income of Medusa Electronics? Is this consistent with the intent of the accounting principles relating to the market and equity methods for intercorporate investments? Explain.
2. Comment on the ethical issues in the arrangements between Hans Rasmussen and Alex Renalda.

Collaborative Learning Exercise

11-60 International Perspective on Consolidation

Form groups of four to six students. Each student should pick a country from the following list:

Australia	Japan
France	Sweden
Germany	United Kingdom
Italy	

Find out the policy on consolidating financial statements in the country you select. If possible, find out when consolidated statements were first required and what criteria are used to determine what subsidiaries should be consolidated.

Meet as a group and share your information. What generalizations can you draw from the policies you found? Propose explanations for the differences you find among countries. Discuss the effect of consolidation policies on comparisons of financial statements across countries.

Analyzing and Interpreting Financial Statements

11-61 Financial Statement Research

Select five companies in any industry. Review each company's financial statements to determine whether an acquisition occurred during the most recent year. For each acquisition, identify as much as possible concerning each of the following:

1. Did the company use cash or stock?
2. What percentage of the target was purchased?
3. Can you determine whether the acquired company was previously either a customer or a supplier of the acquiring company? If so, which one?

11-62 Starbuck's Annual Report

Starbuck's includes the following items on its balance sheet for the year ended September 28, 2003 and September 29, 2002 (amounts in millions). Assume securities involved no purchases or sales except for long-term investments which were acquired during 2003. Also, assume that their 2002 year-end values equaled their cost.

	2003	2002
Short-term investments—Available-for-sale securities	128.9	217.3
Short-term investments—Trading securities	20.2	10.4
Long-term investments—Available-for-sale securities	136.2	– 0 –
Equity and other investments	144.3	102.5

1. The investments are carried at fair value, except for the equity investments. Give the amount of net unrealized gain or loss in each of the first three investment accounts as of year-end 2003.
2. Estimate the effect on 2003 earnings before tax from changes in value of the investments that are accounted for as Available-for-sale securities.
3. Estimate the effect on 2003 earnings before tax from changes in value of the investments that are accounted for as Trading Securities.
4. Consult the footnotes in the appendix to determine why the goodwill account increased in 2003.

11-63 Analyzing Financial Statements Using the Internet

Go to www.ford.com to locate the Ford home page. Select *The Company* and click on *Investor Information*. Then, select the most recent annual report.

    Answer these questions about Ford.

1. What business segments do the consolidated financial statements of Ford include? How are the operations of these segments interrelated?
2. What information does Ford provide about its marketable securities shown on the consolidated balance sheets? Can you tell which ones are classified as trading securities?
3. Did Ford report any goodwill? Why would Ford want to pay more than the value of the net assets of a company it acquired?

Financial Statement Analysis

CHAPTER 12

LEARNING OBJECTIVES

After studying this chapter, you should be able to:

1. Locate and use sources of information about company performance.

2. Analyze the performance of a company using trend analysis, common-size financial statements, and segment disclosures.

3. Use basic financial ratios to guide your thinking.

4. Evaluate corporate performance using various metrics, including ROA, ROE, and EVA.

5. Calculate EPS when a company has preferred stock or dilutive securities.

6. Understand the nature of nonrecurring items and how to adjust for them.

7. Use financial information to help assess a company's value.

Eli Lilly **is a well-respected company whose primary** activities are the discovery, development, manufacture, and sale of pharmaceutical products. Although you may not be familiar with the company, you have probably heard of Prozac, one of its blockbuster drugs. During the 24 months from January 1, 2001 to December 31, 2002, Lilly's shares traded as low as $47.91 and as high as $90.23. *The Wall Street Journal* reported a closing price of $63.50 on December 31, 2002, up 32.5% from the low of $47.91. As of January 1, 2001, Lilly was selling at a price-earnings (P-E) ratio of almost 33. By December 31, 2002, the P-E ratio had fallen to a little over 25, a drop of more than 24%. Although earnings declined over this same 2-year time period, the earnings decline from the end of fiscal 2001 to the end of fiscal 2002 was only 11.4%. What caused earnings to decline? What caused investor sentiment to change?

In prior chapters, we concentrated on how to collect financial data and how to prepare and evaluate financial statements. In financial statement analysis, we interpret these financial data to more fully understand the story they tell about the company. However, understanding Eli Lilly requires more than just understanding its financial statements. You must be attuned to economywide, industrywide, and firm-specific factors. You must understand economywide forces such as the rate of inflation, demographic shifts, interest rate changes, and unemployment. For example, the 2000 census figures revealed that aging Baby Boomers pushed the nation's median age to 35.3, the highest age in U.S. history. The number of Americans in the 45 to 54 age bracket increased by 50% over the number in the 1990 census, whereas the number of people 85 and older increased 38%. These facts suggest increased sales for the pharmaceutical industry, given that demand for

Researchers at Eli Lilly seek answers for many of the world's medical needs. Eli Lilly's financial statements, which reflect the results of research and development, testing, manufacturing, and marketing activities, provide important information to investors and other users. In this chapter, we expand our understanding of financial statement analysis.

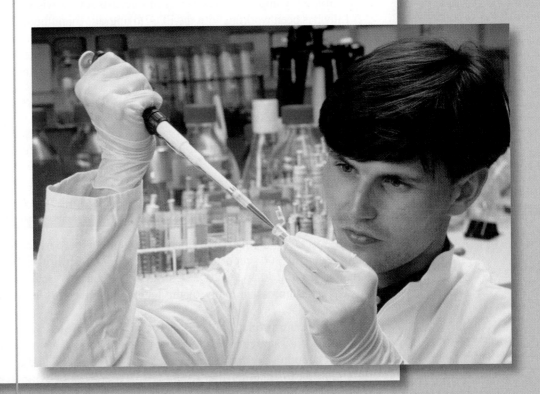

health care products and pharmaceuticals increases with the aging of the population. However, at the industrywide level, pharmaceutical products face increasing price pressures. At both the national and state level, government officials continue to take actions to reduce pharmaceutical prices and limit the ability of firms in the industry to enforce patent rights. In addition, company health plans are forcing patients to purchase lower-priced generic drugs. So, although product demand is likely to increase, product prices may rise more slowly or may actually decline.

At the firm-specific level, one of the major challenges faced by Lilly during 2001 and 2002 was the loss of patent protection for their dominant product, Prozac. This loss was so significant that some followers of the pharmaceutical industry predicted in 2000 that Lilly would not survive without a major business combination. The impact of the loss is evident from reading the management discussion & analysis (MD&A) section of the 2002 annual report, which states that sales of Prozac fell 63% during fiscal 2002. In addition, in early 2001, the U.S. Food and Drug Administration (FDA) expressed concerns about quality control and processes in some of the company's manufacturing facilities. These concerns delayed approval of several new drugs in Lilly's pipeline, resulting in lower than expected revenue.

Financial analysis addresses some of the concerns of investors and industry watchers. Total sales for 2002 decreased 4% from 2001. However, excluding sales of Prozac from both years, sales of other products increased 8%. A number of new products entered the pipeline in late 2002 and early 2003, setting the stage for improved performance. An investor trying to forecast future sales must consider this change in product mix. Due to the demands of these new product launches, marketing and administrative expenses increased in 2002 and are likely to continue to rise in 2003. At the same time, R&D expenses declined in dollar amount in 2002 but held steady as a percent of sales. Overall, Lilly lowered its combined marketing and R&D expenses by 1% relative to 2001.

Another important statistic is that 41% of Lilly's sales in 2002 came from overseas business, up from 36% in 2001. Although sales in the United States decreased by 11%, sales outside the United States increased 9%. Separate forecasts of domestic and international growth and profitability improve the accuracy of forecasts for the whole company.

Lilly has been working with the FDA to upgrade manufacturing and quality operations in both domestic and foreign facilities and has continued to develop new products. Have they been successful? *Financial Executive* published an interview with Eli Lilly CFO Charles Golden in September 2003. Let's see what he had to say:

> *We started planning for the expiration of the (Prozac) patent in late 1996. We planned for this financially, knowing what a strain it would have on the company in terms of cash flow and on our income statement. We had an understanding of what we had to do in terms of accelerating products through our pipeline. We're just coming out from under the shadow of the Prozac patent expiration. However, so far this year we've launched three new products. Our first quarter results show that sales increased by 13% and our earnings increased as well.*

In fact, Lilly's 10-Q (quarterly financial statements) report to the SEC for the 6 months ending June 30, 2003 reported net sales of $5,977.6 million, an increase of 12% over the 6 months ending June 30, 2002. Can Lilly sustain this trend? The analysis methods in this chapter summarize many of the techniques investors use to answer this and other questions.

People perform financial analysis for different reasons. Suppliers want to see if a customer can afford a price hike. Customers want to know if a company will still be around in a year to honor a warranty. Managers, creditors, investors, and the CEO's mother all have their reasons for reading the statements. Regardless of your interest in the company, **financial statement analysis** involves using financial data to assess some aspect of

financial statement analysis
Using financial data to assess a company's performance.

a company's performance. Our focus is on the investor. Investors read financial statements either to check on their current investments or to plan future investments. They analyze these statements and other material to determine whether their beliefs about the company have been borne out and to develop expectations about the future.

How do we use financial statements to forecast the future? We begin with a solid understanding of the company's past performance. Throughout the book we have shown you various ratios and other tools of analysis, so you should have some understanding of how to do it. This chapter integrates the tools you have already seen and teaches you several new ones as we focus on the techniques investors use to improve their investment decisions. ▪

Sources of Information About Companies

Publicly available information takes many forms. The now familiar annual report is one form, known for its completeness and its reliability, given the attestation of an independent third-party auditor. In addition to the financial statements we have already seen (income statement, balance sheet, statement of cash flows, and statement of stockholders' equity), annual reports usually contain:

OBJECTIVE 1

Locate and use sources of information about company performance.

1. Footnotes to the financial statements
2. A summary of the accounting policies used
3. Management's discussion and analysis (MD&A) of the financial results
4. The auditor's report
5. Management's report on its responsibility for the financial statements
6. Management's report on internal controls
7. Comparative financial data for a series of years
8. Narrative information about the company

These sections of the annual report are important to financial analysis. Observe that at the bottom of each financial statement is language that directs you to the footnotes. Some analysts and other financial statement users read the footnotes and the MD&A before examining the financial statements themselves. This provides a context for interpreting the numbers. The Starbucks 10-K information included with this book provides examples of each of the items listed.

In addition to the annual reports distributed to shareholders, companies also prepare reports for the SEC. Form 10-K may contain information not included in the annual report, although many companies now provide the full 10-K to shareholders. Form 10-Q includes quarterly financial statements, so it provides more timely, although less complete, information than does the annual report. Companies issue proxy statements in connection with shareholder meetings. These statements contain useful information such as the qualifications of board members, executive compensation and stock option awards, and audit fee disclosures. The SEC requires other reports for specific events, such as the issuance of common shares or debt. All SEC filings are available to investors, most of them on the World Wide Web. See the SEC Web site (www.sec.gov) for easy access to Edgar, the SEC electronic information source. Also, many companies include links to their SEC filings from their own Web pages.

Both annual reports and SEC filings are issued well after the events being reported have occurred. You can find more timely information in periodic company press releases, which provide the public with news about company developments, including the following:

1. Changes in personnel
2. Changes in dividends
3. Issuance or retirement of debt

4. Acquisition or sale of assets or business units
5. New products
6. New orders
7. Changes in production plans
8. Financial results

The Internet explosion has made it possible for the general public to gain almost immediate access to company press releases, which are often available on company Web sites. In addition, many companies routinely hold conference calls with security analysts to discuss new developments, and they make these calls accessible to investors via Webcasts. Numerous online services compile and sell databases of press releases and other corporate information. One such service is factiva.com, a joint venture of **Reuters** and **Dow Jones and Company**. Investors also rely on articles in the general financial press such as *The Wall Street Journal, Business Week, Forbes, Fortune,* and *Barron's.* Trade and industry-specific publications are other useful information sources. For example, *The Industry Standard* and *Red Herring* concentrate on news about young dynamic companies and high-tech industries. Many of these publications make their articles available to subscribers via the Internet. Services such as **Value Line, Moody's Investor's Services,** and **Standard and Poor's (S&P)** provide investors with useful information, as do credit agencies such as **Dun & Bradstreet**. In addition, stockbrokers prepare company analyses for their clients, and private investment services and newsletters supply analysts' reports and stock recommendations to their subscribers.

The Internet is changing the way investing is done. Investors can now purchase and sell securities electronically without ever talking to a broker. Many Internet browsers provide continuous information about security prices and access to analysts' reports on various industries and securities. Much of this information is free, but some requires the investor to have a brokerage account with the firm or to subscribe to a fee-based service. However, the Internet can also quickly spread false rumors as illustrated in the Business First box on page 539.

Investors should always get information before they invest, and the sources we have described provide plenty. Of course, some investors may request even more information. Banks or other creditors making multimillion-dollar loans may ask for a set of projected financial statements or other estimates of predicted results, known as **pro forma statements.** Not every investor needs this level of detail. There is so much information available to the public that wading through it all is not easy. Although we can gain much information from other sources, our discussion focuses on analyzing the information contained in the financial statements themselves.

pro forma statements
A set of projected financial statements or other estimates of predicted results.

Objectives of Financial Statement Analysis

Different types of investors expect different types of returns. If you are a stockholder, you expect an increase in the value of the stock you hold. If you have invested in a company with a history of paying dividends, you also expect a dividend. If you have loaned the firm money, you expect to receive interest and the return of your loan principal. Although the types of returns they expect are different, equity investors and creditors both risk not receiving those returns. Therefore, both stockholders and creditors use financial statement analysis to (1) predict their expected returns and (2) assess the risks associated with those returns.

short-term liquidity
An organization's ability to meet current payments as they become due.

long-term solvency
An organization's ability to generate enough cash to repay long-term debts as they mature.

The primary concern of creditors is short-term liquidity and long-term solvency. **Short-term liquidity** refers to how much cash a company has on hand to meet current payments, such as interest, wages, and taxes, as they become due. **Long-term solvency** refers to a company's ability to generate cash to repay long-term debts as they mature.

Web sites and focused business newscasts have increased the speed with which information reaches the markets. This change allows investors access to more information and enables them to act more quickly. This question remains: Is every news item "news"? Many companies post press releases to their Web sites. In addition, companies provide press releases to news wires such as PR Newswire or Internet Wire, which distribute the releases to subscribing news agencies such as CNBC or the New York Times. These in turn distribute the news via TV or newspaper. When individual investors or institutional investors see surprising news, they act quickly, buying or selling as the information dictates.

On Friday, August 25, 2000, some investors were hurt badly by a fraudulent news release about Emulex, a designer, developer, and supplier of networking products. Emulex stock closed on Thursday at $113. Just before the market opened on Friday, a press release appeared on Internet Wire indicating that the company was restating its earnings for the quarter from a profit of 25 cents to a loss of 15 cents. The release also said that earnings for the last 2 years would be revised and that the CEO had resigned. The stock dropped rapidly in response to this news. By the time the California-based company could respond to the news (about 7:00 A.M. Pacific Time, 10:00 A.M. Eastern Time), the stock had fallen to $28.50, down 75%. At the company's request, the NASDAQ halted trading in the stock. Trading resumed after 1 P.M. Eastern Time at a price near the prior close after the company assured the markets that the "news" was false. People reassessed their beliefs about the company and the stock closed for the day at $106. Investors made and lost billions of dollars during the day, and the people who sold at $28.50 were the big losers. The people who bought at $28.50 tripled their money in one day.

Mark Jakob, the perpetrator of the hoax, netted $241,000 in profit on trading in Emulex stock. Jakob, a former employee of Internet Wire, used his inside knowledge of how Internet financial news services work to mastermind the hoax. On July 25, 2001, Mr. Jakob agreed to pay $455,642 to settle the SEC civil suit filed against him and a few days later he was sentenced to 44 months in prison. The courts threw out a shareholder lawsuit against Internet Wire and Bloomberg, concluding that they were victims of the hoax, not perpetrators.

Our markets work only because such events are rare. In this case, Internet Wire seems to have forwarded a "press release" and others picked it up and responded to falling share prices by emphasizing the "news" surrounding the price fall. A lot of damage was done before the company had a chance to correct the record. The lesson for all is clear. It is not enough to simply repeat what others have said. The premier news agencies should confirm such explosive news with the company or with the other sources responsible.

Sources: Berenson, A., "On Hair-Trigger Wall Street, A Stock Plunges on Fake News," *New York Times*, August 26, 2000, p. A1; WSJ Staff Reporter, "Emulex Stock Saboteur Agrees to Pay $455,642 to Settle SEC Civil Suit," *The Wall Street Journal*, July 25, 2001, p. B4; Mulligan, T. S. and K. Alexander, "Web Hoax Puts O.C. Company's Stock in a Dive: Shares in Costa Mesa's Emulex Corp. Plunged After a Phony Item Spread Damaging Charges," *Los Angeles Times*, June 15, 2001, p. 1.

In contrast, equity investors are more concerned with profitability and future security prices. Why? Because dividend payments depend, in part, on how profitable operations are, and stock prices depend on the market's assessment of the company's future prospects. Investors gain when they receive dividends and when the value of their securities rise. Rising profits spur both events and declining profits have negative implications for both dividend policy and stock prices. Lilly's stock price declined as sales and income fell after the expiration of the Prozac patent. However, it continued to pay dividends. A struggling company may elect to terminate its dividend. For example, American Greetings has a very long history of paying dividends. In fiscal years 2001 and 2002, the company experienced significant net losses and engaged in major restructuring activities. As part of its retrenchment efforts, the company suspended its dividend after the second quarter of fiscal 2002, paying only $26.6 million for the year, compared with $51.2 million in 2000 and $52.7 million in 2001. No dividends were distributed in fiscal 2003. Not all successful companies pay dividends. For example, despite their enormous profitability, Microsoft did not pay a dividend until 2002.

Profitability is important not only to equity investors, but also to creditors. Why? Because the profitable operations that allow for dividends and drive stock prices to higher levels also provide the cash to repay loans and finance growth. Therefore, both creditors and equity investors are interested in a company's future profitability. If their concern is with the future, what is the value of analyzing prior period financial statements, which deal solely with past events? Trends in past sales, operating expenses, and net income often continue, so financial statement analysis of past performance is often a good indictator of future performance.

Evaluating Trends and Components of the Business

OBJECTIVE 2

Analyze the performance of a company using trend analysis, common-size financial statements, and segment disclosures.

Thorough analysis of financial statement information requires the use of a variety of different tools. The next two sections discuss two of the most popular techniques—trend analysis and common-size financial statements. A third technique, ratio analysis, should already be familiar because you have encountered ratios in several earlier chapters. Nevertheless, a later section of this chapter consolidates and adds to your knowledge of ratio analysis. We apply each technique to the same company, Eli Lilly and Company, as we demonstrate the application of analysis techniques.

Trend Analysis

Annual reports contain balance sheets for the current and previous year and the other financial statements for the current and previous 2 years. In addition, they show the amounts of key financial items for at least the last 5 years and often for 10. In evaluating trends, we may or may not find these numbers to be adequate. Supplemental sources provide much longer and richer access to information by archiving and adjusting older data. For example, many colleges and universities have Compustat PC, a CD-ROM database that provides 20 years of financial information extracted from the financial statements. Mergent Online is a subscriber database that provides Internet access to complete company financial data, along with other information. Many free online databases such as Reuters MultexInvestor and Yahoo! offer historical records of select financial performance measures and, of course, it is possible to access prior year's SEC filings at www.sec.gov.

trend analysis
An analysis technique that compares financial trends and changes from one year to the next and identifies patterns that have occurred in the past.

The essence of **trend analysis** is to compare financial trends and changes from one year to the next and identify predictable patterns that have occurred in the past. You then ask why that trend exists and whether you expect it to continue. If sales have been growing steadily but inventories have not, can this continue, or will future inventory growth require substantial additional investment? If inventories have been growing steadily but sales have not, why is the company buying so much inventory?

Trend analysis also prompts investors to ask themselves what could cause the trends to end. The early 2000s saw an unprecedented decline in interest rates as the Federal Reserve Bank attempted to jump-start the slumping economy. As the economy recovers, the Federal Reserve Bank is likely to raise interest rates. Rising interest rates hurt many industries. Banks are hurt because they must pay more for the money that they lend. Automobile manufacturers are hurt because car buyers face higher car payments when interest rates rise and therefore buy fewer cars. The same analysis follows for builders of new houses. In contrast, rising interest rates often help companies such as The Home Depot, which serves the home owners' needs for home improvement materials. Why? Because people who would like to move to a nicer home but conclude that interest rates

	For the Year Ended December 31, 2002	For the Year Ended December 31, 2001	Increase (Decrease)	
			Amount	Percentage*
Net sales	$11,077.5	$11,542.5	($465.0)	(4.0%)
Cost of sales	2,176.5	2,160.2	16.3	0.8%
Gross margin	8,901.0	9,382.3	(481.3)	(5.1%)
R&D	2,149.3	2,235.1	(85.8)	(3.8%)
Marketing and administrative	3,424.0	3,417.4	6.6	0.2%
Acquired in-process R&D	84.0	190.5	(106.5)	(55.9%)
Asset impairment and other site charges	—	121.4	(121.4)	(100.0%)
Operating expenses	5,657.3	5,964.4	(307.1)	(5.1%)
Operating income	3,243.7	3,417.9	(174.2)	(5.1%)
Other income, net	293.7	280.7	13.0	4.6%
Less: Interest expense	(79.7)	(146.5)	(66.8)	(45.6%)
Nonoperating income	214.0	134.2	79.8	59.5%
Income before tax	3,457.7	3,552.1	(94.4)	(2.7%)
Income tax	749.8	742.7	7.1	1.0%
Income before extraordinary item	2,707.9	2,809.4	(101.5)	(3.6%)
Extraordinary item (loss)	—	(29.4)	29.4	(100.0%)
Net income	$ 2,707.9	$ 2,780.0	($72.1)	(2.6%)
Basic earnings per share				
Income before extraordinary item	$ 2.51	$ 2.61	($0.10)	(3.8%)
Extraordinary item	$ 0.00	($0.03)	$0.03	(100.0%)
Net income	$ 2.51	$ 2.58	($0.07)	(2.7%)
Diluted earnings per share				
Income before extraordinary item	$ 2.50	$ 2.58	($0.08)	(3.1%)
Extraordinary item	$ 0.00	($0.03)	$0.03	(100.0%)
Net income	$ 2.50	$ 2.55	($0.05)	(2.0%)

*Percentage column numbers cannot be added.

Note: Dividends per share, $1.27 and $1.15, respectively. For publicly held companies, there is a requirement to show EPS on the face of the income statement, but it is not necessary to show dividends per share.

Exhibit 12-1

Eli Lilly and Company

Statement of Income (Dollars in millions, except per share data and percentages)

are too high often decide to remodel their existing home. These examples illustrate how you might think about trends in sales and profits in particular industries.

To see how trend analysis works, let's examine the income statements and balance sheets of Eli Lilly as shown in Exhibits 12-1 and 12-2. The first two columns show Lilly's information for 2002 and 2001. The third column shows the dollar amount of the change in each item from 2001 to 2002. Finally, the fourth column shows the percentage change, computed as follows:

$$\text{Percentage change 2001 to 2002} = \frac{2002 \text{ amount} - 2001 \text{ amount}}{2001 \text{ amount}} \times 100$$

For example, Lilly's net sales decreased by $465 million or 4%:

$$\text{Percentage change} = \frac{\$11,077.5 - \$11,542.5}{\$11,542.5} \times 100 = (4.0\%)$$

	December 31, 2002	December 31, 2001	Increase (Decrease) Amount	Percentage*
Cash	$ 1,945.9	$ 2,702.3	($756.4)	(28.0%)
Short-term investments	1,708.8	1,028.7	680.1	66.1%
Accounts receivable	1,670.3	1,406.2	264.1	18.8%
Other receivables	403.9	289.0	114.9	39.8%
Inventories	1,495.4	1,060.2	435.2	41.0%
Deferred income taxes	331.7	223.3	108.4	48.5%
Prepaid expenses	248.1	229.2	18.9	8.2%
Total current assets	7,804.1	6,938.9	865.2	12.5%
Prepaid pension	1,515.4	1,102.8	412.6	37.4%
Investments	3,150.4	2,710.9	439.5	16.2%
Sundry	1,279.1	1,149.1	130.0	11.3%
Other assets	5,944.9	4,962.8	982.1	19.8%
Property, plant, and equipment, net	5,293.0	4,532.4	760.6	16.8%
Total assets	$19,042.0	$16,434.1	$2,607.9	15.9%
Short-term borrowings	$ 545.4	$ 286.3	$ 259.1	90.5%
Accounts payable	676.9	624.1	52.8	8.5%
Employee compensation	231.7	381.9	(150.2)	(39.3%)
Dividends payable	375.8	341.0	34.8	10.2%
Income taxes payable	1,761.9	2,319.5	(557.6)	(24.0%)
Other liabilities	1,471.8	1,250.2	221.6	17.7%
Total current liabilities	5,063.5	5,203.0	(139.5)	(2.7%)
Long-term debt	4,358.2	3,132.1	1,226.1	39.1%
Other noncurrent liabilities	1,346.7	995.0	351.7	35.3%
Total noncurrent liabilities	5,704.9	4,127.1	1,577.8	38.2%
Common stock	702.1	702.7	($0.6)	(0.1%)
Additional paid-in capital	2,610.0	2,610.0	0.0	0.0%
Retained earnings	8,500.1	7,411.2	1,088.9	14.7%
Employee benefit trust & deferred costs	(2,758.3)	(2,764.1)	5.8	(0.2%)
Accumulated other comprehensive loss	(670.8)	(748.4)	77.6	(10.4%)
Treasury stock	(109.5)	(107.4)	(2.1)	2.0%
Total shareholders' equity	8,273.6	7,104.0	1,169.6	16.5%
Total liabilities and shareholders' equity	$19,042.0	$16,434.1	$2,607.9	15.9%

*Percentage column numbers cannot be added.

Exhibit 12-2
Eli Lilly and Company Balance Sheets
(Dollars in millions, except percentages)

At the same time, Lilly's cost of sales increased $16.3 million or 0.8%:

$$\text{Percentage change} = \frac{\$2,176.5 - \$2,160.2}{\$2,160.2} \times 100 = 0.8\%$$

You can add or subtract the dollar change amounts to obtain meaningful subtotals. However, you must use care when considering the effect of increases or decreases on revenue and expense accounts. Increases in revenues and increases in expenses have offsetting effects on net income. In Exhibit 12-1, the decline of $465 million in Net Sales is compounded by the increase in Cost of Sales of $16.3 million. Although the sign of the change in Net Sales is negative and the sign of the change in Cost of Sales is positive, they both contribute to a decrease in gross margin and net income. As a result, the gross margin declined by $481.3 million (5.1%). Similarly, total operating expenses decreased by $307.1 million. This caused operating income to decline by $174.2 million, an amount less than the $481.3 million decline in gross margin. Note that although you can add the changes in dollars as you move down the column, you cannot add the changes in percentage terms.

Finally, nonoperating activities generated income of $134.2 million in 2001 and income of $214.0 million in 2002. This $79.8 million increase in nonoperating income helps offset the $174.2 million decline in operating income. Do not be fooled by the change amounts in the nonoperating section of the income statement. Other Income increased from $280.7 million to $293.7 million, resulting in a $13.0 million (or 4.6%) increase. Interest Expense, which we deduct from Other Income in Exhibit 12-1, declined $66.8 million, from $146.5 million to $79.7 million, hence, the amount and percentage are both negative. Because the reduction in Interest Expense increases income, the total change in nonoperating income is an increase of $13.0 million + $66.8 million = $79.8 million. The decline in operating income offset by the increase in nonoperating income results in a net decrease in income before taxes of $174.2 million − $79.8 million = $94.4 million.

As an aside, in its income statement, Eli Lilly does not distinguish between operating and nonoperating revenues and expenses. We made the distinction in Exhibit 12-1 to enhance discussion. Some analysts might take exception to the classification in Exhibit 12-1 and prefer to treat Acquired In-Process R&D and Asset Impairment and Other Site Charges as nonoperating items. Operating and nonoperating classifications are not universally agreed upon. When you are comparing companies, it is important to recognize differences in classification.

We need both dollar and percentage changes to identify trends and understand their true meaning. For example, although the sales decrease of $465 million is larger than the $174.2 million decrease in operating income, the percentage decrease is actually smaller, (4.0%) compared with (5.1%). Similarly, in Exhibit 12-2, the 90.5% increase in Short-term Borrowings seems large, but the dollar increase of $259.1 million is much smaller than the change in many other accounts.

Although it is always possible to compute and interpret dollar changes, some percentage changes are not meaningful. Look at Exhibit 12-1. Eli Lilly includes two items on the 2001 income statement that do not appear on either the 2002 or the 2000 income statements (2000 income statement not shown): Asset Impairment and Other Site Charges totaling $121.4 million and Extraordinary Loss of $29.4 million. (We explain these items in more detail later in this chapter.) The percentage decrease in these items between 2001 and 2002 is 100%. If you try to compute the percentage increase between 2000 and 2001, the denominator of the percentage change calculation is zero and the percentage is undefined. Another problem arises when a company reports a negative dollar amount in one time period and a positive amount in the comparison period. For example, a company may net interest revenue and interest expense together on the income statement. In one year, the net amount might result in income, and in the other year it might net to an expense. It is not meaningful to compute a percentage change in this case. Also, remember that unlike the dollar amounts of change, you cannot add or subtract the percentage changes to obtain subtotals.

Changes in dollar amounts and percentages help analysts see patterns. Although recognizing patterns is key, understanding what caused those patterns is even more important. In the Eli Lilly example, analysis of the balance sheet in Exhibit 12-2 reveals that inventories increased 41.0%, accounts receivable increased 18.8%, and net property, plant and equipment increased 16.8%. Companies often acquire new property and equipment to meet increased sales demand. Inventories might increase because sales levels have jumped and managers want to be sure they have sufficient product to deliver to the customer. Similarly, increased sales activity typically results in increased accounts receivable. Therefore, increases in these three asset accounts might lead you to conclude that the company is expanding, and you might expect sales and net income to also display increases. Exhibit 12-1 reveals that Lilly actually experienced a 4% decrease in net sales and a 2.6% decline in net income. Are there alternative explanations for the changes in the balance sheet accounts? Consider inventory. Inventory levels may climb when demand for the product falls unexpectedly. Why? Because products produced to meet anticipated demand remain on the shelves when demand falls short of expectations. With respect to accounts receivable, a downturn in the economy may slow collections of existing receivables without a corresponding increase in sales. Finally, it takes time for a new plant or manufacturing equipment to ramp up to full production and begin to generate revenue. In other words, the growth in sales revenue often follows the period of acquisition of new property or equipment.

management discussion and analysis (MD&A)
A required section of the annual report that concentrates on explaining the major changes in operating results, liquidity, and capital resources.

What explains this apparent inconsistency between Lilly's asset growth and sales? The answer to such a question often reveals a specific company strategy or some characteristic of the market. Where would you look for answers? Analysts often look to a section of the company's annual report called the **management discussion and analysis** (often called the **MD&A).** The MD&A concentrates on explaining the major changes in the company's operating results, liquidity, and capital resources. The SEC dictates its contents, and expansion of the required disclosures has caused space devoted to the MD&A to increase dramatically in recent years. The MD&A includes, but is not limited to, disclosures about a company's capital resources and liquidity, including off-balance sheet arrangements and capital expenditures; the results of operations, including a discussion of trends in sales and expenses and an explanation of any unusual or infrequent events; disclosures about contractual obligations and commitments and trading activities; and discussion of critical accounting estimates and the adoption of new accounting policies. For example, Eli Lilly's 2002 MD&A discusses the company's policies, estimates, and assumptions with regard to "sales rebates and discounts and their impact on revenue recognition, product litigation liabilities and other contingencies, pension and retiree medical benefit costs, and the recoverability of deferred tax assets." Because many financial statement numbers are estimates, the investor must read this information carefully. The Starbucks 10-K report that accompanies this book provides an example of MD&A disclosures.

Let us look at what we can learn from Lilly's MD&A. As you already know, Lilly's sales revenue fell due to the loss of patent protection for Prozac. Slower than expected roll out of new products did not generate enough sales to offset the decline in Prozac sales. However, the MD&A explains that sales of new products did increase in December 2002, resulting in increased receivables. Similarly, inventories increased in part due to increased inventory requirements for these new products. The MD&A also indicates that expenditures for property and equipment in 2002 were more than in 2001 as the company continued to invest in manufacturing, R&D, and related infrastructure for the new products. These explanations imply that the decline in 2002 sales was a temporary one and that growth in new product sales will improve sales levels in 2003.

What additional questions arise from analyzing trends in Lilly's financial statements? Here are a few. Why did cash decrease by 28% while short-term investments increased by 66.1%? Has the company changed its short-term investing strategy? Why did current liabilities decrease 2.7% while long-term liabilities increased 38.2%? Has the company changed its financing strategy? Why did current assets increase by 12.5% while current liabilities decreased by 2.7%? Has there been a change in working capital management? The answers to these questions say a lot about how

	For the Year Ended December 31				
	2002	**2001**	**2000**	**1999**	**1998**
Income statement data					
Net sales	$11,077.5	$11,542.5	$10,862.2	$10,002.9	$ 9,236.8
Cost of sales	2,176.5	2,160.2	2,055.7	2,098.0	2,015.1
Gross margin	8,901.0	9,382.3	8,806.5	7,904.9	7,221.7
R&D	2,149.3	2,235.1	2,018.5	1,738.6	1,738.9
Other costs and expenses	3,294.0	3,595.1	2,929.3	2,920.9	2,817.8
Income from continuing operations					
before tax and extraordinary items	3,457.7	3,552.1	3,858.7	3,245.4	2,665.0
Income taxes	749.8	742.7	800.9	698.7	568.7
Income from:					
Continuing operations before extraord. item	2,707.9	2,809.4	3,057.8	2,546.7	2,096.3
Discontinued operations	—	—	—	174.3	8.8
Extraordinary item (loss)	—	(29.4)	—	—	(7.2)
Net income	$ 2,707.9	$ 2,780.0	$ 3,057.8	$ 2,721.0	$ 2,097.9
Earnings per share	2.50	2.55	2.79	2.46	1.87
Dividends per share	1.27	1.15	1.06	0.95	0.83
Balance sheet data (as of December 31)					
Current assets	$ 7,804.1	$ 6,938.9	$ 7,943.0	$ 7,055.5	$ 5,406.8
Current liabilities	5,063.5	5,203.0	4,960.7	3,935.4	4,607.2
Property, plant, and equipment	5,293.0	4,532.4	4,176.6	3,981.5	4,096.3
Total assets	19,042.0	16,434.1	14,690.8	12,825.2	12,595.5
Long-term debt	4,358.2	3,132.1	2,633.7	2,811.9	2,185.5
Shareholders' equity	8,723.6	7,104.0	6,046.9	5,013.0	4,429.6

Exhibit 12-3
Eli Lilly and Company
Five-Year Financial Summary (Dollars in millions, except per share data)

management runs a company, how it will perform in the future, and whether it would be a good investment.

As indicated earlier, an analyst might note that Lilly's sales decreased 4.0% while cost of sales increased by 0.8%, causing a 5.1% decline in gross margin. A declining gross margin is not good news. When relationships do not look as good as expected, the issue is whether a crisis exists. When relationships look better than expected, the question is whether the company can sustain this situation. To see how trends develop over time, analysts often look at several years of financial information. Exhibit 12-3 shows a 5-year summary of key items for Lilly, which enables you to compute a longer trend. For example, percentage changes in sales are:

2002

$$\frac{\$11,077.5 - \$11,542.5}{\$11,542.5} \times 100 = (4.0\%)$$

2001

$$\frac{\$11,542.5 - \$10,862.2}{\$10,862.2} \times 100 = 6.3\%$$

2000

$$\frac{\$10,862.2 - \$10,002.9}{\$10,002.9} \times 100 = 8.6\%$$

1999

$$\frac{\$10,002.9 - \$9,236.8}{\$9,236.8} \times 100 = 8.3\%$$

It appears that the decline in sales in 2002 is unusual. In fact, subsequent issuance of the 2003 financial statements indicates that sales rose 13.6% over 2002 levels.

By applying the present value techniques of Chapter 9, we can compute the
compound annual growth rate (CAGR) in sales for the 4-year period. The CAGR is
the year-over-year growth rate over a specified period of time. In this case, it is the
annual rate at which sales must grow to increase from the initial level of $9,236.8 to
that at the end of the period, $11,077.5. The 4-year CAGR for Lilly is 4.65%. We
obtained this precise value with a calculator. However, you can use the tables in
Chapter 9 to approximate this value. The future value multiple is 2002 sales divided
by 1998 sales, or ($11,077.5 ÷ $9,236.8) = 1.1993. In Table 9A-1, p. 420, the future
value factor for 4 years for 4% is 1.1699 and for 5% is 1.2155. The observed value of
1.1993 falls near the midpoint of this range but closer to 1.2155, so the CAGR must
be closer to 5% than to 4%. The 4.65% value we computed qualifies. This rate may
seem low for a major pharmaceutical company. Given the short time period analyzed
here, the impact of a single observation can have significant impact on the CAGR. If
you compute the CAGR for the 3 years from 1998 to 2001, deleting the decline in
sales in 2002, it increases to 7.71%. If you use the CAGR for purposes of forecasting
the company's future performance, you must exercise caution.

Common-Size Statements

To make it easier to evaluate a company's performance over time or to compare
companies that differ in size, we often analyze income statements and balance sheets

using **common-size statements** in which we express the components as relative
percentages. Lilly's common-size statements appear in Exhibit 12-4, side by
side with the income statements from Exhibit 12-1 and condensed balance sheets
from Exhibit 12-2.

The income statement percentages are based on sales equal to 100%. We express
each element of the income statement as a percentage of sales. In 2001, Lilly's gross
margin was 81.3%, falling to 80.4% in 2002. To better understand this gross margin,
we might compare it with a specific competitor's values or with industry averages.
This small decline in Lilly's gross margin may not be alarming, but it would be interesting to determine if the margins of other firms in the industry are following a similar trend or if Lilly's decline is unusual. Although the use of common-size financial
statements facilitates the comparison of different size firms, remember that differences other than size may need to be considered. For example, a company's choice of
inventory cost flow assumption effects the reported gross margin. A company using
LIFO in a rising input price environment typically reports a higher cost of goods sold
than a company using FIFO, everything else equal. A higher cost of goods sold results
in a lower gross margin.

The behavior of each expense in relation to changes in total revenue is often revealing. That is, which expenses go up or down as sales fluctuate? For example, between
2001 and 2002 Cost of Sales and Marketing and Administrative Expenses increased, both
in absolute dollar terms and as a percentage of sales. Why? In the MD&A, Lilly explains
that the decrease in Gross Margin "was attributed primarily to the decline in sales of
Prozac, a higher margin product, and increased costs associated with current Good
Manufacturing Practices improvements, costs associated with capacity increases for certain growth and new products, and higher inventory losses." The increase in Marketing
and Administrative Expenses is attributed to the costs of new product launches. R&D
costs decreased slightly in dollar amount (from $2,235.1 million to $2,149.3 million) but
stayed stable as a percentage of sales, 19.4% in both years. This is one of the highest
R&D to sales percentages in the industry. A modest decline in R&D spending for 1 year
is not cause for concern. However, R&D is the lifeblood of a pharmaceutical company
and any significant decrease would raise a red flag to investors. Lilly knows that analysts
track R&D closely and offers the following explanation for the decline: "R&D expenses

	For the Year Ended December 31			
	2002		**2001**	
Statement of Income				
Net sales	$11,077.5	100.0%	$11,542.5	100.0%
Cost of sales	2,176.5	19.6%	2,160.2	18.7%
Gross margin	8,901.0	80.4%	9,382.3	81.3%
R&D	2,149.3	19.4%	2,235.1	19.4%
Marketing and administrative	3,424.0	30.9%	3,417.4	29.6%
Acquired in-process R&D	84.0	0.8%	190.5	1.7%
Asset impairment and other site charges	—	0.0%	121.4	1.1%
Operating expenses	5,657.3	51.1%	5,964.4	51.7%
Operating income	3,243.7	29.3%	3,417.9	29.6%
Other income, net	293.7	2.7%	280.7	2.4%
Less: Interest expense	(79.7)	(0.7%)	(146.5)	(1.3%)
Nonoperating income	214.0	1.9%	134.2	1.2%
Income before tax	3,457.7	31.2%	3,552.1	30.8%
Income tax	749.8	6.8%	742.7	6.4%
Income before extraordinary item	2,707.9	24.4%	2,809.4	24.3%
Extraordinary gain (loss)	—	0.0%	(29.4)	(0.3%)
Net income	$ 2,707.9	24.4%	$ 2,780.0	24.1%

	December 31			
	2002		**2001**	
Balance Sheet				
Cash	$ 1,945.9	10.2%	$ 2,702.3	16.4%
Short-term investments	1,708.8	9.0%	1,028.7	6.3%
Other current assets	4,149.4	21.8%	3,207.9	19.5%
Property, plant, and equipment	5,293.0	27.8%	4,532.4	27.6%
Other assets	5,944.9	31.2%	4,962.8	30.2%
Total assets	$19,042.0	100.0%	$16,434.1	100.0%
Current liabilities	5,063.5	26.6%	5,203.0	31.7%
Noncurrent liabilities	5,704.9	30.0%	4,127.1	25.1%
Total liabilities	10,768.4	56.6%	9,330.1	56.8%
Shareholders' equity	8,273.6	43.4%	7,104.0	43.2%
Total liabilities and shareholders' equity	$19,042.0	100.0%	$16,434.1	100.0%

Note: Some percentages' are off by 0.1% due to rounding.

Exhibit 12-4
Eli Lilly and Company
Common-Size Statements (in millions, except percentages)

decreased 4 percent due primarily to lower late-stage clinical trial costs as more products were awaiting regulator approval."

The balance sheet percentages in Exhibit 12-4 are based on total assets equal to 100%. We refer to them as **component percentages** because they measure each component of the financial statements as a percentage of the total. As with the income statement, you must look for changes in balance sheet relationships. For example, Lilly's Cash has decreased from $2,702.3 million or 16.4% of total assets in 2001 to $1,945.9 million or 10.2% of total assets in 2002. This represents a significant change in liquidity. Is this cause for concern? If you combine Cash with Short-Term Investments, the concern is somewhat mitigated. The combination of these two components equals $3,731 million or 22.7% of total assets in 2001 and $3,654.7 million or 19.2% of total assets in 2002. Noncurrent Liabilities increased as a percentage of total assets. What is the cause of the change? Lilly issued almost $1,260 million in new long-term debt in 2002.

component percentages
Elements of financial statements that express each component as a percentage of the total.

INTERPRETING FINANCIAL STATEMENTS

Common-size financial statements are useful in comparing companies that are significantly different in size. However, when you engage in comparisons across companies, you must consider the accounting choices made by the companies in arriving at the numbers presented on the financial statements. Name three accounting choices that impact the comparability of financial statements. You may need to think back to previous chapters to respond to this question.

Answer

1. Inventory cost flow assumption. For example, the use of LIFO versus FIFO can have a significant effect on cost of goods sold reported on the income statement and inventory values reported on the balance sheet.

2. Depreciation method. The use of straight-line versus accelerated depreciation methods can have a significant effect on the income statement and on property, plant, and equipment values on the balance sheet.

3. Lease classification. A lease agreement structured as a capital lease will increase both assets and liabilities relative to a lease structured as an operating lease. Income statement values also vary because an operating lease results in rent expense, whereas a capital lease results in depreciation expense and interest expense.

Segment Reporting

Our analysis of trends and common-size statements has focused on the company as a whole. However, it is often useful to analyze individual segments of the business. A required footnote to financial statements gives us information on the sales, profits, and assets of segments of a company's business.

When employing financial analysis techniques, analysts often consider the different business and geographic segments of a company's activities. Eli Lilly operates in one significant business segment—pharmaceutical products. Although they have an animal health business segment, the operations of that segment are not material and share many of the same economic and operating characteristics as pharmaceutical products. As a result, Lilly combines the animal health operations with pharmaceutical products for segment reporting purposes. In contrast, Merck and Company, a competitor of Eli Lilly's, reports the operations of two segments: Merck Pharmaceutical, which produces pharmaceutical products for treating humans, and Medco Health, which provides pharmacy benefit management services. In fact, Merck decided in early 2003 to divest its Medco Health division to allow it to concentrate more fully on pharmaceuticals. Eli Lilly made a similar decision years ago when it sold Elizabeth Arden, a cosmetics subsidiary. Both Lilly and Merck operate internationally, so they also report results by geographic segments.

Exhibit 12-5 is an excerpt from Eli Lilly's 2002 segment disclosures. Although Lilly operates in only one reportable segment, pharmaceutical products, it reports sales by type of drug. For example, sales of drugs in the neurosciences group declined from $5,157.6 million (47.5% of net sales) in 2000 to $4,668.3 million (42.1% of net sales) in 2002. This reflects the previously mentioned decline in sales of Prozac. The product line reports support the assertion that sales in other product lines (endocrinology, oncology, animal health, and cardiovascular) are increasing. In addition, Lilly reports sales activity and the distribution of long-lived assets by geographic segment. Note that 41% of Lilly's 2002 sales were foreign, up from 36.2% in 2001 and 35.5% in 2000. Clearly, if you want to forecast Lilly's future performance, you must understand not only economic and demographic trends in the United States, but also trends around the globe.

As mentioned previously, Merck reported multiple segments in 2002. Panel A of Exhibit 12-6 displays total Sales, Income Before Taxes, Net Income After Taxes, and Return

	Year Ended December 31					
	2002		**2001**		**2000**	
Net sales—to unaffiliated customers						
Neurosciences	$ 4,668.3	42.1%	$ 5,328.2	46.2%	$ 5,157.6	47.5%
Endocrinology	3,444.6	31.1%	3,103.5	26.9%	2,583.5	23.8%
Oncology	893.1	8.1%	739.1	6.4%	580.5	5.3%
Animal health	693.1	6.3%	686.1	5.9%	668.5	6.2%
Cardiovascular	624.9	5.6%	593.4	5.1%	587.9	5.4%
Anti-infectives	577.4	5.2%	749.5	6.5%	894.3	8.2%
Other pharmaceutical	176.1	1.6%	342.7	3.0%	389.9	3.6%
Net sales	$11,077.5	100.0%	$11,542.5	100.0%	$10,862.2	100.0%
Geographic Information						
Net sales—to unaffiliated customers						
United States	$ 6,536.1	59.0%	$ 7,364.3	63.8%	$ 7,002.9	64.5%
Western Europe	2,155.4	19.5%	1,953.1	16.9%	1,773.9	16.3%
Other foreign countries	2,386.0	21.5%	2,225.1	19.3%	2,085.4	19.2%
	$11,077.5	100.0%	$11,542.5	100.0%	$10,862.2	100.0%
Long-lived assets						
United States	$ 4,725.1	73.9%	$ 4,015.4	75.7%	$ 3,621.0	75.0%
Western Europe	997.1	15.6%	767.9	14.5%	735.3	15.2%
Other foreign countries	673.3	10.5%	519.6	9.8%	472.1	9.8%
	$ 6,395.5	100.0%	$ 5,302.9	100.0%	$ 4,828.4	100.0%

Exhibit 12-5
Eli Lilly and Company
Segment Information
(In millions, except percentages)

Exhibit 12-6
Merck and Company
*Consolidated and
Segment Data
(In millions, except
percentages)*

Panel A: Consolidated Income Statement Data and Return on Sales Information

	For the year ended December 31		
	2002	**2001**	**2000**
Sales	$51,790.3	$47,715.7	$40,363.2
Income before taxes	$10,213.6	$10,402.6	$ 9,824.1
Net income after taxes	$ 7,149.5	$ 7,281.8	$ 6,821.7
Before-tax return on sales	19.7%	21.8%	24.3%
After-tax return on sales	13.8%	15.3%	16.9%

Panel B: Segment Disclosures (all figures shown before taxes)

	Merck Pharmaceutical	Medco Health	All Other	Total
Year Ended December 31, 2002				
Segment revenues	$20,130.0	$33,433.5	$1,244.5	$54,808.0
Segment profits	12,722.8	741.1	1,110.8	14,574.7
Return on sales	63.2%	2.2%	89.3%	26.6%
Year Ended December 31, 2001				
Segment revenues	$19,731.5	$29,693.4	$1,265.9	$50,690.8
Segment profits	12,199.9	731.4	977.5	13,908.8
Return on sales	61.8%	2.5%	77.2%	27.4%
Year Ended December 31, 2000				
Segment revenues	$18,577.3	$23,319.6	$1,211.6	$43,108.5
Segment profits	11,563.6	683.0	924.8	13,171.4
Return on sales	62.2%	2.9%	76.3%	30.6%

on Sales as reported in Merck's 2002 annual report. These aggregate figures cannot answer questions such as: What contribution did each segment make to Merck's total sales? What contribution did each segment make to Merck's net income? What caused the decline in Merck's return on sales? Are sales of one segment driving the decline or is the company experiencing reduced profitability in all segments?

Panel B of Exhibit 12-6 shows Merck's segment disclosures from the 2002 annual report. Sales and profits are broken into three segments: Merck Pharmaceutical, Medco Health, and All Other. One of the first things you may notice is that total segment revenues and total segment profits (reported before tax) do not agree with the total sales and before tax income figures in panel A. The income statement reports 2002 sales of $51,790.3 million and before-tax income of $10,213.6 million, whereas the segment disclosures reflect total sales of $54,808 million and total profits of $14,574.7 million. Why? FASB guidance requires that segment data be presented in a manner consistent with the way in which the company manages its businesses. For internal management purposes, Merck recognizes some revenues that are not recognizable under GAAP; hence, they show higher revenues in the segment disclosures. Also for internal reporting, Merck does not allocate all expenses to the segments resulting in higher profits in the segment disclosures. Merck provides reconciliations (not shown) of their segment numbers to the income statement numbers to clarify the differences.

The segment revenue and profit information reveals that all the segments are not equally profitable. The before-tax return on sales of Medco Health, the segment that sells prescription drugs through managed prescription drug programs, is extremely low relative to the returns reported by the other segments. In addition, the return on sales reported for that segment declined from 2.9% in 2000 to 2.2% in 2002. The return on the Merck Pharmaceutical segment improved slightly from 62.2% in 2000 to 63.2% in 2002. The remaining segment, referred to as "All Other," is much smaller and contributes little in terms of total sales dollars. However, the return on sales jumped from 76.3% in 2000 to 89.3% in 2002.

On August 5, 2003, Merck announced its intention to spin off the Medco Health segment by distributing new Medco stock to existing Merck shareholders. Many investors believe Merck is better off without Medco, partly because the Justice Department is investigating the pharmacy benefits management industry. This spin-off will make Merck's financial statements more comparable to Lilly's, with each having just one major segment.

What about geographic segments? Merck reports that U.S. sales constituted 81.6%, 83.6%, and 83.9% of total sales in 2002, 2001, and 2000, respectively. Similar to Lilly, Merck is experiencing greater growth in their international segments.

INTERPRETING FINANCIAL STATEMENTS

In 2002, 59% of Lilly's $11,077.5 million in sales were domestic sales and 41% were foreign sales. Suppose you predicted domestic sales to decline 2% and foreign sales to grow 4%. What would be your prediction of sales for the year 2003?

2. Foreign sales equal:
   (.41 × $11,077.5 × 1.04) = $4,723.4 million
3. Projected sales would be $11,128.4 for a weighted-average growth rate of about 0.5%.

Answer
1. Domestic sales equal:
   (.59 × $11,077.5 × .98) = $6,405.0 million

Financial Ratios

Although many analysis methods exist, the cornerstone of financial statement analysis is the use of ratios. Exhibit 12-7 groups some of the most popular ratios into four categories. You have encountered most of these ratios in earlier chapters, as indicated in the second column (a dash in the column means that the ratio is being introduced in this chapter for the first time). We provide this summary to avoid the need to search for definitions in prior material.

We focus on the use of ratios by investors. However, managers also use ratios to guide, measure, and reward workers. If managers compensate workers for actions that make the company more profitable, workers are likely to do the right thing. Thus, some companies give workers a bonus if the company generates a return on equity (ROE) in excess of a predetermined benchmark or if earnings per share (EPS) exceed a specific number.

Given recent corporate scandals where companies manipulated accounting records to inflate earnings, many companies are broadening their incentive programs to include nonaccounting measures as well as accounting numbers. For example, **Duke Power Company** decided that profit may not be the right measure for rewarding employees. Suppose profit increases because you raise more capital and expand the company. Should the workers necessarily earn more? Duke Power decided to reward workers based on two factors: success in meeting goals and ROE. For one worker, the goal might be reduced injuries, and for another, improved customer service. However, everyone earns more for meeting ROE targets. ROE is a good measure of efficiency because it can be improved by increasing profitability and also by increasing the efficiency with which assets are employed.

Evaluating Financial Ratios

No single ratio by itself provides a valid basis for assessing a company's financial performance. Rather, it is important to examine a set of ratios, to perform other types of analyses, and to seek out nonfinancial information describing the firm's activities. That said, the focus of this section is the use of financial ratios. The easy part of ratio analysis is the computation of the numerical values. Once you have computed a set of ratios, you must decide if the ratios indicate good, average, or poor performance. There are three main types of comparisons for evaluating financial ratios: comparisons (1) with a company's own historical ratios (called **time-series comparisons**), (2) with general rules of thumb or **benchmarks**, and (3) with ratios of other companies or with industry averages (called **cross-sectional comparisons**).

A few words of caution about these three types of comparisons. When performing a trend analysis or comparing a company's ratios in a time-series analysis, you must be aware of structural shifts in the company. For example, major acquisitions or divestitures cause the financial statements of a company to be difficult to compare across time. Consider the merger of **AOL** and **Time Warner** in early 2000. Time Warner was a media conglomerate whose activities included a cable television system servicing a significant percentage of U.S. households, publishing, music and entertainment, and film libraries. At the time of the merger, AOL was the nation's largest Internet service provider. The financial statements of the combined enterprise bore little resemblance to the financials of either of the original companies.

The use of benchmarks has the advantage of being easy to implement. However, rules of thumb vary from industry to industry and are susceptible to change over time. For example, the traditional rule of thumb for the current ratio has been 2 to 1 or higher. Improvements in working capital management have made it possible for many companies to operate with a much lower current ratio. A current ratio of 1 may be sufficient for a company with strong and stable cash flows, whereas a company with weak cash flows should maintain a higher current ratio.

OBJECTIVE 3
Use basic financial ratios to guide your thinking.

time-series comparisons
Comparisons of a company's financial ratios with its own historical ratios.

benchmarks
General rules of thumb specifying appropriate levels for financial ratios.

cross-sectional comparisons
Comparisons of a company's financial ratios with the ratios of other companies or with industry averages.

Typical Name of Ratio	Introduced in Chapter	Numerator	Denominator	Using Appropriate Lilly Numbers Applied to December 31 of Year	
				2002	**2001**
Short-term liquidity ratios					
Current ratio	4	Current assets	Current liabilities	$7,804.1 \div 5,063.5 = 1.54$	$6,938.9 \div 5,203.0 = 1.33$
Quick ratio	4	Current assets minus inventories	Current liabilities	$(7,804.1 - 1,495.4) \div 5,063.5 = 1.25$	$(6,938.9 - 1,060.2) \div 5,203.0 = 1.13$
Accounts receivable turnover	6	Sales	Average accounts receivable	$11,077.5 \div [\tfrac{1}{2}(1,670.3 + 1,406.2)] = 7.2$	$11,542.5 \div [\tfrac{1}{2}(1,406.2 + 1,630.7)] = 7.6$
Average collection period (in days)	6	365	Accounts receivable turnover	$365.0 \div 7.2 = 50.7$	$365.0 \div 7.6 = 48.0$
Inventory turnover	7	Cost of goods sold	Average inventory at cost	$2,176.5 \div [\tfrac{1}{2}(1,495.4 + 1,060.2)] = 1.7$	$2,160.2 \div [\tfrac{1}{2}(1,060.2 + 883.1)] = 2.2$
Long-term solvency ratios					
Total-debt-to-total-assets	9	Total liabilities	Total assets	$(5,063.5 + 5,704.9) \div 19,042.0 = 56.6\%$	$(5,203.0 + 4,127.1) \div 16,434.1 = 56.8\%$
Total-debt-to-total-equity	9	Total liabilities	Stockholders' equity	$(5,063.5 + 5,704.9) \div 8,273.6 = 130.2\%$	$(5,203.0 + 4,127.1) \div 7,104.0 = 131.3\%$
Interest coverage	9	Earnings before interest and taxes	Interest expense	$(3,457.7 + 79.7) \div 79.7 = 44.4$	$(3,552.1 + 146.5) \div 146.5 = 25.2$
Profitability ratios					
Return on common stockholders' equity (ROE)	4,11	Net income	Average common stockholders' equity	$2,707.9 \div [\tfrac{1}{2}(8,273.6 + 7,104.0)] = 35.2\%$	$2,780.0 \div [\tfrac{1}{2}(7,104.0 + 6,046.9)] = 42.3\%$
Gross profit rate or percentage	4	Gross profit or gross margin	Sales	$(11,077.5 - 2,176.5) \div 11,077.5 = 80.4\%$	$(11,542.5 - 2,160.2) \div 11,542.5 = 81.3\%$
Return on sales	4	Net income	Sales	$2,707.9 \div 11,077.5 = 24.4\%$	$2,780.0 \div 11,542.5 = 24.1\%$
Asset turnover	—	Sales	Average total assets	$11,077.5 \div [\tfrac{1}{2}(19,042.0 + 16,434.1)] = 62.5\%$	$11,542.5 \div [\tfrac{1}{2}(16,434.1 + 14,690.8)] = 74.2\%$
EBIT to sales	—	Earnings before interest and taxes	Sales	$(3,457.7 + 79.7) \div 11,077.5 = 31.9\%$	$(3,552.1 + 146.5) \div 11,542.5 = 32.0\%$

Ratio	Data required	Formula	2002	2001
Return on assets (ROA)	—	Earnings before interest and taxes ÷ Average total assets	(3,457.7 + 79.7) ÷ [$\frac{1}{2}$(19,042.0 + 16,434.1)] = 19.9%	(3,552.1 + 146.5) ÷ [$\frac{1}{2}$(16,434.1 + 14,690.8)] = 23.8%
Earnings per share (EPS)	2	Net income less dividends on preferred stock, if any ÷ Average common shares outstanding	2,707.9 ÷ 1,076.9 = $2.51	2,780.0 ÷ 1,077.4 = $2.58
Market price & dividend ratios				
Price-earnings (P-E)	2	Market price of common share (assume $63.50 and $78.54) ÷ Earnings per share	63.50 ÷ 2.51 = 25.3	78.54 ÷ 2.58 = 30.44
Book value per common share	10	Common stockholders' equity ÷ Number of common shares outstanding	8,273.6 ÷ 1,122.4 = $7.37	7,104.0 ÷ 1,123.3 = $6.32
Market-to-book	10	Market price of common share ÷ Book value per common share	63.50 ÷ 7.37 = 8.62	78.54 ÷ 6.32 = 12.43
Dividend-yield	2	Dividends per common share ÷ Market price of common share	1.27 ÷ 63.50 = 2.00%	1.15 ÷ 78.54 = 1.46%
Dividend-payout	2	Dividends per common share ÷ Earnings per share (EPS)	1.27 ÷ 2.51 = 50.60%	1.15 ÷ 2.58 = 44.57%

Note: Year 2000 data required (in millions): Accounts receivable, $1,630.7; Inventory, $883.1; Stockholders' equity, $6,046.9; and Total assets, $14,690.8. Number of common shares outstanding required (in millions) at December 31, 2002 and December 31, 2001 were 1,122.4 and 1,123.3, respectively.

Exhibit 12-7

Some Typical Financial Ratios. Applied to Eli Lilly and Company (see Exhibits 12-1 and 12-2 on pages 541 and 542 for data) (*$ in millions, except per share data*)

Cross-sectional comparisons require the identification of comparable companies or a set of norms for a specific industry. On the surface, this may appear straightforward. However, identification of similar companies or the appropriate industry is often difficult. Consider Berkshire Hathaway, Inc., which is a holding company comprised of many subsidiaries engaged in diverse business activities. One of Berkshire Hathaway's largest business segments is property and casualty insurance. Their holdings in this area include GEICO, the sixth largest auto insurer in the United States, and General Re, one of the four largest reinsurers in the world. Therefore, it might seem reasonable to compare Berkshire Hathaway to other insurance companies. However, further investigation of Berkshire Hathaway's business holdings reveals that they also own three jewelry companies, four furniture retailers, several finance and financial products companies, a newspaper publisher, seven apparel and footwear companies, a candy manufacturer, and numerous other companies in various industries. Although many companies operate in multiple industries, Berkshire Hathaway is an extreme example. Segment disclosure of the type discussed previously provides some information about different segments, however, the information is limited in scope. (For more on Berkshire Hathaway see the Business First box on page 555.)

How can we find comparable companies? The government has developed the North American Industry Classification System (NAICS). Historically, companies were classified according to the Standard Industry Classification (SIC) system. Both of these systems assign industry codes to companies based on their business activities. Several financial information services use these classification systems to provide average values for selected financial ratios and representative financial statements. The Risk Management Association (formerly Robert Morris Associates), Dun & Bradstreet (D&B), and Standard and Poor's have provided these averages for many years. In addition, numerous online financial service providers compile industry information. Yahoo!Finance, Hoover's Online, and Reuters MultexInvestor are examples. Regardless of the service you use to gather industry data, be alert to differences in computing ratios. Because there are no standards for financial ratio formulas except for EPS, you must know the computational formula employed before using such ratios.

Let's examine some specific ratios by comparing those for Eli Lilly in Exhibit 12-7 with both industry norms and the performance of specific competitors. The ratios shown in the following table have all been discussed in previous chapters. D&B provides the following industry ratios based on 67 companies in the pharmaceutical industry:

Dun & Bradstreet Ratios

	Current Ratio	Quick Ratio	Average Collection Period (days)	Total Liabilities to Stockholders' Equity (%)	Return on Sales (%)	Return on Stockholders' Equity (%)
67 Companies						
Upper quartile	5.0	2.8	34.7	21.7	9.5	17.6
Median	3.3	1.8	51.5	45.0	1.1	5.4
Lower quartile	1.9	0.7	67.5	95.2	(87.1)	(23.4)
Lilly*	1.5	0.7	50.7	130.2	24.4	35.2

*Ratios are from Exhibit 12-7 with the exception of the quick ratio. Exhibit 12-7 computes the quick ratio as [(Current assets − Inventories) ÷ Current liabilities]. D&B computes the quick ratio as [(Cash + Accounts receivable + Marketable securities) ÷ Current liabilities]. In this comparison, Lilly's quick ratio is computed using the D&B formula. Consult Exhibit 12-7 for an explanation of the components of each ratio.

D&B calculates the ratios for each firm in the industry sample and ranks the individual ratios from best to worst. The ratio ranked in the middle is the median. The upper quartile is the ratio ranked halfway between the median and the best value. The lower quartile

Warren Buffet, Chairman of **Berkshire Hathaway**, is one of the most successful and well-known investors in the world. He is number 2 on the *Forbes Magazine* 2003 list of the 400 richest people, and his wealth derives from his skill as a manager and investor. In the early 1990s, Mr. Buffett wrote one of only three letters supporting mandatory expensing of stock options received by the Congressional committee investigating the accounting treatment. His view did not carry the day then, but current practice is moving in that direction.

In addition to information provided in the financial statements, footnotes, and MD&A of the Berkshire Hathaway annual report, followers of the company rely on Mr. Buffett's annual letter to his shareholders. This annual letter has become one of the best reads for accountants and investors anywhere. The full text of his letters written since 1977 is available at www.berkshirehathaway.com/letters/letters.html.

You may find the following excerpts from his 22-page letter in 2002 interesting.

On Pro Forma Earnings:

I have another caveat to mention about last year's results. If you've been a reader of financial reports in recent years, you've seen a flood of "pro-forma" earnings statements—tabulations in which managers invariably show "earnings" far in excess of those allowed by their auditors. In these presentations, the CEO tells his owners "don't count this, don't count that—just count what makes earnings fat." Often, a forget-all-this-bad-stuff message is delivered year after year without management so much as blushing.

We've yet to see a pro-forma presentation disclosing that audited earnings were somewhat high. So let's make a little history: Last year, on a pro-forma basis, Berkshire had **lower** *earnings than those we actually reported.*

That is true because two favorable factors aided our reported figures. First, in 2002 there was no megacatastrophe, which means that Berkshire (and other insurers as well) earned more from insurance than if losses had been normal. . . . Secondly, the bond market in 2002 favored certain strategies we employed in our finance and financial products business.

Sooooo. . . . "except for" a couple of favorable breaks, our pre-tax earnings last year would have been about $500 million less than we actually reported. We're happy, nevertheless, to bank the excess. As Jack Benny once said upon receiving an award: "I don't deserve this honor,—but, then, I have arthritis, and I don't deserve that either."

On Management:

We continue to be blessed with an extraordinary group of managers, many of whom haven't the slightest financial need to work. They stick around though: In 38 years, we've never had a single CEO of a subsidiary elect to leave Berkshire to work elsewhere. Counting Charlie, we now have six managers over 75, and I hope that in four years that number increases by at least two (Bob Shaw and I are both 72). Our rationale: "It's hard to teach a new dog old tricks."

On Accounting:

Three suggestions for investors: First, beware of companies displaying weak accounting. If a company still does not expense options, or if its pension assumptions are fanciful, watch out. When managements take the low road in aspects that are visible, it is likely they are following a similar path behind the scenes. There is seldom just one cockroach in the kitchen. . . . Second, unintelligible footnotes usually indicate untrustworthy management. If you can't understand a footnote or other managerial explanation, it's usually because the CEO doesn't want you to. Enron's descriptions of certain transactions **still** *baffle me. . . . Finally, be suspicious of companies that trumpet earnings projections and growth expectations. Businesses seldom operate in a tranquil, no-surprise environment, and earnings simply don't advance smoothly. . . . Charlie and I not only don't know today what our businesses will earn* **next year**—*we don't even know what they will earn* **next quarter.** *We are suspicious of those CEOs who regularly claim they do know the future—and we become downright incredulous if they consistently reach their declared targets. Managers that always promise to "make the numbers" will at some point be tempted to* **make up** *the numbers.*

Source: Berkshire Hathaway Web site

is the ratio ranked halfway between the median and the worst value. The concept of best and worst must be viewed with caution. Different analysts may have different ideas about what is good and what is bad. For example, a short-term creditor might think that a very high current ratio is good because it means the assets are there to repay the debt. From an investor's perspective, however, a very high current ratio may indicate that the company is maintaining higher levels of inventory and receivables than it should. Let us take a look at how analysts would interpret some of the main types of ratios.

When compared with the D&B ratios, Lilly is in the lower quartile of the current and quick ratios, both of which measure short-term liquidity. They collect their receivables at about the same rate as the median firm in the industry. An additional ratio that would be useful in assessing Lilly's short-term liquidity is the inventory turnover ratio. Unfortunately, D&B does not provide industry norms for this ratio. With regard to long-term solvency, Lilly has significantly higher liabilities than more than 75% of the firms in the comparison set. Typically, companies with heavy debt in relation to ownership capital are in greater danger of suffering net losses or even insolvency when business conditions sour. Why? Because even when revenues decline, interest expenses and maturity dates do not change.

Lilly is in the upper quartile of the two net income-based profitability ratios reported in the table, return on sales and ROE. Lilly's ROE of 35.2% is far above the industry median of 5.4%. We analyze the reasons for Lilly's superior profitability performance later in the chapter.

Overall, Lilly does not perform like the median firm in the industry. What could cause Lilly's ratios to differ from the norms reported by D&B? D&B defines the industry classification broadly, including 67 pharmaceutical companies in their statistics. These firms include companies such as Lilly, Pfizer, and Merck that are engaged in full-cycle pharmaceutical activities, including the discovery, development, manufacturing, and marketing of pharmaceutical products. However, the set also includes much smaller firms that are engaged primarily in the discovery phase, as well as firms that are engaged primarily in manufacturing and marketing. Perhaps we should compare Lilly with companies that are more similar to it.

When compared with ratios for Bristol-Myers Squibb (BMY), Schering-Plough (SGP), and Pfizer (PFE), three similar companies, Lilly's (LLY) ratios are much more in line. You can see that the choice of comparable firms can alter your perception of a company's relative performance. The use of these specific competitors also allows us to compute inventory turnover ratios for comparison purposes.

Specific Competitor Ratio Comparisons

	Current Ratio	Quick Ratio	Average Collection Period (days)	Inventory Turnover (times)	Total Liabilities to Stockholders' Equity (%)	Return on Sales* (%)	Return on Stockholders' Equity* (%)
BMY	1.2	0.9	70.1	3.9	177.4	11.2	22.5
SGP	1.7	1.2	64.5	2.23	73.6	19.4	25.9
PFE	1.3	0.9	59.7	1.6	132.4	28.4	48
LLY	1.5	0.7	50.7	1.7	130.2	24.4	35.2

* Income is after-tax income before extraordinary items, discontinued operations, and cumulative effect of changes in accounting method.

Does the calculation of ratios provide easy answers for the investor? Generally not. The process of analysis involves understanding why a company performs better or worse than its peer group. For example, let's focus on short-term liquidity ratios and consider possible explanations for variation in these ratios. Suppose your company has an average receivables collection period that is much longer than the industry median of 51.5 days. One explanation might be that the company offers longer credit terms than those of its peers as a way to attract customers. An alternative explanation is that many firms in the industry give large discounts for cash purchases, whereas your company does not. A company with many cash sales may have a short average collection period for total sales, even though there are long delays in receiving payments for items sold on credit. Unfortunately, it may be difficult for an investor to obtain information on credit terms or the percentage of sales that were made on credit.

In addition to comparing ratios at a single point in time, changes in a company's ratios over time alert investors and creditors to problems. For example, a decrease in inventory turnover may suggest that a company's sales staff is no longer doing a very good job or that the company's products have fallen out of favor with the buying public. An alternative to the "sales are falling" explanation is the "inventory is rising" explanation. Manufacturing may be producing inventory at a pace beyond what current buyers want. Alternatively, a company may stockpile inventory in anticipation of price increases or inventory shortages. In both cases, inventory builds faster than sales and turnover falls. However, one explanation for rising inventory (overmanufacturing) is cause for concern, whereas the other may represent good inventory planning.

In this section, we focused primarily on liquidity and solvency ratios. Now we turn our attention to ratios used to assess the role of operating performance and financing decisions in the overall success of the company.

Operating Performance and Financing Decisions

On pages 162-164 of Chapter 4, you learned about several ratios used to measure profitability: return on sales (also called the net profit margin ratio), return on common stockholders' equity (ROE or ROCE), and return on assets (ROA). Both operating performance and financing decisions affect these measures of profitability. **Financial management** is concerned with where the company gets cash and how it uses that cash to its benefit. **Operating management** is concerned with the day-to-day activities that generate revenues and expenses. In many scenarios, it is useful to focus on operating efficiency and financing decisions separately. We begin with a discussion of a version of ROA that measures a company's operating performance independent of how it finances those operations. We then consider the impact of debt versus equity financing on the return to investors, using ROE. We expand on the traditional ROE calculation with a discussion of Economic Value Added (EVA), introduced by Stern Stewart and Company. Finally, no discussion of financing alternatives is complete without consideration of income tax effects and alternative measures of financing risk.

OBJECTIVE 4

Evaluate corporate performance using various metrics, including ROA, ROE, and EVA.

financial management
Decisions concerned with where the company gets cash and how it uses that cash to its benefit

operating management
Decisions concerned with the day-to-day activities that generate revenues and expenses.

Operating Performance

In general, we evaluate the overall success of an investment by comparing investment returns with the amount of investment we initially made:

$$\text{Rate of return on investment} = \frac{\text{Income}}{\text{Invested capital}}$$

However, there are several possible definitions of income and invested capital. The appropriate definition of these terms depends on how we intend to use the rate of return measure. In various settings, we find it useful to define income differently, sometimes as net income, sometimes as income from operations, and sometimes as earnings before interest and taxes (**EBIT**). We may also define invested capital differently, sometimes as stockholders' equity and other times as total capital provided by both debt and equity sources. These choices are determined by the purpose of the analysis. For example, an investor in common stock would be more concerned about the ROE (Net income ÷ Average common stockholders' equity), whereas a lender (who has first claim on the resources generated by the company) is more concerned with how effectively the company uses its total assets to generate returns for all suppliers of capital (EBIT ÷ Average total assets).

EBIT
Earnings before interest and taxes.

Suppose we are interested in assessing a firm's use of assets independently of how it financed those assets. In this case, neither return calculation introduced in Chapter 4 is appropriate. If we are interested in assessing this on a pretax basis, we should use pretax ROA, calculated as:

$$\text{Pretax ROA} = \frac{\text{EBIT}}{\text{Average total assets}} \qquad (1)$$

Alternatively, an analyst might be interested in measuring ROA after taxes but independent of financing. In this case, the ROA calculation would be:

$$\text{After-tax ROA} = \frac{[\text{After-tax net income} + \text{Interest expense } (1 - \text{tax rate})]}{\text{Average total assets}}$$

The denominator of both ROA calculations is average total assets, those claimed by all providers of capital (stockholders and debt holders). The numerators include income available to both debt and equity holders. Because net income measures only income available to equity holders, after paying interest to debt holders, we adjust net income by adding back interest expense, either before or after taxes.

As you can see, ROA has multiple definitions in practice, depending on the numerator and denominator used in its calculation. Our discussion focuses on the version of ROA defined in equation 1. We could use the more precise term **pretax and preinterest return on total assets** to distinguish this particular ROA, but the terminology would be cumbersome. Thus, for the remainder of this chapter, we use ROA to mean only the formula in equation 1.

To further explore ROA, we can decompose the right side of equation 1 into two important ratios:

pretax and preinterest return on total assets
A version of ROA defined as earnings before interest and taxes divided by average total assets.

$$\frac{\text{EBIT}}{\text{Average total assets}} = \frac{\text{EBIT}}{\text{Sales}} \times \frac{\text{Sales}}{\text{Average total assets}} \qquad (2)$$

Exhibit 12-8 displays these relationships for Lilly for 2002.

The first term on the right side of equation 2 is a variation of return on sales, which we refer to as the **EBIT-to-sales ratio**, and the second term is the **total asset turnover** ratio. Thus, for 2002 we can express the equation as:

EBIT-to-sales ratio
Earnings before interest and taxes divided by sales.

Return on total assets	=	EBIT-to-sales	×	Total asset turnover
19.9%	=	31.9%	×	0.625 times

total asset turnover (asset turnover)
Sales divided by average total assets.

This equation highlights that the EBIT-to-sales and total asset turnover ratios each contribute to the rate of return on total assets. Firms can achieve the same ROA with different combinations of EBIT-to-sales and total asset turnover ratios. Understanding the industry provides insights. Companies in some industries have heavy fixed-capacity constraints, lengthy time to add new manufacturing capacity, and barriers that prevent new firms from entering the industry, allowing existing firms to charge high prices. Utilities and communications firms are traditional examples. These industries are likely to display high EBIT-to-sales ratios and relatively low total asset turnover ratios. Companies in other industries have few barriers to entry, intense competition, and commodity-like products. Firms in these industries generally have low EBIT-to-sales ratios and high total asset turnover ratios. Grocery stores are a good example.

Just as decomposing the ROA helps understand what drives the operating performance of a company, we can apply a similar decomposition to ROE. In this case, the numerator is net income and the invested capital is average common stockholders' equity. Why use income after taxes and interest in this computation? Because the numerator should represent the income that is available to common stockholders. The company must pay both interest and taxes before there is any return remaining for stockholders.

Exhibit 12-8
Major Ingredients
of Return on Total
Assets

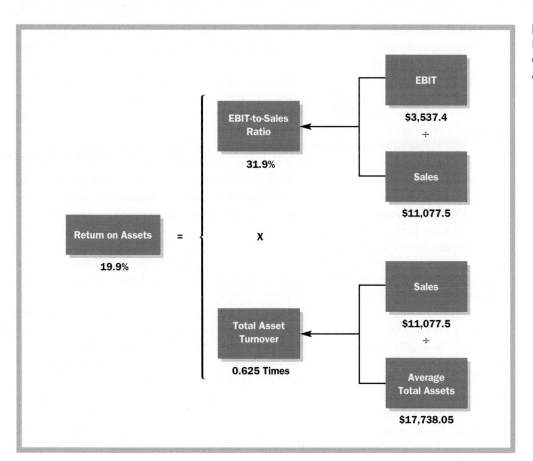

In addition to the return on sales (here with after-tax earnings in the numerator) and total asset turnover, the decomposition has a third component called leverage, which emphasizes the effect of debt on ROE. Some analysts call this decomposition the DuPont analysis because a talented group of financial analysts working at DuPont developed it many years ago. The decomposition is:

$$\begin{aligned} \text{ROE} &= \text{Return on sales} \times \text{Total asset turnover} \times \text{Financial leverage} \\ &= \frac{\text{Net income}}{\text{Sales}} \times \frac{\text{Sales}}{\text{Average total assets}} \times \frac{\text{Average total assets}}{\text{Average stockholders' equity}} \end{aligned}$$

For Eli Lilly, in 2002 the ROE decomposes as follows:

		ROE	=	Return on Sales	×	Total asset turnover	×	Financial leverage
		35.2%	=	24.4%	×	0.625	×	2.307

The introduction of financial leverage in the computation of ROE leads to a discussion of financing decisions.

Financing Decisions

Good financial performance requires an appropriate balance of debt and equity financing. In addition to deciding how much debt is appropriate, a firm must choose how much to borrow short term and how much to borrow by issuing bonds or other longer-term debt. Companies must repay or refinance short-term debt quickly. When a borrower encounters trouble and cannot repay, it becomes difficult to refinance. Lenders prefer healthy, profitable borrowers, not troubled ones. Such problems are especially severe during periods when interest rates are rising because each new refinancing occurs at a higher interest rate, and the cash flow needed to cover interest payments increases.

It is best for companies to finance long-term investments with long-term capital: long-term debt or stock. Debt is often a more attractive vehicle to companies than is common stock because (1) they can deduct interest payments but not dividends for income tax purposes, and (2) the present shareholders retain ownership rights to voting and profits. Most companies have a combination of long-term debt and stockholders' equity. We call the total of long-term financing the **capitalization**, or simply the **capital structure,** of a corporation. Suppose a company has long-term debt (bonds payable) and common stock as its capital structure. The common shareholders enjoy the benefits of all income in excess of interest expense and taxes.

Trading on the equity (also referred to as using **financial leverage, leveraging**, or in the United Kingdom, **gearing**) means using money borrowed at fixed interest rates to try to enhance the rate of return on common stockholders' equity. There are costs and benefits to shareholders from trading on the equity. The costs are interest payments and increased risk, and the benefits are the larger returns to the common shareholders—as long as over-all income is large enough.

To illustrate, imagine companies A, B, and C shown in Exhibit 12-9. Each is in the same industry, with $80,000 of assets and with the same ROA each year. However, the annual ROA varies from 20% in year one, to 10% in year two, and 5% in year three. The three companies have chosen very different capital structures. Company A has no debt, Company B has $30,000 in debt, and Company C has $60,000 in debt. Company B pays 10% interest, whereas the more heavily indebted Company C must pay 12%. How do the shareholders fare in these three companies in different years?

Exhibit 12-9 summarizes the results. The first column gives the income before interest expense. To focus clearly on financial leverage, this example ignores taxes. Recall from equation 1 that we calculate the return on assets as:

$$\text{ROA} = \frac{\text{EBIT}}{\text{Average total assets}}$$

capitalization (capital structure)
Stockholders' equity plus long-term debt.

trading on the equity (financial leverage, leveraging, gearing)
Using borrowed money at fixed interest rates with the objective of enhancing the rate of return on common stockholders' equity.

	(1) Income Before Interest Expense (ROA × Assets)*	(2) Interest Expense (Debt × Interest Rate)†	(3) Net Income (1) − (2)	(4) Stockholders' Equity	(5) Return on Equity (3) ÷ (4)
Year one: 20% ROA					
Company A	$16,000	$ 0	$16,000	$80,000	20%
Company B	16,000	3,000	13,000	50,000	26%
Company C	16,000	7,200	8,800	20,000	44%
Year two: 10% ROA					
Company A	$ 8,000	$ 0	$ 8,000	$80,000	10%
Company B	8,000	3,000	5,000	50,000	10%
Company C	8,000	7,200	800	20,000	4%
Year three: 5% ROA					
Company A	$ 4,000	$ 0	$ 4,000	$80,000	5%
Company B	4,000	3,000	1,000	50,000	2%
Company C	4,000	7,200	(3,200)	20,000	(16%)

*All three companies have $80,000 in assets.
†Company A, no debt; Company B, $30,000 in debt at 10%; Company C, $60,000 in debt at 12%.

Exhibit 12-9
Trading on the Equity Effects of Debt on Rates of Return

Therefore, EBIT equals ROA times average total assets. In this instance, we assume the same ROA for each firm in a given year, but we vary the ROA from one year to the next. We can calculate EBIT each year by multiplying ROA for the year times the constant asset level of $80,000. The interest expense differs by company because each has a different level of debt, but for a given company it does not change from year to year. Our primary concern is the effect of financial leverage on the ROE.

What do we learn from Exhibit 12-9? First, a debt-free, or unlevered, company has identical ROA and ROE. Note that equity-financed, unlevered Company A's ROE and ROA are identical in years 1, 2, and 3: 20%, 10%, and 5%, respectively. Second, when a company with debt has an ROA greater than its interest rate, ROE exceeds ROA. This situation is called *favorable financial leverage* and describes both companies B and C in year one. They earn 20% on their assets and pay either 10% or 12% on their debt. The earnings in excess of the interest cost increase earnings available to shareholders.

Year two is interesting because Company B has an ROA of 10%, which equals its interest rate. Thus, like Company A, Company B has a ROE of 10%. In contrast, Company C experiences unfavorable financial leverage. Because its 10% ROA is less than its 12% interest cost, its ROE falls sharply to 4%. Year three further stresses the effects of financial leverage in years when the company performs poorly. When ROA falls noticeably below the firm's interest cost, ROE also falls sharply. Company B's ROE falls to 2%, whereas the more highly leveraged Company C faces a loss year and negative ROE.

When a company is unable to earn at least the interest rate on the money borrowed, the ROE is lower than it would be for a debt-free company. If earnings are low enough that the company cannot pay the interest and principal payments on debt, it may be forced into bankruptcy. The possibility of bankruptcy increases the risk to the common stockholders even more than it does to debt holders. Remember, debt holders collect their claims before stockholders do.

Obviously, the more stable the income, the less dangerous it is to trade on the equity. Therefore, industries that have traditionally been regulated, such as electric, gas, and telephone companies, tend to have a much heavier proportion of debt than do manufacturers of computers or high-tech companies. Historically, these regulated companies have had a stable customer base and were somewhat protected from competition. Government regulations helped assure that prices would be sufficiently high to ensure a profit. The breakup of AT&T as the dominant national phone company and current efforts to deregulate electric utilities have produced changes in these historical patterns of financial leverage. Many utilities still have debt levels left over from their stable, regulated past. However, deregulation has made their returns much less stable. Thus, you find many utilities today perched at the edge of bankruptcy. The prudent use of debt is part of intelligent financial management.

Economic Value Added

We calculate ROA and ROE directly from the financial statements. They measure performance by relating an income statement number to investment levels reported in the balance sheet. **Economic Value Added (EVA)** is a related performance measure, developed and trademarked by Stern Stewart and Company, that measures the residual wealth of a company after deducting its cost of capital from operating profit. The idea is that a firm must earn more than it pays for capital if it is to increase in value. This is like saying that a firm must earn more than the interest expense on borrowing for borrowing to be favorable. When we refer to capital in EVA, we are referring to all capital, both debt and equity. The cost of that capital is a weighted average of interest cost and the returns required by equity investors. Let us assume that this weighted average cost of capital is 10%. Furthermore, assume that a company has $1 million in capital. Then the company is adding value if its net operating profit after tax exceeds 10% of $1 million, or $100,000.

Economic Value Added (EVA)
Measure of the residual wealth of a company after deducting its cost of capital from operating profit.

If the net operating profit after tax were $120,000, for example, we would calculate the EVA as $120,000 − $100,000 = $20,000. If this firm were generating only $70,000 of net operating profit after tax, we would say that EVA was a negative $30,000 ($70,000 − $100,000). The latter company is losing value. If such losses are expected to continue it would be preferable to dissolve the company and return the capital to the creditors and owners. In applying EVA, managers often make adjustments to the accounting results reported under GAAP because they believe GAAP does not always reflect true economic value. Without exploring all such adjustments, we consider one, R&D expenditures. Although accounting rules require most companies to expense R&D immediately, all agree that it has some economic value and that the expensing procedure is a conservative approach. EVA proponents argue that it is better to arbitrarily assume a 5-year life than no life, and they restate the financial statements accordingly. You saw an example of this type of restatement on page 358 in Chapter 8. As a reminder, suppose a company spent $50,000 on R&D each year and had been doing so for 15 years. If the company capitalized this $50,000 each year and assigned a 5-year life to the resulting asset, after the first four years annual amortization of R&D in the income statement would be $50,000. Whether the $50,000 is expensed each year as R&D expense or as amortization expense, net income is the same after the first four years. However, both assets and stockholders' equity will be higher if the expenditure is capitalized and amortized.

Many companies have adopted EVA as an internal management tool, including Coca-Cola, Best Buy, Herman Miller, and Molson. They believe that this procedure helps them allocate, manage, and redeploy scarce capital resources such as heavy equipment, working capital, and real estate. Eli Lilly includes a calculation of EVA in its financial highlights. Its EVA analysis indicates that Lilly added $1.075 billion dollars of value in 2002.

Income Tax Effects of Financing Decisions

Because interest payments, but not dividends, are deductible by the company for income tax purposes, if all other things are equal, the use of debt is less costly to the corporation than is equity. Consider raising additional capital of $10 million either through long-term debt or through preferred stock. Typically preferred stock is part of shareholders' equity, and any dividends paid to preferred stockholders are not deductible for income tax purposes. Furthermore, the rate of preferred dividends is usually higher than the rate of interest on long-term debt because the preferred stockholders have a greater risk due to their lower priority claim on the total assets of a company. Assume an interest rate of 10% for debt, a preferred dividend rate of 11%, and an income tax rate of 40%. Exhibit 12-10 shows the effects on net income of electing to raise capital through long-term debt versus preferred stock.

When you examine Exhibit 12-10, you should note three points:

1. Interest is tax deductible, so its after-tax cost can be considerably less than that of dividends on preferred stock (6% versus 11%). In other words, using debt makes net income attributable to common shareholders substantially higher.
2. Interest is an expense, whereas preferred dividends are not. Therefore, using preferred shares makes net income higher ($3 million versus $2.4 million). Note that trading on the equity can benefit the common stockholders by the issuance of either long-term debt securities or preferred stock, provided that the additional assets generate sufficient earnings.
3. Failure to pay interest is an act of bankruptcy, which gives creditors rights to control or liquidate the company. The consequences of failure to pay dividends are less severe.

Measuring Safety

Investors in debt securities want to be sure that the company's future operations will easily provide enough cash to cover scheduled payments of interest and principal. Debt securities

Exhibit 12-10
Income Tax Effects of
Financing Decisions

	$10 Million Long-Term Debt	$10 Million Preferred Stock
Income before interest expense (assumed)	$5,000,000	$5,000,000
Interest expense at 10% of long-term debt	$1,000,000	—
Income before income taxes	$4,000,000	$5,000,000
Income tax expense at 40%	1,600,000	2,000,000
Net income	$2,400,000	$3,000,000
Dividends to preferred shareholders at 11%	—	1,100,000
Net income available to common stockholders	$2,400,000	$1,900,000
Pretax cost of capital raised	10%	11%
After-tax cost of capital raised		
$600,000* ÷ $10,000,000	6%	
$1,100,000 ÷ $10,000,000		11%

*Interest expense	$1,000,000	
Income tax savings because of interest deduction:		
.40 × $1,000,000	400,000	
Interest expense after tax savings	$ 600,000	

often have provisions aimed at reducing investor risk, such as the right to repossess assets or the right to receive payment before common stockholders. However, because such provisions kick in only when the company is in danger of defaulting on the loans, they are nowhere near as valuable as a pattern of growing earnings. Bondholders prefer to avoid the trouble and costs of foreclosure or bankruptcy litigation. They would much rather have a steady stream of interest and repayments of principal provided by a company with good, steady earnings. They do not want to be in the position of **Enron**'s bondholders, waiting several years after the company declared bankruptcy and then receiving only pennies for each dollar owed them.

Debt-to-equity ratios, discussed in Chapter 9, are popular measures of risk. However, they do not focus directly on the major concern of the holders of long-term debt: the ability of the company to make interest payments and repay debt on schedule. The interest coverage-ratio, calculated as EBIT divided by interest expense, focuses on interest-paying ability. In Exhibit 12-7, interest coverage for Lilly is 44.4 times in 2002.

A rule of thumb or benchmark for debt investors is that the interest coverage should be at least five times, even in the poorest year in a span of 7 to 10 years. The numerator in this ratio does not deduct income taxes because interest expense is deductible for income tax purposes. In effect, we calculate income taxes as a periodic "claim" on earnings, after deducting interest. This tax-deductibility feature is a major reason companies use bonds much more widely than they use preferred stock.

Prominence of Earnings per Share

Throughout this text, we regard earnings as a basic reporting element in the financial statements. We often express earnings on a per share basis (EPS), and EPS is itself a component in the price-earnings ratio. Up to this point, though, we have kept EPS simple by considering only common stock. In reality, EPS can be a bit more complicated. We now turn to several issues that complicate the computation of EPS: changes in the number of common shares outstanding during the year, the presence of preferred stock, and the existence of convertible securities.

OBJECTIVE 5

Calculate EPS when a company has preferred stock or dilutive securities.

Weighted-Average Shares and Preferred Stock

When the outstanding shares are all common stock, the primary complication is the calculation of weighted-average shares in the following equation (numbers assumed):

$$\frac{\text{Earnings per share}}{\text{of common stock}} = \frac{\text{Net income}}{\text{Weighted-average number of common shares outstanding during the period}}$$

$$= \frac{\$1,000,000}{800,000} = \$1.25$$

How would we calculate the 800,000 weighted-average shares in the denominator? Suppose 750,000 shares were outstanding at the beginning of a fiscal year, and the company issued 200,000 additional shares 3 months before the end of the fiscal year. The weighted average is based on the number of months that the shares were outstanding during the year. We can do the basic computation in two different ways:

750,000 × Weighting of 12/12	=	750,000		750,000 × 9/12	=	562,500
200,000 × Weighting of 3/12	=	50,000	or	950,000 × 3/12	=	237,500
Weighted-average shares		800,000				800,000

In this example, the number of shares outstanding rose because the company issued additional shares. This might have occurred because executives exercised stock options and acquired more shares. Alternatively, the company might have issued a block of additional shares to outside investors at the current market price. The number of shares could also decline during the year if the company purchases shares for the treasury or retires shares.

A second complication arises if shares of nonconvertible preferred stock are outstanding. To compute the earnings applicable to common stock, we deduct the dividends on preferred stock for the current period, even if the company does not pay the dividends (figures assumed):

$$\frac{\text{Earnings per share}}{\text{of common stock}} = \frac{\text{Net income} - \text{Preferred dividends}}{\text{Weighted-average number of common shares outstanding during the period}}$$

$$= \frac{\$1,000,000 - \$200,000}{800,000} = \$1.00$$

Further, to ensure comparability of historical summaries of EPS, we must adjust for changes in capitalization structure, for example, stock splits and stock dividends. As an example, Eli Lilly's Web site indicates that Lilly's common stock has split eight times since 1955, with the most recent two-for-one stock split occurring in 1997. In the 1997 annual report, Lilly reports 1996 EPS of $1.39. If you look at the 1996 annual report, the EPS reported is $2.78. Why did Lilly adjust the 1996 EPS when they published the 1997 annual report? Because the investor wants to be able to compare the year-to-year performance in terms of the current number of shares. Because each 1996 share outstanding counts as two 1997 shares, Lilly adjusted the 1996 EPS to allow meaningful comparisons.

Basic and Diluted EPS

EPS calculations become a bit more complex when companies have convertible securities, stock options, or other financial instruments that holders can exchange for, or convert into, common shares. For example, suppose that a firm has outstanding preferred stock that is convertible into common stock.

Convertible preferred stock at 5%, $100 par, each share convertible into two common shares	100,000 shares
Common stock	1,000,000 shares

The basic EPS computation follows (numbers assumed):

Computation of earnings per share	
Net income	$10,500,000
Less preferred dividends	500,000
Net income available to common stockholders	$10,000,000
Earnings per share of common stock	
$10,000,000 ÷ 1,000,000 shares	$ 10.00

However, note the effect on EPS if the preferred shareholders converted, that is, exchanged their preferred shares for common stock. EPS will be "diluted," or reduced. We can calculate EPS as if conversion had occurred at the beginning of the period. No preferred dividends would be paid, but there would be 200,000 more shares outstanding:

Net income	$10,500,000
less preferred dividends	0
Net income available to common stockholders	$ 10,500,000
Earnings per share of common stock—assuming	
conversion $10,500,000 ÷ 1,200,000 shares	$ 8.75

The dilution of common stock caused by the conversion is $10.00 − $8.75 = $1.25 per share. Diluted EPS assumes the conversion of all potentially dilutive securities. In 2002, Eli Lilly reported basic EPS of $2.51 and diluted EPS of $2.50. The small difference in the two EPS measures indicates that Lilly had few potentially dilutive securities.

INTERPRETING FINANCIAL STATEMENTS

You are considering an investment in a company, and as part of your analysis you decide to compute P-E and dividend–payout ratios. When you examine the company's income statement you find that it reports both basic and diluted earnings per share figures, and they are significantly different. Which earnings per share figure should you use in your ratio computations and why?

Answer

You should use basic earnings per share in the dividend-payout ratio. The market price represents the value of a share of stock currently outstanding and dividends are paid on outstanding shares. So the earnings per share used should reflect the shares actually outstanding, not the number of shares that would be outstanding if potentially dilutive securities were converted to common stock. The answer is not so obvious for the P-E ratio. If you think conversion is likely and will therefore reduce your claims to future net income, you might want to use diluted EPS.

Disclosure of Nonrecurring Items

One of the goals of financial statement analysis is to evaluate or estimate a firm's future prospects. When predicting the future, we need to distinguish the elements of the current financial statements that reflect recurring aspects of the firm from those that represent one-time events or items that are not likely to continue. These nonrecurring items fall into four major categories: special items, extraordinary items, discontinued operations, and changes in accounting principle. The income statement of Mattel, Inc. in Exhibit 12-11 illustrates three of the four categories, with related numbers in bold italic type.

OBJECTIVE 6

Understand the nature of nonrecurring items and how to adjust for them.

Exhibit 12-11
Mattel, Inc. and
Subsidiaries
*Consolidated
Statements of
Operations (Dollars in
thousands, except per
share data)*

	For the year ended December 31	
	2002	**2001**
Net sales	$4,885,340	$4,687,924
Cost of sales	2,524,353	2,538,990
Gross profit	2,360,987	2,148,934
Advertising and promotion expenses	552,502	543,554
Other selling and administrative expenses	1,050,344	964,239
Amortization of goodwill	—	46,121
Restructuring and other charges	***24,600***	***15,700***
Operating income	733,541	579,320
Interest expense	113,897	155,132
Interest (income)	(17,724)	(15,481)
Other nonoperating expense, net	15,871	9,659
Income from continuing operations before income taxes	621,497	430,010
Provision for income taxes	166,455	119,090
Income from continuing operations	455,042	310,920
Discontinued operations		
Gain on disposal of discontinued business, net of tax	***27,253***	—
Income before cumulative effect of change in accounting principles	482,295	310,920
Cumulative effect of change in accounting principles, net of tax	***(252,194)***	***(12,001)***
Net income	$ 230,101	$ 298,919
Basic earnings (loss) per share of common stock		
Income from continuing operations	$ 1.04	$ 0.72
Gain from discontinued operations	0.06	—
Cumulative effect of change in accounting principles	(0.58)	(0.03)
Net income	$ 0.52	$ 0.69
Diluted earnings (loss) per share of common stock		
Income from continuing operations	$ 1. 03	$ 0.71
Gain from discontinued operations	0.06	—
Cumulative effect of change in accounting principles	(0.57)	(0.03)
Net income	$ 0.52	$ 0.68

Special Items

special items
Revenues or expenses that are large enough and unusual enough to warrant separate disclosure.

Special items are revenues or expenses that are large enough and unusual enough to warrant separate disclosure on the income statement. These items typically appear among operating expenses, with any necessary discussion or explanation in the footnotes. Examples include the impairment of property, plant, and equipment; impairment of goodwill; and restructuring charges. Special items represent the most frequent of the four categories of nonrecurring items and usually the one with the biggest magnitude as a percent of sales. Since the mid-1980s, about 38% of major companies' annual reports contained special items, and the median ratio of special items to total sales was 2.3%.

Companies have considerable flexibility in deciding when to treat something as a special item. Recently, the most common special item has been restructuring charges. A restructuring occurs when a firm decides to substantially change the size, scope, or location of a part of the business. It often involves relocation, plant closings, and reductions in personnel. The company typically incurs costs over an extended period of time, often several years. Prior to 2003, GAAP required companies to estimate and record the total cost of the restructuring activity when management initially committed to the restructuring. As a result of this estimation process, managers frequently used restructuring activities to manage earnings. In some cases, management included current and future operating expenses in the restructuring charge, thereby reducing ordinary operating expenses. Given that the market often ignores special items in assessing a company's financial performance, the company would appear stronger. In other cases, management intentionally overstated the restructuring charge in the first year. Restructuring expense is offset with a liability on the balance sheet. In subsequent years, the company reversed the excess restructuring charge, reducing the liability and recognizing income. In 2002, the FASB issued a new pronouncement that requires companies to recognize restructuring charges and the related liability when incurred in most cases. This ruling should eliminate much of the earnings management that has surrounded restructuring activities. For more discussion of earnings management see the Business First box on page 570.

Mattel reported Restructuring and Other Charges as a separate line item on its income statements for both 2001 and 2002. Although not shown in Exhibit 12-11, Mattel also recorded restructuring charges in 2000. How would an analyst use this information to project future income from continuing operations? If the analyst believes the restructuring charge is truly unusual and is unlikely to recur in future years, he or she might ignore the expense of $24.6 million ($15.7 million) in 2002 (2001) in projecting the future. The analyst would base projections on 2002 income from continuing operations before deducting restructuring charges: $621.5 million + $24.6 million or $646.1 million in 2002 and $430.0 million + $15.7 million or $445.7 million in 2001.

Notice that because companies report special items with other expenses, they report such items on a before-tax basis. These items reduce pretax income and therefore reduce income tax expense. If we assume a 40% tax rate, the special item reported in 2002 reduced pretax income by $24.6 million and therefore reduced the tax provision by 40% of $24.6 million, or $9.84 million. The special item's after-tax effect would be $24.6 million − (.40 × $24.6 million) = $14.76 million. In estimating future net income, the analyst would add back $14.76 million to reported after-tax net income.

In 2002, however, life would not be quite that easy for the equity analyst trying to assess the future earnings of Mattel. For one thing, Mattel reported restructuring costs in each of the last 3 years in amounts ranging from $15.7 million to $24.6 million. Although it is important to highlight these costs, it is not obvious that they are unusual and nonrecurring. The evidence is exactly the opposite. The footnote that describes these costs occupies two full pages in the 2002 annual report and classifies the costs as severance and other compensation costs, asset write-downs, and lease termination costs.

An analyst might conclude that costs of this type will continue in future years and therefore base future predictions on the $621.5 million of income from continuing operations without adding back these special items. Adjustment would be more appropriate for a company that had not experienced such costs in prior years, but is making what appears to be a one-time reduction in workforce levels and asset values.

Extraordinary Items

Extraordinary items result from events that are both unusual in nature and infrequent in occurrence. Write-downs of receivables, inventories, and intangibles are ordinary items, as are gains or losses on the sale or impairment of fixed assets. Why? Because they represent ordinary business risks. The effects of a strike and many foreign currency revaluations are

extraordinary items
Items that are unusual in nature and infrequent in occurrence that are shown separately, net of tax, in the income statement.

also ordinary items. However, the financial effects of an earthquake or government expropriation are generally extraordinary items. Interestingly enough, we do not consider the effects of most floods as extraordinary. Why not? Because most floods occur in areas that are prone to certain amounts of flooding; thus, a flood in such locations is not an unusual occurrence. Accountants treat an event or transaction as ordinary unless the evidence clearly supports its classification as extraordinary.

We exclude extraordinary items from regular operating income calculations. We present each event or item that is considered extraordinary on a separate line on the income statement. These items are reported net of tax, which means that the figure presented includes any tax effect the item might have.

Until 2003, most extraordinary items arose from the early extinguishment of long-term debt. The FASB required early debt extinguishments to be treated as extraordinary, although they did not truly meet the definition. Perhaps the goal was to prevent companies from using decisions to redeem debt early to affect the amounts being reported as ordinary income. For example, in the absence of this rule, companies could redeem debt at a gain when operating results were poor. Following a change in FASB guidance, the majority of early debt extinguishments will no longer qualify for extraordinary item treatment. With the change in accounting, the number of extraordinary items appearing in financial statements is likely to decline considerably.

A tragic illustration of an extraordinary charge occurred several years ago as the result of criminal tampering with Tylenol capsules. People died as a result of cyanide being put into the product. The manufacturer, Johnson & Johnson (J&J), took immediate action to pull all Tylenol products from store shelves while tracing the source of the problem. J&J reported the following on its income statement ($ in millions):

Earnings before extraordinary charge	$146.5
Extraordinary charge—costs associated with the withdrawal of Tylenol capsules (less applicable tax relief of $50.0)	50.0
Net earnings	$ 96.5

More recently, consider the terrorist attacks of September 11, 2001. The FASB's Emerging Issues Task Force (EITF) decided that, although the events of September 11 were definitely extraordinary, treating the financial effects of those events as extraordinary items would not be an effective means of communicating with stockholders. In a news release on October 1, 2001, the EITF observed "that the economic effects of the events were so extensive and pervasive that it would be impossible to capture them in any one financial statement line item." Therefore, the losses associated with the terrorist attacks were not treated as extraordinary.

Discontinued Operations

discontinued operations
The termination of a business segment. The results are reported separately, net of tax, in the income statement.

Discontinued operations occur when a company disposes of (i.e., closes or sells) an entire segment of the business, not just a single plant, location, or product line. To qualify as a discontinued segment, the assets and business activities must be physically and operationally distinguishable from the remaining entity. As discussed earlier, many large companies have several discrete business segments. For example, PepsiCo has a beverage business and a snack food business. If PepsiCo sells one of the product lines in its snack food business, the sale would not qualify as a discontinued operation. However, if it sold all its snack food business, the transaction would be treated as a discontinued operation. If a company discontinues any segment, it should report the results of continuing operations separately from those of discontinued operations, although it must still report both on the income statement. Companies must report any gain or loss from the disposal of a segment of a business with the related results of discontinued operations and not as an extraordinary item. Like extraordinary items, discontinued operations are shown on the income statement net of tax.

In comparative income statements over multiple years, the statements must show the income or loss of the discontinued segment's operations separately for all years in which that segment operated. Otherwise, the company's current financial status, which no longer includes the discontinued segment, would not be comparable to its past financial status. Because income statements reflect 3 years of comparative data, in the year a company makes the decision to discontinue a segment, it reports the effect separately for the current year and restates the prior 2 years to isolate the operations of the discontinued segment. The company is not required to make adjustments for periods prior to those shown in the 5-year or 10-year comparative statements. When evaluating a firm's income patterns through time, an analyst may need to estimate the amount of income attributable to discontinued operations in years prior to those restated by the company.

In Exhibit 12-11, Mattel discloses the income statement effects of the sale of its Consumer Software segment. The company actually sold the segment at a loss of $601.1 million in fiscal 2000. However, the terms of the sale called for Mattel to "receive future consideration." Mattel received that consideration in 2002, resulting in a gain of approximately $27.3 million, net of tax. The combined net loss on disposition of the segment was $601.1 million − $27.3 million = $573.8 million.

Changes in Accounting Method

Generally, when the FASB issues a new pronouncement, prior period financial statements are not restated. A company uses the new rule to compute income in the year it adopts the new standard. In addition, the effect of the change on all previous years' income is aggregated into a single number and reflected on the income statement. Companies report the cumulative effect of a change in accounting method net of tax and separate it from ongoing operations in the same section of the income statement that contains discontinued operations and extraordinary items. Such a change in reporting for derivative instruments affected many U.S. companies in 2001. In 2002, a new FASB rule on accounting for goodwill caused many companies to realize a one-time charge to income. Exhibit 12-11 reflects the impact of both of these accounting changes on Mattel's reported net income. The adoption of the new rule on derivatives resulted in a reduction of $12.0 million in 2001 net income. The impact of the change in accounting for goodwill was much more significant, reducing 2002 net income by more than 50%, from $482.3 million to $230.1 million.

A company can also elect to change to a preferred GAAP method. Such voluntary changes in accounting method may also result in the recognition of a cumulative effect adjustment.

International Issues

Internationally, a variety of factors complicate financial statement analysis. Throughout the text, we consider differences in accounting methods used. In addition, we should stress the obvious but easily forgotten differences in the language of reporting and the currency of measurement. For example, most U.S. analysts cannot read financial statements in Japanese and do not readily "have a feel for" the value of yen versus dollars. Last, but not least, is the fact that different structures for security markets, different tax laws, and different preferences among citizens of different countries all affect the relative value of financial assets.

MANAGERIAL MANIPULATION OF ACCOUNTING INFORMATION

Financial statement analysis relies on published financial statements. These statements are prepared by managers and assessed by third-party auditors to assure they "fairly present" the economic circumstances of the company. Investors assess share prices in relationship to a firm's earnings and rely on revenue growth and earnings growth as signs of health and value. They examine patterns to assure that margins are maintained while revenue grows and that revenue and earnings grow in a smooth, persistent manner.

You have learned that many judgments enter into preparation of financial statements. Some are legitimate choices among alternatives, such as accelerated versus straight-line depreciation. We refer to managers' choices among alternative amounts and procedures as *earnings management* when the choices are made to either mislead investors or to affect other outcomes. Managers' compensation contracts may reward them for earnings growth, and boards of directors may award bonuses to management when share prices rise. However, managers may face limitations via bond covenants and other restrictions when earnings fall, targets are not met, or various financial ratios deteriorate. These pressures can cause managers to shade the truth in order to report amounts that make them richer or otherwise better off.

Auditors cannot identify and prevent every such attempt to manage earnings. Infrequently, managers engage in elaborate illegal frauds that are difficult or impossible to detect. More frequently, managers make choices that push the boundaries of GAAP. Auditors must decide whether the choices cause the financial presentations to be presented unfairly. Several of the huge bankruptcies of recent years including Enron and WorldCom involved allegedly misleading financial statements. Courts became involved both in determining whether the auditors should have known about the misstatements and in assessing legal penalties. As you know, Enron contributed to the dissolution of Arthur Andersen, previously one of the top five accounting firms in the world.

What portions of the financials are most exposed to manipulation? In more recent years, the most frequent abuse cited by the SEC is the overstatement of revenues due to recognition of revenue before the dual "earned and recognized" test is met. Many SEC releases, FASB statements, and EITF actions attempt to clarify the rules on revenue recognition, especially with regard to new practices and technology. For example, the Internet explosion created exchanges of advertising that challenged existing GAAP.

In a study in *The Accounting Review*, earnings management was found to be even more frequently associated with reserves. Reserves are liability accounts that arise when provisions are recognized in the earnings statements for costs that will be settled in the future. Examples considered in the study include the allowance for bad debts and the recognition of restructuring costs associated with the future closing of plants and termination of employees. Managers decide how large to make the provision. If managers want higher earnings they can underestimate the provision, and if they want lower earnings they can overestimate it. Overestimates create an excessive reserve. Sometime in the future, management can "decide" the reserve is too large. This decision leads to a reduction of the liability and an offsetting increase in earnings in the year of the reversal. Arthur Levitt, a former chairman of the SEC, referred to these reserves as "cookie jar" reserves because the company reversed the reserve whenever it got hungry for earnings.

Sources: Nelson, Elliott, and Tarpley, "Evidence from Auditors about Managers' and Auditors' Earnings Management Decisions," *The Accounting Review*, 2002 Supplement; Speech by Arthur Levitt at New York University, September 28, 1998, New York, NY.

Valuation Issues

OBJECTIVE 7

Use financial information to help assess a company's value.

Accounting data are critically important to deciding on the value of a company. We have already examined a number of ratios that help in this effort. Exhibit 12-12 presents fundamental price and valuation information gathered from MultexInvestor as of November 9, 2003. Subsequent to November 9, 2003, MultexInvestor became part of Reuters. Information such as that found in Exhibit 12-12 is available at http://www.investor.reuters.com as of this writing. Information provided by Reuters is similar to that provided by many financial services. When using information gathered from outside sources, be sure you thoroughly understand the items reported. For example, the Price/Book ratio and all the ratios listed in the Financial Condition category in Exhibit 12-12 are based on figures from the most recent quarterly financial statements.

PRICE AND VALUATION

Ticker Symbol	Current Price	52-Week Range	Beta	EPS	Price-Earnings
LLY	$ 60.80	52.77–71.40	.37	$2.33	26.45
BMY	$ 27.25	20.74–29.21	.50	$1.21	21.78
PFE	$ 31.45	26.95–36.92	.44	$0.71	44.99
SGP	$ 16.65	14.16–23.75	.42	$0.75	21.66

Ticker Symbol	Price/Sales	Price/Book	Price/Cash Flow	Analyst Rating
LLY	5.69	7.95	21.94	2.8
BMY	2.68	5.32	15.81	3.1
PFE	5.79	3.55	37.49	2.0
SGP	2.58	2.92	16.05	3.1

GROWTH TRENDS

Ticker Symbol	Latest Annual Revenue (mil)	1-yr Revenue Growth	5-yr Revenue Growth	Latest Annual EPS	1-yr EPS Growth	5-yr EPS Growth
LLY	$11,077.5	−4.03%	6.76%	$2.50	−3.11%	6.98%
BMY	$18,119.0	0.73%	1.64%	$1.06	0.67%	−7.78%
PFE	$32,373.0	11.54%	11.10%	$1.46	24.14%	26.34%
SGP	$10,180.0	4.28%	8.48%	$1.34	1.59%	6.59%

Ticker Symbol	Annual Dividend/Share	Dividend Yield	5-yr Dividend Growth Rate
LLY	$1.34	2.18	10.88%
BMY	$1.12	4.24	8.06%
PFE	$0.60	1.88	18.06%
SGP	$0.68	4.21	12.76%

FINANCIAL CONDITION

Ticker Symbol	Total Debt/Equity	Current Total Debt (mil)	Current Ratio	Quick Ratio	Current Inventory Turnover	Current Receivable Turnover
LLY	0.58	$ 5,022.0	1.56	1.03	1.59	5.82
BMY	0.87	$ 8324.0	1.26	0.91	4.14	5.76
PFE	0.21	$14,924.0	1.57	1.13	1.49	4.54
SGP	0.23	$ 1,878.0	1.71	1.16	2.09	5.11

MANAGEMENT EFFECTIVENESS

Ticker Symbol	Return on Assets	5-yr Avg. Return on Assets	Return on Equity	5-yr Avg. Return on Equity	Revenue/ Employee (000s)	Income/ Employee (000s)
LLY	13.23%	18.45%	30.21%	46.67%	$ 268.2	$ 57.6
BMY	9.3%	15.66%	25.33%	34.26%	$433.9	$56.8
PFE	8.8%	16.55%	12.32%	36.07%	$365.8	$38.4
SGP	14.6%	20.99%	13.65%	39.13%	$301.7	$38.4

SHARE INFORMATION

Ticker Symbol	Market Cap (mil)	Shares Outstanding (mil)	% Held by Institutions
LLY	$ 69,026.5	1,122.5	69.29%
BMY	$51,179.0	1,938.6	64.11%
PFE	$ 248,380.4	7,786.22	65.49%
SGP	$ 23,742.3	1,469.2	73.65%

Data as of November 9, 2003.
Source: MultexInvestor.

Exhibit 12-12
Fundamentals of Pharmaceutical Industry
Eli Lilly (LLY), Bristol-Myers Squibb (BMY), Pfizer (PFE), and Schering-Plough (SGP)

Many of the other reported values, such as the P-E ratio, ROA, ROE, and the 1-year growth rates are based on the most recent four quarters. In this case, the most recent four quarters ended on September 30, 2003. As a result, the values for Eli Lilly do not necessarily correspond to those values reported in Exhibit 12-7, which used data from the most recent fiscal year, ended December 31, 2002.

The information in Exhibit 12-12 is for four pharmaceutical companies identified by ticker symbol: Eli Lilly (LLY), Bristol-Myers Squibb (BMY), Pfizer (PFE), and Schering-Plough (SGP). Valuation techniques are beyond the scope of this textbook, and we do not attempt to reach conclusions regarding the appropriateness of the reported stock prices. Rather, our intent is to demonstrate that some of the information needed for valuation is readily available and related to the outputs of financial statement analysis. Reviewing this information gives us an opportunity to emphasize the importance of financial information in valuation and to explain a few common ratios and values that we have not given significant attention. We begin by briefly describing and comparing some of the information in Exhibit 12-12. Then we elaborate on the P-E and Price to Earnings Growth (PEG) ratios.

Some Basic Comparisons

The four pharmaceutical stocks trade at very different prices, and all have shown significant share price variation during the period from November 2002 to November 2003. LLY and PFE are trading in the middle of their 52-week price ranges, whereas BMY is trading near the high end and SGP is trading near the low end of its range. Beta is a measure of how closely the stock of the company follows general market conditions. A value of one indicates the stock moves proportionally to the market. None of these stocks appear to move with the market. For example, on a typical day, if the market moved up 10%, BMY would be expected to move up only 5%, whereas LLY would move only 3.7%.

The EPS of the four companies are widely divergent. The two companies with the most similar EPS are PFE at $0.71 and SGP at $0.75. However, the market has priced these stocks very differently, resulting in PFE having a P-E ratio of 44.99, whereas SGP's P-E ratio is less than one-half of PFE's at 21.66. The table also includes items that relate price to sales, to book value, and to cash flow.

The Growth Trends portion of Exhibit 12-12 gives growth rates for 1 and 5 years for revenue and EPS, and a 5-year growth rate for dividends. It shows the most recent annual revenue, EPS, and dividend figures to provide a sense of the size differences among the companies. PFE is by far the largest of the four with respect to revenues. The data in the Financial Condition section of the exhibit are, with the exception of current total debt, outputs of ratio analysis. You should be familiar with all five of the ratios in this section. MultexInvestor defines debt as both short- and long-term debt, but does not include operating liabilities such as accounts payable and accrued expenses. Note the differences in capital structure. BMY has a total-debt-to-equity ratio of .87, whereas PFE's ratio is only .21.

The Management Effectiveness portion of Exhibit 12-12 shows significant differences in the return on assets and return on equity numbers for the four firms. For example, the ROE for the most recent 12 months ranges from 12.32% for PFE to 30.21% for LLY, a difference of about 18 percentage points. As expected, when you look at the 5-year average ROE, the spread is reduced, dropping to about 12 percentage points (46.67% for LLY and 34.26% for BMY). This highlights the importance of considering more than 1 year's performance.

In the final set of information, you see that PFE is much larger than the other three companies with respect to market capitalization. PFE's market capitalization, the total market price of its outstanding shares, is more than 10 times larger than that of SGP. Institutional investors hold more than 50% of the shares of all four companies. These institutional share-holders are sophisticated investors such as pension funds and insurance companies.

So what might an analyst conclude? There are always more questions. What is the company planning? How many new products are in the pipeline? How are competitors changing the industry dynamics? How will current state and national efforts to reduce drug prices impact the industry? Analysts would pursue answers to these and other questions before reaching a conclusion. MultexInvestor does provide some information about analysts' views on these stocks. See the Analyst Rating in the Price and Valuation section of Exhibit 12-12. A rating of 1 indicates a buy recommendation, 2 indicates that analysts expect the stock to outperform the market, 3 is interpreted as a hold recommendation, 4 suggests the stock will underperform the market, and 5 is a sell recommendation. From the analysts' perspective, PFE is viewed most favorably. The other three stocks are hovering at slightly above or slightly below a ranking of 3.

Price-Earnings Ratios and Growth

The P-E ratio is a useful valuation tool. It relates the price of a company's stock to the earnings it is generating. Some would argue that low P-E stocks might be undervalued and high P-E stocks might be overvalued. This is the view of analysts called "value investors." These investors seek securities that the market is currently undervaluing. They would not blindly buy low P-E stocks, but would use low P-E as a screen to identify securities that are likely candidates for purchase. They would then consider many other factors in determining the best investments.

The opposite view is that the best investments are growth stocks. "Growth investors" believe that high P-E stocks are likely to be high-growth stocks. The price is "high" because investors see strong growth prospects ahead. Again, the growth investor would use high P-Es to identify a group of stocks to evaluate more carefully.

Who is right? How do we relate P-E ratios to growth? When are we paying too much for future growth? As of September 2003, the average P-E on stocks in the S&P 500 was about 24. Although this was high relative to long-term norms of around 14 or 15, it was down from recent levels, which peaked at more than 48. The P-E ratios for the four pharmaceutical companies range from 21.66 to 44.99.

One way to relate P-E ratios directly to earnings growth rates is the **price-earnings growth (PEG) ratio.** To compute the PEG ratio, we divide the P-E ratio by the earnings growth rate. We can calculate the P-E ratio and the earnings growth rate based on historical earnings, current earnings, or forecasted earnings. Many analysts prefer a current P-E ratio and a forecasted 5-year earnings growth rate. Due to the variation in computational methods, information sources report widely different numbers.

price-earnings growth (PEG) ratio
Price-earnings ratio divided by the earnings growth rate.

Consider Genentech, a biotechnology company that discovers, develops, manufactures, and markets biotherapeutics. In July 2003, Genentech was trading at about $78 per share. The P-E ratio based on estimated earnings for the next 12 months was a hefty 69. This seems very high relative to an S&P norm of 24. The estimated 3- to 5-year annual earnings growth rate was 23%, resulting in a PEG ratio of 3.0. How do we interpret the PEG ratio? A PEG ratio greater than 1.0 indicates that the stock may be overvalued or that the market expects future EPS growth to be greater than that currently reflected in the analysts' consensus forecast EPS. Growth stocks typically have a PEG ratio greater than one because investors are willing to pay more for a stock that they expect to grow rapidly. Stocks with a PEG ratio less than 1.0 may be undervalued, or the market may believe the earnings growth estimate reflected in the consensus forecast is too high. What are norms for the PEG ratio? *Forbes* (July 28, 2003) reported: "Based on estimated earnings for the next 12 months and estimated annualized earnings growth over the next three to five years, the S&P 500 and NASDAQ carry PEG ratios of 1.4 and 2.1, respectively." The Motley Fool Web site (www.fool.com) provides its own investment advice on using the PEG ratio:

.50 or less	Buy
.50 to .65	Look to buy
.65 to 1.00	Hold
1.00 to 1.30	Look to sell
1.30 to 1.70	Consider shorting
Over 1.70	Short

With a PEG ratio of 3.0, Genentech falls into the category where the Motley Fool recommends shorting the stock. This means selling stock you don't own, promising to deliver it at some future date. If the price falls, you can buy the stock before you need to deliver it for less than the price you will receive on the sale, making a potentially large profit.

How do the four pharmaceutical companies compare on the PEG ratio? The following information comes from the NASDAQ Web site because MultexInvestor does not report a PEG ratio in its ratio summary:

LLY	1.563
BMY	1.954
PFE	1.015
SGP	4.555

The PEG ratio of SGP is extremely high and might serve as a warning to prospective investors. Thus, the PEG ratio helps inform our analysis, but like all the other ratios we have examined, it is just a tool to help focus our attention.

Relating Cash Flow and Net Income

Although this chapter focuses on evaluating a company's performance based on various earnings metrics (e.g., EPS, P-E, PEG), we would be remiss if we did not mention the important role of cash flow. In fact, many valuation models use estimated cash flows, not forecasted earnings. Both net income and cash flow from operations are positive for the healthiest of firms. However, there are four logical possible combinations of positive and negative net income and cash flow from operations, and it is useful to think about what they might mean.

Relationship	1	2	3	4
Cash flow from operations	+	+	−	−
Net income	+	−	+	−

In relationship one, the two positive values confirm the profitability of the company. In the fourth case, the uniform negative values are again in agreement. When either of these patterns appears and continues for multiple periods, the implications are straightforward.

What about relationship 2? This is common in some industries. Consider high capital investment industries with large depreciation charges or rapidly growing companies in capital-intensive industries. If a company uses a declining-balance depreciation method, large depreciation charges may create losses even though operating cash flow is positive. One might examine several years to assess the pattern. Another example is real estate, where the economic returns to the company include both current operating performance and appreciation of the underlying property. The accounting model does not record appreciation in real estate, so it does not appear in the income statement. Thus, you could have negative net income even though cash flow was sufficient to cover all expenses and the investment was appreciating consistently.

Relationship 3 is often a red flag for trouble, but may also represent the case of a rapidly growing firm. The difference between cash flow from operations and net income is depreciation and accruals of current assets and liabilities. A very rapidly growing firm may be investing heavily in inventory for new stores and granting credit to new customers with the result that inventories and accounts receivable are growing very quickly. This may be a very good situation as long as the sales demand does not outpace the company's ability to meet customer demand and pay its current obligations. We also observe this pattern in cases where sales revenue is not growing quickly, but inventory and accounts receivable are increasing. This situation tends to indicate bad management, slow-moving merchandise, and failure to manage credit. This pattern often precedes bankruptcy.

Analysts often use the relationship between cash flow from operations and net income as one of a set of indicators that address the issue of earnings quality. Earnings quality is not a well-defined or well-understood concept. However, one of the attributes of high-quality earnings that many analysts agree on is that revenues not be recognized prematurely and expenses not be deferred inappropriately. In some cases, companies may, intentionally or unintentionally, engage in accounting choices that lower the quality of earnings numbers. For example, by capitalizing costs that it should have expensed, WorldCom reported higher earnings than it should have. As a result, although earnings were higher in dollar magnitude, the quality of those earnings was lower. There is no single means to assess earnings quality. However, one ratio that some analysts use is a comparison of cash flow from operations to net income. We would expect this ratio to be consistently greater than one. Why? Because net income includes an expense for depreciation, but cash flow from operations does not contain the related cash outflow. (The cash outflow is an investing activity.) If the ratio is significantly less than one, this may be an indication of low-quality earnings and a pending cash flow crisis.

Summary Problem for Your Review

PROBLEM

Exhibit 12-13 contains a condensed balance sheet and income statement for Nautica Enterprises, Inc. The company that began almost 20 years ago with a six-item outerwear collection of clothing has expanded to include a wide assortment of fashion-oriented men's apparel, and now has three distinct brands and a significant international presence.

1. Compute the following ratio for 2003: (a) current ratio, (b) quick ratio, (c) average collection period, (d) inventory turnover, (e) total-debt-to-total-assets, (f) return on sales, and (g) ROE. Define the quick ratio as current assets minus inventories divided by current liabilities. In part (e) define total debt as total liabilities.
2. Compare your computed values with the values that follow for Nike.

Nike 2003	
Current ratio	2.32
Quick ratio	1.57
Average collection period	66.6
Inventory turnover	4.37
Total-debt-to-total-assets	.41
Return on sales	.04
ROE	.12

SOLUTION

1. a. Current ratio = Current assets ÷ Current liabilities

$$= 297{,}795 \div 106{,}555 = 2.79$$

   b. Quick ratio = (Current assets − Inventories) ÷ Current liabilities

$$= 210{,}165 \div 106{,}555 = 1.97$$

Consolidated Balance Sheets (Dollars in thousands, except per share data)

	March 1, 2003	March 2, 2002
Assets		
Current assets		
Cash and cash equivalents	$ 82,953	$ 45,814
Short-term investments	—	6,350
Accounts receivable—net of allowances		
of $45,432 in 2003 and $42,525 in 2002	98,713	89,736
Inventories	87,630	66,443
Prepaid expenses and other current assets	3,428	5,599
Deferred tax benefit	22,229	18,912
Assets held for sale	2,842	2,842
Total current assets	297,795	235,696
Property, plant and equipment at cost—less		
accumulated depreciation and amortization	96,427	111,327
Goodwill, at cost	30,054	31,328
Other intangibles, at cost—less accumulated amortization	34,972	35,489
Other Assets	8,879	8,230
Total assets	$468,127	$422,070
Liabilities and stockholders' equity		
Current liabilities		
Current maturities of long-term debt	$ 754	$ 754
Accounts payable—trade	34,690	30,402
Accrued expenses and other current liabilities	57,017	44,037
Income taxes payable	14,094	9,289
Total current liabilities	106,555	84,482
Long-term debt—net	13,567	14,321
Interest rate swap liability	1,779	687
Total long-term liabilities	15,346	15,008
Stockholders' equity		
Preferred stock—par value $.01; authorized,		
2,000,000 shares; no shares issued	—	—
Common stock—par value $.10; authorized,		
100,000,000 shares; issued, 45,136,000 shares		
in 2003 and 44,718,000 shares in 2002	4,514	4,472
Additional paid-in capital	96,216	93,546
Retained earnings	406,105	385,407
Accumulated other comprehensive income (loss)	(1,287)	(1,862)
Common stock in treasury at cost; 11,534,000 shares		
in 2003 and 11,498,000 shares in 2002	(159,322)	(158,983)
	346,226	322,580
Total liabilities and stockholders' equity	$468,127	$422,070

Exhibit 12-13
Nautica Enterprises, Inc. and Subsidiaries

Exhibit 12-13
Continued

Consolidated Statement of Earnings (Dollars in thousands, except per share data)

	Year Ended March 1, 2003	Year Ended March 2, 2002	Year Ended March 3, 2001
Net sales	$ 693,715	$ 692,092	$ 627,731
Cost of goods sold	397,348	407,677	367,171
Gross profit	296,367	284,415	260,560
Selling, general, and administrative expenses	254,933	249,593	196,927
Special charges	16,282	14,442	—
Net royalty income	(9,329)	(7,860)	(8,779)
Operating profit	34,481	28,240	72,412
Other income			
Investment income	604	1,471	3,075
Interest expense	(1,968)	(1,959)	(156)
Earnings before provision for income taxes	33,117	27,752	75,331
Provision for income taxes	12,419	10,493	29,228
Net earnings	$ 20,698	$ 17,259	$ 46,103
Net earnings per share of common stock			
Basic	$ 0.62	$ 0.52	$ 1.45
Diluted	$ 0.60	$ 0.50	$ 1.39

c. Average collection period = (Average accounts receivable $\times$ 365) $\div$ Sales

$$= [((98,713 + 89,736) \div 2) \times 365] \div 693,715$$

$$= 49.6$$

d. Inventory turnover = Cost of goods sold $\div$ Average inventory

$$= 397,348 \div [(87,630 + 66,443) \div 2]$$

$$= 5.16$$

e. Total-debt-to-total assets = Total liabilities $\div$ Total assets

$$= (\text{Total assets} - \text{Stockholders' equity}) \div \text{Total assets}$$

$$= (468,127 - 346,226) \div 468,127$$

$$= .26$$

f. Return on sales = Net income $\div$ Sales

$$= 20,698 \div 693,715$$

$$= .0298 \text{ or almost } 3\%$$

g. ROE = Net income $\div$ Average stockholders' equity

$$= 20,698 \div [(346,226 + 322,580) \div 2]$$

$$= .06190 \text{ or } 6.2\%$$

2. Nautica has higher current and quick ratios for higher short-term liquidity. This could also suggest that current assets are excessive. Accounts receivable levels are more favorable for Nautica than for Nike, given the shorter collection period. Nautica also turns its inventory over faster than Nike. Nautica has less debt. Although Nautica performs better with respect to short-term liquidity and has a lower debt-to-assets ratio, it does not perform as well as Nike with respect to the return on sales or ROE ratios.

Highlights to Remember

1 **Locate and use sources of information about company performance.** Financial and operating information is available from many sources, including company Web sites, the financial business press, analyst reports, and financial services companies. Various regulations in the United States require the issuance of annual reports and govern their content. In addition, publicly traded companies must disclose particular information by filing 10-K, 8-K, and other forms with the SEC on a periodic basis.

2 **Analyze the performance of a company using trend analysis, common-size financial statements, and segment disclosures.** Companies provide financial information to aid investors in assessing the risk and return of a potential investment. Creditors are particularly concerned about the solvency and liquidity of the issuer, whereas equity investors are more interested in profitability. Numerous tools are available to assist both creditors and equity investors. Trend analysis is a form of financial statement analysis that concentrates on changes in the financial statements through time. It involves comparing relationships for a period of years or quarters. We can construct common-size financial statements by expressing the elements of the balance sheet as a percentage of total assets and the elements of the income statement as a percentage of total revenue. Common-size statements enhance the ability to compare one company with another or to conduct a trend analysis over time. Segment disclosures allow analysis of separate business units.

3 **Use basic financial ratios to guide your thinking.** Basic financial ratios allow us to put numbers in perspective. By relating one part of the financial statements to another, ratios facilitate questions such as "Given the change in revenues, was the change in accounts receivable reasonable?" and "Is the company's inventory level, given its size, comparable to industry norms?" The chapter reviews the ratios presented throughout the text. Liquidity ratios deal with the immediate ability to make payments. Solvency ratios deal with the longer-term ability to meet obligations. Creditors often incorporate such ratios into debt covenants to protect lenders' rights. Investors use profitability ratios to assess operating efficiency and performance.

4 **Evaluate corporate performance using various metrics, including ROA, ROE, and EVA.** Return on assets (ROA) is a type of return on investment that relates earnings before interest and taxes (EBIT) to total assets. We can subdivide ROA into return on sales times total asset turnover. Return on equity (ROE) is the most fundamental profitability ratio for equity investors because it relates income to the shareholders' investment. We can subdivide ROE into the return on sales, total asset turnover, and financial leverage. EVA refers to Economic Value Added. It compares a company's adjusted earnings number with the minimum amount that it should have earned given the total capital in use. If the adjusted earnings exceeds the required return, calculated as the weighted-average cost of capital times the capital in use, then the company has added economic value during the period.

5 **Calculate EPS when a company has preferred stock or dilutive securities.** Earnings per share (EPS) is a fundamental measure of performance. This chapter introduces some complexities in calculating EPS. Because preferred shares receive preference as to dividends, we deduct preferred dividends from earnings in the numerator. Because shares outstanding may change during the year, the denominator is the weighted-average number of shares outstanding over the year. The presence of options and convertible securities creates a potential to issue new shares that dilute current shareholders' interests. Therefore, companies report both basic and diluted EPS when significant options and conversion features exist.

6 **Understand the nature of nonrecurring items and how to adjust for them.** Special items, extraordinary items, discontinued operations, and accounting changes are categories of unusual and possibly nonrecurring items. Separately disclosing these allows analysts to refine forecasts of future performance based on current operations. Income statements include special items with other expenses on a before-tax basis, but identify them separately. In contrast, income statements show extraordinary items, discontinued items, and the cumulative effect of change in accounting method separately, below earnings from operations and net of their individual tax effects.

7 **Use financial information to help assess a company's value.** To assess a company's valuation, you can use actual performance information reported by one of the readily available data providers. These sources report ratio values along with additional performance measures, including price-to-sales, price-to-book, and price-to-earnings. Analysts may see an investment opportunity when a company stands out on measures including ROA and ROE and is growing quite rapidly, but is not the highest priced based on P-E, price-to-sales, and price-to-book ratios.

Accounting Vocabulary

asset turnover, p. 558	EBIT-to-sales ratio, p. 558	operating management, p. 557
benchmarks, p. 551	Economic Value Added (EVA),	pretax and preinterest
capital structure, p. 560	p. 561	return on total assets
capitalization, p. 560	extraordinary items, p. 567	p. 558
common-size statements,	financial leverage, p. 560	price-earnings growth (PEG)
p. 546	financial management, p. 557	ratio, p. 573
component percentages, p. 547	financial statement analysis,	pro forma statements, p. 538
compound annual growth rate	p. 536	short-term liquidity, p. 538
(CAGR), p. 546	gearing, p. 560	special items, p. 566
cross-sectional comparisons,	leveraging, p. 560	time-series comparisons,
p. 551	long-term solvency, p. 538	p. 551
discontinued operations,	management discussion	total asset turnover, p. 558
p. 568	and analysis (MD&A),	trading on the equity, p. 560
EBIT, p. 557	p. 544	trend analysis, p. 540

Assignment Material

Questions

12-1 Why do decision makers use financial statement analysis?

12-2 In addition to the basic financial statements, what information is usually presented in a company's annual report?

12-3 Give at least three sources of information for investors besides a company's annual report.

12-4 "Financial statements report on history. Therefore, they are not useful to creditors and investors who want to predict future returns and risk." Do you agree? Explain?

12-5 How do information demands of creditors differ from those of equity investors?

12-6 "It's always a bad sign when revenues increase at a faster percentage rate than does net income." Do you agree? Explain.

12-7 Suppose you wanted to evaluate the financial performance of **IBM** since the mid-1990s. What factors might affect the comparability of a firm's financial ratios over such a long period of time?

12-8 How do common-size statements aid comparisons with other companies?

12-9 What information is presented in the MD&A section of annual reports?

12-10 Ratios are often grouped into four categories. What are the categories?

12-11 Suppose you compared the financial statements of an airline and a grocery store. Which would you expect to have the higher values for the following ratios: debt-to-equity ratio, current ratio, inventory turnover ratio, accounts receivable turnover ratio, and ROE? Explain.

12-12 Name three types of comparisons that are useful in evaluating financial ratios.

12-13 Suppose you worked for a small manufacturing company and the president said that you must improve your current ratio. Would you interpret this to mean that you should increase it or decrease it?

12-14 Suppose the current ratio for your company changed from 2 to 1 to become 1.8 to 1. Would you expect the level of working capital to increase or to decrease? Why?

12-15 Suppose you work for a small local department store that manages its own accounts receivable with a private charge card. Your boss has told you to improve the average collection period from 30 to 20 days. How would you go about this? What are the risks in your proposal that might affect the company negatively?

12-16 Distinguish between operating management and financial management.

12-17 What two measures of operating performance are combined to give return on total assets as defined in this chapter?

12-18 "Trading on the equity means exchanging bonds for stock." Do you agree? Explain.

12-19 "Borrowing is a two-edged sword." Do you agree? Explain.

12-20 Why are companies with heavy debt in relation to ownership capital in greater danger when business conditions sour?

12-21 "The tax law discriminates against preferred stock and in favor of debt." Explain.

12-22 "Any company that has income before interest and taxes greater than its interest expense is a relatively safe investment for creditors." Do you agree? Explain.

12-23 What causes the "dilution" in diluted EPS?

12-24 How does the accounting for special items differ from the accounting for extraordinary items?

12-25 "Separate reporting of the results of discontinued operations aids predicting future net income." Do you agree? Explain.

12-26 Suppose you wanted to compare the financial statements of Colgate-Palmolive and Procter & Gamble. What concerns might you have in comparing ratios for the two companies?

Critical Thinking Questions

12-27 EVA

Your CEO has heard a lot about EVA as a management tool. This officer understands that the basic concept is to calculate an estimate of true economic profit by subtracting an appropriate charge for the firm's cost of capital from its operating profit. However, the CEO wonders why focusing on EVA is any better than focusing on ROE. Can you help explain the concept?

12-28 Assessing Value

Your accounting teacher has been talking about how important accounting numbers are in valuing a firm, and yet many of the people you know who invest are always talking about growth as the important measure. Who is right?

12-29 Investment Advice on the Internet

Your friend Barry just called to say that you should consider investing in ABC Company because the high-flying chat room on the Internet had 20 buy recommendations posted and not a single sell recommendation. Barry says that the chat room has examples of investments recommended there that have doubled in value in just a few months. What do you think?

12-30 Which P-E

Your investment advisor called to suggest buying ABC Company and noted that its P-E was only 20 and the rest of the companies in its industry had P-Es of around 28. You looked in *The Wall Street Journal* and found they reported a P-E of 32 for ABC Company and an average P-E of around 30. How can you make sense of this?

Exercises

12-31 Common-Size Statements

Following are condensed income statements for Lowe's and The Home Depot for the year ended January 31, 2003 and February 2, 2003, respectively:

	Lowe's (in millions)
Total revenues	$26,491
Cost of sales	18,465
Gross profit	8,026
Selling, general, and administrative	4,730
Store opening costs	129
Depreciation	626
Interest expense	182
Income before income taxes	2,359
Provision for income taxes	888
Net income	$ 1,471

	The Home Depot (in millions)
Total revenues	$58,247
Cost of sales	40,139
Gross profit	18,108
Selling & store operating expenses	11,180
Pre-opening costs	96
General and administrative	1,002
Interest and investment income	(79)
Interest expense	37
Income before income taxes	5,872
Provision for income taxes	2,208
Net income	$ 3,664

1. The companies do not use exactly the same account titles. Align the accounts across the two companies in the manner you believe to be most appropriate. Then prepare common-size income statements for Lowe's and The Home Depot.
2. Compare the two companies by using the common-size statements.

12-32 Computation of Ratios

Procter & Gamble, the giant consumer products company, included the income statement and balance sheets in Exhibit 12-14 in its 2003 annual report. Additional information includes average common shares outstanding of 1,296 million in 2003 and market price per share of $88.30 at its fiscal year end of June 30, 2003. The company paid $125 million in dividends to preferred stockholders during the year ended June 30, 2003. Dividends of $1.64 per share were paid on common stock.

Compute the following ratios for 2003:

1. Current ratio
2. Quick ratio (use current assets − inventories as the numerator)
3. Average collection period
4. Total-debt-to-total-assets (define total debt as total liabilities)
5. Total-debt-to-equity (define total debt as total liabilities)
6. Interest coverage
7. Return on common stockholders' equity

8. Gross profit rate
9. Return on sales
10. Asset turnover
11. Return on assets
12. EPS (basic)
13. P-E ratio
14. Dividend-yield ratio (for common stock)
15. Dividend-payout ratio (for common stock)
16. Market-to-book value

12-33 Common Stock Ratios and Book Value

The Ebert Corporation has issued 450,000 shares of 9% preferred stock with a $100 par value and 10 million shares of $1 par value common stock. The current market price of the common is $24, and the latest annual dividend rate per common share is $2 per share. Common treasury stock consists of 500,000 shares costing $8 million. The company has $150 million of additional paid-in capital, $20 million of retained earnings, and $12 million of investments in affiliated companies. Net income for the current year is $20 million.

Compute the following:

1. Total stockholders' equity
2. Common P-E ratio
3. Common dividend-yield percentage
4. Common dividend-payout percentage
5. Book value per share of common

Exhibit 12-14
Procter & Gamble
Company and
Subsidiaries
*(In Millions, Except
per Share Data)*

CONSOLIDATED BALANCE SHEETS

	June 30	
	2003	**2002**
Assets		
Current assets		
Cash and cash equivalents	$ 5,912	$ 3,427
Investment securities	300	196
Accounts receivable	3,038	3,090
Inventories	3,640	3,456
Deferred income taxes	843	521
Prepaid expenses and other receivables	1,487	1,476
Total current assets	15,220	12,166
Property, plant, and equipment		
Buildings	4,729	4,532
Machinery and equipment	18,222	17,963
Land	591	575
	23,542	23,070
Accumulated depreciation	(10,438)	(9,721)
Net property, plant, and equipment	13,104	13,349
Goodwill and other intangible assets		
Goodwill	11,132	10,966
Trademarks and other intangibles	2,375	2,464
Net goodwill and other intangible assets	13,507	13,430
Other noncurrent assets	1,875	1,831
Total assets	$43,706	$40,776
Liabilities and shareholders' equity		
Current liabilities		
Accounts payable	$ 2,795	$ 2,205
Accrued and other liabilities	5,512	5,330
Taxes payable	1,879	1,438
Debt due within 1 year	2,172	3,731
Total current liabilities	12,358	12,704
Long-term debt	11,475	11,201
Deferred tax liability	1,396	1,077
Other noncurrent liabilities	2,291	2,088
Total liabilities	27,520	27,070
Shareholders' investment		
Convertible Class A preferred stock,		
stated value $1 per share, 600 shares authorized	1,580	1,634
Nonvoting Class B preferred stock,		
stated value $1 per share, 200 shares authorized	—	—
Common stock, stated value $1 per share;		
5,000 shares authorized; shares outstanding:		
1,297.2 shares in 2003 and 1,300.8 shares in 2002	1,297	1,301
Additional paid-in capital	2,931	2,490
Reserve for Employee Stock Option Plan debt retirement	(1,308)	(1,339)
Accumulated other comprehensive income	(2,006)	(2,360)
Retained earnings	13,692	11,980
Total shareholders' equity	16,186	13,706
Total liabilities and shareholders' equity	$43,706	$40,776

Exhibit 12-14
Continued

CONSOLIDATED STATEMENTS OF EARNINGS

	For the Years Ended June 30	
	2003	**2002**
Net sales	$43,377	$40,238
Cost of products sold	22,141	20,989
Marketing, research, administrative, & other	13,383	12,571
Operating income	7,853	6,678
Interest expense	561	603
Other nonoperating income, net	(238)	(308)
Income before income taxes	7,530	6,383
Provision for income taxes	2,344	2,031
Net income	$ 5,186	$ 4,352

12-34 Rate-of-Return Computations

1. Sapporo Company reported a 5% EBIT-to-sales ratio, a 9% rate of return on total assets, and 2 billion yen of total assets. Compute (a) EBIT, (b) total sales, and (c) total asset turnover.
2. Glasgow Corporation reported £900 million of sales, £48 million of EBIT, and a total asset turnover of four times. Compute (a) total assets, (b) the EBIT-to-sales ratio, and (c) the rate of return on total assets.
3. Compare the two companies.

12-35 Return on Assets

The Home Depot, Inc. is the leading retailer in the home improvement industry and ranks among the largest retailers in the United States. Some data from the company's financial statements for the years ended February 1, 2004 and February 2, 2003 ($ in millions):

	2003	2004
Sales	$58,247	$64,816
Earnings before interest and taxes	5,909	6,905
Interest expense	37	62
Provision for taxes	2,208	2,539
Net income	3,664	4,304
Property, plant, and equipment, net	17,168	20,063
Total assets	30,011	34,347
Stockholders' equity	19,802	22,407

1. Compute The Home Depot's rate of return on total assets for the year ended February 1, 2004.
2. Compute the EBIT-to-sales ratio and total asset turnover for the year ended February 1, 2004. Show how these two ratios determine the return on total assets.

12-36 Trading on the Equity

In all years under consideration Bayol Company has assets of $600 million, bonds payable of $300 million, and stockholders' equity of $300 million. The bonds bear interest at 10% per annum. Carmody Company, which is in the same industry, has assets of $600 million and stockholders' equity of $600 million in each year. Prepare a comparative tabulation of Carmody Company and Bayol Company for each of the 3 years. Show income before interest, interest, net income, ROA, and ROE. The income before interest for both companies was: year one, $60 million; year two, $30 million; and year three, $90 million. Ignore income taxes. Show all monetary amounts in millions of dollars. Comment on the results.

12-37 Using Debt or Equity

The O'Hare Corporation is trying to decide whether to raise additional capital of $80 million through a new issue of 12% long-term debt or of 10% preferred stock. The income tax rate is 40%. Compute net income less preferred dividends for these alternatives. Assume income before interest expense and taxes is $20 million. Show all dollar amounts in thousands. What is the after-tax cost of capital for debt and for preferred stock expressed in percentages? Comment on the comparison. Compute the interest-coverage ratio for the first year.

12-38 Debt versus Preferred Stock

In 2003, Hamilton Corporation had earnings before taxes and interest of $8,495 million. Long-term debt was $18,463 million. The company had no preferred stock outstanding, although 10 million shares were authorized.

Suppose $8,000 million of preferred stock with a dividend rate of 11% had been issued instead of $8,000 million of the long-term debt. The debt had an effective interest rate of 7%. Assume the income tax rate is 40%.

Compute net income and net income attributable to common shareholders under (a) the current situation with $18,463 million of long-term debt and no preferred stock, and (b) the assumed situation with $8,000 million of preferred stock and $10,463 million of long-term debt.

12-39 Earnings per Share

Tribune Company, publisher of many newspapers and owner of the Chicago Cubs baseball team, had net income of $442,992 thousand and paid preferred dividends of $25,130 thousand in 2002. An average of 301,932 thousand common shares were outstanding during the year.

1. Compute Tribune's earnings per common share in 2002.
2. Suppose all preferred stock was convertible into 35,000 shares of common stock. Compute diluted earnings per common share.

12-40 EPS and Interest-Coverage Ratio Computations

Baltimore Shipping Company has outstanding 500,000 shares of common stock, $5 million of 8% preferred stock, and $8 million of 10% bonds payable. Its income tax rate is 40%.

1. Assume the company has $6 million of income before interest and taxes. Compute (a) EPS and (b) number of times bond interest has been earned.
2. Assume $3 million of income before interest and taxes, and make the same computations.

12-41 Nonrecurring Items

Conagra Foods, Inc. is one of the country's largest food service suppliers, offering packaged and frozen foods. Conagra's 35 brands include Banquet, Chef Boyardee, Hunt's, and Healthy Choice. The company's 2003 income statement ended with the following four lines (in millions):

Income from continuing operations	$840.1
Income (loss) from discontinued operations, net of tax	(69.2)
Cumulative effect of changes in accounting	3.9
Net income	$774.8

Suppose the operations in place at the end of the year continued into the next year with exactly the same results as before. What net income would you expect Conagra to report in the next year? Explain.

12-42 Interpretation of Changes in Ratios

Consider each of the following as an independent case:

a. Increase in cash dividends
b. Decrease in interest coverage
c. Increase in return on sales
d. Increase in the P-E ratio
e. Reduction in accounts receivable turnover
f. Increase in current ratio

Required

1. From the point of view of a manager of the company, indicate which of these items indicate good news and which indicate bad news. Explain your reasoning for each.
2. Would any of these items be viewed differently by an investor than by a manager? If so, which ones? Why?

Problems

12-43 Common-Size Statements

(Alternate is 12-50.) Price-Break and Low-Cost are both discount store chains. Condensed income statements and balance sheets for the two companies are shown in Exhibit 12-15. Amounts are in thousands.

Exhibit 12-15

Financial Statements
for Price-Break
and Low-Cost
(Dollars in thousands)

INCOME STATEMENTS

	Price-Break	Low-Cost
	Year Ended December 31, 20X9	
Sales	$905,600	$491,750
Cost of sales	602,360	301,910
Gross profit	303,240	189,840
Operating expenses	184,130	147,160
Operating income	119,110	42,680
Other revenue (expense)	(21,930)	6,270
Pretax income	97,180	48,950
Income tax expense	38,870	19,580
Net income	$ 58,310	$ 29,370

BALANCE SHEETS

	Price-Break		Low-Cost	
	December 31		December 31	
	20X9	20X8	20X9	20X8
Assets				
Current assets				
Cash	$ 9,100	$ 10,700	$ 8,200	$ 6,900
Marketable securities	8,300	8,300	4,100	3,800
Accounts receivable	36,700	37,100	21,300	20,500
Inventories	155,600	149,400	105,100	106,600
Prepaid expenses	17,100	16,900	8,800	8,400
Total current assets	226,800	222,400	147,500	146,200
Property and equipment, net	461,800	452,300	287,600	273,500
Other assets	14,700	13,900	28,600	27,100
Total assets	$703,300	$688,600	$463,700	$446,800
Liabilities and stockholders' equity				
Liabilities				
Current liabilities (summarized)	$ 91,600	$ 93,700	$ 61,300	$ 58,800
Long-term debt	156,700	156,700	21,000	21,000
Total liabilities	248,300	250,400	82,300	79,800
Stockholders' equity	455,000	438,200	381,400	367,000
Total liabilities and stockholders' equity	$703,300	$688,600	$463,700	$446,800

Required

1. Prepare common-size statements for Price-Break and Low-Cost for 20X9.
2. Compare the financial performance for 20X9 and financial position at the end of 20X9 for Price-Break with the performance and position of Low-Cost. Use only the statements prepared in requirement 1.
3. Calculate and compare ROE for the two firms.

12-44 Financial Ratios

(Alternate is 12-46.) This problem uses the same data as problem 12-43, but it can be solved independently. Price-Break and Low-Cost are both discount store chains. Condensed income statements and balance sheets for the two companies are shown in Exhibit 12-15. Amounts are in thousands.

Additional information:
- Cash dividends per share: Price-Break, $2.00; Low-Cost, $1.50.
- Market price per share: Price-Break, $30; Low-Cost, $40.
- Average shares outstanding for 20X9: Price-Break, 15 million; Low-Cost, 7 million.

1. Compute the following ratios for both companies for 20X9: (a) current, (b) quick, (c) accounts receivable turnover, (d) inventory turnover, (e) total-debt-to-total-assets, (f) total-debt-to-total-equity, (g) ROE, (h) gross profit rate, (i) return on sales, (j) asset turnover, (k) pretax return on assets, (l) EPS, (m) P-E, (n) dividend-yield, and (o) dividend-payout. Total debt includes all liabilities. Assume all sales are on credit.

2. Compare the liquidity, solvency, profitability, and market price and dividend ratios of Price-Break with those of Low-Cost.

12-45 Trend Analysis

Krispy Kreme Doughnuts, Inc. is a specialty retailer of doughnuts. The income statements and balance sheets (slightly modified) for the years ended February 3, 2002 and February 2, 2003 are in Exhibit 12-16.

1. Prepare an income statement and balance sheet for Krispy Kreme that has two columns, one showing the amount of change between 2002 and 2003 and the other showing the percentage of change.

2. Identify and discuss the most significant changes between 2002 and 2003.

Exhibit 12-16
Krispy Kreme
Doughnuts, Inc
*Years Ended February
3, 2002 and February
2, 2003 (Dollars in
thousands, except per
share data)*

CONSOLIDATED BALANCE SHEETS	2003	2002
Assets		
Current assets		
Cash and cash equivalents	$ 32,203	$ 21,904
Short-term investments	22,976	15,292
Accounts receivable	46,319	38,682
Inventories	24,365	16,159
Prepaid expenses	3,478	2,591
Income taxes refundable	1,963	2,534
Deferred income taxes	9,824	4,607
Total current assets	141,128	101,769
Property, plant, and equipment, net	202,558	112,577
Investments	11,215	16,100
Intangible assets	48,703	16,621
Other assets	6,883	8,309
Total assets	$410,487	$255,376
Liabilities and Stockholders' Equity		
Current liabilities		
Accounts payable	$ 14,055	$ 12,095
Bank overdraft	11,375	9,107
Accrued expenses	30,956	30,600
Current maturities of long-term debt	3,301	731
Total current liabilities	59,687	52,533
Long-term debt	49,900	3,912
Deferred income taxes	9,849	3,930
Other long-term obligations	12,506	4,843
Total long-term liabilities	72,255	12,685
Minority interests	5,193	2,491
Stockholders' equity		
Common stock, no par value		
Authorized—100,000 (2002) and 300,000 (2003)		
Issued—54,271 (2002) and 56,295 (2003)	173,112	121,052
Unearned compensation	(677)	(2,766)
Accumulated other comprehensive income (loss)	(1,486)	456
Retained earnings	102,403	68,925
Total stockholders' equity	273,352	187,667
Total liabilities and stockholders' equity	$410,487	$255,376

Exhibit 12-16
Continued

CONSOLIDATED STATEMENT OF OPERATIONS

	For years ended	
	February 2, 2003	February 3, 2002
Total revenues	$491,549	$394,354
Operating expenses	381,489	316,946
General and administrative expenses	28,897	27,562
Depreciation and amortization expenses	12,271	7,959
Arbitration award	9,075	—
Income from operations	59,817	41,887
Interest income	1,966	2,980
Interest expense	(1,781)	(337)
Equity loss in joint ventures	(2,008)	(602)
Minority interest	(2,287)	(1,147)
Loss on sale of property and equipment	(934)	(235)
Income before taxes	54,773	42,546
Provision for taxes	21,295	16,168
Net income	$ 33,478	$ 26,378
Basic earnings per common share	$ 0.61	$ 0.49
Earnings per common share assuming dilution	$ 0.56	$ 0.45

12-46 Financial Ratios

(Alternate is 12-44.) This problem uses the same data as 12-45, but it can be solved independently. Krispy Kreme Doughnuts, Inc. was incorporated on December 12, 1999 and has been one of the success stories of the early 2000s. Two recent income statements and balance sheets are in Exhibit 12-16. Krispy Kreme paid no dividends. Additional data are:

- Market price per share, February 2, 2003: $30.41
- Average common shares outstanding, 55,093,000

Compute the following ratios for Krispy Kreme for the year ending February 2, 2003: (a) current, (b) quick, (c) average collection period, (d) total-debt-to-total-assets, (e) total-debt-to-total-equity, (f) ROE, (g) return on sales, (h) asset turnover, (i) return on total assets, (j) EPS, (k) P-E and (l) market-to-book. Total debt includes all liabilities. Assume all sales are on credit.

12-47 Trend Analysis and Common-Size Statements

Ryan Company furnished the condensed data shown in Exhibit 12-17.

1. Prepare a trend analysis for Ryan's income statements and balance sheets that compares 20X3 with 20X2.
2. Prepare common-size income statements for 20X3 and 20X2 and common-size balance sheets for December 31, 20X3 and December 31, 20X2 for Ryan Company.
3. Comment on Ryan Company's performance and position for 20X3 compared with 20X2.

12-48 Financial Ratios

Consider the data for Ryan Company in Exhibit 12-17.

1. Compute the following ratios for each of the last 2 years, 20X2 and 20X3:
   a. Percentage of net income to stockholders' equity (ROE)
   b. Gross profit rate
   c. Percent of net income to sales
   d. Ratio of total debt to stockholders' equity
   e. Inventory turnover
   f. Current ratio
   g. Average collection period for accounts receivable

Exhibit 12-17
Ryan Company
*Balance Sheets and
Income Statements
(in Thousands)*

	December 31		
	20X3	**20X2**	**20X1**
Cash	$ 30	$ 25	$ 20
Accounts receivable	90	70	50
Merchandise inventory	80	70	60
Prepaid expenses	10	10	10
Land	30	30	30
Building	70	75	80
Equipment	60	50	40
Total assets	$370	$330	$290
Accounts payable	$ 50	$ 40	$ 30
Taxes payable	20	15	10
Accrued expenses payable	15	10	5
Long-term debt	45	45	45
Paid-in capital	150	150	150
Retained earnings	90	70	50
Total liab. and stk. eq.	$370	$330	$290

	Year Ended December 31	
	20X3	**20X2**
Sales (all on credit)	$800	$750
Cost of goods sold	440	410
Operating expenses	300	295
Pretax income	60	45
Income taxes	20	15
Net income	$ 40	$ 30

2. For each of the following items, indicate whether the change from 20X2 to 20X3 for Ryan Company seems to be favorable or unfavorable, and identify the ratios you computed previously that most directly support your answer. The first two items that follow are given as an example.
   a. Return to owners, favorable, a
   b. Gross profit rate, unchanged, b (declined from 45.3% to 45%, could answer unfavorable)
   c. Ability to pay current debts on time
   d. Collectibility of receivables
   e. Risks of insolvency
   f. Salability of merchandise
   g. Return on sales
   h. Overall accomplishment
   i. Coordination of buying and selling functions
   j. Screening of risks in granting credit to customers

12-49 Computation of Financial Ratios

The financial statements of the Ito Company are shown in Exhibit 12-18.
    Compute the following for the 20X8 financial statements.

1. Pretax return on total assets.
2. Divide your answer to number 1 into two components: EBIT-to-sales ratio and total asset turnover.
3. After-tax rate of return on total assets. Be sure to add the after-tax interest expense to net income.
4. Rate of return on total stockholders' equity including returns to both common and preferred stockholders. Did the preferred and common stockholders benefit from the existence of debt? Explain fully.
5. Rate of return on common stockholders' equity. This ratio is the amount of net income available for the common stockholders, divided by total stockholders' equity less the par value of

Exhibit 12-18
The Ito Company
(Yen in Millions)

BALANCE SHEETS

	December 31	
	20X8	**20X7**
Assets		
Current assets		
Cash	¥ 2,000	¥ 2,000
Short-term investments	—	1,000
Receivables, net	5,000	4,000
Inventories at cost	11,000	8,000
Prepayments	1,000	1,000
Total current assets	¥19,000	¥16,000
Plant and equipment, net	22,000	23,000
Total assets	¥41,000	¥39,000
Liabilities and Stockholders' Equity		
Current liabilities		
Accounts payable	¥10,000	¥ 6,000
Accrued expenses payable	500	500
Income taxes payable	1,500	1,500
Total current liabilities	¥12,000	¥ 8,000
8% bonds payable	¥10,000	¥10,000
Stockholders' equity		
Preferred stock, 12%, par value $100 per share	¥ 5,000	¥ 5,000
Common stock, $5 par value	4,000	4,000
Premium on common stock	8,000	8,000
Unappropriated retained earnings	1,000	3,000
Reserve for plant expansion	1,000	1,000
Total stockholders' equity	¥19,000	¥21,000
Total liab. and stk. eq.	¥41,000	¥39,000

STATEMENT OF INCOME AND RECONCILIATION OF RETAINED EARNINGS

		Year Ended December 31, 20X8
Sales (all on credit)		¥44,000
Cost of goods sold		32,000
Gross profit on sales		¥12,000
Other operating expenses		
Selling expenses	¥ 5,000	
Administrative expenses	2,000	
Depreciation	1,000	8,000
Operating income		¥ 4,000
Interest expense		800
Income before income taxes		¥ 3,200
Income taxes at 40%		¥ 1,280
Net income		¥ 1,920
Dividends on preferred stock		600
Net income for common stockholders		¥ 1,320
Dividends on common stock		3,320
Net income retained		¥ (2,000)
Unappropriated retained earnings, December 31, 20X7		3,000
Unappropriated retained earnings, December 31, 20X8		¥ 1,000

preferred stock. Did the common stockholders benefit from the existence of preferred stock? Explain fully.

6. Calculate inventory turnover. How would Ito have been helped if they had been able to maintain the level of inventory from 20X7?

12-50 Common-Size Statements

(Alternate is 12-43.) Exhibit 12-19 contains slightly modified income statements and balance sheets of Minnesota Mining and Manufacturing Company (3M), a multinational company with sales of more than $16.3 billion.

1. Prepare common-size statements for 3M for 2001 and 2002.
2. Comment on the changes in component percentages from 2001 to 2002.

12-51 Liquidity Ratios

Exhibit 12-19 contains the slightly modified income statements and balance sheets of Minnesota Mining and Manufacturing Company (3M), maker of Scotch brand tapes.

1. Compute the following ratios for 2002: (a) current, (b) average collection period, and (c) inventory turnover.
2. Assess 3M's liquidity compared with the following industry averages from Reuters MultexInvestor, Reuters classifies 3M in the conglomerates industry, which includes firms as diversified as General Electric, ITT, Raytheon, and Tyco.

Current ratio	1.56 times
Average collection period	107.6 days
Inventory turnover	6.19 times

12-52 Solvency Ratios

Exhibit 12-19 contains slightly modified income statements and balance sheets of Minnesota Mining and Manufacturing Company (3M), a diversified manufacturing company with operations in the United States and 51 other countries.

1. Compute the following ratios for 2002: (a) total-debt-to-total-assets and (b) total-debt-to-total-equity. To be consistent with the source of industry data, define total debt as short-term debt and long-term debt only.
2. Assess 3M's solvency compared with the following industry averages from Reuters MultexInvestor.

Total-debt-to-total-assets	Not available
Total-debt-to-total-shareholders'-equity	248.0%

12-53 Profitability Ratios

Exhibit 12-19 contains slightly modified income statements and balance sheets of Minnesota Mining and Manufacturing Company (3M), a technology company with more than 100 technologies. A corporate objective is for significant sales to be generated by new products introduced in the last 5 years. Average common shares outstanding in 2002 totalled 390 million.

1. Compute the following ratios for 2002: (a) ROE, (b) gross profit rate, (c) return on sales, (d) EBIT-to-sales, (e) asset turnover, (f) ROA (with net income in the numerator), (g) ROA (with EBIT in the numerator), and (h) EPS.
2. Assess 3M's profitability in 2002 compared with the following industry averages from Reuters MultexInvestor.

Return on stockholders' equity	20.24%
Gross profit rate	45.4%
Return on sales (Net income ÷ Sales)	9.64%
EBIT-to-sales ratio	16.26%
Asset turnover	0.51 times
Return on assets (Net income ÷ Assets)	4.71%
Return on assets (EBIT ÷ Assets)	8.3%
Earnings per share	Not available

Exhibit 12-19
Minnesota Mining
and Manufacturing
Company (3M) and
Subsidiaries
*(Dollars in millions,
except per share data)*

CONSOLIDATED STATEMENT OF INCOME

	Years Ended December 31	
	2002	**2001**
Net sales	$16,332	$16,054
Operating expenses		
Cost of goods sold	8,496	8,749
Selling, general, and administrative expenses	3,720	4,036
Research, development, and related expenses	1,070	1,084
Other expense (income)	—	(88)
Total	13,286	13,781
Operating income	3,046	2,273
Other income and expense		
Interest expense	80	124
Interest income	(39)	(37)
Total	41	87
Income before income taxes and minority interest	3,005	2,186
Provision for income taxes	966	702
Minority interest	65	54
Net income	$ 1,974	$ 1,430
Weighted-average common shares outstanding—basic	390.0	394.3
EPS—basic	$ 5.06	$ 3.63
Weighted-average common shares outstanding—diluted	395.5	399.9
EPS—diluted	$ 4.99	$ 3.58

CONSOLIDATED BALANCE SHEET

At December 31	**2002**	**2001**
Assets		
Current assets		
Cash and cash equivalents	$ 618	$ 616
Accounts receivable—net	2,527	2,482
Inventories	1,931	2,091
Other current assets	983	1,107
Total current assets	6,059	6,296
Investments	238	275
Property, plant, and equipment—net	5,621	5,615
Intangible assets	2,167	1,250
Other assets	1,244	1,170
Total assets	$15,329	$14,606
Liabilities and Stockholders' Equity		
Current liabilities		
Short-term debt	$ 1,237	$ 1,373
Accounts payable	945	753
Payroll	411	539
Income taxes	518	596
Other current liabilities	1,346	1,248
Total current liabilities	4,457	4,509
Long-term debt	2,140	1,520
Other liabilities	2,739	2,491
Total liabilities	9,336	8,520
Stockholders' equity—net	5,993	6,086
Shares outstanding—2002: 390,195,681		
2001: 391,303,636		
Total liabilities and stockholders' equity	$15,329	$14,606

12-54 Market Price and Dividend Ratios

Exhibit 12-19 contains slightly modified income statements and balance sheets of Minnesota Mining and Manufacturing Company (3M), a leader in bringing new technology-based products to the market. In 2002, 3M paid cash dividends of $2.48 per share, the market price was $123.30 per share and EPS was $5.06.

1. Compute the following ratios for 2002: (a) P-E, (b) dividend-yield, (c) dividend-payout, and (d) market-to-book value.
2. Assess 3M's market price and dividend ratios compared with the following industry averages from Reuters MultexInvestor.

Price-earnings	23.5
Dividend-yield	2.2%
Dividend-payout	45.1%
Market-to-book value	4.09

12-55 Time-Series Analysis

The 3M balance sheets in Exhibit 12-19 show intangible assets of $2,167 million in 2002 and $1,250 million in 2001. Additional disclosures reveal the following detail about intangible assets, in millions:

	2002	2001
Goodwill	$1,898	$1,012
Other intangible assets	269	238
Intangible assets	$2,167	$1,250

1. Goodwill increased $886 million or 87.5% from 2001 to 2002. What does this increase tell you about the activities of 3M during the year ended December 31, 2002?
2. Suppose you calculated various ratios for 3M for the year ended December 31, 2002. If you worked problems 12-51 through 12-54 you actually calculated many ratios. This problem does not require use of specific computations. However, you might review problems 12-51 through 12-54 as a reminder of the ratios that might be impacted. Assume you have been asked to compute these same ratios for 2001. Would the increase in goodwill and the activities implied by that increase, complicate the comparison of ratios over the 2 years in question? If so, why?

12-56 Income Ratios and Asset Turnover

The following data are from the 2002, 2001, and 2000 annual reports of McDonald's Corporation. There are more than 27,000 McDonald's restaurants in 120 countries. Dollar amounts are in millions.

	2002	2001	2000
Rate of return on stockholders' equity	10.0%	17.5%	21.0%
EBIT-to-sales ratio	13.2%	18.1%	23.4%
Total asset turnover (Sales ÷ Average assets)	.66	.67	.67
Average total assets	$23,252.5	$22,109.5	$21,333.5
Interest expense	$ 374.1	$ 452.4	$ 429.9
Income tax expense	$ 670.0	$ 693.1	$ 905.0

1. Complete the following condensed income statements for 2002 and 2000. Round to the nearest million.

	2002	2000
Sales	$?	$?
Operating expenses	?	?
EBIT	$?	$?
Interest expense	?	?
Pretax income	$?	$?
Income tax expense	?	?
Net income	$?	$?

2. Compute the following for 2002 and 2000:
   a. Return on total assets
   b. Net income-to-sales ratio
   c. Average stockholders' equity

3. Compare the values for 2002 with 2000.

12-57 Income Ratios and Asset Turnover

Nicoletti Company included the following data in its 2003 annual report to stockholders (amounts in millions except for percentages):

Net income	$1,480
Total assets	
Beginning of year	$5,936
End of year	$8,798
Net income as a percentage of	
Total revenue	46%
Average stockholders' equity	51%

You calculated a tax rate of 39% for Nicoletti. Using this data, compute the following values for 2003:

1. Net income as a percentage of average total assets
2. Total revenues
3. Average stockholders' equity
4. Asset turnover, using two different approaches

12-58 Industry Identification

Exhibit 12-20 presents common-size financial statements and selected ratio values for eight companies from the following industries:

1. Department store
2. Pharmaceutical
3. Petroleum
4. Newspaper
5. Grocery
6. Consumer products
7. Utility
8. Home building

Use your knowledge of general business practices to match the industries to the company data.

12-59 Choosing Potential Investments Among Delivery Companies

Exhibit 12-21 on page 595 presents some financial information for United Parcel Service (UPS) and FedEx. Which do you believe is the preferred investment based on this information gathered in the fall of 2003? Be prepared to defend your answer.

12-60 Choosing Potential Investments Among Retailers

Exhibit 12-22 on pages 596–597 presents some financial information for Wal-Mart, Target, JCPenney, and Kohl's. Which do you believe is the preferred investment based on this information gathered in the fall of 2003? Be prepared to defend your answer.

12-61 EVA at Briggs & Stratton

Briggs & Stratton Corporation is the world's largest maker of air-cooled gasoline engines for outdoor power equipment. The company's engines are used by the lawn and garden equipment industry. According to a recent annual report, "management subscribes to the premise that the value of Briggs & Stratton is enhanced if the capital invested in the company's operations yields a cash return that is greater than that expected by the providers of capital."

	A	B	C	D	E	F	G	H
	%	%	%	%	%	%	%	%
Balance sheet								
Cash & marketable securities	3.71	1.28	1.67	1.32	0.00	1.21	1.57	3.54
Current receivables	14.52	15.73	18.30	7.90	3.87	2.94	0.00	17.09
Inventories	10.78	7.95	19.23	0.97	2.48	22.62	34.90	11.62
Other current assets	11.20	1.96	2.73	2.93	0.69	1.85	0.67	3.20
Total current assets	40.20	26.92	41.93	13.12	7.04	28.62	37.14	35.45
Net property, plant, & equip.	48.14	61.39	43.22	36.93	84.64	49.91	1.41	32.37
Other noncurrent assets	11.66	11.69	14.86	49.95	8.31	21.47	61.45	32.18
Total assets	100.00	100.00	100.00	100.00	100.00	100.00	100.00	100.00
Current liabilities	46.90	32.30	21.91	14.38	9.35	36.31	29.84	24.90
Long-term liabilities	16.70	26.43	48.69	36.37	50.64	50.87	51.85	45.43
Stockholders' equity	36.40	41.27	29.40	49.25	40.02	12.82	18.31	29.68
Total liabilities & stockholders' eq.	100.00	100.00	100.00	100.00	100.00	100.00	100.00	100.00
Income statement								
Revenue	100.00	100.00	100.00	100.00	100.00	100.00	100.00	100.00
Cost of sales	20.58	54.41	61.71	53.56	32.11	72.80	76.81	51.57
Gross profit	79.42	45.59	38.29	46.44	67.89	27.20	23.19	48.43
Interest expense	1.21	0.68	3.15	1.19	5.28	1.42	6.39	1.14
R & D	13.21	0.77	0.00	0.00	0.00	0.00	0.00	0.00
Selling, general, & admin.	35.89	8.09	27.25	37.48	23.03	21.19	11.79	31.50
Other expenses (income)	(0.43)	27.00	0.50	(8.66)	9.57	(0.15)	1.05	1.09
Depreciation & amortization	3.38	4.60	3.40	0.00	13.35	2.09	1.56	3.10
Income taxes	6.25	2.85	1.73	7.37	6.04	1.11	0.91	3.95
Net Income	19.91	1.60	2.26	9.06	10.62	1.54	1.49	7.65
Ratios								
Current ratio	0.86	0.83	1.91	0.91	0.75	0.79	1.24	1.42
Long-term debt as % of equity*	11.80	27.49	124.44	30.64	75.70	314.43	274.09	96.08
Return on sales	19.80	1.62	2.26	9.05	10.63	1.53	1.49	7.65
ROA	21.34	2.62	1.90	6.72	4.79	4.75	1.22	9.75
ROE	58.42	6.28	6.34	13.56	12.27	46.69	8.08	31.37
Inventory turnover	2.20	9.83	2.88	32.45	5.66	10.05	2.33	5.62
Times interest earned	22.62	7.54	2.27	14.8	4.16	2.86	1.38	11.18

*Note that this is the ratio of long-term-debt-to-equity, not long-term-liabilities-to-equity.

Exhibit 12-20
Common Size Statements in Eight Industries
(Columns May Not Add Due to Rounding)

The following data are from Briggs & Stratton's 2003 annual report (thousands of dollars):

	2003	2002
Adjusted operating profit	$ 160,339	$ 115,352
Cash taxes	27,833	22,903
Invested capital	1,183,689	1,176,483
Cost of capital	8.4%	8.7%

1. Compute the EVA for Briggs & Stratton for 2002 and 2003.
2. Did Briggs & Stratton's overall performance improve from 2002 to 2003? Explain.

PRICE AND VALUATION

Ticker Symbol	Current Price	52-Week Range	Beta	EPS	Price-Earnings
FDX	76.90	47.70–78.05	0.80	$2.64	29.23
UPS	73.14	53.00–73.8	0.48	$3.12	23.46

Ticker Symbol	Price/Sales	Price/Book	Price/Cash Flow	Analyst Rating
FDX	1.03	3.13	10.86	2.7
UPS	2.53	6.18	16.91	2.6

GROWTH TRENDS

Ticker Symbol	Latest Annual Revenue (mil)	1-yr Revenue Growth	5-yr Revenue Growth	Latest Annual EPS	1-yr EPS Growth	5-yr EPS Growth
FDX	$22.487.0	9.12%	7.22%	$2.78	14.46%	10.42%
UPS	$31,272.0	3.14%	6.85%	$2.90**	35.38%	28.63%

Ticker Symbol	Annual Dividend/Share	Dividend Yield	5-yr Dividend Growth Rate
FDX	$0.20	0.26	0.0
UPS	$1.00	1.37	N/C*

FINANCIAL CONDITION

Ticker Symbol	Total Debt/Equity	Current Total Debt (mil)	Current Ratio	Quick Ratio	Current Inventory Turnover	Current Receivable Turnover
FDX	.29	$2,095.0	1.26	1.03	72.7	8.72
UPS	.31	$4,069.0	1.73	1.47	N/A*	7.09

MANAGEMENT EFFECTIVENESS

Ticker Symbol	Return on Assets	5-yr Avg. Return on Assets	Return on Equity	5-yr Avg. Return on Equity	Revenue/ Employee (000s)	Income/ Employee (000s)
FDX	5.39%	5.63%	11.37%	12.76%	$169.5	$6
UPS	13.34%	10.27%	28.62%	22.92%	$ 91.39	$9.88

SHARE INFORMATION

Ticker Symbol	Market Cap (mil)	Shares Outstanding (000s)	% Held by Institutions
FDX	$22,938.7	298,290	78.8%
UPS	$82,309.0	1,125,360	31.0%

Source: Reuters MultexInvestor
Data as of November 9, 2003.
*N/A, not available; N/C, not calculable.
** Based on income excluding extraordinary item.

Exhibit 12-21
Investments in Delivery Companies
FedEx Corporation (FDX) and United Parcel Service Incorporated (UPS)

PRICE AND VALUATION

Ticker Symbol	Current Price	52-Week Range	Beta	EPS	Price-Earnings
TGT	39.05	25.60–41.80	1.12	$1.83	21.27
KSS	50.65	46.18–71.70	1.13	$1.85	28.11
JCP	23.28	15.57–25.55	0.70	$1.16	19.99
WMT	58.12	46.25–60.20	0.86	$1.92	30.44

Ticker Symbol	Price/Sales	Price/Book	Price/Cash Flow	Analyst Rating
TGT	0.78	3.52	12.08	2.4
KSS	1.86	4.65	20.95	1.9
JCP	0.21	1.03	6.45	3.1
WMT	1.03	5.99	20.85	2.1

GROWTH TRENDS

Ticker Symbol	Latest Annual Revenue (mil)	1-yr Revenue Growth	5-yr Revenue Growth	Latest Annual EPS	1-yr EPS Growth	5-yr EPS Growth
TGT	$ 43,917.0	10.27%	9.82%	$1.82	20.35%	16.29%
KSS	$ 9,120.3	21.79%	24.41%	$1.91	28.84%	32.81%
JCP	$ 17,633.0	1.07%	1.24%	$1.29**	294.03%	−9.79%
WMT	$244,524.0	12.23%	15.62%	$1.81	21.42%	18.37%

Ticker Symbol	Annual Dividend/Share	Dividend Yield	5-yr Dividend Growth Rate
TGT	$0.28	0.72%	7.78%
KSS	$0.00	0.0%	N/C*
JCP	$0.50	2.16%	−25.23%
WMT	$0.36	0.62%	17.32%

FINANCIAL STRENGTH

Ticker Symbol	Total Debt/Equity	Current Total Debt (mil)	Current Ratio	Quick Ratio	Current Inventory Turnover	Current Receivable Turnover
TGT	1.18	$11,855.0	1.72	0.83	6.28	8.98
KSS	0.28	$ 1076.6	2.74	1.03	3.67	10.23
JCP	0.91	$ 5,828.0	2.12	0.80	4.29	44.82
WMT	0.60	$25,607.0	0.98	0.17	7.49	168.8

MANAGEMENT EFFECTIVENESS

Ticker Symbol	Return on Assets	5-yr Avg. Return on Assets	Return on Equity	5-yr Avg. Return on Equity	Revenue/ Employee (000s)	Income/ Employee (000s)
TGT	5.83%	6.62%	17.97%	20.08%	$148.9	$ 5.5
KSS	10.54%	11.02%	18.40%	19.14%	$508.1	$33.4
JCP	1.98%	0.50%	5.43%	1.16%	$141.3	$ 1.5
WMT	9.12%	9.11%	21.45%	21.96%	$179.5	$ 6.2

Exhibit 12-22
Comparisons of Retailers
Target (TGT), Kohl's (KSS), JCPenney (JCP), and Wal-Mart (WMT)

		SHARE INFORMATION		
Ticker Symbol	Market Cap (mil)	Shares Outstanding (000s)	% Held by Institutions	
TGT	$ 35,399.1	910,800	85.7%	
KSS	$ 17,622.0	339,470	80.8%	
JCP	$ 6,304.2	271,850	96.6%	
WMT	$255,249.0	4,369,200	36.1%	

Source: Reuters MultexInvestor
Data as of November 9, 2003.
*N/C, not calculable
** Excludes extraordinary items.

Exhibit 12-22
Continued

12-62 Comparing EVA for Two Companies

In November 2004, the following relationships held for two companies in the medical devices industry. Which would you expect to have the larger EVA in 2003? Why?

	Company A	Company B
Share price	$87.75	$88.00
EPS	$ 2.45	$ 2.46
P-E	31.3	31.5
PEG ratio	2.5	2.4
Book value per share	$ 5.69	$ 4.60
Shares outstanding (billions)	2.3	1.1

12-63 MD&A and Ethics

If certain conditions are met, the SEC requires companies to disclose information about future events that are reasonably likely to materially affect the firms' operations. Many companies are understandably reluctant to disclose such information. After all, positive predictions may not materialize and negative predictions may unduly alarm the investors. What ethical considerations should a company's managers consider when deciding what prospective information to disclose in the MD&A section of the annual report?

Collaborative Learning Exercise

12-64 Operating Return on Total Assets

Form groups of four to six students. Each student should choose an industry (a different industry for each student in the group) and pick two companies in that industry. Compute the following for each of the companies:

1. EBIT-to-sales ratio
2. Total asset turnover
3. Return on total assets

Get together as a group and list the industries and the three ratios for each company in the industry. Examine how the ratios differ between the two companies within each industry compared with the differences between industries. As a group, prepare two lists of possible explanations for the differences in ratios. The first list should explain why ratios of two companies within the same industry might differ. The second list should explain why ratios differ by industry.

Analyzing and Interpreting Financial Statements

12-65 Financial Statement Research

Choose two companies in each of two industries.

Calculate the ROA, ROE, and return on sales for each of the companies. Compare and contrast the two companies in each industry and the averages for each industry.

12-66 Analyzing Starbucks' Annual Report

Use the financial statements and notes of Starbucks in the appendix to respond to the questions that follow:

1. Calculate ROE for the year ended September 28, 2003. Compare it with the value for the year ended September 29, 2002.
2. Calculate the current ratio for the year ended September 28, 2003 and compare it with the value for the year ended September 29, 2002.
3. Calculate total-debt-to-total-assets for the year ended September 28, 2003. Compare it with the value for the year ended September 29, 2002.

12-67 Analyzing Financial Statements Using the Internet

Go to www.boeing.com to locate Boeing's home page. Select Investor. Click on Current Annual Reports. Click on Financials.

Answer the following questions about Boeing:

1. What is Boeing's dividend policy?
2. Where does Boeing report geographic segment information? What segments exist? Which is the largest? Which is experiencing the greatest percentage growth?
3. Calculate Boeing's total-debt-to-equity ratio for the last 2 fiscal years. What is the trend? What effect does additional debt financing have on net income, and on EPS?
4. What is the amount of Boeing's EPS for the most recent fiscal year? What factors influenced the change from the last period to the current period?

Starbucks
10–K

Appendix

(excerpted)

UNITED STATES SECURITIES AND EXCHANGE COMMISSION
Washington, DC 20549
Form 10-K

☑ **ANNUAL REPORT PURSUANT TO SECTION 13 OR 15(d) OF
THE SECURITIES EXCHANGE ACT OF 1934
For the fiscal year ended September 28, 2003**

or

❏ **TRANSITION REPORT PURSUANT TO SECTION 13 OR 15(d) OF
THE SECURITIES EXCHANGE ACT OF 1934
For the transition period from   to   .**

Commission file number: 0-20322

Starbucks Corporation

(Exact Name of Registrant as Specified in its Charter)

Washington	**91-1325671**
(State or other jurisdiction of incorporation or organization)	*(IRS Employer Identification No.*
2401 Utah Avenue South Seattle, Washington 98134	**98134**
(Address of principal executive offices)	*(Zip Code)*

Selected Financial Data

In thousands, except earnings per share and store operating data

The following selected financial data have been derived from the consolidated financial statements of Starbucks Corporation (the "Company"). The data set forth below should be read in conjunction with "Management's Discussion and Analysis of Financial Condition and Results of Operations," the section "Certain Additional Risks and Uncertainties" in the Company's annual report on Form 10-K and the Company's consolidated financial statements and notes thereto.

As of and for the fiscal year ended[1]	Sept 28, 2003 (52 Wks)	Sept 29, 2002 (52 Wks)	Sept 30, 2001 (52 Wks)	Oct 1, 2000 (52 Wks)	Oct 3, 1999 (53 Wks)
RESULTS OF OPERATIONS DATA					
Net revenues:					
Retail	$3,449,624	$2,792,904	$2,229,594	$1,823,607	$1,423,389
Specialty	625,898	496,004	419,386	354,007	263,439
Total net revenues	4,075,522	3,288,908	2,648,980	2,177,614	1,686,828
Operating income[2]	424,713	316,338	280,219	212,190	156,641
Internet-related investment losses[3]	—	—	2,940	58,792	—
Gain on sale of investment[3]	—	13,361	—	—	—
Net earnings[2]	$ 268,346	$ 212,686	$ 180,335	$ 94,502	$ 101,623
Net earnings per common share-diluted[2][4]	$ 0.67	$ 0.54	$ 0.46	$ 0.24	$ 0.27
Cash dividends per share	—	—	—	—	—

BALANCE SHEET DATA

Working capital	$ 315,326	$ 310,048	$ 148,661	$ 146,568	$ 135,303
Total assets[2]	2,729,746	2,214,392	1,783,470	1,435,026	1,188,578
Long-term debt (including current portion)	5,076	5,786	6,483	7,168	7,691
Shareholders' equity[2]	$2,082,427	$1,723,189	$1,374,865	$1,148,212	$ 960,887

STORE OPERATING DATA[5]

Percentage change in comparable store sales:[6]

United States	9%	7%	5%	9%	6%
International	7%	1%	3%	12%	8%
Consolidated	8%	6%	5%	9%	6%

Stores opened during the year:[7]

United States					
Company-operated stores	506	503	498	388	394
Licensed stores	315	264	268	342	42
International					
Company-operated stores	96	111	149	96	53
Licensed stores	284	299	293	177	123
Total	1,201	1,177	1,208	1,003	612

Stores open at year end:

United States(8)					
Company-operated stores	3,779	3,209	2,706	2,208	1,820
Licensed stores	1,422	1,033	769	501	159
International					
Company-operated stores	767	671	560	411	315
Licensed stores	1,257	973	674	381	204
Total	7,225	5,886	4,709	3,501	2,498

(1) The Company's fiscal year ends on the Sunday closest to September 30. All fiscal years presented include 52 weeks, except fiscal 1999, which includes 53 weeks.

(2) Amounts have been retroactively adjusted for the effect of the application of the equity method of accounting for the Company's additional equity ownership interests in Austria, Shanghai, Spain, Switzerland and Taiwan. See Notes to Consolidated Financial Statements (Note 2).

(3) See Notes to Consolidated Financial Statements (Notes 4 and 7).

(4) Earnings per share data for fiscal years presented above have been restated to reflect the two-for-one stock splits in fiscal 2001 and 1999.

(5) Store operating data reflects Canada within the international category.

(6) Includes only Company-operated stores open 13 months or longer.

(7) Store openings are reported net of closures.

(8) United States stores open at fiscal 2003 year end include 43 Seattle's Best Coffee ("SBC") and 21 Torrefazione Italia Company-operated stores and 74 SBC franchised stores.

Management's Discussion and Analysis of Financial Condition and Results of Operations

General

Starbucks Corporation's fiscal year ends on the Sunday closest to September 30. Fiscal years 2003, 2002 and 2001 each had 52 weeks. The fiscal year ending on October 3, 2004, will include 53 weeks.

Acquisitions

On July 14, 2003, the Company acquired Seattle Coffee Company ("SCC") from AFC Enterprises, Inc. SCC includes the Seattle's Best Coffee® and Torrefazione Italia® brands, which complement the Company's existing portfolio of products. The results of operations of SCC are included in the accompanying consolidated financial statements from the date of purchase. The $70 million all-cash purchase transaction generated goodwill of approximately $43 million and indefinite-lived intangibles, consisting of trade names and recipes, of approximately $13 million. Pro forma results of operations have not been provided, as the amounts were not deemed material to the consolidated financial statements of Starbucks.

During fiscal 2003, Starbucks increased its equity ownership to 50% for its international licensed operations in Austria, Shanghai, Spain, Switzerland and Taiwan, which enabled the Company to exert significant influence over their operating and financial policies. For these operations, management determined that a change in accounting method, from the cost method to the equity method, was required. This accounting change included adjusting previously reported information for the Company's proportionate share of net losses as required by Accounting Principles Board Opinion No. 18, "The Equity Method of Accounting for Investments in Common Stock."

As shown in the table below, the cumulative effect of the accounting change to the equity method resulted in reductions of net earnings of $2.4 million and $0.9 million for the 52 weeks ended September 29, 2002, and September 30, 2001, respectively (in thousands, except earnings per share):

	52 weeks ended	
	Sept 29, 2002	Sept 30, 2001
Net earnings, previously reported	$215,073	$181,210
Effect of change to equity method	(2,387)	(875)
Net earnings, as restated	$212,686	$180,335
Net earnings per common share-basic: Previously reported	$ 0.56	$ 0.48
As restated	$ 0.55	$ 0.47
Net earnings per common share-diluted: Previously reported	$ 0.54	$ 0.46
As restated	$ 0.54	$ 0.46

Additionally, a reduction of net earnings for the effects of the accounting change prior to fiscal 2001 of $0.2 million was recorded.

Reclassifications

During the fiscal first quarter of 2004, the Company realigned its resources to better manage its rapidly growing operations. In connection with this process, classification of operating expenses within the consolidated statements of earnings was evaluated using broad-based definitions of retail, specialty and general and administrative functions. As a result, management determined that certain functions not directly supporting retail or non-retail operations, such as executive, administrative, finance and risk management overhead primarily within international operations, would be more appropriately classified as "General and administrative expenses" than as store or other operating expenses. Accordingly, amounts in prior year periods have been reclassified to conform to current year classifications.

Results of Operations—Fiscal 2003 Compared to Fiscal 2002

The following table sets forth the percentage relationship to total net revenues, unless otherwise indicated, of certain items included in the Company's consolidated statements of earnings:

Fiscal year end	Sept 28, 2003 (52 Wks)	Sept 29, 2002 (52 Wks)	Sept 30, 2001 (52 Wks)
STATEMENTS OF EARNINGS DATA			
Net revenues:			
Retail	84.6%	84.9%	84.2%
Specialty	15.4	15.1	15.8
Total net revenues	100.0	100.0	100.0
Cost of sales including occupancy	41.4	41.0	42.0
Store operating expenses[1]	40.0	39.7	38.9
Other operating expenses[2]	22.6	21.4	17.3
Depreciation and amortization expenses	5.8	6.3	6.2
General and administrative expenses	6.0	7.1	6.8
Income from equity investees	0.9	1.0	1.0
Operating income	10.4	9.6	10.6
Interest and other income, net	0.3	0.3	0.4
Internet-related investment losses	0.0	0.0	0.1
Gain on sale of investment	0.0	0.4	0.0
Earnings before income taxes	10.7	10.3	10.9
Income taxes	4.1	3.8	4.1
Net earnings	6.6%	6.5%	6.8%

(1) Shown as a percentage of retail revenues.
(2) Shown as a percentage of specialty revenues.

Consolidated Results of Operations

Net revenues for the fiscal year ended 2003 increased 23.9% to $4.1 billion from $3.3 billion for the corresponding period in fiscal 2002. During the fiscal year ended 2003, Starbucks derived approximately 85% of total net revenues from its Company-operated retail stores. Retail revenues increased 23.5% to $3.4 billion for the fiscal year ended 2003, from $2.8 billion for the corresponding period of fiscal 2002. This increase was due primarily to the opening of 602 new Company-operated retail stores in the last 12 months, comparable store sales growth of 8% driven almost entirely by increased transactions and the July 2003 acquisition of 49 Seattle's Best Coffee and 21 Torrefazione Italia stores. Management believes increased customer traffic continues to be driven by new product innovation, continued popularity of core products, a high level of customer satisfaction and improved speed of service through enhanced technology, training and execution at retail stores.

The Company derived the remaining 15% of total net revenues from its Specialty Operations. Specialty revenues increased $129.9 million, or 26.2%, to $625.9 million for the fiscal year ended 2003, from $496.0 million for the corresponding period in fiscal 2002. Of the total growth, expanded Starbucks retail licensing operations provided $70.3 million, or 54.1%, broader distribution and additional accounts in food-service provided $24.5 million, or 18.9%, and an increase in the grocery and warehouse club business provided $22.0 million, or 16.9%.

Cost of sales and related occupancy costs increased to 41.4% of total net revenues in fiscal 2003, from 41.0% in fiscal 2002. The increase was primarily due to higher green coffee costs and a shift in specialty revenue mix to lower margin products. The Company's green coffee costs reached an historic low for Starbucks in the second and third fiscal quarters of 2002 and have gradually increased since then. These increases were partially offset by leverage gained on fixed occupancy costs distributed over an expanded revenue base.

Store operating expenses as a percentage of retail revenues increased to 40.0% in fiscal 2003, from 39.7% in fiscal 2002, primarily due to higher payroll-related and advertising expenditures. Payroll-related costs have increased primarily due to an increase in the number of partners who qualify for the Company's medical and vacation benefits. Advertising expenditures increased in fiscal 2003 due to promotions for new and existing products. These increases were partially offset by lower provisions for asset impairment for international Company-operated retail stores in 2003 as compared to the prior year.

Other operating expenses (expenses associated with the Company's Specialty Operations) were 22.6% of specialty revenues in fiscal 2003, compared to 21.4% in fiscal 2002, primarily due to higher payroll-related expenditures to support the continued development of the Company's foodservice distribution network and international infrastructure, including regional offices and field personnel.

Depreciation and amortization expenses increased to $237.8 million in fiscal 2003, from $205.6 million in fiscal 2002, primarily due to opening 602 Company-operated retail stores in the last 12 months and the refurbishment of existing Company-operated retail stores.

General and administrative expenses increased to $244.6 million in fiscal 2003, compared to $234.6 million in fiscal 2002, which included an $18.0 million charge for the litigation settlement of two California class action lawsuits. Excluding the litigation charge, general and administrative expenses increased $28.0 million from the comparable period in fiscal 2002 due to higher payroll-related expenditures and costs related to the acquisition of Seattle Coffee Company. General and administrative expenses as a percentage of total net revenues decreased to 6.0% in fiscal 2003, compared to 7.1% in fiscal 2002.

Operating income increased 34.3% to $424.7 million in fiscal 2003, from $316.3 million in fiscal 2002. The operating margin increased to 10.4% of total net revenues in fiscal 2003, compared to 9.6% in fiscal 2002 primarily due to leverage gained on fixed costs spread over an expanding revenue base, partially offset by higher green coffee costs, as discussed above.

Income from equity investees was $38.4 million in fiscal 2003, compared to $33.4 million in fiscal 2002. The increase was mainly attributable to continued strong results by The North American Coffee Partnership, the Company's 50 percent owned ready-to-drink partnership with the Pepsi-Cola Company, from expanded product lines, lower direct costs and manufacturing efficiencies. Partially offsetting this increase was the Company's proportionate share of the net losses of Starbucks Japan, Ltd. ("Starbucks Japan") in fiscal 2003, compared to a net profit in fiscal 2002, primarily due to lower average sales per store.

Net interest and other income, which primarily consists of interest income, increased to $11.6 million in fiscal 2003, from $9.3 million in fiscal 2002. The growth was a result of increased interest received on higher balances of cash, cash equivalents and liquid securities during fiscal 2003, compared to the prior year, and gains realized on market revaluations of the Company's trading securities, compared to realized losses on this portfolio in the prior year.

The Company's effective tax rate for fiscal 2003 was 38.5% compared to 37.3% in fiscal 2002 as a result of a shift in the composition of the Company's pretax earnings in fiscal 2003. Operations based in the United States had higher pretax earnings and comprised a higher proportion of consolidated pretax earnings during fiscal 2003. In addition, international operations, which are in various phases of development, generated greater nondeductible losses than anticipated. Management expects the effective tax rate to be 38.0% for fiscal 2004.

Operating Segments

Segment information is prepared on the basis that Company's management internally reviews financial information for operational decision making purposes. Starbucks revised its segment reporting into two distinct, geographically based operating segments: United States and International. This change was in response to internal management realignments in the fiscal first quarter of 2004 and management's evaluation of the requirements of SFAS No. 131, "Disclosures about Segments of an Enterprise and Related Information."

United States

The Company's United States operations ("United States") represent 86% of retail revenues, 81% of specialty revenues and 85% of total net revenues. Company-operated retail stores sell coffee and other beverages, whole bean coffees, complementary food, coffee brewing equipment and merchandise. Non-retail activities within the United States include: licensed operations, foodservice accounts and other initiatives related to the Company's core businesses.

International

The Company's international operations ("International") represent the remaining 14% of retail revenues, 19% of specialty revenues and 15% of total net revenues. International sells coffee and other beverages, whole bean coffees, complementary food, coffee brewing equipment and merchandise through Company-operated retail stores in Canada, the United Kingdom, Thailand and Australia, as well as through licensed operations and foodservice accounts in these and other countries. Because International operations are in an early phase of development and have country-specific regulatory requirements, they require a more extensive administrative support organization, compared to the United States, to provide resources and respond to business needs in each region.

Segment Results of Operations

The following tables summarize the Company's results of operations by segment for fiscal 2003 and 2002 (in thousands):

Fiscal year ended September 28, 2003	United States	% of United States Revenue	International	% of International Revenue	Unallocated Corporate	Consolidated
Net revenues:						
Retail	$2,965,618	85.4%	$484,006	80.3%	$ —	$3,449,624
Specialty	506,834	14.6	119,064	19.7	—	625,898
Total net revenues	3,472,452	100.0	603,070	100.0	—	4,075,522
Cost of sales and related occupancy costs	1,363,267	39.3	322,661	53.5	—	1,685,928
Store operating expenses	1,199,020	40.4(1)	180,554	37.3(1)	—	1,379,574
Other operating expenses	119,960	23.7(2)	21,386	18.0(2)	—	141,346
Depreciation and amortization expenses	167,138	4.8	38,563	6.4	32,106	237,807
General and administrative expenses	45,007	1.3	44,352	7.4	155,191	244,550
Income from equity investees	28,484	0.8	9,912	1.6	—	38,396
Operating income	$ 606,544	17.5%	$ 5,466	0.9%	$(187,297)	$ 424,713

Fiscal year ended September 29, 2002	United States	% of United States Revenue	International	% of International Revenue	Unallocated Corporate	Consolidated
Net revenues:						
Retail	$2,425,163	85.7%	$367,741	79.8%	$ —	$2,792,904
Specialty	403,090	14.3	92,914	20.2	—	496,004
Total net revenues	2,828,253	100.0	460,655	100.0	—	3,288,908
Cost of sales and related occupancy costs	1,114,535	39.4	235,476	51.1	—	1,350,011
Store operating expenses	961,617	39.7(1)	148,165	40.3(1)	—	1,109,782
Other operating expenses	87,718	21.8(2)	18,366	19.8(2)	—	106,084
Depreciation and amortization expenses	142,752	5.0	34,069	7.4	28,736	205,557
General and administrative expenses	33,928	1.2	35,007	7.6	165,646	234,581
Income from equity investees	19,182	0.7	14,263	3.1	—	33,445
Operating income	$ 506,885	17.9%	$ 3,835	0.8%	$(194,382)	$ 316,338

(1) Shown as a percentage of retail revenues.
(2) Shown as a percentage of specialty revenues.

United States

United States total net revenues increased by $644.2 million, or 22.8%, to $3.5 billion in fiscal 2003 from $2.8 billion in fiscal 2002. United States retail revenues increased $540.5 million, or 22.3%, to $3.0 billion, primarily due to the opening of 506 new Company-operated retail stores in fiscal 2003 and comparable store sales growth of 9%. The increase in comparable store sales was almost entirely due to higher transaction volume. Management believes increased customer traffic continues to be driven by new product innovation, continued popularity of core products, a high level of customer satisfaction and improved speed of service through enhanced technology, training and execution at Company-operated retail stores.

United States specialty revenues increased by $103.7 million, or 25.7%, to $506.8 million in fiscal 2003. Of the total growth, expanded retail licensing operations provided $50.0 million, or 48.2%, broader distribution and additional accounts in foodservice provided $24.5 million, or 23.6%, and an increase in the grocery and warehouse club business provided $22.0 million, or 21.2%.

Operating income for the United States increased by 19.7% to $606.5 million in fiscal 2003, from $506.9 million in fiscal 2002. Operating margin decreased to 17.5% of related revenues from 17.9% in the prior year, primarily due to higher green coffee costs and payroll-related expenditures, partially offset by fixed occupancy costs spread over an expanding revenue base.

International

International total net revenues increased by $142.4 million, or 30.9%, to $603.1 million in fiscal 2003, from $460.7 million in fiscal 2002. International retail revenues increased $116.3 million, or 31.6%, to $484.0 million, primarily due to the opening of 96 new Company-operated retail stores in fiscal 2003 and comparable store sales growth of 7%. The increase in comparable store sales was almost entirely due to higher transaction volume and reflects the improved operational execution in the United Kingdom market.

International specialty revenues increased $26.1 million, or 28.1%, to $119.1 million in fiscal 2003, primarily due to the addition of 284 new licensed stores and resulting increases in royalty revenues from and product sales to those licensees.

Operating income for International increased by 42.5% to $5.5 million in fiscal 2003, from $3.8 million in fiscal 2002. International operating margin increased to 0.9% in fiscal 2003, from 0.8% in fiscal 2002, primarily due to lower provisions recorded for retail store asset impairment and disposals of $3.7 million in fiscal 2003 compared to $13.9 million in fiscal 2002. This was partially offset by International's proportionate share of net losses in Starbucks Japan and a shift in sales mix to lower margin products. Excluding Canadian operations, operating losses increased by 11.1% to $18.5 million in fiscal 2003, compared to an operating loss of $16.7 million in fiscal 2002.

Unallocated Corporate

Unallocated corporate expenses pertain to functions, such as executive management, administration, tax, treasury and information technology infrastructure, that are not specifically attributable to the Company's operating segments and include related depreciation and amortization expenses. Unallocated general and administrative expenses decreased to $155.2 million in fiscal 2003, from $165.6 million in fiscal 2002, primarily due to an $18.0 million litigation settlement in fiscal 2002. Depreciation and amortization expenses increased to $32.1 million in fiscal 2003, from $28.7 million in fiscal 2002, primarily due to expanded support facilities and capital spending for information technology enhancements. Total unallocated corporate expenses as a percentage of total net revenues decreased from 5.9% in fiscal 2002 to 4.6% in fiscal 2003.

Liquidity and Capital Resources

The Company had $350.0 million in cash and cash equivalents and short-term investments at the end of fiscal 2003. Working capital as of September 28, 2003, totaled $315.3 million compared to $310.0 million as of September 29, 2002. Total cash and cash equivalents and liquid investments increased by $158.8 million during fiscal 2003 to $486.2 million. The Company intends to use its available cash resources to invest in its core businesses and other new business opportunities related to its core businesses. The Company may use its available cash resources to make proportionate capital contributions to its equity method and cost method investees, depending on the operating conditions of these entities. Depending on market conditions, Starbucks may acquire additional shares of its common stock.

Cash provided by operating activities in fiscal 2003 totaled $566.4 million and was generated primarily by net earnings of $268.3 million and non-cash depreciation and amortization expenses of $259.3 million.

Cash used by investing activities in fiscal 2003 totaled $499.3 million. This included net capital additions to property, plant and equipment of $357.3 million mainly related to opening 602 new Company-operated retail stores, remodeling certain existing stores and purchasing land and constructing the Company's new roasting and distribution facility in Carson Valley, Nevada. The Company used $69.9 million of cash for the acquisition of the Seattle Coffee Company. The net activity in the Company's marketable securities portfolio during fiscal 2003 used $53.8 million of cash. Excess cash was invested primarily in investment-grade securities. During fiscal 2003, the Company made equity investments of $47.3 million in its international investees, excluding the effects of foreign currency fluctuations, as Starbucks increased its ownership stake in several international markets.

Cash provided by financing activities in fiscal 2003 totaled $30.8 million. This included $107.2 million generated from the exercise of employee stock options and the sale of the Company's common stock from employee stock purchase plans. As options granted under the Company's stock plans are exercised, the Company will continue to receive proceeds and a tax deduction; however, neither the amounts nor the timing thereof can be predicted. During fiscal 2003, the Company used $75.7 million to purchase 3.3 million shares of its common stock in accordance with authorized repurchase plans. Share repurchases are at the discretion of management and depend on market conditions, capital requirements and such other factors as the Company may consider relevant. As of September 28, 2003, there were approximately 14.6 million additional shares authorized for repurchase.

Cash requirements in fiscal 2004, other than normal operating expenses, are expected to consist primarily of capital expenditures related to the addition of new Company-operated retail stores as Starbucks plans to open approximately 625 Company-operated stores, remodel certain existing stores and enhance its production capacity and information systems. While there can be no assurance that current expectations will be realized, management expects capital expenditures in fiscal 2004 to be in the range of $450 million to $475 million.

Management believes that existing cash and investments as well as cash generated from operations should be sufficient to finance capital requirements for its core businesses through 2004. New joint ventures, other new business opportunities or store expansion rates substantially in excess of those presently planned may require outside funding.

The following table summarizes the Company's contractual obligations and borrowings as of September 28, 2003, and the timing and effect that such commitments are expected to have on the Company's liquidity and capital requirements in future periods (in thousands):

| | | Payments due by Period | | | |
Contractual obligations	Total	Less than 1 year	1–3 years	3–5 years	More than 5 years
Long-term debt obligations	$ 5,076	$ 722	$ 1,483	$ 1,538	$ 1,333
Operating lease obligations	2,259,434	293,912	554,662	486,657	924,203
Purchase obligations	319,430	211,884	104,831	2,715	—
Total	$2,583,940	$506,518	$660,976	$490,910	$925,536

Starbucks expects to fund these commitments primarily with operating cash flows generated in the normal course of business.

Coffee Prices, Availability and General Risk Conditions

The supply and price of coffee are subject to significant volatility. Although most coffee trades in the commodity market, coffee of the quality sought by Starbucks tends to trade on a negotiated basis at a substantial premium above commodity coffee prices, depending upon the supply and demand at the time of purchase. Supply and price can be affected by multiple factors in the producing countries, including weather, political and economic conditions. In addition, green coffee prices have been affected in the past and may be affected in the future by the actions of certain organizations and associations that have historically attempted to influence commodity prices of green coffee through agreements establishing export quotas or restricting coffee supplies worldwide. The Company's ability to raise sales prices in response to rising coffee prices may be limited, and the Company's profitability could be adversely affected if coffee prices were to rise substantially.

The Company enters into fixed-price purchase commitments in order to secure an adequate supply of quality green coffee and bring greater certainty to the cost of sales in future periods. As of September 28, 2003, the Company had approximately $287.2 million in fixed-price purchase commitments which, together with existing inventory, is expected to provide an adequate supply of green coffee through calendar 2004. The Company believes, based on relationships established with its suppliers in the past, that the risk of non-delivery on such purchase commitments is low.

In addition to fluctuating coffee prices, management believes that the Company's future results of operations and earnings could be significantly impacted by other factors such as increased competition within the specialty coffee industry, fluctuating dairy prices, the Company's ability to find optimal store locations at favorable lease rates, increased costs associated with opening and operating retail stores and the Company's continued ability to hire, train and retain qualified personnel, and other factors discussed under "Certain Additional Risks and Uncertainties" in the "Business" section of the Company's annual report on Form 10-K for the fiscal year ended September 28, 2003.

Financial Risk Management

The Company is exposed to market risk related to foreign currency exchange rates, equity security prices and changes in interest rates.

Seasonality and Quarterly Results

The Company's business is subject to seasonal fluctuations. Significant portions of the Company's net revenues and profits are realized during the first quarter of the Company's fiscal year, which includes the December holiday season. In addition, quarterly results are affected by the timing of the opening of new stores, and the Company's rapid growth may conceal the impact of other seasonal influences. Because of the seasonality of the Company's business, results for any quarter are not necessarily indicative of the results that may be achieved for the full fiscal year.

Application of Critical Accounting Policies

Critical accounting policies are those that management believes are both most important to the portrayal of the Company's financial condition and results, and require management's most difficult, subjective or complex judgments, often as a result of the need to make estimates about the effect of matters that are inherently uncertain. Judgments and uncertainties affecting the application of those policies may result in materially different amounts being reported under different conditions or using different assumptions.

Starbucks considers its policies on impairment of long-lived assets to be most critical in understanding the judgments that are involved in preparing its consolidated financial statements.

Impairment of Long-Lived Assets

When facts and circumstances indicate that the carrying values of long-lived assets may be impaired, an evaluation of recoverability is performed by comparing the carrying value of the assets to projected future cash flows in addition to other quantitative and qualitative analyses. For goodwill and other intangible assets, impairment tests are performed annually and more frequently if facts and circumstances indicate goodwill carrying values exceed estimated reporting unit fair values and if indefinite useful lives are no longer appropriate for the Company's trademarks. Upon indication that the carrying value of such assets may not be recoverable, the Company recognizes an impairment loss as a charge against current operations. Property, plant and equipment assets are grouped at the lowest level for which there are identifiable cash flows when assessing impairment. Cash flows for retail assets are identified at the individual store level. Long-lived assets to be disposed of are reported at the lower of their carrying amount or fair value, less estimated costs to sell. Judgments made by the Company related to the expected useful lives of long-lived assets and the ability of the Company to realize undiscounted cash flows in excess of the carrying amounts of such assets are affected by factors such as the ongoing maintenance and improvements of the assets, changes in economic conditions and changes in operating performance. As the Company assesses the ongoing expected cash flows and carrying amounts of its long-lived assets, these factors could cause the Company to realize material impairment charges.

Consolidated Statements of Earnings

In thousands, except earnings per share

Fiscal year ended	Sept 28, 2003	Sept 29, 2002	Sept 30, 2001
Net revenues:			
Retail	$3,449,624	$2,792,904	$2,229,594
Specialty	625,898	496,004	419,386
Total net revenues	4,075,522	3,288,908	2,648,980
Cost of sales including occupancy costs	1,685,928	1,350,011	1,112,785
Store operating expenses	1,379,574	1,109,782	867,957
Other operating expenses	141,346	106,084	72,406
Depreciation and amortization expenses	237,807	205,557	163,501
General and administrative expenses	244,550	234,581	179,852
Income from equity investees	38,396	33,445	27,740
Operating income	424,713	316,338	280,219
Interest and other income, net	11,622	9,300	10,768
Internet-related investment losses	—	—	2,940
Gain on sale of investment	—	13,361	—
Earnings before income taxes	436,335	338,999	288,047
Income taxes	167,989	126,313	107,712
Net earnings	$ 268,346	$ 212,686	$ 180,335
Net earnings per common share-basic	$ 0.69	$ 0.55	$ 0.47
Net earnings per common share-diluted	$ 0.67	$ 0.54	$ 0.46
Weighted average shares outstanding:			
Basic	390,753	385,575	380,566
Diluted	401,648	397,526	394,349

See Notes to Consolidated Financial Statements.

Consolidated Balance Sheets

In thousands, except share data

Fiscal year ended	Sept 28, 2003	Sept 29, 2002
ASSETS		
Current assets:		
Cash and cash equivalents	$ 200,907	$ 99,677
Short-term investments – Available-for-sale securities	128,905	217,302
Short-term investments – Trading securities	20,199	10,360
Accounts receivable, net of allowances of $4,809 and $3,680, respectively	114,448	97,573
Inventories	342,944	263,174
Prepaid expenses and other current assets	55,173	42,351
Deferred income taxes, net	61,453	42,206
Total current assets	924,029	772,643
Long-term investments – Available-for-sale securities	136,159	—
Equity and other investments	144,257	102,537
Property, plant and equipment, net	1,384,902	1,265,756
Other assets	52,113	43,692
Other intangible assets	24,942	9,862
Goodwill	63,344	19,902
TOTAL ASSETS	$2,729,746	$2,214,392
LIABILITIES AND SHAREHOLDERS' EQUITY		
Current liabilities:		
Accounts payable	$ 168,984	$ 135,994
Accrued compensation and related costs	152,608	105,899
Accrued occupancy costs	56,179	51,195
Accrued taxes	54,934	54,244
Other accrued expenses	101,800	72,289
Deferred revenue	73,476	42,264
Current portion of long-term debt	722	710
Total current liabilities	608,703	462,595

Deferred income taxes, net	33,217	22,496
Long-term debt	4,354	5,076
Other long-term liabilities	1,045	1,036
Shareholders' equity:		
Common stock and additional paid-in capital – Authorized, 600,000,000 shares; issued and outstanding, 393,692,536 and 388,228,592 shares, respectively, (includes 1,697,100 common stock units in both periods)	959,103	891,040
Other additional paid-in-capital	39,393	39,393
Retained earnings	1,069,683	801,337
Accumulated other comprehensive income/(loss)	14,248	(8,581)
Total shareholders' equity	2,082,427	1,723,189
TOTAL LIABILITIES AND SHAREHOLDERS' EQUITY	$2,729,746	$2,214,392

See Notes to Consolidated Financial Statements.

Consolidated Statements of Cash Flows

In thousands

Fiscal year ended 2001	Sept 28, 2003	Sept 29, 2002	Sept 30, 2001
OPERATING ACTIVITIES:			
Net earnings	$268,346	$212,686	$180,335
Adjustments to reconcile net earnings to net cash provided by operating activities:			
Depreciation and amortization	259,271	221,141	177,087
Gain on sale of investment	—	(13,361)	—
Internet-related investment losses	—	—	2,940
Provision for impairments and asset disposals	7,784	26,852	11,044
Deferred income taxes, net	(5,932)	(6,088)	(6,068)
Equity in income of investees	(22,813)	(19,584)	(14,838)
Tax benefit from exercise of non-qualified stock options	36,590	44,199	30,899
Net accretion of discount and amortization of premium on marketable securities	5,996	—	—
Cash provided/(used) by changes in operating assets and liabilities:			
Inventories	(64,768)	(41,379)	(19,704)
Prepaid expenses and other current assets	(12,861)	(12,460)	(10,919)
Accounts payable	24,990	5,463	54,117
Accrued compensation and related costs	42,132	24,087	12,098
Accrued occupancy costs	4,293	15,343	6,797
Deferred revenue	30,732	15,321	19,594
Other operating assets and liabilities	(7,313)	5,465	12,923
Net cash provided by operating activities	566,447	477,685	456,305
INVESTING ACTIVITIES:			
Purchase of available-for-sale securities	(323,331)	(339,968)	(184,187)
Maturity of available-for-sale securities	180,687	78,349	93,500
Sale of available-for-sale securities	88,889	144,760	46,931
Purchase of Seattle Coffee Company, net of cash acquired	(69,928)	—	—
Net additions to equity, other investments and other assets	(47,259)	(15,841)	(17,424)
Distributions from equity investees	28,966	22,834	16,863
Net additions to property, plant and equipment	(357,282)	(375,474)	(384,215)
Net cash used by investing activities	(499,258)	(485,340)	(428,532)
FINANCING ACTIVITIES:			
Proceeds from issuance of common stock	107,183	107,467	59,639
Principal payments on long-term debt	(710)	(697)	(685)
Repurchase of common stock	(75,710)	(52,248)	(49,788)
Net cash provided by financing activities	30,763	54,522	9,166
Effect of exchange rate changes on cash and cash equivalents	3,278	1,560	(174)
Net increase in cash and cash equivalents	101,230	48,427	36,765
CASH AND CASH EQUIVALENTS:			
Beginning of period	99,677	51,250	14,485
End of the period	$200,907	$ 99,677	$51,250
SUPPLEMENTAL DISCLOSURE OF CASH FLOW INFORMATION:			
Cash paid during the year for:			
Interest	$ 265	$ 303	$ 432
Income taxes	$140,107	$105,339	$47,690

See Notes to Consolidated Financial Statements.

Consolidated Statements of Shareholders' Equity

In thousands, except share data

	Common Stock Shares	Amount	Additional Paid-In Capital	Retained Earnings	Accumulated Other Comprehensive Income/(Loss)	Total
Balance, October 1, 2000	376,315,302	$376	$750,496	$ 408,316	$(10,976)	$1,148,212
Net earnings	—	—	—	180,335	—	180,335
Unrealized holding gains, net	—	—	—	—	2,087	2,087
Translation adjustment	—	—	—	—	3,481	3,481
Comprehensive income						185,903
Exercise of stock options, including tax benefit of $30,899	6,289,892	6	77,555	—	—	77,561
Sale of common stock	813,848	1	12,976	—	—	12,977
Repurchase of common stock	(3,375,000)	(3)	(49,785)	—	—	(49,788)
Balance, September 30, 2001	380,044,042	380	791,242	588,651	(5,408)	1,374,865
Net earnings	—	—	—	212,686	–	212,686
Unrealized holding losses, net	—	—	—	—	(1,509)	(1,509)
Translation adjustment	—	—	—	—	(1,664)	(1,664)
Comprehensive income						209,513
Equity adjustment related to equity Investee transaction	—		39,393	—	—	39,393
Exercise of stock options, including tax benefit of $44,199	9,830,136	10	135,465	—	—	135,475
Sale of common stock	991,742	1	16,190	—	—	16,191
Repurchase of common stock	(2,637,328)	(3)	(52,245)	—	—	(52,248)
Balance, September 29, 2002	388,228,592	388	930,045	801,337	(8,581)	1,723,189
Net earnings	—	—	—	268,346	—	268,346
Unrealized holding losses, net	—	—	—	—	(4,426)	(4,426)
Translation adjustment	—	—	—	—	27,255	27,255
Comprehensive income						291,175
Exercise of stock options, including tax benefit of $35,547	8,019,604	8	129,100	—	—	129,108
Sale of common stock, including tax benefit of $1,043	743,340	1	14,664	—	—	14,665
Repurchase of common stock	(3,299,000)	(3)	(75,707)	—	—	(75,710)
Balance, September 28, 2003	393,692,536	$394	$998,102	$1,069,683	$ 14,248	$2,082,427

See Notes to Consolidated Financial Statements.

Notes to Consolidated Financial Statements

Years ended September 28, 2003, September 29, 2002, and September 30, 2001

Note 1: Summary of Significant Accounting Policies

Description of Business

Starbucks Corporation (together with its subsidiaries, "Starbucks" or the "Company"), purchases and roasts high-quality whole bean coffees and sells them, along with fresh, rich-brewed coffees, Italian-style espresso beverages, cold blended beverages, a variety of complementary food items, coffee-related accessories and equipment, a selection of premium teas and a line of compact discs primarily through its Company-operated retail stores. Starbucks sells coffee and tea products through other channels, and, through certain of its equity investees, Starbucks also produces and sells bottled Frappuccino® and Starbucks DoubleShot™ coffee drinks and a line of premium ice creams. These non-retail channels are collectively known as "Specialty Operations." The Company's objective is to establish Starbucks as the most recognized and respected brand in the world. To achieve this goal, the Company plans to continue rapid expansion of its retail operations, to grow its Specialty Operations and to selectively pursue other opportunities to leverage the Starbucks brand through the introduction of new products and the development of new channels of distribution.

Principles of Consolidation

The consolidated financial statements reflect the financial position and operating results of Starbucks, which includes wholly owned subsidiaries and investees controlled by the Company.

Investments in entities which the Company does not control, but has the ability to exercise significant influence over operating and financial policies, are accounted for under the equity method. Investments in entities in which Starbucks does not have the ability to exercise significant influence are accounted for under the cost method.

All significant intercompany transactions have been eliminated.

Fiscal Year-End

The Company's fiscal year ends on the Sunday closest to September 30. The fiscal years ended September 28, 2003, September 29, 2002, and September 30, 2001, each included 52 weeks. The fiscal year ending on October 3, 2004, will include 53 weeks.

Estimates and Assumptions

The preparation of financial statements in conformity with accounting principles generally accepted in the United States of America requires management to make estimates and assumptions that affect the reported amounts of assets, liabilities, revenues and expenses. Actual results may differ from these estimates.

Cash and Cash Equivalents

The Company considers all highly liquid instruments with a maturity of three months or less at the time of purchase to be cash equivalents.

Cash Management

The Company's cash management system provides for the reimbursement of all major bank disbursement accounts on a daily basis. Checks issued but not presented for payment to the bank are reflected as a reduction of cash and cash equivalents on the accompanying consolidated financial statements.

Short-term and Long-term Investments

The Company's short-term and long-term investments consist primarily of investment-grade marketable debt and equity securities as well as bond and equity mutual funds, all of which are classified as trading or available-for-sale. Trading securities are recorded at fair value with unrealized holding gains and losses included in net earnings. Available-for-sale securities are recorded at fair value, and unrealized holding gains and losses are recorded, net of tax, as a separate component of accumulated other comprehensive income. Available-for-sale securities with remaining maturities less than one year are classified as short-term, and all other available-for-sale securities are classified as long-term. Unrealized losses are charged against net earnings when a decline in fair value is determined to be other than temporary. Realized gains and losses are accounted for on the specific identification method. Purchases and sales are recorded on a trade date basis.

Fair Value of Financial Instruments

The carrying value of cash and cash equivalents approximates fair value because of the short-term maturity of those instruments. The fair value of the Company's investments in marketable debt and equity securities as well as bond and equity mutual funds is based upon the quoted market price on the last business day of the fiscal year. For equity securities of companies that are privately held, or where an observable quoted market price does not exist, the Company estimates fair value using a variety of valuation methodologies. Such methodologies include comparing the security with securities of publicly traded companies in similar lines of business, applying revenue multiples to estimated future operating results for the private company and estimating discounted cash flows for that company. For further information on investments, see Notes 4 and 7. The carrying value of long-term debt approximates fair value.

Inventories

Inventories are stated at the lower of cost (primarily moving average cost) or market. The Company records inventory reserves for obsolete and slow-moving items and for estimated shrinkage between physical inventory counts. Inventory reserves are based on inventory turnover trends, historical experience and application of the specific identification method.

Property, Plant and Equipment

Property, plant and equipment are carried at cost less accumulated depreciation. Depreciation of property, plant and equipment, which includes assets under capital leases, is provided on the straight-line method over estimated useful lives, generally ranging from two to seven years for equipment and 30 to 40 years for buildings. Leasehold improvements are amortized over the shorter of their estimated useful lives or the related lease life, generally 10 years. The portion of depreciation expense related to production and distribution facilities is included in "Cost of sales and related occupancy costs" on the accompanying consolidated statements of earnings. The costs of repairs and maintenance are expensed when incurred, while expenditures for refurbishments and improvements that significantly add to the productive capacity or extend the useful life of an asset are capitalized. When assets are retired or sold, the asset cost and related accumulated depreciation are eliminated with any remaining gain or loss reflected in net earnings.

Goodwill and Other Intangible Assets

At the beginning of fiscal 2003, Starbucks adopted SFAS No. 142, "Goodwill and Other Intangible Assets." As a result, the Company discontinued amortization of its goodwill and indefinite-lived trademarks and determined that provisions for impairment were unnecessary. Impairment tests are performed annually on June 1 and more frequently if facts and circumstances indicate goodwill carrying values exceed estimated reporting unit fair values and if indefinite useful lives are no longer appropriate for the Company's trademarks. Had the nonamortization provision of SFAS No. 142 been applied to fiscal 2002 and fiscal 2001, net earnings would have been $214.7 million and $182.2 million, respectively, as compared to net earnings, as shown in Note 2, of $212.7 million and $180.3 million, respectively. Basic earnings per share for fiscal 2002 would have increased to $0.56 per share from $0.55 per share, while diluted earnings per share would have remained unchanged. Basic earnings per share for fiscal 2001 would have increased to $0.48 per share from $0.47 per share, while diluted earnings per share would have remained unchanged. Definite-lived intangibles, which mainly consist of contract-based patents and copyrights, are amortized over their estimated useful lives. For further information on goodwill and other intangible assets, see Note 9.

Long-lived Assets

When facts and circumstances indicate that the carrying values of long-lived assets may be impaired, an evaluation of recoverability is performed by comparing the carrying value of the assets to projected future cash flows in addition to other quantitative and qualitative analyses. Upon indication that the carrying value of such assets may not be recoverable, the Company recognizes an impairment loss by a charge against current operations. Property, plant and equipment assets are grouped at the lowest level for which there are identifiable cash flows when assessing impairment. Cash flows for retail assets are identified at the individual store level.

Revenue Recognition

In most instances, retail store revenues are recognized when payment is tendered at the point of sale. Revenues from stored value cards are recognized upon redemption. Until the redemption of stored value cards, outstanding customer balances on such cards are included in "Deferred revenue" on the accompanying consolidated balance sheets. Specialty revenues, which consist of sales of coffee and tea products to customers other than through Company-operated retail stores, are generally recognized upon shipment to customers, depending on contract terms. Initial non-refundable fees required under licensing agreements are earned upon substantial performance of services. Royalty revenues based upon a percentage of sales and other continuing fees are recognized when earned. Arrangements involving multiple elements and deliverables are individually evaluated for revenue recognition. Cash payments received in advance of product or service revenue are recorded as deferred revenue. Consolidated revenues are net of all intercompany eliminations for wholly owned subsidiaries and for licensees accounted for under the equity method based on the Company's percentage ownership. All revenues are recognized net of any discounts.

Advertising

The Company expenses costs of advertising the first time the advertising campaign takes place, except for direct-to-consumer advertising, which is capitalized and amortized over its expected period of future benefit, generally six to twelve months. The Company had no capitalized direct-to-consumer advertising costs as of September 28, 2003, due to its exit from these business activities. Net capitalized direct-to-consumer advertising costs were $0.8 million as of September 29, 2002, and are included in "Prepaid expenses and other current assets" on the accompanying consolidated balance sheet. Total advertising expenses, recorded in "Store operating expenses" and "Other operating expenses," on the accompanying consolidated statements of earnings totaled $49.5 million, $25.6 million and $28.8 million in 2003, 2002 and 2001, respectively.

Store Preopening Expenses

Costs incurred in connection with the start-up and promotion of new store openings are expensed as incurred.

Rent Expense

Certain of the Company's lease agreements provide for scheduled rent increases during the lease terms or for rental payments commencing at a date other than the date of initial occupancy. Minimum rental expenses are recognized on a straight-line basis over the terms of the leases.

Stock-based Compensation

The Company maintains several stock option plans under which incentive stock options and non-qualified stock options may be granted to employees, consultants and non-employee directors. Starbucks accounts for stock-based compensation using the intrinsic value method prescribed in Accounting Principles Board ("APB") Opinion No. 25, "Accounting for Stock Issued to Employees," and related interpretations. Accordingly, because the grant price equals the market price on the date of grant, no compensation expense is recognized by the Company for stock options issued to employees.

In December 2002, the Financial Accounting Standards Board ("FASB") issued SFAS No. 148, "Accounting for Stock-Based Compensation – Transition and Disclosure," which amends SFAS No. 123, "Accounting for Stock-Based Compensation." SFAS No. 148 pro-vides alternative methods of transition for voluntary change to the fair value method of accounting for stock-based compensation. In addition, SFAS No. 148 requires more prominent disclosures in both annual and interim financial statements about the method of accounting for stock-based employee compensation and the effect of the method used on reported results. Starbucks adopted the annual and interim disclosure requirements of SFAS No. 148 as of September 30, 2002.

Had compensation cost for the Company's stock options been recognized based upon the estimated fair value on the grant date under the fair value methodology allowed by SFAS No. 123, as amended by SFAS No. 148, the Company's net earnings and earnings per share would have been as follows (in thousands, except earnings per share):

Fiscal year ended	Sept 28, 2003	Sept 29, 2002	Sept 30, 2001
Net earnings	$268,346	$212,686	$180,335
Deduct: stock-based compensation expense determined under fair value method, net of tax	37,436	37,447	40,535
Pro forma net income	$230,910	$175,239	$139,800
Earnings per share:			
Basic – as reported	$ 0.69	$ 0.55	$ 0.47
Basic – pro forma	$ 0.59	$ 0.45	$ 0.37
Diluted – as reported	$ 0.67	$ 0.54	$ 0.46
Diluted – pro forma	$ 0.58	$ 0.44	$ 0.36

As required by SFAS No. 123, the Company has determined that the weighted average estimated fair values of options granted during fiscal 2003, 2002 and 2001 were $8.31, $6.48 and $8.98 per share, respectively.

In applying SFAS No. 123, the impact of outstanding stock options granted prior to 1996 has been excluded from the pro forma calculations; accordingly, the 2003 pro forma adjustments are not necessarily indicative of future period pro forma adjustments.

Foreign Currency Translation

The Company's international operations use their local currency as their functional currency. Assets and liabilities are translated at exchange rates in effect at the balance sheet date. Income and expense accounts are translated at the average monthly exchange rates during the year. Resulting translation adjustments are recorded as a separate component of accumulated other comprehensive income/(loss).

Income Taxes

The Company computes income taxes using the asset and liability method, under which deferred income taxes are provided for the temporary differences between the financial reporting basis and the tax basis of the Company's assets and liabilities.

Stock Split

On April 27, 2001, the Company effected a two-for-one stock split of its $0.001 par value common stock for holders of record on March 30, 2001. All applicable share and per-share data in these consolidated financial statements have been restated to give effect to this stock split.

Earnings Per Share

The computation of basic earnings per share is based on the weighted average number of shares and common stock units outstanding during the period. The computation of diluted earnings per share includes the dilutive effect of common stock equivalents consisting of certain shares subject to stock options.

Recent Accounting Pronouncements

In November 2002, the Emerging Issues Task Force reached a consensus regarding Issue No. 02–16, "Accounting by a Customer (Including a Reseller) for Certain Consideration Received from a Vendor." Issue No. 02–16 provides guidance for classification in the reseller's statement of earnings for various circumstances under which cash consideration is received from a vendor by a reseller. The provisions of Issue No. 02–16 apply to all agreements entered into or modified after December 31, 2002. Issue No. 02–16 did not have a material impact on the Company's consolidated financial statements.

In April 2003, SFAS No. 149, "Amendment of Statement 133 on Derivative Instruments and Hedging Activities," was issued. In general, this statement amends and clarifies accounting for derivative instruments, including certain derivative instruments embedded in other contracts, and for hedging activities under SFAS No. 133. This statement is effective for contracts entered into or modified after June 30, 2003, and for hedging relationships designated after June 30, 2003. The adoption of SFAS No. 149 did not have an impact on the Company's consolidated financial statements or disclosures.

In May 2003, SFAS No. 150, "Accounting for Certain Financial Instruments with Characteristics of both Liabilities and Equity," ("SFAS No. 150") was issued, which requires that certain financial instruments be accounted for as liabilities. The financial instruments affected include mandatorily redeemable stock, certain financial instruments that require or may require the issuer to buy back some of its shares in exchange for cash or other assets, and certain obligations that can be settled with shares of stock. SFAS No. 150 is effective for all financial instruments entered into or modified after May 31, 2003, and must be applied to the Company's existing financial instruments effective June 30, 2003, the beginning of the first fiscal period after June 15, 2003. The adoption of SFAS No. 150 did not have an impact on the Company's consolidated financial statements or disclosures.

Reclassifications

During the fiscal first quarter of 2004, the Company realigned its resources to better manage its rapidly growing operations. In connection with this process, classification of operating expenses within the consolidated statements of earnings was evaluated using broad-based definitions of retail, specialty and general and administrative functions. As a result, management determined that certain functions not directly supporting retail or non-retail operations, such as executive, administrative, finance and risk management overhead primarily within international operations, would be more appropriately classified as "General and administrative expenses" than as store or other operating expenses. Accordingly, amounts in prior year periods have been reclassified to conform to current year classifications.

Note 2: Acquisitions

On July 14, 2003, the Company acquired Seattle Coffee Company ("SCC") from AFC Enterprises, Inc. SCC includes the Seattle's Best Coffee® and Torrefazione Italia® brands, which complement the Company's existing portfolio of products. The results of operations of SCC are included in the accompanying consolidated financial statements from the date of purchase. The $70 million all-cash purchase transaction generated goodwill of approximately $43 million and indefinite-lived intangibles, consisting of trade names and recipes, of approximately $13 million. Pro forma results of operations have not been provided, as the amounts were deemed immaterial to the consolidated financial statements of Starbucks.

During fiscal 2003, Starbucks increased its equity ownership to 50% of its international licensed operations in Austria, Shanghai, Spain, Switzerland and Taiwan, which enabled the Company to exert significant influence over their operating and financial policies. For these operations, management determined that a change in accounting method, from the cost method to the equity method, was required. This accounting change included adjusting previously reported information for the Company's proportionate share of net losses as required by APB Opinion No. 18, "The Equity Method of Accounting for Investments in Common Stock."

As shown in the table below, the cumulative effect of the accounting change to the equity method resulted in reductions of net earnings of $2.4 million and $0.9 million for the 52 weeks ended September 29, 2002, and September 30, 2001, respectively. Additionally, a reduction of net earnings for the effects of the accounting change prior to fiscal 2001 of $0.2 million was recorded (in thousands, except earnings per share):

	52 weeks ended	
	Sept 29, 2002	Sept 30, 2001
Net earnings, previously reported	$215,073	$181,210
Effect of change to equity method	(2,387)	(875)
Net earnings, as restated	$212,686	$180,335
Net earnings per common share—basic: Previously reported	$ 0.56	$ 0.48
As restated	$ 0.55	$ 0.47
Net earnings per common share—diluted: Previously reported	$ 0.54	$ 0.46
As restated	$ 0.54	$ 0.46

Note 3: Cash and Cash Equivalents

Cash and cash equivalents consist of the following (in thousands):

Fiscal year ended	Sept 28, 2003	Sept 29, 2002
Operating funds and interest-bearing deposits	$187,118	$88,697
Money market funds	13,789	10,980
Total	$200,907	$99,677

Note 4: Short-Term and Long-Term Investments

The Company's short-term and long-term investments consist of the following (in thousands):

September 28, 2003	Amortized Cost	Gross Unrealized Holding Gains	Gross Unrealized Holding Losses	Fair Value
Short-term investments – available-for-sale securities:				
United States government agency obligations	$ 3,672	$ 1	$ —	$ 3,673
State and local government obligations	125,121	115	(4)	125,232
Total	$128,793	$116	$ (4)	$128,905
Short-term investments – trading securities	21,268			20,199
Total short-term investments	$150,061	—	—	$149,104
Long-term investments – available-for-sale securities:				
State and local government obligations	$131,021	$421	$ (32)	$131,410
Mortgage-backed securities	4,804	14	(69)	4,749
Total long-term investments	$135,825	$435	$(101)	$136,159

September 29, 2002	Amortized Cost	Gross Unrealized Holding Gains	Gross Unrealized Holding Losses	Fair Value
Short-term investments – available-for-sale securities:				
State and local government obligations	$155,471	$244	$(16)	$155,699
United States government agency obligations	2,406	4	—	2,410
Mutual funds	32,000	211	—	32,211
Commercial paper	26,982	—	—	26,982
Total	$216,859	$459	$(16)	$217,302
Short-term investments – trading securities	13,210			10,360
Total short-term investments	$230,069	—	—	$227,662

For available-for-sale securities, proceeds from sales were $88.9 million, $144.8 million and $46.9 million, in fiscal years 2003, 2002 and 2001, respectively. Gross realized gains from the sales were $0.3 million and $1.7 million in 2003 and 2002, respectively. There were no gross realized losses in 2003 or 2002, and gross realized gains and losses were not material in 2001. Long-term investments generally mature between one and three years.

During fiscal 2001, the Company recognized a loss of $0.9 million on its investment in the common stock of Liveworld, Inc. (previously known as Talk City, Inc.), due to impairments that were determined by management to be other than temporary. There were no similar losses in fiscal 2003 or 2002.

Trading securities are comprised mainly of marketable equity mutual funds designated to approximate the Company's liability under the Management Deferred Compensation Plan, a defined contribution plan. The corresponding deferred compensation liability of $20.4 million in fiscal 2003 and $10.4 million in fiscal 2002 is included in "Accrued compensation and related costs" on the accompanying consolidated balance sheets. In fiscal 2003 and 2002, the changes in net unrealized holding gains (losses) in the trading portfolio included in earnings were $1.8 million and ($1.3) million, respectively.

Note 5: Derivative Financial Instruments

Cash Flow Hedges

Cash flow derivative instruments hedge portions of anticipated product and royalty revenues denominated in Japanese yen and Canadian dollars. During fiscal years 2003, 2002, and 2001, derivative gains (losses) of ($1.7) million, $2.9 million, and $1.7 million, respectively, were reclassified to revenues. As of September 28, 2003, existing forward foreign exchange contracts had accumulated net derivative losses of $0.4 million, net of taxes, in other comprehensive income ("OCI") and will expire within 24 months. Of the amount in OCI, $0.3 million of net derivative losses will be reclassified into net earnings within 12 months. No significant cash flow hedges were discontinued during fiscal years 2003, 2002 or 2001.

Net Investment Hedges

Net investment derivative instruments hedge the Company's equity method investment in Starbucks Coffee Japan, Ltd. These forward foreign exchange contracts expire within 14 months and are intended to minimize foreign currency exposure to fluctuations in the Japanese yen. As a result of using the spot-to-spot method, the Company recognized net gains of $1.4 million, $1.8 million and $1.4 million during the fiscal years 2003, 2002 and 2001, respectively. In addition, the Company had accumulated net derivative losses of $3.8 million, net of taxes, in OCI as of September 28, 2003.

Note 6: Inventories

Inventories consist of the following (in thousands):

Fiscal year ended	Sept 28, 2003	Sept 29, 2002
Coffee:		
Unroasted	$167,674	$128,173
Roasted	41,475	35,770
Other merchandise held for sale	83,784	65,403
Packaging and other supplies	50,011	33,828
Total	$342,944	$263,174

As of September 28, 2003, the Company had committed to fixed-price purchase contracts for green coffee totaling approximately $287.2 million. The Company believes, based on relationships established with its suppliers in the past, that the risk of non-delivery on such purchase commitments is low.

Note 7: Equity and Other Investments

The Company's equity and other investments consist of the following (in thousands):

Fiscal year ended	Sept 28, 2003	Sept 29, 2002
Equity method investments	$134,341	$ 94,620
Cost method investments	7,210	5,715
Other investments	2,706	2,202
Total	$144,257	$102,537

Equity Method

The Company's equity investees and ownership interests are as follows:

Fiscal year ended	Sept 28, 2003	Sept 29, 2002
The North American Coffee Partnership	50.0%	50.0%
Starbucks Ice Cream Partnership	50.0%	50.0%
Starbucks Coffee Korea Co., Ltd.	50.0%	50.0%
Starbucks Coffee Austria GmbH	50.0%	19.5%
Starbucks Coffee Switzerland AG	50.0%	19.5%
Starbucks Coffee Espana, S. L.	50.0%	18.0%
President Starbucks Coffee Taiwan Limited	50.0%	5.0%
Shanghai President Coffee Co.	50.0%	5.0%
Starbucks Coffee France SAS	50.0%	—
Starbucks Coffee Japan, Ltd.	40.1%	40.1%
Coffee Partners Hawaii	5.0%	5.0%

The Company has licensed the rights to produce and distribute Starbucks branded products to two partnerships in which the Company holds a 50% equity interest. The North American Coffee Partnership with the Pepsi-Cola Company develops and distributes bottled Frappuccino® and Starbucks DoubleShot™ coffee drinks. The Starbucks Ice Cream Partnership with Dreyer's Grand Ice Cream, Inc. develops and distributes premium ice creams. The remaining entities in which the Company is an equity investee operate licensed Starbucks retail stores, including Coffee Partners Hawaii, which is a general partnership.

During fiscal 2003, Starbucks increased its ownership of its licensed operations in Austria, Shanghai, Spain, Switzerland and Taiwan. The carrying amount of these investments was $21.7 million more than the underlying equity in net assets due to acquired goodwill, which is not subject to amortization in accordance with SFAS No. 142. Goodwill will be evaluated for impairment in accordance with APB Opinion No. 18, "The Equity Method of Accounting for Investments in Common Stock." For additional information on these equity ownership increases, see Note 2.

On October 10, 2001, the Company sold 30,000 of its shares of Starbucks Coffee Japan, Ltd. ("Starbucks Japan") at approximately $495 per share, net of related costs. In connection with this sale, the Company received cash proceeds of $14.8 million and recorded a gain of $13.4 million on the accompanying consolidated statement of earnings. The Company's ownership interest in Starbucks Japan was reduced from 50.0% to 47.5% following the sale of the shares. Also on October 10, 2001, Starbucks Japan issued 220,000 shares of common stock at approximately $495 per share, net of related costs, in an initial public offering in Japan. In connection with this offering, the Company's ownership interest in Starbucks Japan was reduced from 47.5% to 40.1%. Starbucks recorded "Other additional paid-in capital" on the accompanying consolidated balance sheet of $39.4 million, reflecting the increase in value of its share of the net assets of Starbucks Japan related to the stock offering. As of September 28, 2003, the quoted closing price of Starbucks Japan shares was approximately $153 per share.

The Company's share of income and losses is included in "Income from equity investees" on the accompanying consolidated statements of earnings. Also included is the Company's proportionate share of gross margin resulting from coffee and other product sales to, and royalty and license fee revenues generated from, equity investees. Revenues generated from these related parties, net of eliminations, were $68.0 million, $67.7 million and $48.9 million in fiscal 2003, 2002 and 2001, respectively. Related costs of sales, net of eliminations, were $35.7 million, $37.9 million and $30.3 million in fiscal 2003, 2002 and 2001, respectively.

Cost Method

Starbucks has equity interests in entities to develop Starbucks retail stores in other Chinese markets, Puerto Rico, Germany, Mexico, Chile and Greece. Starbucks has the ability to acquire additional interests in its cost method investees at certain intervals during each respective development period. Depending on the Company's total percentage ownership interest and its ability to exercise significant influence, additional investments may require the retroactive application of the equity method of accounting.

Depending on investee operating conditions, Starbucks may contribute capital resources to its equity method and cost method investees in proportion to the Company's ownership.

Other Investments

Starbucks has investments in privately held equity securities that are recorded at their estimated fair values.

Note 8: Property, Plant and Equipment

Property, plant and equipment are recorded at cost and consist of the following (in thousands):

Fiscal year ended	Sept 28, 2003	Sept 29, 2002
Land	$ 11,414	$ 11,310
Buildings	64,427	30,961
Leasehold improvements	1,311,024	1,131,382
Roasting and store equipment	613,825	516,129
Furniture, fixtures and other	375,854	282,068
	2,376,544	1,971,850
Less accumulated depreciation and amortization	(1,049,810)	(814,427)
	1,326,734	1,157,423
Work in progress	58,168	108,333
Property, plant and equipment, net	$1,384,902	$1,265,756

Note 9: Other Intangible Assets and Goodwill

As of September 28, 2003, indefinite-lived intangibles were $23.3 million and definite-lived intangibles were $1.6 million, net of accumulated amortization of $0.9 million. As of September 29, 2002, indefinite-lived intangibles were $8.9 million and definite-lived intangibles were $1.0 million, net of accumulated amortization of $0.4 million. Indefinite-lived intangibles increased by $14.4 million during fiscal 2003, primarily due to the acquisition of Seattle Coffee Company. During fiscal 2003 and 2002, amortization expense for definite-lived intangibles was $0.4 million and $0.1 million, respectively. Amortization expense is estimated to be $0.3 million for each of the next five fiscal years.

During fiscal 2003, goodwill increased by approximately $43.4 million primarily due to the acquisition of the Seattle Coffee Company. There were no acquisitions during fiscal 2002, and no impairment was recorded during fiscal 2003 or 2002. The following table summarizes goodwill by operating segment (in thousands):

Fiscal year ended	Sept 28, 2003	Sept 29, 2002
United States	$60,965	$17,705
International	2,379	2,197
Total	$63,344	$19,902

Note 10: Long-Term Debt

In September 1999, the Company purchased the land and building comprising its York County, Pennsylvania, roasting plant and distribution facility. The total purchase price was $12.9 million. In connection with this purchase, the Company assumed loans totaling $7.7 million from the York County Industrial Development Corporation. The remaining maturities of these loans range from 6 to 7 years, with interest rates from 0.0% to 2.0%.

Scheduled principal payments on long-term debt are as follows (in thousands):

Fiscal year ending	
2004	$ 722
2005	735
2006	748
2007	762
2008	776
Thereafter	1,333
Total principal payments	$5,076

Starbucks has a $20.0 million unsecured revolving credit agreement with a bank, which matures in March 2004. There have been no borrowings under this agreement.

Note 11: Leases

The Company leases retail stores, roasting and distribution facilities and office space under operating leases expiring through 2027. Most lease agreements contain renewal options and rent escalation clauses. Certain leases provide for contingent rentals based upon gross sales.

Rental expense under these lease agreements was as follows (in thousands):

Fiscal year ended	Sept 28, 2003	Sept 29, 2002	Sept 30, 2001
Minimum rentals – Retail	$237,742	$200,827	$150,510
Minimum rentals – Other	22,887	19,143	16,033
Contingent rentals	12,274	5,415	4,018
Total	$272,903	$225,385	$170,561

Minimum future rental payments under non-cancelable lease obligations as of September 28, 2003, are as follows (in thousands):

Fiscal year ending	
2004	$ 293,912
2005	284,401
2006	270,261
2007	253,944
2008	232,713
Thereafter	924,203
Total minimum lease payments	$2,259,434

Note 12: Shareholders' Equity

In addition to 600.0 million shares of authorized common stock with $0.001 par value per share, the Company has authorized 7.5 million shares of preferred stock, none of which was outstanding at September 28, 2003.

During fiscal 2003, the Starbucks Board of Directors authorized management to repurchase shares under any of the Company's programs pursuant to a contract, instruction or written plan meeting the requirements of Rule 10b5-1 (c) (1) of the Securities Exchange Act of 1934.

Pursuant to the Company's authorized share repurchase programs, Starbucks acquired 3.3 million shares at an average price of $22.95 for a total cost of $75.7 million during fiscal 2003, and acquired 2.6 million shares at an average price of $19.81 for a total cost of $52.2 million in fiscal 2002. All share repurchases were effected through either Morgan Stanley & Co. Incorporated or Citigroup Global Markets, Inc. As of September 28, 2003, there were approximately 14.6 million additional shares authorized for repurchase. Share repurchases were funded through cash, cash equivalents and available-for-sale securities and were primarily intended to help offset dilution from stock-based compensation and employee stock purchase plans.

Comprehensive Income

Comprehensive income includes all changes in equity during the period, except those resulting from transactions with shareholders and subsidiaries of the Company. It has two components: net earnings and other comprehensive income. Accumulated other comprehensive income/(loss) reported on the Company's consolidated balance sheets consists of foreign currency translation adjustments and the unrealized gains and losses, net of applicable taxes, on available-for-sale securities and on derivative instruments designated and qualifying as cash flow and net investment hedges. Comprehensive income, net of related tax effects, is as follows (in thousands):

Fiscal year ended	Sept 28, 2003	Sept 29, 2002	Sept 30, 2001
Net earnings	$268,346	$212,686	$180,335
Unrealized holding gains on available for sale securities, net of tax provision of $53, $231, and $434 in 2003, 2002, and 2001, respectively	142	394	738
Unrealized holding gains/(losses) on cash flow hedges, net of tax benefit/(provision) of $804, ($1,066), and ($683) in 2003, 2002 and 2001, respectively	(1,369)	1,815	1,163
Unrealized holding gains/(losses) on net investment hedges, net of tax benefit/(provision) of $1,903, $415, and ($109) in 2003, 2002, and 2001, respectively	(3,241)	(706)	186
Reclassification adjustment for (gains)/losses realized in net earnings, net of tax benefit/(provision) of ($41), $1,769, and $0 in 2003, 2002, and 2001, respectively	42	(3,012)	—
Net unrealized gain/(loss)	(4,426)	(1,509)	2,087
Translation adjustment	27,255	(1,664)	3,481
Total comprehensive income	$291,175	$209,513	$185,903

Expanded foreign-currency based operations in Europe and Canada and the change in value from translating foreign currency exchange rates to the United States dollar have resulted in a favorable translation adjustment during fiscal 2003, compared to an unfavorable translation adjustment in fiscal 2002.

Note 13: Employee Stock and Benefit Plans

Stock Option Plans

The Company maintains several stock option plans under which the Company may grant incentive stock options and non-qualified stock options to employees, consultants and non-employee directors. Stock options have been granted at prices at or above the fair market value on the date of grant. Options vest and expire according to terms established at the grant date.

The following summarizes all stock option transactions from October 1, 2000, through September 28, 2003:

	Shares Subject to Options	Weighted Average Exercise Price Per Share	Shares Subject to Exercisable Options	Weighted Average Exercise Price Per Share
Outstanding, October 1, 2000	41,889,726	$ 9.55	20,330,740	$ 7.82
Granted	9,907,292	20.48		
Exercised	(6,289,892)	7.45		
Cancelled	(2,496,195)	14.22		
Outstanding, September 30, 2001	43,010,931	12.13	24,407,135	9.16
Granted	10,262,709	15.79		
Exercised	(9,830,136)	9.29		
Cancelled	(2,983,701)	15.15		
Outstanding, September 29, 2002	40,459,803	13.55	20,975,598	11.07
Granted	9,537,730	21.10		
Exercised	(8,019,604)	11.69		
Cancelled	(2,912,483)	17.90		
Outstanding, September 28, 2003	39,065,446	$15.47	20,888,694	$12.55

As of September 28, 2003, there were 28.2 million shares of common stock available for issuance pursuant to future stock option grants. Additional information regarding options outstanding as of September 28, 2003, is as follows:

Range of Exercise Prices		Options Outstanding			Options Exercisable	
		Shares	Weighted Average Remaining Contractual Life (Years)	Weighted Average Exercise Price	Shares	Weighted Average Exercise Price
$ 2.87	–	$ 5.88	1,665,970	1.85	$ 4.83	1,665,970	$ 4.83
6.73	–	11.63	12,017,544	4.63	9.98	11,287,641	9.89
11.88	–	14.80	7,863,648	7.53	14.40	2,961,643	13.87
15.34	–	20.64	14,224,022	8.08	20.20	3,941,931	19.89
20.76	–	28.87	3,294,262	8.59	22.98	1,031,509	22.38
$ 2.87	–	$28.87	39,065,446	6.69	$15.47	20,888,694	$12.55

Note 14: Income Taxes

A reconciliation of the statutory federal income tax rate with the Company's effective income tax rate is as follows:

Fiscal year ended	Sept 28, 2003	Sept 29, 2002	Sept 30, 2001
Statutory rate	35.0%	35.0%	35.0%
State income taxes, net of federal income tax benefit	3.6	3.4	3.8
Valuation allowance change from prior year	1.4	(0.6)	1.0
Other, net	(1.5)	(0.5)	(2.4)
Effective tax rate	38.5%	37.3%	37.4%

The provision for income taxes consists of the following (in thousands):

Fiscal year ended	Sept 28, 2003	Sept 29, 2002	Sept 30, 2001
Currently payable:			
Federal	$140,138	$109,154	$ 91,750
State	25,448	16,820	17,656
Foreign	8,523	5,807	3,198
Deferred tax asset, net	(6,120)	(5,468)	(4,892)
Total	$167,989	$126,313	$107,712

Deferred income taxes or tax benefits reflect the tax effect of temporary differences between the amounts of assets and liabilities for financial reporting purposes and amounts as measured for tax purposes. The Company will establish a valuation allowance if it is more likely than not these items will either expire before the Company is able to realize their benefits, or that future deductibility is uncertain. Periodically, the valuation allowance is reviewed and adjusted based on management's assessments of realizable deferred tax assets. The valuation allowances as of September 28, 2003, and September 29, 2002, were related to losses from investments in foreign equity investees and wholly owned foreign subsidiaries. The net change in the total valuation allowance for the years ended September 28, 2003, and September 29, 2002, was an increase of $7.0 million and a decrease of $2.3 million, respectively. The tax effect of temporary differences and carryforwards that cause significant portions of deferred tax assets and liabilities is as follows (in thousands):

Fiscal year ended	Sept 28, 2003	Sept 29, 2002
Deferred tax assets:		
Equity and other investments	$ 17,576	$ 15,270
Capital loss carry forwards	4,578	6,077
Accrued occupancy costs	15,706	14,597
Accrued compensation and related costs	20,533	12,726
Other accrued expenses	22,410	16,608
Foreign tax credits	14,103	10,199
Other	7,084	6,971
Total	101,990	82,448
Valuation allowance	(13,685)	(6,720)
Total deferred tax asset, net of valuation allowance	88,305	75,728
Deferred tax liabilities:		
Property, plant and equipment	(49,419)	(50,819)
Other	(10,650)	(5,199)
Total	(60,069)	(56,018)
Net deferred tax asset	$ 28,236	$ 19,710

As of September 28, 2003, the Company had foreign tax credit carryforwards of $14.1 million with expiration dates between fiscal years 2004 and 2008. The Company also had capital loss carryforwards of $11.9 million expiring in 2006. Taxes currently payable of $30.5 million and $32.8 million are included in "Accrued taxes" on the accompanying consolidated balance sheets as of September 28, 2003, and September 29, 2002, respectively.

Note 15: Earnings per Share

The following table represents the calculation of net earnings per common share-basic (in thousands, except earnings per share):

Fiscal year ended	Sept 28, 2003	Sept 29, 2002	Sept 30, 2001
Net earnings	$268,346	$212,686	$180,335
Weighted average common shares and common stock units outstanding	390,753	385,575	380,566
Net earnings per common share–basic	$ 0.69	$ 0.55	$ 0.47

The following table represents the calculation of net earnings per common and common equivalent share – diluted (in thousands, except earnings per share):

Fiscal year ended	Sept 28, 2003	Sept 29, 2002	Sept 30, 2001
Net earnings	$268,346	$212,686	$180,335
Weighted average common shares and common stock			
units outstanding	390,753	385,575	380,566
Dilutive effect of outstanding common stock options	10,895	11,951	13,783
Weighted average common and common equivalent			
Shares outstanding	401,648	397,526	394,349
Net earnings per common share – basic	$ 0.67	$ 0.54	$ 0.46

Options with exercise prices greater than the average market price were not included in the computation of diluted earnings per share. These options totaled 0.6 million, 1.8 million and 0.9 million in fiscal 2003, 2002 and 2001, respectively.

Note 16: Related Party Transactions

Prior to January 2003, a member of the Company's Board of Directors served as a board member of, and owned an indirect interest in, a privately held company that provides Starbucks with in-store music services. Starbucks paid $0.7 million, $3.0 million and $2.3 million to the privately held company for music services during fiscal 2003, 2002 and 2001, respectively, while the related party relationship existed.

In April 2001, three members of the Board of Directors and other investors, organized as The Basketball Club of Seattle, LLC (the "Basketball Club"), purchased the franchises for The Seattle Supersonics and The Seattle Storm basketball teams. An executive officer of the Company, Howard Schultz, owns a controlling interest in the Basketball Club. Starbucks paid approximately $0.7 million, $0.7 million and $0.3 million during fiscal 2003, 2002 and 2001, respectively, for team sponsorships and ticket purchases while the related party relationship existed. Terms of the team sponsorship agreements did not change as a result of the related party relationship.

Note 17: Commitments and Contingencies

The Company has unconditionally guaranteed the repayment of certain yen-denominated bank loans and related interest and fees of an unconsolidated equity investee, Starbucks Coffee Japan, Ltd. There have been no modifications or additions to the loan guarantee agreements since the Company's adoption of FIN No. 45. The guarantees continue until the loans, including accrued interest and fees, have been paid in full. The maximum amount is limited to the sum of unpaid principal and interest amounts, as well as other related expenses. These amounts will vary based on fluctuations in the yen foreign exchange rate. As of September 28, 2003, the maximum amount of the guarantees was approximately $11.8 million.

Coffee brewing and espresso equipment sold to customers through Company-operated and licensed retail stores, as well as equipment sold to the Company's licensees for use in retail licensing operations, are under warranty for defects in materials and workmanship for a period ranging from 12 months to 24 months. The Company establishes a reserve for estimated warranty costs at the time of sale, based on historical experience. The following table summarizes the activity related to product warranty reserves during fiscal 2003 and 2002 (in thousands):

Fiscal year ended	Sept 28, 2003	Sept 29, 2002
Balance at the beginning of the fiscal year	$1,842	$1,090
Provision for warranties issued	2,895	3,128
Warranty claims	(2,510)	(2,376)
Balance at the end of the fiscal year	$2,227	$1,842

The Company is party to various legal proceedings arising in the ordinary course of its business, but it is not currently a party to any legal proceeding that management believes would have a material adverse effect on the consolidated financial position or results of operations of the Company.

Note 18: Segment Reporting

Segment information is prepared on the basis that Company's management internally reviews financial information for operational decision making purposes. Starbucks revised its segment reporting into two distinct, geographically based operating segments: United States and International. This change was in response to internal management realignments in the fiscal first quarter of 2004 and management's evaluation of the requirements of SFAS No. 131, "Disclosures about Segments of an Enterprise and Related Information."

United States

The Company's United States operations ("United States") represent 86% of total retail revenues, 81% of specialty revenues and 85% of total net revenues. Company-operated retail stores sell coffee and other beverages, whole bean coffees, complementary food, coffee brewing equipment and merchandise. Non-retail activities within the United States include: licensed operations, foodservice accounts and other initiatives related to the Company's core businesses.

International

The Company's international operations ("International") represent the remaining 14% of retail revenues, 19% of specialty revenues and 15% of total net revenues. International sells coffee and other beverages, whole bean coffees, complementary food, coffee brewing equipment and merchandise through Company-operated retail stores in Canada, the United Kingdom, Thailand and Australia, as well as through licensed operations and food-service accounts in these and other countries. Because International operations are in the early phase of development and have country-specific regulatory requirements, they require a more extensive administrative support organization, as compared to the United States, to provide resources and respond to business needs in each region.

The accounting policies of the operating segments are the same as those described in Note 1. Operating income represents earnings before "Interest and other income, net," "Gain on sale of investment" and "Income taxes." No allocations of corporate overhead, interest or income taxes are made to the segments. Identifiable assets by segment are those assets used in the Company's operations in each segment. Unallocated corporate assets include cash and investments, unallocated assets of the corporate headquarters and roasting facilities, deferred taxes and certain other intangibles. Management evaluates performance of segments based on direct product sales and operating costs.

The table below presents information by operating segment (in thousands):

Fiscal year ended	United States	International	Unallocated Corporate	Total
Fiscal 2003:				
Total net revenues	$3,472,452	$603,070	$ —	$4,075,522
Earnings/(loss) before income taxes	606,544	5,466	(175,675)	436,335
Depreciation and amortization	167,138	38,563	32,106	237,807
Income from equity investees	28,484	9,912	—	38,396
Equity method investments	16,919	117,422	—	134,341
Identifiable assets	1,161,512	383,324	1,184,910	2,729,746

Fiscal 2002:				
Total net revenues	$2,828,253	$460,655	$ —	$3,288,908
Earnings/(loss) before income taxes	506,829	3,891	(171,721)	338,999
Depreciation and amortization	142,752	34,069	28,736	205,557
Income from equity investees	19,182	14,263	—	33,445
Equity method investments	18,519	76,101	—	94,620
Identifiable assets	957,127	332,411	924,854	2,214,392
Fiscal 2001:				
Total net revenues	$2,298,563	$350,417	$ —	$2,648,980
Earnings/(loss) before income taxes	400,878	21,138	(133,969)	288,047
Depreciation and amortization	113,945	24,162	25,394	163,501
Income from equity investees	12,668	15,072	—	27,740
Equity method investments	21,652	35,043	—	56,695
Identifiable assets	901,680	245,169	636,621	1,783,470

The tables below represent information by geographic area (in thousands):

Fiscal year ended	Sept 28, 2003	Sept 29, 2002	Sept 30, 2001
Net revenues from external customers:			
United States	$3,472,452	$2,828,253	$2,298,563
Foreign countries	603,070	460,655	350,417
Total	$4,075,522	$3,288,908	$2,468,980

Revenues from foreign countries are based on the location of the customers and consist primarily of retail revenues from the United Kingdom and Canada as well as specialty revenues generated from product sales to international licensees. No customer accounts for 10% or more of the Company's revenues.

Fiscal year ended	Sept 28, 2003	Sept 29, 2002	Sept 30, 2001
Long-lived assets:			
United States	$1,544,300	$1,202,652	$1,064,385
Foreign countries	261,417	239,097	187,146
Total	$1,805,717	$1,441,749	$1,251,531

Assets attributed to foreign countries are based on the country in which those assets are located.

Note 19: Quarterly Financial Information (Unaudited)

Summarized quarterly financial information in fiscal 2003 and 2002 is as follows (in thousands, except earnings per share):

	First	Second	Third	Fourth
2003 quarter:				
Net revenues	$1,003,526	$954,206	$1,036,776	$1,081,014
Operating income	120,834	85,494	106,019	112,366
Net earnings	78,363	52,031	68,356	69,596
Net earnings per common share – diluted	$ 0.20	$ 0.13	$ 0.17	$ 0.17
2002 quarter:				
Net revenues	$ 805,335	$783,217	$ 835,158	$ 865,198
Operating income	92,000	48,444	87,091	88,803
Net earnings	67,709	31,741	55,556	57,680
Net earnings per common share – diluted	$ 0.17	$ 0.08	$ 0.14	$ 0.14

Management's Responsibility for Financial Reporting

The management of Starbucks Corporation is responsible for the preparation and integrity of the financial statements included in this Annual Report to Shareholders. The financial statements have been prepared in conformity with accounting principles generally accepted in the United States of America and include amounts based on management's best estimates and judgments where necessary. Financial information included elsewhere in this Annual Report is consistent with these financial statements.

Management maintains a system of internal controls and procedures designed to provide reasonable assurance that transactions are executed in accordance with proper authorization, transactions are properly recorded in the Company's records, assets are safeguarded, and accountability for assets is maintained. The concept of reasonable assurance is based on the recognition that the cost of maintaining the system of internal accounting controls should not exceed benefits expected to be derived from the system. Internal controls and procedures are periodically reviewed and revised, when appropriate, due to changing circumstances and requirements. In addition, the Company's internal audit department assesses the effectiveness and adequacy of internal controls on a regular basis and recommends improvements when appropriate. Management considers the internal auditors' and independent auditors' recommendations concerning the Company's internal controls and takes steps to implement those that are believed to be appropriate in the circumstances.

Independent auditors are appointed by the Company's Audit and Compliance Committee of the Board of Directors and ratified by the Company's shareholders to audit the financial statements in accordance with auditing standards generally accepted in the United States of America and to independently assess the fair presentation of the Company's financial position, results of operations and cash flows. Their report appears in this Annual Report.

The Audit and Compliance Committee, all of whose members are outside directors, is responsible for monitoring the Company's accounting and reporting practices. The Audit and Compliance Committee meets periodically with management, the independent auditors and the internal auditors, jointly and separately, to review financial reporting matters as well as to ensure that each is properly discharging its responsibilities. The independent auditors and the internal auditors have full and free access to the Committee without the presence of management to discuss the results of their audits, the adequacy of internal accounting controls and the quality of financial reporting.

/s/ ORIN C. SMITH
ORIN C. SMITH
president and
chief executive officer

/s/ MICHAEL CASEY
MICHAEL CASEY
executive vice president,
chief financial officer and chief administrative officer

Independent Auditors' Report

To the Board of Directors and Shareholders of Starbucks Corporation Seattle, Washington

We have audited the accompanying consolidated balance sheets of Starbucks Corporation and subsidiaries (the "Company") as of September 28, 2003, and September 29, 2002, and the related consolidated statements of earnings, shareholders' equity and cash flows for the years ended September 28, 2003, September 29, 2002 and September 30, 2001. These financial statements are the responsibility of the Company's management. Our responsibility is to express an opinion on these financial statements based on our audits.

We conducted our audits in accordance with auditing standards generally accepted in the United States of America. Those standards require that we plan and perform the audit to obtain reasonable assurance about whether the financial statements are free of material misstatement. An audit includes examining, on a test basis, evidence supporting the amounts and disclosures in the financial statements. An audit also includes assessing the accounting principles used and significant estimates made by management, as well as evaluating the overall financial statement presentation. We believe that our audits provide a reasonable basis for our opinion.

In our opinion, such consolidated financial statements present fairly, in all material respects, the financial position of the Company as of September 28, 2003, and September 29, 2002, and the results of its operations and its cash flows for the years ended September 28, 2003, September 29, 2002, and September 30, 2001, in conformity with accounting principles generally accepted in the United States of America.

/s/ DELOITTE & TOUCHE LLP
DELOITTE & TOUCHE LLP
Seattle, Washington
December 19, 2003

accelerated depreciation Any depreciation method that writes off depreciable costs more quickly than the ordinary straight-line method based on expected useful life.

account A summary record of the changes in a particular asset, liability, or owners' equity.

account format A classified balance sheet with the assets at the left.

account payable A liability that results from a purchase of goods or services on open account.

accounting The process of identifying, recording, and summarizing economic information and reporting it to decision makers.

accounting controls The methods and procedures for authorizing transactions, safeguarding assets, and ensuring the accuracy of the financial records.

accounting system A set of records, procedures, and equipment that routinely deals with the events affecting the financial performance and position of the entity.

accounts receivable (trade receivables, receivables) Amount owed to a company by customers as a result of delivering goods or services and extending credit in the ordinary course of business.

accounts receivable turnover Credit sales divided by average accounts receivable.

accrual basis Accounting method that recognizes the impact of transactions on the financial statements in the time periods when revenues and expenses occur.

accrue To accumulate a receivable or payable during a given period, even though no explicit transaction occurs, and to record a corresponding revenue or expense.

accumulated deficit A more descriptive term for retained earnings when the accumulated losses plus dividends exceed accumulated income.

accumulated depreciation (allowance for depreciation) The cumulative sum of all depreciation recognized since the date of acquisition of an asset.

adjustments (adjusting entries) End-of-period entries that assign the financial effects of implicit transactions to the appropriate time periods.

administrative controls All methods and procedures that facilitate management planning and control of operations.

affiliated company A company that has 20% to 50% of its voting shares owned by another company.

aging of accounts receivable An analysis that considers the composition of year-end accounts receivable based on the age of the debt.

allowance for uncollectible accounts (allowance for doubtful accounts, allowance for bad debts, reserve for doubtful accounts) A contra asset account that measures the amount of receivables estimated to be uncollectible.

allowance method Method of accounting for bad debt losses using estimates of the amount of sales that will ultimately be uncollectible and a contra asset account, allowance for doubtful accounts.

American Institute of Certified Public Accountants (AICPA) The principal professional association in the private sector that regulates the quality of the public accounting profession.

amortization When referring to long-lived assets, it usually means the allocation of the costs of intangible assets to the periods that benefit from these assets.

annual report A document prepared by management and distributed to current and potential investors to inform them about the company's past performance and future prospects.

annuity Equal cash flows to take place during successive periods of equal length.

assets Economic resources that a company expects to help generate future cash inflows or help reduce future cash outflows.

audit An examination of a company's transactions and the resulting financial statements.

audit committee A committee of the board of directors that oversees the internal accounting controls, financial statements, and financial affairs of the corporation.

auditor A person who examines the information used by managers to prepare the financial statements and attests to the credibility of those statements.

auditor's opinion (independent opinion) A report describing the scope and results of an audit. Companies include the opinion with the financial statements in their annual reports.

authorized shares The total number of shares that may legally be issued under the articles of incorporation.

available-for-sale securities Investments in equity or debt securities that are not held for active trading but may be sold before maturity.

bad debt recoveries Accounts receivable that were written off as uncollectible but then collected at a later date.

bad debts expense The cost of granting credit that arises from uncollectible accounts.

balance The difference between the total left-side and right-side amounts in an account at any particular time.

balance sheet (statement of financial position) A financial statement that shows the financial status of a business entity at a particular instant in time.

balance sheet equation   Assets 5 Liabilities 1 Owners' equity

bargain purchase option   A provision that the lessee can purchase the asset from the lessor at the end of the lease for substantially less than the asset's fair value.

basket purchase   The acquisition of two or more types of assets for a lump-sum cost.

benchmarks   General rules of thumb specifying appropriate levels for financial ratios.

board of directors   A body elected by the shareholders to represent them. It is responsible for appointing and monitoring the managers.

bond discount (discount on bonds)   The excess of face amount over the proceeds on issuance of a bond.

bond premium (premium on bonds)   The excess of the proceeds over the face amount of a bond.

bonds   Formal certificates of debt that include (1) a promise to pay interest in cash at a specified annual rate, plus (2) a promise to pay the principal at a specific maturity date.

book of original entry   A formal chronological record of how the entity's transactions affect the balances in pertinent accounts.

book value (net book value, carrying amount, carrying value)   The balance of an account shown on the books, net of any contra accounts. For example, the book value of equipment is its acquisition cost minus accumulated depreciation.

book value per share of common stock   Stockholders' equity attributable to common stock divided by the number of shares outstanding.

call premium   The amount by which the redemption price of a callable bond exceeds face value.

call price (redemption price)   The price at which an issuer can buy back a callable preferred stock or bond, which is typically 5% to 10% above the par value.

callable   A characteristic of bonds or preferred stock that gives the issuer the right to redeem the security at a fixed price.

callable bonds   Bonds subject to redemption before maturity at the option of the issuer.

capital lease   A lease that transfers most all the risks and benefits of ownership to the lessee.

capital stock certificate (stock certificate)   Formal evidence of ownership shares in a corporation.

capitalization (capital structure)   Owners' equity plus long-term debt.

capitalize   To add a cost to an asset account, as distinguished from expensing the cost immediately.

cash basis   Accounting method that recognizes the impact of transactions on the financial statements only when a company receives or pays cash.

cash discounts   Reductions of invoice prices awarded for prompt payment.

cash dividends   Distributions of cash to stockholders that reduce retained earnings.

cash equivalents   Highly liquid short-term investments that a company can easily and quickly convert into cash, such as money market funds and Treasury bills.

cash flows from financing activities   The section of the statement of cash flows that helps users understand management's financing decisions.

cash flows from investing activities   The section of the statement of cash flows that helps users understand management's investing decisions.

cash flows from operating activities   The first major section of the cash flow statement. It helps users evaluate the cash impact of management's operating decisions.

certificates of deposit   Short-term obligation of banks.

certified public accountant (CPA)   In the United States, a person earns this designation by meeting standards of both knowledge and integrity set by a State Board of Accountancy. Only CPAs can issue official opinions on financial statements in the United States.

charge   A word often used instead of debit.

chart of accounts   A numbered or coded list of all account titles.

chief executive officer (CEO)   The top manager in an organization.

classified balance sheet   A balance sheet that groups the accounts into subcategories to help readers quickly gain a perspective on the company's financial position.

close the books   Preparing the ledger accounts to record the next period's transactions by making closing entries that summarize all balances in the revenue and expense accounts and transferring the balances to retained earnings.

commercial paper   A short-term debt contract issued by prominent companies that borrow directly from investors.

common stock   Par value of the stock purchased by common shareholders of a corporation.

common-size statements   Financial statements in which components are expressed in relative percentages.

comparability   Conformity across companies with respect to policies and procedures.

compensating balances   Required minimum cash balances on deposit when money is borrowed from banks.

component percentages   Elements of financial statements that express each component as a percentage of the total.

compound annual growth rate (CAGR)   Year-over-year growth rate over a specified period of time.

compound entry   A transaction that affects more than two accounts.

compound interest   The interest rate multiplied by a changing principal amount. The unpaid interest is added to the principal to become the principal for the new period.

conservatism   Selecting the methods of measurement that yield lower net income, lower assets, and lower stockholders' equity.

consistency   Conformity from period to period with unchanging policies and procedures.

consolidated statements Combinations of the financial positions and earnings reports of the parent company with those of various subsidiaries into an overall report as if they were a single entity.

contingent liability A potential liability that depends on a future event arising out of a past transaction.

contra account A separate but related account that offsets or is a deduction from a companion account. An example is accumulated depreciation.

contra asset A contra account that offsets an asset.

convertible A characteristic of bonds or preferred stock that gives the holder the right to exchange the security for common stock.

convertible bonds Bonds that may, at the holder's option, be exchanged for other securities.

copyrights Exclusive rights to reproduce and sell a book, musical composition, film, and similar creative items.

corporate proxy A written authority granted by individual shareholders to others to cast the shareholders' votes.

corporation A business organization that is created by individual state laws.

correcting entry A journal entry that cancels a previous erroneous entry and adds the correct amounts to the correct accounts.

cost-benefit A criterion that states that an accounting system should be changed when the expected additional benefits of the change exceed its expected additional costs.

cost of goods available for sale Sum of beginning inventory plus current year purchases.

cost of goods sold (cost of sales, cost of revenue) The original acquisition cost of the inventory that a company sells to customers during the reporting period.

cost valuation Process of assigning specific historical costs to items counted in the physical inventory.

credit An entry or balance on the right side of an account.

creditor A person or entity to whom a company owes money.

cross-referencing The process of numbering or otherwise specifically identifying each journal entry and each posting.

cross-sectional comparisons Comparisons of a company's financial ratios with the ratios of other companies or with industry averages.

cumulative A characteristic of preferred stock that requires that undeclared dividends accumulate and must be paid in the future before common dividends.

current assets Cash and other assets that a company expects to convert to cash or sell or consume during the next 12 months or within the normal operating cycle if longer than 1 year.

current liabilities Liabilities that fall due within the coming year or within the normal operating cycle if longer than 1 year.

current ratio (working capital ratio) Current assets divided by current liabilities.

cutoff error Failure to record transactions in the correct time period.

data processing The totality of the procedures used to record, analyze, store, and report on chosen activities.

date of record The date that determines which shareholders will receive a dividend.

days to collect accounts receivable (average collection period) 365 divided by accounts receivable turnover.

debenture A debt security with a general claim against all assets, instead of a specific claim against particular assets.

debit An entry or balance on the left side of an account.

debt-to-equity ratio Total liabilities divided by total shareholders' equity.

debt-to-total-assets ratio Total liabilities divided by total assets.

declaration date The date the board of directors declares a dividend.

deferred income tax liability An obligation arising because of predictable future taxes, to be paid when a future tax return is filed.

depletion The process of allocating the cost of natural resources to the periods in which the resources are used.

depreciable value The amount of the acquisition cost to be allocated as depreciation over the total useful life of an asset. It is the difference between the total acquisition cost and the estimated residual value.

depreciation The systematic allocation of the acquisition cost of long-lived or fixed assets to the expense accounts of particular periods that benefit from the use of the assets.

depreciation schedule The listing of depreciation amounts for each year of an asset's useful life.

dilution Reduction in stockholders' equity per share or earnings per share that arises from some changes among shareholders' proportional interests.

direct method A method for computing cash flows from operating activities that subtracts operating cash disbursements from cash collections to arrive at cash flows from operations.

discontinued operations The termination of a business segment. The results are reported separately, net of tax, in the income statement.

discount amortization The spreading of bond discount over the life of the bonds as interest expense.

discount rates Interest rates used to compute present values.

discounted values Another name for present values.

discounting The process of finding the present value.

dividend arrearages Accumulated unpaid dividends on preferred stock.

dividend-payout ratio Common dividends per share divided by earnings per share.

double-declining-balance (DDB) method A common form of accelerated depreciation. It is computed by doubling the straight-line rate and multiplying the resulting DDB rate by the beginning book value.

double-entry system   The method usually followed for recording transactions, whereby every transaction always affects at least two accounts.

early extinguishment   When a company chooses to redeem its own bonds before maturity.

earnings per share (EPS)   Net income divided by average number of common shares outstanding during the period.

EBIT   Earnings before interest and taxes.

EBIT-to-sales ratio   Earnings before interest and taxes divided by sales.

Economic Value Added (EVA)   Measure of the residual wealth of a company after deducting its cost of capital from operating profit.

effective interest amortization (compound interest method)   An amortization method that uses a constant interest rate.

entity   An organization or a section of an organization that stands apart from other organizations and individuals as a separate economic unit.

equity method   Accounting for an investment at acquisition cost, adjusted for the investor's share of dividends and earnings or losses of the investee subsequent to the date of investment.

expenditures   Purchases of goods or services, whether for cash or credit.

expenses   Decreases in owners' equity that arise because a company delivers goods or services to customers.

explicit transactions   Observable events such as cash receipts and disbursements, credit purchases, and credit sales that trigger nearly all day-to-day routine entries.

extraordinary items   Items that are unusual in nature and infrequent in occurrence that are shown separately, net of tax, in the income statement.

F.O.B. destination   Seller pays freight costs from the shipping point of the seller to the receiving point of the buyer.

F.O.B. shipping point   Buyer pays freight costs from the shipping point of the seller to the receiving point of the buyer.

face amount   The loan principal or the amount that a borrower promises to repay at a specific maturity date.

fair market value   The value of an asset based on the price for which a company could sell the asset to an independent third party.

FASB Statements   Name for the FASB's rulings on GAAP.

financial accounting   The field of accounting that serves external decision makers, such as stockholders, suppliers, banks, and government agencies.

Financial Accounting Standards Board (FASB)   The private sector body that is responsible for establishing GAAP in the United States.

financial management   Decisions concerned with where the company gets cash and how it uses that cash to its benefit

financial statement analysis   Using financial data to assess a company's performance.

financing activities   A company's transactions that obtain resources as a borrower or issuer of securities or repay creditors and owners.

financing decisions   Decisions concerned with whether to get cash or repay debt.

finished goods inventory   The accumulated costs of manufacture for goods that are complete and ready for sale.

firm-specific risk   The risk that the firm will not repay the loan or will not pay the interest on time.

first-in, first-out (FIFO)   This method of accounting for inventory assigns the cost of the earliest acquired units to cost of goods sold.

fiscal year   The year established for accounting purposes, which may differ from a calendar year.

Form 10-K   A document that U.S. companies file annually with the Securities and Exchange Commission. It contains the companies' financial statements.

franchises (licenses)   Privileges granted by a government, manufacturer, or distributor to sell a product or service in accordance with specified conditions.

free cash flow   Generally defined as cash flows from operations less capital expenditures.

freight in (inward transportation)   An additional cost of the goods acquired during the period, which is often shown in the purchases section of an income statement.

future value   The amount accumulated, including principal and interest.

general journal   The most common example of a book of original entry; a complete chronological record of transactions.

general ledger   The collection of accounts that accumulate the amounts reported in the major financial statements.

generally accepted accounting principles (GAAP)   The term that applies to all the broad concepts and detailed practices to be followed in preparing and distributing financial statements. It includes all the conventions, rules, and procedures that together comprise accepted accounting practice.

going concern (continuity)   A convention that assumes that ordinarily an entity persists indefinitely.

goodwill   The excess of the cost of an acquired company over the sum of the fair market value of its identifiable individual assets less the liabilities.

gross profit (gross margin)   The excess of sales revenue over the cost of the inventory that was sold.

gross profit percentage (gross margin percentage)   Gross profit (sales 2 cost of goods sold) divided by sales.

gross sales   Total sales revenue before deducting sales returns and allowances.

held-to-maturity securities   Debt securities that the investor expects to hold until maturity.

holding gain (inventory profit)   Increase in the replacement cost or other measure of current value of the inventory held during the current period.

impaired   When an asset ceases to have economic value to the company at least as large as the book value of the asset.

implicit interest (imputed interest)   An interest expense that is not explicitly recognized in a loan agreement.

implicit transactions   Events (such as the passage of time) that do not generate source documents or visible evidence of the event. We do not recognize such events in the accounting records until the end of an accounting period.

improvement (betterment, capital improvement)   An expenditure that is intended to add to the future benefits provided by an existing fixed asset.

imputed interest rate   The market interest rate that equates the proceeds from a loan with the present value of the loan payments.

income (profits, earnings)   The excess of revenues over expenses.

income statement (statement of earnings, operating statement)   A report of all revenues and expenses pertaining to a specific time period.

indirect method   A method for computing cash flows from operating activities that adjusts the previously calculated accrual net income from the income statement to reflect only cash receipts and cash disbursements.

inflation premium   The extra interest that investors require because the general price level may increase between now and the time they receive their money.

intangible assets   Contractual or legal rights or economic benefits, such as franchises, patents, trademarks, copyrights, and goodwill, that are not physical in nature.

interest   The cost the borrower pays the lender to use the principal.

interest-coverage ratio   Pretax income plus interest expense divided by interest expense.

interest rate   A specified percentage of the principal. It is used to compute the amount of interest.

interim periods   The time spans established for accounting purposes that are less than 1 year.

internal control   System of checks and balances that ensures all actions occurring within the company are in accordance with organizational objectives.

International Accounting Standards Board (IASB)   An international body established to develop, in the public interest, a single set of high-quality, understandable, and enforceable global accounting standards.

inventory   Goods held by a company for the purpose of sale to customers.

inventory shrinkage   Inventory reductions from theft, breakage, or losses of inventory.

inventory turnover   The cost of goods sold divided by the average inventory held during the period.

investing activities   Transactions that acquire or dispose of long-lived assets.

investing decisions   Decisions that include the choices to (1) acquire or dispose of plant, property, equipment, and other long-term productive assets, and (2) provide or collect cash as a lender or as an owner of securities.

invoice   A bill from the seller to a buyer indicating the number of items shipped, their price, and any additional costs (such as shipping) along with payment terms, if any.

issued shares   The aggregate number of shares sold to the public.

journal entry   An analysis of the effects of a transaction on the accounts, usually accompanied by an explanation.

journalizing   The process of entering transactions into the journal.

last-in, first-out (LIFO)   This inventory method assigns the most recent costs to cost of goods sold.

lease   A contract whereby an owner (lessor) grants the use of property to a second party (lessee) for rental payments.

leasehold   The right to use a fixed asset for a specified period of time, typically beyond 1 year.

leasehold improvement   Investments by a lessee in items that are not permitted to be removed from the premises when a lease expires, such as installation of new fixtures, panels, walls, and air-conditioning equipment.

ledger   The records for a group of related accounts kept current in a systematic manner.

lessee   The party that has the right to use leased property and makes lease payments to the lessor.

lessor   The owner of property who grants usage rights to the lessee.

liabilities   Economic obligations of the organization to outsiders, or claims against its assets by outsiders.

LIFO layer (LIFO increment)   A separately identifiable additional segment of LIFO inventory.

LIFO liquidation   A decrease in the physical amount in inventory causing old, low LIFO inventory acquisition costs to become the cost of goods sold, resulting in a high gross profit.

LIFO reserve   The difference between a company's inventory valued at LIFO and what it would be under FIFO.

limited liability   A feature of the corporate form of organization whereby corporate creditors (such as banks or suppliers) ordinarily have claims against the corporate assets only, not against the personal assets of the owners.

line of credit   An agreement with a bank to provide automatically short-term loans up to some preestablished maximum.

liquidating value   A measure of the preference to receive assets in the event of corporate liquidation.

liquidation   Converting assets to cash and paying off outside claims.

liquidity   An entity's ability to meet its immediate financial obligations with cash and near-cash assets as those obligations become due.

long-lived asset   An asset that a company expects to provide services for more than 1 year.

long-term-debt-to-total-capital ratio   Total long-term debt divided by total shareholders' equity plus total long-term debt.

long-term liabilities   Obligations that fall due beyond 1 year from the balance sheet date.

long-term solvency   An organization's ability to generate enough cash to repay long-term debts as they mature.

lower-of-cost-or-market method (LCM)   A comparison of the current market price of inventory with historical cost derived under one of the four primary methods and choosing the lower of the two as the inventory value.

management accounting   The field of accounting that serves internal decision makers, such as top executives, department heads, college deans, hospital administrators, and people at other management levels within an organization.

management discussion and analysis (MD&A)   A required section of the annual report that concentrates on explaining the major changes in the income statement, liquidity, and capital resources.

management reports   Explicit statements in annual reports of publicly held companies that management is responsible for all audited and unaudited information in the annual report.

market method   Method of accounting for trading securities changes affect the income statement; for available-for-sale securities a valuation allowance appears in owners' equity.

market rate   The rate available on investments in similar bonds at a moment in time.

marketable securities   Any notes, bonds, or stocks that can readily be sold.

market-to-book ratio   Market value per share divided by book value per share.

matching   The recording of expenses in the same time period that we recognize the related revenues.

materiality   A convention that asserts that an item should be included in a financial statement if its omission or misstatement would tend to mislead the reader of the financial statements under consideration.

minority interests   The outside shareholders' interests, as opposed to the parent's interests, in a subsidiary corporation.

mortgage bond   A form of long-term debt that is secured by the pledge of specific property.

multiple-step income statement   An income statement that contains one or more subtotals that highlight significant relationships.

negotiable   Legal financial contracts that can be transferred from one lender to another.

net income (net earnings)   The remainder after deducting all expenses from revenues.

net loss   The difference between revenues and expenses when expenses exceed revenues.

net sales   Total sales revenue reduced by sales returns and allowances.

neutrality   A quality of information meaning that it is objective and free from bias.

nominal interest rate (contractual rate, coupon rate, stated rate)   A contractual rate of interest paid on bonds.

nonmonetary exchange   An exchange of goods or services in which the assets or liabilities exchanged are not cash.

notes payable   Promissory notes that are evidence of a debt and state the terms of payment.

open account   Buying or selling on credit, usually by just an "authorized signature" of the buyer.

operating activities   Transactions that affect the purchase, processing, and selling of a company's products and services.

operating cycle   The time span during which a company uses cash to acquire goods and services, which in turn it sells to customers, who in turn pay for their purchases with cash.

operating decisions   Decisions that are concerned with the major day-to-day activities that generate revenues and expenses.

operating expenses   A group of recurring expenses that pertain to the firm's routine, ongoing operations.

operating income (operating profit, income from operations)   Gross profit less all operating expenses.

operating lease   A lease that should be accounted for by the lessee as ordinary rent expenses.

operating management   Decisions concerned with the day-to-day activities that generate revenues and expenses.

other postretirement benefits   Benefits provided to retired workers in addition to a pension, such as life and health insurance.

outstanding shares   Shares remaining in the hands of shareholders.

owners' equity   The owners' claims on an organization's assets, or total assets less total liabilities.

paid-in capital   The total capital investment in a corporation by its owners both at and subsequent to the inception of business.

paid-in capital in excess of par value (additional paid-in capital)   When issuing stock, the difference between the total amount the company receives for the stock and the par value.

par value (stated value)   The nominal dollar amount printed on stock certificates.

parent company   A company owning more than 50% of the voting shares of another company, called the subsidiary company.

participating   A characteristic of preferred stock that provides increasing dividends when common dividends increase.

partnership   A form of organization that joins two or more individuals together as co-owners.

patents   Grants by the federal government to an inventor, bestowing (in the United States) the exclusive right for 20 years to produce and sell a given product, or to use a process.

payment date   The date dividends are paid.

pensions   Payments to former employees after they retire.

percentage of accounts receivable method   An approach to estimating bad debts expense and uncollectible accounts at year-end using the historical relations of uncollectibles to accounts receivable.

percentage-of-completion method Method of recognizing revenue on long-term contracts as production occurs.

percentage of sales method An approach to estimating bad debts expense and uncollectible accounts based on the historical relations between credit sales and uncollectibles.

period costs Items supporting a company's operations for a given period. We record the expenses in the time period in which the company incurs them.

periodic inventory system The system in which the cost of goods sold is computed periodically by relying solely on physical counts without keeping day-to-day records of units sold or on hand.

permanent differences Revenue or expense items that are recognized for tax purposes but not recognized under GAAP, or vice versa.

perpetual inventory system A system that keeps a running, continuous record that tracks inventories and the cost of goods sold on a day-to-day basis.

physical count The process of examining and identifying all items in inventory. We then value the inventory by assigning a specific cost to each item.

posting The transferring of amounts from the journal to the appropriate accounts in the ledger.

preemptive rights The rights to acquire a pro rata amount of any new issues of capital stock.

preferred stock Stock that offers owners different rights and preferential treatment.

present value The value today of a future cash inflow or outflow.

pretax and preinterest return on total assets Earnings before interest and taxes divided by average total assets.

pretax income Income before income taxes.

price-earnings growth (PEG) ratio Price-earnings ratio divided by the earnings growth rate.

price-earnings (P-E) ratio Market price per share of common stock divided by earnings per share of common stock.

principal The amount borrowed or the amount to be repaid.

private accountants Accountants who work for businesses, government agencies, and other nonprofit organizations.

private placement A process whereby bonds are issued by corporations when money is borrowed from a few sources, not from the general public.

privately owned A corporation owned by a family, a small group of shareholders, or a single individual, in which shares of ownership are not publicly sold.

pro forma statements A set of projected financial statements or other estimates of predicted results.

product costs Costs that are linked with revenues and are charged as expenses when the related revenue is recognized.

profitability The ability of a company to provide investors with a particular rate of return on their investment.

promissory note A written promise to repay principal plus interest at specific future dates.

protective covenant (covenant) A provision stated in a bond, usually to protect the bondholders' interests.

public accountants Accountants who offer services to the general public on a fee basis, including auditing, tax work, and management consulting.

publicly owned A corporation that sells shares in its ownership to the public.

purchase order A document that specifies the items ordered and the price to be paid by the ordering company.

quick ratio (acid test ratio) Variation of the current ratio that removes less liquid assets from the numerator. Perhaps the most common version of this ratio is (current assets – inventory)/current liabilities.

rate of return The amount an investor earns expressed as a percentage of the amount invested.

rate of return on common equity (ROE) Net income less preferred dividends divided by average common equity.

raw material inventory Includes the cost of materials held for use in the manufacturing of a product.

real interest rate The return that investors demand because they are delaying their consumption.

receiving report A document that specifies the items received by the company and the condition of the items.

recognition A test for determining whether to record revenues in the financial statements of a given period. To be recognized, revenues must be earned and realized.

reconcile a bank statement To verify that the bank balance for cash is consistent with the accounting records.

recoverability test A test for asset impairment that compares the total expected future net cash flows from the use of the asset and its eventual disposal with the net book value of the asset.

relevance The capability of information to make a difference to the decision maker.

reliability A quality of information that assures decision makers that the information captures the conditions or events it purports to represent.

replacement cost The cost at which an inventory item could be acquired today.

report format A classified balance sheet with the assets at the top.

reserve Has one of three meanings: (1) a restriction of dividend-declaring power as denoted by a specific subdivision of retained earnings, (2) an offset to an asset, or (3) an estimate of a definite liability of indefinite or uncertain amount.

residual value (terminal value, disposal value, salvage value, scrap value) The amount a company expects to receive from disposal of a long-lived asset at the end of its useful life.

restricted retained earnings (appropriated retained earnings) Any part of retained earnings that may not be reduced by dividend declarations.

restricted stock Stock paid to employees that generally has constraints such as not being able to sell it until it vests and then generally being able to sell it only back to the company at the current market price.

restructuring   A significant makeover of part of the company typically involving the closing of plants, firing of employees, and relocation of activities.

retailer   A company that sells items directly to the public, to individual buyers.

retained earnings (retained income)   Total cumulative owners' equity generated by income or profits.

return on assets ratio (ROA)   Net income divided by average total assets.

return on common stockholders' equity ratio (ROE or ROCE)   Net income divided by invested capital (measured by average common stockholders' equity).

return on sales ratio   (net profit margin ratio) Net income divided by sales.

revenues (sales, sales revenues)   Increases in owners' equity arising from increases in assets received in exchange for the delivery of goods or services to customers.

sales allowance (purchase allowance)   Reduction of the original selling price.

sales returns (purchase returns)   Products returned by the customer.

Sarbanes-Oxley Act   A law passed by the U.S. Congress in 2002 that gave the government a larger role in regulating the audit profession

Securities and Exchange Commission (SEC)   The government agency charged by the U.S. Congress with the ultimate responsibility for authorizing the GAAP for companies whose stock is held by the general investing public.

short-term debt securities   Largely notes and bonds with maturities of 1 year or less.

short-term equity securities   Capital stock in other corporations held with the intention to liquidate within 1 year as needed.

short-term investment   A temporary investment in marketable securities of otherwise idle cash.

short-term liquidity   An organization's ability to meet current payments as they become due.

simple entry   An entry for a transaction that affects only two accounts.

simple interest   The interest rate multiplied by an unchanging principal amount.

single-step income statement   An income statement that groups all revenues and then lists and deducts all expenses without drawing any intermediate subtotals.

sinking fund   A pool of cash or securities set aside for meeting certain obligations.

sinking fund bonds   Bonds that require the issuer to make annual payments to a sinking fund.

sole proprietorship   A business with a single owner.

source documents   The supporting original records of any transaction.

special items   Revenues or expenses that are large enough and unusual enough to warrant separate disclosure.

specific identification method   This inventory method concentrates on the physical linking of the particular items sold with the cost of goods sold that we report.

specific write-off method   This method of accounting for bad debt losses assumes all sales are fully collectible until proved otherwise.

statement of cash flows (cash flow statement)   One of the basic financial statements that reports the cash receipts and cash payments of an entity during a particular period and classifies them as financing, investing, and operating flows.

statement of income and retained earnings   A statement that includes a statement of retained earnings at the bottom of an income statement.

statement of retained earnings   A statement that lists the beginning balance in retained earnings, followed by a description of any changes that occurred during the period, and the ending balance.

statement of stockholders' equity   A statement that shows all changes during the year in each stockholders' equity account.

stock dividends   Distribution to stockholders of a small number of additional shares for every share owned without any payment to the company by the stockholders.

stock options   Special rights usually granted to executives to purchase a corporation's capital stock.

stock split   Issuance of additional shares to existing stockholders for no payments by the stockholders.

stockholders' equity (shareholders' equity)   Owners' equity of a corporation. The excess of assets over liabilities of a corporation.

straight-line depreciation   A method that spreads the depreciable value evenly over the useful life of an asset.

subordinated debentures   Debt securities whose holders have claims against only the assets that remain after satisfying the claims of other general creditors.

subsidiary   A corporation owned or controlled by a parent company through the ownership of more than 50% of the voting stock.

T-account   Simplified version of ledger accounts that takes the form of the capital letter T.

tangible assets (fixed assets, plant assets)   Physical items that can be seen and touched, such as land, natural resources, buildings, and equipment.

tax rate   The percentage of taxable income paid to the government.

temporary differences (timing differences)   Differences between net income and taxable income that arise because some revenue and expense items are recognized at different times for tax purposes than for financial reporting purposes.

times interest earned (interest coverage)   Income before interest expense and income taxes divided by interest expense.

time-series comparisons Comparisons of a company's financial ratios with its own historical ratios.

total asset turnover (asset turnover) Sales divided by average total assets.

trade discounts Reductions to the gross selling price for a particular class of customers.

trademarks Distinctive identifications of a manufactured product or of a service taking the form of a name, a sign, a slogan, a logo, or an emblem.

trading on the equity (financial leverage, leveraging, gearing) Using borrowed money at fixed interest rates with the objective of enhancing the rate of return on common stockholders' equity.

trading securities Current investments in equity or debt securities held for short-term profit.

transaction Any event that both affects the financial position of an entity and that an accountant can reliably record in money terms.

treasury stock A corporation's issued stock that has subsequently been repurchased by the company and not retired.

trend analysis An analysis technique that compares financial trends and changes from one year to the next and identifies patterns that have occurred in the past.

trial balance A list of all accounts in the general ledger with their balances.

turnover A synonym for sales or revenues in many countries outside the United States.

U.S. Treasury obligations Interest-bearing notes, bonds, and bills issued by the U.S. government.

uncollectible accounts (bad debts) Receivables determined to be uncollectible because debtors are unable or unwilling to pay their debts.

underwriters A group of investment bankers that buys an entire bond or stock issue from a corporation and then sells the securities to the general investing public.

unearned revenue (revenue received in advance, deferred revenue) Represents payments from customers who pay in advance for goods or services to be delivered at a future date.

unit depreciation A depreciation method based on units of service or units of production when physical wear and tear is the dominating influence on the useful life of the asset.

useful life The Shorter of the physical life or the economic life of an asset.

validity (representational faithfulness) A correspondence between the accounting numbers and the objects or events those numbers purport to represent.

verifiability A quality of information meaning that it can be checked to ensure it is correct.

vested options Options for which the holders have the power to exercise their options.

weighted-average method This inventory method computes a unit cost by dividing the total acquisition cost of all items available for sale by the number of units available for sale.

wholesaler An intermediary that sells inventory items to retailers.

work in process inventory Includes the cost incurred for partially completed items, including raw materials, labor, and other costs.

working capital The excess of current assets over current liabilities.

write-down A reduction in the recorded historical cost of an item in response to a decline in value.

yield to maturity The interest rate at which all contractual cash flows for interest and principal have a present value equal to the current price of the bond.

zero coupon bond A bond or note that pays no cash interest during its life.

PHOTO CREDITS

Chapter 1. Page 2 — AP/Wide World Photos

Chapter 2. Page 46 — PhotoEdit

Chapter 3. Page 90 — PhotoEdit

Chapter 4. Page 138 — AP/Wide World Photos

Chapter 5. Page 182 — Getty Images, Inc. – Allsport Photography

Chapter 6. Page 230 — Corbis/Bettmann

Chapter 7. Page 278 — The Image Works

Chapter 8. Page 334 — Getty Images, Inc. – Image Bank

Chapter 9. Page 382 — Corbis/Bettmann

Chapter 10. Page 440 — AP/Wide World Photos

Chapter 11. Page 488 — AP/Wide World Photos

Chapter 12. Page 534 — Phototake NYC

Exhibit 6-3. Page 250 — © "2004" by RMA- The Risk Management Association. All rights reserved. No part of this table may be reproduced or utilized in any form or by any means, electronic or mechanical, including photocopying, recording or by any information storage and retrieval system without permission in writing from RMA- The Risk Management Association. Please refer to www.rmahq.org for further warranty, copyright and use of data information.

Exhibit 7-4. Page 287 — © "2004" by RMA, The Risk Management Association. All rights reserved. No part of this table may be reproduced or utilized in any form or by any means, electronic or mechanical, including photocopying, recording or by any information storage and retrieval system without permission in writing from RMA, The Risk Management Association. Please refer to www.rmahq.org for further warranty, copyright and use of data information.

Exhibit 11-2. Pages 490–491 — Ford Motor Company